EMPLOYMENT LAW

EMPLOYMENT LAW

Gillian Phillips MA (Cantab), LLM, Solicitor, Part-time Employment Judge,
Employment Tribunals

Karen Scott LLB, LLM, Solicitor, Part-time Employment Judge,
Employment Tribunals

Published by

College of Law Publishing,
Braboeuf Manor, Portsmouth Road, St Catherines, Guildford GU3 1HA

British Library Cataloguing-in-Publication Data

A catalogue record for this book is available from the British Library.

ISBN 978 1 915469 23 6

Typeset by Style Photosetting Ltd, Mayfield, East Sussex

Tables and index by Moira Greenhalgh, Arnside, Cumbria

Preface

This book has been written primarily for students of an Employment Law and Practice elective. It covers a number of important areas of individual employment law, although it does not deal with trade union law or collective agreements.

For the sake of brevity, the masculine pronoun is used to include the feminine.

The law is stated as at 1 October 2022, although some later developments have been referred to where possible.

We express our thanks to the many previous authors and contributors to this book. In particular, we would like to remember Peter Rumbelow, who oversaw the early editions of this book and whose legacy remains. We would also like to express our thanks to the Employment Law team at the University of Law for their comments on previous editions of this book. Though we benefitted enormously from their advice, all errors are strictly of our own making. Thanks too to John Moore, formerly of Bevan Brittan LLP.

Thanks as always to David Stott for his help and guidance.

GILLIAN PHILLIPS
KAREN SCOTT

Contents

PREFACE   v

TABLE OF CASES   xi

TABLE OF STATUTES   xli

TABLE OF SECONDARY LEGISLATION AND CODES OF PRACTICE   xlvii

INTRODUCTORY NOTE   liii

TABLE OF ABBREVIATIONS   lxxi

Chapter 1		THE CONTRACT OF EMPLOYMENT	1
	1.1	Introduction	1
	1.2	Background	2
	1.3	The relationship of employer and employee	10
	1.4	The contract of employment	37
	1.5	Implied terms	40
	1.6	Terms implied by statute	40
	1.7	Terms implied by common law	40
	1.8	Written contracts	46
	1.9	Variation of contractual terms	68
	1.10	Human Rights Act 1998	72
	1.11	Protection of wages	73
	1.12	Working Time Regulations 1998	77
	1.13	Checklists	98
	1.14	Further reading	99
		Summary	100
Chapter 2		TERMINATION OF THE CONTRACT OF EMPLOYMENT – WRONGFUL DISMISSAL	101
	2.1	Introduction	101
	2.2	Wrongful dismissal (dismissal in breach of contract)	103
	2.3	Termination of contract	104
	2.4	Employee's remedies for wrongful dismissal	111
	2.5	Employer's remedies	117
	2.6	Checklist	119
	2.7	Further reading	119
		Summary	119
Chapter 3		DISMISSAL – ELIGIBILITY TO PRESENT A STATUTORY CLAIM	121
	3.1	Introduction	121
	3.2	Eligibility factors	121
	3.3	Employees only	122
	3.4	Dismissal	122
	3.5	Continuous employment	129
	3.6	Excluded classes	134
	3.7	Jurisdiction	134
	3.8	Contracting out	139
	3.9	Further reading	139
		Summary	140
Chapter 4		REDUNDANCY	141
	4.1	Introduction	141
	4.2	Definition of redundancy	143
	4.3	Presumption of redundancy	147

	4.4	Offers of re-employment	147
	4.5	Change of employer	149
	4.6	Computation of the statutory redundancy payment	150
	4.7	Enforcement	151
	4.8	Consultation	152
	4.9	Case study: redundancy payment, unpaid notice and holiday pay	157
	4.10	Further reading	159
		Summary	160
Chapter 5		UNFAIR DISMISSAL	163
	5.1	Introduction	163
	5.2	Reasons for dismissal	165
	5.3	Fairness of dismissal	171
	5.4	Procedural unfairness	176
	5.5	Other special cases	204
	5.6	Awards for unfair dismissal	219
	5.7	Penalties for employers	236
	5.8	Case study 1: unfair dismissal, redundancy payment and unpaid wages	237
	5.9	Case study 2: unfair dismissal	238
	5.10	Further reading	245
		Summary	245
Chapter 6		PRACTICE AND PROCEDURE, SETTLEMENTS AND OVERLAPPING CLAIMS	249
	6.1	Introduction	249
	6.2	Applications to the employment tribunal	250
	6.3	Time-limits in employment tribunals	255
	6.4	Tribunal Rules	264
	6.5	Settlements	304
	6.6	Alternatives to tribunal proceedings	310
	6.7	Overlapping claims and awards	311
	6.8	Case study: unfair dismissal	314
	6.9	Further reading	331
		Summary	331
Chapter 7		TRANSFER OF UNDERTAKINGS	335
	7.1	Introduction	335
	7.2	When do the 2006 Regulations apply?	336
	7.3	Effect of a relevant transfer	350
	7.4	What the transferee acquires	356
	7.5	Dismissal of an employee because of a relevant transfer	359
	7.6	Post-transfer variations to terms and conditions	363
	7.7	The provision of information and consultation under the 2006 Regulations	366
	7.8	Further reading	370
		Summary	370
Chapter 8		DISCRIMINATION AND EQUAL PAY	375
	8.1	Introduction	375
	8.2	Protected characteristics	379
	8.3	Prohibited conduct	388
	8.4	Unlawful acts of discrimination – in the employment field	392
	8.5	Occupational requirements	395
	8.6	Vicarious liability	397
	8.7	Retirement	403
	8.8	Enforcement and remedies	403
	8.9	Equal pay and the equality clause	412
	8.10	Part-time workers	417
	8.11	Fixed-term employees	419
	8.12	Trade union membership or activities	419
	8.13	Discrimination under the Human Rights Act 1998	420

	8.14	Further reading	421
		Summary	422
Chapter 9		DIRECT DISCRIMINATION	425
	9.1	Introduction	425
	9.2	Direct discrimination	425
	9.3	Gender reassignment and absence from work	436
	9.4	Pregnancy and maternity discrimination	437
	9.5	Burden of proof	439
	9.6	Remedies	443
	9.7	Case study: direct race discrimination claim – burden of proof	444
		Summary	448
Chapter 10		INDIRECT DISCRIMINATION	451
	10.1	Introduction	451
	10.2	Indirect discrimination	451
	10.3	Burden of proof	463
	10.4	Remedies	464
		Summary	464
Chapter 11		HARASSMENT AND VICTIMISATION	467
	11.1	Introduction	467
	11.2	Burden of proof	468
	11.3	Harassment	468
	11.4	Remedies for harassment	474
	11.5	Employers' liability for the acts of employees	474
	11.6	Employers' liability for the acts of third parties	474
	11.7	Protection from Harassment Act 1997	476
	11.8	Case study: harassment	476
	11.9	Victimisation	481
		Summary	484
Chapter 12		AGE DISCRIMINATION	487
	12.1	Introduction	487
	12.2	The protected characteristic	488
	12.3	Prohibited conduct	488
	12.4	Unlawful acts of discrimination	489
	12.5	Occupational requirements	489
	12.6	Direct discrimination	489
	12.7	Indirect discrimination	494
	12.8	Harassment and victimisation	496
	12.9	Exceptions	496
	12.10	Vicarious liability	497
	12.11	Burden of proof	497
	12.12	Practical considerations	497
	12.13	Enforcement and remedies	499
	12.14	Further reading	499
		Summary	500
Chapter 13		DISABILITY DISCRIMINATION	501
	13.1	Introduction	501
	13.2	The protected characteristic	502
	13.3	The meaning of 'disability' and 'disabled person'	502
	13.4	Unlawful discrimination in employment	514
	13.5	Types of discrimination	515
	13.6	Burden of proof	538
	13.7	Vicarious liability	538
	13.8	Enforcement and remedies	538
		Summary	539

Chapter 14   FAMILY-FRIENDLY RIGHTS AND THE RIGHT TO REQUEST FLEXIBLE WORKING   543
 14.1 Introduction   543
 14.2 Maternity leave   544
 14.3 Ordinary and additional maternity leave   544
 14.4 Compulsory maternity leave   548
 14.5 Redundancy during maternity leave   548
 14.6 Protection from detriment short of dismissal   548
 14.7 Automatically unfair dismissal   549
 14.8 Remedies for unfair dismissal   550
 14.9 Redundancy payments   550
 14.10 Wrongful dismissal   550
 14.11 Pregnancy/maternity discrimination   550
 14.12 Other maternity-related rights   551
 14.13 Adoption leave   553
 14.14 Paternity leave   555
 14.15 Parental leave   555
 14.16 Shared parental leave   555
 14.17 Parental Bereavement Leave and Pay   557
 14.18 Payments whilst on furlough   557
 14.19 Right to request flexible working   558
 14.20 Time off to care for dependants   560
 14.21 Further reading   561
 Summary   562

Chapter 15   HUMAN RIGHTS, MONITORING AND DATA PROTECTION   567
 15.1 Human Rights Act 1998 – introduction   567
 15.2 The existing scheme of the Human Rights Act 1998   568
 15.3 Key definitions   569
 15.4 Relevant Convention rights   570
 15.5 Data protection   579
 15.6 Monitoring in the workplace   586
 15.7 Further reading   591
 Summary   591

Appendix 1   STATEMENT OF TERMS AND SERVICE CONTRACT EXAMPLES   593
Appendix 2   CASE STUDY   603
Appendix 3   PRESIDENTIAL GUIDANCE – GENERAL CASE MANAGEMENT   655

INDEX   673

Table of Cases

A

A and B v X, Y and Times Newspapers Ltd (EAT/0113/18)	287
A Fereday v South Staffordshire NHS Primary Care Trust (UKEAT/0513/10)	128
A Ltd v Z (UKEAT/0273/18)	536
A v B [2003] IRLR 405	194
A v Chief Constable of West Midlands Police (UKEAT/0313/14)	483
A v Secretary of State for Justice [2019] IRLR 108	288
AA Solicitors Ltd (t/a AA Solicitors) & Another v Majid (EAT/0217/15)	408, 474
Abadeh v British Telecommunications plc [2001] IRLR 23	509, 512
Abbey Cars (West Horndon) Ltd v Ford (UKEAT/0472/07)	127
Abbey National plc v Robinson [2000] All ER (D) 1884	128
Abbeyfield (Maidenhead) Society v Hart (UKEAT/0016/21)	278
Abellio London Ltd (Formerly Travel London Ltd) v Musse and Others [2012] IRLR 360 (EAT)	353
Abercrombie & Fitch Italia Srl v Bordonaro [2017] IRLR 1018	492
Aberdeen City Council v McNeill [2014] IRLR 114	129
Abernethy v Mott, Hay and Anderson [1974] ICR 323, CA	165
Abertawe Bro Morgannwg University Local Health Board v Morgan [2018] EWCA Civ 640	259, 404, 527
ABM University Local Health Board v Morgan (UKEAT/ 0305/13)	404
ABN Amro Management Services Ltd & Anor v Hogben (UKEAT/0266/09)	490
Abrahall v Nottingham City Council [2018] EWCA Civ 796	47, 129
Abrahams v Performing Rights Society Ltd [1995] IRLR 486	107
Accattatis v Fortuna Group (London) Ltd (ET/3307587/2020)	169, 170, 207
Achbita v G4S Secure Solutions (Case C-157/15)	428
Adams v BT plc (EAT/0342/15)	254, 257
Adams v Kingdom Services Group Ltd (UKEAT/0235/18)	276
Addison Lee Ltd v Gascoigne (UKEAT/0289/17)	23
Adedeji v University Hospitals Birmingham NHS Foundation Trust [2021] EWCA Civ 23	259, 404
Aderemi v London and South Eastern Railway Ltd (UKEAT/0316/12)	507, 508
Adeshina v St George's University Hospitals NHS Foundation Trust and Others (UKEAT/0293/14)	191
Adesokan v Sainsbury's Supermarkets Ltd [2017] EWCA Civ 22	107
Adjei-Frempong v Howard Frank Ltd (UK/EAT/0044/15)	129
Afzal v East London Pizza Ltd (UKEAT/0265/17)	191
Agarwal v Cardiff University [2018] EWCA Civ 1434	75
Age Concern England Case C-388/07 [2009] ICR 1080	493
Ahir v British Airways plc [2017] EWCA 1392	275
Ahmad v UK (1982) 4 EHRR 126	72, 420
Ahmed v Metroline Travel UK Ltd (UKEAT/0400/10)	505
Ahmed v The Cardinal Hume Academies (UKEAT/0196/18)	471, 474
Air Products PLC v Cockram [2018] EWCA Civ 346	493
Airbus UK Ltd v Webb (UKEAT/0453/06); [2008] IRLR 309	185
Airey v Ireland (1979) 2 EHRR 305	572
Aitken v Commissioner of Police of the Metropolis (UKEAT/0226/09); [2012] ICR 78	512, 517
Akzo Coatings plc v Thompson (UKEAT/117/94)	200
Alabaster v Woolwich plc and DWP [2005] IRLR 576	414
Alboni v Ind Coope Retail Ltd [1998] IRLR 131	167, 174
Aleem v E-Act Academy Trust Ltd (UKEAT/0299/20 and 0100/20)	525
Alexander v Home Office [1988] ICR 685	409
Ali v Birmingham City Council (UKEAT/0313/08)	108
Ali v Capita Customer Management Ltd (ET/1800990/2016)	556
Ali v Capita Customer Management Ltd; Hextall v Chief Constable of Lincolnshire Police [2019] EWCA Civ 900	557
Ali v Office of National Statistics [2005] IRLR 201	272
Alidair v Taylor [1978] IRLR 82	107
All Answers Ltd v W [2021] EWCA Civ 6060	509
Allay Ltd v Gehlen (UKEAT/0031/20)	403
Allen and Another v GMB [2008] IRLR 690	461
Allen and Others v Amalgamated Construction (Case C-234/98) [2000] IRLR 119	337, 371
Allen v Flood and Taylor [1898] AC 1	377, 422
Allonby v Accrington and Rossendale College (Case C-256/01) [2004] ICR 1328	29

Allonby v Accrington and Rossendale College and Others [2001] IRLR 364   454, 460
Amaryllis v McLeod (EAT/0273/15)   347
American Cyanamid v Ethicon Ltd [1975] AC 398   118
Amey Services Ltd v Aldridge (UKEAT/0007/16)   273
Amey v Peter Symonds College [2014] IRLR 206   75
Ameyaw v PwC Services Ltd (UKEAT/0244/18)   302
Amicus v Macmillan Publishers Ltd (UKEAT/0185/07)   156
Amnesty International v Ahmed (UKEAT/0447/08), [2009] ICR 1450, [2009] IRLR 884   396, 426, 427, 432, 435
Anderson v Chesterfield High School (UKEAT/0206/14)   231
Anderson v Turning Point Eespro [2019] EWCA Civ 815   267
Andreou v Lord Chancellor's Department [2002] IRLR 728   572
Angard Staffing Solutions Ltd and Another v Kocur (UKEAT/0105/19)   34
Antovic v Montenegro (Application No 70838/13)   576
Anwar v Tower Hamlets College (UKEAT/0091/10)   508
Anyanwu v South Bank Students' Union [2001] IRLR 305, HL   274
Aparau v Iceland Frozen Foods plc [1996] IRLR 119   50
Apelogun-Gabriels v London Borough of Lambeth [2002] IRLR 116   404
Appleyard v FM Smith (Hull) Ltd [1972] IRLR 19   168
Apsden v Webb Poultry & Meat Group (Holdings) Ltd [1996] IRLR 521   180
AQ Ltd v Holden (UKEAT/0021/12)   296
Arcadia Group and Others v Telegraph Media Group Ltd [2018] EWCA Civ 2329; [2019] EWHC 96 (QB);
    [2019] EWHC 223 (QB)   304
Arch Initiatives v Greater Manchester West Mental Health NHS Foundation (EAT/0267/15)   345
Archibald v Fife Council [2004] IRLR 651   520
Argus Media Ltd v Halim [2019] EWHC 42 (QB)   61, 64
Argyll Coastal Services Ltd v Mr I Stirling and Others (UKEATS/0012/11)   347
Arjomand-Sissan v East Sussex Healthcare NHS Trust (EAT/0122/17)   213
Armitage and HM Prison Service v Johnson [1997] IRLR 162   480
Armstrong v Newcastle upon Tyne NHS Hospital Trust [2006] IRLR 124; [2019] EWCA Civ 1112   416
Arnold Clark Automobiles Ltd v Spoor [2017] IRLR 500   167
Arriva London North Ltd v Maseya (UKEAT/0096/16)   275
Arrowsmith v Nottingham Trent University [2011] EWCA Civ 797   297
Arya v London Borough of Waltham Forest (ET/3200/396/11)   384
Asda Stores Ltd v Brierley (UKEAT/0092/16)   414
Aslam and Others v Uber BV (ET/2202550/2015)   23
Asociacion Profesional Elite Taxi (Case C-434/15)   25
Associated Foreign Exchange Ltd v International Foreign Exchange (UK) Ltd [2010] EWHC 1178 (Ch)   61
Astbury v Gist Ltd [2007] All ER (D) 480   32
Astle and Others v Cheshire County Council and Another [2005] IRLR 12   341
Aston v The Martlet Group Ltd (UKEAT/02274/18)   484
Atkinson v Community Gateway Association (UKEAT/0457/12)   129, 574
Atlantic Air Ltd v Holt (UKEAT/0602/07)   129
Attorney General v Barker [2000] 1 FLR 759   296
Attorney-General v Blake and Jonathan Cape Ltd [2001] IRLR 36   119
Attridge Law v Coleman [2007] ICR 654; [2008] IRLR 722, ECJ   516
Attwood v Lamont [1920] 3 KB 571   63
Autoclenz Ltd v Belcher [2011] UKSC 41; [2010] IRLR 70, CA   11, 25, 32
Awan v ICTS UK Ltd (UKEAT/0087/18)   180
Aylott v Stockton-on-Tees Borough Council [2010] EWCA Civ 910, [2010] IRLR 994   432, 518
Ayodele v Citylink Ltd [2017] EWCA Civ 1913   442
Aziz v FDA [2010] EWCA Civ 304   405
Azmi v Kirklees Metropolitan Borough Council [2007] IRLR 484   461, 462

B

B v GMC [2018] EWCA Civ 1497   585, 586
BA Ltd v Moore and Botterill [2000] IRLR 296   551
BA plc v Pinaud [2018] EWCA Civ 2427   418
BA plc v Sturmer [2005] IRLR 862   453
Babcock FATA Ltd v Addison [1987] ICR 805, [1987] IRLR 173   229, 231
Babula v Waltham Forest College [2007] EWCA Civ 1154 , [2007] ICR 1026   213, 214
Bache v Essex County Council [2000] ICR 313   291
BAE Systems (Operations) Ltd v Konczak [2017] EWCA Civ 1188   411
Bahad v HSBC Bank plc [2022] EAT 83   275

Bailey and Others v The Home Office [2005] IRLR 369   463

Bailey v Stonewall and others (ET/2202172/2020)   385

Baker v British Gas Services Ltd [2017] EWHC 2302 (QB)   357

Baker v Commissioner of Police of the Metropolis (UKEAT/0201/09/CEA)   273

Bakkali v Greater Manchester Buses (South) Ltd t/a Stage Coach Manchester (UKEAT/0176/17)   470

Balamoody v United Kingdom Central Council for Nursing, Midwifery and Health Visiting [2002] IRLR 288   431

Baldeh v Churches Housing Association of Dudley & District (UKEAT/0290/18)   536

Baldwin v Brighton and Hove City Council [2007] ICR 680   124

Balfour Beatty Power Networks Ltd v Wilcox [2007] IRLR 63   294, 340

Balkaya v Kiesel Abbruch- und Recycling Technik GmbH (Case C-229/14)   23, 154

Ball v First Essex Buses Ltd (ET/3201435/17)   195

Bamsey and Others v Albion Engineering and Manufacturing plc [2004] IRLR 457   87

Banaszczyk v Booker Ltd (UKEAT/0132/15)   507

Bancroft, Mr S v Interserve (Facilities Management) Ltd (UKEAT/0329/12)   169

Bank of Credit and Commerce International SA (in compulsory liquidation) v Ali and Others (No 3) [2002] IRLR 460   114

Bank of Credit and Commerce International SA (in liquidation) v Ali and Others (No 1) [2001] 2 WLR 735   305

Banks v Ablex Ltd [2005] IRLR 357   476

Barber and Others v RJB Mining (UK) Ltd [1999] IRLR 308   82

Barber v Guardian Royal Exchange Assurance Group (Case C-262/88) [1990] 2 All ER 660, [1990] IRLR 240   3

Barbulescu v Romania [2016] ECHR 61   574

Barclays Bank plc v Kapur [1989] IRLR 387   395

Barclays Bank v Various Claimants plc [2020] UKSC 13   399

Barlow v Stone [2012] IRLR 898   403

Barnsley Metropolitan BC v Yerrakalva [2011] EWCA Civ 1255   297

Bartholomew v London Borough of Hackney [1999] IRLR 246   42

Bartholomews Agri Food Ltd v Thornton [2016] EWHC 648 (QB)   61, 63

Barton v Greenwich LBC (UKEAT/0041/14)   211

Barton v Investec Securities Ltd [2003] ICR 1205, [2003] IRLR 332   439, 478

Barton v Royal Borough of Greenwich (UKEAT/0041/14)   215

Base Childrenswear Ltd v Otshudi (UKEAT/0267/18)   409

Base Childrenswear Ltd v Otshudi [2019] EWCA Civ 1648   443

Basildon Academies, The v Amadi and Fox (EAT/0342/14)   46

Basildon and Thurrock NHS Foundation Trust v Weerasinghe [2016] ICR 305   530

Basra v BJSS Ltd (UKEAT/0090/17)   310

Bass Leisure Ltd v Thomas [1994] IRLR 104   143

Bathgate v Technip UK Ltd [2022] EAT 155   308

BBC Scotland v Souster [2001] IRLR 150   380

BBC v Roden (UKEAT/0385/14)   287

BC and Others v Chief Constable Police Service of Scotland [2019] CSOH 48   193, 574

BDW Trading Ltd v Kopec (UKEAT/0197/19)   475

Bear Scotland Ltd v Fulton; Hertel (UK) Ltd v Woods; Amec Group Ltd v Law [2015] IRLR 15   76, 89

Beasley v National Grid (UKEAT/0626/06)   257

Beatt v Croydon Health Services NHS Trust [2017] EWCA Civ 401, [2017] IRLR 748   213, 216

Beattie v Condorrat War Memorial and Social Club (EATS/0019/17)   186

Beckett Investment Management Group Limited v Hall [2007] EWCA Civ 613   62

Beckford v London Borough of Southwark (EAT/0210/14)   408

Beddell v West Ferry Printers [2000] ICR 1263   198

Bellman v Northampton Recruitment Ltd [2017] ICR 543; [2018] EWCA Civ 2214   400

Benkharbouche and Anor v Embassy of the Republic of Sudan [2015] IRLR 301   134, 572

Benkharbouche v Secretary of State for Foreign and Commonwealth Affairs [2017] UKSC 62   572

Bensaid v UK (2001) EHRR 205   574

Bernardone v Pall Mall Services Group and Others [2000] IRLR 487   357

Berriman v Delabole Slate Ltd [1985] ICR 546   362

Bessong v Pennine Care NHS Foundation Trust (UKEAT/0247/18)   475

Bethnal Green and Shoreditch Education Trust v Dippenaar (UKEAT/0064/15)   127, 176

Betsi Cadwaladr University Health Board v Hughes and Others (UKEAT/0179/13)   474

Beynon v Scadden [1999] IRLR 700   298

BHS Ltd v Burchell [1980] ICR 303, [1978] IRLR 379   173, 203

Birmingham City Council v Abdulla and Others [2012] UKSC 47   413, 416

Birmingham City Council v EOC [1989] AC 1155   435

Birtenshaw v Oldfield (UKEAT/0288/18)   535

BIS v Studders (UKEAT/0571/10)   33

Blackbay Ventures Ltd v Gahir [2014] ICR 747, [2014] IRLR 416   210, 214

Bliss v South East Thames Regional Health Authority [1985] IRLR 308   114

Blitz v Vectone Group Holdings Ltd (UKEAT/0253/10)   210
Blockbuster Entertainment Ltd v James [2006] IRLR 630, CA   274
Blundell v Governing Body of St Andrew's Catholic Primary School [2007] IRLR 652   547
BMC Software Ltd v Shaikh (UKEAT/0092/16)   416
BMI Healthcare Ltd v Shoukrey (UKEAT/0336/19)   218
Board of Governors of St Matthias Church of England School v Crizzle [1993] ICR 401   461
Bolch v Chipman [2004] IRLR 140   274
Bold v Brough, Nicholson & Hall Ltd [1964] 1 WLR 201   117
Bolton School v Evans [2006] IRLR 500   214
Booth v Pasta King UK Ltd (ET/1401231/2014)   262
Born London Ltd v Spire Production Services Ltd (UKEAT/0255/16)   357, 366
Boston Deep Sea Fishing and Ice Co v Ansell (1888) 39 Ch D 339   44, 107
Botta v Italy (1998) 26 EHRR 241   574
Botzen v Rotterdamsche Droogdok Maatschappij BV (Case 186/83) [1986] 2 CMLR 50   353
Bougnaoui v Micropole Univers (Case C-188/15)   428
Bournemouth University Higher Education Corporation v Buckland (UKEAT/0492/08)   125
Bournemouth University Higher Education Corporation v Buckland [2010] EWCA Civ 121   173
Bowater v North West London Hospitals NHS Trust [2010] IRLR 331   301
Bowes v Hambleton District Council (ET/2500475/16)   31
Bowyer v Siemens Communications (UKEAT/0021/05)   221
Boxer v Excel Group Services Ltd (ET/3200365/2016)   23
Boyd v Renfrewshire Council [2008] CSIH 36   185
Boyo v Lambeth London Borough Council [1994] ICR 727, [1995] IRLR 50   108, 111
Boyraz v Turkey [2015] IRLR 164   579
Boys and Girls Welfare Society [1996] IRLR 129   193
Brace v Calder and Others [1895] 2 QB 253   115
Braganza v BP Shipping Ltd and Another [2015] UKSC 17   113
Braine v The National Gallery (ET/2201625/2018)   18
Braithwaite and Others v HCL Insurance BPO Services Ltd and Another (EAT/152/14/DM; 0153/14)   495
Brangwyn v South Warwickshire NHS Foundation Trust [2018] EWCA Civ 2235   453
Bray v Monarch Personnel Refuelling (UK) Ltd (ET/1801581/12)   34
Breeze Benton Solicitors v Miss A Weddell (UKEAT/0873/03)   573
Brennan and Others v Sunderland City Council and Others (UKEAT/0286/11)   412
Brennan and others v Sunderland City Council and others [2008] ICR 479   280
Brent v Fuller [2011] ICR 806   301, 302
Brentwood Brothers (Manchester) Ltd v Shepherd [2003] IRLR 364   117
Bressol v Gouvernement de la Communauté Française (Case C-73/08)   461
Brettle, White & Others v Dudley Metropolitan Borough Council (ET/1300537/15)   89
Brighton & Sussex University Hospitals HNS Trust v Akinwunmi (UKEAT/0345/16)   195
British Aerospace plc v Green [1995] IRLR 433   197
British Airways v Starmer [2005] IRLR 862   463
British Coal Corporation v Keeble [1997] IRLR 336   404
British Coal v Keeble [1997] IRLR 336   259
British Council v Jeffrey [2018] EWCA Civ 2253   378
British Gas v Sharma [1991] IRLR 101   407
British Home Stores v Burchell [1978] IRLR 379   193, 242
British Newspaper Printing Corporation (North) Ltd v Kelly [1989] IRLR 222   272
British Nursing Association (BNA) v Inland Revenue [2002] IRLR 480   53
British Transport Commission v Gourley [1955] 3 All ER 796, [1956] AC 185   116, 235, 236
British Transport Police v Norman (UKEAT/0348/14)   404
British Waterways Board v Smith (UKEAT/0004/15)   192, 579
Brookes and Others v Borough Care Services and CLS Care Services Ltd [1998] IRLR 636   336
Brooknight Guarding Ltd v Matei (UKEAT/0309/17)   35
Brown v Controlled Packaging Services Ltd (ET/1402252/98)   83
Brown v Merchant Ferries [1998] IRLR 682   125
Brown v Rentokil Ltd [1998] IRLR 445   437, 551
Browne v Associated Newspapers Ltd [2007] EWCA Civ 295   574
Brumfitt v MOD [2005] IRLR 4   470
BT Managed Services Ltd v Edwards & Another (UKEAT/0241/14)   354, 355
Buchanan v Commissioner of Police of the Metropolis (UKEAT/0112/16)   530
Buchanan v Tilcon Ltd [1983] IRLR 417   198
Bull and Another v Hall and Another [2013] UKSC 73   436
Bullimore v Pothecary Witham Weld Solicitors (No 2) [2011] IRLR 18 (EAT)   408
Bullivant v Ellis [1987] ICR 464   57

Bunce v Skyblue [2005] IRLR 557 — 32
Bunning v GT Bunning & Sons Ltd [2005] EWCA Civ 293 — 128
Burdett v Aviva Employment Services Ltd (UKEAT/0439/13) — 535
Burke v Turning Point Scotland (ETS/4112457/2021) — 510, 512
Burlo v Langley & Carter [2006] EWCA Civ 1778 — 224, 229
Burn v Alder Hey Children's NHS Foundation Trust [2021] EWCA Civ 1791 — 42
Burton and Another v De Vere Hotels [1996] IRLR 596 — 474
Bury Metropolitan Borough Council v Hamilton and Others; Council of the City of Sunderland v Brennan and Others (UKEAT/0413–5/09), [2011] 1 ICR 655 — 415
Bvunzai v Glasgow City Council [2005] CSIH 85 — 443
Byrne Brothers (Formwork) Ltd v Baird and Others [2002] IRLR 96 — 10, 20
Byrne v FT Ltd [1991] IRLR 417 — 276

C

C v Police and Secretary of State for the Home Department (November 2014, IPT/03/32) — 587
CAB Automotive Ltd v Blake and Others (UKEAT/0298/07) — 361
Cable & Wireless plc v Muscat [2006] IRLR 354, CA — 32
Cable Realisations Ltd v GMB Northern [2010] IRLR 42 — 369
Cadent Gas Ltd v Singh (UKEAT/0024/19) — 206
Cadman v Health & Safety Executive [2004] IRLR 971 — 492
Cadogan Hotel Partners Ltd v Ozog (UKEAT/0001/14) — 177, 408, 480
Calmac Ferries Ltd v Wallace & Another (UKEATS/0014/13) — 415
Cambridge and Peterborough Foundation NHS Trust v Crouchman [2009] ICR 1306 — 258
Campbell and Cosans v UK (1982) 4 EHRR 293 — 382
Campbell v Frisbee [2003] ICR 141 — 58, 64
Campbell v Mirror Group Newspapers plc [2004] UKHL 22 — 574
Campbell v OCS Group UK Ltd (UKEAT/0188/16) — 284
Canadian Imperial Bank of Commerce v Beck [2009] EWCA Civ 619, [2009] IRLR 740 — 277, 280
Canniffe v East Riding of Yorkshire Council [2000] IRLR 555 — 402
Canning v NICE (EAT/0241/18) — 198
Cantor Fitzgerald International v Callaghan and Others [1999] IRLR 234 — 124
Caparo Industries v Dickman [1990] 2 AC 605 — 42
Cape v Dring [2019] UKSC 38 — 288
Capek v Lincolnshire County Council [2000] IRLR 590 — 103
Capita Hartshead Ltd v Byard (UKEAT/0445/11) — 198
Capita Health Solutions v BBC and McLean (UKEAT/0034/07) — 356
Capita Translation v Siauciunas (UKEAT/0181/16) — 30
Carillion Services Ltd (In Compulsory Liquidation) and Others v Benson and Others (UKEAT/0026/21/BA) — 156
Carmichael v National Power [2000] IRLR 43 — 14, 28
Carphone Warehouse plc v Martin (UKEAT/0371/12) — 519
Carreras v United First Partners Research (UKEAT/0266/15) — 520
Carsway Cleansing Consultants Ltd v Richards & Cooper Cleaning Services (UKEAT/629/97) — 354
Casamitjana Costa v The League Against Cruel Sports (ET/3331129/2018) — 384
Caspersz v Ministry of Defence (UKEAT/0599/05) — 402
Casqueiro v Barclays Bank plc (UKEAT/0085/12) — 297
Catamaran Cruises Ltd v Williams [1994] IRLR 386 — 204
Catt v English Table Tennis Association [2022] EAT 125 — 22
Cave v Goodwin and Another [2001] EWCA Civ 391 — 518
Cavenagh v Williams Evans Ltd [2012] EWCA Civ 697 — 108
Cavendish Munro Professional Risks Management Ltd v Geduld [2010] IRLR 38 — 210
CD v ST [2014] EUECJ C-167/12 — 438, 553
CEF Holdings Ltd and Another v Mundey and Others [2012] EWHC 1524 (QB) — 64
Celtec v Astley (Case C-478/03) [2005] IRLR 647 — 349
Central and NW London NHS Trust v Ambimbola (UKEAT/0542/08) — 220
Cerberus Software Ltd v Rowley [2001] IRLR 160 — 116
Cetinsoy & Others v London United Busways Ltd (UKEAT/0042/14) — 353
Cex Ltd v Lewis [2007] UKEAT/0013/07 — 227
Chabra v West London Mental Health NHS Trust [2014] ICR 194 — 190
Chacón Navas v Eurest Colectividades SA (Case C-13/05) [2006] IRLR 706 — 503, 514
Chadburn v Doncaster & Bassetlaw Hospital NHS Foundation Trust (UKEAT/0259/14) — 297
Chairman & Governors of Amwell View School v Dogherty [2007] IRLR 198 — 293
Chakki v United Yeast Co Ltd [1982] 2 All ER 446 — 110
Chandhok v Tirkey (UKEAT/0190/14), [2015] ICR 527 — 274, 381

Chandler v Thanet District Council (ET/2301782/14) 262
Charlesworth v Dransfields Engineering Services Ltd (UKEAT/0197/16) 531
Chatfeild-Roberts v Phillips and Another (UKEAT/0049/18) 15, 24
Cheesman v R Brewer Contracts [2001] IRLR 144 340
Cherfi v G4S Security Services Ltd (UKEAT/0379/10) 462
Chesterton Global Ltd v Nurmohamed [2017] EWCA Civ 979 211
CHEZ Razpredelenie Bulgaria (Case C-83/14) 427, 459
Chidzoy v BBC (UKEAT/0097/17) 275
Chief Constable of Avon Constabulary v Chew (UKEAT/503/00), [2001] All ER (D) 101 (Sep) 455
Chief Constable of Dumfries and Galloway Constabulary v Mr C Adams (UKEATS/0046/08) 507
Chief Constable of Greater Manchester Police v Bailey [2017] EWCA Civ 425 428, 483
Chief Constable of Gwent Police v Parsons and another (UKEAT/0143/18) 529
Chief Constable of Lincolnshire Police v Stubbs [1999] IRLR 81 397, 398
Chief Constable of Lothian and Borders Police v Cumming (UKEATS/0077/08) 507
Chief Constable of Norfolk v Coffey [2019] EWCA Civ 1061 512, 513
Chief Constable of Northern Ireland v Agnew [2019] NICA 32 77, 91
Chief Constable of Northumbria Police v Erichsen (UKEAT/0027/15) 233
Chief Constable of West Midlands Police v Gardner (UKEAT/0174/11) 113
Chief Constable of West Midlands Police v Harrod [2015] IRLR 790 460
Chief Constable of West Midlands Police v Harrod and others [2017] ICR 869 197
Chief Constable of West Yorkshire Police v Homer [2009] IRLR 262; [2010] All ER (D) 189; [2013] EQLR 295 495
Chief Constable of West Yorkshire Police v Khan [2001] 1 WLR 1947, [2001] IRLR 830 428, 435, 482
Chief Constable of West Yorkshire v Vento [2001] IRLR 124 430
Chindove v Morrisons Supermarkets plc (UKEAT/0201/13 and UKEAT/0043/14) 129
Chouafi v London United Busways Ltd [2006] EWCA Civ 689 258
Christie v Paul, Weiss, Rifkind, Wharton and Garrison LLP (UKEAT/0137/19) 282
Church v West Lancashire NHS Trust [1998] IRLR 4 147
Citibank NA & Ors v Kirk [2022] EAT 103 490
City of Bradford Metropolitan Council v Arora [1991] IRLR 165, CA 410
City of Oxford Bus Services Ltd v Harvey (UKEAT/0171/18) 463
City of York Council v Grosset [2018] EWCA Civ 1105 531
Clark & Tokely Ltd (t/a Spellbrook Ltd) v Oakes [1998] 4 All ER 353 336
Clark v (1) Clark Construction Initiatives Ltd (2) Utility Consultancy Services Ltd (UKEAT/0225/07) 36
Clark v BET plc and Another [1997] IRLR 348 113
Clark v Fahrenheit 451 (Communications) Ltd (UKEAT/591/99) 47, 104
Clark v Nomura International plc [2000] IRLR 766 113
Clark v Novacold Ltd [1999] IRLR 318 528
Clarke v Telewest Communications plc (ET/1301034/04) 559
Clarks of Hove Ltd v The Bakers' Union [1978] IRLR 366 155
CLFIS (UK) Ltd v Reynolds [2015] EWCA Civ 549 434
Clyde & Co LLP and Another v Bates van Winkelhof [2012] EWCA Civ 1207, [2012] IRLR 992, CA 137, 138, 378
Clyde & Co LLP and Another v Bates van Winkelhof [2014] UKSC 32, [2014] IRLR 641 22, 209
Cobb v Employment Secretary [1989] IRLR 464 460
Cocking v Sandhurst [1974] ICR 650 272
Coldridge v HM Prison Service (UKEAT/0728/04) 256
Coleman v EBR Attridge Law LLP and Another (ET/2303745/2005); (UKEAT/0071/09) 516
Coles v Ministry of Defence (UKEAT/0403/14) 34
Collidge v Freeport plc [2008] EWCA Civ 485 307
Collins v National Trust (ET/2507255/05) 215
Collins v Royal National Theatre Board Ltd [2004] EWCA Civ 144, [2004] IRLR 395 522
Collins v Secretary of State for Trade and Industry (UKEAT/1460/99) 109
Commerzbank AG v Keen [2006] EWCA Civ 1536 113
Commerzbank AG v Rajput (UKEAT/0164/18) 436, 441
Commission for Healthcare Audit and Inspection v Ward (UKEAT/0579/07) 148
Commission v Hungary (Case C-286/12) 489
Commissioner of Police for the Metropolis v Shaw (UKEAT/0125/11) 409
Commissioner of the City of London Police v Geldart (UKEAT/0032/19) 432
Commissioner of the City of London Police v Geldart [2021] EWCA Civ 611 551
Commissioners for HM Revenue and Customs v Atholl House Productions Ltd [2022] IRLR 698 12
Commissioners for HMRC v Jones and Others T/A Holmescales Riding Centre (UKEAT/0458/13) 31
Compass Group UK and Ireland Ltd v Morgan (UKEAT/0060/16) 254
Conisbee v Crossley Farms Ltd (ET/3335357/18) 384
Conn v Sunderland City Council [2007] EWCA Civ 1492 476
Contract Bottling Ltd v Cave (UKEAT/0525/12) 231

Conway v Community Options (UKEAT/0034/12) — 524
Cook v MSHK Ltd and Ministry of Sound Recordings Ltd [2009] EWCA Civ 624 — 107
Cooke v Glenrose Fish Co Ltd [2004] IRLR 866 — 291
Cooper Contracting Ltd v Lindsey (EAT/0184/15) — 228
Co-operative Group v Walker (UKEAT/0087/19) — 416
Copland v UK [2007] ECHR 253 — 574
Coppage & Another v Safetynet Security Ltd [2013] EWCA Civ 1176 — 61
Copsey v WWB Devon Clays Ltd [2005] IRLR 811 — 577
Cordant Security Ltd v Singh & Another (EAT/0144/15) — 394
Cordell v Foreign and Commonwealth Office (UKEAT/0016/11), [2012] ICR 280 — 432, 517, 524
Cornwall County Council v Prater (UKEAT/0055/05); [2006] EWCA Civ 102; [2006] IRLR 362 — 13, 132
Corus UK Ltd v Mainwaring (UKEAT/0053/07) — 189
Cosmeceuticals Ltd v Parkin (UKEAT/0049/17) — 130
Cossington v C2C Rail Ltd (UKEAT/0053/13) — 294
Costain v Armitage (UKEAT/0048/14) — 354
Cotswold Developments Construction Ltd v Williams (UKEAT/0457/05) — 21, 28
Council of the City of Newcastle upon Tyne v Allan and Others [2005] IRLR 504 — 416
Coventry v Lawrence [2015] UKSC 50 — 304
Cowen v Rentokil Ltd (UKEAT/0473/07) — 224
Cowley v Manson Timber Ltd [1995] ICR 367 — 219
Cox v Adecco (UKEAT/0339/19) — 274
Cox v Ministry of Justice [2016] UKSC 10 — 398
Cox v Sun Alliance Life Ltd [2001] IRLR 448 — 43
CPL Distribution Ltd v Todd [2003] IRLR 23 — 353
Craig v Abellio Ltd [2022] EAT 43 — 127
Cranwell v Cullen UKEATS/0046/14 — 253
Crawford and Another v Suffolk Mental Health Partnership NHS Trust [2012] IRLR 402 — 172
Credit Suisse First Boston (Europe) Ltd v Lister [1998] IRLR 700 — 358
Credit Suisse First Boston (Europe) Ltd v Padiachy and Others [1998] IRLR 504 — 358
Crew Employment v Gold (UKEAT/0330/19) — 137
Crisp v Apple Retail UK Ltd (ET/1500258/11) — 192, 292, 578
Croft Vets Ltd v Butcher (UKEAT/0430/12) — 524
Croke v Hydro Aluminium Worcester Ltd [2007] ICR 1303 — 29
Cromwell Garage Ltd v Doran (UKEAT/0369/10) — 441
Cross and Others v BA plc [2005] IRLR 423 — 455
Crowson Fabrics Ltd v Rider and Others [2007] EWHC 2942 (Ch) — 44
Cruickshank v VAW Motorcast Ltd [2002] IRLR 24 — 506, 513
CT Plus (Yorkshire) CIC v Black and Others (UKEAT/0035/16) — 345
Cumbria County Council & Governing Body of Dowdales School v Bates (UKEAT/0398/11 & 0039/13) — 232
Cummins Ltd v Mohammed (UKEAT/0039/20) — 533
Curr v Marks & Spencer plc [2003] IRLR 74 — 133

D

D'Silva v NATFHE (UKEAT/0384/07) — 406
D'Silva v NATFHE [2008] IRLR 412 — 431
Da Costa v Optalis [1976] IRLR 178 — 194
Da'Bell v NSPCC (UKEAT/0227/09) — 408, 480
Dabson v David Cover & Sons (UKEAT/0374/2011) — 200
Dacas v Brook Street Bureau (UK) Ltd [2004] IRLR 358 — 32, 37
Dafiaghor-Olomu v Community Integrated Care (UKEAT/0001/17) — 219
Dafiaghor-Olomu v Community Integrated Care [2022] EAT 84, [2022] IRLR 763 — 232
Dahou v Serco Ltd [2016] EWCA Civ 832 — 206
Dansk Jurist- og Økonomforbund v Indenrigs- og Sundhadsministeriet [2013] EUECJ C-546/11 — 460
Darlington Memorial Hospital NHS Trust v Edwards and Vincent (UKEAT/678/95) — 200
Dattani v Chief Constable of West Mercia Police [2005] IRLR 327 — 406
Davies v Sandwell MBC [2013] EWCA Civ 135 — 173, 185, 270, 290
Dawnay, Day & Co Ltd v Braconier d'Alphen & Others [1997] IRLR 442 — 59
Dawson-Damer v Taylor Wessing LLP [2017] EWCA Civ 74 — 586
Day v Lewisham & Greenwich NHS Trust [2017] EWCA Civ 329 — 29
Day v T Pickles Farms Ltd [1999] IRLR 217 — 552
DB Schenker Rail (UK) Ltd v Doolan (UKEATS/0053/09) — 179
De Belin v Eversheds Legal Services Ltd (ET/1804069/09) — 199
De Keyser Ltd v Wilson [2001] IRLR 324 — 286

De Mota v (1) ADR Network and (2) The Co-operative Group Ltd (UKEAT/0305/16)   254
De Souza v Automobile Association [1986] ICR 514   395
De Souza v Vinci Construction UK Ltd [2017] EWCA Civ 879   409
Deer v University of Oxford [2015] EWCA Civ 52   483
Deer v University of Oxford [2015] ICR 1213   394
Delaney v Staples [1991] IRLR 112, [1992] 1 All ER 944   74, 116
Delaney v Staples [1992] IRLR 191   74
Department for Employment and Learning v Morgan [2016] IRLR 350   37
Department for Work and Pensions v Coulson (UKEAT/0572/12)   225
Department for Work and Pensions v Hall (UKEAT/0012/05)   526
Department of Work and Pensions v Boyers (UKEAT/0282/19)   535
Devlin v UK [2002] IRLR 155   572
Dewhurst v CitySprint UK Ltd (ET/220512/2016)   23
Dewhurst v Revisecatch Ltd t/a Ecourier (ET/2201909/18)   335, 351
DH and Others v The Czech Republic (App No 57325/00)   420
DHL Supply Chain Ltd v Fazackerley (UKEAT/0019/18)   258
Dhunna v Creditsights Ltd [2014] EWCA Civ 1238   137
Digital Equipment Co Ltd v Clements (No 2) [1998] IRLR 134, CA   232
Diosynth Ltd v Thomson [2006] IRLR 284   185
Dixon v GB Eye Ltd (ET/2203642/10)   292
Dizedziak v Future Electronics Ltd (UKEAT/0270/11)   380
DKW Ltd v Adebayo [2005] IRLR 514   443
DL Insurance Services Ltd v O'Connor (UKEAT/0230/17)   534
Dobbie v Felton t/a Feltons Solicitors (EAT/0130/20)   213
Dobson v North Cumbria Integrated Care NHS Foundation Trust (UKEAT/0220/19)   454
Dodd v British Telecommunications [1988] IRLR 16   273
Dominique v Toll Global Forwarding Ltd (UKEAT/0308/13)   534
Donelien v Liberata UK Ltd (UKEAT/0297/14)   536
Donelien v Liberata UK Ltd [2018] EWCA Civ 129, [2018] IRLR 535   526, 536
Donkor v Royal Bank of Scotland (EAT/0162/15)   496
Douglas v Birmingham City Council (UKEAT/0518/02)   213
Douglas v Hello! [2005] EWCA Civ 595   574
Drake International Systems Ltd and Others v Blue Arrow Ltd (EAT/0282/15)   253
Drake International Systems Ltd v O'Hare (UKEAT/0384/03)   198
Drake v Ipsos Mori UK Ltd (UKEAT/0604/11)   12
Dray Simpson v Cantor Fitzgerald Europe [2021] EWCA Civ 559   211, 217
Driskel v Peninsula Business Services Ltd [2000] IRLR 151   478
Drysdale v Department of Transport (The Maritime and Coastguard Agency) [2014] EWCA Civ 1083   265
Duchy Farm Kennels Ltd v Steels [2020] EWHC 1208 (QB)   309
Dugdale v DDE Law Ltd (UKEAT/0169/16)   37
Duncan Webb Offset (Maidstone) Ltd v Cooper and Others [1995] IRLR 633   353
Duncombe and Others v Secretary of State for Children, Schools and Families [2011] UKSC 14;
    [2011] UKSC 36   135, 419
Dunhoe v Support Services Group Ltd (in liquidation) (UKEAT/0102/15)   300
Dunn & Another v AAH Ltd [2010] EWCA Civ 183   107
Dunn v Secretary of State for Justice [2018] EWCA Civ 1998   532
Dunn v University of Lincoln (ET/2601819/17)   384
Dunnachie v Kingston Upon Hull [2004] IRLR 727   223, 229
Dunne v Colin & Avril Ltd (UKEAT/0293/16)   148
DWP v Alan (UKEAT/0242/09)   526, 535
Dykes v Whitbread Group plc [2022] IRLR 499   284
Dynamex Friction Ltd and Another v Amicus and Others [2008] IRLR 515   361
Dziedziak v Future Electronics Ltd (UKEAT/0270/11)   434

E

EAGA plc v Tideswell (UKEAT/0007/11)   173
Eagland v British Telecommunications plc [1992] IRLR 323   40
East Kent Hospitals University NHS Foundation Trust v Levy (UKEAT/0232/17)   108
East Lancs Coachbuilders Ltd v Hilton (UKEAT/0054/06)   166
East London NHS Trust v O'Connor (UKEAT/0113/19)   149
East v Valentine (UKEAT/0325/16)   78
Eastlands Homes Partnership Ltd v Cunningham (UKEAT/0272/13)   184
Eastwood v Magnox; McCabe v Cornwall County Council and Another [2004] IRLR 733   114, 115, 223

EB v BA [2006] EWCA Civ 132 — 441
EB v France (App No 43546/02) — 420
ECM (Vehicle Delivery Service) Ltd v Cox and Others [1999] IRLR 559 — 340
Eddie Stobart Ltd v Moreman [2012] IRLR 356 — 347
Edmund Nuttall Ltd v Butterfield [2006] ICR 77 — 504
Edwards v Chesterfield Royal Hospital NHS Foundation Trust [2010] IRLR 702 — 112
Edwards v Chesterfield Royal Hospital NHS Foundation Trust [2013] UKSC 58 — 223
Edwards v Encirc Ltd (UKEAT/0367/14) — 79
Edwards v Governors of Hanson School [2001] IRLR 733 — 180
EF v AB (UKEAT/0525/13) — 287
Efobi v Royal Mail Group (UKEAT/0203/16); [2019] EWCA Civ 18 — 442
Egg Stores (Stamford Hill) Ltd v Leibovici [1976] IRLR 376 — 109
Eiger Securities LLP v Korshunova (UKEAT/0149/16), [2017] ICR 561, [2017] IRLR 115 — 213, 214, 217
Electronic Data Systems Ltd v Hanbury and Brook Street Bureau (UKEAT/128/00) — 33
Elliot v Whitworth Centre Ltd (UKEAT/0030/13) — 572
Elliott v Dorsett CC (UKEAT/0197/20) — 507
Ellis v Brighton & Hove Golf Club (ET/2301658/2014) — 253
Ellis v Ratcliffe Palfinger Ltd (UKEAT/0438/13) — 561
El-Megrisi v Azad University (IR) in Oxford (UKEAT/0448/08) — 217
EMI Group Electronics Ltd v Coldicott (Inspector of Taxes) [1999] IRLR 630, [1999] STC 803 — 107, 116
Enamejewa v British Gas Trading Ltd (UKEAT/0347/14) — 283
Enfield Technical Services Limited v Payne; Grace v BF Components Limited [2008] IRLR 500 — 7
English v Thomas Sanderson Blinds Ltd [2008] IRLR 342 — 471
Enterprise Liverpool Ltd v Jonas and Others (UKEAT/0112/09) — 273
Enterprise Management Services Ltd v Connect-Up Ltd and Others (UKEAT/0462/10) — 348
Environment Agency v Rowan (UKEAT/0060/07), [2008] IRLR 20 — 453, 518
Equal Opportunities Commission v Secretary of State for Trade and Industry [2007] IRLR 327 — 469
Essa v Laing Ltd [2004] IRLR 313 — 410
Essop v Home Office; Naeem v Secretary of State for Justice [2017] UKSC 27, [2017] IRLR 558 — 391, 457
Eurobrokers Ltd v Rabey [1995] IRLR 206 — 65
Evans v Malley Organisation Ltd [2003] ICR 432, CA — 88
Evans v Xactly Corporation Ltd (UKEAT/0128/18) — 471
Eversheds v De Belin (UKEAT/0352/10) — 438
Eweida & Others v UK [2013] ECHR 37, [2013] IRLR 231 — 420, 456, 462, 577
Eweida v British Airways [2009] IRLR 78 — 456
Exmore Ales Ltd and Another v Herriot (UKEAT/0075/18) — 18
Express and Echo Publications v Tanton [1999] IRLR 367 — 15
Ezsias v North Glamorgan NHS Trust (UKEAT/0399/09), [2011] IRLR 550 — 168, 180, 204
Ezsias v North Glamorgan NHS Trust [2007] EWCA Civ 330 — 285

F

Faccenda Chicken Ltd v Fowler [1986] 1 All ER 617 — 45, 57
Fairhurst Ward Abbotts Limited v Botes Building Limited [2004] IRLR 304 — 340
Faithorn Farrell Timms LLP v Bailey (UKEAT/0025/16) — 309
Faleye and Another v UK Mission Enterprise Ltd (UKEAT/0359/10) — 268
Fallahi v TWI (UKEAT/0140/19) — 185
Fallows v News Group Newspapers (UKEAT/0075/16) — 288
Famatina Development Corporation Ltd, In re [1914] 2 Ch 271 — 41
Fareham College v Walters (UKEAT/0396/08) — 521
Fathers v Pets at Home Ltd and anor (UKEAT/0424/13) — 512
FC Shepherd & Co Ltd v Jerrom [1987] 1 QB 301 — 109
FCO and others v Bamieh [2019] IRLR 736 — 378
FDR Ltd v Holloway [1995] IRLR 400 — 198
Fecitt v NHS Manchester [2012] IRLR 64 — 217
Federación de Servicios de Comisiones Obreras v Deutsche Bank SAE (Case C-55/18) — 80
Federación de Servicios Privados del sindicato Comisiones obreras v Tyco Integrated Security SL (Case C-266/14) — 78
Fenoll v Centre d'aide par le travail 'La Jouvene' (Case C-316/13) [2016] IRLR 67 — 22
Fincham v HM Prison Service (UKEAT/0925/01 and 0991/01) — 211
Finn v British Bung Manufacturing Co Ltd (ET/1803764/21) — 471
First Great Western & Linley v Waiyego (UKEAT/0056/18) — 407
First Leeds v Haigh (UKEAT/0246/07) — 180
Fisher v Hoopoe Finance Ltd (UKEAT/0043/05) — 200
Fitzgerald v University of Kent at Canterbury [2004] IRLR 300 — 131

Flatman v Essex CC (UK/EAT/0097/20)   128
Flowers v East of England Ambulance Trust [2019] EWCA Civ 947   90
FOA, acting on behalf of Karsten Kaltoft v Kommunernes Lansforening (KL) (Case C-354/13) [2015] ICR 322   505, 514
Focus Care Agency Ltd v Roberts, Frudd v The Partington Group Ltd and Royal Mencap Society v Tomlinson-Blake
    (UKEAT/0143/16)   53
Fogarty v UK [2002] IRLR 148   572
Follows v Nationwide Building Society (ET/2201937/18)   427, 516, 537
Foot v Eastern Counties Timber Co Ltd [1972] IRLR 83   168
Forbes v LHR Airport Ltd (UKEAT/0174/18)   193, 400
Ford v Warwickshire CC [1983] ICR 273   132
Foreign and Commonwealth Office v Bamieh [2019] EWCA Civ 803   139
Foreningen af Arbejdsledere I Danmark v Daddy's Dance Hall A/S [1988] IRLR 315   365
Forstater v CGD Europe and others (ET/2200909/19)   382
Forth Valley Healthcare Board v John Campbell (UKEAT/0003/21)   418
Four Seasons Healthcare Ltd v Maughan [2005] IRLR 324   110
Fox Cross Claimants v Glasgow CC [2013] ICR 954   414
Fox, H (Father of G Fox, deceased) v BA plc (UKEAT/0315/14)   453
Franco v Bowling and Co (UKEAT/0280/09)   271
Francovich (Andrea) and Bonifaci (Danila) v Italy (Cases C-6 and 9/90) [1992] IRLR 84   4
Franks v Reuters and Another [2003] IRLR 423   32
Fraser v HLMAD [2006] EWCA Civ 738   102
Frewer v Google UK Ltd & Ors [2022] EAT 34   288
Frewin v Consignia plc [2003] All ER (D) 314 (Jul)   180
Fries (Case C-190/16)   489
Frith Accountants Ltd v Law (EAT/0460/13)   231
Frudd v Partington Group (UKEAT/0240/18)   54
Fulcrum Pharma (Europe) Ltd v Bonassera and Another (UKEAT/0198/10)   198
Fuller v London Borough of Brent [2011] EWCA Civ 267, [2011] IRLR 414   172, 196
Fuller v United Healthcare Services Inc (UKEAT/0464/13)   139
Furlong v Chief Constable of Cheshire Police (ET/2405577/2018)   394
Futty v Brekkes (D & D) Ltd [1974] IRLR 130   123

G

G v Headteacher and Governors of St Gregory's Catholic Science College [2011] EWHC 1452 (Admin)   452, 456
G4S Cash Solutions (UK) Ltd v Powell (UKEAT/0243/15)   525
G4S Justice Services (UK) Ltd v Anstey [2006] IRLR 588   351
GAB Robins v Triggs [2008] IRLR 317   223
Gago v Uneek Clothing Co Ltd (ET/1600212/16)   471
Gale v Northern General Hospital [1994] IRLR 292   353
Gallacher v Abellio Scotrail Ltd (UKEATS/0027/19)   176
Gallacher v Alpha Catering Services [2005] IRLR 102   85
Gallop v Newport CC [2013] EWCA Civ 1583   526
Gamatronic (UK) Ltd v Hamilton [2016] EWHC 2225 (QB)   118
Gan Menachem Hendon Ltd v De Groen (UKEAT/0059/18)   383, 434
Garamukanwa v United Kingdom (Application No 70573/17) [2019] 6 WLUK 109   576
Gareddu v London Underground Ltd (UKEAT/0086/16)   382
Gay v Sophos plc (UKEAT/0452/10)   441
General Billposting Co Ltd v Atkinson [1909] AC 118   47, 58, 64
General Dynamics Information Technology Ltd v Carranza (UKEAT/0107/14)   521
General Vending Services v Schofield (UKEAT/0137/13)   204
Genower v Ealing AHA [1980] IRLR 297   203
GFI Group Inc v Eaglestone [1994] IRLR 119   118
Gibson v Hounslow LBC (UKEAT/0033/18)   216
Gibson v Lothian Leisure (ET/4105009/2020)   170, 208
Gilbank v Miles [2006] IRLR 538   411
Gilham v Ministry of Justice [2017] EWCA Civ 2220; [2019] UKSC 44   19, 22, 35
Gill v El Vino Co Ltd [1983] QB 425   428
Gill v Ford Motor Company Ltd [2004] IRLR 840   76
Gill v SAS Ground Services Ltd (ET/2705021/09)   292
Gillespie v Northern Health and Social Services Board [1996] IRLR 214   552
Gillett v Bridge 86 Ltd (UKEAT/0051/17)   272
Giny v SNA Transport Ltd (UKEAT/0317/16)   254, 268
Girvin v Next Retail Ltd (ET/1900767/05)   559

Gisda Cyf v Barratt [2010] UKSC 41   131, 255
Gladwell v Secretary of State for Trade and Industry [2007] ICR 264, EAT   36
Glasgow City Council and Others v Marshall and Others [2000] 1 WLR 333, [2000] ICR 196   413, 415
Glasgow City Council v UNITE Claimants [2017] CSIH 34   415
Glassford v Royal Mail Group (UKEATS/0012/18)   195
Glaxo Wellcome UK Ltd v Sandoz [2018] EWHC 2747 (Ch)   278
Global Torch Ltd v Apex Global Management Ltd [2013] 1 WLR 2993   287
GLS v Brookes (UKEAT/0302/16)   537
GMB and Amicus v Beloit Walmsley Ltd (in administration) [2004] IRLR 18   152
Gnahoua v Abellio London Ltd (ET/2303661/2015)   178
Godfrey Morgan Solicitors Ltd v Cobalt Systems Ltd [2012] ICR 305   300
Goergiev (Cases C-250/09 and C-268/09)   489
Gogay v Hertfordshire County Council [2000] IRLR 703   114, 187
Gondalia v Tesco Stores (UKEAT/0320/14)   194
Goode v Marks and Spencer plc (UKEAT/0442/09)   210, 213
Goodwin v Patent Office [1999] ICR 302   503
Gordon v J & D Pierce (Contracts) Ltd (UK/EATS/0010/20)   129
Gorfin v Distressed Gentlefolk's Aid Association [1973] IRLR 290   168
Gosden v Lifeline Project Ltd (ET/2802731/2009)   578
Gould v St John's Downshire Hill (UKEAT/0002/20)   388, 434
Gover and Others v Property Care Ltd [2006] EWCA Civ 286   230
Governing Body of Tubbenden Primary School v Sylvester (UKEAT/0527/11)   169
Governing Body of Tywyn Primary School v Aplin (UKEAT/0298/17)   128, 189, 442
Governing Body of X Endowed Primary School v Special Educational Needs and Disability Tribunal (No 1)
    [2009] IRLR 1007   504
Grace v Places for Children (UKEAT/0217/13)   434
Graham v Agilitas IT Solutions Ltd (UKEAT/0212/17)   310
Graham v The Secretary of State for Work & Pensions (Jobcentre Plus) [2012] EWCA Civ 903   173
Grainger plc v Nicholson [2010] IRLR 4   383
Grange v Abellio London Ltd (UKEAT/0130/16)   84
Gratton v Hutton (2003) unreported, 1 July   188
Gray v Mulberry Company (Design) Ltd [2019] EWCA Civ 1720   384
Great Ormond Street Hospital for Children NHS Trust v Patel (UKEAT/0085/07)   220
Greater Glasgow Health Board v Mackay 1989 SLT 729   123
Greco v General Physics UK Ltd (UKEAT/0114/16)   310
Green v London Borough of Barking and Dagenham (UKEAT/0157/16)   200
Green v SIG Trading Ltd (UKEAT/0282/16)   139
Greenaway Harrison Ltd v Wiles [1994] IRLR 380   127
Greenfield v The Care Bureau Ltd [2016] IRLR 62   86
Greenhof v Barnsley Metropolitan Borough Council [2006] IRLR 98   125, 524
Greenwood v NWF Retail (UKEAT/0409/09)   294
Greg O'Cathail v Transport for London [2012] EWCA Civ 1004   302
Griffin v Plymouth Hospital NHS Trust [2014] EWCA Civ 1240   113, 225
Griffiths v Secretary of State for Work and Pensions [2015] EWCA Civ 1265   519, 534
Grimmant v Sweden (Application No 43726/17)   578
Grundy v BA plc [2007] EWCA Civ 1020   456
Guardian News & Media Ltd v Rozanov [2022] IRLR 487   288
Gunton v London Borough of Richmond [2000] IRLR 703   112
Gunton v Richmond-upon-Thames Borough Council [1980] IRLR 321   106
Gurieva v Community Safety Development (UK) Ltd [2016] EWHC 643 (QB)   586
Gwynedd Council v Barratt [2021] EWCA Civ 1322   191, 200

H

Hachette Filipacchi UK Ltd v Johnson (UKEAT/0452/05)   146
Haden Ltd v Cowan [1982] IRLR 314   145
Hadjioannou v Coral Casinos Ltd [1981] IRLR 352   174
Hadley v Baxendale (1854) 9 Exch 341   111
Hafiz and Haque Solicitors v Mullick (UKEAT/0356/14)   300
Hainsworth v Ministry of Defence [2014] EWCA Civ 763   519, 527
Hakim v The Scottish Trade Unions Congress (UKEATS/0047/19)   229
Halford v UK [1997] IRLR 471   574
Hall (Inspector or Taxes) v Lorimer [1994] IRLR 171   11, 16
Hall v Chief Constable of West Yorkshire Police (UKEAT/0057/15)   530, 531

Hall v Durham CC and Ors (UKEAT/0256/14) — 233

Hall v London Lions Basketball Club (UK) Ltd [2021] IRLR 17 — 108

Hall v Woolston Leisure Services Ltd [2000] IRLR 578 — 6

Hall v Xerox UK Ltd (UKEAT/0061/14) — 419

Halpin v Sandpiper Books Ltd (UKEAT/0171/11) — 198

Ham v ESL BBSW Ltd (ET/1601260/2020) — 169, 170, 207

Hammond v Haigh Castle & Co Ltd [1973] ICR 148 — 255

Hampshire County Council v Wyatt (UKEAT/0013/16) — 410

Handley v Tatenhill Aviation Ltd (ET/2603087/2020) — 169, 202

Harden v Wootlif & Anor (UKEAT/0448/14) — 404

Hardie Grant London Ltd v Aspden (UKEAT/0242/11) — 232

Hardman v Mallon [2002] IRLR 516 — 552

Hardy v Balfour Beatty Group Employment Ltd (ET/13066954/14) — 263

Hardy v Tourism South East [2005] IRLR 242 — 152

Hardys & Hansons v Lax [2005] EWCA Civ 846 — 461

Hare Wines Ltd v Kaur [2019] EWCA Civ 216 — 361, 362

Hargreaves v Evolve Housing and Support [2022] EAT 122 — 302

Hargreaves v Governing Body of Manchester Grammar School (UKEAT/0048/18) — 190

Harlow v Artemis International Corporation Ltd [2008] EWHC 1126 (QB) — 46

Harper v Virgin Net Ltd [2004] IRLR 390 — 114

Harpur Trust v Brazel [2022] UKSC 21 — 87, 88, 419

Harris v Academies Enterprise Trust [2015] IRLR 208 — 264, 274

Harrison Bowden Ltd v Bowden [1994] ICR 186 — 361

Harrison v Aryma Ltd (UKEAT/0085/19) — 309

Harrod v Chief Constable of West Midlands Police [2017] EWCA Civ 191 — 495

Hartley v King Edward VI College [2017] UKSC 39 — 75

Harvey v Port of Tilbury (London) Ltd [1999] ICR 1030 — 272

Hashman v Milton Park (Dorset) Ltd (ET/3105555/09) — 383

Hassard v McGrath [1996] NILR 586 — 342

Hawes v Curtis Ltd v Arfan [2012] ICR 1244 — 131

Hawkes v Ausin Group (UK) Ltd (UKEAT/0070/18) — 204

Hawkins v Universal Utilities Ltd t/a Unicom (ET/2501234/12) — 384

Haydar v Pennine Acute Hospitals NHS Trust [2018] EWCA Civ 1435 — 302

Hayden v Cowan [1982] IRLR 314 — 49

Heal v The Chancellor, Masters and Scholars of the University of Oxford and others (UKEAT/0070/19) — 290, 539

Health Development Agency v Parish [2004] IRLR 550 — 296

Heathfield v Times Newspapers Ltd (UKEAT/1305/12) — 473

Heaven v Whitbread Group plc (UKEAT/0084/10) — 130

Hedley Byrne & Co Ltd v Heller & Partners Ltd [1964] AC 465 — 304

Heimann v Kaiser GmbH [2013] IRLR 48 — 97

Helmut Kampelmann and Others v Landschaftsverband Westfalen-Lippe (Cases C-253/96 to 256/96) [1997] ECR I-6907 — 48

Hemdan v Ishmail (UKEAT/0021/16) — 276

Hendricks v Commissioner of Police for the Metropolis [2003] IRLR 96 — 271, 405

Hendy Banks v Fairbrother (UKEAT/0691/04) — 198

Hensman v Ministry of Defence (UKEAT/0067/14) — 535

Herbai v Hungary (Application No 11608/15) [2019] IRLR 159 — 579

Herry v Dudley Metropolitan Council (UKEAT/0100/16), [2017] ICR 610 — 511, 536

Heskett v Secretary of State for Justice (UKEAT/0149/18); [2020] EWCA Civ 1487 — 492, 496

Hewage v Grampian Health Board [2012] UKSC 37 — 441

Hewcastle Catering Ltd v Ahmed [1991] IRLR 473 — 168

Hextall v Chief Constable of Leicestershire Police (ET/2601223/2015) — 556

Higgins v Home Office (UKEAT/0296/14) — 267

High Table Ltd v Horst [1997] IRLR 513 — 144

Hill v C A Parsons & Co Ltd [1972] 1 Ch 305 — 117

Hill v Chappell [2003] IRLR 19 — 87

Hill v Governing Body of Great Tey Primary School (UKEAT/0237/12) — 175

Hill v Lloyds Bank plc (UKEAT/0173, 0174 and 0233/19) — 407, 525

Hinton v University of East London [2005] IRLR 522 — 307

His Highness Sheikh Khalid bin Saqr Al Qasimi v Robinson (UKEAT/0283/17) — 218

Hivac Ltd v Park Royal Scientific Instruments Ltd [1946] Ch 169 — 44

HK Danmark (acting on behalf of Ring) v Dansk almennyttigt Boligselskab (Case C-335/11) [2013] IRLR 571 — 503, 514, 525

HM Chief Inspector of Education, Children's Services and Skills v The Interim Executive Board of Al-Hijrah
    School [2017] EWCA Civ 1426   430
HM Land Registry v Benson (UKEAT/0197/11)   495
HM Prison Service v Johnson [1997] IRLR 162   408
HM Prison Service v Salmon [2001] IRLR 425   410, 480
HM Revenue and Customs v Professional Game Match Officials Ltd [2021] EWCA Civ 1370   13
HMRC v Garau (UKEAT/0348/16)   254
HMRC v Murphy [2022] EWCA Civ 1112   234
HMRC v Stringer [2009] UKHL 31   75, 93
Hodgson v Martin Design Associates Ltd (ET/1806368/19)   471
Holbrook v Queen Mary's Sidcup NHS Trust (ET/1101904/06)   215
Holis Metal Industries Ltd v GMB & Newell Ltd [2008] IRLR 187   339, 349
Holman v Johnson (1775) 1 Cowp 341   6
Holmes v Qinetic Ltd (UKEAT/0206/15), [2016] IRLR 664   177
Home Office v Collins [2005] EWCA Civ 598   523
Home Office v Evans [2008] IRLR 59   144
Home Office v Holmes [1984] 3 All ER 549   452
Home Office v Kuranchie (UKEAT/0202/16)   441
Home Office v Tariq [2010] EWCA Civ 462; [2011] UKSC 35   573
Homer v Chief Constable of West Yorkshire Police [2012] UKSC 15, [2012] IRLR 601   391, 455, 460
Hopkins v Norcross plc [1994] IRLR 18   115
Horizon Security Services Ltd v Ndeze and the PCS Group (UKEAT/0071/14)   347
Horkulak v Cantor Fitzgerald International [2003] IRLR 756; [2004] IRLR 942, [2005] ICR 402   113, 114
Horn v Quinn Walker Securities (ET/2505740/03)   559
Hornfeldt (Case C-141/11)   489
Hospital Medical Group Ltd, The v Westwood [2012] EWCA Civ 1005   21
Hotson v Wisbech Conservative Club [1984] ICR 859   165
Hounga v Allen & Another [2014] UKSC 47   7, 378, 436
Housing Corporation v Bryant [1999] ICR 123   272
Housing Maintenance Solutions Ltd v McAteer and others (UKEAT/0440/13)   350
HSBC (formerly Midland Bank) v Madden; Post Office v Foley [2000] IRLR 827   172, 241
HSBC Asia Holdings BV v Gillespie (UKEAT/0417/10), [2011] IRLR 209   271, 292
Hudson v Plymouth Hospitals NHS Trust (ET/1401148/2014)   252
Hughes v Corps of Commissioners Management Ltd [2011] EWCA Civ 1061   84
Hughes v G and L Jones t/a Graylyns Residential Home (UKEAT/0159/08)   78
Hussain v Acorn Independent College Ltd (UKEAT/0199/10)   132
Hutchins v Permacell Finesse Ltd (in administration) (UKEAT/0350/07)   155
Hyland v JH Barker (North West) Ltd [1985] ICR 861   7

I

I Lab Facilities Ltd v Metcalfe and Others (UKEAT/0224/12)   367
Ibarz v University of Sheffield (UKEAT/0018/15)   299, 300, 419
Ibex Trading Company Ltd v Walton and Others [1994] IRLR 564   360
Ibrahim v HCA International Ltd (UKEAT/0105/18)   211, 213
Iceland Foods Ltd v Stevenson (UKEAT/0309/19)   535
Iceland Frozen Foods Ltd v Jones [1982] IRLR 439   171, 241, 246
iForce v Wood (UKEAT/0167/18)   532
Igen Ltd and Others v Wong [2005] IRLR 258   439, 446
Igweike v TSB Bank Plc (UKEAT/0119/19)   510
Ijomah v Nottinghamshire Healthcare NHS Foundation Trust (UKEAT/0289/19)   284
Imam-Sadeque v Blue Bay Asset Management (Services) Ltd [2012] EWHC 3511 (QB)   44
Impact v Ministry for Agriculture and Food (Ireland) (Case C-268/06) [2008] IRLR 552   4
Industry and Commerce Maintenance v Briffa (UKEAT/021508/07)   98
Initial Electronic Security Systems Ltd v Avdic (UKEAT/0281/05), [2005] ICR 1598   256, 257
Insitu Cleaning Co Ltd v Heads [1995] IRLR 4   470
Instant Muscle Ltd v Khawaja (UKEAT/216/03)   539
International Petroleum Ltd v Osipov (UKEAT/0058/17)   218
International Petroleum Ltd v Osipov [2018] EWCA Civ 2321   209
Interserve FM Ltd v Tuleikyte (UKEAT/0267/16)   438
Iqbal v Metropolitan Police Service & Another (UKEAT/0186/12)   572
IR v JQ (Case C-68/17)   397
Ishaq v Royal Mail Group (UKEAT/0156/16)   127
Ishola v Transport for London [2020] EWCA Civ 112   453, 520

Islington Borough Council v Ladele [2009] ICR 387 — 426
ISS Facility Services NV v Govaerts and Atalian NV (Case C-344/18) — 342
Isteed v London Borough of Redbridge (UKEAT/0442/14) — 301
Istituto nazionale della previdenza social (INPS) v Bruno [2010] IRLR 890 — 418
Iwuchukwu v City Hospitals Sunderland NHS Foundation Trust [2019] EWCA Civ 498 — 443
Ix v WABE eV; MH Muller Handels GmbH v MJ [2021] WLR(D) 399 — 463

J

J v DLA Piper UK LLP (UKEAT/0263/09), [2010] ICR 1052 — 504, 512, 536
JAB and Y v East Sussex CC [2003] EWHC 167 (Admin) — 574
Jack Allen (Sales and Service) Ltd v Smith [1999] IRLR 19 — 59
Jackson Lloyd Ltd and Mears Group plc v Smith and Others (UKEAT/0127/13) — 337
Jackson v Computershare Investment Services plc [2008] IRLR 70 — 350
Jackson v Ghost Inc [2003] IRLR 824, EAT — 136
Jakkhu v Network Rail Infrastructure Ltd (UKEAT/0276/18) — 394
Jakowlew v Nestor Primecare (t/a Saga) and others (UKEAT/0431/14) — 354
James v Eastleigh Borough Council [1990] 2 AC 751, [1990] ICR 554 — 390, 392, 435, 453
James v Gina Shoes Ltd and Ors (UKEAT/0384/11) — 441
James v Greenwich Borough Council [2008] IRLR 302 — 32
James v Redcats (Brands) Ltd [2007] ICR 1006 — 21
James W Cook & Co v Tipper [1990] IRLR 386 — 197
Jeffery v The British Council (UKEAT/0036/16) — 137
Jeremiah v Ministry of Defence [1979] IRLR 436 — 428
Jessemey v Rowstock Ltd and anor [2014] EWCA Civ 185 — 395, 484
Jesudason v Alder Hey Children's NHS Foundation Trust [2020] EWCA Civ 73 — 209, 217
Jet2.com v Denby (UKEAT/0070/17) — 205
JH Finn & Co v Holliday [2013] EWHC 3450 (QB) — 65
JH Walker Ltd v Hussain and Others [1996] IRLR 11 — 411, 452
Jhuti v Royal Mail Group (ET/2200982/2015) — 219
Jhuti v Royal Mail Group Ltd and others (UKEAT/0061/17 & UKEAT/0062/17) — 271
Jilley v Birmingham and Solihull Mental Health NHS Trust (UKEAT/0584/06) — 296, 300
Jimenez v Firmdale Hotels (ET/2203194/2020) — 169
Jinadu v Dockland Buses Ltd (UKEAT/0166/16) — 231
Jinadu v Dockland Buses Ltd (UKEAT/0434/14) — 192
Jinks v London Borough of Havering (UKEAT/0157/14) — 346
Jivraj v Hashwani [2011] UKSC 40 — 30
John Brown Engineering Ltd v Brown and Others [1997] IRLR 90 — 198
John Lewis Partnership v Charman (UKEAT/0079/11) — 256, 257
John Lewis plc v Coyne [2001] IRLR 139 — 193
Johnson Controls Ltd v Campbell and Another (UKEAT/0042/12) — 348
Johnson v Transopco Ltd [2022] EAT 6 — 19
Johnson v Unisys Ltd [2001] IRLR 279 — 112, 114, 127, 223
Jones v Associated Tunnelling Co Ltd [1981] IRLR 477 — 50
Jones v Secretary of State for Business, Innovation and Skills (UKEAT/0238/16) — 292
Jones v Tower Boot Co Ltd [1997] IRLR 168, CA — 398
Jones v University of Manchester [1993] IRLR 218 — 454
Joseph Estorninho v Zoran Jokic t/a Zorans Delicatessen (ET/2301487/06) — 462
Joseph v Royal College of Surgeons of England (ET/2202074/14) — 253
JP Morgan Securities plc v Ktorza (UKEAT/0311/16) — 166
Judge v Crown Leisure Ltd [2005] IRLR 823 — 50
Junk v Kuhnel [2005] IRLR 310 — 152
JV Strong & Co Ltd v Hamill (UKEAT/1179/99) — 127

K

Kapadia v London Borough of Lambeth [2000] IRLR 699 — 509
Kapenova v Department of Health (UKEAT/0142/13) — 461
Kapetanakis v Historical Souvenirs (ET/1601368/2020) — 170
Kapoor v Governing Body of Barnhill Community High School (UKEAT/0352/13) — 298
Kaur Gill v Elegance Beauty (ET/3201878/2020) — 170
Kaur v Leeds Teaching Hospitals NHS Trust [2018] EWCA Civ 978 — 126, 129
Keane v Investigo and Others (UKEAT/0389/09) — 459, 489
Keeping Kids Company v Smith & Others (UKEAT 0057/17) — 155
Kellogg Brown & Root (UK) Ltd v Fitton & Another (UKEAT/0205/16) — 49, 144, 197

Kelly ([2021] EWCA Civ 549)   220
Kelly and Another v The Helsey Group [2013] IRLR 515   153
Kelly v Covance Laboratories Ltd (EAT/0186/15)   434
Kelly v PGA European Tour (UKEAT/0285/18)   220
Kelly v Royal Mail Group Ltd (UKEAT/0262/18)   526
Kelly v Secretary of State for Justice (UKEAT/0227/13)   547
Kelly v University of Southampton (UKEAT/0295/07)   203, 393
Kemeh v Ministry of Defence [2014] EWCA Civ 91   397
Kenny v Hampshire Constabulary [1999] IRLR 76   523
Keppel Seghers UK Ltd v Hinds (UKEAT/0019/14)   29
Key2Law (Surrey) LLP v De'Antiquis [2011] EWCA Civ 1567   337
Khan v Checkers Cars Ltd [2005] 12 WLUK 532   15
Khatun v Winn Solicitors Ltd (ET/2501492/20)   71, 170
Khorochilova v Euro Rep Ltd (UKEAT/0266/19)   505
KHS AG v Schulte [2012] IRLR 156   94
Kidd v Axa Equity and Law Life Assurance Society plc and Another [2000] IRLR 301, HC   42
Kilraine v London Borough of Wandsworth [2018] EWCA Civ 1436   211
Kimberley Group Housing Ltd v Hambley (UKEAT/0489/07)   342
King v Eaton Ltd (No 2) [1998] IRLR 686   230, 231
King v Eaton Ltd [1996] IRLR 199   198
King v Royal Bank of Canada Europe (UKEAT/0333/10)   201
King v The Sash Window Workshop Ltd (Case C-214/16)   86, 91
Kirk v Citibank NA (ET/3200291/18)   471
Kirton v Tetrosyl Ltd [2002] IRLR 840   508
Kleinwort Benson Ltd v Lincoln City Council and Other Appeals [1999] 2 AC 349   76
Klusova v London Borough of Hounslow [2007] EWCA Civ 1127   203
Knapton & Others v ECC Card Clothing Ltd [2006] IRLR 756   228
Knight v BCCP (UKEAT/0413/10)   14
Kocur v Angard Staffing Solutions Ltd [2022] EWCA Civ 189   35
Kocur v Angard Staffing Solutions Ltd and Another [2019] EWCA Civ 1185   34
Koenig v Mind Gym Ltd (UKEAT/0201/12)   130
Komeng v Creative Support Ltd (UKEAT/0275/18)   409
Kong v Gulf International Bank (UK) Ltd [2022] EWCA Civ 941   216
Kontinnen v Finland (1996) 87 DR 68, ECtHR   420
Köpke v Germany (Application No 420/17)   576
Korashi v Abertawe Bro Morgannwg University Local Health Board [2012] IRLR 4   214
Kraft Foods v Hastie (UKEAT/0024/10)   494
Kraus v Penna Plc [2004] IRLR 260   214
Kreuziger v Berlin (Case C-619/16)   86
Kubilius v Kent Foods (ET/3201960/2020)   169
Kucukdeveci v Swedex GmbH & Co KG (Case C-555/07)   4
Kuddus v Chief Constable of Leicestershire Constabulary [2001] UKHL 29   410
Kuehne and Nagel Ltd v Cosgrove (UKEAT/0165/13)   227
Kumari v Greater Manchester Mental Health NHS Foundation Trust [2022] EAT 132   259
Kuzel v Roche Products Ltd [2008] IRLR 530   165, 166, 217
Kwamin and Others v Abbey National plc and other cases [2004] ICR 841   572
Kyndall Spirits v Burns (EAT/29/02)   228
Kynixa Ltd v Hynes and Others [2008] EWHC 1495 (Comm)   44, 119

L

L v K [2021] CSIH 35   194
L v Q Ltd [2019] EWCA Civ 1417   302
L'Anson v Chief Constable of West Yorkshire Police (ET/1804854/09)   383
Ladak v DRC Locums Ltd [2014] ICR D39   295
Ladele v The London Borough of Islington [2010] IRLR 211; [2009] EWCA Civ 1357   433
Lafferty v Nuffield Health (UKEATS/0006/19)   194
Laing v Manchester City Council [2006] IRLR 748   441
Lambe v 186K [2005] ICR 307   230
Lambert v BAT (Investments) Ltd (ET/3100897/08)   496
Lancaster and Duke Ltd v Wileman (UKEAT/0256/17)   131
Land Registry v Houghton UKEAT/0149/14   530
Land Rover v Short (UKEAT/0496/10)   270
Land Securities Trillium Ltd v Thornley [2005] IRLR 765, EAT   124

Landeshauptstadt Kiel v Norbert Jaeger (Case C-151/02) [2003] ECR I-8389, [2003] IRLR 804   78
Lange v Addison Lee Ltd (ET/2208029/2016)   23
Lansing Linde Ltd v Kerr [1991] 1 All ER 418, CA   58
Larsson v Føtex Supermarked (Case C-400/95) [1997] ECR I-2757   438
Lavarack v Woods of Colchester Ltd [1967] 1 QB 278   113
Law Society and Others v Bahl [2003] IRLR 640   431, 442
Lawal v Northern Spirit Ltd [2003] IRLR 538   572
Lawless v Print Plus (Debarred) UKEAT/0333/09/JOJ   227
Lawrence v Regent Office Care Ltd [2003] ICR 1092   414
Laws v London Chronicle Ltd [1959] 2 All ER 285   43
Leach v Office of Communications [2012] EWCA Civ 959   169, 203
Lee v Ashers Baking Co Ltd and Others [2018] UKSC 49   434, 435
Lee v McArthur and Ashers Baking Co Ltd [2016] NICA 39   427
Leeds City Council v Woodhouse [2010] IRLR 625   31, 378, 392
Leeds Dental Team Ltd v Mrs D Rose (UK EAT/0016/13)   178
Leicestershire County Council v Unison [2005] IRLR 920   153
Leisure Leagues UK Ltd v Maconnachie [2002] IRLR 600   87, 112
Lenlyn UK Ltd v Kular (UKEAT/0108/16)   310
Leonard v Southern Derbyshire Chamber of Commerce [2001] IRLR 19   507
Leventhal Ltd v North (UKEAT/0265/04)   198
Lewald-Jezierska v Solicitors in Law Ltd and others (UKEAT/0165/06)   296
Lewis v Motorworld Garages Ltd [1986] ICR 157   126
Liddell's Coaches v Cook (UKEATS/0025/12)   346
Lincolnshire CC v Lupton (EAT/0328/15)   220
Linfood Cash & Carry Ltd v Thompson [1989] IRLR 235   189
Linsley v Commissioners for Her Majesty's Revenue and Customs (UKEAT/1050/18)   525
Lisk v Shield Guardian Ltd (ET/3300873/11)   383
Lister and Others v Hesley Hall Ltd [2001] IRLR 472   398
Lister v Romford Ice and Cold Storage Co Ltd [1957] AC 555   44, 117
Litster v Forth Dry Dock & Engineering Co Ltd [1989] IRLR 161   4, 568
Live Nation (Venues) UK Ltd v Hussain (UKEAT/ 0234/08)   490
Livesey v Parker Merchanting Ltd (UKEAT/0755/03)   398
Lock v British Gas Trading Ltd (Case C-539/12), [2014] ICR 813   56, 88
Lock v Cardiff Railway Co Ltd [1998] IRLR 358   177
Locke v Tabfine Ltd t/a Hands Music Centre (UKEAT/0517/10)   259
Lockwood v DWP & Another [2013] EWCA Civ 1195   490
Lodge v Dignity & Choice in Dying (UKEAT/0252/14)   137
Lofty v Harris t/a First Café (UKEAT/0177/17)   513
Logan v Commissioner of Customs and Excise [2004] IRLR 63   293
Lokhova v Sberbank CIB (UK) Ltd (2015)   407, 474
London Ambulance Service NHS Trust v Small [2009] EWCA Civ 220, [2009] IRLR 563   172, 241
London Borough of Enfield v Sivanandan [2005] EWCA Civ 10   102
London Borough of Hackney v Sivanandan and Others [2013] EWCA Civ 22   412
London Borough of Hammersmith & Fulham v Keable (UKEAT/0333/19)   220
London Borough of Hillingdon v Bailey (UKEAT/0421/12)   521
London Borough of Hillingdon v Gormanley & Others (UKEAT/0169/14)   355
London Borough of Islington v Ladele (UKEAT/0453/08)   433
London Borough of Lewisham v Malcolm [2008] IRLR 700   528
London Borough of Southwark v Afolabi [2003] IRLR 220   404
London Borough of Waltham Forest v Omilaju [2005] IRLR 35   126, 128
London Care Ltd v Henry and Others (EAT/0219/17 and 0220/17)   348
London Probation Board v Kirkpatrick [2005] IRLR 443   133
London Transport Executive v Clark [1981] IRLR 166   122
London Underground Ltd v Bragg (UKEAT/847/98)   507
London Underground Ltd v Edwards [1998] IRLR 364   454
London Underground v Amissah [2019] IRLR 545   35
López Ribalda v Spain (Application Nos 1874/13 and 8567/13), [2019] ECHR 752   574, 576
Lord Chancellor and Secretary of State for Justice and another v McCloud and others; Secretary of State for the
    Home Department and another v Sargeant [2018] EWCA Civ 2844   493
Lovett v Wigan Metropolitan Borough Council [2001] EWCA Civ 12   39
Lowri Beck Services Ltd v Brophy (UKEAT/0277/18)   258
Loxley v BAE Systems Land Systems (Munitions and Ordinance) Ltd [2008] IRLR 853, (UKEAT/0156/08)   494
Lund v St Edmund's School, Canterbury (UKEAT/0514/12)   226
Lustig Prean v UK [1999] IRLR 734   575

Luton Borough Council v Haque (UKEAT/0260/17)   263
Lycée Français Charles de Gaulle v Delambre (UKEAT/0563/10)   407
Lyddon v Englefield Brickwork Ltd (EAT/0301/07)   93
Lyfar v Brighton and Sussex University Hospitals Trust [2006] EWCA Civ 1548   405
Lyons v DWP Jobcentre Plus (UKEAT/0348/13)   438
Lyttle v Bluebird UK Bidco2 (Case C-182/13)   154

M

Ma v Merck, Sharp and Dohme Ltd [2008] EWCA Civ 1426   271
MacCulloch v ICI plc [2008] IRLR 846, (UKEAT/0119/08)   494
Macdonald v Advocate General for Scotland; Pearce v Governing Body of Mayfield Secondary School
  [2003] IRLR 512   475
Machine Tool Industry Research Association v Simpson [1988] ICR 558   258
MacInnes v Gross [2017] EWHC 46 (QB)   37
Mackenzie v Chancellor, Masters and Scholars of the University of Cambridge [2020] IRLR 324   220
Mackereth v DWP [2022] EAT 99   384
Macpherson v BNP Paribas (London Branch) [2004] IRLR 558   297
Madarassy v Nomura International plc [2007] EWCA Civ 33, [2007] ICR 867   275, 415, 439, 478
Maga v Birmingham Roman Catholic Archdiocese Trustees [2010] All ER (D) 141   398
Magoulas v Queen Mary University of London (UKEAT/0244/15)   492
Mahlburg v Land Mecklenburg-Vorpommern [2000] IRLR 276, ECJ   551
Mahmud v BCCI [1998] AC 20, HL   124
Maio Marques da Rosa v Varzim (Case C-306/16)   84
Mairs v Haughey [1994] 1 AC 303   151
Maistry v BBC (ET/1313142/10)   383
Majrowski v Guy's and St Thomas's NHS Trust [2005] IRLR 340, CA; [2006] UKHL 34   476
Mak v Wayward Gallery Ltd (UKEAT/0589/10)   294
Makauskiene v Rentokil Initial Facilities Services (UK) Ltd (UKEAT/0503/13)   273
Malik and Another v BCCI SA (in compulsory liquidation) [1998] AC 20   42, 114, 124, 126
Mallon v AECOM Ltd [2021] IRLR 438   519, 522
Mallone v BPB Industries plc [2002] IRLR 452   113
Managers (Holborn) Ltd v Hohne [1977] IRLR 230   50
Manchester College, The v Mr M Cocliff (UKEAT/0035/10)   419
Mandla and Another v Dowell Lee and Another [1983] 2 AC 548, HL   380, 452
Marathon Asset Management LLP v Seddon & Bridgeman [2017] EWHC 300 (Comm)   64
Mari v Reuters Ltd (UKEAT/0539/13)   128
Market Investigations Ltd v Minister of Social Security [1969] 2 QB 173   11
Marks and Spencer plc v William-Ryan [2005] IRLR 562   257
Marleasing SA v La Comercial Internacional de Alimentacion SA [1990] ECR I-4135   4
Marshall v Southampton and South West Hampshire AHA [1986] QB 401   4
Martin v City and County of Swansea (UKEAT/0253/20)   520
Martin v Devonshires Solicitors (UKEAT/0086/10), [2011] ICR 352   216, 432, 441, 482
Martin v MBS Fastenings (Glynwed) Distribution Ltd [1983] IRLR 198   123
Martin v University of Exeter (UKEAT/0092/18)   510
Martins v Marks and Spencer plc [1998] IRLR 326   442
Martland and Others v Cooperative Insurance Society and Others (UKEAT/0220/07 and 0221/07)   146
Maruko v Versorgungsanstalt der deutschen Bühnen (Case C-267/06)   388
Masih-Rogers v Hammersmith Hairdressing and others (ET/2201248/14)   252
Mathieson v Secretary of State for Work and Pensions [2015] UKSC 47   579
Matthews v Kent and Medway Towns Fire Authority [2006] IRLR 367   417
Mattu v The University Hospitals of Coventry and Warwickshire NHS Trust [2012] IRLR 619   571
Matuszowicz v Kingston upon Hull City Council [2009] EWCA Civ 22   539
Matuz v Hungary [2014] ECHR 1112   578
Max-Planck-Gesellschaft zur Förderung der Wissenschaften eV v Shimizu (Case C-684/16)   86
Mayor and Burgesses of the London Borough of Lambeth v Agoreyo [2019] EWCA Civ 322   125, 187
Mayuuf v Governing Body of Bishop Challenor Catholic Collegiate School and Another (ET/3202398/2004)   462
Mba v Mayor and Burgesses of the London Borough of Merton [2013] EWCA Civ 1562, [2014] IRLR 145   456, 462, 577
MBNA Ltd v Jones (UKEAT/0120/15)   175
Mbubaegbu v Homerton University Hospital NHS Foundation Trust (UKEAT/0218/17)   107, 166
Mbuisa v Cygnet Healthcare Ltd (UKEAT/0119/18)   274, 275
McBride v Falkirk Football Club (UKEATS/0058/10)   126
McBride v Scottish Police Authority [2016] UKSC 27   220
McCafferty v Royal Mail Group (UKEATS/0002/12)   289

McCarrick v Hunter [2013] IRLR 26   346, 347
McCarron v Road Chef Motorways & Others (UKEAT/0268/18)   283
McCartney v Oversley House Management [2006] IRLR 514, (UKEAT/0500/3101)   85
McClintock v Department of Constitutional Affairs [2008] IRLR 29   382, 434
McCoy v McGregor & Sons Ltd, Dixon and Aitken (IT/00237/07)   497
McFarlane v Glasgow City Council [2001] IRLR 7   15
McFarlane v Relate Avon Ltd [2010] ICR 50, EAT   433
McIntosh v Governing Body of St Mark's Primary School (UKEAT/0226/13)   482
McKechnie Plastic Components v Grant (UKEAT/0284/08)   509
McKennitt v Ash [2005] EWHC 3003 (QB)   574
McKie v Swindon College [2011] EWHC 469 (QB)   43
McLeny v MOD (ET/4105347/17)   384
McMeechan v Secretary of State for Employment [1997] ICR 549, [1997] IRLR 353   28, 33
McMillan v Airedale NHS Foundation Trust [2014] EWCA Civ 1031   68, 191
McNeil & Others v Commissioners for HM Revenue & Customs (UKEAT/0183/17)   416
McNicol v Balfour Beatty Rail Maintenance Ltd [2002] EWCA Civ 1074   504
McPherson v BNP Paribas [2004] IRLR 558   299
McTear Contracts Ltd v Bennett & ors (UKEATS/0023/19)   342
McTigue v University Hospital Bristol NHS Foundation Trust (EAT/0354/15)   29, 209
McWilliams v Citibank NA, 19 April 2016   586
Mead-Hill v The British Council [1995] IRLR 478   412
Medcalf v Weatherill [2002] UKHL 27   301
Meechan v Secretary of State for Employment [1997] IRLR 353   13
Meek v City of Birmingham District Council [1987] IRLR 250   294
Mehta v Child Support Agency (UKEAT/0127/10)   282
Meister v Speech Design Carrier Systems GmbH (Case C-415/10) [2012] ICR 1066   441
Melia v Magna Kansei (UKEAT/0339/04)   226
Mendy v Motorola Solutions UK Ltd [2022] EAT 47   274
Mensah v East Hertfordshire Trust [1988] IRLR 531   270
Mercer v Alternative Future Group Ltd (UKEAT/0196/20)   205
Merckx and Neuhuys v Ford Motors Belgium SA [1996] IRLR 467   352
Mervyn v BW Controls Ltd [2020] EWCA Civ 393   266, 291
Metroline Travel Ltd v Stoute (UKEAT/0302/14)   512
Metropolitan Police v Keohane (UKEAT/0463/12)   428
Metropolitan Resources Ltd v Churchill Dulwich Ltd [2009] IRLR 700   345
MG v Dublin City Council (Case C-214/20)   79
Mhindurwa v Lovingangels Care Ltd (ET/3311636/2020)   169, 202
Miah v Axis Security Services Ltd (UKEAT/0290/17)   256
Michalak v Mid Yorkshire Hospitals NHS Trust (ET/1810815/08)   407
Micheldever Tyre Service Ltd v Burrell (UKEAT/0427/12)   482
Mid-Staffordshire General Hospitals NHS Trust v Cambridge [2003] IRLR 566   524
Miles v Linkage Community Trust Ltd (UKEAT/0618/07)   85
Miles v The Royal Veterinary College (ET/2206733/2020)   384
Millam v The Print Factory (London) 1991 Ltd [2007] IRLR 526   337
Miller v Community Links Trust Ltd (UK EAT/0486/07)   256
Ministry of Defence v DeBique (UKEAT/0048/09 and 0049/09)   452, 460
Ministry of Defence v Fletcher (UKEAT/0044/09)   410
Ministry of Defence v Meredith [1995] IRLR 52   410
Ministry of Defence v Wallis [2011] EWCA Civ 231, [2011] ICR 617, CA   135, 136
Ministry of Defence v Wheeler [1998] IRLR 23, CA   232, 449, 464, 479
Mirab v Mentor Graphics (UKEAT/0172/17)   200
Mirror Group Newspapers Ltd v Gunning [1986] IRLR 27   30
Mist v Derby Community Health Services NHS Trust (EAT/0170/15)   253, 255
Mist v Derby Community Health Services NHS Trust (UKEAT/0170/15)   255
Mitchells Solicitors v Funkwerk Information Technologies (UKEAT/0541/07)   300
MITIE Managed Services Ltd v French [2002] IRLR 512   357
Mogane v Bradford Teaching Hospitals NHS Foundation Trust [2022] EAT 139   198
Mohamud v WM Morrison Supermarkets plc [2016] UKSC 11   399
Montanaro v Lansafe (ET/2203148/2020)   169
Montgomery v Johnson Underwood Ltd [2001] IRLR 269   15
Moore v Duport Furniture Products Ltd [1980] IRLR 158, CA   305
Moore v Ecoscape UK Ltd (ET/2417563/20)   170, 208
Moore v Phoenix Product Development Limited (UKEAT/0070/20)   191
Moores v Bude-Stratton Town Council [2000] IRLR 676   42

Moorthy v Commissioners for HMRC [2018] EWCA Civ 847 411
Moorthy v HMRC [2018] EWCA Civ 847 236
Moran v Ideal Cleaning Services Ltd [2014] IRLR 172 34
Morgan v Abertawe BRP Morgannwg University Local Health Board (UKEAT/0114/19) 286, 539
Morgan v The Welsh Rugby Union (UKEAT/0314/10) 200
Morris v John Grose Group Ltd [1998] IRLR 499 361
Morris v Metrolink RATP DEV Ltd [2018] EWCA Civ 1350 205
Morris v Walsh Western UK Ltd [1997] IRLR 562 133
Morrow v Safeway Stores plc [2002] IRLR 9 125
Mortimer v The Golden Holiday Company Ltd and Another (ET/2300983/15) 253
Mostyn v S and P Casuals Ltd (UKEAT/0158/17) 124
Mowat-Brown v University of Surrey [2002] IRLR 235 508
Moxam v Visible Changes Ltd and Another (UKEAT/0267/11) 380
Mruke v Khan [2018] EWCA Civ 280 ..... 124, 381
Muggeridge and Slade v East Anglia Plastics Ltd [1973] IRLR 163 168
Mukoro v IWUGB (UKEAT/0128/19) 291
Munchkins Restaurant Ltd and Another v Karmazyn and Others (UKEAT/0359/09) 128, 412, 470
Murphy v Birrell & Sons Ltd [1978] IRLR 458 133
Murphy v Epsom College [1984] IRLR 271 145
Murray and Another v Foyle Meats Ltd [1999] IRLR 562 ..... 146, 147
Muschett v HM Prison Service [2010] EWCA Civ 25 33
Mutombo-Mpania v Angard Staffing Solutions Ltd (UKEAT/0002/18) 509
Myers v Nottingham City Council (2015) 262

N

Naeem v Secretary of State for Justice (UKEAT/0215/14) 454
Nagarajan v London Regional Transport [1998] IRLR 73, CA; [1999] ICR 877, [1999] IRLR 572, HL 415, 428, 482, 530
Nair v Lagardere Sports and Entertainment UK Ltd [2021] IRLR 54 124
Napotnik v Romania [2021] IRLR 70 579
Nasse v SRC [1979] IRLR 465 280
National Coal Board v Galley [1958] 1 WLR 16 117
National Grid Transmission plc v Wood [2007] All ER (D) 358 32
National Statistics v Ali [2005] ICR 201 388
National Union of Rail, Maritime and Transport Workers v Lloyd [2019] IRLR 897 (EAT) 493
Nationwide Building Society v Niblett (UKEAT/0524/08) 125
Neal v Freightliner Ltd (ET/1315342/2012) 90
Neary v Dean of Westminster [1999] IRLR 288 107
Nethermere (St Neots) Ltd v Gardiner and Another [1984] ICR 612 27
Network Rail Infrastructure Ltd v Crawford [2019] EWCA Civ 269 85
New Century Cleaning Co Ltd v Church [2000] IRLR 27 ..... 74, 75
New ISG Ltd v Vernon [2008] IRLR 115 356
New Star v Evershed [2010] EWCA Civ 870 273
New Testament Church of God, The v Stewart [2007] IRLR 178, (EAT/0293/06) 35
Newbound v Thames Water Utilities Ltd [2015] EWCA Civ 677 ..... 172, 173, 195
Newcastle Upon Tyne Hospitals NHS Foundation Trust v Bagley (UKEAT/0417/11) 519
Newcastle upon Tyne Hospitals NHS Foundation Trust v Haywood [2018] UKSC 22 ..... 40, 104
Newcastle upon Tyne NHS Foundation Trust v Haywood [2017] EWCA Civ 153 105
Newham Sixth Form College v Sanders [2014] EWCA Civ 734 ..... 453, 519
Newland v Simons & Willer (Hairdressers) Ltd [1981] IRLR 359 168
Ngomoto v Carltech Community Services (ET/1304618/2014) 253
NHS Leeds v Larner [2012] EWCA Civ 1034 ..... 93, 94
NHS Manchester v Fecitt and Others [2012] IRLR 641 217
Nicholls v London Borough of Croydon (UKEAT/0003/18 and 0004/18) 338, 342
Nicholson v Grainger plc [2010] IRLR 4 382
Nicolson v Highlandwear Ltd [2010] IRLR 859 299
Niemietz v Germany (1992) 16 EHRR 97 574
Nissa v Waverly Education Foundation Ltd (UKEAT/0135/18) 510
NJ Shuter v Ford Motor Company (ET/3203504/2013) 556
Nogueira v Crewlink and Oscar v Ryanair (Cases C-168/16 and C-169/16) 139
Nolan v Balfour Beatty Engineering Services (UKEAT/0109/11) 258
Noor v Foreign and Commonwealth Office (UKEAT/0470/10) 524
Norbrook Laboratories (GB) Ltd v Shaw (UKEAT/0150/13) 210
Norman v National Audit Office (UKEAT/0276/14) 69

Norris v London Fire and Emergency Planning Authority [2013] IRLR 428   76
North and Others v Dumfries and Galloway Council [2013] ICR 993   414
North Glamorgan NHS Trust v Ezsias [2007] EWCA Civ 330   274
North Riding Garages Ltd v Butterwick [1967] 2 QB 56   145
North West Anglia NHS Foundation Trust v Gregg [2019] EWCA Civ 378   41, 194
North West London Hospitals NHS Trust v Bowater [2011] EWCA Civ 63   172, 578
Northamptonshire County Council v Entwhistle (UKEAT/0540/09)   257
Norton Tool Co Ltd v Tewson [1973] 1 WLR 45   229
Nottingham CC v Meckle [2005] ICR 1   127
Nottingham City Homes Ltd v Brittain (UKEAT/0038/18)   524
Nottingham City Transport Ltd v Harvey (UKEAT/0032/12)   453, 519
Nottingham University v Fishel and Another [2000] IRLR 471   118
Nova Plastics Ltd v Frogatt [1982] IRLR 146   45
Now Motor Retailing Ltd v Mulvihill (UKEAT/0052/15)   189
Nursing and Midwifery Council v Somerville [2022] EWCA Civ 229   22

O

O'Brien v Associated Fire Alarms Ltd [1968] 3 ITR 183   50
O'Brien v Bolton St Catherine's Academy [2017] IRLR 547   180
O'Brien v Ministry of Justice (Case C-393/10)   418
O'Brien v Ministry of Justice [2013] UKSC 6, [2013] ICR 499   11, 19, 22
O'Flynn v Airlinks Airport Coach Company Ltd (UKEAT/0269/01)   575
O'Hanlon v HM Revenue & Customs (UKEAT/0109/06)   525
O'Kelly v Trust House Forte plc [1983] IRLR 369   27
O'Neill v Governors of St Thomas More [1996] IRLR 372   551
O'Sullivan v DSM Demolition Ltd (UKEAT/0257/19)   130
Office Equipment Systems Ltd v Hughes [2018] EWCA Civ 1842   269
Office of National Statistics v Ali [2005] IRLR 201   273
Okedina v Chikale (UKEAT/0152/17); [2019] EWCA Civ 1393   8, 168
Okoro and anor v Taylor Woodrow Construction Ltd and Others [2012] EWCA Civ 1590   405
Okwu v Rise Community (UKEAT/0082/19)   213
Olalekan v Serco Ltd (UKEAT/0189/18)   431
Olayemi v Athena Medical Centre & Another (EAT/0140/15)   408
Olivier v DWP (ET/1701407/13)   383
Olsen v Gearbulk Services Ltd (UKEAT/0345/14)   138, 139
Onyango v Berkeley (EAT/0407/12)   215
Opalkova v Acquire Care Ltd (UKEAT/0056/21)   296
Optical Express Ltd v Williams [2007] IRLR 936   149
Orr v Milton Keynes Council [2011] EWCA Civ 62   174
Osborne Clarke Services v Purohit [2009] IRLR 341   393, 463
Osborne v Capita Business Services Ltd (UKEAT/0048/16)   362
Osinuga v BPP University Ltd [2022] EAT 53   198
Otero Ramos v Servicio Galego de Saúde (Case C-531/15) [2018] IRLR 159   552
Ottino Property Services Ltd v Duncan (UKEAT/0321/14)   346
Outasight VB Ltd v Brown (UKEAT/0253/14)   301
Owen v AMEC Foster Wheeler Energy Ltd [2019] EWCA Civ 822   516

P

P14 Medical Ltd v Mahon [2021] IRLR 39   59, 337
Pacitti Jones v O'Brien [2005] IRLR 889 (Court of Session)   129, 255
Packman t/a Packman Lucas Associates v Fauchon [2012] IRLR 721, (UKEAT/0017/12)   145, 147
Paczkowski v Sieradzka (UKEAT 0111/16)   258
Page v Lord Chancellor and another (UKEAT/0304/18)   482, 483
Page v NHS Trust Development Authority (UKEAT/0183/18)   434, 482
Paggetti v Cobb (UKEAT/136/01)   224
Palfrey v Transco plc [2004] IRLR 916   130
Palmer v Southend on Sea BC [1984] ICR 372   256
Panama v London Borough of Hackney [2003] IRLR 278   188
Panayiotou v Chief Constable of Hampshire Police [2014] IRLR 500   209
Panayiotou v Kernaghan (UKEAT/0436/13)   216
Panesar v Nestlé Co [1980] ICR 144   461
Pannu and Others v Geo W King (in liquidation) and Others (UKEAT/0021/11)   345
Pareek v D Delta Ltd t/a Mira Boiler (ET/3300603/2021)   170, 208

Parfums Givenchy v Finch (UKEAT/0517/09)   200
Park Cakes Ltd v Shumba [2013] EWCA Civ 974   45
Parkins v Sodexho Ltd [2002] IRLR 109   213
Parnaby v Leicester City Council (UKEAT/0025/19)   508, 510, 511
Parsons v Airplus International Ltd (UKEAT/0111/17)   213
PAT Systems v Neilly [2012] EWHC 2609 (QB)   60
Patel and Metcalf v Surrey County Council (UKEAT/0178/16)   210
Patel v Folkestone Nursing Home Ltd [2018] EWCA Civ 1689   191
Patel v Mirza [2016] UKSC 42   6, 8
Paterson v Commissioner of Police of the Metropolis [2007] IRLR 763, (UKEAT/0635/06)   506
Pathan v South London Islamic Centre (UKEAT/0312/13)   404
Patka v BBC (UKEAT/0190/17)   272
Patterson v Castlereagh Borough Council (NIIT/1793/13)   95
Paturel v DB Services (UK) Ltd [2015] EWHC 3659 (QB)   113
Paul v East Surrey District HA [1995] IRLR 305   174
Pay v Lancashire Probation Service [2004] IRLR 129; [2009] IRLR 139, ECtHR   175
Pearce v Merrill Lynch (UKEAT/0067/19)   259
Pemberton v Former Acting Bishop of Southwell and Nottingham (UKEAT/0072/16)   397
Pemberton v Inwood [2018] EWCA Civ 564   397, 473
Pendleton v Derbyshire CC & Another (UKEAT/0238/15)   459
Peninsula Business Service Ltd v Baker (UKEAT/0241/16)   538
Peninsula Business Services Ltd v Donaldson (EAT/0249/15)   546
Pepper v Webb [1969] All ER 216   107
Pereda v Madrid Mouilidad (Case C-277/08)   93
Perkin v St George's Healthcare NHS Trust [2005] EWCA Civ 1174, [2005] IRLR 934   165, 168, 203
Petersen (Cases C-229/08 and C-341/09)   489
Phillips v Alhambra Palace Co [1901] 1 KB 59   110
Phoenix House Ltd v Stockman (No 2) (UKEAT/0284/17)   190
Phoenix House Ltd v Stockman (UKEAT/0264/15)   169
Pickwell and Nicholls v Pro Cam CP Ltd [2016] EWHC 1304 (QB)   63
Piepenbrock v London School of Economics and Political Science [2022] EAT 119   574
Pimlico Plumbers Ltd v Smith [2017] EWCA Civ 51   15, 23
Pimlico Plumbers Ltd v Smith [2018] UKSC 29   11, 23
Pinewood Repro Limited t/a County Print (County Print) v Page (UKEAT/0028/10)   199
Pitcher and Another v The Chancellor, Masters and Scholars of the University of Oxford and Another
    (UKEAT/0083/20 and 0032/20)   494
Planon v Gilligan [2022] EWCA Civ 642   63
Plant v API Microelectronics Ltd (ET/3401454/2016)   193
Plastering Contractors Stanmore Ltd v Holden (UKEAT/0074/14)   22
Plumb v Duncan Print Group Ltd (EAT/0071/15)   93
Plymouth City Council v White (UKEAT/0333/13)   277
Pnaiser v NHS England [2016] IRLR 170   530, 536
Polkey v AE Dayton Services Ltd [1987] ICR 301; [1988] 1 AC 344; [1988] ICR 142   173, 178, 197, 230
Poplar Housing and Regeneration Community Association Ltd v Donoghue [2002] QB 48   569
Portnykh v Nomura International plc (UKEAT/0448/13)   282
Post Office v Burkett [2003] EWCA Civ 748   241, 245
Powell v London Borough of Brent [1987] IRLR 466   117
Powell v Newcastle College Group (ET/2514148/09)   257
Powell v OMV Exploration & Production Ltd [2014] IRLR 80, EAT   137
Power v Panasonic UK Ltd [2003] IRLR 151   504
Preece v JD Wetherspoons plc (ET/2104806/10)   192, 578
Preen v Coolink Ltd and another (ET/1403451/2020)   170, 208
President of the Methodist Conference, The v Preston [2013] UKSC 29   35
Pretty v UK (2002) 35 EHRR 1   574
Price v Powys County Council (UKEAT/0133/20)   554
Price v UK (2001) 34 EHRR 1285   574
Priddle v Dibble [1978] 1 All ER 1058   168
Prigge (Case C-447/09)   489
Private Medicine Intermediaries Ltd v Hodkinson and Others (EAT/0134/15)   125
Prophet Plc v Huggett 2014] EWCA Civ 1013   63
Prosser v Community Gateway Association (ET/2413672/2020)   169
Protectacoat Firthglow Ltd v Szilagyi [2009] EWCA Civ 98, [2009] IRLR 365   32
Provident Financial Group plc v Hayward [1989] ICR 160   65
Prudential plc v Special Commissioner of Income Tax [2013] UKSC 1   278

Pryce v Baxterstorey Ltd [2022] EAT 61   254
Publicis Consultants v O'Farrell (UKEAT/0430/10)   112
Pugh v National Assembly for Wales (UKEAT/0251/06)   405
Pulse Healthcare Ltd v Carewatch Care Services Ltd (UKEAT 0123/12)   28
Punjab National Bank (International) Ltd & Others v Gosain (UKEAT/0003/14)   293
Puthenveetil v Alexander and Another (UKEAT/0407/17)   54

Q

Q v Secretary of State for Justice (UKEAT/0120/19)   175, 576
QBE Management Services (UK) Ltd v Dymoke and Others [2012] IRLR 458   118
Qua v John Ford Morrison Solicitors [2003] IRLR 184   560
Quarcoopome v Sock Shop Holdings Ltd [1995] IRLR 353   273
Quashie v Stringfellows Restaurant [2012] EWCA Civ 1735   30
Quelch v Courtiers Support Services Ltd (ET/3313138/2020)   170
Quintiles Commercial UK Ltd v Barongo (UKEAT/0255/17)   167

R

R (G) v The Governors of X School [2009] EWHC 504 (Admin); [2011] UKSC 30   175, 570
R (Heather and Others) v Leonard Cheshire Foundation and Others [2002] 2 All ER 936   569
R (IWGB) v Central Arbitration Committee [2018] EWHC 3342 (Admin)   25
R (JS) v Secretary of State for Work and Pensions [2015] UKSC 16   579
R (on the application of E) v Governing Body of JFS [2009] UKSC 15, [2010] IRLR 136   390
R (on the application of Elias) v Secretary of State for Defence [2006] IRLR 934   388
R (on the application of Guardian News and Media Ltd) v City of Westminster Magistrates' Court
   [2012] EWCA Civ 420   288
R (on the application of Hottak and Anor) v Secretary of State for Foreign and Commonwealth Affairs and Anor
   [2015] EWHC 1953 (Admin)   138, 378
R (on the application of Miller) v College of Policing and another [2020] EWHC 225 (Admin)   579
R (on the application of Susan Weaver) v London and Quadrant Housing Trust [2008] EWHC 1377 (Admin) 569
R (on the application of T and Others) v Secretary of State for the Home Department and anor [2014] UKSC 35 576
R (on the application of the Independent Workers' Union of Great Britain) v Secretary of State for Work and
   Pensions [2021] IRLR 102   207
R (on the application of the IWGB) v CAC and Roofoods Ltd t/a Deliveroo [2021] EWCA Civ 952   25
R (on the application of Watkins-Singh) v Aberdare Girls' High School and Another [2008] EWHC 1865 (Admin) 452
R v Birmingham City Council, ex p Equal Opportunities Commission [1989] IRLR 173   428
R v Ghosh [1982] 3 WLR 110   194
R v Secretary of State for Education and Employment, ex parte Williamson [2005] UKHL 15, [2005] 2 AC 246   381, 434
Rabal Canas v Nexea Gestation Documental (Case C-392/13)   154
Rackham v NHS Professionals Ltd (UKEAT/0110/15)   267, 270, 284
Radia v Jefferies International Ltd (UKEAT/0007/18)   296, 298
Radia v Jefferies International Ltd (UKEAT/0123/18)   189
Raj v Capita Business Services Ltd and another (UKEAT/0074/19)   442, 471
Raja v Secretary of State for Justice [2010] All ER (D) 134   218
Rajabov v Foreign and Commonwealth Office [2022] EAT 112   139
Rajaratnam v Care UK Clinical Services Ltd (UKEAT/0435/14)   460
Rakova v London North West Healthcare NHS Trust (UKEAT/0043/19)   521
Ramdoolar v Bycity Ltd [2005] ICR 368   551
Ramphal v Department for Transport (UKEAT/0352/14)   190
Ramsay and others v Bowercross Construction Ltd and others (UKEAT/0534/07)   295
Ramsey v Walkers Snack Foods Ltd [2004] IRLR 754   189
Rana v London Borough of Ealing [2018] EWCA Civ 2074   302
Rashid v Asian Community Care Services Ltd (UKEAT/480/99)   547
Ratcliffe Duce & Grammer v Binns (UKEAT/0100/08)   300
Ravat v Halliburton Manufacturing and Services Ltd [2012] UKSC 1   135
Ravisy v Simmons & Simmons LLP (UKEAT/0085/18)   138
RCO Support Services Ltd and Another v Unison and Others [2002] ICR 751   341
Ready Mixed Concrete (South East) Ltd v Minister of Pensions and National Insurance [1968] 1 All ER 433   11, 15, 16
Really Easy Car Credit Ltd v Thompson (UKEAT/0197/17)   438, 551
Redfearn v United Kingdom [2012] ECHR 1878   383, 578
Redman v Devon PCT [2013] EWCA Civ 1110   148
Reed in Partnership Ltd v Fraine (UKEAT/0520/10)   257
Regent Security Services v Power [2008] IRLR 226   364
Reid and Bull Information Systems Ltd v Stedman [1999] IRLR 299   478

Reilly v Sandwell MBC [2018] UKSC 18   173
Rembiszewski v Atkins Ltd (UKEAT/0402/11)   220
Remploy Ltd v Lowen-Bulger (UKEAT/0027/18)   292
Remploy v Brain (UKEAT/0465/10)   259
Rendina v Royston Veterinary Centre Ltd (ET/3307459/2020)   170, 208
Rentplus UK Ltd v Coulson [2022] IRLR 664   226
Re-use Collections Ltd v Sendall and May Glass Recycling Ltd [2014] EWHC 3852 (QB)   66
Revenue and Customs Commissioners v Garau (UKEAT/0348/16)   264
Reyes v Al-Malki [2015] EWCA Civ 32   134
Reyes v Al-Malki & Another [2017] UKSC 61   134
Rhys-Harper v Relaxion Group [2003] IRLR 484   484
Ricardo v Portimão Urbis, EM, SA, in liquidation, Município de Portimão Emarp – Empresa Municipal de Águas
   e Resíduos de Portimão, EM, SA (Case C-416/16)   341, 355
Richardson v Delaney [2001] IRLR 663   116
Richmond Adult Community College v McDougall [2008] ICR 431   509, 513
Richmond Pharmacology v Dhaliwal [2009] ICR 724, [2009] IRLR 336   470, 472
Ridehalgh v Horsefield [1994] 3 WLR 462   300
Rider v Leeds CC (UKEAT/0243/11)   521
Ridge v HM Land Registry (EAT/0485/12)   169
Ridout v TC Group [1998] IRLR 628   536
Rigby v Ferodo [1987] IRLR 516   70
Rihal v London Borough of Ealing [2004] IRLR 642   441
Risby v London Borough of Waltham Forest (EAT/0318/15)   531
RNLI v Bushaway [2005] IRLR 674   32
Robb v Green [1895] 2 QB 315   45, 118
Robert Cort & Son Ltd v Charman [1981] ICR 816   131
Robert Sage Ltd t/a Prestige Nursing Care Ltd v O'Connell and Others (UKEAT/0336/13)   354
Roberts v The Regard Partnership (ET/2104545/09)   177
Robertson v Bexley Community Centre [2003] IRLR 434   404
Robinson v Al Qasimi (UKEAT/0106/19)   168
Robinson v Bowskill (UKEAT/0313/12)   131, 255
Robinson v Department for Work and Pensions [2020] EWCA Civ 859   533
Robinson v Harman (1848) 1 Exch 850   111
Robinson v Tescom Corporation [2008] IRLR 408   70
Robinson-Steele v RD Retail Services and other cases (Case C-131/04)   93
Rock Advertising Ltd v MWB Business Exchange Centres Ltd [2018] UKSC 24   47
Rock Refrigeration Ltd v Jones [1996] IRLR 675   64
Roddis v Sheffield Hallam University (UKEAT/0299/17)   417
Rodgers v Leeds Laser Cutting (ET/1803829/2020)   169
Rodgers v Leeds Laser Cutting [2022] EAT 69   207
Rodrigues v Co-Op Group Ltd (UKEAT/0022/12)   274
Roger Bullivant Ltd v Ellis [1987] ICR 464   45, 64
Rolls Royce plc v Unite the Union [2008] EWHC 2420 (QB); [2009] IRLR 576   199, 494
Römer v Freie und Hansestadt Hamburg (Case C-147/08)   388
Rommelfanger v Germany (1989) 62 DR 151   72
Rooney v Leicester City Council [2021] 10 WLUK 69   439, 505
Rosenbladt (Case C-45/09)   489
Rothwell v Pelikan Hardcopy Scotland [2006] IRLR 24   523
Rotsart de Hertaing v Benoidt SA and IGC Housing Service SA (Case C-305/94) [1997] IRLR 127   349
Royal Bank of Scotland plc v Harrison (UKEAT/0093/08)   560, 561
Royal Mail Group Ltd v Jhuti (UKEAT/0020/16)   405
Royal Mail Group Ltd v Jhuti [2017] EWCA Civ 1632, [2018] ICR 1077, [2018] IRLR 251   174, 217, 271
Royal Mail Group Ltd v Jhuti [2019] UKSC 55   166, 190, 215
Royal Mail Group v CWU [2009] EWCA Civ 1045   369
Royal Mencap Society v Tomlinson-Blake [2018] EWCA Civ 1641   54
Royal National Othopaedic Hospital Trust v Howard [2002] IRLR 849   306
Rubins v Latvia [2015] ECHR 2   578
Russell v College of North West London (UKEAT/0314/13)   537
Russell v Transocean International [2011] UKSC 57, [2011] IRLR 24   86, 87
Ryan v South West Ambulance Services NHS Trust [2021] IRLR 4   495
Rynda (UK) Ltd v Rhijnsburger [2015] EWCA Civ 75   348

S

Saad v Southampton Hospitals NHS Trust (UKEAT/0276/17) — 483
Saavedra v Aceground Ltd [1995] IRLR 198 — 74
Safeway Stores v Burrell [1997] IRLR 200 — 145, 147
Sainsbury's Supermarkets Ltd v Hitt [2003] IRLR 23 — 173, 188, 242
Sajid v Chowdhury [2002] IRLR 113 — 102
Salaberria Sorondo v Academia Vasca de Policia y Emergencias (Case C-258/15) — 397
Salford NHS PCT v Smith (UKEAT/0507/10) — 524
Salford Royal NHS Foundation Trust v Roldan [2010] IRLR 721 — 172, 188
Salmon v Castlebeck Care (Teesdale) Ltd (in administration) and others (UKEAT/0304/14) — 191
Salvesen v Simons [1994] IRLR 52 — 7, 168
Sampanis v Greece (App No 32526/05) — 420
Samsung Semiconductor Europe Ltd v Docherty and Another [2011] CSOH 32 — 119
San Ling Chinese Medicine Centre v Miss Lian Wei Ji (UKEAT/0370/09) — 7
Sanders v Parry [1967] 2 All ER 803 — 45
Sandhu v Jan de Rijk Transport Ltd [2007] EWCA Civ 430 — 123
Sandwell & West Birmingham Hospitals NHS Trust v Westwood (UKEAT/0032/09) — 185, 231
Santamera v Express Cargo Forwarding t/a IEC Ltd [2003] IRLR 273 — 189
Santander UK PLC v Bharaj (UKEAT/0075/20) — 277
Santos Gomes v Higher Level Care Ltd (EAT/0017/16) — 85
Sarkar v West London Mental Health NHS Trust [2010] IRLR 508 — 172
Sarnoff v YZ [2021] EWCA Civ 26 — 271, 276
Sash Window Workshop Ltd & Another v King (EAT/0057/14) — 408
Saunders v OCS Group (UKEAT/0051/09) — 224
Savory and 58 Others v South Western Ambulance Service NHS Foundation Trust and Another (ET/1400119/2016) — 263
SCA Packaging Ltd v Boyle [2009] UKHL 37 — 502, 510
SCA Packaging v Revenue and Customs [2007] EWHC 270 (Ch) — 116
Schrems v Irish Data Protection Commissioner (Case C-362/14) — 590
Schultz-Hoff v Deutsche Rentenversicherung Bund [2009] IRLR 214 — 93
Schwarzenbach and Anor v Jones (UKEAT/0100/15) — 134
Scicluna v Zippy Stitch Ltd [2018] EWCA Civ 1320 — 271
Science Research Council v Nassé [1980] AC 1028 — 277
Science Warehouse Ltd v Mills (EAT/0224/15) — 253
Scott and Co v Richardson (UKEAT/0074/04) — 168
Scott v Kenton Schools Academy Trust (UKEAT/0031/19) — 535
Scott v Russell [2013] EWCA Civ 1432 — 296
Scott v Scott [1913] AC 417 — 287
Scottbridge Construction Ltd v Wright [2003] IRLR 21 — 53
Scottish and Southern Energy plc v Mackay (UKEAT/0075/06) — 524
Scottish Federation of Housing Associations v Jones [2022] EAT 114 — 209
Screene v Seatwave Ltd (UKEAT/0020/11) — 165
Scully UK Ltd v Lee [1998] IRLR 259 — 60
Seahorse Marine Ltd v Nautilus International [2018] EWCA Civ 2789 — 154
Sealy v Consignia plc [2002] IRLR 624 — 256
Seccombe v Reed in Partnership Ltd (UKEAT/0213/20) — 503
Secretary of State for BERR v Neufeld [2009] EWCA Civ 280 — 36
Secretary of State for Business, Energy and Industrial Strategy v Parry [2018] EWCA Civ 672 — 267
Secretary of State for Business, Innovation & Skills v Pengelly & Another (UKEAT/0287/12 & 0312/12) — 152
Secretary of State for Employment v Associated Society of Locomotive Engineers and Firemen (ASLEF) (No 2) [1972] 2 QB 455 — 44
Secretary of State for Employment v Litster [1989] IRLR 161 — 351
Secretary of State for Employment v Spence [1986] IRLR 248, CA — 351
Secretary of State for Justice v Hibbert (UKEAT/0289/13) — 108, 129
Secretary of State for Justice v Plaistow (UKEAT/0016/20 & UKEAT/0085/20) — 407
Secretary of State for Justice v Prospere (UKEAT/0412/14) — 519
Secretary of State for Justice v Windle [2016] EWCA Civ 459 — 11, 17, 30
Secretary of State for Trade and Industry v Bottrill [1999] ICR 592 — 36
Secretary of State for Trade and Industry v Cook and Others [1997] ICR 288 — 356
Secretary of State for Trade and Industry v Rutherford and Another [2006] IRLR 551, HL — 452, 455
Secretary of State for Work and Pensions v Alam [2010] ICR 665 — 536
Secure Care UK Ltd v Mott (UKEAT/0135/20) — 217
Securiplan v Bademosi (UKEAT/1128/02) — 353
Sefton BC v Wainwright (UKEAT/0168/14) — 548

Sejpal v Rodericks Dental Ltd [2022] EAT 91   22, 26
Seldon v Clarkson Wright and Jakes (ET/1100275/07); [2009] IRLR 267, EAT; [2010] IRLR 865, CA;
    [2012] UKSC 16, [2012] IRLR 590   427, 491, 492
Selkent Bus Co v Moore [1996] IRLR 661   272
Senior Heat Treatment Ltd v Bell [1997] IRLR 614   356
Serco Ltd v Lawson and Others [2006] UKHL 3   134, 135
SG&R Valuation Service v Boudrais [2008] EWHC 1340 (QB)   65
Shamoon v Chief Constable of the Royal Ulster Constabulary [2003] ICR 337, [2003] IRLR 285   394, 431, 459, 484
Shanahan Engineering v Unite (UKEAT/0411/09)   153
Sharfugeen v T J Morris Ltd (UKEAT/0272/16)   126
Sharma v Lily Communications Ltd (ET/1800437/21)   169
Sharpe v Bishop of Worcester [2015] EWCA Civ 399, [2015] IRLR 663   11, 35
Shaw v CCL Ltd (UKEAT/0512/06)   125
Sheikholeslami v University of Edinburgh (UKEAT/0014/17)   532
Sheridan v Prospects for People with Learning Disabilities (ET/2901366/06)   397
Sheriff v Klyne Tugs (Lowestoft) Ltd [1999] ICR 1170, [1999] IRLR 481   410, 480
Shields Automotive Ltd v Grieg (UKEATS/0024/10)   297
Shifferaw v Hudson Music Co Ltd (UKEAT/0294/15)   227
Shittu v South London and Maudsley NHS Foundation Trust [2022] EAT 18   231
Shove v Downs Surgical plc [1984] IRLR 17   116
Shrestha v Genesis Housing Association Ltd [2015] EWCA Civ 94   188
Sibley v The Girls Day School Trust, Norwich High School for Girls (UKEAT/1368/01)   547
Sidhu v Aerospace Composite Technology Ltd [2000] IRLR 602   398
Sillifant v Powell Duffryn Timber Ltd [1983] IRLR 91   230
Silvey v Pendragon plc [2001] IRLR 685   113
Simmons v Castle [2012] EWCA Civ 1039   408, 480
Simmons v Castle [2012] EWCA Civ 1288   408
Simoes v De Sede UK Ltd (UKEAT/0153/20)   206
Simpson v Endsleigh Insurance Services Ltd (UKEAT/0544/09)   548
Sindicato de Medicos de Asistencia Publica (SiMAP) v Conselleria de Sanidad y Consumo de la Generalidad Valenciana (Case
    C-303/98) [2000] ECR I-7963, [2000] IRLR 845, ECJ   78
Singh v Metroline West Ltd [2022] EAT 80   124, 126
Sir Benjamin Slade v Biggs [2022] IRLR 216   227
Skyrail Oceanic Ltd v Coleman [1981] ICR 864   479
Slaughter v Breuer [1990] ICR 730   230
Small v Shrewsbury and Telford Hospitals NHS Trust [2017] EWCA Civ 882   218
Smania v Standard Chartered Bank (UKEAT/0181/14)   138
Smart Delivery Ltd v Augustine (UKEAT/0219/18)   15
Smith v Carillion (JM) Ltd [2015] EWCA Civ 209   9, 33
Smith v Churchills Stairlifts plc [2006] IRLR 41   521
Smith v Cognita Schools Ltd (ET/1600884/2021)   170, 208
Smith v Gleacher Shacklock LLP (ET/2202747/2015)   558
Smith v Pimlico Plumbers (Rev1) [2022] EWCA Civ 70   77, 91
Smith v Safeway [1996] ICR 868   457
Smith v Scapa Group plc (ET/2400172/2017)   211, 213
Smith v Trafford Housing Trust [2012] EWHC 3221 (Ch)   292, 578
Smoker v London Fire and Civil Defence Authority [1991] ICR 449   228
Snowball v Gardner Merchant Ltd [1987] IRLR 397   480
SNR Denton UK LLP v Kirwan & Others (UKEAT/0158/12), [2012] IRLR 966   347
Sobczyszyn v Szkola Podstawowa w Rzeplinie (Case C-178/15)   94
Sobhi v Commissioner of Police of the Metropolis (UKEAT/0518/12)   507
Société Général, London Branch v Geys [2013] IRLR 122   43, 105
Sodexho v Gibbons (UKEAT/0318/05)   301
Software 2000 Ltd v Andrews and Others [2007] ICR 82   230
Soh v Imperial College (UKEAT/0350/14)   213
Solectron Scotland Ltd v Roper [2004] IRLR 4   45
Solicitors Regulation Authority v Mitchell (UKEAT/0497/12)   441
Somjee v UK [2002] IRLR 886   572
Sood Enterprises Ltd v Healey (UKEATS/0015/12)   93
South Warwickshire NHS Foundation Trust v Lee and Others (UKEAT/0287/17)   532
South West Yorkshire Partnership NHS Foundation Trust v Jackson (UKEAT/0090/18)   438
South Western Ambulance Service NHS Foundation Trust v King (UKEAT/0056/19)   405, 483
Southampton City College v Randall [2006] IRLR 24   523
Southern Cross Healthcare v Perkins and Others [2010] EWCA Civ 1442   40

Southern v Franks Charlesly & Co [1981] IRLR 278   123
Sovereign House Security v Savage [1989] IRLR 115   123
Spaceman v ISS Mediclean Ltd (UKEAT/0142/18)   206
Spaceright Europe Ltd v Baillavoine and Another [2011] EWCA Civ 1565   361
Sparks v Department for Transport [2015] EWHC 181 (QB); [2016] EWCA Civ 360   69
Spence v Intype Libra Ltd (UKEAT/0617/06)   524
Spencer v Paragon Wallpapers Ltd [1976] IRLR 373   179
Spijkers v Gebroeders Benedik Abattoir CV [1986] ECR 1119, ECJ   339
Spillers-French (Holdings) Ltd v USDAW [1980] ICR 31   155
Spring v Guardian Assurance plc [1994] IRLR 460, [1994] 3 All ER 129   42, 304
St Andrews School v Blundell (UKEAT/0330/09)   408
St Helens Metropolitan Borough Council v Derbyshire [2004] IRLR 851; [2005] EWCA Civ 977; [2007] IRLR 540   482
St Ives Plymouth Ltd v Haggerty (UKEAT/0107/08)   13, 17
St John of God (Care Services) Ltd v Brooks [1992] IRLR 546   204
Stack v Ajar-Tec Ltd [2015] EWCA Civ 46   37
Stadt Wuppertal v Bauer (Case C-569/16)   95
Stanley Cole (Wainfleet) Ltd v Sheridan [2003] IRLR 52   124
Stedman v UK (1997) 23 EHRR CD 168   73, 420
Steel and Morris v The UK [2005] ECHR 103   572
Steer v Stormsure Ltd [2021] EWCA Civ 887   406
Stefanko v Maritime Hotel Ltd (UKEAT/0024/18)   39
Stephenson v Delphi Diesel Systems Ltd [2003] ICR 471   13
Sterling Developments v Pagano (UKEAT/0511/06)   289
Sterling v United Learning Trust (UKEAT/0439/14)   254
Stevens v Northolt High School (ET/3300621/2014)   34
Stevens v University of Birmingham [2015] EWHC 2300 (QB)   177, 178
Stevenson Jordan & Harrson Ltd v McDonald and Evans [1952] 1 TLR 101   11
Stoffel & Co v Grondona [2020] UKSC 42   8
Stojsavljevic v DPD Group (UKEAT/0118/20)   22
Stott v Ralli Ltd (UKEAT/0223/20)   533
Stratford v Auto Trail VR Ltd (UKEAT/0116/16)   185
Strathclyde Regional Council v Wallace [1998] ICR 205   415
Strathclyde Regional Council v Zafar [1998] IRLR 36   442
Stringfellows Restaurants Ltd v Quashie [2013] IRLR 99   13, 17
Stuart Delivery Ltd v Augustine [2021] EWCA Civ 1514, [2022] IRLR 56   22, 26
Stuart Peters v Bell [2009] EWCA Civ 938   229
Stubbes v Trower, Still and Keeling [1987] IRLR 321   49
Sturmey v The Weymouth and Portland BC (UKEAT/0114/14)   492
Sullivan v Bury Street Capital [2021] EWCA Civ 1694   510
Summers v Bundy [2016] EWCA Civ 126   409
Sunderland Polytechnic v Evans [1993] IRLR 196   76
Sunrise Brokers LLP Rodgers [2014] EWHC 2633 (QB)   118
Sunuva Ltd v Martin (UKEAT/0174/17)   296
Superdrug Stores plc v Fannon (UKEAT/1190/96)   559
Susie Radin Ltd v GMB and Others [2004] IRLR 400   153, 155, 369
Sutherland v Network Appliance Ltd [2001] IRLR 12   306
Sutton Oak Church of England School v Whittaker (UKEAT/0211/18)   434
Suzen v Zehnacker Gebaudereinigung GmbH Krankenhausservice [1997] IRLR 255   339, 344
Swanbridge Hire & Sales Ltd v Butler & Others (UKEAT/0056/13)   347
Swania v Standard Chartered Bank (EAT/0181/14)   139
Swann v GHL Insurance Services UK Ltd (ET/2306281/07)   490
Swansea University Pension Scheme Trustees v Williams [2015] IRLR 885   529
Sweetin v Coral Racing [2006] IRLR 252   369
Swiss Re Corporate Solutions Ltd v Sommer [2022] EAT 78   282
Symbian Ltd v Christensen [2001] IRLR 77   65

T

Tabberer v Mears Ltd (UKEAT/0064/17)   364
Taiwo and Onu v Olaigbe and Akwiwu [2016] UKSC 31   380
Talon Engineering Ltd v Smith (UKEAT/0236/17)   189, 190
Tameside Hospital NHS Foundation Trust v Mylott (UKEAT/0352/09 and UKEAT/0399/10)   410, 524
Tanner v DT Kean [1978] IRLR 110   123
Tanveer v East London Bus and Coach Co Ltd (UKEAT/0022/16)   263

Tao Herbs and Acupuncture Ltd v Jin (UKEAT/1477/09) — 223
Tapere v South London and Maudsley NHS Trust (UKEAT/0410/08) — 352
Taplin v Shippam Ltd [1978] ICR 1068 — 218
Tarbuck v Sainsbury's Supermarkets Ltd [2006] IRLR 664 — 524
Tarn v Hughes and Others (UKEAT/0064/18) — 271
Taylor v Connex South Eastern Ltd (UKEAT/1243/99) — 364
Taylor v Jaguar Land Rover Ltd (ET/1304471/2018) — 386
Taylor v Ladbrokes Betting and Gaming Ltd [2017] IRLR 312 — 508
Taylor v OCS Group Ltd [2006] EWCA Civ 702, [2006] IRLR 613 — 191
Taylor v Somerfield Stores Ltd (ETS/107487/07) — 192, 292
Taylor v XLN Telecom (EAT/0383/09) — 410
Tayside Public Transport Co Ltd v Reilly [2012] IRLR 755 — 274
Tees Esk and Wear Valleys NHS Foundation Trust v Aslam [2020] IRLR 495 — 471
Teggert v TeleTech UK Ltd (NIET 00704/11), [2014] IRLR 625 — 192, 292, 578
Teinaz v London Borough of Wandsworth [2002] EWCA Civ 1040, [2002] IRLR 721 — 291, 572
Telephone Information Services Ltd v Wilkinson [1991] IRLR 148 — 299
Tenon FM Ltd v Cawley [2018] EWHC 1972 (QB) — 37
Tera (UK) Ltd v Mr A Goubatchev (UKEAT/0490/08) — 441
Terry v East Sussex County Council [1977] 1 All ER 567 — 168
Tesco Stores Ltd v Element & Ors (UKEAT/0228/20) — 278
Tesco Stores Ltd v Tennant (UK/EAT/0167/19) — 509
TGWU v Morgan Platts Ltd (UKEAT/0646/02) — 155
Thind v Salvesen Logistics Ltd (UKEAT/0487/09) — 283
Thomas Sanderson Blinds Ltd v English (UKEAT/0316/10) — 473
Thomas v Far plc [2007] EWCA Civ 118 — 59, 60
Thomas v Nationwide Building Society (ET/1601342/14) — 263
Thompson v East Dumbartonshire Council (UKEATS/0049/13) — 273
Thompson v London Central Bus Company Ltd (UKEAT/0108/15) — 427, 483
Thompson v Scancrown Ltd (t/a Manors) (ET/2205199/19) — 559
Thorpe v Dul, Brooksby Melton College and Learning Skills Council [2003] ICR 1556 — 31
Three Rivers DC and Others v Bank of England (No 5) [2003] EWCA Civ 474 — 278
Three Rivers District Council and Others v Governor and Company of the Bank of England [2004] UKHL 48, [2004] 3 WLR 1274 — 278
Thyagarajan v Cap Gemini UK plc (UKEAT/0264/14) — 511
Tillman v Egon Zehnder Ltd [2019] UKSC 32 — 61, 62
Tilson v Alstom Transport [2010] EWCA Civ 1038 — 33
Timis Sage v Osipov [2019] IRLR 52 — 209
Timothy James Consulting Ltd v Wilton (UKEAT/0082/14), [2015] ICR 764 — 236, 469
Toal v GB Oils Ltd (UKEAT/0569/12) — 177
Todd v British Midland Airways Ltd [1978] ICR 959 — 135
Todd v Care Concern (UKEAT/0057/2010) — 369
Topic v Hollyland Pitta Bakery (UKEAT/523/11) — 298
Tradition Securities & Futures SA v Alexandre Mouradian [2009] EWCA Civ 60 — 74
Trayhorn v Secretary of State for Employment (UKEAT/0304/16) — 382
Tree v South East Coastal Services Ambulance NHS Trust (UKEAT/0043/17) — 276
Trentside Manor Care Ltd v Raphael [2022] EAT 37 — 278, 280
Trow v Ind Coope (West Midlands) Ltd [1967] 2 QB 899 — 255
TSB Bank plc v Harris [2000] IRLR 157 — 43
TSC Europe (UK) Ltd v Massey [1999] IRLR 22 — 61
TSN v Hyvinvointialan (Case C-609/17) — 93
T-Systems Ltd v Lewis (EAT/0042/15) — 531
Tumenaite v PC Soho Centre Administration Ltd & Anor (ET/2204607/18) — 384
Turner v Sawdon [1901] 2 KB 653 — 41
TW White & Sons Ltd v White (UKEAT/0022/21) — 301
Twenty-four Seven Recruitment Services Ltd v Alfonso (UKEAT/0311/17) — 35
Twist DX Limited & others v Armes & another (UKEAT/0030/20) — 210
Tydeman v Oyster Yachts Ltd [2022] EAT 115 — 107, 222
Tyldesley v TML Plastics [1996] ICR 356 — 415

U

U v Butler and Wilson (UKEAT/0354/13) — 266
Uber BV v Aslam [2021] UKSC 5 — 78
Uber BV v Aslam and Others [2021] UKSC 5 — 24

UBS Wealth Management (UK) Ltd v Vesta Wealth LLP and Others [2008] EWHC 1974 (QB)   61, 64
Uddin v London Borough of Ealing (UKEAT/0165/19)   174, 190
Ullah v London Borough of Hounslow (EAT/0084/16)   264
Underwood v Wincanton plc (UKEAT/0163/15)   213
Unionen v Almega Tjänsteförbunden ISS Facility Services AB (Case C-336/15)   358
Unison v Lord Chancellor [2017] UKSC 51   453
UNITE the Union v Nailard [2019] ICR 28   475
United Bank Ltd v Akhtar [1989] IRLR 507   49
United Lincolnshire Trust v Farren (UKEAT/0198/16)   220
University Hospital North Tees & Hartlepool NHS Foundation Trust v Fairhall (UKEAT/0150/20)   174
University of Dundee v Chakraborty [2022] EAT 150   279
University of Oxford v Humphreys [2000] IRLR 183   356
University of Sunderland v Drossou (UKEAT/0341/16)   222
Urso v Department for Work and Pensions (UKEAT/0045/16)   469
USA v Nolan (Case C-583/10)   153
USA v Nolan [2010] EWCA Civ 1223   153
USA v Nolan [2015] UKSC 63   134
USDAW & Ors v Tesco [2022] EWCA Civ 978   71
USDAW v WW Realisation 1 Ltd (UKEAT/0548/12)   153
Uwhubetine v NHS Commissioning Board England (UKEAT/0264/18)   284

V

Van Gend en Loos v Nederlandse Administratie der Belastingen (Case 26/62) [1963] ECR 1   3
Van Resnburg v Royal Borough Kingston-upon-Thames (UKEAT/0095/07)   276
Various Claimants v Catholic Child Welfare Society [2012] UKSC 56   398
Varnish v British Cycling and UK Sport (UKEAT/0022/20)   18
Vaughan v London Borough of Lewisham & Others (UKEAT/0533/12), [2013] IRLR 713   293, 296
Vaughan v Modality Partnership [2021] IRLR 97   272
Veakins v Kier Islington Ltd [2009] EWCA Civ 1288   476
Vento v Chief Constable of West Yorkshire Police [2003] IRLR 102   408, 480
Veolia Environmental Services UK v Gumbs (UKEAT/0487/12)   405, 441
Vestergaard Frandsen Als and Others v Bestnet Europe Ltd and Others [2009] EWHC 1456 (Ch)   57, 118
Vidal-Hall v Google [2014] EWHC 13 (QB)   574
Ville de Nivelles v Matzak (Case C-518/15)   78
Ville de Nivelles v Matzak [2018] IRLR 457   79
Vining v Wandsworth LBC [2017] EWCA Civ 1092   152
Virgin Media Ltd v Seddington & Eland UKEAT/0539/08   227
Vital Pérez v Ayuntamiento de Oviedo (Case C-416/13) [2015] IRLR 158   397
Vivian v Bournemouth Borough Council (UKEAT/0254/10)   218
Volker Willmeroth v Brosson (Case C-570/16)   95

W

W Devis & Sons Ltd v Atkins [1977] AC 931, HL   167, 173, 223
W Gimber & Sons Ltd v Spurrett (1967) 2 ITR 308   147
Wade v CT Plus Community Interest Company (UKEAT/0510/13)   273
Wade v Sheffield Hallam University (UKEAT/0194/12)   524
Walker v Adams [2001] STC 101   236
Walker v Sita Information Networking Computing Ltd (UKEAT/0091/10)   511
Walker v Sita Information Networking Computing Ltd (UKEAT/0097/12)   505
Wallis v Valentine [2002] EWCA Civ 1034   267
Walls Meat Co Ltd v Khan [1979] ICR 52   257
Walters t/a Rosewood v Barik (UKEAT/0053/16)   77
Walton Centre for Neurology v Bewley (UKEAT/0564/07)   414
Waltons and Morse v Dorrington [1997] IRLR 488   42
Wandsworth London Borough Council v D'Silva [1998] IRLR 193   69
Wang v University of Keele (UKEAT/0223/10)   256
Warburton v Chief Constable of Northamptonshire Police [2022] EAT 42   483
Wardle v Credit Agricole Corporate and Investment Bank [2011] IRLR 604   407
Warner v Armfield Retail & Leisure Ltd (UKEAT/0376/12)   109
Warren v Henlys Ltd [1948] 2 All ER 935   398
Wass v Delta Global Source (UK) Ltd (ET/2600605/15)   262
Wasteney v East London NHS Foundation Trust (EAT/0157/15)   430
Watkins v HSBC Bank plc (UKEAT/0018/18)   524

Watson v Hilary Meredith Solicitors (UKEAT/0092/20) — 280
Way and Another v Crouch [2005] IRLR 603 — 407, 411
Way v Spectrum Property Care Ltd [2015] EWCA Civ 381 — 186
Weathersfield Ltd v Sargent [1999] IRLR 94 — 129, 403
Webb v EMO Air Cargo (UK) Ltd [1993] IRLR 27 — 4, 437
Webster v The Attorney General of Trinidad and Tobago [2015] UKPC 10 — 579
Weddell v Barchester Healthcare Ltd and Wallbank v Wallbank Fox Designs Ltd [2012] EWCA Civ 25 — 398
Wedgewood v Ministergate Hull Ltd (UKEAT/0137/10) — 130
Weeks v Newham College of Further Education (UKEAT/0630/11) — 473
Weir Valves and Controls (UK) Ltd v Armitage [2004] ICR 371 — 275
Welton v Deluxe Retail Ltd (t/a Madhouse) [2013] IRLR 166 — 133
Wentworth-Wood v Maritime Transport Ltd (UKEAT/0184/17) — 301
Wess v Science Museum Group (UKEAT/0120/14) — 128
West London Mental Health NHS Trust v Chhabra [2013] UKSC 60 — 68, 111
West Midlands Transport Executive v Singh [1988] ICR 634 — 441
Western Excavating Ltd v Sharp [1978] QB 761 — 124
Wheeler v Patel [1987] IRLR 211 — 360
Whelan and Another (t/a Cheers Off Licence) v Richardson [1998] IRLR 14 — 224
Whitbread & Co v Mills [1988] IRLR 501 — 191
Whitbread plc (t/a Whitbread Medway Inns) v Hall [2001] EWCA Civ 268, [2001] IRLR 275 — 193
White and Another v Troutbeck SA (UKEAT/0177/12); [2013] EWCA Civ 1171 — 16
Whitehead v EMH Housing (ET/2600493/4/6) — 90
Whiteman v CPS Interiors Ltd (ET/2601103/2015) — 558
Whitham v Club 24 Ltd t/a Ventura (ET/1810462/10) — 292
Whitmar Publications Ltd v Gamage [2013] EWHC 1881 (Ch) — 58
Wiggan v Wooler & Co Ltd (UKEAT/0285/07) — 293
Wilcox v Birmingham CAB Services Ltd (UKEAT/0293/10) — 526
Wilding v British Telecommunications plc [2002] IRLR 524 — 228, 523
Wileman v Minilec Engineering Ltd [1988] IRLR 144 — 478
William Hill Organisation Ltd v Tucker [1998] IRLR 313 — 41, 65
Williams Drabble v Pathway Care Solutions Ltd and Another (ET/2601718/04) — 462
Williams v Alderman Davies Church in Wales Primary School (UKEAT/0108/19) — 128
Williams v Architects Registration Board (Administrative Court, 20 May 2016) — 575
Williams v British Airways plc (Case C-155/10) — 88
Williams v Compair Maxam Ltd [1982] ICR 156, [1982] IRLR 83 — 197, 200
Williams v Leeds Football Club [2015] EWHC 376 (QB) — 108
Williams v Leukaemia and Lymphoma Research (UKEAT/0493/13) — 511
Williams v Meddygfa Rhydbach Surgery (ET/1600487/2016) — 179
Williams v Michelle Brown AM (UKEAT/0044/19/OO) — 210
Williams v Trustees of Swansea University Pension and Assurance Scheme [2017] EWCA Civ 1008 — 529
Willis v Jardine Lloyd Thompson Group plc [2015] AC 9301548 — 61
Willoughby v County Home Care Ltd (ET/1100310/99) — 79
Willow Oak Developments Ltd t/a Windsor Recruitment v Silverwood & Others [2006] IRLR 607 — 168
Wilson v Clayton [2005] IRLR 108 — 236
Wilson v Post Office [2000] IRLR 834 — 165
Wilsons & Clyde Coal Co Ltd v English [1938] AC 57 — 41
Wincanton Group plc v Stone [2013] IRLR 178 — 186
Windle v Secretary of State for Justice [2015] ICR 156 — 19
Window Machinery Sales Ltd t/a Promac Group v Luckey (UKEAT/0301/14) — 228
Wingfield v North Cumbria Mental Health and Learning Disabilities NHS Trust (ET/2510953/05) — 383
Wise Group, The v Mitchell [2005] ICR 896 — 114
WM Morrison Supermarkets plc v Various Claimants [2018] EWCA Civ 2239 — 399
WM Morrison Supermarkets plc v Various Claimants [2020] UKSC 12 — 399
Wood v Capita Insurance Services Ltd [2017] UKSC 24 — 37
Wood v Durham CC (UKEAT/0099/18) — 504
Woodcock v Cumbria Primary Care NHS Trust [2012] EWCA Civ 330, [2012] ICR 1126 — 461, 492, 534
Woodhouse v West North West Homes Leeds Ltd (UKEAT/0007/12) — 482
Woodrup v London Borough of Southwark [2003] IRLR 111 — 512
Woods v Andrea Hawkes (ET/2203304/2020) — 170
Woods v WM Car Services (Peterborough) Ltd [1983] IRLR 413 — 42, 124
Woodward v CPS (ET/1800728/19) — 258
Woodward v Santander UK plc (UKEAT/0250/09) — 281
Worrall v Wilmott Dixon Partnership (UKEAT/0521/09) — 46
Wrexham Golf Club Ltd v Ingham (UKEAT/0190/12) — 198

Wright v Aegis Defence Services (BVI) Ltd and Others (UKEAT 0173/17)   16
Wright v Nipponkoa Insurance (Europe) Ltd (UKEAT/0113/14)   276
Wright v North Ayrshire Council (UKEAT/0017/13), [2014] ICR 77   127, 129
WRN Ltd v Ayris [2008] EWHC 1080 (QB)   61

X

X v Mid Sussex Citizens Advice Bureau [2013] IRLR 146   35
X v Y [2004] IRLR 625   175, 575
X v Y Ltd (UKEAT/0261/17)   279
XC Trains Ltd v CD (UKEAT/0331/15)   461
Xerox Business Services Philippines Inc Ltd v Zeb (UKEAT/0121/16)   365
XR v Dopravni hl m Prahy (Case C-107/19)   79

Y

Yarrow v Edwards Chartered Accountants (UKEAT/0116/07)   87
Yeboah v Crofton [2002] IRLR 634   302, 403
Yerrakalva v Barnsley Metropolitan Borough Council and another [2012] ICR 42   296
Yewens v Noakes (1880) 6 QBD 530   11
YL v Birmingham City Council [2007] UKHL 27   569
York City Council v Grosset [2018] ICR 1492 CA   536
Yorkshire Blood Transfusion Service v Plaskitt [1994] ICR 74   415
Yorkshire Window Company Ltd v Parkes (UKEAT/0484/09)   20
Young v Argos Ltd (ET/1200382/11)   292
Ypourgos Esoterikon and Another v Kalliri (Case C-409/16)   452, 462

Z

Zaman v Kozee Sleep Products Ltd (EAT/0312/10)   369
Zebrowski v Concentric Birmingham Ltd (UKEAT/0245/16)   231
Zulu and Gue v MOD (ET/2205687/2018 and ET 2205688/2018)   402

Table of Statutes

Access to Medical Reports Act 1988 179
Apportionment Act 1870
  s 2 75
Apprenticeships, Skills, Children and Learning Act 2009 31
  s 35 31
Asylum and Immigration Act 1996 5, 393

Children Act 1989 319
  s 20 314
Children Act 2004 319, 326
  s 11 319
  s 47 319, 323
Children and Families Act 2014 553
  s 127(1) 552
Civil Liability (Contribution) Act 1978 412
Companies Act 2006
  ss 188–189 48
Computer Misuse Act 1990 399
Contempt of Court Act 1981
  s 9 290
Contracts (Rights of Third Parties) Act 1999 37
Copyright, Designs and Patents Act 1988 56
Coronavirus Act 2020 285
Courts and Legal Services Act 1990 303
  s 71 295

Data Protection Act 1998 580
  s 55 58, 399
Data Protection Act 2018 8, 43, 576, 580, 585–7, 589, 592
  Part 2, Chapter 2 (ss 6–20) 585
  Part 2, Chapter 3 (ss 21–28) 585
  Part 3 (ss 29–54) 585
  Part 4 (ss 55–71) 585
  s 149 58
  s 184 10
Disability Discrimination Act 1995 3, 501, 503–4, 509–10,
  512–14, 516, 523, 526, 528, 539
  s 1 505
  s 4A 524
  s 68 29
Disability Discrimination Act 2005 501

Employers' Liability (Compulsory Insurance) Act 1969 42
Employment Act 1980
  s 6 193
Employment Act 2002 3, 38, 555, 563
  s 31 232
  s 31(3) 227
  s 31(5) 232
  s 38 40, 226, 232, 236, 247
  s 80 555
  Sch 5 40, 226
Employment Act 2008 54–5
  s 3 176
Employment Protection (Consolidation) Act 1978 3
Employment Relations Act 1999 3, 358, 378
  s 10 177–8, 189, 251

Employment Relations Act 1999 – *continued*
  s 10(1)(b) 178
  s 11 251
  s 12 251
  s 13 251
  s 32(3) 134
Employment Relations Act 2004 3
  s 37 177
  s 38 177
Employment Rights Act 1996 3, 41, 55, 67, 73, 87, 95, 122,
  134, 139, 155, 177, 210, 488, 502, 544, 555
  s 1 38–40, 48–50, 68, 100, 206, 226, 357, 366
  s 1(3)–(4) 98, 100
  s 2(1)–(2) 39
  s 2(6) 39
  s 3 39
  s 3(1)(aa) 39
  s 4 39
  s 7A 39
  s 8 51
  s 11 40
  s 12 40
  Part II (ss 13–27) 73, 100, 142, 250, 289
  s 13 19, 73, 75, 90–1, 206, 259
  s 13(3) 74, 235
  s 14 73–4
  s 14(1) 75
  s 17 74
  s 23 76, 90
  s 23(1)–(2) 76
  s 23(3) 76, 92
  s 23(4A) 52
  s 24 235
  s 24(2) 77
  s 25(4) 77
  s 27 74, 77, 222
  s 27(1)(b) 75–6
  s 27(1)(c) 75–6, 564–5
  s 27(1)(ca) 565
  s 27(1)(cb) 565
  s 27(1)(d)–(j) 75–6
  s 27(2) 74
  s 27A(3) 205
  s 28 41
  s 43(8) 92
  s 43B 209, 214
  s 43B(1) 210, 212–13
  s 43B(1)(a)–(c) 213
  s 43B(1)(d) l, 213
  s 43B(1)(e)–(f) 213
  ss 43C–43F 214
  s 43G 214
  s 43G(2)(c)(i) 215
  s 43K 29
  s 43K(1)(a) 29, 209
  s 43K(1)(b) 29
  s 43K(2) 29

Employment Rights Act 1996 – *continued*
  s 43L(3) 210
  Part V (ss 43M–49A) 251
  s 44 207–8
  s 44(1A)(a)–(b) 207
  s 47B 22, 29, 209, 215, 217–18
  s 47B(2) 29
  s 47C 546, 548, 562–5
  s 47E 559, 563
  s 48 548
  s 48(2) 217
  s 49(6) 29
  s 55 552, 564
  s 55(2)–(3) 552
  s 56 552, 564
  s 57 564
  s 57A 557, 560–1, 563–4
  s 57A(1) 560
  s 57A(1)(d) 560
  s 57A(2)–(5) 560
  s 57B 561, 564
  s 57ZE 552
  s 66 549, 551, 564
  ss 67–69 564
  s 70 564
  s 71 544–5, 549, 564–5
  s 72 548
  s 73 545, 564–5
  s 74 548, 565
  s 75A 553, 565
  s 75B 553
  s 75C 553, 565
  s 75D 553
  s 76 564
  s 80 564
  s 80A 555, 564
  ss 80B–80D 555
  ss 80EA–80EE 557
  s 80F 558, 565
  s 80G 558
  s 80H 558–9, 565
  s 80I 558–9
  s 86 14, 47, 100, 102, 104–6, 119, 131–2, 158, 550
  s 86(1)–(3) 105
  s 86(6) 131
  s 87 224
  s 87(4) 550
  s 88 224
  s 92 171
  s 92(4) 550, 564
  s 92(4A) 564
  s 93 171
  Part X (ss 94–134A) 359
  s 94 122, 163, 245
  s 94(1) 134–7
  s 95 122
  s 95(1)(a) 122–3
  s 95(1)(b) 123
  s 95(1)(c) 123, 164
  s 97 130, 255, 331
  s 97(2) 131
  s 97(3)(b) 106
  s 97(4) 131

Employment Rights Act 1996 – *continued*
  s 98 163, 242, 245, 372–3, 498, 564
  s 98(1) 165, 173–4, 359–61
  s 98(1)(a) 165
  s 98(1)(b) 71, 166
  s 98(2) 165, 173, 240, 247, 327
  s 98(2)(a) 165–6
  s 98(2)(b) 166
  s 98(2)(c) 166, 359–60
  s 98(2)(d) 6, 166, 168
  s 98(3) 173
  s 98(3)(a) 166
  s 98(4) 164, 169, 171, 173–5, 191, 198, 200, 205, 240–2,
    245, 247, 359–62, 372–3, 549–50, 562
  s 99 543, 548–9, 551–2, 561–5
  s 100 207–8, 564
  s 101A 208
  s 103A 29, 209, 215, 218
  s 104 206–7, 564
  s 104(1)(a)–(b) 559
  s 104C 559, 563
  s 104F(1) 205
  s 107 174
  s 108 164
  s 108(1) 130
  s 111 255–6, 331
  s 111A 282, 309–10
  s 111A(3) 309
  s 112(2) 219
  s 112(5) 221
  ss 114–115 219–20
  s 116(1) 219
  s 117 220–1
  s 118 221, 236
  s 119 221
  s 122(1) 221
  s 122(2) 221, 231
  s 122(4) 221
  s 123 223–4, 230, 254
  s 123(1) 222, 231
  s 123(6) 231–2
  s 124(5) 307
  s 126 312
  s 128 218, 253
  s 135 122, 143, 359–61
  s 135(1)(b) 141
  s 136 122
  s 136(1)(a) 122–3
  s 136(1)(b) 123
  s 136(1)(c) 123
  s 136(5) 149
  s 138 149, 160
  s 139 144, 152, 158, 161, 167, 238, 359, 362–4, 550
  s 139(1) 143, 160
  s 139(1)(a)(i) 143, 160
  s 139(1)(a)(ii) 143–4, 160
  s 139(1)(b) 144–7, 160
  s 139(6) 143, 169
  s 141 147, 160
  s 141(2)–(4) 148
  s 145 130, 132, 259
  s 145(5) 132
  s 147 41, 141

Employment Rights Act 1996 – *continued*
  s 147(1) 142
  s 147(2) 142
  ss 148–154 141
  s 155 130, 143
  s 162 150, 158, 160
  s 163 141, 160
  s 163(2) 147
  s 164 151
  s 165 151
  s 166 151
  s 182 36
  s 196 134, 378
  s 196(3) 134
  s 203 305–6, 308
  s 207A 184
  s 207B 252, 254, 261–2
  s 207B(2)(a)–(b) 261
  s 207B(3)–(4) 261–4
  Part XIV, Chapter 1 (ss 210–219) 143
  s 210(5) 132
  s 211(1)(a) 129
  s 212 132–3
  s 212(3)(c) 130, 133
  s 214 143
  s 216 133
  s 218 133, 222
  s 218(2) 336
  s 218(6) 134
  ss 220–225 53
  s 221 88–9, 150, 158
  s 221(2) 222
  s 221(4) 88
  s 222 88
  ss 223–224 88
  s 227 171, 369
  s 229 222
  s 230 2, 14, 19, 28, 36, 73, 86, 250–1
  s 230(1) 11, 28, 98, 122, 377, 544
  s 230(2) 11
  s 230(3) 10–11, 19, 22–3, 28–9, 31, 73, 91, 98
  s 230(3)(b) 21, 23–4, 27, 29
  s 231 134
  s 235 142, 219
  Sch A2 228
Employment Rights (Dispute Resolution) Act 1998 310
  s 4 289
Employment Tribunals Act 1996
  s 3 102–3
  s 3(2) 103
  s 4(3) 289
  s 4(5) 289
  s 6 291
  s 7 267–8
  s 7(4) 322
  s 8 102–3
  s 10 287
  s 11 287
  s 11(1)(b) 287
  s 12 287
  s 12A 236, 301
  s 13 294
  ss 16–17 232

Employment Tribunals Act 1996 – *continued*
  s 18 269, 305
  s 18(1) 260
  s 18(1A) 251
  s 18A 251, 253
  s 18A(1) 253
  s 18A(8) 254
  s 18B 250
  s 18C 269
  s 21 301
  s 21(1) 196
  Part 2A (ss 37A–37Q) 301
Enterprise and Regulatory Reform Act 2013 215, 218, 250, 300, 302, 416
  s 14 309
  s 16 236–7, 301
  s 17 209, 211
  s 64 376
  s 65 475
  s 97 381
  Sch 2 260
Equal Pay Act 1970 3, 412, 414
  s 1 413
Equality Act 2006 395
Equality Act 2010 3, 9, 11, 40, 67–8, 138, 180, 250, 302, 308, 375–7, 416–17, 420, 422–3, 449, 453, 463–4, 483–4, 487–8, 500, 512, 528, 539, 577
  s 4 379, 425, 427, 448, 451, 464, 467, 484, 488–9, 500, 502, 515–16
  s 5 379, 425, 488
  s 5(1) 488
  s 5(2) 488, 496
  s 6 379, 425, 502–3, 538
  s 6(1)–(2) 502–3, 539
  s 6(3) 502, 537
  s 6(3)(b) 537
  s 6(4) 502, 511
  s 7 379, 385–6, 391, 425, 451, 467
  s 7(1) 385
  s 7(2)–(3) 386
  s 8 379, 387, 425, 451
  s 8(1)–(2) 387
  s 8(2)(b) 395
  s 9 379, 381, 425, 451, 467
  s 9(1) 379
  s 9(2)–(5) 380
  s 10 73, 379, 381, 383–4, 425, 451, 467
  s 10(1)–(3) 381
  s 11 379, 425, 451, 467
  s 12 379, 385, 425, 451, 467
  s 12(1)–(2) 385
  s 13 388, 391, 394–5, 425–8, 430, 432, 437–8, 445, 448, 467, 477, 488–9, 512, 515, 529, 539, 541, 554, 563
  s 13(1) 391, 426, 430, 490, 515
  s 13(2) 427, 490, 498
  s 13(3) 515
  s 13(4)–(5) 426
  s 13(6) 426
  s 13(6)(b) 426
  s 13(7)–(8) 426
  s 14 488
  s 14(1) 376
  s 15 516, 519, 528–35, 539, 541

Equality Act 2010 – continued
  s 15(1) 528–9, 535
  s 15(1)(a) 531
  s 15(1)(b) 541
  s 15(2) 529, 535–6
  s 16 386, 388, 436
  s 18 379, 388, 425, 432, 437, 439, 451, 546, 550–2, 562–3
  s 18(1)–(4) 437, 550
  s 18(5) 437–8, 550
  s 18(6) 437, 551
  s 18(7) 437–8, 551
  s 19 388, 451, 459–60, 464, 489, 494, 530, 534, 537, 540–1, 563, 577
  s 19(1) 391, 451, 494, 537
  s 19(2) 451–2, 494, 537
  s 19(2)(b) 458
  s 19(2)(d) 460
  s 20 517–18, 520, 522, 525–6, 528, 539, 541
  s 20(1)–(2) 517
  s 20(3)–(6) 517–18
  s 20(7) 517–18
  s 20(8)–(11) 518
  s 21 517–18, 522, 535, 539, 541
  s 21(1) 518
  s 21(2) 518
  s 22 518, 539, 541
  s 23 430
  s 24 436
  s 26 388, 467–9, 473, 475, 484, 489, 512, 538, 540–1, 552, 563
  s 26(1) 468–71, 477–9
  s 26(1)(a) 468, 473
  s 26(1)(b) 473
  s 26(2) 468–9, 477–9
  s 26(3) 468–9
  s 26(4) 468, 471–2
  s 26(4)(a)–(c) 473
  s 27 388, 481, 485, 489, 538, 541
  s 27(1)–(2) 481
  s 27(2)(d) 483
  s 27(3) 481, 483
  Part 5 (ss 39–83) 388, 403, 412
  s 39 5, 377–8, 392, 394, 422, 469, 489, 563
  s 39(1) 392, 514, 539
  s 39(2) 394, 514, 539
  s 39(2)(a) 394
  s 39(3) 393
  s 39(4) 394
  s 39(7) 394, 515
  s 40 378, 392, 422, 468–9, 475, 489
  s 40(1) 393, 395
  s 40(2)–(4) 475
  s 41 31, 377–8, 392
  ss 42–43 392
  ss 44–45 31, 392
  ss 46–49 392
  s 50 377, 392
  ss 51–52 392
  s 55 540
  s 57 377, 392
  s 60 514
  s 61 498
  Part 5 (ss 39–83), Chapter 3 (ss 64–80) 412

Equality Act 2010 – continued
  s 64(1) 413
  s 65(1)-(2) 414
  s 66 413
  s 66(1) 413
  s 66(2) 412–13
  s 67 413
  s 68 413
  s 69 413–14
  s 70 413, 426
  s 70(1) 394
  s 71 394, 413
  s 79 414
  s 83 35, 392, 488, 502
  s 83(2) 29–31, 377
  s 83(2)(a) 19
  s 105 392
  s 108 377–8, 392, 395, 403, 484–5, 515
  s 108(4) 515
  s 108(7) 395, 484
  s 109 397, 403, 479, 497, 538
  s 109(1) 469
  s 109(3) 469
  s 109(4) 397, 400, 450, 469, 486, 542
  s 110 397, 403
  s 110(1) 469
  s 111 397, 403
  s 112 397
  s 113 403
  Part 9, Chapter 3 (ss 120–126) 499
  s 120 388, 403
  s 121 403
  s 122 403
  s 123 403–4
  s 123(1) 259
  s 123(3) 405
  s 124 403, 406, 479, 499
  s 124(2) 406
  s 124(3) 406
  s 124(4)–(5) 411, 464
  s 124(7) 406
  ss 125–135 403
  s 136 439–40, 442, 449, 464, 468, 478, 538
  s 136(2) 497
  s 137 378
  s 138 406, 440
  s 140B 252, 261
  s 142 412
  s 143 412
  s 147 308
  s 159 393, 514–15
  s 195 386
  s 197 498
  s 212 378, 394, 515, 518
  s 212(1) 469, 507
  s 212(2)–(3) 405
  s 212(5) 469
  s 213 437
  s 214 378
  Sch 1 379, 503, 510
    para 1 508
    para 2 509
    para 2(1) 509

Equality Act 2010 – *continued*
    para 2(1)(b) 509
    para 2(2) 509, 511
    para 3 508
    para 5 512
    para 6 513
    para 8 508, 513
    para 9 513
    para 12 503
  Sch 2
    para 2 511
  Sch 6 392
  Sch 7 498
  Sch 8 527
    Part 3, para 20 518, 525
  Sch 9 383, 386, 498–9
    Part 1
      para 1 395–6, 516
      para 2 396–7
    Part 2 497
      para 10 496
      para 11 496
      para 13 497, 499
      para 14 497
      para 15 497
      para 18 388
  Sch 28 378
European Communities Act 1972 4
  s 2(4) 4
European Union (Withdrawal) Act 2018 4

Financial Services and Markets Act 2000 9, 291

Gender Recognition Act 2004 387

Health and Safety at Work etc Act 1974 42, 337, 551
Human Fertilisation and Embryology Act 2008 555
  s 54 553
Human Rights Act 1998 4–5, 9, 72, 175, 219, 303–4, 311,
  420–1, 567–70, 575, 591
  s 2 568
  s 3 568, 570, 575, 591
  s 4 568, 591
  s 6 72, 303, 568–70, 575
  s 6(3) 569
  s 7 568, 570
  s 7(7) 570
  s 8 568
  Sch 1 *see* European Convention on Human Rights

Immigration Act 2014 5
Immigration, Asylum and Nationality Act 2006 5, 393
  s 15 5, 393
  s 21 5, 393
Income Tax (Earnings and Pensions) Act 2003 107, 116, 411
  s 40 151
  ss 44–47 33
  s 62 116
  Part 6 (ss 386–416) 235
  Part 6, Ch 3 (ss 401–414B) 233
  s 401 116
  s 401(1) 233
  s 406 236, 411

Industrial and Provident Societies Act 1965 157
  s 57 157
Industrial Relations Act 1971 2–3
  s 22 134
  s 27(2) 134
Investigatory Powers Act 2016 586–7, 592

Judgments Act 1833
  s 17 232
Judicial Review and Courts Act 2022 299

Legal Aid, Sentencing and Punishment of Offenders Act
  2012 10, 303
  s 44(6) 408–9
Legal Services Act 2007
  ss 194A–194C 299
Limitation Act 1980
  s 33 259, 404
  s 33(3) 404
Local Government Act 2003 338

Modern Slavery Act 2015 570
  s 8 381

National Minimum Wage Act 1998 40, 51, 55

Parental Bereavement (Leave and Pay) Act 2018 555, 557
Patents Act 1977 56
Pension Schemes Act 1993 39, 56
Pensions Act 2004 337, 358
Police Act 2004 327
Police, Crime, Sentencing and Courts Act 2022
  Part 13 286
Police and Criminal Evidence Act 1984 55
Protection from Harassment Act 1997 476
Public Interest Disclosure Act 1998 29, 207, 209–19, 307,
  577

Race Relations Act 1976 3, 460, 474
  s 4(2)(c) 395
  s 29 395
  s 78 29
Regulation of Investigatory Powers Act 2000 576, 586–7
Rehabilitation of Offenders Act 1974 10, 575

Senior Courts Act 1981
  s 51(7) 300
Sex Discrimination Act 1975 3, 386, 412, 460–1, 547
  s 4A 470
  s 38 395
  s 41 398
  s 82(1) 29–30
Small Business, Enterprise and Employment Act 2015 55
  s 27A 38
Social Security Contributions and Benefits Act 1992 544,
  554
State Immunity Act 1978 572

Trade Union and Labour Relations (Consolidation) Act 1992
  3, 152, 155
  s 137 419
  s 137(1) 419
  s 152 205

Trade Union and Labour Relations (Consolidation) Act 1992
  – continued
  s 152(1) 205
  s 152(1)(b) 205
  s 152(2) 205
  s 153 205
  s 161 205
  s 188 152–4, 156, 160, 169
  s 188(7) 155
  s 198A 152, 370
  s 198B 152
  s 207A 222, 226–7, 411
  s 237 206
  s 238A 206
  s 296 26
  Sch A2 178
Trade Union Reform and Employment Rights Act
  1993 3
Tribunals, Courts and Enforcement Act 2007
  s 27(1)–(4) 303

Welfare Reform Act 2007 232
Work and Families Act 2006 3

Bills
Bill of Rights Bill 2022 5, 568
Worker Protection (Amendment of Equality Act 2010) Bill
  2022 468, 472, 476
Protection from Redundancy (Pregnancy and Family Leave)
  Bill 2022 548

EU primary legislation
European Charter of Fundamental Rights 3–4, 567
  Art 31(2) 95

Treaty on European Union 1992 (Maastricht) 375
  Social Chapter 375
Treaty on European Union (post Lisbon numbering)
  Art 50 2, 4
Treaty on the Functioning of the European Union
  Art 157 (ex 119 EEC/141 EC) 3, 377, 413
  Art 157(1) (ex 119 EEC/141(1) EC) 30

International conventions and agreements
EU-UK Trade and Cooperation Agreement 376
European Convention on Human Rights 4, 302, 420–1,
  567–8, 570, 591
  Art 2 420
  Art 3 176, 421
  Art 4 570
  Art 6 175, 203, 287–8, 303, 570–3, 591
  Art 6(1) 571
  Art 8 9, 175–6, 203, 287–8, 420, 568, 574–6, 586, 591
  Art 8(2) 43, 574
  Art 9 72–3, 381, 420, 430, 456, 576–7, 591
  Art 9(1) 578
  Art 9(2) 382, 578
  Art 10 72, 175, 219, 287–8, 576–9, 591
  Art 10(2) 382, 578
  Art 11 25–6, 152, 208, 579, 591
  Art 14 22, 420, 579, 591
  Protocol 12 420
    Art 1 579
EU–US Privacy Shield (IP/16/216) 590–1
UN Convention on the Rights of Persons with Disabilities
  503

US legislation
Dodd–Frank Wall Street Reform and Consumer Protection
  Act 209

Table of Secondary Legislation and Codes of Practice

ACAS Arbitration Scheme (England and Wales) Order 2001 (SI 2001/1185) 310

Additional Paternity Leave Regulations 2010 (SI 2010/1055)
reg 3(2) 554
reg 34 563

Agency Workers (Amendment) Regulations 2011 (SI 2011/1941) 34

Agency Workers (Amendment) Regulations 2019 (SI 2019/724) 34–5

Agency Workers Regulations 2010 (SI 2010/93) 34, 250
reg 5 35
reg 10 35
reg 11 35
reg 13 34

Civil Procedure Rules 1998 (SI 1998/3132) 265, 299–300
r 3.9 264
Part 31 277–8
r 31.6 278
r 32.1 292

Collective Redundancies and Transfer of Undertakings (Protection of Employment) (Amendment) Regulations 2014 (SI 2014/16) 335–7, 345, 357–9, 362–3, 368, 370–1
reg 3 152

Conduct of Employment Agencies and Employment Businesses (Amendment) Regulations 2014 (SI 2014/3351) 9

Damages-Based Agreements Regulations 2013 (SI 2013/609) 303

Data Protection Act 2018 (Commencement No 1 and Transitional and Saving Provisions) Regulations 2018 (SI 2018/625) 580

Data Protection (Charges and Information) Regulations 2018 (SI 2018/480) 580

Deduction from Wages (Limitation) Regulations 2014 (SI 2014/3322) 74–6, 91

Disability Discrimination Act 1995 (Amendment) Regulations 2003 (SI 2003/1673) 501

Employment Appeal Tribunal (Amendment) Rules 2013 (SI 2013/1693) 302

Employment Appeal Tribunal Rules 1993 (SI 1993/2854)
Schedule 302

Employment Equality (Age) Regulations 2006 (SI 2006/1031) 199, 395, 487, 496, 498
Sch 6 500

Employment Equality (Religion or Belief) Regulations 2003 (SI 2003/1660) 383, 577
reg 3(1)(b) 577

Employment Equality (Sex Discrimination) Regulations 2005 (SI 2005/2467) 463

Employment Protection (Recoupment of Jobseeker's Allowance and Income Support) Regulations 1996 (SI 1996/2349) 232, 480–1

Employment Relations Act 1999 (Blacklists) Regulations 2010 (SI 2010/493) 9, 205

Employment Rights Act 1996 (Coronavirus, Calculation of a Week's Pay) Regulations 2020 (SI 2020/814) 53

Employment Rights Act 1996 (Itemised Pay Statement) (Amendment) Orders 2018 (SI 2018/147) 39

Employment Rights Act 1996 (Protection from Detriment in Health and Safety Cases) (Amendment) Order 2021 (Draft) 207

Employment Rights (Employment Particulars and Paid Annual Leave) (Amendment) Regulations 2018 (SI 2018/1378) 88

Employment Rights (Miscellaneous Amendments) Regulations 2019 (SI 2019/731) 38–9

Employment Tribunals Act 1996 (Application of Conciliation Provisions) Order 2014 (SI 2014/431)
Sch, art 3 260

Employment Tribunals Act 1996 (Tribunal Composition) Order 2012 (SI 2012/988) 289

Employment Tribunals (Constitution and Rules of Procedure) (Amendment) Regulations 2014 (SI 2014/271) 250, 267

Employment Tribunals (Constitution and Rules of Procedure) (Early Conciliation: Exemptions and Rules of Procedure) (Amendment) Regulations 2020 (SI 2020/1003) 249–50, 260, 264, 269

Employment Tribunals (Constitution and Rules of Procedure) (Early Conciliation: Exemptions and Rules of Procedure) (Amendment) Regulations 2021 (SI 2021/1037) 249, 251, 264, 286

Employment Tribunals (Constitution and Rules of Procedure) Regulations 2001 (SI 2001/1171) 295

Employment Tribunals (Constitution and Rules of Procedure) Regulations 2013 (SI 2013/1237) 264–5
Sch 1 see Employment Tribunals Rules of Procedure 2013

Employment Tribunals (Early Conciliation: Exemptions and Rules of Procedure) Regulations 2014 (SI 2014/254)
reg 3 260
reg 3(1) 251
reg 3(1)(c) 252
reg 3(1)(d) 253
Sch 250

Employment Tribunals Extension of Jurisdiction (England and Wales) Order 1994 (1994/1623) 102–3
art 3 104
art 5 104
art 8B 252
art 10 104

Employment Tribunals (Interest on Awards in Discrimination Cases) (Amendment) Regulations 2013 (SI 2013/1669) 411

Employment Tribunals (Interest on Awards in Discrimination Cases) Regulations 1996 (SI 1996/2803) 411

Employment Tribunals (Interest) Order 1990 (SI 1990/479)
art 4 232

Employment Tribunals Rules of Procedure 2004 (SI 2004/1861) 295, 301
r 2(1) 295

Employment Tribunals Rules of Procedure 2004 – *continued*
  r 40(3) 295–7
  r 41(2) 295
Employment Tribunals Rules of Procedure 2013 249–50,
  264, 331
  r 1 293, 298
  r 1(3)(a) 269
  r 2 264–6, 270, 275, 290, 293
  r 2(b) 293
  r 3 265
  r 4 251, 265
  r 4(2) 256
  r 4(3) 268
  r 6 253, 322
  r 8 267–8
  r 10 250, 252–3, 263, 268
  r 10(1) 267
  r 10(1)(b)(iii) 252
  r 12 252, 263, 267–8
  r 12(1)(b) 267
  r 12(1)(e) 268
  r 12(1)(f) 268
  r 12(2A) 268
  r 13 263, 268
  r 13(4) 263
  r 15(2)(d) 274
  r 16 268
  r 17 268
  r 19 268
  r 20 269
  r 26 269
  r 27 267, 269
  r 28 269
  r 29 269, 271, 276, 288, 321–2
  rr 30–40 269
  r 30 289
  r 30(2) 321
  r 31 270–1, 276
  r 32 270–1
  r 34 270
  r 37 270, 273, 286, 322
  r 37(1) 265
  r 37(1)(c) 275
  r 38 270, 283
  r 38(2) 283
  r 39 270, 276, 286
  r 41 292
  r 43 282
  r 46 285, 290
  r 50 287–8, 290, 302
  r 50(2) 288
  r 51 284
  r 52 284
  r 53 270, 286
  r 54 286
  rr 55–56 286
  r 57 289
  r 58 269, 289
  r 59 289
  r 60 293
  r 61 293
  r 62 293

Employment Tribunals Rules of Procedure 2013 – *continued*
  r 62(5) 294
  r 67 293
  rr 70–73 301
  r 74 294, 322
  r 74(1) 299
  r 74(2) 295, 299
  r 75 294–5, 322
  r 76 294–6, 298–300, 322
  r 76(1) 295–6
  r 76(1)(b) 298
  r 76(3) 295
  r 77 294, 300, 322
  r 78 294, 299–300, 322
  r 79 294, 300, 322
  rr 80–82 294, 300, 322
  r 83 294, 322
  r 84 294, 296, 300, 322
  r 85 268
  r 92 271
  r 94 290, 302
Enterprise and Regulatory Reform Act 2013 (Consequential
  Amendments) (Employment) (No 2) Order 2014
  (SI 2014/853) 260
Enterprise and Regulatory Reform Act 2013 (Consequential
  Amendments) (Employment) Order 2014 (SI 2014/386)
  art 2 260
  Schedule 260
Equality Act 2010 (Consequential Amendments, Savings
  and Supplementary Provisions) Order 2010
  (SI 2010/2279)
  art 5 515
Equality Act 2010 (Disability) Regulations 2010
  (SI 2010/2128) 503–4
  reg 5 508
Equality Act 2010 (Equal Pay Audits) Regulations 2014
  (SI 2014/2559) 416
Equality Act 2010 (Gender Pay Gap Information)
  Regulations 2017 (SI 2017/172) 416
Exclusivity Terms in Zero Hours Contracts (Redress)
  Regulations 2015 (SI 2015/2012) 38

Fixed-term Employees (Prevention of Less Favourable
  Treatment) Regulations 2002 (SI 2002/2034) 48, 419
Flexible Working (Eligibility, Complaints and Remedies)
  Regulations 2002 (SI 2002/3236) 563
Flexible Working (Procedural Requirements) Regulations
  2002 (SI 2002/3207) 563
Flexible Working Regulations 2014 (SI 2014/1398) 544,
  558, 565
  reg 6 559

Immigration (Restriction on Employment) (Code of Practice
  and Miscellaneous Amendments) Order 2018
  (SI 2018/1340) 5
Information and Consultation of Employees Regulations
  2004 (SI 2004/3426) 156–7, 370
Investigatory Powers (Interception by Businesses etc for
  Monitoring and Record-keeping Purposes) Regulations
  2018 (SI 2018/356) 586, 592
  reg 3 587
Ionising Radiation Regulations 1985 (SI 1985/1333) 551

Management of Health and Safety at Work Regulations 1999
(SI 1999/3242) 564
reg 3(1) 552
Maternity Allowance, Statutory Maternity Pay, Statutory
Paternity Pay, Statutory Shared Parental Pay and Statutory
Parental Bereavement Pay (Normal Weekly Earnings, etc)
(Coronavirus) (Amendment) Regulations 2020
(SI 2020/450) 557
Maternity and Parental Leave etc and Paternity and
Adoption Leave (Amendment) Regulations 2006
(SI 2006/2041)
reg 15 554
Maternity and Parental Leave etc Regulations 1999
(SI 1999/3312) 544, 562
reg 2(1) 546–7
reg 4 545, 564
reg 4(1) 544
reg 4(2)–(4) 545
reg 5 564
reg 6 564
reg 6(1) 545
reg 6(3) 545
reg 7 564
reg 7(6) 545–6
reg 8 564
reg 9 546, 564
reg 10 548–9, 563–5
reg 11 564
reg 11(1) 546
reg 12 564
reg 12A 546, 549
regs 13–17 564
reg 18 564–5
reg 18(2) 547
reg 19 548, 561
reg 20 548, 552, 561, 563
reg 20(2) 561
reg 20(3) 549
reg 20(3)(a)–(b) 549
reg 20(3)(c) 549, 564
reg 20(3)(d) 549
reg 20(3)(e) 549
reg 20(3)(e)(iii) 561
reg 20(3)(ee) 549
reg 20(3)(eee) 549
reg 20(3)(f)–(g) 549
reg 20(4) 549
reg 20(7) 550

National Minimum Wage (Amendment) Regulations 2016
(SI 2016/68) 51
National Minimum Wage Regulations 1999 (SI 1999/584)
19, 51, 54, 98, 100
reg 15 54
reg 16 54
National Minimum Wage Regulations 2015 (SI 2015/621)
51, 54
Part 3 (reg 7) 51
Part 4 (regs 8–16) 51–2
Part 5 (regs 17–20) 51
reg 27 54
reg 30 53
reg 32 53–4

National Minimum Wage Regulations 2015 – *continued*
reg 37 54
reg 57(3) 54

Parental Bereavement Leave Regulations 2020 (SI 2020/249)
555, 557
Parental Bereavement Pay Regulations 2020 (SI 2020/233)
555
Part-time Workers (Prevention of Less Favourable
Treatment) Regulations 2000 (SI 2000/1551) 19, 22, 97,
250, 417–19
reg 2(1)–(2) 418
reg 2(3) 417
reg 2(4) 417–18
reg 5 417
Paternity and Adoption Leave Regulations 2002
(SI 2002/2788) 544, 553, 555, 563–5
reg 20 553
reg 23 565
reg 26 565
regs 28–29 563
Public Interest Disclosure (Prescribed Persons) Order 2014
(SI 2014/2418) 214

Register of Judgments, Orders and Fines (Amendment)
Regulations 2009 (SI 2009/474) 303
Rules of Procedure (Employment Tribunals) *see* Employment
Tribunals Rules of Procedure 2004 *and* 2013

Shared Parental Leave Regulations 2014 (SI 2014/3050)
544, 555, 563–4
reg 39 565
reg 40 565
Sch 7, para 2 557
Social Security (Miscellaneous Amendments) (No 5)
Regulations 2010 (SI 2010/2429) 232
Statutory Maternity Pay Regulations 1986 (SI 1986/1960)
544
Statutory Parental Bereavement Pay (Administration)
Regulations 2020 (SI 2020/246) 557
Statutory Parental Bereavement Pay (General) Regulations
2020 (SI 2020/233) 557
Statutory Parental Bereavement Pay (Persons Abroad and
Mariners) Regulations 2020 (SI 2020/252) 557
Statutory Paternity Pay and Statutory Adoption Pay
(Administration) Regulations 2002 (SI 2002/2820) 544,
554
Statutory Paternity Pay and Statutory Adoption Pay
(General) Regulations 2002 (SI 2002/2822) 544, 554
Statutory Paternity Pay and Statutory Adoption Pay (Weekly
Rates) Regulations 2002 (SI 2002/2818) 544

Telecommunications (Lawful Business Practice)
(Interception of Communications) Regulations 2000
(SI 2000/2699) 586
Trade Secrets (Enforcement etc) Regulations 2018
(SI 2018/597) 59
Transfer of Employment (Pension Protection) Regulations
2005 (SI 2005/649) 359
Transfer of Undertakings (Protection of Employment)
Regulations 1981 (SI 1981/1794) 4, 335, 337, 343, 360,
362, 568

Transfer of Undertakings (Protection of Employment)
Regulations 2006 (SI 2006/246) 5, 133, 145, 150, 157,
260, 335–73
reg 2 346
reg 2(1) 335, 347, 351, 353
reg 3 338, 341, 371
reg 3(1)(a) 338, 347, 372–3
reg 3(1)(b) 338, 342–7, 372–3
reg 3(1)(b)(i)–(ii) 345
reg 3(1)(b)(iii) 345–6, 348
reg 3(2) 339, 341, 354
reg 3(2A) 345
reg 3(3) 345, 372–3
reg 3(3)(a) 345
reg 3(3)(a)(i) 347
reg 3(3)(a)(ii) 346
reg 3(5) 338
reg 4 337, 350, 352–3, 356, 358, 372–3
reg 4(1) 348, 350–1, 355, 363–4
reg 4(2) 351, 355–6
reg 4(3) 351, 356, 361, 371–3
reg 4(4) 361, 363
reg 4(5) 363–4, 371
reg 4(5)(a) 365
reg 4(5A) 363
reg 4(5B) 363–4
reg 4(5C) 364
reg 4(6) 337, 357, 359
reg 4(7) 355, 371
reg 4(8) 355, 371
reg 4(9) 351–3, 355, 359
reg 4(10) 353
reg 4(11) 351–2, 355
reg 4A 358
reg 5 358
reg 6 358
reg 7 337, 359–61, 364, 372–3
reg 7(1) 351, 359, 363, 366, 371–2
reg 7(2)–(3) 359–60, 363
reg 7(3A) 359, 362
reg 7(4) 360
reg 8 337, 351, 371
reg 9 337, 362, 365, 371
reg 10 337, 358
reg 11 357, 366–7, 370–1
reg 11(4) 366
reg 11(6)–(7) 367
reg 12 251, 357, 366–7, 370–1
reg 12(7) 251
reg 13 366–8, 370
reg 13(2) 367
reg 13(3) 368
reg 13(6) 368
reg 13(7)–(8) 368
reg 13A 368
reg 14 366–7, 370
reg 15 366, 369–70
reg 15(9) 359, 369
reg 16 251, 366, 370
reg 16(1) 251
reg 16(3) 369
reg 19 363

UK General Data Protection Regulation 580, 592
art 4 580–1
art 4(11) 588
art 5 581
art 6 581, 588
art 6(1)(c) 588
art 6(1)(e) 588
art 6(1)(f) 588
art 9 582
art 12 586
art 12(1) 585
art 13 582, 585, 588
art 14 585, 588
art 15 582, 585–6
art 16 582
art 17 582
art 18 582
art 20 582
art 21 582
art 22 582
art 33 582
art 35 583
art 58 583
Unfair Dismissal (Variation of the Limit of Compensatory
Award) Order 2013(SI 2013/1949) 222

Working Time (Coronavirus) (Amendment) Regulations
2020 (SI 2020/365) 86
Working Time Regulations 1998 (SI 1998/1833) 19–20,
26, 40, 49, 55–6, 73, 75, 77–98, 100, 120, 208, 235,
250, 419
reg 2 23, 78, 80, 98
reg 2(1) 27, 91
reg 2(1)(a) 79
reg 4 80–2
reg 4(1) 83
reg 5 82
reg 6 90
reg 9 80
reg 10 81, 83
reg 10(1) 79
reg 11 81, 83–4, 206
reg 12 81, 83–4
reg 12(1) 85
reg 13 81, 88–94
reg 13(1) 86
reg 13(9) 86, 92–4
reg 13(10)–(16) 92
reg 13A 86, 89, 91
reg 14 92, 112, 159
reg 14(2) 94
reg 14(4) 87
reg 14(5) 92
reg 15 87, 98
reg 16 88, 90
reg 16(2) 88
reg 16(3) 89
reg 20(1) 82
reg 30 92, 289
reg 30(1) 85, 93–4
reg 30(5) 90, 93

EU secondary legislation
Decision 2010/48 503
Directive 76/207 (Equal Treatment) 4, 377, 422, 562
Directive 77/187 (Acquired Rights) 4, 335–6, 339, 341, 344, 349, 355, 361, 365, 568
    Art 1(1) 339, 350
    Art 3(2) 366
Directive 79/7 (Equal Treatment in Matters of Social Security)
    Art 7 403
Directive 89/391 (Health and Safety at Work) 207
Directive 92/85 (Pregnant Workers) 438, 545, 552, 562
Directive 93/104 (Working Time) 22, 55, 77, 79–80, 85, 88–9, 93–5
    Art 2 78
    Art 7 88, 91, 93–4
Directive 95/46 (Data Protection) 580, 589
Directive 97/80 (Burden of proof) 440, 478
Directive 97/81 (Part-time Work) 19, 417–18
    cl 4(1) 417
Directive 98/50 (Acquired Rights) 336
Directive 98/59 (Collective Redundancies) 23, 153–4
    Art 1(1)(a) 155
Directive 1991/453 (Proof of Employment) 48
Directive 2000/43 (Race Discrimination) 377, 459
Directive 2000/78 (Equal Treatment in Employment and Occupation) 35, 377, 383, 388, 428, 487, 489, 503, 514, 516, 553
    Art 4(1) 429
    Art 5 528
    Art 6 427, 491
    Art 6(1) 491, 493
Directive 2001/23 (Acquired Rights, Amendment) 335–6
Directive 2002/14 (Information and Consultation in the Workplace) 156, 370
Directive 2006/54 (Equal Treatment, Recast) 469–70
Directive 2008/104 (Agency Workers) 34
Directive 2016/943 (Trade Secrets) 57
Recommendation and Code of Practice on the Dignity of Women and Men at Work (92/131/EEC) 400–1
Regulation 2016/679 (General Data Protection) 580, 590
    Art 2 580
    Art 88 580

Codes of Practice and Guidance
ACAS Code of Practice on Disciplinary and Grievance Procedures 3, 117, 120, 163–4, 166–7, 169, 176–85, 188, 192, 197, 219–20, 226–7, 231, 244, 246–7
    para 1 177
    paras 5–7 181
    paras 8–17 182
    para 18 182, 185
    paras 19–22 183, 185
    paras 23–29 183
ACAS Code of Practice on Discrimination 2009 411, 418, 450, 465, 486, 542
ACAS Code of Practice on Flexible Working 558
ACAS Code of Practice on Settlement Agreements 2013 307, 309–10
ACAS Guidance on changing an employment contract, employer responsibilities 71
ACAS Guidance for employers on employment status 2017 23

ACAS Guidance on gender reassignment discrimination 387
ACAS Guidance on overtime 2018 90
ACAS Guidance on religion and belief 2018 385
ACAS Guidance on shared parental leave; a good practice guide for employers and employees 556
ACAS Guidance on shared parental leave; summary process 556
ACAS Guidance on when and how to suspend employees 187–8
ACAS Guide asking and responding to questions of discrimination in the workplace 406
ACAS revised Guidance how to manage collective redundancies 152–3
BIS Employers' Technical Guide to Shared Parental Leave and Pay 556
BIS Guidance on Age Regulations and their impact on pension schemes 498
BIS Guidance on Agency Workers Regulations 2010 34
BIS Guidance on dependant care leave 560
BIS Guidance on employment rights on the transfer of an Undertaking 335, 339, 341, 346–8, 352–3, 360–2, 364, 367
BIS Guidance explaining requirements to inform and consult employees 156
BIS Guidance on maternity leave 545, 547
EHRC Code of Practice on Employment 5, 9, 376, 378–80, 382, 387, 394, 401–3, 439, 499, 501, 517, 519–20, 522–3, 527, 531–2, 534–6, 538–9, 553
    para 2.6.1 434
    para 4.31 499
    para 10.70 138
EHRC Code of Practice on Equal Pay 376
EHRC Guidance on religion and belief 385
EHRC Guidance on the use of confidentiality agreements, October 2019 308
EHRC Guide to the law and best practice in tackling sexual harassment and harassment at work 467
    para 7 470
    para 7.7 470
EHRC Guide to what equality law means for advertisers 395
EHRC non-statutory core guidance on recruitment 388
ET Presidential Direction of 27 March 2015 76
ET Presidential Direction regarding the listing of Employment Tribunal cases during the Covid-19 pandemic 285
ET Presidential Guidance on the bands for injury to feelings and psychiatric injury 409
ET Presidential Guidance on case management 270
ET Presidential Guidance on judicial assessment
    para 21 284
ET Presidential Guidance Note on alternative dispute resolution, incorporating Guidance on judicial mediation, 22 January 2018 311
ET Presidential Guidance on remote and in-person hearings 285
ET Presidential Guidance on seeking a postponement of hearing 291
ET Presidential Guidance on vulnerable parties and witnesses, 22 April 2020 267
ET Presidential Practice Direction and Presidential Guidance on remote and in-person hearings, September 2020 285, 290

ET Presidential Practice Direction on remote hearings and open justice 285

ET Presidents of England and Wales and Scotland issued joint Presidential guidance on principles to be applied when compensating for pension loss 225

ET Presidents of England and Wales and Scotland issued joint Presidential guidance on taking oral evidence by video or telephone from persons located abroad; April 2022 278, 282

ET Presidents or England and Wales and Scotland Joint Direction regarding the listing of Employment Tribunal cases during the Covid-19 pandemic March 2020 285

Guidance Coronavirus Job Retention Scheme 201–2

Health and Safety at Work Act 1974 Code of Practice 551

HM Equality Office Guidance on recruitment and retention of transgender employees 387

HMRC Guide CWG 2 (2009) Employer's Further Guide to PAYE and NICs 116

Home Office Code of Practice on Preventing Illegal Working 2014 5

Home Office Code of Practice on Preventing Illegal Working 2019 5, 393

Home Office Guidance on employer's right to work checks 393

ICO Code of Practice on SARs (subject access requests) 586

ICO Employment Practices Code 592
Part 1 Recruitment and selection 9
Part 3 587

ICO Guidance on bringing your own devices (BYOD) to work 589

ICO Guidance on the GDPR 580–3, 588

ICO Guidance on transferring data overseas from the UK 589

Immigration, Asylum and Nationality Act Code of Practice 2008 5

LCJ and ET President Practice guidance on remote observation of hearings; new powers 2022 286

ODI Guidance on disability 2011 503–8, 511, 537

Treasury Directions and Guidance on 'usual hours' 73
para 7.2 73
para 7.6 73

Circular

Home Office Circular 5/2005 327

Introductory Note

This Introductory Note sets out some general introductory matters that will inform the succeeding substantive chapters. It will also contain contemporary updates that may change from year to year but can be relevant in any given year and give historic and current context to certain matters.

RESPONSIBLE GOVERNMENT DEPARTMENTS

Responsibility for employment law in England and Wales is currently spread across a number of different government departments, including the Department for Work and Pensions, the Department for Business, Energy and Industrial Strategy (BEIS), the Ministry of Justice and the Home Office.

In June 2009, the Department for Business, Enterprise and Regulatory Reform (DBERR) (the former Department of Trade and Industry (DTI)) became the Department for Business, Innovation and Skills (BIS). A number of the websites referred to in this book were originally DTI/DBERR/BIS websites. In July 2016, BIS and the Department of Energy and Climate Change (DECC) merged to form BEIS. The authors have endeavoured to change web addresses where necessary; in most instances, however, pre-existing DTI/DBERR/BIS website addresses remain operative and will automatically redirect the user to the correct web page. References to DTI/DBERR/BIS are retained where relevant for historical purposes.

COVID-19

The impact of the coronavirus pandemic on individuals and their employment

At the end of March 2020, the UK went into what we now call 'lockdown' as a result of the coronavirus pandemic and the measures introduced by the UK Government to halt the spread of the contagion. This resulted in a number of measures and initiatives from the governments of England, Wales and Scotland, which directly impacted on individuals and their employment. The full detail of the Coronavirus Job Retention Scheme is beyond the scope of this book; there is a short summary of the main measures below, and more detail appears, where relevant, in **Chapter 1** (statutory sick pay), **Chapter 5** (unfair dismissal) and **Chapter 6** (practice and procedure).

Overview

(Main source: House of Commons Library briefing paper on answers to frequently asked questions on the Coronavirus Job Retention Scheme.)

The arrival of the pandemic saw all non-essential retail and hospitality stopped and large numbers of employees forced into working remotely from home. On 11 March 2020, the Chancellor announced that the Government would reimburse small employers (under 250 employees) for any statutory sick pay (SSP) they paid to staff for the first 14 days of sickness. On 13 March, amended SSP regulations came into effect which provided that SSP would be available to anyone self-isolating. On 20 March, in response to the realisation of the full economic impact of the pandemic, and in order to avoid the spectre of mass redundancies as businesses were forced to close their doors, the Government announced the introduction of a coronavirus job retention scheme (CJRS), whereby employers could retain staff on their books, but place them on a paid temporary leave of absence (furloughing), where the Government agreed to pay a proportion of their salary for that period. On 23 March, people were advised not to travel and to work from home unless their work 'absolutely [could not]' be done from home.

As a result of the pandemic and the restrictions brought in to manage it, the UK's economy reportedly fell into the deepest recession for 300 years, and UK GDP fell 19% in the three months to May 2020. According to reports, as of 20 July 2020, over 9.3 million people had been furloughed, from over 1 million different employers in the United Kingdom, as part of the CJRS. At that point in time, just under 150,000 redundancies had been announced. The number of employees on company payrolls fell by 649,000 between March and June. The Government's economics forecaster, the Office for Budget Responsibility, warned that unemployment could more than double by the end of 2020 to the highest levels since the 1980s. Aviation, retail, hospitality and leisure were among the hardest hit sectors.

On 25 March 2020, the Coronavirus Act 2020 received royal assent. Most of it came into effect immediately. This gave the Government discretionary powers (for a two-year period) to limit or suspend public gatherings, to detain individuals suspected to be infected with Covid-19, and to intervene or relax regulations in a range of sectors to limit transmission of the disease. The Act also provided measures to combat the economic effects of the pandemic. It included the power to halt the eviction of tenants, protect emergency volunteers from becoming unemployed, and for the Government to reimburse the cost of statutory sick pay for employees affected by Covid-19 to employers. Section 76 of the Coronavirus Act 2020 stated that 'her Majesty's Revenue and Customs are to have such functions as the Treasury may direct in relation to coronavirus or coronavirus disease'. This was followed by a number of Treasury Directions, the first of which was on 15 April 2020, giving HMRC the responsibility for payments and management of the CJRS. On 26 March 2020, the Government announced a number of proposals aimed at helping self-employed individuals.

The CJRS applied from 1 March 2020 and ended at the end of September 2021. The scheme provided grants to employers during coronavirus related lockdowns, so they could retain and continue to pay staff during such lockdowns, by furloughing employees at 80% of their wages.

The CJRS was a mechanism through which employers could claim money from HMRC. It did not alter existing employment law rights and obligations. As employers are normally liable under the employment contract to pay employees their full wages, even if they cannot provide any work, in most cases, the employment contract needed to be varied to allow employers to furlough an employee on reduced pay. The rules of the CJRS – set out in Treasury Directions – required employers to enter into a full furlough agreement or (after 1 July 2020) a flexible furlough agreement with their employees, setting out the main terms and conditions that would apply during any period of furlough. Agreements had to be incorporated into the employee's employment contract.

It was for employers to decide whether to offer furlough to an employee. Some commentators noted that this could cause problems for zero-hours workers and agency workers whose employers could simply reduce their work to zero without making a claim under the CJRS.

The CJRS sat amongst a range of existing statutory employment rights, including protections from discrimination, from unfair dismissal and rights to consultation in cases of collective redundancies.

Under the CJRS, employers were able to claim a grant covering 80% of the wages for a furloughed employee, subject to a cap of £2,500 a month, and the Government also agreed to cover the employer national insurance and minimum auto-enrolment pension scheme contributions. Those made redundant after 28 February 2020 were able to be re-employed and placed on furlough. Detailed arrangements were also put in place to cover the taking and payment of holidays and sick pay for staff who were furloughed. Furloughing was voluntary and had to be agreed between an employer and an employee in writing. Until the end of June

2020, employees had to be furloughed for a minimum period of three weeks to be eligible for the CJRS.

On 27 March 2020, further details of the furlough scheme were issued, and various guidance documents on how it would operate for employers and employees were published by HMRC (the first were published on 26 and 27 March, but these were updated piecemeal on numerous occasions), along with a Treasury Direction (published on 15 April and updated on 20 May 2020). Where there were contradictions between the HMRC Guidance and the Treasury Direction, the Direction prevailed. Guidance was issued for employers and employees on numerous matters relating to the CJRS, including on whom could be furloughed, how the scheme would operate, as well as information on how to claim through the scheme, and how to calculate wages, etc.

The initial CJRS was backdated to 1 March 2020, and opened to applications on 20 April. The CJRS covered all UK employers who had created and started a PAYE payroll scheme on or before 19 March 2020 (originally 28 February), enrolled for PAYE online and had a UK bank account. This included businesses, charities, recruitment agencies and public authorities. The CJRS was originally due to run from 1 March to 31 May 2020. On 17 April, it was announced that the initial period of three months would be extended to four months, until the end of June, for those on the employer's PAYE on or before 19 March. The CJRS did not amend any existing employment laws, and all existing employment rights continued. It relied in essence on a temporary contractual variation by agreement between the employer and the employee on leave and pay. In some cases, employers were also able to rely on existing contractual terms around lay-off. It did not create a legal right to be furloughed. To qualify, employees had to have been on a PAYE payroll scheme before 19 March 2020 and have a UK bank account. It covered employees, whether salaried or agency, as well as 'limb (b)' workers (see ERA 1996, s 230). Separate to this agreement was an agreement between the employer and HMRC.

On 29 May 2020, the Government announced the extension of the Scheme until 31 October 2020, when it was originally due to close. Further detailed guidance on the changes to the CJRS was published on 12 June. Under the initial CJRS, only employees who were employed on 19 March 2020 on a PAYE payroll notified to HMRC through an RTI submission on or before that date were eligible. Employees who were on a payroll on or before 28 February or 19 March but who stopped working after those dates could be re-employed and furloughed. This change was made to try and cover individuals who changed jobs in February/March and who in some instances missed out under the original rules. The rules did not allow people on furlough to do any other paid work ('revenue generating') for their employer. Staff were allowed to do training. Staff were, however, permitted to get paid work with another employer.

The rules were changed to allow employees who had already been furloughed for a full three-week period prior to 30 June 2020 to be 'flexibly furloughed' from 1 July 2020 – meaning employers could ask employees to work any pattern and claim a CJRS grant for any usual hours not worked. The requirement to be furloughed for a minimum period of three weeks was removed but eligibility still depended on having been furloughed under the original scheme. This meant that employers were able to bring back to work employees who had previously been furloughed, for any amount of time and on any shift pattern, while still being able to claim a grant under the CJRS for any normal hours not worked. For any hours which an employee worked, employers had to pay full wages, tax and national insurance contributions in the usual way. Employers were able to make a claim under the CJRS for the remainder of the employee's 'usual hours' that they were not required to work. Employers were required to keep detailed records of an employee's working hours during any period of flexible furloughing for the purposes of any subsequent audit by HMRC.

The CJRS initially covered 80% of an employee's wages (up to £2,500 per month) as well as employer National Insurance and pension contributions. From 1 August 2020, NICs and pension contributions were not covered. In September and October 2020, the CJRS covered only 70% and 60% of wages, respectively, and employers were required to top up to 80%.

The CJRS was originally due to end on 31 October 2020, when it was supposed to be replaced from 1 November by a Job Support Scheme (JSS), which was due to run until April 2021. However, on 5 November 2020, it was announced that the CJRS would be extended again until 31 March 2021. On 17 December 2020, the CJRS was extended to 30 April 2021. Finally, in March 2021, the CJRS was extended until 30 September 2021, when it ended.

Under the extended CJRS, employers were able to flexibly furlough employees and claim a grant from HMRC for 80% of an employee's wages for any usual hours not worked (up to £2,500 per month or the relevant pro rata amount). Employers had to cover employer NICs and pension contributions. As such, the rules were similar to those in place in August 2020. Under the extended CJRS, employees who were employed on 30 October 2020 on a payroll notified to HMRC on or before that date were eligible. Those who were employed on 23 September but who had stopped working could be re-employed and furloughed. There was no need for an employee to have been furloughed between March and October.

Following the announcement of the further extension in March 2021, the extended CJRS rules continued to apply until 30 June 2021, so until that date they continued to cover 80% of an employee's wages. From 1 July 2021, there was a tapering down, so that the grant only covered 70% of wages and employers were required to top up an additional 10%. From 1 August 2021, the grant covered 60% of wages and employers were required to top up 20%. The furlough scheme closed on 30 September 2021.

SSP

In response to the Covid-19 pandemic, in March 2020 the Government announced that SSP would be payable from day 1, not day 4 of absence, that small employers (less than 250 staff) could recoup the first 14 days of SSP from the Government, and that SSP would be available for anyone self-isolating because of the virus. The revised rules ended in March 2022. To be eligible for SSP, employees must now, in line with previous rules, be sick or incapable of work (see **Chapter 1**). Self-isolation rules in England ended in February 2022 (28 March 2022 in Wales), although the Health Security Agency Guidance recommended that those testing Covid positive should not attend work – that guidance was withdrawn on 1 April 2022 and replaced with 'guidance for people with symptoms of a RTI including covid-19', which remains in place.

Record keeping

Record keeping requirements imposed by the Scheme meant that, as well as furlough agreements, employers must keep records of the following for six years:

- the amount claimed for each employee
- the claim period for each employee
- the claim reference number
- calculations (in case HMRC needs more information about the claim)
- usual hours worked, including any calculations for flexibly furloughed employees
- actual hours worked for flexibly furloughed employees.

Employers were advised to keep evidence to show that their operations had been negatively affected by coronavirus and how it impacted, as well as the effect this had on their workforce, so as to show, for example, the lack of work available, or that an employee was furloughed for another reason arising from coronavirus (for example, they lived with a person who was shielding or they were unable to work due to childcare commitments).

Continuing employment law consequences of the pandemic

Acas publishes advice on coronavirus and various employment-related issues arising, which is available via its website and includes information on:

- attending the workplace
- self-isolation and sick pay
- vaccination issues
- long Covid
- disciplinary and grievance procedures
- holiday and leave
- mental health.

As the President of the Employment Tribunals, Judge Barry Clarke, observes in his contribution to the Senior President of Tribunals' Annual Report 2021:

> ... new claims arise from, among other matters, the operation of the Coronavirus Job Retention Scheme, the regulation of furlough payments and the calculation of associated sums such as holiday pay, the permanent or temporary closure of many workplaces, the legal requirement to maintain safe systems of work, and the treatment of those workers who raise concerns about whether those systems are safe enough. The issues raised have presented significant challenges to employers, trade unions and workers, as well as those who advise them.

The aim of the CJRS was to try to limit redundancies. Employers who used the CJRS continued to owe the same contractual and statutory duties to their employees (though there may be argument about what those duties require an employer to do). As the contract of employment remained in place throughout the furlough period, employees remained in continuous service for statutory continuity purposes. Requirements such as notice continued to be relevant to lockdown terminations. Concerns were expressed that once the CJRS ended, and government financial support was withdrawn, employers would still make staff redundant because of the precarious economic environment. There was nothing in the CJRS to prevent employers reaching agreement with employees to extend the period for which employees were furloughed beyond the end of the CJRS, provided employees continued to agree to being furloughed. Likewise, employers could seek to keep employees on furlough with reduced terms when the CJRS ended, provided employees agreed. However, employers had to bear the costs of this, as they were not able to reclaim salary or other wage costs from the CJRS after it ended. These might have been options as an alternative to redundancy. Employers could also consider options such as using unpaid statutory parental leave or granting unpaid sabbaticals, in an effort to enable employees to remain employed on their books but without pay until the situation improved, in the hope that redundancies could be avoided.

Another option was for employers to seek to change terms and conditions, such as reducing hours of work or pay, but this requires consultation and employee agreement. Any unilateral imposition of reduced hours or pay or dismissal and re-engagement on new terms potentially gives rise to unfair dismissal claims. Dismissals in these circumstances may still be fair, so long as there is a clear business necessity for the change and the employer has followed a fair process (see **Chapter 5**). Dismissal and re-engagement will trigger collective consultation requirements where 20 or more dismissals are proposed (see **Chapter 4**).

If a contractual right to lay off without pay exists (such clauses are rare in practice), this could potentially be relied on by employers, but such provisions are subject to the implied term of trust and confidence, which would mean, for example, that there should still be consultation with employees and reasonable notice to avoid potentially being in breach of contract (see **Chapter 3**). There are also specific statutory provisions which provide a right for employees who have been laid off for four or more consecutive weeks, or six weeks in any 13-week period, to claim a statutory redundancy payment in certain circumstances. However, this requires employees to resign in order to receive their redundancy payment (see **Chapter 4**).

Complaints arising out of the administration of the CJRS also gave rise to claims regarding the rules on the calculation of wages and entitlement to holiday and sick pay (see **Chapter 1**).

Some ill-health conditions put employees at a higher risk of serious illness from Covid-19. In addition to pandemic-related claims alleging detriment or dismissal on health and safety or protected disclosure grounds (under ss 43B(1)(d), 44, 47B, 100 and 103A of the Employment Rights Act 1996) (see **Chapter 5**), employers need to be mindful of potential discrimination issues too (see **Chapter 13**).

Employment tribunal hearings

In his foreword to the 2020 Annual Report, the Senior President of Tribunals, the Rt Hon Sir Ernest Ryder, talked about the huge impact the Covid-19 pandemic had had on tribunal judges, members and staff alike:

> We designed a suite of emergency legislative provisions, rule changes, practice directions and guidance to facilitate that aim. Overnight we changed from paper-based face-to-face hearings to remote hearings by audio and video means, using new technology and a host of innovative workarounds provided by judges and staff alike. A four-phase recovery plan was published using administrative instructions to explain what we wanted to happen.

The new Senior President, the Right Honourable Sir Keith Lindblom, stated in the 2021 report that:

> No annual report in 2021 would be complete without some reflection on the COVID-19 pandemic and its effects on the tribunals system. The tribunals judiciary has shown itself to be remarkably adaptable and resilient in the face of the COVID-19 crisis. Processes had to be changed overnight as the majority of cases were, out of necessity, dealt with remotely, and judiciary and users alike have had to adapt repeatedly to an ever-changing procedural landscape. We have learned much from the pandemic and will continue to do so as we work with Government towards recovery. Some practices we shall probably retain. Video hearings will no doubt perform a larger role in the tribunals than they did before the pandemic. This, in my view, ought to be welcomed. However, I am also clear in my opinion that face-to-face hearings will never, and should never, be completely replaced by remote methods. There are always going to be cases – indeed, many cases – in which a face-to-face hearing is clearly the best form of hearing, and for several reasons. Judges are responsible for, and will make, the decision, taking into account the interests of justice and the particular circumstances of each case.

In his 2022 Annual Report he states in the foreword to the report:

> It has been another busy and productive year for the tribunals. As the restrictions necessitated by Covid-19 have gradually eased, our attention has turned from dealing with the immediate impact of the pandemic to tackling the backlog of cases that has inevitably increased above pre-pandemic levels in several of the tribunal jurisdictions. Progress in modernising the tribunals has continued, bringing with it new systems and ways of working. The tribunals have also continued to adapt to new legislation, including powers to enable hearings to be observed remotely.

During the pandemic, a number of guidance documents, FAQs and advisory notes were issued for the conduct of employment tribunal hearings, and updated as circumstances changed. A complete set of these can be found on the Judiciary website at www.judiciary.uk/coronavirus-covid-19-advice-and-guidance/#tribunals. Some of them are referred to below.

On 18 March 2020, the Presidents of Employment Tribunals (England and Wales and Scotland) issued Joint Guidance on the Conduct of Employment Tribunal Proceedings during the Covid-19 pandemic, and on 19 March a Joint Direction regarding the listing of employment tribunal cases during the Covid-19 pandemic was issued. That Direction was amended, reviewed and updated on a number of occasions. The Direction provided that from 23 March 2020, all in-person tribunal hearings were to be converted to telephone case management hearings and gave 'strong encouragement to Tribunals and parties to use electronic communications methods including skype for business and video conferencing technology where available, to conduct hearings of all kinds, where doing so was compatible with the overriding objective and the requirements of the Rules'. Many employment tribunal hearing centres closed, some were staffed but not open to the public and a handful continued to be operational but subject to social distancing. Many tribunal hearings were cancelled and replaced with telephone case management hearings. Over time, hearings started to be conducted remotely, or as hybrids, with judges at home or in the employment tribunal offices and the parties present remotely. On 1 June 2020, the Presidents of England and Wales and Scotland issued a 'road map', representing their joint – and 'partly aspirational' – plan, designed to increase gradually the number and type of hearings which could take place over the course of 2020 while pandemic-related restrictions remained in place.

In the Minutes for the Employment Tribunals National User Group meeting in June 2020, it was recorded that even before the Covid-19 crisis, there was already a significant backlog of outstanding cases – approximately 30,600 single cases as of March 2020. This was primarily due to the impact of the removal of fees in the employment tribunals in July 2017 (see below and **Chapter 6**). To put this in context, across England, Wales and Scotland, the figure had stood at about 10,000 single cases awaiting determination in March 2017, about 19,000 in March 2018 and about 27,000 in March 2019. The previous peak in the 2009/10 financial year, after the credit crisis, was about 36,000. The backlog had been increased – by about 1% per week – by the coronavirus crisis, such that it amounted to around 36,600 by June 2020. By February 2021, it was reported that the backlog of outstanding cases in England and Wales stood at 51,614 – an increase of 45% compared to the baseline figure pre-Covid. Receipts have outstripped disposals in single claims for every week bar one since September, with 6,550 new claims since Christmas compared with 5,881 dealt with.

On 31 March 2021, Judge Barry Clarke and Judge Shona Simon, Presidents of the Employment Tribunals in England and Wales and Scotland respectively, jointly published a revised 'road map' leading out of the pandemic. They said that reverting to face-to-face hearings would not be enough to tackle the outstanding caseload:

> We must reflect on what we have learned and ensure that we keep hold of the good. The future will involve more, not less, use of technology ... Unlike many other jurisdictions, the pandemic has inflated our caseload (which had been rising for some time anyway since the Supreme Court's judgment in the Unison case in 2017). It follows that a return to pre-pandemic ways of working as restrictions relax is not an option for the employment tribunals.

The average waiting time for hearings is reported in the Minutes for the Employment Tribunals National User Group meeting in January 2022 as follows:

> In broad terms, as at January 2022, all regions could list shorter hearings of 1 to 2 days' duration in 2022. A few (North East, Midlands East, London Central, Wales, and parts of the South East) could even manage the first half of 2022.
>
> For longer hearings, however, the picture was much more varied. The shortest waiting times were in the North East, London Central and Wales, where such cases could generally still be listed and heard before the end of 2022. For other regions, including Midlands East, Midlands West, the South West and most parts of the South East, such cases were now generally being listed in the first half of 2023. The longest waiting times were in London South, London East and the North West, where 3 to 5 day hearing and 5 to 10 day hearings were mostly being listed in the second half of 2023. London South and the North West had now started listing cases lasting ten or more days in 2024. This was obviously a matter of great concern.
>
> The President emphasised that this was an overall picture. There were always exceptions, such as cases that had involved numerous preliminary hearings, been postponed for good reason, or been subject to appeal. The President also repeated a point he had made on earlier occasions: as lengthy hearings fell from the list due to settlement, it was often possible to backfill the list by bringing forward cases that had been listed at later dates.

The latest version of the road map was published in March 2022. Video hearings will remain an 'essential part' of the landscape and, for 2022–23, they will remain the default option for preliminary hearings, applications for interim relief, judicial mediations and final hearings of short track claims. However:

> Final hearings of standard track claims (unfair dismissal) will vary. In most parts of Britain, as the physical estate recovers and requirements for social distancing are removed, we wish them to return in greater numbers to in-person, especially where the case involves significant disputed evidence. This will take time, because recovery will not be uniform. In parts of the country where the backlog is greatest, especially in London and the South East, final hearings of standard track claims will continue to default to video, to enable maximum use of judges in the virtual region. Our firm wish is for final hearings of open track claims (discrimination and whistleblowing) to default to in-person. This is achievable in Scotland, where it will be the default approach. However, it is not achievable in all parts of England and Wales ...

BREXIT

As readers know, on 23 June 2016 the UK voted by 52% to 48% to leave the European Union (EU) (the 'Brexit' vote). Following lengthy negotiations, the UK left the EU at the end of January 2020. The detail of Brexit is beyond the scope of this book, but a summary follows. The UK ceased to be a member of the EU on 31 January 2020. There was a transition period until 31 December 2020 ('IP completion day'), which meant that most EU law continued to apply and the Court of Justice of the European Union (CJEU) continued to have jurisdiction. Areas that derive from EU legislation and may be impacted include TUPE (see **Chapter 7**), redundancy consultation (see **Chapter 4**), working time, holiday pay and agency workers' rights (see **Chapter 1**), as well as discrimination (see **Chapter 8**) and family-friendly rights (see **Chapter 14**).

On 26 June 2018, the European Union (Withdrawal) Act 2018 ('the Withdrawal Act 2018') was passed. The Withdrawal Act 2018 was the main vehicle for implementing Brexit. It repealed the European Communities Act 1972 (which legislated for the incorporation of EU law into the domestic law of the United Kingdom and for the direct effect and supremacy of EU law (see **Chapter 1**)) and ended the authority of EU law and the CJEU within the UK. It transferred into UK law all existing provisions of EU law applicable at this point in time (save the European Charter of Fundamental Rights), meaning that 40 years' worth of EU laws continued to apply and EU law would remain supreme in relation to pre-Brexit UK law. The Withdrawal Act 2018 states that when interpreting *retained EU law* after Brexit, UK courts and tribunals will not be bound by any decisions made on or after IP completion day but 'may have regard to' such decisions 'so far as it is relevant to any matter before the Court or tribunal'. The Withdrawal Act 2018 also (controversially) gives (in s 8) Ministers delegated powers to make secondary legislation (through the use of what is known as a 'Henry VIII' clause – so named from the Statute of Proclamations 1539, which gave King Henry VIII power to legislate by proclamation) to amend any law that does not operate appropriately following the UK's departure from the EU (eg references to EU institutions which no longer have jurisdiction). This allows changes to be made to legislation by Ministers without any parliamentary scrutiny. The Employment Rights (Amendment) (EU Exit) Regulations 2019 made some small technical changes to primary and secondary legislation in this regard.

Under the Withdrawal Act 2018, Parliament was obliged to pass a further Act, the European Union (Withdrawal Agreement) Act 2020 (WAA 2020), to approve and implement into national law the EU–UK Withdrawal Agreement negotiated by Prime Minister Johnson. The WAA 2020 amended the position on retained EU case law after the transition period. Section 6 of the Withdrawal Act 2018 gave CJEU decisions the same status in law as UK Supreme Court decisions, but s 26 of the WAA 2000 amended s 6 to give the Government a power to specify in regulations that certain courts and tribunals are not bound by CJEU cases, or by existing domestic case law on EU-derived rights. The power to depart from pre-Brexit EU case law has been limited to the Court of Appeal and Supreme Court. The test to be applied is the same test that the Supreme Court applies when deciding whether to depart from its own previous decisions. *See Lipton v BA City Flyer* (a non-employment related case) for analysis of the approach the courts should take to retained EU law (paras 54–83). Shortly before his resignation as Brexit Minister, Lord Frost proposed changes to the status of retained EU law by curtailing its primacy over other forms of domestic law (see Catherine Barnard, 'REUL (Retained EU Law) and Lord Frost', *UK in a Changing Europe* Blog, 17 December 2021).

The WAA 2020 introduced an obligation on the Government to confirm, where primary legislation is proposed, that the Act does not weaken workers' rights or to confirm that it does. However, the so-called statement of non-regression applies only in respect of primary legislation (so does not, for example, apply to the UK's Working Time Regulations (see **Chapter 1**)).

The EU–UK Trade and Cooperation Agreement (TCA) was concluded between the EU and the UK on 30 December 2020, and entered into force on 1 May 2021. It sets out preferential arrangements in areas such as the trade in goods and in services, labour and social policy, social security coordination, law enforcement and judicial cooperation. It is underpinned by provisions ensuring a level playing field and respect for fundamental rights. Insofar as respect for the 'level playing field' is concerned, the TCA provides that if either party changes its laws in areas such as social or economic regulations, in a way that is liable to give one party's (UK or EU) businesses an advantage, the other party can impose retaliatory tariffs. If these are found to be excessive by an arbitration panel, then retaliatory action can be taken. The European Union (Future Relationship) Act 2020 gave legal force to the TCA.

The EU and the UK agreed not to reduce present levels of employees' labour and social protection where such reductions of protection could result in damages to trade or investments between the parties. Areas named in the TCA include fundamental labour rights, fair labour and employment conditions, occupational health and safety as well as restructurings. However, some matters, such as alterations to employment conditions without negative effects on trade, may be permissible under the TCA. One area where the UK may seek to dilute current rights originating from the EU is in the context of the Working Time Directive (see below). Other areas that may come under increased scrutiny include the Agency Workers Regulations (see **Chapter 1**), collective consultation requirements (see **Chapter 3**) and Transfers of Undertakings (see **Chapter 7**). Any infringement of these and other 'protection obligations' will be subject to consultation between the EU and the UK and/ or examination and review by a panel of experts. This principle reflects the arrangement of the parties for a 'level playing field for open and fair competition and sustainable development' within key economic areas such as labour and social policy.

On 22 September 2022, the Government published the Retained EU Law (Revocation and Reform) Bill which, in broad terms, proposes that 'the three principles of EU law [will be] turned off from the end of 2023 ... direct effect, supremacy of EU law and the general principles of EU law' (Caspar Glyn KC, ELA, *The Law Society Gazette*,18 November 2022, p 27). EU derived law will no longer need to be interpreted in line with underlying EU law and will be revoked at the end of 2023 (or by June 2026). EU-derived law which applied in the UK was originally preserved and retained by the Withdrawal Act 2018. The Bill will potentially affect some key pieces of secondary employment-related legislation derived from EU law in areas such as health and safety, collective consultation on redundancy and TUPE. The Bill had its second reading in the Commons on 25 October 2022. The Bill sets out two alternatives to revocation:

(1) Postpone the revocation of some EU retained laws, but under the terms of the Bill this is only an option to June 2026.

(2) Replace some EU retained laws with new laws. It is estimated that there could be up to 3,800 laws affected. Replacing those laws by 2023 is considered by most to be impossible.

As Caspar Glyn points out in the *Law Society Gazette* (see above):

> the effect of abolishing [the] three principles [direct effect, supremacy and the general principles of EU law] is, even if the government were to retain every single regulation made from EU law since 1972, to strip dozens of regulations of their well understood and settled meaning from January 2024. ... Holiday pay, when it is not affected by the EU three principles, does not guarantee the same pay on holiday as at work – for instance, all overtime is ignored and only contractual pay is included. Alarmingly, the government has not considered that its bill will also affect the meaning of primary legislation such as the Equality Act 2010.

For example, in R *(on the application of IWGB) v SSWP* [2020] EWHC 3050, the High Court considered an application by the IWGB for a declaration that the United Kingdom had failed properly to transpose into domestic law two EU Directives (Council Directive 89/391/EC on the introduction of measures to encourage improvements in the health and safety of workers at work ('the Framework Directive') and Council Directive 89/656/EC on the minimum health and safety requirements for the use by workers of personal protective equipment at the workplace ('the PPE Directive'), which provided protection to workers as well as employees. The High Court found that the relevant domestic UK legislation protected only 'employees' and made a declaration that the UK Government had failed properly to implement the relevant measures in the Framework and PPE Directives by not offering protection to workers as well (see **Chapter 1**).

In *UQ v Marclean Technologies SLU* (Case C-300/19) the ECJ held that when calculating whether sufficient numbers of at risk employees met the threshold to trigger the obligation to collectively consult (see **Chapter 4**), it was necessary to look backwards as well as forwards over a rolling 90-day period when counting – which contrasts with the UK approach under the TULR(C)A 1992. As the ECJ's judgment pre-dates the end of the Brexit transition period, it will amount to 'retained' EU law after 1 January 2021. As things stand, this means that it will not be possible for Employment Tribunals or the Employment Appeal Tribunal to depart from it, although the Court of Appeal and Supreme Court can do so where they feel 'it is right to do so'. Employment Tribunals asked to consider this point may be urged to find a way to read the decision consistently with the existing UK legislation given the wording of s 188(3) of the TULR(C)A 1992. *Francovich* claims against the Government to the effect that it has not implemented the Directive correctly are no longer possible from 1 January 2021. Parliament could legislate at some point to overrule this ECJ decision if it wanted to do so.

Finally, in *ISS Facility Services NV v Govaerts and Atalian NV* (Case-344/18), the ECJ decided, in the context of the Acquired Rights Directive (see **Chapter 8**), that when a part of a business was split up between multiple transferees, an employee could be transferred to multiple different employers on a transfer. In the UK, currently the thinking is that the employee transfers either to the main transferee or does not transfer at all (which can mean they are then at risk of redundancy).

The Retained EU Law Bill does not, however, affect primary Acts of Parliament, so for example the Equality Act 2010 which contains the framework for anti-discrimination law in the UK would not be affected, save in the way that Caspar Glyn outlines above. It is not yet known, if this Bill were to become law, what the impact on employment rights in the UK could be, but there is concern that unless steps are taken to preserve existing law that will otherwise fall away, the effect could be severe. The TCA envisages a regulatory 'level playing field' and includes reciprocal commitments not to reduce the level of protection for workers as part of the level playing field provisions. This may in practice limit the extent to which the Government diverges from current levels of employment protection, because to do so would risk the EU applying trade sanctions to the UK. Readers will need to keep abreast of developments in this area in the coming months.

The Government's summary of the Retained EU Law Bill can be found at:

https://www.gov.uk/government/news/the-retained-eu-law-revocation-and-reform-bill-2022#:~:text=The%20retained%20EU%20Law%20(Revocation%20and%20Reform)%20Bill%20is%20part,primacy%20to%20Acts%20of%20Parliament

The Public Law project team has published a document setting out its concerns:

https://publiclawproject.org.uk/latest/retained-eu-law-bill-four-ways-its-flawed/?utm_source=rss&utm_medium=rss&utm_campaign=retained-eu-law-bill-four-ways-its-flawed

KEY UK EMPLOYMENT LAW AND PROCEDURE DEVELOPMENTS

Employment law reforms

The Government has indicated, on a number of occasions, its intention to repeal the Human Rights Act 1998 and reform the UK human rights framework so as to deliver on the Government's 2015 election manifesto pledge to introduce a British Bill of Rights and reform human rights law. The then Secretary of State for Justice, Dominic Raab, published the Bill of Rights Bill in summer 2022. In September 2022 the new Prime Minister, Liz Truss, announced that the Government would not be proceeding with the Bill of Rights Bill in its current form. However, Prime Minister Rishi Sunak replaced Liz Truss on 25 October 2022, and the reinstated Dominic Raab has said that the Bill will now be brought forward. Interested readers may find useful Mark Elliot's review of the Bill of Rights Bill at https://publiclawforeveryone.com/2022/06/22/the-uks-new-bill-of-rights/.

Employment tribunal reforms

In January 2019, Sir Ernest Ryder, the Senior President of Tribunals, published a report on the Modernisation of Tribunals, which set out a strategy for the reform of tribunals (including employment tribunals) as part of the wider Courts and Tribunals Modernisation Programme, implemented following the Briggs Review of the Civil Courts Structure in July 2016. The proposals include introducing digital case files, having a library of relevant templates from which standard documents can be produced and digitally recording all proceedings.

In April 2020, the Law Commission published its report on 'Employment Law Hearing Structures', which made 23 recommendations with the aim of improving the ability of employment tribunals to resolve employment disputes effectively and justly in one place. The recommendations include:

- having one single time limit for bringing employment tribunal claims of six months;
- expanding the just and equitable test to extend time for all types of claim;
- introducing flexible deployment of judges to permit employment judges to hear discrimination claims in the civil courts;
- creating a specialist list in the High Court;
- increasing the jurisdiction of employment tribunals to hear claims for damages for breach of contract by employees and counterclaims by employers during the currency of a contract of employment and to hear claims in relation to alleged liability arising after employment has terminated;
- increasing the financial limits on contractual claims from £25,000 to £100,000;
- extension of jurisdiction to hear breach of contract claims from workers as well as employees.

The Department for Business, Energy and Industrial Strategy (BEIS) set out the Government's response to the report in June 2021. The Law Commission's Report is available at www.lawcom.gov.uk/project/employment-law-hearing-structures/. The BEIS response is available at www.lawcom.gov.uk/project/employment-law-hearing-structures/.

Some changes have been introduced to the Employment Tribunal Rules as a result of the Covid-19 pandemic (see **Chapter 6**).

HMCTS will, in due course, replace paper-based processes with digital ones. The reformed system will be rolled out in stages. HMCTS also intends for the replacement platform for CVP, the Video Hearings service, to be rolled out in 2022.

Employment tribunal fees – see also Chapter 6

The Government introduced employment tribunal fees in July 2013. The introduction of fees for claimants in employment tribunals led to a significant drop in the number of cases brought, approaching 70%.

The Government launched a post-implementation review of the fees on 11 June 2015.

The House of Commons Justice Committee published a Report into the effect of employment tribunal fees in June 2016. The Committee concluded that 'the regime of employment tribunal fees has had a significant adverse impact on access to justice for meritorious claims'.

On 31 January 2017, the Government published its post-implementation review of employment tribunal fees. The review concluded that the current system of fees and remissions had been 'generally successfully in meeting the scheme's original objective' and was 'generally working effectively and is operating lawfully'. It stated that 'there is no conclusive evidence that ET fees have prevented people from bringing claims'.

A judicial review brought by Unison against the fees was heard by the Supreme Court in March 2017. Unison's challenge was successful (R (*on the application of UNISON*) *v Lord Chancellor* [2017] UKSC 51). A seven-judge Supreme Court unanimously held that the Fees Order was unlawful *ab initio* and must therefore be quashed. The Supreme Court's conclusion was based on the fact that fees were 'inconsistent with access to justice' and had resulted in a substantial fall in claims being brought. It said that the fees were contrary to the Equality Act 2010 as they disproportionately affected women.

According to figures released by the Ministry of Justice in September 2018, following the abolition of fees in July 2017, tribunal claims increased by 165% in the second quarter of 2018 compared to the same period in 2017. The increase has led to a significant backlog in hearing tribunal claims (between January and March 2019 there was a 40% increase in outstanding caseload over the same period the previous year). From the launch of the fee refund scheme in October 2017 to 30 September 2019, 22,000 applications for refunds were received and 22,000 payments made, with a total value of £18 million.

In June 2018, the Government confirmed that it had launched a review on 'how' it would charge fees in the future. In November, the Ministry of Justice said it was confident that it could find a balance that helps fund the court system while being 'proportionate and progressive'. It therefore appears that it is only a question of time before a new fee scheme is introduced. In June 2020, there were reports that the Ministry of Justice had written to the Law Commission inviting it to 'provide recommendations for creating a coherent system for charging and updating fees in the future'. However, at the time of writing, nothing has been announced.

Employment tribunal awards

Employment tribunal compensation awards are increased each year in line with inflation, based on the September retail price index (RPI). The Employment Rights (Increase of Limits) Order 2022 (SI 2022/182) increased tribunal compensation limits for awards on and after 6 April 2022. The maximum basic award increased to £17,130. The maximum compensatory award for unfair dismissal was raised to £93,878. The maximum amount of a week's pay, used to calculate statutory redundancy payments and various awards including the basic and additional awards for unfair dismissal, was raised to £571. The minimum basic award for certain categories of unfair dismissal increased to £6,959 (see **Chapter 5** in particular).

Other matters

Cyber bullying

A new type of workplace bullying – cyber bullying – has emerged in recent years. Acas defines cyber bullying as 'any form of bullying, harassment or victimisation online'. Cyber bullying can include leaking sensitive personal information about individuals, threatening or abusive comments online, inappropriate comments and the posting of pictures. Although it is not possible to bring an employment tribunal claim in respect of bullying/cyber bullying in isolation, it can generally be tagged on to discrimination, harassment or victimisation claims or constructive or unfair dismissal claims. In July 2017 Acas released guidance on cyber bullying and how it can be dealt with in the workplace. Employers should make sure they have an up-to-date policy in place that deals with cyber bullying, not least because this can happen outside the workplace and can occur through the work email system in and out of working hours.

The gender pay gap

The Equality Act 2010 (Gender Pay Gap Information) Regulations 2017 (SI 2017/172), which require larger public and private sector employers with over 250 employees to publish their gender pay gap figures, came into force in April 2017. The Regulations require private and public sector employers to publish annually six pieces of mandatory information about the pay and bonuses of men and women in their organisations. The Regulations clarify who is covered by the obligation (most workers but not genuinely self-employed workers or, for example, partners in firms). The information must be signed off as accurate by a director and published on the organisation's website, so that it is accessible to staff and the public. The same information must be provided to the Government, which also publishes the details on its gender pay gap website. Acas and the Government Equalities Office have published joint guidance on the new law. The first statistics had to be published by 4 April 2018, and over 10,000 employers submitted data. The median gap was 11.8%. Those employers have to follow through on any initiatives identified to close gender pay gaps. Many reported big gaps between men and women's pay. Figures submitted by 10,428 employers for 2019 showed no significant change: the median gap was 11.9%.

In April 2020, as a result of the Covid-19 pandemic, mandatory gender pay gap reporting in respect of 2019/20 was suspended. Amidst concerns that the pandemic was further entrenching gender inequality, in June 2021, the Equalities and Human Rights Commission (EHRC) announced that due to the pressures faced by employers during the pandemic, employers had until 5 October 2021 to report their gender pay gap information for 2020/21. This is a six-month extension from the original deadline of 4 April 2021 for private businesses with more than 250 employees. The Government confirmed that no enforcement action would be taken against employers if they submitted their reports by 5 October 2021. In 2021, the UK's median gender pay gap fell to 9.8%. On average, women earn just over 15% less than men per hour.

The Taylor Review

In October 2016, Matthew Taylor, chief executive of the Royal Society of the Arts, was tasked with looking at how working practices in the modern economy needed to change in order to keep pace with modern business models. On 11 July 2017, the Taylor Review of Modern Working Practices, which made 53 recommendations, was published. In February 2018, the Government published 'Good Work', its response to the Taylor Review, in which it accepted the vast majority of the recommendations. Alongside this, the Government launched four consultations, seeking views on:

- employment status
- agency worker recommendations
- increasing transparency in the labour market
- enforcement of employment rights recommendations.

In December 2018, drawing on the feedback from these consultations, the Government published its 'Good Work Plan', which it described as the largest upgrade in a generation to workplace rights. The Good Work Plan sets out a number of proposals under three headings – fair and decent work, clarity for employers and workers, and fairer enforcement. As part of the 'fair and decent work' heading, the Government has proposed the abolition of the so-called Swedish derogation in the Agency Workers Regulations (see **Chapter 1**), a reduction in the threshold required to request information and consultation arrangements from 10% to 2% (see **4.8.2**), extending the period that can break continuity of employment from one week to four weeks (see **3.5**), and the right to request a more stable and predictable contract for workers who are working flexibly and have acquired 26 weeks' continuous service.

Under the 'clarity' heading, proposals include extending the holiday pay reference pay period from average pay over 12 weeks to 52 weeks (in force from 6 April 2020 – **see Chapter 1**), the right to a written statement of particulars of employment to be extended to all workers as well as employees from day one (see **1.4**) and expanding the content of the written statement to include work patterns, probationary periods and details of all benefits. The Government has also said that it intends to clarify the distinction between 'workers' and those who are self-employed (see **1.3**). It is also proposed that there should be greater alignment between the tests applied for the purposes of employment rights and taxation. The Government has commissioned independent research to help it formulate these proposals.

Under 'fairer enforcement', the Government has referred to the separate ongoing project to modernise the tribunal system. The maximum penalty for aggravated breach of employment law increased, with effect from April 2019, from £5,000 to £20,000.

One of the many recommendations of the Taylor Review was that the Government should ask the Low Pay Commission (LPC) to review what is known as 'one-sided flexibility' in the labour market – ie where employers expect employees to be flexible by offering variable or zero hours contracts. The LPC published its findings and response in December 2018. It recommended, amongst other things, a right to switch to a contract which reflected normal hours worked, a right to reasonable notice of a work schedule, and compensation for shift cancellations or curtailment without reasonable notice. In July 2019, the Government launched a consultation seeking views on the latter two proposals (the Government said, as part of the Good Work Plan, that it would legislate to introduce a right for all workers to switch to a more predicable work pattern, enforceable through employment tribunals). The consultation closed on 11 October 2019. In the December 2019 Queen's Speech, a new Employment Bill was announced, to 'protect and enhance workers' rights', with the aim of implementing a number of the recommendations of the Good Work Plan. Owing to the impact of the Covid-19 pandemic, the introduction of the Employment Bill was delayed. To the surprise of many, it was not included in the May 2021 Queen's Speech. In July 2022 the Government announced that there would not be any reform to employment status.

However, in June 2021, the Government announced the setting up of a new watchdog to enforce the rights of UK workers. The Government stated in its press release that the plans for the new watchdog come as part of its wider efforts to protect workers' rights, including boosting the minimum wage for around 2 million employees and protecting furloughed workers' parental pay. The watchdog will, it is planned, take on the current responsibilities of three different bodies – the Gangmasters and Labour Abuse Authority, the Employment Agency Standards Inspectorate and HMRC's National Minimum Wage Enforcement – and will be focused on tackling modern slavery; enforcing the minimum wage; and protecting agency workers. The Government stated in its press release that the merging of these responsibilities under one roof would improve enforcement through better coordination and pooling of intelligence and resources. The press release said that the new watchdog will have the ability to 'ensure vulnerable workers get the holiday pay and statutory sick pay they are entitled to – without having to go through a lengthy employment tribunal process'. It is not clear from the press release how this will be achieved. The press release notes that the new body will be established through primary legislation 'when parliamentary time allows'. No timeframe has been provided to date.

In July 2021, the Labour Party announced plans to create a single status of 'worker' to include employees and 'limb (b)' workers who would have rights from the first day of their engagement (see **Chapter 1**). The proposal would remove qualifying periods for some basic employment rights to give workers day one rights in the job. Under the proposals, all workers would receive rights and protections including Statutory Sick Pay (SSP), National Minimum Wage entitlement, holiday pay, paid parental leave, and protection against unfair dismissal. The genuinely self-employed would not be affected. 4.2 million people in the UK are currently classified as self-employed. They do not qualify for sick pay. According to a Trade Union Council report from February 2021, an additional 1.9 million people who are in work are also limited in the ability to claim sick pay when they fall ill. Sick pay only kicks in if someone is sick for at least four days in a row, so someone on SSP will normally receive no payment for the first three days. Additionally, low-paid workers are not entitled to SSP as the 'lower-earnings limit' requires an average income of £123 a week (calculated over their previous eight weeks of earning) for people to qualify. Labour has said it would remove these requirements and extend the statutory provision to everyone. Trade Union Council research from June 2021 found that one in 12 so-called 'key' workers did not qualify for sick pay, including more than a quarter of cleaners (27%) and retail workers (26%), nearly one in 10 teaching assistants (9%) and over one in 20 care workers (6%).

Modern slavery

Research by the International Labour Organization suggests that over 40 million people worldwide are the victims of modern slavery. Modern slavery can include forced labour, bonded labour, human trafficking and prostitution, forced marriage and domestic servitude.

Although public awareness of modern slavery has grown in recent years, victims of trafficking often go unnoticed. A recent modern slavery prosecution saw hundreds of victims recruited from Poland forced to work for food chains supplying some of the UK's leading supermarkets. It is worth noting, although beyond the scope of this texbook, that in addition to the gang masters, trafficked victims may find themselves the subject of criminal prosecutions – see R v VSJ [2017] EWCA Crim 36 and R v GS [2018] EWCA Crim 1824.

The Modern Slavery Act 2015 requires certain organisations to produce and publish an annual statement setting out the steps taken to ensure that no form of modern slavery exists anywhere in its business or its supply chain. The aim is to encourage organisations to take responsibility not only for their own labour force, but also for the use of labour in the organisations that supply goods and services to them. The Act applies to all commercial organisations producing goods or services that do business in the UK and have an annual global turnover of over £36 million. This means that even businesses with a relatively small UK presence can be caught by the requirement. Those organisations covered by the Act have to produce their first statement within six months of the end of the financial year. From 31 March 2019, organisations which have failed to publish a statement are at risk of being named and shamed by the Government. In October 2019, the second CPS Modern Slavery Report was published. The Government published statutory guidance for public authorities in England and Wales and a modern slavery statement on 31 March 2020, and guidance for businesses on modern slavery in the pandemic on 21 April 2020.

Although the details are beyond the scope of this work, in *Basfar v Wong* [2022] UKSC 20, the Supreme Court (by a majority of three to two) held that a diplomat could not rely on Article 31(1)(c) of the Vienna Convention on Diplomatic Relations 1961 to obtain diplomatic immunity to avoid employment tribunal proceedings based around facts which were assumed for the purposes of the application to amount to modern slavery.

Sexual harassment

In March 2018, the Equalities and Human Rights Commission (EHRC) published a report, 'Turning the tables: ending sexual harassment at work', which raises serious concerns about sexual harassment in the workplace. It identified widespread failures by employers and set out a number of recommendations in a call to the Government to take action, including:

- a statutory code of practice, with tribunal discretion to increase compensation by 25% for non-compliance;
- safeguards against employers using confidentiality agreements to prevent the disclosure of past acts of harassment;
- extension of the limitation period for bringing a sexual harassment claim;
- reinstatement of protection from third party harassment (without the requirement to show two previous incidents).

Following a number of high profile harassment claims (such as Zelda Perkins against Harvey Weinstein), non-disclosure agreements came back into the spotlight. In July 2018, the Women and Equalities Select Committee made a number of recommendations on sexual harassment at work, including on the use of non-disclosure agreements.

In December 2018, the Government published its response to these recommendations. It noted the need for more data highlighted by the Select Committee. It also agreed with the Committee that a new statutory Code of Practice should be introduced, to be developed by the Equalities and Human Rights Commission.

In March 2019, the Government published its consultation paper on the better regulation of non-disclosure agreements. The consultation looked at two distinct uses of confidentiality clauses – in contracts of employment (see **Chapter 1**) and in settlement agreements (see **Chapter 6**). The Women and Equalities Committee also published a report on the use of non-disclosure agreements in discrimination cases on 13 June 2019. In July 2021, the Government published its response to its consultation paper. The Government has said it will legislate to introduce a new positive duty upon employers to take 'all reasonable steps' to prevent workplace sexual harassment and will create explicit legal protections from harassment by third parties. The new positive duty would be enforceable by both the EHRC and by individual employees, with employers being made potentially liable if they do not take reasonable steps to prevent harassment in accordance with a statutory code of practice, which the EHRC will be tasked with producing. It also said it would 'look closely' at extending the time limit to bring employment tribunal discrimination claims from three months to six months. No time estimate for the introduction of these proposals has been given.

In October 2019 the Equality and Human Rights Commission issued guidance on the use of non-disclosure agreements to cover up discrimination, harassment and victimisation. While it does not have statutory force, it contains useful guidance. As far as lawyers drafting non-disclosure agreements are concerned, the guidance says that those who advise employers and workers on confidentiality agreements should ensure that they remain up to date with their regulatory obligations and any guidance issued by regulators on the subject.

The SRA published an updated warning notice on 12 December 2019, and Acas published guidance in February 2020. See **Chapter 6** for more details.

Trade union reforms

Although collective rights are beyond the scope of this work, in May 2016, one of the most significant pieces of trade union legislation for many years was passed. The Trade Union Act 2016 includes changes to the way in which lawful industrial action can be voted for. The Act received the Royal Assent on 4 May 2016 and became law in March 2017. In January 2017, the Government published draft regulations giving more details on what constitutes 'important public services' and a revised code of practice on industrial action ballots and notice to employers. Those regulations became law, with effect from 1 March 2017.

The rules require unions to include more detailed information on the ballot paper sent to members. This must now summarise the dispute in enough detail that members can understand what issues are unresolved, the action planned, and the period during which it is expected to take place. Any ballot sent to union members from 1 March 2017 must meet the requirements. Unions must now provide all eligible voters and the employer with certain prescribed information relating to the result of the ballot. In addition to a majority voting in favour, a minimum turnout of 50% of those entitled to vote in now required. In certain essential services (including health, education, fire, border security and transport), at least 40% of those entitled to vote in a ballot must vote in favour of action. Unions will be required to give employers 14 rather than the current 7 days' notice of industrial action. A ballot for strike action will cease to provide a mandate after 6 months (extendable to 9 months if the employer agrees). Ultimately, after a transitional period of 12 months, new trade union members will only have to pay the political levy if they actively opt in to do so. As a measure to tackle intimidation during strike action, it is now a requirement for a union to appoint a supervisor to oversee any picketing for picketing to qualify for protection.

The Conduct of Employment Agencies and Employment Businesses (Amendment) Regulations 2022 (SI 2022/852) came into force on 21 July 2022, allowing agency workers to replace striking workers.

Liz Truss indicated that she would seek to reform trade union laws further if elected as the UK's Prime Minister. She spoke of requiring minimum service levels in 'critical' industries, raising the voting participation threshold to 50% of the workforce and limiting the number of strikes permitted following a successful ballot. She was replaced by Rishi Sunak on 25 October 2022, but it is anticipated that the laws will be enacted by a Sunak Government.

GENERAL

For some years now, there have been common commencement dates for the introduction of employment policy. The two dates for commencement of domestic employment law for which BEIS has responsibility are 6 April and 1 October of each year. BEIS publishes an annual statement of forthcoming employment legislation every January. An e-mail alert system is also available on the BIS website.

In July 2022, Acas released its annual report, including statistics on early conciliation for the period April 2021–March 2022. These show that there were 90,811 requests for early conciliation compared to 114,533 in the previous year. Over this same period, 31,198 of those notifications proceeded to a claim in the employment tribunal. (See **Chapter 6.**)

In June 2022, the Ministry of Justice published Quarterly Tribunal Statistics and Tables for January to March 2022. The report states that:

> Employment Tribunals transitioned to a new database (Employment Case Management) during March to May 2021. It has not been possible to provide full results from both databases during this migration period on a consistent basis. Therefore, Employment Tribunal (ET) data is not available for Q1 2021/22, and as a result we are unable to present data for the full financial year of 2021/22.

In the annual statistics for the year leading up to March 2021, claims went up compared to the same period in the previous year, and continue to show a general upward trend since fees were removed in July 2017 (fees were introduced in July 2013) (191,541 in 2012–13, 105,803 in 2013–14, 61,308 in 2014–15, 83,031 in 2015–16, 88,476 in 2016–17, 109,685 in 2017–18, 121,075 in 2018–19, 103,973 in 2019–20 and 117,926 in 2020–21).

In 2019–20, according to Ministry of Justice annual employment tribunal statistics, the median unfair dismissal award was £6,646 (£6,243 in 2018–19) and the average (mean) award was £10,812 (£13,704 in 2018–19). The median race discrimination award was £8,040 (£7,882 in 2018–19) and the average (mean) award was £9,801 (£12,487 in 2018–19). For sex discrimination claims, the figures were £14,073 (£6,498) and £17,420 (£8,774), for disability claims £13,000 (£12,156) and £27,043 (£28,371), for religious or belief discrimination £0 (£0) and £1,500 (£4,767), for age discrimination £11,791 (£12,365) and £38,794 (£26,148) and for sexual orientation discrimination £9,245 (£0) and 27,936 (£0) respectively. The highest discrimination award was £265,719 in a disability discrimination claim. The highest unfair dismissal award was £118,842. Costs were awarded to the claimant in 47 cases and to the respondent in 130 cases. The maximum costs award was £103,486 and the median was £2,500 (source: Practical Law Company, Thomson Reuters). No average award figures are available for 2020–21 or 2021–22.

For the most up-to-date and detailed analysis of the trends in employment tribunal claims, readers are directed to the quarterly and annual reports (and supporting data files) provided online by the Justice Statistics Analytical Services Division of the Ministry of Justice.

The Employment Rights (Increase of Limits) Order 2022, which reviews various employment compensation limits, came into force on 6 April 2022 to reflect increases in the RPI. Increases for maternity and other statutory pay rates are governed by the Social Security Benefits Uprating Order 2022. Relevant limits are recorded in the chapters which follow.

REFERENCE RESOURCES

At the end of each chapter are listed some additional academic and practical text and reference books. Within chapters, other useful external resources will be flagged where relevant.

Useful information for employees may also be found at <http://www.direct.gov.uk>. The site contains guidance on a number of employment matters, such as starting a new job, pay, employment contracts, work and families, discrimination and redundancy. The site also contains links to guidance on flexible working and maternity rights.

The EHRC has sections on its website <http://www.equalityhumanrights.com> containing guidance on all aspects of discrimination. The website also contains past publications and reports governing disability, gender and race.

The Acas website <http://www.acas.org.uk> provides a series of online publications which are free to download (for example on topics such as discipline and grievances at work, redundancy, stress, flexible working and holiday pay). It also offers a range of e-learning courses.

A number of law firms with employment law practices also provide a range of useful publications and guidance on their websites.

Table of Abbreviations

Legislation

ASCLA 2009	Apprenticeships, Skills, Children and Learning Act 2009
CPR 1998	Civil Procedure Rules 1998
DDA 1995	Disability Discrimination Act 1995
DPA 2018	Data Protection Act 2018
EA 2002	Employment Act 2002
EPA 1970	Equal Pay Act 1970
EP(C)A 1978	Employment Protection (Consolidation) Act 1978
ERA 1996	Employment Rights Act 1996
ERA 1999	Employment Relations Act 1999
ERRA 2013	Enterprise and Regulatory Reform Act 2013
ETA 1996	Employment Tribunals Act 1996
GDPR	General Data Protection Regulation
HRA 1998	Human Rights Act 1998
HSWA 1974	Health and Safety at Work etc Act 1974
ICE Regulations	Information and Consultation of Employees Regulations 2004
ITEPA 2003	Income Tax (Earnings and Pensions) Act 2003
MPLPAL(A)R 2006	Maternity and Parental Leave etc and Paternity and Adoption Leave (Amendment) Regulations 2006
MPLR 1999	Maternity and Parental Leave etc Regulations 1999
NMWA 1998	National Minimum Wage Act 1998
PALR 2002	Paternity and Adoption Leave Regulations 2002
PIDA 1998	Public Interest Disclosure Act 1998
RRA 1976	Race Relations Act 1976
SDA 1975	Sex Discrimination Act 1975
TULR(C)A 1992	Trade Union and Labour Relations (Consolidation) Act 1992

Employment case reports

ICR	Industrial Cases Reports
IRLR	Industrial Relations Law Reports

Other abbreviations

AAL	additional adoption leave
Acas	Advisory, Conciliation and Arbitration Service
AML	additional maternity leave
APL	additional paternity leave
BEIS	Department for Business, Energy and Industrial Strategy
CJEU	Court of Justice of the European Union
CRE	Commission for Racial Equality
DfWP	Department for Work and Pensions
DRC	Disability Rights Commission
DTI	Department of Trade and Industry
EAT	Employment Appeal Tribunal
ECHR	European Convention on Human Rights
ECtHR	European Court of Human Rights
ECJ	European Court of Justice
EDT	effective date of termination (of employment)

EHRC	Equality and Human Rights Commission
EOC	Equal Opportunities Commission
ETO	economic, technical or organisational (reason for dismissal on transfer of an undertaking)
EWC	expected week of childbirth
HMRC	HM Revenue and Customs
HSE	Health and Safety Executive
ICO	Information Commissioner's Office
MA	maternity allowance
NICs	National Insurance Contributions
NMW	national minimum wage
OAL	ordinary adoption leave
OML	ordinary maternity leave
OPL	ordinary paternity leave
PAYE	Pay As You Earn (in relation to Schedule E Income Tax)
PCP	provision, criterion or practice
PILON	payment in lieu of notice
ROET	Regional Office of the Employment Tribunals
RRO	restricted reporting order
S2P	Second State Pension Scheme
SAP	statutory adoption pay
SMP	statutory maternity pay
SOSR	some other substantial reason
SPP	statutory paternity pay
TEU	Treaty on European Union
TFEU	Treaty on the Functioning of the European Union

CHAPTER 1

THE CONTRACT OF EMPLOYMENT

1.1	Introduction	1
1.2	Background	2
1.3	The relationship of employer and employee	10
1.4	The contract of employment	37
1.5	Implied terms	40
1.6	Terms implied by statute	40
1.7	Terms implied by common law	40
1.8	Written contracts	46
1.9	Variation of contractual terms	68
1.10	Human Rights Act 1998	72
1.11	Protection of wages	73
1.12	Working Time Regulations 1998	77
1.13	Checklists	98
1.14	Further reading	99
	Summary	100

LEARNING OUTCOMES

After reading this chapter you will be able to:

- understand and explain the differences between an employee and a worker, and identify which statutory rights apply to which

- understand and explain the difference between a written statement of terms and an employment contract

- identify statutory restrictions on the freedom to contract

- understand how implied terms operate in an employment contract

- list the key terms that *must* be included in a written statement of terms/contract of employment

- list the key additional terms that *may* be included in a written contract of employment, and understand the importance of and the enforceability of restrictive covenants

- understand how the protection of wages legislation works

- understand the Working Time Regulations

- advise as to the enforceability of post-termination duties.

1.1 INTRODUCTION

Employment law in the UK derives from various sources – not only common law and statute, but also codes of practice and European Union (EU) law. In recent years, EU legislation has had a particularly significant influence, in terms both of legislation and judgments of the Court of Justice of the European Union (CJEU).

On 23 June 2016, the UK voted to leave the EU. Article 50 of the Treaty on European Union (TEU) was triggered by the UK Government, and the UK left the EU on 31 January 2020. There was a transition period which ended on 31 December 2020. (See **Introductory Note**.)

Further, quite separately, decisions of the European Court of Human Rights (ECtHR) in Strasbourg (which originates separately from the EU through the Council of Europe) have influenced the development of UK employment law. This book will attempt to explain the impact and effect of all these areas on UK employment law. The main emphasis of this book is on individual employment rights – that is to say, the law that relates to employers and their employees and workers. There is very little commentary on collective areas of labour law such as trade unions, but these areas are touched upon where relevant.

1.2 BACKGROUND

Set out below is a summary of the main sources of employment law and their relevance.

1.2.1 Common law

Prior to the enactment of legislation affecting the relationship of employer and employee, the obligations each owed to the other were largely governed by the law of contract. Case law developed as the courts were called upon to interpret express contractual provisions, and to determine the nature and extent of implied contractual rights and duties. Case law has also developed on the interpretation of statutory provisions, many of which depend on the concept of 'reasonableness'.

This book considers reports of decisions reached by the UK courts and by the employment tribunals, as both forums can be used to determine issues of employment law. Judgments of the ECJ and ECtHR are also referred to, where relevant.

1.2.1.1 Employment tribunals

Employment tribunals have jurisdiction (through statute) to hear claims arising out of breaches of most aspects of the employment relationship, for example unfair dismissal, wrongful dismissal, redundancy payments, discrimination claims, equal pay claims and protection of wages claims (see **6.2.1** for further details). Tribunals also have jurisdiction to hear some claims by workers (eg, claims under the protection of wages legislation – see **1.10** below – and discrimination claims). For the distinction between a worker and an employee, see s 230 of the Employment Rights Act 1996 (ERA 1996) and **1.3** below.

1.2.1.2 The Employment Appeal Tribunal

The Employment Appeal Tribunal (EAT) hears appeals on questions of law from an employment tribunal. Its decisions are binding on employment tribunals. An appeal from the EAT lies to the Court of Appeal and from there to the Supreme Court.

1.2.1.3 The civil courts

In addition to the appellate function of the civil courts, the High Court and county court can hear breach of contract claims (eg wrongful dismissal) (see **Chapter 2**). Further, the civil courts can grant injunctive relief (eg where a restraint of trade clause has been breached, see **1.8.7.1**).

Note that the last House of Lords hearings took place in July 2009. The House of Lords has been replaced by the Supreme Court.

1.2.2 Legislation

The Industrial Relations Act 1971 attempted for the first time to introduce a comprehensive regulatory framework for all aspects of employment law, from collective bargaining to individual rights. Prior to this, employment issues had had to be dealt with in the common law courts under the common law. There were no special provisions or protections. There were no concepts of fairness – an employer was free to dismiss an employee as long as it did so in a contractually correct manner. The 1971 Act introduced the right to complain of 'unfair' dismissal. The majority of individual rights were consolidated, first in the Employment Protection (Consolidation) Act 1978 (EP(C)A 1978) and most recently in the ERA 1996. The 1996 Act was amended by the Employment Relations Acts 1999 and 2004 (ERA 1999 and 2004), the Employment Act 2002 (EA 2002) and the Work and Families Act 2006.

The Trade Union and Labour Relations (Consolidation) Act 1992 (TULR(C)A 1992), as amended by the Trade Union Reform and Employment Rights Act 1993 and the ERA 1999, consolidated all statute law containing trade union and group provisions. In the field of equal pay and discrimination, the Equal Pay Act 1970 (EPA 1970), the Sex Discrimination Act 1975 (SDA 1975), the Race Relations Act 1976 (RRA 1976) and the Disability Discrimination Act 1995 (DDA 1995) have all been repealed and replaced by the provisions of the Equality Act 2010 (see **Chapter 8**).

In addition to statutes there is a plethora of delegated legislation regulating employment law (much of it driven by EU law – see **1.2.4**), which will be referred to where relevant.

1.2.3   Codes of practice

A code of practice is not legally binding and is intended to give guidance to employers on good employment practices. It may, however, be used in evidence. For example, the Advisory, Conciliation and Arbitration Service (Acas) Code of Practice on Discipline and Grievance is often referred to by tribunals (see **Chapter 5**).

1.2.4   European Union law – applicability to Member States

What follows is a brief summary of the position in Member States. The UK is no longer a Member State.

1.2.4.1   Treaty provisions and Regulations

Provisions of EU treaties and EU Regulations which give clear, precise and unconditional rights to individuals are generally directly enforced in national courts because they have direct applicability (see *Van Gend en Loos v Nederlandse Administratie der Belastingen* (Case 26/62) [1963] ECR 1). One important example is Article 157 TFEU (ex Article 119 EEC/141 EC), which provides that 'Each Member State shall ensure that the principle of equal pay for male and female workers for equal work or work of equal value is applied'.

In the case of *Barber v Guardian Royal Exchange Assurance Group* (Case C-262/88) [1990] 2 All ER 660, Article 157 TFEU was applied directly in favour of a man in order to entitle him to the same benefits as a woman under an occupational pension scheme. The scheme was discriminatory as it permitted women to receive a pension from age 50, but men only from age 55. Article 157 TFEU was applied despite the fact that different retiring ages in pension schemes were apparently permitted under the SDA 1975 and the EPA 1970. In equal work cases, Article 157 TFEU is directly effective and overrides inconsistent national law.

1.2.4.2   Directives

A Directive is secondary EU legislation. It is not directly applicable in a Member State but must be implemented by national legislation. However, if a Directive gives clear, precise and unconditional rights to an individual, and the State fails to implement it at all or to implement it properly within the stipulated time frame, the individual has a right to rely on the Directive directly against the State or an emanation of the State. The ECJ looked at the horizontal effect of fundamental rights derived from the EU Charter of Fundamental Rights in *Bauer et al* (Cases C-569/16 and C-570/16) in the context of the right to be paid for untaken leave at the date of termination of employment (see **1.12.5** below).

This means that Directives that have not been properly implemented in a Member State can be directly enforced, but only by employees of the State or of an emanation of the State. This influenced a number of developments in UK employment law. In *Marshall v Southampton and South West Hampshire AHA* [1986] QB 401, a female former employee of the Area Health Authority was able to rely on the Equal Treatment Directive 76/207 in order to challenge contractual retirement ages which discriminated on the grounds of sex. A challenge was possible in this case because the Area Health Authority was found to be an emanation of the State; Ms Marshall would not have been able to rely directly on the Directive if she had been employed in the private sector. (However, see *Kucukdeveci v Swedex GmbH & Co KG* (Case C-555/07) where the general principle of non-discrimination on grounds of age was given effect between individuals by the ECJ.)

The ECJ, in *Impact v Ministry for Agriculture and Food (Ireland)* (Case C-268/06) [2008] IRLR 552, confirmed that public sector employees can bring such claims in employment tribunals as well as in the national courts.

1.2.4.3 Interpretation of national legislation

Employees who cannot rely on direct effect, for example if they work in the private sector, may seek to enforce rights conferred by EU Directives which have not been properly implemented by asking their national courts to interpret their national legislation in the light of the EU Directive (indirect effect).

Section 2(4) of the European Communities Act 1972 (now repealed by the European Union (Withdrawal) Act 2018) provided that 'any enactment passed or to be passed ... shall be construed and have effect subject to [EU law]'. Where UK legislation had been passed to implement an EU Directive, the English courts interpreted the UK legislation so as to comply with EU law. For example, in *Litster v Forth Dry Dock & Engineering Co Ltd* [1989] IRLR 161 (see **7.2.2.3**), the House of Lords (now Supreme Court) put a very strained interpretation on the Transfer of Undertakings (Protection of Employment) Regulations 1981 (SI 1981/1794) in order to make the Regulations comply with the Acquired Rights Directive 77/187, which they were intended to implement. The ECJ held in *Marleasing SA v La Comercial Internacional de Alimentacion SA* [1990] ECR I-4135 that national courts must 'as far as possible' interpret national law in light of EU law, irrespective of whether the national law was adopted before or after the Directive in question. In *Webb v EMO Air Cargo (UK) Ltd* [1993] IRLR 27, the House of Lords followed *Marleasing* and stated that

> it is for a UK court to construe domestic legislation ... so as to accord with the interpretation of [a] Directive as laid down by the European Court, if that can be done without distorting the meaning of the domestic legislation.

1.2.4.4 Action against the State

If a State fails to implement a Directive at all (or incorrectly), an employee who is affected can bring a claim against the State for damages under the principle in *Francovich (Andrea) and Bonifaci (Danila) v Italy* (Cases C-6 and 9/90) [1992] IRLR 84.

1.2.4.5 Brexit

See **Introductory Note** ('Brexit'). The legacy and influence of EU employment law and regulation remains as it is embedded in much UK legislation and case law.

1.2.5 Human Rights Act 1998

The Human Rights Act 1998 (HRA 1998) came into force on 2 October 2000. Courts and tribunals in the UK now have to interpret national law in the light of the rights contained in the European Convention for the Protection of Human Rights and Fundamental Freedoms ('the Convention' or ECHR), and where this is not possible, the High Court is empowered to declare such law incompatible with Convention rights. Employees of public authorities have a direct cause of action against their employer under the Act for contravention of the Act (see **Chapter 15**).

The then Secretary of State for Justice, Dominic Raab, published the Bill of Rights Bill in summer 2022, which if passed would repeal and replace the Human Rights Act 1998. In September 2022 the then Prime Minister, Liz Truss, announced that the Government would not be proceeding with the Bill of Rights Bill in its current form. However, Rishi Sunak replaced her on 25 October 2022, and Dominic Raab, reinstated as Minister of Justice, has said that the Bill will now be brought forward (see **Introductory Note**).

1.2.6 Recruitment and induction

Employers should take care not to discriminate when they advertise jobs. A job applicant can bring a claim against a potential employer for discrimination (Equality Act 2010, s 39) in terms of the arrangements made for recruitment, the terms offered or as a result of a refusal or deliberate failure to offer employment.

1.2.6.1 Immigration, Asylum and Nationality Act 2006 and Immigration Act 2014

For all employees employed on or after 16 May 2014, an employer must undertake required checks before an individual commences working. (For employees employed before 16 May 2014, the position was dealt with by the 2006 Act and a 2008 Code of Practice; and for employees employed before 29 February 2008 by the Asylum and Immigration Act 1996.) An employer is *not* exempt from carrying out checks on employees acquired as a result of a transfer under the Transfer of Undertakings (Protection of Employment) Regulations 2006 (SI 2006/246) (see **Chapter 7**).

Two codes of practice for employers came into effect on 16 May 2014, the first relating to the prevention of illegal working, and the second avoiding unlawful discrimination while preventing illegal working. The Code of Practice on Preventing Illegal Working was updated in January 2019. It sets out the prescribed checks that employers should conduct to avoid a civil penalty in the event of illegal working. It reflects the Immigration (Restriction on Employment) (Code of Practice and Miscellaneous Amendments) Order 2018 (SI 2018/1340) which provides that employers may establish a statutory excuse against liability for an illegal working civil penalty by conducting an online right to work check using the Home Office Online Right to Work Checking Service.

Section 15 of the Immigration, Asylum and Nationality Act 2006 provides that an employer who negligently employs a person subject to immigration control who does not have the right to take employment, shall be guilty of a civil offence. The Act allows employers to avoid a civil penalty if they have carried out specific document checks before they employ the employee. The Act also makes it a criminal offence to employ someone whom the employer knows or has reasonable cause to believe has no permission to work in the UK (s 21). The Government introduced temporary changes during the Covid-19 pandemic (see Home Office and Immigration Enforcement: Coronavirus (Covid-19): right to work checks (30 March 2020)).

An employer who is found to have employed someone illegally may be fined up to £20,000 per individual illegal worker if it has not carried out the necessary checks before employing the person. For knowingly employing an illegal worker, or having 'reasonable cause to believe' a person has no permission to work in the UK, the sanctions are up to five years' imprisonment and unlimited fines.

All UK citizens have the right to work in the UK (from 1 January 2021, the free movement of people within the EU ended in the UK). Otherwise, no one has the right to work in the UK unless they are granted the right to work by the Home Office – generally by a visa which is now based on a points system depending on skills, qualifications, salaries and occupations with shortages.

Asylum seekers can apply for permission to work if they have waited more than 12 months for a decision from the Home Office. All asylum seekers who apply for permission to work and are not considered responsible for the delay are restricted to national shortage occupations. Students, if studying at foundation degree level or above, can work part time during terms, for no more than 20 hours a week. Students, if studying below foundation degree level, can work part time during terms, for no more than 10 hours a week.

Dismissal of an employee on the basis that he does not have the right to work in the UK may involve a consideration of issues relating to whether he has contravened a statutory enactment (ERA 1996, s 98(2)(d)), some other substantial reason and illegality (see **1.2.7** and **Chapter 5** below), as well as discrimination (see **Chapter 8** onwards).

Readers should log on to the Home Office UK Visa and Immigration website <http://ukba.homeoffice.gov.uk> for further detailed guidance (see also **8.4.1**).

Note that the 'Brexit' vote in June 2016 impacted on the ability of employers to employ EU citizens. From 1 January 2021, a new points-based system applies to all non-British/Irish citizens (some EU citizens are eligible to remain under the EU Settlement Scheme of course). The detail is beyond the scope of this book, and readers should refer to <www.gov.uk/guidance/new-immigration-system-what-you-need-to-know> for information.

1.2.6.2 Illegality

There is a long-standing principle that the courts will not assist a party whose case is based upon an unlawful act. In an employment law context, this means that an employee whose contract is illegal may be prevented from asserting their contractual and statutory rights. This principle is the common law doctrine of illegality, which can defeat claims in contract or tort. The doctrine is rooted in public policy. The underlying principle was identified by Lord Mansfield in Holman v Johnson (1775) 1 Cowp 341:

> The objection, that a contract is immoral or illegal as between plaintiff and defendant ... is founded in general principles of policy ... The principle of public policy is this; ex dolo malo non oritur actio. No court will lend its aid to a man who founds his cause of action upon an immoral or an illegal act. If, from the plaintiff's own stating or otherwise, the cause of action appears to arise ex turpi causa, or the transgression of a positive law of this country, there the court says he has no right to be assisted. It is upon that ground the court goes; not for the sake of the defendant, but because they will not lend their aid to such a plaintiff. So if the plaintiff and defendant were to change sides, and the defendant was to bring his action against the plaintiff, the latter would then have the advantage of it; for where both are equally in fault, potior est conditio defendentis.

The correct application of the doctrine of illegality was, until relatively recently, uncertain as to whether courts were required to apply relatively rigid rules, or whether they could adopt a more flexible principle-based approach. The Supreme Court in the 2016 case of Patel v Mirza [2016] UKSC 42 resolved that uncertainty in favour of the more flexible approach. The Court held that the core question for the courts to determine in such a case was whether permitting the claim would be contrary to the public interest, damaging the integrity of the legal system. It identified a 'trio of necessary considerations' when assessing this, namely:

(1)   Identifying the underlying purpose of the prohibition which has been transgressed, and considering whether that purpose would be advanced by providing a defence to the claim.

(2)   Identifying the public policy grounds against granting a defence.

(3)   Considering whether, in the circumstances of the claim, granting the defence and denying the claim would be a proportionate response to the unlawfulness.

There are three categories of case where a contract may be tainted with illegality. These were identified by Peter Gibson LJ in Hall v Woolston Leisure Services Ltd [2000] IRLR 578 (paras 30–31). The judgment also contains a useful run-through of the previous case law in an employment context. The first category is where the contract is entered into with the intention of committing an illegal act. The second is where the contract is expressly or impliedly prohibited by statute. The third category is where the contract was lawful when made but has been performed illegally, and the party seeking the assistance of the court knowingly participated in the illegal performance. In the first two types of cases, case law has established that illegality in these situations generally renders a contract void and unenforceable from the outset. In the first type, the contract may be unenforceable even if the activities do not form part of the contract. In the third, the contract is legal on its face but the illegality may prevent a party from enforcing it. The most common example of the third type in an employment situation often involves some sort of tax fraud. In order to fall within the third category, it is traditionally said that there are two requirements:

(a)   knowledge of the illegal performance; and

(b)   participation in the illegal performance.

Knowledge requires that the employee must have knowledge of the facts which render the performance illegal. However, it is irrelevant whether the party appreciates that what he is doing is illegal: ignorance of the law is no excuse. In *San Ling Chinese Medicine Centre v Miss Lian Wei Ji* (UKEAT/0370/09) the EAT applied *Hall* and upheld the tribunal's decision that the claimant's contract was not tainted by illegality in circumstances where the claimant's work permit *might* be revoked. There was no illegality unless and until the permit *was* revoked.

Participation requires active participation. There are cases in which the courts have held that mere knowledge of the illegality coupled with a failure to do anything about it can constitute participation. In *Hall* it came to the employee's attention that her employers were deceiving the Revenue and not paying the appropriate tax. The Court of Appeal held that this was not sufficient to render the contract an illegal one because there was no illegality by Mrs Hall:

> Her acquiescence in the employer's conduct, which is the highest her involvement in the illegality can be put, no doubt reflects the reality that she could not compel her employer to change its conduct.

In the context of discriminations claims, the Supreme Court considered the issue in *Hounga v Allen* [2014] UKSC 47. The Supreme Court had to consider in what circumstances the defence of illegality should defeat a complaint by an employee that an employer has discriminated against him. The claimant was working illegally in the UK when she was dismissed by her employer. The Court of Appeal had decided that the illegality of the contract of employment formed a material part of the claimant's complaint and that to uphold it would be to condone the illegality. The Supreme Court allowed the appeal and held that entry into the illegal contract and its continued operation provided no more than the context in which the employer perpetrated the discriminatory act. There was not a sufficiently close connection between the illegality and the discrimination claim for the claim to be defeated by illegality. Furthermore, the decision of the Court of Appeal to uphold Mrs Allen's defence of illegality to her complaint ran counter, on the facts, to the public policy against trafficking and in favour of the protection of its victims, according to a majority of the Supreme Court.

In the context of unfair dismissal claims, it was settled law that if the underlying contract of employment was illegal then it was against public policy to allow the claim to be pursued: *Tomlinson v Dick Evans*, applied in *Davidson v Pillay*, cited with approval in *Hall*. Moreover, the employee could not count any period during which he was employed under an illegal contract as part of his period of continuous employment for the purpose of obtaining the requisite continuity to pursue a claim. In *Hyland v JH Barker (North West) Ltd* [1985] ICR 861, continuity was broken by a four-week period during which the employee received a tax-free benefit which both parties knew to be illegal. (See also *Salvesen v Simons* [1994] IRLR 52 and *Enfield Technical Services v Payne; Grace v BF Components Ltd* [2008] IRLR 500.)

However, readers should note the decision in *Patel v Mirza* (above), where the Supreme Court encouraged a more flexible assessment of whether the public interest would be harmed by enforcement of an illegal contract:

> The essential rationale of the illegality doctrine is that it would be contrary to the public interest to enforce a claim if to do so would be harmful to the integrity of the legal system .... In assessing whether the public interest would be harmed in that way, it is necessary a) to consider the underlying purpose of the prohibition which has been transgressed and whether that purpose will be enhanced by denial of the claim, b) to consider any other relevant public policy on which the denial of the claim may have an impact and c) to consider whether denial of the claim would be a proportionate response to the illegality, bearing in mind that punishment is a matter for the criminal courts.

The Supreme Court considered the *Patel* test in *Stoffel & Co v Grondona* [2020] UKSC 42 (a mortgage fraud case). The Supreme Court felt able to determine the case applying the first two stages of the *Patel* test. It held that granting Stoffel a defence would not advance the public policies in favour of criminalising mortgage fraud. On the other hand, denying the claim would harm the victim of the fraud, run counter to other important public policies, and result in the incoherence of the law recognising the existence of a property right but declining to protect it. For those reasons, the Court denied Stoffel's appeal without considering the third limb of the test. However, the Court nevertheless went on to consider the question of proportionality, concluding that denying the claim would be a disproportionate response to the unlawfulness.

The judgment in *Stoffel* does not suggest any change in the Court's approach to illegality since *Patel*, but it does provide an example at Supreme Court level of how the courts will apply the test set out in *Patel*. Illegality can arise in an 'infinite possible variety of cases', which may involve very different policy conditions.

In an employment law context, the effect of *Patel* and *Stoffel* has yet to be determined, but there is an argument that the rather rigid approach previously taken (see above) that a contract tainted with illegality will not be enforced might now be open to challenge. It seems clear therefore that the more flexible policy-based approach will apply to unfair dismissal cases. Readers should have regard to these cases if they are advising on a situation where there is said to be illegality in employment contracts.

In *Okedina v Chikale* (UKEAT/0152/17) (a domestic worker case), the EAT considered the impact of an illegal contract of employment upon an employee's right to bring claims of unfair dismissal, race discrimination and for arrears of pay. It noted that there were two types of illegality which rendered a contract unenforceable from the outset: (i) where the contract is entered into with the intention of committing an illegal act; and (ii) where the contract is expressly prohibited by statute. Neither of these applied here. The EAT noted a third category where a party might be prevented from enforcing a contract lawfully made but later illegally performed. In this case, the employee was not involved in the illegal performance, and as such she was entitled to bring her claims to the tribunal. The Court of Appeal upheld the decision ([2019] EWCA Civ 1393), and the judgment contains an extremely useful, comprehensive review of the defence of illegality.

1.2.6.3   Criminal record and other background checks

Any data that employers acquire as a result of job applications, must be processed fairly in accordance with an employer's obligations (as a data controller) under the Data Protection Act (DPA) 2018 (see **15.5**). There are six data protection principles that apply when processing personal data. These include keeping the data secure, but also that the data should be kept no longer than is necessary, and that any that are retained are accurate, relevant and not excessive. This also applies to data retained/stored after termination of employment.

Some employers may also be tempted to conduct their own background 'research' on applicants via social media. Such searches should be for specific and good reason. Under the

Equality Act 2010, it is unlawful to ask candidates about protected characteristics, whether they are married or plan to have children. Questions should only be asked about health or disability if there are necessary requirements of the job that cannot be met with reasonable adjustments. Age should only be sought on an application form if there are age requirements for the job. These matters can be asked about on separate equality monitoring forms. Drug screening can only be undertaken with an individual's explicit consent, but the use of drug and alcohol tests should be justified as necessary and proportionate (eg safety-critical jobs).

The same data protection principles referred to above will also apply when 'processing' these sorts of data. Part One of the Employment Practices Code on recruitment and selection (see **15.5**) sets out a number of recommendations, a key one of which is that any checks need to be justified by reference to the vacant position, so that the checks conducted on a van driver will be different from those for a senior management position. The Code warns employers against placing reliance on 'information collected from possibly unreliable sources'. The Information Commission has warned employers about using deception, such as claiming to be a friend, in order to access an applicant's social media information. Applicants should be given the opportunity to make representations on the accuracy of the information and any adverse findings.

The Employment Practices Code draws a distinction between obtaining information in order to 'verify' something and obtaining information in order to 'vet' someone. The latter will generally be regarded as a more intrusive act than the former, so it should only be used where there are 'particular and significant risks involved to the employer, clients, customers or others and where there is no less intrusive and reasonably practicable alternative'. In some limited circumstances, such as for those in the financial sector or as regards employees coming into contact with vulnerable individuals, vetting is a legal requirement. The Financial Services and Market Act 2000, for example, requires individuals working in controlled functions, such as senior customer-facing roles, to be 'fit and proper', meeting honesty, competence and financial soundness criteria. The Conduct of Employment Agencies and Employment Business (Amendment) Regulations 2014 (SI 2014/3351) (which came into force in April 2014) require agencies to screen candidates adequately, giving employers information on why they might be unsuitable. Agencies should also pass on any information they later obtain showing that the person might after all be unsuitable, for up to three months.

After *Smith v Carillion (JM) Ltd* [2015] EWCA Civ 209, the Employment Relations Act 1999 (Blacklists) Regulations 2010 (SI 2010/493) now make it unlawful for employers, employment agencies and others to compile, supply or use a blacklist of trade union members or activists for discriminatory purposes such as employment vetting. They also make it unlawful to refuse to employ someone for a set of specified 'prohibited' reasons.

Pre-employment screening can be a legal minefield, not least because data protection and privacy requirements differ from country to country, and in some instances pre-employment screening without consent may be unlawful. Employers need to consider not only the laws of the country where the applicant is to be employed, but also the laws of the country from which the applicant is being considered. Further, job applicants are increasing aware of their data protection and privacy rights. In Europe, Article 8 of the ECHR gives individuals the right to respect for their private and family life, their home and correspondence. In UK law, this right is enshrined in the Human Rights Act 1988 (see **15.4.2**).

Employers should make sure they comply with relevant data protection laws affecting the storage of personal data. Employees and applicants (as well as clients and customers) are entitled to make subject access requests to obtain any personal data that an organisation, including their employer, holds on them. Companies should have policies in place to deal with subject access requests, which have strict time limits (see **15.5**).

If employers want to know whether job applicants have a criminal record, they should have a proper reason for doing so, in terms of the job role. Employers can specifically ask the applicant to declare any criminal record on any application form (but see, regarding spent convictions, **1.2.7**) and/or they can use the Disclosure and Barring Service (formerly the Criminal Records Bureau), which does not disclose spent convictions. A practice had developed of employers circumventing the protection against revealing spent convictions by insisting that job applicants make a data protection subject access request (see **15.5.2**) to get hold of their full criminal record and provide it to the prospective employer. It is a specific criminal offence (DPA 2018, s 184) to require a job applicant (or indeed existing employees) to produce a copy of his criminal record through a subject access request.

1.2.6.4 Rehabilitation of Offenders Act 1974

Job applicants do not generally have to disclose spent convictions. Some excepted professions (eg teachers, healthcare practitioners and lawyers) may have to disclose information about spent convictions, if required. Amendments to the Rehabilitation of Offenders Act 1974, included in the Legal Aid, Sentencing and Punishment of Offenders Act 2012, which came into effect in March 2014, mean that the length of time that it takes for criminal convictions to become 'spent' has been reduced. Where an offender receives a custodial sentence of six months or less, the conviction becomes spent at the end of 24 months from the date the sentence is completed (for a sentence of up to two-and-a-half years, after four years; and for a sentence up to four years, after seven years). A Government White Paper published in July 2020 proposes to reduce the time after which a conviction is spent (see 'A Smarter Approach to Sentencing'). Custodial sentences of more than four years or a public protection sentence never become spent.

A spent conviction or a failure to declare one is not a proper ground for dismissing an employee. The Ministry of Justice has issued guidance on this topic.

1.2.6.5 Guidance on recruitment and induction

Acas has published a number of guides which are helpful in this area. They include 'Recruiting staff', 'Employment references', 'Starting staff: induction', 'Social media' and 'Recruitment and unconscious bias'. (See too **8.4** and **12.12**.)

1.3 THE RELATIONSHIP OF EMPLOYER AND EMPLOYEE

1.3.1 Introduction

Not all persons who perform work for others are employees, ie employed under a contract of service (a name derived from the old-fashioned terminology of master and servant). Some are workers (see **1.3.3**) and some are truly independent contractors who work under a contract *for services*. In marginal cases, it may be difficult to distinguish a contract of service from a contract for services.

The difference is important in practice because, for example, only employees are entitled to redundancy payments or to present a claim of unfair dismissal. Further, there are different income tax regimes. Employees pay income tax, which is deducted at source under the PAYE scheme, whereas independent contractors pay income tax under a different regime. There are also differences in National Insurance contributions (NICs) and entitlement to benefits.

Certain employment-related rights, such as discrimination, are not limited to employees and, increasingly, protections are being applied to 'workers' rather than the more narrow 'employee'. The term 'worker' includes employees but is wider (see ERA 1996, s 230(3)). It can be difficult to distinguish between a worker and an employee, and between a worker and those who are to be regarded as carrying on a business (see *Byrne Brothers (Formwork) Ltd v Baird* [2002] IRLR 96 for a discussion) (see below at **1.3.3**).

The Taylor Review (see Introductory Note) suggested that there should be a new categorisation of 'dependent contractor', who should be given certain basic rights around minimum wage, holiday pay and sickness pay. It is possible that someone who has registered as self-employed for tax purposes may still be a 'worker' for paid holiday entitlement and national minimum wage purposes and also an employee under the Equality Act 2010 where there is an extended definition of 'employee'. No single factor is determinative of status, and a number of factors must be considered (see further below), such as 'personal service', 'control', 'mutuality of obligations', 'integration into the business' and 'who bears the financial risk'. In *Hall (Inspector or Taxes) v Lorimer* [1994] IRLR 171, the Court of Appeal stated that, when determining employment status, the process includes 'paint[ing] a picture from the accumulation of detail', and that approach was confirmed most recently by the Supreme Court in *Pimlico Plumbers Ltd v Smith* [2018] UKSC 29, which held that employment status must be considered on the individual facts of each case and that what actually happens on the ground is more important than the wording of the contract.

1.3.2 Employee

Section 230(1) of the ERA 1996 defines an employee as 'an individual who ... works under ... a contract of employment'. Section 230(2) defines contract of employment as 'a contract of service ... whether express or implied, and (if it is express) whether oral or in writing'. Section 230(3) defines a worker (see **1.3.3**). The definitions of employee and worker both require there to be a contract in existence: see the Court of Appeal in *Secretary of State for Justice v Windle* [2016] EWCA Civ 459. This appears to be an absolute requirement and needs to be determined before any discussion can take place on whether a person is an employee or a worker. For a contract to exist, there must be, expressly or impliedly, an offer, acceptance, consideration and an intention to create legal relations. See too *Sharpe v Bishop of Worcester* [2015] IRLR 663 and *O'Brien v Ministry of Justice* [2013] ICR 499.

Over the years, the courts have formulated a variety of tests to identify the existence of a contract of service. These tests have included the 'control' test (see, eg, *Yewens v Noakes* (1880) 6 QBD 530); the 'integration' test (see, eg, *Stevenson Jordan & Harrson Ltd v McDonald and Evans* [1952] 1 TLR 101); and the 'economic reality' test (see, eg, *Market Investigations Ltd v Minister of Social Security* [1969] 2 QB 173). The 'multiple factor' test advocated by McKenna J in *Ready Mixed Concrete (South East) Ltd v Minister of Pensions and National Insurance* [1968] 1 All ER 433) was approved by the Supreme Court in *Autoclenz v Belcher* [2011] UKSC 41.

McKenna J stated that a contract of service existed if three conditions were fulfilled:

(a) the servant agrees that, in consideration of a wage or other remuneration, he will provide his own work and skill in the performance of some service for his master ('mutuality of obligation', ie on the employer to pay for the work and on the employee to personally do the work ('personal service'));

(b) the servant agrees, expressly or impliedly, that in the performance of that service he will be subject to the other's control in a sufficient degree to make that other master (control);

(c) the other provisions of the contract are consistent with its being a contract of service.

When, if at all, might an express agreement be challenged? This was considered by the Supreme Court in *Autoclenz Ltd v Belcher* (above). The Court of Appeal, in its judgment ([2010] IRLR 70), set out the circumstances in which courts can look behind the express terms of the parties' agreement. The EAT had held that the 20 car valets who worked for Autoclenz at its premises in Derbyshire were not employees but were workers within the meaning of s 230(3) of the ERA 1996. The Court of Appeal disagreed. The terms of the agreement between Autoclenz and the valets provided that:

(a) there was no obligation on the valets to perform any work or for Autoclenz to provide it;

(b)   the valets' services would be engaged from time to time;

(c)   the valets could arrange for a substitute to carry out their valeting duties; and

(d)   the valets paid their own tax and had to purchase their own insurance, uniforms and materials.

However, according to the Court of Appeal, the above terms did not accurately reflect the relationship between the parties:

(a)   the valets were required to notify Autoclenz whether or not they would be turning up for work; and

(b)   whilst there existed a substitution clause, the valets would not, in practice, be permitted to send a substitute in their place and were expected to turn up and provide services in person.

The Court of Appeal, upholding the Employment Judge's decision at first instance, held that the valets were employees. The Court said that tribunals should focus on the actual legal obligations of the parties rather than merely relying on the written terms of an agreement when determining what kind of employment relationship existed. The fact that Autoclenz described the valets as workers and not employees was not conclusive. The tribunal has to consider whether or not the words represent the actual legal obligations of the parties. The Court of Appeal said it was not necessary to find any deliberate intention to deceive. The written terms are always the starting point, but where an issue is raised the tribunal must ask if the parties ever realistically intended or envisaged that its terms would be carried out as written.

The Supreme Court agreed with the Court of Appeal that the individual valets were not self-employed subcontractors and, although it was not necessary for the claims for minimum wage and holiday which only necessitated a finding that the valets were workers, it also upheld the finding that they were 'employees'. The Supreme Court held the real situation trumped what was written in the contract. It was not necessary for the valets to prove a 'sham', in the sense that the parties intended to mislead HM Revenue and Customs (HMRC). The fact that the employer had written a 'substitution clause' into the contracts did not reflect the reality, as everyone expected the valets to carry out their duties personally. The essential question was: What was the true nature of the agreement between the parties? That *might* be what is written down, but was not necessarily so.

There is a helpful review of the legal distinctions between a contract of service and a contract for services in *Drake v Ipsos Mori UK Ltd* (UKEAT/0604/11).

Note that IR35 (legislation that allows HMRC to collect additional payments where a contractor worker is an employee in all but name) covers the situation where a contractor worker operates through an intermediary, such as a limited company, and but for that intermediary the worker would really be an employee. Additional payments must be made (by the client if in the public sector or the medium and large sized private sector; by the intermediary in the private sector where the worker provides services to a small client) to cover income tax and national insurance. In *Commissioners for HM Revenue and Customs v Atholl House Productions Ltd* [2022] IRLR 698, the Court of Appeal reviewed the authorities for determination of employment status in an IR35 case. There is concern about the operation of IR35, such as the danger of overzealous application of the rules, but at the time of writing plans to repeal it have been cancelled.

1.3.2.1   Case law

Mutual obligations

The courts draw a distinction between mutuality on the one hand (which is necessary for there to be a contract at all) and, where there is a contract, the nature of that contract. That will be determined by the *nature* of the mutual obligations: mutual obligations on the employee to work personally for another, and on the employer to pay for the work. There is no reason why a worker should not be employed under a contract of employment for separate engagements, even if of short duration (see *Meechan v Secretary of State for Employment* [1997] IRLR 353 and *Cornwall County Council v Prater* [2006] IRLR 362). However, to establish continuity, the worker will need to establish that a contract continues between assignments (a so called 'umbrella contract'). See *Carmichael* and *Stephenson* (below) and *Stringfellows Restaurants Ltd v Quashie* [2013] IRLR 99 at **1.3.2.2** below. In *St Ives Plymouth Ltd v Haggerty* (UKEAT/0107/08), the issue arose whether the worker had the requisite continuity of employment. The Tribunal found that there was a sufficient mutuality of obligations in the gaps when no work was performed to infer the existence of an umbrella or overarching contract:

> There was an expectation that the claimant would be available for a reasonable amount of work. Her services were valued and frequently called upon. I entirely accept that there was no obligation upon her to accept any particular offer but I am satisfied that had she persistently declined offers of work her name would be removed from the list of casuals. Equally although there was no guaranteed minimum amount of work the claimant had an expectation that she would be offered a reasonable amount of work. If the flow of work had dried up she would undoubtedly have sought work elsewhere. I find that those circumstances are sufficient – just sufficient – to amount to the minimum of mutual obligation between the parties to enable me to find that there was an overarching contract of employment.

The EAT upheld that decision (by majority):

> ... the Tribunal in this case was entitled to find that there was a proper basis for saying that the explanation for the conduct was the existence of a legal obligation and not simply goodwill and mutual benefit. The majority consider that it is important to note that the test is not whether it is necessary to imply an umbrella contract, or whether business efficacy leads to that conclusion. It is simply whether there is a sufficient factual substratum to support a finding that such a legal obligation has arisen. It is a question of fact, not law. The majority place weight on the fact that nowhere does Lord Irvine state that the only proper conclusion for the Tribunal was to find a lack of mutual obligations. The emphasis is on this being a finding that the Tribunal was entitled to make.

It is useful to repeat part of Elias J's judgment in *Stephenson v Delphi Diesel Systems Ltd* [2003] ICR 471:

11   The significance of mutuality is that it determines whether there is a contact in existence at all. The significance of control is that it determines whether, if there a contract in place, it can properly be classified as a contract of service, rather than some other kind of contract.

12   The issue of whether there is a contract at all arises most frequently in situations where a person works for an employer, but only on a casual basis from time to time. It is often necessary then to show that the contract continues to exist in the gaps between the periods of employment. Cases frequently have had to decide whether there is an over-arching contract or what is sometimes called an 'umbrella contract' which remains in existence even when the individual concerned is not working. It is in that context in particular that courts have emphasised the need to demonstrate some mutuality of obligation between the parties but, as I have indicated, all that is being done is to say that there must be something from which a contract can properly be inferred. Without some mutuality, amounting to what is sometimes called the 'irreducible minimum of obligation', no contract exists.

13   The question of mutuality of obligation, however, poses no difficulties during the period when the individual is actually working. For the period of such employment a contract must, in our view, clearly exist. For that duration the individual clearly undertakes to work and the employer in turn undertakes to pay for the work done. This is so, even if the contract is terminable on either side at will. Unless and until the power to terminate is exercised, these mutual obligations (to work on the one hand and to be paid on the other) will continue to exist and will provide the fundamental mutual obligations.

The Court of Appeal relied on this analysis in HM *Revenue and Customs v Professional Game Match Officials Ltd* [2021] EWCA Civ 1370. The Upper Tribunal had held that part-time football referees were independent contractors and not employees. Looking at both mutuality of obligation and control, it held that, while there was an overarching annual contract and a series of separate contracts for each match, mutuality of obligation was missing and so the referees were not engaged under contracts of service by PGMOL. The Court of Appeal held that the Upper Tribunal erred in its approach to the question of mutuality of obligation in the individual contracts and remitted the case for determination as to whether there was sufficient mutuality of obligation in the individual separate contracts for those to be contracts of employment.

Carmichael v National Power [2000] IRLR 43 illustrates this point. Mrs Leese and Mrs Carmichael applied, were interviewed and were told:

> I am pleased to note that you are agreeable to be employed by the CEGB at Blyth 'A' and 'B' Power Stations on a casual as required basis as a station guide.
>
> When your services are required you will be paid at the rate of 376.56 pence per hour being the minimum of Band I of the NJIC Agreement. Your salary will be paid by credit transfer.
>
> Please find enclosed a pre-typed reply letter which should be returned to me confirming your acceptance of this offer together with the completed method of payment form.

The employment tribunal held that their case 'founder[ed] on the rock of absence of mutuality', that is that, when *not* working as guides, they were in no contractual relationship of any kind with the company. The House of Lords agreed and held that the employment tribunal's decision that the 'documents did no more than provide a framework for a series of successive ad hoc contracts of service or for services which the parties might subsequently make; and that when they were not working as guides they were not in any contractual relationship with [the company]' was correct. When they were not working as guides, they were not in employment because the company did not promise to offer work, and the claimants were not agreeing to do work. The contracts did not create mutuality of obligation and therefore could not be contracts of employment. The company was not obliged to provide guide work as might become available in future and they were not obliged to undertake such work when made available.

In *Knight v BCCP* (UKEAT/0413/10), the EAT again emphasised the importance of mutuality – without mutual obligations to offer and to accept work, there can be no employment relationship under s 230 of the ERA 1996. Mr Knight was a licensed private hire driver, who was engaged by the respondent company for just over six weeks between 1 September and 14 October 2008. There was no contractual documentation. He was told that he would receive mileage rates for the work that he did, and that he had to provide his car upon the basis that he paid the insurance as well as the running costs including petrol, maintenance bills and other expenses. He was paid by submitting an invoice based on the company's records. He had to pay his own tax and National Insurance contributions and did not have any set working hours. He worked under the company's control to a degree in that it dictated the dress to be worn, how the car was to be presented, how the claimant was to deal with opening doors and procedure at airports and stations. He received wages only for the occasions when he actually worked. The relationship between the claimant and the company terminated when he was asked to complete a detailed security questionnaire in connection with cars provided for government purposes, and he decided he did not want to disclose the detailed information which it required. The issue before the employment tribunal was whether he was entitled to one week's statutory notice pay under s 86 of the ERA 1996, which necessitated his being an employee. The employment tribunal found that Mr Knight was under no obligation to accept work and the company was under no obligation to offer work to him, and as such, he was not an employee. The EAT upheld the tribunal's decision.

However, the phrase 'mutuality of obligation' does not require the would-be employee to be obliged to work whenever asked by the purported employer. This might involve a factual assessment as to whether any refusal was so extensive as to deny the existence of an obligation to even do a minimum of work (see, for example, *Khan v Checkers Cars Ltd* [2005] 12 WLUK 532).

Personal service

Mr Justice MacKenna noted in *Ready Mixed Concrete (South East) Ltd v Minister of Pensions and National Insurance* [1968] 1 All ER 433 that 'Freedom to do a job either by one's own hands or by another's is inconsistent with a contract of service, although a limited or occasional power of delegation may not be.'

In *Express and Echo Publications v Tanton* [1999] IRLR 367, the Court of Appeal emphasised that, to be a contract of service, a contract had to contain an obligation on the part of the employee to provide his services personally. Generally, therefore, if a worker is entitled to substitute personal service (ie to ask a replacement to do his work) then that will usually demonstrate that the contract is not a contract of service because the worker lacks the obligation required. However, in *McFarlane v Glasgow City Council* [2001] IRLR 7, the EAT said that a lack of personal service is not necessarily conclusive:

> [P]roperly regarded, [the decision in] *Tanton* does not oblige the tribunal to conclude that under a contract of service the individual has, always and in every event ... to personally provide his services.

Whether a power to delegate work to a substitute is determinative may depend on whether the right to delegate is fettered and/or the nature of the duties that may be delegated. In *McFarlane*, the claimant could not unilaterally refuse to work; it was only in circumstances where he was unable to attend that a substitute could be provided, and any substitute had to be approved by the employer. In the circumstances he was an employee.

It is useful to refer to the Court of Appeal decision in *Pimlico Plumbers Ltd v Smith* [2017] EWCA Civ 51. Although the case went up to the Supreme Court (see below), the Court of Appeal helpfully reviewed the existing authorities in relation to personal service in a case about whether plumbers were workers or independent contractors (see **1.3.3** below) and summarised the basic principles (at [84]):

> Firstly, an unfettered right to substitute another person to do the work or perform the services is inconsistent with an undertaking to do so personally. Secondly, a conditional right to substitute another person may or may not be inconsistent with personal performance depending upon the conditionality. It will depend on the precise contractual arrangements and, in particular, the nature and degree of any fetter on a right of substitution or, using different language, the extent to which the right of substitution is limited or occasional. Thirdly, by way of example, a right of substitution only when the contractor is unable to carry out the work will, subject to any exceptional facts, be consistent with personal performance. Fourthly, again by way of example, a right of substitution limited only by the need to show that the substitute is as qualified as the contractor to do the work, whether or not that entails a particular procedure, will, subject to any exceptional facts, be inconsistent with personal performance. Fifthly, again by way of example, a right to substitute only with the consent of another person who has an absolute and unqualified discretion to withhold consent will be consistent with personal performance.

This approach was applied by the EAT in *Chatfeild-Roberts v Phillips and Another* (UKEAT/0049/18), where the claimant, a live-in carer, was held to be an employee notwithstanding a limited right to use a substitute when she was unable to work. See too *Smart Delivery Ltd v Augustine* (UKEAT/0219/18).

Control

In the *Ready Mixed Concrete* case (**1.3.2** above), McKenna J described control as including 'the power of deciding the thing to be done, the way ..., the means ..., the time ... and the place'.

The Court of Appeal, in *Montgomery v Johnson Underwood Ltd* [2001] IRLR 269, confirmed that for a contract of service to exist there had to be control, that control is a separate factor, and no less important than mutuality of obligation when considering whether there is a contract of service. Control requires a general ultimate direct authority over an employee in the performance of his work. Control in itself, however, is not conclusive: an independent contractor can agree to submit himself to the same control as an employee without actually becoming an employee (see, for example, *Ready Mixed Concrete*); and many employees will, by virtue of seniority for example, be subject to very little control.

The EAT confirmed in *White and Another v Troutbeck SA* (UKEAT/0177/12) that the issue of control concerns whether there is, to a sufficient degree, a contractual right of control over the worker, and not whether in practice the worker has day-to-day control of his own work. The EAT's decision was upheld by the Court of Appeal ([2013] EWCA Civ 1171), which emphasised the need to address the cumulative effect of the totality of provisions in any written agreement and all the circumstances of the relationship created by it.

For an application of *Troutbeck*, see *Wright v Aegis Defence Services (BVI) Ltd and Others* (UKEAT 0173/17). The employment tribunal was held in error in its approach to determining employment status 'by reason of its approach to determining whether the relevant Respondent has sufficient control over the Claimant. It did not remind itself that the law was clear that the relevant question is not what practical manifestations there were of control being exercised, but whether under the contract the purported employer had the right to direct the Claimant in what he did.' The claimant worked providing security for the Australian Government at the Australian Embassy in Kabul for a number of years. The employment tribunal judge decided that there was mutuality of obligation in the claimant agreeing to provide personal service to the First Respondent and the First Respondent providing work for him to do; and that there was a requirement for him to provide personal service. However, the judge held that whilst there 'was a level of control exerted over the Claimant, [this was] not sufficient in my view to make the First Respondent "the master" in an employment relationship. I have taken into account the particular type of service being provided by the Claimant and that due to this, sufficient control would have to be applied in order to ensure that the services were carried out in accordance with health and safety and appropriate rules in place, particularly as weapons were to be used.' The EAT held that the employer had the contractual power to direct, and the employee had bound himself to observe that direction. The employment tribunal had been in error when it concentrated upon practical manifestations of day-to-day control and not upon the contractual entitlement. The EAT concluded:

> Examples come to mind of the in-house solicitor who advises an employer on matters of law as to which the employer may be ignorant or much less well informed; or the chauffeur who when driving is subject to the directions of traffic constables and traffic signs and is exercising his skill which his employer may simply not have, or chooses not to perform, delegating the judgements to be exercised to the chauffeur from time to time. Both are plainly employees, and are engaged as such precisely because the employer does not have their particular skills and could not himself do their jobs. Thus, the question does not depend, as the cases make clear, upon the practical demonstration of control by drawing attention to particular instances when control has or has not been exercised, but rather to what is known of or maybe inferred as to the contract between the parties which is said to give rise to the right in the employer to direct in relevant respects.

1.3.2.2   Other matters

An employment tribunal must consider the overall picture. The tribunal should not adopt a 'checklist' approach but consider all aspects, with no single factor being in itself conclusive, and each of which may vary in weight and direction (see eg *Hall v Lorimer* [1994] IRLR 171).

Among matters that may be relevant to consider as to whether the person is an employee are:

(a)   How is the individual paid?

(b)   Who pays tax and National Insurance?

(c)   Who provides the tools and equipment?

(d)   How integral to the business is the individual's role?

(e)   Is the individual paid for sickness and holiday?

(f)   Is the individual subject to the disciplinary and grievance policy?

(g)   Is the individual a member of a company pension scheme?

(h)   Where does the economic risk lie?

(i)   How did the parties view the relationship at the outset

(j)   How was the arrangement terminable?

In *Stringfellows Restaurants Ltd v Quashie* [2013] IRLR 99, the Court of Appeal reinstated an employment tribunal's finding that it had no jurisdiction to hear a claim for unfair dismissal brought by a lap dancer at 'Stringfellows' night club as she was not an employee. The claimant was a lap dancer who was paid entirely from customers' vouchers, which were changed into cash at the end of the night. She had to comply with house rules, including that she was required to work set nights as rostered. There was a dress code and she had to do a certain number of free dances each shift. The employment tribunal decided that she was not an employee, as there was no obligation on the employer to pay her anything.

The employment tribunal found that, in a number of respects, conditions for there to be an employment relationship were met: the supply of her services was personal to the claimant; she could not send a substitute; the employer exercised sufficient control over the claimant for there to be an employment contract. However, while there was also plainly a contract in existence between the parties, as there were some mutual obligations in play (eg to work when rostered and for her to be allowed to dance when at work), the crucial question was not whether there was a contract but whether the contract was a contract of employment. In coming to the conclusion that it was not, the employment tribunal found there was no obligation on the employer to pay the claimant anything, so the claimant took the financial risk, she negotiated her own fees with customers; in the circumstances, she paid the club to give her an opportunity to earn money by dancing. This finding was reinforced by the fact that the terms of the contract involved the claimant being responsible for her own tax and National Insurance, and not being entitled to sick pay or holiday pay.

The EAT reversed the tribunal decision and held that the claimant was an employee and could bring a claim for unfair dismissal. It also held that there was an umbrella contract which covered gaps in the evenings when the claimant did not dance.

The Court of Appeal, in overturning the EAT, looked at the nature of the mutual obligations required for the purposes of a contract of employment. The leading judgment was given by Elias LJ. He revisited his earlier assessment of mutuality in *Stephenson v Delphi* (**1.3.2.1** above) and said that in so far as he had suggested that once some mutuality was shown, the only question was whether there was sufficient control, that was too sweeping: even where the work-wage relationship exists and there is substantial control, there may be other features of the relationship which entitle a tribunal to conclude there was no employment contract, even during individual engagements. In this case, the fact that the employer was under no obligation to pay the dancer and she took the economic risk supported the tribunal's finding that she was not an employee. Given its findings that there was no employment contract during individual engagements, the Court of Appeal did not feel it necessary to look at whether there was an umbrella contract in existence.

In *St Ives Plymouth Ltd v Haggerty* (UKEAT/0107/08), although the EAT upheld the tribunal's conclusion that the claimant was an employee, it added that it would not have given any weight to the fact that she was subject to a disciplinary procedure because that was also consistent with the fair treatment of a casual worker.

In *Secretary of State for Justice v Windle* [2016] EWCA Civ 459, the Court of Appeal held that the absence of an overriding or umbrella contract for a series of assignments or engagements could be crucial: 'the fact that a person supplying services is only doing so on an assignment-to-assignment basis may tend to indicate a degree of independence, or lack or subordination, in the relationship while at work which is incompatible with employee status ...'.

This approach was adopted in *Braine v The National Gallery* (ET/2201625/2018), where a number of artists and art lecturers who worked for the National Gallery were dismissed en masse in October 2017, following a restructuring, without any consultation or receiving any benefits. They argued that they were employees and brought claims including unfair dismissal and discrimination. They argued that although their contracts described them as freelancers, they undertook regular work, were paid and taxed through PAYE, and were subject to appraisals and mandatory training requirements. After training was completed, they served a probationary period of around six months before being added to the freelance roster on a permanent basis. Sometime later they were offered standard terms that stated that there was no obligation for the National Gallery to offer work and they could accept/reject any work offered to them. They were also allowed access to computers and copiers; received overnight expenses; got access to the staff canteen; had invitations to private viewings; and were given staff discounts. They were required to wear the respondent's clothing and were listed as staff in the respondent's directory. They did not have the right to substitute themselves for another person if they were unable to attend work.

Following the usual approach, the employment tribunal looked at the reality of the situation. It held that there was no umbrella contract between assignments and held that the claimants were workers and not employees. Its reasoning was that despite there being no contract of employment – or continuity of employment between jobs – the claimants had to perform the jobs personally, were subject to managerial control and heavily integrated into the gallery. As a result of being workers, the discrimination claims could proceed but the unfair dismissal claims failed as the claimants did not have the requisite employment status.

In *Varnish v British Cycling and UK Sport* (UKEAT/0022/20), a former track and sprint cyclist, who was dropped in 2016 from the elite cycling programme run by British Cycling, argued that she was an employee and sought to bring claims of unfair dismissal, sex discrimination and detriment suffered as a whistleblower. She argued that British Cycling had 'net' control over her and that she was told what to eat, wear and say in public. British Cycling said that funding for athletes was akin to a grant and should not be subject to employment rights and that there was no mutuality of obligation. The EAT agreed with the employment tribunal that there was no mutuality of obligation and ruled that, while there was some control, Ms Varnish was neither an employee nor a worker.

See too *Exmore Ales Ltd and Another v Herriot* (UKEAT/0075/18), where the EAT upheld an employment tribunal's judgment that an accountant for a brewery was an independent contractor until 2011, when she became an employee. The employment tribunal held that the claimant was regarded as 'fully integrated' into the first respondent's business from April 2011 and that it was 'satisfied that there was a mutuality of obligations between the Claimant and the First Respondent from April 2011 onwards and that the First Respondent exercised a high level of control over the Claimant whilst at work'. The mutual obligations were, on the claimant's side, to provide services personally, precluding any substitution, and on the first respondent's side to provide her with work and pay. The judge also found that 'substitution of the Claimant, in the event of her absence from work for whatever reason, would not have been contemplated by the parties'. Finally, the judge said he was not persuaded that the evidence from the second respondent that the claimant was known to refer to herself as a contractor was 'determinative, to any degree, of the Claimant's status'. It was, he said, 'not at all apparent from the evidence as to when the alleged comment had been made by the Claimant. It was certainly not clear that it was being alleged by the Respondents that the Claimant had made such a comment after April 2011.'

1.3.3   Workers

A number of statutory employment protections apply not solely to employees but to a wider class of 'worker' (which includes employees). See, for example, s 13 of the ERA 1996 (relating to deductions from wages – see **1.11** below), the National Minimum Wage Regulations 1999 (SI 1999/584) (see **1.8.3.1** below), the Working Time Regulations 1988 (SI 1988/1833) (see **1.12** below) and the Part-time Workers (Prevention of Less Favourable Treatment) Regulations 2000 (SI 2000/1551) (see **8.10** below).

A worker is defined under s 230(3) of the ERA 1996 to mean

> an individual who has entered into or works under (or where employment has ceased worked under)
>
> (a)   a contract of employment; or
>
> (b)   any other contract, whether express or implied and (if it is express) whether oral or in writing, whereby the individual undertakes to do or perform personally any work or services for another party to the contract whose status is not by virtue of the contract that of a client or customer of any profession or business undertaking carried on by the individual.

The reference to a contract of employment in para (a) above means that an employee is also a worker. The same definition appears in the National Minimum Wage Regulations 1999, the Working Time Regulations 1998 and the Part-time Workers Regulations 2000.

There are thus four requirements that need to be satisfied in limb (b):

(a)   the worker has to be an individual who has entered into or works under a contract;

(b)   with another party for work or services;

(c)   the individual undertakes to do or perform personally the work or services for the other party;

(d)   that other party must not, by virtue of the contract, have the status of a client or customer of any profession or business undertaking carried on by the individual who is to perform the work or services (see on this point *Johnson v Transopco Ltd* [2022] EAT 6).

The Equality Act 2010 uses the term 'employee' rather than 'worker'. Under s 83(2)(a), 'employment' means employment under (i) a contract of employment, (ii) a contract of apprenticeship, or (iii) a contract personally to do work (see **Chapter 8**). The third encompasses 'worker' and goes beyond the definition of employee in s 230 (see further below).

As far as the requirement for a contract is concerned, readers are reminded that there must be an offer, acceptance, consideration and an intention to create legal relations. See *Windle v Secretary of State for Justice* [2015] ICR 156 and *O'Brien v Ministry of Justice* [2013] ICR 499 (where the Supreme Court dispensed with the requirement for a contract, applying the Framework Directive 97/81/EC, which referenced a broader concept of 'employment relationship'). See too *Gilham v Ministry of Justice* [2019] UKSC 44.

As far as the third and fourth requirements are concerned, there are a number of authorities, dealt with below.

Readers should note again the Supreme Court decision in *Autoclenz* (above) where the Court held that

> the ET was entitled to hold that the documents did not reflect the true agreement between the parties and that, on the basis of the ET's findings, four essential contractual terms were agreed: (1) that the valeters would perform the services defined in the contract for Autoclenz within a reasonable time and in a good and workmanlike manner; (2) that the valeters would be paid for that work; (3) that the valeters were obliged to carry out the work offered to them and Autoclenz undertook to offer work; and (4) that the valeters must personally do the work and could not provide a substitute to do so. See in particular, per Aikens LJ at para 97. It follows that, applying the principles identified above, the Court of Appeal was correct to hold that those were the true terms of the contract and that the ET was entitled to disregard the terms of the written documents, in so far as they were inconsistent with them.

In *Byrne Brothers (Formwork) Ltd v Baird* [2002] IRLR 96, the EAT held that a tribunal had not erred in holding that various labour-only subcontractors who worked as carpenters in the construction industry were workers within the meaning of the Working Time Regulations, and had therefore correctly concluded that they were entitled to holiday pay: as the applicants undertook to perform work or services for the company personally, they fell within the definition of 'worker' in limb (b) above, notwithstanding that the contract provided that, in certain circumstances, the services could be provided by someone other than the subcontractor with the prior express agreement of the contractor.

The EAT said, usefully:

> Thus the essence of the intended distinction must be between, on the one hand, workers whose degree of dependence is essentially the same as that of employees and, on the other, contractors who have a sufficiently arms-length and independent position to be treated as being able to look after themselves in the relevant respects.
>
> ...
>
> Drawing [the] distinction [between workers and independent contractors] will involve all or most of the same considerations as arise in drawing the distinction between a contract of service and a contract for services – but with the boundary pushed further in the putative worker's favour. It may, for example, be relevant to assess the degree of control exercised by the putative employer, the exclusivity of the engagement and its typical duration, the method of payment, what equipment the putative worker supplies, the level of risk undertaken etc. The basic effect of limb (b) is ... to lower the pass mark, so that cases which failed to reach the mark necessary to qualify for protection as employees might do so as workers (at 101).

The EAT, following *McFarlane* (**1.3.2.1** above), held that a limited power to appoint a substitute was not inconsistent with an obligation to provide services personally and that the purpose of limb (b) is 'to create an intermediate class of protected worker who is on the one hand not an employee, but on the other hand cannot in some narrower sense be regarded as carrying on a business'. In looking at the policy behind limb (b), the EAT said that it was to extend protection to workers who were 'substantively and economically' in the same position as employees.

The EAT emphasised that what was important were the rights and obligations of the parties *under the contract* and not what happened *in practice*, although that 'may shed light' on the contractual position. The EAT thought that the carpenters in *Byrne* were a good example of the kind of workers for whom the intermediate category in limb (b) was designed. The carpenters were clearly not carrying on a business, and Byrne Brothers were not their clients. There was sufficient mutuality of obligation between the parties for it to be said that there was a contract for services within the meaning of limb (b).

In *Yorkshire Window Company Ltd v Parkes* (UKEAT/0484/09) the EAT helpfully drew the following from the authorities:

> We would draw the following principles from the authorities to which we have referred, (a), the question whether or not a contract provides for the performance of personal services is essentially a matter of construction, (b), the court is concerned with construing the contract, rather than with general policy considerations, (c), the fact that the individual chooses personally to supply the services is irrelevant; the issue is whether he is contractually obliged to do so, (d), the right or obligation to employ a substitute will not necessarily mean that there is no obligation on the part of the 'contractor' to perform personal services unless that right to employ a substitute is unfettered, (e), in cases where the 'contractor' is unable as opposed to unwilling, to carry out specified services, and has accepted an obligation to perform those services, but is unable to do so, and where he himself does not bear the costs of employing a substitute, a limited or occasional power of delegation may not be inconsistent with a contract to provide personal services, (f), a worker holds an intermediate position between an employee and someone who carries on his own business undertaking.

The fourth requirement is there, as Mr Recorder Underhill QC (as he then was) noted in *Byrne Brothers (Formwork) Ltd v Baird and Others* [2002] IRLR 96, to create an intermediate class of protected worker, who is on the one hand not an employee but on the other hand cannot in some narrower sense be regarded as carrying on a business. ... it is sometimes said that the effect of the exception is that the regulations do not extend to the 'genuinely self-employed'; but that is not a particularly helpful formulation since it is unclear how 'genuinely' self-employment is to be defined.

It is clear that not all those who might properly be described as self-employed are engaged in a business undertaking. The question whether the 'worker' carries on a business undertaking of which the 'employer' is a client or customer is, of course, closely linked to the issue of whether the 'worker' provides services personally. It must be determined whether the essence of the relationship is that of a worker or somebody who is employed, albeit in a small way, in a business undertaking. In many cases, it might assist, as Langstaff J suggested in *Cotswold Developments Construction Ltd v Williams* [2006] IRLR 281, para 53, to focus upon 'whether the purported worker actively markets his services as an independent person to the world in general ... or whether he is recruited by the principal to work for that principal as an integral part of the principal's operations'. As Elias J said in *James v Redcats (Brands) Ltd* [2007] ICR 1006, the question is whether the obligation for personal service is the dominant feature of the contractual arrangement or not. If it is, then the contract lies in the employment field; if it is not – if, for example, the dominant feature of the contract is a particular outcome or objective and the obligation to provide personal service is an incidental or secondary consideration – it will lie in the business field and the person concerned will not be a worker.

In *Yorkshire Window Company Ltd v Parkes* (above), the Employment Judge held that the claimant was not an employee because, in particular, he had treated himself as self-employed in relation to VAT and income tax, and prepared accounts on that basis, was entitled to refuse referrals and could elect which leads he wished to pursue. The Judge went on to find, however, that the claimant was a worker because, on the facts, the claimant had to carry out the work personally (there was no unfettered right to provide a substitute) and he was not pursuing a business; the claimant was not conducting a business enterprise of a general character to the benefit of a larger class of beneficiaries. The claimant was required to confine his services to the respondent and did so as the terms of the contract made clear. The EAT upheld the decision.

The Court of Appeal, in *The Hospital Medical Group Ltd v Westwood* [2012] EWCA Civ 1005, had to consider whether a GP who, aside from his job, carried out hair restoration surgery for the respondent's clients on a Saturday morning, was a worker. The claimant brought claims of unlawful deductions, accrued holiday pay and age discrimination. The employment tribunal ruled, applying *Autoclenz v Belcher* (**1.3.2** above), that the claimant was not an employee but that he was a worker within s 230(3)(b) of the ERA 1996. The claimant was 'clearly in business on his own account, and was engaged under a contract for services as a self-employed independent contractor' (para 30). Nevertheless, he was engaged personally to carry out the work himself (as the respondent conceded); he had no right to delegate the work to others; he was engaged by the respondent because of his skills (para 31).

The EAT upheld the decision of the employment tribunal. The EAT said the claimant was not performing work or services for the respondent as a client or customer of any profession or business carried on by him. The Court of Appeal agreed, Maurice Kay LJ commenting that:

> The striking thing about the judgments in *Cotswold* and *Redcats* is that neither propounds a test of universal application. Langstaff J's 'integration' test was considered by him to be demonstrative 'in most cases' and Elias J said that the 'dominant purpose' test 'may help' tribunals 'in some cases' (paragraph 68). In my judgment, both were wise to eschew a more prescriptive approach which would gloss the words of the statute. ... (at [18])

> ... HMG was not just another purchaser of Dr Westwood's various medical skills. Separately from his general practice and his work at the Albany Clinic, he contracted specifically and exclusively to carry out hair restoration surgery on behalf HMG. In its marketing material, HMG referred to him as 'one of our surgeons'. Although he was not working for HMG pursuant to a contract of employment, he was

clearly an integral part of its undertaking when providing services in respect of hair restoration, even though he was in business on his own account. ... (at [19])

Readers are also referred to *O'Brien v Ministry of Justice* [2013] UKSC 6, where the Supreme Court explained its decision (delivered in July 2012) that a part-time Crown Court recorder was a part-time worker for the purposes of the provisions preventing less favourable treatment regarding part-time workers (see **8.10**). The Court of Appeal held in *Gilham v Ministry of Justice* [2017] EWCA Civ 2220 that a District Judge was not a worker. The distinction between the *O'Brien* judge and the *Gilham* judge is that the judge in the former case was relying on the Part-time Workers Regulations 2000 (which derive from European legislation), whereas Ms Gilham was relying on the ERA 1996 (s 47B/whistleblowing), which does not derive from European legislation. However, the Supreme Court held very recently that a judge *can* be a worker for the purposes of the whistleblowing provisions because to exclude would activate Article 14 of the ECHR (right to non-discrimination) unless such exclusion could be justified on the facts. Here there was no legitimate aim and so the District Judge was, on the facts, a worker ([2019] UKSC 44).

The ECJ defined a worker (for the purpose of the Working Time Directive) as someone who pursues real, genuine activities, to the exclusion of activities on such a small scale as to be regarded as purely marginal and ancillary (*Fenoll v Centre d'aide par le travail 'La Jouvene'* (Case C-316/13) [2016] IRLR 67). As Caspar Glyn QC blogged, 'the case potentially opens the door for individuals who fall outside the domestic s 230(3) ERA 1996 definition of worker to bring claims for working time rights derived from EU law'. (See also *Balkaya* below.)

In *Clyde & Co LLP and Another v Bates van Winkelhof* [2014] IRLR 641, the Supreme Court held that an equity partner who spent most of her time on secondment in Tanzania was a worker. As an equity partner, Ms Bates was unable to market her services to anyone other than the LLP, and she played an integral part within the business. The fact that she was not in a subordinate position as regards the LLP was irrelevant. See too *Plastering Contractors Stanmore Ltd v Holden* (UKEAT/0074/14) and *Catt v English Table Tennis Association* [2022] EAT 125.

For a useful case summarising the case law up to and including *Uber*, see *Stojsavljevic v DPD Group* (UKEAT/0118/20).

In *Pimlico Plumbers* (above and below) the Supreme Court held that a limited right of substitution was not inconsistent with worker status. See too *Stuart Delivery Ltd v Augustine* [2022] IRLR 56, where the Court of Appeal held that a courier was a worker, notwithstanding a limited right of substitution to release the slot to another courier already approved by the respondent.

In *Nursing and Midwifery Council v Somerville* [2022] EWCA Civ 229, the Court of Appeal held that a Council panel member who undertook short term assignments can be a 'limb (b) worker' when they are working, without the need for an 'irreducible minimum of obligations' between assignments (there was no requirement to offer or accept future work). It is an important case in this respect.

In *Sejpal v Rodericks Dental Ltd* [2022] EAT 91, the EAT (HHJ Tayler) held that a dentist was a worker. HHJ Tayler started with an analysis of the legal position:

> 7. The entitlement to significant employment protection rights depends on a person being a worker. Deciding whether a person is a worker should not be difficult. Worker status has been the subject of a great deal of appellate consideration in recent years. Worker status has come to be seen as contentious and difficult. But the dust is beginning to settle. Determining worker status is not very difficult in the majority of cases, provided a structured approach is adopted, and robust common sense applied. The starting point, and constant focus, must be the words of the statutes. Concepts such as 'mutuality of obligation', 'irreducible minimum', 'umbrella contracts', 'substitution', 'predominant purpose', 'subordination', 'control', and 'integration' are tools that can sometimes help in applying the statutory test, but are not themselves tests. Some of the concepts will be irrelevant in particular cases, or relevant

only to a component of the statutory test. It is not a question of assessing all the concepts, putting the results in a pot, and hoping that the answer will emerge; the statutory test must be applied, according to its purpose.

HHJ Tayler considered mutuality of obligation, noting that when someone is working, the concept does not assist and takes the same approach to substitution, ie even if substitution is permitted, 'it is hard to see what it has to offer while a person *is* working' (emphasis added). The EAT also considered it arguable that post-*Uber* a person can still be a worker, notwithstanding an unfettered right of substitution.

Note

BIS has published a 'worker' checklist in connection with national minimum wage claims (search 'national minimum wage worker checklist'). In March 2017, Acas published new guidance for employers on employment status.

Finally, note that the ECJ held in *Balkaya v Kiesel Abbruch- und Recycling Technik GmbH* (Case C-229/14) that a director and an unpaid trainee may fall within the concept of 'worker' under the Collective Redundancies Directive (98/59/EC) (see **4.8**). But note that the EU definition of 'worker' is, and has been since 1986, different from that in the UK.

The 'gig economy'

The 'gig economy' has been defined as 'a labour market characterised by the prevalence of short-term contracts or freelance work, as opposed to permanent jobs'. In the gig economy, instead of a regular wage, workers get paid for the 'gigs' they do, such as a food delivery or a car journey. Jobs include courier and delivery services, plumbing and minicab driving. According to a report published by the Trades Union Congress in June 2019, the gig economy has doubled in size since 2016, with gig platforms now employing one in 10 adults. Proponents of the gig economy claim that people can benefit from independence, flexible hours, with control over how much time they can work as they juggle other priorities in their lives. Most of those working in the gig economy are classed as self-employed independent contractors, which has meant that they are not viewed as workers or employees, so have no protection against unfair dismissal, no right to redundancy payments and no right to receive the national minimum wage, paid holiday or sickness pay. The 2017 Taylor Review of Modern Working Practices recommended a new category of 'dependent contractor' to cover these sorts of workers and said that they should be entitled to certain minimum basic rights. In response to a consultation carried out after the Taylor Review on employment status, the Government has said that it intends to clarify the distinction between workers and those who are self-employed.

In the meantime, there have been a number of 'gig economy' cases heard by employment tribunals, which were seeking to determine whether individuals were workers (s 230(3)) or self-employed (see eg *Dewhurst v CitySprint UK Ltd* (ET/220512/2016), *Boxer v Excel Group Services Ltd* (ET/3200365/2016) and *Aslam and Others v Uber BV* (ET/2202550/2015)).

In *Lange v Addison Lee Ltd* (ET/2208029/2016), an employment tribunal ruled that a group of Addison Lee drivers were not self-employed but were workers who were entitled to the national minimum wage and holiday pay. The EAT upheld the employment tribunal's decision. The Court of Appeal ([2021] EWCA Civ 594) refused permission to appeal from the EAT's decision and, following the approach of the Supreme Court in the *Uber* case, held that every time a driver logged on to the Addison Lee app, there was a contract in place.

In *Addison Lee Ltd v Gascoigne* (UKEAT/0289/17), the EAT upheld a tribunal's finding that a cycle courier was a worker within the meaning of reg 2 of the Working Time Regulations 1998 and s 230(3)(b) of the ERA 1996 when he was logged on to the Addison Lee app, and so was entitled to holiday pay. There was mutuality when he was logged on to the app.

In *Pimlico Plumbers Ltd v Smith* [2018] UKSC 29 (not strictly a gig economy case), the Supreme Court got to consider the issues for the first time. It held that a plumber, carrying out plumbing and maintenance work on behalf of the company, was a 'worker'. Mr Smith wore a branded uniform, drove a branded van, carried an identity card and was bound by a number of restrictive covenants regarding his working activities post-termination. The Court of Appeal ([2017] EWCA Civ 51) had previously set out the applicable principles as to the requirement for personal performance:

> Firstly, an unfettered right to substitute another person to do the work or perform the services is inconsistent with an undertaking to do so personally. Secondly, a conditional right to substitute another person may or may not be inconsistent with personal performance depending upon the conditionality. It will depend on the precise contractual arrangements and, in particular, the nature and degree of any fetter on a right of substitution or, using different language, the extent to which the right of substitution is limited or occasional. Thirdly, by way of example, a right of substitution only when the contractor is unable to carry out the work will, subject to any exceptional facts, be consistent with personal performance. Fourthly, again by way of example, a right of substitution limited only by the need to show that the substitute is as qualified as the contractor to do the work, whether or not that entails a particular procedure, will, subject to any exceptional facts, be inconsistent with personal performance. Fifthly, again by way of example, a right to substitute only with the consent of another person who has an absolute and unqualified discretion to withhold consent will be consistent with personal performance. (para 84)

The Court of Appeal held that the employment tribunal was correct to find that, on the proper interpretation of the 2009 agreement, Mr Smith undertook to provide his services personally. The express wording of the agreement between the company and Mr Smith required personal performance by Mr Smith. It provided, for example, in para 2.1 that 'You shall provide such building trade services as are within your skills'; in para 2.2 that 'You shall provide the services for such periods as may be agreed with the company ... The actual days on which you will provide the services will be agreed between you and the company ...'; in para 2.4 that 'you will be competent to perform the work which you agree to carry out', and 'you will promptly correct ... any errors in your work ...'; in para 2.5 that 'If you are unable to work due to illness or injury ... you shall notify the company'; and in para 3.9 that 'You will have personal liability for the consequences of your services to the company' (in all cases emphasis added) and that there was no express right of substitution or delegation. The Court of Appeal also found that the tribunal had legitimately found that there was an umbrella contract that placed a continuing obligation on Mr Smith to make himself available for work. In the view of the Supreme Court, the employment tribunal was entitled on the evidence to conclude that Pimlico Plumbers was not (looking at the extended definition of worker in s 230(3)(b) of the ERA 1996) a 'client or customer' of Mr Smith. See too *Chatfeild-Roberts v Phillips* (UKEAT/0049/18).

In *Uber BV v Aslam and Others* [2021] UKSC 5, the Supreme Court ruled that drivers operating through Uber's platform were workers and not self-employed contractors. Uber argued that Uber BV acted solely as a technology provider with its subsidiary (Uber London in this case) acting as a booking agent for drivers. Uber argued that, when a ride is booked through the Uber app, a contract is thereby made directly between the driver and the passenger whereby the driver agrees to provide transportation services to the passenger. Uber said that it collected payment on behalf of the driver and charged a 'service fee' to the driver for the use of its technology and other services. Uber relied on the wording of its standard written contracts between Uber BV and drivers and between the Uber companies and passengers. Uber also emphasised that drivers were free to work when they wanted and to do as much or as little as they wanted. Uber said this meant that drivers were independent contractors who worked under contracts made with customers and did not work for Uber.

The Supreme Court unanimously dismissed Uber's appeal. Lord Leggatt gave the sole judgment. He said that as there was no written contract between the drivers and Uber London, the nature of their legal relationship had to be inferred from the parties' conduct and there was no factual basis for asserting that Uber London acted as an agent for drivers. The Court said that it is wrong in principle to treat the written agreements as a starting point in deciding whether an individual is a 'worker'. A tribunal should examine the reality of the relationship between the parties and not be bound by what the documentation states. The correct inference was that Uber London contracted with passengers and engaged drivers to carry out bookings for it. The Court considered and explained its previous decision in *Autoclenz Ltd v Belcher* [2011] UKSC 41. The Court said that the purpose of the relevant employment legislation is to give protection to vulnerable individuals who have little or no say over their pay and working conditions because they are in a subordinate and dependent position in relation to a person or organisation which exercises control over their work. This legislation also precludes employers, frequently in a stronger bargaining position, from contracting out of these protections. The judgment emphasised five aspects of the findings made by the employment tribunal which it relied upon as justifying its conclusion that the claimants were working for and under contracts with Uber. Those five factors were:

(1)   Where a ride is booked through the Uber app, it is Uber that sets the fare, and drivers are not permitted to charge more than the fare calculated by the Uber app, so Uber dictates how much drivers are paid for the work they do.

(2)   The contract terms on which drivers perform their services are imposed by Uber and drivers have no say in them.

(3)   Once a driver has logged on to the Uber app, the driver's choice about whether to accept requests for rides is constrained by Uber.

(4)   Uber exercises significant control over the way in which drivers deliver their services.

(5)   Uber restricts communications between passenger and driver to the minimum necessary to perform the particular trip and takes active steps to prevent drivers from establishing any relationship with a passenger capable of extending beyond an individual ride.

Taking these factors together, the Supreme Court said that the transportation service performed by drivers and offered to passengers through the Uber app is very tightly defined and controlled by Uber. Drivers have little or no ability to improve their economic position through professional or entrepreneurial skill. In practice, the only way in which they can increase their earnings is by working longer hours. The Supreme Court also held that the employment tribunal was entitled to find that time spent by the claimants working for Uber was not limited (as Uber argued) to periods when they were actually driving passengers to their destinations, but included any period when the driver was logged onto the Uber app within the territory in which the driver was licensed to operate and was ready and willing to accept trips. The ruling therefore means that Uber drivers were entitled to the national minimum wage from the moment they switched on their app and were available to work. It also means that they were entitled to 5.6 weeks' annual leave each year and would have whistleblowing rights.

(Note that the French Court of Cassation (the highest civil court in France) ruled in March 2020 that Uber drivers were employees. It held that contractual documentation and regulatory compliance are irrelevant when a technology platform exercises tight algorithmic control: the drivers had no choice in determining their client base, terms and conditions and pay. While limited to French law, the reasoning and analysis is of interest and is in line with the 2017 ECJ preliminary decision in *Asociacion Profesional Elite Taxi* (Case C-434/15) where the Court said that Uber was not an information society service but a provider of 'a service in the field of transport'.)

Readers should also note the decision in R *(on the application of the IWGB) v CAC and Roofoods Ltd t/a Deliveroo* [2021] EWCA Civ 952, where the Court of Appeal examined a novel argument which the High Court had allowed to proceed 'with some hesitation' based around the effect of collective bargaining rights in Article 11 of the European Convention on Human Rights. In R *(IWGB) v Central Arbitration Committee* [2018] EWHC 3342 (Admin), the High Court had upheld a November 2017 CAC decision rejecting an application from the Independent Workers Union of Great Britain (IWGB) for collective bargaining rights in respect of Deliveroo riders. The

CAC held that Deliveroo drivers were not workers because they could in fact (it was found) appoint a substitute – so were under no obligation to provide services in person – and there was therefore, on the facts, no personal service, so they did not come within the 'limb (b)' definition in s 296 of the TULR(C)A 1992. This decision meant that the CAC could not proceed with IWGB's application for compulsory recognition in respect of a group of London-based Deliveroo riders. IWGB sought permission to proceed with a judicial review of the CAC's ruling on five grounds, all but one of which the High Court rejected. Following a full hearing on the Article 11 issue, the High Court dismissed the IWGB's appeal. The IWGB appealed to the Court of Appeal. The Court of Appeal focused on the question of whether Deliveroo riders were 'in an employment relationship' and concluded that they were not. The Court of Appeal noted that an obligation of personal service was an 'indispensable feature of the relationship of employer and worker' and not a 'parochial peculiarity' of UK law, and said that was equally so in the context of Article 11. It stated that the key issue was the legal relationship between the parties. The IWGB also sought to raise the potential relevance of the decision of the Supreme Court in the *Uber* case (see above). The Court of Appeal noted that that judgment had not been about personal service, because Uber drivers did not have a right to substitute. The Court noted that the High Court had refused IWGB permission to appeal against the CAC's decision on domestic law arguments such as those considered in the *Uber* case, and concluded that the IWGB's arguments on *Uber* were of limited relevance. It did, however, note that, while applying the *Uber* decision to the facts determined by the CAC would not be straightforward, Deliveroo riders' right of substitution meant that the 'inevitable result' was that the appeal had to fail. In the *Pimlico Plumbers* case (above), the Supreme Court had noted that the 'sole test' in deciding whether someone was a worker was whether there was an obligation of personal performance, and any other test would be an 'inappropriate usurpation' of this. This decision of the Court of Appeal held that where there is a clear and genuine right of substitution, that is determinative. The IWGB was refused permission to appeal to the Supreme Court. However, following the judgment of HHJ Tayler in *Sejpal v Rodericks Dental Ltd* [2022] EAT 91 (see **1.3.3** above), that is in doubt. HHJ Tayer stated:

> It is arguable, post *Uber*, and the focus on statutory interpretation that is now expressly required, that there could be a situation in which despite there being a contractual term that provides an unfettered right of substitution, the reality is that the predominant purpose of the agreement is personal service, so that the person is a worker. It might even be argued that personal service need not be the predominant purpose of the agreement, provided that the true agreement is for the provision of 'any' personal service as required by the statute.

In September 2019, an employment tribunal in Watford referred a number of questions concerning the status of Yodel couriers to the CJEU. One of those questions related to whether a contractual right to use a substitute is fatal to a finding of 'worker' status under the Working Time Regulations 1998. In April 2020, the CJEU issued a 'reasoned order' (Case C-692/19) that where a contractor is genuinely independent and is not subordinate, they are not entitled to holiday pay under the Directive. However, an independent contractor can be a worker if their independence is fictitious. The case will now return to the Watford employment tribunal for a determination on the facts.

While cases in this area will always be fact specific, there is an increasing line of authority emerging that those working in the gig economies, even where technologically novel working practices are used, will more often than not be found to be, at a minimum, workers (with some employment rights) rather than self-employed independent contractors (with none). See *Stuart Delivery Ltd v Augustine* [2021] EWCA Civ 1514 for a decision of the Court of Appeal in a gig economy case, where a moped courier with a very limited power of substitution was held to be a worker.

As noted at **1.3.3**, HHJ Tayler set out a detailed review of the 'worker' case law in *Sejpal*. Readers are advised to read the case.

Zero hours contracts

'Zero hours contracts can be a positive part of work–life balance if they offer genuine two-way flexibility', according to the 2017 Taylor Review of Modern Working Practices.

There is no legal definition of a zero hours contract. If they are freely entered into, they are not illegal under UK domestic law. In a Private Member's Bill introduced by MP Andy Sawford in 2013, the following definition of a zero hours contract was included:

> (1)   A zero hours contract is a contract or arrangement for the provision of labour, which— (a) fails to specify guaranteed working hours, ...

A typical contractual wording might read: 'We are under no obligation to provide work to you at any time and you are under no obligation to accept any work offered by us at any time.'

Zero hours contracts are essentially any contract where an individual works with no stipulation as to minimum hours of work or pay, and often no stipulation about the manner of the work. The individual will only be paid for the hours they actually work. The zero hours label serves, however, as shorthand for a large body of people who work at the unregulated margins of the UK's workforce under a variety of contractual and non-contractual arrangements. Historically, these arrangements were prevalent in areas of female workers and industries such as construction, fishing and docking, but more recently in food service and care, as well as the gig economy cases discussed above. Terms such as 'on call', 'reserve', 'bank', 'casuals', 'regular causals' and 'key-time' intermingle with the more traditional binary and tripartite delineations of employees, workers and the self-employed (or freelance).

In the UK Labour Force Survey (LFS) for the period December 2017 to February 2018, just over 900,000 people or about 2.8% of the workforce said that they were on a zero hours contract. The Business Survey indicated that, as at November 2017, employers said they had issued 1.8 million 'non-guaranteed hours contracts' (NGHCs). The number of contracts actually issued is likely to be larger than this, because, for example, some people will hold more than one such contract. The LFS statistics show that the number of people reporting zero hours did not change much between 2000 and 2012, but from 2012 onwards, the numbers increased rapidly – rising two and half times between 2012 and 2016, from 0.8% of the workforce to 2.8%. The Business Survey figures suggest a 22% increase in contracts issued between 2014 and 2017.

There are often negative concerns around zero hours contracts, including lower earnings, difficulties for planning finances due to the variability of earnings, lack of employment rights and security, and that the choice to turn down work is often in reality 'illusory'. On the other hand, others emphasise the positives that come from the flexibility and lack of ties for both employers and those working under such arrangements.

Trying to analyse and apply legal protections to those on zero hours contracts using the traditional binary or tripartite scheme of employees, workers and the self employed creates difficulties. The absence of any stipulation as to minimum hours and the absence of any future commitment will generally be regarded as indicative of an absence of mutuality of obligations (see eg *Nethermere (St Neots) Ltd v Gardiner and Another* [1984] ICR 612, *Carmichael* (above) and *O'Kelly v Trust House Forte plc* [1983] IRLR 369) and so presents a serious impediment for anyone seeking to argue that there is an employment or even a worker relationship between the parties.

The recent Court of Appeal case of *Nursing and Midwifery Council v Somerville* (above) offers some helpful guidance in a situation where someone is on a zero hours or casual contract, especially where there is no minimum commitment expected of the worker. The claimant sat as a panel member for the Nursing & Midwifery Council (NMC) on its Fitness to Practise panels and brought a claim for unpaid statutory holiday pay. The employment tribunal held that he was a worker within the meaning of s 230(3)(b) of the ERA 1996 and reg 2(1) of the Working Time Regulations 1998 (and so was entitled to holiday pay). The tribunal found that there were a series of individual contracts between the parties each time the claimant agreed to sit on a hearing, for which the NMC agreed to pay him a fee, and that there was also an overarching contract between them in relation to the provision of his services as a panel member. In rejecting his alternative contention that he was an employee under a contract of service, the tribunal decided that there was no irreducible minimum of obligation, as the claimant was not obliged to offer a minimum amount of sitting dates and he was free to withdraw from dates he had accepted. The NMC appealed the conclusion that the claimant was a worker on the basis that an absence of mutuality of obligation in the sense of an absence of an irreducible minimum of obligation was incompatible with a finding of worker status. Following a review of the authorities including the Supreme Court's decision in *Uber*, the EAT found that an irreducible minimum of obligation in the sense relied upon by the NMC was not a prerequisite for satisfying the definitions of worker status, in circumstances where an overarching contract existed between the parties under which the individual agreed to perform services personally and had done so in respect of a series of separate contracts. The absence of an irreducible minimum of obligation could be relevant to the question of whether the client/customer exception applied, but it was not necessarily fatal to a conclusion of worker status. The Court of Appeal upheld that conclusion.

Even if each single individual arrangement could be said to fulfill the s 230 ERA 1996 definition, the difficulty in establishing any sort of global or umbrella contract may mean that there is insufficient continuity to fall within many of the statutory protections. In some instances where the traditional analysis creates obvious difficulties, the courts have started to look at the 'reality' of the arrangement (see for example Lord Hoffman in *Carmichael* ([1999] 1 WLR 2042 at 2050G); Langstaff J in *Cotswold Developments Construction Ltd v Williams* (UKEAT/ 0457/05), where he expressed concern that courts may have misunderstood that mutuality does not deprive the existence of an underlying contract where an employee has the right to refuse work or an employer to withhold it; the Supreme Court in *Autoclenz* (above), giving effect to the parties' 'actual legal obligations'; and *Pulse Healthcare Ltd v Carewatch Care Services Ltd* (UKEAT 0123/12) where the contractual agreement was found not to reflect the true agreement between the parties). In *Haggerty* (above), the EAT found that while there was a zero hours contract, there were 'mutual obligations subsisting between the employer and the employee during the periods when the employee, as a casual worker, was not actually engaged on any particular shift'. This was based on a finding of a long and well-established regular work pattern. It is therefore possible that a zero hours contract could be classified as one of employment, although there may be complications around continuity of service in terms of access to certain rights (see eg *Stephenson and Prater* (above) and *McMeechan v Secretary of State for Employment* [1997] IRLR 353). Even where a zero hours worker is not an employee, they may still be (as indeed the recent gig economy cases indicate) a worker and therefore still have access to some statutory rights in terms of holiday pay, minimum wage legislation etc.

The Taylor Review recommended that individuals working under zero hours contracts who have been in post for 12 months should have the right to request a contract that guarantees hours which better reflect the hours worked. It also suggested that companies beyond a certain size should be required to report on how many such requests they receive, and how many they agree to. In 2019 the Government consulted on measures to address one-sided flexibility. However, in May 2022, the Government announced that Matt Warman MP is to lead another 'Future of Work' review which will be conducted over spring and summer 2022.

1.3.4 Other relevant qualifying definitions

Although the definitions of 'employee' and 'worker' contained in s 230(1) and (3) of the ERA 1996 are the most common definitions of those terms (see **1.3.2** and **1.3.3**), it is important nonetheless to check what definition is relevant to any particular legislation. Set out below are two areas where wider definitions appear.

1.3.4.1 Public Interest Disclosure Act 1998

So far as a claim under the Public Interest Disclosure Act 1998 (PIDA 1998) is concerned (see **5.5.5**), workers have a right not to be subjected to a detriment on the grounds that they have made a protected disclosure (ERA 1996, s 47B). Employees will be regarded as unfairly dismissed if the principal reason for their dismissal is that they made a protected disclosure (ERA 1996, s 103A). Workers who are dismissed for making a protected disclosure must complain, however, that dismissal is a detriment (ERA 1996, s 47B(2)). Different compensation regimes apply: under s 49(6) of the ERA 1996, workers cannot get more than if they had brought a successful unfair dismissal claim. 'Worker' is given an extended definition beyond the standard definition in s 230(3) of the ERA (see s 43K of the ERA 1996). In particular, the definition is extended to cover agency workers (s 43K(1)(a)), and covers those who would be defined as a worker within s 230(3) if the words 'personally or otherwise' were substituted for 'personally' in s 230(3)(b) (see above) (s 43K(1)(b)). Section 43K(2) contains an extended definition of 'employer'. It provides that with regard to agency and similar workers, 'employer' includes the person who substantially determines the terms on which those workers were engaged. The *Clyde & Co* case referred to at **1.3.3** above was a public interest disclosure case.

Section 43K was considered by the EAT in *Croke v Hydro Aluminium Worcester Ltd* [2007] ICR 1303. The EAT concluded that in construing the definition of 'worker' in s 43K, it was appropriate to adopt a purposive approach. Accordingly, where an individual supplied his services to an employment agency through his own company, and the employment agency, in turn, provided the services of that company to an end-user, it may be that in appropriate circumstances the individual is a 'worker' of the end-user for the purposes of s 43K. (See also on this area *Keppel Seghers UK Ltd v Hinds* (UKEAT/0019/14).)

Following *Clyde & Co v Bates* (see **1.3.3**), partners in LLPs can be workers, and accordingly, while they do not have unfair dismissal rights, they do have protection against being subjected to a detriment. In *McTigue v University Hospital Bristol NHS Foundation Trust* (EAT/0354/15) the EAT confirmed that some agency workers come within s 43K(1)(a).

The Court of Appeal considered s 43K in *Day v Lewisham & Greenwich NHS Trust* [2017] EWCA Civ 329. The Court held that words should be read into s 43K to exclude a claim by an employee or worker falling within s 230(3) but allow a claim by the same person under s 43K against a different respondent. In this case a doctor has brought a claim against the Trust and Health Education England (HEE) (a training body). The EAT had upheld the employment tribunal's decision that he was precluded from bringing a claim against the HEE because the Trust was his employer under s 230(3). The Court of Appeal decided that the doctor fell within s 43K notwithstanding his worker relationship with the Trust.

1.3.4.2 Discrimination legislation

By s 83(2) of the Equality Act 2010:

> 'Employment' means ... employment under a contract of employment, a contract of apprenticeship or a contract personally to do work ...

This definition applies to discrimination which is 'because of' any of the protected characteristics (see **Chapter 8**). It is similar, but not identical to the wording that appeared in the old legislation (for example SDA 1975, s 82(1); RRA 1976, s 78; DDA 1995, s 68).

The definition clearly covers employees and workers, and it also extends to individuals who are self-employed, provided that their 'employment' contract obliges them to perform the work personally: in other words, if they are not permitted to sub-contract any part of the work.

The ECJ held in *Allonby v Accrington and Rossendale College* (Case C-256/01) [2004] ICR 1328 that 'the term worker ... cannot be defined by reference to the legislation of the Member States but has a Community meaning. Moreover, it cannot be interpreted restrictively.' It went on to hold that under European law a worker is a person who, for a certain period of time performs services for and under the direction of another person in return for which he receives remuneration, but that the authors of the EC Treaty did not intend the term 'worker', within the meaning of Article 141(1) EC (now Article 157(1) TFEU), to include independent providers of services who are not in a relationship of subordination with the person who receives the services. The question whether such a relationship exists must be answered, said the ECJ, in each particular case having regard to all the factors and circumstances by which the relationship between the parties is characterised.

The UK courts have emphasised that the important question is to ascertain what the dominant objective of the contract was. The Court of Appeal in *Mirror Group Newspapers Ltd v Gunning* [1986] IRLR 27 said the key question was whether the dominant purpose of the contract in that case was the personal execution of any work or labour. It held that the words 'a contract personally to execute any work or labour' (in the extended definition of 'employment' in the SDA 1975, s 82(1)) contemplated a contract the dominant purpose of which is that the party contracting to provide services under it performs personally the work or labour which forms the subject matter of the contract. In *Gunning*, a contract for the distribution of newspapers was not to be considered an 'employment' contract under the discrimination legislation. The dominant purpose of the contract was to secure effective distribution of the paper.

However, according to the Supreme Court in *Jivraj v Hashwani* [2011] UKSC 40, the dominant purpose test is not the key test. The focus must be on the contract and the relationship between the parties. Lord Clarke emphasised the words in the statute 'employment under', and held that

> [an arbitrator's] role is not one of employment under a contract personally to do work. Although an arbitrator may be providing services for the purposes of VAT and he of course receives fees for his work, and although he renders personal services which he cannot delegate, he does not perform those services or earn his fees for and under the direction of the parties as contemplated in ... *Allonby*. He is rather in the category of an independent provider of services who is not in a relationship of subordination with the parties who receive his services ...

An arbitrator appointed by the parties to a dispute was not therefore a worker within the meaning of the discrimination legislation.

In *Secretary of State for Justice v Windle* [2016] EWCA Civ 459, the Court of Appeal held that the claimants did not satisfy the extended definition of employee in s 83(2) of the Equality Act 2010. The claimants were interpreters engaged on an 'as and when' basis to provide interpretation services in courts. They were not obliged to accept work and there was no requirement that they be offered work. It was argued that they were under 'a contract personally to do work'. Underhill LJ said that the test for 'a contract personally to do work' is the same as the test for 'workers' (see **1.3.2**) and agreed with the reasoning in *Quashie v Stringfellows Restaurant* [2012] EWCA Civ 1735 (which found that there was insufficient mutuality of obligation for a lap dancer to be an employee of the club where she worked). The Court decided that although mutuality of obligation between assignments is not a strict requirement for the purposes of meeting the extended definition of 'employee', it is something that can be taken into account. Underhill LJ said:

> [I]t does not follow that the absence of mutuality of obligation outside that period [of the assignment] may not influence, or shed light on, the character of the relationship within it. It seems to me a matter of common sense and common experience that the fact that a person supplying services is only doing so on an assignment-by-assignment basis may tend to indicate a degree of independence, or lack of subordination, in the relationship while at work which is incompatible with the employee status even in the extended sense [under the Equality Act 2010].

Windle was applied in *Capita Translation v Siauciunas* (UKEAT/0181/16). Mr Siauciunas was an interpreter registered with Capita working within the HM Courts Service via a framework agreement to provide his services on an assignment by assignment basis. In considering his status for a discrimination claim, the employment tribunal found that he was an 'employee', applying s 83(2), because he personally provided services and because it held, applying the EAT decision in *Windle*, that a lack of obligation between assignments for Capita to provide work to him and for him to accept work was not relevant. After the employment tribunal's judgment, the Court of Appeal overturned the EAT's decision in *Windle*. Capita's appeal succeeded, following the Court of Appeal in *Windle* that a lack of mutuality of obligation between assignments was relevant when determining employment status. Offers for work could be, and on the facts were, declined, and Mr Siauciunas had never committed himself or been obliged to commit himself to work exclusively for Capita. The case was remitted to a new employment tribunal for further factual investigation.

It seems to the authors that to consider whether there is mutuality of obligation between assignments when determining extended employee 'worker' status seriously undermines the reach of the extended definition of employee in s 83(2) and does not sit well with, for example, the *Uber*, *Pimlico Plumbers* and *Somerville* cases (see **1.3.3** above). *Windle* was not referred to in *Somerville*. Permission to appeal in the *Windle* case was declined, so the case remains, however, as a binding precedent. For the time being, however, the hurdle for proving 'employee' status in the wider s 83(2) sense may be higher than proving worker status under s 230(3) of the ERA 1996 because of *Windle*. The Supreme Court did not need to decide the point in *Pimlico Plumbers*.

Note that s 41 of the Equality Act also protects contract workers from being discriminated against by their principals, ie the client who engages them. Such workers may also be separately protected from discrimination by the agency they work for (if it is their employer) (see s 39 and **8.12**). Sections 44 and 45 protect partners.

For a pre-Equality Act 2010 decision on the meaning of 'contract worker' in discrimination legislation, see *Leeds City Council v Woodhouse* [2010] IRLR 625. There, the Court of Appeal held that an employee of an 'arm's-length' management organisation (which carried out property management for Leeds Council) was a contract worker of the Council.

1.3.5 Apprenticeship

In *Thorpe v Dul, Brooksby Melton College and Learning Skills Council* [2003] ICR 1556, the EAT held that a 'modern' apprenticeship, ie one established under a government-funded scheme, is not a contract of employment, and therefore modern apprentices are not automatically protected by unfair dismissal and other statutory rights. However, the EAT also said that there could also be, on the facts in any case, in addition to the apprenticeship, a contract of employment (see, for example, *Bowes v Hambleton District Council* (ET/2500475/16), where a trainee solicitor succeeded with a complaint of unfair dismissal).

The current statutory scheme for apprenticeships in England and Wales is set out in the Apprenticeships, Skills, Children and Learning Act (ASCLA) 2009. At common law, a contract of apprenticeship was a common law creation distinct from a contract of employment. These 'traditional' apprenticeships have been almost completely replaced by apprenticeships governed by the ASCLA regime. Apprenticeship agreements under the ASCLA 2009 are expressly given (s 35) the status of contracts of service, not the (traditional) status of contracts of apprenticeship. This means that ASCLA apprentices are entitled to all of the same employment rights and protections as an employee. There is a special apprenticeship rate of the national minimum wage (£3.90 per hour as at 1 April 2019).

For a case examining contracts of apprenticeship, see *Commissioners for HMRC v Jones and Others T/A Holmescales Riding Centre* (UKEAT/0458/13).

For readers interested in more information about apprenticeships, there was a very useful article looking at both traditional common law apprenticeships and modern arrangements established under statutory schemes in the IDS Employment Law Brief 1002 (August 2014).

1.3.6   Agency workers

Much of the detail in relation to the status of agency workers is beyond the scope of this book, but this is always a developing area of law (see eg *Franks v Reuters and Another* [2003] IRLR 423, CA; *Dacas v Brook Street Bureau (UK) Ltd* [2004] IRLR 358, CA; *Astbury v Gist Ltd* [2007] All ER (D) 480, *Bunce v Skyblue* [2005] IRLR 557, CA and *RNLI v Bushaway* [2005] IRLR 674; *Cable & Wireless plc v Muscat* [2006] IRLR 354, CA). Agency workers may be employees of the agency, or of the end-user or of neither (see eg *National Grid Transmission plc v Wood* [2007] All ER (D) 358).

In *Dacas* (above), endorsed in *Muscat* (above), the Court of Appeal directed tribunals always to consider the possibility of an implied employment contract between an agency worker and client (or end-user) where there is a triangular relationship between the agency worker, agency and end-user.

The Court of Appeal offered the following guidance to tribunals on when a contract of employment should be implied between the worker and the end-user:

(a)   Where the arrangements between agency, agency worker and end-user are genuine and reflect the actual working relationship – such as where there was no pre-existing employment relationship between the agency, worker and end-user – then it will be a rare case in which the evidence justifies the tribunal implying a contract. Such evidence would need to show that the agency worker is working pursuant to mutual obligations with the end-user, and that these obligations are incompatible with the agency arrangement.

(b)   The mere passage of time does not in itself justify the implication of a contract on the ground of necessity. Something more is required to show that it is necessary to imply a contract.

(c)   It would be more readily open to a tribunal to infer a contract where, as in *Muscat*, the agency arrangement had been superimposed on a pre-existing employment relationship between worker and end-user, although, strictly speaking, the tribunal would be finding that the agency arrangements did not bring the original contract to an end.

The Court of Appeal's view is that whether a contract of employment should be implied between an agency worker and an end-user is a question of fact for the tribunal.

See also *Protectacoat Firthglow Ltd v Szilagyi* [2009] IRLR 365 and the Court of Appeal decision in *Autoclenz Ltd v Belcher* [2010] IRLR 70 (confirmed by the Supreme Court) at **1.3.2** above.

It was hoped that the Court of Appeal would take the opportunity to consider some of the various and conflicting agency decisions when *James v Greenwich Borough Council* [2008] IRLR 302 came before it on appeal. However, Mummery LJ asserted that 'there is no significant difference between the law stated and applied in the decisions of this court and in those of the EAT. It is apparently thought in some quarters that they are in conflict. I do not think so.'

Ms James had a 'Temporary Worker Agreement' with an employment agency, which found her a position as a housing support worker with Greenwich Council. After several years the Council replaced her with another worker supplied by the agency. In response to her claim for unfair dismissal, the Council disputed her legal status as an employee. She was paid by the agency following receipt by the agency from her of completed weekly timesheets. The tribunal found that the Council's Disciplinary Procedure and Grievance Policy did not apply to Ms James and that she was not entitled to benefit from the Council's sick pay or holiday pay provisions applicable to employees. The decisions of both the tribunal and the EAT were that she was not employed by the Council under a contract of service. The Court of Appeal held that the 'real issue' in agency worker cases is whether a contract should be implied between the worker and the end-user in a tripartite situation of worker, agency and end-user, rather than whether the irreducible minimum of mutual obligation exists. Mutuality is important in deciding whether a contract that has been concluded is a contract of employment or some other kind of contract. The correct approach is for an employment tribunal to decide – as a question of fact – whether, applying common law principles, it is necessary to imply a contractual relationship between the agency worker and the end-user client. In many cases, agency workers will fall outside the scope of protection because neither the workers nor the end-users are in any kind of express contractual relationship with each other and it is not necessary to imply one in order to explain the work undertaken by the worker for the end-user. The Court of Appeal held that the EAT in *James* had not erred in holding that the circumstances did not exist which could justify the inference of an implied contract. The provision of work by the local authority, its payments to the agency, and the performance of the work by Ms James were all explained by their respective express contracts with the agency, so it was not necessary to imply the existence of another contract in order to give business reality to the relationship between the parties. The Court of Appeal expressly approved the guidance given in paras 53–61 of the EAT's decision, and readers advising on this topic should therefore also read the EAT's judgment.

Muschett v HM Prison Service [2010] EWCA Civ 25 is yet another example of the difficulties of establishing a contractual relationship between an agency worker and the end-user. The Court of Appeal emphasised that in tripartite arrangements a contract could only be implied between the agency worker and the end-user where it was necessary to do so to reflect the business reality of the situation. To find necessity, it required evidence from which a tribunal could conclude that the agency relationship no longer adequately reflected how the work was actively being performed. The Court of Appeal in this case said the 'meagre collection of facts' relied upon by the claimant could not justify making a finding that the claimant was an employee.

In *Tilson v Alstom Transport* [2010] EWCA Civ 1038, the Court of Appeal was again reluctant to imply a contractual relationship between the agency worker and the end-user. In this case, the ongoing relationship was conducted on the basis that no contract of employment existed (on two occasions, Alstom asked Mr Tilson to become an employee but on each occasion he declined because he preferred to be an independent contractor); and even though there was evidence of a significant degree of integration of an agency worker into an organisation (Mr Tilson was supervised by Alstom's managers and had to apply to his line manager to take holiday; he also supervised Alstom staff), the court held that that was not inconsistent with an agency relationship in which there is no contract between worker and end-user. The Court of Appeal also held that the need to apply to a line manager before taking annual leave was not sufficient to justify the implication of a contract. This case reinforces the position that while it is not impossible to find an employment contract between an agency worker and the end-user (see, for an example, *McMeechan v Secretary of State for Employment* [1997] ICR 549), a contract of employment will not be implied where it is not necessary to do so to explain a working relationship. In many such cases, the 'irreducible minimum' requirement for an employment contract – mutuality of obligation and control exercised by the employer – will not be met. It is also likely that deduction of National Insurance and PAYE in such situations will be regarded as a neutral factor (since ss 44–47 of the Income Tax (Earnings and Pensions) Act 2003 necessitate it). Elias LJ said in *Smith v Carillion (JM) Ltd* [2015] EWCA Civ 209 that 'it is not against public policy for a contractor to obtain services this way, even when the purpose is to avoid legal obligations ... A contract cannot be implied merely because the court disapproves of the employer's conduct.' The only exception may be where there is evidence that both parties have deliberately entered into a sham arrangement to prevent a relationship of employer and employee from arising (see too *BIS v Studders* (UKEAT/0571/10)).

It should be remembered, of course, that even if the agency worker is not an employee, he may still benefit from some protections, eg the anti-discrimination legislation (see **1.3.4.2**), national minimum wage legislation and working time legislation (see, for example, *Electronic Data Systems Ltd v Hanbury and Brook Street Bureau* (UKEAT/128/00)), as a worker.

1.3.6.1   Agency Workers Regulations 2010

Following the coming into force of the EC Directive on conditions for temporary (agency) work (Directive 2008/104/EC) in December 2008, the Agency Workers Regulations 2010 (SI 2010/93), as amended by SI 2011/1941 and SI 2019/724, came into force on 1 October 2011. The Regulations create a right for agency workers to receive the same basic terms and conditions as if they had been directly recruited by the end-user. The detail is beyond the scope of this book. However, a short summary appears below.

The Regulations provide that agency workers (defined as individuals having a contract of employment with the agency or a contract with the agency to perform work and services temporarily) will have equal access to facilities (such as canteen, childcare facilities, vacancy lists etc) and information on job vacancies as direct employees of the end-user from day 1. Otherwise, for the more detailed requirements, such as equal treatment in terms of pay and other basic working conditions (annual leave, rest breaks, rest periods, duration of working time, length of night work – and pregnant agency workers must be allowed to take paid time off for ante-natal appointments), there is a 12-week qualifying period, so short-term agency temps will not qualify for these rights. The 12 weeks do not have to be continuous; there can be breaks between assignments and absences on grounds of, say, sickness or jury service.

The number of hours that the worker has worked during the reference period is calculated differently depending on the type of work done by the worker.

There are four types of work:

(a)   time work;

(b)   salaried hours work;

(c)   output work;

(d)   unmeasured work.

The rules vary according to the type of work done, and readers should consult the Regulations for the detail. For example, lunch breaks will not count as hours worked for time workers but will count for salaried hours workers if they form part of the workers' basic minimum hours under the contract.

In May 2011, the BIS published Guidance on the Agency Workers Regulations 2010. The Guidance seeks to assist in interpreting the Regulations and gives illustrations in relation to issues such as:

•   Who is an agency worker?

•   What terms and conditions are covered by the requirement of equal treatment?

•   Is a comparator needed?

•   How to calculate the 12-week qualifying period

•   Who will be responsible if the Regulations are breached?

There have been relatively few reported cases on the Regulations. See, for example, *Bray v Monarch Personnel Refuelling (UK) Ltd* (ET/1801581/12), *Moran v Ideal Cleaning Services Ltd* [2014] IRLR 172, *Stevens v Northolt High School* (ET/3300621/2014) and *Coles v Ministry of Defence* (UKEAT/0403/14).

In *Kocur v Angard Staffing Solutions Ltd and Another* [2019] EWCA Civ 1185, the Court of Appeal held that the Regulations do not entitle agency workers to work the same number of contractual hours as a comparator. See also the separate but related case of *Angard Staffing Solutions Ltd and Another v Kocur* (UKEAT/0105/19), where the EAT said that reg 13 did not entitle agency workers to apply and be considered for internal vacancies on the same terms as directly recruited employees. The EAT held that this is a right to be notified of the vacancies on the same basis as directly recruited employees, and a right to be given the same level of information about the vacancies as the directly recruited employees, but it does not create a right to be entitled to apply for and be considered for such vacancies. The EAT also looked in this case at the application and effect of reg 5 which entitles agency workers to the same basic working and employment conditions as they would be entitled to had they been directly recruited. The Court of Appeal upheld the decision in *Kocur v Angard Staffing Solutions Ltd* [2022] EWCA Civ 189.

The Court of Appeal gave some useful guidance on apportioning liability for a breach of the Regulations between agency and hirer in *London Underground v Amissah* [2019] IRLR 545.

In *Brooknight Guarding Ltd v Matei* (UKEAT/0309/17), the EAT held that a security guard employed on a zero hours contract was not a permanent employee but was an agency worker under the Regulations. As a result, he was entitled to the same terms and conditions as a comparable employee.

One of the changes proposed by the Government as part of its 'Good Work Plan' (see **Introduction**) was for what is known as the 'Swedish derogation' within the Agency Worker Regulations 2010 to be abolished. The 'Swedish derogation' (regs 10 and 11) permitted a special type of employment contract which allowed for guaranteed pay between gaps in assignments in return for giving up pay parity with permanent staff (see for example *Twenty-four Seven Recruitment Services Ltd v Alfonso* (UKEAT/0311/17)). Government estimates were that as many of 130,000 people were engaged on such contracts. The Taylor Review recommended that the derogation be abolished – the rationale being that this would encourage more employers to take on permanent employees, so providing greater security and certainty. The Agency Worker (Amendment) Regulations 2019 (SI 2019/724) effected this change, which came into force on 6 April 2020. They mean that all agency workers will be entitled to pay parity. From 30 April 2020, all temporary worker agencies must provide workers whose contracts contain a Swedish derogation provision with a written statement telling them that those provisions will no longer apply. Workers asserting their rights under the new Regulations will be protected from detriment and unfair dismissal.

Given that this is a complex and developing area, readers should always ensure that they look at the most up-to-date case law on this topic.

1.3.7 Other categories

In *The New Testament Church of God v Stewart* [2007] IRLR 178, the presumption that all ministers were office holders and not employees was successfully challenged. The Court of Appeal upheld the EAT's decision that a Christian minister was an employee of his church. In *The President of the Methodist Conference v Preston* [2013] UKSC 29, the Supreme Court said that a Methodist minister was not an employee for the purposes of an unfair dismissal claim. Baroness Hale dissented, saying that 'it quacks like a duck and swims like a duck'. The majority, after consideration of the internal arrangements of the Methodist Church, concluded that there was no intention to create legal relations in such cases. The Court of Appeal upheld an employment tribunal decision that there was no contract between a Church of England rector and the Bishop because the relationship was governed by ecclesiastical law and was not a contractual arrangement (*Sharpe v Bishop of Worcester* [2015] EWCA Civ 399). It is clear that each case will depend on its facts. See *Gilham v Ministry of Justice* [2017] EWCA Civ 2220 for a useful discussion of the case law on clergy (although the case concerned a judge) – the Supreme Court has overturned the Court of Appeal's decision (see **1.3.3**).

In *X v Mid Sussex Citizens Advice Bureau* [2013] IRLR 146, the Supreme Court held that the Equal Treatment Framework Directive (2000/78) did not cover a volunteer at a Citizens Advice Bureau, at least when the volunteer's activity was not undertaken pursuant to a contract (and so did not fall within the expanded definition of 'employment' in discrimination legislation; s 83 of the Equality Act 2010, see **1.3.4.2**). The Supreme Court identified nine reasons for rejecting the argument that voluntary activity was covered by the Directive, based around a careful textual analysis of the language used in the Framework Directive, including its French version.

In *Gladwell v Secretary of State for Trade and Industry* [2007] ICR 264, EAT, the EAT held that the fact that a claimant was a company director with a shareholding of 50% did not preclude him from being an employee. Mr Justice Elias commented, 'a majority shareholder will in practice act as the employer, making decisions on behalf of the company, but that does not prevent him being an employee'.

In *Secretary of State for BERR v Neufeld* [2009] EWCA Civ 280, the Court of Appeal had to determine whether a controlling shareholder of a company could also be an employee. Mr Neufeld claimed to have been an employee (under ERA 1996, s 230) of the company for which he worked. The company was insolvent and he claimed that he was entitled as an employee to a payment from the Secretary of State under s 182 of the ERA 1996 (which provides that employees of insolvent employers can recover certain debts from the National Insurance Fund, including up to eight weeks' arrears of pay, notice pay and a basic award in an unfair dismissal claim). He was a controlling shareholder and a director of the company. The tribunal held that Mr Neufeld was not an employee, but the EAT reversed that finding. The Court of Appeal, after reviewing the authorities, confirmed that the leading case on employees, shareholders and directors was *Secretary of State for Trade and Industry v Bottrill* [1999] ICR 592, and that being a controlling shareholder was one factor that had to be taken into account when deciding, in all the circumstances, whether a person was an employee or not, but that there is no reason in principle why a person who was a shareholder and director of a company could not also be an employee of the company under a contract of employment, even if that person had a controlling interest in, or even total control of, the company.

The Court of Appeal in *Neufeld* approved, in essence, the approach taken by the EAT in *Clark v (1) Clark Construction Initiatives Ltd (2) Utility Consultancy Services Ltd* (UKEAT/0225/07). In that case the EAT concluded that 'what we have to do is to look at the whole picture, which we have done. We should balance out all the factors and make a reasoned conclusion'. The EAT listed three circumstances (although not exhaustive ones) in which it said it might be possible for a tribunal to see through what was on its face a legitimate employment contract:

(a)   where the company is itself a sham (ie it is the *alter ego* of the individual) – this would be an 'exceptional' case;

(b)   where the contract was entered into for an ulterior purpose, eg to secure a redundancy payment from the Secretary of State;

(c)   where the parties do not conduct their relationship in accordance with the contract, either because:

    (i)   they never intended to, or

    (ii)   the relationship in practice has ceased to reflect the contractual terms.

The EAT then listed a number of other factors which it said would need to be considered when deciding whether to give effect to the contract.

The Court of Appeal held, on the facts, that Mr Neufeld was an employee. The Court summed up the position as follows:

> In a case in which no allegation of sham is raised, or in which the claimant proves that no question of sham arises, the question ... for the court or tribunal will be whether the claimed contract amounts to a true contract of employment. ... [G]iven that the critical question in cases such as those under appeal is as to whether the putative employee was an employee at the time of the company's insolvency, it will or may be necessary to inquire into what has been done under the claimed contract: there will or may therefore need to be the like inquiry as in cases in which an allegation of sham is made. In order for the employee to make good his case, it may well be insufficient merely to place reliance on a written contract made, say, five years earlier. The tribunal will want to know that the claimed contract, perhaps as subsequently varied, was still in place at the time of the insolvency. In a case in which the alleged contract is not in writing, or is only in brief form, it is obvious that it will usually be necessary to inquire into how the parties have conducted themselves under it.

See also *Stack v Ajar-Tec Ltd* [2015] EWCA Civ 46, where the Court upheld an employment tribunal decision that a director and shareholder who performed part-time work for the respondent company without pay for three years was an employee and a worker. See *Department for Employment and Learning v Morgan* [2016] IRLR 350 and *Dugdale v DDE Law Ltd* (UKEAT/0169/16) for two decisions applying *Neufield*.

1.4 THE CONTRACT OF EMPLOYMENT

The general common law provisions that apply to any assessment of whether a binding and legally enforceable contract exists (ie offer, acceptance, certainty, intention to create legal relations, consideration) apply equally to employment contracts (see *MacInnes v Gross* [2017] EWHC 46 (QB)). Generally, courts adopt an objective approach to interpreting contracts, including employment contracts, but in doing so they rely on a number of 'tools' in order to assess the objective meaning – including the language and commercial implications. Where contracts have been drafted or negotiated by professionals, there may be more willingness to rely on textual analysis, but where contracts are informal or brief or lack skilled professional input, or there is inequality of bargaining position, courts may place greater emphasis on the factual matrix (see eg *Wood v Capita Insurance Services Ltd* [2017] UKSC 24).

Parties to an employment relationship will often, but not always, put the terms and conditions that govern that relationship into writing. However, there is no legal requirement for the contract of employment to be in writing. It may be written, oral or a mixture of both. In some circumstances the court will imply a contract of employment (see, eg, *Dacas v Brook Street Bureau (UK) Ltd* (**1.3.6**)). Where there is no written contract of employment, the law requires employers to provide what is known as a written statement of terms to their employees. In the absence of any written contract, the written statement should set out some minimum details about the terms governing the employment relationship.

Even where there is a written contract that sets out the express terms which govern the relationship, the courts will in certain situations imply additional terms into that contract (see **1.5**). This section and those following consider the written statement of terms, some of the terms which may be implied into a contract of employment, including the regulation of working time and minimum wage legislation, and the principal terms which should be considered for express inclusion in a written contract, including restrictive covenants. The protection of wages is addressed in **1.11**.

Readers should note the Contracts (Rights of Third Parties) Act 1999. The full operation of the Act is beyond the scope of this book, but in outline, the Act reforms the doctrine of privity of contract but expressly provides that no rights are conferred on a third party to enforce any term of an employment contract against an employee. However, the Act does not prevent third parties from enforcing relevant contractual terms against the employer where, for example, the terms of the contract purport to confer a benefit on a third party, eg a company car. The Act must be considered when drafting employment contracts or compromise agreements (see **6.5**).

Where the employer and the employee have agreed the terms of their contract, those terms cannot be changed without both parties agreeing to the changes. In other words, employers cannot unilaterally change the terms and conditions of the contract without possible consequences (see **1.9** below).

It is important for employers to make sure that employees sign their contracts, that the employer keeps copies of signed contracts, as well as any revisions that are agreed to (which may need some form of consideration to be binding). For a case which highlights the dangers for an employer of not doing so, see *Tenon FM Ltd v Cawley* [2018] EWHC 1972 (QB).

1.4.1 Types of contract

The two most common types of employment contract are:

(a)   the indefinite contract – this is a 'continuing' contract which is terminable by either the employer or the employee on giving the requisite period of notice; and

(b)   the 'fixed-term' (or 'limited-term') contract – which provides for employment for a fixed (limited), definite period of time (see **1.8.1.2**).

These contracts may be used whether the contract is for full-time or part-time work.

Increasingly, employers are utilising a variety of non-standard contracts, such as zero hours contracts, in order to achieve flexible working arrangements. Zero hours contracts (see **1.3.3** above) are casual contracts where the hours to be worked are left (deliberately) undefined and unguaranteed, but employees may be required to be available for work at any time or at specified times. The employer is not obliged to offer any minimum amount of work (or pay), effectively putting the employee on call. Section 27A of the Small Business, Enterprise and Employment Act 2015 renders unenforceable any term prohibiting the worker working under another contract or from doing so without consent. The Exclusivity Terms in Zero Hours Contracts (Redress) Regulations 2015 (SI 2015/2012) came into force on 1 January 2016. These provide, inter alia, that dismissal for breach of an exclusivity clause is automatically unfair (see **5.5**), and it is unlawful to subject an employee or worker to a detriment if they work for another employer in breach of such a clause. The Government has announced that it will encourage businesses and unions to develop codes of practice, and has also published 'Zero hours contracts: guidance for employers'.

Note: With effect from 1 September 2013, a new category of employee status was introduced, whereby employees may give up employment rights in return for shares. The detail is beyond the scope of the book, but, in brief, individuals can opt to receive at least €2,000 of shares in return for giving up rights to claim unfair dismissal, the right to a statutory redundancy payment, and the right to request flexible working and time off to study or for training. The employee will have to receive independent advice, paid for by the employer.

1.4.2   Written statement of terms

By s 1 of the ERA 1996 (as amended by the EA 2002 and the Employment Rights (Miscellaneous Amendments) Regulations 2019), before an individual starts work, the employer must give the individual a written statement of terms and conditions. The right to receive a written statement covers workers as well as employees. It relates to the following particulars:

(a)   identity of the parties;

(b)   date employment began;

(c)   date continuous employment began (taking into account any relevant employment with a previous employer);

(d)   whether the contract is subject to a probationary period;

(e)   scale or rate of remuneration and intervals of pay and any fringe benefits;

(f)   hours of work;

(g)   any terms relating to:

    (i)   holidays and holiday pay;

    (ii)   sickness and sick pay;

    (iii)   pensions and pension schemes;

(h)   details of any training that will be provided;

(i)   length of notice required to determine the contract;

(j)   in the case of non-permanent employment, the period for which it is expected to continue or, if it is for a fixed term, the date it is to end;

(k)   job title or a brief description of work;

(l)   place or places of work;

(m)   particulars of any collective agreements which directly affect the terms and conditions of employment;

(n)   where employees are required to work outside the UK for a period of more than one month, the period of such work, currency in which payment is made, benefits provided and terms relating to the return to the UK;

(o)   details of the disciplinary and dismissal rules and grievance procedures (ERA 1996, s 3) (to avoid the procedures becoming contractual in nature, the s 1 statement should make it clear they are not); these can be set out in the body of the particulars, or reference may be made to another reasonably accessible document;

(p)   whether a contracting out certificate is in force (under the Pension Schemes Act 1993).

If there are no particulars to be entered under any of the heads above, that fact must be stated (ERA 1996, s 2(1)).

Although the statement must be given to the employee, it may refer him to a document that is reasonably accessible and which contains full details of the terms relating to pension schemes and dismissal and disciplinary procedures and grievance procedures (ERA 1996, ss 2(2) and 3(1)(aa)).

Any changes in the terms of employment must be notified by the employer in writing within one month of the change (ERA 1996, s 4).

An example of a statement of terms under s 1 may be found in **Appendix 1**.

The EAT held in *Stefanko v Maritime Hotel Ltd* (UKEAT/0024/18) that the statement must be given, even if the employment ends prior to the two-month period of employment required by virtue of s 2(6) of the ERA 1996.

Note that the Employment Rights (Miscellaneous Amendments) Regulations 2019 (SI 2019/731) will, with effect from April 2020, extend the right to a written statement of terms to all workers as well as employees from Day 1 of employment.

The Employment Rights Act 1996 (Itemised Pay Statement) (Amendment) Orders 2018 extends the right to receive an itemised pay statement (or payslip) to all workers and not just employees. They require payslips to state the number of hours being paid where wages vary according to time worked (for example under variable hours or zero hours contracts), either as an aggregate number of hours or as separate figures for different types of work or rate of pay. The Government estimated that some 290,000 workers (1% of the workforce) did not receive a payslip. It hopes that by providing workers with itemised payslips, the greater transparency over how much they are paid and why, will ensure that they are paid correctly. This implements one of the recommendations of the Taylor Review (see Introductory Note).

1.4.2.1   Exceptions

Written contract

If the contract of employment is in writing and contains all the particulars that need to be referred to under s 1 of the ERA 1996, no separate written statement of terms need be given to the employee (ERA 1996, s 7A). (See **1.8** for written contracts.) Employers may decide not to set out the disciplinary and dismissal rules and grievance procedures in the contract to avoid giving the procedures contractual status (see **Chapter 3**).

1.4.2.2   Disputes about the statement

The written statement of terms given by the employer under s 1 of the ERA 1996 merely states what the contract terms are, it is not the contract itself. The employee may dispute the accuracy of the statement, or, alternatively, the employer may fail to give the employee a written statement. In *Lovett v Wigan Metropolitan Borough Council* [2001] EWCA Civ 12, the Court of Appeal confirmed that a s 1 statement did not form part of the contract of employment. An employee did not agree to any variation of existing terms by signing to 'confirm receipt' of the particulars. If it is intended that the s 1 statement is to have contractual force, it must expressly state so and signing must be stated to confirm agreement to the contractual terms. A mere acknowledgement of receipt will be insufficient to bind an employee.

By s 11 of the ERA 1996, where the employer fails to give the employee a written statement as required, or where a dispute arises as to its accuracy, either party may refer the matter to an employment tribunal. The tribunal's duty is to determine what particulars should have been contained in the written statement. The tribunal does not have power to invent terms or impose terms on the parties which had not been agreed between them (*Eagland v British Telecommunications plc* [1992] IRLR 323, CA). See too *Southern Cross Healthcare v Perkins and Others* [2010] EWCA Civ 1442 where the Court of Appeal said that ss 11 and 12 of the ERA 1996 do not give a tribunal rights to construe the terms of the contract or amend the agreement. Such a power can arise only in the context of a breach of contract claim in the civil courts. The only power the tribunal has is to amend the statutory statement so that it corresponds with any written agreement.

The EA 2002 states that the tribunals must award compensation of two to four (gross) weeks' pay (up to the statutory maximum – £571 as at 6 April 2022) to the employee, where the absence of particulars becomes evident upon a successful tribunal claim being brought under any of the tribunal jurisdictions listed in Sch 5 to EA 2002 (which covers most common tribunal complaints) (EA 2002, s 38). There is no free-standing right to claim compensation. The tribunal must award the minimum of two weeks' pay and may, if it considers it just and equitable in the circumstances, award four weeks' pay (ie a maximum of £2,284 as at 6 April 2022) in respect of the failure. The tribunal does not have to make an award if there are exceptional circumstances that make it unjust to make an award.

1.5   IMPLIED TERMS

In certain situations, even where there is a written statement or a written contract, terms will be implied into the contract. Terms may be implied into a contract of employment either at common law, where there is no express term (see **1.7**), or under statute (see **1.6**). The terms of a collective agreement (an agreement between an employer and a trade union) may be incorporated into a contract of employment by implication. Collective agreements are beyond the scope of this book.

In *Newcastle upon Tyne Hospitals NHS Foundation Trust v Haywood* [2018] UKSC 22, the Supreme Court held that a term will be implied into all employment contracts that notice of termination will only start to run from the date the employee receives written notice of their dismissal and has had a reasonable opportunity to read it, if different. This will therefore be the default position unless there is an express contractual clause making clear that, for example, notice is effective from the date of delivery. Contracts will need to set out clearly how notice can be served and when it will be considered to have been received.

1.6   TERMS IMPLIED BY STATUTE

The Working Time Regulations 1998 (see **1.12**) provide an example of terms implied by statute, as does the National Minimum Wage Act 1998 (NMWA – see **1.8.3.1**). The 'equality clause' arising under the Equality Act 2010 (see **8.9.1.1**) is also a term implied by statute.

1.7   TERMS IMPLIED BY COMMON LAW

In addition to terms which are implied by statute, terms may also be implied into a contract by the common law. The principal implied duties are set out below. These may conveniently be divided into employers' duties and employees' duties.

1.7.1 Employers' duties

1.7.1.1 Duty to pay wages and provide work

At common law, the general rule is that an employee has no right to work. Provided that the employer pays the employee, there is no breach of an implied term if the employee is kept idle (*Turner v Sawdon* [1901] 2 KB 653).

There are, however, increasing exceptions to this rule. It has long been established, for example, that workers whose livelihood depends on publicity, for example actors and singers, have the right to work. Similarly, if the employee is paid by commission or is a piece worker, there is an implied duty to provide the employee with work. Furthermore, in *William Hill Organisation Ltd v Tucker* [1998] IRLR 313, the Court of Appeal held that the employee in question had the right to be provided with work during his notice period. The Court of Appeal stated that whether an employee has the right to be provided with work is a 'question of construction of the ... contract in light of its surrounding circumstances'. The Court of Appeal pointed to three factors which, on the facts, supported the right to work:

(a) The employee was in a specific and unique post, both in substance as well as form. The employee was the only senior dealer – he was the person appointed to conduct a new and specialised business.

(b) The skills necessary to the proper discharge of such duties as a senior dealer in spread betting required their frequent exercise.

(c) The terms of the contract itself. The contract provided for the days and hours of work, and specifically imposed on the employee an obligation to work those hours necessary to do the job in a full and professional manner. The court said that if the work was available it was inconsistent with that provision if the employee was bound to draw his pay without doing the work. In addition the contract provided for only a limited power of suspension in narrow circumstances.

Many senior employees will fall within the criteria referred to above, with the result that they will enjoy the right to work (see also **1.8.7.3**). An implied right to work is less likely to be implied into more junior employees' contracts. The Court of Appeal held in *North West Anglia NHS Foundation Trust v Gregg* [2019] EWCA Civ 387 that where a contract does not address pay during suspension, the default should be suspension without pay (see too **5.4.2.2**).

The Government's Coronavirus Job Retention Scheme, whereby staff could be furloughed (ie retained but placed on a temporary paid leave of absence), implicitly recognised the problem of a 'right to work'.

There are a number of statutory provisions which can impact on an employee's right to work and to be paid. For example, the ERA 1996 has provisions relating to lay-offs and short-time working (s 147), which can be used as alternatives to redundancies. There can also be a right in some circumstances to what is known as a guarantee payment (ERA 1996, s 28). The details are beyond the scope of this work, but see **Chapter 4** on redundancy for a little more detail.

1.7.1.2 Duty to indemnify employee

The employer is under a duty to indemnify the employee for expenses and liabilities incurred by the employee in the course of his employment (*In re Famatina Development Corporation Ltd* [1914] 2 Ch 271).

1.7.1.3 Duty to take reasonable care of the employee's safety and working conditions

There are implied contractual duties on the employer to provide adequate plant and premises, competent fellow workers and a safe system of work (*Wilsons & Clyde Coal Co Ltd v English* [1938] AC 57). This duty to take reasonable care of an employee's safety and working conditions extends only to the employee's personal safety, not to safeguarding his property.

The employer also has statutory duties in respect of health and safety imposed by the Health and Safety at Work etc Act 1974 (HSWA 1974). Further, the Employers' Liability (Compulsory Insurance) Act 1969 requires the employer to take out employers' liability insurance for the benefit of his employees.

In *Waltons and Morse v Dorrington* [1997] IRLR 488, a term was implied in favour of a non-smoker in a smoking environment, that the employer should provide and monitor, so far as is reasonably practicable, a working environment which is reasonably suitable for the performance of contractual obligations.

In *Moores v Bude-Stratton Town Council* [2000] IRLR 676, the EAT held that the employer was under a duty to take reasonable steps to protect employees from unacceptable treatment.

The Covid-19 pandemic has put under the spotlight the potential conflict between an employee's obligation to be available for work at a specific location and during a certain time (when a refusal to do as instructed could amount to a breach of the employment contract, with the possibility of disciplinary action or even dismissal) and the health and safety obligations of the employer to provide a safe place of work. Workplaces carry risk, and an employer must take reasonable steps to ensure that the right safeguards and policies are in place before reopening. Employers have a duty of care to look after both the physical and mental health of their staff. Under the Government's Covid-19 return to the office guidance, all businesses have a duty to conduct a Covid-19 risk assessment, and details of how the risks will be mitigated must be available.

1.7.1.4   Duty of mutual trust and confidence

There is a duty of mutual trust and confidence owed by the employer and the employee to each other. As far as the employer is concerned, it was stated in *Woods v WM Car Services (Peterborough) Ltd* [1983] IRLR 413, CA (approved by the House of Lords in *Malik and Another v BCCI SA (in compulsory liquidation)* [1998] AC 20), that employers will not 'without reasonable and proper cause, conduct themselves in a manner calculated or likely to destroy or seriously damage the relationship of mutual confidence and trust between employer and employee'. This is particularly important in the area of constructive dismissal. (See **3.4.3** for further details.)

In *Burn v Alder Hey Children's NHS Foundation Trust* [2021] EWCA Civ 1791, the Court of Appeal expressed, obiter, that there could be an implied term that disciplinary processes will be conducted fairly, which is not conceptually linked to the implied term of trust and confidence.

1.7.1.5   Duty to take reasonable care in giving references

There is an implied term to take reasonable care in compiling or giving a reference and in verifying the information on which it is based. An employer may be liable to the employee or former employee for any economic loss suffered as a result of a negligent misstatement (see *Caparo Industries v Dickman* [1990] 2 AC 605 (re the test to be applied when establishing whether or not a duty of care is owed) and *Spring v Guardian Assurance plc* [1994] IRLR 460 (re references)).

In *Bartholomew v London Borough of Hackney* [1999] IRLR 246, the Court of Appeal held that where an employer decides to give a reference, there is a duty of care to provide a reference that is 'true, accurate and fair' (ie not misleading). By 'fair', the Court of Appeal meant in terms of the overall impression given of the employee, as well as being factually correct in its component parts. In *Kidd v Axa Equity and Law Life Assurance Society plc and Another* [2000] IRLR 301, the High Court rejected an employee's claim that he had a right to a 'full and comprehensive' reference. The court said that the duty owed by a referee is

> not to give misleading information ... whether as a result of the unfairly selective provision of information, or by the inclusion of facts or opinions in such a manner as to give rise to a false or mistaken inference in the mind of a reasonable recipient.

The EAT held in *TSB Bank plc v Harris* [2000] IRLR 157 that an employee was entitled to resign and claim constructive dismissal on the basis that a reference provided to a prospective employer was in breach of the implied duty of mutual trust and confidence. Ms Harris's employer provided a reference limited to the factual history of Ms Harris's employment. It recorded that there had been 17 complaints against her, 15 more than she knew of, and that four of them had been upheld and eight remained outstanding. The reference said nothing about Ms Harris's character, nor her ability to undertake her job.

The EAT upheld the tribunal's decision that Ms Harris had been unfairly constructively dismissed. The employer should have made Ms Harris aware of the complaints before the reference had been given in order to allow her the opportunity to address the damaging information which was on her file. The reference supplied was unfair and misleading, and not prepared with due skill and care. The approach of the EAT was reinforced by the Court of Appeal in *Cox v Sun Alliance Life Ltd* [2001] IRLR 448. The Court emphasised that the duty of care owed by an employer with regard to the provision of a reference is not only to take reasonable care to provide an accurate reference, but also to take reasonable care to provide a fair one. A reference does not generally 'have to provide a full and comprehensive report on all the material facts concerning the subject'.

In *McKie v Swindon College* [2011] EWHC 469 (QB), the High Court held that an employer owed a duty to its former employee to take reasonable care when referring to that former employee in communications with a third party (an email sent by a former employer to a current employer which resulted in the employee's dismissal). This extends the scope of *Spring* to include circumstances beyond that of simply providing a reference. The case is a useful reference for the process that a court will follow in order to determine whether a duty of care is owed.

Employers, especially public authority employers, need to take care that nothing they write when acting as a referee could be taken to amount to an interference with employees' private or family lives, unless one of the exceptions set out in Article 8(2) of the ECHR applies (see **15.4.2**).

The DPA 2018 (see **Chapter 15**) regulates when and how information concerning an employee may be held, obtained and disclosed. An employer who provides a reference will be processing data for the purposes of the DPA 2018. However, the Act excludes the disclosure to employees of references provided for future employment, although employees may be able to obtain the same from the recipient of the reference. It is clear that while there is no common law duty to provide a reference, an employee may be able to see one if it is provided.

1.7.1.6 Duty to notify on termination without notice

In *Société Générale v Geys* [2013] IRLR 122, the Supreme Court held that an employer must notify an employee in clear terms that the contract is ended.

1.7.1.7 Duty to give reasonable notice

Readers are referred to **2.3.3**.

1.7.2 Employees' duties

1.7.2.1 Duty to give personal service

The relationship of employer and employee is a personal one, and the employee may not delegate performance of his duties. This can be crucial in determining whether someone is an employee or not (see **1.3** above).

1.7.2.2 Duty to obey reasonable orders

The employee is under a contractual duty not wilfully to disobey a lawful order (*Laws v London Chronicle Ltd* [1959] 2 All ER 285). Neither must the employee act in a manner designed to frustrate the commercial aspect of the contract. A 'work to rule' may amount to a breach of contract if designed to disrupt work (*Secretary of State for Employment v Associated Society of Locomotive Engineers and Firemen (ASLEF) (No 2)* [1972] 2 QB 455).

See also **1.7.1.3** on the potential conflict between an employee's duty to obey reasonable orders and the employer's health and safety obligations during the Covid-19 pandemic.

1.7.2.3 Duty of reasonable care and indemnity

The employee is under a duty to exercise reasonable care and skill in the performance of his duties. An employee will be in breach of this duty if he performs his duties negligently or incompetently. If an employee is in breach of this duty, he is also liable to indemnify the employer for any loss suffered by the employer by reason of the employee's breach (*Lister v Romford Ice and Cold Storage Co Ltd* [1957] AC 555).

1.7.2.4 Duty of fidelity or good faith

The duty of fidelity or good faith is sometimes referred to as the employee's part of the mutual duty of trust and confidence. The duty consists principally of a number of aspects of confidentiality and non-competition, some of which also apply after employment has ceased (see **1.7.2.6–1.7.2.8** and **1.8.6**).

In *Crowson Fabrics Ltd v Rider and Others* [2007] EWHC 2942 (Ch), the High Court held that employees who had copied customer contact details and sales figures during employment, had not acted in breach of their implied duty of confidentiality because the information was not confidential (it was in the public domain). However, they were held to have breached their duty of fidelity and, in the case of the senior employee, the fiduciary duty (see **2.5.3**).

In *Kynixa Ltd v Hynes and Others* [2008] EWHC 1495 (Comm), the court held that three senior employees had breached their duty of fidelity by deliberately misleading their employer about their intention to work for a competitor, with which they had been in discussions for at least two months prior to departure.

The High Court held that a senior employee breached his contract and fiduciary duties when he helped set up a business that would compete with his employer's business during 'garden leave' (see **1.8.7.3**) (*Imam-Sadeque v Blue Bay Asset Management (Services) Ltd* [2012] EWHC 3511 (QB)).

1.7.2.5 Secret profits

An employee must not make a secret profit. If he does so, he can be compelled to account to his employer for the profit made (*Boston Deep Sea Fishing and Ice Co v Ansell* (1888) 39 Ch D 339) (see **2.5.3**).

1.7.2.6 Competition

In the absence of an express prohibition in the contract, taking a job outside working hours is not necessarily a breach of the employee's duty of fidelity, even where that job involves working for a competitor. Much will depend on how damaging that other employment is to the employer's business.

In *Hivac Ltd v Park Royal Scientific Instruments Ltd* [1946] Ch 169, five skilled manual workers who assembled hearing aids worked for their employer's sole competitor on Sundays. The Court of Appeal held that they were in breach of the implied duty of fidelity because it could not be consistent with their contract of employment for them to do in their spare time something which could potentially inflict such harm on their employers. Clearly, the fact that they worked for the only other competitor in the market was of great significance.

For the employee's duty of fidelity to be breached in this situation, the employee must normally occupy a position where he has access to confidential information or trade secrets such that the employer is at risk of such information being passed to a competitor. Therefore, in *Nova Plastics Ltd v Frogatt* [1982] IRLR 146, an odd-job man who worked for a competitor in his spare time was not in breach of contract.

After employment, the ex-employee may compete with his former employer without restriction. Any restrictive covenant which attempts to restrict such competition is subject to the doctrine of restraint of trade (see **1.8.7**).

1.7.2.7 Conflict of interest and duty

During employment, the employee must not allow his duty of fidelity to his employer to conflict with his personal interest. In particular, an employee who is intending to leave his employment and set up in competition may wish to obtain information from his employer or entice away his employer's customers and staff. It is a breach of the duty of fidelity to make lists of existing customers with the intention of using it after the termination of the employment relationship (*Roger Bullivant Ltd v Ellis* [1987] ICR 464) or even deliberately to memorise such a list for such a purpose (*Robb v Green* [1895] 2 QB 315). It is also a breach of the duty to entice away or agree to work personally for existing customers of the employer, or to induce other employees to break their contracts of employment (*Sanders v Parry* [1967] 2 All ER 803). (See also *Kynixa* at **1.7.2.4** above.)

1.7.2.8 Trade secrets and confidential information

During employment, an employee is in breach of his duty of fidelity if he uses or reveals trade secrets or other information which by its nature is confidential, or which has been impressed upon the employee as being confidential (*Faccenda Chicken Ltd v Fowler* [1986] 1 All ER 617). Such other information which by its nature is confidential would include lists of customers (see **1.7.2.7** above). A particular method of doing work, though not a trade secret, could be confidential information if the employee had been told of its confidentiality. However, information of a trivial or mundane character, or information that is available from public sources, cannot be turned into confidential information, even by an express term of the contract.

See too the statutory definition of trade secrets and the position after employment has ended at **1.8.6** and **1.8.7**.

1.7.3 Other implied terms

As well as the above general terms, which are seen as a necessary part of contracts of employment, terms may also be implied into contracts where the court is satisfied that the term is necessary to give business efficacy to the contract or that the term is so obvious that the parties must have intended it. It is only appropriate to imply a term where, on a consideration of the express terms of the agreement and the facts and circumstances surrounding it, an implication arises that the parties actually intended the term in question to be part of their original contract.

Terms may also be implied (increasingly rarely) where it is the normal custom and practice to include such a term in contracts of that kind. The custom must be 'reasonable, notorious and certain', and the parties must be shown to be applying the term because there is a sense of legal obligation to do so (cf a matter of policy) (*Solectron Scotland Ltd v Roper* [2004] IRLR 4). Implication from custom or usage should only normally be on the basis that it does not conflict with an express term. In *Park Cakes Ltd v Shumba* [2013] EWCA Civ 974, the Court of Appeal reviewed the authorities relating to when a contractual term may be implied from past custom or practice and provided a useful summary of the applicable principles relating to the provision of past benefits.

Lastly, a term may be implied by the courts (albeit rarely) where an intention to include the term (at the time of entering into the contract) is shown by the way the contract has been performed.

1.8 WRITTEN CONTRACTS

Although a contract of employment may be oral, written, or partly oral and partly written, it is advisable in the interests of certainty and to avoid disputes for the contract to be in writing and expressly to set out all the essential terms of the employment. There is no prescribed form for a written contract. An example is set out in **Appendix 1**.

Issues of interpretation or construction of express terms are determined objectively: what would, at the time, objectively have been understood? The subjective views of the parties are technically not relevant (see *The Basildon Academies v Amadi and Fox* (EAT/0342/14)).

One of the practical difficulties that may occur is deciding what documents form part of the contract and give rise to binding terms. For example, is the disciplinary procedure contractual? This may cause problems if an employer wishes to change a policy. Generally speaking, if it is a term of the contract, it cannot be changed unilaterally, ie without the employee's consent (see **1.9**).

In *Harlow v Artemis International Corporation Ltd* [2008] EWHC 1126 (QB), the High Court said that a redundancy policy, referred to in Mr Harlow's contract but contained in a staff handbook, was an express term of the employee's contract, and he was therefore contractually entitled to an enhanced payment under the policy. The policy spoke of 'entitlement', which set it aside from true policies, said the Court. Just because a document is referred to in a contract, though, does not mean it automatically becomes a contractual term. It will depend on the facts. The EAT held in *Worrall v Wilmott Dixon Partnership* (UKEAT/0521/09) that to incorporate a term of a collective agreement into a contract, the term must be brought to the employees' notice or agreed. It said it was not sufficient for the term simply to be in a readily available document, such as a handbook. The EAT held:

> [I]t cannot be right that a party is bound by a contractual document which he has not received merely because it was a document available to him. The fact that a document was available to the claimant does not show that he had notice of its terms or that he had agreed to them.

On the facts, a term in a collective agreement providing for enhanced redundancy pay was held not to have been incorporated into the claimants' contracts, as there was no evidence of it being brought to the claimants' notice or agreed.

Nevertheless, care needs to be taken if an employer wishes to refer the employee to a policy or procedure but wants to remain free to change that policy or procedure at its discretion. (See, eg, clause 17 of the sample Service Contract in **Appendix 1**.) A non-exhaustive list of considerations to take into account when determining whether the provisions of a policy were incorporated into a contract of employment was set out in *Albion Automotive Ltd v Walker* [2002] EWCA Civ 946. That case concerned whether employees who had been made redundant were entitled to enhanced redundancy payments because the employers had made such payments on previous occasions. The employees did not have written contracts of employment. Peter Gibson LJ, with whom the other members of the Court of Appeal agreed, endorsed the submission of the employees' counsel (set out at [15]) that when assessing whether a policy originally produced unilaterally by management had acquired contractual status, a number of considerations are relevant, including the following:

(a)   whether the policy was drawn to the attention of employees;

(b)   whether it was followed without exception for a substantial period;

(c)   the number of occasions on which it was followed;

(d)   whether payments were made automatically;

(e)   whether the nature of communication of the policy supported the inference that the employers intended to be contractually bound;

(f)   whether the policy was adopted by agreement;

(g)   whether employees had a reasonable expectation that the enhanced payment would be made;

(h)   whether terms were incorporated in a written agreement;

(i)   whether the terms were consistently applied.

If a policy is not meant to be contractual, the policy or contract should clearly state this. See also *Bateman v Asda Stores* at **1.4** above.

Note: In *Rock Advertising Ltd v MWB Business Exchange Centres Ltd* [2018] UKSC 24 (a rent arrears case), the Supreme Court upheld the validity of a contractual clause that required any variations to the contract to be in writing and signed. This meant that a subsequent oral agreement to vary the contract was not valid. Employers sometimes try to rely on the assertion that, after a change to a working term or practice is unilaterally introduced, ie without express agreement, it is impliedly accepted if employees continue to work. In *Abrahall v Nottingham City Council* [2018] EWCA Civ 796, the Court of Appeal held that a group of employees, who had continued to work following their employer's imposition of a pay freeze, did not implicitly agree to a variation. The question of what, if any, inferences are to be drawn from continuing to work will depend on the particular circumstances of each case. (See **1.9** below.)

Some of the other principal clauses which should be considered for inclusion in a contract and some points to consider when drafting them are outlined below. The desirability of the clauses and their content will vary depending upon whether the employer or employee is being advised.

1.8.1   Duration clause

1.8.1.1   Indefinite contracts

In a contract for an indefinite term, the duration clause should specify the notice period to be given by the employer and the employee to terminate the contract.

In the case of managerial, professional and other senior employees, it may be appropriate to make the notice period fairly long, for example six months to be given by either party. This is mutually beneficial for employer and employee. It means that the employer should not be deprived of the services of a key employee on short notice and it gives the employee a degree of security. It may be worth considering reducing the notice period in the early stages of employment, to allow earlier termination if either the employer finds the employee unsuitable or the employee dislikes the job. For example, only one month's notice might be required to terminate within one year of commencing employment.

For less skilled employees, it may be appropriate to make the notice period shorter, but it must comply with the statutory minimum required by s 86 of the ERA 1996 (see **2.3.3**). In many cases, the contractual notice period would be the statutory minimum.

If there is no express term in the employment contract as to notice, then a term will be implied that the notice be of 'reasonable length'. In *Clark v Fahrenheit 451 (Communications) Ltd* (UKEAT/591/99), the EAT said that determining what is a reasonable length is a mixed question of law and fact and depends on all the circumstances of the case.

Consideration should also be given to whether to include a pay in lieu of notice (PILON) clause in the contract. This may protect an employer from an unlawful damages claim where a contract is terminated without notice (see **2.3.3**). It gives the employer the option of terminating a contract immediately by making a payment in lieu rather than waiting for the employee to work his notice. This can mean that restrictive covenants remain enforceable, because there has been no breach by the employer (see *General Billposting Co Ltd v Atkinson* [1909] AC 118, below at **1.8.7.2**). However, it is important, where a PILON clause is relied on, that an employer makes this clear and unambiguous (see *Société Général, London Branch v Geys*, at **2.3.3**).

1.8.1.2 Fixed (limited)-term contracts

In the case of key, senior employees, the employer may wish to secure the employee's services for a longer period by entering into a fixed-term contract, for example for a period of five years from a specified date. This will bind both the employer and the employee for the fixed period.

If advising the employer on a fixed-term contract, the following matters should also be considered:

(a)   A clause that permits a fixed-term contract to be lawfully ended before expiry is known as a 'break' clause. The 'break' clause may permit the employer, or the employee, or both to have the right to end the contract by giving notice to the other. If a break clause is inserted, it should comply with the statutory minimum notice periods. For example, if the employer is in a strong enough bargaining position, he may wish to insert a clause under which he can terminate the contract at any time by giving the employee three months' notice. This effectively binds the employee for the full fixed term, but allows the employer to bring the contract to an end by giving notice. If there is no express 'break' clause, then the contract cannot be brought to an end by notice. The statutory minimum notice periods are not relevant in that situation.

(c)   Whether or not there is a break clause dealing with notice, it is advisable to insert a 'termination' clause into a fixed-term contract, under which the employer may terminate the contract without notice on the happening of specified events, such as bankruptcy of the employee. This is a more limited form of 'break' clause. In an indefinite contract, such a clause would not be necessary unless the notice period was very long.

(d)   If the employee is a director of the employer company, fixed-term contracts in excess of two years require the approval of the members of the company, otherwise the contract becomes terminable by reasonable notice (Companies Act 2006, ss 188 and 189).

(e)   It is unlawful to treat employees on fixed-term contracts less favourably than permanent employees without objective justification (Fixed-term Employees (Prevention of Less Favourable Treatment) Regulations 2002 (SI 2002/2034)) (see **8.11**).

1.8.1.3 Continuous employment

Section 1 of the ERA 1996 requires the employee to be informed whether any previous employment is continuous with the current employment and the date of commencement of the period of continuous employment (see **1.4.2**). This would normally be dealt with in the duration clause.

1.8.2 Duties and mobility

The duties and mobility clauses are concerned with defining the job which the employee is engaged to perform and the place or places where he can be required to perform it.

1.8.2.1 Job title

The job title or brief description should be stated to comply with s 1 of the ERA 1996. Although s 1 of the Act requires only the job title, the ECJ held in *Helmut Kampelmann and Others v Landschaftsverband Westfalen-Lippe* (Cases C-253/96 to 256/96) [1997] ECR I-6907 that the Proof of Employment Directive requires the employee to be told the nature of his employment, or be given a brief description of his work. The employer may wish to address matters such as job flexibility, or mobility, within a job description.

1.8.2.2   Duties

Defining duties

From the employer's point of view, the employee's duties should be defined widely. The clause should cover all duties that the employer envisages that the employee may be asked to do, and any possible changes in duties. In the case of a senior manager, for example, the contract could require him to carry out 'such duties as the employer may from time to time direct'. However, even if the duties are widely defined, they will be limited to some extent by the job title. For example, in *Hayden v Cowan* [1982] IRLR 314, the applicant's job title was 'divisional contracts surveyor'. The Court of Appeal held that the employer could not therefore transfer him to any job as a quantity surveyor, despite a term in his contract which stated that he was 'required to undertake, at the direction of the company, any and all duties which reasonably fell within [his] capabilities'.

The duties of junior employees would usually be more narrowly defined. However, the employer must still bear in mind any changes he may wish to make to the employee's duties in the future, so that the changes can be made without the employer being in breach of contract.

How widely duties are defined may be relevant in determining if an employee is redundant (see **4.2.3.2**).

Time devoted to duties

From the employer's point of view, senior employees should be required to devote their whole time and attention to their duties. This does not mean that they have to work 24 hours a day, seven days a week, but it does mean that they are not restricted to specific hours. With junior employees, it is usual to specify the hours to be worked but, if appropriate, the contract should specify that the employee can be compelled to work overtime. Note that the Working Time Regulations 1998 regulate the hours that employees can be required to work (see **1.11**).

Consideration should be given as to whether there should be a term prohibiting the employee from taking part in any other business during employment. In the absence of any express term, an employee is only prohibited from working for a competitor during employment, and only then if he possesses information of a confidential nature (see **1.7.2**). The term prohibiting working for any other business will allow the employer, if appropriate, to obtain an injunction against the employee in the event of breach.

Qualifications

If the employee is required to hold a particular qualification (eg to possess a driving licence), or to pass a test or medical examination, this should be made an express term of the contract. The courts will not imply such a term unless it is necessary to make the contract work (*Stubbes v Trower, Still and Keeling* [1987] IRLR 321).

1.8.2.3   Place of work and mobility

Section 1 of the ERA 1996 requires the place or places of work to be stated (see **1.4.2**). A mobility clause defines the area within which the employee can be required to work. From an employer's perspective, such a clause, particularly for a senior employee, should be drawn widely so that the employer is entitled to change the employee's place of work if necessary. It might, for example, require an employee to work anywhere within the UK. This can be very important when considering the question of redundancy (see **4.2.2**). If the employee will, or may, be required to work elsewhere, a mobility clause should be included. Even where the contract does contain a mobility clause, the court has held that the employer must not exercise that clause in such a manner as to breach the implied duty of trust and confidence (*United Bank Ltd v Akhtar* [1989] IRLR 507). In *Kellogg Brown & Root (UK) Ltd v Fitton & Another* (UKEAT/0205/16), the claimants were dismissed following a workplace closure. The closure was announced in April 2015 and the employees were told they would move in July 2015. The claimants had refused to relocate and they were dismissed. The mobility clause provided:

> The location of your employment is _____ but the company may require you to work at a different location including any new office location of the company either in the UK or overseas either on a temporary or permanent basis. You agree to comply with this requirement unless exceptional circumstances prevail.

The employment tribunal concluded that the mobility clause was too wide and uncertain and had been unreasonably invoked by the respondent.

Furthermore, it may be argued that a mobility clause is indirectly discriminatory on the grounds of sex, on the basis that it is likely to be more difficult for women than men to comply with the requirement to move, as a greater proportion of women are secondary earners (see **Chapter 10**).

Where there is no express mobility clause, the court is very unlikely to imply one where the written particulars state the place of work as required under ERA 1996, s 1. Even if there is no place of work clause, the court may still refuse to imply a mobility clause where there is no need to do so to give the contract business efficacy (*Aparau v Iceland Frozen Foods plc* [1996] IRLR 119).

The implication of a term is a matter for the court or tribunal, and whether or not a term is implied depends upon the intention of the parties, as collected from the words of the agreement and the surrounding circumstances. An implied term will usually be made in two situations: first, where it is necessary to give business efficacy to the contract, and, secondly, where the term implied represents the obvious, but unexpressed intention of the parties (see **1.7.3**).

Whether the court or tribunal will imply a mobility clause into the contract of employment will therefore depend upon the particular contractual relationship of the parties. If the tribunal is prepared to imply a mobility clause into the contract, as a rule of thumb, it may be possible to expect an employee to be mobile within a reasonable daily travelling distance from his home (see *Jones v Associated Tunnelling Co Ltd* [1981] IRLR 477, where the Court of Appeal held that since the employer was in business as a contractor working at different sites, the parties must have envisaged a degree of mobility). In *O'Brien v Associated Fire Alarms Ltd* [1968] 3 ITR 183, the Court of Appeal would not imply a term requiring an employee to move 120 miles. The Court of Appeal held that the only term that could be implied into the employee's contract was that he should be employed within a reasonable distance of his home. In *Managers (Holborn) Ltd v Hohne* [1977] IRLR 230, the EAT implied a term requiring the employee to work anywhere in Central London, since the employee was a commuter and the whole of central London was accessible to her by public transport.

See also **1.7.1.3** on the potential conflict between the requirement to work under a mobility clause and the employer's health and safety obligations during the Covid-19 pandemic.

1.8.2.4   Employee's viewpoint

The above guidelines are expressed from the point of view of the employer. From the employee's viewpoint, it is desirable to have a narrower definition of duties and mobility.

1.8.3   Remuneration, illness and holidays

In order to comply with s 1 of the ERA 1996, terms relating to pay, sickness and sick pay, holidays and holiday pay must be notified to the employee in the contract or s 1 statement.

In *Judge v Crown Leisure Ltd* [2005] IRLR 823, the Court of Appeal held that in order for there to be a legally binding contractual commitment, there must be certainty as to the contractual commitment entered into. Otherwise, a promise amounts to nothing more than a statement of intention. Therefore, on the facts, an employee was not entitled to rely on a promise made at a Christmas party that he would be paid the same as his colleagues 'eventually'.

1.8.3.1 Pay, benefits and commission

The remuneration clause should specify how the employee's remuneration is calculated (eg hourly wage or annual salary) and when payment is due (eg weekly or monthly). The contract should also specify any fringe benefits to which the employee is entitled (eg a company car or medical insurance).

Legislation on payslips means that all employees (ERA 1996, s 8) should receive itemised payslips showing gross and net amounts, and where different amounts are paid in different ways, this must be shown. These rights will be extended to workers from April 2019.

The NMWA 1998 established the legislative framework for the national minimum wage (NMW). The National Minimum Wage Regulations 1999, outlining the detail of the NMW, came into force on 1 April 1999 (now the 2015 Regulations (SI 2015/621), which remade the 1999 Regulations and consolidated amendments). The National Minimum Wage (Amendment) Regulations 2016 (SI 2016/68) came into force on 1 April 2016. These set a 'national living wage' for workers aged 25 and over. The rates change every April. The 2016 Regulations:

(a)   set a rate for the national living wage for those aged 23 and over (£8.91 from 1 April 2021; £9.50 from 1 April 2022; £10.42 from 1 April 2023);

(b)   set a rate for the NMW for those aged 21–22 (£8.36 from 1 April 2021; £9.18 from 1 April 2022; £10.18 from 1 April 2023);

(c)   set modified rates for 18–20-year-olds (£6.56 from 1 April 2021; £6.83 from 1 April 2022; £7.49 from 1 April 2023);

(d)   provided that workers aged below 18 who have ceased to be of compulsory school age qualify for the NMW (£4.62 for such workers from 1 April 2021; £4.81 from 1 April 2022; £5.28 from 1 April 2023);

(e)   exempted non-employed apprentices under 26 in the first year of their apprenticeship. Persons who are workers on specified government schemes at pre-apprenticeship level will not be entitled to the NMW, whether they are employed by the employer or not;

(f)   set rates for employed apprentices under the age of 19, or 19 or above in their first year of apprenticeship (£4.30 from 1 April 2021; £4.81 from 1 April 2022; £5.28 from 1 April 2023);

(g)   set the pay reference period for averaging NMW pay at a maximum of one month;

(h)   determined how to calculate hours worked for which the NMW is payable;

(i)   required employers to issue a statement of the NMW to workers; and

(j)   required employers to keep records.

The Government updated its guidance on the NMW in July 2022: <www.gov.uk/guidance/calculating-the-minimum-wage>.

It is a useful document but readers should always ensure that they consider up-to-date case law. The detail is beyond the scope of this book but the following issues are examples of things to consider:

(a)   The process for determining whether the NMW has been paid is set out in Part 3 of the 2015 Regulations. Part 4 sets out how to determine which payments qualify as remuneration, and Part 5 sets out how to calculate the hours worked for the purposes of the calculation.

(b)   The number of hours that the worker has worked during the reference period is calculated differently depending on the type of work done by the worker.

(c)   On-call or standby time outside normal working hours may be working time.

(d)   The Government Guidance document states:

> For salaried hours work, the hours of work that count for minimum wage purposes include:

- time spent at the workplace working (rest breaks may count as working time for minimum wage purposes if provided for by the worker's contract. In some circumstances, this may include time spent sleeping. See 'Sleep-in' shifts

- time spent at the workplace and required to be available for work – it makes no difference whether or not you actually provide work for that time

- time required to be available for work either on standby or on-call at or near their workplace, unless the worker is at home - however there is an exception if the worker is permitted to sleep during this time and is provided with suitable sleeping facilities (See 'Sleep-in' shifts)

- time spent travelling on business (see Time spent travelling on business)

- time spent training

For time work (paid by the hour), the hours of work that count for minimum wage purposes include:

- time spent at the workplace working, excluding rest breaks

- time spent at the workplace and required to be available for work – it makes no difference whether or not you actually provide work for that time

- time required to be available for work either on standby or on-call at or near their workplace, unless the worker is at home - however there is an exception if the worker is permitted to sleep during this time and is provided with suitable sleeping facilities (see Sleep in shifts)

- time spent travelling on business, or between clients (see Time spent travelling on business)

- under certain circumstances, time when the worker is asleep (see Sleep in shifts)

- time spent training

The time that does not count as working time for minimum wage purposes includes any time spent:

- away from work – even if you pay them for that time – including rest breaks, holidays, sick leave, maternity/paternity/adoption leave, industrial action

- travelling between home and work (unless the worker works whilst travelling) – regardless of whether the worker has a fixed place of work

Example scenarios

You call a time worker into your factory to help with an urgent order, but the delivery is delayed. While the worker is at the factory and required to be available for work you must pay them at least the minimum wage rate for the time – even though they cannot do any work.

However, if the worker is at home waiting for you to call them into work, you do not have to pay them the minimum wage for the time they are at home. They would only be entitled after they have arrived at work and are working or available for work.

For output work, the hours of work over and above any piece/output rate that count for minimum wage purposes include:

- time spent travelling on business (see Travel time for output workers)

- if the worker works from home, time travelling from home to other work premises

- time spent training

For unmeasured work, where the work does not fit the definitions of salaried work, time work or output work, the hours of work that count for minimum wage purposes include:

- time spent travelling on business (see Time spent travelling on business)

- hours specified in a 'daily average' agreement or time actually worked

- time spent training

(e)   Part 4 sets out what payments are and are not permitted to count towards the NMW (eg tips, commission).

(f)   There is a two-year limit on back claims in an action to recover underpayments (ERA 1996, s 23(4A)).

Note that levels of furlough pay under the Coronavirus Job Retention Scheme (CJRS) (see **Introductory Note**) may have taken some employees or workers below the national minimum wage levels, but this would not appear to be unlawful as furlough was about *not* working. But any training done during furlough should have been reimbursed in accordance with national minimum wage levels.

Note too that although the calculation of wages is normally defined by reference to ss 220–225 of the ERA 1996, the impact of furlough under the CJRS is different. For the purposes of the CJRS, when defining what is 'regular pay', the key date is 19 March 2020. Where pay varies, provision is made for an average to be calculated. For more details, refer to the ERA 1996 (Coronavirus, Calculation of a Week's Pay) Regulations 2020, which came into effect on 31 July 2020 and required employers to calculate various statutory payments during the pandemic, including redundancy and notice pay, with reference to a furloughed employee's normal week's pay rather than to their furloughed pay. The Regulations are complex and require careful reading. For example, they only apply in circumstances where the employee is entitled to statutory minimum notice only or to a notice period which is less than a week more than the statutory minimum notice period. So, employees with longer contractual notice periods will not be covered by the Regulations, suggesting that they could be paid on the basis of their furlough pay rather than 'normal' pay.

Sleeping time

Much of the case law around the NWM has concentrated on on-call hours and time when a worker is permitted to sleep. Under the NMW legislation, salaried hours workers and time work workers who are 'on call' are regarded as working when they are available at or near a place of work for the purpose of doing work and are required to be available for such work, unless they are at home. However, when they are provided with suitable facilities for sleeping, only time when they are awake for the purposes of working is treated as time work or salaried work.

In the conjoined cases of *Focus Care Agency Ltd v Roberts*, *Frudd v The Partington Group Ltd* and *Royal Mencap Society v Tomlinson-Blake* (UKEAT/0143/16), the President of the EAT considered all of the then recent appellate case law on the question whether employees who sleep in, in order to carry out duties if required, engage in 'time work' for the full duration of the night shift or whether they are only entitled to the NMW when they are awake and carrying out relevant duties. She considered and rejected a challenge to the approach taken in a number of the earlier decisions on this issue, including *British Nursing Association (BNA) v Inland Revenue* [2002] IRLR 480 and *Scottbridge Construction Ltd v Wright* [2003] IRLR 21. She held that 'a multifactorial evaluation is required. No single factor is determinative and the relevance and weight of particular factors will vary with and depend on the context and circumstances of the particular case.'

In the BNA case, the Court of Appeal had held that nurses providing an overnight telephone service from home were 'working' throughout their shifts so that all their work amounted to time work within reg 30 (as amended), even though they could do what they wished between calls. Regulation 32 (as amended), which deems certain 'on-call' work to be time work, therefore had no application on the facts of the case. The Court observed that:

> No one would say that an employee sitting at the employer's premises during the day waiting for phone calls was only working, in the sense of only being entitled to be remunerated, during the periods when he or she was actually on the phone. Exactly the same consideration seems to me to apply if the employer chooses to operate the very same service during the night-time, not by bringing the employees into his office (which would no doubt impose substantial overhead costs on the employer and lead to significant difficulties of recruitment), but by diverting calls from the central switchboard to employees sitting waiting at home. It was indeed as a continuation of the day-time service that the employer presented the night-time service to his employees and recruited them for that purpose.

In the *Royal Mencap Society* case, the EAT had upheld the tribunal's finding that a care worker who provided care for two vulnerable adults with local authority assessed care plans, specifying 24-hour support, was working for the entirety of her sleep-in shifts. As a result of the EAT's decision, the Government changed its guidance to require all employers to pay the NMW for sleep-in shifts. This has had an enormous impact on social care providers and local authorities. The Government also put in place a social care compliance scheme (SCCS) to assist employers with back pay liabilities.

The EAT's decision was overturned by the Court of Appeal in *Royal Mencap Society v Tomlinson-Blake* [2018] EWCA Civ 1641, which held that such carers were not on call and were only entitled to have sleep-in hours counted for minimum wage purposes when they are, and are required to be, awake for the purpose of performing some specific activity. Underhill LJ reviewed all the previous authorities and held that at least one of them (*Burrow Down*) was wrongly decided. He rejected the multifactorial approach suggested by the EAT and held (at [43]) that since the sleep-in exception (1999 Regulations, regs 15, 16; 2015 Regulations, regs 32, 37) only applies when a worker is 'available for work' and not in cases where the worker is actually working, while it is first necessary to ascertain into which of these two categories a worker who is 'sleeping in' falls, that is an 'unnecessarily elaborate approach' as 'the self-evident intention of the relevant provisions' is to deal comprehensively with the position of sleep-in workers: the draftsperson clearly regarded them as being 'available for work rather than actually working'.

In reaching this conclusion, Underhill LJ distinguished a number of the previous cases (including *BNA* and *Scottbridge*). He found that if a worker is expected to sleep, the time must fall into the 'available for work' provisions. For Underhill LJ, a night watchman falls comfortably on the 'actual work' side of the line. The Court of Appeal's approach was welcomed in some quarters and criticised in others: care providers concerned about potentially vast back pay liabilities welcomed it; those sleep-in carers who provided already relatively low paid work were less pleased. Unison, which supported Tomlinson-Blake's case, lodged an appeal to the Supreme Court, which was heard in February 2020. In March 2021, the Supreme Court handed down its judgment ([2021] UKSC 8), dismissing the claimant's appeal and confirming that a care worker was not entitled to be paid the NMW for all the time that they were on a 'sleep-in' shift. The Supreme Court confirmed that 'sleep-in' time is not 'shift time work' for the purposes of the National Minimum Wage Regulations 1999 and 2015, and it cannot be 'work' in any other sense in the Regulations. In the definition of 'time work', the phrase 'awake for the purposes of working' is composite and cannot be broken up into 'awake' and 'for the purposes of working'. Any time not asleep cannot therefore be 'time work'. If a worker is actually called on to respond to someone's care needs (or any other duties) when on a shift, that time will count as 'time work' and will be subject to the NMW. All the judges decided that *British Nursing* should not be followed as it was not a correct statement of the law for sleep-in shifts. The Court was divided on the reason for this, so *Tomlinson-Blake* cannot be regarded as providing binding case law on whether similar legal arguments on different facts to those in *British Nursing* could be raised again in respect of the home-working exception in the Regulations.

Regulations 27 and 32 only become relevant if the tribunal decides that the worker is not working by being present during the period in question.

See too *Frudd v Partington Group* (UKEAT/0240/18) for a recent EAT case on 'time work'.

Note: Regulation 57(3) contains an exemption for family workers. In *Puthenveetil v Alexander and Another* (UKEAT/0407/17), the EAT held that the employment tribunal had been wrong to say there was no power to disapply the 'family worker' exemption. On remission, the tribunal (ET/2361118/2013) held that the family worker exemption was unlawful and indirectly discriminatory on the basis of sex (the claimant was a domestic worker for the respondents). The respondents relied upon the provision which provides for an exemption for family *and* for workers 'treated as [a member of the family]'). The tribunal concluded that the respondents could not justify the exemption. The Low Pay Commission has recommended that the exemption be removed.

Penalties

With effect from 6 April 2009, with the introduction of the Employment Act 2008, employers have to pay all arrears at the current rate where these are higher than the rate that applied when the underpayment was made. In addition, if an HMRC investigation finds that an employer has underpaid workers, notices of underpayment will require the employer to pay a financial penalty to the Secretary of State within 28 days of service. The penalty is set at 100% of the total underpayment of the NMW. The minimum penalty payable is £100 and the maximum penalty is £20,000 per worker. If the employer complies with the notice within 14 days of its service, the financial penalty will be reduced by 50%. The 2008 Act also gives some new powers to help HMRC inspectors carry out their investigations.

For employers who refuse to cooperate with the above civil regime, criminal proceedings are possible. The fine on conviction for each offence is up to £5,000 (level 5) in the magistrates' court, or an unlimited fine in the Crown Court. The Employment Act 2008 also gives HMRC the power to use the search and seize powers in the Police and Criminal Evidence Act 1984 when investigating criminal offences under the NMWA 1998. The Government has started publishing a list 'naming and shaming' employers who fail to pay workers the NMW. The Government published the latest list in December 2020 naming 139 companies in breach of the rules.

Note: The Small Business, Enterprise and Employment Act 2015 increased the maximum fine to £20,000, and for this to be on a 'per worker' (rather than per employer) basis. The Act came into force on 26 May 2015).

1.8.3.2 Deductions

If deductions are to be made from salary or wages, for example, to repay loans from the employer or, in the case of employees who handle money, to recoup any shortages, the contract should give the employer the right to make such deductions. This is to comply with the requirements of the ERA 1996 and is dealt with in more detail at **1.11**.

1.8.3.3 Sick pay

The contract should state whether the employer pays sick pay (other than statutory sick pay (SSP)). If sick pay is paid, the contract should state the period for which it is payable, how much is payable and whether SSP is deducted in calculating it. An employee who is off sick for a period of more than three consecutive days is entitled to receive SSP from his employer.

This clause should also specify that the employer is entitled to require the employee to provide a medical certificate if absent for more than, say, seven days.

With effect from 6 April 2022, the rate of SSP is £99.35, which is payable for a maximum period of 28 weeks in any three years.

The relationship between holidays and sickness is considered at **1.12.5**.

The Government abolished employers' ability to recover payments of SSP made to their employees on 6 April 2014. This means that now employers pay SSP. The money the Government saves is to be used to set up Health Advisory Centres, aimed at getting employees who are on long-term sick leave back to work. The Fitness for Work Service will provide an occupational health assessment, and will give advice to employees, employers and GPs. Where an employee has been absent from work for four weeks, or is expected to be so absent, due to sickness, he should normally be referred by his GP for an assessment. Following assessment, a Return to Work Plan will be issued. See <fitforwork.org>.

1.8.3.4 Holidays and holiday pay

The clause should specify how many days paid holiday the employee is entitled to each year and when it can be taken. Paid holiday can originate from two different sources: statute and contract. In general, statute lays down minimums, which can be topped up by contract. Note that minimum paid annual leave in the UK is now regulated by the Working Time Regulations 1998 (see **1.12**). The Working Time Directive (93/104) lays down a minimum of four weeks' paid leave. The 1998 Regulations provide an additional minimum for UK workers of 1.6 weeks. The ECJ held in *Lock v British Gas Trading Ltd* (Case C-539/12) that an employee should receive 'normal pay' during his UK statutory annual leave – that is, not limited to bare pay but including compensation for allowances and commission which the employee would have received had he been working during leave (see **1.12.5.3**).

1.8.4 Pension

The contract should specify whether or not the employer has an occupational pension scheme which the employee is entitled to join. An employee cannot be compelled to join an occupational pension scheme and is entitled to enter into a personal pension scheme instead.

If the employer has an occupational pension scheme, there will usually be a contracting out certificate in force under the Pension Schemes Act 1993. If there is no contracting out certificate in force, the employee will be entitled to a second State pension under the Second State Pension Scheme (S2P). An employee who is contracted out of S2P pays lower National Insurance contributions.

Employers must, unless exempt (eg employing fewer than five employees, or offering an occupational pension that all staff can join within a year of starting work), give their employees access to a stakeholder pension scheme.

Since 1 October 2012, there has been a requirement to enrol employees automatically in a pension scheme, and the employer will be obliged to contribute. The new employer duties were introduced over six years. All employers must now comply. Further details may be found at <www.pensionsadvisoryservice.org.uk>.

1.8.5 Inventions and discoveries

In the case of employees who are likely to make discoveries or inventions, for example senior scientific and technical employees, the employer should ensure that the contract provides that any invention or discovery made in the course of employment belongs to the employer.

Such a clause is subject to the provisions of the Patents Act 1977 and the Copyright, Designs and Patents Act 1988. Details of these Acts are beyond the scope of this book but the basic rule is that inventions made in the course of employment belong to the employer. Other inventions belong to the employee and this cannot be varied by agreement. Even if the invention is made in the course of employment, the employee may be entitled to an award of compensation if the invention is of outstanding benefit to the employer.

1.8.6 Confidentiality

The use of confidentiality clauses in the employment context has been brought into sharp focus in the light of the allegations made against Harvey Weinstein in October 2017 and the consequential growth of the #MeToo movement. In March 2019, the UK Government launched a consultation to seek evidence and views on the use of confidentiality clauses in the employment context. That consultation closed on 29 April 2019. It drew a distinction between confidentiality clauses as used in contracts of employment for reasons such as protecting commercially sensitive information and preventing confidential information being shared with competitors (see below), and confidentiality clauses in settlement agreements (see **6.5**).

In July 2019, DBEIS announced that there would be new legislation to 'tackle the misuse of non-disclosure agreements in the workplace'. The proposed new legislation would, it was said, aim to prohibit clauses being used in employment contracts which prevent individuals from disclosing information to the police, regulated health and care professionals or legal professionals, such as a doctor, lawyer or social worker. Employers would need to make clear, in plain English, in the written statement of terms, the limitations of a confidentiality clause, so that individuals fully understand what they are signing and what their rights are. New enforcement measures would be introduced to deal with confidentiality clauses that do not comply with the legal requirements. Maria Miller MP put forward a private members' bill, which had its second reading in May 2022. It is not clear whether and, if so, when the proposals will come into effect.

Confidentiality agreements may legitimately be part of an employment contract or the terms of an engagement, but care needs to be taken as to their drafting and extent.

1.8.6.1   During employment

During employment, there is an implied term that an employee shall not reveal any confidential information (*Faccenda Chicken Ltd v Fowler* [1986] 1 All ER 617 – see **1.7.2.8**). Although there is an implied term that the employee shall not reveal any confidential information, it is advisable, in the case of employees who have access to confidential information, to insert an express term making it clear that they may not reveal such information during employment. Such a clause may also state what information the employer regards as confidential, though mundane information or information already in the public domain cannot be made confidential even by an express clause. The purpose of this clause is to draw the employee's attention to the duty of confidentiality and so to prevent the disclosure of such information.

1.8.6.2   After employment

The courts have traditionally viewed restrictions that limit an employee's future commercial activities after the termination of employment as being in restraint of trade, and for public policy reasons will not enforce such clauses unless they go no further than is reasonably necessary to protect legitimate business interests.

As far as the implied term protecting confidential information is concerned, after employment, only trade secrets and equivalent highly confidential information are protected by the implied term (see *Faccenda Chicken Ltd v Fowler*, **1.8.6.1** above). In *Faccenda Chicken*, the Court of Appeal set out a number of factors to be taken into account to determine whether particular information falls within the category that ought not to be disclosed after the employment has ended (applied recently in *Vestergaard Frandsen Als and Others v Bestnet Europe Ltd and Others* [2009] EWHC 657 (Ch)):

(a)   What was the nature of the employment?

(b)   What was the nature of the information?

(c)   Did the employer tell the employee that he regarded the information as confidential?

(d)   Could the information be easily isolated from the other information which the employee was free to use?

(See too the new Trade Secrets Directive adopted on 27 May 2016 and **1.8.7.1** below.)

On the facts of *Faccenda Chicken Ltd*, although Mr Fowler's knowledge of customers, sales and prices information was confidential and therefore could not be used or even memorised deliberately during employment, it was not confidential information equivalent to a trade secret, and thus his employer was not entitled to an injunction restraining the former employee from using information which he had generally acquired in his employment. If, however, Mr Fowler had made a copy of the list of customers or deliberately memorised it during his employment, that would amount to a breach of the duty of fidelity and the employer would have been able to restrain him from using that information in a competing business after the employment had ended (see, eg, *Bullivant v Ellis* [1987] ICR 464 and *Robb v Green* above – see **1.7.2.7**)

The advent of social media has meant that what is confidential information is not as clear-cut as it once was. For example, if an employee, with his employer's implied or express knowledge, uses Facebook, or Twitter or LinkedIn to communicate with customers or clients, these can be commercially valuable tools. Do those contacts belong to the employer or to the employee? Often, employees use their work e-mail addresses for personal and work purposes – who 'owns' their contacts lists? Employers need to have clear policies regarding these issues. In a recent case, *Whitmar Publications Ltd v Gamage* [2013] EWHC 1881 (Ch), the court issued an interim injunction to Whitmar, requiring its three employees to give Whitmar 'exclusive access, management and control' of four LinkedIn groups, which one of the employees (Wright) had had responsibility for operating in her role at Whitmar. The High Court held that Wright had been 'responsible for dealing with the LinkedIn groups as part of her employment duties at Whitmar', and that they had been 'operated for Whitmar's benefit and promoted its business' using the company's computers. The information in these accounts had been used when the new company set up by the employees had issued a press release, in breach of the duty of good faith.

Data protection law (see **Chapter 14**) may now provide additional protection for employers against employees leaving and taking confidential information with them. The UK's Information Commissioner's Office (ICO) announced in June 2016 that it had brought an enforcement action under s 55 of the Data Protection Act 1998 (now s 149 of the 2018 Act) against an individual who had left to join a competitor and taken a list of over 900 clients with him, including their purchase history and other commercial data. Section 55 makes it an offence for a person to knowingly or recklessly obtain or disclose personal data without the consent of the data controller. The individual concerned pleaded guilty to an offence under s 55 and was fined £300 and ordered to pay just over £400 in costs. While in most cases it will not be possible for an employer to bring a private prosecution itself against a former employee, it can report it to the ICO which has power to investigate and prosecute. A criminal record may serve as a more effective deterrent to an employee than the risk of civil injunction proceedings.

While it is well established that an employer cannot enforce restrictive covenants contained in the contract of employment if he is in repudiatory breach (see *General Billposting Company Ltd v Atkinson* [1909] AC 118 and **1.8.7.5**), it seems likely that any express term relating to confidentiality will continue notwithstanding any repudiation of the contract by the employer and that, in the absence of an express provision, the implied duty will, in any event, continue. Nevertheless, the issue is not beyond doubt (*Campbell v Frisbee* [2003] ICR 141).

1.8.7 Restrictive covenants

In order to prevent unfair competition after employment ends, it is advisable for an employer, where it is possible, rather than relying on the narrow scope of the implied term to protect confidential information, to insert an express restrictive covenant into the employee's contract.

Otherwise, in the absence of an effective restrictive covenant, while an ex-employee may not reveal confidential information, they can compete with the ex-employer, solicit the former customers of the ex-employer and poach its staff.

1.8.7.1 Restraint of trade

A restrictive covenant restraining an ex-employee from working in a competing business or soliciting ex-customers is prima facie void as being in restraint of trade. An employer is not entitled to protect himself against competition as such; he must have an interest to protect.

In order for a restrictive covenant to be enforceable:

(a)   the employer must have a legitimate business interest to protect. Legitimate business interests are:

    (i)   trade secrets or other highly confidential information which 'if disclosed to a competitor, would be liable to cause real or significant damage to the owner of the secret which the owner had tried to limit dissemination of' (*Lansing Linde Ltd v Kerr*

[1991] 1 All ER 418, CA). Readers should note that the Trade Secrets (Enforcement, etc) Regulations 2018 (SI 2018/597) came into force on 9 June 2018 and define trade secrets as information which '(a) is secret in the sense that it is not generally known among, or readily accessible to, persons within the circles that normally deal with the kind of information in question, (b) has commercial value ..., and (c) has been subject to reasonable steps ... to keep it secret';

(ii) trade connections, eg employers' relationships with their customers and clients (goodwill). The employer will have to demonstrate that a breach would result in actual or potential harm to the employer's business (see eg *Jack Allen (Sales and Service) Ltd v Smith* [1999] IRLR 19);

(iii) the employer's interest in maintaining a stable and trained workforce (see eg *Dawnay, Day & Co Ltd v Braconier d'Alphen & Others* [1997] IRLR 442).

A restrictive covenant can be valid only if imposed on a person who has such information, for example a senior technical employee with knowledge of trade secrets, or a manager or salesperson who has knowledge of trade connections.

In *Thomas v Far plc* [2007] EWCA Civ 118, the Court of Appeal held that an employer was entitled to seek to protect its pricing and financial information by way of a non-compete clause in the contract (see **1.8.7.2**).

(b) the restraint must also be reasonable in time and area, and it must be no wider than necessary to protect the employer's business interest (ie, the activity prohibited must be no wider than necessary; see **1.8.7.2**).

A restrictive covenant will not be enforced unless its terms are sufficiently clear.

Note that different outcomes may arise depending on whether the restrictive covenant under consideration is a non-solicitation or non-competition clause as opposed to a confidentiality clause. The type of information that can be protected by a confidentiality clause post termination of employment is information that amounts to a trade secret or other information of an equivalent confidentiality (see *Faccenda Chicken v Fowler* above). An attempt to restrict an employee post termination from using information that is 'merely' confidential is unlikely to succeed (see *P14 Medical Ltd v Mahon* [2021] IRLR 39).

In *Kynixa* (see above at **1.7.2.4**) the High Court upheld terms preventing two employees from competing with their employer ('*in any business competing with the Business*'); from soliciting customers of the employer ('*any person who is, or has been at any time, in the previous 6 months, a customer of the Business*'); and from poaching employees for a period of 12 months ('*solicit or entice away or endeavour to solicit or entice away any consultant, director or employee of the Group engaged in the Business*').

The Court held that the employer

> had a legitimate interest in seeking to prevent the solicitation of its customers. Equally it had a legitimate interest in seeking to prevent solicitation of [employees]. Given the nature of its business, the competitive nature of the market in which it operated, the fact that the ... [Defendants] were well known to the customers of the Claimant and the fact that with some customers, at least, arrangements for the provision of services by the Claimant between ... it and the customer would remain in place for a fixed period time (measured often in two year periods) but then be reviewed ... a restraint lasting twelve months was entirely reasonable. [The Court] also had regard to the fact that the ... Defendants had a choice about whether or not to enter the shareholder agreement [where the terms were contained] and in each case they chose to do so for (potentially) substantial gain ...

The Court also held that the *anti-competition clause was justified*. The defendants were very senior employees and were privy to confidential information which the claimant was justified in seeking to protect.

1.8.7.2   Contents of the clause

Restrictive covenants can cover competition by the ex-employee after the employment ends, the soliciting of (or dealing with) former customers and clients, and also the poaching of former employees. The basic rules set out above apply to all these areas.

Non-competition

The typical non-competition clause prohibits the employee, for a specified number of months or years after the end of the employment, from carrying on or being associated with the business in which the employer is engaged, within a specified number of miles of the employer's premises at which the employee was employed.

The clause must be no wider than is necessary to protect the employer's business:

(a)   The business activity from which the employee is barred must be no wider than the business in which he was employed. In *Scully UK Ltd v Lee* [1998] IRLR 259, the Court of Appeal refused to grant an injunction enforcing a covenant prohibiting an ex-employee from dealing with companies which were not in direct competition with the former employer. Mr Lee worked as a technical sales engineer for Scully, who were involved in the design and manufacture of systems for use in the oil and gas industry. In January 1997, he resigned from Scully and went to work as a sales manager for a company concerned with the supply of fuel distribution products and gauges. The Court of Appeal struck down a clause which prohibited the ex-employee from having any involvement in any business dealing with the type of equipment provided by Scully, on grounds that it extended to non-competing businesses (ie, businesses not involved in the oil and gas industry) and was therefore wider than necessary to protect their legitimate interests in customer connections and confidential information.

(b)   A time restraint in excess of one year can usually be justified only in exceptional circumstances. One year may be too long in some cases, especially if the employer's trade connections are subject to rapid change.

(c)   The area within which the ex-employee is barred from competing must be reasonable. It must not be wider than the area within which the employer did business.

The Court of Appeal held in *Thomas v Far plc* (see **1.8.7.1**) that a clause in the contract of a managing director of a firm of insurance brokers, which prevented him from competing with the company for 12 months, was enforceable. The employee had argued on appeal that the non-solicitation and confidentiality clauses in the managing director's contract adequately protected the employer and that the non-compete clause was unnecessary. The Court of Appeal held that because of the problems of differentiating between confidential and non-confidential information, and the fact that the solicitation of clients was unlikely to be done by the managing director himself, the non-compete clause was necessary to protect the legitimate business interest. It was accepted, on the facts, that the 12-month non-compete clause did not prevent Mr Thomas from acting as an insurance broker in sectors other than social housing, and since most insurance policies in the social housing sector were for longer than 12 months, the 12-month period was reasonable.

It is important to remember to review contracts when employees are promoted. In *PAT Systems v Neilly* [2012] EWHC 2609 (QB), the High Court refused to enforce a 12-month non-compete clause which had been entered into when the employee started employment in a junior role. The court said that the clause had to be assessed at the time it was entered into – because of the employee's very junior role, it was not reasonable to have a 12-month non-complete covenant, so it was unenforceable from the outset, and the promotion could not, absent express agreement to the clause from the employee, make it enforceable.

The High Court also expressed the provisional view that a 12-month non-compete clause was too long on the facts, having regard to the nature of the market in which the claimant operated and the transparent market in which the employer operated.

For recent cases on non-compete clauses, see *Tillman v Egon Zehnder Ltd* [2019] UKSC 32 and *Argus Media Ltd v Halim* [2019] EWHC 42 (QB).

Non-solicitation

The non-solicitation clause will prohibit the employee from seeking business from persons who were customers of the employer within a specified period prior to the employee leaving employment. Such a clause is more likely to be upheld if it is restricted to those customers with whom the employee has had personal contact during a specified period before termination (see, eg, *WRN Ltd v Ayris* [2008] EWHC 1080 (QB) where the term was held to be too wide because it was not restricted to customers with whom the employee had actually dealt). The clause should be no wider than necessary to protect the employer's business. Again, the clause is more likely to be upheld if it is restricted to those persons who were the employer's customers within a comparatively short time prior to the employee leaving. What is reasonable will depend on the nature of the business, eg how often customers come and go.

In *Associated Foreign Exchange Ltd v International Foreign Exchange (UK) Ltd* [2010] EWHC 1178 (Ch) the High Court held that there was insufficient evidence that a non-solicitation restriction of 12 months went no further than was reasonably necessary to protect an employer's legitimate business interests. The contract also contained a six-month non-dealing clause. The High Court refused to grant an injunction to prevent an ex-employee soliciting customers. It said that the non-dealing clause gave the employer adequate protection because the employee in question was not particularly senior and had not played a key part in building up new business for AFEX. Such protection as was sought by the non-solicitation clause would only be appropriate where a business could show that building up a relationship with its potential customers was a long and difficult process involving significant investment in time and money.

In *Coppage & Another v Safetynet Security Ltd* [2013] EWCA Civ 1176, the Court of Appeal upheld a six-month non-solicitation clause which prevented a director approaching anyone who had been a customer of the employer during the director's four-year term of employment. Although not restricted to customers with whom the employee had had personal contact, it was, in the court's opinion, reasonable because the term was 'only' six months and it was a non-solicitation clause and not a non-competition clause. However, in *Bartholomews Agri Food Ltd v Thornton* [2016] EWHC 648 (QB), the High Court refused to award an injunction in a case where the clause was not restricted to customers with whom the employee had been in contact.

Non-poaching

A non-poaching clause will prevent the employee from persuading other employees to go with him to a new employer. Such clauses are probably best restricted to senior employees known to the employee, where the employer has a legitimate interest to protect in the stability of its workforce (see, eg, *TSC Europe (UK) Ltd v Massey* [1999] IRLR 22 and, more recently, *UBS Wealth Management (UK) Ltd v Vesta Wealth LLP and Others* [2008] EWHC 1974 (QB)). Any clause will need to consider how long it will take for an employee's influence to end.

In deciding whether to grant an injunction to prevent an employee from poaching other employees, courts apply a 'balance of convenience test' (see **2.5.2**). For a recent decision on how the balance of convenience test is applied on an interim injunction application invoking the impact of the movements of senior employees on more junior employees left behind, see *Willis v Jardine Lloyd Thompson Group plc* [2015] AC 9301548.

Non-dealing

A non-dealing clause will prevent the employee from dealing with clients even if the clients approach the employee.

In *Beckett Investment Management Group Limited v Hall* [2007] EWCA Civ 613, the Court of Appeal upheld a 12-month non-dealing clause imposed by a holding company, even though on a literal interpretation of the clause the employees were not in breach. Beckett Investment Management Group Ltd (BIMG) was the holding company within a group of companies that provided financial advice. BIMG did not itself provide direct financial advice. This was done by a subsidiary, Beckett Financial Services Ltd (BFS). Hall and Yadev, who were both senior employees employed by BIMG but based at BFS's offices, left to start up their own competing business. Their contracts contained post-termination restrictions preventing them from providing financial advice of a type provided by the Company (defined as BIMG) to certain clients. Hall and Yadev continued to deal with BFS's clients and argued that the non-dealing restriction was unenforceable. The Court of Appeal said that the phrase the business of 'the Company' should be construed as the business undertaken by the subsidiaries. In terms of the length of the restriction, the Court said that 12 months was reasonable having regard to the nature of the financial services business, the seniority of Hall and Yadev, and evidence of an industry standard of 12 months. However, the Court said that a period longer than 12 months would have been unreasonable and unenforceable.

In this case, the clause was trying to protect the business for which the employees were actually working. It is important when drafting such restrictions to ensure that these clauses not only reflect the employee's actual circumstances, but also properly protect the actual business in which they are working.

Enforcement

If the clause is in restraint of trade, either because the employer has no interest to protect or because it is drafted too widely and therefore is unreasonable in time or area, it is void and hence unenforceable.

The 'blue pencil' test

If a clause is drafted too widely and is found to be in restraint of trade, the court may be able to apply the 'blue pencil' test to sever that part of the clause that is too wide and leave the remainder as an enforceable clause. Therefore, if drafting a restrictive covenant, draft for severance so that if one part of a clause is found to be void it can be severed, leaving the remainder valid. The court must be able to sever the offending part by striking a 'blue pencil' through it. The court cannot rewrite the clause (eg by substituting a shorter time-limit).

The Supreme Court in *Tillman v Egon Zehnder* (see above) looked at the circumstances in which the courts can exercise the power to sever unlawful provisions from a restrictive covenant. Egon Zehnder is a head-hunter firm. Ms Tillman worked there from 2003 until her resignation in 2017, to join a competitor. At the time she left, she was co-Global head of a key profit-making division of the business. Her contract of employment included a six-month post-termination non-compete clause, which prohibited her from engaging in or 'being concerned or interested in' any business that competed with the business of Egon Zehnder with which Ms Tillman had been materially concerned at the termination of her employment or for 12 months beforehand. The clause did not include a minimum threshold for a permitted minor shareholding. When she resigned, Ms Tillman made it clear that she would comply with all the restrictions in her contract except for the non-compete clause, which she said was too wide as it prevented her holding even a very small shareholding in a competing business (even though she did not intend to hold any such shareholding for the six-month period of the restriction).

Egon Zehnder was granted an interim injunction in the High Court to enforce the non-compete clause. That was set aside by the Court of Appeal, which, applying a line of previous authorities which stated that severance was only permissible in cases where the provision to be severed was a truly separate obligation (see eg *Attwood v Lamont* [1920] 3 KB 571 and *Scully UK Ltd v Lee* above), declined to sever the words 'interested in' from the clause in order to save it. The Supreme Court overturned the Court of Appeal and reinstated the injunction. The Supreme Court held that the words 'interested in' did prevent Ms Tillman from holding any shares in a competing business and that this rendered the clause too wide to be reasonable. However, it went on to find that the phrase 'interested in' could be severed from the clause, leaving the remainder untouched and therefore narrowing its scope and rendering it enforceable. The Supreme Court also looked at the use of the word 'concerned' and held that it implied some sort of active engagement or involvement in the competing business and it would not be too wide to prohibit that for a period post-termination.

The Supreme Court confirmed (paras 85–87) a three-stage approach:

(a)   Can the unenforceable provision be removed without needing to add to or modify the wording of what remains?

(b)   Are the remaining terms supported by adequate consideration?

(c)   Does the removal of the unenforceable provision change the character of the overall effect of all the post-employment restraints in the contract? (it is for the employer to establish this).

In this case, the Supreme Court answered all three of the questions in the affirmative. Thus, the test for severance now is whether the objectionable words can be deleted without generating any major change in the overall effect of all the post-employment restraints in the contract.

Drafting a series of cumulative restrictions leaving the court to decide where the line should be drawn (eg restraint for three years, followed by restraint for two years, followed by restraint for one year) is very likely to be void for uncertainty and is not recommended. Particular care needs to be taken where there is a transfer of an undertaking (see **7.4.1.1**).

In *Prophet Plc v Huggett* [2014] EWCA Civ 1013, the Court of Appeal, while holding that the wording of a non-compete clause was 'absurd', reiterated that while a court is able to 'blue pencil' (delete) bits of covenants to make them enforceable, it cannot add new words to make effective a provision that is not. While it might be possible to construe an ambiguous covenant in a way that made it enforceable, where the clause was not ambiguous but plain wrong and ineffective, as here, it could not be rescued.

For a recent case where a restrictive covenant was held to be unenforceable on the basis that it was too wide, see *Bartholomews Agri Food Ltd v Thornton* [2016] EWHC 648 (QB). For a case where a covenant was held to be properly drafted and enforceable, see *Pickwell and Nicholls v Pro Cam CP Ltd* [2016] EWHC 1304 (QB).

Mode of enforcement

The employer's remedy when an employee is in breach of an effective restrictive covenant will be an injunction where damages are not an adequate remedy, that is, an injunction to prevent the ex-employee from carrying on a competing business, soliciting customers or poaching staff, whichever is appropriate. The Court of Appeal considered injunctive relief in *Planon v Gilligan* [2022] EWCA Civ 642 and the application of the 'American Cyanamid' rules on interim injunctions. These concentrate on three elements: (i) was there a serious issue to be tried; (ii) would damages be an adequate remedy rather than direct enforcement; and (iii) where does the balance of convenience lie?

The employer may also claim damages if he has suffered pecuniary loss. The employee can be compelled to hand over, for example, copies of lists of customers and details of trade secrets in his possession. See *Roger Bullivant Ltd v Ellis* (at **1.8.6.2** above) and, more recently, *UBS Wealth Management (UK) Ltd v Vestra Wealth LLP* (above), where a business was granted a 'springboard' injunction to prevent a rival business, its founder and four defecting employees from doing business with and attempting to poach clients and other staff. See, most recently, *CEF Holdings Ltd and Another v Mundey and Others* [2012] EWHC 1524 (QB), where the High Court determined a number of issues arising out of an employer's attempts to stop its former employees setting up a rival company. The case set out some important principles in relation to without notice injunctions and the obligation of full and frank disclosure. The court also held that a number of restrictive covenants were too wide and invalid or, in some cases, unnecessary.

Damages awards can be a vexed issue. In *Marathon Asset Management LLP v Seddon & Bridgeman* [2017] EWHC 300 (Comm), the High Court considered the approach to assessing damages in a claim against two former employees who had unlawfully removed approximately 40,000 documents when they resigned to set up a competing business. The court found that the defendants had breached their duties of confidence but had only made very limited use of the documents. Marathon's case was that it did not matter what use was actually made of any of the files or that no loss had been shown: the defendants unlawfully took its confidential information and must pay for the value of what they took. It claimed that £15 million was the appropriate value to be placed on an award of damages. In a 74-page judgment following a nine-day High Court trial, involving factual and expert evidence and 'citation of case law and legal scholarship filling no fewer than 11 volumes', Marathon's arguments were rejected and nominal damages of only £1 were awarded against each of the two defendants. The misuse of confidential information had neither caused Marathon to suffer any financial loss nor resulted in the defendants making any financial gain, so it was hard to see how Marathon could be entitled to any remedy other than an award of nominal damages. It was only if and to the extent that any use was actually made of any of the files that it might be possible to show that any significant benefit was obtained by the defendants from wrongful use of the confidential information.

Effect of wrongful dismissal

If the contract terminates in circumstances where neither party is in breach of contract, or where the employee is rightfully dismissed for his own breach, the restrictive covenant can be enforced by the employer provided it is not void as being in restraint of trade.

However, the House of Lords held in *General Billposting Company Ltd v Atkinson* [1909] AC 118, that an otherwise valid restrictive covenant cannot be enforced if the employee has been wrongfully dismissed by the employer.

Thus, according to *Billposting*, where there is a repudiatory breach of contract by the employer, the employee is released from the obligations under the covenant.

Whilst *Billposting* remains good law (see *Argus Media Ltd v Halim* [2019] EWHC 42 (QB)), it remains unanswered as to whether *Billposting* applies in circumstances where the employer breaches the contract between resignation and termination but the employee only accepts the breach after the employment has ended. Some judges have expressed reservations as to the correctness of the principle (see eg *Rock Refrigeration Ltd v Jones* [1996] IRLR 675). Support for the view that confidentiality covenants can survive wrongful dismissal can be found in *Campbell v Frisbee* [2003] ICR 141.

Note that where the contract expressly provides that payment may be made in lieu of notice, the employer may dismiss the employee without proper notice and still be able to enforce any restrictive covenants (provided they are otherwise reasonable). This is because the employer is not then in breach of contract. This is the principal reason for the inclusion of a pay in lieu of notice provision (see **2.3.3**).

Employee's viewpoint

Ideally, an employee would want to avoid restrictive covenants, or limit them so as not to prejudice his ability to change employment. However, it may be in the employee's interest to agree to a restrictive covenant which is patently too wide and hence unenforceable.

1.8.7.3 'Garden leave' clauses

The term 'garden leave' is used to mean the period of time during which the employee is paid but is required to stay at home rather than attend work. The employer can thus hold the employee to the terms of his contract and prevent him from working for a competitor during the period. The clause will be invoked where either party gives notice of termination but the employer does not want the employee to attend at work during the notice period or to work for a competitor during that period.

A garden leave clause is more likely to be enforceable than a simple restriction precluding the employee joining a competitor for a period post-termination because it ensures that the employee does not suffer financially during the period of garden leave (*Eurobrokers Ltd v Rabey* [1995] IRLR 206). Nevertheless, the clause will not be enforced unless it is a reasonable restraint and the employer can show a legitimate business interest that he is seeking to protect (*Provident Financial Group plc v Hayward* [1989] ICR 160; *Symbian Ltd v Christensen* [2001] IRLR 77; *JH Finn & Co v Holliday* [2013] EWHC 3450 (QB)).

A long period of garden leave may be unduly onerous for an employee, and it is a matter for the court's discretion as to whether and to what extent the provision should be enforced. The court may, if the restraint during garden leave is drafted too widely, 'whittle it down' to something reasonable.

An employer who wishes to be sure that an employee can be sent home on garden leave should ensure that there is an express clause in the employee's contract sanctioning this course of action. This is because, in some cases (see **1.7.1**), the contract may give the employee the right to be provided with work during the notice period, or such a right may be implied and failure by the employer to observe that right may prevent him from relying on the garden leave clause; indeed, it could amount to a breach of contract by the employer (*William Hill Organisation Ltd v Tucker* [1998] IRLR 313).

In *SG&R Valuation Service v Boudrais* (see **1.7.1.1**), the High Court held that an employer can, however, send an employee on garden leave, in the absence of an express contractual right to do so, where there is evidence of actual wrongdoing by the employee (here helping himself to confidential information as part of a planned move to a competitor).

Table 1.1 Solicitation, poaching, competition and confidentiality: summary chart

	Solicitation (clients/customers) or Poaching (fellow employees)	Competition	Confidentiality
During contract (a) *Implied terms*	Not to solicit customers and/or employees of the employer Not to copy list of customers	Must not compete with employer Cannot 'moonlight' for a competitor if causes harm	Respect any confidential information
(b) *Express terms*	To increase employee's duty and/or clarify implied position	To increase employee's duty – eg devote 'full time' clause – to prevent all moonlighting	To clarify implied position – eg to define what counts as confidential information

	Solicitation (clients/ customers) or Poaching (fellow employees)	Competition	Confidentiality
After contract (a) *Implied terms*	No implied term	No implied term	Only 'highly confidential' information/trade secrets are protected
(b) *Express terms*	Covenant protecting legitimate interest (eg, customer connections/ stable workforce). Covenant must be reasonable in terms of (a) the activity prohibited (eg customers with whom employee had personal contact/senior employees known to the employee); and (b) time (eg customers from the last 6 months and for the next 6 months).	Covenant protecting legitimate interest (eg trade secrets) (see *Lansing Linde*). Covenant must be reasonable in terms of (a) the activity prohibited (eg no wider than the business in which employee employed, such as not to work for a competitor); (b) time; and (c) area covered (eg no wider than the area where the employer carries on business).	Covenant protecting legitimate interest (eg trade secrets or other highly confidential information which if disclosed would cause real harm to the employer (*Lansing Linde*)). To clarify the implied position, ie what the employer considers highly confidential information (cannot increase the duty).

1.8.7.4   Reviews

Employers should regularly review their restrictive covenants, to make sure they remain relevant and that the business interests to be protected are properly described. Where new restrictive covenants are imposed, for example where a business is acquired and new employees are merged into existing teams, it will be necessary not only to ensure that the employees agree to any changes but also, in certain situations, for consideration to be paid, in order to ensure that there is an enforceable covenant. In *Re-use Collections Ltd v Sendall and May Glass Recycling Ltd* [2014] EWHC 3852 (QB), Re-use sought to rely on express restrictive covenants to prevent former employees from setting up a competing business. The High Court emphasised that for a binding contract to exist, there needed to be 'consideration', ie some benefit provided in return for the obligation accepted by the employee. In this case, although there had been a pay rise, that had not been awarded in connection with the acceptance of new terms and conditions. Continued employment will be sufficient consideration only if it is dependent on acceptance of the covenants.

1.8.7.5   Government review of 'non-compete clauses'

In May 2016, the Government issued a consultation on whether post-termination restrictions unfairly hinder the free movement of employees or stifle entrepreneurship. When it published its 2018 response to the Taylor Review of Modern Working Practices (see **Introductory Note**), the Government noted that the consensus view to the response was that restrictive covenants were a valuable and necessary tool for employers to use to protect their business interests and did not unfairly impact on an individual's ability to find other work. It concluded then that no further action was required.

In December 2020, the Government launched a new consultation on measures to reform post-termination non-compete clauses in contracts of employment. Its justification for launching a fresh consultation so soon after the last was that Covid-19 had had a profound impact on the labour market. The Government said that, as with its previous consultation, non-compete clauses can act as a barrier by preventing individuals from working for a competing business, or from applying their entrepreneurial spirit to establish a competing business. Employers say that the common law controls on restrictive covenants, enforced through the courts, mean that non-competes are unenforceable unless they are shown to be no more restrictive than reasonably necessary to protect the employer's legitimate business interests. They argue that this approach has stood the test of time and is adaptable to changing economic needs and aspirations.

The consultation proposed two options for reform.

- Option one is to make non-competes enforceable only when mandatory compensation (around 60–80% of the employee's earnings) is paid by the employer for the period that the employee is prevented from working for a competitor or starting their own business. Measures are also suggested to place statutory limits on the length of non-compete clauses.

- Option two proposes banning non-compete clauses completely, along with measures short of an outright ban in the interests of spreading innovation.

The law and practice on non-compete clauses varies around the world. Germany, along with many other European countries, requires compensation as a pre-requisite of an enforceable restrictive covenant, whereas California bans non-compete clauses altogether. The closing date for responses was 26 February 2021.

In the Response submitted by the Employment Lawyers' Association (ELA), there is a detailed and very helpful explanation of the current law; an analysis of the available evidence on the impact of non-compete clauses; a comparison of post-termination restraints in different jurisdictions; and the results of a survey of 128 employers undertaken by ELA via its members. The ELA concludes (with acknowledgement to the summary of the ELA response written by Kerenza Davis, a barrister at Blackstone Chambers) that:

- although the pandemic has had a massive impact on the economy overall, it has seen no evidence of any material change specifically relevant to post-termination restraints;

- in its survey (conducted after the pandemic began), 78% of respondents indicated that a ban on non-compete clauses would have a negative impact on their business;

- there is no clear evidence that the existing regime prevents the Government's stated objectives (boosting innovation, creating jobs and increasing competition) or that the proposed reforms would help to achieve these objectives;

- non-competes can be used by young, innovative businesses to protect themselves from bigger and better established rivals as well as vice versa.

The ELA does acknowledge that there are issues with the current system, particularly in terms of transparency and enforcement, including employees being deterred from challenging unreasonable covenants for fear of potential cost consequences. The ELA makes some proposals to address these issues, including:

- requiring an employer to clear a higher hurdle than the standard 'serious issue to be tried' to secure interim relief in respect of restrictive covenants;

- changing the costs rules for employee competition proceedings to something more favourable to employees;

- introducing a requirement (along the lines of what is required before an individual can waive their statutory rights under the Employment Rights Act 1996 or the Equality Act

2010) that an employee should obtain independent legal advice before agreeing to be bound by a non-compete covenant;

- requiring employers to remind employees on an annual basis of any non-compete clauses that apply to them.

The Government announced in April 2022 that it was still considering responses.

1.8.8 Disciplinary and grievance procedures

Details of disciplinary and grievance procedures may be included to comply with s 1 of the ERA 1996 (see **1.4.2**). If employers wish to have the power, on appeal by an employee, to increase any disciplinary sanction, they will need to reserve that power expressly (see *McMillan v Airedale NHS Foundation Trust* [2014] EWCA Civ 1031 and **5.4.2.2** below).

Note: where a disciplinary procedure forms part of an employee's contract of employment, civil remedies for breach of contract may be used during the course of disciplinary proceedings. In *West London Mental Health NHS Trust v Chhabra* [2013] UKSC 60, the Supreme Court granted an injunction preventing an NHS Trust from holding a disciplinary hearing against the claimant as a result of a number of irregularities in the proceedings against the claimant, which cumulatively rendered the convening of the disciplinary panel unlawful as a material breach of her contract

1.8.9 Surrender of papers

It is common for the employment contract to require the employee, on the termination of the contract, to surrender all notes and documents that he has in his possession which relate to the employer's business.

1.8.10 Other issues

Consideration should be given to inclusion of other clauses in the contract and policy statements, for example:

(a)   a PILON clause (see **Chapter 2**);

(b)   a whistle-blowing policy (see **5.6.5**);

(c)   computer/telephone usage policies (see **15.5.2**);

(d)   an equal opportunities policy (see **Chapter 8**);

(e)   a health and safety policy;

(f)   a maternity, paternity and parental leave policy (see **Chapter 14**);

(g)   a flexible working policy (see **Chapter 14**).

1.9   VARIATION OF CONTRACTUAL TERMS

Where the employer and employee have agreed the terms of their contract, generally speaking those terms cannot be changed without both parties agreeing to the changes. Employers cannot unilaterally change the terms and conditions of the contract without possible consequences. In practice, there are four routes available to an employer who wishes to vary contractual terms:

- mutual agreement;
- through a pre-existing flexibility clause;
- dismissal and re-engagement on new terms (see **Chapter 5**);
- unilateral imposition.

Where an employer wishes to vary the terms of a contract, it is first necessary to identify whether the terms are contractual or not. Where terms are contained in staff handbooks, this can give rise to uncertainty as to the contractual effect of clauses and how to change them. Where terms are not contractual, and subject to a power being provided to allow change, as long as there is a consultation, then, generally speaking, such terms can ultimately be varied without agreement. Where terms are contractual, employers will either need to obtain the express agreement of the employees to any variation, or, in an extreme case, they could terminate the employment and offer to re-employ on the new terms. This might give rise to an unfair dismissal claim (see **Chapter 5**). If employers wish to rely on a clause purporting to give them a power to make unilateral variations to a contact, such a clause will need to be very clear and unambiguous. Even if there is a power to impose changes unilaterally, the employer still needs to consider how changes will be communicated, and it needs to consult about the proposed change. Failure to do so may give rise to a breach of the implied duty of trust and confidence (see **1.7.1.4** and **3.4.3**).

Sometimes, when an employer wants to try to change a term of a policy, it will maintain that the term is not contractual and so consent is not needed (see **1.8**). In *Norman v National Audit Office* (UKEAT/0276/14), an employer imposed changes to sick pay and privilege leave days after unsuccessful negotiations. The terms of the contract contained a clause that said that the conditions of service were 'subject to amendment', and that any significant changes would be notified by management, policy circulars or general orders, changes to employees' particular terms being notified separately. The employment tribunal accepted that the 'subject to amendment' provision permitted the variation. The EAT disagreed: it said that the wording was not sufficiently clear and unambiguous to permit the changes the employer was trying to make; 'subject to amendment' came 'nowhere near' the standard of being clear and unambiguous. The references to amendment and notification raised the possibility of change occurring, and how that would be communicated, but did not establish a clear power to change terms. The EAT also held that the relevant provision was not incorporated into the actual contracts as it was contained in a staff handbook, which largely addressed collective bargaining issues and was not the 'stuff of terms and conditions'.

Mutual agreement is obviously the preferred route, which may involve negotiations through a recognised union or workforce agreement as well as directly with individual employees. Any changes agreed should be recorded and confirmed in writing and, if they relate to any of the matters required to be included in a written statement, they must be confirmed in writing within one month.

It is quite common for employers to include so-called 'flexibility clauses' in contracts, which purport to allow the employer to vary some terms unilaterally, ie without agreement. The courts are generally wary of such clauses, and terms that purport to give employers the right to change any terms of the contract, eg 'the right to vary this contract from time to time', have usually been construed narrowly.

The test as to when express variation or flexibility clauses will be permitted was set out by the Court of Appeal in *Wandsworth London Borough Council v D'Silva* [1998] IRLR 193. The Court said that employers need to use clear and unambiguous language in a contract to be able to rely upon a clause allowing unilateral variation. If the change might produce an unreasonable result, the tribunals must 'seek to avoid such a result'.

Even if such a clause exists, terms must be used in a manner that is not oppressive or capricious. Problems can arise with staff handbooks, which may or may not form part of the contractual terms. If they are contractual, changing them may become problematic.

Careful regard should be had to the contract to see whether the terms are wide enough to allow for the proposed change. Often a contract will permit variations to certain terms, eg hours of work and place of work. However, employers must also have regard to the implied duty of mutual trust and confidence, even where the contractual terms permit a variation. An employer should, for example, consult with employees before introducing changes.

In *Sparks v Department for Transport* [2015] EWHC 181 (QB); [2016] EWCA Civ 360, seven employees who worked for different agencies within the Department of Transport (such as the

DVLA and the Highways Agency) applied to the High Court for a declaration that their employer had breached their contracts of employment by unilaterally imposing a change to the attendance management provisions of what they argued was a contractual staff handbook. In July 2012, following unsuccessful negotiations with the trade unions, the Department of Transport sought to introduce standardised attendance management terms across all its agencies. As some agencies had pre-existing different terms, this had the effect of unilaterally changing some employees' terms of service. The Departmental Staff Handbook for each agency provided as follows:

1.1   Contract of employment

    1.1.1 ... Your terms and conditions of employment include those set out in

        (1)   ...

        (2)   the DfT Departmental Staff Handbook which contains terms and conditions and procedures and guidance applying specifically to you as a Crown employee ...

1.2   The Departmental Staff Handbook

    1.2.1 The Departmental Staff Handbook, as applying to you, sets out many of your terms and conditions. It is the intention of the recognised trade unions ... and of the Crown that all of the provisions of the Departmental Staff Handbook which apply to you and are apt for incorporation should be incorporated into your contract of employment.

    1.2.2 The Departmental Staff Handbook is in two parts:

    Part A contains terms and conditions. Without prejudice to the generality of paragraph 1.2.1 above, all of Part A and all annexes of Part A which apply to you and which are apt for incorporation, will be incorporated into your contract of employment; and

    Part B contains procedures and guidance relevant to your employment relationship with the Crown. Those procedures and guidance can be relevant to the operation of your contractual terms and conditions set out in Part A, but in the event of inconsistency between Part A and Part B it is Part A which prevails.

The High Court held that the terms relating to attendance management were incorporated into the individual employees' contracts and that the Department of Transport's attempts to impose variations on them unilaterally should not be permitted, as the relevant terms provided that any proposals to change the relevant terms and conditions should have been the subject of consultation, 'with a view to reaching agreement'. If no agreement could be reached, the High Court said that 'unilateral changes could then have been made but only if they were not detrimental to the employee'. On the facts, the court found the changes were detrimental. The court also held that certain clauses were not apt for contractual incorporation, for example clauses relating to reporting obligations when sick. The High Court's analysis was upheld by the Court of Appeal: the attendance management provisions were contractual and could only be amended in accordance with the contract.

Where an employer does try to impose a unilateral variation on an employee, an employee has four choices (see *Robinson v Tescom Corporation* [2008] IRLR 408):

(a)   to agree to the variation (either expressly, or by continuing to work without protest);

(b)   to resign and complain of unfair constructive dismissal (see **3.4.3**) and wrongful dismissal (see **Chapter 2**);

(c)   to refuse to work under the new terms and force the employer to take such steps as it thinks are appropriate;

(d)   to stand and sue, ie continue to work under protest and seek damages (either for breach of contract – see for example *Rigby v Ferodo* [1987] IRLR 516 – or, if the breach is so serious as to bring the original contract to an end, unfair dismissal).

In *Robinson v Tescom*, the employee agreed to changes 'under protest', but then refused to work under the new terms and was dismissed. The EAT said the decision to dismiss him was fair because, having agreed (albeit under protest) to the changes, he could not then renege on what he had agreed – he was refusing to obey a lawful and reasonable instruction.

See also *Rock Advertising Ltd v MWB Business Exchange Centres Ltd* and *Abrahall v Nottingham City Council* at **1.8** above.

Note. The Coronavirus Job Retention Scheme (CJRS) (see **Introductory Note**) was essentially based around express agreed variations to contracts of employment by the employer and the employee. The CJRS required that the agreement between employers and employees to place staff on furlough had to be confirmed in writing by the employer. It was also possible to rely on a collective agreement. An agreement to go on furlough is not of itself an agreement to a deduction from wages. In a widely publicised incident during the pandemic, British Gas gave employees notice to end their existing contracts and asked them to agree new terms for lower pay and longer hours. Hundreds refused and their employment was terminated. In January 2021, staff voted to take strike action in response to the attempt to impose the new conditions. In April 2021, it was reported that 500 engineers had lost their jobs after they refused to sign new contracts. In July 2021, it was announced that a new pay and conditions deal, which allowed those sacked the chance to return, had been reached. Other high-profile disputes over the use of fire and rehire tactics during lockdown included British Airways, Go West North and Tesco. In the recent tribunal case of *Khatun v Winn Solicitors* (ET/2501492/2020), the dismissal of a solicitor for refusing to accept new terms during furlough was held to be unfair. While it was accepted that the reason for dismissal was 'some other substantial reason of a kind such as to justify the dismissal of an employee holding the position which the employee held' (ERA 1996, s 98(1)(b)), it was held that the respondent employer had not acted reasonably in relation to her dismissal.

In *USDAW & Ors v Tesco* [2022] EWCA Civ 978, the Court of Appeal overturned a High Court decision to grant an injunction to prevent Tesco from firing and rehiring employees to remove a contractual entitlement to a specific element of their pay called Retained Pay. The High Court found that there was an implied term in the employees' contracts that Tesco could not terminate their contracts in order to remove or reduce the Retained Pay, and so held that an injunction was necessary to prohibit Tesco from implementing those dismissals. The Court of Appeal disagreed with the High Court. It held that a term can only be implied into employment contracts where this is objectively necessary in order to give the contract commercial or practical coherence (business efficacy) or where the need for the term is 'so obvious that it goes without saying', which it said was not the case here. The Court of Appeal added that the appropriate remedy for wrongful dismissal is almost invariably a financial one, and so it was not appropriate to grant an injunction which in effect prevented a private sector employer from dismissing an employee for an indefinite period. This decision confirms that the practice of 'fire and rehire' does remain an option open to employers who seek for business reasons to change terms and conditions of employment.

In June 2021, Acas published a fact-finding paper on the use of 'fire and rehire' practices, where employers dismiss then re-employ workers on changed terms and conditions, or where the prospect of doing so is put to workers during negotiations about changing their terms and conditions. It presented a number of legislative options (including tightening up the law around unfair dismissal; enhancing the requirement and capacity for employment tribunals to scrutinise businesses' rationale for change; protecting continuity of employment; strengthening employers' consultation obligations around proposed dismissals) and non-legislative options (including improved guidance for employers on their legal obligations and good practice; and publishing 'naming and shaming' data). Acas has also published a useful process map for employers who are considering making changes to employees' contracts and/or terms of conditions, and in November 2021 it published guidance for employers on making changes to employment contracts (<www.acas.org.uk/changing-an-employment-contract/employer-responsibilities>).

The Government has indicated that it does not intend to legislate to make the practice of 'fire and rehire' unlawful. However, in March 2022, it announced that a new Statutory Code of

Practice will be published on the use of fire and rehire to bring about changes to employees' terms and conditions. The Code will detail how businesses must hold fair, transparent and meaningful consultations on proposed changes to employment terms and will include practical steps that employers should follow. As a Statutory Code, once in effect, employment tribunals will be required to consider the Code and will have the power to uplift compensation awarded to employees by up to 25% where the Code applies and an employer has unreasonably failed to follow it. No date has been given as to when a draft of the Code will be published. Employers should not, however, overlook the obligation to conduct collective consultation if they propose to make changes to employees' terms and conditions which affect 20 or more employees.

1.10   HUMAN RIGHTS ACT 1998

From a contractual perspective, the individual rights recognised by the HRA 1998 (see **Chapter 15**) may be given greater weight, especially when they have to be balanced against managerial interests. This could be achieved by two routes. First, the courts may be persuaded to accept that those rights are implicitly incorporated into individual contracts of employment. Secondly, if that is a step too far, it may be argued that they are part and parcel of the development of the implied duty of mutual trust and confidence. Thus, even though the HRA 1998 is not directly enforceable between private individuals, if there is a breach of a Convention right, that may give rise to a claim for breach of contract.

Additionally, as courts and tribunals are obliged to act compatibly with the HRA 1998 (s 6), it has also been argued that the HRA 1998 will impact on the construction of terms of the contract of employment, in particular terms relating to confidentiality and restraint of trade, and the HRA 1998 may well limit the 'scope' of 'managerial prerogative' in the context of giving orders and the obligation of an employee to obey (lawful and reasonable) orders.

Note that the current Government gave a manifesto commitment to repeal the HRA 1998 and replace it with a British Bill of Rights. See **Introductory Note**.

Although there is nothing specifically stated in the HRA 1998, it has long been accepted that rights under the ECHR can be waived by contract. The ECtHR's jurisprudence makes it clear, however, that:

(a)   any waiver must be clear and unequivocal;

(b)   simply signing a contract may not amount to a waiver – an employee's attention must be drawn to any specific provision;

(c)   even where there is a waiver in a contract, it is not deemed to be conclusive of the matter; courts will still scrutinise and assess any such waiver.

In *Rommelfanger v Germany* (1989) 62 DR 151, Mr Rommelfanger was a German doctor working in a Catholic hospital. He expressed views on abortion in the press which ran counter to those of the Catholic Church, and was dismissed as a result. In his contract, he had accepted a duty of loyalty to the Catholic Church. It was held that he had accepted a limitation on his freedom of expression but had not thereby deprived himself of the protection of Article 10 of the ECHR. Notwithstanding the contractual limitation, the Court maintains a supervisory jurisdiction to look at the substantive issue and weigh up the competing interests of the employer and employee. The Court will give weight to contractual waivers, but there may be situations where the restriction on the right is too extreme, in which case the Court will interfere. As the Catholic Church was an organisation based on certain fundamental convictions and beliefs which it considered essential, it was entitled to its freedom of expression.

In *Ahmad v UK* (1982) 4 EHRR 126, a local authority teacher complained of constructive dismissal after he was refused permission to attend a mosque during working hours. It was accepted by the Court that his right to exercise his freedom of religion (Article 9) could be limited by contractual obligations such as requirements relating to the hours of work, timetabling etc, provided that his employers did not arbitrarily disregard his freedom of religion.

In *Stedman v UK* (1997) 23 EHRR CD 168, the Commission rejected the employee's claim that her employer had breached Article 9 by requiring her to work on Sundays; the employee was not dismissed because of her religious beliefs but because she refused to work her contractual hours (see now, however, s 10 of the Equality Act 2010 – at **8.2.3**).

1.11 PROTECTION OF WAGES

If an employer fails to pay remuneration due under the employment contract, the employee (or worker – see **1.3** above) will often be able to rely on what is commonly referred to as the 'protection of wages' legislation – set out in Pt II of the ERA 1996. This part of the ERA 1996 expressly includes workers as well as employees within its protections (as defined in s 230). The term 'worker' is wider and expressly encompasses an individual who works under a contract of employment (s 230(3)), and will be used below when describing the protection provided. Workers serving in the armed forces, parliamentary staff and some categories of seamen are exempt. Notice pay is not covered by Pt II and s 14 expressly excludes deductions made in respect of an overpayment of wages or expenses (see **1.11.4** below). The normal remedies for breach of contract are also available in all these situations. Most workers utilise the protection of wages legislation where it is available in addition to or in preference to the normal breach of contract remedies. No qualifying period of service is needed.

It is possible that the furlough arrangements made possible by the Coronavirus Job Retention Scheme (CJRS) may impact, at least in the short term, on unlawful deduction claims. The rules on eligibility, and who could claim for what, were complex and changed over the duration of the CJRS. For example, on 25 June 2020, new Treasury Directions and Guidance came into existence which explained what was meant by 'usual hours'. Paragraph 7.2 of the Treasury Directions defines a variable pay employee as anyone who does not meet the definition of a fixed pay employee in para 7.6 of the Treasury Directions. Government guidance statements may also be relevant. One such says that 'HMRC will not decline or seek repayment of any grant based solely on the particular choice of pay calculation, as long as a reasonable choice is made', which allows room for discretion on decisions that an employer made. These provisions will be relevant when considering how to respond to an unlawful deduction from wages claim arising out of an employer's use of the CJRS.

Readers should also bear in mind that such claims may also arise as a shortfall in holiday pay or a failure to pay the NMW and that workers may have a variety of overlapping legal grounds on which to bring such claims, each of which may have different limits and restrictions applying to them. It may sometimes be necessary to rely on all possible heads of claim. This may be particularly significant where there are relatively short limitation periods for bringing claims. For example, under the ERA 1996 and the Working Time Regulations 1998, claims must generally be brought within three months, whereas for breach of contract claims, there is a six-year limitation period.

Two aspects of the statutory protection for unpaid wages that exist in Pt II of the ERA 1996 are considered below: first, the need for authority before the employer is entitled to make deductions from wages; and, secondly, the method of enforcement by employment tribunals.

1.11.1 Deductions from wages

The basic right given to workers by Pt II of the ERA 1996 is stated in s 13, whereby an employer must not make any deduction from wages unless:

(a) it is authorised by statute (eg Pay As You Earn (PAYE) and National Insurance); or

(b) it is authorised by the worker's contract; or

(c) the worker has previously signified in writing his consent to the making of it. This means that the worker must have agreed to the deduction before the event occurs.

A deduction is defined in s 13(3) as follows:

> Where the total amount of wages paid on any occasion by an employer to a worker employed by him is less than the total amount of wages properly payable by him to the worker on that occasion ... the amount of the deficiency shall be treated ... as a deduction ...

Therefore, if the total amount paid to the worker is less than the total amount properly payable (which will not include pure errors of computation), it will be a deduction.

Non-payment of a sum due may amount to a deduction, provided that the sum relates to a period of employment. Non-payment of wages in lieu of notice after termination of the contract does not therefore fall under the ERA 1996 (*Delaney v Staples* [1991] IRLR 112).

A unilateral reduction in wages may amount to a deduction, as may a non-payment of commission.

An employer may also make deductions where those deductions are covered by one of the exemptions in s 14 (see **1.11.4**).

If the employer wishes to make any deductions from a worker's wages, for example penalties for substandard work or to recoup 'till shortages' from workers handling money, authority to make the deduction should be specified in the contract.

For workers in retail employment, deductions for cash shortages or stock deficiencies must not, except for the final payment of wages, exceed one-tenth of the employee's gross wages (ERA 1996, s 17).

If the employer wishes to make deductions of a type not provided for in the contract, for example, if the employer makes a loan to be repaid by deductions from wages, the worker must give his written consent to the deduction. (In the example given, this would usually be done in the loan agreement.)

1.11.2   What are 'wages'?

The ERA 1996 prohibits deductions from 'wages', and s 27 of the ERA 1996 defines wages as 'any sums payable to the worker [by his employer] in connection with his employment ... including any fee, bonus, commission, holiday pay or other emolument referable to his employment, whether payable under his contract or otherwise'. It includes all statutory pay entitlements, such as sick pay and maternity pay. Lord Browne-Wilkinson in *Delaney v Staples* [1992] IRLR 191 said that:

> ... the essential characteristic of wages is that they are consideration for work done or to be done under a contract of employment. If a payment is not referable to an obligation on the employee under a subsisting contract of employment to render his services it does not in my judgment fall within the ordinary meaning of the word 'wages'.

(See too *New Century Cleaning Co Ltd v Church* [2000] IRLR 27.)

'Wages' has been held to include overtime payments, shift payments, meal and overnight allowances. Tips and service charges may be covered if there is a contractual arrangement for them to be distributed to staff (see eg *Saavedra v Aceground Ltd* [1995] IRLR 198). There is a list of excluded payments in s 27(2) (eg pension payments).

In *Tradition Securities & Futures SA v Alexandre Mouradian* [2009] EWCA Civ 60, the Court of Appeal held that an employee was entitled to bring a claim relating to the amount of his bonus in the employment tribunal under the unlawful deduction from wages provisions because the amount of the bonus was quantifiable according to a precise formula for calculating the bonus.

As stated above, payments in lieu of notice are not wages under ERA 1996, s 27.

Following the EAT's decision in *Bear Scotland* (see **1.12.5.3** below), the Government passed the Deduction from Wages (Limitation) Regulations 2014 (SI 2014/3322), which took effect from

8 January 2015. The Regulations apply to claims presented to the employment tribunal on or after 1 July 2015. Although designed to limit back claims for holiday pay to two years, they also amend the ERA 1996 so that all complaints presented on or after 17 July 2015 of unauthorised deductions from wages can only be brought in respect of deductions occurring within two years of presentation of the claim (but excluding some very specific statutory payments, such as SSP (see **1.8.3.3**) and statutory maternity pay (SMP, see **14.2**), as set out in s 27(1)(b)–(j) of the ERA 1996). The Regulations also amended the Working Time Regulations 1998 by stating that the right to payment in respect of annual leave is not contractual but purely statutory, thus preventing the bringing of contractual claims under the protection of wages legislation for statutory holiday pay claims. This also now overrules one of the findings of the House of Lords in *HMRC v Stringer* [2009] UKHL 31.

One area that can be particularly complex is how you actually calculate what a day's wages are. Where someone is paid an annual salary, should you divide it by 365, or by some lesser fraction to allow for non-working days such as weekends? The Supreme Court had to look at this in *Hartley v King Edward VI College* [2017] UKSC 39. A county court ruled that teachers who had been on strike should have 1/260 of their annual pay deducted for each strike day. Contractually most full-time teachers are directed to work 195 days per year. They also have to undertake work during undirected time. The claimants argued that the proportion to be deducted should be 1/365 for each strike day. The county court followed the decision in *Amey v Peter Symonds College* [2014] IRLR 206 and ruled that the proper deduction should be 1/260. The Court of Appeal held, applying s 2 of the Apportionment Act 1870, that monies are apportioned on the basis that payment accrues daily, but that does not necessarily mean that it accrues at an even rate on each day. In this case, the respondent employer's interpretation of the contract, that pay accrued at a rate of 1/260 on working days and days of paid holiday, rather than 1/365 as contended by the claimant teachers, was correct. That fraction was based on the premise that the teachers' working days were Monday to Friday, and that all work days should be included, even those that did not have to be worked because of holidays. So the formula applied was:

5 working days a week x 52 weeks a year = 260 working days a year

The Supreme Court allowed the appeal and directed that 1/365th should be deducted.

1.11.3 'Properly payable'

The Court of Appeal held in *New Century Cleaning Co Ltd v Church* [2000] IRLR 27 that wages will be 'properly payable' only if the worker has a legal (although not necessarily contractual) entitlement to the wages. In *Hellewell v AXA Services* (**1.11 2** above) the EAT confirmed that the claimants were not entitled to a bonus because the contract was clear – no bonus was payable where the employees had committed gross misconduct. The Court of Appeal held, in *Agarwal v Cardiff University* [2018] EWCA Civ 1434, that the employment tribunal has jurisdiction to construe a contract in order to determine a claim under s 13 of the ERA 1996 not to suffer an unauthorised deduction from wages. In Ms Agarwal's case, in order to decide whether there was a deduction of wages, a tribunal had to decide whether the salary she claimed was properly payable pursuant to a legal obligation. That necessarily meant that it would need to resolve any dispute as to the meaning of the contract relied on.

1.11.4 Exceptions

The burden of proof is on an employer to show that one of the exemptions or exceptions applies.

1.11.4.1 Overpayment of wages or expenses

An employer may make deductions to recover overpayments of wages or expenses previously paid by mistake to the worker (ERA 1996, s 14(1)). Any dispute as to the lawfulness of such a deduction must be resolved in the civil courts. Such overpayments are recoverable unless the employer has led the worker to believe the money was his and the worker changes his position (eg spends the money) and the overpayment was not the worker's fault (*Kleinwort Benson Ltd v Lincoln City Council and Other Appeals* [1999] 2 AC 349).

1.11.4.2 Deductions in respect of industrial action

If the worker is not performing any of his duties, the employer may deduct an amount which represents a fair proportion of his salary. (For some relevant cases, see *Norris v London Fire and Emergency Planning Authority* [2013] IRLR 428, *Sunderland Polytechnic v Evans* [1993] IRLR 196 and *Gill v Ford Motor Company Ltd* [2004] IRLR 840.)

1.11.5 Enforcement

If an employer makes an unauthorised deduction from wages, the worker may present a complaint to an employment tribunal within three months of the payment from which the deduction was made (or within three months of the last in a series of deductions, so allowing a claim to go back more than three months if the underpayments form part of a series). An employment tribunal may still consider a complaint presented outside the time limit if it is satisfied that it was not reasonably practicable for the complaint to be presented before the end of the three-month period, and the claimant has presented it.

Note that the Deduction from Wages (Limitation) Regulations 2014, which took effect from 8 January 2015 (see **1.11.2**), apply to claims that are presented to the employment tribunal on or after 1 July 2015. Although designed to limit back claims for holiday pay to two years, these Regulations also amend the ERA 1996 so that all claims of unauthorised deductions from wages can only be brought in respect of deductions occurring within two years of presentation of the claim (but excluding some very specific statutory payments such as SSP and SMP, as set out in s 27(1)(b)–(j) of the ERA 1996). Where a claim for unpaid holiday pay is made and further deductions are made by the employer, the ET Presidential Direction of 27 March 2015 permits the claimant to apply to amend the claim to add further complaints of alleged non-payment of holiday pay.

Series of deductions

Section 23 of the ERA 1996 provides:

> (1)   A worker may present a complaint to an employment tribunal—
>
>   (a)   that his employer has made a deduction from his wages in contravention of section 13 (including a deduction made in contravention of that section as it applies by virtue of section 18(2)),
>
>   ...
>
> (2)   Subject to subsection (4), an employment tribunal shall not consider a complaint under this section unless it is presented before the end of the period of three months beginning with—
>
>   (a)   in the case of a complaint relating to a deduction by the employer, the date of payment of the wages from which the deduction was made, or
>
>   (b)   in the case of a complaint relating to a payment received by the employer, the date when the payment was received.
>
> (3)   *Where a complaint is brought under this section in respect of—*
>
>   (a)   *a series of deductions or payments, or*
>
>   ...
>
>   *the references in subsection (2) to the deduction or payment are to the last deduction or payment in the series or to the last of the payments so received.* (emphasis added)

Case law on series of deductions

There is no statutory definition of a 'series of deductions'. In *Bear Scotland Ltd v Fulton; Hertel (UK) Ltd v Woods; Amec Group Ltd v Law* [2015] IRLR 15, Langstaff P stated:

> Whether there has been a series of deductions or not is a question of fact: 'series' is an ordinary word, which has no particular legal meaning. As such in my view it involves two principal matters in the present context, which is that of a series through time. These are first a sufficient similarity of subject-matter, such that each event is factually linked with the next in the same way as it is linked with its predecessor; and second, since such events might either be stand-alone events of the same general type, or linked together in a series, a sufficient frequency of repetition. This requires both a sufficient factual, and a sufficient temporal, link.

The EAT decided that a gap of three months between *unlawful* deductions would break the series.

In *Chief Constable of Northern Ireland v Agnew* [2019] NICA 32, the Court of Appeal in Northern Ireland held that a 'series' of unlawful deductions from wages were not interrupted by gaps of more than three months, as long as there was an unlawful act in the series falling within the three-month time limit. *Agnew*, as a Northern Ireland case, is not technically binding in England and Wales, so the dicta in *Bear Scotland* continue to apply. Of course, if there is a gap of more than three months between deductions, it is still open to argue that the time limit in respect of the earlier deductions should be extended under the 'not reasonably practicable' exception (above).

Most recently on the time point, in *Smith v Pimlico Plumbers (Rev)* [2022] EWCA Civ 70, Simler LJ said:

> My strong provisional view is that *Agnew* is correct on this point. With respect to the EAT, the reasoning in *Bear Scotland* drives no support from the express words used in section 23(3) ERA 1996.... There is nothing to suggest that the three-month time limit was intended to restrict or qualify the meaning of a 'series of deductions' ... the word series is an ordinary English word connoting a number of things of a similar or related kind coming one after another. It is a question of fact and degree, based on the evidence, whether deductions are sufficiently similar or related over time to constitute a 'series'.

Where the complaint is upheld, the tribunal will make a declaration and order the employer to pay to the worker the amount of the unauthorised deduction (ERA 1996, s 27). Awards can be made gross, and the employer will be left to apportion what is due to the worker and what has to go to HMRC (see *Walters t/a Rosewood v Barik* (UKEAT/0053/16)). There is no mitigation duty placed on the worker. Section 24(2) of the ERA 1996 permits the tribunal to award a sum for consequential losses too. Alternatively, an employee could pursue a claim for breach of contract in the civil courts. See also the table at **5.6.2.5**.

When a tribunal orders an employer to repay an unauthorised deduction or payment, it cannot be recouped from the worker by any other means (ERA 1996, s 25(4)).

1.12 WORKING TIME REGULATIONS 1998

The Working Time Regulations 1998 (the Regulations) implement the Working Time Directive (93/104).

The Government has issued guidance on the limits of working time and some of the entitlements provided for in the 1998 Regulations (see <http://www.direct.gov.uk>). The guidance explains how the Regulations work and how employers may seek to comply with them – what questions they need to consider and what action they should take. The guidance is intended to be just that, and should not be regarded as a complete or authoritative statement of the law.

Note that the Regulations apply to workers as well as employees (see **1.3**). As the definition of worker encompasses that of employee, that term will be used below. What follows is an introduction to the Regulations.

1.12.1   The nature and scope of the Regulations

1.12.1.1   Working time

The Regulations provide (reg 2) that, in relation to a worker, 'working time' means:

(a)   any period during which he is working, at his employer's disposal and carrying out his activity or duties;

(b)   any period during which he is receiving 'relevant training' (defined as *excluding* training provided by an external provider); and

(c)   any additional period which is to be treated as working time under a relevant agreement.

The Government's guidance gives some examples:

(i)   On-call time will be working time when a worker is required to be at his place of work – when a worker is away from the workplace when on-call, and accordingly free to pursue his leisure activities, on-call time is *not* working time (see *Sindicato de Medicos de Asistencia Publica (SiMAP) v Conselleria de Sanidad y Consumo de la Generalidad Valenciana* [2000] IRLR 845, ECJ). The ECJ confirmed in *Landeshauptstadt Kiel v Jaeger* [2003] IRLR 804 that the three criteria mentioned in (a) above are cumulative. In the *Jaeger* case the ECJ held that on-call time spent at a hospital was working time, even though the doctor was allowed to sleep when not required, because all three criteria in (a) were met.

In *Hughes v G and L Jones t/a Graylyns Residential Home* (UKEAT/0159/08), the EAT held that working time included the period the care worker was on call between 9pm and 8am, seven days a week, during which time she occupied a flat on site at a reduced rent.

In *Ville de Nivelles v Matzak* (Case C-518/15), the ECJ held that stand-by time spent at home by a volunteer fireman, which was within eight minutes' travelling distance of a workplace, was working time.

In *Uber BV v Aslam* [2021] UKSC 5, the Supreme Court upheld the tribunal's decision that working time included all time when the drivers were logged into the Uber app and ready and willing to accept trips.

(ii)   A lunch or rest break spent at leisure will not be working time, although a working lunch would be.

(iii)   Time spent working abroad will be working time.

(iv)   Time spent travelling to and from a place of work is unlikely to be working time as a worker will probably neither be working nor carrying out his duties, but a worker may well be doing both if he is engaged by travel that is required by the job. In *Federación de Servicios Privados del sindicato Comisiones obreras v Tyco Integrated Security SL* (Case C-266/14), the ECJ held that Article 2 of the Directive should be interpreted as meaning that the time spent travelling at the beginning and end of the day by a peripatetic worker who was not assigned to a fixed place of work but was required to travel every day from home to the premises of a different customer of the employer and to return home from the premises of another, different customer (following a route or list that was determined for the worker by the employer the previous day) constituted 'working time' and was not a 'rest period'. So for technicians who do repair or maintenance work, time spent travelling between home and the first and last visits of the day is working time.

Working time includes any period during which the employee is in work, at the employer's disposal (ie legally obliged to obey its instructions) and carrying out his activity or duties for that employer. In *East v Valentine* (UKEAT/0325/16), the claimant was a support worker assisting disabled persons in the community. He had to travel from place to place using his car. At the beginning of a period of work, he would drive directly from his home to the first assignment, and when he finished his last assignment he would drive directly home. The claimant's contract set out working hours and pay and specifically stated that his working hours did not include time taken to travel to and from work. There was also a clause stating that additional hours would generally be taken as time off in lieu. The question arose as to whether this time should be counted as working time. The EAT overruled the employment tribunal's finding based on *Tyco* that there was an unlawful deduction from wages. They said that the Regulations were not concerned with questions of payment. A finding that a journey is working time does not give rise to any statutory right to payment, and moreover the contractual position here was very clear.

(v)   In *Edwards v Encirc Ltd* (UKEAT/0367/14), the EAT overturned an employment tribunal's finding that a trade union shop steward and a health and safety representative were not working when they attended meetings at their workplace between night shifts. In the EAT's view, the tribunal had adopted an unduly restrictive approach to the questions of whether the employees were at their employer's disposal and carrying out their duties when attending the meetings. In September 2013, E, who worked night shifts, attended a health and safety meeting during the day. This meant he had only six hours between the end of the meeting and the start of his next night shift. Likewise, M attended a trade union meeting during the day. He also had a break of six hours between the end of the meeting and the start of his next night shift. Both E and M brought employment tribunal claims arguing that they had been denied their right (see **1.12.4.1**) to 11 hours' consecutive rest in any period of 24 hours (reg 10(1)). The EAT pointed out that in order for workers to be at their employer's disposal, it is not necessary that they be under the employer's specific control and direction. The Directive allows for a broader approach, and can cover the situation where an employer has required an employee to be in a specific place and to hold himself out as ready to work for the employer's benefit. Similarly, there was no requirement that the activity or duties referred to in reg 2(1)(a) must be solely the specified contractual duties. If a worker is engaged in activities that arise from the employment relationship, are for the benefit of the employer and done with the employer's knowledge, at and in an approved time and manner, then this could amount to working time.

In *Ville de Nivelles v Matzak* [2018] IRLR 457, the ECJ held that time spent by firefighters on standby at home (they had to remain at home) and who could be required to report for work within eight minutes was working time. In *XR v Dopravni hl m Prahy* (Case C-107/19), the ECJ (post-Brexit) held that the Working Time Directive 'must be interpreted as meaning that the break granted to a worker (firefighter here) during his or her daily working time, during which the worker must be ready to respond to a call-out within a time limit of two minutes if necessary, constitutes "working time" within the meaning of that provision, where it is apparent from an overall assessment of all the relevant circumstances that the limitations imposed on that worker are such as to affect objectively and very significantly the worker's ability to manage freely the time during which his or her professional services are not required and to devote that time to his or her own interests'. In contrast, in *MG v Dublin City Council* (Case C-214/20) a part-time firefighter's standby time, during which he could be called back to emergency duties in no less than 10 minutes, was held not to constitute working time under the Working Time Directive, as he was permitted to work as a self-employed taxi driver during such periods.

1.12.1.2 Worker

Subject to the exclusions outlined below, the Regulations will apply to individuals over the minimum school leaving age who can be categorised as 'employees' (ie those working under contracts of service or apprenticeship) plus a wider group who undertake to perform personally any work or services (eg freelancers) (see, eg, *Willoughby v County Home Care Ltd* (ET/ 1100310/99)). Those whose work amounts to carrying out business activity on their own account (with whom there is a relationship of client/customer rather than employer) are excluded; such individuals are likely to be paid on the basis of an invoice rather than receiving wages (see discussion at **1.3**).

The Regulations specifically exclude domestic servants in private households from the provisions of working time and night work. However, they are covered by the provisions on rest periods and annual leave.

The Regulations distinguish between 'adult workers' (workers who have attained the age of 18) and 'young workers' (who are over compulsory school age but below the age of 18). Only adult workers are dealt with below.

1.12.1.3   Excluded activities and sectors of activity

Prior to 1 August 2003, most of the entitlements under the Regulations did not apply to workers in air, road, sea, inland waterway and lake transport; sea fishing and other work at sea; and doctors in training. However, since 1 August 2003, the Regulations now generally apply in full to non-mobile workers within these industries.

Regulation 2 defines a mobile worker as 'any worker employed as a member of travelling or flying personnel by an undertaking which operates transport services for passengers or goods by road or air'. The position with regard to mobile workers in these industries is more complicated, and often mobile workers are protected under sector-specific legislation or are only covered by certain parts of the Regulations.

The armed forces and the police and emergency services are partially exempt from the Regulations.

Young workers in the armed forces, the police and emergency services, the aviation sector and the road transport sector, are covered by the young workers provisions in the Working Time Regulations.

The UK Regulations do now apply to junior doctors.

Detailed consideration of the above provisions is beyond the scope of this book.

1.12.1.4   Records

Under the Regulations (reg 9), there is a requirement to keep 'adequate records' to show whether the weekly working time and nightwork limits are being complied with. In *Federación de Servicios de Comisiones Obreras v Deutsche Bank SAE* (Case C-55/18), the CJEU held that the Directive requires Member States to require employers to have a system in place to measure the daily working time of all workers. This necessitated the setting up of an 'objective, reliable and accessible' system for recording the actual number and distribution of hours worked by individual workers each day, as this is the only way to ensure that workers enjoy the rights conferred by the Directive. The CJEU decision means that the UK's Regulations do not properly implement the Directive, and need amending, although this may be affected by Brexit. In the UK, claims for failure to keep records can only by brought by the Health and Safety Executive.

1.12.2   Summary of the limits, rights and duties

Almost all of the rights and limits introduced by the Regulations are subject to exceptions and qualifications. The basic provisions with regard to day workers and adults are summarised below. There are also specific provisions relating to night work and young workers which are outside the scope of this book.

1.12.2.1   Limits on working time

Weekly working time (reg 4)

In a 17-week period (which may be extended), no worker is permitted to work more than an average of 48 hours per week.

1.12.2.2 Adult workers' rights

Daily rest period (reg 10)

Eleven consecutive hours' rest in every 24-hour period. See **1.12.4**.

Weekly rest period (reg 11)

An uninterrupted rest period of not less than 24 hours in each seven-day period (in addition to the daily rest period).

Daily rest period (reg 12)

Twenty minutes' rest break, provided that the working day is longer than six hours.

Annual leave (reg 13)

An entitlement to 5.6 weeks' (ie 28 days for a 5-day per week employee) paid annual leave (see **1.12.5**).

1.12.3 Maximum weekly working time (reg 4)

The Regulations set a limit on the amount of working time which may be undertaken by a worker each week. The general rule is that a worker's working time (including overtime) in any reference period shall not exceed an average of 48 hours for each seven days. An employer is under a positive duty to take all reasonable steps, in keeping with the need to protect the health and safety of workers, to ensure that this limit is not exceeded.

1.12.3.1 'Reference period'

For the purposes of the maximum weekly working time-limits, the reference period which applies in the case of a worker is any period of 17 weeks in the course of his employment (unless a relevant agreement (see below) between an employer and a trade union/workforce representative or an individual stipulates which successive periods of 17 weeks amount to such a reference period). This means that, so long as the employee has not worked more than the average in the 17 weeks preceding and including today, then the rules are not breached. In view of this, employers are well advised to put in place early warning systems to check whether an employee is nearing the limit on each rolling period.

The reference period may also be extended to a period not exceeding 52 weeks, by means of a collective or workforce agreement, for objective or technical reasons or reasons concerning the organisation of work. The 17-week reference period is extended to a 26-week period where a worker is engaged in 'special case' activities (eg security or surveillance, hospitals, prisons, broadcasting, tourism, rail transport) where the worker's activities are intermittent.

1.12.3.2 'Average working time'

A worker's 'average working time' is normally calculated by identifying the number of weeks in the reference period (C) and the aggregate number of hours of working time worked by the worker in that period (A) and dividing A by C to produce an average figure.

However, where a worker will not have worked certain days during the reference period because of, for example, annual leave, sick leave or maternity leave, A will be increased by the number of hours worked immediately after the reference period during the number of working days on which the worker was absent in the reference period (B).

The Regulations contain the following formula for calculating average working time for each seven days during a reference period:

$$\frac{A + B}{C}$$

The Regulations (reg 4) state that:

> A is the aggregate number of hours comprised in the worker's working time during the course of the reference period;
>
> B is the aggregate number of hours comprised in his working time during the course of the period beginning immediately after the end of the reference period and ending when the number of days in that subsequent period on which he has worked equals the number of excluded days during the reference period; and
>
> C is the number of weeks in the reference period.

and that:

> 'excluded days' means days comprised in—
>
> (a)   any period of annual leave taken by the worker in exercise of his entitlement under regulation 13;
>
> (b)   any period of sick leave taken by the worker;
>
> (c)   any period of maternity, paternity, adoption or parental leave taken by the worker; and
>
> (d)   any period in respect of which the limit specified in paragraph (1) did not apply in relation to the worker by reason of the fact that the employer has obtained the worker's agreement as mentioned in paragraph (1).

In *Barber and Others v RJB Mining (UK) Ltd* [1999] IRLR 308, five pit deputies sought and obtained declarations that they need not work beyond the 48-hour average, irrespective of what their contract required. The High Court ruled that the Regulations imposed a contractual obligation on the employer which was enforceable in the High Court.

1.12.3.3   'Unmeasured' working time

The limit on weekly working time does not apply in relation to a worker where, on account of the specific characteristics of the activity in which he is engaged, the duration of his working time is not measured or predetermined, or can be determined by the worker himself.

Essentially, this applies to workers who have complete control over the hours they work and whose time is not monitored or determined by their employer. The Guidance states that an indicator may be if the worker is able to decide when to do his work and for how long.

The Regulations provide the following examples of situations in which this exception may apply (see reg 20(1)):

(a)   managing executives or other persons with autonomous decision-taking powers;

(b)   family workers (eg family members who work in a shop and live in a flat above it); or

(c)   workers officiating at religious ceremonies in churches and religious communities.

Note, however, that where a 'normal' worker voluntarily works in excess of his contractual hours, those extra hours count towards the 48-hour limit.

1.12.3.4   'Opt out' agreements (reg 5)

A worker may agree in writing with his employer that the 48-hour limit on average working time does not apply to him. Such an agreement may either relate to a specified period or apply indefinitely, but the agreement shall always be terminable by the worker giving not less than seven days' notice to his employer in writing (or such other period of notice not exceeding three months specified in the agreement).

An 'opt out' agreement will be binding only if the employer keeps up-to-date records of workers who have agreed to opt out.

The employer cannot make an employee sign an 'opt out' agreement. A worker will be protected against detrimental treatment if he refuses to sign an 'opt out' agreement. If such a refusal leads to an employee's dismissal, that dismissal will be treated as automatically unfair, irrespective of the length of service of the employee concerned (see, for example, *Brown v Controlled Packaging Services Ltd* (ET/1402252/98)).

1.12.3.5 Sanctions

A failure to observe the weekly working time-limit in respect of a worker will render an employer liable to the sanctions and penalties presently available to the Health & Safety Executive (HSE) and local authorities under health and safety legislation. Under this legislation, the HSE/local authorities can issue improvement and prohibition notices. In extreme cases, criminal proceedings may be commenced, and this may lead to unlimited fines.

As employers have a general duty to protect the health and safety at work of their workers, employers could be in breach of this common law duty of care if the weekly working time-limit is exceeded. This common law duty of care is bolstered by the Regulations which contain a statutory duty on an employer to observe the limits on weekly working time. If the employer fails to observe this statutory duty, a worker may enforce it as a civil claim in the courts.

The Regulations also give workers two further rights if they refuse to work in excess of the maximum weekly working time-limit. First, a worker has the right not to be subjected to any detriment by any act, or any deliberate failure to act, by his employer for (inter alia) refusing to work in excess of an average 48 hours per week. Secondly, an employee shall be regarded as unfairly dismissed (irrespective of length of service) if the principal reason for his dismissal is that he has (inter alia) refused to exceed the weekly limit on his working hours (see **Chapter 5**).

Additionally, as the weekly working units underpin contractual rights, an employee will be entitled to enforce these rights through a contract claim in the civil courts. In the *Barber* case (see **1.12.3.2** above), the High Court indicated that a declaration, rather than an injunction, would normally be the appropriate remedy.

Prosecutions for breach have been few. In 2002, Fourboys newsagent was fined £5,000 because the managers worked, on average, 71.3 hours per week. In 2007, a construction company (CFR Group plc) was fined £750 for breaching reg 4(1) on weekly working time limits.

1.12.4 Rest (regs 10, 11, 12)

The rest entitlements provided by the Regulations differ depending upon whether a person is a worker or a young worker. The rest entitlements provided for young workers are more generous than those provided for workers. See reg 10.

1.12.4.1 Daily rest period (reg 10)

An adult worker is entitled to a rest period of at least 11 consecutive hours in each 24-hour period during which he works for the employer. This entitlement is subject to the following exceptions:

(a)   where working time is unmeasured (see **1.12.3.3**);

(b)   where the worker is engaged in one of the 'special case' activities;

(c)   where a shift worker changes shift and cannot take the daily rest period between the end of one shift and the start of the next one;

(d)   where the worker is engaged in activities involving periods of work split up over the day (eg cleaning staff);

(e)   where the right is modified or excluded by a collective or workforce agreement (see **1.12.6**).

Where any of these exceptions applies (other than the unmeasured working time exception), the employer must allow the worker to take an equivalent period of compensatory rest and, in exceptional cases where this is not possible for objective reasons, the employer must afford the worker such protection as may be appropriate in order to safeguard the worker's health and safety.

1.12.4.2   Weekly rest period (reg 11)

Adult workers are entitled to an uninterrupted rest period of not less than 24 hours in each seven-day period. This right is additional to the daily rest entitlement except where objective, technical or work organisation conditions justify incorporating all or part of the daily entitlement into the weekly rest period. Daily rest and weekly rest should be taken consecutively, ie giving an uninterrupted period of 35 hours.

If the employer so determines, the seven-day reference period can be averaged over a reference period of 14 days. In these circumstances, the employer can choose between:

(a)   two uninterrupted rest periods each of not less than 24 hours in each 14-day period; and

(b)   one uninterrupted rest period of not less than 48 hours in each such 14-day period.

The ECJ held in *Maio Marques da Rosa v Varzim* (Case C-306/16) that there is no requirement for a rest day to be at the end of a 7-day period.

The relevant reference period shall be taken to begin at midnight between Sunday and Monday of each week or (as the case may be) every other week unless a relevant agreement provides to the contrary.

The weekly rest entitlement of adult workers is subject to the same exceptions as are outlined in relation to daily rest (**1.12.4.1** above).

1.12.4.3   Daily rest breaks (reg 12)

Most adult workers (except those in some sectors such as merchant shipping, fishing, the police and armed services and certain designated special cases where services need to be performed continuously (caretakers, security guards, doctors, etc) or in certain key industries (gas, electricity, water etc)) are entitled to a daily rest break where their daily working time is more than six hours. The details of this rest break (including its duration and the terms on which it is granted) may be set by a collective or workforce agreement. In the absence of such an agreement, the break must be an uninterrupted period of not less than 20 minutes. The worker shall be entitled to spend this break away from his workstation if he has one.

In *Grange v Abellio London Ltd* (UKEAT/0130/16), the EAT held that even if the worker does not expressly request breaks, employers must provide them, and a claim can be brought if provision is not made. Employers must take active steps to ensure that their working arrangements enable workers to take the requisite rest breaks. Workers cannot be forced to take rest breaks, but they are to be positively enabled to.

This entitlement is subject to the following exceptions:

(a)   where working time is unmeasured;

(b)   where the worker is engaged in one of the 'special case' activities;

(c)   where the right is modified or excluded by a collective or workforce agreement (see **1.12.6**);

(d)   where something unusual happens beyond the employer's control.

Where (b) or (c) applies, the employer must allow the worker to take an equivalent period of compensatory rest and, in exceptional cases where this is not possible for objective reasons, must afford the worker such protection as may be appropriate in order to safeguard the worker's health and safety. In *Hughes v Corps of Commissioners Management Ltd* [2011] EWCA Civ 1061, the Court of Appeal held that there should be a proper uninterrupted break from work during a rest period, of at least 20 minutes, and then considered the approach to be taken in assessing the special case exception.

In *Network Rail Infrastructure Ltd v Crawford* [2019] EWCA Civ 269, Mr Crawford was a signal box worker. He worked in five signal boxes on eight-hour shifts (12 hours on Sundays). When he was working alone, he was not able to take a 20-minute uninterrupted break. He complained that this was in breach of the Regulations. Network Rail permitted rest in 5/10/15-minute chunks during quiet periods. The Court of Appeal said that, in these special cases, there was no reason why the break had to be uninterrupted, so long as the aggregate totalled 20 minutes or more.

In *McCartney v Oversley House Management* [2006] IRLR 514, the EAT held that the on-call time of a live-in employee was working time, and could not therefore count as a 'rest period', even if the employee was entitled to 'rest' while on call.

In *Gallacher v Alpha Catering Services* [2005] IRLR 102, the EAT said a 'break' was a period when employees were not at their employer's disposal.

1.12.4.4 Sanctions

A worker may present a complaint to a tribunal that his employer has not allowed him to exercise his right to a daily/weekly rest period or rest break, or has failed to provide an equivalent period of compensatory rest. Such complaints must be brought within three months of the act or omission complained of, unless the tribunal considers that it was not reasonably practicable to bring the complaint within this period. The EAT confirmed in *Miles v Linkage Community Trust Ltd* (UKEAT/0618/07) that time will run from the date of the refusal by the employer.

In *Grange v Abellio London Ltd* (see **1.12.4.3**) the claimant was told that he would have to work an eight-hour shift without a break, finishing half an hour earlier (previously he received a half-hour break, finishing later). The issue was whether he had been *refused* a break. The EAT held that:

> Adopting an approach that both allows for a common sense construction of Regulation 30(1), read together with Regulation 12(1), and still meets the purpose of the WTD, I consider the answer is thus to be found in the EAT's Judgment in *Truslove*: the employer has an obligation ('duty') to afford the worker the entitlement to take a rest break (paragraph 32 *Truslove*). That entitlement will be '*refused*' by the employer if it puts into place working arrangements that fail to allow the taking of 20 minute rest breaks (*MacCartney*). If, however, the employer has taken active steps to ensure working arrangements that enable the worker to take the requisite rest break, it will have met the obligation upon it: workers cannot be forced to take the rest breaks but they are to be positively enabled to do so.

If the tribunal upholds such a complaint, it must make a declaration to that effect and may also award compensation. The amount of compensation is such as the tribunal considers just and equitable in all the circumstances having regard to the employer's default in refusing to permit the exercise of the worker's entitlement and any loss sustained by the worker as a consequence of that default. Compensation for injury to feelings is not available (*Santos Gomes v Higher Level Care Ltd* (EAT/0017/16)).

The Regulations also provide that a worker has the right not to be subjected to any detriment by any act, or any deliberate failure to act, by his employer on the ground that the worker has refused (or proposed to refuse) to forgo a rest entitlement, has brought proceedings against the employer to enforce such an entitlement or has alleged that the employer has infringed such a right. If this is the principal reason for an employee's dismissal, the dismissal will be treated as unfair (irrespective of the employee's length of service).

1.12.5 Annual leave and holiday pay

The Working Time Directive (93/104) provides for a basic period of four weeks' annual leave per year. The Regulations, however, go further than this for UK workers and provide that a worker is entitled to a minimum of 5.6 weeks' annual leave in each leave year (ie 28 days for full-time employees, ie those who work five days a week). This is effectively to compensate for the eight bank holidays. Thus a UK worker's statutory paid holiday entitlement is made up of:

- four weeks' basic annual leave (20 days for full-time employees) each year (reg 13(1));
- an additional 1.6 weeks' annual leave (eight days for full-time employees) each year (reg 13A).

The usual ERA 1996, s 230 definition applies to employees and workers. Where a worker has irregular working patterns or their shift patterns vary on a weekly basis, it may be more difficult to work out paid holiday entitlement. In *Russell v Transocean International Resources Ltd* [2011] IRLR 24 and *Greenfield v The Care Bureau Ltd* [2016] IRLR 62, pragmatic approaches to calculation were approved.

These basic minimums can also be topped up, enhanced or extended by express contractual terms. Different rules can apply as to how holiday leave is paid and impacted on by termination or sick pay, depending on whether the paid holiday entitlement is basic, additional or contractual. So, for example, while basic paid holiday must be used in the year it accrues or be lost and cannot be paid for in lieu or accrued over from year to year (unless on termination), additional leave can be carried over but cannot be paid in lieu, and any contractual paid holiday above and beyond these minimums can be treated as having been agreed in the contract, so may be able to be carried over or paid in lieu. The general view when looking at paid holiday entitlement is that the basic holiday accrues first, followed by the additional, followed by any contractual entitlement. This can be important because of the different rules that apply (see below for more details).

A worker's leave year will normally be specified in the contract of employment. If not, a 'leave year' starts on 1 October 1998 or, if later, the date on which the worker starts work, and each subsequent anniversary of that date.

Regulation 13(9) provides that:

(a) the leave may only be taken in the leave year in respect of which it is due (but see **1.12.5.3** and **1.12.5.5** and *Kreuziger v Berlin* (Case C-619/16), *Max-Planck-Gesellschaft zur Förderung der Wissenschaften eV v Shimizu* (Case C-684/16) and *King v The Sash Window Workshop Ltd* (Case C-214/16) where the ECJ held that leave can be carried over not only where the employer obstructs the worker taking holiday, including telling a worker that holiday will not be paid holiday where the worker is entitled to paid holiday (and in sickness cases), but also where the employer has not helped the worker to take their holiday, particularly by not providing adequate information (a worker cannot, however, be forced to take a holiday)). Note that the Working Time (Coronavirus) (Amendment) Regulations 2020 provide that, with effect from 26 March 2020, leave can be carried over for two leave years where it was 'not reasonably practicable' for a worker to take some or all of their statutory leave due to the effects of coronavirus on the worker, the employer or wider society. This only applies to the 'basic' four week entitlement;

(b) a worker's leave may not be replaced by a payment in lieu (except at termination of employment) (see **1.12.5.6** below).

Contractual and statutory annual leave will continue to accrue during maternity/adoption, etc leave (see **Chapter 14**).

From 6 April 2020, pay should be calculated over a 52-week average period (it was previously a 12-week average). If there are fixed hours of work, this will equate to the same rate the individual earns for their normal week's work. Where there are no normal working hours, the average earnings calculation must be used.

DBEIS issued new holiday pay guidance which outlines how employers should perform the 52-week average pay calculation for workers without fixed hours or fixed rates of pay. It also provides guidance on calculating holiday pay of term-time workers.

In *Harpur Trust v Brazel* [2022] UKSC 21, the Supreme Court clarified the calculation of holiday for part-year workers and term-time workers (workers who are employed for the year but only work some of the year) and confirmed that the leave entitlement of 5.6 weeks is fixed and not linked to the amount of work done by the worker, even if it produced 'anomalies' in untypical cases. The 5.6 weeks should not be reduced pro rata for workers who are employed for the whole year but only work some weeks. In this case, that meant that a teacher on a term-time-only contract ended up being entitled to proportionately more holiday than comparable full-time employees (see below). Of course a week's pay will vary depending on hours worked (see **1.12.5.3** below).

Note that government guidance confirmed that, under the Coronavirus Job Retention Scheme, annual leave both accrued and could be taken during a period of furlough. May 2020 Guidance suggests that an employer could require an employee to take leave while on furlough.

1.12.5.1 Joiners and leavers

There are special rules relating to joiners and leavers. For joiners, their rights to annual leave are proportionate to the amount of the 'leave year' for which they work. For leavers, workers have a right to be paid in lieu for any untaken leave to which they are entitled. (See *Kreuziger* and *Shimizu* (above) (Cases C-619/16 and C-684/16) for the position upon termination in respect of a worker who has not applied to take leave during the year.)

In *Leisure Leagues UK Ltd v Maconnachie* [2002] IRLR 600, the EAT held that holiday pay should be calculated on the basis of the number of working days in the year and not the number of calendar days. See also *Yarrow v Edwards Chartered Accountants* (UKEAT/0116/07).

The Court of Appeal decided in *Bamsey and Others v Albion Engineering and Manufacturing plc* [2004] IRLR 457 that, when calculating holiday pay, compulsory but non-guaranteed overtime does not need to be taken into account in computing a week's pay.

Regulation 14(4) provides that an employer can recover payment for excess holiday taken by a leaver only if there is express agreement between the employer and employee. That means that if an employer wants to be able to recover compensation from an employee who is leaving and has taken more holiday than that to which he was entitled at the date of termination, this should be provided for in the contract of employment. The EAT confirmed in *Hill v Chappell* [2003] IRLR 19, that an employer cannot use the ERA 1996 to claw back the money.

1.12.5.2 Notice

A worker does not have the right to take leave at any time he chooses. Subject to variation or exclusion by a relevant agreement, a worker is required under reg 15 to give written notice to his employer specifying the dates on which leave is to be taken twice as many days in advance of the earliest day specified in the notice as the number of days to which the notice relates. A similar notice requiring a worker to take leave on particular days may be issued by the employer.

An employer also has the power to issue a notice to a worker requiring him *not* to take leave on particular days. Such a notice must be given to the worker as many days in advance of the earliest day specified in the notice as the number of days to which the notice relates. Again, this right is subject to modification or exclusion by a relevant agreement. (See the decision of the Supreme Court in *Russell v Transocean International* [2011] UKSC 57 on when leave can be taken.)

The ECJ has recently held, in *Shimizu* (above) that the mere fact that a worker did not apply for leave during a given year does not automatically mean that leave is lost and cannot be carried over. An employer must 'diligently' bring it to a worker's attention that leave will be lost; the burden of proof will be on the employer.

1.12.5.3 Calculating holiday pay

A worker is entitled to a 'week's pay' for each week (5.6 weeks) of annual leave (reg 16). Article 7 of the Working Time Directive requires workers to be paid 'normal remuneration' during the holiday to which they are entitled under EU law (ie the basic four weeks). For the purposes of reg 16 of the 1998 Regulations, a 'week's pay' is defined in accordance with the Employment Rights Act 1996 (ss 221–224), subject to modifications introduced by the 1998 Regulations (eg no cap on a week's pay). If the pattern of work is settled and normal, regular working hours are involved, it should be straightforward to calculate normal pay (ERA 1996, ss 221–223). If there are not 'normal' working hours, a 52-week reference period is used (or the number of completed weeks the worker has worked) (ERA 1996, s 224, as amended by reg 16 of the Employment Rights (Employment Particulars and Paid Annual Leave) (Amendment) Regulations 2018). In *Harpur Trust v Brazel* [2022] UKSC 21, the Supreme Court confirmed that all workers are entitled to 5.6 weeks' leave (see **1.12.5** above). Pay for the leave should be calculated in accordance with the formula for a 'week's pay' set out in s 224, so in this case was based on the worker's average pay in the 12 weeks prior to taking leave (now a 52-week reference period), ignoring the weeks for which the worker was not paid anything (by taking earlier weeks (up to 104 weeks) into account).

In 2012, the ECJ, in *Williams v British Airways plc* (Case C-155/10) (see **1.12.5** above), confirmed that a worker must be no worse off financially during annual leave than if he had continued working, and that workers are entitled to their 'normal remuneration' when on holiday. Different considerations may apply where additional or contractual holiday is concerned. In *Williams*, the ECJ had been asked by the UK Supreme Court to consider whether or not 'normal remuneration' during a period of annual leave should include allowances on top of basic pay, in the context of a dispute over how the holiday pay of British Airways pilots, who were paid flying allowances as well as basic pay, should be calculated. The ECJ gave a wider definition to 'normal pay' under the Directive than had previously been assumed. Accordingly, holiday pay was not confined to basic pay but included the supplementary payments for time spent flying, as well as allowances linked to the pilots' professional and personal status. Since *Williams*, tribunals have considered a number of claims concerning whether overtime arrangements, commission and various other financial supplements paid to workers formed part of 'normal remuneration' for the purposes of calculating holiday pay.

Commission payments

By s 221(4), commission or similar payments which vary with the amount of work done are included, but not if they depend on results rather than the amount of work done (*Evans v Malley Organisation Ltd* [2003] ICR 432, CA).

The reasoning in *Williams* (above) was also adopted by the ECJ in *Lock v British Gas Trading Ltd* [2014] ICR 813, a case concerning the right to paid annual leave under Article 7 of the Working Time Directive. In *Lock*, the ECJ held that commission payments that were directly and intrinsically linked to an individual's work must be reflected in the worker's holiday pay. Mr Lock was employed as a sales consultant. He was remunerated by a basic salary plus a sales-based commission payment, which accounted for approximately 60% of his total pay. While he was on holiday, he did not get any commission. When the case returned to the employment tribunal, the tribunal held that it could read the 1998 Regulations compatibly with the EU Directive by adding words to the Regulations. The new words it inserted into reg 16(2) resulted in it reading as below:

> Sections 221 to 224 of the 1996 Act shall apply for the purpose of determining the amount of a week's pay for the purposes of this regulation, save that where these provisions result in a worker not receiving components of pay which form part of his normal remuneration in respect of the period of leave to which he is entitled under regulation 13, the worker shall be deemed to have no normal working hours

and section 224 of the 1996 Act shall apply to that entitlement, subject in either case to the modifications set out in paragraph (3).

Both the EAT (UKEAT/0189/15) and the Court of Appeal ([2016] EWCA Civ 983) upheld the tribunal's decision and dismissed British Gas's appeal, ruling that the 1998 Regulations can be interpreted to provide that calculating 'normal pay' for the four weeks' paid holiday derived from the Working Time Directive must include regular commission payments.

However, the Court of Appeal held that the tribunal's wording went beyond what was needed and rather than reword reg 16(2) said that reg 16(3) should be reworded as follows by adding a new para (e):

(e)   as if, in the case of entitlement under regulation 13, a worker with normal working hours whose remuneration includes results based commission shall be deemed to have remuneration which varies with the amount of work done for the purpose of section 221 [of the ERA 1996].

Overtime

Until the courts decided otherwise, non-guaranteed but compulsory overtime was not included in the calculation for holiday pay. Consequently, overtime at the employer's discretion was not included in the holiday pay calculation.

Following *Williams & Lock* (above), in the joined cases of *Bear Scotland Ltd v Fulton; Hertel (UK) Ltd v Woods; Amec Group Ltd v Law* [2015] IRLR 15, the EAT (Langstaff J, President of the EAT, sitting alone), applying the *Marleasing* principle (see **1.2.4.3** above), considered what constitutes 'normal remuneration' for holiday pay purposes and, if a worker has been underpaid, how far back he can claim. The appeal concerned the decisions of two employment tribunals that supplementary payments normally received by workers, including overtime payments, should count towards holiday pay. The EAT held:

•   Holiday pay must correspond to 'normal' remuneration, which is pay that is normally received, including 'non-guaranteed' overtime, commission and other allowances forming a worker's normal pay (but only in relation to the first four weeks of statutory leave, which are covered by the Working Time Directive).

•   There is, however, limited scope for workers to recover underpayments of holiday pay by way of an unlawful deduction from wages claim.

The EAT concluded therefore that overtime, including non-guaranteed overtime and other allowances 'intrinsically linked to the performance of the tasks' (in this case 'radius allowances' and 'travelling time payments'), must be included when calculating holiday pay.

The decision only applies in relation to basic holiday pay payable in respect of the first four weeks of holiday entitlement (1998 Regulations, reg 13), which derives from the Working Time Directive. While under UK law, workers are entitled to 5.6 weeks' annual leave, only the first four weeks of leave derive from the Directive. The additional 1.6 weeks come under reg 13A and are a matter of UK law only. As reg 13A leave is not derived from the Directive, the wider interpretation of 'normal pay' does not apply here.

While the EAT had ruled (*Bear Scotland*) that compulsory overtime pay should be included when calculating holiday pay, it had not dealt with the issue of payment for voluntary overtime payments until recently. There had been a couple of employment tribunal judgments that had looked at the issue. In *Brettle, White & Others v Dudley Metropolitan Borough Council* (ET/1300537/15) the tribunal helpfully analysed the current position regarding the calculation of holiday pay, what it should include and what counts as a 'regular' payment where voluntary overtime is concerned. The tribunal heard from five lead claimants (there were 56 claimants in total) employed by Dudley Council in the repair and improvement department for social housing. They were all tradesmen with a variety of skills – including plumbers, roofers, electricians and carpenters – each of whom worked different types of voluntary overtime and/or were on stand-by/on-call rotas on a 'regular' basis, receiving payments for these additional hours when worked (but not whilst they were on annual leave). The tradesmen were invited to work on a Saturday on a purely voluntary basis while working on the council's stock of social housing. They also elected to go on standby every four weeks, to deal with emergency call-outs and repairs – again, not at the employer's discretion. The voluntary overtime and on-call rota had been in place for such a period, and with such regularity, that it was argued it had become part of their 'normal work' and accordingly part of their 'normal pay'. The council argued that it did not form part of 'contractual pay'. But the judge ruled that the payment for that work had to be included in the calculation of holiday pay for the first 20 days of annual leave, under reg 13 of the 1998 Regulations. The employment judge emphasised that the question of whether a payment is 'intrinsically linked to normal work, paid in such a manner and with such sufficient regularity to be considered part of normal remuneration' is fact specific (see too *Whitehead v EMH Housing* (ET/2600493/4/6)). The EAT held (UKEAT/0334/16) that voluntary overtime, normally worked, is pay for the purposes of calculating holiday pay. This approach was upheld by the Court of Appeal in *Flowers v East of England Ambulance Trust* [2019] EWCA Civ 947, which said that voluntary overtime was part of normal remuneration if it was paid over a sufficient period. The case is no longer being appealed to the Supreme Court.

(See too the 2018 Acas Guidance on Overtime.)

How far back can a claim be made?

Under the 1998 Regulations, workers can only claim underpayments under reg 13 arising in the three months prior to the presentation of their claim. Where an employer has failed to pay holiday pay under reg 16, the tribunal must order payment of the amount due (reg 30(5)). Claims must be brought within three months beginning with the date payment should have been made.

However, in *HMRC v Stringer* (see **1.12.5** above), the House of Lords established that a failure to pay holiday pay under the 1998 Regulations can also be framed as an unlawful deduction from wages claim, contrary to s 13 of the ERA 1996 (see **1.11** above). A worker can bring a s 13 claim in respect of a 'series of deductions'; in such a case, the claim must be brought within three months of the last deduction in the series (ERA 1996, s 23). It was assumed that using this route allowed claimants to link together a series of underpayments in order to bring a backdated claim, regardless of the length of time that had elapsed between each deduction. This decision meant that if workers brought a claim under the protection of wages provisions of the ERA 1996 for a series of deductions of wages, there would be more flexibility on time restrictions than there would be if a claim were brought under the 1998 Regulations. In the employment tribunal case of *Neal v Freightliner Ltd* (ET/1315342/2012) (which was settled before an appeal to the EAT was heard), the tribunal allowed a worker to claim for underpayments going back to 2007 when his employment began.

However, the EAT in *Bear Scotland* (above) (and confirmed in UKEATS/0010/16) concluded that the workers could *not* claim any consequent holiday underpayment as forming part of a series of deductions of wages where *more than* three months had elapsed between the 'deductions'. The EAT stated that 'any series punctuated from the next succeeding series by a gap of more than three months is one in respect of which the passage of time has extinguished the jurisdiction to consider a complaint that it was unpaid'. This analysis thus severely restricts the amount of time that a worker may potentially look back at as the chances of a worker having a long (if any) series of untaken reg 13 leave over a number of years is likely to be minimal. At the end of November 2014, Unite announced that it was not pursuing an appeal in the *Bear Scotland* case, so the position remains that other than cases where there has not been a three-month break period between leave periods, most claims will have been restricted. As *Bear Scotland* conflicts with other (non-binding), higher authority on the meaning of 'series', it is, however, likely to be an area that is revisited by the courts sooner rather than later (see below).

In any event, following the EAT's decision in *Bear Scotland* and the joined cases, the Government introduced legislation to 'reduce potential costs to employers and give certainty to workers on their rights following the recent court decisions on holiday pay'. The Deduction from Wages (Limitation) Regulations 2014 took effect from 8 January 2015, and apply to claims presented to the employment tribunal on or after 1 July 2015. Designed to limit back claims for holiday pay to two years, these Regulations also amended the 1998 Regulations by stating that the right to payment in respect of annual leave is not contractual but purely statutory, thus preventing the bringing of contractual claims for statutory holiday pay (see **1.11.5**).

However, the ECJ in *King v The Sash Window Workshop Ltd* (Case C-214/16) (a case referred to the ECJ by the Court if Appeal following an employment tribunal decision to award £25,000 in respect of untaken holiday stretching back 13 years, Mr King's claim having been brought as a series of unlawful deductions under s 13 of the ERA 1996, and pre-dating the 2014 Regulations) held that workers' denied paid holiday can carry over their four weeks' statutory entitlement indefinitely and be paid in lieu of the entire accrued untaken entitlement on termination.

In this case, the employer wrongly classed Mr King as self-employed and therefore maintained that he had no right to paid holidays. As a result, he did not take most of his holiday entitlement from 1999 to 2012 (over 24 weeks'). The ECJ said it did not matter that the worker had not put in holiday requests. It also said that Article 7 of the Directive had to be interpreted as precluding national provisions which prevent a worker from carrying over and/or accumulating until termination paid annual leave rights.

This decision (although it only applies to the basic four weeks under reg 13 and not to the additional eight days in the UK under reg 13A) runs directly counter to the decision of the EAT in *Bear Scotland* (above) and obviates the two-year backstop implemented by the 2014 Regulations. The case was referred back to the Court of Appeal and was listed for hearing in late November 2018. Unfortunately it settled, leaving the situation in respect of the two-year backstop rule uncertain.

In another case, *Chief Constable of Northern Ireland v Agnew* [2019] NICA 32, the Court of Appeal in Northern Ireland held that a 'series' of unlawful deductions from wages were not interrupted by gaps of more than three months where the series of deductions related to holiday pay. This conflicts with the formulation of the EAT in *Bear Scotland*, which stated that a gap of three months would break the series. *Agnew*, as a Northern Ireland case, is not technically binding in England and Wales, so the dicta in *Bear Scotland* continue to apply.

Most recently on this point, in *Smith v Pimlico Plumbers (Rev1)* [2022] EWCA Civ 70, the Court of Appeal upheld an appeal against the EAT's decision that Mr Smith's holiday pay claim was out of time (see too **1.11.5** above). Mr Smith took periods of leave from time to time, but these were always unpaid, as the employer maintained he was self-employed (see **1.3.3** for the Supreme Court's decision that Mr Smith was a worker). The Supreme Court held that Mr Smith undertook to 'perform [his services] personally'. Accordingly he was a 'worker' within the meaning of s 230(3) of the ERA 1996 and reg 2(1) of the Working Time Regulations 1998. The tribunal held that the claim was presented out of time because Mr Smith's last period of (unpaid) leave ended on 4 January 2011; the respondent ought to have paid him for that period of leave on 5 February 2011 when Mr Smith received his payslip for that month; and he was therefore obliged to present a claim by 4 May 2011 at the latest, but did not present his claim until 1 August 2011, nearly three months after the expiry of the relevant deadline. The tribunal rejected Mr Smith's argument that the decision in *King v The Sash Window Workshop Ltd* (above) entitled him to bring, on the termination of his engagement, a claim in respect of all unpaid annual leave accrued throughout his engagement with the respondent, both taken and untaken. The EAT upheld that decision. The EAT concluded, in agreement with the employment tribunal, that the principles established in *King* were limited to cases of leave not taken.

The Court of Appeal held that:

(a)   although the factual context was a worker who had not taken all the leave to which he was entitled, the answers given by the CJEU rest on principles with a broader reach and, in my judgment, are to be read as extending to cover workers who have taken leave but have not been paid for it in the circumstances described. It followed that that the principles established in *King* did apply to Mr Smith's claim, and therefore the claim was not made outside the relevant time limits.

(b)   obiter that *Bear Scotland* was wrongly decided and that *Agnew* is preferred. Lady Justice Simler stated:

> My strong provisional view is that *Agnew* is correct on this point. With respect to the EAT, the reasoning in *Bear Scotland* derives no support from the express words used in section 23(3) ERA. The existence of a three-month time limit for bringing claims is a weak basis for inferring that Parliament did not intend to link similar payments occurring more than three months apart: see [81]. Nor is there anything in the history or background to the legislation that supports this reasoning. It is not an approach that has been applied in relation to other similar limitation provisions based on a series, for example, section 43(8) ERA. Had this been Parliament's intention, it could and should quite easily have been stated expressly.

The Court of Appeal also suggested amended wording for regs 13, 14 and 30 of the 1998 Regulations to reflect the effect of *King*. Clearly, the wording proposed is not binding as the Court of Appeal has no power to draft Regulations, but it is helpful to set out its wording:

Appendix to judgment

13   Entitlement to annual leave

...

(9)   Leave to which a worker is entitled under this regulation may be taken in instalments, but—

(a)   subject to the exceptions in paragraphs (10) and (11), *(14) and (15), and (16)*, it may only be taken in the leave year in respect of which it is due, and

(b)   it may not be replaced by a payment in lieu except where the worker's employment is terminated.

(10)   Where in any leave year it was not reasonably practicable for a worker to take some or all of the leave to which the worker was entitled under this regulation as a result of the effects of coronavirus (including on the worker, the employer or the wider economy or society), the worker shall be entitled to carry forward such untaken leave as provided for in paragraph (11).

(11)   Leave to which paragraph (10) applies may be carried forward and taken in the two leave years immediately following the leave year in respect of which it was due.

(12)   An employer may only require a worker not to take leave to which paragraph (10) applies on particular days as provided for in regulation 15(2) where the employer has good reason to do so.

(13)   For the purpose of this regulation 'coronavirus' means severe acute respiratory syndrome corona-virus 2 (SARS-CoV-2).

(14)   *Where in any leave year a worker was unable or unwilling to take some or all of the leave to which the worker was entitled under this regulation because he was on sick leave, the worker shall be entitled to carry forward such untaken leave as provided for in paragraph (15).*

(15)   *Leave to which paragraph (14) applies may be carried forward and taken in the period of 18 months immediately following the leave year in respect of which it was due.*

(16)   *Where in any leave year an employer (i) fails to recognise a worker's right to paid annual leave and (ii) cannot show that it provides a facility for the taking of such leave, the worker shall be entitled to carry forward any leave which is taken but unpaid, and/or which is not taken, into subsequent leave years.*

14   Compensation related to entitlement to leave

...

(5)   Where a worker's employment is terminated and on the termination date he remains entitled to leave in respect of any previous leave year which carried over under regulation 13(10) and (11),

(14) *and* (15), *or* (16), the employer shall make the worker a payment in lieu of leave equal to the sum due under regulation 16 for the period of such leave.

30 **Remedies**

(1) A worker may present a complaint to an employment tribunal that his employer—

    (a) has refused to permit him to exercise any right he has under—

        (i) regulation 10(1) or (2), 11(1), (2) or (3), 12(1) or (4), 13 or 13A;

        (ii) regulation 24, in so far as it applies where regulation 10(1), 11(1) or (2) or 12(1) is modified or excluded; [...]

        (iii) regulation 24A, in so far as it applies where regulation 10(1), 11(1) or (2) or 12(1) is excluded; or

        (iv) regulation 25(3), 27A(4)(b) or 27(2); or

    (b) has failed to pay him the whole or any part of any amount due to him under regulation 14(2), 14(5) or 16(1).

    ....

(5) Where on a complaint under paragraph (1)(b) an employment tribunal finds that an employer has failed to pay a worker in accordance with regulation 14(2), 14(5) or 16(1), it shall order the employer to pay to the worker the amount which it finds to be due to him.

1.12.5.4 'Rolled-up' holiday pay

The ECJ held in *Robinson-Steele v RD Retail Services and other cases* (Case C-131/04) that it is contrary to the Working Time Directive for a payment for annual leave to be made in the form of payments staggered over the year and paid together with remuneration for work done, rather than in the form of a payment in respect of a specific period during which the worker actually takes leave.

Notwithstanding that ruling in 2006, rolled-up holiday pay continues for many workers. Current UK Government guidance states: 'Holiday pay should be paid for the time when annual leave is taken. An employer cannot include an amount for holiday pay in the hourly rate. ... If a current contract still includes rolled-up pay, it needs to be re-negotiated.' However, where it continues it would appear that, so long as payments are clearly identified as holiday pay, an employer is entitled to offset rolled-up holiday pay against a claim by a worker for his holiday entitlement (see *Lyddon v Englefield Brickwork Ltd* (EAT/0301/07)).

1.12.5.5 Annual leave and sickness

The analysis below is relevant to the four weeks' annual leave entitlement under the Working Time Directive (different considerations may apply in respect of additional leave beyond four weeks, which is not derived from the Directive and which is dependent on contractual provisions (*TSN v Hyvinvointialan* (Case C-609/17)) – see *Sood Enterprises Ltd v Healey* (UKEATS/0015/12)). Article 7, as implemented by reg 13 of the 1998 Regulations, provides that an employee is entitled to paid annual leave of at least four weeks. Regulation 13(9) of the Regulations provides that annual leave may only be taken in the leave year in respect of which it is due. However, the following principles can be distilled from domestic and European case law:

(1) A sick employee must be permitted to take annual leave whilst sick (*HMRC v Stringer*).

(2) An employee who is permitted to take paid annual leave during a period of sick leave cannot be required to do so (*Pereda v Madrid Mouilidad* (Case C-277/08); *Plumb v Duncan Print Group Ltd* (EAT/0071/15)).

(3) The Working Time Directive does not preclude national legislation or practices which prevent an employee from taking paid annual leave during a period of sickness absence provided, however, that the worker has the opportunity to take annual leave at a later date or be paid for it if the employment relationship ends before the employee can take the leave (*Schultz-Hoff v Deutsche Rentenversicherung Bund* [2009] IRLR 214; see too *NHS Leeds v Larner* [2012] EWCA Civ 1034).

(4)   EU law does not confer an unlimited right to carry over periods of annual leave to subsequent years. The Working Time Directive, at most, only requires that employees on sick leave are able to take annual leave within a period of 18 months of the end of the leave year in respect of which the annual leave arises. Consequently, reg 13(9) of the Regulations is to be read as permitting a worker to take annual leave within 18 months of the end of the leave year in which it accrued (or be entitled to payment on termination for the paid annual leave), where the worker was unable or unwilling to take annual leave because he was on sick leave and, as a consequence, did not exercise his right to annual leave (*Plumb v Duncan Print Group Ltd*). A year is too short a period. National law restricting the period to 15 months is acceptable (*KHS AG v Schulte* [2012] IRLR 156).

(5)   A worker who becomes unfit during annual leave must be allowed to take the part of the annual leave that coincides with sickness at a later date and to carry it forward to the next holiday year if unable to use it (*Pereda v Madrid Mouilidad* and *Sobczyszyn v Szkola Podstawowa w Rzeplinie* (Case C-178/15)).

(6)   In *NHS Leeds v Larner* [2012] EWCA Civ 1034, the Court of Appeal commented, on an obiter basis, that reg 14(2) (which allows for payment, on termination, in respect of untaken but accrued holiday during the last year of employment) could be read and interpreted (so as to comply with Article 7 of the Directive) to include a provision requiring an employer to make a payment on termination in respect of any untaken holiday pay from a previous holiday year which was rolled over due to sickness. Under reg 30(1), a worker can bring a claim for any amount which is unpaid but due under reg 14(2).

Where the employer in question is the state or an emanation of the state (see **1.2.4.2**), the employee will be able to rely on the direct effect of Article 7 of the Working Time Directive. In other cases the court will be asked to interpret domestic law in line with EU law. The Court of Appeal suggested in *Larner* (above) that reg 13 could be construed in line with Article 7.

Leave to which a worker is entitled under the Working Time Directive may only be taken in the leave year in respect of which it is due, 'save that it may be taken within 18 months of the end of that year where the worker was unable or unwilling to take it because he was on sick leave and, as a consequence did not exercise his right to annual leave' (*Plumb v Duncan Print Group Ltd* (above)).

1.12.5.6   Annual leave and maternity/paternity leave

As employment rights are protected in the UK while on maternity/paternity leave (see **Chapter 14**), paid holiday will continue to accrue. Generally, this will be taken before or after the maternity/paternity leave period. This applies to both statutory and contractual annual leave entitlements. (See the ECJ case of *Tribunalul Botosani v Dicu* on the ability of EU States' laws to disapply the accrual of annual leave during parental leave, distinguishing it from maternity leave and sickness, for which the Working Time Directive does not presuppose that the worker is actually at work.)

1.12.5.7   Summary of current state of affairs on annual leave in the UK

Generally statutory annual leave must be taken in the year in which it falls due and cannot be carried forward. Case law has established that where someone is on sick leave, maternity leave or has not been permitted to take annual leave, their holiday continues to be due and accrue. Case law now suggests that untaken holiday cannot be carried forward indefinitely and should be limited to 18 months after the end of the holiday year in question (see above). This only applies to the four weeks' annual leave mandated by the Directive, and different considerations will apply to the additional 1.6 weeks allowed under UK law and any separate express contractual holiday pay provisions, which will be governed by the terms of the contract.

When calculating how much an employee should be paid in respect of annual leave, it is necessary to work out what a 'week's pay' means. Where a worker has 'normal working hours' and is on a fixed salary, this is a fairly straightforward exercise. Where the worker receives variable pay depending on the amount of work he does or when he does it, a week's pay is averaged out over the previous 52 weeks. Both guaranteed and non-guaranteed contractual overtime payments, as well as commission payments, should be included. There is nothing in principle that appears likely to prevent voluntary overtime, at least where this is worked regularly (so as to constitute work 'normally carried out' and amount to an 'appropriately permanent feature' so as to form part of a worker's 'normal hours'), from also having to be taken into account (see *Patterson v Castlereagh Borough Council* (NIIT/1793/13). Likewise, any payments that are linked to productivity, and travel time payments that exceed expenses incurred and so amount to additional taxable remuneration. These sums only apply when calculating the four weeks to which employees are entitled under the Working Time Directive.

Workers can only bring claims for holiday pay in the employment tribunal. Claims can be brought either under the Regulations, or as a series of unlawful deductions from wages under the ERA 1996. However, claims under the Working Time Directive have to be brought within three months of the date of the last payment. A gap of more than three months will not restrict a 'series' claim under the unlawful deductions for wages provisions in the ERA 1996 (see *Agnew* above). Any claims for statutory annual holiday pay issued after 1 July 2015 can in any event only go back a maximum of two years.

Note. In a recent CJEU judgment (in the joined cases of *Stadt Wuppertal v Bauer* (Case C-569/16) and *Volker Willmeroth v Brosson* (Case C-570/16)), the horizontal direct effect of the right to be paid annual leave enshrined in Article 31(2) of the Charter of Fundamental Rights of the EU was invoked in a worker/private employer context. Generally, Directives cannot be invoked in private disputes (unless they are implemented accordingly in national law) (see **1.2.4.2**). As the UK has now left the EU, and so is no longer bound by the Charter, the implications of *Bauer* are unlikely to have any impact.

Holiday pay – summary of relevant case law

	ECJ	SC	CA	EAT	ET
On call	SiMAP (C-303/98) [2000] IRLR 845, paras 48–49; Grigore (C-258/10), para 53; Jaeger (C-151/02) [2003] IRLR 804, para 63; Matzak (C-518/15)			Hughes (UKEAT/0159/08)	
Travelling to work	Tyco Integrated Security (C-266/14)			Valentine (UKEAT/0325/16)	
Normal remuneration/ week's pay	Williams (C-155/10)			Bear Scotland (UKEATS/ 0047/13)	
Commission payments	Williams (C-155/10); Lock [2014] ICR 813		Evans [2003] ICR 432; Lock [2016] EWCA Civ 983		
Overtime	Hein (C-385/17)		Peacock [1973] ICR 273; Patterson [2015] IRLR 721; Flowers [2019] EWCA Civ 947	Bear Scotland (UKEATS/ 0047/13); Willetts (UKEAT/0334/16)	Brettle (ET/1300537/15); Whitehead (ET/2600493/4/ 6)
Sickness	Pereda (C-277/08); Schultz-Hoff [2009] IRLR 214; Sobczyszyn (C-178/15); Hyinvointialan (C-609/17)	Stringer [2009] UKHL 31	Larner [2010] EWCA Civ 1034	Plumb (UKEAT/0071/15); Sood Enterprises (UKEATs/ 0015/12)	
Calculation/entitlement	Bollacke (C-118/13); Hein (C-385/17); Bauer (C-569/16 and C-570/16)	Stringer [2009] UKHL 31 Harpur Trust v Brazel [2022] UKSC 21			
Limitations on back pay: Deduction from Wages (Limitation) Regulations 2016	King (C-214/16)		Smith v Pimlico Plumbers [2022] EWCA Civ 70	Bear Scotland (UKEATS/ 0047/13)	Neal (ET/1315342/2012)
Rolling up	Robinson-Steele (C-131/04)				

1.12.5.8   Zero hours contracts

In *Heimann v Kaiser GmbH* [2013] IRLR 48, the ECJ ruled that national legislation could provide for workers on zero hours contracts to be entitled to be paid annual leave on a pro rata basis, since their situation was analogous to that of part-time workers. Accordingly, claimants do not accrue untaken annual leave during the period of their zero hours arrangement.

1.12.5.9   Bank holidays

This is another potentially vexed area. Some employers only give the benefit of bank or public holidays if the holiday in question falls on a day when the worker would normally be at work. However, this may be in breach of the Part-Time Workers Regulations 2000 (see **8.10**) because some part-time workers (generally those who do not work on Mondays or whose working days are variable) could be treated less favourably than comparable full-time workers. In general it is simplest to give part-time workers a pro rata entitlement to public holidays, regardless of which days they normally work.

1.12.5.10   Holidays and discrimination

While most Christian festivals such as Christmas and Easter are provided for as public holidays, there is no such provision for non-Christian festivals. This may lead to requests in some businesses for a large volume of days off at the same time, outside the designated public holidays. Employers need to be wary of avoiding putting employees of particular religions or beliefs at a disadvantage if they refuse such requests. They will need to ensure they are acting reasonably in how they deal with such requests. Similar issues can arise in regard to request for leave during school holidays in respect of possible indirect sex discrimination claims. See by way of illustration the approach of the EAT in *Garreddu v London Underground Ltd* (see **8.2.3.1** below).

1.12.5.11   Sanctions

The sanctions for failing to provide a worker with paid annual leave are very similar to the sanctions that are imposed in respect of a breach of a worker's rest entitlements outlined at **1.12.4.4** above. However, where the complaint is of failure to provide due pay for a period of annual leave or pay in lieu of untaken leave on termination of employment, the tribunal must order payment of the amount due by the employer. (See the chart at **5.6.2.5**.)

1.12.5.12   Law Society practice note

The Law Society has a useful practice note on its website about holiday entitlement, advising on calculating entitlement to paid annual leave, how entitlement is affected by working part time, for a fixed term or on a temporary contract, and the difference between contractual and statutory entitlement.

1.12.6   Relevant agreements

The Regulations enable workers and employers to enter into agreements to establish the way in which some of the working time rules apply to their own workplaces. Provision is made for the following agreements which, collectively, are referred to as 'relevant agreements':

(a)   workforce agreements, ie agreements with workforce representatives;

(b)   collective agreements with independent recognised trade unions;

(c)   written agreements, ie any other agreement in writing which is legally enforceable between the worker and his employer.

1.12.6.1   Which rights/limits can be modified or excluded?

The main situation in which a written agreement between a worker and his employer can be utilised is to modify or exclude the limits on weekly working time.

Collective or workforce agreements can be used (inter alia) to modify or exclude the following rights:

(a)   length of night work;

(b)   daily and weekly rest periods; and

(c)   rest breaks.

In each case where a collective or workforce agreement is utilised to modify or exclude these rights, the employer must allow the worker wherever possible to take an equivalent period of compensationary rest and, if this is not possible for objective reasons, must afford the worker such protection as may be appropriate in order to safeguard the worker's health and safety.

In *Industry and Commerce Maintenance v Briffa* (UKEAT/021508/07), the EAT held that the basic requirements in reg 15 could be varied or excluded by a contractual term which covered the position and was legally enforceable as a relevant agreement under reg 2.

1.12.6.2   Workforce agreements: the legal requirements

The Regulations lay down detailed provisions with regard to a valid workforce agreement. For example, the agreement has to be in writing, and it cannot last longer than five years.

1.13   CHECKLISTS

1.13.1   Terms and conditions

(1)   Is the individual an employee or a worker? For the definition of 'employee' see s 230(1) of the ERA 1996; for the definition of 'worker' see s 230(3) of the 1996 Act.

(2)   Within two months of starting employment, employers must give their employees a written statement of the main terms of their contract.

(3)   There are certain key terms that *must* be included in a written statement of terms and conditions (see ERA 1996, s 1(3)–(4)).

(4)   Consider whether to include other express terms as well (see **1.4** and **Appendix 1**).

(5)   Check that any restrictive covenants are reasonable in terms of time and area, and are necessary to protect the employer's business interests.

(6)   Check that the National Minimum Wage Regulations and Working Time Regulations are not being broken.

(7)   Check that the employee signs and returns the statement/contract, and that both the employer and the employee have copies.

1.13.2   Summary of basic working time rights, enforcement and exceptions

SUMMARY OF BASIC WORKING TIME RIGHTS

Maximum working week	48 hours/week
Daily break	20 minutes/6 hours
Daily rest	11 hours/24 hours
Weekly rest	24 hours/7 days
Paid annual leave	5.6 weeks/52 weeks

ENFORCEMENT

	Health & Safety etc	Declaration and Compensation	No Detriment	Unfair Dismissal
WORKING WEEK	✓		✓	✓
NIGHT WORK	✓		✓	✓
REST PERIODS		✓	✓	✓
REST BREAKS		✓	✓	✓
ANNUAL LEAVE		✓	✓	✓

EXCEPTIONS

	Written Agreement	Unmeasured Working Time	Special Case Activities	Shift/Split Period Workers	Collective/ Workforce Agreements
WORKING WEEK	✓	✓			
NIGHT WORK		✓	✓		✓
REST PERIODS		✓	✓	✓	✓
REST BREAKS		✓	✓		✓
ANNUAL LEAVE					

1.14 FURTHER READING

Harvey, *Industrial Relations and Employment Law* (LexisNexis), Divs A, B and C.

Lewis, *Employment Law – an adviser's handbook*, 14th edn (LAG, 2022).

Selwyn's Law of Employment, 22nd edn (OUP, 2022).

Blackstone's Employment Law Practice, 10th edn (OUP, 2019).

Bowers, *A Practical Approach to Employment Law*, 9th edn (OUP, 2017), chs 1–6.

Duggan, *Contracts of Employment* (2 vols), 4th edn (Duggan Press, 2019).

TUC, *Your Rights at Work*, 6th edn (Kogan Page, 2021).

SUMMARY

This chapter has looked at the various sources of UK employment law (common law, statute, codes of practice and EU law (**1.2** and **1.4**)). It has identified that there are some important differences between employees, workers and those who work for themselves as far as statutory protections are concerned. Certain rights, such as unfair dismissal and the right to a redundancy payment, apply only to employees; others (eg the National Minimum Wage Regulations and the Working Time Regulations) apply to a wider category of worker (**1.3**).

Section 1 of the ERA 1996 provides that employers must give their employees a written statement of the main terms of their contract (**1.4** and **Appendix 1**). A statement of terms and conditions is not a contract, but it does confirm the main express terms of the employment contract. It is not definitive of the entire contract, but it does provide an evidential basis of the most important terms.

Contracts of employment, where both sides agree the terms, may be written or oral, but it is sensible to put them in writing. Even where there is a written contract with express terms, statute and the courts will sometimes imply terms into a contract (**1.4**). The most important implied term is that of mutual trust and confidence. Where this term is broken, it may entitle either side to bring the relationship to an end. If an employer breaches it, it may entitle an employee with the requisite period of continuous employment to resign and claim constructive unfair dismissal (**3.4.3**).

The contract should, as a minimum, deal with all the matters set out in s 1(3) and (4) of the ERA 1996. This includes pay, job description, hours of work, place of work and whether the employee can be made to move, holiday, pension and sickness provisions, the length of notice that needs to be given by either side to terminate the arrangement (s 86 of the ERA 1996 sets out certain minimum notice periods), disciplinary and grievance procedures, and the obligations of confidentiality that an employee owes his employer (**1.4–1.8, Appendix 1**). It is also possible to include terms which protect an employer's business after the employee has left. These terms are known as restrictive covenants. They may be expressly included in a contract, so long as they are reasonable in terms of time and area and are necessary to protect the employer's business interests (**1.8.7**).

The protection of wages legislation set out in Pt II of the ERA 1996 protects an employee if an employer fails to pay the proper wages due under the contract, and prevents an employer from making deductions from an employee's wages unless they are authorised (**1.11**). For claims presented after 1 July 2015, there is a maximum of two years' deductions that can be claimed (**1.11.2**).

The Working Time Regulations 1998 set out maximum weekly working hours and provide for certain minimum rights to have breaks and paid annual leave (**1.12**). For claims presented after 1 July 2015, there is a maximum of two years' back pay that can be claimed.

CHAPTER 2

TERMINATION OF THE CONTRACT OF EMPLOYMENT – WRONGFUL DISMISSAL

2.1	Introduction	101
2.2	Wrongful dismissal (dismissal in breach of contract)	103
2.3	Termination of contract	104
2.4	Employee's remedies for wrongful dismissal	111
2.5	Employer's remedies	117
2.6	Checklist	119
2.7	Further reading	119
	Summary	119

LEARNING OUTCOMES

After reading this chapter you will be able to:

- describe and understand the differences between a claim of wrongful dismissal based on a breach of contract and the statutory claim of unfair dismissal, and the remedies that are available for wrongful dismissal

- explain when a wrongful dismissal claim arises

- understand the main ways in which a contract of employment may come to an end and the relevance of notice periods

- understand the significance of constructive dismissal

- understand the relevant principles to apply when calculating an employee's damages following a wrongful dismissal

- understand what remedies are available to an employer if an employee is in repudiatory breach of contract.

2.1 INTRODUCTION

Before considering in detail three of the main potential claims an employee might have on termination of a contract of employment (wrongful dismissal (see **2.2**), unfair dismissal (see **Chapter 5**) and the right to a redundancy payment (see **Chapter 4**)), it is useful to have a preliminary overview of these claims.

2.1.1 Wrongful dismissal (breach of contract)

This is a common law contractual claim for breach of contract, which may be brought by workers or employees, based *solely* on the fact that the dismissal by the employer was in breach of contract. The remedy is therefore damages for breach of contract.

For example:

(a) termination of the contract with no notice or short notice (see **2.3.3**); or

(b) where the employee/worker establishes he has been constructively dismissed (see **2.3.5**); or

(c) termination of the contract before the expiry of a limited term where there is no break clause (see **2.3.8**).

A breach of contract claim can be brought in the civil courts or in the employment tribunal. However, an employment tribunal's contract jurisdiction is limited (Employment Tribunals Act (ETA) 1996, ss 3 and 8; Employment Tribunal's Extension of Jurisdiction Order 1994). In *London Borough of Enfield v Sivanandan* [2005] EWCA Civ 10, the Court of Appeal held that where a breach of contract claim is struck out (as opposed to being withdrawn – see *Sajid v Chowdhury* [2002] IRLR 113) by an employment tribunal, it is an abuse of process to re-issue it in the civil courts. Even if a claim is withdrawn, it may be an abuse of process to re-issue it if the claim in the employment tribunal covered the same facts and was worth less than £25,000. If a claim is withdrawn but it is intended to pursue the claim in the civil courts, the claimant should tell the employment tribunal that that is the reason the claim is being withdrawn.

There is no limit to the amount of damages recoverable in a court action, although there is a restriction on tribunal awards. This is currently £25,000. Breach of contract claims can be brought in a tribunal where the claim follows termination of the employment together with a claim for unfair dismissal. Claimants need to be aware, though, that if they bring a high-value breach of contract claim in the tribunal, they will not be permitted to seek to recover any excess over £25,000 in the civil courts. The Court of Appeal, in *Fraser v HLMAD* [2006] EWCA Civ 738, said that once the claimant had lodged an ET1 claim form, which included a claim for breach of contract for wrongful dismissal, the claims had 'merged' and there was no independent claim left which he could pursue. The Court of Appeal said that claimants wishing to bring high-value breach of contract claims should do so in the civil courts, unless they are willing to limit damages to £25,000. In April 2020, the Law Commission published its report on 'Employment Law Hearing Structures', which made 23 recommendations with the aim of improving the ability of employment tribunals to resolve employment disputes effectively and justly in one place. The recommendations include introducing flexible deployment of judges to permit employment judges to hear discrimination claims in the civil courts; increasing the jurisdiction of employment tribunals to hear claims for damages for breach of contract by employees and counterclaims by employers during the currency of a contract of employment and to hear claims in relation to alleged liability arising after employment has terminated; increasing the financial limits on contractual claims from £25,000 to £100,000; and an extension of the jurisdiction to hear breach of contract claims from workers as well as employees.

Limitation periods for bringing claims in the tribunal and courts are also different (see **2.2**).

When considering a breach of contract claim, no account is taken of the reasonableness of an employer's action in terminating the contract. This allows employers to write in contractual provisions entitling them to terminate the contract and dismiss the employee without facing any common law claim for breach of contract (the contractual notice period must not be shorter than the statutory minimum period required by s 86 of the ERA 1996 – see **2.3.3**). So, for example, if an employer dismisses an employee with the correct notice, generally no claim for breach of contract will arise. To redress the balance, in the 1960s, statute began to intervene in the hitherto unfettered rights of the employer. In particular, concepts of fairness and reasonableness were introduced. Two statutory rights given to the employee are the right to claim unfair dismissal and/or the right to claim a redundancy payment on termination.

Note that workers and employees with less than a year's service will also be entitled to bring a claim for unpaid notice if their contract is terminated with insufficient notice (but note that ERA 1996, s 86 – relating to minimum notice periods – applies only to employees).

2.1.2 Unfair dismissal

This is a statutory claim that can be brought only by certain employees who satisfy eligibility criteria. It can be brought only before an employment tribunal.

The success of the claim does not rest on the issue of breach of contract. The tribunal looks instead into whether or not there was a fair reason for dismissal and at the reasonableness of the employer's actions.

A successful applicant may receive a basic award of compensation calculated in accordance with a set formula. In addition, he may receive a compensatory award to compensate for actual financial loss suffered (in a similar way to an award of damages for breach of contract). This compensatory award is subject to a maximum limit, which was £78,962 as at 6 April 2016 (note the limit is subject to revision in February each year – the Secretary of State can, each year, increase or decrease that sum in accordance with the Retail Price Index).

2.1.3 Redundancy payment

This is another statutory claim, which is in the nature of a reward for past services; it is compensation for the loss of a secure job rather than for future financial losses.

The claimant must, again, be eligible and the claim is pursued (where necessary) in the employment tribunal.

The payment is calculated in accordance with a set formula, which is the same as the basic award formula for unfair dismissal.

2.1.4 Conclusion

There is overlap, in terms of the remedy afforded to an employee, between the three claims, which is considered after looking in detail at each of them (see **6.8**).

The remainder of this chapter deals with the common law claim of wrongful dismissal in breach of contract.

The statutory claims of unfair dismissal and redundancy payments are dealt with in **Chapters 3–5**.

2.2 WRONGFUL DISMISSAL (DISMISSAL IN BREACH OF CONTRACT)

At common law, an employee (or worker) will have a claim for damages against his employer if the employer has dismissed him in breach of contract. This breach of contract claim is known as the claim for 'wrongful dismissal'. See **2.3** for when termination of the contract amounts to a breach of contract (ie gives rise to a wrongful dismissal claim). If there is no dismissal, there cannot be a claim for wrongful dismissal. Instead, there would be a general breach of contract claim.

This claim may be pursued in the civil courts or in the employment tribunal.

In the courts, the limitation period is six years and there is no upper limit on the level of damages which may be awarded. If the claim is worth less than £5,000 and is pursued in the county court, it will automatically be referred to the small claims track.

If a wrongful dismissal claim is pursued in the employment tribunal, there are certain preconditions (ETA 1996, ss 3 and 8; Employment Tribunal's Extension of Jurisdiction Order 1994):

(a) the claim *must* be for breach of a contract of employment or other contract connected with employment and must arise or be outstanding on the *termination* of employment. In *Capek v Lincolnshire County Council* [2000] IRLR 590, the Court of Appeal held that tribunals have no jurisdiction to hear claims for breach of contract which are lodged prior to the termination of the employee's contract (ETA 1996, s 3(2));

(b) the only remedy available is compensation;

(c) the employment tribunal will not be able to award more than £25,000 in respect of a contract claim (1994 Order, art 10);

(d) the tribunal cannot hear all claims arising out of an alleged breach – for example claims relating to contractual terms of confidentiality and restrictive covenants are excluded (1994 Order, arts 3, 5);

(e) the employer will be able to raise a counterclaim (alleging that the employee has also breached the contract of employment);

(f) the claim will have to be brought within three months of termination (see **6.3.6**).

2.3 TERMINATION OF CONTRACT

2.3.1 Introduction

At common law, the contract of employment may come to an end in a number of ways. Only if the termination amounts to a breach of contract by the employer will the employee be entitled to claim damages for wrongful dismissal. The main ways in which an employment contract can come to an end are set out below.

2.3.2 Termination by agreement

The parties may at any time agree to bring the contract to an end. Neither party will be in breach of contract and no claim for wrongful dismissal will arise.

2.3.3 Termination by notice

A contract of employment for an indefinite term may be terminated by either party giving the other proper notice. Provided proper notice is given, the contract will terminate with no liability for breach of contract, whatever the reason for the termination. If the contract is ended by the employer with proper notice, there can be no wrongful dismissal claim by the employee because the employer has acted within the terms of the contract.

In *Newcastle upon Tyne Hospitals NHS Foundation Trust v Haywood* [2018] UKSC 22, the Supreme Court held that a term will be applied into all employment contracts that notice of termination will only start to run from the date the employee received written notice of their dismissal and has had a reasonable opportunity to read it, if different. This will be the default position unless there is an express contractual clause making clear that, for example, notice is effective from the date of delivery.

This rule applies only to contracts for an indefinite term. In the absence of a 'break' clause, limited-term contracts cannot be terminated by notice.

If the contract contains an express term stating the period of notice to be given by either party, then a party giving shorter notice to terminate will be in breach of contract, subject to **2.3.4**. If an expressly agreed period of notice is shorter than the statutory minimum period required by ERA 1996, s 86 (see below), the longer statutory minimum period must be given. The parties should agree the period of notice when the contract is entered into.

In the absence of an express term, it is an implied term of every indefinite contract of employment that it can be terminated by reasonable notice given by either party. What period is reasonable will depend on the facts of each case. The more senior the employee, the longer the period of notice required. The courts have held, for example, that three months was a reasonable period of notice for a salesman and an airline pilot, but only one week was required in the case of a milk carrier. In *Clark v Fahrenheit 451 (Communications) Ltd* (UKEAT/591/99), the EAT held that an employee's seniority and status and the employer's financial position are to be taken into account in determining what is a reasonable period of notice. Clearly, a reasonable amount must not be less than the statutory minimum.

When advising employers on reasonable periods of notice, it must be remembered that for senior, highly-skilled employees, reasonable notice can be quite long. For professional employees such as solicitors, accountants, highly-skilled technical employees, scientists or middle-managers, reasonable notice is likely to be in the region of three to six months. For a very senior employee, such as a managing director, it could be 12 months. For the unskilled and semi-skilled employee, reasonable notice is unlikely to exceed the statutory minimum period required by ERA 1996, s 86. The problem should be avoided by incorporating expressly agreed periods of notice into the employees' contracts.

Where a contract of employment is terminable by notice, s 86 of the ERA 1996 lays down the statutory minimum period of notice which must be given to employees. The statutory minimum period prevails over any shorter contractual period. However, as the parties may agree longer periods, any contractual provisions should be checked as, if these are more beneficial to the employee, they will override the statutory minimum. In *Newcastle upon Tyne NHS Foundation Trust v Haywood* [2017] EWCA Civ 153, the Court of Appeal held that notice of termination of employment is given when the employee actually receives the notice, because the contents of the letter had to be communicated to the employee. So the day a letter was written or the day it was posted or the day the letter arrived at the claimant's house were not relevant (see also **3.5.2.1**).

The statutory minimum period of notice required to be given by an employer under s 86(1) is:

Period of continuous employment	Notice
1 month to 2 years	1 week
2 years to 12 years	1 week for each year
12 years plus	12 weeks

The only statutory minimum notice required to be given by an employee is one week's notice after one month's continuous employment (s 86(2)).

See **3.5** for the meaning of continuous employment. Either party may waive notice (s 86(3)).

Sometimes the employer will terminate a contract without notice or with short notice but give the employee a payment in lieu of the notice period due ('PILON'). What is the effect of such a payment? There are two possibilities (the second of which is the norm):

(a)   The employee accepts the PILON, although there is no provision in the contract permitting such a payment, and agrees, expressly or impliedly, to waive the requirement for notice. In this case there will either be no breach by the employer, or the breach has been waived by the employee for consideration. In either case, there will be no liability for wrongful dismissal.

(b)   The employer pays the employee in lieu of notice, but there is no provision in the contract permitting such a payment to be made and the employee, while taking the money, does not accept the payment as waiving his right to notice. In this case the employer is in breach of contract and technically the employee could claim wrongful dismissal. However, unless the payment in lieu of notice is significantly less than the damages likely to be awarded (see **2.4.1**), the claim would not be worth pursuing in financial terms.

In *Société Générale, London Branch v Geys* [2013] IRLR 122, the Supreme Court settled a long-running question as to whether a party's repudiation of a contract of employment itself automatically terminates the contract, or whether the contract comes to an end only when the other party accepts the repudiation (the elective theory). The elective theory is in accordance with the general common-law rule that a repudiated contract is not terminated unless and until the repudiation is accepted by the innocent party. This is primarily because it would be manifestly unjust to allow the wrongdoer to determine a contract by a repudiatory breach where the innocent party wished to affirm the contract for good reason. The effect of the automatic theory of termination is to reward the wrong-doer.

The Supreme Court favoured the elective theory, by a 4:1 majority. The claimant was the managing director at a bank. His contract had a clause saying it could be terminated after three months' notice. The staff handbook provided that the bank reserved the right to terminate the employment at any time with immediate effect by making a payment in lieu of notice. The contract gave the claimant an entitlement to a termination payment, under which, if his contract terminated after 31 December 2007, he would receive a figure calculated by reference to his salary in 2006 and 2007. If his employment terminated before that date, his termination payment was to be calculated by reference to two earlier years, when his salary was much lower. So it was a key issue as to whether the contact terminated in 2007 or 2008.

At a meeting on 29 November 2007, the claimant was given a letter informing him that his employment was being terminated 'with immediate effect'. No reference was made to the PILON clause, so this appeared on its face to be a repudiatory breach of contract. On 18 December, the bank paid a sum into the claimant's bank account that would have satisfied the PILON clause, but again there was no reference to the PILON clause. The claimant became aware of the payment at some point before the end of December, and on 2 January 2008 the claimant told the bank that he was affirming his contract. On 4 January, the bank wrote to the claimant for the first time making express reference to an intention to make the payment pursuant to the PILON clause and terminate his contract with effect from 29 November 2007. Under the contract, notices were deemed to be received on the second day after posting, ie on 6 January. The claimant therefore argued that his contract was not actually terminated until that date. The bank argued that the contract was terminated on 29 November or, in the alternative, on 18 December. The High Court accepted the claimant's argument, but the Court of Appeal decided that the correct date was 18 December. The Supreme Court decided that the elective theory of termination was correct, so that the bank's breach of contract did not actually terminate the claimant's contract unless or until it was accepted by the claimant (which it was not), thus preferring the line of authority in cases such as *Gunton v Richmond-upon-Thames Borough Council* [1980] IRLR 321. That meant that the contract terminated on 6 January, when the bank lawfully terminated the claimant's contract by validly exercising the PILON clause. However, the Supreme Court rejected the suggestion (of Buckley LJ in *Gunton*) that a court could easily infer acceptance: real acceptance was required in the sense of a conscious intention to bring the contract to an end or doing an act inconsistent with its continuation.

The Supreme Court rejected the suggestion that the payment into the claimant's account amounted to the exercise of the PILON clause. The Court emphasised the need for notices to be given in clear and unambiguous terms; thus it was not sufficient to make the payment in lieu, the employee also had to receive a clear and unambiguous notice that the payment had been made in exercise of the right to terminate under the PILON clause. Even if writing is not required by the contract, a sensible employer will give notice in writing; otherwise notice can be given by a clear verbal statement to the effect that the contract is at an end.

It therefore follows that:

(a)   the elective theory applies equally to repudiatory breaches by an employee;

(b)   there is no difference in principle between a resignation and a dismissal – the elective theory applies in all instances;

(c)   a justified summary dismissal (as opposed to a repudiatory breach) will still be effective to bring a contract an end;

(d)   for the purpose of the effective date of termination (EDT), which is a statutory concept, s 97(3)(b) of the ERA 1996 provides that the EDT is 'the date when the contract of employment was terminated by the employer' (plus any statutory notice required by s 86 of the ERA 1996) (see **3.5.2.1**). Although this was not discussed by the Supreme Court, the Court of Appeal did consider this and held that the EDT would not necessarily be the same date as the repudiatory acceptance, so could precede that date.

Note: Where a contract expressly allows the employer to terminate the contract either by notice or by making a payment in lieu of notice, the dismissal does not become wrongful even if the employer fails to make the payment. The employee's claim in this situation is for a sum due under the contract (a debt owed), *not* for damages for breach of contract (*Abrahams v Performing Rights Society Ltd* [1995] IRLR 486, CA). Because the sum is for the recovery of a debt, the employee is not under a duty to mitigate losses. By contrast an employee who brings a claim for wrongful dismissal is under a duty to mitigate losses (see **2.4**).

A PILON paid under the terms of the contract is always regarded as an 'emolument' from that employment and will be chargeable to income tax (*EMI Group Electronics Ltd v Coldicott (Inspector of Taxes)* [1999] IRLR 630, CA). Thus, such payments are not treated as falling within the Income Tax (Earnings and Pensions) Act 2003 exemption relating to termination payments up to £30,000 (see **2.4.1.8**).

Readers should consult the latest information on the HMRC website when giving advice on the tax implications of termination payments (www.hmrc.gov.uk).

2.3.4   Dismissal for employee's breach – 'summary dismissal'

If the employee commits a repudiatory breach of contract, the employer is entitled to treat the contract as discharged, ie to dismiss the employee without notice. In *Tydeman v Oyster Yachts Ltd* [2022] EAT 115, HHJ Taylor stated:

> 'Gross misconduct' is a term of art at common law. It does not appear in the statutory provisions that deal with the assessment of compensation for unfair dismissal. It is a contractual assessment turning on whether an individual has acted in a manner that fundamentally breaches their contract of employment so that the employer is entitled to accept the breach and terminate the contract without being required to rely on a contractual notice provision, and so can dismiss summarily without notice. Typically, gross misconduct involves dishonesty, disobedience or incompetence on the part of the employee: see Harvey at [443.04]. It is not always an easy test to apply as there is no rule of law that sets out the degree of misconduct that will justify summary dismissal. The more recent approach has been to focus on whether there has been an undermining of mutual trust and confidence so that the employer is entitled to dismiss the employee: see *Mbubaegbu v Homerton University Hospital NHS Foundation Trust* UKEAT/0218/17/JOJ, a decision of Choudhury J, in which reliance was placed on the decision in *Neary v Dean of Westminster* [1999] IRLR 288 (see particularly paragraphs 22 and 32–33).

Any repudiatory breach of an express or implied term by the employee will justify the employer dismissing without notice. Non-exhaustive examples would include revealing trade secrets, wilful disobedience of lawful orders, theft from the employer or other gross misconduct and negligence if sufficiently serious. The crucial factor is the seriousness of the breach. It must be repudiatory (or fundamental), ie sufficiently serious to entitle the employer to treat the contract as discharged. In cases of gross negligence, the test is whether the negligent dereliction of duty was 'so grave and weighty' (*Neary v Dean of Westminster* [1999] IRLR 288). For two examples, see (misconduct) *Pepper v Webb* [1969] All ER 216 and (performance) *Alidair v Taylor* [1978] IRLR 82. In *Dunn & Another v AAH Ltd* [2010] EWCA Civ 183, the Court of Appeal held that an employee who had failed to follow instructions to report risk of fraud to HQ over a five-month period had so undermined the duty of trust and confidence by virtue of his wilful neglect of duty that the employer could accept the breach of contract and dismiss without notice. See too *Adesokan v Sainsbury's Supermarkets Ltd* [2017] EWCA Civ 22.

When dealing with a suspected repudiatory breach, the employer must reserve its position so as not to waive the breach if it does not intend to take immediate disciplinary action (see *Cook v MSHK Ltd and Ministry of Sound Recordings Ltd* [2009] EWCA Civ 624). Otherwise it will be deemed to have affirmed the contract (and waived the breach).

Dismissal without notice can be justified by discovery of sufficient grounds *after* dismissal has taken place. In *Boston Deep Sea Fishing and Ice Co v Ansell* (1888) 39 Ch D 339, the misconduct of a managing director in taking bribes was discovered only after his dismissal. The tribunal held that the employer could rely on the latter acquired knowledge to justify the decision summarily to dismiss the employee. For a recent example, see *Williams v Leeds Football Club* [2015] EWHC 376 (QB). However, the Court of Appeal held in *Cavenagh v Williams Evans Ltd* [2012] EWCA Civ 697 that the employer could not rely on after-discovered gross misconduct in circumstances where it had already agreed to make a contractual payment in lieu of notice.

If the employer is mistaken about the seriousness of the breach and dismisses without notice in circumstances where he is not entitled to, the employer will have dismissed in breach of contract and be liable for wrongful dismissal (see **2.3.3**). It will be for the tribunal (or court) to decide whether the conduct amounted to a repudiatory breach of contract. In theory the employee has a choice whether to accept the breach or waive it, but in practice an employee has little choice but to accept the breach because he cannot perform his duties (*Boyo v Lambeth London Borough Council* [1995] IRLR 50).

2.3.5 Resignation and constructive dismissal

Normally, an employee who resigns will have no claim for wrongful dismissal. This is because it is the employee, not the employer, who has terminated the contract. For an example of how difficult it will be for an employee to claim that his unambiguous words of resignation amount to a dismissal, see *Ali v Birmingham City Council* (UKEAT/0313/08). Indeed, if the employee does not give proper notice or terminates a fixed-term contract before its expiry date, it is the employee who will be in breach of contract.

However, if the employer commits a repudiatory breach of an express or implied term of the contract of employment, the employee is entitled to accept the breach, resign and treat the contract as discharged. This is known as a constructive dismissal. The employee must leave within a reasonable time of the breach, otherwise he may be taken to have affirmed the contract and waived the breach. If the employee can establish that he has been constructively dismissed, he will have a claim for wrongful dismissal (dismissal in breach of contract). Note that an employer cannot avail itself of a contractual notice period to try to limit any damages (see *Hall v London Lions Basketball Club (UK) Ltd* [2021] IRLR 17).

Note that the employer's breach must be repudiatory; a minor breach will not entitle the employee to leave and claim that he has been constructively dismissed. Note too that the date of the resignation may be relevant as to when time starts to run to bring an employment tribunal claim. If an employee resigns without notice, the employment will end there and then, and time will start to run; the employer does not need to 'accept' the resignation, nor is he obliged to give the employee a 'cooling-off period', though some employers do so (see, eg, *Secretary of State for Justice v Hibbert* (UKEAT/0289/13)).

See **3.4.3** for details of constructive dismissal.

In *East Kent Hospitals University NHS Foundation Trust v Levy* (UKEAT/0232/17) the EAT held that giving notice does not automatically amount to an unambiguous act of resignation. The claimant was made a conditional offer of a new role within the same NHS trust. She sent a letter giving one month's notice for the old job. The conditional offer was later withdrawn and the claimant sought to withdraw her notice. The NHS trust refused, her employment ended and she brought an unfair dismissal claim. The tribunal found the wording of the notice to be ambiguous and concluded that the letter was merely signifying an intention to move jobs. The EAT agreed.

2.3.6 Frustration

If the contract of employment is frustrated, it terminates automatically by operation of law. Neither party will be in breach and neither party will have a claim against the other, other than for wages due to the date of frustration. Frustration occurs where, without the fault of either party, some event occurs which prevents performance of the contract. The event must not have been provided for by the contract. The principal events which may frustrate a contract of employment are as follows.

2.3.6.1 The death of either party

The death of the employee clearly frustrates the contract. The death of a sole trader employer will also frustrate the contract. However, if the employees are re-employed by the personal representatives of the deceased, or the business is transferred to another employer who re-employs the employees, continuity of employment will usually be preserved (see **3.5.5**).

2.3.6.2 Illness or injury of the employee

Long-term or permanent illness or injury which prevents the employee from performing his duties *may* frustrate the contract. Factors which will be taken into account in deciding whether or not a contract is frustrated include:

(a)   the nature of the work;

(b)   the length of employment;

(c)   the nature, length and effect of the illness or injury;

(d)   the need for the work to be done and the need for a replacement to do it; and

(e)   whether in all the circumstances a reasonable employer could be expected to wait any longer (*Egg Stores (Stamford Hill) Ltd v Leibovici* [1976] IRLR 376);

(f)   how likely it is that the employee will return to work.

The terms of the contract must also be considered. If the contract makes provision for a period of absence due to ill-health, then the contract would not be frustrated if the employee was likely to return to work within that period.

In practice, especially with contracts terminable by notice, the courts and employment tribunals are extremely reluctant to find that a contract has been frustrated. The effect of holding that a contract is frustrated deprives the employee of any remedy that he might have had if he had been dismissed. Nevertheless, in rare cases the court may find that the contract has been frustrated. In *Collins v Secretary of State for Trade and Industry* (UKEAT/1460/99), the EAT held that a contract had been frustrated by an employee's long-term illness. Of particular relevance, on the facts, was the length of time the employee was off work (three years) and the unlikeliness of any return to work.

In *Warner v Armfield Retail & Leisure Ltd* (UKEAT/0376/12), the EAT held that, in the case of a disabled person, before the doctrine of frustration can apply there is an additional factor which must be considered over and above the factors set out above – namely whether the employer is in breach of its duty to make reasonable adjustments (see **Chapter 13**). While there is something which it is reasonable to expect the employer to do, the doctrine of frustration cannot apply. On the facts, the tribunal having found no breach of the duty to make reasonable adjustments, the tribunal's decision that the contract had been frustrated was upheld.

2.3.6.3 Imprisonment of the employee

A problem arises when a contract is terminated on the imprisonment of an employee. The employer will allege frustration and termination by operation of law. The employee will argue that he has been dismissed, frustration not being applicable as imprisonment constitutes 'self-induced frustration'. This would give the employee a potential claim for wrongful dismissal, even though in the majority of cases the dismissal would be justified.

The Court of Appeal in *FC Shepherd & Co Ltd v Jerrom* [1987] 1 QB 301 decided the imprisoned employee had no claim. Balcombe LJ found that the frustrating event was the actual imposition of the sentence, not the misconduct by the employee, but Lawton and Mustill LJJ held that the rule against reliance on self-induced frustration only meant that neither party could rely on his own misconduct to establish a defence of frustration. But since the employer was relying on the employee's fault, that requirement was satisfied and thus frustration could succeed.

In *Chakki v United Yeast Co Ltd* [1982] 2 All ER 446, the EAT held that certain elements need to be considered when deciding whether or not a prison sentence has frustrated the contract of employment. It distinguished between a situation where a sentence of imprisonment was a cause of 'instantaneous' frustration of a contract of employment and one where it was merely a 'potentially frustrating event' depending on the time at which frustration occurred, being the time at which the parties became aware of the cause and the likely outcome of the interruption and had to decide on a future course of action. The EAT said:

> [I]t seems to us that in some cases a sentence of imprisonment will be similar to an accident or an illness and thus a potentially frustrating event rather than a cause of instantaneous frustration. It has to be recognised, however, that a sentence of imprisonment differs from an accident to an illness in that, unless and until it is varied on appeal, the length of the employee's absence and the affect on the contract of employment is immediately predictable. One has therefore to try to find that moment at which the question of frustration or not has to be determined.

In *Four Seasons Healthcare Ltd v Maughan* [2005] IRLR 324, the EAT held that frustration requires that there should be some outside event or extraneous change of situation, not foreseen or provided for by the parties within the contract. The EAT commented, in a situation where there was a detailed disciplinary procedure in the employment contract which made specific reference to the misconduct which the claimant had been dismissed over (namely physical abuse directed towards residents), 'it seems to us that the presence of such a detailed disciplinary procedure should indeed ... inhibit us from being too ready to find in favour of frustration'. In this case, therefore, the contract was not frustrated until the custodial sentence made its performance impossible. Thus, a very short custodial sentence might not have the effect of frustrating a contract.

2.3.7 Partnerships and companies

The dissolution of a partnership or the winding up of a company may terminate the employees' contracts.

2.3.7.1 Partnerships

Usually, a change of partners where the employer is a partnership will have no effect on the employees' contracts of employment.

However, if the contract is of a personal nature, ie the identity of the partners is material to the contract, then if the relevant partner leaves, the employee's contract will automatically be terminated (*Phillips v Alhambra Palace Co* [1901] 1 KB 59). If the partner leaves voluntarily (eg by retirement), there will be a wrongful dismissal of the employee unless proper notice was given. If the partner dies, the employee's contract will be frustrated. In practice, it is rare for the contract to be of a personal nature, the usual rule being that a change of partners does not affect the employee's contract.

Even if an employee's contract is terminated in such circumstances, there will be no break in the continuity of his employment if he is re-employed by the new partners (see **3.5.5**).

2.3.7.2 Companies

An order for the compulsory winding up of a company and a resolution to wind up an insolvent company will usually terminate the employees' contracts automatically. Dismissal will be wrongful unless proper notice is given. The making of an administration order or the appointment of a receiver by debenture holders would not normally terminate employees' contracts.

2.3.8   Limited-term contracts

At common law, a limited-term contract expires by effluxion of time at the end of the term. For example, a contract for a limited term of three years commencing on 1 February 2013 will come to an end on 31 January 2016 with no liability on either party if it is not renewed.

There is no implied term allowing a party to terminate a limited-term contract before its expiry date. If the employer or employee terminates a limited-term contract, with or without notice, before its expiry date, there will be a breach of contract unless:

(a)   the other party is in repudiatory breach of the contract; or

(b)   there is express power in the contract allowing early termination (a 'break' clause) (see below); or

(c)   the termination is by mutual agreement.

One or both parties (often only the employer) may be able to terminate the contract before the end of the limited term if the contract contains a 'break' clause. A 'break' clause allows a party to bring the contract to an end within the limited term, usually by giving notice. The 'break' clause may, for example, allow the employer to terminate in any circumstances by giving the employee, say, six months' notice, or it may allow termination in specific circumstances only (eg on the employee's bankruptcy or long-term illness) (see **1.8.1.2**).

2.4   EMPLOYEE'S REMEDIES FOR WRONGFUL DISMISSAL

In practice, the employee/worker who is wrongfully dismissed will usually have little choice but to accept the dismissal. It is virtually unheard of for a court to grant an injunction to prevent a dismissal, but it may depend on the precise terms of the contract. In *West London Mental Health NHS Trust v Chhabra* [2013] UKSC 60, the Supreme Court granted an injunction, preventing the Trust from holding a disciplinary hearing into matters said by the Trust to constitute 'gross misconduct' (see **1.8.8**), because this was not in accordance with the contractual disciplinary procedure. The employee/worker may then claim damages for wrongful dismissal against the employer.

2.4.1   Damages for wrongful dismissal

2.4.1.1   Introduction

Damages for wrongful dismissal are damages for breach of contract. They are governed by the normal rules of the law of contract:

(a)   the loss claimed must not be too remote, ie it must either arise naturally from the breach or be such as may reasonably be supposed to have been in the contemplation of both parties at the time of contract, as the probable result of the breach (*Hadley v Baxendale* (1854) 9 Exch 341);

(b)   the measure of damages, for loss which is not too remote, is the sum required to put the claimant, so far as money can, in the same position as if the contract had been performed (*Robinson v Harman* (1848) 1 Exch 850).

In *Boyo v Lambeth London Borough Council* [1994] ICR 727, CA, it was held that the correct measure of damages following the employer's repudiatory breach of contract was the amount the employee would be entitled to receive if dismissed in accordance with the terms of the contract. See also *Société Général, London Branch v Geys* at **2.3.3** above.

In the case of wrongful dismissal, damages are usually assessed as follows.

2.4.1.2   Loss of net wages

The starting point in calculating damages in the case of a contract for an indefinite term is the salary or wages that the employee/worker would have earned during the proper notice period.

In the case of a fixed-term contract it would be the salary for the remainder of the fixed term. There is an exception in the case of a fixed term where the employer was entitled to terminate under a 'break' clause, in which case it is the salary which would have been earned during the period of notice due under the 'break' clause.

Note that there is a danger in using the term 'ex gratia'. In *Publicis Consultants v O'Farrell* (UKEAT/0430/10) Mrs O'Farrell's contract entitled her to three months' notice of termination. The letter of dismissal said she would be paid statutory redundancy pay, holiday pay and a sum which, although equivalent to three months' gross salary, was said to be an ex gratia payment. An issue arose (in her successful unfair dismissal claim) as to whether she was entitled to receive three months' notice pay as damages for her dismissal without notice. The EAT said she was. The starting point in any exercise of the construction of documents must be with the words the parties have used. An 'ex gratia' payment is, on its ordinary construction, a payment made freely and not under obligation. Further, the *contra proferentem* rule meant that, as this was the company's own unilateral document, if it was ambiguous it had to be read with 'the construction least favourable to the author'.

Where an employer fails to follow a contractual disciplinary procedure, the employee is generally only entitled to receive compensation for the wages he would have received during the course of the disciplinary procedure (see *Gunton v London Borough of Richmond* [2000] IRLR 703) plus any contractual notice. This remains the case even if the employee is able to show that the disciplinary process, if followed, would have meant that the employee was not dismissed. This is because, at common law, employers are entitled to dismiss on notice without proper cause. The only recourse for an employee in this situation is to bring an unfair dismissal claim (see **Chapter 5**).

The Court of Appeal held in *Edwards v Chesterfield Royal Hospital NHS Foundation Trust* [2010] IRLR 702 that compensation for reputational damage caused by a flawed disciplinary procedure might be recovered 'at large' as it was not caused by the dismissal but rather by failure to follow an express contractual disciplinary procedure, if that failure led to the misconduct finding and the resultant inability to secure permanent NHS employment. The Court therefore permitted a claim for £4 million loss of earnings to proceed. The Court of Appeal rejected a submission that the principles laid down by the House of Lords in *Johnson v Unisys Ltd* [2001] IRLR 279 (see **2.4.1.5** and **5.6.2.2**) precluded recovery of the lossed claimed. *Unisys* does not apply where there is a breach of an express contractual term – it restricts compensation to the unfair dismissal regime where what is said to cause the loss is the manner of dismissal.

Edwards was appealed to the Supreme Court. A majority of the Supreme Court overruled the Court of Appeal's decision. The majority held that breach of contract claims for an alleged failure to follow an express disciplinary process could not proceed: as the claims for financial loss caused by damage to reputation were inextricably linked to the dismissal process, they fell within the exclusion indentified by the House of Lords in *Johnson v Unisys* and unfair dismissal was the appropriate claim. (There is an excellent and detailed analysis of the case and its significance in IDS Employment Law Brief No 943, February 2012, at p 3 onwards.)

2.4.1.3   Accrued holiday pay

Under the employee's contract and/or the Working Time Regulations 1998, reg 14, the employee/worker will be entitled to payment in lieu of any holiday to which he was entitled but had not yet taken, subject to a maximum of two years' back pay (see **1.12.5**).

In *Leisure Leagues UK Ltd v Maconnachie* [2002] IRLR 600, the EAT gave guidance on calculating holiday pay. The EAT held that the correct method of calculating holiday pay for a worker with regular hours and an annual salary is to divide the worker's annual salary by the number of working (not calendar) days in a year, multiplied by the number of days' leave the worker has outstanding (see **1.12.5**).

2.4.1.4 Additional loss

In addition to such lost salary or wages, the employee/worker may claim damages for loss of other benefits to which he was entitled under the contract. This would cover lost commission in the case of employees/workers remunerated wholly or partly by commission. It would also cover loss of fringe benefits such as a company car and also loss of pension rights if the employee/worker was entitled to a pension. In *Silvey v Pendragon plc* [2001] IRLR 685, the Court of Appeal held that an employee who was wrongfully dismissed 12 days short of his 55th birthday was entitled to claim damages for loss of significant pension rights that would have accrued when he attained the age of 55.

Loss of pension entitlement may in some cases involve a large sum, and it can be difficult to calculate this loss. There are two forms of pension loss which may be suffered: the loss of the pension position earned to the date of dismissal, and loss of future pension opportunity. Usually the sum lost will be based on the amount of employee's and employer's contributions made to a future pension. Where an employee/worker is close to retirement, the court may look at the cost of purchasing an annuity to produce the pension lost by the employee/worker.

The Government Actuary's Department (GAD) had produced guidelines to assist in calculating pension loss, the latest (third) edition being produced in 2003. The Court of Appeal, in *Griffin v Plymouth Hospital NHS Trust* [2014] EWCA Civ 1240, called for there to be an updated version of the guidelines, but in 2015 they were withdrawn on the basis that they were out-of-date. The guidelines had drawn a helpful distinction between money purchase schemes and final salary schemes, and set out two approaches to calculating future pension losses – a simplified approach and a substantial loss approach. The former was for use where there was either a money purchase scheme or a final salary scheme where there was a relatively short period of continuing pension loss. The substantial loss approach was for use only in cases concerning final salary schemes where there was long-term or whole career loss. A working group of Employment Judges produced a consultation paper in March 2016 to review the 2003 guidelines. The consultation closed on 20 May 2016.

The EAT's decision in *Chief Constable of West Midlands Police v Gardner* (UKEAT/0174/11) provides a useful discussion of the various approaches to pension loss calculation.

The employee/worker is only awarded damages for loss of benefits to which he was entitled under the contract. Thus, the established orthodoxy has always been that an employee/worker will not generally be awarded damages for loss of a discretionary contractual payment which he might have expected to receive, such as a Christmas bonus or an annual salary increase (*Lavarack v Woods of Colchester Ltd* [1967] 1 QB 278). However, in *Clark v BET plc and Another* [1997] IRLR 348, the employee successfully argued that, although his contract only entitled him to an annual salary increase 'by such amount as the board shall in its absolute discretion decide', this term amounted to a contractual obligation to increase his salary each year. The court said that contractual provisions relating to salary increases must be interpreted realistically and not on the basis that any discretion would have been exercised to give the employee the least possible benefit. Similar reasoning was applied in respect of a 'discretionary' bonus scheme entitlement under his contract of employment. Similarly in *Clark v Nomura International plc* [2000] IRLR 766, Burton J held that it was a breach of contract for an employer to exercise discretionary powers in a manner that was irrational or perverse. The Court of Appeal's decision in *Mallone v BPB Industries plc* [2002] IRLR 452 confirms that an employer must not exercise its discretion in an irrational manner (see also *Horkulak v Cantor Fitzgerald International* [2004] IRLR 942, *Commerzbank AG v Keen* [2006] EWCA Civ 1536 and *Paturel v DB Services (UK) Ltd* [2015] EWHC 3659 (QB)). Readers should also note the Supreme Court's decision in *Braganza v BP Shipping Ltd and Another* [2015] UKSC 17, where the Court applied *Wednesbury* unreasonableness to death benefits in an employment case. In that case the Supreme Court held that, although the decision not to pay a widow death in service benefit was not 'arbitrary, capricious or perverse', it was unreasonable in the *Wednesbury* sense, having been formed without taking relevant matters into account. Whether the same approach might be taken to bonus cases remains to be seen, but the Court indicated that might not be the case at para 57 of its judgment:

> In cases such as *Clark v Nomura International Plc*, *Keen v Commerzbank AG* and *Horkulak v Cantor Fitzgerald International* [2005] ICR 402 the courts have reviewed contractual decisions on the grant of performance-related bonuses where there were no specific criteria of performance or established formulae for calculating a bonus. In such cases the employee is entitled to a bona fide and rational exercise by the employer of its discretion. The courts are charged with enforcing that entitlement but there is little scope for intensive scrutiny of the decision-making process. The courts are in a much better position to review the good faith and rationality of the decision-making process where the issue is whether or not a state of fact existed, such as whether an employee's wilful act caused his death.

Damages may also be claimed for the loss of opportunity to earn tips in occupations where tips are usual (eg in the case of waiters and waitresses).

An employee cannot claim damages for breach of contract in respect of a loss of opportunity to bring an unfair dismissal claim (see **Chapter 5**). (See, eg, *The Wise Group v Mitchell* [2005] ICR 896.) The Court of Appeal held in *Harper v Virgin Net Ltd* [2004] IRLR 390 that an employee dismissed in breach of contract with less than one year's service, cannot claim damages for wrongful dismissal on the basis that she lost the chance of recovering unfair dismissal compensation that she would have received if she had been given her *contractual* notice of termination. Brooke LJ stated:

> I do not consider it is open to the courts, through the machinery of an award of damages for wrongful dismissal, to rewrite Parliament's scheme and to place a financial burden on employers which Parliament decided not to impose on them.

Chadwick LJ added that Parliament

> did not – as it easily could have done – postpone the effective date of termination to whichever should be the later of the expiry of the periods of contractual or statutory notice. That must be seen as a deliberate policy choice.

The other reason given for the decision is the need to be consistent with the House of Lords decision in *Johnson v Unisys Ltd* [2001] IRLR 279 (as explained in *Eastwood and Another v Magnox Electric plc* [2004] IRLR 733) (see below and **5.6.2.2**). These cases are authority for the rule that damages for breach of contract cannot include losses arising out of the fact and manner of dismissal.

2.4.1.5 Pecuniary loss only

Damages can usually be claimed for pecuniary loss only, so damages cannot generally be claimed for loss of future prospects or injured feelings (*Bliss v South East Thames Regional Health Authority* [1985] IRLR 308).

In *Malik v BCCI; Mahmud v BCCI* [1997] IRLR 462, HL, it was held that an employee might be entitled to 'stigma' damages, for example where the employer's business was conducted in a wholly dishonest manner which affected the employees' future prospects because of the stigma attaching to their reputations. The Court of Appeal's decision in *Bank of Credit and Commerce International SA (in compulsory liquidation) v Ali and Others (No 3)* [2002] IRLR 460 confirms that loss of employment prospects is almost impossible to prove without strong evidence, preferably from prospective employers.

The House of Lords held in *Johnson v Unisys Ltd* [2001] IRLR 279 that a claimant cannot recover contractual damages for psychiatric illness arising from the dismissal. Their Lordships distinguished the *Malik* case on the basis that that claim arose from a breach of the implied term of trust and confidence *during* the employment relationship; it did not arise on dismissal. Similarly, in *Gogay v Hertfordshire County Council* [2000] IRLR 703, the Court of Appeal held that the employer was in breach of the implied term of trust and confidence when it suspended an employee pending further investigation of a disciplinary charge, because it had no reasonable grounds for suspending her. Mrs Gogay was able to recover damages at common law for psychiatric injury on the facts, because the loss arose from breach of the implied duty of trust and confidence *during* the subsistence of the employment relationship.

The House of Lords in *Eastwood v Magnox; McCabe v Cornwall County Council and Another* [2004] IRLR 733, two cases concerning the overlap between common law claims for damages for breach of trust and confidence, and the statutory unfair dismissal regime, held that a distinction must be drawn between those cases where the employer has breached the term of trust and confidence *prior* to the dismissal – for which an (unlimited) common law claim can be brought – and cases where the *decision* to dismiss amounts to a breach of trust and confidence. These latter cases fall within the statutory unfair dismissal regime, and are therefore subject to the cap on compensation which cannot be circumvented by bringing a breach of contract claim in the civil courts. Lord Nicholls recognised the artificiality of the distinction but said it was nevertheless a distinction that had to be observed. At para 28 of his judgment he said:

> In the ordinary course ... an employer's failure to act fairly in the steps leading to dismissal does not of itself cause the employee financial loss. The loss arises when the employee is dismissed and it arises by reason of his dismissal. Then the resultant claim for loss falls squarely within the *Johnson* exclusion area. ... Exceptionally financial loss may flow directly from the employer's failure to act fairly when taking steps leading to dismissal. Financial loss flowing from suspension is an instance ... [and] cases ... when an employee suffers financial loss from psychiatric or other illness caused by his pre-dismissal unfair treatment.

The existence of such an exclusion area may mean that in some cases a continuing course of conduct, such as a disciplinary process followed by dismissal, may need to be chopped up artificially. Where financial losses flow directly from a pre-dismissal action, that can give rise to a cause of action which arises independently from the dismissal. Lord Nicholls noted two instances where problems will arise: financial losses flowing from suspension without pay and financial losses (as occurred in these two cases) flowing from psychiatric illness caused by pre-dismissal unfair treatment. He said that in such cases 'the employee has a common law cause of action which precedes, and is independent of, his subsequent dismissal'. He went on to note that in some circumstances an employer would be better off dismissing an employee than suspending him.

2.4.1.6 Duty to mitigate

The employee is under a duty to mitigate his loss. Once the employment is terminated, he must take steps to obtain suitable alternative employment. He will be in breach of this duty if he refuses a reasonable offer of re-employment. The employee is not entitled to damages in respect of any loss that has been mitigated or would have been mitigated but for the employee's breach of duty (*Brace v Calder and Others* [1895] 2 QB 253).

The employee is only under a duty to accept reasonable offers of re-employment, not any other job offered. For example, there would be no need to accept an offer involving serious demotion. If the old employer offers to re-engage the employee, the employee would be in breach of his duty to mitigate if he failed to accept, provided that the job offered was reasonable and there was still a relationship of mutual trust and confidence between employer and employee.

2.4.1.7 Benefits reducing loss

If the employer has paid money in lieu of notice to the employee, this will be taken into account in assessing the damages awarded. Certain other benefits received by the employee which reduce his loss will also be set against the damages awarded, for example, jobseeker's allowance and income support. If a pension becomes payable during the period for which damages are claimed, this does not reduce the damages awarded (*Hopkins v Norcross plc* [1994] IRLR 18, CA). The rule on pensions is based on public policy.

Overlap with redundancy payments and awards of compensation for unfair dismissal are dealt with at **6.7**.

2.4.1.8   Tax and National Insurance contributions

The basic rule is that income tax and NICs that would have been paid on the wages or salary, if earned, are deducted in assessing damages (*British Transport Commission v Gourley* [1956] AC 185; *Shove v Downs Surgical plc* [1984] IRLR 17). Damages are therefore generally awarded in respect of loss of *net* earnings. This puts the employee in the position as though the contract had been performed.

However, the effect of the Income Tax (Earnings and Pensions) Act 2003 (ITEPA 2003) has to be considered. Guidance on the Act may be found in the HMRC guide CWG2 (2009), *Employer's Further Guide to PAYE and NICs*. It is available on HMRC's website <http://www.hmrc.gov.uk/guidance/cwg2.pdf>. An employer is exempt from paying tax on termination payments, including damages for wrongful dismissal, which do not exceed £30,000 (ITEPA 2003, s 401). The exemption applies only if the payment is not otherwise subject to tax under any other head; only then can it be taxed as a termination payment. This means considering whether the payment is a contractual payment made in return for services (see, eg, *Delaney v Staples* [1992] 1 All ER 944 and *SCA Packaging v Revenue and Customs* [2007] EWHC 270 (Ch)). If the payment or benefit is earnings from the employment, tax is due under s 62 of the ITEPA 2003 (and there is no £30,000 exemption). As the employee receives only his net loss of earnings, it is therefore the employer who benefits from the rule. Termination payments exceeding £30,000 are subject to income tax on the excess over £30,000. Therefore, if the damages for wrongful dismissal exceed £30,000, the award of damages will have to be grossed up to compensate the employee for the double tax that the employee will have to pay. Note, however, that pure damages for breach of contract in a tribunal are subject to a £25,000 jurisdictional limit. In reality, damages for breach of contract in a tribunal claim will need to be grossed up only where other awards, such as compensation for unfair dismissal, take the award over £30,000 (see **5.7.2.2**).

For example, in the case of *Shove v Downs Surgical plc* (above), the court assessed the ex-employee's total loss as being £70,300. The court deducted an element for failure to mitigate and accelerated receipt (see **2.4.1.9** below), giving a net loss of £60,729. Damages of £88,447 were therefore payable by the employer to ensure that, after paying tax, the ex-employee was left with £60,729 in his hands, the remainder going to the Revenue.

Note that where the contract of employment contains an express PILON provision, the £30,000 tax and the unlimited NICs exemption will not be available in respect of the sum paid by way of compensation or for wrongful dismissal (see *EMI Group Electronics Ltd v Coldicott (Inspector of Taxes)* [1999] IRLR 630 and *Cerberus Software Ltd v Rowley* [2001] IRLR 160). This is because HMRC takes the view that, in such cases, the pay in lieu is due under the contract and is not, therefore, a true severance payment (see **2.3.3**). In practice, this means that awards for unpaid notice pursuant to a PILON clause should always be paid grossed up, because they are taxable as earnings and are not covered by the £30,000 exemption.

Where there is no PILON clause, even if a payment is made, termination without notice is strictly speaking still a breach of contract and the payment does not therefore flow from the contract. Note that the tax position where a contract is terminated without notice and there is a discretion to give a PILON is complex and beyond the scope of the book (see *Richardson v Delaney* [2001] IRLR 663, the Revenue's Tax Bulletin 63, February 2003 and the Revenue's Employment Income Manual 12800 (updated 2010)). (See though **5.6.2.5** and see also **Table 5.1.**)

2.4.1.9   Accelerated receipt

In the majority of cases, any award of damages for wrongful dismissal will be made after the employee's contract could have been properly terminated by the employer. In this situation, no question of accelerated receipt arises.

However, in the case of a long fixed-term contract, the employee may receive his damages before he would have earned some of the salary that they represent. In this case, a deduction will be made from the damages as the accelerated receipt will allow the employee to invest the money (eg in an annuity) and obtain a return on it (*Bold v Brough, Nicholson & Hall Ltd* [1964] 1 WLR 201). In *Brentwood Brothers (Manchester) Ltd v Shepherd* [2003] IRLR 364, the Court of Appeal questioned whether the 5% discount rate normally applied by tribunals remained appropriate in 2004, given that the discount in personal injury cases was by then 2.5%. The court also held that any deductions should be done on the basis of an appropriate percentage deduction year on year and not one single deduction. A Government consultation on the personal injury discount rate closed on 7 May 2013. In August 2014, the Ministry of Justice said that it would appoint a panel of experts to review the rate, with a report due in April 2015. No report has yet been published.

2.4.1.10 Adjustment to an award for unreasonable failure to follow Acas Code of Practice

Note that the Employment Tribunal cannot award an Acas uplift to wrongful dismissal damages (see **Chapter 5**).

2.4.2 Other remedies

The employee will usually have little choice but to accept dismissal and claim monetary compensation. The courts will not award specific performance of contracts of employment, nor will they usually issue an injunction restraining the employer from terminating the employment in breach of contract. In exceptional circumstances the courts have granted an injunction, the effect of which is to keep the contract alive until proper notice would have expired, but the employer was not required to allow the employee to do work during the period covered by the injunction (*Hill v C A Parsons & Co Ltd* [1972] 1 Ch 305). Occasionally, the courts will grant an interim injunction restraining an employer from dismissing an employee (eg pending an appeal hearing). Such an injunction can be granted only if there is sufficient mutual trust and confidence between employer and employee (*Powell v London Borough of Brent* [1987] IRLR 466). These remedies are exceptional and details are beyond the scope of this book.

2.5 EMPLOYER'S REMEDIES

If the employee is in repudiatory breach of contract, the employer may dismiss him without notice ('summarily') (see **2.3.4**). Other remedies available to the employer include damages, injunction and account of profit.

2.5.1 Damages

Any breach of contract by the employee theoretically entitles the employer to claim damages. In practice, it is a remedy which employers rarely pursue.

(a) An employee may be in breach of contract by resigning without giving proper notice or leaving before a fixed-term contract has expired. The usual measure of damages in such cases would be the additional cost of providing a substitute to do the work (*National Coal Board v Galley* [1958] 1 WLR 16). The remedy is not usually worth pursuing because the amount involved would usually be too small.

(b) If an employer suffers loss by reason of the employee's negligence, the employer may be entitled to an indemnity from the employee (see *Lister v Romford Ice and Cold Storage Co Ltd* [1957] AC 555, at **1.7.2.3**). The remedy is rarely pursued, partly because it can lead to bad industrial relations and also because the employer is often insured against the loss. The employee may, anyway, have insufficient funds to meet a substantial award of damages.

(c) Damages might be an appropriate remedy where the employer has suffered loss by reason of the employee's breach of the duty of good faith, for example where the employee has revealed trade secrets or competed with the employer's business. In *Gamatronic (UK) Ltd v Hamilton* [2016] EWHC 2225 (QB), two employees set up a rival firm during their employment. The employer sought to recover the employees' salaries for the period of breach (they were still employed). The judge rejected the claim to recover salaries. There was no causal connection between the wrongful acts and the loss claimed (the salaries paid) and no failure of consideration. The evidence failed to establish that the employees failed to dedicate proper time and attention to their work for Gamatronic.

2.5.2 Injunction

An injunction may be awarded to an employer to restrain certain actions of an employee where damages would be an inadequate remedy:

(a)   It may be used to restrain or prevent breaches of the duty of fidelity, for example by restraining an employee from using or revealing trade secrets. In *Robb v Green* [1895] 2 QB 315, an employee who had made a list of customers was ordered to deliver up the list and was restrained by injunction from copying it.

(b)   It is the appropriate remedy to enforce a valid restrictive covenant after employment, by restraining the employee from working in contravention of it (see **1.8**).

(c)   Where an employee is required by contract to give a period of notice, the employer might obtain an injunction to prevent him from breaching that term by taking up a new position before expiry of his contractual notice period.

In deciding whether and to what extent to grant an injunction the court will apply the 'balance of convenience' test (*American Cyanamid v Ethicon Ltd* [1975] AC 398). The court will take into account the following factors:

(a)   actual or potential damage to the employer's business (eg loss of important clients who may follow the employee);

(b)   inconvenience (financial and other) to the employee;

(c)   whether the employee has given an adequate undertaking to abide by the contract;

(d)   no more relief should be granted than is absolutely necessary – any injunction need not necessarily be for the full contractual period (*GFI Group Inc v Eaglestone* [1994] IRLR 119).

For a decision which provides a useful analysis of the general principles on injunctions, see *Vestergaard Frandsen Als and Others v Bestnet Europe Ltd and Others* [2009] EWHC 1456 (Ch) and *QBE Management Services (UK) Ltd v Dymoke and Others* [2012] IRLR 458.

In *Sunrise Brokers LLP Rodgers* [2014] EWHC 2633 (QB), the High Court granted Sunrise an injunction that meant that Mr Rodgers had to abide by his contract until the expiry of his notice period. There was no obligation on Sunrise to put him on garden leave (see **1.8.7.3**), and as Mr Rodgers refused to come into work, Sunrise was not obliged to pay him. The High Court also issued an injunction holding Mr Rodgers to the terms of his restrictive covenants.

Where the employer is not at fault and an employee has walked out, refusing to pay the recalcitrant employee will not allow him to argue that the employer is in breach.

2.5.3 Action for account of profits

Usually in breach of contract claims the measure of damages is the loss suffered by the claimant, and not the profit made by the respondent. Account of profits is, however, assessed on the profits made by the respondent. Until recently, an action for account of profits was available as a remedy only in the special case where there is a breach of the implied duty of good faith, by using the employer's confidential information to make a secret profit (see **1.7.2.5**), or breach of a fiduciary duty (see *Nottingham University v Fishel and Another* [2000] IRLR 471, where the High Court confirmed that the employment relationship is not a fiduciary one but that fiduciary duties may arise from the relationship, *Kynixa Ltd v Hynes and Others* [2008] EWHC 1495 (Comm), where the High Court held that the company director owed a fiduciary duty and that a second employee was also subject to a fiduciary duty by virtue of her senior status as a clinical services manager, and *Samsung Semiconductor Europe Ltd v Docherty and Another* [2011] CSOH 32, where the Court of Session held that a QA manager who worked with the employer's most important customer was subject to a fiduciary duty). In *Attorney-General v Blake and Jonathan Cape Ltd* [2001] IRLR 36, it was held that exceptionally a respondent may be required, as a remedy for breach of contract, to pay over to the claimant the profits received from the breach, even where the claimant has suffered no financial loss as a result of the breach and the wrongdoer is not in breach of a fiduciary duty. The House of Lords said a useful guide, although not exhaustive, is whether the employer had a legitimate interest in preventing the employee's profit-making activity and, hence, in depriving him of a profit.

2.6 CHECKLIST

(1) How did contract end – has there been a breach of contract by employer?

(2) Can employer raise employee's conduct as defence to a wrongful dismissal claim? (Remember after-acquired knowledge can be used.)

(3) Is contract for a fixed term or terminable on notice?

(4) What was employee's net pay?

(5) Are there any factors which will increase/decrease starting point?

(6) Are damages in excess of £30,000? If so, consider the tax position.

2.7 FURTHER READING

Textbooks dealing with termination at common law include:

Harvey, *Industrial Relations and Employment Law* (LexisNexis), Div A.

Duggan, *Wrongful Dismissal and Breach of Contract*, 2nd edn (Duggan Press, 2019).

Duggan, *Contracts of Employment*, 4th edn (Duggan Press, 2019).

Lewis, *Employment Law – an adviser's handbook*, 14th edn (LAG, 2022).

Selwyn, *Law of Employment*, 22nd edn (OUP, 2022).

Blackstone's Employment Law Practice, 10th edn (OUP, 2019).

SUMMARY

This chapter has looked at the differences between the breach of contract claim known as wrongful dismissal and the statutory claim of unfair dismissal, and at the extent to which they may overlap (**2.1, 2.2**). Provided that a contract is terminated in accordance with any express or implied terms (eg s 86 of the ERA 1996 sets out minimum periods of notice), neither party will be in breach of contract. The chapter has looked at the main ways in which a contract of employment may come to an end and the relevance of notice periods (**2.3**). It has also considered when a summary dismissal claim may be justified (**2.3.4**). It explains the principles to be applied when calculating an employee's damages following a wrongful dismissal (**2.4**) and the remedies available to an employer if an employee is in repudiatory breach of contract (**2.5**). A flowchart summarising wrongful dismissal and breach of contract claims is set out in **Figure 2.1** below.

Figure 2.1 Flowchart: Wrongful Dismissal/Breach of Contract Claims

1.   Has there been a dismissal?

- actual dismissal
- constructive dismissal
  - — Employer commits a repudiatory/fundamental (not minor) breach of express/implied term so that employee is entitled to resign in response (with or without notice) and treat the contract as discharged
  - — Employee must resign within a reasonable time of the breach in response to the breach

NB Expiry of a limited-term contract is not a dismissal for the purposes of wrongful dismissal

Time limit

Claim in employment tribunal within 3 months of dismissal

Claim in civil court within 6 years of dismissal

NO → **No claim**

YES ↓

2.   Is the dismissal wrongful?

- actual dismissal with no notice or insufficient notice unless justified by the employee's repudiatory breach (gross misconduct)

NB 1. Look at contractual notice period – must not be less than statutory minimum

2. Consider impact of a PILON clause

OR

- dismissal *before* the expiry of a limited term unless
  - — in accordance with terms of a break clause
  - — justified by the employee's repudiatory breach (gross misconduct)*

*__NB__ Employee's after-discovered but pre-dismissal misconduct may justify dismissal without notice – *Boston Deep Sea Fishing v Ansell*

OR

- constructive dismissal – the employer's repudiatory breach renders the dismissal wrongful

NO

YES ↓

3.   Compensation: damages for breach of contract

Normal contractual damages rules (*Hadley v Baxendale*; loss of *net* wages) for proper notice period or until end of limited term (unless break clause)

PLUS any additional *contractual* losses (eg commission, pension, health insurance, car, bonuses, holiday pay, etc)

Reducing factors

payments made (eg payment in lieu)

certain benefits

duty to mitigate

accelerated receipt

Employment tribunal – maximum award £25,000

Civil court – no maximum

NB Overlapping claims – damages for wrongful dismissal will be set off against any overlapping unfair dismissal compensatory award (usually the 'immediate loss of earning' element) arising from the same dismissal

NB Compensation may be:

- Increased by up to 25% for an unreasonable failure to follow the Acas Code of Practice
- Decreased by up to 25% for an unreasonable failure to follow the Acas Code of Practice

(Consider too bringing a claim under the Working Time Regulations for unused statutory leave on termination in the absence of a contractual right to payment for unused holiday on termination.)

CHAPTER 3

Dismissal – Eligibility to Present a Statutory Claim

3.1	Introduction	121
3.2	Eligibility factors	121
3.3	Employees only	122
3.4	Dismissal	122
3.5	Continuous employment	129
3.6	Excluded classes	134
3.7	Jurisdiction	134
3.8	Contracting out	139
3.9	Further reading	139
	Summary	140

LEARNING OUTCOMES

After reading this chapter you will be able to:

- list the eligibility factors that must be satisfied before a person may bring a claim for unfair dismissal and/or a redundancy payment
- explain the difference between an actual and a constructive dismissal
- understand the significance of the non-renewal of a fixed-term contract
- understand the importance of continuity of employment
- calculate continuous employment
- explain when an employment tribunal will not have jurisdiction to hear a claim of unfair dismissal and/or for a redundancy payment.

3.1 INTRODUCTION

In addition to the common law claim for wrongful dismissal (see **Chapter 2**), there are two further claims that may be available to an employee on termination of his employment. These claims arise as a result of statutory rights given to an employee, namely, the right to a redundancy payment and the right not to be unfairly dismissed.

These claims differ from wrongful dismissal in many respects, most notably because not every employee is eligible to present a claim for redundancy or unfair dismissal. In this chapter, we consider the eligibility requirements for both statutory claims.

3.2 ELIGIBILITY FACTORS

In order to claim a redundancy payment or to pursue a complaint of unfair dismissal, a person must:

(a) be an employee;

(b) have been dismissed;

(c) have been continuously employed for the requisite period;

(d)   not be within an excluded class.

In certain situations, a person may be unable to bring a claim for jurisdictional reasons.

Each of these issues will be considered in more detail below.

3.3 EMPLOYEES ONLY

The claimant must be an employee (ERA 1996, ss 94, 135). An employee is defined as 'an individual who ... works under ... a contract of employment' (ERA 1996, s 230(1)). The self-employed, workers and independent contractors are excluded from entitlement (see **1.3**).

3.4 DISMISSAL

The fact that the contract has terminated does not in itself give rise to a statutory claim.

In order to be entitled to a redundancy payment or to claim unfair dismissal, an employee must show (ie has the burden of proving) that he has been 'dismissed' within the meaning of the legislation. An employee who resigns, leaves by mutual agreement, or whose contract is frustrated has not been dismissed and is not eligible to pursue a statutory claim.

The word 'dismissal' for the purpose of unfair dismissal and redundancy payments is defined by ss 95 and 136 of the ERA 1996, respectively, and differs in one important respect from the common law definition (see (b) below).

Under ERA 1996, dismissal may arise in one of three ways:

(a)   the contract is terminated by the employer; or

(b)   a limited term expires without being renewed; or

(c)   the employee is constructively dismissed.

The following paragraphs consider each of these situations in detail.

3.4.1 The contract is terminated by the employer – actual dismissal

An employee is treated as dismissed if 'the contract under which he is employed ... is terminated by the employer (whether with or without notice)' (ERA 1996, ss 95(1)(a) and 136(1)(a)).

(a)   This includes the most common of the three dismissal situations – where the employer simply gives the employee notice in accordance with the terms of the contract.

(b)   It also covers the situation where the employer terminates the contract without notice, ie he dismisses summarily. In this case, even though the dismissal may have been provoked by the employee's conduct, it is the employer's action in treating the contract as discharged which terminates the contract and thus constitutes dismissal.

> **EXAMPLE**
>
> If an employee is absent without leave and the employer refuses to allow him to return to work, this will operate as a dismissal (*London Transport Executive v Clark* [1981] IRLR 166, CA).

(c)   Occasionally, there is some doubt as to whether there has been a dismissal or a resignation where the words used by the employer are ambiguous.

> **EXAMPLE**
>
> The employer may use the words 'get lost' (or something even less polite) in an argument with the employee. If the employee takes him at his word, can he claim to have been dismissed?

> If the words used by the employer are ambiguous, then the test is to consider how the words would have been understood by the reasonable listener. The test is an objective one and the question of whether or not there has been a dismissal must be considered in light of all the surrounding circumstances (*Southern v Franks Charlesly & Co* [1981] IRLR 278). There is one authority (*Tanner v DT Kean* [1978] IRLR 110) for the proposition that the intention of the speaker is the relevant test, but none of the other cases supports this view.
>
> In *Futty v Brekkes (D & D) Ltd* [1974] IRLR 130, a foreman had a conversation with an employee which ended with the foreman saying 'if you don't like the job, you can f*** off'. The employee left and claimed that he had been dismissed. The tribunal decided that there was no dismissal, but only a 'general exhortation'.
>
> However, note that in appropriate circumstances, speaking to an employee in a disrespectful manner may, through the employer's breach of the implied term of mutual trust and confidence, constitute a constructive dismissal (see **3.4.3**).

(d)   There are cases where the employer will offer the employee a 'choice' – resign or be dismissed. If the employee chooses to resign, as this has been forced upon him by his employer, it will be treated as a dismissal by his employer (see, eg, *Martin v MBS Fastenings (Glynwed) Distribution Ltd* [1983] IRLR 198, CA).

In *Sandhu v Jan de Rijk Transport Ltd* [2007] EWCA Civ 430, an employee was summoned to a meeting and informed that his contract would be ended. He agreed severance terms in the meeting. Both the employment tribunal and the EAT held that he had resigned. The Court of Appeal overturned that finding. The Court said that resignation involves some degree of negotiation, discussion and genuine choice on the part of the employee. In this case, the employee had had no advance knowledge of what was to be discussed in the meeting, no time to take advice and no opportunity for reflection. The Court said he was not negotiating freely and had therefore been dismissed.

3.4.2   A limited term expires without being renewed or is ended early

Unlike the position at common law, the non-renewal of a limited-term contract is treated as a dismissal for the purpose of pursuing the statutory claims.

(a)   An employee is treated as dismissed if 'he is employed under a limited-term contract and that contract terminates by virtue of the limiting term without being renewed under the same contract' (ERA 1996, ss 95(1)(b) and 136(1)(b)).

(b)   A limited-term contract may contain a 'break' clause under which one party, usually the employer, is entitled to terminate by giving notice before the term expires. If such a contract expires by effluxion of the limited term and the contract is not renewed, the employee is treated as being dismissed under this subsection. If the employer terminates the contract by giving notice under the 'break' clause, the employee is dismissed under s 95(1)(a) or s 136(1)(a) (see **3.4.1**).

3.4.3   The employee is constructively dismissed

Generally, an employee will not be regarded as having been dismissed if he resigns (but see *Southern v Franks Charlesly & Co* [1981] IRLR 278, *Sovereign House Security v Savage* [1989] IRLR 115 and *Greater Glasgow Health Board v Mackay* 1989 SLT 729). However, an employee is to be treated as dismissed if 'the employee terminates the contract under which he is employed (with or without notice) in circumstances in which he is entitled to terminate it without notice by reason of the employer's conduct' (ERA 1996, ss 95(1)(c) and 136(1)(c)). The test is whether, on the facts, in all the circumstances the employer so conducts itself as to destroy or seriously undermine the relationship of trust and confidence between it and the employee without reasonable or probable cause. Conduct can take the form of a failure to do something or positively doing something (see *Nair v Lagardere Sports and Entertainment UK Ltd* [2021] IRLR 54).

(a) An employee who leaves in such circumstances is said to be constructively dismissed. In order for an employee to treat himself as constructively dismissed within this provision, the employer's conduct must either amount to a significant breach going to the heart of the contract, or show that the employer no longer intends to be bound by one or more of the essential terms of the contract. The employee is then entitled to treat the contract as discharged at common law (*Western Excavating Ltd v Sharp* [1978] QB 761, CA). The test is an objective one; whether the employer intended to breach the contract or not is irrelevant.

(b) A breach of an express term of the contract by the employer can amount to such a constructive dismissal. Examples would include:

   (i) *Failure to pay/reduction of pay*

   A unilateral reduction in pay will amount to repudiation of the contract. This would include, for example, reduction in fringe benefits or refusal to pay overtime at overtime rates. In *Cantor Fitzgerald International v Callaghan and Others* [1999] IRLR 234, the Court of Appeal emphasised the importance of pay in any contract of employment; it said there was a crucial distinction between an employer's failure to pay or delay in paying agreed remuneration, perhaps due to a mistake or oversight, which would 'not necessarily' go to the root of the contract, and a deliberate refusal to do so, which the Court said would undermine the whole basis of the contract. See, more recently, *Mostyn v S and P Casuals Ltd* (UKEAT/0158/17) and *Singh v Metroline West Ltd* [2022] EAT 80.

   (ii) *Pay below the national minimum wage*

   Where an employee is paid well below the national minimum wage, that may amount to such an obvious and egregious breach as to amount to a clear repudiatory breach (see *Mruke v Khan* [2018] EWCA Civ 280).

   (ii) *Job description*

   A fundamental change in the nature of the job will amount to repudiation if there is no term allowing the employer to make such a change. In *Land Securities Trillium Ltd v Thornley* [2005] IRLR 765, EAT, it was held that there was a repudiatory breach when the employer moved the employee from a 'hands on' role to a managerial position, because the contract of employment did not include that flexibility for the employer. In so deciding, the EAT stated that the tribunal should look not only at the claimant's job description, but also at the work she actually did. Although her contract said that the claimant 'would perform to the best of [her] abilities … any other duties which may reasonably be required of [her]', this, said the EAT, imposed a requirement of reasonableness on any request by the employer.

(c) A significant breach of an implied term by the employer will entitle the employee to treat himself as constructively dismissed. There is implied into contracts of employment a term that employers will not 'without reasonable and proper cause, conduct themselves in a manner calculated or likely to destroy or seriously damage the relationship of confidence and trust between the employer and employee' (*Woods v WM Car Services (Peterborough) Ltd* [1983] IRLR 413, CA; see also *Malik v BCCI*; *Mahmud v BCCI* [1998] AC 20, HL and *Baldwin v Brighton and Hove City Council* [2007] ICR 680). This is known as the duty of trust and confidence.

This duty is very wide in its application. Employers have been held to be in breach of this duty by, for example, making unjustified accusations of theft on scant evidence, making unjustified allegations that an employee was incapable of doing his job and falsely telling an employee who wanted a transfer that no vacancies were available. In *Stanley Cole*

(Wainfleet) Ltd v Sheridan [2003] IRLR 52, the EAT upheld the tribunal's decision that the unjustified imposition of a final written warning amounted to a repudiatory breach entitling the employee to resign and claim she had been unfairly constructively dismissed; and in *Greenhof v Barnsley Metropolitan BC* [2006] IRLR 98, the EAT held that a serious breach of the employer's duty to make reasonable adjustments (see **Chapter 13**) amounted to a breach of the implied duty of trust and confidence (see also *Shaw v CCL Ltd* (UKEAT/0512/06), where the employer's actions, which amounted to sex discrimination, were held to breach the implied duty (discrimination against an employee will usually amount to a repudiatory breach)). In *Private Medicine Intermediaries Ltd v Hodkinson and Others* (EAT/0134/15), the EAT upheld a tribunal decision that an employer committed a repudiatory breach by raising performance concerns during a period of sick leave, and that the claimant has been constructively unfairly dismissed. (The case demonstrates the need for a sensitive approach when contacting absent employees.) Performance issues and grievances should, as far as possible, be dealt with separately.

If an employer acts in an unreasonable way there may be a breach of this duty, but the test remains that in *Western Excavating Ltd v Sharp* (see (a) above). The employer's conduct has to amount to a repudiatory breach of contract. In *Brown v Merchant Ferries* [1998] IRLR 682, the Court of Appeal accepted that if the employer's conduct is seriously unreasonable, this may provide evidence that there has been a repudiatory breach of contract but, on the facts, held that the conduct in question fell far short of a repudiatory breach by the employer. Mere unreasonable behaviour is not enough.

In *Morrow v Safeway Stores plc* [2002] IRLR 9, the EAT held that the employment tribunal had erred in holding that although a manager's conduct in giving the applicant a public reprimand amounted to a breach of the implied contractual term of trust and confidence, it was not sufficiently serious to amount to a repudiation entitling the applicant to resign and claim constructive dismissal. The EAT held that where an employer breaches the implied term of trust and confidence, that breach is 'inevitably' fundamental, and thus such a breach goes to the root of the contract and amounts to a repudiatory breach, entitling the employee to resign and claim constructive dismissal. If the employer's conduct is insufficiently serious, there is no breach of the implied term. The EAT remitted the case for re-hearing: was the breach sufficiently serious or not?

In *Mayor and Burgesses of the London Borough of Lambeth v Agoreyo* [2019] EWCA Civ 322, the Court of Appeal held that the suspension of a teacher, following allegations that she had used unreasonable force against pupils, did not breach the implied term of trust and confidence. Suspension to allow a fair investigation will not breach the implied term. The test is whether there is reasonable and proper cause to suspend and whether the act of suspension destroys or seriously damages the relationship of trust and confidence.

For some years there was a debate about the relevance of the 'range of reasonable responses' test used in determining whether a dismissal was fair or unfair (see **Chapter 5**) when determining whether an employee has been constructively dismissed. In *Bournemouth University Higher Education Corporation v Buckland* (UKEAT/0492/08) the EAT held that the band of reasonable responses test is *not* relevant when considering whether an employee has been constructively dismissed. At this stage, held the EAT, the only question for the tribunal is whether the employer had conducted himself in a manner calculated or likely to destroy or seriously damage the employment relationship (although as the EAT stated in *Nationwide Building Society v Niblett* (UKEAT/0524/08), it is perhaps 'difficult to envisage circumstances in which an employer will be in breach of the implied term of trust and confidence unless the employer's conduct has been unreasonable').

The Court of Appeal upheld the *Buckland* decision ([2010] EWCA Civ 121) and held that the only question for the tribunal in determining a constructive dismissal is whether the employer had without reasonable or proper cause conducted himself in a manner calculated or likely to destroy or seriously damage the employment relationship; the range of reasonable responses test should be relevant only when considering whether or not the dismissal (be it actual or constructive) is fair or unfair (see **Chapter 5**). The Court of Appeal also said it was clear as a matter of general contract law that an anticipatory breach of contract could be withdrawn at any time up to the moment of acceptance, but once a repudiatory breach had been committed the defaulting party had 'crossed the Rubicon' and was unable to retreat, ie the breach cannot be cured; the other party could then elect whether or not to accept the breach.

In *Singh v Metroline West Ltd* [2022] EAT 80, the EAT held that there was a deliberate decision not to pay full company sick pay to which the claimant was entitled. There was a substantial reduction in the claimant's weekly earnings. That was a fundamental breach of contract.

In *RDF Media Group v Clements* [2008] IRLR 207, the High Court gave a very clear explanation of the implied term of trust and confidence (see paras 100–106). Importantly, the High Court held that an employee was not constructively dismissed because he himself was in repudiatory breach of the mutual obligation of trust and confidence. He could not therefore rely on the employer's later breach of the obligation. This applies even where the employer only subsequently finds out about the employee's breach.

The duty not to act in a manner likely to undermine trust and confidence was looked at again by the EAT in *McBride v Falkirk Football Club* (UKEATS/0058/10). The claimant was the Club's under-19s team manager. He resigned after his right to pick his team was arbitrarily removed after an Academy Director was appointed. The tribunal implied into his contract a term that he would relinquish his right to pick his team once an Academy Director was appointed, and on that basis found no breach of contract by the Club, and rejected his claim for constructive dismissal. The EAT, in overturning the employment tribunal's decision and substituting a finding of constructive dismissal, said that the test to be applied in trust and confidence cases was to be judged from an objective standpoint, so that an employer could not rely upon factors in a particular industry – such as 'an autocratic style of management' being 'the norm in football' – as a defence to a breach of the implied term of trust and confidence. The EAT also held that a term ought not to be implied into a contract of employment which contradicted an express term or which was imprecise, unnecessary or not obvious. Useful guidance on when to imply terms in a contact is set out at paras 54 and 55.

For a case where the employer was held to have reasonable and proper cause for its conduct, see *Sharfugeen v T J Morris Ltd* (UKEAT/0272/16).

(d)   In some instances, while an act may not of itself be sufficiently serious, it is possible to look at the cumulative effect of a number of minor breaches, through what is known as the 'last straw' doctrine. In *London Borough of Waltham Forest v Omilaju* [2005] IRLR 35, the Court of Appeal (referring to *Malik v BCCI* [1998] AC 20 and *Lewis v Motorworld Garages Ltd* [1986] ICR 157) restated that 'the last action of the employer which leads to the employee leaving need not itself be a breach of contract'. In *Omilaju*, the 'straw that broke the camel's back' was, looked at objectively, perfectly reasonable, justifiable and permissible conduct. What is clear is that a last straw must not be 'utterly trivial' or innocuous and must contribute something to the breach, and an entirely innocuous act cannot be a final straw.

Most recently, in *Kaur v Leeds Teaching Hospitals NHS Trust* [2018] EWCA Civ 978, the Court of Appeal again restated the general principles to be applied in last straw cases and what questions a tribunal should ask itself, namely:

(1   What was the most recent act (or omission) on the part of the employer which the employee says caused, or triggered, his or her resignation?

(2)   Has he or she affirmed the contract since that act?

(3)   If not, was that act (or omission) by itself a repudiatory breach of contract [ie entitling the employee to treat the contract as at an end]?

(4)   If not, was it nevertheless a part ... of a course of conduct comprising several acts and omissions which, viewed cumulatively, amounted to a (repudiatory) breach of [the implied term of trust and confidence]? (If it was, there is no need for any separate consideration of a possible previous affirmation ...)

(5)   Did the employee resign in response (or partly in response) to that breach?

In *Kaur*, given that the employer's disciplinary procedure had been perfectly properly applied, there could be no 'last straw' and hence no constructive dismissal. The Court of Appeal also confirmed in *Kaur* that, in relying on previous acts, an employee claiming constructive dismissal could rely on a previously affirmed repudiatory breach where there were then subsequent breaches, based on the cumulative effect of all the breaches. A final straw will revive the opportunity to resign; otherwise an employee who soldiers on and does not object at the first opportunity would lose their right to rely on all conduct up to that point, which would not be right.

See too *Craig v Abellio Ltd* [2022] EAT 43 and (g) below.

(e)   A threat to change terms and conditions, and to dismiss an employee if he does not accept the changes, may amount to a constructive dismissal even if the employee resigns before implementation of the changes. The employer's threats could amount to anticipatory breach of contract (*Greenaway Harrison Ltd v Wiles* [1994] IRLR 380). See also *Buckland* (above).

(f)   It is not possible to argue that the *manner* of a dismissal is a breach of the implied term of trust and confidence. The House of Lords, in *Johnson v Unisys Ltd* [2001] IRLR 279, was unwilling to develop the common law to imply a contractual term that an employer must carry out a dismissal in good faith, given the existence of the statutory unfair dismissal regimes which specifically cover the process of dismissal. (This decision also had implications for what damages may be recovered in a wrongful dismissal claim – see **2.4.1.5** and **5.6.2.2**.) The EAT held in *Bethnal Green and Shoreditch Education Trust v Dippenaar* (UKEAT/0064/15) that subjecting an employee to capability proceedings with no reasonable and proper cause amounted to a repudiatory breach.

(g)   It is important to determine, once a repudiation has been established, whether 'the repudiatory breach played a part in the dismissal' (see *Abbey Cars (West Horndon) Ltd v Ford* (UKEAT/0472/07). However, it is an error of law to look for 'the' effective cause, ie the principal or main cause (see *Wright v North Ayrshire Council* [2014] ICR 77). The EAT referred to *Nottingham CC v Meckle* [2005] ICR 1 in *Wright*, where the Court of Appeal stated:

> The proper approach, therefore, once a repudiation of the contract by the employer has been established, is to ask whether the employee has accepted that repudiation by treating the contract of employment as at an end.

So even if an employee leaves for a whole host of reasons, he can still claim constructive dismissal if the repudiatory breach is one of the factors relied on. (See *Ishaq v Royal Mail Group* (UKEAT/0156/16) for a case where the tribunal's decision that the real reason for resignation was to avoid disciplinary proceedings and not in response to the employer's breach was upheld by the EAT.)

It is possible to look to the cumulative effects of the employer's actions (see above). The final act may not in itself amount to a repudiatory breach of contract but could be the 'last straw' entitling the employee to claim constructive dismissal. Where there is a series of incidents, none of which individually amounts to a serious breach but which together amount to a breach of the implied duty of trust and confidence, if the employee continues to work, any implied waiver of the breach will be conditional upon there being no repetition of the breach (*JV Strong & Co Ltd v Hamill* (UKEAT/1179/99)). Where there is a series of incidents, the employee's response has to be measured from the last incident. In *Abbey National plc v Robinson* [2000] All ER (D) 1884, the EAT found that an employee was entitled to claim constructive dismissal when she resigned almost a year after a breach of contract by her employers. There was a series of incidents culminating with the 'last straw' (the withdrawal of a job offer) and her resignation was tendered shortly after that last incident.

Note that, according to the Court of Appeal in *London Borough of Waltham Forest v Omilaju* (above), the final straw must contribute something to that breach, although what it adds may be relatively 'insignificant'. If the alleged final straw is an entirely innocuous act (here, a justified refusal to pay) on the part of the employer, this cannot be the last straw.

However, that does not mean that all previous conduct by an employer is irrelevant. In *Williams v Alderman Davies Church in Wales Primary School* (UKEAT/0108/19), the EAT held that 'so long as there has been conduct which amounts to a fundamental breach [and the breach has not been affirmed] and the employee does resign at least partly in response to it, constructive dismissal is made out. That is so even if other, more recent, conduct has also contributed to the decision to resign.' The EAT confirmed in *Flatman v Essex CC* (UK/EAT/0097/20) that an employer cannot 'cure' a breach once committed.

(h)   Founded as it is on the contractual concept of repudiatory breach, the employee must leave within a reasonable period following the breach to avoid being taken as having affirmed the contract and waived the breach. In *Bunning v GT Bunning & Sons Ltd* [2005] EWCA Civ 293, the employer had breached the claimant's contract when it failed to carry out adequate risk assessments when the claimant said she was pregnant. However, the Court of Appeal held that she waived the breach when she accepted an alternative job with the employer. In *The Governing Body of Tywyn Primary School v Aplin* (UKEAT/0298/17), the EAT held that appealing against a disciplinary decision did not amount to affirming an employment contract; rather such action amounts to giving the employer the opportunity to remedy the breaches.

How long is too long is a question of fact. In *Munchkins Restaurant Ltd and Another v Karmazyn and Others* (UKEAT/0359/09), the waitresses in question put up with the employer's conduct for several years. The tribunal made the point that in its view the waitresses were migrant workers with no certainty of continued employment, save at Munchkins; that there were considerations of convenience for one; that they were constrained by financial and in some cases parental pressure; that they had the fear that they might not obtain other work; that they had the comfort of one manager acting as a cushion until she left; and that they managed, therefore, to find a balance between conduct which was unwelcome and unlawful and the advantages which their job gave them. It was not therefore, according to the EAT, completely beyond the scope of reason to think that women in this particular situation should behave as they did.

Mere delay by itself (unaccompanied by any express or implied affirmation of contract) does not constitute affirmation of the contract, but if it is prolonged it may be evidence of an implied affirmation. In *Mrs A Fereday v South Staffordshire NHS Primary Care Trust* (UKEAT/0513/10), the claimant invoked the grievance procedure, which resulted in a decision adverse to her on 13 February 2009, but she only resigned by a letter dated 24 March 2009. The EAT upheld the employment tribunal's decision that the respondent had repudiated the contract of employment but that the claimant had affirmed the contract by her delay. The EAT held that the employment tribunal was entitled to take the prolonged delay of nearly six weeks between the grievance decision and the claimant's resignation as an implied affirmation, bearing in mind that the claimant was expecting or requiring the respondent (the employer) to perform its part of the contract of employment by paying her sick pay. See also *Mari v Reuters Ltd* (UKEAT/0539/13) (where the EAT set out the case law and relevant principles of law on the question of affirmation and the significance of accepting sick pay), *Wess v Science Museum Group* (UKEAT/0120/14) (where the EAT said that delay alone might be neutral, but where terms had an immediate impact, affirmation was more likely to be found) and the Court of Appeal's decision in *Abrahall v Nottingham City Council* [2018] EWCA Civ 796, where employees who had continued working two years after a pay freeze was imposed were held not to have accepted the variation.

Delay is one of many factors to which the tribunal may have regard to when deciding whether the contract has been affirmed. Other relevant factors might be illness (see,eg, *Chindove v Morrisons Supermarkets plc* (UKEAT/0201/13 and UKEAT/0043/14)), whether a grievance has been raised (see *Gordon v J & D Pierce (Contracts) Ltd* (UK/EATS/0010/20) where the EAT held that exercising a right to raise a grievance or a right of appeal should not be taken as affirmation), whether there are ongoing discussions as to whether or not some accommodation might be reached, etc. The important question is, in the end, whether, in all the circumstances, the employee's conduct had demonstrated an intention to continue the contract. See too *Adjei-Frempong v Howard Frank Ltd* (UK/EAT/0044/15) and *Kaur v Leeds Teaching Hospitals NHS Trust* [2018] EWCA Civ 978.

(i) The employee's acceptance of the breach must be unambiguous and unequivocal (see *Atlantic Air Ltd v Holt* (UKEAT/0602/07), but it need not be communicated to the employer. The Court of Appeal, in *Weathersfield v Sargeant* [1999] IRLR 94, stated that the fact that an employee left her employment without giving a reason at the time did not preclude her from claiming that she had been constructively dismissed, although such conduct would usually make it more difficult to obtain such a finding. The Court rejected the notion that there could be no acceptance of a repudiation unless the employee told the employer at the time that he was leaving because of the employer's repudiatory conduct. The EAT held in *Wright v North Ayrshire Council* (UKEAT/0017/13) that the issue is whether the breach 'played a part in the [resignation]'. The repudiatory breach need not be the only cause but must be 'an' (cf 'the') effective cause of the resignation. The fact that an employee had other non-repudiatory reasons would not vitiate the acceptance of the repudiation.

(j) The date of the resignation and whether it is with or without notice may be important when establishing the effective date of termination for the purpose of bringing an unfair dismissal claim (see **3.5.1** and **6.3.1**). In *Secretary of State for Justice v Hibbert* (UKEAT/0289/13), the EAT held that a claimant's letter of resignation was immediate and unambiguous, and did not include a four-week period of notice. This meant that her unfair dismissal claim was out of time. Where the resignation is clear, the employer does not need to accept the resignation, nor is it obliged to offer a 'cooling-off period' where a resignation is made in the heat of the moment (though many employers do as good practice).

(k) A prior repudiatory breach by an employee will not prevent that employee from claiming constructive dismissal – even if he might have been dismissed for gross misconduct if the employer had known of it. Under employment law principles, an unaccepted repudiation has no effect. However, the misconduct will be relevant to remedy (see *Aberdeen City Council v McNeill* [2014] IRLR 114 and *Atkinson v Community Gateway Association* (UKEAT/0457/12).

3.5 CONTINUOUS EMPLOYMENT

In order to be eligible to present a statutory claim, the claimant must have the requisite period of 'continuous employment' prior to the dismissal.

In calculating periods of continuous employment, a month means a calendar month and a year means 12 calendar months. If, for example, an employee commenced employment on 20 April 2019 and worked continuously for his employer from that date, his period of two years' continuous employment is complete on 19 April 2021. (See, eg, *Pacitti Jones v O'Brien* [2005] IRLR 889.) Section 211(1)(a) of the ERA 1996 provides that a period of continuous employment begins 'with the day on which the employee starts work'. Unofficial work prior to the formal start date is unlikely to count towards a period of continuous employment (see *Koenig v Mind Gym Ltd* (UKEAT/0201/12) and *O'Sullivan v DSM Demolition Ltd* (UKEAT/0257/19).

Continuous employment usually means working for the same employer without a break. Sometimes, employment can be regarded as continuous in spite of short breaks (ERA 1996, s 212(3)(c) (see **3.5.3**)). Sometimes, time spent with a previous employer may be added on (eg where there are 'associated employers', such as teachers within one local education authority who work for different schools).

3.5.1 Periods of employment required

3.5.1.1 Unfair dismissal

From 6 April 2012, for employees who start work on or after that date, to be entitled to present a complaint of unfair dismissal, the dismissed employee must have been continuously employed for a period of not less than two years, starting on the date that employment commenced and ending on the 'effective date of termination' (EDT) (ERA 1996, s 108(1)).

It is advisable for employers to review the employment of new employees well before they have been continuously employed for two years. This will enable an employer to dismiss an unsatisfactory employee with proper notice, before he becomes entitled to present a complaint of unfair dismissal. However, note that even if an employee does not have the necessary length of service, he is eligible to present other claims, for example a claim for discrimination if relevant on the facts (see **Chapters 8** and **13**).

Exceptionally, an employee does not need a qualifying period of continuous employment to present an unfair dismissal claim, for example an employee who is dismissed for trade union reasons (**5.5.1**), for having stopped work on health and safety grounds (**5.5.4**), for having asserted a statutory right (**5.5.3**) or because she is pregnant (**Chapter 14**).

3.5.1.2 Redundancy payment

To be entitled to claim a redundancy payment, the dismissed employee must have been employed for a period of not less than two years, starting on the date that employment commenced and ending on the 'relevant date' (ERA 1996, s 155). See further **Chapter 4**.

3.5.2 Calculating continuous employment

3.5.2.1 Unfair dismissal and the effective date of termination

The EDT is defined by ss 97 and 145 of the ERA 1996 to mean:

(a) for an employee whose contract is terminated by notice, whether given by the employer or employee, the date on which that notice expires. In *Palfrey v Transco plc* [2004] IRLR 916, the EAT said that the employee's EDT was his leaving date as agreed with the employer, and not the termination date given in the notice of dismissal (see also *Wedgewood v Ministergate Hull Ltd* (UKEAT/0137/10);

(b) for an employee whose contract is terminated without notice, the date on which termination takes effect (see *Heaven v Whitbread Group plc* (UKEAT/0084/10), the Court of Appeal's decision in *Société Général, London Branch v Geys* at **2.3.3** above and more recently *Cosmeceuticals Ltd v Parkin* (UKEAT/0049/17)); and

(c) for an employee with a limited-term contract which expires without renewal, the date on which the term expires.

Dismissals, resignations and EDT can often be complex matters to ascertain in practice (see, eg, *Secretary of State for Justice v Hibbert* at **3.4.3(i)** above). As a rule of thumb, the EDT is the last day on which the employee worked for the employer.

Note that:

(a)   if an employee is dismissed without notice but given wages in lieu, the EDT is still the date the employee was told to go (see, eg, *Robert Cort & Son Ltd v Charman* [1981] ICR 816);

(b)   with a constructive dismissal, where the employee resigns the EDT is the date of departure, ie the employee's acceptance of the repudiation. Where an employee resigns and gives notice, the EDT will be the date the notice expires.

The Court of Appeal held that the EDT is a statutory construct and cannot be fixed by agreement between the parties (*Fitzgerald v University of Kent at Canterbury* [2004] IRLR 300).

The EDT may be important in determining whether an employee has presented a case to a tribunal within the requisite time-limits (see **6.3**). In *Gisda Cyf v Barratt* [2010] UKSC 41, the Supreme Court held that the EDT of an employee dismissed for gross misconduct was the date she opened and read the letter from her employer, informing her of her dismissal. See also *Robinson v Bowskill* (UKEAT/0313/12) and *Cosmeceuticals Ltd v Parkin* (above). The position is the same under the common law (see **2.3.3** above).

In *Hawes v Curtis Ltd v Arfan* [2012] ICR 1244, it was accepted that an altered decision on an appeal against dismissal might change the EDT, for example where the appeal expressly varied the date on which termination took effect.

Extension of EDT in special circumstances

The main purpose of this rule is to ensure that employers do not deprive employees of their statutory rights by wrongfully dismissing them without notice just before they reach the qualifying period to present a claim of unfair dismissal.

In circumstances where the employee is entitled to a statutory minimum period of notice under s 86 of the ERA 1996 (see **2.3.3**), if he is dismissed without notice or with less notice than the statutory minimum, for certain purposes his EDT will be extended by the statutory minimum period of notice to which he was entitled but did not receive (ERA 1996, s 97(2)):

(a)   The EDT is extended only by the statutory minimum period of notice, not by any longer contractual period to which he may have been entitled.

(b)   The EDT is extended only if the employee was entitled to notice. It is not extended if a limited-term contract terminates (except under a 'break' clause), or if an employer is entitled to dismiss the employee without notice (ERA 1996, s 86(6)). In *Lancaster and Duke Ltd v Wileman* (UKEAT/0256/17), the EAT emphasised that where there is a genuine entitlement to summarily dismiss, an employee cannot rely on the deeming provisions in s 86 of the ERA 1996 to get to two years' qualifying service. In this case, Ms Wileman was dismissed for gross misconduct with no notice, two days before her two-year anniversary. No process was carried out before her dismissal and there was no right of appeal. The tribunal extended her period by adding in the statutory minimum one week's notice and found that she was unfairly dismissed. The EAT overturned this because the tribunal had not made any finding as to whether Ms Wileman has been guilty of gross misconduct, such that the s 86(6) provision would apply. There needed to be a wrongful dismissal claim for the additional week to be added.

(c)   A constructively dismissed employee is also entitled to extend the EDT by the statutory minimum period for the purposes of bringing an unfair dismissal claim (see (d) below). The statutory minimum period of notice that would have been due from the employer had the employer terminated, will start to run from the date that the employee gave notice (ERA 1996, s 97(4)).

(d)   The EDT is extended only for some purposes, such as the qualification period to present an unfair dismissal claim, the calculation of awards for such a claim and entitlement to be given a written statement of reasons for dismissal (see **5.2.3**). It does not extend the EDT for the purposes of extending the time-limits to present claims.

> **EXAMPLE**
>
> Natalie commenced employment on 2 April 2019. There is no break in her continuity of employment. Her employer wrongfully dismissed her without notice on 30 March 2021. On this date she had been continuously employed for more than one month but less than two years. Under s 86 of the ERA 1996 she was entitled to one week's statutory minimum notice (see **2.3.3**). Her EDT is extended by one week to 7 April 2021 (the seven days' notice starts on 31 March and expires on 7 April), which gives her the necessary two years' continuous employment to present an unfair dismissal claim.

3.5.2.2 Redundancy payments and the relevant date

The relevant date is defined by ERA 1996, s 145 in exactly the same way as the EDT is for unfair dismissal (see **3.5.2.1** above).

Extension of the relevant date in special circumstances

Again, the rules are designed to prevent an employer wrongfully dismissing an employee just before he reaches the qualifying period for presenting a redundancy payment claim. Points (a), (b) and (d) at **3.5.2.1** above apply to extension of the relevant date also (s 145(5)).

Point (c) above does not apply. The relevant date will be extended by the statutory minimum period to which the employee is entitled but did not receive, but only where there is an actual dismissal by the employer. The relevant date is *not* extended by the statutory minimum period for the purposes of making a redundancy payment claim where the employee has been constructively dismissed.

> **EXAMPLE**
>
> George commenced employment on 2 April 2019. There is no break in his continuity of employment. He resigns on 30 March 2021, alleging that he has been constructively dismissed. On this date he has been employed for just less than two years. Although, under ERA 1996, s 86, he is entitled to one week's statutory minimum notice, the relevant date will *not* be extended by the statutory minimum period. He is not eligible to claim a redundancy payment.

3.5.3 Continuity of employment

Periods of employment must be continuous. If a period of employment is broken so that it is not continuous with a later period, the employee will commence a new period of employment after the break, starting again at week one. He will not be able to add the old period of employment to the new.

There is a presumption in favour of the employee that employment is continuous (ERA 1996, s 210(5)). This may, however, be rebutted by the employer.

A week counts towards the period of continuous employment if in that week the employee actually works or the employee's relationship with the employer is governed by a contract.

Weeks during which the employee is *not employed* under a contract of employment do not count. However, such weeks *will* count in the following circumstances (ERA 1996, s 212):

(a)   if the employee is absent due to sickness, injury, pregnancy or confinement up to a maximum of 26 weeks;

(b)   if there is a temporary cessation of work (see *Cornwall County Council v Prater* (UKEAT/0055/05)) (the case was appealed to the Court of Appeal on different grounds; there was no appeal on this point ([2006] IRLR 362) and *Ford v Warwickshire CC* [1983] ICR 273, HL (applied in *Hussain v Acorn Independent College Ltd* (UKEAT/0199/10)));

(c)   if the employee is absent in circumstances where, by arrangement or custom, the employee is regarded as continuously in employment (see *Curr v Marks & Spencer plc* [2003] IRLR 74 for a decision of the Court of Appeal on this issue).

It is necessary to rely on these provisions to preserve continuity only where there is no continuing contract of employment. If there is a subsisting contractual relationship, continuity of employment will be preserved, even though the employee does not work due to, for example, sickness or holiday or maternity leave. If an employee is reinstated following an unfair dismissal finding, continuity will be assumed as if there had been no dismissal.

For a recent decision considering the statutory construction of s 212 of the ERA 1996, see the EAT's decision in *Welton v Deluxe Retail Ltd (t/a Madhouse)* [2013] IRLR 166, which looked at the situation where there was a gap of just over a week between the claimant ending work at one of the employer's stores and starting work at another.

Note that continuity is a statutory concept. In *London Probation Board v Kirkpatrick* [2005] IRLR 443, the EAT held that it was open to an employer and an employee to arrange (under ERA 1996, s 212(3)(c)) that absence from work could count towards continuity of employment and that reinstatement could qualify as such an arrangement. The EAT in *Welton* disagreed with this analysis, preferring the line of authority in *Murphy v Birrell & Sons Ltd* [1978] IRLR 458 and *Morris v Walsh Western UK Ltd* [1997] IRLR 562, that an 'arrangement' had to exist beforehand, or arise contemporaneously with the relevant absence from work; it could not be made retrospectively to cure gaps in employment. This is because the wording of the section is in the present tense, 'he *is* regarded as *continuing in* the employment of his employer' (emphasis added).

3.5.4   Industrial action

Industrial action does not break continuity of employment, but days during which the employee is on strike or locked out by the employer do not count in computing the length of employment (ERA 1996, s 216).

This is achieved by postponing the beginning of the period of continuous employment by the number of days between the last working day before the strike or lockout and the day on which work was resumed.

EXAMPLE

An employee, whose continuous employment commenced on 6 September 2020, goes on strike at lunchtime on Friday 6 November 2021. She resumes work on Tuesday 10 November 2021. Her period of continuous employment will now be treated as beginning on 11 September 2020. It is postponed by the four days (ie 6, 7, 8, 9 November 2021) between the last working day before the strike (5 November 2021) and the day work resumed (10 November 2021). The days 8 and 9 November are 'lost' by the employee, even though they are a Saturday and Sunday and not working days.

3.5.5   Change of employer

The basic rule is that for employment to be continuous, it must be with the same employer. A change of employer will break continuity (ERA 1996, s 218).

Although a change of employer breaks continuity, a change of job with the same employer will not break it.

In the following circumstances, continuity of employment is preserved despite a change of employer:

(a)   there is a transfer of an undertaking within TUPE 2006 (see **Chapter 7**);

(b)   on the death of an employer, the employee is employed by the personal representatives of the deceased;

(c)   there is a change of partners who are the employers;

(d)   the new employer is an associated employer of the old employer (ERA 1996, s 218(6)). Employers are associated if one is a company of which the other has control, or if both are companies of which a third person has control (ERA 1996, s 231). Therefore, if an employee is moved between companies within a 'group', his continuity will be preserved (see the EAT's decision in *Schwarzenbach and Anor v Jones* (UKEAT/0100/15)).

3.6   EXCLUDED CLASSES

The ERA 1996 excludes certain classes of employee from entitlement to the statutory claims. For example, members of the armed forces, the police service and 'share' mariners are excluded from the right to present a claim of unfair dismissal. Crown employees, 'share' mariners and certain domestic servants employed by close relations are not entitled to redundancy payments. Diplomatic and state immunity may also protect certain classes of employees (see eg *Reyes v Al-Malki* [2015] EWCA Civ 32, *Benkharbouche and Anor v Embassy of the Republic of Sudan* [2015] IRLR 301 and *USA v Nolan* [2015] UKSC 63). Further details of these exclusions may be found in Harvey, *Industrial Relations and Employment Law* (Butterworths), Division C. The Supreme Court held in *Reyes v Al-Malki & Another* [2017] UKSC 61 that embassy employees do not have immunity from claims brought by their domestic staff.

3.7   JURISDICTION

Many employers have mobile or globally based workforces. Generally speaking, employees who ordinarily work in Great Britain will be protected under UK employment laws. For peripatetic employees, their bases will normally be regarded as their place of work. The contract may be relevant here, although courts tend to focus on the actual position in practice rather than on what the contract says, if there is a conflict.

In cases where there is a foreign element, for example expatriate employees working abroad for a UK company, or employees who spend some, but not all, of their time working abroad, the question arises whether a tribunal has jurisdiction to hear the case at all or whether it should be heard in a foreign court.

The right of an employee not to be unfairly dismissed by his employer is embodied in s 94(1) of the ERA 1996. When the right not to be unfairly dismissed first made its appearance (as s 22 of the Industrial Relations Act 1971), it was accompanied by a provision (s 27(2)) which said that s 22 did not apply 'to any employment where under his contract of employment the employee ordinarily works outside Great Britain'. When the legislation was consolidated, ultimately in ERA 1996, the geographical limitation for unfair dismissal claims appeared in s 196(3) under the heading 'Employment outside Great Britain'.

Section 196 of the ERA 1996 provided, inter alia, that the unfair dismissal provisions of the Act did not apply in relation to employment during any period when the employee was working outside Great Britain, unless the employee ordinarily worked in Great Britain for the same employer, or his contract was governed by the law of England and Wales (or Scotland). However, the whole of s 196 was repealed by s 32(3) of the ERA 1999, with effect from 25 October 1999. This repeal left uncertain the extent to which tribunals had jurisdiction to hear unfair dismissal claims under s 94(1) (which simply states that an employee has the right not to be unfairly dismissed by his employer).

It has therefore been left to the courts to imply whatever geographical limitations seem appropriate to the substantive right. Read literally, s 94(1) of the ERA 1996 applies to any individual who works under a contract of employment anywhere in the world. Nonetheless, as pointed out by the House of Lords in the leading case, *Serco Ltd v Lawson and Others* [2006] UKHL 3, it is inconceivable that Parliament was intending to confer rights upon employees working in foreign countries and having no connection with Great Britain. The argument has been over what those limitations should be. In the absence of statutory guidance, guidance on the developing domestic law principles of territoriality and jurisdiction in the enforcement of employment law rights has been provided by the appellate courts. There are now a number of important authorities on this issue of the legislative reach of s 94(1).

Some issues were resolved by the House of Lords in *Serco Ltd v Lawson and Others* [2006] UKHL 3. Hoffmann LJ, giving the judgment, identified three categories of case:

(a) where the employee was working in Great Britain at the time of the dismissal (so long as that was not a casual visit) – he said that this was the 'normal' case and s 94(1) would generally apply;

(b) the peripatetic employee – where the 'commonsense [approach] of treating the base' as the place of employment would apply (see *Todd v British Midland Airways Ltd* [1978] ICR 959); and

(c) expatriate employees – where there would have to be 'unusual' or 'exceptional' circumstances for an employee to be protected under British employment law.

Two examples were given:

(i) an employee posted abroad by a British employer for the purposes of a business carried on in Britain,

(ii) an employee of a British employer operating in a British enclave in a foreign country.

Lord Hoffmann said that there might be other examples of employees who 'have equally strong connections with Great Britain and British employment law' but that he could not think of any.

In *Duncombe and Others v Secretary of State for Children, Schools and Families* [2011] UKSC 36, the Supreme Court held that teachers working abroad in schools in Europe and employed by a UK government department were protected under the expatriate employee category identified in *Serco* above because they were another example of employees who have equally strong connections with Britain – the employees' employment had an overwhelmingly closer connection to Britain than anywhere else. The factors that were important were that the Government employed the employees; their contracts were governed by English law; they were employed in international enclaves and it would be anomalous if a teacher employed by the British Government working in a European school in England were protected but these employees working in a school in another country were not.

Lady Hale, delivering the judgment of the Supreme Court remarked (para 8) that it was a mistake to try to torture the circumstances of one employment to make them fit one of the examples given, for 'they are merely examples of the application of the general principle'. She went on to say:

> In our view, these cases do form another example of an exceptional case where the employment has such an overwhelmingly closer connection with Britain and with British employment law than with any other system of law that it is right to conclude that Parliament must have intended that the employees should enjoy protection from unfair dismissal.

In *Ravat v Halliburton Manufacturing and Services Ltd* [2012] UKSC 1 and *Ministry of Defence v Wallis* [2011] EWCA Civ 231, the courts considered the extent to which, if at all, an employment tribunal can go beyond the three categories of case identified by Lord Hoffmann in *Serco*. In *Wallis*, the Court of Appeal upheld the tribunal's decision that the claimants fell within the expatriate category of employee, making it clear that each case must be decided on its own facts. The fact that the claimants were recruited by the MoD, were eligible for the posts as dependants of serving members of the army posted abroad and were employed on terms governed by English law were all factors which meant that the claimants had 'clear, firm, sound connections with Britain'. In *Ravat*, the Supreme Court, on an appeal from the Scottish

Court of Session (which was divided as to the extent to which it was possible to depart from Lord Hoffman's categories), held that a British citizen who lived in England but worked in Libya on what was known as a commuter or rotational basis (he worked 28 days in Libya, then was in England for 28 days), could bring an unfair dismissal claim. He was employed by Halliburton Manufacturing and Services Ltd, a UK subsidiary of Halliburton Inc, a US company. The work he carried out was for the benefit of a German subsidiary of Halliburton Inc. He was paid in sterling and paid UK tax. At the time of his dismissal he was working in Libya. The Supreme Court held that he had sufficiently strong connections with Great Britain to be able to bring a claim of unfair dismissal in England.

In a unanimous judgment, Lord Hope pointed out that Mr Ravat did not fit into any of the three categories identified by Lord Hoffmann in *Serco*. He was not working in Great Britain at the time of his dismissal. He was not a peripatetic employee. He was not working abroad as an expatriate in a political or social British enclave. Nor had he been posted abroad to work for a business conducted in Great Britain, as he was commuting from his home in Preston and the company for whose benefit he was working in Libya was a German company.

Lord Hope referred to the warning given by Lady Hale in *Duncombe* against adopting too restrictive an approach to the problem, and concluded:

> The question in each case is whether section 94(1) applies to the particular case, notwithstanding its foreign elements. Parliament cannot be taken to have intended to confer rights on employees having no connection with Great Britain at all. The paradigm case for the application of the subsection is, of course, the employee who was working in Great Britain. But there is some scope for a wider interpretation, as the language of section 94(1) does not confine its application to employment in Great Britain ... the starting point needs to be more precisely identified. It is that the employment relationship must have a stronger connection with Great Britain than with the foreign country where the employee works. The general rule is that the place of employment is decisive. But it is not an absolute rule. The open-ended language of section 94(1) leaves room for some exceptions where the connection with Great Britain is sufficiently strong to show that this can be justified. The case of the peripatetic employee who was based in Great Britain is one example. The expatriate employee, all of whose services were performed abroad but who had nevertheless very close connections with Great Britain because of the nature and circumstances of employment, is another. But it does not follow that the connection that must be shown in the case of those who are not truly expatriate, because they were not both working and living overseas, must achieve the high standard that would enable one to say that their case was exceptional. The question whether, on given facts, a case falls within the scope of section 94(1) is a question of law, but it is also a question of degree. The fact that the commuter has his home in Great Britain, with all the consequences that flow from this for the terms and conditions of his employment, makes the burden in his case of showing that there was a sufficient connection less onerous. Mr Cavanagh said that a rigorous standard should be applied, but I would not express the test in those terms. The question of law is whether section 94(1) applies to this particular employment. The question of fact is whether the connection between the circumstances of the employment and Great Britain and with British employment law was sufficiently strong to enable it to be said that it would be appropriate for the employee to have a claim for unfair dismissal in Great Britain.

On the facts, the factors that pointed to a sufficiently close connection with Britain were:

(a)   Mr Ravat's home was in Britain;

(b)   he was paid in sterling;

(c)   he was treated as a commuter under his employer's assignment policy; and

(d)   his contract was stated to be subject to UK law.

A number of other appellate decisions have examined this vexed area in the unfair dismissal context. These include:

•   *Ministry of Defence v Wallis* [2011] ICR 617, CA – spouses of UK military personnel, based in Germany, working at an international school; held, they were subject to the employment tribunal's jurisdiction.

- *Clyde & Co LLP and Another v Bates van Winkelhof* [2012] IRLR 992, CA – an LLP partner in a London-based law firm, who was based in and worked mainly in Tanzania but who retained property in the UK and visited regularly – 100 days a year (78 work/22 personal) – brought whistleblowing and sex discrimination claims; held, was subject to the employment tribunal's jurisdiction.

- *Dhunna v Creditsights Ltd* [2014] EWCA Civ 1238 – an employee of the London office of a US-based company was permanently relocated to Dubai, where he worked for the benefit of the US-based business in Dubai; the employment tribunal held that there was insufficient connection with the UK; the EAT allowed his appeal but the Court of Appeal restored the tribunal's finding.

- *Powell v OMV Exploration & Production Ltd* [2014] IRLR 80, EAT – the claimant worked for an Isle of Man company, which was ultimately owned by a German company; there was no place of business in the UK and the administration of the company was based in Austria; the claimant worked for three weeks abroad and then 'rested' for one week in the UK; in total, over the period for which he was employed, from November 2010 until February 2012 when his contract was terminated, he worked a total of 20 full working days in the UK; the employment tribunal held he fell outside its territorial jurisdiction scope; the EAT dismissed the claimant's appeal.

- *Lodge v Dignity & Choice in Dying* (UKEAT/0252/14) – the EAT found that an Australian citizen, who was not an expatriate and had not been posted abroad, who was employed as head of finance for a UK company and who worked remotely in Australia for family reasons, was entitled to pursue unfair dismissal and whistleblowing claims in the UK. The fact that she was a 'virtual employee' in Australia rather than a 'physical employee' in London did not mean she fell outside the protection of the UK courts.

- *Jeffery v The British Council* (UKEAT/0036/16) – the EAT found that an expatriate (UK citizen) employee who had worked abroad for the British Council for over 20 years, latterly as a teaching centre manager in Bangladesh, who did not have a home in the UK and returned to the UK only to visit his parents, was entitled to bring claims of constructive unfair dismissal and whistleblowing to an employment tribunal. His contract was governed by English law, and he was entitled to a civil service pension.

- *Crew Employment v Gold* (UKEAT/0330/19) – the EAT found that a US resident, who was the captain of a superyacht, which was registered in the Caymans and owned by a Guernsey company, was entitled to bring a claim for unfair dismissal because the 'effective' owner of the yacht was a Mr Borodin, who lived in the UK, and who determined the itineraries for the yacht, whose sailings were mostly to and from the UK. Mr Borodin had interviewed and recruited the claimant, promoted him and gave him instructions. Relying on *Jeffery*, the EAT held that there was a sufficiently strong connection with the UK.

Although each case ultimately is determined on its own facts, the following principles may be derived from the decisions:

(a)   The essential question for the tribunal to ask itself is: 'Does s 94(1) of the ERA 1996 apply to the employee in question?' This is a question of law and degree on the facts (*Ravat* (paras 28, 29)).

(b)   The starting point and general rule is that the place of employment is decisive (*Serco* (para 11); *Ravat* (para 27); *Dhunna* (para 50); *Bates*, CA (para 92)), but the open-ended language of s 94(1) leaves room for some exceptions (*Serco*).

(c)   It is not necessary to try to fit each case within one of the examples given by Lord Hoffmann in *Serco* (*Duncombe* (para 8)).

(d)   For an exception to apply, as a minimum, the connection of an employee with Great Britain/the UK and with British/UK employment law must be 'sufficiently strong' as 'to enable it to be said that Parliament would have regarded it as appropriate for the Tribunal to deal with the claim' (*Ravat* (para 35)).

(e)   Where the employee concerned is peripatetic or an 'international commuter' who commutes from a UK base, a 'sufficiently strong' connection test applies (*Ravat* (paras 28, 29, 33, 35); *Dhunna* (para 50); *Powell* (paras 47, 48). See also *Olsen v Gearbulk Services Ltd* (UKEAT/0345/14), where a Danish citizen carrying on an international role in Switzerland with a Bermudan company subject to Bermudan law and jurisdiction, who spent just under half his working time in the UK, was not permitted to bring an unfair dismissal claim in the UK.

(f)   The two further examples given by Lord Hoffmann in *Serco* as exceptional cases are:

   (i)   an employee who is posted abroad by a British employer for the purposes of a business carried on in Great Britain; and

   (ii)   an expatriate employee of a British employer, who is operating within what amounts to an extra-territorial British enclave in a foreign country.

(g)   Although Lord Hoffmann described the two examples given at (f) above as 'expatriate' examples, a distinction is now drawn between 'expatriate' cases, where the employee in fact maintains some work or personal link to the UK/Great Britain, and 'true expatriate' cases, where the employee works and lives wholly abroad;

(h)   There is a more onerous test for a 'true' expatriate employee who works and lives outside Great Britain/the UK, where there must be an 'especially strong' connection (see, eg, *Duncombe* (para 8); *Ravat* (paras 28, 29, 33).

(i)   There is no need, in the 'sufficiently strong' connection cases, for any comparative exercise to be applied between the UK/Great Britain and the other jurisdiction.

Note: The Equality Act 2010, which deals with discrimination claims, is silent as to its territorial scope (see para 15 of the Explanatory Notes). Paragraph 10.70 of the EHRC's Statutory Code of Practice on Employment (see **Chapter 8**) states that discrimination protection in employment is required 'when there is a sufficiently close link between the employment relationship and Great Britain'. This therefore requires a similar approach to that for unfair dismissal when determining if an employment tribunal has jurisdiction to hear a claim.

In *Clyde & Co LLP and Another v Bates van Winkelhof* (above), the Court of Appeal upheld an employment tribunal's decision with regard to jurisdiction and agreed that it was right to apply the *Serco* test of a *sufficiently* strong connection to Great Britain to discrimination claims. Elias LJ did say that, in cases where the employee works *wholly* abroad (on the facts the employee lived and/or worked for part of the time in Great Britain), a comparative approach would be appropriate to decide where the stronger connection is. Ms Bates van Winkelhof's connection with Great Britain was found to be sufficiently strong to overcome the fact that she was based in Tanzania. For a contrasting case, see the EAT's decision in *Ravisy v Simmons & Simmons LLP* (UKEAT/0085/18), where the claimant was an equity partner of a UK LLP but worked almost exclusively in France, had chosen to be paid in euros into a French bank account and paid tax in France. Her visits to London were ad hoc, infrequent and generally short.

In *R (on the application of Hottak and Anor) v Secretary of State for Foreign and Commonwealth Affairs and Anor* [2015] EWHC 1953 (Admin), the High Court held that there was no jurisdiction to hear claims brought by Afghan interpreters working with the British military in Afghanistan, who were employed by the British Government. The Court of Appeal upheld the decision and confirmed that the same test (in *Lawson*) applies to discrimination claims ([2016] EWCA Civ 438).

In *Smania v Standard Chartered Bank* (UKEAT/0181/14), the EAT said that the test for territorial jurisdiction in a claim alleging dismissal or detriment based on a protected disclosure is the same test as for ordinary unfair dismissal. It upheld an employment tribunal decision that it had no jurisdiction to hear a whistleblowing claim by an Italian banker who lived and worked in Singapore, and whose head office was based in Great Britain. See also *Fuller v United Healthcare Services Inc* (UKEAT/0464/13) and *Foreign and Commonwealth Office v Bamieh* [2019] EWCA Civ 803. The law on territorial jurisdiction continues to be a live issue. Other recent cases have included *Fuller v United Healthcare Services Inc* (UKEAT/0464/13) (US employee on assignment in London), *Swania v Standard Chartered Bank* (EAT/0181/14) (Italian banker living and working in Singapore), *Olsen v Gearbulk Services Ltd* (UKEAT/0345/14), *Green v SIG Trading Ltd* (UKEAT/0282/16) and the joined cases of *Nogueira v Crewlink and Oscar v Ryanair* (Cases C-168/16 and C-169/16) decided by the CJEU in September 2017. The CJEU said that jurisdiction could not be displaced by clauses in a contract so as to prevent proceedings being brought in the State where the employee habitually works.

In *Foreign and Commonwealth Office v Bamieh* [2019] EWCA Civ 803, the Court of Appeal held that a public interest disclosure detriment claim against co-workers could not be brought in the employment tribunal because there was not a sufficient Great Britain close connection between the workers. Whether there would have been a sufficiently strong connection to Great Britain if the claim had been brought against the employer itself was not discussed.

In *Rajabov v Foreign and Commonwealth Office* [2022] EAT 112, the EAT dismissed an appeal against the employment tribunal's decision that a former employee of the British Embassy in Tajikistan did not have territorial jurisdiction over his claim for unfair dismissal, because the appellant's employment had a closer connection with Tajikistan:

> ... the tribunal noted a number of factors which, in its view, tended to show that the appellant's employment was more closely connected with Tajikistan than with Great Britain (§28). These included that the governing law of the contract was that of Tajikistan, the appellant's residence was in Tajikistan, the appellant had been locally recruited and he was taxed and made social security contributions in Tajikistan. The tribunal then noted two factors which tended in the other direction: that the employer clearly has connections with the UK government and an assertion made by the appellant that he had been told that he would be protected by UK laws relating to whistleblowing should he raise concerns about financial wrongdoing (§30). The tribunal had found that it would not accept that assertion of the appellant, which had not been included in his witness statement and about which he had not been cross-examined (§19). The tribunal decided that even if it were to accept that assertion, it, and the point about connection with the UK government, were 'of little weight' and did not outweigh the factors which supported there being a stronger connection with Tajikistan. Therefore, the tribunal did not have territorial jurisdiction to hear the claim (§31).

That reasoning was upheld.

3.8 CONTRACTING OUT

Any provision purporting to contract out of the employee's rights under the ERA 1996 is void except in so far as it is permitted by the Act (see eg **6.5**).

3.9 FURTHER READING

Textbooks dealing with eligibility include:

Selwyn's Law of Employment, 22nd edn (OUP, 2022).

Harvey, *Industrial Relations and Employment Law* (LexisNexis), Div DI.

Lewis, *Employment Law – an adviser's handbook*, 14th edn (LAG, 2022).

Duggan, *Unfair Dismissal: Law, Practice and Precedents*, 2nd edn (Duggan Press, 2019).

SUMMARY

This chapter has looked at two statutory claims which might be available to an employee on the termination of his employment in addition to the common law claim for wrongful dismissal covered in **Chapter 2** – unfair dismissal and/or for a redundancy payment. It has covered eligibility to present these claims to an employment tribunal. In order to claim a redundancy payment or pursue a complaint of unfair dismissal a person must be an employee (**1.3**), must have been dismissed (actually, constructively or on the expiry of a fixed-term contract) (**3.4**), must have the requisite two years' continuous employment (**3.5**) and must not fall within any of the excluded classes (**3.6**). Additionally, the tribunal must have the necessary jurisdiction to hear the claim (**3.7** and **6.2.1**).

It is therefore sensible always to check the following matters in order to determine if someone is eligible to bring a claim:

(1)   commencement date;

(2)   EDT;

(3)   no break;

(4)   starting date in the event of industrial action;

(5)   two years' service.

CHAPTER 4

REDUNDANCY

4.1	Introduction	141
4.2	Definition of redundancy	143
4.3	Presumption of redundancy	147
4.4	Offers of re-employment	147
4.5	Change of employer	149
4.6	Computation of the statutory redundancy payment	150
4.7	Enforcement	151
4.8	Consultation	152
4.9	Case study: redundancy payment, unpaid notice and holiday pay	157
4.10	Further reading	159
	Summary	160

LEARNING OUTCOMES

After reading this chapter you will be able to:

- describe the three different definitions of redundancy

- explain how an employee may make a redundancy payment claim

- explain when an employee may lose his entitlement to a redundancy payment

- calculate a redundancy payment.

4.1 INTRODUCTION

An eligible employee, dismissed by reason of redundancy, will be entitled, at a minimum, to a statutory redundancy payment from his employer (ERA 1996, s 163). The contract of employment may provide for more generous payments. *Note:* where an employee is dismissed by reason of redundancy, this may *also* give rise to potential wrongful dismissal and/or unfair dismissal claims (see **Chapters 2** and **5**). The right to claim a redundancy payment is a separate right, which will arise irrespective of whether the dismissal is unfair or wrongful. Note that women on maternity leave have special protection in a redundancy situation (see **14.5**). Only employees are entitled to a redundancy payment.

A redundancy payment is in the nature of a reward for past services, and so an eligible employee is entitled to receive the full payment even when he manages to find another job immediately.

Often the employer accepts that the employee is redundant and will simply calculate the amount of the redundancy payment and make payment without the need for any formal application to an employment tribunal. However, where there is a dispute over the right to receive the payment or over the correct amount, an application will need to be made and the tribunal will determine these matters.

Redundancy payments can also arise where there has been a lay-off or temporary cessation of work or short-time working has been imposed by the employer (ERA 1996, s 135(1)(b)). The provisions relating to this are contained in ss 147–154 of the ERA 1996. It is a complex area and considered only in brief here.

Laying off staff or offering short-time working can help avoid making staff redundant. Subject to certain statutory conditions, where there is a temporary shortage of work or insufficient finance to fund full-time employment and there is a contractual right, employers can 'lay off' an employee (ie ask them to stay at home or take unpaid leave) when they temporarily cannot give them paid work.

Section 147(1) of the ERA 1996 states that an employee has been laid off for a week where:

- their employment contract provides that pay is dependent on their employer providing them with work that they are employed to do, but
- they are not entitled to remuneration for that week because their employer has not provided them with work.

Employees should get full pay during lay-offs unless their contract provides for unpaid or reduced pay or it is agreed otherwise.

'Short-time' working is where an employee's hours are reduced or they are paid less than half a week's pay.

Section 147(2) of the ERA 1996 sets out the statutory definition of 'short-time working'. An employee will be determined to be on 'short-time working' where the work that they are provided by their employer under their contract of employment has diminished, which results in their remuneration for the week being less than half a week's pay. The normal statutory definition of a 'week' is set out in s 235 of the ERA 1996.

Employees continue to accrue holiday in the usual way during lay-offs and short-time working.

While employees are laid off or put on short-time working, they might be eligible for universal credit or jobseeker's allowance.

The Acas guide, 'Lay-offs and short-time working', suggests that where an employer seeks to impose a lay-off or short-time working where there is no contractual right to do so, and there has been no express consent, an employee's options are to:

- choose to accept the breach of contract and treat the contract as continuing, while claiming a statutory guarantee payment;
- sue for damages for breach of contract in the civil court or, in certain circumstances, at an employment tribunal;
- claim before an employment tribunal that there has been an unlawful deduction of wages under Part II of the ERA 1996;
- claim that the employer's action amounted to a dismissal (constructive or otherwise), giving rise to potential claims for unfair dismissal and/or redundancy pay.

Employees can be entitled to a guarantee payment if they are not provided with a full day's work during time they would normally be expected to work. The maximum statutory payment is £30 a day for 5 days (£150) in any 3 months. For employees who usually earn less than £30 a day, they should get their normal day rate. Some contracts may provide for more generous guarantee payments.

Where a lay-off or short-time working runs for more than 4 weeks in a row or for 6 or more weeks in a 13-week period, where no more than 3 weeks are in a row, employees can apply for redundancy and claim a redundancy payment. An employee will have to resign to claim redundancy in this way.

For more detail, see the Acas note at <www.acas.org.uk/lay-offs-and-short-time-working>.

4.1.1 Eligibility

Before advising on the right to a redundancy payment, eligibility must be checked. Employees must have two years' continuous service 'by the relevant date' before they are eligible to claim a redundancy payment (ERA 1996, s 155). Note that there are a number of circumstances where the general rules on continuity set out in Chapter I of Part XIV of the ERA 1996 (see **3.5**) do not apply in redundancy cases (see eg ERA 1996, s 214). There must also, of course, be a dismissal (see **3.4** for the definition of dismissal).

4.1.2 Redundancy

The next point to consider is whether the situation which led to the dismissal fits the statutory definition of redundancy. In other words, is the reason for the dismissal redundancy? If it is not, there will be no right to a redundancy payment. The scope of the definition is considered below at **4.2**.

4.2 DEFINITION OF REDUNDANCY

Section 135 of the ERA 1996 sets out that an employer shall pay a redundancy payment to an employee if the employee is (a) dismissed by reason of redundancy, or (b) is eligible by reasons of being laid off or kept on short-time working. This chapter focuses on the former aspect of the entitlement. The latter is beyond the scope of this work.

The definition of redundancy is contained in s 139(1) of the ERA 1996:

> For the purposes of this Act an employee who is dismissed shall be taken to be dismissed by reason of redundancy if the dismissal is wholly or mainly attributable to—
>
> (a) the fact that his employer has ceased or intends to cease—
>
> > (i) to carry on the business for the purposes of which the employee was employed by him, or
> >
> > (ii) to carry on that business in the place where the employee was so employed, or
>
> (b) the fact that the requirements of that business—
>
> > (i) for employees to carry out work of a particular kind, or
> >
> > (ii) for employees to carry out work of a particular kind in the place where the employee was employed by the employer,
>
> have ceased or diminished or are expected to cease or diminish.

Section 139(6) of the ERA 1996 states that the words 'cease' and 'diminish' mean cease and diminish either permanently or temporarily and for whatever reason, so redundancy includes a situation where the business needs for an employee's work have *temporarily* diminished.

Looking at this definition, it may be seen that redundancy occurs in three main situations: job redundancy, place of work redundancy and employee redundancy (our labels). Each of these is now considered in turn.

4.2.1 Cessation of business – 'job redundancy'

Within s 139(1)(a)(i) of the ERA 1996, an employee who is dismissed by reason of the closure of the employer's business will be dismissed by reason of redundancy. This will be the case whether the cessation of business is permanent or temporary.

4.2.2 Cessation or reduction in work at place of employment – 'place of work redundancy'

Here, *the place* where the employee is employed is being relocated (ERA 1996, s 139(1)(a)(ii)). This sounds a simple proposition, but there were, in the past, difficulties in determining whether 'place of work' is where the employee *could be required to work according to the contract of employment* (the 'contractual' test), or alternatively where the employee *actually* works (the 'factual' test). In *Bass Leisure Ltd v Thomas* [1994] IRLR 104, the EAT held that an employee's place of work, for the purposes of redundancy, is a question of 'fact', taking into account where the employee 'actually' worked.

The decision was approved by the Court of Appeal in *High Table Ltd v Horst* [1997] IRLR 513. The applicants were all employed as waitresses by High Table, who provided in-house catering services for city companies. The three applicants had always worked at Hill Samuel, but their contracts did contain a mobility clause. Hill Samuel reduced their requirements and the three applicants were dismissed. The Court held that for the purposes of redundancy, an employee's place of work was not to be decided solely by reference to the contract of employment regardless of where the employee actually worked. The place where the employee was employed for the purposes of s 139(1)(a)(ii) was to be established by a factual inquiry, taking into account the employee's fixed place or changing places of work and any contractual terms which might assist.

The Court said that if an employee had worked in only one location under his contract of employment for the purposes of the employer's business (as was the case, on the facts, in *High Table*), it defied common sense to widen the extent of the place where he was so employed merely because of the existence of the mobility clause. However, if the work of the employee for the employer had involved a change of location, then the contract of employment might be helpful to determine the extent of the place where the employee was employed.

Thus the position is as follows:

(a)   if an employee has worked in only one location, that is his place of work, regardless of any mobility clause in his contract;

(b)   if an employee has worked from several locations, the place of work is still to be established by a factual enquiry, taking into account any contractual terms that might assist in evidencing his place of work, for example a mobility clause.

4.2.2.1   Mobility clauses in the context of a 'place of work' redundancy situation

As noted above, when considering an employee's 'place' of work, the existence of a contractual mobility clause is irrelevant to that particular analysis where the employee worked in one location only.

However, mobility clauses are nevertheless still relevant when considering whether an employee is entitled to a redundancy payment on the facts, even if you have established that there is a redundancy situation within the meaning of s 139. This is because the cause of the dismissal must still be established. To be entitled to a redundancy payment, the employee's dismissal must have been caused by the redundancy situation. Whilst a mobility clause is not always relevant to identifying the place of work (see above), it is still a valid term of the contract. If an employee has a mobility clause in his contract, but refuses to obey a lawful request from his employer to move in accordance with the contractual term, then the dismissal may be due to the employee's misconduct rather than the underlying redundancy situation which has given rise to the need to implement the mobility clause (see *Home Office v Evans* [2008] IRLR 59 and *Kellogg Brown & Root (UK) Ltd v Fitton* (UKEAT/0205/16) (see also **1.8.2.3**)).

4.2.3   Reduction in requirement for employees to do work of a particular kind – 'employee redundancy'

An employee is dismissed by reason of redundancy within s 139(1)(b) of the ERA 1996 if the reason for his dismissal is that the requirement for employees to do work of a particular kind has ceased or diminished either permanently or temporarily. This will clearly cover the situation where the dismissed employee's own job has disappeared through lack of work, but the section also covers other situations, some of which may not be so obvious.

4.2.3.1 Surplus employees

If the requirement for employees to do the work is reduced, even though the same amount of work is still being done, this will come within the ambit of the section.

EXAMPLES

(a) Initial overstaffing may mean fellow employees can absorb the work done by the dismissed employee.

(b) New technology means that some employees are dismissed and replaced by machines.

(c) A reorganisation of work methods may produce a more efficient system requiring less manpower so some employees are dismissed.

(d) The work carried out by an employee may be done in fewer hours, so the employer seeks to reduce the employee's hours (not the overall employee headcount). The employee does not agree and is dismissed (see *Packman v Fauchon* (UKEAT/0017/12)).

(e) An independent contractor may be taken on to do the same work, for example instead of employing an office cleaner the employer may engage the services of a cleaning company, and the cleaner therefore will be dismissed. Note in this example the effect of the Transfer of Undertakings (Protection of Employment) Regulations 2006 (see **Chapter 7**).

4.2.3.2 Work of a particular kind

What if a change in the nature of a job leads to the dismissal of an employee? Will the dismissal be by reason of redundancy? If the nature of the work has changed fundamentally so that work of a particular kind has ceased or diminished, even though it has been replaced by different work, this will amount to redundancy. For example, in *Murphy v Epsom College* [1984] IRLR 271, as a result of the installation of a new heating system, a plumber was replaced by a heating technician and was held to have been made redundant. The dismissal was for redundancy because the employer no longer needed to carry out work of the particular kind done by him. However, a mere reallocation of duties or introduction of new methods will not amount to redundancy. See, for example, *North Riding Garages Ltd v Butterwick* [1967] 2 QB 56, where no redundancy situation arose when a garage manager was asked to sell cars in addition to his other duties.

The contract test or the function test?

Historically, there have been two conflicting tests used for determining whether work of a particular kind has ceased or diminished: the contract test and the function test. The contract test focused on how the duties of the employee were *defined* in the contract of employment. The function test focused on the duties *actually performed* by the employee. Historically, the contract test prevailed.

According to the contract test, if duties are narrowly defined as the actual job being carried out by the employee, and that job has gone, the employee is redundant. However, if the duties are widely defined in the contract, whilst the job performed by that employee may have gone, there may be other available jobs he could still be required to perform under his contract. In this case his dismissal will not be by reason of redundancy if the alternative job is offered (*Haden Ltd v Cowan* [1982] IRLR 314). According to the function test, if the actual job carried out by the employee has gone, the employee is redundant regardless of whether, under his contract, he could be required to do other work.

However, the EAT held in *Safeway Stores v Burrell* [1997] IRLR 200 that neither the contract nor the function test should be applied. Judge Peter Clark held that the test to establish whether or not a redundancy situation existed under s 139(1)(b) should be a three-stage process:

(1)   Was the employee dismissed? If so,

(2)   Had the requirements of the employer's business for employees to carry out work of a particular kind ceased or diminished, or were they expected to cease or diminish? If so,

(3)   Was the dismissal of the employee caused wholly or mainly by that state of affairs?

In determining at stage (2) whether there was a true redundancy situation, the only question to be asked is whether there was a diminution/cessation in the employer's requirements for *employees* (not the applicant) to carry out work of a particular kind, or an expectation of such a diminution/cessation in the future. The terms of the applicant's contract are irrelevant to that question.

The House of Lords confirmed in *Murray and Another v Foyle Meats Ltd* [1999] IRLR 562 that neither the contract nor the function test is determinative of the matter.

Their Lordships approved the reasoning and conclusion of Judge Peter Clark in the *Safeway* case above (see stages (2) and (3) in *Safeway* above). Lord Irvine held that the definition of redundancy in s 139(1)(b)

> is ... simplicity itself [and] asks two questions of fact. The first is ... whether the requirements of the business for employees to carry out work of a particular kind have diminished. The second ... is whether the dismissal is *attributable*, wholly or mainly to that state of affairs. This is a question of causation. (emphasis added)

Thus, the dismissal of an employee may be attributable to a diminution in the employer's need for employees, irrespective of the terms of the contract or the function which the employee performed. The causal connection between the need for fewer employees to carry out work of a particular kind and the dismissal of the employee is a matter of fact, not law. Clearly at stage (3), contractual terms which allow the employer to move the employee from one job to another (flexibility clauses) may be a relevant fact to take into account. If an employee is asked, for example, to move to another job (under his contractual terms) and refuses, then the dismissal may be due to the employee's misconduct rather than the underlying redundancy situation.

As commentators have pointed out (see Rubenstein [1997] IRLR 197, [1999] IRLR 505), the weakness of the approach in *Safeway* and *Murray* is that no weight is given to the words 'work of a particular kind'. However, the commentator considers that this is also the strength of the House of Lords decision. By directing the focus on causation, a dismissal will now be by reason of redundancy if it is attributable to the business's diminished need for employees to do work of a particular kind. In *Martland and Others v Cooperative Insurance Society and Others* (UKEAT/0220/07 and 0221/07), the EAT held that the words 'work of a particular kind' referred to the generic type of job, not the specific terms and conditions, so where financial advisers were dismissed and immediately offered re-engagement on new terms and conditions, the dismissals were not for redundancy but for some other substantial reason. The job was essentially the same, albeit that time spent selling was to increase by 50% and commission paid was to be reduced.

It is clear, then, that not all re-organisations will amount to redundancies. The restructuring must, to fall within the statutory definition, entail a reduction in the number of employees required to work of a particular kind. If, for example, the employer dismisses employees and replaces them with less well-paid employees, that will not amount to a redundancy situation.

The EAT also considered the three-stage test in *Hachette Filipacchi UK Ltd v Johnson* (UKEAT/0452/05). The employee had moved to a new position within the company as a project director, 'revitalising' a magazine published by the company. Her old job was filled. Subsequently, the company decided to end production of the magazine in question and the employee was dismissed. The EAT agreed with the employment tribunal that she had been dismissed by reason of redundancy applying the three-stage test: she had been dismissed; the employer's requirements for a project director had ceased; and her dismissal had been caused wholly or mainly by that state of affairs.

In *Packman t/a Packman Lucas Associates v Fauchon* [2012] IRLR 721, the EAT confirmed that if the amount of work is reduced then the definition of redundancy can be satisfied, even if the headcount of employees is not reduced. The EAT said:

> A redundancy situation under section 139(1)(b) either exists or it does not. It is open to an employer to organise its affairs so that its requirement for employees to carry out particular work diminishes. If that occurs, the motive of the employer is irrelevant to the question of whether the redundancy situation exists.

4.2.3.3 'Bumping'

'Bumping' occurs where employee A's job disappears. However, employee A is moved to do employee B's job and it is B who is dismissed. In *W Gimber & Sons Ltd v Spurrett* (1967) 2 ITR 308, it was held that the dismissal of B was by reason of redundancy within what is now s 139(1)(b) of the ERA 1996. Work of 'a particular kind', ie A's work, has ceased.

In *Church v West Lancashire NHS Trust* [1998] IRLR 4, the EAT decided it was not bound by *Gimber v Spurrett* and held that dismissal of a 'bumped' employee was not by reason of redundancy. The EAT held that 'work of a particular kind' within ERA 1996, s 139(1)(b) meant work of a particular kind that the *dismissed* employee was employed to do. However, the EAT stated in *Safeway Stores v Burrell* [1997] IRLR 200 that bumping dismissals may be dismissals by reason of redundancy, and the House of Lords confirmed in *Murray and Another v Foyle Meats Ltd* [1999] IRLR 562 that the wording of s 139(1)(b) can include 'bumping' redundancies. Thus, although the House of Lords did not expressly overrule *Church*, it should not be followed in future 'bumping' cases.

'Bumping' may also be relevant to the issue of whether a dismissal by reason of redundancy is fair or unfair (see **5.3**).

4.3 PRESUMPTION OF REDUNDANCY

In many cases there will be no dispute as to whether or not the employee is redundant. However, if the employer will not accept the claim and the employee refers the matter to an employment tribunal, there is a presumption that the dismissal was by reason of redundancy (ERA 1996, s 163(2)). The presumption applies only in the case of a claim for a redundancy payment and may be rebutted by the employer showing that the reason for the dismissal was not redundancy but was for another reason, such as misconduct.

4.4 OFFERS OF RE-EMPLOYMENT

A redundancy payment is intended to compensate the employee for loss of his job with that employer. Therefore, if the employee is re-employed by his employer, or by an associated employer, he does not need compensation and may not be entitled to a redundancy payment.

Section 141 of the ERA 1996 therefore provides that if the employee is offered a job, he may lose his entitlement to a redundancy payment.

4.4.1 Offers to renew or re-engage

An offer to renew is the offer of the employee's old job back where, for example, the employer secures a new customer and finds that work is beginning to increase again.

An offer of re-engagement involves an offer of a different job with the same or an associated employer.

Even if dismissed by reason of redundancy, an employee will lose his entitlement to a redundancy payment if he unreasonably refuses an offer of suitable alternative employment made in accordance with the provisions of s 141 of the ERA 1996.

4.4.1.1   The offer

By s 141(2)–(4) of the ERA 1996, an employee is not entitled to a redundancy payment if he unreasonably refuses an offer, whether oral or written:

(a)   made by his employer or an associated employer; and

(b)   made before the contract of employment comes to an end;

(c)   to re-employ him in the same or some other suitable employment;

(d)   provided that the renewal or re-engagement is to take effect within four weeks of the end of the original contract.

The employer's offer must comply with all the above requirements, otherwise the employee will be entitled to a redundancy payment, even if he unreasonably refuses it.

4.4.1.2   Acceptance of the offer

If the employee accepts an offer made in accordance with the provisions set out above, the employee is treated as though he had not been dismissed. Thus his continuity of employment is not broken but, as there is deemed to have been no dismissal, there is no entitlement to a redundancy payment. This will be the case whether or not the alternative employment was 'suitable'.

4.4.1.3   Rejection of the offer

If the employee rejects the offer then the question of whether or not he is entitled to a redundancy payment turns on two issues:

(a)   suitability of the alternative offered; and

(b)   the reasonableness of the employee's refusal.

If the alternative offered was unsuitable, the employee will be entitled to a redundancy payment without more analysis. However, if the alternative is suitable, then the second issue must be considered. If the employee has unreasonably refused suitable alternative employment, the right to the redundancy payment is lost.

(a)   The alternative employment has to be suitable for the particular employee and is ultimately a question for the employment tribunal to decide using an objective test. The key factors are pay, nature of duties, status, hours and place. The question is whether the new job is substantially equivalent to the old job. In *Commission for Healthcare Audit and Inspection v Ward* (UKEAT/0579/07), the EAT held that a tribunal is entitled to have regard to the degree of suitability of a job when deciding if a refusal is reasonable. So, if a new job offer is overwhelmingly suitable, it may be easier for the employer to show that a refusal was unreasonable than if suitability is less obvious.

(b)   When looking at the reasonableness of a refusal, a subjective test is used, taking into account personal circumstances, for example domestic circumstances.

Even if a job is deemed suitable, a particular employee may still be reasonable to refuse it. In *Redman v Devon PCT* [2013] EWCA Civ 1110, the Court of Appeal confirmed that the reasonableness or otherwise of an employee's refusal depends on factors personal to the employee and the test is therefore subjective. The case was remitted to the tribunal for reconsideration of whether the employee's refusal to work in a hospital, having worked in the community for 30 years, was reasonable. The EAT held in *Dunne v Colin & Avril Ltd* (UKEAT/0293/16) that an employee can rely at tribunal stage on a reason for refusal that he or she has not raised expressly with the employer when refusing the offer.

4.4.1.4   Trial period

It may be difficult for the employee to decide whether or not the alternative employment offered is suitable. The employer may also have doubts as to the employee's suitability for the new job. To assist both parties to decide whether the new employment is suitable, s 138 of the ERA 1996 provides that there may be a 'trial period' of four weeks (calendar weeks), beginning with the date on which the employee starts work under the new contract.

In *Optical Express Ltd v Williams* [2007] IRLR 936, the claimant was a manager in charge of a dental clinic. The dental clinic closed and a redundancy situation arose. The claimant was offered an alternative position as manager of an optical store. Whilst she did not consider the post suitable, she accepted a four-week trial period, in accordance with the provisions of s 138 of the ERA 1996. The claimant gave notice to terminate the contract two weeks after the four-week trial period had expired. An employment tribunal upheld her claim for a redundancy payment and stated she had a 'common law' reasonable period in addition to the statutory trial period because this was a constructive dismissal case (her employers were in breach of the implied term of trust and confidence by imposing on her a new contract which was clearly unsuitable). The EAT allowed the appeal and held that where there is an offer and acceptance of a new contract of employment by reference to the four-week trial period in s 138, the claimant could not claim a redundancy payment unless within the trial period she exercised the rights given by s 138 to terminate the contract. It is now clear that where an acceptance of alternative employment is made under the statutory trial period scheme, the employee must give notice of termination within the 4-week statutory trial period in order to receive a redundancy payment.

If either the employer or the employee terminates the contract during the statutory trial period for a reason connected with the change, the original dismissal by reason of redundancy will revive. Whether or not the employee is then entitled to a redundancy payment still turns on whether the alternative employment offered was suitable. However, there will now be evidence available from the trial period.

(a)   There is no 'trial period' if there is no change in the terms of employment, ie if the only change is in the identity of the employer.

(b)   If the new employment involves retraining, the parties may agree, before the employee starts work under the new contract, to extend the trial period. The agreement must specify the date on which the extended period ends.

The EAT considered when the period starts in *East London NHS Trust v O'Connor* (UKEAT/0113/19).

4.5   CHANGE OF EMPLOYER

4.5.1   Death, etc, of employer

Exceptionally, by s 136(5) of the ERA 1996, where any act by or affecting an employer terminates the contract of employment by operation of law, such termination takes effect as termination by the employer. The effect of this is that if a business closes down by virtue of the death of the employer or dissolution of a partnership then, although at common law the contract may be frustrated, it will be treated as a dismissal for the purposes of redundancy payments. Thus, an eligible employee will, if the business ceases or his job comes to an end, be entitled to a redundancy payment.

This provision may not apply if the employee continues in his job. If he is employed by the personal representatives on the death of an employer, or if there is effectively only a change in partners despite a dissolution of the partnership, the employee will not be dismissed and there will be continuity of employment (see **3.5.5**).

4.5.2   Associated employer

If an employee is re-employed by an associated employer, this will be a re-engagement within **4.4.1**. See **3.5.5** for the definition of associated employer.

4.5.3 Transfer of undertakings

A business closure should be distinguished from a transfer of the business to a new employer. In the latter situation the employees will usually be transferred to the new employer without being dismissed, so the employee will not be entitled to a redundancy payment. This is by virtue of the Transfer of Undertakings (Protection of Employment) Regulations 2006 (see **Chapter** 7).

4.6 COMPUTATION OF THE STATUTORY REDUNDANCY PAYMENT

A redundancy payment is computed by applying a formula based on an age factor, length of service and a 'week's pay' (ERA 1996, s 162). It is not based on loss suffered.

(a)   Working *back* from the date of termination of employment, the employee is entitled to:
  (i)   one-and-a-half weeks' *gross* pay for each complete year of continuous employment in which the employee was 41 or over;
  (ii) one week's *gross* pay for each earlier year in which the employee was 22 or over (but under 41);
  (iii) half a week's *gross* pay for each earlier year.

(b)   The total number of years to be taken into account is subject to a maximum of 20.

(c)   A 'week's pay' is calculated in accordance with ERA 1996, s 221. In the majority of cases where there is a normal weekly wage, a week's pay would be the *gross* basic pay to which the employee was entitled in the week ending with the dismissal, subject to a statutory maximum of £571 (at 6 April 2022). The current maximum statutory redundancy payment is £17,130 (from 6 April 2022).

EXAMPLE 1

Doris is aged 63 when dismissed in November 2022 by reason of redundancy. Her normal retiring age is 65. She has been continuously employed for 35 years and her gross basic week's pay in her last week was £575.

Her redundancy payment will be:

1½ × 20 (years) × £571 = £17,130.

This is the maximum possible redundancy payment.

The number of years is 20, not 35, as this is the maximum.

The age factor is 1½ as all years that count are aged 41 or over – taking the most 'valuable' year first, ie working back from the date of dismissal.

The 'week's pay' is the maximum of £571, not the £575 actually earned.

EXAMPLE 2

Ron is aged 43 when dismissed by reason of redundancy in November 2022. He has been continuously employed for just over 6 years and his gross basic week's pay in his last week was £580. The statutory cap on a week's pay will be applied.

His redundancy payment will be:

1½ × 2 years × £571 (= £1,713) (ie for ages 42 and 41)

plus 1 × 4 years × £571 (= £2,284) (ie for ages 40, 39, 38, 37) giving a total of £3,997.

The age factor is 1½ for the 2 complete years worked after the 41st birthday and 1 for the other 4 years.

EXAMPLE 3

Jack is aged 24 when dismissed by reason of redundancy in November 2022. He has been continually employed for 8 years and his gross basic week's pay in his last week was £400.

His redundancy payment will be:

1 × 2 × £400 (= £800) (ie for ages 23 and 22)

½ × 6 × £400 (= £1,200) (ie for ages 21, 20, 19, 18, 17, 16)

giving a total of £2,000.

The age factor is 1 for 2 complete years worked after the 22nd birthday and ½ for the 6 years between 18 and 21.

A redundancy payment is compensation for loss of employment and not deferred pay (see *Mairs v Haughey* [1994] 1 AC 303) so it is not taxable as income unless it exceeds the £30,000 tax-free allowance under s 40 of the ITEPA 2003.

Note: The Business Link website <http://www.businesslink.gov.uk> features an interactive redundancy payment calculator. Select Employment and Skills; Redundancy and Dismissal; Calculate the statutory redundancy pay due to your employee. See also <calculatemyredundancy.com>.

4.7 ENFORCEMENT

4.7.1 Employer's liability

The person primarily liable to pay a redundancy payment is the employer. In the majority of cases the employer will simply make the payment without dispute. When the employer makes a statutory redundancy payment, he must give the employee a written statement of how the amount has been calculated (ERA 1996, s 165). The employee can then check its accuracy.

4.7.2 Reference to employment tribunal

If the employer fails to make a payment or there is a dispute about the amount, the employee may refer the matter to an employment tribunal. There is a time limit which must be observed.

By s 164 of the ERA 1996, an employee is not entitled to a redundancy payment unless, within six months of the dismissal:

(a)   a payment is agreed and made; or

(b)   he has given the employer written notice of the claim; or

(c)   a question as to the right to, or amount of, the payment has been referred to an employment tribunal; or

(d)   a complaint of unfair dismissal has been presented to the employment tribunal.

An employment tribunal may, if it considers it just and equitable that the employee should receive a redundancy payment, extend the time-limit to 12 months from dismissal, but employees should regard the six months' time-limit as strict.

It is not necessary to refer the matter to an employment tribunal within six months of dismissal, provided written notice of the claim has been given to the employer within that time.

4.7.3 Employer's insolvency

Where an employee is entitled to a statutory redundancy payment from his employer, but the employer is declared legally insolvent and the redundancy payment remains unpaid, the employee may apply for payment out of the National Insurance Fund to the Redundancy Payment Office (RPO) using Form RP1 (available at <http://www.insolvency.gov.uk>). The RPO, if satisfied that the employee is entitled to the payment, will make the payment out of the Fund (ERA 1996, s 166). The RPO then has a statutory right to recover the amount of the payment from the employer. The employee must have claimed the payment from his employer within the relevant time-limit, and the payment must have been owed when the employer became insolvent (see *Secretary of State for Business, Innovation & Skills v Pengelly & Another* (UKEAT/0287/12 & 0312/12) (see **4.7.2**).

4.8   CONSULTATION

4.8.1   Duty to consult representatives

4.8.1.1   The duty to consult under TULR(C)A 1992, s 188

What follows is a very brief introduction to the collective provisions, which are set out in the Trade Union and Labour Relations (Consolidation) Act 1992 (TULR(C)A 1992). In April 2014, Acas published revised Guidance entitled *How to manage collective redundancies*. The Guidance is intended to make it easier for employers to understand the law on collective redundancies. It includes a useful flow chart and case studies, as well as a checklist and sample selection matrix.

Where an employer is proposing to dismiss as redundant 20 or more employees at one establishment (but see below as to what is meant by 'establishment' and whether that limitation is lawful) within a period of 90 days or less, he should consult the 'appropriate representatives' (representative of any independent trade union which is recognised, or elected employee representatives) of any employees who may be affected by the proposed dismissals or measures taken in connection with the dismissals, unless there are special circumstances that mean it is not reasonably practicable to consult (see *GMB and Amicus v Beloit Walmsley Ltd (in administration)* [2004] IRLR 18) (TULR(C)A 1992, s 188, as amended). In *Hardy v Tourism South East* [2005] IRLR 242, the EAT confirmed that the s 188 duty to consult applies even when the employer intends to offer alternative employment to the majority of employees, thereby bringing the number actively dismissed below 20. The employer must also inform the Secretary of State (Form HR1). Failure to do so is a criminal offence.

Regulation 3 of the Collective Redundancies and Transfer of Undertakings (Protection of Employment) (Amendment) Regulations 2014 (SI 2014/16), inserted new ss 198A and 198B into TULR(C)A 1992. These provide that the statutory obligation to consult over collective redundancies may be discharged by a prospective employer where the redundancy dismissals are consequent on a TUPE transfer (see **Chapter 7**). The Government considered that it made practical sense to allow a transferee to consult affected employees before a transfer, about redundancies that might occur after the transfer, even though at that stage they were still employees of the transferor.

Redundancy has a different meaning, for the purposes of this consultation exercise, from the s 139 definition set out in **4.2** above. Here, redundancy is defined as a 'dismissal for a reason not related to the individual concerned or for a number of reasons all of which are not so related'. This definition will also, therefore, include a reorganisation where an employer gives notice to end existing terms and offer new terms of employment, and is therefore wider than the s 139 definition.

Fixed-term employees are excluded from the scope of collective redundancy consulation where their fixed-term contract will expire on an agreed date within the redundancy period.

Under UK law, officers in the police service are also excluded from the collective consultation rights. However, in *Vining v Wandsworth LBC* [2017] EWCA Civ 1092, the Court of Appeal ruled that this exclusion infringed their right to association under Article 11 of the ECHR.

Consultation must begin in good time. In particular, if 100 or more employees are to be dismissed at one establishment within a 90-day period, the employer must consult at least 45 days before the first dismissal is to take effect; otherwise, for at least 20 but fewer than 100 employees, he must consult at least 30 days before the first dismissal takes effect. Employers should ensure that the consultation period has ended before giving notice of dismissal to those employees who are to be dismissed by reason of redundancy (see *Junk v Kuhnel* [2005] IRLR 310 and *Leicestershire County Council v Unison* [2005] IRLR 920). Even if there are good reasons for shortening the 30-day consultation period, the obligation to consult remains (see *Shanahan Engineering v Unite* (UKEAT/0411/09)).

The obligation to consult includes consulting about ways of avoiding dismissals, reducing the numbers of employees to be dismissed and mitigating the consequences of those dismissals. In *UK Coal Mining Ltd v National Union of Mineworkers (Northumberland Area)* (UKEAT/0397/06), the EAT held that the duty to consult includes consultation over the business reason(s) for a closure. The decision overturned 15 years of established authority. The Court of Appeal referred the matter to the ECJ in *USA v Nolan* [2010] EWCA Civ 1223. The issue arose as to whether collective consultation should have started when the US Government was proposing to close a UK army base in Hampshire, so that redundancies might be said to be foreseeable or inevitable, or did it only have to consult after the decision to close had been taken? The ECJ held (*USA v Nolan* (Case C-583/10)) that it had no jurisdiction to respond to the reference because the Collective Redundancies Directive (98/59/EC) excludes employees of public administrative bodies. In October 2015, the Supreme Court handed down its judgment in *USA v Nolan*. However, it did not deal with the consultation issue, which awaits prior determination by the Court of Appeal. The Supreme Court determined that the relevant UK legislation did apply to the base in the UK and so the US Government was under a duty to consult; even if the decision to dismiss was made in Washington, the dismissals related to the base in the UK. Further, as the US had not invoked state immunity early in the proceedings, it was now prevented from relying on it. In the meantime, employers would be advised to follow *UK Coal Mining*.

Employers who recognise a trade union *must* consult with representatives of that trade union; they cannot choose to consult with elected employee representatives. If there is no recognised trade union, the employer must arrange for employee representatives to be elected and *must* consult with them.

The employer must disclose the reasons for the redundancies, numbers and descriptions of the employees to be made redundant and the method of selection. The consultation must consider the possibility of avoiding or reducing the redundancies and mitigating their effects.

The Court of Appeal stated in *Susie Radin Ltd v GMB and Others* [2004] IRLR 400 that the obligation set out in s 188 placed an 'absolute obligation on the employer to consult, and to consult meaningfully'. This means that the employer must disclose the reasons for the redundancies, the number and description of employees to be made redundant, and the method of selection. See also *Kelly and Another v The Helsey Group* [2013] IRLR 515.

What amounts to an 'establishment' is a fact-sensitive issue. The Acas Guidance notes that the Court of Justice of the European Union (CJEU) indicated that 'establishment' means 'depending on the circumstances, the unit to which the workers made redundant are assigned to carry out their duties'. The Guidance sets out some useful questions that might be asked in order to clarify what amounts to an 'establishment' for these purposes:

- Is it a distinct entity?
- Does it have a degree of permanence and stability?
- Does it have the ability to carry out the tasks it has been assigned?
- Does it have a workplace, technical means and organisational structure to carry out work assigned?

The Guidance suggests that an establishment can be made up of more than one place, but distinct entities do not need to have geographical separation, legal, economic, financial, administrative, technological or managerial autonomy or independence.

In *USDAW v WW Realisation 1 Ltd* (UKEAT/0548/12), the EAT struck out the words 'at any one establishment' from the definition in s 188 of TULR(C)A 1992, on the basis that it was an incorrect transposition of the Collective Redundancies Directive (98/59/EC). The case was based around the closure of a number of Woolworths and Ethel Austin stores. In both instances, administrators argued that each store was a separate establishment, and so sought to limit the impact of the obligation to consult on a collective basis: a large number of employees were employed at stores with fewer than 20 employees (3,233 Woolworths employees out of a total of 4,400, and 720 Ethel Austin employees out of a total workforce of 1,210). No consultation was undertaken (not uncommon in insolvencies), but only those employees at larger establishments would be entitled to a protective award (see **4.8.1.2** below). The employment tribunal found that 'establishment' meant each individual shop, so while staff at shops with 20 or more staff were entitled to a protective award, staff at the smaller stores were not. The EAT reviewed the wording of the Collective Redundancies Directive and held that the UK wording did not uphold the Directive's core objective of protecting workers' rights. This meant that where it was proposed to dismiss 20 or more employees, it did not matter if they were located at different stores. The Secretary of State appealed the EAT judgment. The Court of Appeal decided to refer the case to the ECJ, to clarify whether the 20 or more redundancies have to be at the same establishment, and also whether the relevant provisions of the Directive have direct effect.

In April 2015, the ECJ, following the Advocate General's Opinion in February, ruled that the definition of 'establishment' in s 188 of the TULR(C)A 1992 does comply with the EU Collective Redundancies Directive, and employers are not therefore required to aggregate dismissals across all establishments. The ECJ confirmed that the Directive does allow establishments to be treated separately for the purposes of the 20-employee threshold for collective consultation. This effectively overrules the finding of the EAT, and means that employers with multiple sites can rely on the position as it was before the EAT's ruling and approach any future consultation exercises over collective redundancies and dismissals on a more local basis. The ECJ was concerned to apply a consistent approach, ruling that 'establishment' must be given the same meaning throughout the EU (in contrast to the earlier Opinion of the Advocate General, who thought that it was up to the national courts to reach a national definition). According to the ECJ, 'establishment' means 'the entity to which the workers are assigned to carry out their duties'. The Advocate General talked in terms of 'local employment unit'. It is not essential that the unit in question is endowed with a management that can independently effect collective redundancies. An establishment may consist of a distinct entity having a certain degree of permanence and stability, which is assigned to perform given tasks and has a workforce, technical means and organisational structure allowing for that. The entity may be a part of an undertaking and does not need to have autonomy – whether legal, economic, administrative or technological – in order to be an 'establishment'. In light of these factors, the ECJ concluded that where an undertaking comprises several entities meeting the criteria for 'establishment', it is the entity to which the workers made redundant are assigned to carry out their duties that constitutes the 'establishment' for collective consultation purposes. The ECJ said that it is up to the UK courts to decide if each Woolworth store was an 'establishment'. Determining the unit will be normally be a question of fact for a tribunal. The ECJ has formally referred the 'Woolworths' case back to the Court of Appeal for it to decide whether, in light of the clarification now given, the employment tribunal was correct in finding that the stores to which the employees made redundant were assigned were separate 'establishments'. The ECJ has confirmed the approach it took in the 'Woolworths' case in two further decisions: *Lyttle v Bluebird UK Bidco2* (Case C-182/13) and *Rabal Canas v Nexea Gestation Documental* (Case C-392/13).

The Court of Appeal held in *Seahorse Marine Ltd v Nautilus International* [2018] EWCA Civ 2789, where the business was the supply of labour to ships, that each ship (not all ships) was the 'establishment' (which is in line with the 'Woolworths' case).

Note that the Collective Redundancies Directive talks about 'workers' being 'employed'. In *Balkaya v Kiesel Abbruch- und Recycling Technik GmbH* (Case C-229/14), the ECJ held that 'worker' could include a director and an unpaid trainee when deciding whether an obligation to consult arose. The Court stated that the concept of worker in Article 1(1)(a) of the Directive could not be defined by reference to the legislation of the Member States but had to be given an autonomous and independent meaning. Otherwise, the methods for calculation of the thresholds would be within the discretion of the Member States, which would allow the latter to alter the scope of the Directive and thus to deprive it of its full effect.

4.8.1.2   Protective award

If the employer fails to consult in accordance with the TULR(C)A 1992 provisions, the trade union, elected employee representatives or affected employees may present a complaint to an employment tribunal. If the complaint is well founded, the tribunal must make a declaration to that effect and may make a 'protective award' of wages per employee for such 'protected period' as the tribunal considers just and equitable. A protective award is an award of pay to the employees affected by the failure to consult properly.

A protective award can be awarded where more than 20 employees are made redundant from one location within specific timeframes. The statutory requirement is that where 20–100 employees are at risk of redundancy, the employer must consult at least 30 days prior to the redundancies taking effect. Where over 100 employees are concerned, the consultation period must start 90 days prior to the redundancies taking effect. The protective award for failure to consult is fixed at a maximum of 90 days' actual pay per individual employee. Where the employer is insolvent, the protective award is one of the payments guaranteed by the Secretary of State under the Employment Rights Act 1996.

The maximum 'protected period' is 90 days. In *TGWU v Morgan Platts Ltd* (UKEAT/0646/02) the EAT ruled that the starting point for tribunals in calculating protective awards should be the maximum period. From there the tribunal should then consider whether there are reasons for reducing the amount. On the facts of the case there were not, as the company had failed to consult at all. Once a protective award is made, relevant employees are entitled to one week's gross pay for each week of the 'protected period'. The award is not capped. Where there is a total failure to consult and no 'special circumstances' (see below), the protective award should be the maximum 90 days' pay per employee (see *Hutchins v Permacell Finesse Ltd (in administration)* (UKEAT/0350/07)).

For many years the courts treated protective awards as compensatory in nature (see, for example, *Spillers-French (Holdings) Ltd v USDAW* [1980] ICR 31), but in *Susie Radin Ltd v GMB* [2004] IRLR 400 the Court of Appeal held that the purpose of the protective award was to punish the employer and should act as an effective sanction and deterrent. The Court held that the starting point is the maximum 90 days, which should be reduced only where there are mitigating circumstances.

It is a defence to a claim for a protective award for the employer to show that '... there [were] special circumstances which render[ed] it not reasonably practicable for the employer to comply with [the duty to consult]' (TULR(C)A 1992, s 188(7)). In *Clarks of Hove Ltd v The Bakers' Union* [1978] IRLR 366, the Court of Appeal held that 'special circumstances' had to be something out of the ordinary and uncommon, such as a sudden disaster, not insolvency. In *Keeping Kids Company v Smith & Others* (UKEAT 0057/17), the EAT upheld a claim for protective awards from various employees for KKC's failure to inform and consult as required. On 12 June, KKC applied for a government grant and included a restructuring plan which envisaged half of its posts being deleted but with no specific posts being identified. On 29 July, the government offered the extra funding sought. On 30 July, it became public knowledge that the police were investigating certain safeguarding issues. On 3 August, the government told KKC that the grant was withdrawn and demanded repayment. On 5 August, KKC closed with all the employees being dismissed. Although KKC had planned to consult on the redundancies, the withdrawal of funding meant that it could no longer do so. The claimants, who numbered over 140, believed that they were entitled to their 90 days' gross pay protective awards and initiated tribunal claims, which the tribunal upheld. The EAT held that the tribunal was entitled to find that, as of 12 June, there was a 'proposal to dismiss' that might affect all of KKC's staff, not simply those specifically identified. This was a clear, albeit provisional, intention to dismiss for redundancy, and the potential impact this might have was on all staff. The EAT rejected KKC's argument that it did not have enough information to comply with its obligations to engage in 'meaningful consultation' until it had heard back from the government about its grant application. The EAT upheld the tribunal's decision that the 'special circumstances' defence did not apply on these facts. The sudden and unexpected disaster of the withdrawal of the government's grant, which derailed its plans, was not sufficient for the defence to apply. The EAT did allow one aspect of KKC's appeal, overturning the tribunal's award of the full 90 days' protective award. Although the events of 30 July did not amount to a 'special circumstances' defence, the EAT said they were relevant to the assessment of the appropriate award – and the tribunal had failed to recognise this. It will be interesting to see if the Covid-19 pandemic results in any claims for protective awards, and if so whether any employers will try to argue for the application of the 'special circumstances' defence.

In *Carillion Services Ltd (In Compulsory Liquidation) and Others v Benson and Others* (UKEAT/0026/21/BA), the EAT upheld the tribunal's decision that there were no special circumstances on the facts. Compulsory liquidation was not such a circumstance in this case.

Note that if an employee also brings and wins an unfair dismissal claim, the amount of the protective award will be deducted from that award.

4.8.2 Information and Consultation Regulations 2004

Directive 2002/14 gives employees in the covered undertakings a right to be informed about the undertaking's economic situation, informed and consulted about employment prospects, and informed and consulted with a view to reaching agreement about decisions likely to lead to substantial changes in work organisation or contractual relations, including, but not limited to, collective redundancies and transfers (see **Chapter 7**).

The Information and Consultation of Employees Regulations 2004 (SI 2004/3426) (ICE Regulations) apply to undertakings employing 50 or more employees. They require employers to set up information and consultation arrangements to ensure that employees are consulted on a wide range of matters. However, the obligations are triggered only on a valid request from at least 10% of employees.

The detail of the ICE Regulations is beyond the scope of this book, but note that where there is an overlap between the duty under the ICE Regulations and the duty to consult under s 188 (**4.8.1.1** above), the ICE obligations cease to apply once the employer informs the representatives in writing that he will comply with his s 188 duty. BIS has produced a guide for explaining the requirements to inform and consult employees, which is available on its website.

The EAT is empowered to award penalties of up to £75,000 for breaches of the ICE Regulations. In *Amicus v Macmillan Publishers Ltd* (UKEAT/0185/07), Macmillan were fined £55,000 for failing to comply with the Regulations. This was the first penalty so awarded. The EAT took into account the following factors in imposing the penalty:

(a)   the fact that the legislation had clearly been ignored;

(b)   Macmillan had committed other breaches of the legislation, including a failure to provide information;

(c)   Macmillan had unacceptably 'dragged its feet' in dealing with the employee request;

(d)   Macmillan had not adequately explained its failure to comply.

The EAT concluded that a penalty of £55,000 was appropriate as it would deter other employers from adopting a similarly 'cavalier' attitude to their obligations, but the breach in this case was not sufficiently grave to warrant the maximum penalty. The EAT in its decision commented that employers must recognise the importance of the rights under the ICE Regulations and that the provisions must be complied with.

See also **Chapter** 7, at **7.7**, which deals with the (similar but not identical) collective consultation requirements under the 2006 TUPE Regulations.

4.8.3 Duty to notify Secretary of State

Where 20 or more redundancies are proposed there is a duty to notify the Secretary of State of the proposals. Notification is made on form HR1 (available at <http://www.insolvency.gov.uk>).

4.8.4 Unfair dismissal

Failure to consult with individual employees about proposed redundancies can render the dismissals unfair (see **5.4.2.3**). Redundant employees in such circumstances may be able to bring claims for a redundancy payment and unfair dismissal.

4.9 CASE STUDY: REDUNDANCY PAYMENT, UNPAID NOTICE AND HOLIDAY PAY

Facts

(1)   R was an independent working men's club. It was not for profit and was registered under the Industrial and Provident Societies Act (IPSA) 1965 with the Financial Services Authority. Its members and employees were governed by the rules of the Club. The premises from which the Club operated were leased to the Club under a full maintenance and repairing lease.

(2)   C was employed by R as a bar steward/cleaner. She started work with R in September 2004. She continued to work for R until her dismissal on 28 April 2021. Over that period, she worked approximately 40 hours a week every week, apart from when she took holidays. She was paid £10.00 an hour and took home a net weekly wage of £320 (gross £400).

(3)   On or around 28 April 2021, C was informed by a member of R's committee that the Club was in severe financial difficulties and was being wound up. The committee member gave C 48 hours' notice. She was paid one week's notice. She was informed that there was no money to pay her any redundancy payment or any other outstanding monies due to her, such as in respect of untaken but accrued holiday. A subsequent letter received by C indicated that there had been mismanagement at R for several years, and that because of the parlous financial state of R, it had been shut down. Rent had not been paid for several months and various suppliers were owed money. The premises were being advertised for sale. It did not appear that any steps had been taken with regard to liquidating R. All the committee members had resigned.

(4)   Under the provisions of the IPSA 1965, Ch 12, s 57, no individual officer, member or servant is personally liable for any of the debts of the Club. The situation therefore remains somewhat in limbo as far as the legal status of R is concerned. On the face of it, it appears to be insolvent.

(5)   At the time of the termination of her employment, C, who was aged 57 as at the date of her dismissal, had achieved some 13 years' continuous employment. She was disappointed that none of the committee members had expressed any concerns about her situation and appeared to feel no moral responsibility towards her predicament, notwithstanding that they appeared to have been aware of the Club's difficulties for some time.

Claims

(6)   In her ET1, C brings claims of unpaid notice, breach of contact, unpaid wages and unpaid holiday pay. She also seeks a redundancy payment. She did not complain about unfair dismissal.

Evidence

(7)   C appeared before the Employment Judge (sitting alone) and gave evidence. She produced various items of paperwork, including letters from the Insolvency Service relating to her claim. She also had with her the originals of her pay slips. Although a committee member had submitted a brief ET3/Response Form, which said that R had been wound up, no one appeared for R at the hearing.

Issues

(8)   Although C had a long service record with R, she had not included a claim for unfair dismissal in her ET1. This omission was discussed at a Case Management Discussion (CMD). The notes of this recorded that C said she had not realised she could bring such a claim. By the time the CMD took place, it was over four and half months since the termination of C's contract. The Employment Judge found as a preliminary issue that any claim for unfair dismissal would amount to a new claim, that it was not implicit from the matters set out in the ET1, that it was out of time and that there was nothing to suggest that it was not reasonably practicable for the claim to have been made within the time limit, ignorance of the law per se being no defence (see **Chapter 8**).

(9)   On that basis, the Tribunal had to determine the following matters:

   (a)   Was C an employee of R?

   (b)   Was C entitled to a redundancy payment; and if so, to how much?

   (c)   Had C been paid her proper notice?

   (d)   Had C been paid the holiday pay due on the termination of her employment?

Findings

(10)   On the basis of the evidence before it, the Employment Judge found as follows:

   (a)   C was an employee of R. Although she had no written contract, this was not a difficult issue on the facts. C had worked regularly for R for nearly 14 years. There was no issue that she expected to work each week and expected to be paid for her work. She gave evidence about the hours she worked, from whom she took instructions, that the materials she used, for example, to clean were all provided by R, that she had had her PAYE and National Insurance deducted from her wages, and that she had been paid for her holidays. She produced her wage slips to support this.

   (b)   C was entitled to a redundancy payment, as the reason for her dismissal was clearly a reason that fell within the definition in s 139 of the ERA 1996, namely, the closure of the business. C had 13 years' completed service at the date of her dismissal; as she was aged 41 and over for the duration of her employment with R, she was entitled to one and a half week's gross pay for each completed year of continuous service (ERA 1996, ss 162 and 221): 13 x 1.5 x £400 = £7,800. R was ordered to pay to C the sum of £6,240 in respect of a redundancy payment.

   (c)   R was in breach of C's contract of employment by failing to give her proper notice or to pay her due notice entitlement. Although R paid C one week's notice, under s 86 of the ERA 1996, the statutory minimum period of notice required to be given to an employee with 12 years' plus service is 12 weeks' notice. C is therefore entitled to be paid for 11 weeks' notice at her net weekly wage (£320) per week: 11 x £320 = £3,520. R is ordered to pay damages to C in the sum of £3,520 (net).

(d)   C's complaint that R had failed to pay holiday pay due on the termination of the employment was well founded. Regulation 14 of the Working Time Regulations allows an employee to be paid in lieu of any accrued but untaken holiday as at the date of dismissal. As at the date of her dismissal, C had 15 days' holiday accrued and due. C is therefore due payment in respect of 15 days' holiday, calculated on the basis of an eight-hour working day and a net weekly wage of £320 (8 hours x £8.00 (net)) = £64.00 per day rate x 15 = £960 (net). R is ordered to pay to C the sum of £960 (net).

Note: Given that R has been wound up/appears to be insolvent, and that there are no apparent assets, C is unlikely to be able to get any money back from R. In this sort of case, C would be able to make a claim from the National Insurance Fund, by completing Form RP1, in respect of any redundancy pay, unpaid wages (up to a maximum of eight weeks), holiday pay (up to a maximum of six weeks), notice pay (one week after one calendar month's service, rising to one week per year of service up to a maximum of 12 weeks, but new earnings will be taken into account), and any basic award for unfair dismissal. To qualify for a redundancy payment, C will need to show that she has been made redundant, has worked continuously for her employer for two years or more, and that she either made a written claim to her employer for her redundancy payment, or made a complaint to an employment tribunal, within six months of her dismissal. She will be able to attach the Tribunal's decision as evidence of these matters. There is a current limit of £544 (at April 2021) a week on the amount C can claim for her weekly pay.

4.10   FURTHER READING

Textbooks covering redundancy include:

Selwyn's Law of Employment, 22nd edn (OUP, 2022).

See also:

Harvey, *Industrial Relations and Employment Law* (LexisNexis), Div E.

Lewis, *Employment Law – an adviser's handbook*, 14th edn (LAG, 2022).

Blackstone's Employment Law Practice, 10th edn (OUP, 2019).

McMullen, *Redundancy: Law and Practice*, 4th edn (OUP, 2021).

Acas has produced a helpful redundancy process map for employers, which is available at <https://company-180825.frontify.com/d/9XEi1YzDsXxS/n-a#/employers-process-maps/acas-resources-redundancy-process-map>.

SUMMARY

This chapter has set out the mechanisms for making a claim for a redundancy payment. A redundancy payment is in the nature of a reward for past services. Where there is a dispute over the right to receive a redundancy payment or over the amount due, an employment tribunal has jurisdiction to determine the matter (**4.3**). Employees must be eligible to bring a claim. They must have at least two years' continuous service and there must also be a dismissal by reason of redundancy (**3.4**).

The definition of 'redundancy' is contained in s 139(1) of the ERA 1996. Redundancy occurs in three main situations: job redundancy (ie where the business closes down – ERA 1996, s 139(1)(a)(i)); place of work redundancy (ie where there is a cessation or reduction in work *at the place* where the employee works – ERA 1996, s 139(1)(a)(ii)); and employee redundancy (ie there is a reduction in the requirement for employees to do work of a particular kind – ERA 1996, s 139(1)(b)) (**4.2**).

An eligible employee, dismissed by reason of redundancy, will be entitled, at a minimum, to a statutory redundancy payment from his employer (ERA 1996, s 163). The contract of employment may provide for more generous payments.

If the employee is offered a suitable alternative job by his employer, which he unreasonably refuses, he may lose his entitlement to a redundancy payment (ERA 1996, s 141). It is possible to have a trial period of four weeks in order to determine whether the job is suitable (ERA 1996, s 138) (**4.4**). If a business is sold as a going concern, so that employees are not dismissed, they may not be entitled to a redundancy payment (see **Chapter 7** on the transfer of undertakings).

A redundancy payment is calculated by applying a formula based on age, length of service and 'a week's pay' (ERA 1996, s 162) (**4.6**).

Where an employee is dismissed by reason of redundancy, this may also give rise to wrongful (**Chapter 3**) and/or unfair dismissal (**Chapter 5**) claims. The right to claim a redundancy payment is a separate right that will arise irrespective of whether the dismissal is unfair.

Under s 188 of the Trade Unions and Labour Relations (Consolidation) Act 1992, obligations are imposed on employers to consult appropriate employee representatives (**4.8**).

In summary, in each case, consider the following.

- Is the employee eligible (**3.4**)?
- Has there been a dismissal (**3.4**)?
- Do the circumstances fit the statutory definition of redundancy (**4.2**)?
- Was the dismissal caused by the redundancy situation?
- Has there been a suitable offer of alternative employment (**4.4**)?
- Is the employee reasonable in refusing this (**4.4**)?

A flowchart showing the redundancy payment system is set out at **Figure 4.1** below.

Figure 4.1 Flowchart: Redundancy payments

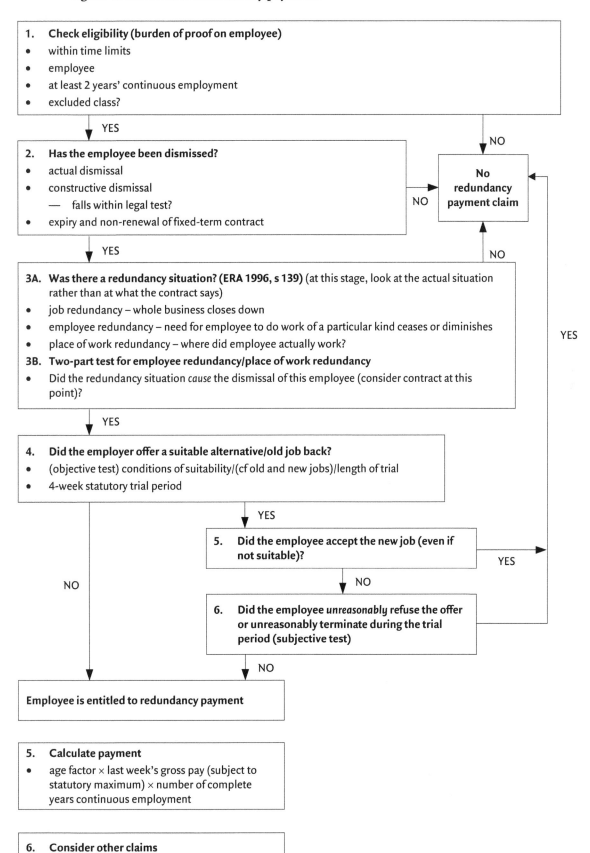

CHAPTER 5

UNFAIR DISMISSAL

5.1	Introduction	163
5.2	Reasons for dismissal	165
5.3	Fairness of dismissal	171
5.4	Procedural unfairness	176
5.5	Other special cases	204
5.6	Awards for unfair dismissal	219
5.7	Penalties for employers	236
5.8	Case study 1: unfair dismissal, redundancy payment and unpaid wages	237
5.9	Case study 2: unfair dismissal	238
5.10	Further reading	245
	Summary	245

LEARNING OUTCOMES

After reading this chapter you will be able to:

- describe the statutory claim of unfair dismissal and how it differs from wrongful dismissal
- list the potentially fair reasons for dismissal set out in ERA 1996, s 98 and understand their ambit
- understand the different procedural steps that should normally be followed before dismissal, depending on the reason for dismissal
- understand the relevance of the Acas Code of Practice on Disciplinary and Grievance Procedures
- understand the significance of *BHS v Burchell* in a misconduct case
- explain and apply the range of reasonable responses test
- be aware of the relevant maximum for unfair dismissal awards, and understand and be able to apply the relevant principles for calculating damages for unfair dismissal.

5.1 INTRODUCTION

In the UK, every eligible employee has the right not to be unfairly dismissed by his employer (ERA 1996, s 94). Note that, although much employment law in Europe is underpinned by common principles, very significant differences exist when it comes to dismissals. Do not assume that following UK principles will necessarily be sufficient when dismissing employees based abroad. International law firm CMS (now CMS Cameron McKenna Nabarro Olswang) issued in February 2018 two helpful guides to dismissal – one relating to Europe (covering 24 countries, plus Russia) and one relating to China, Singapore and UAE.

At common law, an employer can dismiss any employee whenever he chooses, whether he has any good reason or not. Provided he gives full notice and otherwise complies with the contract, the employee has no remedy. Even where the contract is breached, the award of damages is often relatively small (see **Chapter 2**).

In order to give a measure of protection against dismissal at the whim of the employer, the statutory claim of unfair dismissal introduced the concept of fairness into termination of contracts of employment. The employer must be able to show not only that he had a good reason to dismiss, but also that he acted fairly in, for example, the way in which he handled the dismissal.

5.1.1 Eligible employee

See **Chapter 3** for details of eligibility, but check in particular that the individual is an employee (not a worker) and has the necessary two years' continuous employment (ERA 1996, s 108), as relevant. (There are exceptions where the dismissal is for a reason relating to, for example, trade union membership, health and safety, or on the grounds of pregnancy. These exceptions are dealt with at **5.5**).

5.1.2 Dismissal

The employee must have been dismissed. See **3.4** for the definition of dismissal.

Where an employee intends to rely on s 95(1)(c) of the ERA 1996 – constructive dismissal – rather than on actual dismissal, he should consider using the grievance procedure set out in the Acas Code of Practice on Disciplinary and Grievance Procedures (see **5.4.1** below) before he resigns, or before he submits the ET1. A failure to follow the Code, where it applies, gives tribunals a discretionary power to increase or decrease awards by up to 25%, if they consider that the employer's/employee's failure to comply with the Code was unreasonable.

The Code sets out the process for dealing with grievances, which is as follows:

- Let the employer know the nature of the grievance.
- Hold a meeting with the employee to discuss the grievance.
- Allow the employee to be accompanied at the meeting.
- Decide on appropriate action.
- Allow the employee to take the grievance further if not resolved.
- Overlapping grievance and disciplinary cases: where an employee raises a grievance during a disciplinary process, the disciplinary process may be suspended temporarily in order to deal with the grievance. Where the grievance and disciplinary cases are related, it may be appropriate to deal with both issues concurrently.

To complement the Code, Acas has published guidance. Tribunals cannot adjust awards on account of any failure to follow the guidance, neither are they required to have regard to the guidance.

Where there is an actual dismissal, an employer should also consider the Code (see **5.4.1**). A failure to follow the Code gives tribunals a discretionary power to increase or decrease awards by up to 25% if they consider that the employer's/employee's failure to comply with the Code was unreasonable.

5.1.3 Potentially fair reason for dismissal

The onus is on the employer to show that the dismissal is for one of the five permitted reasons (see **5.2**). If the employer cannot show that the dismissal was for one of these permitted reasons, the dismissal will be unfair.

5.1.4 Fairness

Where the reason for the dismissal falls within one of the five permitted reasons, the tribunal must then go on to decide whether the employer acted reasonably in all the circumstances under ERA 1996, s 98(4) (see **5.3**) in dismissing this employee for this reason.

5.1.5 Remedies

Remedies are dealt with at **5.6**.

5.2 REASONS FOR DISMISSAL

The employer must be able to establish that the only or principal reason for the dismissal was a potentially fair reason. The burden of proof is on the employer, but it is not a heavy burden to discharge (see *Kuzel v Roche Products Ltd* [2008] IRLR 530). If he is unable to show that the dismissal was for one of the five permitted reasons, the dismissal will be held to be unfair. This is the case whether there is an actual or a constructive dismissal. Where the employee is basing his claim on a constructive dismissal, the reason for the dismissal given by the employer will be the reason for which the employer allegedly breached the contract.

The employer should try to ensure that he states the correct reason for dismissal on the ET1 to avoid being at risk of the dismissal being held to be unfair. However, the employment tribunal will seek to discover the real reason for dismissal, and if the employer has made a genuine mistake in how it has labelled the reason but the factual basis for the dismissal is clear to the employee, the tribunal can ignore an incorrect label. In *Abernethy v Mott, Hay and Anderson* [1974] ICR 323, CA, the employee refused to relocate and was dismissed for redundancy. The tribunal held that the employee was actually fairly dismissed for incapability. The Court of Appeal upheld the fairness of the dismissal, since the facts were clear to the employee at the time of the dismissal and the employer should not be penalised for attaching the wrong legal label.

In *Wilson v Post Office* [2000] IRLR 834, the Court of Appeal confirmed that the characterisation of the reason for a dismissal is a matter of legal analysis, and that since this was not a case in which the employer had tried to change the nature of the case, it was open to the EAT to say that the dismissal was to be characterised as for SOSR when it was originally formulated by the employer in terms of capability. So, where an employer wrongly labels the reason for dismissal, but still seeks to justify the dismissal on factual grounds made clear at the time of dismissal, he will not be bound by the wrong label. (See also *Screene v Seatwave Ltd* (UKEAT/0020/11).)

However, different considerations apply where the employer seeks to change the factual basis of the dismissal. In *Hotson v Wisbech Conservative Club* [1984] ICR 859, the EAT allowed an appeal by Ms Hotson, a club barmaid dismissed for gross inefficiency, because the real reason was suspected dishonesty, which went beyond a mere change of label. The allegation of dishonesty should have been put to the employee at the outset, to allow her to answer it. See too *Screene v Seatwave* (above) (where the EAT said a tribunal was entitled to make its decision on the basis of what it considered to be the real reason for dismissal) and *Perkin v St George's Healthcare NHS Trust* [2005] IRLR 934 (at **5.4.2.5** below).

Thus, provided the factual basis of the employer's argument is adhered to, it should not matter that the wrong reasons are pleaded. However, it would be good practice for an employer to state the reason for dismissal expressly, and, where there is a genuine uncertainty as to which of the reasons apply, state in the alternative. But reasons should not be stated in the alternative unless there is genuine uncertainty, because s 98(1)(a) requires the employer to show the reason or, if more than one, the principal reason.

5.2.1 The five permitted reasons

By s 98(1) and (2) of the ERA 1996, in determining whether a dismissal is fair or unfair, it is for the employer to establish the only or principal reason for the dismissal, and that it is a reason falling within the following:

(a) relating to the capability or qualifications of the employee to do work of the kind which he was employed to do (s 98(2)(a)); or

(b)   relating to the conduct of the employee (s 98(2)(b)); or

(c)   that the employee was redundant (s 98(2)(c)); or

(d)   that the employee could not continue to work in the position held without contravening some statutory provision (s 98(2)(d)); or

(e)   there was some other substantial reason (SOSR) that could justify the dismissal of an employee holding the position that employee held (s 98(1)(b)).

In *Kuzel v Roche Products Ltd* [2008] IRLR 530, the Court of Appeal confirmed that the burden is on the employer to show the reason for dismissal; but that where the employee asserts there was a different reason, the employee must produce some evidence of that. Where there is such evidence, it will be for the employer to show that the potentially fair reason was, in fact, the principal reason (see also *East Lancs Coachbuilders Ltd v Hilton* (UKEAT/0054/06)). It will then be for the tribunal to consider the evidence and make a finding of fact.

Note also *Royal Mail Group Ltd v Jhuti* [2019] UKSC 55, where the Supreme Court held that where a person 'in the hierarchy of responsibility' determines that the employee should be dismissed for a reason, but 'hides it behind an invented reason' which the decision maker (innocent of any improper motive) adopts, the 'reason for the dismissal is the hidden reason, rather than the invented reason'.

5.2.2   The ambit of the five reasons

This section deals with the ambit or scope of each of the five reasons. If the employer shows the dismissal is for one of these reasons, it has overcome the first hurdle. However, showing the reason does not of itself make the dismissal fair. The employment tribunal still has to decide whether the employer acted reasonably in dismissing the employee for that reason. We shall look at how fairness relates to these reasons in more detail below (see **5.4**).

5.2.2.1   Capability and qualifications

Section 98(2)(a) provides that an employer may fairly dismiss an employee for a reason that 'relates to the capability or qualifications of the employee for performing work of the kind which he was employed by the employer to do'. Capability is defined in s 98(3)(a) as 'capability assessed by reference to skill, aptitude, health or any other physical or mental quality'. There is always the potential for a degree of overlap between conduct and capability.

The incapability or lack of qualification for which the employee is dismissed must relate to the work which the employee was employed to do. Incapability within the provision may be incapability to do the job by virtue of incompetence, or an inherent inability to perform the job. It also extends to the inability of the employee to do his job by reason of illness or injury. Therefore sickness of an employee is a reason which may justify dismissal, even where that illness has been caused by the employer (see **5.4.2.1**).

Note: The Acas Code of Practice on Disciplinary and Grievance Procedures 2015 covers culpable (ie incompetent) poor performance dismissals but not ill health dismissals.

5.2.2.2   Conduct

The 'conduct' reason (s 98(2)(b)) may cover conduct of virtually any sort, but it would usually be misconduct within the employment. The EAT confirmed in *JP Morgan Securities plc v Ktorza* (UKEAT/0311/16) that there is no requirement for the conduct to be culpable. Of course, culpability or otherwise may be relevant to reasonableness (see **5.3**). It would include, for example, a range of conduct, from minor incidents (such as bad time-keeping) through to more serious matters such as disobedience of orders, breach of the duty of fidelity, dishonesty, fighting, sexual harassment or absence without permission. Conduct does not need to be gross, as opposed to serious, to be a fair dismissal. In *Mbubaegbu v Homerton University Hospital NHS Foundation Trust* (UKEAT/0218/17), the EAT upheld an employment tribunal's decision that multiple alleged breaches, even absent a single act of gross misconduct, could amount to a fair dismissal. A 'series of acts, demonstrating a pattern of conduct' could be of 'sufficient seriousness to undermine the relationship of trust and confidence'. See also *Quintiles Commercial UK Ltd v Barongo* (UKEAT/0255/17).

To minimise his potential liability for unfair dismissal, the employer should have a comprehensive set of disciplinary rules (see **Chapter 1** and the Acas Code of Practice on Disciplinary and Grievance Procedures at **5.4.2.2** below) that differentiate between the sorts of conduct regarded as minor or serious, and which set out how such incidents will be treated and what the possible consequence may be. The distinction between misconduct and gross misconduct can be important: generally speaking, only gross misconduct will justify summary dismissal, ie dismissal without notice, and one incident of a minor nature would not usually justify dismissal as a sanction, whereas a series of minor incidents or repeatedly bad behaviour could be expected to do so. What is important is that it is made clear to the employee what sort of response can be expected following particular sorts of misconduct. The exact nature of the employer's disciplinary rules and procedures will depend on the size of the organisation. Larger firms should have a comprehensive set of detailed rules and procedures which should be carefully followed (although a minor deviation will not necessarily lead to a finding of unfair dismissal). A smaller firm may have a much less formal procedure, although it should still ensure that there is a fair investigation and a reasonable sanction. Note that a dismissal for gross misconduct can be unfair (see, for example, *Arnold Clark Automobiles Ltd v Spoor* [2017] IRLR 500).

Dismissal for misconduct outside employment, such as criminal offences committed elsewhere, will also come within this reason, but for such a dismissal to be fair the outside misconduct must usually have an effect on the employment relationship (see **5.4.2.2** below). For example, if a cashier is charged with a motoring offence, this would have no employment implications. However, a charge of theft clearly could have.

In order for the employer to rely on misconduct to justify a dismissal, the misconduct must have been known to the employer at the time of dismissal. He cannot rely on subsequently discovered misconduct to justify the dismissal (*W Devis & Sons Ltd v Atkins* [1977] AC 931, HL). For example, an employee is dismissed because his employer does not like him. After he leaves, his employer discovers that he has been submitting bogus expense claims. The employer cannot rely on this conduct when giving his reason for the dismissal.

However, note that it is at the point of actual dismissal beyond which after-acquired knowledge cannot be taken into account. The employer is entitled to take into account factors that occur until dismissal, even after notice of termination has been given (*Alboni v Ind Coope Retail Ltd* [1998] IRLR 131, CA), both in determining the reason for the dismissal and whether the employer acted reasonably in the circumstances in treating it as a sufficient reason for dismissal. Note also that after-acquired knowledge may affect the amount of compensation an employee may receive (see **5.6.2**).

5.2.2.3 Redundancy

As we have seen, a dismissal by reason of redundancy may give rise to a claim for a redundancy payment (see **Chapter 4**). However, redundancy is also a potentially fair reason for dismissing an employee. If an employer does not handle a redundancy situation fairly, that can give rise, separately, to an unfair dismissal claim (see **5.4.2.3**). The definition of redundancy has already been dealt with, and the same definition in ERA 1996, s 139 applies here (see **4.2**).

Redundancy dismissals are not covered by the Acas Disciplinary and Grievance Code.

5.2.2.4 Contravention of a statutory provision ('illegality')

For more details on the long-standing principle that the courts will not assist a party whose case is based upon an unlawful act, see **1.2.6.2**. In an employment law context, this means that an employee whose contract is illegal may be prevented from asserting their contractual and statutory rights.

Contravention of a statutory provision (s 98(2)(d)) covers the situation where it becomes illegal by statute either for the employee to work in the position held, or for the employer to employ the employee in it. The burden of proving illegality is on an employer.

One of the more common types of dismissal for this reason is the dismissal of the driver of a motor vehicle who is disqualified by a court from driving because of a motoring offence (see, eg, *Appleyard v FM Smith (Hull) Ltd* [1972] IRLR 19). Another common situation that arises is where employers fail to pay an employee's tax and/or National Insurance (see for example *Newland v Simons & Willer (Hairdressers) Ltd* [1981] IRLR 359, *Hewcastle Catering Ltd v Ahmed* [1991] IRLR 473 and *Salvesen v Simons* [1994] IRLR 52). In *Robinson v Al Qasimi* (UKEAT/0106/19) the claimant worked for the respondent from 2007 to 2017. Until 2014 she was paid gross, having agreed to be responsible for the tax, which she failed to do. From mid-2014 the respondent made deductions to cover tax and national insurance while her status was in dispute. A tribunal rejected her claims for wrongful and unfair dismissal on the basis that she had participated in the illegal performance of the contract by not paying tax between 2007 and 2014. This was overturned by the EAT as from mid-2014 she had not participated in illegality.

Another area is the employment of someone who is in the UK illegally, or who does not have permission to work. See **1.2.6** for more analysis and the recent case of *Okedina v Chikale* (UKEAT/0152/17), which re-emphasised that an employer will not be able to avoid liability on a contract which is performed illegally by it (eg because appropriate tax deductions were not made) if the employee is not complicit in those acts.

5.2.2.5   Some other substantial reason

Some other substantial reason is not limited by the four reasons above. The employer may show any substantial reason outside the four above as the reason for the dismissal of an employee holding the position held, but the onus of proof is on the employer to show that it is a substantial reason that could justify the dismissal. Provided the reason is not 'whimsical, unworthy or trivial', it will suffice. In *Scott and Co v Richardson* (UKEAT/0074/04), Mr Scott carried out debt recovery services and decided to introduce shift work. Mr Richardson refused to accept the proposed change to his contract of employment on the basis that he should continue to be paid overtime for working in the evening. He was dismissed. The EAT held that what the employer had to demonstrate to the tribunal was that it reasonably believed/ concluded that the reorganisation of working hours had advantages – it was not necessary to go beyond that to see whether it did have those advantages. In this case there was a commercial reason for carrying out the reorganisation, and the EAT said the tribunal was bound to find that the employer had shown that the reason for dismissal was for some other substantial reason.

It is not possible to give a comprehensive list of other reasons which may justify dismissal, but reasons which have been held to be a potentially fair reason for dismissal include refusal to accept a reorganisation affecting working hours (*Muggeridge and Slade v East Anglia Plastics Ltd* [1973] IRLR 163 and *Scott and Co v Richardson* (UKEAT/0074/04)), replacement by a better qualified employee (*Priddle v Dibble* [1978] 1 All ER 1058), end of genuine temporary employment (*Terry v East Sussex County Council* [1977] 1 All ER 567), dismissal because of a clash of personalities between employees (*Gorfin v Distressed Gentlefolk's Aid Association* [1973] IRLR 290; see also *Perkin v St George's Healthcare NHS Trust* [2005] EWCA Civ 1174), marriage of an employee to a competitor, where there was a real risk of a leak of trade secrets (*Foot v Eastern Counties Timber Co Ltd* [1972] IRLR 83), refusal of employees to accept a new restraint of trade clause in their contracts (even if the clause was unreasonable) (*Willow Oak Developments Ltd t/a Windsor Recruitment v Silverwood & Others* [2006] IRLR 607), loss of trust and confidence in the employee, in exceptional cases (*Ezsias v North Glamorgan NHS Trust* [2011] IRLR 550 and

Governing Body of Tubbenden Primary School v Sylvester (UKEAT/0527/11)), risk of damage to the employer's reputation (*Leach v Office of Communications* [2012] EWCA Civ 959), third-party pressure (*Mr S Bancroft v Interserve (Facilities Management) Ltd* (UKEAT/0329/12)) and a series of repeated short absences where health is not the issue as far as the employer is concerned (see *Ridge v HM Land Registry* (EAT/0485/12)).

Note: Not all 'some other substantial reason' dismissals are covered by the Acas Code of Practice on Disciplinary and Grievance Procedures (see *Phoenix House Ltd v Stockman* (UKEAT/0264/15)).

5.2.2.6   Unfair dismissal and Covid-19

Although the full details of the (now ended) Coronavirus Job Retention Scheme (CJRS) are beyond the scope of this work, there is a summary in the **Introductory Note**. Guidance issued by the Government on the CJRS made clear that, for furloughed staff, usual employment law and employee rights applied, including protection from unfair dismissal and discrimination.

There is unlikely to be a one-size-fits-all answer to potential unfair dismissal claims arising from the pandemic, which created some novel employment circumstances. Matters such as an employer's decision to dismiss rather than furlough under the CJRS, or to dismiss after the CJRS because of the financial implications of the pandemic on its business, will come under scrutiny.

The most likely reason for dismissals is redundancy which, as stated above, is a potentially fair reason for dismissal. Employees with two or more years' service can potentially claim unfair dismissal. An employee ostensibly dismissed on the grounds of 'redundancy' may bring an unfair dismissal claim alleging that in fact they were dismissed for a different or unlawful reason. It will therefore be necessary to determine whether there is a genuine redundancy situation (see **4.2** above). Section 139(6) of the ERA 1996 states that redundancy includes a situation where the business need for an employee's work has *temporarily* diminished. If there is a potentially fair reason for dismissal, it will still be necessary to consider whether the dismissal was fair in all the circumstances (applying ERA 1996, s 98(4)) and that a fair process was followed. In particular, if challenged, employers will have to show that selection pools and criteria used to select for redundancy were fair, objective and reasonable; were not directly or indirectly discriminatory; that (in addition to any collective consultation obligations under TULR(C)A 1992, s 188) staff were warned and consulted about them before they were finalised; and the employer took reasonable steps to consider whether it could 'redeploy' or find alternative employment for the employee (see **5.4.2.3** below). One issue that may arise when considering fairness (see below for more details) is whether an employer should have considered or offered the option of being furloughed, remembering that there was no 'right' to be furloughed.

Those treated as unable to work due to diagnosis with Covid-19 will usually be placed on sick leave until they are fit to return to work. At that point, they will be treated the same as other employees.

The October 2021 IDS Employment Brief (no 1142) contained a useful summary of a number of Covid-19-related employment tribunal cases (which are not binding). They included unfair dismissal (see by way of example *Accattatis v Fortuna Group (London) Ltd* (ET/3307587/2020), *Montanaro v Lansafe* (ET/2203148/2020) and *Kubilius v Kent Foods* (ET/3201960/2020)), redundancy (*Mhindurwa v Lovingangels Care Ltd* (ET/3311636/2020) and *Handley v Tatenhill Aviation Ltd* (ET/2603087/2020)), automatic unfair dismissal on health and safety grounds (*Ham v ESL BBSW Ltd* (ET/1601260/2020) and *Rodgers v Leeds Laser Cutting* (ET/1803829/2020)), discrimination (*Prosser v Community Gateway Association* (ET/2413672/2020) and *Jimenez v Firmdale Hotels* (ET/2203194/2020)) and entitlement to discretionary commission payments during furlough (*Sharma v Lily Communications Ltd* (ET/1800437/21)). The EAT dismissed the claimant's appeal in the *Rodgers* case, holding, on the facts, that the employment tribunal had not erred when it decided that the claimant's dismissal was not automatically unfair pursuant to s 100(1)(d) of the ERA 1996 (he failed to return to work because of concerns related to the coronavirus pandemic). The tribunal had decided that Mr Rodgers had been fairly dismissed, as he had been unable to establish a reasonable belief in a serious and imminent workplace danger. That finding was upheld.

A number of unfair dismissal claims have focused on the serious and imminent danger language in s 100 of the ERA 1996 (see **5.5.4** below). In *Khatun v Winn Solicitors Ltd* (ET/ 2501492/20), the tribunal found that a solicitor's dismissal for refusing to agree to changes to her employment contract following a downturn in work at the start of the Covid-19 pandemic was unfair. In *Rendina v Royston Veterinary Centre Ltd* (ET/3307459/2020), a veterinary nurse was held to have been automatically unfairly dismissed by reason of her raising health and safety concerns. See too *Preen v Coolink Ltd and another* (ET/1403451/2020), *Quelch v Courtiers Support Services Ltd* (ET/3313138/2020) and *Ham v ESL BBSW Ltd* (ET/1601260/2020). In *Pareek v D Delta Ltd t/a Mira Boiler* (ET/3300603/2021), the claimant, who worked as an administrator for a boiler and central heating service company, worked in a small office with two other people, with no space for appropriate social distancing. Neither hand sanitisers nor face masks were provided by the respondent. The staff wore no masks, and the ventilation was inadequate. The office window could only be opened if the temperature was uncomfortably high. They could not do anything to rearrange the small office. The claimant's dismissal was held to have been automatically unfair under s 100 of the ERA 1996. The tribunal also held that the dismissal was ordinarily unfair under s 98. The employers had provided no evidence to support conduct being the reason for dismissal, nor had it followed a fair procedure.

In *Gibson v Lothian Leisure* (ET/4105009/2020), the claimant was employed by the respondent as a chef. In the second week of March 2020, the claimant was put on furlough. Up to that point he had had no problems at work. When he was asked to return to 'help out for a bit' towards the end of lockdown, the claimant raised the vulnerability of his father. No PPE was provided and when the claimant raised that, he was told to 'shut up and get on with it'. He was subsequently dismissed on the pretext of a reorganisation. The tribunal held that the claimant was automatically unfairly dismissed because he reasonably believed that this was a serious and imminent danger, leading him to raise concerns regarding the lack of PPE. See too *Smith v Cognita Schools Ltd* (ET/1600884/2021) where the tribunal held that there was not an objective serious and imminent risk to the claimant's health by a student not asking permission before removing a mask for a drink, particularly bearing in mind the clear acceptance of the claimant that students could have a drink, removing their masks to do so, if they did ask permission. The respondent followed all advice of the Welsh Government and the claimant's classroom allowed for her to be two metres away from her students. The door was open, and the room was therefore well ventilated.

In *Moore v Ecoscape UK Ltd* (ET/2417563/20), the tribunal held that the claimant was not unfairly dismissed, in circumstances where she had significant concerns about being required to leave her home rather than specific concerns about the workplace.

A number of cases have concerned employees attempting to argue that they should have been furloughed instead of being asked to work. The tribunal decisions have confirmed that, as stated in the government guidance, the decision as to whether to place an employee on furlough rested with the employer, and the employee had no legal right to insist on being furloughed (see for example *Woods v Andrea Hawkes* (ET/2203304/2020), *Kapetanakis v Historical Souvenirs* (ET/1601368/2020) and *Accattatis v Fortuna Group (London) Ltd* (ET/3307587/2020)). In *Kaur Gill v Elegance Beauty* (ET/3201878/2020), a tribunal found that a failure to pay an employee while on furlough was an unlawful deduction from wages (see **1.11** above).

5.2.3 Statement of reasons for dismissal

An employee who has been continuously employed for at least two years (or one year if employed by the employer before 6 April 2012) is entitled to request that he be provided by his employer, within 14 days of the request, with a written statement of the reason for his dismissal (ERA 1996, s 92). The statement is admissible in evidence in any proceedings. If a woman is dismissed while pregnant or during her maternity leave period, she is entitled, without prior request, to a written statement (see **14.9.2**).

If the employer unreasonably fails to comply with the request or the particulars given are inadequate or untrue, the employee may present a complaint to an employment tribunal. The time-limit to present the complaint is the same as that for a complaint of unfair dismissal (see **6.3.1**), generally three months from the EDT (see **3.5**). If the complaint is well founded, the tribunal must order the employer to pay the employee two weeks' pay (gross) (ERA 1996, s 93). There is no upper limit on a week's pay for this purpose (ERA 1996, s 227).

5.3 FAIRNESS OF DISMISSAL

Once the employer has shown that the reason for the dismissal falls within one of the permitted reasons, the tribunal must then decide whether the employer has acted reasonably within s 98(4) of the ERA 1996 in dismissing the employee for that reason.

In practice, it is usually relatively easy for the employer to show the reason for the dismissal. Persuading the tribunal that he has acted reasonably on the evidence presented may be more difficult.

By s 98(4) of the ERA 1996, the tribunal must decide whether the dismissal was fair or unfair, having regard to the reason shown by the employer, *and* whether, in the circumstances (including the size and administrative resources of the employer's undertaking), the employer acted reasonably or unreasonably in treating that reason as a sufficient reason for dismissing the employee; *and* that question shall be determined in accordance with equity and the substantial merits of the case. It is not for the tribunal to decide if the employee did do what was alleged, nor is it for the tribunal to decide what it would have done: the test is an objective one.

5.3.1 ERA 1996, s 98(4): general

Each case will turn on its own facts, but there are a number of principles the tribunal must follow in determining reasonableness.

5.3.1.1 Has the employer acted reasonably?

In *Iceland Frozen Foods Ltd v Jones* [1982] IRLR 439, the EAT summarised the correct approach for the tribunal to adopt in answering the question posed by s 98(4) of the ERA 1996:

(a) the starting point should always be the words of s 98(4) themselves;

(b) in applying the section an employment tribunal must consider the reasonableness of the employer's conduct, not simply whether they (the members of the employment tribunal) consider the dismissal to be fair;

(c) in judging the reasonableness of the employer's conduct an employment tribunal must not substitute its decision as to what is the right course to adopt for that of the employer;

(d) in many (though not all) cases there is a band of reasonable responses to the employee's conduct within which one employer might reasonably take one view, another quite reasonably take another;

(e) the function of the employment tribunal, as an industrial jury, is to determine whether in the particular circumstances of each case the decision to dismiss the employee fell within the band of reasonable responses that a reasonable employer might have adopted. If the dismissal falls within the band, the dismissal is fair: if the dismissal falls outside the band, it is unfair.

The question for the tribunal to determine, therefore, is whether the respondent's decision to dismiss the employee fell within the band (or range) of reasonable responses of a reasonable employer. It is sufficient that a reasonable employer would regard the circumstances as a sufficient reason for dismissing – it is not necessary that all reasonable employers would dismiss in those circumstances. However, the tribunal should be careful to not substitute its own view for what the employer should have done, for this would be an error in law which is appealable. Provided that the tribunal does not fall into this error, almost any decision may be justified, because it is for the tribunal to determine what a reasonable employer could or should have done. In *London Ambulance Service NHS Trust v Small* [2009] IRLR 563 the Court of Appeal held that the tribunal substituted its view of the facts for that of the employer. It is useful to quote from the judgment:

41.　The ET ought to have confined its consideration to facts relating to the Trust's handling of Mr Small's dismissal: the genuineness of the Trust's belief and the reasonableness of the grounds of its belief about the conduct of Mr Small at the time of the dismissal. Instead, the ET introduced its own findings of fact about the conduct of Mr Small, including aspects of it that had been disputed at the disciplinary hearing. For example, the ET found that the daughter, who did not give evidence to the ET, had not told Mr Small that her mother was hypertensive and diabetic. Further, on the point whether Mr Small had done a risk assessment before asking the patient to walk, the ET held that there was no evidence that he had failed to carry out a risk assessment, but Mr Suter gave evidence to the ET that the crucial issue before the disciplinary panel was that Mr Small had not carried out a proper patient assessment, before the decision was made.

42.　The ET used its findings of fact to support its conclusion that, at the time of dismissal, the Trust had no reasonable grounds for its belief about Mr Small's conduct and therefore no genuine belief about it. By this process of reasoning the ET found that the dismissal was unfair. In my judgment, this amounted to the ET substituting itself and its findings for the Trust's decision-maker in relation to Mr Small's dismissal.

43.　It is all too easy, even for an experienced ET, to slip into the substitution mindset. In conduct cases the claimant often comes to the ET with more evidence and with an understandable determination to clear his name and to prove to the ET that he is innocent of the charges made against him by his employer. He has lost his job in circumstances that may make it difficult for him to get another job. He may well gain the sympathy of the ET so that it is carried along the acquittal route and away from the real question – whether the employer acted fairly and reasonably in all the circumstances at the time of the dismissal.

See *Fuller v London Borough of Brent* [2011] EWCA Civ 267, *Crawford and Another v Suffolk Mental Health Partnership NHS Trust* [2012] IRLR 402 and *Newbound v Thames Water Utilities Ltd* [2015] EWCA Civ 677 for decisions of the Court of Appeal finding that there was no error of law and that a reasonable employment tribunal could find that dismissal was outside the range of reasonable responses.

The approach set out in *Iceland* was re-stated by the Court of Appeal in the joined cases *HSBC (formerly Midland Bank) v Madden; Post Office v Foley* [2000] IRLR 827, CA, and in *London Ambulance Service NHS Trust v Small* [2009] EWCA Civ 220. In *Sarkar v West London Mental Health NHS Trust* [2010] IRLR 508 and *Salford Royal NHS Foundation Trust v Roldan* [2010] IRLR 721, the Court of Appeal appeared to endorse a more interventionist approach by employment tribunals when applying the range of reasonable responses test. In *Roldan*, the Court of Appeal said that the tribunal had been entitled to find that the dismissal was unfair, given the conflict in evidence which meant that the Trust should have investigated the issues in more depth. In *North West London Hospitals NHS Trust v Bowater* [2011] EWCA Civ 63, the Court of Appeal upheld an employment tribunal's decision that the decision to dismiss could not possibly be within the band of reasonable responses. The employee had made a lewd comment, but one that 'a large proportion of the population would consider ... to be merely humorous'. The Court said (at [26]):

It is important that, in cases of this kind, the EAT pays proper respect to the decision of the ET. It is the ET to whom Parliament has entrusted the responsibility of making what are, no doubt sometimes, difficult and borderline decisions in relation to the fairness of dismissal. An appeal to the EAT only lies on a point of law and it goes without saying that the EAT must not, under the guise of a charge of perversity, substitute its own judgment for that of the ET.

In *Graham v The Secretary of State for Work & Pensions (Jobcentre Plus)* [2012] EWCA Civ 903 (a conduct case), the Court said (at [36]) that

the ET must then decide on the reasonableness of the response by the employer. In performing the latter exercise, the ET must consider, by the objective standards of the hypothetical reasonable employer, rather than by reference to the ET's own subjective views, whether the employer has acted within a '*band or range of reasonable responses*' to the particular misconduct found of the particular employee. If the employer has so acted, then the employer's decision to dismiss will be reasonable. However, this is not the same thing as saying that a decision of an employer to dismiss will only be regarded as unreasonable if it is shown to be perverse. The ET must not simply consider whether they think that the dismissal was fair and thereby substitute their decision as to what was the right course to adopt for that of the employer. The ET must determine whether the decision of the employer to dismiss the employee fell within the band of reasonable responses which '*a reasonable employer might have adopted*'. An ET must focus its attention on the fairness of the conduct of the employer at the time of the investigation and dismissal (or any internal appeal process) and not on whether in fact the employee has suffered an injustice.

The Court of Appeal confirmed in *Davies v Sandwell MBC* [2013] EWCA Civ 135, that the fairness of a decision to dismiss for misconduct, which relies on a previous final warning, should be assessed under s 98(4) principles; but that in assessing reasonableness, while a tribunal may assess whether the final warning was issued in good faith or was 'manifestly inappropriate', it is not the tribunal's function to re-hear earlier internal disciplinary proceedings.

Note that the 'range of reasonable responses' test applies not just to the substantive reason for the dismissal, but also to the procedural aspects of the employer's actions. In *Sainsbury's Supermarkets Ltd v Hitt* [2003] IRLR 23, the Court of Appeal held that the range of reasonable responses test applied as much to whether a reasonable investigation had been carried out as it does to the reasonableness of the decision to dismiss for the conduct reason. The Court of Appeal confirmed this in *Bournemouth University Higher Education Corporation v Buckland* [2010] EWCA Civ 121.

For a useful discussion of some of the authorities, see *EAGA plc v Tideswell* (UKEAT/0007/11) and, more recently, *Newbound v Thames Water Utilities Ltd* [2015] EWCA Civ 677.

In *Reilly v Sandwell MBC* [2018] UKSC 18, the Supreme Court held that it was fair to dismiss a school head teacher for failing to disclose a close relationship with a man convicted of making indecent images of children. The employment tribunal held that the dismissal was procedurally unfair (due to technical failures in the appeal process) but that the reason for dismissal was a fair and sufficient reason (conduct) for dismissal. It directed (i) a 90% reduction in any compensation in accordance with the approach endorsed in *Polkey v AE Dayton Services Ltd* [1988] 1 AC 344 (see below), and (ii) a 100% reduction due to blameworthy conduct. The Supreme Court raised some doubt about the relevance of the test in *BHS Ltd v Burchell* [1980] ICR 303 (see below) to s 98(4) (as opposed to s 98(1)–(3) – reason and belief) but ultimately concluded:

[N]o harm has been done by the extravagant view taken of the reach of [that] judgment ... In effect it has been considered only to require the tribunal to inquire whether the dismissal was within a range of reasonable responses ... and had been preceded by a reasonable amount of investigation.

5.3.1.2   Matters known to the employer

The employer must generally justify the decision to dismiss on the basis of the information known to him at the time of dismissal (*W Devis & Sons Ltd v Atkins* [1977] AC 931, HL). See also

Alboni v Ind Coope Retail Ltd [1998] IRLR 131, CA (see **5.2.2.2**). The Court of Appeal held in *Orr v Milton Keynes Council* [2011] EWCA Civ 62 that 'known to the employer' means facts known to the decision maker or facts that he could reasonably acquire through the appropriate disciplinary procedure.

The Court of Appeal in *Royal Mail Ltd v Jhuti* [2017] EWCA Civ 1632 (a whistleblowing case) gives some useful examples at paras 60–63. Underhill LJ opined that where the 'manipulation' is carried out by somebody very senior, there might be a case for attributing the motivation to the employer. The Supreme Court agreed and held ([2019] UKSC 55) that where a manager engineers a dismissal and 'fools' a dismissing officer, the 'hidden reason' is the principal reason for the dismissal, even if the dismissing officer was unaware of it. The reason operating in the mind of the manager could be imputed to the employer. In *Uddin v London Borough of Ealing* (UKEAT/0165/19), the EAT said that this approach applied not only to the reason for the dismissal (ie ERA 1996, s 98(1)) but also to the fairness under s 98(4). In *Uddin*, the reason relied upon was not invented, but material information was not shared with the decision maker, which could be relevant to fairness. Most recently, the EAT, in *University Hospital North Tees & Hartlepool NHS Foundation Trust v Fairhall* (UKEAT/0150/20) provided a reminder of the limitations of the *Jhuti* approach.

5.3.1.3 Size of the undertaking

The tribunal must take into account the size and administrative resources of the undertaking. An employer with a small workforce might, for example, find it more difficult than a larger firm to find other employees to do the work of an employee who is absent sick for a long period. This might justify a dismissal and replacement of a sick employee in circumstances where a large firm would not be acting reasonably. A small firm is also less likely to have suitable alternative employment for employees who lose their own jobs through redundancy. A small firm may also have less formal disciplinary and consultation procedures than a large one.

5.3.1.4 Does the reason justify dismissal?

The tribunal must decide whether dismissal was within a range of reasonable responses. Would a reasonable employer have demoted or suspended instead?

5.3.1.5 Pressure on the employer

In deciding whether the employer acted reasonably, the tribunal must not take into account any pressure put on the employer, by way of industrial action or the threat of industrial action, to dismiss the employee (ERA 1996, s 107).

5.3.1.6 Breach of contract

The fact that a dismissal is in breach of contract will not of itself render it unfair. The test is whether the employer acted reasonably.

5.3.1.7 Equitable considerations

A long-serving employee deserves more consideration before dismissal. For example, an employee with 20 years' service who is convicted of an offence of dishonesty unrelated to his employment, might be demoted to a position which would not give him an opportunity for breach of trust rather than be dismissed.

5.3.1.8 Consistency

The employer should consider how previous similar situations have been dealt with in the past. Nevertheless, it will be rare that the circumstances of one employee are truly comparable with those of another. In *Hadjioannou v Coral Casinos Ltd* [1981] IRLR 352, the EAT said that inconsistency of treatment would be relevant only in limited circumstances. In *Paul v East Surrey District HA* [1995] IRLR 305, the Court of Appeal held that the employee's dismissal was fair on the ground that there was a clear and rational basis for distinguishing between the cases of the two employees. For a recent decision on consistency of treatment, see *MBNA Ltd v Jones* (UKEAT/0120/15).

5.3.1.9 Human rights

Although the Human Rights Act 1998 (HRA 1998) is only directly effective between victims and public authorities (see **Chapter 15**), for employees pursuing their private sector employers for unfair dismissal, the HRA 1998 may be used to 'shape and determine' the outcome of the claim. In *Pay v Lancashire Probation Service* [2004] IRLR 129, the EAT agreed that the ERA 1996, s 98(4) must be read in a way which is compatible with human rights. However, on the facts, the EAT decided that the activities in which the applicant was involved (performing in fetish clubs and merchandising of products connected with bondage, domination and sado-masochism; photographs were available on the Internet of him involved in these activities) were not private, and that the interference with freedom of expression was justified and accordingly there was no infringement of the applicant's rights under Articles 8 or 10 (freedom of expression) of the ECHR. Mr Pay was a probation officer who worked with sex offenders. The EAT said that the interference with Article 10 was justified on the facts because of the competing interests of the employer to protect its reputation and maintain public confidence. Dismissal was a proportionate response.

In *X v Y* [2004] IRLR 625, the Court of Appeal dealt with the question of whether tribunals must take account of the HRA 1998 (in this case Article 8 of the Convention) when deciding unfair dismissal claims brought against private sector employers. The majority of the Court of Appeal held that Article 8 was not engaged. Mummery LJ went on to state that there should be no difference in approach, whether the employer is private or public sector. He said the Convention had an 'oblique' effect rather than a horizontal one, and that the right to respect for private life 'blended' with the law on unfair dismissal, but without creating new private law causes of action against private employers. (See *Hill v Governing Body of Great Tey Primary School* (UKEAT/0237/12) and *Q v Secretary of State for Justice* (UKEAT/0120/19).) See **15.4.2**.

It has also been suggested that Article 6 (the right to a fair hearing) might apply to internal disciplinary hearings. In *R (G) v The Governors of X School* [2011] UKSC 30, the Supreme Court held that Article 6 *may* be engaged in internal disciplinary hearings where the consequences of an internal disciplinary proceeding were sufficiently linked to the determination of an individual's civil rights to practise his chosen profession (in the sense of having a 'substantial influence or effect' on the outcome of a subsequent process which is determinative of civil rights (in this case the outcome of the Independent Safeguarding Authority's process, which could have meant that the claimant's name was added to the register)).

Statutory provisions obliged the school, when it made a serious finding of misconduct, to make a reference to what became the Independent Safeguarding Authority (ISA) (originally the Secretary of State) to consider whether the claimant should be should be placed on the 'children's barred list' and prevented from working with children in the future. Under this statutory framework, the claimant would have a right to legal representation before the ISA; and if dissatisfied with its decision, there was a right of appeal. Applying that test to the facts, the fact that ISA was required by statutory provisions and published guidance to 'exercise its own independent judgment both in relation to finding facts and making an assessment of their gravity and significance', before forming a view as to whether G should be placed on the barred list, was significant in the Supreme Court's view. The Supreme Court considered that the governors' determination that G had been guilty of gross misconduct would *not* have a 'substantial influence or effect' on the ISA's decision-making process. It followed that G's Article 6 rights were not engaged at the internal disciplinary stage, but only at the subsequent ISA hearing (see further **15.4.1**).

Other rights may be of relevance, for example an excessively long period of suspension could amount to inhuman or degrading treatment or punishment under Article 3; or unjustified surveillance of an employee before or as part of an investigation process in a disciplinary matter may be a breach of the right to respect for private life under Article 8 (see **15.4.2**).

5.4 PROCEDURAL UNFAIRNESS

An employer may be justified in dismissing an employee for the substantive reason, but the dismissal may still be unfair if the employer does not follow a fair procedure in reaching the decision to dismiss. There can be different procedural requirements, depending on the reason for the dismissal. These matters are dealt with in more detail in **5.4.2** in relation to each of the different reasons for dismissal.

In *Gallacher v Abellio Scotrail Ltd* (UKEATS/0027/19) the EAT emphasised that the absence of any procedure does not automatically mean a dismissal will be unfair. In this case, there was a breakdown in relations between the claimant and her manager at a difficult period for the respondent's business. The claimant's manager decided, after consulting with HR, to dismiss her at an appraisal meeting with no procedure, forewarning or right of appeal. The tribunal found the dismissal to be fair, holding that the decision to dismiss without any procedure was within the band of reasonable responses in the particular circumstances, because any further action would have been futile. The EAT declined to overturn the decision, holding that although it will be rare, this was one of those rare cases where it was open to the tribunal to conclude that dismissal without any procedure was within the band of reasonable responses. The EAT cautioned however that:

> Dismissals without following any procedures will always be subject to extra caution on the part of the Tribunal before being considered to fall within the band of reasonable responses.

5.4.1 Codes of practice

Any relevant Code (for example, the Acas Code of Practice on Disciplinary and Grievance Procedures, available at <http://www.acas.org.uk>) should be considered by the tribunal. If the employer fails to comply with the Code, that will be taken into account by the tribunal when deciding fairness. It may also have an effect on the amount of compensation awarded.

The Acas Code of Practice on Disciplinary and Grievance Procedures (latest version March 2015) is intended to provide basic practical guidance on the key procedural principles that underpin the handling of disciplinary and grievance situations at work. It sets down minimum standards only.

The key points to note are:

- A failure to follow the Code will not in itself make a dismissal automatically unfair, but tribunals can adjust awards by up to 25% for any unreasonable failure to comply with any of its provisions (EA 2008, s 3).
- The Code applies to disciplinary and grievance matters, but the text also refers to performance issues, suggesting that the disciplinary procedure guidance should also be applied to handling capability dismissals. Note that while misconduct involves culpable conduct, poor performance is capable of involving both culpable and non-culpable conduct. Where poor performance is the result of genuine ill health or injury, the Code will not apply. The position will be different where ill health leads to a failure to comply with a sickness absence procedure or is not believed to be genuine. In these sort of cases there is culpable conduct which it will be appropriate to investigate under the Code.
- If the employer purports to dismiss for a culpability-related reason, the Code applies even if a tribunal does not accept that reason as genuine (see *Bethnal Green and Shoreditch Education Trust v Dippenaar* (UKEAT/0064/15)).

- The Code does not apply to other dismissals, such as redundancy, the termination of a fixed-term contract and cases of medical incapability (*Holmes v Qinetic Ltd* (UKEAT/0206/15), although it would apply to allegations of misuse of a sickness system. Employers will be required to satisfy a tribunal that the termination procedure is fair according to the general fairness principles set out in the ERA 1996 and case law (see **5.4.2.3**).
- The Code does not require employees to submit a grievance before bringing a tribunal claim, but employees who unreasonably fail to do this may suffer a reduction in any tribunal award of up to 25%. Note that grievances must be in writing, so the Code does not apply to oral grievances (*Cadogan Hotel Partners Ltd v Ozog* (UKEAT/0001/14)).

The Acas Code is not legally binding, but its provisions will be taken into account by employment tribunals where appropriate when deciding whether a dismissal is fair or unfair. In *Lock v Cardiff Railway Co Ltd* [1998] IRLR 358, the EAT emphasised (it was dealing with the old Acas Code) the importance of tribunals examining and taking into account the Acas Code. Not to do so would amount to a misdirection of law.

The Acas Code applies to disciplinary situations, and para 1 states that 'disciplinary situations include misconduct and poor performance', so it is also applicable in a capability dismissal.

The Code sets out the process for disciplinary matters, which is as follows:

- Establish the facts of each case.
- Inform the employee of the problem.
- Hold a meeting with the employee.
- At that meeting, allow the employee to be accompanied.
- Decide on the appropriate action.
- Provide the employee with an opportunity to appeal.

(See **5.4.2.1** and **5.4.2.2** below for further detail.) While an employer may lay down its own procedures, it will need to ensure that these meet the minimum standards of the Acas Code.

Under s 10 of the ERA 1999, workers have a statutory right to be accompanied at a disciplinary hearing. This right applies only where the worker 'reasonably requests' the presence of a companion. Where the worker's request is reasonable, the employer must permit the companion to attend (see eg *Roberts v The Regard Partnership* (ET/2104545/09)). Note that while the worker may choose whom he wishes to accompany him, his choice of companion is limited under s 10 to trade union officials or fellow workers. Some organisation will, however, permit a wider choice of companion in their disciplinary procedures. There may be limited circumstances where the employee asks to be accompanied by a person other than a colleague or trade union representative and where a denial of such a request could amount to a breach of trust and confidence (see *Stevens v University of Birmingham* [2015] EWHC 2300 (QB)).

Note that by virtue of ss 37 and 38 of the ERA 2004 (amending s 10 of the ERA 1999), employers must now allow a companion who accompanies an employee to a disciplinary hearing to address the hearing to put an employee's case, to sum up that case and to respond on the employee's behalf. However, the companion is not entitled to answer questions on the worker's behalf. If the employer fails to tell the employee of his right to be accompanied to a disciplinary hearing, or does not allow a companion to attend, this can be taken into account when considering fairness (see Acas Code of Practice at **5.4.1** below). (Note that these provisions also apply to workers – see **1.3.3**.)

Two cases have considered the right to be accompanied. In *Toal v GB Oils Ltd* (UKEAT/0569/12), the claimant requested that he be accompanied at a grievance hearing by a member of his trade union. The manager refused to allow the union member to attend, because he considered that he might prejudice the hearing. The claimant asked another union member to represent him. The grievance was not upheld and the claimant complained to an employment tribunal under s 10. The EAT, overturning the decision of the tribunal, held that the claimant had an absolute right to choose his companion: the use of the word 'reasonably' in s 10(1)(b) applied to the right to request to be accompanied but not to the choice of companion. Although the Acas Code (see below) suggests that 'it would not normally be reasonable for workers to insist on being accompanied by a companion whose presence would prejudice the hearing', the Code was not an available aid to the interpretation of a statute. The Acas Code has twice been amended in the light of this decision. In *Gnahoua v Abellio London Ltd* (ET/ 2303661/2015), however, a tribunal confirmed that in such a case, where a nominated companion was within the statutory categories but was otherwise unsuitable, only nominal damages may be appropriate.

In *Leeds Dental Team Ltd v Mrs D Rose* (UK EAT/0016/13), the claimant wanted to be accompanied to a disciplinary hearing by the former owner of the dental practice. The respondent refused: the claimant went off sick and then resigned, bringing a constructive unfair dismissal claim, including the refusal to allow her to be accompanied by the former owner. The tribunal held that the respondent's refusal was unreasonable and contributed to a breach of trust and confidence. There was no breach of s 10 on the facts, but the refusal contributed to a breach of trust and confidence. (See too *Stevens v University of Birmingham* [2015] EWHC 2300 (QB), where the High Court held it was unfair for the University to refuse the claimant a companion of his choosing, and that amounted to a breach of the implied term of trust and confidence, such that the claimant was entitled to a declaration that he had permission to be accompanied by his choice of person.)

As noted above, a failure to follow the Code, where it applies, gives tribunals a discretionary power to increase or decrease the unfair dismissal award (and presumably other awards that also arise out of the disciplinary process or dismissal on grounds of misconduct or capability, eg claims of unlawful discrimination, wrongful dismissal, unlawful deduction of wages) by up to 25%, if they consider that the employer's/employee's failure to comply with the Code was unreasonable. It is for the tribunal to decide what uplift (or reduction) would be just and equitable. The full list of claims to which this regime applies is set out in Sch A2 to TULRCA 1992.

To complement the Code, Acas has published guidance. Tribunals cannot adjust awards on account of any failure to follow the guidance, neither are they required to have regard to the guidance. However, it is anticipated that in many cases tribunals will refer to the guidance to assist them in determining whether the employer's handling of misconduct and poor performance matters has complied with general principles of fairness. For that reason, when dealing with disciplinary matters, employers and their advisers should read the relevant section of the guidance and ensure that they comply with it.

5.4.2 Procedural unfairness: particular reasons

The general principles dealt with in **5.3.1** apply to dismissals for any reason. However, where procedural unfairness is concerned, particular reasons may require a particular procedural approach (see below).

The application of an unfair procedure can render a dismissal unfair even though compliance with a fair procedure would have produced the same result of dismissal (*Polkey v AE Dayton Services Ltd* [1987] ICR 301). However, the fact that compliance would have still led to dismissal may be taken into account when considering compensation (a '*Polkey*' deduction) (see **5.6.2.2**).

5.4.2.1 Capability and qualifications

The approach to capability and qualifications should vary depending on whether the incapability is due to incompetence or sickness. The Acas Code covers poor performance/ incompetence.

Incompetence

Before dismissing any employee for incompetence, an employer should normally have met with the employee, warned the employee about his standard of work and given him the opportunity to improve. Where appropriate, adequate training should have been given and review periods set down. In some cases, for example where an employee has been moved to a job beyond his capabilities, the employer should consider whether it is possible to move the employee to a job within his capabilities. Acas gives the following example in the guidance:

> A member of staff in accounts makes a number of mistakes on invoices to customers. You bring the mistakes to his attention, make sure he has had the right training and impress on him the need for accuracy but the mistakes continue. You invite the employee to a disciplinary meeting and inform him of his right to be accompanied by a colleague or employee representative. At the meeting the employee does not give a satisfactory explanation for the mistakes so you decide to issue an improvement note setting out: the problem, the improvement required, the timescale for improvement, the support available and a review date. You inform the employee that a failure to improve may lead to a final written warning.

In *Williams v Meddygfa Rhydbach Surgery* (ET/1600487/2016), an employment tribunal decision, the tribunal found that Mrs Williams had been constructively unfairly dismissed when she was bullied during a mishandled performance management process. Following various personnel changes, Mrs Williams, who had been employed for 30 years, was considered to have been over-promoted and was no longer well regarded by some of the practice. During a performance meeting, one of the doctors raised his voice and banged his fist on the table. Mrs Williams brought a grievance and, when it was not upheld, resigned. The employment tribunal found that the performance management had not been properly carried out and she had been bullied. This is a first instance decision and could be appealed, but it serves as a reminder of the importance of dealing with performance management issues in a structured and measured way.

Readers should always have regard to the guidance produced by Acas (see the overview chart reproduced at **5.4.2.2**).

Sickness

The Acas Code does not explicitly cover dismissals by reason of ill-health, but the guidance produced by Acas includes a section dealing with ill-health absences, which employers would be well advised to read.

Absence may be due to sickness or may be a misconduct issue, which means that different procedural considerations may arise and may be appropriate.

An employee may be fairly dismissed for long-term sickness. The nature and likely duration of the illness and the length of service of the employee are relevant, as are the needs of the employer. A key employee or an employee in a small firm may need to be replaced by an employer more quickly than a less vital employee or one in a larger firm. Ultimately, the test is whether the employer could reasonably be expected to wait any longer for the employee (*Spencer v Paragon Wallpapers Ltd* [1976] IRLR 373).

The employer should consult with the employee concerning the nature and likely length of the illness, seek medical advice relating to the condition of the employee and consider whether suitable alternative employment can be offered. Under the Access to Medical Reports Act 1988, the written consent of an employee is required before the employer can obtain a medical report from the employee's specialist or doctor. The medical practitioner must be responsible for the clinical care of the individual. For this reason, reports prepared by occupational doctors are normally exempt. Warnings would not normally be appropriate, but an employee who takes a large number of short breaks for illness could be warned about his attendance record.

The EAT held in *DB Schenker Rail (UK) Ltd v Doolan* (UKEATS/0053/09) that where there is a conflict in medical evidence, the employer need only show that it acted within the range of reasonable responses when preferring the evidence of one expert over another. The decision to dismiss in capability cases is a managerial one for the employer and not a medical one for doctors.

According to the EAT in *Edwards v Governors of Hanson School* [2001] IRLR 733, if an employer has

> acted maliciously, or wilfully caused an employee incapacitating ill-health, we see no reason why dismissal, however fair the ultimate procedures in themselves, should not lead to a finding of unfair dismissal.

This may mean that a dismissal of an employee on long-term sick absence caused by bullying and mismanagement at work may be unfair.

In *Frewin v Consignia plc* [2003] All ER (D) 314 (Jul), the EAT stated that, when considering the fairness of a dismissal, a tribunal is entitled to take into account whether the incapacity was caused by the employer. The EAT said that

> the weight to be attached to that factor would depend on all the circumstances of the case. In some instances, the existence of causation could render the decision to dismiss unfair; in other cases it might not. Thus the existence of a causative link would not require the conclusion that the decision to dismiss had been unfair or raise any presumption of unfairness. It was merely a factor to be considered and weighed in the balance.

In *First Leeds v Haigh* (UKEAT/0246/07), the EAT held that a capability dismissal will normally be unfair if an employer fails to take reasonable steps to ascertain whether an employee is entitled to an ill-health retirement (see also *Apsden v Webb Poultry & Meat Group (Holdings) Ltd* [1996] IRLR 521).

In *O'Brien v Bolton St Catherine's Academy* [2017] IRLR 547, the claimant had been off work for over a year, and there was no evidence that she would be fit to return in the foreseeable future, if at all, when the decision to dismiss was taken. However, the position had changed by the time of the appeal hearing. There was now evidence, albeit not unproblematic, that she was fit to return to work at once. The Court of Appeal held that it was open to the tribunal to hold that it was unreasonable for the school to disregard that new evidence without at least a further assessment by its own occupational health advisers. The dismissal was therefore unfair.

The impact of the disability discrimination provisions of the Equality Act 2010 should always be considered in relation to an ill-health dismissal. This area is considered further in **Chapter 13**. In *Awan v ICTS UK Ltd* (UKEAT/0087/18) the dangers of dismissing an employee for incapacity where they have a contractual entitlement to long-term disability benefits or permanent health insurance were made clear.

Care is needed when dealing with employees with drug or alcohol problems. It will be important to determine at an early stage whether the issue should be dealt with as a capability or as a misconduct issue. This may be determined by reference to any disciplinary policies, and whether the drug or alcohol problem impacts on the employee's performance at work.

5.4.2.2   Conduct

As mentioned previously, the type of misconduct may vary greatly, from incidents of a minor nature (eg bad time-keeping) to gross misconduct (eg theft or divulging trade secrets).

It is important, however, to determine what the real reason for the dismissal is – for example, if the reason for the dismissal is a breakdown in trust and confidence caused by the employee's behaviour, an employer does not need to follow its contractual conduct dismissal procedure (see *Ezsias v North Glamorgan NHS Trust* (UKEAT/0399/09)). In *Ezsias*, the EAT upheld the tribunal's decision that Mr Ezsias had been fairly dismissed for 'some other substantial reason' where Mr Ezsias' behaviour had led to relationships in the department breaking down (see **5.4.2.5**).

The important feature here, when considering the reasonableness of the employer's actions, is how he handled the situation.

The Acas guidance gives an overview on 'Handling discipline', as shown in **Figure 5.1**.

Figure 5.1   Handling discipline – an overview

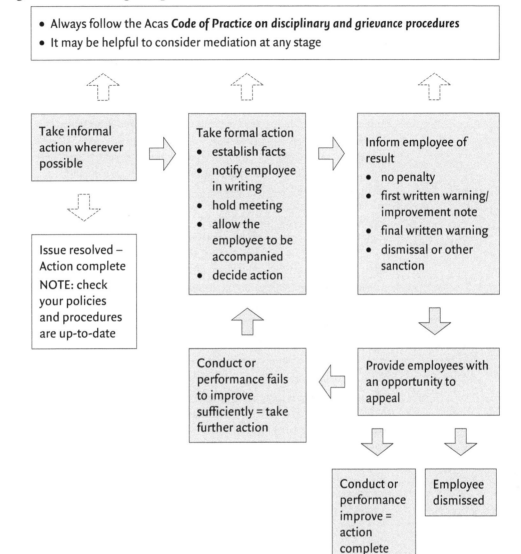

Source: Acas, *Discipline and grievances at work*

An extract from the Code follows:

> Keys to handling disciplinary issues in the workplace
>
> **Establish the facts of each case**
>
> 5.   It is important to carry out necessary investigations of potential disciplinary matters without unreasonable delay to establish the facts of the case. In some cases this will require the holding of an investigatory meeting with the employee before proceeding to any disciplinary hearing. In others, the investigatory stage will be the collation of evidence by the employer for use at any disciplinary hearing.
>
> 6.   In misconduct cases, where practicable, different people should carry out the investigation and disciplinary hearing.
>
> 7.   If there is an investigatory meeting this should not by itself result in any disciplinary action. Although there is no statutory right for an employee to be accompanied at a formal investigatory meeting, such a right may be allowed under an employer's own procedure.

8. In cases where a period of suspension with pay is considered necessary, this period should be as brief as possible, should be kept under review and it should be made clear that this suspension is not considered a disciplinary action.

Inform the employee of the problem

9. If it is decided that there is a disciplinary case to answer, the employee should be notified of this in writing. This notification should contain sufficient information about the alleged misconduct or poor performance and its possible consequences to enable the employee to prepare to answer the case at a disciplinary meeting. It would normally be appropriate to provide copies of any written evidence, which may include any witness statements, with the notification.

10. The notification should also give details of the time and venue for the disciplinary meeting and advise the employee of their right to be accompanied at the meeting.

Hold a meeting with the employee to discuss the problem

11. The meeting should be held without unreasonable delay whilst allowing the employee reasonable time to prepare their case.

12. Employers and employees (and their companions) should make every effort to attend the meeting. At the meeting the employer should explain the complaint against the employee and go through the evidence that has been gathered. The employee should be allowed to set out their case and answer any allegations that have been made. The employee should also be given a reasonable opportunity to ask questions, present evidence and call relevant witnesses. They should also be given an opportunity to raise points about any information provided by witnesses. Where an employer or employee intends to call relevant witnesses they should give advance notice that they intend to do this.

Allow the employee to be accompanied at the meeting

13. Workers have a statutory right to be accompanied by a companion where the disciplinary meeting could result in:
    - a formal warning being issued; or
    - the taking of some other disciplinary action; or
    - the confirmation of a warning or some other disciplinary action (appeal hearings).

14. The statutory right is to be accompanied by a fellow worker, a trade union representative, or an official employed by a trade union. A trade union representative who is not an employed official must have been certified by their union as being competent to accompany a worker. Employers must agree to a worker's request to be accompanied by any companion from one of these categories. Workers may also alter their choice of companion if they wish. As a matter of good practice, in making their choice workers should bear in mind the practicalities of the arrangements. For instance, a worker may choose to be accompanied by a companion who is suitable, willing and available on site rather than someone from a geographically remote location.

15. To exercise the statutory right to be accompanied workers must make a reasonable request. What is reasonable will depend on the circumstances of each individual case. A request to be accompanied does not have to be in writing or within a certain timeframe. However, a worker should provide enough time for the employer to deal with the companion's attendance at the meeting. Workers should also consider how they make their request so that it is clearly understood, for instance by letting the employer know in advance the name of the companion where possible and whether they are a fellow worker or trade union official or representative.

16. If a worker's chosen companion will not be available at the time proposed for the hearing by the employer, the employer must postpone the hearing to a time proposed by the worker provided that the alternative time is both reasonable and not more than five working days after the date originally proposed.

17. The companion should be allowed to address the hearing to put and sum up the worker's case, respond on behalf of the worker to any views expressed at the meeting and confer with the worker during the hearing. The companion does not, however, have the right to answer questions on the worker's behalf, address the hearing if the worker does not wish it or prevent the employer from explaining their case.

Decide on appropriate action

18. After the meeting decide whether or not disciplinary or any other action is justified and inform the employee accordingly in writing.

19. Where misconduct is confirmed or the employee is found to be performing unsatisfactorily it is usual to give the employee a written warning. A further act of misconduct or failure to improve performance within a set period would normally result in a final written warning.

20. If an employee's first misconduct or unsatisfactory performance is sufficiently serious, it may be appropriate to move directly to a final written warning. This might occur where the employee's actions have had, or are liable to have, a serious or harmful impact on the organisation.

21. A first or final written warning should set out the nature of the misconduct or poor performance and the change in behaviour or improvement in performance required (with timescale). The employee should be told how long the warning will remain current. The employee should be informed of the consequences of further misconduct, or failure to improve performance, within the set period following a final warning. For instance that it may result in dismissal or some other contractual penalty such as demotion or loss of seniority.

22. A decision to dismiss should only be taken by a manager who has the authority to do so. The employee should be informed as soon as possible of the reasons for the dismissal, the date on which the employment contract will end, the appropriate period of notice and their right of appeal.

23. Some acts, termed gross misconduct, are so serious in themselves or have such serious consequences that they may call for dismissal without notice for a first offence. But a fair disciplinary process should always be followed, before dismissing for gross misconduct.

24. Disciplinary rules should give examples of acts which the employer regards as acts of gross misconduct. These may vary according to the nature of the organisation and what it does, but might include things such as theft or fraud, physical violence, gross negligence or serious insubordination.

25. Where an employee is persistently unable or unwilling to attend a disciplinary meeting without good cause the employer should make a decision on the evidence available.

Provide employees with an opportunity to appeal

26. Where an employee feels that disciplinary action taken against them is wrong or unjust they should appeal against the decision. Appeals should be heard without unreasonable delay and ideally at an agreed time and place. Employees should let employers know the grounds for their appeal in writing.

27. The appeal should be dealt with impartially and wherever possible, by a manager who has not previously been involved in the case.

28. Workers have a statutory right to be accompanied at appeal hearings.

29. Employees should be informed in writing of the results of the appeal hearing as soon as possible.

The Acas Guidance gives the following examples:

---

1. An employee in a small firm makes a series of mistakes in letters to one of your key customers promising impossible delivery dates. The customer is upset at your firm's failure to meet delivery dates and threatens to take his business elsewhere.

   You are the owner of the business and carry out an investigation and invite the employee to a disciplinary meeting. You inform her of her right to be accompanied by a colleague or an employee representative.

   Example outcome of meeting

   At the meeting the employee does not give a satisfactory explanation for the mistakes and admits that her training covered the importance of agreeing realistic delivery dates with her manager. During your investigation, her team leader and section manager told you they had stressed to the employee the importance of agreeing delivery dates with them before informing the customer. In view of the seriousness of the mistakes and the possible impact on the business, you issue the employee with a final written warning. You inform the employee that failure to improve will lead to dismissal and of her right to appeal.

> **Example outcome of meeting in different circumstances**
>
> At the meeting, the employee reveals that her team leader would not let her attend training as the section was too busy. Subsequently the team leader was absent sick and the employee asked the section manager for help with setting delivery dates. The manager said he was too busy and told the employee to 'use her initiative'. Your other investigations support the employee's explanation. You inform the employee that you will not be taking disciplinary action and will make arrangements for her to be properly trained. You decide to carry out a review of general management standards on supervision and training.
>
> 2.   A member of your telephone sales team has been to lunch to celebrate success in an exam. He returns from lunch in a very merry mood, is slurring his speech and is evidently not fit to carry out his duties. You decide to send him home and invite him in writing to a disciplinary meeting setting out his alleged behaviour of gross misconduct for which he could be dismissed. Your letter includes information about his right to be accompanied by a colleague or an employee representative. At the meeting he admits he had too much to drink, is very apologetic and promises that such a thing will not happen again. He is one of your most valued members of staff and has an exemplary record over his 10 years service with you. You know that being unfit for work because of excessive alcohol is listed in your company rules as gross misconduct. In view of the circumstances and the employee's record, however, you decide not to dismiss him but give him a final written warning. You inform the employee of his right to appeal.

Note: The Guidance is not the same as the Code and is not statutorily binding; although it can still be referred to in terms of fairness, breaches of it do not count for s 207A purposes (see **5.6.2**).

Some principles derived from case law

Characterisation of the misconduct

As mentioned above (**5.2.2.2**), it is important that employers correctly characterise misconduct, in particular if it is said to be gross misconduct, as this may trigger different procedural routes in any disciplinary policy, but will also be relevant as to whether a decision to dismiss is reasonable. It will also have implications for wrongful dismissal (see **Chapter 2**). Ultimately, to dismiss for gross misconduct, an employee's conduct has to be so serious that it warrants dismissal without prior warnings and without notice.

This was considered by the EAT in the case of *Eastlands Homes Partnership Ltd v Cunningham* (UKEAT/0272/13), where Mr Cunningham had been a caretaker in a care home for the elderly, run by the respondent housing association, for 32 years. He had an exemplary record. One of the tenants left his entire estate to Mr Cunningham and his wife. Mr Cunningham's wife was appointed sole executor of his will. The respondent's code of conduct prevented employees accepting gifts worth more than £50, but also stated that any gifts must be approved by the management. Mr Cunningham failed to notify the respondent of his inheritance until after a disciplinary investigation had begun. He was dismissed for gross misconduct on the basis of a serious breach of trust occasioned by his non-disclosure. The employment tribunal said that the dismissal was unfair and wrongful. The EAT allowed the respondent's appeal. The EAT said that the tribunal had failed to analyse the misconduct or the respondent's approach to that misconduct, in terms of whether it was capable of amounting to gross misconduct or whether it was reasonable for the respondent to believe it was gross misconduct.

In most cases of misconduct, notice (or, if the contract so provides, payment in lieu) should still be given in accordance with the contract. However, in the case of gross misconduct, this amounts to a repudiation of the contract by the employee, entitling the employer to terminate without notice or give payment in lieu (see **Chapter 2**).

Note that where a tribunal finds that the conduct justifying a dismissal was not gross misconduct, so as not to justify summary dismissal (ie without notice), this will not (necessarily) mean that the dismissal is unfair, although it may mean that the dismissal is wrongful if no notice was given.

Warnings

The Acas Code of Practice provides for a graduated system of warnings. Warnings are a critical part of the disciplinary and dismissal process. Depending on the seriousness of the misconduct, they may be oral, written or final. Warnings should usually have some sort of fixed time-limit. For serious misconduct, however, it may be appropriate to skip the imposition of a first written warning and, for gross misconduct, to dismiss without warning (see paras 18–22 of the Code, above). In *Sandwell & West Birmingham Hospitals NHS Trust v Westwood* (UKEAT/0032/09), the EAT held that the question of what amounts to gross misconduct is a mixed question of law and fact: as a matter of law it connotes deliberate wrongdoing or gross negligence. Thus tribunals must consider the character of the conduct and whether it was so serious as to amount to gross misconduct (see above).

In *Davies v Sandwell MBC* [2013] EWCA Civ 135, the Court of Appeal held that it is not open to the Employment Tribunal (ET) to re-open a warning. Rather, 'the function of the ET is to apply the objective statutory test of reasonableness to determine whether the ... warning was a circumstance, which a reasonable employer could reasonably take into account ...' The Court of Appeal agreed that it is relevant for the ET to consider 'whether the final warning was issued in good faith, whether there were prima facie grounds for following the warning procedure and whether it was manifestly inappropriate to issue the warning'. The test for looking behind a written warning applies to both conduct and capability warnings. The EAT in *Fallahi v TWI* (UKEAT/0140/19) applied *Sandwell* and noted the limited scope for going behind a final written warning when considering fairness. A tribunal has to judge the reasonableness of the dismissal in all the circumstances, not simply whether the final warning was reasonable or appropriate. Although the warning is a relevant factor, it is only one of many. In this case, which concerned a capability dismissal, where there was a history of performance issues, the tribunal was entitled to find that the warning was not 'manifestly inappropriate' and so was within the range of reasonable responses test. However, in conduct cases, a final warning can leave an employee at risk of dismissal for misconduct unrelated to that which led to a final written warning, so in such cases the 'validity' of the final warning will still be crucial.

It is clear that where a previous warning has expired, it may not be taken into account in a case in which, but for the previous warning, the employer would not have shown a reason for dismissing the employee (*Diosynth Ltd v Thomson* [2006] IRLR 284). However, the Court of Appeal confirmed in *Airbus UK Ltd v Webb* [2008] IRLR 309 that an expired warning may be taken into account where the expired final warning was not the reason, or the principal reason, shown for dismissal, but rather its relevance was to whether the range of reasonable responses to the later misconduct included dismissal for that misconduct. It might also be relevant where an allegation of inconsistent treatment is raised by the employee. The absence of previous misconduct and of a final warning may provide a reason for imposing a lesser penalty on another employee. (See too *Stratford v Auto Trail VR Ltd* (UKEAT/0116/16).)

If an employee is at risk of dismissal, he must be told of this in advance of the hearing, otherwise the dismissal may be unfair. See, for example, *Boyd v Renfrewshire Council* [2008] CSIH 36. Mr Boyd was summarily dismissed for gross misconduct in 'deliberately and wilfully' taking an unauthorised break and failing to complete his work. The tribunal found that the dismissal was unfair because it had not been alleged until after the disciplinary hearing that Mr Boyd's actions were 'wilful', nor had there previously been any mention of gross misconduct or the possibility of dismissal. The tribunal's decision was upheld by the Court of Session.

In *Way v Spectrum Property Care Ltd* [2015] EWCA Civ 381, the Court of Appeal looked at whether, where an employee alleges that a previous warning was in bad faith, there is any obligation on the employer or the employment tribunal to reconsider that. The claimant was dismissed for misconduct in December 2013. Previously, in December 2010, he had been given a final 12-month written warning and informed of his right of appeal against the imposition of the warning. He said he was told not to appeal, as there was a risk it could end up with dismissal. The warning letter stated that the claimant needed to be familiar with the policies and procedures in the Staff Handbook. Both before and after the December 2010 warning (which was not connected to sending e-mails), the claimant had sent 'inappropriate' e-mails, which were not in accordance with the staff policies and procedures. Management carried out a general crackdown on inappropriate e-mail usage, and judged this employee's e-mails to fall into a 'red' category, which meant that they were regarded as warranting a final warning (as opposed to a gold warning, which would have meant that they were sufficiently serious to initiate the gross misconduct disciplinary process, or an amber warning, which would have resulted only in a letter of concern). However, because the claimant was already on a final written warning, it was decided there should be a disciplinary hearing, as a result of which the claimant was dismissed. At his appeal, he raised what he said was the bad faith of the previous warning. That contention was rejected. The employment tribunal and the EAT both found the dismissal to be fair, relying principally on the live final written warning. The claimant appealed. The Court of Appeal referred to *Davies v Sandwell* (above), which held that the essential principle is that it is legitimate for an employer to rely on a final warning when deciding to dismiss for a further offence, provided that it was issued in good faith, there were at least prima facie grounds for imposing it and it must not have been manifestly inappropriate to issue it. The Court also referred to *Wincanton Group plc v Stone* [2013] IRLR 178, where the EAT gave specific guidance to tribunals (para 37) to the effect:

> If a tribunal is not satisfied that the first warning was issued for an oblique motive or was manifestly inappropriate or, put another way, was not issued in good faith nor with prima facie grounds for making it, then the earlier warning will be valid. If it is so satisfied, the earlier warning will not be valid and cannot and should not be relied upon subsequently.

The Court of Appeal said that the fact that the claimant had been given a final warning was highly relevant to the reasonableness or otherwise of any subsequent decision to dismiss him, as it meant that he had been found guilty of misconduct and had been warned that a further act of misconduct meant he was likely to be dismissed. The warning had therefore taken him a step further down the disciplinary road to dismissal. The Court of Appeal went on to say, however, that where a warning is given in bad faith, it should not be taken into account in deciding whether there is, or was, sufficient reason for dismissing an employee. It was not reasonable for an employer to take into account such a warning; and it would not be in accordance with equity or the substantial merits of the case to do so. Whether a warning was given in bad faith was a matter of fact, which a tribunal would, in an appropriate case, have to determine for itself on the evidence. The tribunal could not therefore rely on the employer's own assessment of the position. For a recent application of the 'manifestly inappropriate' test being applied (and failing), see *Beattie v Condorrat War Memorial and Social Club* (EATS/0019/17).

Suspension

When someone is the subject of a serious allegation of misconduct at work, their employer may decide to suspend them whilst it undertakes an investigation. The usual reasons given for suspending employees include the seriousness of the misconduct, a severe breakdown of working relationships, or a belief that the employee could compromise the integrity of the investigation in some way. If someone is suspended, they remain employed and should continue to be paid, but they do not have to attend work or undertake any usual contractual duties.

Before taking a decision to suspend, employers must carefully consider all of the circumstances and be sure that suspension is an appropriate action to take. It must consider other options, such as working from home or being transferred to another area of the business. Acas advises that it is normally best for an employer to avoid suspending an employee during a disciplinary investigation. Suspension cannot realistically be viewed as a 'neutral act' and will inevitably reflect on an employee's character or ability to carry out their role. As such, employers must show that there is a 'reasonable and proper cause' for suspension. Before any suspension commences, employers are advised to send a letter setting out the reason for the suspension, the proposed length of the suspension, the employee's rights and obligations during the suspension and a point of contact, and make clear that the purpose of the suspension is to investigate and is not an assumption of guilt.

In October 2022, Acas published updated guidance on when and how to suspend employees and the process that should be adopted. Readers should refer to this where appropriate, bearing in mind that it is not legally binding.

Depending on all the facts, an employer may wish to suspend the employee pending the outcome of an investigation. So long as the employer is not under an obligation to provide the employee with work (see **1.7.1.1**), he will not normally be acting in breach of contract to suspend the employee with pay. Clearly, if there is a contractual clause allowing for suspension with pay, there can then be no argument about breach of the right to be provided with work.

In *Gogay v Hertfordshire County Council* [2000] IRLR 703 (see **2.4.1.5**), the Court of Appeal upheld the High Court's finding that suspension of an employee was in breach of the implied duty of trust and confidence. The woman employee had been suspended (on full pay under a contractual clause) pending the outcome of an investigation. The letter sent to the employee said that 'the issue to be investigated is an allegation of sexual abuse by a young person in our care'. In the event, the investigation concluded that there was no case to answer and that the child had never said anything which might be construed as an allegation of abuse. The Court of Appeal says that it does not inevitably follow that an employee should be suspended merely because there are reasonable grounds for an investigation. There are other options open to an employer, such as transfer. There must be reasonable and proper cause for a suspension. In the case of *Mayor and Burgesses of the London Borough of Lambeth v Agoreyo* [2019] EWCA Civ 322, the Court of Appeal considered whether suspension of a teacher for child protection reasons was a breach of trust and confidence (see **3.4.3** above). It held on the facts that it was not, as the school had reasonable and proper cause for the suspension. Explanations given at the time should be considered, along with alternatives to suspension.

Factors to consider before suspending include:

- How serious is the alleged offence?
- Are fuller preliminary investigations appropriate before suspending?
- Are there risks if an employee remains (theft, damage, repeat, danger to others)?
- Might the employee influence the investigation (influence witnesses, remove evidence)?
- What is the employee's role, length of service, disciplinary record?
- How have others been treated?
- Are there alternatives available?

The Acas guidance makes it clear that suspension with pay may be considered for certain cases such as gross misconduct or where relationships have broken down, or where it is considered that there is a risk to an employer's property or responsibilities to others. However, the guidance emphasises that such suspension should be imposed only after careful consideration and should be reviewed to ensure that it is not unnecessarily protracted.

While on suspension, employees should be kept informed as to the ongoing reasons for it and its likely length, which should be kept as short as possible. Employees should receive their normal salary. As far as possible, the suspension should be kept confidential. If a suspension has been unfairly imposed or inappropriately handled, it may contribute to arguments that a dismissal was unfair. In extreme circumstances, it may give rise to grounds to seek an injunction to force the employer to end the suspension; or an employee could resign and claim 'constructive dismissal' (see **Chapter 3**).

Investigations

The Acas Code sets out that an employer should establish the facts of each case. This means that, generally speaking, before there is a disciplinary hearing, an employer will need to carry out an investigation into the alleged misconduct. Depending on the size of the organisation, it is preferable for different people to carry out the investigation and the hearing. The employer should carry out the investigation as quickly as possible.

An investigation may require the employer to interview the employee and get his account of the incident, and also to interview any witnesses or others involved in the incident. The employer should try to take notes of any such interviews. It may be appropriate for an employer to examine any physical evidence that may exist, for example where something is recorded on CCTV.

The employer should consider the results of the investigation and decide whether it is appropriate to proceed to a disciplinary hearing. Where the matter is to proceed to a hearing, the employer should normally make any notes of interview and other evidence relied upon available to the employee before the hearing.

The Court of Appeal considered the scope of a reasonable investigation in a conduct dismissal in *Shrestha v Genesis Housing Association Ltd* [2015] EWCA Civ 94. The claimant contended, when challenged over allegations of inflating his expenses, that there was an obligation on his employer to investigate in full all the defences he advanced. The Court of Appeal said such an approach would add an 'unwarranted gloss' to the range of reasonable responses test. Any investigation should be looked at as a whole. Employers must consider those defences that are advanced, but whether and to what extent it is necessary to carry out a specific inquiry into each of them will depend on the circumstances. On the facts in this case, the assessment, that the claimant's explanations were not plausible, was a reasonable assessment in the circumstances, with the result that it was unnecessary for the employer to pursue any further inquiries into the claimant's explanations.

The Court of Appeal held, in *Sainsbury's Supermarkets Ltd v Hitt* [2003] IRLR 23, that the range of reasonable responses test 'applies as much to the question of whether the investigation into the suspected misconduct was reasonable in all the circumstances as it does to ... the decision to dismiss'. In *Gratton v Hutton* (2003) unreported, 1 July, the EAT emphasised that the test is not whether further investigation might reasonably have been carried out but whether the investigation which *had* been carried out could be regarded by a reasonable employer as adequate. Furthermore, the Court of Appeal held in *Panama v London Borough of Hackney* [2003] IRLR 278 that the employer's failure to obtain evidence to support an allegation of misconduct meant that it neither had reasonable grounds for its belief, nor had it carried out as much investigation into the matter as was reasonable in all the circumstances.

In *Salford Royal NHS Foundation Trust v Roldan* [2010] IRLR 721, the Court of Appeal confirmed that when carrying out an investigation into allegations of gross misconduct, employers should take into account the gravity of the potential consequences for an employee. This may mean a more thorough investigation is required in cases where there are potentially significant consequences for the employee if he loses his job. In *Roldan*, the employee, who was a nurse, lost her work permit and consequently her right to stay in the UK, and also became the subject of a criminal investigation by the police.

An investigation need not necessarily be recorded in writing, although a written record of witnesses' evidence is generally required (*Now Motor Retailing Ltd v Mulvihill* (UKEAT/0052/15)).

For a recent case on investigations, see *The Governing Body of Tywyn Primary School v Aplin* (UKEAT/0298/17). In *Radia v Jefferies International Ltd* (UKEAT/0123/18), an employer relied on findings of an employment tribunal and did not hold an investigation. The claimant was given the opportunity to comment and raise issues at the disciplinary hearing. The EAT held that relying on the employment tribunal findings as a basis for dismissal was within the range of reasonable responses in the particular circumstances.

Conduct of the hearing

Section 10 of the Employment Relations Act 1999 provides for an employee to be accompanied and requires an employer to agree to a request to postpone a hearing where the rescheduled date is within five days of the original date. However, an unreasonable refusal to agree to a longer postponement may render a dismissal procedurally unfair (see *Talon Engineering Ltd v Smith* (UKEAT/0236/17)).

In *Ramsey v Walkers Snack Foods Ltd* [2004] IRLR 754 the EAT confirmed that it is possible to have a fair procedure where witnesses for the employer insist on anonymity because, on the facts, there was a very real fear of reprisals against the witnesses. In *Linfood Cash & Carry Ltd v Thompson* [1989] IRLR 235 the EAT set out guidelines to assist in balancing the need for a fair hearing with protecting witnesses. In outline, the employer should ensure that the information given by the informant is reduced into writing, noting key facts such as date, time and place, clarity of observation, circumstantial evidence, such as the reason for the presence of the informer and why certain small details are memorable, whether the informant has suffered at the hands of the accused or has any other reason to fabricate, whether from personal grudge or any other reason.

Further investigation can then take place, including inquiries into the character and background of the informant, or any other information which may tend to add or detract from the value of the information. If the employer is satisfied that the fear is genuine then a decision will need to be made whether or not to continue with the disciplinary process. If it is to continue, it is best if, at each stage of the process, the member of management responsible for the hearing should himself interview the informant and satisfy himself that weight is to be given to the information. The written statement of the informant, if necessary with omissions to avoid identification, should be made available to the employee and his representatives. Full and careful notes should be taken during all stage of the disciplinary process, and if evidence from an investigating officer is to be taken at a hearing, it should, where possible, be prepared in a written form.

The tribunal will want to make clear findings as to the extent of the respondent's investigation into the reasons why the informant is insisting on anonymity, and then carry out a balancing act between the respondent's perceived need to protect the identity of the informant and natural justice that the claimant should know sufficiently the nature of the case against him, applying the band of reasonable responses test.

The EAT confirmed that there is 'no rule of law which renders it incumbent on an employer, when dismissing an employee for misconduct ... [to give] the employee who is liable to be dismissed the opportunity to cross-examine the person making the complaint' (*Santamera v Express Cargo Forwarding t/a IEC Ltd* [2003] IRLR 273).

In *Corus UK Ltd v Mainwaring* (UKEAT/0053/07) the EAT held that there is no obligation to take a witness statement from an employee who 'tips off' an employer about a malingering employee, where the employer subsequently relies on his own evidence (eg, video/medical) before dismissing.

In *Hargreaves v Governing Body of Manchester Grammar School* (UKEAT/0048/18) the EAT held that it was within the band of reasonable responses for an employer not to disclose to a disciplinary panel evidence from potential witnesses, who said that they had seen nothing. The tribunal was entitled to conclude that the employer had conducted a fair investigation and that the dismissal was not unfair.

Care needs to be taken as to who the decision maker is – ie who takes the actual decision to dismiss. This would usually be a manager. Managers may need, on occasions, to take advice from human resources (HR) about the process and any issues that arise during the hearing. If the manager's decision is improperly influenced by HR, it is likely that this will render any dismissal unfair (see *Chabra v West London Mental Health NHS Trust* [2014] ICR 194 and *Ramphal v Department for Transport* (UKEAT/0352/14)). An investigating or disciplinary officer is entitled to call on advice from HR, but HR must limit advice to questions of law, procedure and/or process; HR should avoid straying into areas of culpability and appropriateness of sanctions.

Note also *Royal Mail Group Ltd v Jhuti* [2019] UKSC 55, where the Supreme Court held that where a person 'in the hierarchy of responsibility' determines that the employee should be dismissed for a reason, but 'hides it behind an invented reason' which the decision maker (innocent of any improper motive) adopts, the 'reason for the dismissal is the hidden reason, rather than the invented reason'. See too *Uddin v London Borough of Ealing* (UKEAT/0165/19).

Note. Employees need to be careful if they covertly record meetings with employers. In *Phoenix House Ltd v Stockman (No 2)* (UKEAT/0284/17), the employer contended, after it was disclosed by the employee during her employment tribunal case that she had covertly recorded a meeting, that her compensation should be reduced on 'just and equitable grounds' and under *Polkey* (see **5.6.2.2**). The respondent said that, had it known about this, it would have dismissed the claimant for gross misconduct. The tribunal reduced the compensation award by 10% to reflect the circumstances relating to the covert recording. The EAT, in considering this, set out observations on when covert recordings might be misconduct: in general, employers and employees should say if they intend to record meetings and not to do so, except in the most pressing of circumstances, will be misconduct. The intention behind and the nature of what is recorded will be important.

Failure to attend a hearing

An employer may be faced with an employee who is unable or refuses to attend a disciplinary hearing by reason of ill-health. This can cause a dilemma for the employer, who may be keen to get the hearing dealt with quickly. It may be sensible in this situation to ask the employee to produce a note from his GP to the effect that he is not fit to attend the hearing (a 'fit note' stating that the employee cannot work may not be sufficient). Alternatively, an employer might ask its occupational health department to assess the employee. Other options, such as a telephone hearing or a hearing at a neutral venue near the employee's home, or allowing the employee to make written submissions, should be considered where appropriate. If none of these options is possible, the employer should consider adjourning the hearing for a short period. Ultimately, it may be necessary to go ahead in the employee's absence. Tribunals will expect the employer to explain why it went ahead and what efforts were made to get the employee to attend, and to have a full note of the hearing. The employer should also take great care to make sure that the decision, especially if it is one of dismissal, is communicated properly to the employee.

In *Talon Engineering Ltd v Smith* (UKEAT/0236/17), the EAT held that the employment tribunal was entitled to conclude that a refusal to postpone a hearing for two weeks to allow Mrs Smith's union representative to accompany her was, in the circumstances, outside the range of reasonable responses. Although the employer had complied with the rules governing the right to be accompanied, this did not automatically mean that the dismissal was procedurally fair.

Right of appeal

The employee should have the right to appeal against any disciplinary action taken. In *Afzal v East London Pizza Ltd* (UKEAT/0265/17), the EAT emphasised that the whole dismissal process, including an appeal, was relevant to the question of fairness (see too *Radia* above). There has been some discussion over the years as to whether an appeal can remedy procedural defects at the initial hearing. Most appeals are not a full rehearing of all the facts and evidence but tend to be reviews of what has gone before. The conventional wisdom was that procedural defects at the initial hearing could only be cured by an appeal which took the form of a full rehearing (which was a matter of substance not label – see, for example, *Whitbread & Co v Mills* [1988] IRLR 501). However, the Court of Appeal in *Taylor v OCS Group Ltd* [2006] EWCA Civ 702 disapproved of that approach, and said that the essential question, when deciding whether a dismissal is fair under ERA 1996, s 98(4), is whether the employer acted reasonably. The Court held that where a first hearing is defective, the appeal can cure the defect if the appeal is comprehensive, and that the distinction drawn in previous case law between reviews and rehearings is not helpful. According to Smith LJ, 'what matters is not whether the internal appeal was technically a rehearing or a review but whether the disciplinary process as a whole was fair'. In *Adeshina v St George's University Hospitals NHS Foundation Trust and Others* (UKEAT/0293/14), the EAT held that procedural defects were cured at an appeal hearing and thus rendered a dismissal fair.

In *Patel v Folkestone Nursing Home Ltd* [2018] EWCA Civ 1689, the Court of Appeal, applying *Salmon v Castlebeck Care (Teesdale) Ltd* (UKEAT/0304/14), found that an appeal, which had overturned an earlier dismissal finding, revoked the dismissal and reinstated the employee who was therefore prevented from bringing unfair and wrongful dismissal claims.

In *McMillan v Airedale NHS Foundation Trust* [2014] EWCA Civ 1031, the Court of Appeal held that as a right to appeal against a disciplinary sanction is for the employee's benefit, an increase in sanction would be permitted only if there was an express term in the employment contract allowing this. In McMillan the claimant, a hospital consultant, was disciplined and given a final written warning, following a finding of misconduct. She appealed against the sanction. The appeal panel upheld the finding (after a rehearing) and took steps to reconvene to consider the appropriate sanction. The claimant withdrew her appeal and sought an injunction to prevent the appeal panel considering sanctions. The High Court held:

(a)   that the appeal panel could not, in the absence of express contractual power, impose a more severe sanction;

(b)   because the appeal was withdrawn, the appeal panel could not reconvene to consider sanctions.

An injunction was granted. The Court of Appeal rejected the hospital's appeal and upheld the High Court's decision. Underhill LJ did accept that there was nothing wrong in principle with an employer's reserving an express power to increase sanctions on appeal.

The EAT held in *Adeshina v St George's University Hospitals NHS Foundation Trust and Others* (UKEAT/0293/14) that it endorsed the Acas advice that the person hearing the appeal be more senior to the original decision taker but that, on the facts, a less senior member of a panel of three (where the other two were more senior) did not render the decision unfair.

An appeal will normally be part of a fair procedure, but not invariably so. The relevant circumstances should always be taken into account. See *Moore v Phoenix Product Development Limited* (UKEAT/0070/20) for an example of a case where the lack of an appeal did not render a dismissal unfair – the respondent company was a small organisation, relations between the parties had broken down, the claimant held a senior position and was unrepentant. The tribunal was right to find that an appeal would have been futile, and that was one of the relevant circumstances to be taken into account when considering the fairness of the dismissal. See too *Gwynedd Council v Barratt & Another* [2021] EWCA Civ 1322, where the Court of Appeal upheld the employment tribunal's finding that the lack of appeal was substantively and procedurally unfair on the facts.

Dealing with grievances during a disciplinary process

It can often be a vexed issue for an employer whether a disciplinary process should be put on hold where an employee issues or has an on-going grievance. Employers can be wary of what might be seen as a delaying tactic. The Acas Code provides that the disciplinary process 'may' be temporarily suspended in order to deal with a grievance. The Acas Guidance suggests that where a grievance is raised during a meeting, 'it may sometimes be appropriate' to stop the meeting. An important consideration may be the extent to which the grievance and the disciplinary process are related or arise out of the same facts, or where the grievance is directed against an individual who is involved in the disciplinary process. It is in any event sensible for an employer in this situation, who does not suspend the disciplinary process, to keep a note of why it was not considered appropriate to do so.

The issue of whether the disciplinary process should be suspended was considered by the EAT in *Jinadu v Dockland Buses Ltd* (UKEAT/0434/14). Ms Jinadu was a bus driver for the respondent. Her driving was considered to be below standard and she was instructed to arrange a driving assessment. She did not do so and was eventually dismissed for gross misconduct. She appealed against the decision to dismiss her. The appeal was adjourned to allow her to take her assessment, as a result of which she was required to undertake some corrective training. She failed the training and the appeal was reconvened. At the appeal hearing, Ms Jinadu made various complaints, including of discrimination, against a number of members of the respondent's management. Her appeal against dismissal failed, on the basis of her failure to display an adequate standard of driving and the interests of public safety. An employment tribunal rejected her claim for unfair dismissal. She appealed to the EAT. One of the grounds of appeal was that the respondent should have considered suspending the disciplinary process while Ms Jinadu's grievances were considered. This ground was rejected by the EAT, although it gave no reasons for this. (Ms Jinadu succeeded in her appeal on other grounds.)

Social media

Social media have increasingly become relevant in unfair dismissal cases (see Acas research paper, *Workplaces and Social Networking – the Implications for Employment Relations* at <http://www.acas.org.uk>). Employers often use information posted on Facebook and other social media sites as evidence of employees' wrongdoing. This can give rise to a question whether employers should be entitled to rely on such evidence (have they, for example, breached their employee's privacy in accessing the information, or are they interfering with an employee's right to free speech – see **Chapter 15**), but there may also be issues about the employee's use of social media sites during working hours and about what the employer regards as other inappropriate use of social media by staff, even if outside the workplace.

In *Taylor v Somerfield Stores Ltd* (ETS/107487/2007), a supermarket warehouse employee was dismissed for posting video footage on YouTube which captured a colleague hitting another colleague with a plastic bag full of plastic bags in one of the employer's warehouses. The footage did not show who the employees were but did reveal the uniforms they were wearing. The footage was taken down after three days and had only eight hits while it was up, three of which were by the supermarket's managers after they discovered the footage was online. The supermarket held a disciplinary process and dismissed the employee for bringing the supermarket into disrepute and breaching health and safety rules. The employment tribunal found there was no evidence to indicate that the supermarket had been brought into disrepute and found the dismissal unfair. (See also *Teggert v TeleTech UK Ltd* (NIET/00704/11), *Preece v JD Wetherspoons plc* (ET/2104806/10) and *Crisp v Apple Retail UK Ltd* (ET/1500258/11).)

The EAT held in *British Waterways Board v Smith* (UKEAT/0004/15) that it was fair to dismiss on the facts for derogatory comments made about the employer on Facebook. (In August 2016, a policeman (PC Graham Wise), who tweeted abuse about celebrities, was summarily dismissed by Cleveland Police after being found guilty of gross misconduct.) What is important is that employers have a policy on social networking, treat 'electronic behaviour' consistently with 'non-electronic behaviour' and react reasonably to issues around social networking.

In *Plant v API Microelectronics Ltd* (ET/3401454/2016), an employment tribunal held that the dismissal of a long-serving employee with a clean disciplinary record who had made derogatory remarks over social media about her employer was fair. There was a social media policy, the claimant was aware of it and what it entailed. See also *BC and Others v Chief Constable Police Service of Scotland* [2019] CSOH 48 (WhatsApp group chats held not to be private).

In *Forbes v LHR Airport Ltd* (UKEAT/0174/18) (a discrimination case), the EAT held that the posting of an offensive image on a private Facebook account was not done in the 'course of employment' so the employer was not liable. If the right to freedom of expression is raised (see eg *Teggert v TeleTech*), it cannot be used to harass or damage a colleague.

See '"I Lost My Job Over a Facebook Post – Was That Fair?" Discipline and Dismissal for Social Media Activity', 2019 *International Journal of Comparative Labour Law and Industrial Relations* (31 October 2018) for a good account of this area (available to download on SSRN at <https://papers.ssrn.com/sol3/papers.cfm?abstract_id=3276055>) and 'Principles into Practice: Protecting Offensive Beliefs in the Workplace', Amir Paz-Fuchs (<www.uklabourlawblog.com/2020/02/12>).

Suspected misconduct: the approach in *British Home Stores v Burchell* [1978] IRLR 379

What if the employer *suspects* misconduct by an employee? Does he have to be able to prove the employee did the act? An employer can still be fair in dismissing, provided the tribunal is satisfied that:

(a) the employer had a genuine belief in guilt (this is really relevant to the reason for the dismissal);

(b) the employer had reasonable grounds upon which to base the belief; and

(c) the employer carried out a reasonable investigation.

Note: The burden of proof in relation to (b) and (c) is a neutral one, but (as a result of s 6 of the Employment Act 1980) the onus of proof (with regard to the reason for dismissal) lies on the employer. The first of the three elements of *Burchell* is relevant to reason, *not* reasonableness.

In *Boys and Girls Welfare Society* [1996] IRLR 129, the EAT said *BHS v Burchell* was inappropriate if there was no conflict on the facts, for example the employee admitted or did not dispute his guilt. Nevertheless, in *Whitbread plc (t/a Whitbread Medway Inns) v Hall* [2001] IRLR 275, the Court of Appeal made it clear that even where misconduct is admitted (so that an employer does not need to prove that it had reasonable grounds for its belief), an employer is still under a duty to follow a fair procedure, such as hearing explanations and considering other penalties besides dismissal (unless the offence is so heinous that a reasonable employer following good industrial practice could conclude that no explanation or mitigation would make any difference to the decision to dismiss). In *John Lewis plc v Coyne* [2001] IRLR 139, an employment tribunal held that a dismissal for making personal telephone calls (which was not denied), in breach of company rules, was unfair because the employer had failed to investigate the seriousness of the offence, including the purpose of the calls, whether there was any element of personal crisis and whether or not the conduct was persistent.

Criminal offences

An issue which sometimes causes difficulties for employers is whether they can fairly dismiss an employee when the employee is charged with, but not convicted of, a criminal offence, particularly when the employee denies guilt. This should be grounds for dismissal only where it has employment implications. For example:

(a)   Was the offence committed in the course of employment?

(b)   Was it an offence of dishonesty?

(c)   Was the employee in a position of trust?

(d)   Is the employee to be detained in custody?

What is the position where the offence is not related to the employment, but the employer is concerned about its reputation when the employee is arrested and/or charged with, but ultimately not convicted of, a criminal offence? The EAT in *Lafferty v Nuffield Health* (UKEATS/ 0006/19) held, in what it called 'quite a difficult case', that such a dismissal could be fair. The claimant was a hospital porter with a long, unblemished service record with the respondent. His duties included transporting anaesthetised patients. He was charged with a serious sexual offence unconnected with work, which he denied. The respondent dismissed the claimant before any trial, on the basis that there was a risk to its reputation from continuing to employ the claimant when he had access to vulnerable patients. The tribunal found that the dismissal, for some other substantial reason, was fair. The EAT helpfully reviewed the law on dismissals involving unproven allegations of criminal conduct. It said that an employer faced with information about alleged criminal conduct by an employee should not take that information at face value, but should make some inquiry of its own into the circumstances. On the facts of this case, the claimant's job did provide the opportunity for him to commit the kind of act that he was charged with. The EAT accepted that there was a risk of reputational damage for the respondent, which was a charity.

In *L v K* [2021] CSIH 35, a case heard by the Scottish Court of Session, the Court held that it was not unfair to dismiss a teacher who had been suspected but not charged of possessing indecent images of children. The reason for the dismissal was that, whilst it could not be proved that the teacher had downloaded the images, the fact that he may have done gave risk to a safeguarding concern, reputational risk and a breakdown in trust. The employment tribunal found that the teacher had been fairly dismissed for some other substantial reason, a decision upheld by the Court of Session, which held that in some circumstances it will be reasonable for an employer to dismiss someone who may be innocent if there is a genuine and substantial reason to justify the dismissal.

The outcome of any subsequent criminal proceedings does not necessarily have any bearing on the issue of reasonableness. For example, in *Da Costa v Optalis* [1976] IRLR 178, the employee in question was dismissed from his job as a bookkeeper for not keeping proper accounts. He was later prosecuted but was acquitted. The employment tribunal held his dismissal to have been fair. The issues involved were different, as was the standard of proof to be applied.

An employer does not have to delay a disciplinary process pending the outcome of any police investigation or criminal proceedings. He may, however, decide to suspend the employee pending the decision of the criminal court. For a recent case, see the Court of Appeal decision in *North West Anglia NHS Foundation Trust v Gregg* [2019] EWCA Civ 378. In *A v B* [2003] IRLR 405, the EAT emphasised that 'the investigator ... should focus no less on any potential evidence that may exculpate or at least point to the innocence of the employee as he should on the evidence directed toward proving the charges against him'.

The EAT held in *Gondalia v Tesco Stores* (UKEAT/0320/14) that an Employment Judge had not erred when, in considering the fairness of a dismissal for allegedly dishonest conduct, he did not apply the criminal law test for dishonesty (known as the 'Ghosh test': *R v Ghosh* [1982] 3 WLR 110). The appropriate question is whether the employer acted reasonably in treating the alleged dishonesty as a sufficient reason for dismissal.

With regard to employees with drug or alcohol problems, it may need to be initially considered whether this amounts to a capability (ie health) issue or one of conduct. The nature of the employer's business might be relevant here and whether the drugs/alcohol affect the performance of an individual at work. It is important that employers' policies are clear about what course of action will be taken in what circumstances: consumption of drugs or alcohol will not automatically be gross misconduct (see *Ball v First Essex Buses Ltd* (ET/3201435/ 17) and *Glassford v Royal Mail Group* (UKEATS/0012/18)).

Absence

Dealing with an employee's absence can be a complicated issue. In the first instance it can be important that an employer makes the right decision as to whether to treat absence as a conduct issue or as a capability issue. If the latter is appropriate, then a different procedure will need to be adopted from that which would be applied if the absence was a misconduct issue (see **5.4.2.1** above). Persistent lateness or absence may be a conduct issue, as would unauthorised absences and late returns from holiday. These may be properly dealt with under disciplinary processes.

In *Brighton & Sussex University Hospitals HNS Trust v Akinwunmi* (UKEAT/0345/16), the claimant, who was a consultant neurosurgeon, was dismissed after he took 20 months of unauthorised absence following complaints made about him by colleagues. There was a long and complicated history of tit-for-tat complaints. The hospital undertook a number of investigations and reports during the absence. The tribunal accepted that the hospital genuinely believed that the claimant's 20-month unauthorised absence was misconduct and that it had reasonable grounds for that belief. The key issue, however, was whether it was within the band of reasonable responses for them to dismiss the claimant for that reason. The tribunal found that the claimant had been unfairly dismissed. In its view, the situation here was similar to that of an employee who is disciplined for failing to obey a reasonable management instruction. What the hospital did not do during the absence was have any meaningful contact with the claimant. The tribunal found it had made no real efforts to address the claimant's concerns about his colleagues, and as such it had been reasonable for the claimant to refuse to return. In effect the tribunal viewed this as a reasonable failure by the claimant to follow an unreasonable management instruction. The EAT upheld the tribunal's decision. The case is a cautionary tale about dismissals for absence. While unauthorised absence can often be a straightforward misconduct issue – on the face of it an unauthorised absence of over a year would be thought to be a straightforward case for a fair dismissal finding – employers still need to look at the reason for the absence and, where it is or appears to be work-related, they will need to adopt appropriate processes to try to resolve it.

Summary

In coming to a decision whether a conduct dismissal is unfair, a tribunal has to consider not just the reason given by the employer for the dismissal, but whether it was a genuinely held reason, as well as whether dismissal was within the range of reasonable responses of a reasonable employer and whether a fair procedure was followed. This can involve the tribunal making findings of fact on the evidence as it is presented to it.

The Court of Appeal, in the case of *Newbound v Thames Water Utilities Ltd* [2015] EWCA Civ 677, looked in detail at when an employment tribunal was justified in finding that a decision to dismiss on the grounds of conduct was unfair (and also at when such a finding can be challenged on appeal). Mr Newbound was dismissed by Thames Water for misconduct after 34 years of service. He was employed to maintain Thames Water's water assets, including valves known as 'penstocks', which open and close sewers. During a complex, though routine, maintenance operation, which was supervised by others more senior, the claimant and a contractor carried out an inspection without wearing breathing apparatus, which was required for health and safety reasons. This was reported and an investigation was carried out. The claimant was not interviewed as part of the investigation. Possible charges of gross misconduct were identified against the claimant and another less experienced but more senior employee. In the event, gross misconduct charges were laid against the claimant and misconduct charges against the other employee. The claimant was told the nature of the charge and was suspended on full pay. Further investigations were carried out, including into the claimant's record and history. The claimant was not interviewed as part of this investigation. A disciplinary hearing found that he had committed a serious infringement of health and safety rules that amounted to gross misconduct. He was summarily dismissed for this, and it was later added that there was also some other substantial reason as there was a 'loss of trust and confidence'. (The Court of Appeal felt that although this was added as an 'afterthought', and was not an allegation that the claimant had had to meet before, nothing turned on this in that it was 'simply another label attached to the same set of facts'). The claimant appealed against the decision to dismiss him, acknowledging that there had been an error of judgement on his part, but stated that he was sorry and was willing to undergo refresher training. He also referred to his 34 years of service. The decision to dismiss him was upheld. The other employee received a 12-month written warning and had to undergo some additional training.

The claimant decided to issue a claim for unfair dismissal. He sought assistance from his trade union. The union refused to support him and, in a letter to him expressed in 'trenchant' terms, said that because he had been dismissed for 'a very significant and potentially very dangerous breach of health and safety, to both you and others ... the failure to abide by the requirements as set out by the on site briefing is totally damning'. At some point this letter came into the possession of the employers, who made use of it in the tribunal proceedings when cross-examining the claimant. The employment tribunal judge did not mention this in his judgment, but said during the hearing that the views expressed in it could not be binding on him. (The Court of Appeal said that the judge was right to ignore the views expressed in the letter.)

The employment tribunal found that the claimant had been unfairly dismissed but held that he had made a 40% contribution to his dismissal (which impacted on the compensation he was awarded – see **5.6.2.2**). It was accepted that the reason for the dismissal was conduct. The employment tribunal judge expressed some concerns about the investigation but held that, overall, it was reasonable. (That finding was not challenged before the Court of Appeal.) The crucial question for the judge was 'whether the respondent acted reasonably or unreasonably in treating the claimant's conduct as a sufficient reason for dismissal, a question to be decided having regard to equity and the substantial merits of the case'. On the facts, the judge concluded that 'no reasonable employer would have dismissed the employee in the circumstances and that the decision to terminate his employment was perverse'. He also relied on the disparate treatment between the two employees.

The employers appealed to the EAT, which allowed their appeal and dismissed the claimant's claim. The EAT held, inter alia, that the judge had 'failed to consider the reasonableness of the gravity with which' the employer viewed the claimant's conduct. It criticised the judge for relying on the evidence that was given at the hearing before him, rather than on the evidence that was before the employer when taking the decision to dismiss. The EAT found he had 'impermissibly substituted his view of the importance' of a number of factors. On the disparate treatment point, the EAT held that this was 'erroneously based on the EJ's own view of the relative culpability' of the two employees.

The claimant appealed to the Court of Appeal. One of the issues for the Court was the extent to which appellate courts could interfere with the findings of an employment tribunal, the only legal basis for an appeal from an employment tribunal being on a question of law (ETA 1996, s 21(1)). One consequence of this is that a finding of primary fact by an employment tribunal cannot be overturned on appeal unless there is no evidence to support it (*Fuller v London Borough of Brent* [2011] IRLR 414). The Court found that the employment tribunal judge was entitled to reach the conclusions that he had, that he made no error of law and that the EAT should not have interfered with his decision. With regard to the judge's reliance on the claimant's length of service, the Court held that 'the fact that Mr Newbound was an employee of 34 years' service with a clean disciplinary record was a factor the judge was fully entitled to take into account: it would have been extraordinary if he had not done so'. On the disparity of treatment issue, the Court held that there had rarely been 'such an obvious case of unjustified disparity'.

This case is a very useful and recent point of reference as to how an employment tribunal approaches an unfair dismissal case. It is well worth a read.

5.4.2.3 Redundancy

There is a well-established principle that a tribunal will not investigate the commercial and economic reasons behind the decision giving rise to making redundancies (other than to satisfy itself that the reason for dismissal genuinely was redundancy) (see *James W Cook & Co v Tipper* [1990] IRLR 386 and *Chief Constable of West Midlands Police v Harrod and others* [2017] ICR 869). It will be interesting to see, in Covid-19 related cases, how far tribunals will go when checking decisions by employers.

(The Acas Code of Practice on Disciplinary and Grievance Procedures does not apply to redundancy dismissals, but there is an Acas advisory booklet on handling redundancy.)

Where a dismissal is for redundancy, the tribunal must be satisfied that it was reasonable to dismiss *that* employee by reason of redundancy. It is not enough to show that it was reasonable to dismiss *an* employee (*Williams v Compair Maxam Ltd* [1982] IRLR 83).

In *Kellogg Brown & Root (UK) Ltd v Fitton & Another* (UKEAT/0205/16), the claimants were dismissed following a workplace closure. The closure was announced in April 2015 and the employees were told they would move in July 2015. The claimants had refused to relocate and they were dismissed.

The mobility clause provided:

> The location of your employment is _____ but the company may require you to work at a different location including any new office location of the company either in the UK or overseas either on a temporary or permanent basis. You agree to comply with this requirement unless exceptional circumstances prevail.

The tribunal asked whether the instruction had been legitimate – in the sense that it was a valid contractual requirement – and concluded that it was not; whether the instruction was reasonable, again concluding that it was not; finally, whether the refusal was reasonable, concluding that it was (the claimants faced an additional 100 mile commute each day, one had brought a property near to his former workplace and did not have a car (although a car share might be possible), and the other had worked near to his home town for the respondent for 25 years, would soon be 64 and was due to retire a year later). The judgment cites and applies *United Bank Ltd v Akhtar* (see above at **1.8.2.3**). The tribunal concluded that the dismissals were unfair.

The essence of a fair redundancy dismissal is (1) fair selection (fair criteria applied fairly), (2) warning and consultation, and (3) consideration of alternative employment (*Williams*). In *Polkey v AE Dayton Services Ltd* [1988] ICR 142, HL, it was stated that in the case of redundancy, the employer will not normally act reasonably unless he:

(a) warns and consults any employees affected or their representatives;

(b) adopts a fair basis on which to select for redundancy, ie identifies an appropriate pool from which to select, and uses objective criteria and applies those criteria fairly (see *British Aerospace plc v Green* [1995] IRLR 433, CA); and

(c) takes such steps as may be reasonable to avoid or minimise redundancy by redeployment within his own organisation.

In *Osinuga v BPP University Ltd* [2022] EAT 53, the EAT held that 'the three [*Williams*] issues (fair consultation, fair selection and reasonable search for alternative employment) must be addressed [by the tribunal] ... unless the parties exclude them by agreement'.

The EAT reminded us that the statutory words matter and that case law guidance remains that – guidance. The question is always whether the decision to dismiss was fair within the statutory wording of s 98(4) of the ERA 1996 (see *Canning v NICE* (EAT/0241/18)).

See also *Buchanan v Tilcon Ltd* [1983] IRLR 417, *FDR Ltd v Holloway* [1995] IRLR 400, *John Brown Engineering Ltd v Brown and Others* [1997] IRLR 90 and *King v Eaton Ltd* [1996] IRLR 199. Where a trade union is involved, readers should refer to *Williams and Others v Compair Maxam Ltd* (above).

Issues of fairness and reasonableness still need to be judged by reference to the 'range of reasonable responses' test (see *Beddell v West Ferry Printers* [2000] ICR 1263). In *Drake International Systems Ltd v O'Hare* (UKEAT/0384/03), the EAT emphasised that tribunals should not impose their own views as to the reasonableness of the selection criteria or the implementation of the criteria: the correct question was whether the selection was one that a reasonable employer acting reasonably could have made. One of the tricky areas in redundancy is how an employer determines the 'pool' of employees that is being considered for redundancy, even if it might be thought that only one role is being lost and that there should therefore be a pool of just one. Employers need to consult about the pool and to consider whether there are other employees occupying similar roles who should be included in it.

In *Hendy Banks v Fairbrother* (UKEAT/0691/04) the EAT confirmed that the 'range of reasonable responses' test applied when deciding whether an employer had acted reasonably in selecting a pool for redundancy, ie the group of employees from which those to be made redundant will be selected. The tribunal must first decide whether the pool selected by the employer fell within a 'range of reasonable responses'. In *Wrexham Golf Club Ltd v Ingham* (UKEAT/0190/12) the EAT held that it can be reasonable to focus upon a single employee without developing a pool or even considering developing a pool. In *Leventhal Ltd v North* (UKEAT/0265/04) the EAT upheld a decision that a redundancy dismissal was unfair (on the facts) because the employer had not considered 'bumping' (see also *Fulcrum Pharma (Europe) Ltd v Bonassera and Another* (UKEAT/0198/10)) (see **4.2.3.3**). However, in *Halpin v Sandpiper Books Ltd* (UKEAT/0171/11) the EAT held that it was not unreasonable not to 'bump' another employee and that a pool of one was reasonable. (See also *Capita Hartshead Ltd v Byard* (UKEAT/0445/11), where the EAT held that a redundancy dismissal was unfair where the employer used a selection pool of one.) In *Fulcrum Pharma (Europe) Ltd v Bonassera*, the EAT said that the following factors should be considered when assessing whether others should be included in a pool, where one post is being made redundant:

- whether there is a vacancy
- how different the jobs are
- how different the salaries are
- the relative lengths of service of those holding the jobs
- the qualifications of the employee in danger of redundancy.

In *Mogane v Bradford Teaching Hospitals NHS Foundation Trust* [2022] EAT 139, the EAT looked at whether it was fair for an employer making redundancies to decide on a pool of one employee without prior consultation and said that it was not. The claimant was one of a number of nurses employed on a succession of fixed-term contracts. Her post was selected as 'at risk' for redundancy on the basis that her funding was coming to an end. The EAT overturned the tribunal's judgment, substituting a finding of unfair dismissal because it said consultation should have taken place prior to the decision on a 'pool of one' being made, when the employee could still, potentially, have influenced the outcome. Whilst a pool of one can be fair in appropriate circumstances, it should not be considered without prior consultation, where there is more than one employee. The EAT held that in circumstances where the choice of criteria adopted to select for redundancy had 'the practical result that the selection is made by that decision itself', consultation should take place prior to that decision being made. It said it was not 'within the band of reasonable responses, in the absence of consultation, to adopt one criterion which simultaneously decides the pool of employees and which employee is to be dismissed'. Furthermore, the EAT said that the implied term of trust and confidence requires that employers will not act arbitrarily towards employees in the methods of selection for redundancy. The EAT restated long-established principles about consultation from cases such as *Williams* and *Polkey*, but commentators have suggested that ruling out initial pools of one on principle would lead to employers artificially widening pools to cover staff not genuinely at risk and suggested that the case is hard to reconcile with the Court of Appeal's decision in *British Aerospace v Green*, which was not cited in the judgment, and the statement there (Waite LJ) that 'the concept of fairness, when applied to the selection process for redundancy, is incapable of being expressed in absolute terms. There are no cut and dried formulae and no short cuts.'

Ultimately, the test is whether the employer has 'genuinely applied its mind' to the composition of the pool and whether the dismissal fell within the range of reasonable responses. The *Capita* case contains a useful summary of the law on redundancy selection.

Having decided upon the pool for selection, the employer must then fairly select for redundancy. There is no one fair method of selection. Last in, first out ('LIFO') is sometimes used as a basis for selection, but following the introduction of the Employment Equality (Age) Regulations 2006 there was concern that LIFO was potentially age discriminatory against younger employees who were presumed to have less service. Both the Acas guide on 'Age in the Workplace' and the Government guide 'Age Positive' counsel against the use of LIFO, although the High Court in *Rolls Royce plc v Unite the Union* [2008] EWHC 2420 (QB) held that including length of service as part of a matrix of selection criteria was not unlawful. LIFO may also be potentially sex discriminatory. However, there are advantages to it, not least that it is completely objective. Where there is a contractual procedure, an employer should follow it.

Some of the selection criteria commonly used include:

(a)   skills or experience;

(b)   standard of work performance or aptitude for work;

(c)   attendance or disciplinary record.

In *De Belin v Eversheds Legal Services Ltd* (ET/1804069/09) the employment tribunal held that a decision to inflate the billing score of a woman on maternity leave was discriminatory on the ground of sex. The decision was upheld by the EAT (UKEAT/0352/10).

Having drawn up fair objective selection criteria, as the Acas booklet on handling redundancies makes clear, 'the selection will still be unfair if those criteria are carelessly or mistakenly applied'.

One of the most difficult questions for tribunals is the extent to which they should examine the marking that has been applied in a selection exercise. It is clear that one of the requirements for fair consultation in a redundancy exercise involves giving an employee sufficient information about and explanation for his scoring so that he understands them and has a meaningful chance to comment on and challenge the scores.

In *Pinewood Repro Limited t/a County Print (County Print) v Page* (UKEAT/0028/10), the employer agreed the selection criteria (attendance, quality, productivity, abilities, skills, experience, disciplinary record and flexibility) with the trade union, ensured that the scoring was carried out by two senior managers and gave the employee a right to appeal his selection for redundancy, but did not explain to Mr Page why he had received lower scores than the two other people in the selection pool. Mr Page was provided with a copy of his scores; he queried why he had been marked down for 'abilities, skills and experience' given his level of qualifications and 27 years' experience. He also queried why he had been marked down for flexibility as he was 'as flexible as the next man'. He was given no explanation as to how the scores had been arrived at, being told only that 'we believe that the scores given by the assessors are responsible and appropriate'. On appeal he was told that the employers were 'satisfied that the scoring was factual and correct'.

A tribunal found that Mr Page had been unfairly dismissed. The EAT upheld its decision and took the opportunity to review the relevant authorities and, whilst cautioning against an impermissible 'microscopic analysis' of scoring by tribunals, indicated that, particularly with subjective criteria, employees should have sufficient information to understand their scores and an opportunity to challenge them.

It is also important that employers make (and keep) written notes of why a particular score was awarded and what it was based on: the EAT in *Page* was critical of the 'complete absence of comments on the scoring sheet'. In *Dabson v David Cover & Sons* (UKEAT/0374/2011), the EAT emphasised, however, that when assessing the fairness of selection for redundancy, the marks awarded in the selection exercise should be investigated only in exceptional circumstances such as bias or obvious mistake.

The employer should always consider whether there are any alternative vacancies before implementing redundancies. The duty requires employers not only to look for a different post but more generally to 'consider possible alternative solutions' (*Williams*), which may include alternatives on worse terms and conditions or part-time or self-employed possibilities, as well as short-term working and temporary lay-offs. In *Parfums Givenchy v Finch* (UKEAT/0517/09), the EAT said that this included seeing 'if any assistance could be given to an employee'. It may be necessary for an employer, when considering whether a dismissal for redundancy is within the 'range of reasonable responses' test, to consider 'bumping' (see **4.2.3.3** above): *Mirab v Mentor Graphics* (UKEAT/0172/17), and it may not be necessary for the employee to have specifically raised this. An employer should provide information about the financial prospects of alternative positions (*Fisher v Hoopoe Finance Ltd* (UKEAT/0043/05).

The EAT held in *Morgan v The Welsh Rugby Union* (UKEAT/0314/10) that it was fair to apply subjective criteria, such as by interviewing applicants, when deciding whom to appoint to a suitable alternative vacancy where there were multiple applicants. The 'classic' redundancy guidance set out in *Williams v Compair Maxam Ltd* [1982] ICR 156 does not apply where redundant employees are applying for a new and different role. The principles in *Williams* apply to selection for redundancy not selection for a new role, even where redundancies arise in consequence of such a process. The EAT accepted that in new role cases after a reorganisation, the employer's decision must of necessity be forward looking and may involve something more like an interview process than the application of selection criteria. In that case, *Morgan* directs tribunals back to an 'unvarnished' s 98(4) reasonableness test. Note, however, the EAT's decision in *Green v London Borough of Barking and Dagenham* (UKEAT/0157/16), a case in which the tribunal had taken the view that it was inappropriate to apply the redundancy fairness rules in *Williams* (above) because this was, they thought, a '*Morgan v Welsh RFU* case'. The EAT held that the case was not on all fours with *Morgan* because the nature of the work had not changed significantly; and even if it had been, it was not clear that the tribunal had considered the s 98(4) reasonableness test. See also *Akzo Coatings plc v Thompson* (UKEAT/117/94), *Darlington Memorial Hospital NHS Trust v Edwards and Vincent* (UKEAT/678/95) and *Gwynedd Council v Barratt* [2021] EWCA Civ 1322 (where the posts were effectively for the same or substantially the same job and where the lack of availability of an appeal against the decision to make the employees redundant, while not determinative on its own of unfairness, was held to be a relevant factor in determining whether the dismissal was unfair).

As cases such as *Williams* and *Polkey* make clear, procedural fairness is as key in a redundancy context as it is in an unfair dismissal case. Even if a fair selection process is adopted, factors such as whether an appeal was allowed will still need to be taken into account when determining fairness. This was emphasised recently by the Court of Appeal in the *Barratt* case, which followed a tribunal's finding that the teacher claimants were unfairly dismissed, a finding upheld by the EAT and by the Court of Appeal. The claimants were dismissed when their school closed and a new one opened on the same site, and where there was no consultation over the closure and no appeal offered and their applications for new roles at the new school were unsuccessful. The Court of Appeal noted that while it would be wrong to find a dismissal unfair following a fair process *only* because of the lack of an appeal procedure, a tribunal has to have regard to all the relevant circumstances, which will include any appeal, opportunity to be consulted or to grieve about the process. The Court restated the classic principles found in *Williams* and *Polkey* as setting out the obligations on an employer making redundancies.

Note that there are some special cases:

(a) It is automatically unfair to select an employee for redundancy for a 'trade union' reason (see **5.5.1** for details).

(b) It is automatically unfair to select an employee for redundancy because she is pregnant. There are also special rules concerning offers of alternative employment to pregnant employees (see **14.9**).

The tribunal will also take into account whether or not the employer has complied with his statutory duties to consult (see **4.8**).

A tribunal's findings of fact may also be relevant as regards compensation. If an employer dismissed an employee without consultation, a tribunal must take account of the possibility of alternative employment arising during the period of consultation (see *King v Royal Bank of Canada Europe* (UKEAT/0333/10)).

Covid-19

Government Guidance issued with reference to the Coronavirus Job Retention Scheme (see Introductory Note) indicated that employees could be made redundant while on furlough, or afterwards. The note for employees stated '*your employer can still make you redundant while you're on furlough or afterwards*', and the note for employers stated '*when the government ends the scheme [employers] must make a decision, depending on [their] circumstances, as to whether employees can return to their duties [and] if not, it may be necessary to consider termination of employment (redundancy)*'. The Guidance is clear that, whilst on furlough (and afterwards), employees still had the same employment rights, including in relation to redundancy rights and protection from unfair or discriminatory dismissal.

There were a number of additional logistical issues which would not normally arise for consideration, where staff were furloughed or working remotely from home, including how to consult with such staff individually and/or collectively, as appropriate. This may have had to be done by video call or conference call or in writing. Employers may have needed to build extra time into the consultation process to allow for any logistical difficulties which may have arisen. Employees needed to be given the right to be 'accompanied' to redundancy meetings (if that was normal practice), even if such meetings were carried out remotely or virtually. Employers therefore had to consider how best to enable this.

If employers are seeking to relying on the potentially fair reason of redundancy to justify dismissals because of coronavirus, whether of staff on furlough or not, they will have to be able to show that, as with any redundancy dismissal, selection pools and criteria were fair, objective and reasonable; were not directly or indirectly discriminatory; and that staff were consulted about them before they were finalised. Automatically selecting employees for redundancy purely on the basis that they have been furloughed could be problematic. Fairness will depend on the particular circumstances of each case, including the size, resources and financial position of the employer. At each stage, the tribunal will ask whether the employer's conduct fell within the band of reasonable responses. The possibility of recourse to the Scheme may play into all three of the key procedural requirements. For example, in the case of an employer which decided to furlough some employees and dismiss others, the tribunal will need to ascertain that the employer applied fair and reasonable selection criteria in deciding which employees should fall into each category. If staff were put on furlough because they had caring responsibilities, or were shielding for health reasons, subsequently pooling and/or selecting these employees for redundancy could constitute indirect discrimination based on sex, disability or age.

Redundancy dismissals may be unfair if they take place in circumstances where an employer did not properly consider alternatives, which will most likely include, where available, consideration of retaining employees on furlough. There is potential for an argument that it would be unfair to make employees redundant while the government-funded furlough Scheme was available as an alternative. The latest date that an individual could be put on furlough for the first time was 10 June 2021. This means that anyone who was not furloughed by that date cannot raise this unfairness argument, because furlough was no longer available as an alternative. From August onwards, employers had to start making increased levels of contributions towards employee wage costs, and the affordability of this may be a reason which employers could advance for making redundancies rather than continuing furlough from this date. Employers may need to have waited (taking their financial position into consideration) until the Scheme came to an end, and/or the organisation was able to claim decreased staff costs under the Scheme, before effecting any redundancies.

Where unfair dismissal claims based on a failure to furlough succeed, the question of compensation will depend on whether a tribunal finds that even if there were procedural failings – for example there was a failure to consult on the Scheme – the employer would still have decided to dismiss rather than use the Scheme. If it is found that the failure to rely on the Scheme was unreasonable, an employee may be able to argue for a larger award. The precise amount of any award will depend on a what would have happened if the employee had been furloughed rather than dismissed. In *Mhindurwa v Lovingangels Care Ltd* (ET/3311636/2020) an employment judge held that employers had a duty to actively consider furlough when making someone redundant, and the absence of a reasonable explanation for not furloughing made the dismissal unfair. However, in *Handley v Tatenhill Aviation Ltd* (ET/2603087/2020), an employment judge found that dismissing an employee despite the existence of the Scheme did not make the dismissal unfair.

Employees being made redundant are entitled to redundancy pay (assuming they have two or more years' service), their contractual notice period (or pay in lieu), and any accrued but untaken annual leave (or pay in lieu). The Government announced (31 July 2020) that when calculating redundancy pay, this should be calculated on the basis of 100% of normal pay and not any reduced furloughed pay. Employees are probably likewise entitled to be paid their full salary during their notice period, even if they have only been receiving the relevant percentage of furlough pay during furlough, although this may depend on whether the notice period is contractual or statutory. Any outstanding untaken annual leave should also be paid at the full rate of pay (bearing in mind that annual leave continued to accrue during furlough leave). Employees who were made redundant whilst on furlough were entitled to notice of termination in accordance with their contracts. Note that employers cannot reclaim any payment made in lieu of notice or annual leave under the furlough Scheme. They could claim a furlough grant for the cost of any annual leave taken during the notice period, of up to 80% (or 70% or 60%) salary subject to the relevant monthly cap. This leave had to be topped up by the employer to the rate of the employee's full (pre-furlough) salary.

5.4.2.4 Contravention of a statutory provision

If it becomes illegal for an employee to continue in his employment because to do so would contravene a statutory provision, dismissal will often be fair. However, the employer should consider whether it is possible to redeploy the employee to another job. For example, if a driver has been disqualified from driving, is there any suitable alternative job, such as vehicle maintenance, that he could do without a driving licence? For two cases in this area, see *Kelly v University of Southampton* (UKEAT/0295/07) and *Klusova v London Borough of Hounslow* [2007] EWCA Civ 1127. (See **1.2.6**.)

5.4.2.5 Some other substantial reason

The natures of 'some other substantial reason' dismissals are so varied that no specific rules can be laid down. The general principles must be followed and, in particular, the dismissal must be within the reasonable range of responses. For example, in a business reorganisation which involves making changes to certain terms and conditions, the employer must weigh the commercial needs of the business against the detriment suffered by individual employees.

In *Genower v Ealing AHA* [1980] IRLR 297, the applicant was a general administrative assistant in the supplies department of a hospital. In order to solve a problem of corruption, the respondent decided to move certain grades of employees to different posts at different hospitals. The applicant was ordered to become a purchasing officer at another hospital quite outside the terms of his contract. The EAT held that the applicant's resignation amounted to a constructive dismissal but that the dismissal was fair: the respondent had initiated an internal reorganisation with the intention of preventing corruption.

It is clear from the authorities that where it is sought to justify a dismissal as being for some other substantial reason, there must be some kind of pressure on the employer; it is not enough for an employer simply to say that it is convenient or helpful to carry out a business reorganisation or that to do so would reduce employment costs. It is often appropriate to consider the procedural aspects in a similar way to that suggested in *Polkey* (see **5.4.2.3**).

In *Perkin v St George's Healthcare NHS Trust* [2005] EWCA Civ 1174 the Court of Appeal said employers were entitled to dismiss employees for having a difficult personality even if they were technically good at their jobs. The Court of Appeal held that the three-stage test set out in *BHS Ltd v Burchell* [1978] IRLR 379 (see **5.4.2.2** above) applies when dismissing an employee for some other substantial reason (a breakdown in trust and confidence). The tribunal will have to determine whether the employer had reasonable grounds following a reasonable investigation for deciding that trust and confidence has been damaged.

The EAT also counselled employment tribunals to be on the lookout, in cases of this kind, to see whether an employer is using the rubric of 'some other substantial reason' as a pretext to conceal the real reason for the employee's dismissal.

In *Leach v Office of Communications* [2012] EWCA Civ 959, the Court of Appeal upheld a tribunal's decision that an employee had been fairly dismissed, for 'some other substantial reason' on the basis of a breakdown of trust and confidence, after the police had disclosed to the employer credible but untested allegations that the employee had committed child sex offences. The employer had adopted a sufficiently critical approach to the allegations and had not accepted them at face value. Even though the claimant had denied all of the allegations at a disciplinary hearing, the risk of damage to the employer's reputation was sufficient to justify dismissal. Arguments based on Articles 6 and 8 of the ECHR (which was directly applicable to Ofcom as a public authority employer) were also rejected. The EAT had upheld the tribunal's findings, but Mr Justice Underhill had stated that the EAT did not find the terminology of 'trust and confidence' particularly helpful. He observed 'a growing trend among parties to employment litigation to regard the invocation of "loss of trust and confidence" as an automatic solvent of obligations', which it is not. The Court of Appeal also noted that the duty of trust and confidence was an obligation at the heart of the employment relationship, and was not a convenient label to stick on any situation in which the employer feels let down by an employee or which the employer can use as a valid reason for dismissal whenever a conduct reason is unavailable or inappropriate. Courts are particularly aware that reliance by employers on 'trust and confidence' carries a danger of omitting the procedural safeguards that would apply to a conduct dismissal (see, eg, *Ezsias v North Glamorgan NHS Trust* [2011] IRLR 550, where the EAT pointed out that tribunals must be alert to employers using 'some other substantial reason' as a pretext for dismissal when conduct is the real concern).

In *General Vending Services v Schofield* (UKEAT/0137/13), the employer wanted, for business reasons, to make changes to the terms and conditions of its engineers, which would lead, amongst other things, to a reduction in salary. Twenty to 30 employees accepted the new terms. Mr Schofield did not, and he was dismissed, being offered re-engagement on the new terms. His claim succeeded before the employment tribunal, on the basis that he was reasonable in rejecting the changes. The EAT overturned the decision, stating that just because the employee is reasonable, that does not mean that the employer was unreasonable in dismissing. The EAT held that 'while the reaction of employees was a relevant matter which an employer would take into account, it could not be decisive'. It added that the number of employees who agree to a change could be persuasive (see, eg, *Catamaran Cruises Ltd v Williams* [1994] IRLR 386 and *St John of God (Care Services) Ltd v Brooks* [1992] IRLR 546).

In *Bancroft v Interserve* (**5.2.2.5** above), the EAT confirmed that where an employee is dismissed as a result of third-party pressure, the dismissal will be fair if the employer has done everything he reasonably can to avoid or mitigate the injustice brought about by the stance of the client, by trying to get the client to change his mind or, if that is not possible, by trying to find alternative work for the employee.

In *Bancroft*, Interserve had a contract with the Home Office to provide catering at a bail hostel. Mr Bancroft was a chef at the hostel but fell out with the hostel manager. Following a disciplinary hearing, Mr Bancroft was given a warning. However, relying on a term on the contract, the Home Office asked for Mr Bancroft to be replaced. No inquiry was made as to whether the request was justified and no efforts were made to persuade the Home Office to change its mind. Mr Bancroft was offered an alternative, but with more traveling, fewer hours and less pay, which he refused. He was dismissed for 'some other substantial reason'. The employment tribunal found the dismissal fair.

The EAT said that the tribunal had not asked the right question: was there any injustice to Mr Bancroft, and whether Interserve had done 'everything they could to mitigate the injustice'? As the tribunal had not explored why Interserve had not looked into the relationship between Mr Bancroft and the hostel manager, the EAT send the case back to the tribunal to consider again in light of the EAT's conclusions.

In *Hawkes v Ausin Group (UK) Ltd* (UKEAT/0070/18), the EAT held that the employer's failure to hold a meeting with the claimant before deciding to dismiss him for 'some other substantial reason' did not render the dismissal unfair: these cases are different from misconduct cases, and on the evidence, even had a meeting taken place, it would have made no difference to the outcome. In a 'some other substantial reason' case, the procedure to be followed to ensure a fair dismissal will depend on the facts. In *Hawkes*, the employer was a small employer with four employees.

5.5 OTHER SPECIAL CASES

There is a number of other special cases where the normal rules relating to unfair dismissal are varied. In summary, these are:

(a)   pregnancy or maternity-related dismissals (see **Chapter 14**);

(b)   dismissal for trade union reasons (see **5.5.1**);

(c)   selection for redundancy based on either of the above (see **5.4.2.3** and **5.5.1**);

(d)   dismissal following industrial action (see **5.5.2**);

(e)   dismissal for asserting a statutory right (see **5.5.3**);

(f)   health and safety dismissals (see **5.5.4**);

(g)   some dismissals on transfer of a business (see **Chapter** 7);

(h)   dismissal by reason of political opinions or affiliation (see **5.5.5**);

(i)   dismissals where the worker has made a protected disclosure (see **5.5.6**);

(j)   if the reason for the dismissal relates to a prohibited list (ERA 1996, s 104F(1)) (there is a statutory prohibition on compiling trade union blacklists – see Employment Relations Act 1999 (Blacklists) Regulations 2010);

(k)   dismissals where an employee is dismissed because of a breach of an exclusivity clause rendered unenforceable by s 27A(3) of the ERA 1996 (see **1.4.1**).

In the case of pregnancy or maternity-related dismissals, dismissals for trade union reasons (or selection for redundancy on either of these grounds), dismissals for asserting a statutory right, health and safety dismissals, some dismissals for a reason connected with a transfer of a business and dismissals for making a protected disclosure, the dismissal will be 'automatically' unfair. This means that once the tribunal has established that the reason for the dismissal falls under one of these heads, it will not have to go on to consider the reasonableness of the decision under s 98(4).

5.5.1 Dismissals for trade union reasons

The general principle is that an employee is free to join a trade union or not to join as he chooses. Consequently, it is unfair to dismiss any employee either because he is or because he is not a member of a trade union or because of involvement in union activities (see *Jet2.com v Denby* (UKEAT/0070/17).

By s 152(1) of TULR(C)A 1992:

> ... the dismissal of an employee [is] unfair if the reason for it ... was that the employee—
>
> (a)   was, or proposed to become, a member of an independent trade union, or
>
> (b)   had taken part, or proposed to take part, in the activities of an independent trade union at an appropriate time, or
>
> (c)   was not a member of any trade union, or of a particular trade union ... or [refused] to become or remain a member.

An 'appropriate time' within s 152(1)(b) above is either outside working hours or within them at a time to which the employer has agreed (s 152(2)). 'Activities of an independent trade union' would cover such matters as union meetings. It does not extend to industrial action. The Court of Appeal held in *Morris v Metrolink RATP DEV Ltd* [2018] EWCA Civ 1350 that misconduct did not, on the facts, take the conduct outside the scope of 'trade union activities' for the purpose of s 152.

For a recent case on what falls within the scope of 'trade union activities', see the EAT in *Mercer v Alternative Future Group Ltd* (UKEAT/0196/20).

No qualifying period of continuous employment is necessary to bring a claim within this section because employees would be at risk of dismissal for these reasons shortly after commencing employment.

It is automatically unfair to select an employee for redundancy for one of the reasons within s 152 of TULR(C)A 1992 listed above (TULR(C)A 1992, s 153).

Where a complaint is made that the dismissal was on trade union membership grounds, the applicant may also seek interim relief (TULR(C)A 1992, s 161) (ie an injunction to preserve the status quo until a full hearing: in effect reinstatement until final judgment).

As to burden of proof, see *Kuzel* at **5.5.6.4** (confirmed in *Dahou v Serco Ltd* [2016] EWCA Civ 832), and for a recent case see *Cadent Gas Ltd v Singh* (UKEAT/0024/19).

5.5.2 Industrial action

Industrial action includes strikes and other industrial action (eg a 'work to rule') by employees and lock-outs by the employer. The right of the employee to present a complaint of unfair dismissal depends whether the industrial action is 'unofficial' or 'other' ('official') industrial action. Basically, industrial action is 'official' if either:

(a)   authorised or endorsed by a trade union; or

(b)   none of those taking part is a member of a trade union.

5.5.2.1 Unofficial industrial action

By s 237 of the TULR(C)A 1992, if at the time of his dismissal the employee was taking part in unofficial industrial action, the employment tribunal has no jurisdiction to hear a complaint of unfair dismissal. This is not to say that the dismissal is fair, but merely that the employee is not eligible to present a claim. This means that in the event of unofficial strikes and other unofficial industrial action, the employer can select employees, such as the ringleaders of the strike, for dismissal without fear of a claim for unfair dismissal.

5.5.2.2 Other industrial action

All employees taking part in official strike action are protected from dismissal during the first 12 weeks of the strike action. There is no qualifying period of employment. Section 238A of the TULR(C)A 1992 provides that a dismissal will be automatically unfair if the reason (or, if more than one, the principal reason for the dismissal) is that the employee took 'protected' industrial action, provided the dismissal occurred within the 12-week period, or if after that period the employee was dismissed when they had ceased to take part in the action, or if the dismissal occurs after the 12-week period, but the employer had not taken proper steps for the purposes of resolving the dispute.

5.5.3 Dismissal for asserting a statutory right

5.5.3.1 ERA 1996, s 104

It is unfair to dismiss an employee (or to select for redundancy) because:

(a)   he has brought proceedings against an employer to enforce a relevant statutory right; or

(b)   he has alleged that the employer has infringed a right of his which is a relevant statutory right.

'Relevant statutory rights' include, for example, claims under s 13 of the ERA 1996 (protection of wages) or a claim to a written statement of terms under ERA 1996, s 1.

No qualifying period of continuous employment is necessary.

Such a claim must be based on an assertion that there has already been a breach, not that there may be a breach in the future (see *Spaceman v ISS Mediclean Ltd* (UKEAT/0142/18)). The issue of when a breach occurs was considered by the EAT in *Simoes v De Sede UK Ltd* (UKEAT/0153/20) in the context of working 14 consecutive days in breach of reg 11 of the Working Time Regulations 1998. The question arose whether it was necessary for the employee to have worked the shift that would give rise to the breach. The claimant did the shift (which was cover for a colleague on holiday) after having initially protested, and she was later dismissed by reason of her earlier protest. Applying *Spaceman*, the tribunal dismissed her automatic unfair dismissal claim as, at the time of the complaint, the breach had not yet occurred. The EAT allowed the appeal and a finding of automatic unfair dismissal was substituted. The EAT held that the matter crystalised when she was instructed to work. Distinguishing *Spaceman*, the assertion was not an allegation of future or intended breach, but instead the instruction itself constituted a breach of her statutory rights.

Note: there is some scope for an overlap with a public interest disclosure claim (see **5.5.5** below). Section 104 does not cover breaches of contractual obligations (unless it is a wages claim) but the PIDA 1998 might cover this. Section 104 does not cover detriments.

5.5.4 Health and safety dismissals

5.5.4.1 ERA 1996, s 100

It is unfair to dismiss an employee who 'stops the job' on health and safety grounds. No period of continuous employment is required. (For Covid-19-related cases, see, amongst others, *Ham v ESL BBSW Ltd* (ET/1601260/2020), *Rodgers v Leeds Laser Cutting* [2022] EAT 69, *Accattatis v Fortuna Group (London) Ltd* (ET/3307587/2020) and further below.)

Section 44(1A)(a) and (b) of the ERA 1996 provide that employees and workers should not to be subjected to any 'detrimental' act, or failure to act, by their employer on the basis that they left or refused to return to work or took appropriate steps to protect themselves because they believed they were in serious and imminent danger. In order for the protection to apply, an employee or worker:

(a)   must reasonably believe;
(b)   that they, or other persons, were in serious and imminent danger;
(c)   which they could not reasonably have been expected to avert,

and so they left, proposed to leave, or did not return to, work. They will also be protected if they took 'appropriate steps' to protect themselves or other persons in these circumstances.

In *R (on the application of the Independent Workers' Union of Great Britain) v Secretary of State for Work and Pensions* [2021] IRLR 102, the Administrative Court held that the UK had failed properly to implement the EU Framework Directive 89/391 in s 44 and s 100 in respect of 'limb (b)' workers. The Employment Rights Act 1996 (Protection from Detriment in Health and Safety Cases) (Amendment) Order 2021 extended the protections for health and safety-related detriments to workers from 31 May 2021.

The s 44 ERA 1996 right was rarely used before last year but is now being used frequently by employees and workers who are anxious about travelling to, or being in, work during the coronavirus pandemic.

The question of whether an employee or worker had the required 'reasonable belief' is partly subjective as the tribunal will consider what was in their mind at the relevant time. The tribunal will then apply an objective test, considering whether it was reasonable for them to hold that belief in the circumstances. The protection under s 44 is only triggered if they can show that they have suffered a 'detriment' either as the result of an action taken or not taken by their employer and that the action/inaction was on the ground that they took the protected action.

One question which arose out of the Covid-19 pandemic was whether staff would be protected if they refused to work during the pandemic. An employment tribunal is likely to take into account relevant scientific advice about transmission of the virus at the time the refusal to work occurred, the particular risks applying in the workplace (and whether the employer had conducted a risk assessment), and the risks to the individual who was allegedly in danger (such as any particular vulnerability to the virus). It would also be likely to consider any steps the employer has taken to reduce the risks and the extent to which there was discussion between the employer and the employees. Imminence is likely to require a sufficient closeness in time and possibly space between the employee and the specific risk; a potential or hypothetical risk is unlikely to be sufficient. It is worth noting that s 44 also applies to dangers which 'other people' are exposed to, which may mean that employees who have vulnerable family members and refuse to attend work can be protected under s 44.

A detriment is anything which is disadvantageous to the employee and might cover a decrease in pay, the loss of an opportunity or promotion, the withdrawal of certain benefits or being moved to a different role or department. Whatever the detriment is, it must be shown to be significantly influenced by their protected conduct.

For example, if an employee or worker refuses to attend work because there is an imminent and serious danger of contracting Covid-19 and they are subsequently furloughed on reduced pay, the employee may have grounds to say that the employer has breached s 44 if they can show that their being placed on furlough on reduced pay was because of their refusal to attend work. An employer may defeat such a claim if it can show, for example, that regardless of the refusal to attend work, the employer had decided to place them on furlough and can provide evidence for this (for example, because they furloughed staff in the same position who did not refuse to attend work on those grounds and there were clear wider business reasons for placing those staff on furlough).

Dismissing an employee for an act covered by s 44 is automatically unfair under s 100 of the ERA 1996. There is no cap on compensation where an employee is found to have been automatically unfairly dismissed for health and safety reasons under s 100, unlike in ordinary unfair dismissal claims. It is also possible for an employee to bring an unfair dismissal claim under s 100 before they reach two years' service. Tribunals can make financial awards for successful detriment claims under s 44. It is also possible for tribunals to make injury to feelings awards.

Employees may alternatively be able to claim protection via a health and safety whistleblowing action (see below).

See the following cases by way of some examples arising out of the pandemic:

- *Rendina v Royston Veterinary Centre Ltd* (ET/3307459/2020) – automatically unfair dismissal because the claimant had raised with her employer issues of concern she reasonably believed were harmful or potentially harmful to health and safety, namely the potential spread of the coronavirus;
- *Pareek v D Delta Ltd t/a Mira Boiler* (ET/3300603/2021) – automatically unfair dismissal and detriment because the claimant had raised health and safety concerns which ended with him no longer being required by the respondent to work;
- *Preen v Coolink Ltd and another* (ET/1403451/2020) – automatically unfair dismissal because the claimant was refusing to do routine work because of genuine concerns, following the lockdown rules, about protecting the health of himself and others;
- *Gibson v Lothian Leisure* (ET/4105009/2020) – the claimant was dismissed because in circumstances of danger which he reasonably believed to be serious and imminent he took steps to protect his father by raising the issue of PPE.

See too *Smith v Cognita Schools Ltd* (ET/1600884/2021) and *Moore v Ecoscape UK Ltd* (ET/2417563/20).

5.5.4.2 ERA 1996, s 101A

It is unfair to dismiss an employee for refusal to work in breach of the Working Time Regulations 1998.

5.5.5 Political dismissals

Following the case of *Redfearn v UK* in the ECtHR (see **Chapter 8**), where the Court ruled that the UK had not sufficiently implemented Article 11 of the ECHR (the right of assembly), the requirement for a qualification period was removed where someone claims he has been dismissed by a reason or principal reason that relates to the employee's political opinions or affiliations. This does not make dismissals on this ground automatically unfair; it simply means that no qualifying period is required. The Government could have dealt with the effect of *Redfearn* by allowing a free-standing claim for unlawful discrimination on political grounds, but chose instead to create a further exception to the qualifying period. For a recent case, where 'relates to' is given a narrow interpretation, see *Scottish Federation of Housing Associations v Jones* [2022] EAT 114.

5.5.6 Public Interest Disclosure Act 1998

5.5.6.1 Introduction

The PIDA 1998, often referred to as the 'whistleblower's charter', introduced special rights and protections for workers who disclose wrongdoing by their employers to a third party in specific circumstances. It was introduced after a series of disasters (such as the Zeebrugge ferry, Piper Alpha oil platform and the Clapham rail crash) which highlighted the need for a law to protect workers who 'blew the whistle' in the public interest.

The PIDA 1998 aims to promote better relations between employers and their workforce over wrongdoing in the workplace, and to end the so-called 'cover-up culture', so that workers are not scared to tell their bosses or others about problems relating to matters such as health and safety or criminal activities for fear of being dismissed or victimised. The Act assumes that whistleblowing is in the public interest. This approach offers some protection to whistleblowers but does little to encourage them. Some commentators have argued that the UK should adopt a similar approach to that in the USA (see the Dodd-Frank legisation), which permits a percentage of any fine imposed to be paid to the whistleblower and has encouraged the flow of information to US regulators.

The provisions of the PIDA 1998 apply not just to employees and workers but also to third-party contractors whose work is controlled by an employer. (See **1.3.4.1** for the definition of a 'worker' in a PIDA claim. Members of an LLP are workers for these purposes – see *Clyde & Co LLP and Another v Bates van Winkelhof* [2014] UKSC 32 – and some agency workers may be covered (ERA 1996, s 43K(1)(a) – see *McTigue v University Hospital Bristol NHS Foundation Trust* (EAT/0354/15).)

The Act does not create a general right for all whistleblowing. Only certain categories of information will be protected in certain situations. Claims under the PIDA 1998 may be brought in respect of treatment which subjects the claimant to a detriment (ERA 1996, s 47B) (for recent detriment cases, see *Panayiotou v Chief Constable of Hampshire Police* [2014] IRLR 500, *Timis Sage v Osipov* [2019] IRLR 52 and *Jesudason v Alder Hey Children's NHS Foundation Trust* [2020] EWCA Civ 73) and, in respect of employees only, for unfair dismissal (ERA 1996, s 103A). A claim may therefore relate both to treatment during the employment relationship and to the termination of it. For a case on the significance of a detriment claim to that of a dismissal claim, see *International Petroleum Ltd v Osipov* [2018] EWCA Civ 2321: in particular, there is a lower causation hurdle for a detriment claim (significant influence rather than principal reason), but there is no reasonable steps defence and available remedies are different. In *International Petroleum Ltd v Osipov*, Mr Osipov was able to claim that his dismissal was both unfair and a detriment.

This section of the book deals with dismissal claims, whether by an employee or a worker, and is meant only as an introduction to what is a complex topic.

In order to assess whether a dismissal/detriment falls within the PIDA 1998, the following matters will need to be considered:

(1) Is there a qualifying disclosure (ERA 1996, s 43B (as amended by the Enterprise and Regulatory Reform Act 2013, s 17)):

- Has there been a disclosure of information?

- Does the worker believe that the disclosure is made in the public interest (a subjective test)?
- Is that belief reasonable?
- Does the worker believe that the disclosure tends to show one of the relevant failures?
- Is that belief reasonable?

See *Williams v Michelle Brown AM* (UKEAT/0044/19/OO).

(2)   Was that disclosure made to an appropriate person?

(3)   Was that disclosure the reason or principal reason for the dismissal or did it materially influence the detrimental treatment?

See below for more details on each of these areas. In *Blackbay Ventures Ltd v Gahir* [2014] IRLR 416 and *Patel and Metcalf v Surrey County Council* (UKEAT/0178/16), the EAT gave some guidance to tribunals when considering how to approach a protected disclosure case. It is important that each disclosure is properly identified along with each failure, that disclosures are not 'lumped together' and that specific findings are made with reference to each disclosure. A tribunal should be careful not to substitute its own view of whether a disclosure was in the public interest. Linden J stated in *Twist DX Limited & others v Armes & another* (UKEAT/0030/20) that:

> it is important for the ET to identify which limb, or limbs, of the definition (i.e. subsections (a)-(f)) are relevant, as this will affect the next, 'reasonableness', question. If the claimant says that they believed that the disclosed information tended to show that criminal offences were being, or were likely to be, committed, it is the reasonableness of that belief which must be considered. Likewise, if they say they believed that it tended to show that a legal obligation had been, or was likely to be, breached, the information should also be examined in context with a view to deciding whether such a belief was reasonable.

5.5.6.2   Qualifying disclosure

Disclosure of information

The word 'disclosure' is not defined in the ERA 1996; the phrase is intended, however, to have a wide reach. The question is to be determined in the light of the statute itself – whether there is a disclosure of *information*. The disclosure has to show or tend to show something that comes within the section (s 43B(1)). An employee simply has to communicate the information by some effective means in order for the communication to constitute a disclosure of the information. There is no requirement in the legislation that the disclosure needs to be in writing. However, there is room for disagreement where broad communications, especially verbal conversations, are relied upon, not least because of the evidential issues that can arise where a conversation is disputed.

There is also no need for the disclosure to be of information that is formerly unknown or secret (s 43L(3)): telling someone something they already know can be a disclosure. It is clear that a disclosure of information must convey some sort of factual information that goes beyond a mere allegation or opinion (*Cavendish Munro Professional Risks Management Ltd v Geduld* [2010] IRLR 38). In *Geduld*, the court said that a disclosure was the 'giving of information' and the 'conveying of facts'. *Geduld* was followed in *Goode v Marks and Spencer plc* (UKEAT/0442/09) where a distinction was sought to be drawn between information and an allegation. In *Blitz v Vectone Group Holdings Ltd* (UKEAT/0253/10), the EAT held that there was no disclosure of information in an email that was interpreted as seeking advice and requesting information rather than supplying it. In *Norbrook Laboratories (GB) Ltd v Shaw* (UKEAT/0150/13), the EAT accepted that concerns raised in separate documents over a number of days with different individuals may be taken together to form a disclosure of information where the earlier disclosures help to explain the meaning of subsequent disclosures. However, it is not sufficient to say that two disclosures can be associated with each other to add up to protected disclosures (see *Barton v Greenwich LBC* (UKEAT/0041/14) and *Fincham v HM Prison Service* (UKEAT/0925/01 and 0991/01)). As summarised in *Norbrook* at [22], 'two communications can, taken together, amount to a protected disclosure. Whether they do is a question of fact.'

Most recently, the Court of Appeal in *Dray Simpson v Cantor Fitzgerald Europe* [2021] EWCA Civ 559 considered a number of key whistleblowing components, including: when a protected disclosure can be made by a composite collection of more than one disclosure; the meaning of 'information'; the relevance of trade knowledge to 'reasonable belief'; the meaning of 'reasonable'; the 'public interest' test; and the reason for dismissal and 'tainted decisions' (eg when a person compiling an investigation report is motivated by a public interest disclosure but the decision maker is not). In regard to the latter point (where the Supreme Court's decision in *Royal Mail v Jhuti* – see below – had not been handed down when the case was in the EAT), the Court confirmed that the 'tainted decision' doctrine applied by the Supreme Court in *Jhuti* was difficult to apply outside of the facts of *Jhuti*. On the point about whether the collective effect of disclosures amounts to a protected disclosure even if on their own the disclosures do not have this status (as per *Norbrook* above), the Court said that aggregation of disclosures was entirely fact dependent and was only needed where one disclosure embedded within it another one, or referenced back to it. The Court confirmed that the leading case regarding public interest remains *Chesterton Global* and said that that decision provided an accurate summary of the law.

Otherwise, the case provides nothing by way of new law, but the Court of Appeal's judgment and the earlier EAT judgment (UKEAT/0016/18) provide a useful summary and discussion of a number of key components of whistleblowing legislation and are a recommended read.

Whether something is an allegation or a fact continues to cause difficulties, not least because the margins between the two can be fine and they can be intertwined. In *Kilraine v London Borough of Wandsworth* [2018] EWCA Civ 1436, the Court of Appeal, while declining to give comprehensive guidance on what constituted a disclosure, said that there should be no rigid distinction applied between 'information' and 'allegations' and held that an allegation could constitute 'information', but words that were too general and devoid of factual content would not do so (eg saying 'the windows 'have not been cleaned for two weeks' discloses information, whereas saying 'you are in breach of health and safety law', without more, is not sufficient). Words that would otherwise fall short can, however, be boosted by context or surrounding circumstances. *Kilraine* had not been mentioned in the employment tribunal's judgment in *Dray Simpson* (by then *Kilraine* had been heard by the EAT but not the Court of Appeal), and it was argued therefore that the tribunal had failed to follow it. The Court of Appeal rejected this ground and focused on the factual findings made.

Public interest

What matters is that the claimant's (subjective) belief was (objectively) reasonable.

Disclosures must be in the 'public interest' to qualify. This was added by the Enterprise and Regulatory Reform Act 2013, s 17, to ensure that all disclosures are in the public interest, so as to avoid workers using this section to raise concerns about private or personal employment rights such as a breach of their own contracts (see *Parkins v Sodexho*, above). (See *Smith v Scapa Group plc* (ET/2400172/2017) and *Ibrahim v HCA International Ltd* (UKEAT/0105/18).) However, public interest is not defined, and employees may still try to argue that complaints about breaches of their contracts do pass the test. In *Chesterton Global Ltd v Nurmohamed* [2017] EWCA Civ 979, the Court of Appeal had the opportunity to consider the application of the 'public interest' test. An employment tribunal had found that a complaint by an employee about the misstatement of costs and liabilities in his employer's accounts, which could have had an impact on his and other colleagues' bonuses, was a disclosure of information. The employment tribunal concluded that while the claimant was motivated by self-interest, he was also concerned about financial probity and the wider interests of his colleagues. In the tribunal's view, this was a sufficiently large section of the public for the claimant reasonably to believe that his disclosure was in the public interest. The tribunal said it was not necessary for the disclosure to be of interest to the entirety of the public. The EAT, upholding the tribunal's decision, said that s 43B(1) of the 1996 Act imposes a subjective test, since it asks whether the claimant had a reasonable belief (at the time of making the disclosure) in two matters:

(a)   that his disclosure was in the public interest; and

(b)   that the disclosure tended to show that one of the five relevant failures had occurred or was likely to occur (see below).

The Court of Appeal upheld that reasoning. It held:

27.   First, and at the risk of stating the obvious, ... [t]he tribunal thus has to ask (a) whether the worker believed, at the time that he was making it, that the disclosure was in the public interest and (b) whether, if so, that belief was reasonable.

36.   The statutory criterion of what is 'in the public interest' does not lend itself to absolute rules, still less when the decisive question is not what is in fact in the public interest but what could reasonably be believed to be. I am not prepared to rule out the possibility that the disclosure of a breach of a worker's contract of the *Parkins v Sodexho* kind may nevertheless be in the public interest, or reasonably be so regarded, if a sufficiently large number of other employees share the same interest. I would certainly expect employment tribunals to be cautious about reaching such a conclusion, because the broad intent behind the amendment of section 43B(1) is that workers making disclosures in the context of private workplace disputes should not attract the enhanced statutory protection accorded to whistleblowers – even, as I have held, where more than one worker is involved. But I am not prepared to say never. In practice, however, the question may not often arise in that stark form. The larger the number of persons whose interests are engaged by a breach of the contract of employment, the more likely it is that there will be other features of the situation which will engage the public interest.

37.   Against that background, in my view the correct approach is as follows. In a whistleblower case where the disclosure relates to a breach of the worker's own contract of employment (or some other matter under section 43B(1) where the interest in question is personal in character), there may nevertheless be features of the case that make it reasonable to regard disclosure as being in the public interest as well as in the personal interest of the worker .... The question is one to be answered by the Tribunal on a consideration of all the circumstances of the particular case, but [counsel for the employee's] fourfold classification of relevant factors which I have reproduced ... above may be a useful tool. As he says, the number of employees whose interests the matter disclosed affects may be relevant, but that is subject to the strong note of caution which I have sounded in the previous paragraph.

The four factors the Court referred to are:

(1)   the numbers in the group whose interests the disclosure served;

(2)   the nature of the interests affected and the extent to which they are affected by the wrongdoing disclosed – a disclosure of wrongdoing directly affecting a very important interest is more likely to be in the public interest than a disclosure of trivial wrongdoing affecting the same number of people, and all the more so if the effect is marginal or indirect;

(3)   the nature of the wrongdoing disclosed – disclosure of deliberate wrongdoing is more likely to be in the public interest than the disclosure of inadvertent wrongdoing affecting the same number of people;

(4)   the identity of the alleged wrongdoer: 'the larger or more prominent the wrongdoer (in terms of the size of its relevant community, ie staff, suppliers and clients), the more obviously should a disclosure about its activities engage the public interest' – though this should not be taken too far.

On the facts, given that numbers affected were high; the misstatements in the accounts were to the tune of £2 million–£3 million; the wrongdoing concerned deliberate falsification of accounts; and the employer was a national estate agent and a major player in the London property market, the disclosures were in the public interest.

The guidance in *Chesterton* was followed in *Underwood v Wincanton plc* (UKEAT/0163/15) when the EAT held that the test can be satisfied by a group of employees raising a matter specific to their conditions of employment.

The approach of the Court of Appeal in *Chesterton* suggests that the introduction of the element of 'public interest' imposes a relatively low threshold for a claimant. A disclosure will qualify for protection as long as the belief in its public interest is reasonable (see *Okwu v Rise Community* (UKEAT/0082/19)). It does not have to be 'in the public interest' so long as the claimant reasonably believes it is.

For cases since *Chesterton*, see *Parsons v Airplus International Ltd* (UKEAT/0111/17) (the EAT said that a disclosure made purely out of self-interest could not constitute sufficient grounds for a reasonable belief that the disclosures were made in the public interest), *Smith v Scapa Group plc* (ET/2400172/2017) and *Ibrahim v HCA International Ltd* (UKEAT/0105/18) and also *Dray Simpson* (above).

In *Dobbie v Felton t/a Feltons Solicitors* (EAT/0130/20), the EAT held that whilst the worker must have a belief that the disclosure is in the public interest, that does not have to be their predominant motive in making it, if it has to be part of their motive at all.

Reasonable belief

The Court of Appeal gave general guidance in *Babula v Waltham Forest College* [2007] EWCA Civ 1154 as to what is meant by 'reasonable belief'. It held that there may be a qualifying disclosure even if the employee is wrong, so long as the belief was reasonable in the circumstances at the time of the disclosure. Further guidance was provided on this in *Goode v Marks and Spencer plc* (UKEAT/0442/09). In *Soh v Imperial College* (UKEAT/0350/14) the EAT held that what matters is whether there is a reasonable belief that the *information being disclosed* shows one of the wrongdoings in paras (a)–(f) of s 43B(1) of the ERA 1996 (not whether there is a reasonable belief that the colleague had (in this case) failed to comply with a legal obligation). The Court of Appeal held in *Beatt v Croydon Health Services NHS Trust* [2017] EWCA Civ 401 that the belief of the decision maker as to whether the disclosure is protected is irrelevant when deciding whether the disclosure is protected. See also *Chesterton Global Ltd v Nurmohamed* (below) and *Dray Simpson* (above).

Relevant failures

There are limits on the matters about which an employee may complain. The PIDA 1998 inserts a provision into the ERA 1996 (s 43B(1)), which provides that a 'qualifying disclosure' means any disclosure of information which in the reasonable belief of the worker (see above) tends to show wrongdoing of one or more of the following kinds (past, present or future) of 'relevant failures':

(a)   a criminal offence (see *Babula v Waltham Forest College* [2007] EWCA Civ 1154);

(b)   a failure to comply with a legal obligation (see *Parkins v Sodexho Ltd* [2002] IRLR 109, *Douglas v Birmingham City Council* (UKEAT/0518/02); *Eiger Securities LLP v Korshunova* (UKEAT/0149/16), *Ibrahim v HCA International Ltd* (UKEAT/0105/18) and *Arjomand-Sissan v East Sussex Healthcare NHS Trust* (EAT/0122/17));

(c)   a miscarriage of justice;

(d)   the health and safety of any individual is endangered;

(e)   the environment is being damaged;

(f)   information relating to any of the above areas is being deliberately concealed.

The disclosure does not need to spell out the source of the wrong relied upon in strict legal language, nor to spell it out at all in a case where it is, from the context, obvious that a breach of some legal obligation/a criminal offence would be involved (*Bolton School v Evans* [2006] IRLR 500; *Blackbay Ventures Ltd v Gahir* [2014] ICR 747; *Eiger Securities LLP v Korshunova* [2017] IRLR 115). In *Bolton*, the general nature of the obligation and that it had a legal basis was readily apparent. The Court of Appeal made it clear in *Babula v Waltham Forest College* [2007] ICR 1026 that it does not matter whether the claimant is right or not, or even whether the legal obligation exists or not, although whether it does or does not may be relevant to the reasonableness of the claimant's belief that the information disclosed tends to show a relevant breach (*Twist* above). What must be established is that the claimant (considering the claimant's personal circumstances/professional knowledge (*Korashi v Abertawe Bro Morgannwg University Local Health Board* [2012] IRLR 4)) had a reasonable belief that the information disclosed 'tended to show' that someone had failed, was failing or was likely to fail to comply with one of the matters set out in s 43B. Reasonableness has both a subjective and objective element.

'Tends to show' is a lower hurdle than having to believe that the information 'does' show the relevant breach or likely breach (*Twist*). The word 'likely' appears in the section in connection with future failures only, not past or current failings where what is required is that the worker reasonably believes that the information disclosed 'tends to show' actual failures. Where what is in issue is a likely future failure, the EAT in *Kraus v Penna Plc* [2004] IRLR 260 held that 'likely' in this context means 'probable or more probable than not'. On that point, *Kraus* was not overruled by *Babula* and remains good law.

5.5.6.3   Relevant person and procedure

In order to qualify for protection, there is a tiered disclosure regime:

(a)   a disclosure to an employer or (where the failure related to a person other than an employer) to that other person (s 43C);

(b)   a disclosure to a legal adviser in the course of obtaining legal advice (s 43D);

(c)   where the employer is appointed under any statute by a Minister of the Crown, a disclosure to a Minister of the Crown (s 43E);

(d)   a disclosure to a prescribed person under s 43F. (Details of prescribed bodies and the matters in respect of which they are prescribed are set out in the Public Interest Disclosure (Prescribed Persons) Order 2014 (SI 2014/2418) (as last amended in 2022). The list includes bodies such as HMRC, the HSE and the Office for Environmental Protection.)

These four methods of disclosure are very specific. In addition, there are two much more general provisions which impose more complex tests:

(a)   A disclosure, reasonably believing that the information disclosed is substantially true, which is not made for personal gain, where the employee reasonably believes that if he discloses the information to his employer or a prescribed person he will suffer a detriment, or he has previously made a disclosure of substantially the same information to the employer or the prescribed person. In deciding whether it is reasonable for the employee to make the disclosure, the Act lays down a number of circumstances that should be borne in mind, including the identity of the person to whom the disclosure is made, the seriousness of the relevant failure and how the employer responded to the earlier disclosure (s 43G).

(b)   A disclosure of 'exceptionally serious' material such as merits bypassing one of the other procedures.

In *Goode v Marks and Spencer plc* (**5.5.5.2** above), one of the reasons Goode's claim failed was because the tribunal found that his disclosure to the media was different from his internal expressions of concern and did not therefore satisfy the test for the wider disclosure under s 43G(2)(c)(i), which requires a worker to have 'previously made a disclosure of substantially the same information to his employer'.

In *Collins v National Trust* (ET/2507255/05), C was able to avail himself of the 'exceptionally serious circumstances' provisions, such that his disclosure to a local newspaper of a confidential report about dangers on a public beach was protected. (Compare this to the circumstances in *Holbrook v Queen Mary's Sidcup NHS Trust* (ET/1101904/06).)

In *Barton v Royal Borough of Greenwich* (UKEAT/0041/14), the EAT upheld an employment tribunal's decisions that:

(a)   a disclosure to the Information Commissioner's Office (ICO) by an employee, although a qualifying disclosure, was not protected because it was made to an external body, so needed to satisfy the higher standard of 'reasonable belief' that the information was substantially true. As the employee had taken no steps to verify the information before contacting the ICO, he was not able to satisfy that requirement;

(b)   the call the employee made to the ICO did not convey 'information' (it was seeking advice) and so was not a protected disclosure.

Employers should have an appropriate disclosure policy in their staff handbooks so as to avoid whistleblowing cases reaching the tribunal. This should ensure they receive early notification of any problems. Since April 2010, claimants bringing a whistleblowing claim against their employer can tick a box on the claim form, requesting that the tribunal forward details of their whistleblowing allegations to the appropriate regulator for investigation.

Until 2013, there was a good faith requirement for disclosures. The ERRA 2013 removed the good faith requirement for a disclosure. However, tribunals now have a power to reduce compensation by 25% if a disclosure was not in good faith.

In *Onyango v Berkeley* (EAT/0407/12), the EAT held that a claimant could rely on a post-termination protected disclosure in a claim brought under s 47B of the ERA 1996 (the right not to be subjected to a detriment on the ground that he had made a protected disclosure), as long as the disclosure preceded the related detriment.

5.5.6.4   Causation

The disclosure must be the reason or principal reason for the dismissal (or, for detriment, 'materially influenced the action of the employer'). Section 103A of the ERA 1996 requires that the protected disclosure be 'the reason (or, if more than one reason, the principal reason) for the dismissal'. In *Royal Mail Group Ltd v Jhuti* [2019] UKSC 55, the Supreme Court considered when a dismissal decision will be treated as connected with whistleblowing. The claimant made a protected disclosure to her line manager, who then misled the person who made the decision to dismiss. The tribunal dismissed the claim, finding that the disclosures were not the reason for the dismissal. The EAT found that the dismissal was automatically unfair within s 103A of the ERA 1996, holding that a decision made in ignorance of true facts due to 'manipulation by someone in a management position' can be attributed to the employer of both of them. The Court of Appeal held that the dismissal was fair because the dismissing officer was not aware of the protected disclosures. The Supreme Court agreed with the EAT and held that the 'hidden reason' was the principal reason for dismissal. Notwithstanding the ignorance of the decision maker, the hidden motive could be attributed to the employer.

In *Jhuti*, the situation was one which the Supreme Court described as 'extreme' and 'not … common'(at [41]). The dismissal decision had been taken in good faith by a manager based on evidence of poor performance presented by the claimant's line manager. However, the tribunal found that the line manager had dishonestly constructed the evidence of poor performance in response to a protected disclosure made by the employee. At [60], the Supreme Court concluded as follows:

> 60. In searching for the reason for a dismissal for the purposes of section 103A of the Act, and indeed of other sections in Part X, courts need generally look no further than at the reasons given by the appointed decision-maker. Unlike Ms Jhuti, most employees will contribute to the decision-maker's inquiry. The employer will advance a reason for the potential dismissal. The employee may well dispute it and may also suggest another reason for the employer's stance. The decision-maker will generally address all rival versions of what has prompted the employer to seek to dismiss the employee and, if reaching a decision to do so, will identify the reason for it. In the present case, however, the reason for the dismissal given in good faith by Ms Vickers turns out to have been bogus. If a person in the hierarchy of responsibility above the employee (here Mr Widmer as Ms Jhuti's line manager) determines that, for reason A (here the making of protected disclosures), the employee should be dismissed but that reason A should be hidden behind an invented reason B which the decision-maker adopts (here inadequate performance), it is the court's duty to penetrate through the invention rather than to allow it also to infect its own determination. If limited to a person placed by the employer in the hierarchy of responsibility above the employee, there is no conceptual difficulty about attributing to the employer that person's state of mind rather than that of the deceived decision-maker.

The Supreme Court's judgment in *Jhuti* is not authority for a wider principle that where an individual has manipulated the actions of other employees in order to retaliate against a claimant for making a protected disclosure, that motivation is to be attributed to the individual who takes the decision to dismiss or subjects the individual to a detriment – save where the manipulation in fact amounts to a situation within the ratio of *Jhuti* (ie where there has been dishonest presentation of facts to the decision-maker so that the ostensible reason for the decision-maker's action is an 'invention').

Even if someone makes a protected disclosure, they will not be immune from disciplinary action, but care will need to be taken to make clear that grounds for disciplinary action are genuinely separable from the making of the protected disclosure (see *Martin v Devonshires Solicitors* (UKEAT/0086/10), *Panayiotou v Kernaghan* (UKEAT/0436/13) and *Gibson v Hounslow LBC* (UKEAT/0033/18)).

In *Beatt v Croydon Health Services NHS Trust* [2017] IRLR 748, the issue in dispute before the Court of Appeal, it having been accepted that Mr Beatt had made protected disclosures, was whether he could succeed in his claim when the employer did not believe he had made a protected disclosure. The Court distinguished between two questions: (1) Was the making of the disclosure the reason/principal reason for the dismissal?; (2) Was the disclosure in question a protected one? The first question requires a finding as to what was in the decision maker's mind; the second does not. Therefore if the disclosure was the reason for the dismissal, and it was found by the tribunal to be protected, then the claim would succeed.

In *Kong v Gulf International Bank (UK) Ltd* [2022] EWCA Civ 941, the Court of Appeal upheld the tribunal's decision that the Bank's Head of Legal had subjected the claimant to a detriment materially influenced by the protected disclosure (that claim was time-barred) but that the principal reason for the claimant's dismissal was not the protected disclosure about the template, but that she had questioned the Head of Legal's professional competence. The tribunal found that this was a separate reason related to her conduct and that she was not dismissed because of her protected disclosure. Although the protected disclosure and the criticisms made of the Head of Legal's competence were connected, the tribunal properly distinguished them. The EAT had upheld the tribunal's decision that they did not impute to the respondent the motivation of the Head of Legal, who had not participated in the decision to dismiss. That reasoning was upheld by the Court of Appeal:

> The employment tribunal reached the conclusion that the principal reason why the claimant was dismissed was what the decision-makers perceived as the seriously inappropriate way in which she had challenged [the Head of Legal's] competence/integrity (which reinforced concerns that they already had about a lack of emotional intelligence in dealing with colleagues) and was not the fact that she had

made protected disclosures. Both as a matter of common sense and on the authorities that was a legitimate distinction in principle, and the tribunal considered with evident care how it applied in the present case. Its decision was unquestionably open to it on the evidence. The fact that the tribunal found that the claimant had not in fact behaved in a way which justified her dismissal does not mean that it was required to find that the dismissal decision was taken on the proscribed ground.

See too *Osipov* (below).

See too, on causation, *Jesudason v Alder Hey Children's NHS Foundation Trust* [2020] EWCA Civ 73, where the Court of Appeal held that the employer was not motivated by the protected disclosures but rather to minimise harm from the protected disclosures to reassure patients (a fine line in many cases and a question of fact), and the Court of Appeal in *Dray Simpson* (at **5.5.6.2** above), which looked at the reason for dismissal and 'tainted decisions' (the Supreme Court's decision in *Jhuti* had not been handed down when the case was decided by the EAT). The Court confirmed in *Dray Simpson* (above) that the 'tainted decision' doctrine applied by the Supreme Court in *Jhuti* was difficult to apply outside of the facts of *Jhuti* and reinforces the narrow application of the 'tainted decision' concept applied in other cases.

In a case where the claimant has made multiple disclosures, the question is whether the cumulative impact was the principal reason for the dismissal (*El-Megrisi v Azad University (IR) in Oxford* (UKEAT/0448/08)). The employment tribunal must be careful to ensure that it restricts its deliberations to the causal effect of proven protected disclosures, where some but not all complaints have succeeded (*Secure Care UK Ltd v Mott* (UKEAT/0135/20)).

In detriment cases, the test is whether the protected disclosure *materially influences* the employer's treatment of the whistleblower. That, as the Court of Appeal noted in *NHS Manchester v Fecitt and Others* [2012] IRLR 641, means that there are different tests. See too *Eiger Securities LLP v Korshunova* (UKEAT/0149/16).

5.5.6.5   Burden of proof

Employees will be treated as having been automatically unfairly dismissed where the reason or principal reason for the dismissal was that they made a protected disclosure. There is no continuous employment requirement. However, the employee's continuity of employment will still matter.

If the employee has the requisite continuity of employment to bring an 'ordinary' unfair dismissal claim, the burden of proving the reason for the dismissal is on the employer to show that he had a potentially fair reason for the dismissal. There is no burden on the employee to disprove the reason put forward by the employer, but he will have to produce some evidence supporting the positive case that he was dismissed by reason of making a protected disclosure. It will then be for the tribunal to consider the evidence as a whole and make findings of fact on the basis of the direct evidence and/or by reasonable inferences from primary facts established by the evidence (*Kuzel v Roche Products Ltd* [2008] IRLR 530). In *Royal Mail Group Ltd v Jhuti* [2017] EWCA Civ 1632, the Court of Appeal confirmed that it is only the mental processes of the dismissing officer that are relevant; if that person was not aware of proceedings, the dismissal could not be by reason of those disclosures.

Where an employee does not have the requisite continuous employment required for an 'ordinary' unfair dismissal claim, the burden of proof is on the employee to prove that the protected disclosure was the employer's reason or principal reason for the dismissal (see the EAT's reasoning on this in *Kuzel* (UKEAT/0516/06). In a detriment case, the worker must prove that he made the relevant disclosure and prove the detrimental treatment. The employer then has to prove another reason for the treatment. If it does not prove another reason, the tribunal must conclude that it was by reason of the protected disclosure.

In dismissal cases, the standard of proof is different from that in detriment cases (s 48(2)/s 47B – see *Fecitt v NHS Manchester* [2012] IRLR 64; where a worker alleges that he was dismissed by reason of making a protected disclosure, he will need to rely on the detriment provisions because only employees are able to allege unfair dismissal). See also *International Petroleum Ltd v Osipov* (UKEAT/0058/17) which looks at a number of issues, including when an individual decision maker can be sued by the whistleblower, the approach to burden of proof and inference drawing as well as various issues on remedies in a whistleblowing context.

5.5.6.6   Vicarious liability

The ERRA 2013 includes a provision making employers vicariously liable when their employees victimise a whistleblowing colleague. This came into effect on 25 June 2013. There is a defence for an employer of having taken all reasonable steps to prevent such treatment.

5.5.6.7   Enforcement and remedies

The usual three-month time limit applies for bringing a claim (see **6.3.1**). Where the employee is dismissed, time runs from the date of dismissal. Where the complaint is one of detrimental treatment, this can sometimes be problematic where the act complained of and the detriment occur on different dates – see *Vivian v Bournemouth Borough Council* (UKEAT/0254/10). Where this happens, time runs from the date of the act which has been done on the ground that the worker has made a protected disclosure, not the later date of the detriment suffered as a result. In this case, the act was placing the employee in the redeployment pool, and time ran from that act, not from the consequences of that act. However, it may be found not to have been reasonably practicable to bring the complaint until the detriment occurred, so the claim may be admissible if it is brought within a further reasonable period (see **6.3.1**).

Since April 2010 claimants have been invited to tick a box on the ET1 (see **Chapter 6**) indicating whether their claim includes protected disclosure allegations and, if so, whether the claimant wishes the tribunal to refer the allegation on to the relevant authority.

In whistleblowing cases, there is the possibility of 'interim relief' (ERA 1996, s 128). An employee who has been dismissed can ask the tribunal to order the employer to continue to pay his wages through to trial (and any subsequent appeal). An order may be made where the employment judge considers the employee is 'likely to succeed'. 'Likely' means having a 'pretty good chance' of success (see *Taplin v Shippam Ltd* [1978] ICR 1068, *Raja v Secretary of State for Justice* [2010] All ER (D) 134 and *His Highness Sheikh Khalid bin Saqr Al Qasimi v Robinson* (UKEAT/0283/17)).

Where an individual makes the decision to dismiss, in a whistleblowing case, then they may be personally liable (as well as the employer) for all losses arising (*International Petroleum Ltd and Others v Osipov and Others* (UKEAT/0058/17)).

Where an employee has made a protected disclosure and is dismissed for that reason, that is an automatically unfair dismissal (ERA 1996, s 103A). No qualifying period of service will be necessary to bring a claim. There are no limits on the amounts which may be awarded by way of compensatory award, and the tribunal may award reinstatement/re-engagement. It is also unlawful to subject an employee who has made a protected disclosure to any other detriment (ERA 1996, s 47B). That will include dismissal for workers. There is an express provision making it unlawful to contract out of the PIDA 1998. Note that damages will be awarded on different bases, depending on whether the claim is for a detriment (akin to a discrimination claim) or unfair dismissal (unfair dismissal principles will apply). Thus, in detriment cases, compensation can include compensation for injury to feelings. The ERRA 2013 gives tribunals a power to reduce compensation by 25% if a disclosure was not given in good faith.

See *Small v Shrewsbury and Telford Hospitals NHS Trust* [2017] EWCA Civ 882 for a recent case on damages awards in whistleblowing cases. The Court of Appeal recognised in this case that bringing a whistleblowing claim may be 'career-ending' and said that a tribunal should consider whether to award long-term loss of earnings in such cases, even if not specifically raised by the claimant. The EAT looked at how an employment tribunal should assess the calculation of life-long damages in a whistleblowing case in *BMI Healthcare Ltd v Shoukrey*

(UKEAT/0336/19). The tribunal, having upheld his whistleblowing detriment claim, awarded the claimant, a gynaecologist who worked for a private hospital provider, loss of earnings of £880,302 based upon 10 years of career losses. The respondent appealed on the grounds that the tribunal had failed properly to consider: (i) the extent to which the claimant's losses were caused by the detriments; (ii) the possibility that the hospital would close in the future; (iii) the possibility that the claimant's career would not have progressed as claimed; and (iv) whether it would be reasonable to expect the claimant to relocate to mitigate his loss. The EAT upheld all four appeal grounds and remitted the claim to a new tribunal panel to reassess the claimant's loss of earnings. See too *Jhuti v Royal Mail Group* (ET/2200982/2015) (above) where the tribunal awarded compensation for unfair dismissal and detriment in a whistleblowing case, including loss of earnings to retirement, psychiatric injury, £40,000 for injury to feelings and aggravated damages and a very small uplift for breach of the Acas Code, taking into consideration the substantial financial value of the award as a whole.

5.5.6.8 Human Rights Act 1998

Article 10 of the ECHR, as incorporated by the HRA 1998, contains a right to freedom of expression. That includes the right to hold opinions, and to give and receive information and opinions. That right is subject to balancing restrictions such as are necessary in a democratic society. There is considerable overlap between this and the protection offered by the PIDA 1998. However, Article 10 may provide assistance in areas which are not deemed to be 'protected disclosures' under the 1998 Act.

5.6 AWARDS FOR UNFAIR DISMISSAL

The remedies available for an unfairly dismissed employee are either:

(a)   reinstatement or re-engagement; or

(b)   compensation.

Section 112(2) of the ERA 1996 requires an employment tribunal to explain to a successful complainant what awards are available by way of reinstatement and re-engagement, and when they may be made, and to ask the complainant if he wants such an order to be made. The wording is mandatory. A failure to comply with s 112(2) does not render the decision void, but it does make it voidable, depending on whether the failure caused injustice and unfairness (see *Cowley v Manson Timber Ltd* [1995] ICR 367).

5.6.1 Reinstatement and re-engagement

If the employee wants his job back, he may ask for reinstatement (ERA 1996, s 114) or re-engagement (ERA 1996, s 115). Reinstatement is to his old job as though he had not been dismissed. Re-engagement is in a different job with the same employer, his successor or an associated employer. The EAT held in *Dafiaghor-Olomu v Community Integrated Care* (UKEAT/0001/17) that a 'successor employer' does not include a relevant TUPE transfer where there is no change in ownership, because the definition of successor in s 235 of the ERA 1996 requires a change in legal ownership of the undertaking itself. Reinstatement or re-engagement orders are very rare, occurring in less than 1% of unfair dismissal cases that were successful at tribunal.

5.6.1.1 Availability of the order

In deciding whether to make an order for reinstatement or re-engagement, the tribunal must take into account:

(a)   whether the complainant wishes to be reinstated or re-engaged;

(b)   whether it is practicable for the employer to comply with the order;

(c)   whether it would be just to make the order where the complainant has caused or contributed to his dismissal (ERA 1996, s 116(1)).

Where a tribunal orders re-engagement, the terms must be specified with a degree of detail and precision (*Lincolnshire CC v Lupton* (EAT/0328/15)).

The order will not be made unless the employee asks for it. When considering whether to make such an order, the relevant time to assess practicability is the time of the hearing or when the order is to take effect, not the position at the time of dismissal (see *Great Ormond Street Hospital for Children NHS Trust v Patel* (UKEAT/0085/07), *Rembiszewski v Atkins Ltd* (UKEAT/0402/11) and *Dafiaghor-Olomu v Community Integrated Care* (above)). It is unlikely to be made if the employee substantially contributed to his own dismissal. In practice, few reinstatement or re-engagement orders are made. Those which are made are often found where the employer is a large organisation such that it is practical to order the employee to return. Where, as is often the case, the employment relationship is permanently damaged, an order will not be made. It is the employer's view of trust and confidence, tested by the tribunal as to its genuineness and rational foundation, that matters. (See, for example, *Central and NW London NHS Trust v Ambimbola* (UKEAT/0542/08) and *Kelly v PGA European Tour* (UKEAT/0285/18) where the EAT held that the existence of mutual trust and confidence was a relevant factor in terms of both conduct and capability dismissals when addressing the issue of practicability of compliance. The Court of Appeal upheld the decision in *Kelly* ([2021] EWCA Civ 549).)

In *McBride v Scottish Police Authority* [2016] UKSC 27, the Supreme Court emphasised that the only obligation under s 114 was that a claimant be restored to their contractual employment. Reinstatement terms cannot alter contractual terms of employment, but reinstatement does not require the recreation of the precise factual conditions at the point of dismissal. The judgment contains a useful analysis of the principles applicable to reinstatement, as does *United Lincolnshire Trust v Farren* (UKEAT/0198/16).

In *London Borough of Hammersmith & Fulham v Keable* (UKEAT/0333/19), the EAT stated:

> In our view, it does not automatically follow, particularly in an organisation as large as the Council, that because the dismissing officer ... genuinely believed that the Claimant had been guilty of misconduct, that the Council, as an employer, had lost trust and confidence in him. Similarly, and self-evidently, it does not automatically follow that because an employer decides to dismiss an employee for conduct, that decision later being found to be an unfair one, that reinstatement is impracticable. If that were the case, the primary remedy of reinstatement would very rarely be able to be made.

On the facts, notwithstanding that the claimant had been dismissed for serious misconduct arising from a breach of the Code of Conduct and had brought the Council into disrepute, the employment tribunal was entitled to find that it was practicable for the claimant to be reinstated.

5.6.1.2   Contents of the order

Where the tribunal orders reinstatement in the old job, it will make consequential orders that the employee be paid arrears of pay, maintains seniority and maintains pension rights (ERA 1996, s 114).

Where the tribunal orders re-engagement in a different job, it will make consequential orders relating to the nature of employment, remuneration, arrears of pay, seniority and pension rights (ERA 1996, s 115).

5.6.1.3   Non-compliance with order

If an order for reinstatement or re-engagement is made but not complied with by the employer, the employer cannot be compelled to reinstate or re-engage the employee (*Mackenzie v Chancellor, Masters and Scholars of the University of Cambridge* [2020] IRLR 324). The tribunal must then make an award of compensation in favour of the employee instead (ERA 1996, s 117). Section 117 provides for an award of compensation, and also the making of an additional award of compensation, unless the employer satisfies the tribunal that it was not practicable to comply with the order. Practicability of compliance is thus assessed at two separate stages: a provisional determination at the first stage (see **5.6.1**), and a second conclusive determination, with the burden on the employer at the second stage (under s 117).

This award of compensation will consist of a basic, compensatory and additional award.

The basic award is calculated in the usual way (see **5.6.2.1**).

The compensatory award will be assessed in the same way as usual, but instead of being limited to £93,878 or 52 weeks' gross pay (whichever is the lower) (see **5.6.2.2**), the limit will be the higher of £93,878 (as at 6 April 2022) or the value of the employee's arrears of pay and benefits which should have been paid to him under the original order for reinstatement or re-engagement. The amount of any award already made under s 112(5) shall be deducted from any compensation awarded under s 117.

For example, if the reinstatement order required the employer to pay the employee the sum of £94,500 by way of arrears of pay and the employer fails to comply, the compensatory award will be £94,500 not £93,878.

Lastly, the tribunal must make an additional award unless the employer can satisfy the tribunal that it was not practicable to comply with the reinstatement or re-engagement order. The employer could put forward new evidence to show this. If the tribunal makes an additional award, this will be an amount equivalent to between 26 and 52 weeks' gross pay. A week's pay is subject to a maximum of £571 as at 6 April 2022.

5.6.2 Compensation

If the tribunal considers that the complaint is well founded, but no order for reinstatement or re-engagement is made, it must make an award of compensation. The award will consist of two elements:

(a) the basic award; and

(b) the compensatory award (ERA 1996, s 118).

5.6.2.1 Basic award

The basic award is generally calculated in the same way as a redundancy payment, by applying the formula based on age factor, length of service and one week's pay. The same maximum of 20 years' service and £571 (as at 6 April 2022) for one week's pay applies (ERA 1996, s 119). (See **4.6** for details.) A gross weekly figure is used (subject to the maximum cap). The maximum basic award is currently £17,130 (since 6 April 2022).

There are, however, a number of differences between the calculations of the basic award and a redundancy payment:

(a) In certain circumstances, such as where an employee is unfairly dismissed for being a member of a trade union or refusing to be a member of one, or where a health and safety official is dismissed, the basic award is subject to a minimum, which is £6,959 as at 6 April 2022.

(b) The basic award may be subject to reduction. Section 122(1) and (2) provide that the basic award may be reduced by such sum as is just and equitable having regard to the claimant's unreasonable refusal to accept an offer of reinstatement and/or the claimant's pre-dismissal conduct (even if the conduct did not contribute to the dismissal).

Redundancy payments should also be deducted from the basic award. Note that in *Bowyer v Siemens Communications* (UKEAT/0021/05) the EAT held that a payment made by an employer which purported to be a redundancy payment, but which was not in fact because there was no redundancy situation, could not be set off against the basic award in an unfair dismissal claim. Such a payment could be offset (under ERA 1996, s 122(4)) only where the true reason for the dismissal was redundancy. (In practice, this will have an impact only where the compensatory award exceeds the statutory cap, as usually such sum will be set off against the compensatory award.)

Note, when calculating the basic award, that age, length of continuous service and pay are all artificially defined by statute. This contrasts with the approach to the compensatory award which is almost entirely discretionary. Thus the approach to the calculation of the two awards is necessarily different. The formula for a week's pay is set out in s 229 of the ERA 1996. For continuity of the period of employment, regard needs to be had to s 218 of the ERA 1996.

Determining what amounts to a week's pay can sometimes be a complicated process. In the context of the calculation of the basic award, it is subject to a statutory cap. But it may still require some complex working out – especially where employees work on flexible hours, or where their pay includes a rate for overtime or holiday pay. Note also that the TULR(C)A 1992, s 207A increase for breach of a Code of Practice (see below) only applies to the compensatory award, not the basic award.

5.6.2.2 Compensatory award

Unlike the basic award, which is based on a formula, the compensatory award is designed to compensate the employee for the loss that he has suffered.

By s 123(1) of the ERA 1996, the compensatory award consists of 'such amount as the tribunal considers just and equitable in all the circumstances having regard to the loss sustained by the complainant in consequence of the dismissal in so far as that loss is attributable to action taken by the employer'.

For a useful walk through some of the key issues on calculating compensation (conduct, misconduct, gross misconduct, contribution and *Polkey* reductions), see *Tydeman v Oyster Yachts Ltd* [2022] EAT 115 (para 35 onwards).

Maximum award

The compensatory award is subject to a maximum, which is £93,878 (from 6 April 2022) or 52 weeks' gross pay (whichever is the lower) (Unfair Dismissal (Variation of the Limit of Compensatory Award) Order 2013 (SI 2013/1949)). So, for example, if an employee was earning £46,000 per annum, the cap will be £46,000. This maximum is applied *after* any reductions have been made (see 'Reducing factors' below).

In the context of calculating the compensatory element of an award, a week's pay is not subject to any limit (as it is for calculating the basic award). Where an employee receives non-variable pay for their working hours, the amount of a week's pay is 'the amount that is payable by the employer' under the contract. In *University of Sunderland v Drossou* (UKEAT/0341/16), the EAT upheld a tribunal decision that a week's pay could include the employer's pension contributions – even though this was paid into a pension fund and the employee did not receive it as income in hand. For example, an employee earns £1,000 per week gross and his employer contributes £150 into a pension scheme each week. If pension contributions are not included, the maximum award would be £52,000 (£1,000 x 52 weeks). If the pension is included then the maximum award would be £59,800 (£1,150 x 52 weeks). The EAT noted that the wording of s 221(2) of the ERA 1996 is different from the wording in s 27 (unlawful deductions from wages claims). Whereas the wording of s 27 ('sums payable to the worker') would rule out including a pension contribution, s 221(2) refers to wages as 'sums payable to the worker'. This can make a significant difference to an award, and would appear to cover other financial rewards.

Note that the maximum does not apply to whistleblowing cases or to dismissals for asserting statutory rights.

Note: The £93,878 maximum applies only to the compensatory element of the award. A claimant could therefore receive £93,878 (or, if less, 12 months' pay) plus a basic award of up to £17,130 (as at 6 April 2022).

In *Tao Herbs and Acupuncture Ltd v Jin* (UKEAT/1477/09), the EAT confirmed that it was not appropriate when assessing compensation under s 123 of the ERA 1996 to take account of the employer's ability to pay (even if it would mean the business went into liquidation): the prime consideration is the loss suffered by the claimant.

In *W Devis & Sons Ltd v Atkins* [1977] AC 931 the dismissal of an abattoir manager was held to be unfair, but because the employer subsequently discovered information suggesting that the employee had been dishonest during his employment, the court held that it was just and equitable to order no compensatory award.

Whether an employee can recover non-economic loss was the subject of discussion in *Johnson v Unisys Ltd* [2001] IRLR 279. The employee received the maximum compensatory award from a tribunal. He then made a claim for breach of contract in the county court, claiming that his dismissal without a fair hearing was in breach of the duty of trust and confidence, and that this breach resulted in his having a mental breakdown. He sought damages for this. His claim was dismissed on two grounds. First, because the implied duty of trust and confidence was said to be inappropriate to the termination of the employment relationship (see **2.4.1.5**) and, secondly, because the employee had already exercised his statutory right to claim unfair dismissal. In the course of his judgment, Lord Hoffmann commented that while 'in the early days' the compensatory award was only there to compensate financial loss, that was

> too narrow a construction. The emphasis is upon the tribunal awarding such compensation as it thinks just and equitable. So I see no reason why in an appropriate case it should not include compensation for distress, humiliation, damage to reputation in the community or to family life.

However, in *Dunnachie v Kingston Upon Hull* [2004] IRLR 727, the House of Lords unanimously held that damages for non-economic loss are *not* recoverable for unfair dismissal, and that s 123 of the ERA 1996 only allows a tribunal to award financial losses. Thus it is not possible to recover damages for injury to feelings as part of unfair dismissal compensation. This overrides the Court of Appeal's decision (see [2004] IRLR 287).

Dunnachie was heard by the House of Lords at the same time as *Eastwood v Magnox; McCabe v Cornwall County Council and Another* [2004] IRLR 733, two cases concerning the overlap between common law claims for damages for breach of trust and confidence, and the statutory unfair dismissal regime. In these cases the House of Lords confirmed that a common law claim for breach of the implied term of trust and confidence will be allowed for events leading up to the dismissal, but not for the dismissal itself (because that would amount to a circumvention of the statutory cap placed on compensation for unfair dismissal) (see further **2.4.1.5**). So the employee who suffers psychiatric harm arising out of the events leading up to dismissal cannot recover damages for the loss suffered as part of his unfair dismissal claim because such a loss does not flow from the dismissal, but he might be able to bring a personal injury claim and/or a claim for breach of contract in the civil courts for such pre-dismissal loss. Damages for losses arising out of breach of an implied term flowing from the dismissal are only recoverable in an employment tribunal (where the cap on damages applies).

The Supreme Court confirmed that the so-called *Johnson* exclusion area also applies to cases in which the breach relied upon is of an express contractual term (*Edwards v Chesterfield Royal Hospital NHS Foundation Trust* [2013] UKSC 58). Therefore, an employee who is dismissed cannot bring proceedings for breach of contract based on a failure to follow contractual disciplinary procedures because that would, according to the Supreme Court, undermine the statutory unfair dismissal regime (see **Chapter 2**).

In *GAB Robins v Triggs* [2008] IRLR 317 (an unfair constructive dismissal claim), the Court of Appeal held, applying *Johnson* and *Eastwood*, that in assessing the claimant's loss of earnings for unfair dismissal purposes, no regard could be had to losses which flowed from the bullying that led to her taking time off ill and subsequently resigning, and which resulted in reduced earning capacity thereafter. Regard must be had, for the purposes of s 123 of the ERA 1996, only to losses flowing from the dismissal (by which time the claimant was already ill). The claimant's reduced earning capacity by reason of her illness was not a loss suffered 'in consequence of the dismissal'. Rather, it was caused by the bullying, and therefore the claimant could recover damages in respect of it only by bringing a separate claim at common law, such as for psychiatric injury.

A tribunal must, in deciding whether to make a compensatory award (see *Saunders v OCS Group* (UKEAT/0051/09)):

(a)   identify what loss the employee has suffered at the date of dismissal; and then

(b)   decide whether the employer's action (in dismissing the employee) caused the loss.

Heads of loss

Compensation will usually be assessed under the following main heads:

(a)   Immediate loss of net earnings to which the employee was entitled, from the date of dismissal to the date of the hearing or until the employee finds a new job, if earlier (provided that job is higher-paid). In *Whelan and Another (t/a Cheers Off Licence) v Richardson* [1998] IRLR 14, the EAT said, when calculating unfair dismissal compensation, that the applicant should be compensated for all losses arising from the date of dismissal until the date on which higher-paid alternative employment is found.

In *Burlo v Langley & Carter* [2006] EWCA Civ 1778, the Court of Appeal dealt with the principles for calculating compensation during an employee's notice period. Ms Burlo worked as a nanny for Mr Langley and Ms Carter. Her employment was subject to a written contract which provided for eight weeks' notice of termination on either side. The contract also provided that, during periods of sickness, the employers would pay 'sickness benefit in accordance with government statutory sick pay legislation'. Following an argument about money, Ms Burlo threatened to resign. Mr Langley said that she would be required to work her notice. Ms Burlo continued at work, but some days later she had a car accident and was provided with a sick note to say that she would be off work for several weeks. In the meantime, her employers engaged another nanny and wrote saying that they would not now require Ms Burlo to work out her notice. Ms Burlo brought a number of claims in the employment tribunal, including claims for wrongful and unfair dismissal. Both these claims succeeded. The tribunal assessed damages for the notice period at £3,440 (eight weeks at her normal weekly wage). They did not explain why they held that the damages should be based on the normal weekly wage rather than on the statutory sick pay to which the employee would have been entitled whilst off sick under her contract of employment. The Court of Appeal held that if Ms Burlo had not been dismissed, she would have received statutory sick pay during her period of absence. Consequently, statutory sick pay was the correct measure of her weekly loss during the notice period. Note, however, that where an employee is entitled only to statutory minimum notice, the employer must pay full pay during the notice period, even where the employee is off work sick (ERA 1996, ss 87 and 88).

In *Paggetti v Cobb* (UKEAT/136/01), the EAT held that when assessing the compensatory (and basic) awards, the tribunal must have regard to the minimum wage.

(b)   Future loss of net earnings to which the employee was entitled from the date of hearing until the employee obtains new employment. No award will be made under this head if the employee is permanently re-employed in an equally well remunerated job at the date of hearing. If he loses that new job, the tribunal will have to assess whether the chain of causation has been broken (*Cowen v Rentokil Ltd* (UKEAT/0473/07)). If the employee takes a less well-paid job, he will be compensated for the difference in pay for such period as the tribunal thinks appropriate in the circumstances. If the employee remains unemployed at this date, the tribunal will have to estimate if and when the employee is likely to be re-employed. Compensation for future loss of earnings is not limited to the employee's contractual notice period. The tribunal will take into account local employment conditions, the skills of the employee, his age and general employability. If an employee could and would have worked beyond the age of 65, compensation may be awarded for potential loss of earnings after 65. If evidence shows that the employee would shortly have lost his job anyway, due, for example, to redundancy, compensation will be limited.

(c)   Loss of pension rights and net fringe benefits from the date of dismissal to the date at (b) above. The value of lost pension rights is very difficult to calculate, and depends on a number of factors, such as the duration of the loss, the type of scheme, the benefits paid and the benefits receivable on retirement. There are two main approaches – a simplified approach and a substantial approach. Where there is a defined contribution scheme, calculation should be relatively straightforward, since the loss will be the value of the contributions that have not been paid. Where there is a defined benefit scheme, the position will be more complicated to assess, and may depend on whether an individual is able to transfer the value of his pension to a new fund. The detail of these approaches is beyond the scope of this work. In *Department for Work and Pensions v Coulson* (UKEAT/ 0572/12), the EAT upheld a pension award reflecting compensation for the pension the claimant would have received if she had remained in employment until her retirement (the claimant was 42 at the date of dismissal). See the Court of Appeal's decision in *Griffin v Plymouth Hospital NHS Trust* [2014] EWCA Civ 1240 for a more recent consideration of the calculation of pension loss.

The *Compensation for Loss of Pension Rights* booklet (the Fourth Edition of the Third Revision should be used) sets out the approach to be adopted in calculating pension losses. The booklet sets out that there should be a default assumption that as far as state pension rights were concerned, there were no losses. As far as occupational pensions are concerned, there should be two possible approaches, depending on whether a case is simple or complex. The Judicial Pensions Working Group has also produced a shorter *Basic Guide to Compensation for Pension Loss*. In simple cases (usually defined contribution or money purchase schemes), the value should be calculated using the amount of lost employer future service contributions from the date of dismissal, taking account where appropriate of any mitigation. In complex cases, such as loss of defined benefit rights for a substantial period of time (in the absence of any agreement between the parties on pension loss), pension loss should be determined using factors set out in what are known as the Ogden tables (actuarial table commonly used to assess compensation in personal injury cases), valued by expert actuaries. Following publication of this booklet in March 2016, the Presidents of Employment Tribunals in England and Wales and Scotland have issued Presidential Guidance on the principles to be applied when compensating for pension loss, applying from 10 August 2017. The principles adopt the approach set out in the booklet. Readers are advised to refer to this Guidance and the booklet when advising on calculating pension losses.

(d)   Loss of statutory rights. The loss of accrued redundancy rights is compensated for by the basic award, but the tribunal will order a sum for the loss of the right to bring an unfair dismissal claim for one year. Conventionally, this sum is £400–£500.

The employee may exceptionally also be awarded up to half-a-week's net pay for each week of the statutory minimum period of notice to which he had been entitled at the end of employment. For example, an employee with 20 years' service would have been entitled to the maximum 12-week notice period. He may be awarded ½ × 12 × net weekly pay (ie six weeks) to compensate for the loss of this. This payment will be made only in exceptional circumstances, because it depends on the double contingency that the employee will get a new job and be dismissed from it before building up the same period of notice. More often than not, a tribunal will simply award the £400–£500 above for loss of statutory rights.

(e)   Expenses in looking for work; removal expenses incurred in taking up a new job.

(f)   A premium for delayed payment may be awarded (the reverse of accelerated receipt – see 'Reducing factors' below) (*Melia v Magna Kansei* (UKEAT/0339/04)).

Compulsory increase of the compensatory award

Section 38 of the EA 2002 states that a tribunal must award compensation to an employee where, upon a successful claim being made under any of the jurisdictions listed in Sch 5 to the EA 2002 (which include unfair dismissal), it becomes apparent that the employer was in breach of his duty to provide full and accurate written particulars (under ERA 1996, s 1). This is not a free-standing claim, it is dependent upon a claim under one of the listed jurisdictions being successful. The tribunal must award the minimum amount of two weeks' pay and may, if it considers it just and equitable, in the circumstances, award a higher amount of four weeks' pay (subject to the maximum of £571 (as at 6 April 2022)). This is on top of any award the tribunal might already have made in respect of the main claim. The tribunal does not have to make any award if there are exceptional circumstances that would make it unjust or inequitable to make an award or increase an award.

Discretionary increase of compensation

Where there has been an unreasonable failure by the employer to comply with the Acas Code, the tribunal has power to increase compensation by up to 25% (TULR(C)A 1992, s 207A). It should be noted that this adjustment option does not apply to the basic award.

Note also that uplifts can only be applied to employees and not workers (see *Local Government Yorkshire v Shah* (UKEAT/0587/11)).

In *Rentplus UK Ltd v Coulson* [2022] IRLR 664, HHJ Tayler set out guidance on the application of the Acas uplift. Tribunals should, he said, ask the following questions (para 19):

(a)   *Is the claim one which raises a matter to which the Acas Code applies?* The Code applies to all cases where an employee's alleged actions or omissions involve culpable conduct or performance on his part that requires correction or punishment (Simler J in *Holmes v Qinetiq Ltd*). HHJ Tayler stated that it is not necessary that the claimant is guilty of misconduct or is providing poor performance. If an employer believes that an employee has stolen money, but is wrong, it would be very surprising if that meant that the Acas Code did not apply because as a matter of fact there was not a disciplinary situation. There is a disciplinary situation because the employer believes that there may be misconduct; that is why the employee should have the benefit of the safeguards of a fair procedure that accords with the Acas Code. The protection of the Acas Code is particularly important for innocent employees. He stated that the Code should be applicable to all categories of dismissal where there is a culpability/disciplinary reason for the dismissal. It does not therefore apply to ill-health dismissals.

Note that because s 207A only 'bites' on claims where the relevant Code of Practice applies, and because the only Code of Practice published to date does not apply to dismissals by reason of redundancy or where the dismissal was as a result of the expiry of a fixed-term contract, no adjustment will be made to redundancy payment awards or unfair dismissal awards where the reason for the dismissal was redundancy or expiry of a fixed-term contract.

The EAT held in *Lund v St Edmund's School, Canterbury* (UKEAT/0514/12) that the Code applies to 'some other substantial reason' dismissals where the reason related to the employee's behaviour. The claimant was dismissed because the school had lost confidence in him as a result of the claimant's actions at work. The EAT held that 'his claim concerned the conduct on his part which led the school to consider whether he should be dismissed, even if it was not his conduct but the effect of his conduct ... which was the ultimate reason for his dismissal'.

(b)   *Has there been a failure to comply with the Acas Code in relation to that matter?* HHJ Taylor stated that:

> A similar approach will generally be appropriate to that adopted under the previous uplift provisions set out in section 31(3) of the Employment Act 2002; see the approach of Underhill J (president) in *Lawless v Print Plus (Debarred)* UKEAT/0333/09/JOJ:
>
> > (4) The circumstances which will be relevant will inevitably vary from case to case and cannot be itemised, but they will certainly include: (a) whether the procedures were ignored altogether or applied to some extent (see *Virgin Media Ltd v Seddington & Eland* UKEAT/0539/08, at paragraph 20); (b) whether the failure to comply with the procedures was deliberate or inadvertent; and (c) whether there are circumstances which may mitigate the blameworthiness of the failure. Those factors are sometimes embraced under the labels of the 'culpability' or 'seriousness' of the failure.
> >
> > (5) Provided a tribunal has directed itself appropriately, this Tribunal will be very slow to interfere with its exercise of discretion: *Cex Ltd v Lewis* [2007] UKEAT/0013/07.

He also concluded that if an employer acts in bad faith and pretends to apply an appropriate procedure, that cannot amount to compliance with the Acas Code.

(c)   *Was the failure to comply with the Acas Code unreasonable?* In *Kuehne and Nagel Ltd v Cosgrove* (UKEAT/0165/13) HHJ Eady QC stated, albeit obiter:

> 52. Equally, I do not need to say anything about the ACAS uplift point, save that I would add that I would have found an error of law here in the Employment Judge's failure to correctly direct himself that a breach would need to be unreasonable.

(d)   *Is it just and equitable to award an uplift because of the failure to comply with the Acas Code and, if so, by what percentage, up to 25%?* In *Sir Benjamin Slade v Biggs* [2022] IRLR 216 at [77], Griffith J said:

> In future, when considering what should be the effect of an employer's failure to comply with a relevant Code under s 207A of TULRCA, tribunals might choose to apply a four-stage test, in order to navigate the various points which I have been considering in this appeal:
>
> (i)   Is the case such as to make it just and equitable to award any ACAS uplift?
>
> (ii) If so, what does the ET consider a just and equitable percentage, not exceeding although possibly equalling, 25%?
>
> Any uplift must reflect 'all the circumstances', including the seriousness and/or motivation for the breach, which the ET will be able to assess against the usual range of cases using its expertise and experience as a specialist tribunal. It is not necessary to apply, in addition to the question of seriousness, a test of exceptionality.
>
> (iii) Does the uplift overlap, or potentially overlap, with other general awards, such as injury to feelings; and, if so, what in the ET's judgment is the appropriate adjustment, if any, to the percentage of those awards in order to avoid double-counting?
>
> (iv) Applying a final sense-check, is the sum of money represented by the application of the percentage uplift arrived at by the ET disproportionate in absolute terms and, if so, what further adjustment needs to be made?

HHJ Tayler upheld the tribunal's uplift of 25% in this case. The tribunal had decided that the procedure adopted by the respondent before dismissing the claimant, ostensibly for redundancy, was a total sham. The employment tribunal did not therefore err in awarding an Acas uplift of 25%.

In *Shifferaw v Hudson Music Co Ltd* (UKEAT/0294/15) the employment tribunal dealt with the uplift issue as follows:

> 65. ... Whilst we rejected ... some other complaints of failure to comply with the ACAS code, we found unreasonable failure to comply in relation to James De Wolfe having not been an independent person to deal with the Claimant's grievance. We considered that this was a serious failure because he was the person considering her whole grievance and she was not given a right of appeal. The just and equitable

uplift was more than the 10% proposed by [the respondent]. However, there were *some* measures taken to address her concerns internally, and other complaints had not succeeded before us [tribunal's emphasis]. Overall, within the statutory range of 0% to 25%, we considered a 20% uplift would be fair in this case.

There was no challenge to that decision. The EAT held that where there are concurrent unfair dismissal and wrongful dismissal claims, it is a matter for the judge's discretion whether the uplift should be applied from the date of dismissal or from the end of the notice period (wrongful dismissal is not included in Sch A2). The case was remitted for the judge to determine that question. In the authors' opinion, the uplift ought to apply to the unfair dismissal compensatory award from the date of dismissal. In such cases wrongful dismissal damages would become a notional award (see **6.7.1**).

Reducing factors

Note that early pension payments should *not* be deducted from the compensatory award (*Smoker v London Fire and Civil Defence Authority* [1991] ICR 449, followed in *Knapton & Others v ECC Card Clothing Ltd* [2006] IRLR 756).

(a)   Mitigation

The employee is under a duty to mitigate his loss by taking reasonable steps to obtain alternative employment. Compensation will not be awarded for any loss that should have been mitigated but was not (*Kyndall Spirits v Burns* (EAT/29/02)). The burden of raising and proving an unreasonable failure to mitigate is on the employer. In practice, an employee should keep records of his job applications to show the tribunal that he has tried to mitigate his loss. Where an employee turns down an offer of employment, the ultimate question for the tribunal is whether he acted unreasonably in turning it down. The tribunal must consider all the surrounding circumstances (*Wilding v British Telecommunications plc* [2002] IRLR 524). Failure to mitigate can reduce the compensatory award but not the basic award. Similarly, if the employee has secured an alternative job by the time of the hearing, wages from that new job will be taken into account. The EAT held in *Window Machinery Sales Ltd t/a Promac Group v Luckey* (UKEAT/0301/14) that the tribunal should ask first what steps were reasonable for the claimant to have taken; secondly, whether the claimant did take reasonable steps; and thirdly, to what extent, if any, the claimant would have actually mitigated the loss if he had taken those steps; and that the burden of proof is on the employer at all stages.

In *Cooper Contracting Ltd v Lindsey* (EAT/0184/15), the EAT summarised the following principles as being relevant when assessing mitigation of loss:

(1)   It is not for the employee to prove that they mitigated their loss: the burden of proof is on the employer.

(2)   If the employer does not address the issue of mitigation, the Tribunal need not consider it.

(3)   If the employer does raise the issue, it must prove that the employee acted unreasonably; the employee does not have to show that what they did was reasonable. While it might be reasonable for an employee to accept the most lucratively paid job, it is not necessarily unreasonable for them to accept a lesser paid job due to a preference for the nature of that particular role: 'there may come a time in a person's working life when some types of work are no longer appropriate ... Mr Lindsey's evidence was that he preferred to be his own boss having had the experience of employment with the Respondent. It is very much his own choice.'

(4)   The employee does not have to take all reasonable steps to mitigate their loss. If such a position were adopted, an employer would be able to argue that an employee's compensation should be reduced on the basis of a single reasonable step not taken.

(5) Ultimately, it is the Tribunal's view of what is unreasonable in all the circumstances that matters, which can include the views and wishes of the employee.

(6) It is not for the claimant to be put on trial when looking at mitigation of loss; they are not the party at fault in the proceedings.

In *Hakim v The Scottish Trade Unions Congress* (UKEATS/0047/19), the EAT held that if a specific percentage reduction is to be applied because of a failure to mitigate, the tribunal should be in a position to justify the adoption of its approach, especially if it is a 'crude' one. In this case, it had evidence by which it could have fixed the date when the claimant should have regained employment and could have calculated a differential wage loss, but instead it applied an unscientific 30% reduction. The EAT held that this had not been a logical approach.

The Court of Appeal in *Burlo* (see 'Heads of loss' above) looked closely at the decision of the National Industrial Relations Court (Sir John Donaldson presiding) in *Norton Tool Co Ltd v Tewson* [1973] 1 WLR 45. It said that *Norton Tool* settled two basic points of law on the calculation of compensation for unfair dismissal in an actual dismissal. First, compensation could not be awarded for injury to feelings. (*Norton Tool* was expressly approved on this point by the House of Lords in *Dunnachie v Kingston upon Hull City Council* (see above).) Secondly, where an employer summarily dismissed an employee in a situation where notice should have been given but was not, an employee was entitled to be awarded compensation for wages in lieu of notice without any deduction for wages which were actually earned, or could have been earned, with an alternative employer during the notice period. In *Babcock FATA Ltd v Addison* [1987] ICR 805, the employer had challenged (unsuccessfully) *Norton Tool* on the wages in lieu of notice point. Although the employer won its appeal on the particular facts in *Babcock*, the Court of Appeal in that case were unanimous in not accepting the contention that *Norton Tool* was wrong in holding that the employee should not have to give credit for the wages that he had received from alternative employment during the period of notice. It was argued in *Burlo* that the House of Lords in *Dunnachie* had impliedly overruled the *Norton Tool* principle that credit need not be given by an employee for other earnings during the notice period. The Court of Appeal said that issue had to be left for another case to determine, but in the meantime a claimant should not have to give credit for monies earned during the notice period. The Court of Appeal in *Stuart Peters v Bell* [2009] EWCA Civ 938 held that this principle does not apply to a constructive dismissal. In a constructive dismissal case, credit has to be given for wages earned during the notice period.

(b) *Accelerated receipt for future loss of earnings*

See **2.4.1.9** for a discussion of this reducing factor.

(c) *Ex gratia payments made by the employer to the employee*

(d) *'Polkey' deductions*

One of the factors that a tribunal has to consider when assessing compensation where there have been procedural failings in the dismissal process, is whether the employee would still have been dismissed if a proper procedure had been followed. If the tribunal concludes that even if a fair procedure had been followed, dismissal would still have occurred, then that can sound in the compensation that is awarded. Such a conclusion can have two main effects:

(i) on the period of time over which compensation is awarded; and

(ii) on the actual amount,

in that a percentage reduction (up to 100%) may be made by the tribunal to take account of the tribunal's assessment of the likelihood that dismissal would still have occurred. An employment tribunal's task, when deciding what compensation is just and equitable for future loss of earnings in these circumstances, will almost inevitably involve a consideration of uncertainties. What the tribunal has to do is to 'construct, from evidence not speculation, a framework which is a working hypothesis about what would have happened had the [employer] behaved differently and fairly' (*Gover and Others v Property Care Ltd* [2006] EWCA Civ 286).

In *Polkey v AE Dayton Services Ltd* [1988] ICR 142, the House of Lords ended what was known as the 'no difference' rule, which had allowed procedurally irregular dismissals to be ruled as fair where it could be shown that carrying out a proper procedure would have made no difference to the outcome. Their Lordships said this was not relevant to fairness, but it would sound in the assessment of damages because s 123 of the ERA 1996 refers to 'such amount as the tribunal considers just and equitable in all the circumstances'. Lord Mackay of Clashfern approved the remarks of Browne-Wilkinson J in *Sillifant v Powell Duffryn Timber Ltd* [1983] IRLR 91, at 92:

> Where in the circumstances known at the time of the dismissal, it was not reasonable for the employer to dismiss without giving an opportunity to explain, but facts subsequently discovered or proved ... show that the dismissal was in fact merited, compensation would be reduced to nil. Such an approach ensures that an employee who could have been fairly dismissed does not get compensation.

Lord Bridge also approved the remarks of Browne-Wilkinson J at 96:

> There is no need for an 'all or nothing' decision; if the industrial tribunal thinks there is a doubt whether or not the employee would have been dismissed, this element can be reflected by reducing the normal amount of compensation by a percentage representing the chance that the employee would still have lost his employment.

In *Lambe v 186K* [2005] ICR 307, the Court of Appeal considered how tribunals should approach the question of compensation in cases where a dismissal might have occurred in any event. Giving the judgment of the Court, Wall LJ (at 323) cited with approval the judgment of Lord Prosser in the Court of Session in *King v Eaton Ltd (No 2)* [1998] IRLR 686. The procedure by which an applicant was made redundant in *King* was found to be unfair, and the issue was whether the applicant would have been made redundant had a fair procedure been followed. Lord Prosser stated (at para 19):

> It seems to us that the matter will be one of impression and judgment, so that a tribunal will have to decide whether the unfair departure from what should have happened was of a kind which makes it possible to say, with more or less confidence, that the failure made no difference, or whether the failure was such that one cannot sensibly reconstruct the world as it might have been.

Wall LJ stated that the formulation 'provides tribunals with a straightforward and sensible yardstick with which to approach such cases'. At para 60, Wall LJ adopted that approach and stated:

> [That] approach to the facts of the instant case leads us to the conclusion that on the evidence available to it, the Tribunal was entitled to conclude that in the Appellant's case, whilst both the process of selection for redundancy and the absence of consultation was unfair, it was unlikely that the Appellant would have found alternative employment with the Respondent or any of its associated companies at the conclusion of an extended period of consultation. The Tribunal was entitled to find that what the Appellant wanted was his job back, and that he was not willing to consider the alternative offered by the Respondent, which the Tribunal found was both a promotion and commanded a higher income. In short, this was not a case in which it was impossible for the Tribunal sensibly to reconstruct the world as it never was: the Tribunal was entitled to come to the conclusion that an extended period of consultation should have taken place, but that at the end of it, the Appellant would still have left the Respondent's employment.

Where a fair procedure would have delayed an otherwise inevitable dismissal, compensation will be awarded for the time the procedure would have taken to conduct properly (see, for example, *Slaughter v Breuer* [1990] ICR 730).

In *Software 2000 Ltd v Andrews and Others* [2007] ICR 825, Elias J reviewed and summarised the principles to be extracted from all the authorities on *Polkey*.

The EAT confirmed in *Zebrowski v Concentric Birmingham Ltd* (UKEAT/0245/16) that, in summary, tribunals have three *alternative* options when assessing how long a period to make an award for:

- to find that it is 100% certain that the employee would have been dismissed by the end of a particular period and so limit compensation to that period (see *O'Donoghue* above and *Shittu v South London and Maudsley NHS Foundation Trust* [2022] EAT 18);

- to find that the employment relationship would have continued unaffected for a certain period but thereafter there was a percentage chance that the employee would have ceased to be employed (see, for example, *Frith Accountants Ltd v Law* (EAT/0460/13));

- to assess the percentage likelihood of the employment terminating in any event.

Polkey deductions may be made whether the dismissal is substantively unfair or procedurally unfair, although it will be easier to assess if the failure is procedural (*King v Eaton Ltd (No 2)* [1998] IRLR 686). For decisions considering a *Polkey* reduction (i) in a redundancy situation, where there was a procedurally unfair dismissal, see *Contract Bottling Ltd v Cave* (UKEAT/0525/12), and (ii) in an unfair dismissal case, see *Anderson v Chesterfield High School* (UKEAT/0206/14).

(e) *Discretionary reduction in compensation*

Where there has been an unreasonable failure by the employee to comply with the Acas Code, a reduction of up to 25% is possible. (See the discussion above of the discretionary increase of compensation.)

(f) *Contributory fault*

If the tribunal finds that the complainant caused or contributed to his dismissal (this must be pre-dismissal conduct), the compensatory award *must* be reduced by such proportion as it considers just and equitable (ERA 1996, s 123(6)). If the employee substantially contributed to his own dismissal, this will mean a substantial percentage reduction in the awards, even of 100%, leaving the employee with a finding of unfair dismissal but no compensation. This is usually relevant only in misconduct dismissals. It is unusual in capability dismissals, for example on health grounds, where the employee is not culpable or blameworthy (but see *Jinadu v Dockland Buses Ltd* (UKEAT/ 0166/16) where the claimant's compensatory (and basic) award was reduced by 75% in a capability case). The tribunal does not necessarily need to reduce basic and compensatory awards by the same percentage, but it often does so in practice. The question for the tribunal is whether, in a misconduct case, the claimant was in fact guilty of the blameworthy or culpable conduct which to any extent caused or contributed to the dismissal. The employer's conduct is irrelevant (*Sandwell & West Birmingham Hospitals NHS Trust v Westwood* (UKEAT/0032/09), but tribunals must consider mitigating factors before making a reduction.

(g) *Pre-dismissal misconduct discovered after dismissal*

The tribunal, in deciding what amount is just and equitable, may take into account any misconduct of the employee discovered after dismissal and reduce both the basic and compensatory awards accordingly (ss 122(2) and 123(1)). Post-dismissal conduct is not relevant.

(h) *Contractual redundancy payments in excess of the basic award.*

(i) *Payments in lieu – compensatory award only*

If the employee receives a payment in lieu of notice or an ex gratia payment from his employer, this will be taken into account in assessing his compensation (*Babcock FATA Ltd v Addison* [1987] IRLR 173, CA).

(j)   Conduct of the employee post dismissal, in so far as it might breach the chain of causation when considering future loss (see *Cumbria County Council & Governing Body of Dowdales School v Bates* (UKEAT/0398/11 & 0039/13).

Order of compensatory award adjustments

The correct order of adjustments once the net loss is calculated is (see *Ministry of Defence v Wheeler* [1998] IRLR 23, CA, and *Digital Equipment Co Ltd v Clements (No 2)* [1998] IRLR 134, CA):

(a)   deduct payments in lieu/ex gratia payments made by the employer (for a recent case, see *Dafiaghor-Olomu v Community Integrated Care* [2022] EAT 84, [2022] IRLR 763);

(b)   deduct sums earned by the employee from new employment, or make deductions (notional earnings) by reason of a failure to mitigate;

(c)   deduct benefits other than jobseeker's allowance and income support (see also **5.6.2.4** below);

(d)   make any *Polkey* deduction;

(e)   reduce the award or increase by up to 25% for a failure to comply with the Acas Code;

(f)   add in any award for sums awarded for failure to provide written particulars of employment (EA 2002, ss 31 and 38) (s 31(5));

(g)   make any contributory fault deduction/deduction for misconduct discovered after dismissal (ERA 1996, s 123(6));

(h)   deduct contractual redundancy payment made by the employer which is in excess of basic award;

(i)   gross up (if appropriate) (see *Hardie Grant London Ltd v Aspden* (UKEAT/0242/11) for authority on when to gross up a compensatory award in a case of unfair dismissal to allow for tax when the statutory cap applies – the authors think, with respect, that the decision is probably wrong, but, unless and until it is overruled, it must be applied);

(j)   apply statutory cap of £93,878 (as at 6 April 2022) (if appropriate).

5.6.2.3   Interest

Interest may be awarded on compensation for unfair dismissal. It begins to run from the day after the decision is sent to the parties. However, if the amount is paid in full within 14 days, no interest is payable.

The current rate of interest is set out in s 17 of the Judgments Act 1833 and Article 4 of the Employment Tribunals (Interest) Order 1990 (SI 1990/479). Since 1 April 1993, this rate has been 8% per annum.

5.6.2.4   Recoupment of social security benefits

The Employment Protection (Recoupment of Jobseeker's Allowance and Income Support) Regulations 1996 (SI 1996/2349) (as amended and updated by the Welfare Reform Act 2007 and the Social Security (Miscellaneous Amendments) (No 5) Regulations 2010 (SI 2010/2429)) allow the Government to recoup jobseeker's allowance, income support and (from 1 November 2010) income-related employment and support allowance (IRESA) paid to an employee who gets an unfair dismissal award of compensation. These benefits received by the employee are not deducted by the tribunal in computing the compensatory award. (*Note:* Contributory employment and support allowance is not covered by the recoupment regulations.)

The Employment Tribunals Act 1996 (ETA 1996), ss 16 and 17 operate as follows:

(a)   where the employee has received jobseeker's allowance, income support or IRESA between the EDT and the hearing, the tribunal designates the 'immediate loss of earnings' part of the award as the 'prescribed element' and notifies the Department for Work and Pensions (DfWP);

(b)   the employer withholds the 'prescribed element' from the employee until notified by the DfWP of the amount of jobseeker's allowance, income support and IRESA to be recouped (up to the maximum of the 'prescribed element');

(c)   the amount to be recouped is then paid by the employer to the DfWP and any balance of the 'prescribed element' paid to the employee.

EXAMPLE

Whilst awaiting a hearing, the employee receives income support *totalling* £1,500. The tribunal awards compensation of £10,000.

£2,000 of this represents immediate loss of wages (the 'prescribed element').

The employer pays £8,000 to the employee immediately and tells DfWP that he has retained £2,000.

DfWP tells the employer to account for £1,500.

The employer pays £1,500 to DfWP and £500 to the employee.

Note: the recoupment regulations do not apply to settlements.

5.6.2.5   Taxation

If an award is made for termination of employment that exceeds £30,000 (including the basic award), it is subject to taxation (see Income Tax (Earnings and Pensions) Act 2003, Ch 3, Pt 6, s 401(1)). This covers payments for 'being' an employee, including emoluments from the employer and rewards for services past, present and future. Any awards over £30,000 should therefore be grossed up to ensure that the net loss is actually paid to the claimant (see **2.4.1.8**). The EAT explains how to calculate the grossed up figure in *Hall v Durham CC and Ors* (UKEAT/0256/14) and confirms in *Chief Constable of Northumbria Police v Erichsen* (UKEAT/0027/15) that since pension loss is assessed on a gross basis, that loss should not be grossed up. National insurance contributions also have to be paid on termination payments over £30,000.

The only awards that should be grossed up are those that are calculated using a net weekly pay figure, ie:

•   the compensatory element of an award;

•   damages for wrongful dismissal;

•   financial losses suffered as a result of unlawful discrimination.

The following heads of loss will *not* be grossed up:

•   any awards that have been calculated as a gross figure (when tax will be deducted either before the employee receives the payment (if they are still employed) or on the employee's own self-assessment (if they are no longer employed));

•   any other awards calculated as a gross figure (eg the basic award and additional award);

•   awards which are not taxed (eg psychiatric injury).

A detailed explanation of how taxation impacts in practice on tribunal awards is beyond the scope of this work, but a summary chart is set out in **Table 5.1** below. Tribunals generally make awards that reflect a claimant's losses, but should take into account when doing so any prospective tax liability. From 6 April 2011, employers must deduct PAYE from post-termination payments at the appropriate marginal rate.

Readers should note that, from 6 April 2018, significant changes were introduced by legislation to the tax treatment of termination payments to ensure that payments in respect of the contractual notice period will be taxable, even if the employee does not work the notice period, ensuring that NICs due on sums above £30,000 will be payable and clarifying that the exception does not apply to termination payments relating to injury to feelings awards. In essence, the new rules treat all employment contracts as if they contain a payment in lieu of notice (PILON) clause, so that the basic pay the employee would have received during the notice period will be taxed as earnings (and subject to income tax and national insurance contributions). The £30,000 exemption will remain potentially available for any balance which is genuinely compensation for loss of office. Payments for injury to feelings (except where the injury amounts to a psychiatric injury or other recognised medical condition) will fall outside the injury payments exemption.

The stated aims of the April 2018 changes were to make the taxation of termination payments simpler for both employees and employers to understand and operate, clearer and more certain, fairer and not unduly expensive to implement and operate.

The distinction between contractual/customary termination payments from the employer, such as holiday pay (which are taxable), and non-contractual ones, such as statutory redundancy pay (which currently are not subject to tax), was retained. In responses at the time to a draft of the proposals, it was pointed out that to change this state of affairs would involve a considerable amount of legislative changes, which would increase complexity. However, the changes made clear that only payments directly relating to termination were exempt, and reference would need to be made to the contractual terms and conditions of employment in order to ascertain which payments are contractual. The excess of any non-contractual payments over £30,000 is taxable, and the £30,000 threshold was retained.

Note that the rules on taxation are not just relevant to tribunal awards but also apply to sums paid by way of settlement of employment disputes. In *HMRC v Murphy* [2022] EWCA Civ 1112, the Court of Appeal held that a full settlement sum was taxable as earnings despite being partly used for the payment of legal fees. The Court said that a settlement sum will not cease to be taxable in full just because the recipients may use some of the money to pay their legal fees and an insurance premium covering costs associated with their legal claim. The claimant was a police officer employed by the Metropolitan Police Service who, along with other officers, commenced a group claim against the Met in respect of unpaid overtime and allowances. In May 2016, a settlement agreement was reached with the police officers. When the settlement sum was paid, the Met applied PAYE to the whole settlement sum, including a proportion of the settlement sum which was to pay a lawyer's success fee and an insurance premium. An officer challenged the taxation of the settlement sum on the basis that the sum paid to his lawyer and for the insurance premium were not earnings. The Court of Appeal found that given that the settlement sum was predominantly a reimbursement of sums which would have been taxable as employee income, the appropriate analysis was that the sum was taxable in full. It is therefore important to give careful consideration to the structure of any settlement sum and the associated tax treatment of payments agreed.

> **EXAMPLE**
>
> Suppose a tribunal awards £50,000 as the compensatory element of an award for unfair dismissal. HM Revenue and Customs regards this as taxable as a termination payment. The first £30,000 is tax free (if statutory redundancy has also been paid or there is a basic award, this would also count towards the £30,000 figure). The remaining £20,000 is taxed as income. What tax rate is applicable will depend on what the employee has already earned in the tax year. If his total gross earnings in the year do not exceed £42,385, the appropriate tax rate will be 20%. The compensatory element of the award will need to be grossed up (which will provide a figure of £25,000 (20,000 ÷ 0.8)). Then add back in the £30,000. The tribunal will need to award £55,000 to the employee to ensure that the employee is left, after the employer pays the tax due on £25,000 (being £5,000), with the true net loss of £50,000.

Table 5.1 Taxation of tribunal awards

Type of Award	Gross/Net	Explanation
Unlawful deduction from wages [ERA 1996, s 24] (see **1.11.1**)	Gross (but see wording in ERA 1996, s 13(3)) NI is also payable	Wages. This is deferred remuneration; it is a contractual payment which is taxable in the hands of the employee. It is not a payment on termination and does not come within the £30K exemption.
Unpaid holiday pay (whether under contract or under WTR) (see **1.12.5**)	Gross NI is also payable	Wages. This is deferred remuneration; it is a contractual payment which is taxable in the hands of the employee. It is not a payment on termination and does not come within the £30K exemption.
Unpaid notice: (a) PILON clause (see **2.4.1.8**)	(a) Gross NI is also payable	(a) This is a contractual payment which is taxable in the hands of the employee. It is not a payment on termination and does not come within the £30K exemption.
(b) No PILON clause	(b) Net (after notional deduction of tax and NICs)	(b) (This will be rare due to changes introduced from April 2018 – see above.) Where there is no PILON clause, this will not be a contractual payment but rather is damages for breach of contract. Damages are generally awarded in respect of net loss of earnings as this puts the employee in the same position as if the contract had been performed. An employee is exempt from paying tax on termination payments, including damages for wrongful dismissal, which do not exceed £30K. This sum should be included as part of the £30K exemption as it is a payment on termination under IT(EP)A 2003, Pt 6. Sums in excess of £30K will need to be grossed up.
Damages for wrongful dismissal (such as genuine compensation for loss of office (over and above any notice pay)) – generally calculated on basis of a sum equal to the wages payable during the contractual notice period (see **2.4**) (See *British Transport Commission v Gourley* [1955] 3 All ER 796)	Net (after notional deduction of tax and NICs)	This is not a contractual payment but rather is damages for breach of contract. An employee is exempt from paying tax on termination payments, including damages for wrongful dismissal, which do not exceed £30K. This sum should therefore be included as part of the £30K exemption as it is a payment on termination. NB: there is a £25K jurisdictional limit on tribunal awards for breach of contract, so in reality this will require grossing up only where other awards, such as compensation for unfair dismissal, take the award over £30K.

Type of Award	Gross/Net	Explanation
Employment Act 2002, s 38 payment (see **5.6.2.2**)	Gross (subject to the weekly pay cap)	This is not wages and therefore is not normally taxable. Not included within the £30K exemption.
UD reinstatement or re-engagement (where arrears of wages etc will have to be paid)	Net	The Court of Appeal in *Wilson v Clayton* [2005] IRLR 108 said this was not earnings but a payment in consequence of dismissal. An employee is exempt from paying tax on termination payments which do not exceed £30,000. This sum should be included as part of the £30,000 exemption.
UD basic award and compensation award (ERA 1996, s 118) (see **5.6.2.1** and **5.6.2.2**)	The basic award is calculated using gross figures. The compensatory award is calculated using net figures (after notional deduction of tax and NI).	Not taxable *unless* in excess of £30K exemption, when will have to gross up the compensatory element which exceeds £30K before applying the cap. (See *British Transport Commission v Gourley* [1955] 3 All ER 796.)
Compensation award for unlawful discrimination – treated as statutory tort (see **8.13.2.1**)	Net (after notional deduction of tax and NI)	Not taxable unless in excess of £30K exemption, when will have to gross up the amount which exceeds £30K. (See *Walker v Adams* [2001] STC 101.)
Discrimination – injury to feelings and personal injury award (ITEPA 2003, s 406) (see *Moorthy v HMRC* [2018] EWCA Civ 847 and *Timothy James Consulting Ltd v Wilton UK* (EAT/0082/14)) (see **8.8.2.2**)	Simple figure awarded	If the injury to feelings award relates to conduct before termination then it is not earnings, is not taxable and does not need to be grossed up. Prior to April 2018, if an injury to feelings award arose out of the termination of employment then it was not taxable. From April 2018, payments arising out of termination of employment will be exempt only if they relate to a psychiatric injury or other recognised medical condition.

5.7 PENALTIES FOR EMPLOYERS

Section 16 of the ERRA 2013 introduced, from 6 April 2014, financial penalties for employers who lose a claim (see ETA 1996, s 12A). Any penalty goes to the Government, not to the claimant. A penalty may be imposed where the employer's breach has 'one or more aggravating features'. The level of penalty is subject to a minimum of £100 and (since 6 April 2019) a maximum of £20,000. Very few awards have been made.

If a financial award has been made to a claimant, the penalty will be half the total award made by the tribunal (subject to the maximum level). A 50% reduction will be applied if the penalty is paid within 21 days.

The penalty is designed to encourage employers to take their legal responsibilities seriously. There is no definition of what amounts to an aggravating feature. The Government's Explanatory Note to s 16 of the ERRA 2013 states that a tribunal may be more likely to find aggravating features where the employer's actions were deliberate or committed with malice, the employer was an organisation with a dedicated human resources department, or the employer repeatedly breaches the employment rights. It therefore appears that the penalty is not intended to be applied where there is 'inadvertent error'.

Even if a tribunal finds an aggravating feature, it will still have a discretion whether to impose a penalty, taking into account factors such as size, duration of the breach, the behaviour of the parties and ability to pay. (See too **6.4.10.5**)

5.8 CASE STUDY 1: UNFAIR DISMISSAL, REDUNDANCY PAYMENT AND UNPAID WAGES

Facts

(1)   R ran a graphic design agency employing a number of designers. C was employed by R as a senior designer. On 1 October 2021, C was given her wage cheque for September. That cheque bounced. By 13 October 2021, the entire workforce, including C, had been sent home on full pay. The workshop was closed. R indicated to its workforce that the company expected a payment and that wages would be honoured. There was considerable uncertainty amongst the members of the workforce as to what was happening, and other than as indicated below, there appears to have been no formal notification to C either of the fact that she was being made redundant, or of when she was being made redundant. C was born on 2 February 1994. She worked for R between June 2019 and October 2021. Her ET1 was dated 28 October 2021. In her ET1, C says that on 28 October 2021 she phoned R to ask what was happening and was told that she was being made redundant. Her basic wage was £30,000 per annum. Her normal working week was 40 hours.

Claims

(2)   C complained in her ET1 of unfair dismissal, and that R had not paid her wages and/or had not paid the notice pay and/or outstanding holiday pay to which she was entitled by her contract.

Evidence

(3)   Oral evidence was heard on oath from C, who produced a bundle of papers relating to her claim, including payslips and her contract of employment. C confirmed that she had not been paid for September or October, and that she had not been given any notice. Her contract confirmed that she was entitled to one month's notice of termination.

Findings

(4)   The decision of the tribunal was that C was unfairly dismissed by R, and that she was entitled to a redundancy payment and wages in breach of contract.

Reasons

(5)   There was some confusion over the effective date of termination for C. One of her colleagues had received a letter confirming that his last date of employment was 20 October 2021, although C had not received such a letter. As C had submitted her ET1 on 30 October 2021, two days after she had been told she was being made redundant, the tribunal concluded that 28 October was the appropriate date from which to assume that the employment relationship with R had ended.

(6)   The tribunal (which heard the claim in February 2022) concluded that:

(a)   this was a genuine redundancy situation in accordance with s 139 of the ERA 1996, and that redundancy was the reason for C's dismissal;

(b)   as C had two years' service, she was entitled to complain of unfair dismissal and was entitled to a redundancy payment;

(c)   on the basis of the evidence, her dismissal was unfair. Notwithstanding that there had been some communication with her on 13 October, when she had been sent home on full pay, after that date she was not given any further information about the company's situation and had to find things out for herself. On that basis, there had not been proper, adequate or reasonable warning or consultation. There was clearly no attempt to consider any help or assistance with regard to alternative employment. However, as it was clear that even had there been proper warning, consultation, etc, it was highly likely that C would still have been dismissed, the tribunal made a 100% Polkey reduction in respect of the compensatory element of the unfair dismissal award;

(d)   unauthorised deductions had been made from C's wages, in that she had not been paid money properly due and payable in respect of wages, as set out below; further, the tribunal found as fact that R had failed to pay notice pay and holiday pay to which C was entitled.

(e)   in addition, C was owed overtime in respect of hours worked in September.

Remedy

(7)   R was order to pay C:

Unpaid wages awards:

Four weeks' (gross) salary for September	£2,500.00
Four weeks' (gross) salary for October	£2,500.00
September overtime (gross) (45 hours at time and a half) (best estimate)	£3,750.00

Wrongful dismissal award:

Four weeks' salary in lieu of notice (net)	£2,000.00

Holiday pay:

Ten days' unpaid leave (gross)	£1,153.84
TOTAL	£11,903.84

In addition, C was entitled to a redundancy payment/unfair dismissal basic award of 1 x 2 x £544 (max gross week's pay as at date of calculation) = £1,088. There was no compensatory element to this award in the light of the Polkey finding.

GRAND TOTAL	£12,991.84

All the amounts detailed above have been calculated gross unless otherwise stated. Where a sum is stated to be gross, the respondent will account to HMRC directly in respect of tax and National Insurance due thereon as is appropriate.

5.9 CASE STUDY 2: UNFAIR DISMISSAL

Facts

(1)   C commenced employment with R (Isle of Sodor Train Company (ISTC)) on 3 December 2010, as a Revenue Protection Assistant based at Sodor Town station. He was summarily dismissed with effect from 3 October 2020, as result of an incident on Sodor Town station on 10 September 2020, when he was accused by a customer of having taken money for two single tickets valued at £5.80, and failing to issue either a receipt or tickets. V (Group Revenue Protection Manager, Isle of Sodor) conducted an investigation into the incident. C was interviewed on 11, 16, 19 and 23 September. He was suspended on basic pay pending the investigation. In addition, W (Senior Revenue

Protection Inspector), X (Senior Revenue Protection Inspector), Y (Acting Senior Revenue Protection Inspector) and Z (RO2, Sodor Town) were interviewed.

(2)   At the conclusion of the investigatory process, C was invited, by letter dated 23 September, to attend a disciplinary hearing. C was told that he was being charged under para 9 of the ISTC Disciplinary Procedure 'with the following irregularity of gross misconduct', namely, of misappropriating £5.80 of Isle of Sodor Trains' monies. That letter informed C of his right to be accompanied at the disciplinary hearing. C's representative was sent all the relevant paperwork.

(3)   A disciplinary hearing was held on 2 and 3 October. H, Group Station Manager, Sodor Town, conducted it. C was accompanied by a trade union representative. Z was called by C to give evidence on his behalf. The hearing was adjourned to enable H and C's trade union representative to view some CCTV footage. At the conclusion of the disciplinary process, H found that:

(a)   money was taken from the customers;

(b)   the ticket issuing machine was switched off;

(c)   no tickets were issued;

(d)   the money that was taken was not accounted for and that 'no credible reason has been given for not issuing the tickets', and that 'Therefore I believe that C took the money and did not intend to issue the tickets thereby misappropriating ISTC monies'.

H found that the charge was proved, and he decided that C should be dismissed with immediate effect. H confirmed his decision in writing in a letter dated 3 October. That letter also set out details of the right to appeal against the decision.

(4)   C appealed against:

(a)   the severity of the punishment; and

(b)   the interpretation of the facts by H.

N, Retail Manager, Isle of Sodor, heard the appeal on 10 October. C was again accompanied by his trade union representative. N upheld the decision to dismiss C. N believed that 'it has been proven beyond doubt that C intentionally pocketed the £5.80 by making a conscious decision not to issue the tickets'. His decision was confirmed in writing by letter dated 10 October.

(5)   C's contract refers at para 17 to 'Disciplinary and other rules'. At para 2.1, disciplinary procedures are stated to apply to '(f) misconduct or negligence' and '(l) irregularities involving cash'. Procedure Agreement 4 is headed 'Discipline' and an Annex contains the relevant agreed procedure. This allows, inter alia, for witnesses to be called and for the employee to be accompanied. Paragraph 9 states that in cases of 'exceptionally grave misconduct which may warrant summary dismissal' the usual procedure shall not apply. Paragraph 17 of C's contract stated that ISTC may

> at any time ... dismiss without notice, or suspend from duty, and after inquiry, dismiss without notice, or suspend from duty as a disciplinary measure an employee for certain offences including but not limited to ... (c) misconduct or negligence ... (e) cash procedure irregularities (f) a serious or repeated breach of the rules.

Claims

(6)   C complained of unfair dismissal. He said in his ET1 Claim Form (box 11) that he believed his dismissal was unfair because 'the company did not properly and thoroughly investigate the matter because they clearly did not take into account all the information I gave them regarding the incident'. C seeks reinstatement. R, in its ET3 Claim Form, maintained that C's dismissal was fair and, in the alternative, that if it were to be found that the dismissal was unfair, that C's own conduct caused or contributed to his dismissal.

Evidence

(7) Disclosure took place in the usual way and paginated bundles were prepared which included extracts from C's personal file, extracts from the ISTC Disciplinary Procedure, other rules and regulations, Procedure Agreement 4, plus papers relating to C's dismissal and a Schedule of Loss from C setting out his claim for compensation.

(8) Although standard directions were made for the exchange of witness statements prior to the hearing, and witness statements were provided by R to C prior to the hearing, C did not provide one. Although R complained about this failure, in the circumstances the tribunal felt that in the light of the pre-litigation correspondence R was well aware of C's case and the grounds of his complaint. As such the tribunal did not believe R had been prejudiced by this failure. On the basis that there was little information in the ET1 about C's case, it was agreed that the tribunal would first of all read the relevant documents and that C would present his evidence first. C, who was not legally represented at the hearing but was assisted by his brother, read out as his evidence-in-chief a letter that he had written to the RMT Regional Organiser dated 21 November, which set out his complaints in some detail. In addition, the tribunal had written statements, on R's side, from P (Group Revenue Protection Manager, Isle of Sodor), who conducted the final part of the investigation, H (Group Station Manager, Sodor Town, who conducted the disciplinary hearing) and N (Retail Manager, Isle of Sodor, who heard C's appeal). Oral evidence was given on oath by all witnesses, except P who affirmed.

(9) At the hearing, all witnesses who gave oral evidence were cross-examined and the tribunal had the opportunity to ask questions of them. C also submitted a written statement from Ms A, whose evidence he wanted the tribunal to take into account, but who was unable to give oral evidence. Although R pointed out that it had not had advance notice of this, having had the opportunity over a short adjournment to consider the contents of the statement, R did not object to the tribunal reading Ms A's statement; nevertheless, R reminded the tribunal that it had not had the opportunity to cross-examine Ms A.

(10) There was some discussion during the case about whether the tribunal should see CCTV footage, stills of which had been available at the time of the investigation and the footage of which was viewed as part of the disciplinary hearing. Although both sides agreed that it might be of assistance for the tribunal to see the CCTV in the presence of the parties, unfortunately there was a problem getting the equipment to work and it was not possible to view it during the hearing. After discussion it was agreed that the tribunal would watch the CCTV footage in chambers.

(11) At the conclusion of the evidence, both sides made oral submissions on liability and remedy. All these matters were taken into consideration by the tribunal before reaching its decision.

The issues to be decided

(12) The principal issue for the tribunal to determine was whether the dismissal was fair within s 98(4) of the ERA 1996:

  (a) What was the reason for C's dismissal?

  (b) Was this a potentially fair reason for dismissal?

  (c) Was the dismissal substantively fair?

  (d) Was the dismissal procedurally fair?

  (e) Depending on the outcome, a remedy might need to be considered.

Submissions

(13) On behalf of C it was submitted that, on the facts, even if the dismissal was for the potentially fair reason of conduct under s 98(2) of the ERA 1996, R did not act

reasonably in treating that as a sufficient reason for dismissal under s 98(4) of the 1996 Act. Procedurally, C said that R did not acknowledge C's denial and did not accept the counter-evidence that was produced. In particular, it was submitted that R's investigation was flawed, and that it did not properly and thoroughly investigate the matter in that:

(a)   it was neither full nor impartial;

(b)   evidence was not examined, or was improperly concluded;

(c)   it was at best based on assumptions and speculation; and

(d)   it did not take into account all the information C gave to R.

It was submitted that it was unfair to dismiss on suspicion of misconduct without a full examination of the evidence. C said that there was no evidence that he deliberately set out to steal money from the company; there was no evidence that, as per the charge, funds had been misappropriated – no search was made of C and what money was found was in the float bag, which in the event contained more than it should have done because of money added by C. C says that it is not possible to conclude that 'no stone was left unturned in getting to the bottom of the facts'.

(14)   R's representative submitted that the reason for the dismissal was a potentially fair reason, namely, misconduct, and that procedurally R had done all that it should have done. R submitted that it honestly believed that C was guilty of misappropriating £5.80; that there were reasonable grounds for that belief following a reasonable investigation; and that dismissal was within the range of reasonable responses, as C was in a position of trust. In the alternative, it was submitted that if the tribunal found that the dismissal was unfair, then C's conduct caused or contributed to his dismissal and any award should be reduced by 100% to zero.

The law

(15)   Where there is a potentially fair reason for dismissal, the tribunal must decide whether the employer acted reasonably or unreasonably in treating that as a sufficient reason for dismissal. The material statutory provisions are set out in s 98(4) of the ERA 1996, which, so far as relevant, read as follows:

> (4)   Where the employer has fulfilled the requirements of subsection (1), the determination of the question whether the dismissal is fair or unfair (having regard to the reason shown by the employer—
>
> (a)   depends on whether in the circumstances (including the size and administrative resources of the employer's undertaking) the employer acted reasonably or unreasonably in treating it as a sufficient reason for dismissing the employee, and
>
> (b)   shall be determined in accordance with equity and the substantial merits of the case.

(16)   Tribunals should not, when considering these matters, look at what they would have done but should judge, on the basis of the range of reasonable responses test, what the employers actually did. The appropriate test is whether the dismissal of the applicant lay within the range of conduct that a reasonable employer could have adopted.

(17)   The Court of Appeal in the joined cases of *HSBC (formerly Midland Bank) v Madden; Post Office v Foley* [2000] IRLR 827, reiterated that the correct approach for a tribunal to adopt was that set out by the EAT in *Iceland Frozen Foods Ltd v Jones* [1982] IRLR 439, namely, that it was not for a tribunal to substitute its own view as to an employer's conduct and that tribunals should determine in each case whether the decision to dismiss fell within the 'band of reasonable responses' which a reasonable employer might have adopted towards the employee's conduct. That approach was re-emphasised by the Court of Appeal in *Post Office v Burkett* [2003] EWCA Civ 748 and most recently in *London Ambulance Service NHS Trust v Small* [2009] EWCA Civ 220.

(18)   Section 98 does not require the dismissing employer to be satisfied, on the balance of probabilities, that the employee whose conduct is in question has actually done what he or she is alleged to have done. The EAT, in *British Home Stores v Burchell* [1978] IRLR 379, held that where an employer *suspects* misconduct, a dismissal can still be fair provided that the employer (i) had a genuine belief in guilt; (ii) had reasonable grounds upon which to base that belief; and (iii) carried out a proper investigation.

(19)   The Court of Appeal in *Sainsbury's Supermarkets Ltd v Hitt* [2003] IRLR 23, held that the range of reasonable responses test

>   applies as much to the question of whether the investigation into suspected misconduct was reasonable in all the circumstances as it does to other procedural and substantive aspects of the decision to dismiss a person from his employment for a conduct reason. ... The objective standards of the reasonable employer must be applied to all aspects of the question whether an employee was fairly and reasonably dismissed. ... The objective standard ... did not require [the employer] to carry out further investigations of the kind which the tribunal majority considered ought to have been carried out. ... The purpose of the investigation was not to establish whether or not the applicant was guilty of the alleged theft but whether there were reasonable grounds for the employer's belief that there had been misconduct on his part to which a reasonable response was to dismiss him.

(20)   The test to be applied in a case of suspected misconduct is not whether further investigation should have been carried out, or whether more could have been done, but whether the investigation that had been carried out could be regarded by a reasonable employer as adequate. Even in the most serious of cases, it is unrealistic and inappropriate to require the standards and safeguards of a criminal trial, but a careful and conscientious investigation of the facts is necessary, and the person carrying out the investigation should focus carefully on the potential evidence, particularly if it points towards innocence, as opposed to concentrating on evidence which goes to prove the charges being made. In these sorts of cases, the more grave the charges and the potential impact of dismissal, the more rigorous the process that is required.

The tribunal's findings

(21)   The unanimous decision of the tribunal was that C was fairly dismissed by reason of conduct. C was a Revenue Inspection Assistant. Trust and integrity are at the heart of such a role. The tribunal believed that in that circumstances, the dismissal of C for the offence charged was within the range of reasonable responses, and that this accordingly was a fair dismissal.

(22)   The tribunal found that C's dismissal was for the potentially fair reason of conduct. The dismissal was a result of the employer's belief that C had appropriated money.

(23)   The tribunal then considered s 98(4) of the ERA 1996. Since no burden of proof exists on either party to establish the reasonableness or unreasonableness of a dismissal under s 98(4), this is a question for the tribunal to determine 'neutrally'. The tribunal is not able to re-hear the evidence or to re-examine C's case. In particular, it is not for the tribunal to determine whether C is guilty or innocent. This was emphasised most recently by the Court of Appeal in *London Ambulance Service v Small*, where the Court reiterated that a tribunal must review the fairness of the employer's decision to dismiss, not substitute its own view on the facts. The Court of Appeal said the tribunal should have concentrated on the employer's handling of the dismissal rather than making its own findings about Small's conduct.

(24)   The tribunal considered the following questions:

(a)   *Did R have a genuine belief that C had behaved in the manner alleged?* In the tribunal's judgment, having heard the evidence of H, who conducted the disciplinary interview, and N, who conducted the appeal, and having read and considered the investigatory interviews, R did have a genuine belief that C had behaved in the manner charged. In particular, R believed he had misappropriated the ticket money.

(b) *Did R have reasonable grounds for that belief?* In the tribunal's judgment, R did have reasonable grounds for that belief. The tribunal noted that:

   (i)   the initial allegation came from a customer;

   (ii)   there was no dispute that C had taken money from the customer;

   (iii) there was no conclusive evidence that C had issued or attempted to issue any tickets: the customer said he had not; the ticket issuing machine 'bleed and print' did not show that any tickets had been issued; the CCTV was inconclusive on this point;

   (iv)   C had altered his account of what had happened: initially he said that he had issued tickets and had then disposed of them in a plastic rubbish bag – a subsequent search did not produce the tickets; subsequently he said that he must have been confused and had not issued the tickets; later still he said he had not taken any money, or that he must have returned it all to the customer;

   (v)   C said initially that his ticket issuing machine was switched off because he had 'just' returned from a toilet break – the CCTV showed him at the barrier for an unbroken period of 30 minutes before the incident;

   (vi)   C failed to do a full cashing-up when asked to do 'an end of shift' and to cash up – he did only a partial cash-up: in particular, he did not remove his float before cashing up; his shift sheet should have shown a surplus of £5.80 but did not.

The tribunal considered that each explanation C gave was examined in full by R. An employer is not obliged to accept a denial, neither is it obliged to accept counter-evidence; what it must do is give it due consideration. The tribunal believes R did this.

C questioned whether there was sufficient evidence of 'intent'. He said that the CCTV appeared to show him trying to issue a ticket. In fact, the tribunal felt that the CCTV was inconclusive on this. H found that 'the money that was taken was not accounted for', that 'no credible reason has been given for not issuing the tickets' and that 'Therefore I believe that C took the money and did not intend to issue the tickets thereby misappropriating ISTC monies'. In answer to a question from C in cross-examination about this, H said he concluded 'intent' because 'no attempt was made to issue a ticket'. In *Post Office v Burkett*, the Court of Appeal said that the crucial question was whether the Post Office's response to the facts before it was reasonable. The question whether there were reasonable grounds for an honest belief had to be answered not by reference to the tribunal's own objective views formed subsequently, but by reference to its assessment of what it was open to a reasonable employer to conclude on the material before it. In the tribunal's judgment, there were sufficient grounds for H to reach the conclusion that he did. C was 'charged' with misappropriating £5.80. Disciplinary hearings are not criminal hearings. The issue for R was, put simply, whether it felt C had made an innocent mistake or not in taking money and not issuing a ticket. It concluded that he had not. In the tribunal's judgment, R was entitled to reach that conclusion on the evidence before it.

(c) *Did R conduct an investigation which was fair and proportionate having regard to the employer's capacity and resources?* This was at the heart of the way C framed his initial complaint – namely, that ISTC did not 'properly and thoroughly investigate the matter because they clearly did not take into account all the information I gave them regarding the incident'. Although there was no attempt made to contact the initial complainant or to elicit a statement from him, in the tribunal's judgment the investigation conducted was fair, full and thorough. There is no obligation as matter of law to turn over every stone. The tribunal concluded that R operated a fair, adequate and reasonable procedure. C was interviewed on a number of occasions. Any matters raised by him in his interviews were followed up and checked. Z was interviewed, all the Revenue Inspection Officers who were involved in the initial process were questioned, and the CCTV was considered. The disciplinary appeal was adjourned to allow C's representative to look at the CCTV footage (as opposed to the stills) and Z gave evidence. In a situation where an employee's livelihood is at stake and the allegation is a serious one, there is a heightened obligation on an employer as to the thoroughness of its investigation. The tribunal had no doubt that this investigation met that standard. In the tribunal's judgment there was a reasonable investigation.

(d) *Other procedural shortcomings.* In addition to the areas identified above, the tribunal looked at whether there were any procedural or other lapses by ISTC. One matter the tribunal considered was the so-called 'Paragraph 9 Summary Procedure'. The Tribunal looked at this against the Acas Code of Practice, which emphasised that workers should be aware of the likely consequences of breaking rules. The tribunal noted that there was no specific list of offences or examples of matters which would amount to serious (or 'exceptionally gross') misconduct, and thus no indication as to precisely when the para 9 procedure would be invoked. Paragraph 9 (which deals with the procedure in cases of 'exceptionally grave misconduct which may warrant summary action') stated that the 'usual' procedure shall not apply. Paragraph 12 contained a list of 'recordable punishments', of which the last was dismissal. Paragraph 17 of C's contract stated that R might

> at any time ... dismiss without notice, or suspend from duty, and after inquiry, dismiss without notice, or suspend from duty as a disciplinary measure an employee for certain offences including but not limited to ... (c) misconduct or negligence ... (e) cash procedure irregularities (f) a serious or repeated breach of the rules.

Overall, while the tribunal felt that the position could have been spelled out more clearly, in its judgment R's procedure did make clear to C that a possible consequence of misconduct was summary dismissal – the letter summoning C to interview contained a heading that alerted him to this. While the tribunal felt it might be preferable to identify some examples of serious misconduct – as opposed to less serious misconduct – so that the procedure and the possible consequences would be very clearly set out, it did not feel that this was sufficient *per se* to render the dismissal unfair.

The tribunal examined the initial letter informing C that he was to attend a disciplinary hearing, which did not contain any specific mention of the possible consequences of the disciplinary action that was to be taken. It contained a heading, 'Clause 9 Summary Procedure', and it then specified that the charge was considered to amount to gross misconduct. The Clause 9 Summary Procedure states that the usual procedure shall not apply in cases of 'exceptionally grave misconduct, which may warrant summary action'. Again while the tribunal felt it would have been preferable if this letter had set out the possible consequences of the proposed action, bearing in mind that it was not for the tribunal to substitute its own views, it did not feel, either in isolation or taken with the other matters set out here, that this rendered the dismissal procedurally unfair. Both C and his representative appeared to understand the Clause 9 Procedure and its significance.

In general, subject to the above, the tribunal had no criticisms about the way in which the investigatory process or the actual disciplinary hearing were conducted. There was a long, detailed and thorough investigation. The tribunal felt that C was aware of the accusations made against him in advance, and that he was given a proper opportunity to know the case against him and to state his case. It noted that he was entitled to and did call Z at the disciplinary hearing. It also noted that a representative accompanied C to both the disciplinary and the appeal hearings. The tribunal heard no evidence that made it doubt that those conducting the disciplinary hearing and the appeal were anything other than independent, or that they acted in anything but good faith.

(e) *The substantive decision to dismiss – was it within the range of responses of a reasonable employer in the circumstances?* The Court of Appeal, in *Post Office v Burkett* [2003] EWCA Civ 748, said that the crucial question for a tribunal was whether an employer's response to the facts before it was reasonable. The real question in these cases is whether R acted fairly and reasonably in all the circumstances at the time of the dismissal. If satisfied of R's fair conduct of the dismissal in those respects, the tribunal then has to decide whether the dismissal of C was a reasonable response to the misconduct. In all the circumstances, the tribunal held that decision of H to dismiss C, albeit over a very small sum of money, could not be said to fall outside the range of reasonable responses. The tribunal felt that given that C was in a position of trust in handling money as a Revenue Inspection Assistant, the misconduct that R believed him to have committed amounted to serious dishonesty. Contributory fault arises for decision only if it is established that the dismissal was unfair. As the tribunal had concluded the dismissal was fair, there was no need for it to consider contribution or remedy.

5.10 FURTHER READING

Textbooks include:

Lewis, *Employment Law – an adviser's handbook*, 14th edn (LAG, 2022).

Harvey, *Industrial Relations and Employment Law* (LexisNexis), Div D1.

Selwyn's Law of Employment, 22nd edn (OUP, 2022).

Blackstone's Employment Law Practice, 10th edn (OUP, 2019).

Gray (ed), *Employment Tribunal Remedies Handbook 2022–23* (Bath Publishing).

Duggan, *Unfair Dismissal: Law, Practice and Precedents*, 2nd edn (Duggan Press, 2019).

Lewis, *Whistleblowing: Law and Practice*, 4th edn (OUP, 2022).

SUMMARY

At common law, provided the employer gives the correct notice and otherwise complies with the terms of the contract, he may dismiss any employee he chooses, whether he has a good reason or not (see **Chapter 2**). The statutory claim of unfair dismissal introduced the concept of reasonableness into the termination of contracts of employment. Now every eligible employee (see **Chapter 3**) has a statutory right not to be unfairly dismissed by his employer under s 94 of the ERA 1996.

An employer must be able to establish that the only or principal reason for the dismissal was one of five potentially fair reasons as listed in s 98 of the ERA 1996 (conduct, capability, redundancy, illegality and some other substantial reason) (**5.2**).

Once an employer has shown the existence of one of the five permitted reasons, the tribunal must then decide if the employer acted reasonably, as defined by s 98(4) of the ERA 1996, having regard to the reason shown by the employer, in dismissing the employee (**5.3**).

When deciding whether the dismissal was fair or unfair, in addition to having regard to the reason, the tribunal should also have regard to all the circumstances, including the Acas Code of Practice on Disciplinary and Grievance Procedures (**5.4.1**) and the size and administrative resources of the employer, as well as to equity and the substantial merits of the case. Each case will ultimately turn on its own facts, but tribunals will generally look at both the substantive reason for the dismissal and any appropriate procedure (**5.4**). The test is ultimately one of reasonableness, and tribunals will ask themselves whether the dismissal was within the range of responses of a reasonable employer (see *Iceland Frozen Foods Ltd v Jones* [1982] IRLR 439 (**5.3.1.1**)).

There are a number of special cases where the normal rules relating to unfair dismissal either do not apply or are varied (**5.5**).

The remedies available for unfair dismissal are either reinstatement or re-engagement (together with any consequential awards relating to arrears of pay, etc), or compensation. Awards which exceed £30,000 are subject to income tax and may need to be grossed up to ensure that the net loss is actually paid to the claimant (**5.6**).

In summary, the following questions should be asked:

- Do any of the special rules apply (**5.5**)?
- Is the employee eligible (**Chapter 3**)?
- Has there been a dismissal (**3.4**)?
- Is there a potentially fair reason (**5.2**)?
- Has the employer acted reasonably (**5.3** and **5.4**)?
- Has the employee asked for reinstatement or re-engagement (**5.6.1**)?
- How much will the basic award be (**5.6.2.1**)?
- What are the relevant heads of compensatory award (**5.6.2.2**)?
- Are there any relevant increasing factors?
- Are there any relevant reducing factors?

Figure 5.2 Flowchart: Unfair Dismissal

---

1. Eligibility (burden of proof on employee)
- time limits (3 months (less 1 day) from EDT)
- employee
- 2 years' service (for employees employed by current employer on or after 6 April 2012; 1 year for all others)
- not excluded class

---

2. Dismissal (burden of proof on employee)
- expiry and non-renewal of limited-term contract or
- actual dismissal or
- constructive dismissal

NB Definition in *Western Excavating v Sharp*

---

3. Reason for dismissal (ERA 1996, s 98(2)) (burden of proof on employer)
- what is the main reason for the dismissal?
- does that reason fall within one of the five potentially fair reasons?

NB If reason is redundancy, consider claim for both unfair dismissal and a redundancy payment

---

4. Consider fairness of dismissal (ERA 1996, s 98(4))

Test – range of reasonable responses (Iceland Frozen Foods)

Question of fact for tribunal
- size and administrative resources of employer
- equity
- sufficiency of the reason given by the employer
- substantial merits
- procedure (depends on reason)
- Acas Code if conduct/capability

---

5. Remedies
- reinstatement (old job back)
- re-engagement (job elsewhere in business)
- compensation
  — basic award: age factor (½/1/1½) x gross weekly pay (max £571 from 6 April 2022) x number of complete years service (max 20 years) (EA 2002, s 38)
  — compensatory award (consider heads of loss/deductions) (max £93,878 or 52 weeks' gross pay from 6 April 2022)
    immediate loss of net earnings etc
    future losses including pension
    mitigation; other deductions (*Polkey*/contribution)

NB Award (basic and compensatory) can be increased or decreased by up to 25% for unreasonable failure to follow Acas Code

---

6. Consider other claims
- redundancy payment/wrongful dismissal/discrimination

NB Employee cannot be compensated twice for same loss

CHAPTER 6

PRACTICE AND PROCEDURE, SETTLEMENTS AND OVERLAPPING CLAIMS

6.1	Introduction	249
6.2	Applications to the employment tribunal	250
6.3	Time-limits in employment tribunals	255
6.4	Tribunal Rules	264
6.5	Settlements	304
6.6	Alternatives to tribunal proceedings	310
6.7	Overlapping claims and awards	311
6.8	Case study: unfair dismissal	314
6.9	Further reading	331
	Summary	331

LEARNING OUTCOMES

After reading this chapter you will be able to:

- describe the relevant employment tribunal procedures for bringing a claim, from submitting a claim form to the giving of a judgment
- understand the different time-limits that apply to tribunal claims
- explain the options that are available other than bringing a tribunal claim
- describe the different ways in which claims may be settled
- understand the significance of overlapping claims.

6.1 INTRODUCTION

This chapter deals with the procedure for making a claim to the employment tribunal and, in outline, the hearing of a complaint by the tribunal. It also covers settlement and overlapping claims.

Employment tribunal procedure is governed primarily by the Employment Tribunals Rules of Procedure 2013, as contained in Sch 1 of the Employment Tribunals (Constitution and Rules of Procedure) Regulations 2013 (SI 2013/1237). These have been amended on a number of occasions, including by the Employment Tribunals (Constitution and Rules of Procedure) (Early Conciliation: Exemptions and Rules of Procedure) (Amendment) Regulations 2020 (which made a number of wide-ranging amendments to the 2013 Rules, with effect from 8 October 2020), and most recently by the Employment Tribunals (Constitution and Rules of Procedure) (Early Conciliation: Exemptions and Rules of Procedure) (Amendment) Regulations 2021.

6.2 APPLICATIONS TO THE EMPLOYMENT TRIBUNAL

6.2.1 Jurisdiction

The following claims may all be brought by presenting a complaint to the employment tribunal:

(a) unfair dismissal;

(b) claims of discrimination on the grounds of sex, race, religion or belief, disability, sexual orientation and age from employees and job applicants (Equality Act 2010);

(c) equal pay;

(d) complaints that unlawful deductions from wages have been made under Pt II of the ERA 1996 (these claims may also be brought in the county court);

(e) redundancy payments;

(f) complaints in relation to maternity rights, paternity rights, adoption leave rights, parental rights, dependant rights and flexible working rights;

(g) complaints in relation to failure to provide written reasons;

(h) complaints of victimisation because an employee has exerted any of his statutory rights;

(i) certain claims for damages for breach of contract, including (subject to a maximum award of £25,000) wrongful dismissal (contractual claims may also be brought in the county court);

(j) complaints under the Part-time Workers (Prevention of Less Favourable Treatment) Regulations 2000;

(k) complaints under some provisions of the Working Time Regulations 1998;

(l) complaints under the Agency Workers Regulations 2010.

The above list is not exhaustive. In most instances, these claims must be brought by employees, although there are some exceptions (eg, claims under the protection of wages legislation (see **1.10**) and discrimination claims) where claims by workers can be dealt with. For the distinction between a worker and an employee, see s 230 of the ERA 1996 and **1.1.1** and **1.3**.

6.2.2 Mandatory pre-claim Early Conciliation

6.2.2.1 Introduction

Anyone considering bringing an employment tribunal claim must make an Early Conciliation notification to Acas, to see whether the dispute can be resolved through conciliation. The legislative framework for the Early Conciliation scheme is contained in the ERRA 2013. The details of the scheme itself are set out in the Schedule to the Employment Tribunals (Early Conciliation: Exemptions and Rules of Procedure) Regulations 2014 (SI 2014/254) (the Early Conciliation Regulations). The scheme came into effect on 6 April 2014, but only became mandatory for claims presented on or after 6 May 2014. The 2013 Employment Tribunals Rules of Procedure (see **6.4**) were amended to provide for the rejection of claims in accordance with the Early Conciliation scheme. Rule 10 now provides (added by the Employment Tribunal (Constitution and Rules of Procedure) (Amendment) Regulations 2014 (SI 2014/271)) that a tribunal shall reject a claim if it does not contain either an Early Conciliation number, or confirmation that the Early Conciliation proceedings do not apply to the claim or that an exemption applies. The scheme does not affect Acas's pre-existing duty to conciliate claims that were already in the system (see **6.5.2**). Some minor changes were made to the 2014 Early Conciliation Rules of Procedure with effect from 1 December 2020, under the Employment Tribunals (Constitution and Rules of Procedure) (Early Conciliation: Exemptions and Rules of Procedure) (Amendment) Regulations 2020. Readers should make sure they have access to the most up-to-date version.

The details of the scheme are set out in ss 18A and 18B of the ETA 1996. These are the key stages of the compulsory Early Conciliation scheme:

(a) the prospective claimant must send information to Acas in the 'prescribed manner', ie via the prescribed form or via the telephone using a prescribed number;

(b) a Conciliator will make contact with the claimant;

(c) the Conciliator must try to promote settlement within the 'prescribed period' of one month (subject to a maximum extension of two weeks);

(d) if at any time the Conciliator concludes it is not possible to reach settlement, or time expires, a certificate is issued;

(e) the claimant cannot start most claims without the certificate.

Acas has published a guidance note on how Early Conciliation will work, available at <http://www.acas.org.uk/media/pdf/h/o/Early-Conciliation-explained.pdf>.

Employers will also be able to use Early Conciliation if they believe there is a workplace dispute that is likely to lead to 'relevant' tribunal proceedings. Relevant proceedings are listed in s 18(1A) of the ETA 1996. There are two areas that are not expressly included in the list:

(a) the right to be accompanied under ss 10–13 of the ERA 1999 (but this appears to be indirectly incorporated, as Part V of the ERA 1996 is included in the s 18 list); and

(b) claims under regs 12 and 16 of the Transfer of Undertakings (Protection of Employment) Regulations 2006, but the view is that these claims are indirectly covered via the Regulations (see regs 12(7) and 16(1)).

There are some exceptions to the requirement to make an Early Conciliation notification: for example, if many people are making a claim against the same employer and one person has already made a request to Acas about the same issue, other potential claimants may not have to. The full list of exemptions is set out in reg 3(1) of the Early Conciliation Regulations.

6.2.2.2 Procedure

Tribunal claims will not be accepted unless the complaint has been referred to Acas and a conciliation certificate issued. There is a prescribed notification form. The easiest way to access this is through the Acas website at <http://www.acas.org.uk/earlyconciliation>. The notification form asks for basic contact details for the claimant and the employer. Claimants need to take care to include the correct name of their employer, as the name of the employer on any subsequent ET1 will need to correspond to the name on the form. If the names are different, this could lead to the claim being rejected by the tribunal. Rule 4 of the 2014 Early Conciliation Regulations originally said that if there is more than one prospective respondent, a separate form must be presented for each. However, with effect from 1 December 2021, a new statutory instrument, the Employment Tribunals (Constitution and Rules of Procedure) (Early Conciliation: Exemptions and Rules of Procedure) (Amendment) Regulations 2021, changes the 2014 early conciliation rules to allow more than one respondent's name to be included on a single Early Conciliation notification form.

When Acas receives an Early Conciliation notification form, it will contact the sender and check whether the claimant wants to proceed with Early Conciliation. If he does, Acas will then approach the employer. According to the Acas guidance, a Conciliator will aim to make contact with both parties by the end of the following working day, to explore with them how the potential claim might be resolved. If a Conciliator cannot contact either of the parties, or the prospective claimant does not wish to proceed with conciliation, the case will be closed and an Early Conciliation certificate will be issued to the prospective claimant. This will allow the prospective claimant to progress his claim. Likewise, if the prospective respondent is not willing to participate, the prospective claimant will be informed and a certificate issued.

The initial period of Early Conciliation is intended to last for up to one calendar month. However, if both parties agree, the period may be extended by a further 14 days. In September 2020, the Government published regulations to make changes to the Early Conciliation procedure. One of the changes which will come into force on 1 December 2020 is to increase the Early Conciliation period to six weeks (but remove the possibility of extension). If after this period the matter has not been resolved, the Conciliation will end and the claimant will be free to make a tribunal claim. The formal certificate that Early Conciliation has finished will include a unique reference number. Claimants will need to include this when issuing their claim form/ET1 to prove that they have complied with the Early Conciliation notification requirement. Failure to include the unique reference number will result in the claim being rejected (see **6.2.2.5** below). If settlement is reached, this will be recorded using an Acas settlement document (known as a COT3 – see **6.5.1** below).

6.2.2.3   Time-limits

In order to allow time for Early Conciliation to take place, changes have been made (eg ERA 1996, s 207B, Equality Act 2010, s 140B and Employment Tribunals Extension of Jurisdiction (England and Wales) Order 1994, art 8B) to the usual time-limits within which an employee must bring an employment tribunal claim. These time-limits are dealt with in detail at **6.3** below, but the usual three or six calendar months (depending on the type of claim) are suspended (ie the clock is stopped) during the conciliation period. Even if a the time-limit would normally expire less than a month after the end of the conciliation period, a claimant will have a full month (not one month less one day, as originally suggested by HM Courts & Tribunals Service Booklet T420) from when he receives the certificate to lodge his claim with the employment tribunal office. This will mean that where a claimant approaches Acas towards the end of the normal maximum limitation period, he will be able to have up to two and a half months longer to bring a claim (the one-month initial period, the two-week extension, plus a further month after it ends). See **6.3.7.1** for a detailed analysis of how Early Conciliation will affect time-limits.

6.2.2.4   Errors

Rules 10 and 12 provide that a claim form will be rejected where the form has no Early Conciliation number, if the form does not confirm that an Early Conciliation exemption applies. Until October 2020 an employment judge had a discretion to accept a claim where it contained a 'minor' error (in relation to names and addresses). From 8 October 2020 an employment judge can accept a form that contains 'an error' and can accept a form where the Early Conciliation number on the Early Conciliation certificate is different to the one on the form due to the claimant's error. A claim form must be rejected if it does not contain an Early Conciliation number at all (if there is no applicable and stated exemption).

6.2.2.5   Cases

In the years since Early Conciliation was introduced, there have been a number of cases, many of them at first instance, that have considered the interpretation of some of the key provisions. (For cases on Early Conciliation time-limits see **6.3.7.1** below.) While first instance decisions are not binding on other tribunals, they are still a useful reference point.

In *Masih-Rogers v Hammersmith Hairdressing and others* (ET/2201248/14) (heard on 2 October 2014), the claimant's Early Conciliation certificate only referred to the second respondent, not the first. The Employment Judge concluded that Rule 10(1)(b)(iii) of the Tribunal Rules had not been complied with and that there was no jurisdiction to consider the claimant's complaint.

In *Hudson v Plymouth Hospitals NHS Trust* (ET/1401148/2014) (heard on 9 October 2014), an employment tribunal considered what was meant by reg 3(1)(c) (which provides that a claimant can claim an exemption where his 'employer has already been in touch with Acas').

There had been preceding discussions at Acas between the claimant's representative and the employer about two other, similar cases. The claimant's case was not actually discussed. No Early Conciliation certificate had been obtained. The employment tribunal held that the respondent had not contacted Acas in connection with this dispute and struck out the claimant's claim for want of jurisdiction.

In *Ngomoto v Carltech Community Services* (ET/1304618/2014) (heard on 16 October 2014) an employment tribunal considered what was meant by reg 3(1)(d) (which provides that a claimant can claim an exemption where his 'claim contains an application for interim relief'). The claimant had issued a claim of automatically unfair dismissal on the grounds of public interest disclosure, and had included an application for interim relief under s 128 of the ERA 1996. No Early Conciliation certificate had been obtained. The employment tribunal held (somewhat controversially) that there was no basis in law for the interim relief application but as it was genuinely made, there was jurisdiction to hear the claim.

Section 18A(1) of the ETA 1996 provides that before a claim is presented 'relating to any matter', information must be provided to Acas 'about that matter'. Does 'matter' require a full detailed particularisation of the specific dispute and the legal basis for the claim, or might this be a more broad-brush reference? In *Ellis v Brighton & Hove Golf Club* (ET/2301658/2014) (heard on 30 January 2015), the date of the Early Conciliation certificate was 22 June 2014. This was obtained two days before the claimant's employment was terminated, ostensibly by reason of redundancy. The employer argued that the unfair dismissal claim that the claimant sought to bring could not be covered by the Early Conciliation certificate as it pre-dated the dismissal. The Employment Judge looked at matters in the round and said that the Early Conciliation certificate could only be said to have been obtained in connection with the likely termination of employment, and it did not matter that the prospect of redundancy as the reason had not previously been raised. The claimant had complied with the requirements of Rule 10 and the tribunal had jurisdiction to hear the claim. See too *Mortimer v The Golden Holiday Company Ltd and Another* (ET/2300983/15); *Science Warehouse Ltd v Mills* (EAT/0224/15); *Drake International Systems Ltd and Others v Blue Arrow Ltd* (EAT/0282/15); and *Mist v Derby Community Health Services NHS Trust* (EAT/0170/15).

In *Joseph v Royal College of Surgeons of England* (ET/2202074/14) (heard on 27 February 2015), the claimant brought claims of unfair dismissal and discrimination on the grounds of race and age. The employer sought to argue that because the Early Conciliation process had not considered a number of the specific allegations relied upon, the claimant should not be able to bring those claims. The Employment Judge noted that the conciliation process itself was confidential, and it was not appropriate for the tribunal to know all the details of that process. The Employment Judge concluded that 'matter' must be interpreted broadly, without any detailed particularisation of the facts.

In *Cranwell v Cullen* UKEATS/0046/14 (heard by the EAT on 20 March 2015), the claimant's claims of sexual harassment and other demeaning treatment were rejected because she had not obtained an Early Conciliation certificate from Acas before making the claim. She found the very thought of conciliation on the facts of her claim problematic, as it would involve her talking to someone who had treated her in the manner she described. Further, she said that her former employer had been subject to a court order which prohibited him from contacting her. So, she said, she simply could not conciliate with him. She had ticked the box indicating that she was exempt from Early Conciliation. However, none of the exemptions applied to her and the tribunal rejected her claim on that basis. She appealed. The EAT dismissed her appeal. Although it was sympathetic, it ruled that s 18A of the ETA 1996 imposed a mandatory obligation. This was reinforced by Rule 10 of the Tribunal Rules, which makes it clear that a tribunal must reject a claim if the Early Conciliation details are not included in the claim. Rule 6 (which deals with irregularities and failures to comply with the Rules) could not be construed as 'entitling the Tribunal to avoid having to satisfy an obligation which is placed upon the Tribunal itself in absolute and strict terms'.

Several cases have confirmed that a claim will be rejected if the Early Conciliation number is omitted or incorrect (eg *Sterling v United Learning Trust* (UKEAT/0439/14); *Adams v BT plc* (EAT/0342/15)) (see **6.3.1** below). In *Giny v SNA Transport Ltd* (UKEAT/0317/16), an error was made in the name of the respondent during the Early Conciliation process. The error was corrected when the claim was issued. The EAT applied the two-stage test and rejected the claimant's application for reconsideration:

(1)   Is it a minor error? No – the claim will be rejected.

(2)   If it is a minor error, is it in the interests of justice to allow the claim to go ahead?

In this case, the EAT felt that the error was not minor.

In *Compass Group UK and Ireland Ltd v Morgan* (UKEAT/0060/16), the EAT held that an Early Conciliation certificate could still be valid for events that occurred after the certificate had been issued, in this case a constructive dismissal after a disability discrimination claim. This is likely to be the case unless the matters in dispute at the time of the certificate were wholly different to those arising thereafter.

In *De Mota v (1) ADR Network and (2) The Co-operative Group Ltd* (UKEAT/0305/16) the claimant named two respondents on one form, and Acas issued a certificate naming both. Rule 4, however, requires a separate form for each prospective respondent. An employment tribunal held that it lacked jurisdiction to hear the claim because the certificate was improperly issued. The EAT allowed the claimant's appeal and said that the Acas certificate was sufficient to give jurisdiction, notwithstanding the error.

In *HMRC v Garau* (UKEAT/0348/16), the EAT said that issuing a second Early Conciliation certificate in the same matter does not extend time to make a claim.

In *Pryce v Baxterstorey Ltd* [2022] EAT 61, the claimant submitted an ET1 the same day that she was dismissed. She had not applied to Acas first. When she realised the error, she applied to Acas and obtained the number. She then emailed the tribunal asking it to append this to her claim. That was done but a judge later dismissed the claim for lack of jurisdiction on the basis that the employment tribunal had no jurisdiction to consider it by virtue of s 18A(8) of the Employment Tribunals Act 1996, because she did not have an Acas Early Conciliation certificate when she started her claim. The decision was upheld on appeal. HHJ Shanks said: 'This, I regret to say, is the kind of case that gives the law a bad name.' He suggested that the claimant should submit a fresh claim and ask for an extension of time in the light of the facts, though whether to grant this would be very much in the discretion of the tribunal.

6.2.2.6   Summary

Below is a summary of some of the main principles that have emerged from these cases:

- Claimants only have to commence the Early Conciliation process once; provided there is a certificate, tribunals will not usually look behind it.

- The 'stop the clock' provisions (ERA 1996, s 207B) only apply to the first period of conciliation.

- Claimants (probably) can take the benefit of the 'stop the clock' provisions that provide them with the longest time to issue their claim.

- If a claimant fails to commence Early Conciliation until after the normal limitation period for bringing a claim, they will need to get an extension of time from the tribunal (under ERA 1996, s 123).

- If the claimant does not commence Early Conciliation before issuing their claim, they will not be able to proceed with it.

- Getting the name of an employer wrong will not necessarily invalidate an Early Conciliation certificate.

- A separate Early Conciliation certificate is needed for each respondent. However, it is not necessary for a claimant to go through the Early Conciliation process again before applying to amend an existing claim to include a new respondent (*Mist v Derby Community Health Services NHS Trust* (UKEAT/0170/15)).

6.2.3 Insolvency

Where a winding-up order has been made, no action or proceedings can be started or continued without the leave of the insolvency court. The liquidator, when appointed, will become the appropriate party, and any proceedings which will be against the company in liquidation will be stayed. If there is a creditors' voluntary winding up, any proceedings will continue. If there is an administration order, no legal proceedings can be started or continued without the consent of the administrator or the court's permission.

6.3 TIME-LIMITS IN EMPLOYMENT TRIBUNALS

Time-limits differ depending upon the complaint. The main limits are set out below. A claimant who fails to present a claim in time will generally lose the right to bring the claim, although there are escape clauses. Time-limits go to a tribunal's jurisdiction, so they are not simply matters of procedure that the parties can waive. There are two types of escape clause – that it is 'not reasonably practicable' to present the claim in time, or that it is 'just and equitable' to grant an extension. These are discussed in more detail below.

6.3.1 Unfair dismissal

The time-limits for an unfair dismissal claim are set out in s 111 of the ERA 1996. The complaint must normally be presented to the tribunal within three months starting with the 'effective date of termination' (EDT), or within such further period as the tribunal considers reasonable where it was not reasonably practicable for the complaint to be presented within three months (ERA 1996, s 111). The EDT for this purpose is the basic EDT as defined by s 97 of the ERA 1996 (see **3.5.2**). It is not extended where the employee did not receive the statutory minimum period of notice (see **3.5.2**). The three months start with (ie includes) the EDT (see *Trow v Ind Coope (West Midlands) Ltd* [1967] 2 QB 899 and *Hammond v Haigh Castle & Co Ltd* [1973] ICR 148). This effectively means three months less a day (see *Pacitti Jones v O'Brien* [2005] IRLR 889 (Court of Session)).

In *Gisda Cyf v Barratt* [2010] UKSC 41, the Supreme Court held that in a summary dismissal, the EDT would be the date the employee actually learned of the decision to dismiss. In the case, Barratt dismissed Mrs Syf in a letter, delivered by recorded delivery and signed for by her son, on 30 November 2006. She was expecting the decision letter to arrive, but was away at the time it arrived as her sister was giving birth, and as a result she did not actually open the letter until 4 December. She subsequently presented an unfair dismissal claim on 2 March. If the EDT was the date the letter was sent and received, namely 30 November, then her unfair dismissal claim was out of time. If it was the date she read it, 4 December, then her unfair dismissal claim would have been presented in time. The Supreme Court held that the EDT was 4 December, ie when she actually read the letter. It held that she should not be criticised for wanting the letter to remain at home unopened, instead of asking her son to read to her, as its contents were private. There was nothing to indicate that she had deliberately not opened the letter or gone away to avoid reading it. The Supreme Court stated that, on policy grounds, it was desirable to interpret the time-limit legislation in a way favourable to the employee, and that strict contractual laws concerning termination of contracts should not displace the statutory framework. In *Robinson v Bowskill* (UKEAT/0313/12) the EAT held that this also applies where the dismissal is communicated through a third party.

In *Wang v University of Keele* (UKEAT/0223/10), the EAT held that, unless a contract specifically provides otherwise, contractual notice, whether oral or written, runs from the day after the notice is given.

The complaint should actually be received by the appropriate Regional Office of the Employment Tribunals (ROET) within the appropriate time-limit. For example, s 111 of the ERA 1996 provides that an unfair dismissal claim must be presented (although a tribunal does have the power to extend the period where it was not 'reasonably practicable' to present the complaint within three months – see below) 'before the end of the period of three months beginning with the effective date of termination'. So, if an employee is dismissed on 15 January, his claim form must arrive at ROET before midnight on 14 April. If an employee is dismissed on 30 November, his claim must be presented by 28 February.

Where the normal three-month time-limit expires on a non-working day (such as a Saturday, Sunday or bank holiday), care will need to be taken to ensure that the claim reaches the tribunal beforehand. Rule 4(2) of the Rules of Procedure *cannot* be relied upon to extend the date to the next working day (see *Miah v Axis Security Services Ltd* (UKEAT/0290/17)).

The time-limit for presenting a complaint of unfair dismissal should be regarded as strict. Claim forms may be delivered not only by post but also by hand, by fax and by e-mail. Generally speaking, it is up to the party (or his solicitor) to make sure that the claim form is received within the relevant time-limit.

The tribunal's discretionary power in s 111 of the ERA 1996 to extend the time-limit is subject to a two-part test. First, the tribunal must be satisfied that it was not reasonably practicable for the claim to be presented in time. Secondly, the tribunal must be satisfied that the claim was presented within such further period as the tribunal considers reasonable. In *Palmer v Southend on Sea BC* [1984] ICR 372, the Court of Appeal said that 'reasonably practicable' does not mean reasonably or physically possible but rather something like 'reasonably feasible'. The determination of what is reasonably practicable is a question of fact for the tribunal (see *Miller v Community Links Trust Ltd* (UK EAT/0486/07). The burden of proof is on the claimant. In all cases the question is what is reasonable.

In *Sealy v Consignia plc* [2002] IRLR 624, the Court of Appeal held that in determining whether it is reasonably practicable for a claim to have been presented in time, a complainant is entitled to rely on the 'ordinary course of post', such that a letter sent by first class post may be assumed to be delivered on the second day after it was posted (excluding weekends and bank holidays), and if it does not so arrive, it may be regarded (for the purposes of an application to extend) as not reasonably practicable for the complaint to be presented in time. The current line of authority stands for three propositions: first, that 'where a claimant does an act within the period prescribed, which in the ordinary event would result in the complaint being made within the specified period, and that is prevented from having its normal and expected result by some unforeseen circumstance', the 'escape clause' is available; secondly, that if the condition is satisfied, it does not matter why the complainant has waited until the last moment; and, thirdly, that the question whether the condition has been satisfied is a question of fact, to be determined by the tribunal on the evidence before it. (See also *Coldridge v HM Prison Service* (UKEAT/0728/04) and *John Lewis Partnership v Charman* (UKEAT/0079/11), where the EAT held it was not reasonably practicable for a claimant to present his unfair dismissal claim in time because he was awaiting the outcome of an internal appeal.)

Where a claim form is sent by e-mail, a claimant is entitled to assume that it will be delivered at the tribunal within an hour (unless there is an indication that it has not been received, such as a bounce-back message). In *Initial Electronic Security Systems Ltd v Avdic* (UKEAT/0281/05), the EAT held the *Consignia* 'escape route' is also available where a claim form is served by e-mail (so long as the claimant sends it at least an hour before midnight on the day time expires). If an e-mail is not received then a tribunal should assume that it was not reasonably practicable for the complaint to be presented in time, and consider whether the claimant acted reasonably promptly in re-submitting the claim form, once he realised it had not been received.

General guidance on e-mail transmission was set out by the EAT in *Initial Electronic Security Systems Ltd v Audic* [2005] ICR 1598. *Beasley v National Grid* (UKEAT/0626/06) is an illustration of how strictly the time-limits are enforced. In that case, the EAT upheld a tribunal decision not to accept an unfair dismissal claim which was presented by e-mail 88 seconds late. The employment tribunal held that it was 'reasonably practicable' to present the claim in time. The claimant knew on 5 May 2006 that the three-month period expired on 6 May 2006, but he misread the e-mail address of place to which the claim form had to be sent and sent it at 23.44 on 6 May 2006 to 'qsi' and not to the correct address, which was 'gsi'. The claim form was returned to the claimant at 23.45 and he sent a test message (rather than the claim form) to the correct address at 23.57 on 6 May 2006. The claimant then sent the claim form to the correct address so that it arrived at 00.01 and 28 seconds on 7 May 2006, ie late. The EAT held that the tribunal had considered the reasonable practicability issue properly, taking into account all relevant matters: it had considered whether the claimant knew of the three-month period; the steps taken by him to ensure that the claim was brought in time; and the impediments preventing him from bringing the claim within the prescribed three-month period. The Court of Appeal refused leave to appeal.

For a contrasting case to *Beasley* (above), see *Powell v Newcastle College Group* (ET/2514148/09).

The remedy of unfair dismissal is considered to be sufficiently well known that ignorance of the remedy will not be accepted as an excuse (see *Reed in Partnership Ltd v Fraine* (UKEAT/0520/10). Generally, the question in all cases is whether the claimant ought to have known of his rights. In *John Lewis Partnership v Charman* (UKEAT/0079/11), the EAT upheld a decision of the employment tribunal that because the claimant was 'young and inexperienced', and prior to his dismissal he knew nothing about employment tribunals or any right to claim for unfair dismissal, it was not reasonably practicable for him to have presented his claim in time. The starting-point, said the EAT, is that if an employee is reasonably ignorant of the relevant time-limits it cannot be said to be reasonably practicable for him to comply with them. The EAT held in *Adams v BT plc* (EAT/0342/15) that, while the employment tribunal was correct to reject a claim for unfair dismissal where the Early Conciliation number was wrong, the tribunal should have accepted the claim when re-presented (out of time), because it was not reasonably practicable to re-present the claim in time as the claimant was not aware of the need to re-present the claim until she was advised of the error in the first claim. (See too *Walls Meat Co Ltd v Khan* [1979] ICR 52.)

What of carelessness by the employee or his adviser? Generally, this will not be sufficient. If the employee's solicitor misses the time-limit, the tribunal will not extend it, unless there are wholly exceptional circumstances, such as the claimant and the solicitor being misled by the employer as to a material factual matter. Where a professional adviser is careless, this could lead to a negligence claim by the employee against his solicitor if the tribunal does not exercise its discretion to extend time.

In *Marks and Spencer plc v William-Ryan* [2005] IRLR 562, the Court of Appeal held that the employment tribunal had been entitled to find that it had not been reasonably practicable for a claimant to present her unfair dismissal claim within three months because she had received misleading information from her employer, who had advised her that she could not present a claim until she had been through the employer's appeal procedure. Whilst the employee had sought advice from a CAB, the nature of the advice was to seek to resolve the matter with her employer, and the CAB had not advised about making a claim in the Employment Tribunal.

In *Northamptonshire County Council v Entwhistle* (UKEAT/0540/09), however, the EAT held that an employment tribunal had erred in finding that it was not reasonably practicable for a claimant to present his unfair dismissal claim in time in circumstances where his solicitor had been negligent; notwithstanding erroneous advice from the employer, the solicitor should have known the limitation period and filed the claim in time. The EAT said that:

> ... the Judge was right not to read Lord Phillips' endorsement of the *Dedman* principle in *Williams-Ryan* as meaning that in no case where a claimant has consulted a skilled adviser and received wrong advice about the time limit can he claim that it was not reasonably practicable for him to present his claim in time. It is perfectly possible to conceive of circumstances where the adviser's failure to give the correct advice is itself reasonable. Waller LJ made this very point in *Riley*: see at page 336 B. The paradigm case, though not the only example, of such circumstances would be where both the claimant and the adviser had been misled by the employer as to some material factual matter (for example something bearing on the date of dismissal, which is not always straightforward). ...

> ... in a case where a claimant has consulted skilled advisers the question of reasonable practicability is to be judged by what he could have done if he had been given 'such [advice] as they should reasonably in all the circumstances have given him': see the judgment of Brandon LJ in the *Walls* case quoted at para. 5 (3) above. It necessarily follows from the finding of negligence that Mr Lee did not give the Claimant the advice which he should reasonably, in all the circumstances, have given him.

In *Paczkowski v Sieradzka* (UKEAT 0111/16), the claimant was told, by three separate advisers (the CAB, Acas and her local trade union adviser), that she could not bring an unfair dismissal claim without two years' service. The tribunal had concluded that it was not reasonably practicable for the claimant to lodge her claim in time. The EAT remitted the case to the tribunal to determine whether the advice given to the claimant was reasonable in the particular circumstances of this case and – at the same time – was the information provided by the claimant and specific questions raised by her also reasonable? The tribunal could, held the EAT, only arrive at a final conclusion on that question once it had made findings as to the actual instructions given and questions asked as to the status of the advisers and advice received. In *DHL Supply Chain Ltd v Fazackerley* (UKEAT/0019/18), the EAT said that it was not reasonably practicable for an employee to present a claim for unfair dismissal in time, where the delay was due to erroneous advice from Acas. The position is different for erroneous advice from a solicitor or adviser. Acas is a government agency which should not be offering advice. In *Lowri Beck Services Ltd v Brophy* (UKEAT/0277/18), the claimant suffered from severe dyslexia and difficulties understanding information. He relied upon his brother to present his tribunal claim. His brother misunderstood the date of dismissal and presented the ET1 out of time. The EAT held that the mistake was one of fact not law. The question was whether the brother's belief was reasonable: the tribunal had concluded it was and so was entitled to conclude that it had not been reasonably practicable to present the claim in time.

The discovery of new relevant facts can give grounds for an extension of time (see *Machine Tool Industry Research Association v Simpson* [1988] ICR 558 and *Cambridge and Peterborough Foundation NHS Trust v Crouchman* [2009] ICR 1306). Illness of the claimant may also be a relevant factor (see *Chouafi v London United Busways Ltd* [2006] EWCA Civ 689).

Even if a claimant satisfies a tribunal that it was not reasonably practicable to present a claim within the three-month time-limit, the tribunal must still go on to consider whether the claim was presented within such further period as it considers reasonable. The length of any further period will be determined by the facts in any given case. In *Nolan v Balfour Beatty Engineering Services* (UKEAT/0109/11), the EAT said that tribunals must bear in mind the surrounding context, including the primary time-limit and the general principle that litigation should be progressed efficiently and without delay. Tribunals should then go on to consider all the circumstances of a particular case, including what the claimant did; what he or she knew, or reasonably ought to have known, about time-limits; and why it was that the further delay had occurred. The basic rule is that tribunals expect claimants who present a claim late to act to rectify the delay as soon as they become aware of it. In *Marks and Spencer plc v William-Ryan* (above), the Court of Appeal emphasised the importance of considering what a claimant knew and what knowledge she should have had, had she acted reasonably. In *Woodward v CPS* (ET/

1800728/19), an employment tribunal held that while ill health had made it not reasonably practicable to submit an unfair dismissal claim within the initial three-month time-limit, the further delay, which included making an appeal against the dismissal, meant that the claim was not presented within a reasonable further period. (See too *Pearce v Merrill Lynch* (UKEAT/0067/19).)

For two cases where a delay of several months beyond the initial three months was still held to be reasonable, see *Remploy v Brain* (UKEAT/0465/10) and *Locke v Tabfine Ltd t/a Hands Music Centre* (UKEAT/0517/10).

6.3.2 Redundancy payments

An employee will lose his entitlement to a redundancy payment unless, before the end of a period of six months beginning with the 'relevant date', the employee has, where no payment has been made, made a claim in writing to the employer for the payment or presented a claim to the tribunal. The 'relevant date' is defined by s 145 of the ERA 1996 (see **3.5.2**).

6.3.3 Discrimination

Any complaints of discrimination must be brought within three months starting with the date the act or actions to which the complaint relates took place, or such other period as the tribunal considers just and equitable (Equality Act 2010, s 123(1)). (This is considered further at **8.8**.) This gives the tribunal a wide discretion to consider whether to allow in a claim out of time. See the decisions in *Abertawe Bro Morgannwg University Local Health Board v Morgan* [2018] EWCA Civ 640 and *Adedeji v University Hospitals Birmingham NHS Foundation Trust* [2021] EWCA Civ 23, where the Court of Appeal explored the principles behind extending time-limits in discrimination cases. In *Adedaji*, the Court said it was not helpful for a tribunal when considering an extension of time for a discrimination claim to focus on the factors in s 33 of the Limitation Act 1980. The court reviewed a number of cases involving the Limitation Act factors cited in *British Coal v Keeble* [1997] IRLR 336 and said that:

> The best approach for a tribunal in considering the exercise of the discretion under section 123(1)(b) [Equality Act 2010] is to assess all the factors in the particular case which it considers relevant to whether it is just and equitable to extend time, including in particular, 'the length of, and the reasons for, the delay'. If it checks those factors against the list in *Keeble*, well and good; but I would not recommend taking it as the framework for its thinking.

In *Kumari v Greater Manchester Mental Health NHS Foundation Trust* [2022] EAT 132, the EAT held that the potential merits of a proposed complaint, which is not plainly so weak that it would fall to be struck out, are not necessarily an irrelevant consideration when deciding whether it is just and equitable to extend time, or whether to grant an application to amend. However, if the tribunal weighs in the balance against the claimant its assessment of the merits formed at a preliminary hearing, that assessment must have been properly reached by reference to identifiable factors that are apparent at the preliminary hearing, and taking proper account, particularly where the claim is one of discrimination, of the fact that the tribunal does not have all the evidence before it, and is not conducting the trial. This tribunal had properly done that.

6.3.4 Equal pay

There is, in practice, no time-limit for a claim in respect of the ongoing operation of an equality clause whilst still in employment. A claim should be brought within six months of the employee leaving that employment.

6.3.5 Deductions from wages

The time-limit for presenting a claim for unlawful deduction of wages (ERA 1996, s 13) is three months starting with the date of the deduction, or later if it was not reasonably practicable for the claim to be presented in time (see **6.3.1** for more details on the application of this approach).

6.3.6 Wrongful dismissal

The time-limit for presenting a claim for wrongful dismissal is three months starting with the EDT, or later if it was not reasonably practicable for the claim to be presented within the time-limit (see **6.3.1**).

6.3.7 Acas Early Conciliation – effect on time-limits

One of the consequences of the requirements around Early Conciliation is that if there are problems which cause delay, they can impact on time-limits and may mean that claims are submitted out of time (see **6.2.2.3**).

The new system of mandatory Acas Early Conciliation applies to claims presented on or after 6 May 2014. The list of relevant proceedings is set out in s 18(1) of the ETA 1996. The claims to which Early Conciliation does not apply are set out in reg 3 of the Early Conciliation Regulations 2014, but it will apply to all of the most common claims.

6.3.7.1 Early Conciliation

When a claimant contacts Acas, this will 'pause' the time-limit for presenting his claim to a tribunal from the date Acas is notified. This pause (from December 2020) can be for up to six weeks. The time-limit will start to run again when the claimant receives his formal acknowledgement (the Certificate) that Early Conciliation has finished. Once Early Conciliation has ended, the claimant will have at least one calendar month in which to present his claim. If a claimant was already out of time for making a tribunal claim when requesting Early Conciliation, he will still be late afterwards. Provisions to extend time have been inserted into primary and secondary legislation by:

- Sch 2 to the ERRA 2013;
- art 3 of and the Schedule to the Employment Tribunals Act 1996 (Application of Conciliation Provisions) Order 2014 (SI 2014/431);
- art 2 of and the Schedule to the ERRA 2013 (Consequential Amendments) (Employment) Order 2014 (SI 2014/386);
- the ERRA 2013 (Consequential Amendments) (Employment) (No 2) Order 2014 (SI 2014/853), which amended TUPE 2006 with effect from 20 April 2014;
- Employment Tribunals (Amendment) Regulations 2020.

In the first instance, the Early Conciliation period simply stops the clock, and any time between contacting Acas and the issuing of the certificate will be added to the original three-month time-limit to present the claim. However, there are circumstances where the impact can be longer, and a claimant will have at least a calendar month within which to present a claim.

The guide below is provided by the Citizens' Advice Bureau:

If you want to go to a tribunal – working out the new deadline

You'll need to calculate the deadline for making the claim.

Because you've been through early conciliation, you'll have given yourself more time to make a tribunal claim. You'll have at least 1 month after the end of early conciliation to make your claim, but you may have more.

It's important to make sure you work out what the new deadline is so that you don't miss it.

To work out the new deadline for making your claim, the first thing you should do is work out your original deadline. For most claims, this will be 3 months minus 1 day from the date of the thing you're complaining about. If your claim is for statutory redundancy pay or equal pay, it's 6 months minus 1 day.

Then you need:

- the date on which you contacted Acas to start early conciliation
- the date on which you received the early conciliation certificate

If your original deadline for making a tribunal claim is more than 1 month away when you get the certificate, count the number of days from the day after you contacted Acas up to and including the day you received your certificate. Add that number to the original deadline, starting the day after the original deadline.

For example, you get your early conciliation certificate on 1 February and your original deadline is 3 March - more than 1 month away. If early conciliation takes 11 days, you have to get your tribunal claim in by midnight on 14 March.

If the original deadline has passed or is 1 month or less away when you get the certificate, add 1 month to the date when you receive your early conciliation certificate. That's your new deadline.

For example, your original deadline is 6 October. You receive your early conciliation certificate on 17 September. You must get your tribunal claim in by midnight on 17 October.

As mentioned above (**6.2.2.3**), changes have been made to time-limits to allow time for Early Conciliation to take place. The unfair dismissal and other time-limits (see **6.3.1**) are now subject to the provisions of s 207B of the ERA 1996, s 140B of the Equality Act 2010 etc. There has, however, been considerable uncertainty as to the interpretation and effect of these time-limits. There are, as illustrated below, many traps for the unwary. Many of the cases discussed below are first instance cases, and first instance decisions are not binding on other tribunals, though they are still, nonetheless, a useful reference point.

EXAMPLE 1

EDT 22 June 2020

Acas contacted (Day A) 18 July 2020 (ERA 1996, s 207B(2)(a))

EC cert issued by email (Day B) 18 August 2020 (ERA 1996, s 207B(2)(b))

Original time-limit 3 months less a day = 21 September 2020

Time between Day A and Day B = 31 days (begin with day after Day A and end with Day B)

ET1 presented 18 October 2020

Apply s 207B(3) ERA 1996: time started running before Acas Early Conciliation entered into so the full 31 days of the clock will be 'stopped' = 21 September plus 31 days = 22 October 2020 revised deadline.

Claim was presented in time.

Note. Section 207B(4) does not need to be relied upon on these facts because 22 October (the extended time limit) does *not* fall within Day A and 1 month of Day B (18 September).

Note that if the claimant contacts Acas before the limitation clock starts to tick (eg if in the above example the claimant contacted Acas before 22 June), only the period of Early Conciliation that occurs on or after 22 June (when the limitation clock started) will count.

EXAMPLE 2

EDT 22 June 2020

Acas contacted (Day A) 12 September 2020

EC cert issued (Day B) 19 September 2020

Original time-limit 3 months less a day = 21 September 2020

Time between Day A and Day B = 7 days

ET1 presented 18 October 2020

Apply s 207B(3) ERA 1996: time started running before Acas Early Conciliation entered into so the full 7 days of the clock will be 'stopped' = 21 September plus 7 days = 28 September revised deadline.

Claim seems to have been presented out of time

BUT

s 207B(4) applies on the facts, because 28 September 2020 (the 207B(3) time-limit) falls within Day A and 1 month of Day B (19 October). The time-limit is extended by 1 month from the date of the certificate and so the claim is in time.

In *Booth v Pasta King UK Ltd* (ET/1401231/2014) (heard in October 2014), the tribunal looked at the effect of s 207B of the ERA 1996. The claimant was dismissed on 2 April 2014. He sought to bring an unfair dismissal claim, and his ET1 was therefore due on or before 1 July 2014. He made contact with Acas on 21 May 2014 (day A). He received the Early Conciliation certificate on 21 June 2014 (day B). He submitted his ET1 on 24 July 2014. Under s 207B(3) (as relied upon by the claimant), 'the period beginning with the day after day A (22 May) and ending with Day B (21 June) is not be counted'. On this basis, 31 days could be discounted, leaving a date of 1 August. However, under s 207B(4) (as relied upon by the employer), 'if a time limit set by a relevant provision would (if not extended by this subsection) expire during the period beginning with day A (21 May) and ending one month after day B (21 July), the time limit expires instead at the end of that period'. On this basis, the last date for filing the ET1 was 21 July. The question for the tribunal was which, if either, subsection prevailed. The Employment Judge determined that Parliament could not have intended that a claimant should fail to have the benefit of s 207B(3) just because s 207B(4) was also available. She determined that the two provisions should not be read or applied in isolation, and held that the claim was in time. (See too *Wass v Delta Global Source (UK) Ltd* (ET/2600605/15).)

In *Chandler v Thanet District Council* (ET/2301782/14), the claimant was dismissed on 14 May 2014. He sought to bring an unfair dismissal claim, and his ET1 was due on or before 13 August 2014. He made contact with Acas on 8 May 2014. He received the Early Conciliation certificate on 7 June 2014 (day B). He submitted his ET1 on 10 September 2014. Argument focused on whether the time spent in Early Conciliation prior to the termination date (some five days) should be counted. The employer argued that they should not. On this basis, only 25 days could be counted, leaving a final date of 8 September. The claimant argued that all 30 days should be counted. The Employment Judge determined in favour of the claimant, finding that the period for submitting the claim was extended to 13 September, and therefore that the claim had been presented in time. Section 207B of the ERA 1996 should be interpreted so that time spent in Early Conciliation should always in effect be added on to the normal time-limit, even where the Early Conciliation period starts before time begins to run. Some commentators have said that s 207B does not easily support the employment judge's interpretation. Until the issue is resolved by appellate authority, claimants would be advised to be cautious about relying on it, but the same approach was also adopted by another tribunal in *Myers v Nottingham City Council* (2015).

In *Thomas v Nationwide Building Society* (ET/1601342/14) (heard in October 2014), no Early Conciliation certificate had been obtained, and the claim was rejected at the first stage sift under Rules 10 and 12. The claimant applied for a reconsideration under Rule 13. At a preliminary hearing to consider this, a later Early Conciliation certificate was presented. The employment tribunal held (somewhat controversially) that this remedied the defect and that there was therefore jurisdiction to hear the claim. Rule 13(4) provides that in a case where the original rejection was correct but the defect has been rectified, the claim shall be treated as presented on the date that the defect was rectified. In this case, the Employment Judge held that the claim should be treated as if presented at the date the defect was rectified (7 October, which was the date when Early Conciliation was completed) and listed a further hearing to consider whether the claim was out of time.

The EAT considered the meaning of 'one month *after*' (s 207B(4)) in *Tanveer v East London Bus and Coach Co Ltd* (UKEAT/0022/16). The claimant contacted Acas on 18 June 2015 and received the Early Conciliation certificate on 30 June 2015. The claim was issued on 31 July 2015. The issue was: 'what was "one month after"'? The employment tribunal concluded that one month was a calendar month, which meant that time expired on 30 July 2015. On appeal, the claimant argued that a calendar month meant that time expired on the last day of the calendar month, ie 31 July 2015, because the language of 'one month *after*' differs from the usual language (within the relevant period beginning with a date). The EAT disagreed and held that time expired on the corresponding date, ie 30 July 2015.

In *Hardy v Balfour Beatty Group Employment Ltd* (ET/13066954/14), the relationship between s 207B(3) and (4) was again considered. The claimant was dismissed on 15 July 2014. He sought to bring claims of unfair dismissal, non-payment of holiday pay and breach of contract, and his ET1 was therefore due on or before 14 October 2014. He made contact with Acas on 2 October 2014 (day A). He received the Early Conciliation certificate on 16 November 2014 (day B). Under s 207B(3), this stopped the clock for 45 days, which extended the period to 28 November. He submitted his ET1 on 22 December. However, under s 207B(4) (as relied upon by the claimant), the revised limitation period (28 November) would fall during the period beginning with day A (2 October) and ending one month after day B (16 December). On this basis, the last date for filing the ET1 was 16 December. So on either basis, the claim appeared to have been filed out of time. The claimant sought to argue that the two sections were cumulative, and he could therefore add the 45 days to day B, thus extending the period until 31 December. The Employment Judge disagreed with this analysis. If the extended date under s 207B(3) falls *within* day A and day B, s 207B(4) is engaged. The 45 days in s 207B(3) must be added to day B and not to the original limitation period. Section 207B(4) can be relied upon where the circumstances in s 207B(3) might be disadvantageous.

In *Luton Borough Council v Haque* (UKEAT/0260/17), a case which again concerned the relationship between s 207B(3) and (4), the effective date of termination was 20 June 2016. The claimant went to Acas on 22 July 2016 (Day A). The Early Conciliation certificate was issued on 22 August 2016 (Day B). The three months statutory time-limit therefore expired on 19 September 2016. The period of conciliation was 31 days. The claim form was presented on 18 October 2016. A dispute arose as to whether the 31 days period of conciliation extended the time limit from 19 September to 20 October (ie 31 days after 19 September) or whether the effect of s 207B(4) meant that time expired one month after Day B, ie 22 September (in which case the claim would be out of time). The employment tribunal ruled that the claimant's claims had been presented in time and should proceed to a full hearing. The respondent appealed. The EAT referred the case to a full hearing in an effort to resolve the ambiguity of the approach to the relationship between s 207B(3) and (4). In its judgment on allowing the appeal to go to a full hearing, the EAT referred to *Booth v Pasta King UK Ltd* (above) and *Savory and 58 Others v South Western Ambulance Service NHS Foundation Trust and Another* (ET/1400119/2016). In its substantive judgment (UKEAT/0180/17), the EAT said that the statutory provisions are to be applied sequentially and not as alternatives. First, the time-limit is extended by the period of conciliation. Next (and only if the time-limit would then expire prior to a month after Day B), the time-limit expires at the end of that month. Subsection (3) applies in every case. By contrast, subsection (4) expressly applies only in the circumstances to which it refers: the EAT therefore found that the claimant's claims has been presented in time.

In *Ullah v London Borough of Hounslow* (EAT/0084/16) the EAT confirmed that the statutory provisions did not require the period between date A and B to be added to the usual limitation period: they did not deal with 'adding time at all'; they only provided that time was 'not to be counted'. Therefore, 'whatever part of the usual time limit would run between A and B is ignored when reckoning the expiry of 3 months'.

In *Revenue and Customs Commissioners v Garau* (UKEAT/0348/16), the EAT held that there is no provision for a second certificate to be issued, and therefore such second certificate that was issued could have no effect on the time-limit.

Discrimination claims

Note that in discrimination claims, there will be different time-limits for acts of discrimination relied upon where there are multiple allegations. Where the last act of discrimination is in time, the easiest way to work out which alleged acts are out of time is to count back from Day A (day the claimant contacted Acas). So if, for example, Day A is 3 April 2020, any act which occurred on or after 4 January is within time, assuming the ET1 is presented in time. Earlier acts may be part of continuing acts, or an extension to bring in the earlier acts may be granted (see **Chapter 8**).

6.4 TRIBUNAL RULES

The practice and procedure of employment tribunals is governed by the Employment Tribunals (Constitution and Rules of Procedure) Regulations 2013, which came into force on 29 July 2013. Schedule 1 sets out the Tribunal Rules of Procedure. These have been amended on a number of occasions, including by the Employment Tribunals (Constitution and Rules of Procedure) (Early Conciliation: Exemptions and Rules of Procedure) (Amendment) Regulations 2020 (which made a number of wide-ranging amendments to the 2013 Rules, with effect from 8 October 2020), and most recently by the Employment Tribunals (Constitution and Rules of Procedure) (Early Conciliation: Exemptions and Rules of Procedure) (Amendment) Regulations 2021.

Rule 2 states that the 'overriding objective' of the Rules is to enable tribunals to deal with cases fairly and justly. This includes, so far as practicable:

(a)   ensuring the parties are on an equal footing;

(b)   dealing with the case in ways that are proportionate to the complexity and importance of the issues;

(c)   avoiding unnecessary formality and seeking flexibility in the proceedings;

(d)   avoiding delay, so far as compatible with a proper consideration of the issues; and

(e)   saving expense.

The parties have a duty to assist the tribunal in furthering the overriding objective. Tribunals are obliged to apply the overriding objective when interpreting every rule or exercising any power.

In *Harris v Academies Enterprise Trust* [2015] IRLR 208, the EAT compared the wording of the overriding objective as it appeared in the Employment Tribunal Rules and as it was worded in rule 3.9 of the Civil Procedure Rules (CPR) 1998. The claimant brought a number of claims against the Trust, including for whistleblowing, disability discrimination, victimisation and harassment. Witness statements were due to be exchanged on 19 February 2014, and a full hearing had been listed to start on 3 March 2014. The employer applied for an extension of time to exchange witness statements, but this was refused. On 26 February, the claimant applied for an unless order (see **6.4.5.6**). The Employment Judge did not make the order but stated that she was considering striking out the ET3/response under Rule 37(1) because of non-compliance with the original order to exchange witness statements (see **6.4.5.5**). At the beginning of the hearing on 3 March, the claimant applied to strike out the response. The Employment Judge accepted that there had been a failure to comply with a tribunal order and that the employer had acted unreasonably in not providing the witness statements, but noted that the overriding objective in the Tribunal Rules required tribunals to deal with cases fairly and justly, and went on to assess the relative prejudice to each of the parties. Having done so, the Employment Judge did not consider it appropriate to strike out the ET3/response, on the basis that it would not be proportionate, and the case was adjourned to the following Monday.

The claimant's appeal was dismissed by the EAT. The EAT noted that the correct approach was to focus on the consequences of default before determining the proportionate response. The EAT noted that there were differences between the wording of the overriding objective in the CPR 1998 and in the Employment Tribunal Rules, and concluded, 'Though, it seems to me, there is much of principle that applies to both, it would be a mistake to suggest that the CPR applied in the tribunals in the same way as they apply in the civil courts.' The EAT held that the concept of justice in the employment tribunal was wider than simply reaching a fair decision; it also involves delivering justice within a reasonable time, and dealing with a case in a way which ensures that other cases are not deprived of their own fair share of resources.

Rule 3 states that the tribunal shall, whenever practicable and appropriate, encourage the use of alternative means to settle the dispute.

Rule 4 sets out the rules on 'calculating time limits' for any act required under the Rules in Sch 1. (See eg **6.4.3** below.) The tribunal has a wide discretion to extend or shorten time-limits.

6.4.1   Litigants in person

A key area where the overriding objective comes into play is when dealing with unrepresented parties or litigants in person. Employment tribunals are accustomed to dealing with litigants in person. In 1995, the Woolf Report noted, 'All too often the litigant in person is regarded as a problem for judges and for the court system rather than a person for whom the system of civil justice exists.'

In March 2013, the Master of the Rolls issued practice guidance on dealing with litigants in person applicable to courts, and a judicial working group was established, chaired by Mr Justice Hickinbottom, which reported in July 2013 (*The Judicial Working Group on Litigants in Person: Report*). The Hickinbottom Report reiterated what the Woolf Report had noted, namely, that it is the court's or tribunal's duty to ensure that litigants have every reasonable opportunity to present their case, without assisting them with it.

The starting point for any consideration of this area is Rule 2 of the Employment Tribunal Rules and the overriding objective. The Court of Appeal in *Drysdale v Department of Transport (The Maritime and Coastguard Agency)* [2014] EWCA Civ 1083 provided some guidance on how employment tribunals should apply the overriding objective in the context of litigants in person. Mr Drysdale was represented by his wife during his employment tribunal proceedings. During the hearing, Mrs Drysdale, with her husband's apparent consent, asked that the claim be withdrawn. The tribunal asked her if her husband agreed and she confirmed that he did. The tribunal then dismissed the claim. The respondent employer then made a costs application, and Mr and Mrs Drysdale walked out after an acrimonious exchange. They subsequently appealed against the dismissal, challenging whether the tribunal had taken adequate steps to ensure that Mr Drysdale had taken a properly considered decision to withdraw the claim.

The Court of Appeal set out (at para 49) a number of general principles:

(a) It is desirable for courts generally, and employment tribunals in particular, to provide appropriate assistance to litigants in the formulation and presentation of their case.

(b) What level of assistance or intervention is 'appropriate' depends upon the circumstances of each particular case, including whether the litigant is represented or not, whether any representative is legally qualified and, in any case, the apparent level of competence and understanding of the litigant and/or his representative.

(c) The appropriate level of assistance or intervention is constrained by the overriding requirement that the tribunal must at all times be, and be seen to be, impartial as between the parties, and that injustice to either side must be avoided.

(d) How much assistance or intervention is appropriate is for the judgment of the tribunal hearing the case, and for the tribunal's assessment and 'feel' for what is fair in all the circumstances of the specific case. Rigid obligations or rules of law should be avoided.

(e) There is a wide margin of appreciation available to a tribunal in assessing such matters, and an appeal court will not normally interfere with the tribunal's exercise of its judgment in the absence of an act or omission on the part of the tribunal which no reasonable tribunal, properly directing itself on the basis of the overriding objective, would have done/omitted to do, and which amounts to unfair treatment of a litigant.

A difficult area for tribunals is the extent to which they should intervene or assist in a litigant in person's presentation of their case and the extent of help that can be offered to formulate and present their cases. Such decisions have to made bearing in mind the overriding objective in Rule 2 (see above) to deal with cases fairly and justly. In the recent case of *Mervyn v BW Controls Ltd* [2020] EWCA Civ 393, the Court of Appeal gave guidance on the status of a List of Issues, as well as the level of assistance that a tribunal can provide to litigants in person. The Court ruled that in cases where at least one party is unrepresented, courts must step in if litigants in person are mistakenly pursuing the wrong case and should intervene to clarify issues which arise on pleadings and confirm which claims have been conceded. Marion Mervyn brought an unsuccessful claim for unfair dismissal. The Court of Appeal found she had advanced the wrong case. In her claim form, Mervyn had ticked the box next to the words, 'I was unfairly dismissed (including constructive dismissal).' Her particulars of claim included allegations 'which to any employment lawyer would seem to indicate a case of constructive dismissal'. Mervyn maintained that she was 'dismissed', and the employment tribunal subsequently found that her complaint of unfair dismissal failed. She said that her first case management hearing, conducted by telephone, 'went too fast' and was confusing. The EAT noted that judges must be 'careful not to invent a case for a litigant' but said that tribunals have a duty to ensure that a litigant in person understands the nature of their claim. Where a litigant in person has decided not to advance a claim, the tribunal 'should be confident [they have] done so advertently'. Lord Justice Bean in the Court of Appeal agreed that it was good practice for tribunals to consider at the start of a hearing, where at least one party has no lawyer, whether issues drawn up at a case management conference reflect the points in dispute. He said: 'I do not think, with respect, that it was enough for the tribunal simply to ask at the start of the substantive hearing whether the parties confirmed the previous list of issues.' It would not have amounted to a 'step into the factual and evidential arena' for the tribunal to have said that it seemed to them that there was an issue as to whether Ms Mervyn had been dismissed or had resigned.

In *U v Butler and Wilson* (UKEAT/0354/13), the EAT considered a tribunal's approach to adjournment, where the claimant wanted time to collect his papers from a nearby printing shop and to challenge the dismissal of his case in his absence because he arrived late. The right to a fair hearing may require a judge to adjourn a hearing even without an application from a party. The EAT held that the Employment Judge had failed to properly exercise her case management powers to adjourn in order to permit the claimant an opportunity to reflect on what course he wished to pursue. Furthermore, the tribunal had been in error in not explaining to the claimant that he had an option to make a written application for a review rather than proceeding immediately with an oral application. It was an important factor that the tribunal knew that the claimant was disabled with post-traumatic stress disorder and episodic psychosis, which should have been taken into account when making case management decisions. The EAT held:

> Anyone conducting a judicial or quasi-judicial hearing confronted with a person who is plainly unwell would necessarily and obviously adjourn the hearing for a brief time to enable them to recover sufficiently to present their case, or their evidence, if possible during the course of the hearing.

A distinction between *Drysdale* and *Butler and Wilson* is that, in the latter case, it could not be said the claimant was 'participating effectively' in his hearing.

In *Rackham v NHS Professionals Ltd* (UKEAT/0110/15) the EAT makes reference to ground rules hearings, a pre-trial process involving all the parties and the judge which can be used to assist any party or witness who may be vulnerable and address any issues that might arise so as to ensure that all parties can participate effectively in the hearing – including setting out 'ground rules' before their evidence is given. See the Presidential Guidance on Vulnerable Parties and Witnesses, issued on 22 April 2020, and the Advocate's Gateway, which provides free access to practical, evidence-based guidance on vulnerable witnesses and defendants. (See also *Anderson v Turning Point Eespro* [2019] EWCA Civ 815.)

6.4.2 The claim (Rule 8)

The complaint must be made in writing on the prescribed claim form ET1. (Only the official ETS versions of the forms are acceptable – they can be downloaded from <http://www.employmenttribunals.gov.uk>.) The ET1 *must* contain the following information:

(a)   each claimant's name;

(b)   each claimant's address;

(c)   each respondent's name;

(d)   each respondent's address;

(e)   details relating to Early Conciliation, including the Early Conciliation number.

Rule 10(1) states that if a claim is not presented on the prescribed form, or where the claim does not include the minimum information referred to above or does not contain an early conciliation number or confirmation that one is not required, it will be rejected. (Rule 10(1) was amended by the Employment Tribunals (Constitution and Rules of Procedure) (Amendment) Regulations 2014 (SI 2014/271) to bring it up to date with regard to the early conciliation procedure, and further changes came into force on 8 October 2020 to provide greater discretion to judges where an ET1 contains clerical errors.)

Rule 12 states that a claim form may be referred to an Employment Judge, and the Judge can strike out a claim, if it appears that (a) a tribunal has no jurisdiction to consider the claim or part of it, or (b) if it cannot sensibly be responded to or is an abuse of process. This then effectively allows the Employment Judge to conduct a preliminary 'sift' of the claim. In *Higgins v Home Office* (UKEAT/0296/14), the claimant sought to bring an unfair constructive dismissal claim six years after the employment relationship ended. The employment tribunal rejected the claim as an abuse of process under the sifting procedure in Rule 12. The EAT said that striking out a valid claim as an abuse of process should be the last resort (see *Wallis v Valentine* [2002] EWCA Civ 1034). Claims should only be rejected in the sift in the most plain and obvious cases; borderline cases should be dealt with under Rule 27 (no reasonable prospect of success). As the tribunal had failed to appreciate that the claimant may have had significant mental health issues, the case was remitted back to a fresh tribunal to reconsider it under Rule 12 and under Rule 27. In *Secretary of State for Business, Energy and Industrial Strategy v Parry* [2018] EWCA Civ 672, the Court of Appeal considered the scope and ambit of Rule 12(1)(b), which allows for rejection of a claim without a hearing. It held that the rejection of a claim under Rule 12(1)(b) is not a 'determination of proceedings' within s 7 of the Employment Tribunals

Act 1996. Rule 12 has to be read with Rule 8, which states that proceedings only commence when a completed claim form is presented. Further, a rejection is not a determination – it is a judicial act of a different quality which does not go to the substance of the claim or the quality of the issues.

Rule 12 also make provision for the rejection of a defective claim including:

> (f) one which institutes relevant proceedings and the name of the respondent on the claim form is not the same as the name of the prospective respondent on the early conciliation certificate to which the early conciliation number relates.

Rule 12(2A) states that the claim (or part of it):

> shall be rejected if the Judge considers that the claim, or part of it, is of a kind described in sub-paragraph (e) or (f) of paragraph (1) unless the Judge considers that the claimant made an error in relation to a name or address and it would not be in the interests of justice to reject the claim.

In *Giny v SNA Transport Ltd* (UKEAT/0317/16), the claimant's Early Conciliation Certificate named the respondent as a 'Mr A' (the correct name was 'SNA Ltd', of whom Mr A was the director). The claimant gave the correct address. He subsequently took legal advice and the ET1 was issued in the correct name. The tribunal struck the claim out under Rule 12(1)(f), considering that this was not a minor error and declining to exercise its discretionary power that it would not be in the interests of justice to reject the claim. The EAT held that this was a decision that the tribunal could properly come to, having applied the two-stage test. The rule has now been amended to remove the word 'minor' and the authors think that the decision would now be different.

A claimant may apply under Rule 13 for reconsideration of a decision to reject a claim form under Rules 10 or 12, if he considers the rejection erroneous or if the notified defect can be rectified.

The form should be sent to the appropriate ROET. The complaint must be received at the ROET within the relevant time-limit (see **6.3** above). Generally, as a matter of practice, claims will be held in the 'relevant' tribunal region for the claimant's postcode – work or home. However, there is no 'right' for a claimant to have a case heard in a particular region (see *Faleye and Another v UK Mission Enterprise Ltd* (UKEAT/0359/10)). Requests for transfers between regions are purely a matter, subject to any injustice, of discretion for an Employment Judge to determine.

A complaint may be posted, delivered by hand or sent electronically (see Rule 85). (See also **6.3.1**.)

A copy of the complaint will be sent by the ROET to the employer and to Acas.

6.4.3   Response (Rule 16)

The employer should file a response on prescribed form ET3. Rule 16 states that if a response is not presented on the prescribed form, or where the response does not include all the required information or it is received outside the required time-limit, the response shall be rejected (the respondent can apply for reconsideration of that decision under Rule 19 if he considers the rejection erroneous).

The form should be submitted within 28 days of the date on which the ET1 was sent by the tribunal to the respondent. Rule 4(3) states that:

> where any act must or may be done within a certain number of days of or from an event, the date of that event shall not be included in the calculation. For example, a response shall be presented within 28 days of the date on which the respondent was sent a copy of a claim: if the claim was sent on 1st October, the last day for presentation of the response is 29th October.

A copy of the response will be sent to all parties.

Rule 17 states that the following information must be provided:

(a)   respondent's full name;

(b)   respondent's full address;

(c)   whether or not the respondent wishes to resist the claim in whole or in part; and

(d)   if the respondent wishes to resist, on what grounds.

Rule 20 allows the respondent to apply for an extension of time within which to submit his ET3. The application for an extension must be made in accordance with Rule 20. Any application should set out reasons why an extension is sought.

Where a respondent fails to enter a response within the time-limits (or to apply for an extension under Rule 20) a tribunal judge shall decide whether a determination can be made and, if it can, issue a judgment. Otherwise a hearing will be listed. Even where a respondent is barred from contesting liability (for example because it fails to present a response in time), it should normally be able to participate in a remedy hearing (*Office Equipment Systems Ltd v Hughes* [2018] EWCA Civ 1842).

6.4.4   Initial consideration (Rule 26)

Once a claim form and response have been received, an Employment Judge will conduct an initial consideration of the case. The Employment Judge may make a case management order, or list the case for a preliminary or final hearing, or propose mediation or some other form of dispute resolution; or (Rule 27), if the Employment Judge considers that there is no jurisdiction to hear the claim, or that it or a part of it has no reasonable prospect of success, he may dismiss the claim or part of it (subject to giving the claimant the opportunity to make written representations explaining why it should not be dismissed). Rule 28 contains similar powers with regard to dismissing a response.

Note that in a change to the rules, a notice of final hearing may be issued before the ET3 is received, provided the date of hearing is no sooner than 14 days after the response is due (Rule 58) (amended by SI 2020/1003).

Tribunals use three 'tracks' to manage and list cases – short, standard and open. Short track cases include breach of contract and notice pay, Wages Act, holiday pay and redundancy payment claims. These cases are often listed fairly speedily, without any case management hearing, with basic directions, including the preparation of a schedule of loss. Unfair dismissal claims generally fall into the standard track, and discrimination and multi-day cases are listed in the open track. In both of the latter instances, they will usually be listed for a case management hearing (see below) to set out directions for the full hearing, identify issues and any preliminary matters that go to the jurisdiction of the tribunal to hear the claim.

A copy of the claim form and response will normally be sent to Acas by the tribunal, because Acas has a statutory duty to endeavour to promote settlement under most employment protection legislation (ETA 1996, s 18, as amended). Section 18C, which came into force on 6 April 2014, provides that Acas is under a duty to conciliate where a claim has been presented to an employment tribunal, provided it is requested to do so by the parties or it considers there is a reasonable prospect of achieving a settlement.

6.4.5   Case management (Rules 29 to 32)

Rule 29 is headed 'Case management orders' and states that an employment tribunal 'may at any stage of the proceedings, on its own initiative or on application, make a case management order'. The particular powers identified in the following rules do not restrict that general power. A case management order may vary, suspend or set aside an earlier case management order where that is necessary in the interests of justice, and in particular where a party affected by the earlier order did not have a reasonable opportunity to make representations before it was made. The term 'case management order' in Rule 29 is defined in Rule 1(3)(a) as '... an order or decision of any kind in relation to the conduct of proceedings, not including the determination of any issue which would be the subject of a judgment'. Rules 30–40 set out a number of miscellaneous case management and other powers of the Tribunal, which include rules on disclosure of documents (Rule 31), attendance of witnesses (Rule 32), addition, substitution and removal of parties (Rule 34), striking out (Rule 37), unless orders (Rule 38) and deposit orders (Rule 39).

Rule 2 reminds tribunals that the overriding object of the Rules is to enable tribunals to deal with cases fairly and justly. Case management powers need to be exercised to ensure that evidence is kept within 'reasonable bounds'. Case management is aimed at achieving this objective. It will aim to identify what the issues are between the parties (see eg *Mensah v East Hertfordshire Trust* [1988] IRLR 531), what the relevant areas of law may be, what orders need to be made in order to ensure the case is properly prepared, with the correct documents and witnesses in place, and any arrangements for the hearing, including the length, location and dates. It will also identify any adjustments that may be needed to make sure a fair hearing takes place (see the guidance in *Rackham v NHS Professionals Ltd* (UKEAT/0110/15)) and will look at the possibilities for alternative dispute resolution. In *Davies v Sandwell MBC* [2013] EWCA Civ 135, Lewison LJ said:

> As a newcomer to this field, I cannot believe that it was intended that a claim for unfair dismissal should take some four weeks to hear, with witnesses producing witness statements hundreds of pages long and being subjected to cross-examination for days on end. In our case aspects (b), (c) and (d) of the overriding objective seem to have been largely forgotten. The function of the ET [in an unfair dismissal case] is a limited one. It is to decide whether the employer acted reasonably in dismissing the employee. It is not for the ET to conduct a primary fact-finding exercise. It is there to review the employer's decision. Still less is the ET there to conduct an investigation into the whole of the employee's employment history. The ET itself commented in this case that much of the evidence that it heard was irrelevant to the issues it had to decide. But irrelevant evidence should be identified at the case management stage and excised. It should not be allowed to clutter up a hearing and distract from the real issues. The ET has power to do this and should not hesitate to use it. The ET also has power to prevent irrelevant cross-examination and, again, should not hesitate to exercise that power. If the parties have failed in their duty to assist the tribunal to further the overriding objective, the ET must itself take a firm grip on the case. To do otherwise wastes public money; prevents other cases from being heard in a timely fashion, and is unfair to the parties in subjecting them to increased costs and, at least in the case of the employer, detracting from his primary concern, namely to run his business. An appellate court or tribunal (whether the EAT or this court) should, wherever legally possible, uphold robust but fair case management decisions.

Under the Rules, the Employment Judge has wide case management powers. The Employment Judge may, for example, strike out a claim (Rule 37) (see **6.4.5.2**), make an unless order (Rule 38) (see **6.4.5.7**) or order a deposit (Rule 39) (see **6.4.5.3**), If there is a hearing, it will be a preliminary hearing (Rule 53) (see **6.4.6.1**). Preliminary hearings are normally in private (unless they involve the determination of a preliminary issue or consideration to strike out a claim or response which must be decided at a public hearing). The Employment Judge may require:

(a)   a party to provide additional information;

(b)   a party to disclose documents;

(c)   a party to provide written answers to questions;

(d)   attendance of witnesses;

(e)   provision and exchange of witness statements.

An example of a pro forma template agenda for a case management discussion at a preliminary hearing is set out at the end of **Appendix 3**, along with the detailed (and helpful) Guidance issued by the President of the Employment Tribunals. One important process that is conducted at a preliminary case management hearing is to set out a list of issues, which should be agreed if possible between the parties. In *Land Rover v Short* (UKEAT/0496/10), the EAT noted that agreed lists of issues were usually of considerable assistance to tribunals and contributed to the natural justice requirements that a party should know the case it has to meet. The Court of Appeal in *Scicluna v Zippy Stitch Ltd* [2018] EWCA Civ 1320 held that an agreed list of issues is 'the road map by which the judge is to navigate his or her way to a just determination', and departure from it should only occur in exceptional circumstances. The EAT held that it is not open to the employment tribunals to limit the issues a claimant can pursue (subject to claims being struck out, which will be rare in discrimination claims (see **6.4.5.2**)) (*Tarn v Hughes and Others* (UKEAT/0064/18). See too *Royal Mail Group Ltd v Jhuti* [2018] ICR 1077, where the EAT made clear that tribunals are not required to stick 'slavishly' to agreed lists of issues if to do so would prevent them from hearing and determining the case in accordance with the law and evidence.

The EAT held in *Jhuti v Royal Mail Group Ltd and others* (UKEAT/0061/17 & UKEAT/0062/17) that the appointment of a litigation friend is possible as part of case management in cases where otherwise a litigant who lacks capacity to conduct litigation would have no means of accessing justice or achieving a remedy for a legal wrong. Where there is legitimate reason to doubt a litigant's capacity to litigate, that issue must be addressed.

The 'reasonable bounds' test

In *Hendricks v Commissioner of Police for the Metropolis* [2003] IRLR 96, Ms Hendricks' discrimination claim related to most of her 11 years at the force, involving nearly 100 specific allegations against 50 or so officers. The Court of Appeal stated that there must be close case management in lengthy discrimination cases, with agreed lists of issues and attempts to keep the proceedings within 'reasonable bounds' by concentrating on the most serious and most recent allegations. This approach was endorsed by the EAT in *HSBC Asia Holdings BV v Gillespie* (UKEAT/0417/10), which held that tribunals have wide discretionary case management powers and gave, obiter, guidance on the issue of pursuing 'sample' claims. It stated that there was no reason in principle why a tribunal could not hive off claims which it regarded as secondary or repetitive or otherwise unnecessary to a second hearing, allowing it to focus on claims considered to be more key.

However, there are limits to this. In *Tarn v Hughes* (UKEAT/0064/18), there were over 40 acts of discrimination alleged, requiring determination of 180 issues. The employment tribunal ordered Dr Tarn to select a sample of the 10 most recent and serious allegations to pursue. The EAT said that the order was perverse. While the tribunal has wide case management powers, limiting the claim in this way might undermine a just determination of the case. Claims should only be limited in exceptional cases. A tribunal has no power to prevent a claimant pursuing a properly arguable claim, even if it forms one of many similar claims (see *Ma v Merck, Sharp and Dohme Ltd* [2008] EWCA Civ 1426 and *Franco v Bowling and Co* (UKEAT/0280/09)).

In *Sarnoff v YZ* [2021] EWCA Civ 26, the Court of Appeal held that the power of the employment tribunal to make disclosure orders against parties derived from its general case management powers under Rule 29, and that Rule 31 was concerned only with disclosure against non-parties.

6.4.5.1 Applications to amend

There is nothing in the Rules dealing specifically with amendments. Such applications may give rise to subsidiary considerations about whether claims are made in time. One alternative to seeking to amend an existing claim is to issue a new claim and, if necessary, apply for permission to present it out of time (see **6.3.1** for time-limits and extensions). However, claimants need to remember that under the Early Conciliation rules (**6.2.2**), before a claim is brought an Early Conciliation certificate must be obtained. It is not clear how this will apply to an application to amend a pre-existing claim, where there is a new cause of action not covered by any existing certificate. Rule 92 requires that when parties send a communication to the tribunal (except an application under Rule 32), they will send a copy to all other parties.

The principal authorities with regard to amendments are *Cocking v Sandhurst* [1974] ICR 650, *British Newspaper Printing Corporation (North) Ltd v Kelly* [1989] IRLR 222, *Selkent Bus Co v Moore* [1996] IRLR 661, *Housing Corporation v Bryant* [1999] ICR 123, *Harvey v Port of Tilbury (London) Ltd* [1999] ICR 1030, *Ali v Office of National Statistics* [2005] IRLR 201 and most recently *Vaughan v Modality Partnership* [2021] IRLR 97.

The EAT in *Selkent* stated a number of general principles which it said were applicable to the amendment of tribunal claims:

> (4)   Whenever the discretion to grant an amendment is invoked, the tribunal should take into account *all* the circumstances and should balance the injustice and hardship of allowing the amendment against the injustice and hardship of refusing it.

> (5)   What are the relevant circumstances? It is impossible and undesirable to attempt to list them exhaustively, but the following are certainly relevant:

>> (a)   *The nature of the amendment*

>> Applications to amend are of many different kinds, ranging, on the one hand, from the correction of clerical and typing errors, the additions of factual details to existing allegations and the addition or substitution of other labels for facts already pleaded to, on the other hand, the making of entirely new factual allegations which change the basis of the existing claim. The tribunal have to decide whether the amendment sought is one of the minor matters or is a substantial alteration pleading a new cause of action.

>> (b)   *The applicability of time limits*

>> If a new complaint or cause of action is proposed to be added by way of amendment, it is essential for the tribunal to consider whether that complaint is out of time and, if so, whether the time limit should be extended under the applicable statutory provisions ...

>> (c)   *The timing and manner of the application*

>> An application should not be refused solely because there has been a delay in making it. There are no time limits laid down in the Rules for the making of amendments. The amendments may be made at any time – before, at, even after the hearing of the case. Delay in making the application is, however, a discretionary factor. It is relevant to consider why the application was not made earlier and why it is now being made: for example, the discovery of new facts or new information appearing from documents disclosed on discovery. Whenever taking any factors into account, the paramount considerations are the relative injustice and hardship involved in refusing or granting an amendment. Questions of delay, as a result of adjournments, and additional costs, particularly if they are unlikely to be recovered by the successful party, are relevant in reaching a decision.

In *Vaughan*, HH Judge James Tayler emphasised that the 'core test' when considering applications to amend is the balance of injustice and hardship to each party in either refusing or allowing an application to amend. He went on to say that the factors set out by the EAT in *Selkent* are examples and 'should not be taken as a checklist to be ticked off to determine the application, but are factors to take into account in conducting the fundamental exercise of balancing the injustice or hardship of allowing or refusing the amendment'. He advised that the best approach might be to put the *Selkent* factors to one side and to start by considering what will be the 'real practical consequences of allowing or refusing the amendment. If the application to amend is refused how severe will the consequences be, in terms of the prospects of success of the claim or the defence; if permitted what will be the practical problems in responding?'

Even in the most extreme case, ie where there is a finding that, as 'a new' claim, that claim would be out of time (allowing for the relevant 'escape clause'), the authorities do not suggest that that would be fatal to an application to amend. Conversely, the fact that an amendment could be commenced as a new claim within the time-limit, while a significant feature, is not conclusive in favour of granting an application (see *Gillett v Bridge 86 Ltd* (UKEAT/0051/17) and *Patka v BBC* (UKEAT/0190/17)).

The Court of Appeal in *Office of National Statistics v Ali* [2005] IRLR 201 considered an appeal relating to an application to amend an ET1. The claim form alleged direct racial discrimination. Even though there was an argument about whether it included some aspects of indirect racial discrimination, it did not allege the indirect racial discrimination upon which the employee wished to rely. The details of complaint in the ET1 clearly referred to race as the reason for the treatment of which complaint was made. Mr Ali was originally unrepresented. After counsel was instructed, an application to amend the ET1 was made specifying the basis of a claim for indirect discrimination. The employment tribunal took the view that the ET1 raised the issue of whether there was something about the respondent's recruitment practice which had the effect of excluding black people and concluded that the ET1 included a claim of indirect race discrimination and no amendment was required. The Court of Appeal (Waller LJ) held, at para 39:

> In my view the question whether an originating application contains a claim has to be judged by reference to the whole document. That means that although box 1 may contain a very general description of the complaint and a bare reference in the particulars to an event (as in *Dodd v [British Telecommunications* [1988] IRLR 16]), particularisation may make it clear that a particular claim, for example for indirect discrimination, is not being pursued. That may at first sight seem to favour the less particularised claim as in *Dodd*, but such a general claim cries out for particulars and those are particulars to which the employer is entitled so that he knows the claim he has to meet. An originating application which appears to contain full particulars would be deceptive if an employer cannot rely on what it states. I would for my part think that insofar as *Quarcoopome [v Sock Shop Holdings Ltd* [1995] IRLR 353] suggests to the contrary it should not be followed. Therefore I would hold that paragraph 25A seeks to bring into the proceedings a new claim.

For other decisions on amendment see, for example, *Baker v Commissioner of Police of the Metropolis* (UKEAT/0201/09/CEA), *Enterprise Liverpool Ltd v Jonas and Others* (UKEAT/0112/09), *Thompson v East Dumbartonshire Council* (UKEATS/0049/13), *Wade v CT Plus Community Interest Company* (UKEAT/0510/13) and *Makauskiene v Rentokil Initial Facilities Services (UK) Ltd* (UKEAT/0503/13). In *New Star v Evershed* [2010] EWCA Civ 870, the Court of Appeal held that adding a public interest disclosure claim to an unfair dismissal claim with similar facts did not require 'wholly different evidence' such that the application to amend should be refused. The claimant sought to add an 'automatic' unfair constructive dismissal claim by asserting that the reason, or principal reason, for his dismissal was that he had made a protected disclosure and that it was a 'whistle-blowing' claim. He had made allegations about being bullied in the context of his unfair dismissal claim, where he argued that it contributed to the intolerable atmosphere causing him to resign. Although the respondent said the allegations were irrelevant to the unfair dismissal claim, they had not been struck out and remained part of the case. The Court of Appeal accepted that this was not a mere 're-labelling' and specific findings would have to be made about the individual components of the public interest disclosure claim; but it upheld the reasoning of the EAT that there was a substantial overlap in the issues. The EAT held in *Amey Services Ltd v Aldridge* (UKEAT/0007/16) that the time issue must, where relevant, be decided before determining the amendment application.

6.4.5.2 Striking out

Rule 37 states that a claim or response may be struck out at any stage of the proceedings if:

(a)   the claim or response is scandalous, vexatious or has no reasonable prospects of success;

(b)   the manner in which proceedings have been conducted by the claimant or respondent is scandalous, unreasonable or vexatious;

(c)   the claimant or respondent has failed to comply with any tribunal orders;

(d)   the claim has not actively been pursued;

(e)   it is not possible to have a fair hearing of the claim.

In *Mendy v Motorola Solutions UK Ltd* [2022] EAT 47, the EAT held that determining a strike-out application at a private hearing without giving the claimant a proper opportunity to make representations is an error of law.

It is a matter for the tribunal's judgment whether a claim is struck out. In *Blockbuster Entertainment Ltd v James* [2006] IRLR 630, CA, it was held that a power to strike out was a 'draconic power not to be too readily exercised'. See too *Tayside Public Transport Co Ltd v Reilly* [2012] IRLR 755 (Court of Session), *Rodrigues v Co-Op Group Ltd* (UKEAT/0022/12), *Harris v Academies Enterprise Trust* [2015] IRLR 208 and most recently *Mbuisa v Cygnet Healthcare Ltd* (UKEAT/0119/18). In *Cox v Adecco* (UKEAT/0339/19), the EAT said that before making a strike out or similar order (such as a deposit order), it was important that reasonable steps were taken by the tribunal to identify the claims, and the issues in the claims: 'You can't decide whether a claim has reasonable prospects of success if you don't know what it is.' The Employment Judge should read the pleadings and any core documents that set out the claimant's case and not just ask the claimant to say what their claims were. A less draconian alternative to striking a claim out may be for a deposit to be ordered to be paid (see below), where the test for making such an order is lower than for strike out.

The power to strike out a claim on the ground that it has no reasonable prospect of success should only be exercised in rare circumstances (*Tayside Public Transport Co Ltd v Reilly*). It should not be struck out where the central facts are in dispute (see *North Glamorgan NHS Trust v Ezsias* [2007] EWCA Civ 330). In *Ezsias*, Maurice Kay LJ stated (at [29]) that:

> It would only be in an exceptional case that an application to an employment tribunal will be struck out as having no reasonable prospect of success when the central facts are in dispute. An example might be where the facts sought to be established by the claimant were totally and inexplicably inconsistent with the undisputed contemporaneous documentation. The present case does not approach that level.

The EAT stated in *Bolch v Chipman* [2004] IRLR 140 (a case under the previous rules) that:

(1) There must be a conclusion by the Tribunal not simply that a party has behaved unreasonably but that the proceedings have been conducted by or on his behalf unreasonably.

(2) Assuming there be a finding that the proceedings have been conducted scandalously, unreasonably or vexatiously, that is not the final question so far as leading on to an order that the Notice of Appearance must be struck out.

(3) Once there has been a conclusion, if there has been, that the proceedings have been conducted in breach of Rule 15(2)(d), and that a fair trial is not possible, there still remains the question as to what remedy the tribunal considers appropriate, which is proportionate to its conclusion. It is also possible, of course, that there can be a remedy, even in the absence of a conclusion that a fair trial is no longer possible, which amounts to some kind of punishment, but which, if it does not drive the defendant from the judgment seat (in the words of Millett J) may still be an appropriate penalty to impose, provided that it does not lead to a debarring from the case in its entirety, but some lesser penalty.

Discrimination cases should, say the courts, rarely be struck out. In *Anyanwu v South Bank Students' Union* [2001] IRLR 305, HL, Lord Steyn stated:

> For my part such vagaries in discrimination jurisprudence underline the importance of not striking out such claims as an abuse of the process except in the most obvious and plainest cases. Discrimination cases are generally fact-sensitive, and their proper determination is always vital in our pluralistic society. In this field perhaps more than any other the bias in favour of a claim being examined on the merits or demerits of its particular facts is a matter of high public interest.

This does not mean that discrimination cases can never be struck out. The EAT in *Chandhok v Tirkey* [2015] ICR 527, citing *Anyanwu*, said (at [20]):

> This stops short of a blanket ban on strike-out applications succeeding in discrimination claims. There may still be occasions when a claim can properly be struck out—where, for instance, there is a time bar to jurisdiction, and no evidence is advanced that it would be just and equitable to extend time; or where, on the case as pleaded, there is really no more than an assertion of a difference of treatment and

a difference of protected characteristic which (per Mummery LJ in *Madarassy v Nomura International plc* [2007] ICR 867, para 56):

> only indicate a possibility of discrimination. They are not, without more, sufficient material from which a tribunal 'could conclude' that, on the balance of probabilities, the respondent had committed an unlawful act of discrimination.

Or claims may have been brought so repetitively concerning the same essential circumstances that a further claim (or response) is an abuse. There may well be other examples, too: but the general approach remains that the exercise of a discretion to strike out a claim should be sparing and cautious.

The position was also considered by the Court of Appeal in *Ahir v British Airways plc* [2017] EWCA 1392, where Underhill LJ stated (at [16]):

> Employment tribunals should not be deterred from striking out claims, including discrimination claims, which involve a dispute of fact if they are satisfied that there is indeed no reasonable prospect of the facts necessary to liability being established, and also provided they are keenly aware of the danger of reaching such a conclusion in circumstances where the full evidence has not been heard and explored, perhaps particularly in a discrimination context. Whether the necessary test is met in a particular case depends on an exercise of judgment.

See *Chidzoy v BBC* (UKEAT/0097/17) for a recent case on striking out a claim on the unreasonable conduct ground.

In *Arriva London North Ltd v Maseya* (UKEAT/0096/16), Simler J stated there is nothing automatic about a decision to strike out. Rather, a tribunal is required to exercise a judicial discretion by reference to the appropriate principles.

The EAT urged caution to be exercised where a case is badly pleaded, for example by a litigant in person, in *Mbuisa v Cygnet Healthcare Ltd* (UKEAT/0119/18).

Rule 37(1)(c) provides that a Tribunal may strike out a claim on grounds that include that the claimant has not complied with an order of the Tribunal. In *Weir Valves and Controls (UK) Ltd v Armitage* [2004] ICR 371, the EAT considered the approach to be taken where an application to strike out (in that case, the response rather than the claim) is made on the grounds of breach of an order. The case was decided under the earlier Rules, but the approach remains applicable. In para 16 of its judgment, the EAT stated that, where there was no breach of an order (for example, where unreasonable conduct alone was in issue), the crucial and decisive question will generally be whether a fair trial of the issues is still possible. However (para 17), where breach of an order is relied upon, the EAT said that the guiding consideration is the overriding objective, as set out in Rule 2, namely to enable employment tribunals to deal with cases fairly and justly. The EAT continued:

> This [ie the overriding objective] requires justice to be done between the parties. The court should consider all the circumstances. It should consider the magnitude of the default, whether the default is the responsibility of the solicitor or the party, what disruption, unfairness or prejudice has been caused and, still, whether a fair hearing is still possible. It should consider whether striking out or some lesser remedy would be an appropriate response to the disobedience.

In *Bahad v HSBC Bank plc* [2022] EAT 83, the EAT stated:

> The approach that should be adopted to applications to strike out is of extremely long standing. From the House of Lords to the EAT, the appellate courts have for many years urged caution in striking out discrimination and public interest disclosure claims. Yet, on occasions employment tribunals having directed themselves that it is an extraordinary thing to do, strike out claims that are far from unusual. Experienced employment judges may sometimes feel that it is pretty clear that a claim will not succeed at trial and wish to save the expense and, possibly, the distress to the claimant of a failed claim. But that is what deposit orders were designed for. To strike out a claim the employment judge must be confident that at trial, after all the evidence has come out, it is almost certain to fail, so it genuinely can be said to have no reasonable prospects of success at a preliminary stage, even though disclosure has not taken place and no witnesses have given evidence. When discrimination claims succeed it is often because of material that came out in disclosure and because witnesses prove unable to explain their actions convincingly when giving evidence.

6.4.5.3   Requirement to pay a deposit (Rule 39)

Rule 39 allows for a party to be ordered to pay a deposit of up to £1,000 in order to continue to take part in proceedings, where the Employment Judge considers any argument or allegation in a claim or response has 'little reasonable prospect of success'. This test is a lower one than for making a strike out order. Elias J in *Van Resnburg v Royal Borough Kingston-upon-Thames* (UKEAT/0095/07) remarked that this test provided 'greater leeway' than an order for strike out, particularly where there is doubt over facts rather than law. The wording of the rule allows deposit orders to be made in relation to individual 'allegations or arguments'. Before ordering a deposit to be paid, the Employment Judge must make reasonable enquiries as to the party's ability to pay (see, for example, *Hemdan v Ishmail* (UKEAT/0021/16)). Where applications are made for deposit orders in regard to a number of individual aspects of a claim or response, the tribunal must at the end 'stand back and look at the total sum awarded and consider the question of proportionality before finalising the orders made' (*Wright v Nipponkoa Insurance (Europe) Ltd* (UKEAT/0113/14)).

The Employment Judge must set out their grounds for making such an order and give a copy of the document recording their reasons to the parties, and explain to the party against whom the order is made the potential consequences of the order. If the party does not pay the deposit by the date specified on the order, the claim or response will be struck out. A deposit order cannot be made merely because the claimant's case is unclear (*Tree v South East Coastal Services Ambulance NHS Trust* (UKEAT/0043/17)). See too *Adams v Kingdom Services Group Ltd* (UKEAT/0235/18).

6.4.5.4   Additional information

A request for additional information should first be made directly to the other party before seeking an order from the tribunal. A tribunal may order a party to the proceedings to provide additional information about the grounds upon which they rely and of any facts or contentions relevant thereto, and it may impose a time-limit by which the order is to be complied with.

The aim of written answers is to identify and narrow the issues; they need not be confined to amplification of the grounds upon which the party relies and are thus wider in scope than additional information. A similar approach is likely to be taken to such requests in the civil courts, so 'fishing' questions, for example, will not be allowed, neither will questions which relate solely to the evidence which a party intends to adduce. They are unlikely to be ordered where other procedural processes would be more appropriate, for example a request for additional information or a request for disclosure.

The purpose of additional information is to remedy any deficiency in the case stated in the claim or response form, in order that the parties will know in advance reasonable details of the nature of the complaints that each side is going to make at the hearing. For example, additional information may be ordered about a vague allegation such as 'the claimant failed to perform her duties satisfactorily'.

See *Byrne v FT Ltd* [1991] IRLR 417 for the basic principles to consider when applying for such orders.

6.4.5.5   Disclosure of documents (Rules 29 and 31)

In *Sarnoff v YZ*, [2021] EWCA Civ 26, the Court of Appeal held that the power of the employment tribunal to make disclosure orders against parties derived from its general case management powers under Rule 29 and that Rule 31 was concerned only with disclosure against non-parties.

The power to order disclosure is discretionary. Again, a request should first be made to the other party before seeking an order. The tribunal has powers similar to those of the county court in ordering disclosure and inspection (CPR 1998, Part 31; see **Civil Litigation, Chapter 11**). Part 31 of the CPR 1998 provides for disclosure of:

(a)   the documents on which a party relies; and

(b)   the documents which:

    (i)   adversely affect a party's own case,

    (ii)   adversely affect another party's case, or

    (iii)   support another party's case.

Disclosure is not, therefore, solely dependent on relevance but rather whether the document is one on which a party relies, adversely affects their own or another party's case, or supports another party's case (see Linden J in *Santander UK PLC v Bharaj* (below)).

The main purpose of the disclosure and inspection stage of the litigation process is to enable the parties better to evaluate the strength of their opponent's case in advance of the trial. The parties have to reveal to each other the documents which have a bearing on the disputed issues in the case. The process is intended to promote settlements and therefore a saving in costs. It ensures that the parties are not taken by surprise at the trial and that the court has all relevant information in order to do justice between the parties.

As far as the CPR 1998 have been discussed in the employment context, the House of Lords in *Science Research Council v Nassé* [1980] AC 1028 set out the basic principles. Since then, the Court of Appeal held in *Canadian Imperial Bank of Commerce v Beck* [2009] IRLR 740 that:

> the test is whether or not an order for [disclosure] is necessary for fairly disposing of the proceedings. Relevance is a factor, but is not, of itself, sufficient to warrant the making of an order. The document must be of such relevance that disclosure is necessary for the fair disposal of the proceedings. Equally, confidentiality is not, of itself, sufficient to warrant the refusal of an order and does not render documents immune from disclosure. 'Fishing expeditions' are impermissible.

In the case of *Plymouth City Council v White* (UKEAT/0333/13), the EAT said that the sequence in a disclosure application is as follows:

(1)   The Judge must first consider if the document sought is relevant (if it is not, then it will not be ordered to be disclosed).

(2)   If it is relevant, the next question is whether it is necessary for the fair trial of the case for it to be ordered to be disclosed. Where there is objection, the Judge should examine the document itself so as to consider whether or not in a contention that it is confidential it should still be disclosed.

(3)   If the document is relevant and necessary and is to be disclosed, the Judge should consider whether there is a more nuanced way of disclosing the material so as to respect confidentiality [in this case, for example, there was an issue of child protection] and the Judge may then decide to order the document to be disclosed wholly or partially, usually by the system now known as redaction.

(4)   The disclosure Judge, having read the disputed documents should not conduct the full hearing unless the parties agree.

That basic approach was reiterated by the EAT in *Santander UK PLC v Bharaj* (UKEAT/0075/20), albeit with a caveat as to the use of the word 'relevant'. The EAT said that when an employment tribunal is considering whether to order specific disclosure of documents, it must decide whether the documents sought satisfy the test in Part 31 of the CPR 1998. While it may be convenient to use 'relevant' as shorthand for documents that must be disclosed, the word 'relevant' does not actually appear in the rule. In *Bharaj*, an employment tribunal made an order for disclosure of a number of specific documents created by Santander. The employment judge indicated that the nature of these documents suggested they were potentially relevant. Santander did not disclose any documents, stating that none of the documents were relevant to Ms Bharaj's claim. Ms Bharaj applied to strike out Santander's defence, arguing that Santander had not complied with the order for disclosure. The employment tribunal refused her strike-out application. Santander appealed the specific disclosure order. It argued that the tribunal had made an order for disclosure without first determining whether the documents were relevant. The EAT allowed the appeal. It held that an employment judge can only order specific disclosure of documents in accordance with CPR 1998, r 31.6. The judge must decide which documents or categories of documents meet the CPR 1998 test. It will then need to decide whether disclosure is necessary for a fair disposal of the proceedings. The applicant for a specific disclosure order must put materials before the tribunal to establish the case for a disclosure order, and the tribunal may hear evidence from the parties on this issue. In some cases, a tribunal might need to read the documents, but that is not always required. See too the recent case of *Tesco Stores Ltd v Element & Ors* (UKEAT/0228/20) where it was again emphasised that the guiding principle for disclosure is not simply relevance but whether a document is one on which a party relies, adversely affects their own or another party's case, or supports another party's case.

The Employment Tribunal Presidents of England and Wales and Scotland issued joint Presidential guidance on taking oral evidence by video or telephone from persons located abroad in April 2022: <www.judiciary.uk/wp-content/uploads/2015/03/Presidential-guidance-evidence-from-abroad-April-2022.pdf>.

Privilege

There are some circumstances in which a party will not have to allow the other party to inspect a disclosed document. One of those is where a party relies on the document being protected by legal professional privilege. The rules on privilege are also the same as those that apply in the civil courts. In brief, there are two types of legal professional privilege (which can be lost under the 'iniquity' principle – see *Abbeyfield (Maidenhead) Society v Hart* (UKEAT/0016/21) and below):

(a)   *Advice privilege*

Communications passing between a party and their legal advisers, or between a party's legal advisers, are privileged from inspection, provided they are written by or to the solicitor in their professional capacity and for the sole or dominant purpose of obtaining legal advice or assistance for the client. 'Legal advice' is not confined to telling the client the law; it includes information passed by solicitor to client, or vice versa, so that advice may be sought and given, and it includes advice about what should prudently and sensibly be done in the relevant legal context. Privilege is normally restricted to legally qualified advisers. In *Prudential plc v Special Commissioner of Income Tax* [2013] UKSC 1, the Supreme Court had identified that, for the purposes of legal advice privilege, a lawyer means either a barrister, solicitor or a member of the Institute of Legal Executives, and a solicitor must hold a current practising certificate.

Communications between an employer and, for example, a firm of HR advisers are not covered by legal advice privilege. In *Trentside Manor Care Ltd v Raphael* [2022] EAT 37, the advisers were not a firm of solicitors but had an HR and Employment Law advice team, headed by solicitors, in which all but one of the managers were legally qualified. The individual client advisers were not qualified. There can be privilege where, for example, a firm of solicitors is involved, and the advice falls to be treated as the advice of the lawyer concerned. But that was not the case on the facts. See further below.

Privilege does not extend without limit to all solicitor/client communications. The range of assistance given by solicitors to their clients has greatly broadened in recent times; for example, many solicitors now provide investment advice to clients. The scope of legal professional privilege has to be kept within reasonable bounds. See further *Three Rivers District Council and Others v Governor and Company of the Bank of England* [2004] UKHL 48, [2004] 3 WLR 1274. Nor does it extend to communications with third parties (see the (criticised) case of *Three Rivers DC and Others v Bank of England (No 5)* [2003] EWCA Civ 474 (between an employee and the company lawyer) and *Glaxo Wellcome UK Ltd v Sandoz* [2018] EWHC 2747 (Ch)). In *Prudential* (above), the House of Lords declined to extend the privilege to accountants who had given specialist tax advice even though they were a firm of professionals, and the privilege would have attached to precisely the same advice given by a solicitor.

The privilege extends to communications between a party and their solicitor's employee or agent, and also to communications between a party and a solicitor in their service, for example a solicitor to a government department or in a legal department of a commercial enterprise. The privilege also covers instructions and briefs to counsel, counsel's opinions, and counsel's drafts and notes.

There is an exception to legal advice privilege where 'sharp practice' or iniquity is involved. In X v Y Ltd (UKEAT/0261/17), the EAT held that an email sent by a lawyer to a client containing legal advice on the dismissal of an employee crossed the threshold of iniquity because it was in fact advice on how to use redundancy to cloak an unfair and discriminatory dismissal. As such, the advice was not protected by legal advice privilege. However, the Court of Appeal held that the employment tribunal had been right to strike out parts of the claim on the basis that they referred to an email which was privileged. The Court concluded that the advice was advice given 'day in, day out' by lawyers and disagreed with the EAT that the advice was iniquitous (see *Curless v Shell International Ltd* [2019] EWCA Civ 1710).

In *University of Dundee v Chakraborty* [2022] EAT 150, the EAT found that a first version of a grievance investigation report did not retrospectively attract legal professional privilege because it had been subsequently reviewed by lawyers. The claimant had raised a grievance which included allegations of harassment, bullying, discrimination and racial abuse, which was investigated and a report was prepared by a member of the University's academic staff. Their first version of the report was reviewed by external legal advisers and, as a result of their advice, changes were made to it. When tribunal proceedings were commenced by the claimant, the University disclosed the amended report, which had a note on it stating it had been amended and reissued following independent legal advice. Disclosure was sought of the first version of the report. The EAT rejected the submission that if disclosure of this was ordered, it could then be compared to the final version, and it would be possible to infer what the legal advice had been. The EAT held that the first version of the report was not privileged and there was no principle of law which would permit the document to attract legal privilege retrospectively.

(b) *Litigation privilege*

(i) Communications passing between the solicitor and a third party are privileged from production and inspection only if:

(1) they come into existence after litigation is contemplated or commenced (see *Director of the Serious Fraud Office v ENRC Ltd* [2018] EWCA Civ 2006 where the Court of Appeal held that criminal proceedings were reasonably contemplated when ENRC initiated an investigation into allegations made by a whistleblower); and

(2) they are made with a view to the litigation, either for the sole or dominant purpose of obtaining or giving advice in regard to it, or for obtaining evidence to be used in it. In the ENRC case (above) the Court of Appeal held that the notes of employee interviews were made with the dominant purpose of avoiding and/or dealing with litigation and met the test.

Examples of documents which may come within this head of privilege are a report from an expert obtained by a solicitor with a view to advising their client about existing or contemplated litigation, or witness statements obtained by a solicitor for the purpose of existing or contemplated litigation.

(ii)   Communications between the client and a third party are privileged if the sole or dominant purpose for which they were produced was to obtain legal advice in respect of existing or contemplated litigation, or to conduct, or aid in the conduct, of such litigation. It must be the case that litigation was reasonably in prospect at the time when the document was brought into existence, and that the sole or dominant reason for obtaining the document was to enable solicitors to advise as to whether a claim should be made or resisted, or to have it as evidence.

Where a client is not an individual, this form of privilege is also applied to communications between individuals within that organisation. Thus, a memorandum sent by one partner of a firm to another would be privileged if it was prepared for the dominant purpose of obtaining legal advice in respect of existing or contemplated litigation, or to aid the conduct of such litigation.

In *Scotthorne v Four Seasons Conservatories (UK) Ltd* (UKEAT/0178/10) the EAT decided that litigation privilege extended to protect advice given by a firm of employment law consultants to the employees and that the claimant did not have the right to inspect such communications. The EAT considered that legal advice given by non-legally qualified staff was not covered by legal advice privilege.

In *Trentside Manor Care Ltd v Raphael* [2022] EAT 37, the EAT held that tribunals should not order a party to disclosure documents to another party's legal representative where privilege is contested. The claimant applied for disclosure of communications between her employer and their advisers. The respondent claimed that such documents were protected by both litigation privilege and legal advice privilege. The advisers were not a firm of solicitors, but were an HR and Employment Law advice team, headed by solicitors, and in which all but one of the managers was legally qualified. However, the individual client advisers were not. The EAT held that it was not an appropriate exercise of the tribunal's discretion to make an order for the contested documents to be provided to the claimant's representatives (on the basis that they would not show the documents to the claimant herself) to determine the privilege issues. Privilege protects the relevant party from being required to disclose documents to anyone at all, and if documents had been provided to the claimant's solicitors or counsel this would almost certainly have created an irreconcilable conflict of interest. The respondent had in fact refused to comply with the order, and the tribunal had subsequently directed the respondent to provide the documents to the tribunal itself for the sight only of the judge deciding the issue. That decision was not challenged; but the EAT observed that such an order should be made only as a matter of last resort.

Waiver of privilege

The privilege is the client's and not the solicitor's, and therefore it may be waived by the client but not by the solicitor. Once a copy of a privileged document is served on the other side, the privilege is waived. Waivers cannot be selective if that would create a misleading impression or lead to unfairness. There is a well-established principle that a waiver of privilege on a specific matter applies to all material relevant to it: there should be no 'cherry picking'. But otherwise, there is no unfairness in disclosing privileged material relating to specific issues. See *Brennan and others v Sunderland City Council and others* [2008] ICR 479 and, most recently, *Watson v Hilary Meredith Solicitors* (UKEAT/0092/20) for cases on waiving privilege; in *Watson*, the EAT conducted a helpful review of the leading authorities on the subject.

Confidentiality

If one party is seeking the disclosure of documents which the other side regards as being of a confidential nature (eg references, assessments, etc), the judge should inspect the documents in order to satisfy themselves that disclosure is necessary. The judge will usually order disclosure where the content of the document is relevant and necessary to dispose of the case fairly (see, eg, *Nasse v SRC* [1979] IRLR 465; *Canadian Imperial Bank of Commerce v Beck* [2009]

EWCA Civ 619). If appropriate, parts of the documents may be covered up (redacted), for example the name of an employee.

Voluntary disclosure

There is no general duty of disclosure in the absence of an order. However, if voluntary disclosure is made, there is a duty not to be selective by withholding documents and creating a false impression.

Without prejudice communications

In general, without prejudice communications are not disclosable. One exception to that rule is where there is unambiguous impropriety. See *X v Y Ltd* (above).

In *Woodward v Santander UK plc* (UKEAT/0250/09), the EAT, after considering the leading modern authorities concerning the without prejudice rule and the policy underlying the rule (namely that parties should not be discouraged from settling their disputes by fear that something said in the course of negotiations might be used against them) went on to hold:

58.   Reading the judgment in *Mezzotero* as a whole, we do not think that it establishes any new exception to the without prejudice rule. In paragraph 38 Cox J expressly stated that she would regard the employer's alleged conduct as an exception to the without prejudice rule 'within the abuse principle'....

59.   We doubt whether Cox J intended to say that it was unnecessary, in a discrimination case, to find unambiguous impropriety. We appreciate that paragraph 38 of her reasons, in which she refers to 'the unattractive task of attaching different levels of impropriety to fact sensitive allegations of discrimination', can be read in that way. But Cox J went on to say that she regarded the employer's alleged conduct as 'within the abuse principle'.

60.   We would observe that the policy underlying the 'without prejudice' rule applies with as much force to cases where discrimination has been alleged as it applies to any other form of dispute. Indeed the policy may be said to apply with particular force in those cases where the parties are seeking to settle a discrimination claim.

61.   Discrimination claims often place heavy emotional and financial burdens on claimants and respondents alike. It is important that parties should be able to settle their differences (whether by negotiation or mediation) in conditions where they can speak freely. A claimant must be free to concede a point for the purposes of settlement without the fear that if negotiations are unsuccessful he or she will be accused for that reason of pursuing the point dishonestly. A respondent must be free to adhere to and explain a position, or to refuse a particular settlement proposal, without the fear that in subsequent litigation this will be taken as evidence of committing or repeating an act of discrimination or victimisation. And it is idle to suppose that parties, when they participate in negotiation or mediation, will always be calm and dispassionate. They should be able, within limits, to argue their case and speak their mind.

62.   What are the limits? To our mind they are best stated in terms of the existing exception for impropriety. This exception, as we have seen, applies only to a case where the Tribunal is satisfied that the impropriety alleged is unambiguous. It applies only in the very clearest of cases. A court or Tribunal is therefore required to make a judgment as to whether the evidence which it is sought to adduce meets this test. Words which are unambiguously discriminatory will of course fall within the exception: see the example given by Cox J at para 37 of *Mezzotero*.

63.   It may at first sight seem unattractive, given the fact sensitive nature of discrimination cases, to exclude any evidence from which an inference of discrimination could be drawn. But it would have a substantial inhibiting effect on the ability of parties to speak freely in conducting negotiations if subsequently one or other could comb through the content of correspondence or discussions (which may have been lengthy or contentious) in order to point to equivocal words or actions in support of (or for that matter in order to defend) an inference of discrimination. Parties should be able to approach negotiations free from any concern that they will be used for evidence-gathering, or scrutinised afterwards for that purpose.

64.   We therefore reject Mr Bacon's submission that there ought to be a wider exception to the without prejudice rule where discrimination is alleged. We do not think such an exception is

consistent with the policy behind the rule. We cannot see any workable basis for applying such an exception while preserving the parties' freedom to speak freely in conducting negotiations.

In *Swiss Re Corporate Solutions Ltd v Sommer* [2022] EAT 78, the EAT allowed an appeal against a tribunal finding of unambiguous impropriety thereby allowing a 'without prejudice' letter to be admissible in evidence. The EAT held that the 'without prejudice' protection was not removed from the letter from the employer to the claimant which contained exaggerated allegations by the employer against the employee. Mr Justice Bourne stated that '[w]here there was an arguable basis for the allegations, an Employment Judge at a preliminary hearing without oral evidence was not in a position to rule that the letter amounted to "unambiguous impropriety"'.

In *Portnykh v Nomura International plc* (UKEAT/0448/13), the employment tribunal held that the without prejudice rule did not apply as there was no 'dispute' in existence when certain correspondence was entered into. The EAT disagreed. It held, looking at the factual matrix prior to the exchange of correspondence, that there was clearly a dispute in existence: if an employer announces an intention to dismiss an employee for misconduct, and there are then discussions about an alternative manner of dismissal, there is either a present dispute or the potential for a future dispute.

These cases highlighted the problems which can arise where termination discussions take place when there is no existing dispute. As a result, the Government inserted a new provision (s 111A) into the ERA 1996 to extend 'without prejudice' protections to make it easier for employers to make 'without prejudice' offers to employees. See **6.5.4** below.

6.4.5.6 Witnesses

Tribunals almost invariably order that the parties' representatives prepare witness statements for the witnesses, and such statements stand as the witnesses' evidence-in-chief. The general rule (Rule 43) is that witness statements should not be read out but should be taken as read. In a case pre-dating the introduction of that rule, the President of the EAT gave guidance on the practice of reading out witness statements in tribunals. In *Mehta v Child Support Agency* (UKEAT/ 0127/10) he said that very often reading witness statements aloud 'achieves nothing of value' and 'wastes the time of tribunal and the parties', but that sometimes it might be helpful to read out a statement or part of a statement if matters might need clarifying or elucidation, or to help 'settle' an individual before he is cross-examined. He suggested that where both parties were represented, a procedure should be agreed. Where a party is not represented, a tribunal should ensure that they understand the implications of what is proposed. Tribunals were cautioned against having a policy of not allowing a claimant to read out their statement – the appropriate procedure should be decided on a case by case basis at the tribunal's discretion. The tribunal will also usually order that statements are exchanged on an agreed date. Further detail may be found in **Civil Litigation, Chapter 12**.

The power to order disclosure and to issue witness orders is discretionary. The tribunal will normally need to be satisfied that the witness's evidence/document is sufficiently relevant.

For a case on when an order compelling a witness to attend may be issued, see *Christie v Paul, Weiss, Rifkind, Wharton and Garrison LLP* (UKEAT/0137/19).

Joint Presidential guidance was issued in April 2022 on the taking of oral evidence by video or telephone from persons located abroad. Employment tribunals must have regard to the guidance, but they are not bound by it. See <www.judiciary.uk/wp-content/uploads/2015/03/ Presidential-guidance-evidence-from-abroad-April-2022.pdf>.

6.4.5.7   Unless orders

Rule 38 gives a tribunal powers to make an unless order, whereby if an order is not complied with by a specified date, the claim or response will automatically be dismissed. Rule 38(2) allows such orders to be set aside if it is in the interests of justice to do so.

In *McCarron v Road Chef Motorways & Others* (UKEAT/0268/18), HHJ Auerbach noted that:

> ... potentially the Rule 38 regime can give rise to as many as three decision points for the Tribunal. Firstly, a decision as to whether or not to make an Unless Order, and, if so, in what terms. Secondly, a decision as to whether to give written notice to the parties confirming that the Order has bitten, and a dismissal has occurred. As to that, although it is well-established that non-compliance with an Unless Order will have the effect of causing the relevant claim to be treated as dismissed without any need for further Order by the Tribunal, nevertheless, there may be an issue as to whether there has been non-compliance. If there is, a Judge will have to make some sort of determination as to whether there has, and hence whether a notice is to be issued. That determination is itself potentially amenable to appeal.

He also made the point that a claim should only be treated as dismissed for non-compliance when it can be said without doubt that on a strict reading of the Order there has indeed been such non-compliance, not merely on the basis of what might be said to be the spirit, but not in fact the letter of the Order.

In *Enamejewa v British Gas Trading Ltd* (UKEAT/0347/14), the EAT looked at the approach to be taken to an application to revoke an unless order made under Rule 38(2). The claimant was dismissed for gross misconduct in January 2013. He claimed that he had been wrongfully and unfairly dismissed, and that he had also been the subject of discrimination on the ground of race. The employers disputed all of his claims. A case management discussion took place on 4 June 2013, and the case was listed for a hearing in December 2013. Following an argument between the parties about what was to be included in the agreed bundle, the employers' solicitor applied for an unless order requiring the claimant to provide his witness statement by 27 November. On 21 November, the claimant was told to disclose his witness statement 'forthwith'; if he did not, an 'unless order' would be made on 22 November. On 22 November, the employers' solicitors said that the claimant had not provided the witness statement. On 27 November, an unless order was made to the effect that both sides were to exchange witness statements by 12 noon on 29 November; and unless that happened, 'the claim or response as appropriate shall stand dismissed without further order'. On 29 November, at 11.33 am, the employers' solicitors emailed their witness statements to the claimant. The claimant emailed his witness statement to the employers' solicitors at 12.08, eight minutes after the deadline. At 12.19, the employers' solicitors emailed the tribunal, pointing out that the claimant had not complied with the unless order and inviting the tribunal to treat the claim as struck out without further order. On 3 December, the employment tribunal stated that the claimant's complaints had been dismissed and cancelled the hearing. The claimant's application for a review was rejected. The claimant appealed. The EAT said that while the reasons for making an unless order in the first place are 'highly relevant factors', they are not only factors to consider when reviewing an unless order under Rule 38(2). Those factors can include events that have occurred subsequent to the making of the order, such as, for example, a sudden incapacity or power failure. As Underhill J (the EAT President) observed in *Thind v Salvesen Logistics Ltd* (UKEAT/0487/09):

> The tribunal must decide whether it is right, in the interests of justice and the overriding objective, to grant relief to the party in default notwithstanding the breach of the unless order. That involves a broad assessment of what is in the interests of justice, and the factors which may be material to that assessment will vary considerably according to the circumstances of the case and cannot be neatly categorised. They will generally include, but may not be limited to, the reason for the default, and in particular whether it is deliberate; the seriousness of the default; the prejudice to the other party; and whether a fair trial remains possible. The fact that an unless order has been made, which of course puts the party in question squarely on notice of the importance of complying with the order and the consequences if he does not do so, will always be an important consideration. Unless orders are an

important part of the tribunal's procedural armoury (albeit one not to be used lightly), and they must be taken very seriously; their effectiveness will be undermined if tribunals are too ready to set them aside. But that is nevertheless no more than one consideration. No one factor is necessarily determinative of the course which the tribunal should take. Each case will depend on its own facts.

The EAT remitted the case to the same Employment Judge, to reconsider in the light of the approach to the law set out by it.

A claim should only be struck out for non-compliance with an unless order when, qualitatively, there has been material non-compliance (see *Uwhubetine v NHS Commissioning Board England* (UKEAT/0264/18)). In that case, the Judge gives some useful guidance about the making and enforcing of unless orders. See too *Ijomah v Nottinghamshire Healthcare NHS Foundation Trust* (UKEAT/0289/19) and *Dykes v Whitbread Group plc* [2022] IRLR 499.

6.4.5.8 Judicial assessment and mediation

Employment Judges can suggest to the parties at a case management hearing that the case be referred to judicial assessment. Likewise, if the parties agree, a case can be referred to judicial mediation (see **6.6**).

Mediation involves bringing the parties together with an employment tribunal judge who will try to assist the parties to resolve their dispute. Mediation is private and confidential.

Judicial assessment is an impartial and confidential assessment by an Employment Judge, at an early stage of the proceedings, of the strengths and weaknesses of parties' claims.

Judicial assessment will generally be offered at the first case management hearing after the issues have been clarified and case management orders made. Paragraph 21 of the Presidential Guidance states:

> If the parties consent, the Employment Judge may then give an assessment of the liability and/or remedy aspects of the case. It will be made clear that the assessment is provisional and that the Employment Tribunal hearing the case may come to a different view. In conducting the assessment the Employment Judge must make it clear that they are assessing the case on the state of the allegations and not evaluating the evidence, which has not been heard or seen, and assessing provisionally the risks as to liability and, typically, brackets of likely compensation on remedy. The Employment Judge will encourage parties to approach the process with an open mind and to be prepared to enter into the assessment pragmatically and to be receptive and listen to the Employment Judge's views.

6.4.5.9 Withdrawal (Rules 51 and 52)

Rule 51 permits a claimant to withdraw all or part of a claim at any time, subject to costs.

Rule 52 provides that where a claim has been withdrawn, a tribunal shall issue a judgment dismissing it (which means that the claimant cannot bring a further claim against the employer raising the same complaint) unless the claimant indicates a wish to reserve a right to bring a further claim, or the tribunal believes it is not in the interests of justice to issue a judgment. Claimants need to be careful about the impact of a dismissal, which will prevent them from bringing a claim in the civil courts. The EAT reiterated the obligation on the tribunal to ensure that the withdrawal is clear and unambiguous before dismissing a claim in *Campbell v OCS Group UK Ltd* (UKEAT/0188/16).

6.4.6 Hearings – general

In *Rackham v NHS Professionals Ltd* (UKEAT/0110/15), the EAT looked at the tribunal's obligation to make reasonable adjustments to ensure that a claimant (with Asperger's syndrome and anxiety) was able to access and fully participate in the proceedings. The EAT said that when considering whether proposed adjustments were fair and reasonable, this had to be judged by reference to both parties, proportionality and making sure the hearing proceeded. The autonomy of the disabled person (including parties, witnesses and lawyers) is of great importance, and those who have disabilities are entitled to have their voice listened to. This will probably mean in practice that any reasonable adjustments need to be worked out (and agreed if possible) in advance of the commencement of the substantive hearing.

There are two different types of hearing that may be held: preliminary and final. The text below deals with preliminary hearings. The final hearing is examined at **6.4.7**.

The Court of Appeal held in *Ezsias v North Glamorgan NHS Trust* [2007] EWCA Civ 330 that where there are facts in dispute, it would be exceptional for a case to be struck out without hearing the evidence at a full merits hearing. Only if the facts alleged by the claimant disclose no arguable case should it be struck out.

Like many courts, following the Covid-19 pandemic and the subsequent restrictions, employment tribunals moved as best as they could to online modes of working wherever possible. Unlike many courts and tribunals, which needed specific legislation under the Coronavirus Act 2020, to allow them to use video hearings, Rule 46 of the Employment Tribunal Rules already provided that hearings could be conducted, in whole or in part, by use of electronic communication (including by telephone) provided that the Tribunal considers that 'it would be just and equitable to do so' and provided that 'the parties and members of the public attending the hearing are able to hear what the Tribunal hears and see any witness as seen by the Tribunal *so far as practical*' (our emphasis – inserted in September 2020). A complete set of Guidance, FAQs and Advisory Notes on remote hearings can be found on the Judiciary website at <www.judiciary.uk/coronavirus-covid-19-advice-and-guidance/#tribunals>.

On 19 March 2020, the Presidents of Employment Tribunals (England and Wales and Scotland) issued a Joint Direction regarding the listing of Employment Tribunal cases during the Covid-19 pandemic. That Direction was subsequently amended, reviewed and updated on a number of occasions. The Direction provided 'strong encouragement to Tribunals and parties to use electronic communications methods including skype for business and video conferencing technology where available, to conduct hearings of all kinds, where doing so is compatible with the overriding objective and the requirements of the Rules'.

Many employment tribunal hearing centres closed during lockdown. Initially all hearings scheduled after lockdown were converted to telephone case management hearings. On 1 June 2020, the Presidents of England and Wales and Scotland issued a 'road map', representing their joint – and 'partly aspirational' – plan, designed to increase gradually the number and type of hearings which could take place over the course of 2020 while pandemic-related restrictions remain in place. The Government gradually rolled out the use of a web-based platform, Cloud Video Platform (CVP), for remote and hybrid hearings in a number of jurisdictions, including employment tribunals. Over time, judicial mediations and simple full hearings started to be conducted remotely, or as hybrids, with Judges at home or in the employment tribunal offices and the parties present remotely, with a view to trying to relist multi-track cases.

The President of Employment Tribunals (England and Wales) issued a Practice Direction (<www.judiciary.uk/wp-content/uploads/2013/08/14-Sept-2020-SPT-ET-EW-PD-Remote-Hearings-and-Open-Justice.pdf>) and Presidential Guidance (<www.judiciary.uk/wp-content/uploads/2013/08/14-Sept-2020-SPT-ET-EW-PG-Remote-and-In-Person-Hearings-1.pdf>) on remote and in-person hearings in September 2020. The Practice Direction was issued in response to the Covid-19 pandemic. Readers should refer to the Practice Direction, which provides for wholly remote, partly remote (or in the tribunal) and sets out Directions about inspection of witness statements by observers, observation of a hearing and inspection of documents. The Presidential Guidance confirms that the format of the hearing is a judicial decision but that, of course, the parties can express their views. Helpfully, it sets out the factors that the judge might take into account and gives guidance as to the parties' responsibilities, electronic and printed documents, other safety measures and recording of the proceedings (it is a criminal offence to do so). An updated 'road map' for listing and hearing cases was issued in March 2022 (<www.judiciary.uk/wp-content/uploads/2013/08/ET-road-map-31-March-2022-final.pdf>).

From 28 June 2022, courts and tribunals were given new powers to allow reporters and other members of the public to observe hearings remotely. Part 13 of the Police, Crime, Sentencing and Courts Act 2022, which came into force on that date, contains provisions that allow specified courts and tribunals to make video or audio transmissions available to individuals who wish to observe court proceedings. The provisions apply to all courts across England and Wales and all UK tribunals (except for devolved tribunals in Wales, Scotland and Northern Ireland). This will therefore more clearly facilitate the remote observation of proceedings in employment tribunals (as well as in the Employment Appeal Tribunal). These provisions are specifically about *observing* proceedings remotely rather than *participating* in proceedings remotely. They give judges the powers to allow (i) the direct transmission of proceedings to identified individuals who have requested access to a hearing; and (ii) remote observation at designated live-stream premises (ie an overspill room). A judge will need to consider a number of factors when deciding whether to allow remote observation. Before making such a direction, the court must be satisfied that (a) it would be in the interests of justice to make it; (b) there is capacity and technological capability to enable transmission; and (c) giving effect to the direction would not create an unreasonable administrative burden. There is a list of mandatory considerations including the need for open justice; the timing of any access request and its impact on the business of the court; any issues that might flow from observation by people outside the UK; and any impact which the making or withholding of such a direction, or its terms, might have upon (i) the content and quality of the evidence; (ii) public understanding; (iii) the ability of the media and public to observe and scrutinise; and (iv) the safety and right to privacy of any person involved with the proceedings. In June 2022, the Lord Chief Justice and the Senior President of Tribunals issued practice guidance on the new powers: <www.judiciary.uk/guidance-and-resources/practice-guidance-on-remote-observation-of-hearings-new-powers/>.

6.4.6.1 Preliminary hearings (Rules 53–56)

Preliminary hearings are interim hearings, which should be held in private (unless they are determining any preliminary issue or whether to strike out a claim). Rule 53 allows the Employment Judge, at a preliminary hearing, amongst other things, to:

(a)   conduct a preliminary consideration of the claim and make a case management order;

(b)   determine preliminary issues (eg an issue as to whether the claim was brought in time, or whether the claimant has sufficient continuity of service or whether the employee was dismissed). The Employment Judge can give judgment at the hearing on preliminary matters, which may result in the proceedings being struck out so that a final hearing is no longer required (see Rule 37 below);

(c)   decide whether to order expert evidence. In *Morgan v Abertawe BRP Morgannwg University Local Health Board* (UKEAT/0114/19), the EAT held that tribunals should first decide if the evidence is reasonably required and only go on to consider the form if so (see also *De Keyser Ltd v Wilson* [2001] IRLR 324);

(d)   consider whether to strike out a claim (see **6.4.8.2** below);

(e)   order payment of a deposit under Rule 39 (see **6.4.8.4** below);

(f)   explore the possibility of settlement;

(g)   conduct a judicial assessment of the case (if the parties agree) (from 3 October 2016).

Rule 54, as amended by the Employment Tribunals (Constitution and Rules of Procedure) (Early Conciliation: Exemptions and Rules of Procedure) (Amendment) Regulations 2021, states that:

a preliminary hearing may be directed by the Tribunal on its own initiative at any time or as the result of an application by a party. The Tribunal shall give the parties reasonable notice of the date of the hearing and in the case of a hearing involving any preliminary issues at least 14 days' notice shall be given and the notice shall specify the preliminary issues that are to be, or may be, decided at the hearing.

6.4.6.2 Privacy and restrictions on disclosure (Rule 50)

Tribunals, like most courts, should hold most of their proceedings in open court (see ECHR, Article 6 and **6.4.14**). The principle that justice should be open is one of the foundations of the common law (see eg *Scott v Scott* [1913] AC 417 and *Global Torch Ltd v Apex Global Management Ltd* [2013] 1 WLR 2993) and applies as much to employment tribunals as to any other court. Rule 50, however, permits a tribunal at any stage of the proceedings to make an order to prevent or restrict the public disclosure of any aspect of the proceedings, if it considers it necessary in the interests of justice or in order to protect the Convention rights of any person. This gives a tribunal very wide powers to hold hearings or part of hearings in private, and to give anonymity to parties, witnesses and others.

The ETA 1996, ss 10–12 also give tribunals powers to make restricted reporting orders (RROs) in cases involving national security, confidential information, sexual offences or misconduct and disability. For a good summary of the case law to date, see *A and B v X, Y and Times Newspapers Ltd* (UKEAT/0113/18).

An order can prevent publication of the name of the applicant (or respondent, or other persons affected by the allegation, including the alleged perpetrators) or any other matter that is likely to lead to the identification of the individual in question. The RRO can last until the tribunal's written decision is sent to the parties. The order can include making the judgment anonymous. Any further restriction thereafter will have to be justified under the 'strictly necessary' common law test, 'balancing' as appropriate Convention (ECHR) rights of open justice (Article 6), privacy (Article 8) and freedom of expression (Article 10). Where an allegation of a sexual offence is involved, the central register (see **6.4.12**) may be altered to delete any 'identifying material'.

In *EF v AB* (UKEAT/0525/13), the EAT overturned an employment tribunal's refusal to extend an RRO following the bringing of tribunal proceedings by a former employee for constructive dismissal and sexual harassment. The claims involved lurid revelations and allegations of sexual misconduct made against a senior manager and his wife. The tribunal made an RRO under Rule 50 and s 11(1)(b) of the ETA 1996, preventing a number of individuals, and various corporate respondents, from being identified until the determination of liability and remedy. The tribunal also made a register deletion order, because the proceedings involved allegations of sexual offences. Meanwhile, the Chief Executive Officer (CEO) obtained an interim injunction in the High Court restraining the claimant from making the allegations public. The High Court privacy proceedings were then stayed pending the outcome of the tribunal case. The claims were eventually dismissed in their entirety, the tribunal finding them wholly without merit. The tribunal ordered that the RRO remain in force in respect of four individuals. However, it refused to make the RRO permanent in respect of the CEO and others and the corporate respondents. It referred to the 'substantial public interest' in the issues raised by the case, and applying the balancing test found that the interests of open justice outweighed the right to respect for private life under Article 8 of the ECHR. The CEO appealed and the EAT allowed the appeal. The EAT found that the tribunal had erred in considering that there was a public interest in the claimants' identities being revealed, and in giving weight to the right of other employees to know what was going on. The EAT held that the tribunal erred in concluding that the 'public interest' outweighed the CEO's right to privacy.

In *BBC v Roden* (UKEAT/0385/14), the EAT overturned an RRO that had been made at the conclusion of employment tribunal proceedings. The claimant had been dismissed after his employer had been informed that serious allegations of a sexual nature had been made against him in relation to young men with whom he had been in contact in the course of his work. He brought a claim for unfair dismissal. The employment tribunal made an order granting anonymity to the claimant throughout the hearing, because the allegations of serious sexual assaults would be raised at the hearing but, as they were not in issue, the tribunal would not have an opportunity to make a specific finding that the allegations were not proved, which would affect the claimant's reputation. In finding against the claimant on his substantive claim, the tribunal found that he had misled his employer about an earlier incident and that this was a fundamental breach of his employment contract. The BBC applied to set aside the earlier RRO. The employment tribunal refused this application. The central plank of the Employment Judge's reasoning was that the public would conclude that the claimant was guilty of the allegations. The BBC appealed to the EAT. It submitted that the Employment Judge had failed to properly balance the claimant's Article 8 rights against the principles of open justice and freedom of expression, and that as a result the anonymity order constituted a disproportionate and unlawful interference with those competing rights. It further contended that the Judge had failed to take account of relevant considerations and took account of irrelevant ones. The EAT agreed, holding that the anonymity order constituted a disproportionate and unlawful interference with the principle of open justice and the strong public interest in full publication. The decision in *EF v AB* (above) is an example of the same principles being applied to produce the opposite result, as the Article 8 rights of the parties in that case, and the lack of any discernible public interest, were found to outweigh the rights of freedom of expression under Article 10 and open justice under Article 6. The judgment in *Roden* provides a helpful summary of the principles relevant to anonymity applications, and is a useful reference point for consideration of the issues involved in these sorts of cases.

For a more recent case on Rule 50, see *TYU v ILA Spa Ltd* (UKEAT/0236/20), where the EAT, in overturning a tribunal decision to refuse an anonymity order in respect of a third party referred to in tribunal proceedings brought by two of her relatives, conducted a comprehensive review of the legal authorities around Article 8 privacy rights and the balancing exercise. See too *Fallows v News Group Newspapers* (UKEAT/0075/16) (a case relating to Elton John's hairdresser) where the employment tribunal, upheld by the EAT, and applying the balancing exercise, declined to make an order, and *A v Secretary of State for Justice* [2019] IRLR 108 where the EAT confirmed that there is no power to remove a judgment from the Public Register, save in national security cases, and which also contains useful guidance on the Rule 50 balancing exercise.

In *Frewer v Google UK Ltd & Ors* [2022] EAT 34, the respondent applied under Rules 29 and 50 of the Tribunal Rules for the names of its clients to be replaced with numerical codes. The tribunal ordered anonymity and that commercially sensitive information be redacted. The EAT allowed the appeal. It held that it was an error of law to require the anonymisation of clients without having regard to the right to freedom of expression under Article 10 of the European Convention on Human Rights (see Rule 50(2)) and/or to the cases that explain that the public interest would normally require the naming of those involved. The EAT ordered that the respondent's application for redaction be remitted to the tribunal. Readers are advised to read the judgment. It contains a useful summary of the principles involved.

There is a developing area of law to the effect that documents referred to in open court, including but not limited to witness statements and skeleton arguments, should be made available to the media on request (see R (on the application of Guardian News and Media Ltd) v City of Westminster Magistrates' Court [2012] EWCA Civ 420, Cape v Dring [2019] UKSC 38 and Guardian News & Media Ltd v Rozanov [2022] IRLR 487).

The House of Commons Justice Committee published a report on 1 November 2022 entitled 'Open justice: court reporting in the digital age'. See also **6.4.12** (publication of judgments online).

6.4.7 The final hearing (Rules 57–59)

6.4.7.1 Preparation for the final hearing

The date, time and place of the hearing will be fixed, and a notice of hearing sent to the parties. Before the date has been fixed, the parties will be asked for dates to avoid. The parties should then ensure that their witnesses will be available.

Before the hearing the parties should prepare a bundle of documents for use at the hearing. The tribunal will often direct who is responsible for preparing the bundle. It should include all correspondence and other documents on which the parties intend to rely, arranged in correct sequence and numbered consecutively. It is desirable, wherever possible, that there should be an agreed bundle. At least six bundles should be available at the hearing, one for each member of the tribunal, one for each side and one for use by the witnesses. Some tribunals ask for the bundle to be lodged in advance of the hearing, others prefer it to be brought to the tribunal on the day of the hearing.

6.4.7.2 Postponement

A new Rule 30 provides that applications to postpone the hearing must be made as soon as possible after the need arises, and that applications made less than seven days before the hearing is due to begin can only be granted where the parties consent, and it is appropriate to allow the parties to settle their dispute by agreement or otherwise in accordance with the overriding objective, or the application was necessitated by fault of the other party or there are exceptional reasons. Costs may follow (see **6.4.9**).

6.4.7.3 Constitution of the tribunal

The Employment Tribunals Act 1996 (Tribunal Composition) Order 2012 (SI 2012/988) allows an Employment Judge to hear unfair dismissal cases sitting alone. Employment Judges were already able to sit alone in certain circumstances, for example in cases brought under Pt II of the ERA 1996 (protection of wages), reg 30 of the Working Time Regulations (holiday pay entitlement) or where the parties consented to this (ETA 1996, s 4(3)). Section 4(5) of the ETA 1996 still provides that, in certain circumstances, an Employment Judge may order a hearing by a full panel, including where there is a likelihood of a dispute arising on the facts. Section 4(5) also provides that the views of any of the parties should be taken into account.

The EAT expressed some reservations about judges sitting alone, in *McCafferty v Royal Mail Group* (UKEATS/0002/12). Mr McCafferty was a postman with 19 years' service, who had been dismissed for gross misconduct by reason of alleged dishonesty. The lay members of the tribunal found the dismissal fair. The Employment Judge, in the minority, considered that the dismissal was unfair. On appeal, the decision of the majority that the dismissal was fair was upheld. Lady Smith pointed out that the lay members of the employment tribunal reached their conclusion drawing on their 'valuable common sense'. Lady Smith remarked that this underlines the need to give careful consideration to any views expressed by parties as to whether proceedings should be heard by an Employment Judge and members. The EAT decided in *Sterling Developments v Pagano* (UKEAT/0511/06) that the Employment Judge need not consider s 4(5) before hearing a case alone where neither party made representations.

There is also provision in the ETA 1996 (as amended by s 4 of the Employment Rights (Dispute Resolution) Act 1998) for hearings to be heard by a tribunal judge and one member where the parties consent.

6.4.7.4 The hearing

Subject to Rules 50 and 94, the final hearing shall be in public. It can determine liability and/or remedy and/or costs.

Post the Covid-19 pandemic, while some cases will revert back to socially distanced hearings in person, many cases will be heard remotely or as hybrids, with Judges at home or in the employment tribunal offices and the parties present remotely. Rule 46 of the Employment Tribunal Rules provides that hearings can be conducted, in whole or in part, by use of electronic communication (including by telephone) provided that the Tribunal considers that 'it would be just and equitable to do so' and provided that 'the parties and members of the public attending the hearing are able to hear what the Tribunal hears and see any witness as seen by the Tribunal'.

Approved platforms, in particular the web-based Cloud Video Platform (CVP), are being used for remote and hybrid hearings in a number of jurisdictions including employment tribunals. While a full discourse on the conduct of remote court sittings is beyond the scope of this text, those conducting and appearing in such hearings will need to adapt to new ways of working and presenting cases. Document management will need to be considered – will it be by reference to a hard copy of the documents (and the authorities) or will these be referenced by way of electronic bundles only, and if so, how? How will witnesses be sworn (those conducting a case may need to ensure ready access to the appropriate religious book). The strength of available internet connection may need to be investigated. Issues around open justice and ensuring access for vulnerable users and those less able to use technology all need to be taken account of. A Practice Direction on remote hearings and accompanying presidential guidance on the conduct of remote and in-person hearings during the pandemic in England and Wales was issued in September 2020 (see **6.4.6**).

Tribunals need to ensure that hearings are conducted in accordance with the overriding objective in Rule 2. In *Davies v Sandwell MBC* [2013] EWCA Civ 135, Mummery LJ said:

> Much of the evidence given at the first hearing was of little or no relevance to unfair dismissal, which was the only claim. The ETs are responsible for ruling on what is relevant and what is irrelevant. The parties and their representatives are under a duty to co-operate with the ETs by sticking to relevant issues, evidence and law. The ETs are not obliged to read acres of irrelevant materials nor do they have to listen, day in and day out, to pointless accusations or discursive recollections which do not advance the case. On the contrary, the ETs should use their wide-ranging case management powers, both before and at the hearing, to exclude what is irrelevant from the hearing and to do what they can to prevent the parties from wasting time and money and from swamping the ET with documents and oral evidence that have no bearing, or only a marginal bearing, on the real issues.

Hearings should only be permitted to be recorded by litigants in very rare circumstances, and only then under strict limits, held the EAT in *Heal v Oxford University* (UKEAT/0070/19). Section 9 of the Contempt of Court Act 1981 makes it a contempt of court 'to use in court, or bring into court for use, any tape recorder or other instrument for recording sound, except with the leave of the court'. It is a criminal offence to publish any such recording, and courts do not have power to give permission to publish any authorised recording. In *Heal*, the claimant said that his disabilities, which included dyslexia and dyspraxia, made it difficult for him to make a contemporaneous note of proceedings, and asked for permission to record his tribunal hearing. The tribunal directed that the application to record proceedings be made at a case management preliminary hearing, and the claimant appealed on the ground that it ought to have been decided before the preliminary hearing. The EAT dismissed the claimant's appeal. The EAT, acknowledging that s 9 of the 1981 Act gives a tribunal a discretion to allow a litigant to record proceedings, said that such permission should normally only be granted if there is a complete or partial inability to take contemporaneous notes, which results in a substantial disadvantage to the litigant. The EAT emphasised that even where such a recording is permitted, the tribunal's written notes of evidence remained the conclusive record of the hearing (although this might change if official digital recording of proceedings becomes routine). A possible alternative for a person in the claimant's position is to allow time at the end of each witness's evidence for the recording to be played back, to allow the litigant to formulate his questions and/or submissions.

6.4.7.5 Representation

The parties may appear in person, or be represented by a friend or any other person they desire, a union representative or a professional adviser (see ETA 1996, s 6) (see *Bache v Essex County Council* [2000] ICR 313 for a case on the right to appoint a representative of choice). In England and Wales, public funding is not available for representation at the hearing, although a solicitor may advise prior to the hearing under the Legal Help scheme (subject to the usual restrictions). Note that under the Financial Services and Markets Act 2000, non-lawyers are prohibited from representing or advising claimants and charging them a fee, unless they are formally registered with and regulated by the Regulated Claims Management Service. Breach of the registration requirements is punishable by up to two years in prison. Free representation does not need to be regulated. A party is not obliged to attend a hearing and a tribunal may hear a case in a party's absence without further inquiry (see *Cooke v Glenrose Fish Co Ltd* [2004] IRLR 866).

6.4.7.6 Adjournments

Occasionally, there will last minute requests for the adjournment of a hearing. While this can be frustrating for the other party and for the tribunal, care must be taken when deciding whether to accede to such an application. In *Mukoro v IWUGB* (UKEAT/0128/19), the EAT held that an employment tribunal had been wrong to refuse an adjournment and to strike out the claim where the claimant employee needed emergency dental treatment on the date and time fixed for the hearing of the respondent employer's application to strike out her claim for discrimination and other matters. The employer opposed the adjournment, arguing that the lack of medical evidence and procedural history suggested that the application could be regarded with suspicion. The tribunal judge refused any further adjournment and also struck out the claim on the ground that a fair hearing was no longer possible. The EAT (applying the Court of Appeal decision in *Teinaz v Wandsworth LBC* [2002] EWCA Civ 1040) referred to the Presidential Guidance on seeking a postponement of a hearing, and noted that a party or witness being unable to attend for medical reasons was a stated example of 'exceptional circumstances', and the Guidance explained how an employment judge should respond. If a party was unable to attend the hearing through no fault of their own, an adjournment had to be granted, and it would be a denial of justice not to do so because it would mean that the claimant would have no opportunity to resist a striking out order. The EAT also added that strike out had to be a proportionate response, and cases alleging abuse of process or discrimination were only to be struck out in the most obvious and plainest of cases (applying *James v Blockbuster Entertainment Ltd* and *Anyanwu v South Bank Students Union* above).

6.4.7.7 Opening the case

A tribunal is not obliged to stick to the list of issues decided at a case management hearing (*Mervyn v BW Controls Ltd* [2020] EWCA Civ 393).

The case will usually be opened by the side with the burden of proof for the first point in issue: for example, if it is alleged that the applicant has been constructively dismissed, the applicant will open. If there is no dispute as to dismissal, the respondent will open. Some tribunals will hear an opening speech, others prefer to hear witnesses immediately. There is generally no formal right to make an opening speech. An opening speech should briefly outline the facts (indicating areas of dispute), introduce the evidence and summarise the legal principles involved. In practice, opening speeches are very rare.

6.4.7.8   Presentation of evidence

Witnesses may give evidence under oath or by affirming. Pursuant to Rule 41, the rules of evidence are not strictly applicable. Rule 41 provides, inter alia:

> The tribunal shall seek to avoid undue formality and may itself question the parties or any witness so far as appropriate in order to clarify the issues or elicit the evidence. The tribunal is not bound by any rule of law relating to the admissibility of evidence in proceedings before the courts.

Therefore, for example, the tribunal can hear hearsay evidence. It is a matter for the tribunal to decide the weight to attach to such evidence. Often the witness will have signed a written statement, and this may be used as evidence-in-chief. The tribunal can, and very often will, order the exchange of statements before the hearing (see **6.4.4.5** above). Since April 2012, the general rule is that witnesses should not read out statements (see also **6.4.4.5** above). The tribunal may or may not allow supplementary questions by the witness's representative. This is then followed in the usual way by cross-examination and re-examination. The tribunal may intervene and ask questions of a witness at any time. This frequently happens.

Where a tribunal grants a witness order to a party, it should normally copy that to the other side (see *Jones v Secretary of State for Business, Innovation and Skills* (UKEAT/0238/16); Rules 32 and 60).

The overarching rule that governs the admissibility of evidence, including the making of witness attendance orders (see *Remploy Ltd v Lowen-Bulger* (UKEAT/0027/18)), is relevance. For further information, see **Civil Litigation**.

Increasingly, parties seek to rely on social media content as evidence in employment disputes: it may be used to undermine the evidence of a witness or a party (see, eg, *Gill v SAS Ground Services Ltd* (ET/2705021/09), *Young v Argos Ltd* (ET/1200382/11), *Teggert v TeleTech UK Ltd* (NIET/00704/11) and *Dixon v GB Eye Ltd* (ET/2203642/10)). Evidence of disparaging or offensive remarks about an employer, its products or a colleague may be produced (see, eg, *Whitham v Club 24 Ltd t/a Ventura* (ET/1810462/10), *Crisp v Apple Retail UK Ltd* (ET/1500258/11), *Taylor v Somerfield Stores Ltd* (ETS/107487/07) and *Smith v Trafford Housing Trust* [2012] EWHC 3221 (Ch)). Such content may not be in standard documentary form – it may be electronically stored, it may comprise screen shots, it may be available because a user has not paid much attention to his privacy settings, so that his personal information is accessible – but none the less it should still be included in any disclosure if it is material to the case.

Another evidential matter that is becoming increasingly common in tribunal hearings centres around the admissibility of covert recordings. Often employees record exchanges or conversations or even disciplinary hearings on mobile devices. Rule 41 gives tribunals very broad powers to 'regulate their own procedure', stating:

> The Tribunal may regulate its own procedure and shall conduct the hearing in the manner it considers fair, having regard to the principles contained in the overriding objective. The following rules do not restrict that general power. The Tribunal shall seek to avoid undue formality and may itself question the parties or any witnesses so far as appropriate in order to clarify the issues or elicit the evidence. The Tribunal is not bound by any rule of law relating to the admissibility of evidence in proceedings before the courts.

This Rule gives tribunals a very wide discretion in relation to the admissibility and exclusion of evidence. The EAT held in *HSBC Asia Holdings BV v Gillespie* [2011] IRLR 209 that, despite the absence of any express power, tribunals have the same powers as a civil court (see CPR 1998, r 32.1) with regard to the exclusion of evidence.

Tribunals will normally look first at whether any covert evidence that is sought to be admitted is relevant or material to any of the issues in the case. If it is, the tribunal will then move on to consider whether to exercise its discretion to admit or exclude that evidence. Even if evidence is relevant, tribunals have a discretion to exclude it.

One consideration that they will balance when deciding whether to exercise their discretion to admit such evidence is the public policy in preserving the integrity and confidentiality of employers' private deliberations. This has led, in some instances, to a distinction being drawn between recordings of hearings or discussions in 'public', ie when the employee is present, and deliberations that occur in 'private'. In *Chairman & Governors of Amwell View School v Dogherty* [2007] IRLR 198, the EAT held that 'no ground rule could be more essential to ensuring a full and frank exchange of views between members of the adjudicating body ... than the understanding that their deliberations would be conducted in private and remain private'.

Tribunals also have to bear in mind Rule 2 (see **6.4** above) which sets out that the 'overriding objective' is to 'enable Employment Tribunals to deal with cases fairly and justly'. The public interest in preserving private discussions will be balanced, for example, against the benefit of the tribunal having before it all the relevant evidence, particularly if there is a factual dispute between the parties that the evidence could help resolve. In *Amwell*, the EAT stated that:

> The balance between the conflicting public interests might well have fallen differently if the claim had been framed in terms of unlawful discrimination, where the decision was taken by a panel which gave no reasons for its decision, and where inadvertent recording of private deliberations (or the clear account of one of the panel members participating in those deliberations) had produced the only evidence – and incontrovertible evidence – of such discrimination.

On the other hand, Rule 2(b) provides that cases should be dealt with in ways that are proportionate to the complexity and importance of the issues. In *Vaughan v London Borough of Lewisham & Others* (UKEAT/0533/12), an employment tribunal refused to allow the claimant to produce 39 hours' worth of covert recordings of meetings between her, her colleagues and managers over the course of a year. The EAT, upholding the tribunal's decision, referred to the importance of proportionality and the need for a focused and selective application. The EAT said that it might have been different if the claimant 'produc[ed] the transcripts and the tapes of the material on which she wishe[d] to rely, and accompan[ied] them with a clear explanation of why they are said to be relevant'.

In *Punjab National Bank (International) Ltd & Others v Gosain* (UKEAT/0003/14), the claimant made allegations of sex discrimination, sexual harassment and constructive dismissal. She had made secret recordings of both the public and private parts of her grievance and disciplinary hearings. She alleged that the recordings contained evidence that inappropriate comments and considerations had occurred during the private parts of the employer's discussions. The evidence was admitted by the employment tribunal. On appeal, the EAT upheld that decision.

In *Wiggan v Wooler & Co Ltd* (UKEAT/0285/07), the EAT said that it will be rare for a case to be dismissed at half-time on the ground that it has no reasonable prospect of success (see the Court of Appeal decision in *Logan v Commissioner of Customs and Excise* [2004] IRLR 63).

6.4.7.9 Closing the case

Closing speeches may be made by the parties; whoever opened the case will make the final closing speech. The purpose of a closing speech is to review the evidence and to remind the tribunal of the relevant law.

6.4.7.10 The decision

The tribunal will then give its decision, with reasons (Rules 60–62). Rule 1 sets out the definitions of 'order', 'decision' and 'judgment'. A judgment is a decision which finally determines any part of a claim, including jurisdictional issues. The tribunal may give an oral decision immediately with oral reasons, or may follow an oral decision with written reasons. If the tribunal gives oral reasons for its decision, the parties may apply for written reasons. In complex cases, a decision may be reserved to a later date. The decision is formally recorded in a central register held at the Central Office of the Employment Tribunals in Bury St Edmunds (Rule 67). This register has been open to the public since February 2017. Sometimes a tribunal will adjourn at this stage to allow the parties to reach an agreement on quantum. Failing this, evidence will be heard relating to losses, etc (if not already dealt with in examination-in-chief during the hearing). Practice varies as to when the tribunal will hear evidence relating to quantum at the same time as liability.

Where there has been a hearing, an employment tribunal decision which is a judgment must (Rule 62(5)):

(a)   identify the issues which the tribunal has determined;

(b)   state the findings of fact relevant to the issues which have been determined;

(c)   concisely identify the relevant law;

(e)   state how that law has been applied to the findings of fact in order to decide the issues; and

(f)   where the judgment includes a financial award, include a table or other means of showing how the amount or sum has been calculated.

A failure to do this will amount to an error of law (see *Balfour Beatty Power Networks Ltd v Wilcox* [2007] IRLR 63). In *Meek v City of Birmingham District Council* [1987] IRLR 250, Bingham LJ (see in particular paras 8 to 12) provided useful guidance on the minimum requirements as to what should be contained in an employment tribunal judgment (a case decided under the old rules). Paragraph 8 stated as follows:

> It has on a number of occasions been made plain that the decision of an Industrial Tribunal is not required to be an elaborate formalistic product of refined legal draftsmanship, but it must contain an outline of the story which has given rise to the complaint and a summary of the Tribunal's basic factual conclusions and a statement of the reasons which have led them to reach the conclusion which they do on those basic facts. The parties are entitled to be told why they have won or lost. There should be sufficient account of the facts and of the reasoning to enable the EAT or, on further appeal, this court to see whether any question of law arises; and it is highly desirable that the decision of an Industrial Tribunal should give guidance both to employers and trade unions as to practices which should or should not be adopted.

In other words, tribunals must provide a sufficient outline of the complaint along with a summary of its conclusions and its reasons for reaching those conclusions, so that the parties have enough detail to be able to work out why the decision was made. In *Greenwood v NWF Retail* (UKEAT/0409/09) the EAT re-examined whether a tribunal's written reasons were sufficient. The EAT made it clear that an employment tribunal is required, amongst other things, to decide relevant facts and how those facts should be applied to the law, and that a failure to do so will amount to an error of law. The EAT commented that the 'constituent parts [of a judgment] will need to be more than a formal statement paying lip service to the subparagraphs of the rule'. See also, eg, *Mak v Wayward Gallery Ltd* (UKEAT/0589/10) and *Cossington v C2C Rail Ltd* (UKEAT/0053/13).

6.4.8   Awards

See **5.6** and **8.8** for the calculation of awards. The sum payable is due within 14 days of the judgment. Interest is payable (at 8%) from the day after the decision day, unless paid within 14 days. Unpaid awards must be enforced through the courts (see also **6.4.1.3**).

6.4.9   Costs

Costs are defined as 'fees, charges, disbursements or expenses incurred by or on behalf of the receiving party'. Unlike much civil litigation, costs do not follow the event in employment tribunals.

Although costs are not often awarded against the losing party in tribunal cases, there are limited powers to make costs orders (ETA 1996, s 13 and Rules 74–84 of the Tribunal Rules). Costs orders can be made where a party is legally represented or represented by a lay representative. A legal representative is defined as a person who has a general qualification within the meaning of s 71 of the Courts and Legal Services Act 1990 (Rule 74(2)). Tribunals also have a power to make preparation time orders where a party is not legally represented (see **6.4.9.3**). (See *Ladak v DRC Locums Ltd* [2014] ICR D39 and *Ramsay and others v Bowercross Construction Ltd and others* (UKEAT/0534/07).)

The Tribunals Service Quarterly Report for April–June 2020, published by the Ministry of Justice, shows that the total number of costs orders (not including preparation time or wasted costs orders) had decreased from 889 in 2013/14 to 177 in 2019/20, less than 0.2% of the total number of cases in the Tribunal system. The median award remains at around £2,500 and the average in the same period was £5,664.

Three sorts of costs orders may be made:

(a)   costs orders (**6.4.9.1** and **6.4.9.2**);

(b)   preparation time orders (**6.4.9.3**); and

(c)   wasted costs orders (**6.4.9.4**).

6.4.9.1   Costs orders

Employment tribunals are established under, and derive their powers from, regulations made under statute (see **Chapter 1**). It has been a consistent feature of those regulations that the power to make an order containing an award of costs against a party to proceedings before an employment tribunal has been subject to a restriction relating to conduct. Formerly, the power could only be exercised if, in the opinion of the tribunal, the party had acted frivolously or vexatiously in bringing or conducting the proceedings. The threshold was subsequently lowered by the addition of the words 'or otherwise unreasonably', and it was later further reduced by the addition of conduct that was abusive or disruptive. The Employment Tribunals (Constitution and Rules of Procedure) Regulations 2001 (SI 2001/1171) continued the trend towards a reduction of the threshold by including:

(a)   cases where the bringing or conducting of the proceedings by a party had been misconceived; and

(b)   cases where it was the conduct of the proceedings by the party's *representative* that had been vexatious, abusive, disruptive or otherwise unreasonable.

The rules on costs were further developed by the 2004 Tribunal Rules (SI 2004/1861). Rule 41(2) stated that a 'tribunal or Employment Judge may have regard to the paying party's ability to pay when considering whether it or he shall make a costs order or how much that order should be'. Rule 2(1) also provided that the term 'misconceived' (see (a) above – which appeared in Rule 40(3)), 'includes having no reasonable prospect of success'. The 2013 Rules (SI 2013/1237) made yet further changes by removing the second part of Rule 40(3) ('or the bringing or conducting of the proceedings by the paying party has been misconceived') and replacing it with the second limb of Rule 76(1), namely, that costs might be awarded where a 'claim or response had no reasonable prospect of success'. Underhill J, in his Review of Employment Tribunal Rules in June 2012, said that he saw 'no case for changing the substantive criteria for the award of costs'. As such, it is unlikely that this latter change was intended to make a substantive difference to the threshold test.

The general powers to make costs orders are now set out in Rule 76. Costs orders (including fees) may be made where a party is legally represented or represented by a lay representative. An unrepresented party can make a claim for a preparation time order (see below). Witness expenses come within the definition of 'costs order' in Rule 75, but they are dealt with separately in Rule 76 and different considerations apply. The circumstances in which a tribunal *must* make a costs order are set out in Rule 76(3): a tribunal *must* make a costs order against a respondent in an unfair dismissal case where reinstatement or re-engagement is in issue and a hearing has to be postponed because of the respondent's failure to adduce evidence about the availability of the suitable employment. There is no definition of what constitutes 'costs' in Rule 76. The EAT in *Sunuva Ltd v Martin* (UKEAT/0174/17) said that costs orders can be awarded in respect of costs incurred before a claimant receives the ET3 Response.

Under Rule 76(1) a tribunal *may* make a costs order in a wide variety of circumstances, as mentioned above, where it considers that a party (or that party's representative) has acted vexatiously (see *Attorney General v Barker* [2000] 1 FLR 759 and *Scott v Russell* [2013] EWCA Civ 1432), abusively, disruptively or otherwise unreasonably (see *Yerrakalva v Barnsley Metropolitan Borough Council and another* [2012] ICR 42) in bringing or conducting the proceedings (note that conduct prior to proceedings being commenced, or in the case of a respondent, from the date of filing an ET3, cannot found a costs order – see *Health Development Agency v Parish* [2004] IRLR 550) or any claim or response had no reasonable prospect of success (see *Radia v Jefferies International Ltd* (UKEAT/0007/18) and *Opalkova v Acquire Care Ltd* (UKEAT/0056/21), or an unfair dismisal hearing was postponed on the application of a party less than seven days before the hearing was due to begin. Rule 76 therefore provides a gateway as to when a costs (or preparation time) order can be made. A tribunal must first establish whether the power to award costs exists and then decide whether to exercise that discretion (*Lewald-Jezierska v Solicitors in Law Ltd and others* (UKEAT/0165/06)).

If a tribunal concludes that the commencement or pursuit of the claim was vexatious, abusive, disruptive or otherwise unreasonable, or had no reasonable prospect of success (see further below), then the tribunal must proceed to consider whether to make a costs order. However, it is not *obliged* to make a costs order – that process is discretionary. At this stage a tribunal may, but is not obliged to, take into account, both in terms of whether to make an order at all and, if so, the amount, the paying party's means (Rule 84).

In *AQ Ltd v Holden* (UKEAT/0021/12), the EAT said, at para 41:

> The threshold tests in Rule 40(3) are the same whether a litigant is or is not professionally represented. The application of those tests should, however, take into account whether a litigant is professionally represented. A tribunal cannot and should not judge a litigant in person by the standards of a professional representative. Lay people are entitled to represent themselves in tribunals; and, since legal aid is not available and they will not usually recover costs if they are successful, it is inevitable that many lay people will represent themselves. Justice requires that tribunals do not apply professional standards to lay people, who may be involved in legal proceedings for the only time in their life. As Mr Davies submitted, lay people are likely to lack the objectivity and knowledge of law and practice brought by a professional legal adviser. Tribunals must bear this in mind when assessing the threshold tests in Rule 40(3). Further, even if the threshold tests for an order for costs are met, the tribunal has discretion whether to make an order. This discretion will be exercised having regard to all the circumstances. It is not irrelevant that a lay person may have brought proceedings with little or no access to specialist help and advice.

But Judge Richardson continued:

> This is not to say that lay people are immune from orders for costs: far from it, as the cases make clear. Some litigants in person are found to have behaved vexatiously or unreasonably even when proper allowance is made for their inexperience and lack of objectivity.

Until 2004, there was no express provision about tribunals taking into account the paying party's means. Cases decided under the Tribunal Rules prior to 2004 need to be treated with some caution, as there was at that time no express requirement, nor provision of any machinery, for an inquiry into a party's means.

The current power is now set out in Rule 84 of the 2013 Rules, but it is still entirely a matter for the tribunal's discretion whether to take ability to pay into account (see *Vaughan v Lewisham LBC* [2013] IRLR 713). In *Jilley v Birmingham and Solihull Mental Health NHS Trust* (UKEAT/0584/06), the EAT considered the exercise by a tribunal of its discretion, under what was then Rule

40(3) of the 2004 Rules, whether to take into account the paying party's ability to pay. It held that if a tribunal decides not to do so, it should say why:

> If it decides to take into account ability to pay, it should set out its findings about ability to pay, say what impact this has had on its decision whether to award costs or on the amount of costs, and explain why. Lengthy reasons are not required. A succinct statement of how the Tribunal has dealt with the matter and why it has done so is generally essential. The Tribunal has no absolute duty to do so. … In many cases it will be desirable to take means into account before making an order; ability to pay may affect the exercise of an overall discretion, and this course will encourage finality and may avoid lengthy enforcement proceedings. But there may be cases where for good reason ability to pay should not be taken into account: for example, if the paying party has not attended or has given unsatisfactory evidence about means. A question for the Tribunal in this case will be whether to take into account means given that in any event it has no power to do so in respect of the first proceedings. It may or may not be desirable to do so; it will depend on the submissions which are made to the Tribunal. If the Tribunal decides not to take means into account, it should express that conclusion, and say why. If the Tribunal decides to take means into account, it will then need to set out its findings about ability to pay, decide whether to make a costs order at all in the light of the paying party's means, and if it does what the order should be; and it give succinct reasons for its conclusions.

In the case of *Arrowsmith v Nottingham Trent University* [2011] EWCA Civ 797, it was held that a costs order need not be confined to sums the party could pay, as it might well be that the party's circumstances would improve in the future. In *Chadburn v Doncaster & Bassetlaw Hospital NHS Foundation Trust* (UKEAT/0259/14), the EAT reviewed the legal framework and principles that should be considered when assessing the means of the paying party. It held that a costs award can still be made against a party who cannot afford to pay, if it is reasonable to believe that that party's financial situation might improve in the future: as the tribunal did not have to take the paying party's financial position into account at all when making a costs order, it must be able to take account of other matters.

The exercise of the tribunal's discretion is not dependent upon the existence of any causal nexus between the conduct relied upon and the costs incurred (*Macpherson v BNP Paribas (London Branch)* [2004] IRLR 558.). In *Barnsley Metropolitan BC v Yerrakalva* [2011] EWCA Civ 1255, the Court of Appeal had to look at the relationship between causation and the costs awarded, where a 100% costs order had been made in the respondent employer's favour. In *Yerrakalva*, the claimant's conduct in the proceedings was held to be unreasonable, which gave the employment tribunal jurisdiction to order costs. However, the Court of Appeal said, it did not follow that the claimant should pay all the Council's costs of the entire proceedings. The employment tribunal had rejected some of the Council's criticisms of the claimant. It had also criticised the Council for making more of a meal than was necessary to respond to the claimant's case. Those factors, the Court of Appeal said, are relevant to how the cost's discretion should be exercised, and operated against a 100% order in the Council's favour. Mummery LJ said:

> The vital point in exercising the discretion to order costs is to look at the whole picture of what happened in the case and to ask whether there has been unreasonable conduct by the claimant in bringing and conducting the case and, in doing so, to identify the conduct, what was unreasonable about it and what effects it had.

In *Casqueiro v Barclays Bank plc* (UKEAT/0085/12) (a case on wasted costs, looking at which costs or what part of the costs had been caused by the unreasonable conduct of the claimant), Slade J (at [22]–[23]) suggested that if a party wished to rely on limited evidence of his means, that evidence should be submitted with some level of formality: 'He should make a statement with supporting evidence for such an argument, such statement and documentation should be disclosed to the Respondent three weeks before any hearing and he should tender himself for cross-examination.' In *Shields Automotive Ltd v Grieg* (UKEATS/0024/10), the EAT said that where a tribunal has decided to have regard to a party's means, it is required to look at his whole means, and that included his capital resources.

When considering an application for costs on the basis that a claim or response had no reasonable prospect of success, under Rule 76(1)(b), a tribunal should consider each statutory cause of action separately. In *Opalkova v Acquire Care Ltd* (above), the ET1 contained six causes of action. The Tribunal found in favour of the claimant in three of six claims. One was conceded before trial, two succeeded at trial and three were dismissed. The claimant, who was unrepresented, sought a preparation time order on the basis that the responses to each of the three claims that succeeded had no reasonable prospect of success. This was refused by the tribunal. The EAT reviewed the definitions of 'claim' and 'complaint' in Rule 1 and confirmed that 'claim', in the context of an application for a costs or preparation time order, meant each separate cause of action was to be considered, rather than adopting an overview of the prospects of success of the entire ET1 or ET3:

> Accordingly, in rule 76 where reference is made to a response having no reasonable prospect of success, I consider that means the response made to each of the claims brought by the claimant, rather than the entirety of the response set out in the ET3 response form to all of the claims brought by the claimant in the ET1 claim form.

Determining that a claim or response did not have a reasonable prospect of success or that a claimant or respondent acted unreasonably in bringing/defending the claim is a threshold test that, if successful, results in the tribunal then having a discretion to make a costs or preparation time order. For each separate cause of action, there are three questions to determine:

(1)   (Objectively analysed when the claim/response was submitted) did it have no reasonable prospects of success; or alternatively at some later stage as more evidence became available, was a stage reached at which the claim/response ceased to have reasonable prospects of success?

(2)   At the stage that the claim/response had no reasonable prospects of success, did the claimant/respondent know that was the case?

(3)   If not, should the claimant/respondent have known that the claim/response had no reasonable prospect of success?

In summary, when considering a costs application, a tribunal must ascertain whether a party has acted vexatiously, abusively, disruptively or otherwise unreasonably either in bringing the proceedings (or part), or in the way the proceedings (or part) have been conducted; or whether the claim had no reasonable prospect of success. If any one or more of these threshold triggers is met then the tribunal must go on to consider whether to make a costs order, but is not obliged to make one. When exercising its discretion as to whether to make a costs order, the tribunal may, but is not obliged to, have regard to the paying party's ability to pay. Where the tribunal has decided to make a costs order, again it may, but is not obliged to, have regard to the paying party's ability to pay in determining the amount of the award.

As far as what might amount to unreasonable conduct, in *Topic v Hollyland Pitta Bakery* (UKEAT/523/11), HHJ Burke QC said (at [27]) that lies do not automatically lead to a finding of unreasonableness, but no lies do not mean there cannot be unreasonableness; it is necessary to '[l]ook at the whole picture bearing in mind that costs are rarely awarded in the [employment tribunal]'. In *Kapoor v Governing Body of Barnhill Community High School* (UKEAT/0352/13), the EAT held that an employment tribunal was wrong to find that a claimant had conducted her case unreasonably, such as to warrant a costs award against her, on the simple basis that she had given false evidence: the case had to be considered as a whole, including, for example, the fact that the school's efforts to have the claim struck out had not always found favour. *Beynon v Scadden* [1999] IRLR 700 is authority for the proposition that a litigant should be expected to take stock of matters once all evidence is disclosed and the weaknesses of a complaint are identified. To carry on after a fundamental weakness is revealed, may amount to unreasonableness. Likewise, a refusal of an offer to settle might form the basis of unreasonableness. See also *Radia v Jefferies International Ltd* (UKEAT/0007/18).

In *Nicolson v Highlandwear Ltd* [2010] IRLR 859, the EAT allowed an appeal against a tribunal's refusal to award costs against an employee, where the tribunal found it was open to an employee to pursue an unfair dismissal claim purely in order to obtain a 'simple finding' of unfair dismissal 'without the objective of obtaining money'. The EAT pointed out that the ET1 form specified only three remedies and, unlike a discrimination claim, there was no provision for a declaration as a remedy. Commentators have pointed out that an employee may bring a claim to clear his name. It is also, arguably, inconsistent with *Telephone Information Services Ltd v Wilkinson* [1991] IRLR 148, where the EAT held that an employer's offer to pay the maximum unfair dismissal compensation did not render it frivolous or vexatious for the employee to continue the claim when unfairness was not admitted.

The Court of Appeal offered some advice to tribunals when deciding whether to make costs orders in late withdrawal cases, in *McPherson v BNP Paribas* [2004] IRLR 558 (decided under the 2004 Rules but still of assistance). Mr McPherson had withdrawn his tribunal claim about two weeks before the hearing, citing ill-health. There were doubts about the extent of his ill-health. He had also failed to comply with a number of tribunal orders. The tribunal and the EAT held that the late withdrawal, when taken against the background of his non-compliance with tribunal orders, amounted to unreasonable conduct. He was ordered to pay all of BNP Paribas's costs. The Court of Appeal agreed that Mr McPherson had acted unreasonably, but allowed his appeal to the extent that it varied the amount of costs he should have to pay. It held (Mummery LJ) that

> it would be legally erroneous if, acting on a misconceived analogy with the CPR, tribunals took the line that it was unreasonable conduct for employment tribunal claimants to withdraw claims and that they should accordingly be made liable to pay all the costs of the proceedings. It would be unfortunate if claimants were deterred from dropping claims by the prospect of an order for costs on withdrawal, which might well not be made against them if they fought on to a full hearing and failed. ... withdrawal could lead to a saving of costs. Also, ... notice of withdrawal might in some cases be the dawn of sanity and the tribunal should not adopt a practice on costs, which would deter applicants from making sensible litigation decisions. On the other side, ... tribunals should not follow a practice on costs, which might encourage speculative claims, by allowing applicants to start cases and to pursue them down to the last week or two before the hearing in the hope of receiving an offer to settle, and then, failing an offer, dropping the case without any risk of a costs sanction. The solution lies in the proper construction and sensible application of rule [76 (the relevant rule under the 2013 Rules)]. The crucial question is whether, in all the circumstances of the case, the claimant withdrawing the claim has conducted the proceedings unreasonably. It is not whether the withdrawal of the claim is in itself unreasonable.

The EAT decided in *Ibarz v University of Sheffield* (UKEAT/0018/15) that employment tribunal fees can be reimbursed to the claimant, even if they were paid by the claimant's trade union. (There is an EAT decision to the contrary, but the authors' view is that this decision is correct.)

Note that the Judicial Review and Courts Act 2022 provides that tribunals (and the EAT) can now make pro bono costs orders. The money is to go to a prescribed charity providing such representation. This change is effected by adding new ss 194A–194C to the Legal Services Act 2007. The power applies where a party was represented by a legal representative and that representation was provided free of charge, in whole or in part. In deciding whether to make a costs order, the tribunal must have regard to whether, had the representation not been provided free of charge, it would have made a costs order and, if so, what the terms of the order would have been. The charity prescribed for these purposes is Access to Justice.

6.4.9.2 Amount of costs (Rule 78)

Costs include fees, disbursements or expenses incurred by or on behalf of a party in relation to the proceedings (Rule 74(1)). They can include the costs of an in-house employed lawyer (see Rule 74(2)).

A costs order can be made against a respondent in respect of issue and hearing fees, even if they have been paid by a third party such as a trade union or insurance company (see *Ibarz v University of Sheffield* (UKEAT/0018/15)).

The costs ordered will either be a specified sum summarily assessed not exceeding £20,000, an agreed sum or a sum assessed by detailed assessment carried out by the county court or tribunal (which may exceed £20,000) (Rule 78). Rule 84 states that a tribunal may have regard to the paying party's ability to pay when considering (i) whether to make a costs order, or (ii) how much it should be, but there is no absolute duty to take this into account (see *Jilley v Birmingham and Solihull Mental Health NHS Trust* (UKEAT/0584/06)). Readers are referred to **Civil Litigation** for further details. The employment tribunal will have regard to the CPR 1998 and their accompanying practice directions and, for summary assessment, the 'Guideline Rates'.

6.4.9.3 Preparation time orders

Tribunals have the power to make 'preparation time orders' (Rules 76–79), where parties are not legally represented, in respect of carrying out preparatory work relating to but not including the hearing. The grounds for making such orders are the same as for a costs order (Rule 76). The Rules allow a rate of £42 per hour (from 6 April 2022; the amount increases by £1 each year) (up to a maximum of £20,000), in the same circumstances in which costs orders may be made. This may include time spent by the party (or its employees). Rule 79 deals with the assessment of preparation time orders.

Where a party is represented for only part of the proceedings, the tribunal can award costs and preparation time orders (see *Dunhoe v Support Services Group Ltd (in liquidation)* (UKEAT/0102/15)).

The ERRA 2013 enables tribunals to award both preparation time orders and witness expenses to litigants in person. This became effective from 25 June 2013.

6.4.9.4 Wasted costs orders (Rules 80–82)

Rule 80 permits tribunals to make a 'wasted costs' order against a party's representative (except not-for-profit representatives) as a result of 'any improper, unreasonable or negligent act or omission' by the representative. In *Mitchells Solicitors v Funkwerk Information Technologies* (UKEAT/0541/07), the EAT said that the threshold for a wasted costs order was high. The representative must not only have acted improperly, unreasonably or negligently, but must also have lent assistance to proceedings which amount to an abuse of process. Rule 80 is based on the wasted costs provision set out in s 51(7) of the Senior Courts Act 1981 for civil courts. The Court of Appeal's guidance on s 51(7), as set out in *Ridehalgh v Horsefield* [1994] 3 WLR 462, is therefore relevant and should be consulted.

In *Ratcliffe Duce & Grammer v Binns* (UKEAT/0100/08), the EAT confirmed that a wasted costs order cannot be made against a solicitor simply because the employment tribunal thinks that the client's pursuance of his claim is unreasonable and that the solicitor should have known that it was. The EAT repeated the three-stage test in *Ridehalgh* (above):

(1)   Has the legal representative of whom complaint is made acted improperly, unreasonably, or negligently?

(2)   If so, did such conduct cause the applicant to incur unnecessary costs?

(3)   If so, is it in the circumstances just to order the legal representative to compensate the applicant for the whole or any part of the relevant costs?

(See *Godfrey Morgan Solicitors Ltd v Cobalt Systems Ltd* [2012] ICR 305 for useful guidance.)

In *Hafiz and Haque Solicitors v Mullick* (UKEAT/0356/14), the EAT held that an employment tribunal erred in making a wasted costs order against a solicitor based on an inference that an unrealistic schedule of loss produced by the solicitor gave the claimant unreasonable expectations and prevented the claim's being settled earlier. The relevant principles were set out by the House of Lords in *Medcalf v Weatherill* [2002] UKHL 27, which emphasised the difficulties faced by a representative responding to an allegation of negligent conduct in circumstances where legal professional privilege prevented the representative from revealing details of the instructions given and the material provided by the client. The EAT said that tribunals should be 'very slow' to make wasted costs orders in cases where legal professional privilege prevented a representative from revealing details of the client's instructions.

In *Isteed v London Borough of Redbridge* (UKEAT/0442/14) the EAT again repeated the three-stage test set out in *Ridehalgh* (above) and held that the tribunal had focused only on question (1) and had not addressed the causation question. The tribunal must conduct a rigorous examination of the conduct in question and identify the improper, unreasonable or negligent acts relied upon. Mere allegations will not suffice (see *Wentworth-Wood v Maritime Transport Ltd* (UKEAT/0184/17)).

6.4.9.5 Financial penalties on employers that lose at tribunal

From April 2014, employment tribunals have the power to impose a penalty of up to £20,000 on a losing respondent employer, payable to the Secretary of State, where the employer's breach of the employee's rights 'has one or more aggravating features' (Enterprise and Regulatory Reform Act 2013, s 16, introducing s 12A into the Employment Tribunals Act 1996). 'Aggravating features' is not defined, although the explanatory notes to the 2013 Act provide non-exhaustive examples. If a financial award is made against the employer, the penalty must be 50% of that, subject to the £20,000 (since April 2019) maximum penalty. The employer can pay only 50% of the penalty if he pays within 21 days. By 2017, just £17,704 had been paid under the scheme (Margot James, then Business Minister).

In April 2016, a new Part 2A was inserted into the Employment Tribunals Act 1996 and came into force to introduce a new scheme for warning and penalising employers who fail to pay tribunal or settlement sums under a COT3. The penalty is 50% of the unpaid sum to a maximum of £5,000. Interest will accrue on the penalty. The penalty is payable to the Government (not the party awarded the sum due). In December 2018, BEIS introduced a scheme to name employers who fail to pay employment tribunal awards of £200 or more. However, names have not yet been released.

6.4.10 Reconsideration of tribunal decisions (Rules 70–73)

A party may, within 14 days, ask for decisions and judgments of the tribunal to be reconsidered where it is in the interests of justice. The tribunal can also reconsider of its own initiative. See *Sodexho v Gibbons* (UKEAT/0318/05) for a decision about tribunals' powers of reconsideration (decided under the 2004 Rules but still helpful) and *Outasight VB Ltd v Brown* (UKEAT/0253/14) (decided under the new Rules). Most recently, the EAT provided guidance on the procedure for reconsideration applications in *TW White & Sons Ltd v White* (UKEAT/0022/21).

6.4.11 Appeals to the EAT

An appeal may be made from a decision of the employment tribunal, on a point of law only, to the EAT (ETA 1996, s 21). As with employment tribunals, the EAT must guard against substituting its own subjective response to an employer's conduct (see *Brent v Fuller* [2011] ICR 806). The EAT must pay proper regard to the decision of the employment tribunal, 'to whom Parliament has entrusted the responsibility of making what are, no doubt sometimes, difficult and borderline decisions' (see *Bowater v North West London Hospitals NHS Trust* [2010] IRLR 331).

Determining what is the difference between a question of law and findings of fact and inference is crucial but difficult: an error of law can be found if a tribunal fails to make a finding of fact where there is uncontroverted evidence, or has made a finding contrary to all the evidence. But there is no error of law where some evidence points one way and some evidence points another way (see *Yeboah v Crofton* [2002] IRLR 634 and *Brent v Fuller* [2011] ICR 806). Nor may an appellant try to reargue factual issues.

The procedures of the EAT are governed by rules in the Schedule to the Employment Appeal Tribunal Rules 1993 (SI 1993/2854), which have been amended on a number of occasions, most recently by the Employment Appeal Tribunal (Amendment) Rules 2013 (SI 2013/1693), to bring them into line with changes to the Employment Tribunal Rules. Any appeal must be made within 42 days after written reasons are sent out by the tribunal. The EAT's time-limit is enforced strictly (see, eg, the Court of Appeal's decision in *Greg O'Cathail v Transport for London* [2012] EWCA Civ 1004). In *Haydar v Pennine Acute Hospitals NHS Trust* [2018] EWCA Civ 1435, the Court of Appeal refused to extend time for a claimant to submit his appeal, after his original was lost in the post. When the employment tribunal sends out judgments to parties, it refers in its standard letter to a booklet entitled 'The judgment', which says that a party appealing should make a check with the EAT if no acknowledgement of the appeal is received within seven days. The claimant waited six weeks before checking with the EAT, and the Court of Appeal found that the claimant had failed to check with the EAT soon enough and his delay was serious and significant. However, in *Rana v London Borough of Ealing* [2018] EWCA Civ 2074, where the tribunal failed to send a judgment to the correct address, the Court of Appeal said that this was a situation where the discretion to allow an appeal 'out of time' should be exercised. Responses are due 28 days after notification of the appeal. The EAT confirmed in *Hargreaves v Evolve Housing and Support* [2022] EAT 122 that if the tribunal makes a correction to its judgment, the 42-day time limit continues to flow from the date of the original decision and not from the date of the correction, *unless* a new decision is issued in substitution for the old, and replacing it entirely.

In July 2021, a new electronic filing system came into operation at the EAT, which enables parties to lodge their appeals with the EAT, upload documents and access all their appeals. It provides an additional method of lodging documents; it is not compulsory, although it may become so for professionally represented parties in the future. The new system is known as CE-File. An explanatory guidance note has been issued by the President of the EAT.

A Practice Direction dealing with EAT procedure came into force on 19 December 2018. The Rules set out instructions as to the documents to be submitted when lodging an appeal, improve the procedures for weeding out unmeritorious appeals, and contain costs rules for the EAT, in line with the costs rules for employment tribunals.

Previously, most EAT cases were determined by a panel consisting of a judge and lay members. The ERRA 2013, which received Royal Assent on 25 April 2013, requires all EAT cases to be heard by a judge alone, unless a judge orders otherwise or any order specifies that certain proceedings are to be heard by a panel. The change applies to all EAT hearings that started on or after 27 June 2013.

6.4.12 The public tribunal register

Claims which are settled are not matters of public knowledge. Since late 2016, all employment tribunal judgments (including preliminary hearing decisions and written reasons) go online (see <www.gov.uk/employment-tribunal-decisions>). There are only two exceptions – national security (Rule 94) or the interests of justice necessary to protect Convention (ECHR) rights (Rule 50).

In *Ameyaw v PwC Services Ltd* (UKEAT/0244/18), the EAT emphasised the importance of open justice, which included the principle that cases are held in public and judgments are publically available. It would only rarely be the case that no judgment at all would be published. As the hearing was conducted in open court, without anonymity there was no reasonable expectation of privacy. Just because the public record might be painful or humiliating did not mean it should not be made public. The Court of Appeal agreed in *L v Q Ltd* [2019] EWCA Civ

1417. Other than in cases involving national security, judgments must be published on the register.

6.4.13 Enforcement

Employment tribunals are not responsible for enforcement of an award. This must be done in the civil courts as if it were a county court judgment.

Section 27(1)–(4) of the Tribunals, Courts and Enforcement Act 2007, which came into force on 1 April 2009, removed the previous requirement to register unpaid tribunal awards before they could be treated as enforceable. Claimants may go directly to the county court (or High Court) for enforcement. Form N322B, which is available on the court services website at <http://www.hmcourts-service.gov.uk>, needs to be completed to allow enforcement of a decision or an Acas settlement (Form COT3).

Employers or individuals who fail to pay employment tribunal or EAT awards in England and Wales, will now be added to the *Register of Judgments, Orders and Fines* once enforcement proceedings are brought against them (Register of Judgments, Orders and Fines (Amendment) Regulations 2009 (SI 2009/474)).

6.4.14 Funding

Apart from paying privately, there are a number of other options:

(a) *Legal aid*. This is only available for complaints under the Equality Act 2010, and is subject to complex financial conditions and does not cover advocacy in the employment tribunal (but does so in the EAT). For further information, see the Legal Aid, Sentencing and Punishment of Offenders Act 2012.

(b) *Damages-based agreements*. These are arrangements whereby the representative takes an agreed percentage of the damages the client receives, up to a maximum of 35% (excluding disbursements which can be charged on top). Readers should refer to the Damages-Based Agreements Regulations 2013 (SI 2013/609) and the Courts and Legal Services Act 1990 (amended 2013).

(c) Conditional fee agreements. Readers should refer to the Courts and Legal Services Act 1990 (amended 2013). Success fees cannot be recovered from the opponent.

For a good overview of the above types of funding, see **Civil Litigation** at **2.4**.

6.4.15 Human Rights Act 1998

Under Article 6 of the ECHR, everyone is entitled, 'in the determination of his civil rights and obligations', to 'a fair and public hearing within a reasonable time by an independent and impartial tribunal established by law'. Any party to an employment-related dispute, whether it takes place in the courts or before a tribunal, is therefore entitled to a fair trial. Case law from Strasbourg has suggested, however, that employment disputes may not come within the definition of 'civil rights and obligations' because they are essentially concerned with private rights. Nonetheless, under the HRA 1998, courts and tribunals are obliged to act compatibly with the HRA 1998 (s 6), and therefore, when determining an employment dispute between private parties, will still have to apply Convention rights.

Inherent in the concept of a fair trial is equality of arms between the parties. This may render the lack of legal representation in employment tribunal proceedings open to challenge, although because such proceedings are set up to be conducted in a practical and straightforward manner, without undue formality, such a challenge may not succeed. The ECtHR has held that the unavailability of legal assistance in respect of complex issues is a breach of the principles of a fair trial. The Scottish Executive made a decision to make public funding available in some circumstances to individuals pursuing employment cases in Scotland amid fears that a failure to do so is in contravention of Article 6. Public funding is available where the claimant can show that his claim is arguable and too complex for him to litigate without assistance. The Lord Chancellor stated on 5 July 2001 that he was 'confident' that the public funding in England and Wales is fully compliant with the ECHR. (See too the judgment of the Supreme Court in *Coventry v Lawrence* [2015] UKSC 50.)

Readers should refer to **Chapter 15** for cases involving the HRA 1998.

6.5   SETTLEMENTS

Many complaints are settled without a hearing. In the first quarter of 2018–19, for example, 69% of all cases were withdrawn or settled before a full hearing. 25% were settled through Acas. Only 8% of cases were determined at a final hearing by the tribunal. The usual terms of settlement involve the employee agreeing not to start or proceed with a claim in consideration of the employer making a monetary payment and sometimes agreeing to provide a reference. Employers should be careful when providing a reference in these circumstances. A negligent reference that causes loss may be actionable by the recipient (*Hedley Byrne & Co Ltd v Heller & Partners Ltd* [1964] AC 465) or by the employee (*Spring v Guardian Assurance plc and Others* [1994] 3 All ER 129) (see **1.7.1.5**). Even in cases where the employer has a reasonable chance of success, it may be worth settling to avoid the cost of a tribunal hearing. This is a commercial decision to be taken by the employer. The effect of the recoupment regulations is also avoided (see **5.7.2.4**).

There has been a lot of controversy about the use and contents of confidentiality provisions or 'gagging clauses' in internal NHS whistleblower cases and #MeToo sexual harassment and abuse claims. In March 2018, the Solicitors Regulation Authority (SRA) issued a warning notice about use of non-disclosure agreements that they must not be used to prevent disclosure of otherwise reportable conduct, or as a means of 'exerting' inappropriate influence over people not to make disclosures which are protected by statute or reportable to regulators or law enforcement agencies. The SRA warns that failure to comply with the notice may lead to disciplinary action (see <www.sra.org.uk/solicitors/guidance/warning-notices/use-of-non-disclosure-agreements-ndas--warning-notice/>). The issue came into focus in the case of *Arcadia Group and Others v Telegraph Media Group Ltd* [2018] EWCA Civ 2329; [2019] EWHC 96 (QB); [2019] EWHC 223 (QB).

In March 2019, the Government launched a consultation to seek evidence and views on the use of confidentiality clauses in the employment context. That consultation closed on 29 April 2019. It drew a distinction between confidentiality clauses as used in contracts of employment (generally for legitimate reasons, such as protecting commercially sensitive information and preventing confidential information being shared with competitors (see **1.8.7**)) and confidentiality clauses as used in settlement agreements, where it was noted that, in a minority of cases, these were being used to silence workers, and to cover up criminal acts in the workplace, including sexual harassment, assault, as well as discrimination. Separately, in June 2019, the Woman and Equalities Parliamentary Select Committee published its report into the use of confidentiality clauses.

In July 2019, DBEIS announced that there would be new legislation to 'tackle the misuse of non-disclosure agreements in the workplace'. While it was noted that non-disclosure clauses could be used for a number of legitimate purposes, it was acknowledged that there was evidence that a minority of employers were misusing such clauses. The proposed new legislation will seek to prohibit clauses being used in employment contracts to prevent individuals from disclosing information to relevant authorities and individuals (see **1.8.6**). As far as the use of such clauses in settlement agreements is concerned, the Government proposes to extend current legislation so that individuals signing non-disclosure agreements will get independent legal advice to cover the nature and limitations of any confidentiality clause and the disclosures the individual is still entitled to make. Any clause in a settlement agreement that does not meet the new wording requirements will be void in its entirety.

These proposed reforms form part of a wider response to sexual harassment in the workplace (see **Introduction**). It is not clear when these proposals will come into effect.

In August 2019, the Law Society launched a new public education initiative to help the public understand their rights when faced with non-disclosure agreements. It also published a leaflet on 'NDAs and confidentiality agreements – what you need to know as a worker'. This points out that confidentiality agreements may be part of an employment contract or the terms of an engagement (see **1.8.6**) but also that confidentiality clauses are often contained in settlement agreements which resolve disputes between employers and workers. The leaflet advises of the importance of getting independent legal advice on any clause that places legal restrictions on workers.

In October 2019, the EHRC issued its own guidance on the use of confidentiality agreements. This does not have any statutory force but is a useful resource in determining good practice in this area, and readers are referred to it for more detailed guidance. See too *Duchy Farm Kennels Ltd v Steels* (below at **6.5.3**) for the impact of a breach of a confidentiality clause in a settlement agreement. Such clauses may need to be expressly described as 'conditions' to make the settlement obligations unenforceable.

6.5.1 ERA 1996, s 203

Section 203 of the ERA 1996 provides that any provision in an agreement is void in so far as it purports to exclude or limit the operation of any of the provisions of the Act, or to preclude a person from bringing any proceedings under the Act before an employment tribunal (this prevents an employee waiving their statutory rights – such as relating to unfair dismissal, redundancy payment, discrimination or holiday pay), unless:

(a)   a conciliation officer has taken action under s 18 of the ETA 1996; or

(b)   a written agreement (a 'settlement agreement') is entered into.

Other than by involving Acas, a settlement agreement is therefore the only way in which an employee can effectively waive any statutory claims. Although it is not legally necessary to use this route to waive purely contractual disputes (such as breach of contract, notice, contractual holiday pay), it makes sense to include everything in one document.

6.5.2 Acas settlements

Conciliation officers are designated by Acas. Where a complaint is presented to a tribunal, it is the duty of the Secretary of the Tribunals to send copies of all documents to an appropriate conciliation officer. The officer's duties are to promote a settlement and ensure that both parties understand its effect. He does not have a duty to ensure that the settlement is fair (*Moore v Duport Furniture Products Ltd* [1980] IRLR 158, CA). He must be involved in promoting the settlement. He will not merely 'rubber-stamp' an agreement already reached between the parties. Any settlement achieved in this way is recorded on a COT3. A COT3 will be a legally binding and enforceable contract.

Note that personal injury claims cannot be settled through Acas, but if both parties agree, waivers in respect of existing claims can be included in the agreement.

It is common practice to exclude all possible claims by the employee in return for the settlement. However, care should be taken in drafting. In *Bank of Credit and Commerce International SA (in liquidation) v Ali and Others (No 1)* [2001] 2 WLR 735, the House of Lords held that a COT3 agreement containing a general release under which the employee accepted an additional payment on being dismissed for redundancy which was expressed as being 'in full and final settlement of all or any claims whether under statute, common law or in equity of whatsoever nature that exists or may exist' did not preclude a claim for 'stigma' damages which the parties could not have contemplated at the time the agreement was signed because the decision in *Malik* was not handed down until some eight years later. The House of Lords held that clear language leaving no scope for doubt is needed for an employee to be held to have intended to surrender rights and claims of which they were unaware and could not have been aware. Similarly, in *Royal National Othopaedic Hospital Trust v Howard* [2002] IRLR 849, the EAT held that an agreement settling a complaint of sex discrimination which was stated to be 'in full and final settlement ... of all claims which the applicant may have against the respondent' did not preclude her from bringing a victimisation claim later. The EAT held that, if such a result is intended, the language must be absolutely clear and leave no room for doubt that the agreement relates to future claims.

6.5.3   Settlement agreements

In order for a settlement agreement to be binding it must comply with the following conditions:

(a)   it must be in writing, identify the adviser, relate to the particular complaint and state that the relevant statutory conditions are satisfied,

(b)   the employee or worker must have received advice from a relevant independent adviser as to the terms and effect of the proposed agreement and, in particular, its effect on his ability to pursue his rights before an employment tribunal, and

(c)   there must be in force, when the adviser gives the advice, a contract of insurance, or an indemnity provided for members of a profession or professional body, covering the risk of a claim by the employee or worker in respect of loss arising in consequence of the advice.

A person is a relevant independent adviser:

(a)   if he is a qualified lawyer;

(b)   if he is an officer, official, employee or member of an independent trade union who has been certified in writing by the trade union as competent to give advice and as authorised to do so on behalf of the trade union;

(c)   if he works at an advice centre (whether as an employee or a volunteer) and has been certified in writing by the centre as competent to give advice and as authorised to do so on behalf of the centre; or

(d)   if he is a person of a description specified in an order made by the Secretary of State, eg a Fellow of the Institute of Legal Executives employed by a solicitors' practice.

However, a person is not a relevant independent adviser:

(a)   if he is employed by or is acting in the matter for the other party or a person who is connected with the other party;

(b)   in the case of a person within (b) or (c) above, if the trade union or advice centre is the other party or a person who is connected with the other party;

(c)   in the case of a person within (c) above, if the complainant makes a payment for the advice received from him; or

(d)   in the case of a person within (d) above, if any condition specified in the order in relation to the giving of advice by persons of that description is not satisfied.

A qualified lawyer is a barrister or solicitor who holds a practising certificate.

The conditions are applied strictly, such that if any one of the conditions is not satisfied the agreement is not binding.

Note: The settlement agreement must relate to a 'particular complaint'; a settlement agreement which seeks to exclude all possible claims will fall foul of ERA 1996, s 203, which contains restrictions on contracting out of statutory rights. In *Sutherland v Network Appliance Ltd* [2001] IRLR 12, the applicant's employment with the respondent was settled on agreed terms by way of a settlement agreement. The terms stated that the settlement was in 'full and final settlement of any claims you may have against the company'. The EAT confirmed that the agreement was void in respect of statutory claims but held that the agreement was enforceable to the extent that it contained a compromise of contractual claims. Thus a settlement agreement must only seek to settle those statutory claims which have already been raised (either by presentation to the tribunal or raised by the employer prior to the issue of proceedings). The Court of Appeal gave guidance on settlement agreements in *Hinton v University of East London* [2005] IRLR 522. Smith LJ stated that it is not adequate for settlement agreements to use 'a rolled up expression such as "all statutory rights"'. Instead the particular proceedings must be identified, 'either by a generic description such as "unfair dismissal" or by reference to the section of the statute giving rise to the claim'. She agreed with Mummery LJ's statement that 'it is good practice for the particulars of the nature of the allegations and of the statute under which they are made or the common law basis of the alleged claim to be inserted in the ... agreement in the form of a brief factual and legal description'. Readers should pay careful attention to this case when drafting settlement agreements.

Where an agreement is concluded either through a conciliation officer or as a settlement agreement, any proceedings will normally be adjourned generally. If the employer complies with the agreement, the employee is barred from continuing with his complaint. If the employer does not comply with the agreement, the employee can either return to the tribunal to continue with the complaint, or sue for breach of contract in the county court or High Court or the tribunal itself.

In *Collidge v Freeport plc* [2008] EWCA Civ 485, the Court of Appeal held that an employer was entitled to withhold payment under a settlement agreement where the employee was in breach of a warranty he had given in the agreement, whereby the employee stated that he knew of no circumstances which would amount to a repudiatory breach of contract.

Where a settlement does not bind an employee, any sums paid under it will be taken into account by the tribunal in making any award. However, as a result of s 124(5) of the ERA 1996, the maximum compensatory award (£78,335 as at April 2015) must be applied after all deductions have been made.

Whatever method of settlement is used, the employee's adviser should ensure that any personal injury claims or claims arising out of employment pension benefits are expressly excluded from the settlement. There is an ongoing, unresolved, debate as to whether future rights can be settled using a settlement agreement.

On 29 July 2013, Acas published a Statutory Code of Practice on Settlement Agreements. Failure to follow the Code will not automatically make an employer liable, but tribunals can take the guidance into account. The Code states that as a general rule, a minimum of 10 calendar days should be given for parties to consider terms and take independent advice. It also states that it would be best practice at such meetings to allow employees to be accompanied by a work colleague or trade union official. The Code includes a basic model form of settlement agreement. Typically, such an agreement will look to contain provisions relating to:

- any contractual payments due up to and on termination;
- any ex gratia payment as compensation for loss of employment and/or in consideration for the waiver/withdrawal of claims;
- an express waiver;
- provisions as to any ongoing confidentiality obligations.

Care should be taken to ensure that such clauses are drafted so as not to be seen as preventing individuals from raising legitimate public interest or safety concerns, such as those listed in the Public Interest Disclosure Act 1998 (see **Chapter 5**). The EHRC has suggested that such clauses should not be used in public sector settlements;

- provisions as to any ongoing restrictive covenants;
- practical provisions, such as payments into pensions;
- contributions to legal fees;
- indemnities regarding the tax treatment of any payments (it will usually be the obligation of the employee to declare payments to HMRC).

In October 2019, the EHRC issued its own guidance on the use of confidentiality agreements. While it does not have statutory force, it contains useful practical guidance and recommendations for employers. Readers should also look out for any further regulatory guidance from the Solicitors Regulation Authority and the Law Society. This is also an area where legislation may be forthcoming following the Government's recent consultation on the use and abuse of non-disclosure agreements (see Introductory Note).

Note, in *Solomon v University of Hertfordshire*, that the EAT, in an obiter comment, said that an offer of £500 plus VAT to allow an employee to take full advice on a settlement offer, while sufficient to cover advice on the 'terms and effect' (ERA 1996, s 203), was 'wholly unrealistic' for a solicitor to advise on the merits of the claim and the likely award of compensation, which 'would require reading and consideration on a quite different scale'.

Care must be taken when drafting settlement agreements that they do not infringe certain statutory requirements. In *Bathgate v Technip UK Ltd* [2022] EAT 155, the EAT refused to allow an employer to rely on a settlement agreement that was concluded before the claimant knew whether or not he had a claim. The claimant claimed he had been discriminated against on the ground of his age when his employer decided not to pay him a pension payment because of his age. The respondent said that the claimant had settled any claim he might have for age discrimination when he had accepted a redundancy package which among other things waived his right to claim for age discrimination. The employment tribunal's ruling that on ordinary contractual principles he had lawfully settled his claim was overturned by the EAT. It relied upon s 147 of the Equality Act 2010 which did not permit settlement of claims before they had arisen and said that on a sound construction of the words 'the particular complaint', the Equality Act 2010 limited settlement to claims that were known to the parties. Lord Summers decided:

> [The claimant] signed away his right to sue for age discrimination before he knew whether he had a claim or not. While that may be possible at common law, the [Equality] Act restricts parties' ability to do so. ... [T]he inclusion of a claim in a [settlement] agreement defined merely by reference to its legal character or its section number does not satisfy the language of [the Equality Act]. The words 'the particular complaint' suggest that Parliament anticipated the existence of an actual complaint or circumstances where the grounds for a complaint existed. I do not consider that the words 'the particular complaint' are apt to describe a potential future complaint.

Conclusion

In order to comply with the above requirements, non-disclosure agreements in sexual harassment and discrimination settlements should:

- make it clear to workers that they still maintain some disclosure rights even when they sign a non-disclosure agreement;
- spell out the non-disclosure agreement's limitations and the types of disclosures that are not prohibited by it; and
- ensure that workers receive independent legal advice specifically on any confidentiality provisions and their limitations.

Many types of clauses are either already prohibited by Solicitor Regulation Authority rules or will most likely be prevented by the Government's proposed new legislation, for example wording which:

- limits or restrict a worker's rights to discuss a matter with the police or report a crime without fear of reprisal;

- improperly threatens litigation or other adverse consequences, or otherwise exerts inappropriate influence over a worker to stop them making disclosures which are protected by statute, or reportable to regulators or law enforcement agencies;

- impedes a worker from making protected disclosures to protect the public interest (whistleblowing);

- deters a person from cooperating with a criminal investigation or prosecution; or

- seeks to improperly influence disclosure or cooperation.

In *Duchy Farm Kennels Ltd v Steels* [2020] EWHC 1208 (QB), the High Court found that a former employee's breach of a confidentiality clause in an Acas-conciliated settlement agreement did not entitle Duchy Farm to cease settlement payments which has been provided for in the agreement as it was not a condition. The confidentiality clause in that case was held to be an 'intermediate term' and the breach was not so serious as to amount to a repudiatory breach. Confidentiality clauses tend to be generically included in such agreements. If confidentiality is considered to be of significant importance, it may be necessary to expressly stipulate that it is a condition of the agreement and make provision for any breach.

6.5.4 Pre-termination negotiations – protected conversations

The ERRA 2013 included a new provision in the ERA 1996 (s 111A) to make it easier for employers to make settlement offers to employees without this being admissible in subsequent unfair dismissal proceedings. Claims for automatically unfair dismissal are excluded by s 111A(3) (see *Harrison v Aryma Ltd* (UKEAT/0085/19) for a case where the employee alleged that she was dismissed because she was pregnant). The relevant provision (s 14) came into force on 29 July 2013 and inserted a new s 111A into the ERA 1996. Before this section was introduced, the common law 'without prejudice' rule prevented any statement made during a 'without prejudice' discussion from being used in a court or a tribunal (see **6.4.5.5** on without prejudice communications). Section 111A of the ERA 1996 allows greater flexibility, so that confidential discussions may be initiated as a means of negotiating the ending of an employment relationship without the need for an 'existing dispute', with such discussions being protected from disclosure unless there has been improper behaviour. Where a valid settlement agreement is concluded, an employee will be unable to bring an employment tribunal claim. Where a settlement agreement is not concluded, such that an employee can still bring a claim, s 111A will exclude evidence about termination discussions in unfair dismissal cases. An employer is therefore able to make an offer to 'pay off' an employee before any performance management or disciplinary proceedings have started, and before any dispute has arisen between them. Such offers are admissible in evidence in discrimination claims and any claims of automatically unfair dismissal, and also admissible if anything 'improper' is said or done. The Acas Statutory Code gives guidance on what might constitute improper behaviour, including:

- bullying and intimidation through the use of aggressive behaviour or offensive words

- putting undue pressure on a party, eg by not giving reasonable time for consideration

- saying that if a settlement proposal is rejected, the employee will be dismissed.

The first appellate judgment on s 111A was given by the EAT in *Faithorn Farrell Timms LLP v Bailey* (UKEAT/0025/16). The EAT noted that case law on 'without prejudice' discussions was not applicable to pre-termination negotiations, and s 111A had to be read on its own terms. Claims not covered by s 111A (eg discrimination) would still be governed by normal 'without prejudice' principles, so evidence may be admitted for a discrimination claim but remain excluded regarding unfair dismissal. The EAT held that the protection of s 111A is broader than it is for 'without prejudice' communications, in that it covers not just the content of a protected conversation but also the fact of them taking place. It would also cover an employer's internal discussions about a protected conversation. Section 111A did not allow for any waiver of the protection, although it noted that the 'improper behaviour' exception was broader than the 'unambiguous impropriety' test required to admit 'without prejudice' communications. See also *Greco v General Physics UK Ltd* (UKEAT/0114/16) and *Lenlyn UK Ltd v Kular* (UKEAT/0108/16) for two other cases looking at the impact of this provision. The EAT held in *Graham v Agilitas IT Solutions Ltd* (UKEAT/0212/17) that an employer cannot seek to use the s 111A shield in relation to part of a discussion but at the same time seek to rely on other parts of the same discussion to raise disciplinary allegations. In *Basra v BJSS Ltd* (UKEAT/0090/17), the EAT held that there is an exception to the general rule that pre-termination discussions cannot be referred to, namely where the date of the termination is in dispute:

> The chronological dividing line between what is, and what is not, admissible ... lies on the point at which the contract is terminated. ... where there is a dispute as to whether or not the contract was terminated on a particular date, the Tribunal would not be in a position to say what evidence should be excluded until that dispute is determined.

Acas has published a code of practice on settlement agreements which includes guidance on how to carry out settlement negotiations.

6.5.5   Recording the settlement

Once a claim has been presented, this needs to be withdrawn by the claimant in one of two ways:

(a)   the terms of the settlement may be recorded and registered with the employment tribunal on Form COT3. This is the usual method used where a settlement is reached after a conciliation officer has taken action;

(b)   alternatively, the claimant may merely decide to withdraw his claim to the tribunal, for example in compliance with a settlement agreement. Form COT4 can be used for this purpose, or a letter to the tribunal will suffice.

6.6   ALTERNATIVES TO TRIBUNAL PROCEEDINGS

Acas was given power to run a statutory arbitration scheme, as an alternative to the employment tribunal for unfair dismissal cases, by the Employment Rights (Dispute Resolution) Act 1998. The ACAS Arbitration Scheme (England and Wales) Order 2001 (SI 2001/1185) is intended to be 'confidential, informal, relatively fast and cost-efficient'. Procedures are 'non-legalistic' and flexible. Awards are final, with very limited opportunity to appeal. The scheme applies only to unfair dismissal complaints or claims under the flexible working law (see **14.19**). Full details of the scheme, including a guide to the scheme, may be found on the Acas website <http://www.acas.org.uk>. To use the scheme, both the employer and the employee must agree to enter into voluntary arbitration. An Acas officer will listen to the arguments of both sides and decide whether compensation should be awarded and, if so, how much.

The arbitrator cannot deal with 'jurisdictional matters' (eg whether the worker was an employee; whether the complaint was presented in time; or whether the employee has sufficient continuity of service). A dispute is referred to arbitration by the parties entering into an arbitration agreement. A waiver form under which the parties agree to arbitration and waive the right to return to the employment tribunal must accompany the agreement. If the employee withdraws from the scheme his claim is dismissed. The employer cannot unilaterally withdraw from the scheme.

Once the parties have agreed to arbitration the procedure in outline is as follows.

At least 14 days before the arbitration hearing each party must send to the Acas Arbitration Section:

(a)   a written statement of case;

(b)   supporting documents;

(c)   a list of witnesses.

In deciding whether the dismissal was fair or unfair, the arbitrator must have regard to general principles of fairness and good conduct rather than legal rules. He must still apply EU law and the HRA 1998. Witnesses cannot be cross-examined by the parties; it is for the arbitrator to establish facts.

The arbitrator's decision must identify the reason for dismissal, the main considerations taken into account in reaching the decision, state the decision, the remedy awarded and the date it was made. Awards are binding and there is generally no right of appeal.

As indicated above (see **6.4.5.8**), Employment Judges can suggest to the parties at the case management discussion that the case be referred to judicial mediation. Judicial mediation is voluntary and provides parties to an employment tribunal claim with a confidential, alternative settlement option that tries to avoid the need for a full merits hearing. Over 65% of cases mediated reach a successful conclusion on the day. It operates in addition to, and not as a substitute for, the role of Acas or privately negotiated settlements. A Presidential Guidance Note on Alternative Dispute Resolution, incorporating Guidance on Judicial Mediation, was issued on 22 January 2018. It sets out details as to the rationale and the procedure to be adopted for judicial mediation of a claim. The judicial mediation takes place in private. A trained Employment Judge acts as an impartial mediator to try to help the parties to resolve their dispute. This judge will not hear the case if the mediation fails.

The principal criteria which identify cases as being suitable for judicial mediation are:

(a)   a full hearing has been fixed for the substantive issues of at least three days in length;

(b)   the case will often involve at least one element of discrimination – cases where a claimant is still employed may be particularly suitable;

(c)   the claims are generally single claims, but occasionally judicial mediation can incorporate small multiples (ie two or three claimants);

(d)   there must be no proceedings in other jurisdictions; and

(e)   there must be no insolvency involved.

If a settlement is achieved, the terms are agreed in writing. The parties may finalise the settlement terms by entering into a compromise agreement or by using a COT3 Form if Acas is involved. The Law Society has now published a Practice Note to support judicial mediation. This is available at <http://www.lawsociety.org.uk/productsandservices/practicenotes/judicialmediation.page>.

Acas also offers a pre-claim conciliation scheme. The details are available on the Acas website (see above).

6.7   OVERLAPPING CLAIMS AND AWARDS

A dismissed employee may have more than one potential claim against his employer. For example, a dismissal that is both unfair and without proper notice or within a fixed term may give rise to both an unfair dismissal claim and a wrongful dismissal claim. If an employee is unfairly selected for redundancy, he will be entitled to a redundancy payment and be able to present an unfair dismissal claim. All three claims of wrongful dismissal, redundancy payment and unfair dismissal would be available to the employee unfairly dismissed without proper notice by reason of redundancy.

6.7.1 Wrongful and unfair dismissal

The wrongful dismissal claim is a breach of contract action which may be brought as a court action or pursued in an employment tribunal. The unfair dismissal claim is pursued only in an employment tribunal. Both may be pursued. In the case of a less well-paid employee who is entitled to only a short period of notice, the unfair dismissal claim is usually more advantageous, as compensation for future loss may extend beyond the employee's notice period.

If both claims are brought, and both succeed, the basic principle is that compensation will not be awarded for the same loss twice. The tribunal will deduct the breach of contract damages awarded from the compensatory award for unfair dismissal.

6.7.2 Redundancy payment and unfair dismissal

The redundancy payment will be set against the unfair dismissal award. Usually it will simply offset the basic award, but if it exceeds the basic award (eg because the basic award has been reduced by contributory fault) the remainder will reduce the compensatory award. The excess redundancy payment should be deducted *after* the other deductions (eg for contributory fault) have been made (see **5.6.2.2**).

6.7.3 Redundancy payment and wrongful dismissal

Since a redundancy payment is a reward for past services, and a wrongful dismissal payment is an award for future loss, a redundancy payment is not taken into account in awarding damages for wrongful dismissal.

6.7.4 A discriminatory dismissal

If a person is dismissed for reasons relating to a protected characteristic, such as sex or race, this is not automatically unfair but, in practice, will often be found to be unfair.

A claim for unfair dismissal may be pursued alongside a discrimination claim. Discrimination awards are not subject to any maximum figure and may include an award in respect of injured feelings. In addition, no eligibility conditions need be satisfied. As against this, the award for unfair dismissal includes a basic award in addition to compensation. Alternatively, re-engagement or reinstatement may be ordered. If both claims are pursued, s 126 of the ERA 1996 provides that compensation cannot be awarded again in respect of any loss or other matter which has already been taken into account in dealing with the other claim. (See **Chapters 8–13** for further details of discrimination claims.)

6.7.5 Compensation

The general rule of the compensation regime is that the employee cannot be compensated twice for the same *financial* loss.

1. Compensation in respect of time spent at work
• unfair dismissal basic award
• redundancy payment
• no other regimes
NB Employee will not be paid both

> **2.   Compensation in respect of actual losses**
> - unfair dismissal compensatory loss to date of employment tribunal hearing
> - wrongful dismissal damages (eg notice)
> - discrimination pecuniary loss claims to date of employment tribunal hearing
>
> **NB**   Employee can recover these only once

> **3.   Compensation in respect of future losses**
> - unfair dismissal compensatory loss from date of employment tribunal hearing
> - discrimination future pecuniary loss claims from date of hearing
>
> **NB**   Employee can recover these only once

See further the diagram set out below.

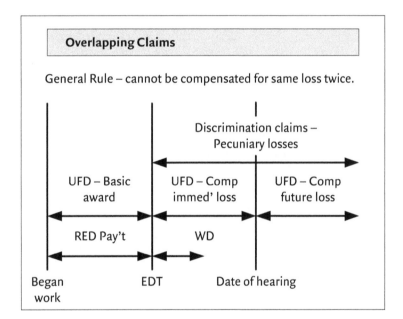

Overlapping Claims

General Rule – cannot be compensated for same loss twice.

Discrimination claims –
Pecuniary losses

UFD – Basic
award

UFD – Comp
immed' loss

UFD – Comp
future loss

RED Pay't

WD

Began
work

EDT

Date of hearing

6.8　CASE STUDY: UNFAIR DISMISSAL

(1)　Chronology and facts

(2)　Particulars of response

(3)　Tribunal orders

(4)　Witness statement

(5)　Judgment

IN THE GUILDSHIRE EMPLOYMENT TRIBUNAL　　　　CASE NUMBER: 1234/2021

BETWEEN

MRS JANE MINNERY　　　　　　　　Claimant

- and -

GUILDSHIRE PRIMARY CARE TRUST ('PCT')　　　　Respondent

CHRONOLOGY of
EVENTS

NUMBER	EVENT	DATE
1	Claimant commences employment with the Respondent	08/09/2014
2	Claimant's daughter made allegations of child abuse – Claimant's children taken into care	26/01/2021
3	Claimant's children voluntarily accommodated per Section 20 of the Children Act 1989	29/01
4	Claimant contacts acting senior nurse manager to notify Respondent of need to take emergency annual leave – no mention of superseding allegations	29/01
5	A one-week sick note is received by the Respondent from the Claimant	05/02
6	A further ten-day sick note received by the Respondent from the Claimant	09/02
7	Case Conference meeting – children placed on the Child Protection Register for emotional and physical abuse & Respondent notified	09/02 14/02
8	Claimant informed of her suspension by the Respondent	15/02
9	Children returned to the family home	22/02
10	Guildshire Police state that no criminal prosecution will be taken against the Claimant but that a notation will be made on the Criminal Records Bureau register.	01/03
11	Dr Francis meets with Claimant to assess the Claimant's fitness/competence to work	30/04
12	Dr Francis' investigations recommend Claimant is dismissed	21/05
13	Disciplinary panel meeting chaired by the PCT's Group Manager for Children's Services	02/07
14	Written confirmation of outcome of Disciplinary hearing	10/07
15	Claimant notifies the Respondent of her wish to appeal against the disciplinary panel's decision to dismiss her	17/07
16	Appeal panel hearing chaired by the PCT's Director of Children Services	07/09

NUMBER	EVENT	DATE
17	Written confirmation of outcome of Appeal hearing	10/09
18	Proceedings commenced in Tribunal. The Claimant alleges unfair dismissal on the grounds that: • Insufficient evidence presented to the hearing to justify dismissal • Decision based primarily on suspicion rather than evidence of wrongdoing • PCT's decision based on the CRB notation but those who presented the PCT's case could not say how long it would remain on file • The allegation of abuse was retracted • It was not true that the claimant did not have an insight on how personal life would impact on job – the claimant outlined that she would use reflection, support of colleagues and supervision, along with policies and procedures to deal with similar child protection issues. • No formal warnings given • Previous good service not taken into account	05/10
19	Tribunal Hearing: The Tribunal had an agreed bundle of documents The Tribunal had Witness Statements from the Claimant on her own behalf; and from Dr M Francis, Consultant Paediatrician for the PCT; the PCT's Group Manager of Children's Services who chaired the disciplinary hearing; and the PCT's Director of Children Services who chaired the appeal hearing.	17–19/2/ 2022

Tribunal's findings of fact

1. The Claimant began her employment with the Respondent in September 2014, starting as a student health visitor. She qualified in August 2015. The Claimant's line manger told Dr Francis, the Trust's consultant paediatrician, that she had always found the Claimant to be hardworking, reliable and flexible. She assessed the Claimant as being a good colleague.

2. The Claimant has two daughters who live with her.

3. On 12 January 2021 the Claimant spoke to her line manager about allegations that had been made against her by her daughter which involved allegations of physical abuse, being hit with a belt by her mother.

4. Social services wrote to the Respondent on 14 February, reporting that both the Claimant's daughters had been removed from the family home on 26 January due to allegations of physical harm made by one daughter. The children had been placed on the Child Protection Register under categories of 'physical harm and emotional abuse' on 9 February.

5. The Respondent suspended the Claimant on 15 February. The decision to suspend was made because of the serious nature of the allegations. The Claimant remained on full pay and was told that the suspension was a neutral act, not disciplinary.

6. Dr Francis was asked by the Respondent to investigate. By the time he met with the Claimant her children had returned home, and the Claimant had signed a written

agreement saying she would not cause emotional harm to her daughters and that she would work in partnership with the authorities.

7. Dr Francis interviewed the Claimant's line manager, the council's social worker and the Claimant.

8. The social worker told Dr Francis that she was concerned about the Claimant's perception of child abuse and physical chastisement. The Claimant was, she said, still attributing her actions to her upbringing and culture.

9. Dr Francis noted that no criminal charges were brought against the Claimant but that the investigation carried out by the police would appear as a notation on the Criminal Records Bureau record.

10. Dr Francis interviewed the Claimant on 30 April. He asked her about her practice as a health visitor. He then asked her about the recent events and for her assessment of how the incident would affect her work. The Claimant said that she did not think that it would affect her work, and that children were the priority in the service and that she would not impose her own values on her work. The Claimant told Dr Francis that her daughter had retracted her allegations, but there was no evidence of this. The Claimant appeared to think, Dr Francis notes, that if this was the case then there was no issue for the Respondent to take up with her.

11. Dr Francis recommended dismissal for the following reasons:

    (i)   The Claimant's refusal fully to accept responsibility for the offence that had occurred, instead attempting to justify her action because of her culture, knowing full well, through her child protection and health visitor training, that this was not acceptable. Instead the Claimant continued to focus on issues relating to her being misconstrued and misrepresented in the child protection investigation.

    (ii) The Claimant's unwillingness to acknowledge that the events which occurred in her private life would impact on her work and practice as a health visitor.

    (iii) His concern that the Claimant's experiences would affect her attitude and her ability to work jointly with agencies involved in child protection investigations, and in particular with social services.

    (iv) His concern that because of the issues raised in the investigation, the Claimant's duty to assess risks and make appropriate referrals to social services where there were child protection concerns might be affected, as this was dependent not just on her knowledge but also on her attitude. The concern was that it would be difficult for any manager to have confidence that the Claimant was making the correct decisions and taking appropriate actions, especially in child protection cases, given the independent way that health visitors work.

12. Dr Francis was also concerned about whether the Claimant could maintain her credibility among her colleagues and other professionals if they became aware of events that had occurred, and that the Respondent would be taking a risk if it continued to employ her as a health visitor. Should there be any other child protection issues in connection with the Trust's clients, where her judgment was called into question because of this background, the Respondent could be seen to be at fault.

13. Dr Francis also produced a document entitled: 'Management case relating to Jane Minnery'. The risks were listed as follows:

    1. 'The welfare, safety and health of children must always be paramount. This is an overriding responsibility of Guildshire PCT.

    2. As a health visitor [the Claimant] will present a risk to the children and families she will be working with because her current knowledge and attitude could impair her judgment and her ability to manage cases appropriately.

3.   The organisation will be at risk if it continues to employ a health visitor who has been the executor of child abuse, and whose CRB check will contain a notification of this abuse.'

14.   The Claimant was told in a letter dated 4 June that there would be a disciplinary hearing on 26 June to consider her dismissal due to the Claimant's conduct, and in light of the need to protect children and of the risk to the children and the PCT.

15.   The Claimant was told that the hearing could result in the termination of her employment, and that she was entitled to be accompanied to the hearing by a trade union representative or friend or colleague. The disciplinary hearing took place on 2 July, not 26 June, at the Claimant's request as she wanted to go on holiday to recover from the trauma of recent events.

16.   At the hearing Dr Francis presented the Respondent's case, summarising its concerns as that the Claimant had not seen the problem that he was trying to highlight to her when he had questioned her. He said that she was unable to make the connection between what she had experienced personally and how it could possibly affect her ability to do her job. He did not believe she was capable of being credible to other professionals, and he thought that it could be a problem employing someone carrying a CRB notation. For this reason she should be dismissed, he said. The Respondent made it clear to the Claimant that it was not concerned with the details surrounding her children's being taken into care. The Respondent was only concerned with its duty to protect clients from potential harm and with how what had happened had affected the Claimant's ability to carry out her job. The Respondent had to investigate that risk.

17.   The Claimant's representative asked the Claimant a series of questions to enable her to give answers which would deal with the Respondent's apparent concerns. The Claimant confirmed that she would follow the Respondent's policies and procedures should she have to deal with a child at risk. She did not explain how that would work in practice. The Claimant confirmed that she did not feel compromised as a health visitor since the incident.

18.   The Respondent wrote the Claimant a letter of dismissal dated 10 July. The reasons given for the decision to dismiss were:

   •   It has been deemed not suitable for you to continue in your role as a health visitor due to 'some other substantial reason'. That is, given the PCT's overriding responsibility to protect its clients, the potential risk of employing a frontline health visitor with a CRB notation for physical and mental abuse of children outweighs the arguments to continue to employ you in that capacity.

   •   For the same reason it has been deemed not suitable for the PCT to offer you alternative employment within adult services as a 'Registered General Nurse'. The Claimant was offered an administrative post.

19.   The Claimant was told that her employment would be terminated with three months' notice, and she was told of her right to appeal within 21 days. Otherwise the dismissal would take effect from date of the hearing, 2 July.

20.   The Claimant did appeal on 17 July. The appeal hearing was heard on 7 September. The central theme in the appeal was that as no evidence of wrongdoing had ever been presented against her, she should not have been dismissed. The Claimant relied heavily upon the absence of any formal finding of guilt against her as a result of the investigation carried out by the police and social services. She also stated that allegations by family members had subsequently been retracted, which should have made a difference to the outcome of the disciplinary hearing.

21   The CRB notation was discussed at the appeal hearing. The Respondent confirmed that it had relied on the police and social services investigation, which had concluded that there was insufficient evidence for a criminal prosecution but that there was enough for a CRB notation, which reflected the seriousness of the allegations.

22. The appeal panel decided as follows:

- The panel had serious concerns about the impact of Jane Minnery working with vulnerable children and her lack of insight.
- The appeal hearing considered whether she was suitable for a clinical alternative and decided (like the disciplinary panel) that the risks were too great.
- The panel had confidence in the professional advice that personal behaviour impacts on professional behaviour, and confirmed that as a health visitor advising on child protection, there would be a risk.
- The panel did not have confidence in the level of the Claimant's acceptable behaviour in parenting.

23. It had been noted during the hearing that the Claimant would not be supervised unless she reported a case to her team leader. As a band 7 employee she would be expected to assist with supervising junior staff and to have an in-depth knowledge of child protection matters, and to take a lead role in resolving those issues within families.

24. The appeal panel confirmed the disciplinary panel's decision on 10 September. The panel had reviewed the earlier decision to ensure it was fair and reasonable, taking into account the facts and circumstances.

25. It had been apparent to the appeal panel that the Claimant lacked insight into how her private behaviour could impact on her professional ability to make objective decisions about vulnerable children. The advice the panel had received was that the Claimant's conduct towards her children could not be separated from the risks presented by her continuing to work as a health visitor. The Respondent has to be responsible for children in the borough, and the children's needs remain paramount.

26. The appeal panel therefore agreed with the panel that the risks in continuing to employ the Claimant as a health visitor were too high.

IN THE GUILDSHIRE EMPLOYMENT TRIBUNAL   CASE NUMBER: 1234/2021

BETWEEN

MRS JANE MINNERY   Claimant

- and -

GUILDSHIRE PRIMARY CARE TRUST   Respondent

_____
PARTICULARS OF RESPONSE
_____

1. The Respondent is a Primary Care Trust commissioning and providing health services to members of the general public in the Guildshire area.

2. It is admitted that the Claimant was employed as a Health Visitor by the Respondent from September 2014 to July 2021. It is admitted that the Claimant was dismissed. It is not admitted that the dismissal was unfair.

3. Unless admitted in these Particulars of Response the Respondent denies all of the Claimant's allegations.

4. The Respondent has an overriding duty and responsibility to protect members of the public, especially children, who use the services it commissions or provides. That duty includes ensuring that any employee who comes into contact with children presents no risk of harm. Section 11 of the Children Act 2004 places a statutory duty on NHS bodies, amongst others, to make arrangements to safeguard and promote the welfare of children. Statutory guidance was first issued in 2005 and revised guidance was published in April 2007. The NHS bodies that are covered by this statutory duty include Strategic Health Authorities, NHS Trusts, NHS Foundation Trusts and Primary Care Trusts.

5. As part of its overriding duty to protect the welfare of children the Respondent has to ensure that staff coming into contact with children present no risk in themselves to the children who are referred to services operated or commissioned by the Respondent. It is averred that this overriding duty is such that the Respondent must also consider any potential risk to service users and act accordingly.

6. As stated above the Claimant was employed by the Respondent as a Health Visitor. In that role she regularly came into contact with vulnerable children. In February 2020 it was brought to the Respondent's attention that a Child Protection Section 47 investigation had been undertaken by Social Services together with a police investigation in respect of the Claimant's two children. Both children were put on the Child Protection Register and placed in foster care.

7. Although the police subsequently confirmed that no further action would be taken against the Claimant, they made a notation with the Criminal Records Bureau ('CRB'). The Claimant's two children were returned to her care in due course.

8. Because of the Respondent's overriding duty subject to the Children Act 2004 and also the Children Act 1989 ('The welfare, safety and health of children must always be paramount'), the Respondent considered it imperative to initiate an investigation into the Claimant's conduct and professional suitability to be in contact with children. The investigation was undertaken by Dr Francis, Consultant Paediatrician. The Claimant was invited by letter dated 4 June to a disciplinary hearing.

9. The disciplinary hearing took place on 2 July and the Claimant was notified of the outcome by letter dated 10 July. The panel concluded that the Claimant was unable to continue in her role as a Health Visitor due to its overriding duty to protect clients, and the potential risk of continuing to employ a health visitor with a CRB notation for physical and emotional abuse outweighed arguments to continue to employ her in that role. Equally the Respondent did not consider it suitable to continue to employ the Claimant as a Registered General Nurse within the Adult Service, and as such the

Claimant's contract as a health visitor with the Respondent would terminate three months from 2 July. The Respondent offered to re-deploy the Claimant into an administrative post.

10. The Claimant appealed the decision of the disciplinary panel by letter dated 17 July. An appeal hearing took place on 7 September. The appeal panel upheld the decision of the disciplinary panel and the Claimant was notified of that decision by letter dated 10 September.

11. The Human Resources Manager subsequently had a telephone conversation with the Claimant and discussed vacant posts within the Respondent. The posts included a clerical officer post and a post as a personal assistant. It was left for the Claimant to express an interest in either post but the Claimant failed to do so. The Claimant would certainly have been appointed to the clerical officer position if she had confirmed she wanted that post.

12. In all the circumstances the Respondent maintains that the dismissal was fair. The Respondent denies that the Claimant was unfairly dismissed as alleged and denies that the Claimant is entitled to the relief sought or at all.

Advocate & Co
Solicitor for the Respondent
19 October 2021

IN THE GUILDSHIRE EMPLOYMENT TRIBUNAL   CASE NUMBER: 1234/2021

BETWEEN

MRS JANE MINNERY   Claimant

- and -

GUILDSHIRE PRIMARY CARE TRUST   Respondent

CASE MANAGEMENT ORDER

Employment Tribunal Rules of Procedure 2013 Rule 29

TO ALL PARTIES

Employment Judge Hazel has made the following Orders on his own initiative. Under Rule 29 any party affected by the Order may apply to have it varied or revoked. Such an application must be made in writing to this office before the date ordered for compliance and must include reasons for the application. All parties are required by Rule 30(2) to provide all other parties in writing with the information set out in that Rule.

ORDERS

1. **DISCLOSURE OF DOCUMENTS:**
    On or before **29th November 2021** each party shall send to the other a list of the documents in their possession or control relevant to the claims and to the grounds of resistance. Additionally, the Claimant shall send to the Respondent a 'schedule of loss', ie a written statement of what is claimed, including a breakdown of the sums concerned showing how they are calculated; and the Claimant's list of documents should include any documents relevant to the schedule of loss.

2. **INSPECTION OF DOCUMENTS:**
    If either party requests a copy of any document on the other party's list, that other party shall provide a clear photocopy within 14 days of the request. Alternatively, that other party shall allow the requesting party on reasonable notice and at a reasonable time to inspect the original documents on the list and to make photocopies of them. That inspection shall take place where the documents are normally situated, but the parties may agree that inspection shall take place at some other convenient location. The provision of copies in compliance with this order shall entitle the supplying party to reimbursement of reasonable copying expenses, but not to delay or withhold provision of the copies pending such reimbursement.

3. **BUNDLE OF DOCUMENTS:**
    For the Hearing, the parties shall agree a bundle of documents limited to those which are relevant to the determination by the Tribunal of the issues in the case. Because it appears likely that the Respondent has most of the original documents, the Respondent shall create the bundle unless the parties specifically agree otherwise. On or before **20th December 2021** the Claimant shall notify the Respondent of the relevant documents to be included on behalf of the Claimant. On or before **8th January 2022** the Respondent shall provide to the Claimant a clear, indexed, paginated copy of the bundle, assembled in chronological order (save in respect of formal policies or procedures, which may be placed together) and containing all the relevant documents which any party wishes to be included. The Respondent shall also bring 4 copies to the Hearing (3 for the Tribunal and one for any witness).

4.   **WITNESS STATEMENTS:**

Not later than **7 days** before the hearing the parties shall exchange written witness statements (including one from a party who intends to give evidence). The witness statement should set out all of the evidence of the relevant facts which that witness intends to put before the Tribunal. If it is intended to refer to any document, the witness statement should refer to page/s in the agreed bundle. A failure to comply with this order may result in a witness not being permitted to give evidence because it has not been disclosed in a witness statement; or in an adjournment of the hearing and an appropriate order for costs caused by such adjournment. Each party shall bring 4 copies of any such witness statement to the hearing. The Claimant's statement should contain evidence relevant to the schedule of loss.

5.   **HEARING TIME:**

The case will be listed for a **3 days** hearing on the Judge's estimate of the time required for it. That estimate is intended to include the time needed for considering the oral and written evidence; each party's closing statements; the consideration and delivery of the judgment of the Tribunal; and consideration and judgment on remedy, if arising. The Tribunal will require the case to be completed within the time allocated to it and the parties must now consider the question, whether that time is adequate. If you consider that the hearing may require a time longer than that which has been set aside for it, you must write to the Tribunal as soon as possible, giving your own estimate of the time required, with reasons, and with an indication of the extent of the witnesses and documents which constitute the evidence in the case.

Notes:

(1)   Any person who without reasonable excuse fail to comply with an order to which s 7(4) of the Employment Tribunals Act 1996 applies shall be liable on summary conviction to a fine of £1,000.00.

(2)   Under Rule 6, if this order is not complied with, the Tribunal may take such action as it considers fair and just which may include (a) waiving or varying the requirement; (b) striking out the claim or response, in whole or part, in accordance with Rule 37; (c) barring or restricting a party's participation in the proceedings; and/or (d) awarding costs under Rules 74–84.

(3)   You may apply under Rule 29 for this order to be varied, suspended or set aside.

IN THE GUILDSHIRE EMPLOYMENT TRIBUNAL   CASE NUMBER: 1234/2021

BETWEEN

MRS JANE MINNERY   Claimant

- and -

GUILDSHIRE PRIMARY CARE TRUST   Respondent

WITNESS STATEMENT OF
DR MIKE FRANCIS

I, Dr Mike Francis MAKE OATH AND SAY as follows:

1. I am employed as a Consultant Paediatrician by Guildshire Primary Care Trust. The statements made within this witness statement are based upon facts within my own knowledge, save where I have indicated the source of my information or belief. Where matters are not directly within my knowledge, I believe them to be true.

2. I was appointed as the Designated Doctor for Child Protection for Guildshire in 2000 and continue to hold that post. I have worked in the speciality of paediatrics for 24 years, and I have had a significant experience managing cases where child abuse is suspected. In the last 13 years as Consultant Paediatrician and Designated Doctor for Child Protection, I have led the service strategically in the field of safeguarding children. I provide advice and supervision to clinicians, social workers and other professionals, and also to senior management within the health organisations locally.

3. I make this statement in support of the Respondent in respect of the claim that has been commenced by the Claimant in the Employment Tribunal alleging unfair dismissal.

4. I was asked by the Head of Children's Services for the Respondent to undertake an investigation surrounding allegations of physical abuse that had been made about the Claimant by her children. I wrote to the Claimant on 23 March 2021 informing her of my role and explaining that as part of my investigation I would be obtaining information about the allegations from Guildshire County Council Social Services and the section 47 investigation that had been completed. (A section 47 investigation requires the Local Authority to make enquiries when a child is suspected to be suffering, or likely to suffer, significant harm, in order to enable the Local Authority to decide whether it should take any action to safeguard and promote the welfare of the child.) I told the Claimant that as part of the investigation I would need to interview the relevant people concerned, which included herself, and I would write to her in due course to arrange a date for that interview. I told her she would be able to be accompanied by a trade union representative, work colleague or friend at the interview. I gave her my contact details so that she could contact me if she had any queries. (p52 Hearing Bundle)

5. I arranged to meet the Claimant on 19 April, but she cancelled that appointment two days beforehand (p55) and we eventually met on 30 April. The Claimant was accompanied at the meeting by her representative from the Royal College of Nursing, and notes were taken by my personal assistant.

6. At the start of the meeting I again confirmed that I had been asked to conduct an investigation by the Respondent and explained the reasons for the investigation, ie that it had been alleged that the Claimant had physically abused her children. I told her that I would prepare a report following our meeting which would be sent to her prior to being finalised, and at that point she would be asked to sign a copy of the final version.

7. The Claimant told me that after qualifying as a health visitor she was offered a substantive post as a health visitor with the Respondent. She said that her caseload was heavy, but she received support from the senior health visitors with whom she worked and also her manager and supervisor.

8.   I explored with the Claimant the allegations and what had happened afterwards. She told me that she understood that the allegations had to be investigated but said that she felt what she had told the social worker had been misconstrued. One of the allegations that had been made was that she had hit her children with a belt. The Claimant told me that she had been asked by the social worker if she had ever hit her children with a belt but she said that the children were only ever smacked on their bottoms with the hand. She did concede that in the culture she came from, using a belt as a means of punishment was acceptable, but she said that through her health visitor training she had realised that was not the way forward. She was concerned that the report prepared by social services incorrectly conveyed what had been discussed and what she had said at the child protection conference when she and her partner had been interviewed by the Senior Practitioner, Child Protection Investigation Team, although she did accept that she had been given an opportunity to check the report and correct any inaccuracies. I took it that she had objected to the report, but she confirmed that the comments she had been concerned about were still in the report, so I presume that the social worker felt that the report was an accurate reflection of what had been discussed.

9.   The Claimant also told me that she did not consider that the allegations about abuse, and the fact that her children had been taken into care, would affect her work as a health visitor. She told me that the children with whom she came into contact through her work were her priority, and she assessed each case on the evidence and merits, and not according to her personal beliefs or cultural background. The notes of my meeting with the Claimant are at page 68.

10. Also as part on my investigation I interviewed the Claimant's immediate line manager (p66); the social worker who conducted the investigation into the abuse allegations (p71); and I also reviewed the Child Protection Conference report (p80) prepared by the social worker; and liaised with Guildshire Police (p86).

11. When I interviewed the social worker on 19 April, she confirmed that she had not had any contact with the Claimant's family prior to the allegations, although one of her colleagues had been involved previously. She explained that the Claimant had acknowledged hitting her children with her hand and had in the past hit the elder daughter with a belt, but there had been no physical signs of abuse on either of the children, although the elder daughter had told her school that she was afraid to go home as she might be beaten. This had been mentioned to teachers at the school on a number of occasions but it was the first time that social services had been involved, and the referral by the school was prompted by the elder daughter alleging, on 26 January, that the Claimant had grabbed her around the neck and shaken her several times. Whilst the social worker confirmed that the elder daughter had subsequently stated that the smacking by hand and belt at home had stopped, she did not say that it had never happened; and the social worker felt that the daughter was intelligent and articulate, and had been reliable and consistent in the accounts that she had given.

12. The social worker told me that the Claimant had said that she (the Claimant) had been treated in the same manner at home when she was a child, ie hit with a belt, and that such chastisement was culturally acceptable. She said that the Claimant told her that following her health visitor training, she realised that type of behaviour was wrong, although the social worker suspected that it was possible that the abuse had continued after that point in time. Although the Claimant, when she was interviewed during the child protection conference on 8 February, confirmed that she had smacked both children in the past and had used a belt on the hands of the elder child, and appeared to have taken responsibility for her actions, that acknowledgement and acceptance for that type of punishment was subsequently retracted by the Claimant. However, when the Claimant's children were interviewed on 26 April, the social worker was told that the smacking by belt and hand had stopped, which would suggest to me that at some point in time in the past the Claimant had used a belt to punish her children.

13. As a result of the initial Child Protection Conference, it was recommended that the Claimant and her partner should attend meetings and parenting courses, to which they agreed. The fact that the Claimant had two jobs also probably contributed to the stress that the Claimant was under, and would not have helped with the Claimant's attempts to cope with her children at home. I was told that the next review was due on 26 April (p87), but at the time of our meeting the children remained on the Child Protection Register, although there were no active concerns about their welfare at that time. I explained to the council's social worker that my concerns were around the Claimant's ability to care for her children without using physical violence or emotional pressure. I also had some concerns about the advice that she would give to clients, and whether she could properly decide when a referral was necessary if there were child protection concerns.

14. I met the claimant's line manager on 2 May. She confirmed that she first met the Claimant when the Claimant was training to be a health visitor, and she became her line manager in August 2014. She told me that although she did not monitor the Claimant's work each day, when the Claimant was sick her cases were allocated to other health visitors who did not discover any issues with the management of her cases. She found the Claimant to be hard-working and reliable.

15. Her line manager confirmed that health visitors worked independently and effectively managed themselves, but they could contact their line managers if there were problems, specifically with child protection issues. I asked her to explain how the Claimant could be monitored or supervised if she came back into practice. She was unable to explain how such monitoring would take place as it was not something that had happened before. I explained that I had concerns about the Claimant's attitude towards Social Services which could perhaps affect her willingness to report appropriate child protection issues.

16. In addition to interviewing the above-named witnesses, I also carefully studied the initial Child Protection Conference report (p80), which was appendix 7 of my report. The report confirmed that following the allegations made on 26 January, the Claimant's two daughters were made subjects of a Police Protection Order and placed in local authority care. On 29 January the Claimant and her partner agreed to the children remaining in foster care, and then proposed that the children should be placed with family members rather than remaining in foster care, which happened on 6 February. The report noted that both the Claimant and her partner had admitted physically chastising their children, which included smacking the children's bottoms with their hands and hitting the elder child on the hand with a belt, but later commented that it was not illegal to chastise children reasonably.

17. The report noted that both the Claimant and her partner agreed to sign a parental agreement, by which they agreed not to use any form of physical chastisement at any time against their children in the family home. In addition, the Claimant and her partner accepted that disciplining their children by the use of physical chastisement was not acceptable and could not continue.

18. The report also noted that although the Claimant and her partner had admitted using a belt to chastise their elder daughter, that admission was retracted to some extent later by the Claimant, as it was reported that, according to her, there had been a misunderstanding in relation to the use of the belt and she had not used it for two years to punish her elder daughter.

19. The report recommended that the children should be placed on the Child Protection Register under the category of Physical Abuse, and whilst it was proposed that the children should be returned to the family home on a gradual basis, they should be closely monitored by professionals to ensure their safety, and the Claimant and her partner were to attend a parenting course, amongst other requirements.

20. I also contacted Guildshire Police to determine if any formal charges had been made against the Claimant and her partner, and I was informed that they had not been cautioned

and there was insufficient evidence to proceed with a criminal prosecution. I was told, however, that the incident would show up on a CRB check, but whether or not the information was released would depend upon the nature of the job for which the Claimant applied (p54). I was also subsequently informed by the social worker that the children had been removed from the Child Protection Register as they were no longer considered to be at risk of harm, and the Claimant and her partner had agreed to cooperate with the Child Protection Plan, and the children were classified as Children in Need (p87).

21.   In the light of the evidence that I had gathered, the witnesses I had interviewed, including the Claimant, and the report from the Initial Child Protection Conference, I had to decide whether or not I considered the Claimant presented a risk to clients, and children in particular, if she was allowed to resume her job as a health visitor. I felt that the Claimant was not able to accept responsibility for her actions in relation to her children, and continued to deny that she had done anything wrong when I interviewed her. The Claimant was of the view that as her children had been returned to her then that was evidence that there had not been any abuse and that nothing wrong had occurred. I could not see any degree of reflection about the events that had happened, which is what I would have expected, and especially from somebody working as a health visitor.

22.   Although the Claimant's children had been returned to her, this did not mean that there was no risk, or no continuing risk, or that there had not been any abuse. I must explain that child protection issues are based on the balance of probabilities. Initially the balance of probabilities in this case was that the children had either been significantly harmed, or were at risk of significant harm. Subsequently, when the children's names were removed from the register, it was felt that the risks were not as high as previously because of the work that had gone into the case.

23.   Upon concluding my investigation I had to consider whether or not I could recommend that the Claimant should be allowed to return to her job as a health visitor, albeit with supervision, or if I should recommend that she could not work with vulnerable clients, particularly children. I felt that the Claimant would need extensive supervision, and I came to the conclusion that as health visitors by the nature of the job work on their own a lot, it would have been difficult to be entirely confident that the Claimant did not pose a risk to children, either through failing to identify a risk or by condoning practices that she might have considered to be acceptable. I came to the conclusion that this was too high a risk to accept. The Children Act 2004 (p162) places a statutory obligation to promote and safeguard the welfare of children. Not only did I believe that to have allowed the Claimant to return to her position as a health visitor would have put that duty in jeopardy, but fundamentally I believe that my duty, and that of the Respondent, is to try to address the imbalances that exist when children are involved. The overriding duty of the Respondent, and its employees, is to protect and safeguard the welfare of children generally, and especially those considered to be at risk. It was my professional opinion that to return the Claimant to her role as a health visitor would have meant that the Respondent would not have been fulfilling its obligations and duty to protect the welfare of children, and as such I had to recommend that the Claimant should be dismissed from her position as a health visitor.

24.   I prepared a Management Statement of Case (p90) for the hearing, and on the basis of the risks I had assessed as to allowing the Claimant to continue to work as a health visitor, I recommended that she should be dismissed from that post. I presented the Management Case at the hearing on 2 July. I had no further involvement with the matter after that date save for my involvement as a witness for the Respondent in respect of the claim brought by the Claimant in the Employment Tribunal.

I confirm that the contents of this my witness statement are true.

Signed:

Date:

Judgment of the Employment Tribunal

The unanimous decision of the Tribunal is that the Claimant's dismissal was for some other substantial reason and was fair and reasonable in the circumstances.

REASONS

1.   The Claimant brought a claim of unfair dismissal against the Respondent. The Respondent resisted her complaint.

EVIDENCE

2.   The Tribunal had before it an agreed bundle of documents. The Tribunal had witness statements from the Claimant on her own behalf; and from Dr Francis, Consultant Paediatrician, Mr Y, Group Manager Children's Services and Z, Director of Adult and Children Services; all on behalf of the Respondent.

ISSUES

3.   The tribunal had to determine the following issues:
     (a)   the reason for the Claimant's dismissal
     (b)   whether the reason fell within one of the permitted reasons under s 98(2) ERA 1996, and if so;
     (c)   whether the Respondent had conducted a reasonable investigation on which to base its beliefs with regard to the Claimant;
     (d)   whether it was reasonable in all the circumstances for the Respondent to treat it as a sufficient reason for dismissing the Claimant.

FINDINGS OF FACT [see the facts at pp 278–281 above]

LAW

4.   The tribunal needs to consider the reason for the Claimant's dismissal and whether that reason is one that is proved by the employer; as the burden is on the employer to show the reason for the dismissal and that it is a reason falling under sub-section (2) of section 98 ERA 1996 or some other substantial reason of a kind such as to justify the dismissal of an employee holding the position which the employee did.

5.   It is the Respondent's case that they dismissed for SOSR.

6.   In order to prove that the dismissal has been for SOSR, the Respondent would need to prove that it is a substantial reason and thus not frivolous or trivial.

7.   If the tribunal decides that the reason for dismissal is proven by the employer and that it is one of the reasons set out in section 98(2) ERA 1996, then the tribunal needs to decide if it was fair and reasonable in all the circumstances. The tribunal has to decide whether taking into account all the relevant circumstances, including the size and administrative resources of the employer's undertaking and the substantial merits of the case, the employer has acted reasonably treating that reason as a sufficient reason for dismissing the employee. In determining this, the tribunal has to be mindful not to substitute its views for that of the employer.

8.   The tribunal is also aware of the Police Act and the Home Office Circular 5/2005 entitled 'Criminal Records Bureau: Local checks by police forces for the purpose of enhanced disclosure'.

APPLYING THE LAW TO THE FACTS:

Was the dismissal unfair?

9.   In our judgment Dr Francis' investigation was thorough and fair. In conducting his investigation Dr Francis interviewed the Claimant after interviewing most of the

witnesses. The brief that he was given by the Respondent was properly focused in that he was not concerned with the details of what occurred between the Claimant's daughter and herself so much as with the Claimant's reaction to what had happened and her perspective on it, given the nature of her duties as a health visitor. After Dr Francis saw the Claimant he met her line manager who was supportive of the Claimant and stated that in her opinion the Claimant had been hard-working, reliable as a colleague and flexible whenever cover was required in managing their caseload.

10. The line manager confirmed that health visitors work independently, self-supervising on the whole, and that they would be monitored only if there were issues of concern.

11. When Dr Francis met the Claimant he asked her wide-ranging questions which allowed her the opportunity to give her version of the incident, and also to discuss broadly how the incident might affect her practice and influence her thinking or how she would work to ensure it did not do.

12. In our view Dr Francis was correct not to reinvestigate the child's allegations. As the Claimant's employer the Respondent's only interest in the situation would be how what has occurred in the Claimant's private life affects her ability to do her job. In order to do so, it was able to rely on the findings and judgment of the police and social services after their investigation into the child's allegations.

13. The social services and the police had decided that the children needed to be placed on the Register, even for a short period of time. Also, that although the children were returned to the family eventually, work needed to be done with both parents around parenting issues thrown up by the incident, and this occurred over a number of weeks from the date of the incident.

14. Lastly, the Respondent was aware from information provided by the police that there would be a notation on any Criminal Records Bureau disclosure that was obtained in respect of the Claimant in relation to working with children or vulnerable adults.

15. From those circumstances it was quite right for the Respondent to accept the fact that the Claimant had behaved in such a way toward her daughter that it warranted a CRB notation, even if there had been no conviction at the magistrates' court.

16. The disciplinary hearing was a hearing in which the Respondent balanced the risks involved in continuing to employ the Claimant (who it was aware, and which was noted in the minutes, had a good record prior to this incident and who would now have a CRB notation if a search were made); and the risks posed to the children in need within its catchment area, being the need to protect the safety of children, the risk to children and the risk to the PCT. The Respondent is entitled to weigh up those risks.

17. It was noted that if the Claimant was a new applicant for a job as a health visitor, with a CRB notation for physical and emotional abuse of her own children she would not have been employed. The difference is that the Claimant is an existing employee with a previous unblemished record. As she was a longstanding employee, it was the Respondent's duty to treat the Claimant fairly and reasonably, and to consider in the light of her previous employment with the Respondent whether or not that outweighed the risks.

18. In our judgment the Respondent was also entitled to take into consideration some of the inconsistencies in the evidence which was given by the Claimant to the Respondent in interviews and at the hearing. The Claimant stated that she used to condone chastisement with a belt, but that she stopped doing so when she undertook health visitor training and learnt this was not a suitable way to discipline her children. However, the Claimant became a qualified health visitor three years before the incident but she stated that she stopped using the belt against her children only two years prior to the incident. That would mean she continued to use the belt even after she completed her training, and therefore challenges her earlier statement.

19. The Claimant also stated during the course of the internal proceedings that she no longer believed that physical chastisement of children was appropriate. However, in her answer to Dr Francis at the investigatory interview, she stated that she would not impose her own values on her work and that each case was to be judged on its own merit and not on her beliefs. This would tend to suggest that she continues to believe that that method of discipline is still appropriate but that she is endeavouring to keep those beliefs to herself. There is a significant difference between the two positions.

20. In presenting her case to the Respondent at the disciplinary and appeal hearing and at the tribunal Hearing, the Claimant appeared to be suggesting that the fact that there was no evidence of abuse, that there had been no conviction at the magistrates' court, and that the children were returned to her and removed from the at risk register, meant that the Respondent should not have considered that anything significant had occurred but should instead consider that everything had, in effect, 'gone back to normal'. This would suggest to the Respondent that the Claimant did not appreciate that the fact that this had occurred at all would give the Respondent cause for concern.

21. The Respondent is therefore, in the tribunal's judgment, correct in its judgment that it could not have any confidence that the Claimant's personal opinions had in fact changed with regard to the correct methods for disciplining children. Instead it appears that the Claimant was going to keep her personal feelings to herself, which is different and less reliable.

22. The Respondent's real concern was that if the Claimant did not consider that whatever was happening with a particular child was wrong or was inappropriate, she was unlikely even to be aware that she had condoned it, and would not have flagged it up for advice from anyone.

23. When questioned about how she saw issues in her personal life affecting her work, the Claimant's answer was that there were policies and procedures that dealt with those issues. This answer demonstrated that she was not aware of a potential conflict between her apparent beliefs and the duties of the job.

24. The Respondent weighed up its duty towards the Claimant and the risks involved in continuing to employ her. The risks outweighed any duty towards her as a longstanding employee with no previous disciplinary record and a good work record, and this is why the decision was made to dismiss her.

25. It is therefore our judgment that the decision to dismiss was for some other substantial reason and that it was reasonable in all the circumstances that it should be considered as an appropriate reason for dismissing the Claimant.

26. The Respondent not only took into account the CRB notation but also took into consideration the Claimant's attitude to the existence of the notation, the investigation by social services and the police, and the effect of the whole incident on her practice. The claimant showed that she had failed to analyse the situation in a way which showed she appreciated the risks that faced the Respondent.

27. The Respondent was not weighing up the risk that the Claimant might abuse children; this was not the issue. The issue was that she might observe something in her work that should give her cause for concern and cause her to report the family to the authorities, but that she would not do so because she would not consider what she had observed as wrong or worrying. There were concerns that if she harboured personal views that physical chastisement of children with a belt or a hand was actually acceptable in her 'culture' or otherwise, she would not take up the issue with the family or her employers, as appropriate, and as required by the Respondent in satisfaction of its duties to protect children in its care.

28. The Claimant's job required her to work independently. The Respondent therefore had to be reassured that she would be able to perform her duties professionally and without any personal issues clouding matters. And even though the Claimant states that she

would not allow them to do so, the possibility that she might still hold those beliefs reasonably gave the Respondent cause for concern.

29. The Respondent is an independent organisation and is entitled to come to its own decision based on the facts. The Respondent's decision to dismiss that Claimant for some other substantial reason was fair and reasonable in the circumstances, and although it was unfortunate, considering the Claimant's unblemished work record up until that date, it was not unfair.

Signed

....

Employment Judge

Judgment sent to the Parties on

....

and entered on the Register

....

For Secretary of the Tribunals

6.9 FURTHER READING

Lewis, *Employment Law: an adviser's handbook*, 14th edn (LAG, 2022).

Cunningham and Reed, *Employment Tribunal Claims – Tactics and Precedents*, 4th edn revised (LAG, 2013).

Blackstone's Employment Law Practice, 10th edn (OUP, 2019).

Mather, *Settlement Agreements* (ebook, 2021).

SUMMARY

A wide range of different statutory claims may be brought by presenting a complaint to an employment tribunal (**6.2**). In most instances these claims must be brought by employees, but some claims by workers may also be dealt with (**1.3** and **6.2**). There are a number of different time-limits within which claims to tribunals must be submitted, depending upon the nature of the complaint. Care needs to be taken with these rules as the time-limits are relatively short (in most cases three months) and enforced strictly (**6.3**). For example, an unfair dismissal claim must normally be presented within three months starting with the effective date of termination (EDT – see **3.5.2**), or within such further period as the tribunal considers reasonable where it was not reasonably practicable for the complaint to be presented within three months (ERA 1996, s 111). The EDT for these purposes is the basic EDT defined by ERA 1996, s 97.

Since May 2014, claimants must make an early notification to Acas, to see whether the claim can be resolved through conciliation. If a settlement is not possible, a certificate will be issued, which is needed before a claim can be lodged at a tribunal. See **6.2.2**.

The practice and procedure of employment tribunals is governed by Rules set out in Sch 1 to the Employment Tribunals (Constitution and Rules of Procedure) Regulations 2013. These cover such matters as the form and substance of the claim form (ET1) and the response (ET3), case management, ancillary applications for information or documents, preliminary hearings and costs (**6.4**).

Many employment tribunal claims are settled without a hearing. Settlements, to be binding, may be negotiated either through an Acas conciliation officer or via a compromise agreement (**6.5**).

There are options other than bringing tribunal proceedings, including using ADR, the Acas statutory scheme and judicial mediation (**6.6**).

A dismissed employee may have more than one potential claim against an employer, eg unfair dismissal, wrongful dismissal and a redundancy payment claim. However, as a general rule an employee cannot be compensated twice for the same financial loss (**6.7**).

The following practical steps should be taken when bringing a claim:

- Consider whether to bring the claim in the tribunal or in a civil court (see **Chapter 1**).
- Check that the tribunal has jurisdiction. There is a list of all the tribunal jurisdictions at <http://www.employmenttribunals.gov.uk/FormsGuidance/jurisdictionList.htm>.
- Check time-limits. For example, for unfair dismissal, a claim must be received by the tribunal within three months starting with the EDT (or within such further period as the tribunal considers reasonable in all the circumstances: ERA 1996, s 111). In discrimination cases or complaints relating to non-payment of wages or holiday pay, the three-month period begins when the matter complained about happened. This may mean that time can start running in some cases before termination of employment. There are special rules for equal pay and redundancy payment claims.

- Notify Acas for Early Conciliation. Obtain a certificate.

- Submit the claim on the approved ET1 form and ensure all required information is provided.

- If the claim is posted (it is also possible to send it using a downloadable pdf via the employment tribunals website), the postcode for the place where the employee normally worked should be used to identify the correct tribunal office address to use. If the employee has never worked for the respondent, identify the correct tribunal office postal address by using the postcode for the place where the matter being complained about happened. There is a list on the employment tribunal website which indicates the correct tribunal office: <http://www. employmenttribunals.gov. uk/Documents/HearingCentres/Postcodelist_1st April2010.pdf>.

- Once the tribunal office has received and accepted the claim, it will give it a case number. If the claim is accepted, the tribunal office will send a letter to confirm this, together with a booklet about what the next steps are. At the same time, the tribunal office will send the respondent a copy of the claim form together with a form [ET3] for its response. In most cases, the tribunal office will also send a copy of the claim to Acas. The forms and guidance notes are available on the employment tribunal website.

- If the claim is not accepted, the tribunal office will return the form with a letter explaining the reason why the claim has not been accepted and what action needs to be taken. In these cases it will be very important to ensure that the form is resubmitted within the time limits.

- The response form and guidance notes are available on the employment tribunal website. If a response is not on the approved form, is not received within the specified time limit, or does not contain: (i) the employer's full name and address; (ii) whether the employer wants to defend all or part of the claim; and (iii) the grounds on which the claim is being defended, it will not be accepted.

- If the response is not accepted, it will be returned by the tribunal office. In these cases it will be very important to ensure that the form is resubmitted within the time-limits.

- If the response is accepted, a copy will be sent to the claimant.

- If no proper response is received within 28 days, the tribunal judge shall decide whether, on the material available (including further information requested), a determination can be made; and if so, judgment will be issued. Otherwise a hearing will be fixed. The respondent will be entitled to participate in a hearing only to the extent permitted by a judge, unless and until an extension of time is granted.

- A respondent should consider whether it wishes to make a counterclaim. Any such counterclaim must be made within six weeks of receiving the copy of the claim from the tribunal office. If a counterclaim is being made, the tribunal office can be asked to send the appropriate form.

- Once the claim and response have been received and accepted, the parties need to consider whether there are any issues they want to be dealt with or any orders which should be made before the claim should proceed further. The tribunal may give directions or orders on a variety of matters (see **6.4.5**), including further information, documents and witnesses. If a party decides that it needs more information or documents from the other party, it should first ask for these to be provided voluntarily by writing to the other party, giving a reasonable time limit for responding. If matters do not get resolved voluntarily, a party should write to the tribunal and ask the tribunal to issue an order.

- The final hearing will determine whether the claim succeeds or fails (ie on liability) and, if it succeeds, what remedy is appropriate. A full hearing will normally be conducted by an Employment Judge sitting alone, unless the case involves a claim of discrimination, in which case there will also be two non-legal members.

- A preliminary hearing (see **6.4.6.1**) can be held to determine jurisdictional issues, for example: (i) whether the claim or response should be struck out; (ii) questions of entitlement to bring or defend a claim; (iii) if either side's case appears weak, whether a deposit needs to be paid and, if so, how much, before that side can go ahead. This type of hearing is normally held in public before an Employment Judge sitting alone, but may also be held over the phone.

- In a straightforward case, the tribunal will issue, of its own motion, a short set of directions to help the parties prepare for the substantive hearing. In a more complex case, the tribunal may hold a preliminary hearing to deal with any outstanding matters. It may be held over the phone or in person. It is normally held in private. A preliminary hearing will normally seek to: (i) clarify the issues in the case; (ii) decide what orders should be made about matters such as documents and witnesses; and (iii) decide the time and length of the main hearing. The time and length of the main hearing will be given automatically in the standard directions.

- The length of time allocated to a case includes time for: (i) the substantive hearing on liability; (ii) any issues or evidence on remedy; and (iii) the tribunal to deliberate and deliver a judgment. Hearing dates are postponed only where there is a good reason and/or it is in the interests of justice to postpone a hearing.

- All or part of a claim (or responses) may be withdrawn at any time before or during the hearing, by telling the tribunal and the other parties in writing. Withdrawals should be done as soon as possible.

- If a case settles before the hearing, the parties should let the tribunal office know as soon as possible.

- Prior to the hearing it will be necessary for the parties to prepare and agree between them a bundle of documents for use at the hearing (see **6.4.7.1**). This is usually done by the respondent. It will also be necessary for the parties to have prepared witness statements for their witnesses and to have provided copies of these in advance in accordance with any case management directions to the other party. Signed copies must be brought to the tribunal.

- See **6.4.7.4** for the conduct of the main hearing, **6.4.9** for the rules on costs, and **6.4.10** and **6.4.11** for reconsiderations and appeals.

CHAPTER 7

TRANSFER OF UNDERTAKINGS

7.1	Introduction	335
7.2	When do the 2006 Regulations apply?	336
7.3	Effect of a relevant transfer	350
7.4	What the transferee acquires	356
7.5	Dismissal of an employee because of a relevant transfer	359
7.6	Post-transfer variations to terms and conditions	363
7.7	The provision of information and consultation under the 2006 Regulations	366
7.8	Further reading	370
	Summary	370

LEARNING OUTCOMES

After reading this chapter you will be able to:

- explain when the Transfer of Undertakings (Protection of Employment) Regulations 2006 (as amended) apply
- identify what constitutes a 'relevant transfer'
- list and understand the *Spijkers* factors
- understand the effect of a 'relevant transfer' and who is covered by it
- describe the implications of dismissals connected to a transfer
- explain the impact of a transfer on an employer's ability to vary the terms of a contract of employment
- be aware of the requirements to inform and consult under the Regulations.

7.1 INTRODUCTION

In this chapter, we consider the protection afforded to employees (and probably also workers – see reg 2(1) and *Dewhurst v Revisecatch Ltd t/a Ecourier* (ET/2201909/18)), when there is a transfer of a business, by the Transfer of Undertakings (Protection of Employment) Regulations 2006 (SI 2006/246) ('the 2006 Regulations'), which replaced the 1981 Regulations (SI 1981/1794), and the Collective Redundancies and Transfer of Undertakings (Protection of Employment) (Amendment) Regulations 2014 (SI 2014/16) ('the 2014 Amendment Regulations'), which came into force in January 2014. The Regulations implement the European Acquired Rights Directive (77/187/EEC) of 1977 as amended in 2001.

The BIS Guide, *Employment Rights on the Transfer of an Undertaking* (January 2012), as amended to take account of the 2014 Amendment Regulations – available at <https://www.gov.uk/government/publications/tupe-a-guide-to-the-2006-regulations> – summarises the effect of the Regulations as follows:

> Broadly speaking, the effect of the Regulations is to preserve the continuity of employment and terms and conditions of any employees who are transferred to a new employer when a relevant transfer takes place. This means that employees employed by the previous employer (the 'transferor') when the transfer takes effect automatically become employees of the new employer (the 'transferee') on the

same terms and conditions (except for certain occupational pensions rights). It is as if their contracts of employment had originally been made with the transferee employer. However, the Regulations provide some limited opportunity for the transferee or transferor to vary the terms and conditions of employment contracts in a range of stipulated circumstances, even though the sole or principal reason for the variation is the transfer.

... The Regulations can apply regardless of the size of the transferred business: so the Regulations equally apply to the transfer of a large business with thousands of employees or of a very small one (such as a shop, pub or garage). The Regulations also apply equally to public or private sector undertakings and whether or not the business operates for gain, such as a charity.'

The 2006 Regulations were introduced to comply with various EC Directives concerning the transfers of undertakings. The main Directives are:

(a)   the Acquired Rights Directive (77/187/EC);

(b)   the Acquired Rights Directive (98/50/EC);

(c)   the Acquired Rights Amendment Directive (2001/23/EC).

As part of the Government's plans to deregulate business, in January 2013 it issued a consultation on reforming the 2006 Regulations. In November 2013, it published draft Regulations to implement a number of proposed amendments. These (the 2014 Amendment Regulations) became effective in January 2014. They include:

•   changes to the definition of 'entailing changes in the workforce' to include a change in location (see **7.5.3**)

•   amendments which are meant to make it easier for an employer to change employees' terms and conditions (see **7.6**).

At common law in the UK, the transfer of an undertaking by one employer to another automatically terminates the employee's contract of employment, ie there is a dismissal. In this situation the reason for the dismissal will generally be redundancy (as the employer's requirement for employees to do work of a particular kind has ceased or diminished). Should the undertaking's new owner require the employee's services, he will offer a new contract of employment, and can do so on whatever terms he likes. Depending on the timing of the dismissal, the employee may still retain continuity in this situation (see ERA 1996, s 218(2) and *Clark & Tokely Ltd (t/a Spellbrook Ltd) v Oakes* [1998] 4 All ER 353). The 2006 Regulations altered the legal position by providing that where there is a 'relevant transfer', there will not be any automatic termination of the contract of employment. There will not be a dismissal simply because there is a transfer. In that situation, the employee will transfer with the undertaking and will be employed by the new owner under his original contract. If there are any dismissals, whether actual or constructive, and whether before or after the transfer, if those dismissals are connected with the transfer, they will be automatically unfair unless, effectively, there is a genuine redundancy situation (see **7.5** below).

7.2   WHEN DO THE 2006 REGULATIONS APPLY?

7.2.1   Applicability

The 2006 Regulations contain a number of exclusions and limitations. The most important ones are as follows:

(a)   There must be a transfer from one person to another; consequently, there must be a change in the employer, not merely in the ownership. The 2006 Regulations do not, therefore, apply to share sale transfers or where a purchaser buys a majority shareholding in a company, thereby gaining control. This is because there is no change in the identity of the employer. (See *Brookes and Others v Borough Care Services and CLS Care Services Ltd* [1998] IRLR 636, EAT, for confirmation of this principle.) A transfer which is caught by the Regulations can occur alongside or after a share sale (see, for example,

Millam v The Print Factory (London) 1991 Ltd [2007] IRLR 526 and *Jackson Lloyd Ltd and Mears Group plc v Smith and Others* (UKEAT/0127/13)).

The ECJ in *Allen and Others v Amalgamated Construction* (Case C-234/98) [2000] IRLR 119 ruled that the then applicable 1981 Regulations were capable of applying to transfers between two companies belonging to the same group, or where one subsidiary subcontracts work to another, provided the transfer involves the transfer of an 'economic entity' (see **7.2.2**). By way of guidance, the Regulations have been found to apply to mergers, sale of part of a going concern, changes of franchisee, sale of a sole trader's business or partnership. The Regulations do not apply to transfers of assets only. (See *Jackson Lloyd Ltd and Mears Group plc v Smith and Others* (UKEAT/0127/13).) For example, on insolvency the receiver may break up the business and sell off its assets to various buyers, the plant to one buyer and the premises to another.

Only a transfer of an undertaking or a service provision change (see **7.2.2**) will be covered by the 2006 Regulations.

(b)   The EAT, in *Holis Metal Industries v GMB* [2008] IRLR 187, confirmed that the Regulations can apply where the ownership of a company is transferred to a company operating outside the EU.

(c)   There are special provisions regarding insolvency (regs 8 and 9) which are beyond the scope of this book, but where there are bankruptcy or insolvency proceedings (but not administration proceedings – see *Key2Law (Surrey) LLP v De'Antiquis* [2011] EWCA Civ 1567), contracts of employment will not be transferred automatically.

(d)   Regulation 4 (automatic transfer of contract of employment together with all rights and liabilities (see **7.3.1** and **7.4**)) does not apply to rights under or in connection with an occupational pension scheme (reg 10). For this purpose, any provisions of an occupational scheme which do not relate to benefits for old age, invalidity or survivors are treated as not being part of the pension scheme, with the result that these benefits will be transferred. Some pension protection is now afforded to employees transferred by virtue of the Pensions Act 2004 (see **7.4.1.3**).

(e)   Regulation 4 (above) also does not transfer any liability of any person to be prosecuted for, convicted of and sentenced for any criminal offence. So, for example, if the transferor is liable to be prosecuted for breach of the HSWA 1974, that liability cannot pass to the transferee on the transfer of a business (reg 4(6)).

(f)   Regulation 7 (dismissals connected to the transfer are automatically unfair unless economic, etc reason (see **7.5**)) applies only to employees who satisfy the usual qualifying conditions for unfair dismissal protection (see **Chapter 3**), for example two years' continuous employment (see **7.5**).

(g)   The 2006 Regulations apply to England, Wales, Scotland and Northern Ireland; the 2014 Regulations do not apply to Northern Ireland.

(h)   Whether the 2006 Regulations apply to 'workers' (as opposed to employees) is not clear. The IWGB is supporting a claim alleging that a worker's contract transferred to CitySprint under the Regulations.

Note: In determining whether a transfer has taken place, the court will look at the substance and not the form of a transfer. Courts are alert to the fact that an employer might try to deprive employees of the protection of the 2006 Regulations by failing to mention or acknowledge that a transfer is taking place. There need not necessarily be any documentation formally recording a transfer. Even if either party fails to comply with consultation and notification requirements (see below), that does not mean that a transfer did not take place (see *P14 Medical Ltd v Mahon* [2021] IRLR 39).

7.2.2 A relevant transfer – reg 3

The 2006 Regulations apply only to what are known as 'relevant transfers', which may occur in a wide range of situations. There are two broad categories of relevant transfers: business transfers (reg 3(1)(a)); and service provision changes (reg 3(1)(b)). Some transfers will comprise both a business transfer and a service provision change. The two definitions are not mutually exclusive – as long as one definition is satisfied, it does not matter if the other one is not.

We shall look at both types of relevant transfer in more detail below.

Regulation 3 also endeavours to clear up some areas where there had previously been uncertainty. It makes clear that the 2006 Regulations:

(a)   apply to public and private undertakings engaged in economic activities, whether or not they are operating for gain;

(b)   can apply to a transfer or service provision change howsoever effected, notwithstanding:

    (i)   that the transfer of an undertaking, business or part of an undertaking or business situated in the UK pre-transfer is governed or effected by the law of a country or territory outside the United Kingdom, or that the service provision change is governed or effected by the law of a country or territory outside Great Britain;

    (ii)   that the employment of persons employed in the undertaking, business or part transferred, or, in the case of a service provision change, persons employed in the organised grouping of employees, is governed by any such law.

As far as a business transfer is concerned (see **7.2.2.1** below), the 2006 Regulations apply so long as the undertaking itself (comprising, amongst other things, premises, assets, fixtures and fittings, and goodwill as well as employees) is situated in the UK; and so far as a service provision change is concerned, provided there is an organised grouping of employees situated in the UK immediately before the service provision change (therefore if an employee is part of team but works abroad, that should not prevent the Regulations from applying; but if the whole team worked abroad, that would fall outside the definition);

(c)   apply to a transfer of an undertaking, business or part of an undertaking or business (which may also be a service provision change) where persons employed in the undertaking, business or part transferred ordinarily work outside the UK, provided, of course, that the undertaking itself is situated in the UK immediately before the transfer;

(d)   do *not* apply to an administrative reorganisation of public administrative authorities or the transfer of administrative functions between public administrative authorities (reg 3(5)). For a recent case on what constitutes the exercise of public authority (as well as reviewing existing European and UK case law on whether there is an economic activity), see *Nicholls v London Borough of Croydon* (UKEAT/0003/18 and 0004/18). (*Note*: many such transfers are in fact covered by similar protection under other statutes, eg the Local Government Act 2003 applies in relation to the reorganisation of service provision within local government. See the Cabinet Office Statement of Practice, 'Staff Transfers in the Public Service' for more details.)

Regulation 3 also provides that:

(e)   a relevant transfer may be effected by a series of two or more transactions;

(f)   a relevant transfer may take place whether or not any property is transferred to the transferee by the transferor.

7.2.2.1 Business transfers

Under reg 3(1)(a), a business transfer is 'a transfer of an undertaking, business or part of an undertaking or business situated immediately before the transfer in the United Kingdom to another person where there is a transfer of an economic entity which retains its identity'. Regulation 3(2) defines 'economic entity' as 'an organised grouping of resources which has the objective of pursuing an economic activity, whether or not that activity is central or ancillary'. The expression 'organised grouping of resources' is derived from *Suzen v Zehnacker Gebaudereinigung GmbH Krankenhausservice* [1997] IRLR 255.

At the heart of this definition is the principle that to qualify as a business transfer, the identity of the employer must change. This is why the Regulations do not apply to transfers by share takeover because, when a company's shares are sold to new shareholders, there is no transfer of a business or undertaking – the same company continues to be the employer.

The key ECJ case outlining the general tests to be applied in determining whether there is a business transfer is *Spijkers v Gebroeders Benedik Abattoir CV* [1986] ECR 1119, ECJ. In *Spijkers*, the transferor owned and ran a slaughterhouse. The business came to an end, whereupon the premises, certain goods and all employees bar Mr Spijkers were transferred to the transferee. It was held that the fact that there was a break in time between the old business ceasing and the new one starting, and the lack of a transfer of goodwill, did not prevent the application of the Acquired Rights Directive. The Court said:

> It appears from the general structure of Directive 77/187 and the wording of Article 1(1) that the Directive aims to ensure the continuity of existing employment relationships in the framework of an economic entity irrespective of a change of owner. It follows that the decisive criterion for establishing the existence of a transfer within the meaning of the Directive is whether the entity in question retains its identity.
>
> Consequently, it cannot be said that there is a transfer of an enterprise business or part of a business on the sole ground that its assets have been sold. On the contrary, in a case like the present, it is necessary to determine whether what has been sold is an economic entity which is still in existence, and this will be apparent from the fact that its operation is actually being continued or has been taken over by the new employer, with the same economic or similar activities.
>
> To decide whether these conditions are fulfilled it is necessary to take account of all the factual circumstances of the transaction in question, including the type of undertaking or business in question, the transfer or otherwise of tangible assets such as buildings and stocks, the value of intangible assets at the date of transfer, whether the majority of the staff [in terms of numbers or skills] are being taken over by the new employer, the transfer or otherwise of the circle of customers and the degree of similarity between activities before and after the transfer and the duration of any interruption in those activities. It should be made clear, however, that each of these factors is only a part of the overall assessment which is required and therefore they cannot be examined independently of each other.

So, from *Spijkers* and later ECJ decisions, we may state that the decisive criterion for establishing the existence of a transfer within the meaning of the Directive is whether the entity in question retains its identity after the transfer. The key question is whether there is a transfer of an economic entity that retains its identity.

In *Holis Metal Industries Ltd v GMB* (see **7.2.1**), the EAT held that the 2006 Regulations might apply to a transfer from the UK to a non-UK country; the test is the same – is there an economic entity and has it transferred?

Is there an economic entity?

Regulation 3(2) defines 'economic entity' as 'an organised grouping of resources which has the objective of pursuing an economic activity, whether or not that activity is central or ancillary'. The reference to 'economic' appears to suggest that the 'undertaking' being transferred does need to have some sort of cost centre.

The BIS Guide says that 'the economic entity test ... means the Regulations apply where there is an identifiable set of resources (which includes employees) ... and that set of resources retains its identity after the transfer'.

The definition applies to the transfer not just of an undertaking but also of part of an undertaking. An illustration is *Fairhurst Ward Abbotts Limited v Botes Building Limited* [2004] IRLR 304, where an operation was split into two geographical units when it was re-tendered, and it was held that there were transfers to each of the two successful new contractors.

Even though it pre-dates the 2006 Regulations, the domestic authority that gives the best general guidance on whether there has been a business transfer is *Cheesman v R Brewer Contracts* [2001] IRLR 144 (approved by the Court of Appeal in *Balfour Beatty Power Networks Ltd v Wilcox* [2007] IRLR 63).

In *Cheesman*, when looking at the question whether there was an undertaking, the EAT said that:

(a)   there needs to be found an economic entity, which is stable and discrete and whose activity is not limited to performing one specific works contract, an organised grouping of wage earners and assets enabling the exercise of an economic activity;

(b)   the entity must be sufficiently structured and autonomous but will not necessarily have significant assets;

(c)   in certain sectors the entity can essentially be based on manpower;

(d)   the identity of the entity emerges from factors such as its workforce, management staff, the way work is organised and operating methods.

In *Fairhurst Ward Abbotts Ltd* (above), the Court of Appeal confirmed that there is no requirement that the part of an undertaking transferred is itself a separate economic entity in the hands of the transferor; it is enough if part of a larger stable economic entity is identified for the first time as a separate economic entity on the occasion of the transfer separating a part from the whole.

This is therefore essentially a factual exercise. Once it has been determined that an entity exists, it is then necessary to ask 'Has that entity transferred?'

Has that entity transferred?

The *Spijkers* factors (see above) are particularly pertinent here. The decisive criterion established by *Spijkers* is whether 'the entity in question retains its identity'. This may be ascertained by looking at whether its operations are continued or resumed after the transfer. *Spijkers* laid down seven factors that tribunals should consider:

(a)   the type of undertaking or business;

(b)   the transfer or otherwise of tangible assets such as building, equipment and stocks;

(c)   the value of intangible assets at the date of transfer (eg goodwill);

(d)   whether the majority of the staff (in terms of numbers or skills) are being taken over by the new employer;

(e)   the transfer or otherwise of the circle of customers;

(f)   the degree of similarity between activities before and after the transfer;

(g)   the duration of any interruption in those activities.

The ECJ in *Spijkers* emphasised that all factors must be taken into account and that 'they cannot be examined independently of each other'.

The EAT confirmed in *Cheesman* (above) that where an economic entity can function without assets, the lack of assets transferred does not preclude a transfer; and where no staff are transferred, the reasons why may be relevant. (In *ECM (Vehicle Delivery Service) Ltd v Cox and Others* [1999] IRLR 559, the Court of Appeal held that the tribunal was entitled to have regard to the reasons why the employees were not taken on by the transferee – namely because it wished to avoid the (old) Regulations applying.)

The EAT overturned the decision of the tribunal that there was no transfer where the workforce of the transferor was not taken on. A tribunal should ask itself which, if any, of these factors are present. If the answer is all of (or in some cases several of) the above factors, it is generally going to be safe to assume that there has been a transfer of a stable economic entity.

The BIS Guidance suggests that 'resources' in reg 3(2) includes not only tangible and intangible assets but also employees. It is unclear how the reg 3(2) definition will work where only part of a large business is transferred, as it may be difficult to ascertain (particularly if resources are shared by different parts of the business) whether resources transferred were part of an 'organised grouping' capable of satisfying the reg 3 requirement. The Guidance states that in this situation the resources in question do not need to be used exclusively by the part of the business being transferred for the 2006 Regulations to apply.

For useful case law on the implications of the transferee not taking on former employees, see *RCO Support Services Ltd and Another v Unison and Others* [2002] ICR 751 and *Astle and Others v Cheshire County Council and Another* [2005] IRLR 12.

In *Ricardo v Portimão Urbis, EM, SA, in liquidation, Município de Portimão Emarp – Empresa Municipal de Águas e Resíduos de Portimão, EM, SA* (Case C-416/16), the CJEU examined whether a decision by a local Portuguese council to wind up its trading company and continue its activities by other means, was a transfer of an undertaking within the meaning of the Acquired Rights Directive (ARD).

The claimant, Mr Ricardo, was a director of the trading company, which had responsibility for all tourist matters, including street trading and cultural services. The Council decided to wind it up. At the time of the winding up, Mr Ricardo had been (at his request) on unpaid leave for three years. Some of the activities were taken over by the Council itself and the remainder of its activities were outsourced to another entity, Emarp (of which the Council was also the sole shareholder). There was an arrangement to transfer the staff to the Council and Emarp, but Mr Ricardo was not included in those plans. He was informed that his employment would end on the final closure of the trading company. He therefore brought a claim on the basis that there had been a transfer of an undertaking.

Where a transfer relates to public authorities, it is necessary to examine whether there is a transfer of an economic entity (ie of an undertaking engaged in economic activities) or an administrative reorganisation of public administrative authorities or the transfer of administrative functions between public administrative authorities. The first of these is a transfer of an undertaking. The latter two are not. In the *Portimão Urbis* case, the CJEU looked at these distinctions:

> The Court has made clear in that regard that the notion of economic activity encompasses any activity consisting in offering goods or services on a given market. Activities which fall within the exercise of public powers are excluded as a matter of principle from classification as economic activity. However, services which are carried out in the public interest and without a profit motive and are in competition with those offered by operators who seek to make a profit may be classified as economic activities for the purposes of [the ARD].

In this case, the Court considered that the various activities engaged in by the Council did not fall within the exercise of public powers, and were capable of being classified as economic activities for the purposes of the ARD:

> It is necessary in this regard to consider all the facts characterising the transaction at issue in the main proceedings, including, in particular, the type of undertaking or business in question, whether or not its tangible assets, such as buildings and movable property, are transferred, the value of its intangible assets at the time of the transfer, whether or not the majority of its employees are taken over by the new employer, whether or not its customers are transferred, the degree of similarity between the activities carried on before and after the transfer, and the period, if any, for which those activities were

suspended. However, all those circumstances are merely single factors in the overall assessment which must be made and cannot therefore be considered in isolation.

Ultimately this will be a matter for national courts to decide. This was recently looked at in *Nicholls v London Borough of Croydon* (UKEAT/0003/18) where the EAT provides a useful summary of the elements to be considered in a public sector transfer case.

In *ISS Facility Services NV v Govaerts and Atalian NV* (Case C-344/18), the ECJ held that an employment contract can be divided between different transferees in proportion to the tasks performed providing the division is possible and does not worsen the employee's working conditions or adversely affect their rights. Ms Govaerts was the project manager for cleaning contracts with the city of Ghent which were divided into three lots. The ECJ found that the Directive did not prevent the employee's contract being split. The decision goes against previous UK case law on splitting employment across multiple transferees, which holds that the employee either goes to the part of the business they are 'most closely connected' with (see eg *Kimberley Group Housing Ltd v Hambley* (UKEAT/0489/07) where the EAT was scathing about the employment tribunal's conclusion that there could be a transfer to two employers proportionate to the volume of work taken over by each transferee) or, if the employee's duties are spread across individual parts of the undertaking in a more disparate manner, then the employee cannot be said to be assigned to any part transferred, leading to no transfer and a likely redundancy by the transferor employer (see eg *Hassard v McGrath* [1996] NILR 586). If followed, this decision will lead to some potentially very difficult practical questions, as it will often be hard to 'split' employees' day to day work between different employers, not least if the two transferees do not agree on the relevant split. If the employee objects or the splitting is impossible in practice, then it is likely that the transferees will be regarded as having terminated the contract. In those circumstances, the transferees will be liable for the termination of employment of the employee, whether the liability arises as a result of the employee resigning or of the transferee(s) making the decision to dismiss. This means that all transferees will potentially be liable for notice payments, unfair dismissal claims and, potentially, redundancy costs. Given that such terminations would inevitably be by reason of the transfer, the risk for transferees is that these dismissals would be automatically unfair unless an 'ETO' (eg redundancy) reason can be argued.

In the case of *McTear Contracts Ltd v Bennett & ors* (UKEATS/0023/19), the EAT considered the application of *Govaerts* in a situation where there were two transferees in the context of a service provision change. North Lanarkshire Council re-tendered the work for replacement of kitchens within its social housing properties. Previously, all such work had been carried out by a single contractor, Amey Services Ltd. A group of Amey's employees worked exclusively on providing the services. Mr Bennett and his colleagues were split into two teams who generally worked independently of each other and contained the full range of trades necessary to fit kitchens, with each team working across the geographical area covered by the contract. When the work was re-tendered, it was split into two separate lots based on geographical lines (north and south) which were awarded to two new contractors, McTear Contracts Ltd and Mitie Property Services Ltd. Amey took the view that the 2006 Regulations (TUPE) would apply to the transfer of the services. In order to assess which employees should transfer to which new contractor, Amey looked at the geographical areas in which each team had worked in the previous 12 months and aligned these with the area covered by the two lots. As a result, Amey concluded that one team broadly corresponded to Lot 1 and the other team corresponded to Lot 2. Both McTear and Mitie took on certain of Amey's employees but not all of them, on the basis that they argued TUPE did not apply. Those Amey employees who were not taken on brought tribunal claims. The tribunal decided that there had been service provision changes under TUPE (applying reg 3(1)(b)) from Amey to McTear and Mitie and that all the employees transferred in accordance with Amey's allocation of them. In so doing, it held itself bound by previous authority that any transferring employees had to transfer to one or other transferee and ruled out the possibility of any employee transferring to both transferees. Both transferees appealed, relying on *Govaerts*, arguing that the tribunal had got it wrong as regards the allocation of employees.

On appeal, the EAT considered whether the approach taken by the tribunal was correct, taking into account the ECJ's decision in *Govaerts*. While the EAT accepted that there was no requirement to apply *Govaerts* to a service provision change under TUPE (which is unique to the UK), it was persuaded that having different approaches depending on whether it was a business transfer (which would have to follow *Govaerts*) or a service provision change (which did not) was not ideal. On that basis, the EAT decided that *Govaerts* could apply to a service provision change. The EAT held that:

> there is no reason in principle why an employee may not, following such a transfer, hold two or more contracts of employment with different employers at the same time, provided the work attributable to each contract is clearly separate from the work of the other(s) and is identifiable as such. The division along geographical lines, of work previously carried out under a single contract into two new contracts is, in principle, a situation where there could properly be found to be different employees on different jobs.

The EAT therefore set aside the tribunal's decision on the allocation of the employees and remitted the case back to the same tribunal to reconsider in light of *Govaerts*. Following Brexit, UK courts could depart from *Govaerts*, but this can only be done at Court of Appeal level or higher, unless there is legislative intervention from the government. For the time being, transferee employers involved in outsourcings and business acquisitions should investigate carefully the extent to which they have adequate indemnity protection against such outcomes.

7.2.2.2 Service provision changes

Background

As noted earlier, the most typical situation where the 2006 Regulations apply is the sale of a business as a going concern. Regulation 3(1)(b) was included in the 2006 Regulations in order to reduce the previous uncertainty which had existed in the 1981 Regulations about whether changes in service provision contracting would be captured by the Regulations or not.

Since the early 1980s, one of the developing trends within the public and private sector has been to externalise service functions, such as cleaning, catering, maintenance and IT systems, support and development. In this way, a particular organisation can concentrate its efforts on the core business, leaving ancillary services to those better equipped and qualified to provide them. Further, it allows businesses to deal more effectively with fluctuating demand for support services. Such externalisation has often involved contracting out, a process where the ancillary function which the organisation no longer wishes to manage is awarded, by contract, to another organisation. Contracting out is one of the most common 'atypical' transfer situations.

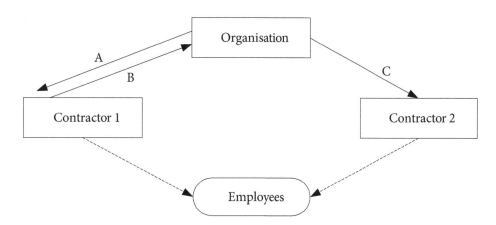

'First generation' contracting out occurs where the organisation awards a contract for some ancillary function to contractor 1 (arrow A). 'Second (third, fourth, etc) generation' contracting out occurs where an organisation ends a contract with one contractor (arrow B), and awards it to another (arrow C). Here, there is no contract between contractor 1 and contractor 2. The Regulations were, eventually, held to be capable of applying to all these scenarios.

When determining whether a business had retained its identity before and after the transfer, the courts focused on the nature of the activity rather than on the nature of the business. For example, on the contracting out of a canteen, the courts focused on whether *a* canteen existed after the transfer, rather than on whether *the* canteen (ie substantially the same business as before) existed after the transfer. In this way, it was not easy to see circumstances in which contracting out would fall outside the scope of the Acquired Rights Directive, and hence the Regulations, because where an organisation contracts out services, by definition, those activities will be continued or resumed by the (new) contractor.

In *Suzen v Zehnacker Gebaudereinigung GmbH Krankenhausservice* [1997] IRLR 255, the ECJ held that the Directive did not apply to the dismissal of a cleaner. Mrs Suzen was employed by Zehnacker as a cleaner at secondary church-run school, whose premises Zehnacker had contracted to clean. Mrs Suzen was dismissed along with seven other cleaners at the school when Zehnacker lost the contract. She claimed that the dismissal was automatically unfair, relying upon the Acquired Rights Directive.

The ECJ determined that the Directive did not apply to a change of contractor if there was no accompanying transfer from one undertaking to another of significant tangible or intangible assets, or taking over by the new employer of a major part of the workforce, in terms of their numbers and/or skills, assigned by the transferor to the performance of the contract:

> The decisive criterion for establishing the existence of a transfer within the meaning of the Directive is whether the entity in question retains its identity, as indicated inter alia by the fact that its operation is actually continued or resumed ...

> For the Directive to be applicable, however, the transfer must relate to a stable economic entity whose activity is not limited to performing one specific works contract. The term entity thus refers to an organised grouping of persons and assets facilitating the exercise of an economic activity which pursues a specified objective ... the fact that the service provided by the old and new awardees of a contract is similar does not therefore support the conclusion that an economic entity has been transferred. An entity cannot be reduced to the activity entrusted to it ... the mere loss of a service contract to a competitor cannot therefore by itself indicate the existence of a transfer within the meaning of the Directive.

The ECJ felt able to come to this conclusion on the same authority as it had done in *Spijkers* (see **7.2.2.1**), namely, whether the entity in question retains its identity. This is because the factors to be taken into account in determining whether the entity in question retains its identity are varied and may be applied by the courts at their discretion. In *Suzen*, the decisive criterion applied was whether there was an accompanying transfer from one undertaking to another of significant tangible or intangible assets *or* taking over by the new employer of a major part of the workforce (in terms of numbers or skills), ie *Suzen* sets a minimum precondition in these situations.

The 2006 Regulations aim to clear up most, if not all, of the previous uncertainties by including an express provision that the 2006 Regulations will apply to a 'service provision change'.

Service provision changes

Regulation 3(1)(b) states that a service provision change may exist in any one of three possible situations, provided that certain specified conditions are satisfied. The three situations are:

(a)   *activities cease to be carried out by a person ('a client') on his own behalf and are carried out instead by another person on the client's behalf ('a contractor') – outsourcing or contracting out (ie client to contractor) (reg 3(1)(b)(i));*

(b)   *activities cease to be carried out by a contractor on a client's behalf (whether or not those activities had previously been carried out by the client on his own behalf) and are carried out instead by another person ('a subsequent contractor') on the client's behalf – second generation contracting (ie contractor to contractor) (reg 3(1)(b)(ii)); or*

(c)   *activities cease to be carried out by a contractor [or sub-contractor] or a subsequent contractor on a client's behalf (whether or not those activities had previously been carried out by the client on his own behalf) and are carried out instead by the client on his own behalf – insourcing or contracting back in-house (ie contractor to client) (reg 3(1)(b)(iii)).*

Note: The 2014 Amendment Regulations inserted a new reg 3(2A) into the 2006 Regulations, which reads:

> References in paragraph (1)(b) to activities being carried out instead by another person are to activities which are fundamentally the same as the activities carried out previously.

While this is mainly cosmetic, in that it reflects existing case law (see, eg, *Metropolitan Resources Ltd v Churchill Dulwich Ltd* [2009] IRLR 700, below), it is intended to assist in the definition of 'activities' in reg 3(1)(b) by making it clear that the activities pre- and post-change must be fundamentally or essentially the same.

The EAT confirmed in *Arch Initiatives v Greater Manchester West Mental Health NHS Foundation* (EAT/0267/15) that a service provision change does not require the whole of the service carried out by the transferor to transfer (see analysis below).

The preconditions which must be satisfied (reg 3(3)) are that:

(a)   immediately before the service provision change:

(i)   there is an organised grouping of employees situated in Great Britain which has as its principal purpose the carrying out of the activities concerned on behalf of the client,

(ii)   the client intends that the activities will, following the service provision change, be carried out by the transferee other than in connection with a single specific event or task of short-term duration; and

(b)   the activities concerned do not consist wholly or mainly of the supply of goods for the client's use. If there is a mixture, the service element will need to be predominant. (See *Pannu and Others v Geo W King (in liquidation) and Others* (UKEAT/0021/11) for a case in which the EAT upheld a decision that this exclusion applied.)

The wording of reg 3(3)(a) does not therefore cover transactions where there is no identifiable group of employees dedicated to meeting one client's needs.

Analysis

A service provision change will occur when a client who engages a contractor to do work on its behalf is either:

(a)   reassigning such a contract; or

(b)   bringing the work 'in-house'.

In *CT Plus (Yorkshire) CIC v Black and Others* (UKEAT/0035/16), the appellant ran a 'park-and-ride' service under a contract with the local council. The second respondent decided to run a commercial service on the same route, using its own staff and buses, without a subsidy from the Council. As a result, the Council (the first respondent) terminated its contract with the appellant. The appellant contended that the second respondent was a subsequent contractor carrying out the same activities 'on the client's behalf', the Council being the client. The

Employment Judge found that the second respondent was not carrying out the activities on the 'client's' (the local council's) behalf, but as a commercial venture on its own behalf. The EAT agreed. 'Client' means an organisation that is in a position to carry out activities either itself or by commissioning them from others to carry out those activities on its behalf. The Council had not commissioned the second respondent's services.

Note that reg 2 provides that 'contractor' includes subcontractors. It has nonetheless been a matter of some contention as to whether the 2006 Regulations protect the interests of subcontractors in the event of a service provision change. In *Jinks v London Borough of Havering* (UKEAT/0157/14), the EAT had to consider the interpretation of the word 'client'. Havering Council had contracted with a third party (S) to operate an ice rink and car park. S subcontracted the running of the car park to another company (R). The subcontract ended when the Council transferred the car park to a local NHS Trust. The question arose whether there was a relevant transfer of the running of the car park operation to the Council, so that R's staff, including the claimant, who wanted to bring an unfair dismissal claim, transferred to the Council's employment. The employment tribunal found that the Council was the client of S, not R, and that there was no service provision change as the client must be the same both before and after the transfer. As there was no contractual relationship between the Council and R, the activities could not be 'carried on behalf of the client'. The EAT disagreed and adopted a wider interpretation of 'client'. It said that the question that should be asked was: On whose behalf was the car park being run? The identification of the 'client' is a question of fact, not law, and the EAT said that there can be more than one client in any given case. A strict legal or contractual relationship was not essential. Regulation 3(1)(b)(iii) must be read with reg 2: R was in reality carrying out activities 'on behalf' of the Council. The case was remitted to the employment tribunal to reconsider. In *Ottino Property Services Ltd v Duncan* (UKEAT/0321/14), the EAT also confirmed that the references to 'a client' and 'the client' in reg 3(1)(b) not only applied to a single client, but could also apply where there was a change in the provision of activities carried out on behalf of a group of clients. There are two provisos to this: (i) the identity of the clients must remain the same before and after the service provision change (see *McCarrick v Hunter* [2013] IRLR 26); and (ii) the clients must be able to demonstrate (reg 3(3)(a)(ii)) a common intention.

It will *not* be a service provision change if:

(a)   the contract is wholly or mainly for the supply of goods for the client's use (eg client engages a contractor to supply sandwiches and drinks to its canteen every day to sell on to staff) (see *Pannu* (above)); or

(b)   the activities are carried out in connection with a single specific event or a task of short-term duration. This suggests that where something is a 'one-off' job it will not be covered by the 2006 Regulations. There is a lack of clarity in the drafting of this exception. This wording may be read in one of two ways: either the exclusion applies to an activity (an 'event' or 'task') that is a one-off job *and* is of short duration, or it applies where the service activity in question is either a single specific event *or* a task of short-term duration.

The BIS Guidance supports the former interpretation, giving as an example two hypothetical contracts covering security for the Olympic Games. The first contract concerns the provision of security advice to the event organisers and covers a period of several years running up to the event. The second contract concerns hiring staff to protect athletes during the Games themselves. Both contracts are one-off in the sense that they relate to the holding of a specific event. The first contract runs for a significantly longer period than the second and would be covered by the Regulations, but the second would not.

This issue was considered by the EAT in *Liddell's Coaches v Cook* (UKEATS/0025/12), with the EAT disagreeing with the BIS Guidance: the phrase, it said, must be considered disjunctively. A single specific event did not need to be of short-term duration. The EAT looked at this again in *Swanbridge Hire & Sales Ltd v Butler & Others* (UKEAT/0056/13). The EAT held, disagreeing with *Lidell*, that the phrase 'short term' qualifies single events as well as tasks. Slade J's decision in *Swanbridge* is supported by the President of the EAT and should, for the moment, be preferred to that in *Lidell* (see *SNR Denton UK LLP v Kirwan & Others* (UKEAT/0158/12)). *Swanbridge* was applied by the EAT in *Horizon Security Services Ltd v Ndeze and the PCS Group* (UKEAT/0071/14).

(c)   the client is not the same client. In *McCarrick v Hunter* [2013] IRLR 26, the Court of Appeal upheld the EAT's decision that there cannot be a service provision change in circumstances in which the client changes as well as the service provider: the client must be the same throughout. This was the first case in which the Court of Appeal considered the definition of a service provision change in reg 3(1)(b). (See also *SNR Denton UK LLP v Kirwan & Others* [2012] IRLR 966 for a similar analysis and *Horizon* (above).)

Note: These are exceptions to reg 3(1)(b). Regulation 3(1)(a) may still apply in such situations, facts permitting.

Under reg 3(3)(a)(i), for there to be a service provision change, there does not have to be an 'economic entity' before the alleged transfer, so long as there is an organised grouping of employees and the other tests above are met. The term 'organised grouping of employees' is probably best summarised by the word 'team' (but note it is also stated that a single employee can satisfy the test – reg 2(1)). The EAT held in *Argyll Coastal Services Ltd v Mr I Stirling and Others* (UKEATS/0012/11) that the phrase 'organised grouping of employees' 'connotes a number of employees ... organised for the purpose of carrying out activities ... who work as a team'. Further, it does not matter whether the new contractor takes on any of the old contractor's employees; the transferee cannot now seek to argue that the 2006 Regulations do not apply because he did not take on any employees. So long as the same activities are carried out for the client before and after the transfer, there is a transfer.

The EAT gave helpful guidance on the concept of an 'organised grouping of employees' in *Eddie Stobart Ltd v Moreman* [2012] IRLR 356:

> The paradigm of an 'organised grouping' is indeed the case where employees are organised as 'the [Client A] team', though no doubt the definition could in principle be satisfied in cases where the identification is less specific .

In *Amaryllis v McLeod* (EAT/0273/15) the EAT, referring to the *Moreman* case, said that what must be focused on was what the grouping of employees were doing immediately before the transfer, and not what happened historically. It is not enough that a department carries out significant work for a client – as the EAT said in *Moreman*, 'the regulation does not merely say that employees should in their day-to-day work in fact (principally) carry out the activities in question; it says that carrying out those activities should be the (principal) purpose of an "organised grouping to which they belong".'

Where the grouping comes about by virtue of 'coincidences of working patterns', that is unlikely to be enough – there needs to be an element of planning and deliberate organisation (see *Ceva Freight*, below).

The BIS Guidance offers the following analysis:

> This is intended to confine the Regulations' coverage to cases where the old service provider (ie the transferor) has in place a team of employees to carry out the service activities, and that team is essentially dedicated to carrying out the activities that are to transfer (though they do not need to work exclusively on those activities but carrying them out for the client does need to be their principal purpose). It would therefore exclude cases where there was no identifiable grouping of employees or where it just happens in practice that a group of employees works mostly for a particular client. This is because it would be unclear which employees should transfer in the event of a change of contractor, if

there was no such grouping. For example, if a contractor was engaged by a client to provide, say, a courier service, but the collections and deliveries were carried out each day by various different couriers on an ad hoc basis, rather than by an identifiable team of employees, there would be no 'service provision change' and the Regulations would not apply. It should be noted that a 'grouping of employees' can constitute just one person as may happen when the cleaning of small business premises is undertaken by a single person employed by a contractor.

In *Enterprise Management Services Ltd v Connect-Up Ltd and Others* (UKEAT/0462/10), the EAT set out a useful statement of the law:

> (2)   The expression 'activities' is not defined in the Regulations. Thus the first task for the Employment Tribunal is to identify the relevant activities carried out by the original contractor: see *Kimberley*, para 28; *Metropolitan*, paras 29–30. That was the issue on appeal in *OCS*, where the Appellant's challenge to the activities identified by the Employment Tribunal failed.
>
> (3)   The next (critical) question for present purposes will be whether the activities carried on by the subsequent contractor after the relevant date ... are fundamentally or essentially the same as those carried on by the original contractor. Minor differences may properly be disregarded. This is essentially a question of fact and degree for the Employment Tribunal (*Metropolitan*, para 30).
>
> (4)   Cases may arise (eg [*Clearsprings*]) where the division of services after the relevant date, known as fragmentation, amongst a number of different contractors means that the case falls outside the service provision change regime, as explained in *Kimberley* (para 35).
>
> (5)   Even where the activities remain essentially the same before and after the putative transfer date as performed by the original and subsequent contractors, [a service provision charge] will only take place if the following conditions are satisfied:
>
> > (i)   there is an organised grouping of employees in Great Britain which has as its principal purpose the carrying out of the activities concerned on behalf of the client;
> >
> > (ii)   the client intends that the transferee post-service provision change will not carry out the activities in connection with a single event of short-term duration;
> >
> > (iii) the activities are not wholly or mainly the supply of goods rather than services for the client's use. ...
>
> (6)   Finally, by reg 4(1) the Employment Tribunal must decide whether each Claimant was assigned to the organised grouping of employees.

The statement of law set out in *Enterprise Management Services Ltd* (above) was endorsed in *Johnson Controls Ltd v Campbell and Another* (UKEAT/0042/12). The EAT added that the identification of 'activity' is critical in many cases and that tribunals must be careful to ensure that they do not take too narrow a view of that term. The EAT said that

> if for instance the activity performed by a given employee is after a service provision change to be performed by two or three employees in the transferee or, in a 3(1)(b)(iii) situation, by the client itself, then it may well be that the approach of the Tribunal should recognise that the same activity may well be carried on, though it is performed now by three people rather than by the one person who earlier performed it.

In *Rynda (UK) Ltd v Rhijnsburger* [2015] EWCA Civ 75, the Court of Appeal upheld an employment tribunal decision that a single employee was an organised grouping that carried out the activity of management of a portfolio of commercial properties in The Netherlands. A deliberate decision had been taken by the transferor before the transfer, to organise the employee to work on these properties. See also *Robert Sage v O'Connell* (above), where the EAT overturned a tribunal's finding that an employee who was prohibited from working for a client, X (because he was suspended) was assigned to the group of employees working with X. The EAT held that as the employee was prohibited from working with the group of employees who were subject to the service provision change, that employee could not be said to be 'assigned' to that group.

In *London Care Ltd v Henry and Others* (EAT/0219/17 and 0220/17) the EAT confirms that fragmentation must be considered when deciding whether the activities taken on by the new contractors are essentially the same as those carried out by the previous contractor (see

Kimberley above). Only then will it be possible to ascertain whether there is an organised grouping of employees with the principal purpose of carrying out the activities.

7.2.2.3 Cross-border transfers of undertakings

There has long been uncertainty about whether the Directive/Regulations apply in relation to the transfer of a UK-based business even if the purchaser is outside the European Union. This was looked at by the EC Commission, which reported on 18 June 2007. It did not reach a definitive conclusion! In *Holis Metal Industries Ltd v GMB & Newell Ltd* [2008] IRLR 187, the EAT said the UK Regulations could apply transnationally.

7.2.2.4 Time of transfer

Practically speaking, a transfer of an undertaking may extend over a period of time rather than being an event staged to take place for the purposes of the Acquired Rights Directive and the 2006 Regulations at any one particular moment in time. However, the legal requirement for certainty, so as to be able to identify, at the least, the date when a transfer took place, may conflict with practical realities. Sometimes the point of transfer is expressly pinpointed in sale documentation or otherwise agreed by the parties, but if it is not, tribunals have to identify as best they can when the actual transfer took place. The date of transfer may be important.

The ECJ considered the 'time' of transfer in *Celtec v Astley* (Case C-478/03) [2005] IRLR 647, where it had to decide whether a relevant transfer could be a gradual process occurring over a period of several years. The ECJ ruled that the use of the word 'date' (singular) in the Acquired Rights Directive, combined with the need for legal certainty, meant that the claimants in that case had to be able to point to a specific date on which they said the transfer occurred. A transfer *cannot* occur over a period of time (see paras 32–36). The ECJ went on to find:

> 29. ... [T]he reference to 'date of a transfer' in [the Acquired Rights Directive] is designed to identify the workers who may rely on the protection established by that provision. That protection therefore covers workers assigned to the unit affected by the transfer whose contract of employment or employment relationship is in force on the 'date of a transfer' and not those who have ceased to be employed by the transferor on that date (see Case 19/83 *Wendelboe and Others* [1985] ECR 457, paragraphs 13 and 15) or those who were engaged by the transferee after that date (see *Ny Mølle Kro*, cited above, paragraphs 24 to 26).
>
> 30. Both the choice of the word 'date' and reasons of legal certainty indicate that, in the mind of the Community legislature, the workers entitled to benefit from the protection established by [the] Directive must be identified at a particular point in the transfer process and not in relation to the length of time over which that process extends.
>
> ...
>
> 36. In those circumstances, the term 'date of a transfer' in [the Directive] must be understood as referring to the date on which responsibility as employer for carrying on the business of the unit in question moves from the transferor to the transferee.

In support of that interpretation, the Court observed, first, that the Acquired Rights Directive gives the Member States the option of providing that, after the date of transfer, the transferor is to be liable, alongside the transferee, for the obligations arising from a contract of employment or employment relationship. Such a rule implies that in any event those obligations are transferred to the transferee on the date of the transfer (*Rotsart de Hertaing v Benoidt SA and IGC Housing Service SA* (Case C-305/94) [1997] IRLR 127, para 23).

Lastly, the Court considered that to allow the transferor or transferee the possibility of choosing the date from which the contract of employment or employment relationship is transferred would amount to allowing employers to derogate, at least temporarily, from the provisions of the Directive, whereas those provisions are mandatory, and it is thus not possible to derogate from them in a manner unfavourable to employees (*Rotsart de Hertaing*, paras 17 and 25).

Having established that the Directive refers to a transfer taking place on a particular date, the ECJ went on to consider the issue of how that date was to be identified. The ECJ referred to Article 1(1) of the Acquired Rights Directive, which refers to the change in the legal or natural person responsible for carrying on the business and who continues or resumes the operation. The ECJ concluded that what was significant was to identify 'the date on which responsibility as employer for carrying on the business of the unit in question moves from the transferor to the transferee'.

Following the ECJ's ruling that a relevant transfer cannot take place over a period of time but only on a specific date, the House of Lords gave its opinion on the actual facts in *Celtec*. The House of Lords had to decide whether the date of the transfer was the date the employees were originally seconded. Their Lordships found that there was a deemed transfer of the claimants' contracts to the Training and Enterprise Council at the date of the original secondment, even though for three years the claimants thought they were civil service employees. This was when responsibility for carrying on the business had passed to the transferee.

The EAT followed *Celtec* in *Housing Maintenance Solutions Ltd v McAteer and others* (UKEAT/0440/ 13). That case concerned a contract for the repair and maintenance of housing association properties in Liverpool. The housing association terminated its contract with its existing contractor on 9 June 2011. Staff were made redundant and told that their contracts terminated on that date. The housing association began the process of setting up a subsidiary company, Housing Maintenance Solutions Ltd, to carry out the role. Housing Maintenance Solutions Ltd did not start operating until 1 July 2011. A number of employees brought claims for unfair dismissal, unpaid wages during the interval, and a failure to inform and consult. A key issue was the identity of the employer between 9 June and 1 July. The employment tribunal said the transfer took place on 9 June 2011 because that was the date that Housing Maintenance Solutions Ltd 'accepted responsibility for the claimants as employees'. The EAT disagreed and said that the date of transfer was the date when management responsibility for the employer's business transferred. The legal assumption of responsibility for the employees occurs on the date of transfer and not vice versa. The case was remitted to the employment tribunal to determine the date of the transfer.

In all cases, in determining when a relevant transfer takes place it will be essential to consider when responsibility for carrying on the business or service had transferred from one entity to another. In practice, if the transfer is a sale of a business and there is a gap between exchange of contracts and completion, it will be the date of completion which is the date of transfer for the purposes of reg 4.

7.3   EFFECT OF A RELEVANT TRANSFER

Once it has been established that a relevant transfer has occurred, it is necessary to consider what effect that has on the employment relationship.

7.3.1   Automatic transfer of contracts of employment

Regulation 4(1) of the 2006 Regulations provides:

> Except where objection is made under paragraph (7), a relevant transfer shall not operate so as to terminate the contract of employment of any person employed by the transferor and assigned to the organised grouping of resources or employees that is subject to the relevant transfer, which would otherwise be terminated by the transfer, but any such contract shall have effect after the transfer as if originally made between the person so employed and the transferee.

In other words, an employee's contract of employment does not end by reason of the transfer; instead the contract will be transferred from the old employer to the new on the existing terms and conditions, and with the employee's existing continuity of service (see *Jackson v Computershare Investment Services plc* [2008] IRLR 70). (Employees do, however, have the right to object to the transfer of their contracts (see **7.3.2.3**).) Note that the reference to employees is likely to include workers too (see reg 2(1) and *Dewhurst v Revisecatch Ltd t/a Ecourier* (ET/2201909/18)). Note too that where there is a pre-transfer dismissal, that dismissal is effective and contracts do not then transfer. Liability for the dismissal *may* transfer (see **7.3.2**).

In *G4S Justice Services (UK) Ltd v Anstey* [2006] IRLR 588, the EAT held that employees who had been dismissed for gross misconduct but who had an internal appeal pending at the date of a relevant transfer had their employment preserved only for the purpose of the appeal. If the appeal failed, the dismissal stood and the employees would not have been employed immediately before the transfer. If the appeal succeeded and the dismissal was set aside then it 'vanished', and the employees would be treated as if they were employed immediately before the transfer, so they continued in employment with the transferee.

Regulation 4(2) states that on the completion of a relevant transfer:

(a)   all the transferor's rights, powers, duties and liabilities under or in connection with any such contract shall be transferred by virtue of this regulation to the transferee; and

(b)   any act or omission before the transfer is completed, of or in relation to the transferor in respect of that contract or a person assigned to that organised grouping of resources or employees, shall be deemed to have been an act or omission of or in relation to the transferee.

The employees, in other words, have the same rights against the transferee as they had against the transferor and their continuity of employment is not affected by the transfer.

Regulation 8 sets out the position in respect of insolvent businesses. The detail is beyond the scope of this book.

7.3.2   Who is covered by reg 4(1)?

Regulation 4(3) states that any reference

to a person employed by the transferor and assigned to the organised grouping of ... employees that is subject to a relevant transfer, is a reference to a person so employed immediately before the transfer, or who would have been so employed if he had not been dismissed in the circumstances described in regulation 7(1) ...

Regulation 4(3) clearly applies to all employees employed by the transferor immediately before the transfer. In *Secretary of State for Employment v Spence* [1986] IRLR 248, CA, the Court of Appeal said that the phrase 'immediately before' means at the precise moment of transfer.

However, reg 4(3) of the 2006 Regulations also applies to employees who would have been so employed had they not been unfairly dismissed in the circumstances described in reg 7(1) (see **7.5**). This statutory provision encapsulates the House of Lords' judgment in *Secretary of State for Employment v Litster* [1989] IRLR 161. In that case the employees were dismissed one hour before the transfer. The House of Lords made it clear that a transferee may still be liable for any claims arising out of a pre-transfer dismissal, and reg 4(3) preserves that rule. This means that a transferee cannot circumvent the 2006 Regulations by insisting that the transferor dismiss some or all of the workforce prior to completion.

Thus a relevant transfer will:

(a)   transfer the contracts of anyone who is employed by the transferor immediately before the relevant transfer and who is assigned to the relevant group of employees that is the subject of the transfer. Their contracts of employment will transfer to the transferee and they will be employed by the transferee under the terms and conditions of those contracts;

(b)   pass liability for any pre-transfer dismissals falling within the circumstances described in reg 7(1) to the transferee. In other words, the transferee will be liable for any claims arising out of pre-transfer dismissals (actual or constructive (see reg 4(11)), or 'deemed' (see reg 4(9)) – see **7.3.2.1**) if those dismissals were by reason of the transfer, and those dismissals will be automatically unfair (see **7.5**) unless there is an economic, technical or organisational reason entailing changes in the workforce. Although the dismissal is effective (see **7.6**) and the employee is therefore not employed by the transferee, all rights, duties, and liabilities relating to his previous employment will transfer in addition to the claim of unfair dismissal, including, for example, any wrongful dismissal claim or any claim for discrimination.

7.3.2.1 Meaning of dismissal

Dismissal includes actual and constructive dismissal (see reg 4(11) at **7.3.2.3**). However, the term also includes, for the purpose of the 2006 Regulations, 'deemed' dismissal. This is because reg 4(9) provides that

> where a relevant transfer involves or would involve a substantial change in working conditions to the material detriment of a person whose contract of employment is or would be transferred under paragraph (1) [of reg 4], such an employee may treat the contract of employment as having been terminated, and the employee shall be treated for any purpose as having been dismissed by the employer.

The wording in reg 4(9) is wider than the meaning of constructive dismissal, where the employee must prove that he resigned as a result of a repudiatory breach of contract (see **Chapter 3**). The regulation will apply even when there is no fundamental breach of contract.

The BIS Guidance suggests that a substantial change in working conditions is likely to include a major relocation of the workplace which makes it difficult or much more expensive for an employee to travel, or the withdrawal of a right to a tenured post.

The EAT considered the meaning of reg 4(9) in *Tapere v South London and Maudsley NHS Trust* (UKEAT/0410/08). The EAT pointed out that there are two components to reg 4(9):

(a)   a 'substantial change in working conditions';

(b)   'to the material detriment of a person whose contract of employment is ... transferred'.

The EAT held that the term 'working conditions' should be interpreted widely following the decision of the ECJ in *Merckx and Neuhuys v Ford Motors Belgium SA* [1996] IRLR 467. In that case, salesmen were transferred to a new dealership at a different workplace without any guarantee as to client base or sales figures, so that there was potential for an adverse impact on commission. These components were regarded by the ECJ as 'working conditions'. The phrase therefore applies, according to the EAT, to contractual terms and conditions as well as physical conditions. On the facts, therefore, a change of workplace was a change to 'working conditions'. The question of whether it is a change of substance is, according to the EAT, a question of fact, and the employment tribunal will need to consider the nature, as well as the degree, of the change in order to decide whether it is substantial. The character of the change is likely to be the most important aspect of determining whether the change is substantial. In *Merckx*, the ECJ regarded the change as substantial because it was a change in remuneration. The EAT gave another example: a change in the method of salary payment. Moving from cash payment to bank, or from weekly to monthly payment would be a change of substance, even if the amount of remuneration was not altered. Therefore a change of workplace, on the facts, is also a change of substance.

On the phrase 'material detriment', the EAT held that 'material' simply means not trivial or fanciful, and that what has to be considered is the impact of the proposed change from the employee's point of view. On the facts of *Tapere* the change of location meant potential disruption to child-care arrangements and a longer journey, or an altered journey involving travelling on the M25, which the appellant did not find attractive. The tribunal should ask whether the employee regarded those factors as detrimental and, if so, whether that was a reasonable position for the employee to adopt. On the facts the claimant was therefore deemed to have been dismissed under reg 4(9).

In *Abellio London Ltd (Formerly Travel London Ltd) v Musse and Others* [2012] IRLR 360 (EAT), the EAT held that a move from north to south of the river in London (six miles) was substantial and that an increase in the working day of one to two hours was a material detriment, and that it was irrelevant that the contract contained a mobility clause. There was therefore a reg 4(9) dismissal, notwithstanding that there was no breach of contract. *Cetinsoy & Others v London United Busways Ltd* (UKEAT/0042/14) involved the transfer of a bus route from one company to another. As with the *Abellio* case, the transfer resulted in a move to a different depot. Although the contract specified that the employees should work at various locations, that did not include the new depot. The EAT upheld the employment tribunal decision that while the requirement to work at the new depot was a breach of contract, it was not a fundamental (repudiatory) breach. Furthermore, the move (which added between 30 minutes' and 60 minutes' travelling time a day) did not involve a substantial change in working conditions and was not to the material detriment of the employees.

Note that an employee who resigns in reliance on reg 4(9) cannot make a claim for notice pay. The employee should give notice and work it out (reg 4(10)).

7.3.2.2 Employees whose contracts would 'otherwise have been terminated by the transfer'

Those employees whose contracts would not be terminated by the transfer do not come within reg 4. This may, for example, apply to an employee who is retained by the transferor and redeployed in some other part of his operation within the terms of the employee's contract or with his consent. Such redeployment should take place before the transfer.

Where part of a business is transferred, employees will not be affected by reg 4 if they did not work in the part transferred. Even employees who perform duties in relation to the part transferred (eg administrative duties) will not be covered unless they are assigned to the part transferred, ie the organised grouping.

The question of whether an employee is assigned to the relevant grouping is a question of fact. The 2006 Regulations do not provide much by way of assistance as to what is meant by 'assigned'. Regulation 2(1) provides that it means 'assigned other than on a temporary basis'. For the time being, therefore, existing domestic and European case law will still be relevant. See, for example, *Securiplan v Bademosi* (UKEAT/1128/02) and *Gale v Northern General Hospital* [1994] IRLR 292. In general the case law confirms that where the employee was assigned is a matter of overall impression for the tribunal. This may often be decided as a mathematical question of how the employee spent most of his time, but sometimes a different approach may be called for.

The BIS Guidance suggests that in determining whether an assignment is temporary, factors such as 'the length of time the employee has been there and whether a date has been set by the transferor for his return or re-assignment to another part of the business or undertaking' should be taken into account.

Regard should also be had to the test laid down in *Botzen v Rotterdamsche Droogdok Maatschappij BV* (Case 186/83) [1986] 2 CMLR 50, ECJ. The ECJ said, in summary, that the test is whether there is a transfer of the part of the undertaking to which the employees 'were assigned and which formed the organisational framework within which their employment relationship took effect'.

Useful guidance on the *Botzen* test was given by the EAT in *Duncan Webb Offset (Maidstone) Ltd v Cooper and Others* [1995] IRLR 633. Factors which should be taken into account include how much time was spent on different parts of the business, how much value has been given to each part, what the contract said about the employee's duties, and how the cost of the employee was shared between the various parts of the business.

Further guidance may be found in the Court of Appeal decision in *CPL Distribution Ltd v Todd* [2003] IRLR 23. In *Argyll Coastal Services Ltd* (see **7.2.2.2** above), the EAT confirmed that involvement in carrying out the activity will not necessarily mean that the employee was assigned to the organised group, eg where the employee was covering for a colleague. In BT *Managed Services Ltd v Edwards & Another* (UKEAT/0241/14), the EAT held that an employee on long-term sick leave with no possibility of returning to work was not assigned to an organised grouping and so his employment did not transfer. Although it was a question of fact in each case, here he did not contribute to the 'economic activity' of the grouping (reg 3(2)), was unlikely to do so in the future, and a mere administrative connection was insufficient to constitute assignment.

In *Carsway Cleansing Consultants Ltd v Richards & Cooper Cleaning Services* (UKEAT/629/97), the EAT held that an employer could not 'off-load' an unwanted employee by deliberately moving him to a part of the undertaking that the employer knew was about to be transferred. The EAT held that such an act was fraudulent and, accordingly, void. The employee was not 'employed in the part of the undertaking' being transferred.

In *Jakowlew v Nestor Primecare (t/a Saga) and others* (UKEAT/0431/14), the EAT considered whether the client can determine who is assigned to the organised grouping. In a previous case (*Robert Sage Ltd t/a Prestige Nursing Care Ltd v O'Connell and Others* (UKEAT/0336/13)), the EAT had held that this issue is to be determined by asking the question: Where would the employee be required to work immediately before the transfer? While the terms of any contract plays a part in answering that question, in some cases the contract can be superseded by the practical situation. In *Sage*, the EAT had held that as the employee had been prohibited from undertaking work with the organised group immediately before the transfer, and that prohibition was permanent, she could not be regarded as being assigned to it. *Jakowlew* asked the same question, but came to a different conclusion on the facts. N was a contractor who employed the claimant in providing care services. E was the client. The contract between N and E came to an end on 30 June 2013, and W took it over from 1 July 2013. The claimant was told that her employment would transfer from N to W. However, from February 2013, the claimant had, with others, been suspended for disciplinary reasons. The contract between N and E provided that E had the right to reject staff it considered unsuitable. E was concerned about the continued employment of the suspended employees, and on 19 June, E told N that it did not want the three suspended employees to continue working on its contract. N refused this request, saying that it was vexatious and not valid. On 27 June, three days before the transfer, the claimant was disciplined and given a final written warning. After the transfer, N reviewed the situation; it decided that E's request was valid and hence that the claimant should have been taken off the contract. As a result, it said that the claimant was not transferred. N had lost two contracts with E, and as a result had closed its office, so was in a position to make straightforward redundancies. The claimant was made redundant by N in September 2013. The claimant issued proceedings against both N and W, claiming that she was assigned to the organised grouping of employees that had transferred from N to W. The employment tribunal held that E's request was effective and that, as at the date of the transfer, this meant that the claimant was not assigned to the organised grouping. The EAT allowed the claimant's appeal and held that it was up to the employer, not the client, to decide who was assigned where. At the time of the transfer the claimant was no longer suspended and remained working for N: N had not accepted E's demand for the employee to be removed from the contract.

In *Kimberley Group Housing v Hambley* (above at **7.2.2.2**) the EAT held that there may be a transfer to more than one transferee under the Regulations. On the facts there were two overlapping contracts post-transfer, providing for activities done pre-transfer by one provider. By analogy with *Duncan Webb* above, the EAT found that the transferor's employees transferred to the transferee taking over the majority of the services, in this case Kimberley which took over 79% of the activities performed in one area and 97% in the other area of the country. See also *Costain v Armitage* (UKEAT/0048/14).

For a useful analysis of the tribunal's role in assessing whether an employee is 'assigned', see *London Borough of Hillingdon v Gormanley & Others* (UKEAT/0169/14). The EAT upheld a tribunal's decision that an employee on long-term sick leave who had been off sick for more than five years was not assigned to the group that transferred because there was, on the tribunal's findings, no prospect of the employee returning (BT *Managed Services Ltd v Edwards & Another* (UKEAT/0241/14)).

In *Ricardo v Portimão Urbis, EM, SA, in liquidation, Município de Portimão Emarp – Empresa Municipal de Águas e Resíduos de Portimão, EM, SA* (Case C-416/16), the CJEU had to consider whether the claimant, Mr Ricardo, who was a director of a local council's trading company, which was being wound up by the Council and its activities continued by other means, was covered by the concept of 'employee' within the meaning of the Acquired Rights Directive (ARD) such that his employment contract should transfer. Mr Ricardo had been (at his request) on unpaid leave for three years. There was an arrangement to transfer the staff to the Council and a new entity, but Mr Ricardo was not included in those plans. He was informed that his employment would end on the final closure of the trading company. The Court noted that any person who is considered to be an employee under the relevant national employment will be covered, so their employment contract will exist at the date of the transfer. Portuguese legislation provides that whilst an employment contract is suspended, the rights, obligations and safeguards of parties who are not required to be in active service are maintained. Therefore, said the Court, in such a case, the ARD will protect an employee who is not actually performing his duties because his employment contract is suspended.

7.3.2.3   The employee's right of objection

In the UK, employees can object to the transfer of their employment contract. If they do this, their employment is treated as terminated by operation of law and there is no dismissal.

Regulation 4(7) states:

> Paragraphs (1) and (2) shall not operate to transfer the contract of employment and the rights, powers, duties and liabilities under or in connection with it of an employee who informs the transferor or the transferee that he objects to becoming employed by the transferee.

Under reg 4(8):

> Subject to paragraphs (9) and (11), where an employee so objects, the relevant transfer shall operate so as to terminate his contract of employment with the transferor but he shall not be treated, for any purpose, as having been dismissed by the transferor.

And under reg 4(11):

> Paragraphs (1), (7), (8) and (9) are without prejudice to any right of an employee arising apart from these Regulations to terminate his contract of employment without notice in acceptance of a repudiatory breach of contract by his employer.

The transfer of the contract of employment and rights, powers, duties and liabilities under and in connection with it, will not occur if the employee informs the transferor or the transferee that he objects to becoming employed by the transferee. In that event, the transfer will terminate the employee's contract of employment with the transferor, but he will not be treated for any purpose as having been dismissed by the transferor, ie he will be regarded as having resigned (reg 4(7) and (8)) unless the reason for the objection is that the transfer will involve a significant and detrimental change in working conditions (reg 4(9)) (see **7.3.2.1** above), or the employee is alleging constructive dismissal (reg 4(11)). Therefore, if an employee exercises this right, he will lose all his rights against both the transferor and the transferee, unless he has been caused to resign by a change in working conditions or a breach of contract by his employer. Interestingly, the Court of Appeal has held that as the effect of the objection was that the contract of employment did not transfer to the transferee, neither did liability for any claims flowing from a constructive or reg 4(9) dismissal, which therefore remain with the transferor. In a case of this type, reg 4(3)/*Litster* does not apply to transfer liability (*University of Oxford v Humphreys* [2000] IRLR 183, CA).

There is nothing to prevent an employee in this situation being re-engaged by the transferee on new terms, although his continuity would be broken.

The right of employees to object to a transfer of their employment on a business transfer was also considered in *Senior Heat Treatment Ltd v Bell* [1997] IRLR 614. In this case, the employer decided to move its Heat Treatment Department to a vacant factory and new employer six miles away. The employees were given the following options:

(a)   transfer to the new factory and new employer;

(b)   opt out of the transfer and receive a payment equivalent to statutory redundancy pay, pay in lieu of notice and a further ex gratia sum.

The employees were given a form on which to state their preference. Having ticked the box objecting to the transfer, they received payments in accordance with the severance package. However, they had *already* signed employment contracts with the new employer and then turned up for work for the new employer the following Monday. When they were dismissed 10 months later, they claimed unfair dismissal and/or redundancy payments in the employment tribunal.

When the case reached the EAT, it was found that on the peculiar facts of this case the former employees were entitled to count their employment before the transfer towards their continuity of service, and as a result they had two years' service and could bring claims in the employment tribunal. The reasoning was that the employees had already signed contracts with the new employer before they completed the forms provided by their old employer. As a result, the EAT found they had not objected to the transfer even though they had said they wished to 'opt out' of it.

Opting out was also considered by the EAT in *Capita Health Solutions v BBC and McLean* (UKEAT/0034/07). The BBC transferred its occupational health unit to an outside contractor. Mrs McLean 'objected' and 'resigned' on the day before the transfer, stating that she would work 'a period of secondment' with the contractor while she served out her notice. The employment tribunal said that on the facts, Mrs McLean had not objected and her contract still transferred. The EAT agreed. Regulation 4 states that an objection will stop a transfer occurring and end the contract. There is no provision for working out notice. If Mrs McLean had objected successfully, she could not have continued as the BBC's employee.

It is now clear that neither the general application of the automatic transfer principle nor the existence of the employee's right to object is subject to a precondition that employees have knowledge of both the fact of a transfer and the identity of the transferee (*Secretary of State for Trade and Industry v Cook and Others* [1997] ICR 288, EAT).

Note that according to the High Court, employees may object after a transfer where they do not know the identity of the transferee pre-transfer, so long as they do so promptly (see *New ISG Ltd v Vernon* [2008] IRLR 115). In this case the High Court, interpreting the 2006 Regulations purposively, made it clear that where the identity of the buyer is not known until the sale is completed, the right to object would be meaningless if it could be exercised only pre-sale.

7.4   WHAT THE TRANSFEREE ACQUIRES

The transferee inherits those employees employed by the transferor on their existing terms and conditions, assuming that they do not object (reg 4(2)).

Equally, the transferred employee has no right to insist that he be given the benefit of any superior terms and conditions enjoyed by the transferee's existing staff. In addition, the transferee inherits the legal responsibilities for any employees dismissed by reason of the transfer or for a reason connected with the transfer, where no ETO reason exists (see **7.5.2** below).

7.4.1 Rights transferring – employees employed immediately before the transfer

The transferee inherits all the employees employed immediately before the transfer, together with all the contracts of employment of the transferred employees. The transferee cannot pick and choose which employees to take on. The only exceptions to this are where:

(a)   employees are 'temporarily' assigned to the 'organised grouping' (see **7.3.2.1**);

(b)   the employee has objected (see **7.3.2.2**).

The transferee also inherits all the accrued rights and liabilities connected with the contract of the transferred employee (except for criminal liabilities (reg 4(6)) and some benefits under an occupational pension scheme (see **7.4.1.3**)).

If, for example, the transferor was in arrears with wages at the time of the transfer, the employee can sue the transferee as if the original liability had been the transferee's. The transferor is relieved of his former obligations without any need for the employee's consent. All liability for tortious claims, for example personal injury claims, will also pass to the transferee whether the accident happens before the transfer or after the transfer but due to the pre-transfer negligence of the transferor (*Bernardone v Pall Mall Services Group and Others* [2000] IRLR 487, CA and *Baker v British Gas Services Ltd* [2017] EWHC 2302 (QB)). Note that where an entitlement is inextricably linked to the identity of the transferor (eg profit-sharing schemes), the employee's post-transfer entitlement, according to the EAT in *MITIE Managed Services Ltd v French* [2002] IRLR 512, is to participate 'in a scheme of substantial equivalence'.

Equally, the transferee may sue an employee for a breach of contract committed against the transferor prior to transfer.

The transferee will also inherit all the statutory rights and liabilities which are connected with the individual contract of employment, for example unfair dismissal, redundancy and discrimination.

Regulations 11 and 12 contain provisions requiring the transferor to notify the transferee in writing of 'liability' information about an employee who is 'assigned to the organised grouping of employees or resources that is the subject of a relevant transfer'. This includes providing details of the identity and age of the employee, the particulars of employment (ERA 1996, s 1), and information relating to disciplinary and grievance procedures involving the employee. If a transferor fails to provide this information in whole or part, the transferee may complain to an employment tribunal, which may award compensation of not less than £500 per employee (see **7.7**).

In *Born London Ltd v Spire Production Services Ltd* (UKEAT/0255/16), a transferor incorrectly stated that a Christmas bonus was non-contractual, when it turned out to be contractual. The question arose as to whether this was a breach of reg 11, such as to give rise to a compensation claim. The employment tribunal found that the claim had no reasonable prospect of success, and the EAT agreed. Even assuming that the bonus was contractual, all reg 11 requires is for particulars of employment to be provided as defined by s 1 of the ERA 1996. That did not impose a requirement to state whether a bonus was contractual or not. Saying that the bonus was non-contractual went further than the particulars required to be provided by reg 11. The way to avoid this sort of problem is a practical one: the transferee could have undertaken more due diligence on the question of whether remuneration was contractual or not. If the warranties and indemnities had covered this, then the transferee might have had a contractual claim against the transferor under the transfer contract.

The 2014 Amendment Regulations, which came into force on 31 January 2014, made changes to reg 11, so that the deadline for notification of employee information is increased from not less than 14 days before the transfer to not less than 28 days before the transfer. This will assist incoming contractors and transferees by giving them more information earlier about the employees they will be taking on.

The transferred employee's period of continuous employment will date from the beginning of his period of employment with the transferor, and the statutory particulars of terms and conditions of employment, which every employer is obliged to issue, must take account of any continuity enjoyed by virtue of the Regulations.

7.4.1.1   Restrictive covenants

In the case of restrictive covenants, these will normally be expressed in terms of protecting customers of the transferor. In essence, following the transfer of an undertaking a restrictive covenant should be read as being enforceable by the transferee, but only in respect of customers of the transferor who fall within the protection. (Great care needs to be taken if restrictive covenants are re-drafted post-transfer. See *Credit Suisse First Boston (Europe) Ltd v Padiachy and Others* [1998] IRLR 504 and *Credit Suisse First Boston (Europe) Ltd v Lister* [1998] IRLR 700.)

7.4.1.2   Collective agreements

Under the 2006 Regulations, any collective agreements made with a union by the transferor are deemed to have been made by the transferee (reg 5). Further, the transferee is deemed to recognise the trade union to the same extent as did the transferor (reg 6). In effect, the transferee steps into the shoes of the transferor. Neither the 2006 Regulations nor the general law prevent the employer from seeking to derecognise the union entirely, or from amending the basis of the recognition. This lack of an effective remedy undermines the protection given to trade unions on a relevant transfer. Note that the ERA 1999 contains detailed statutory procedures for the recognition and de-recognition of trade unions for collective bargaining. The procedures are beyond the scope of this book.

In *Unionen v Almega Tjänsteförbunden ISS Facility Services AB* (Case C-336/15), the ECJ confirmed that employees cannot be made subject to less favourable working conditions than those applicable prior to a transfer and that a transferee is required to take into account service with the transferor when calculating notice periods. Four employees with long service transferred to ISS. After some years of service with ISS they were all made redundant. At the date of redundancy all had total service with the transferor and ISS in excess of 10 years. However, they had all only been employed for periods between two and six years with ISS (the transferee) since the transfer. Both the transferor and transferee were parties to a collective agreement, which gave different periods of notice depending on the length of service of the particular employee. This provided for extended notice in cases where length of service exceeded 10 years and the employee was aged over 55 years. Under Swedish law, compliance with collective agreements entered into by the transferee was only required for one year after the transfer. The ECJ stated that although one year had passed, so ISS was entitled for economic reasons not related to the transfer to no longer continue to observe the original terms and conditions, no amendments had been made to the terms and conditions of the collective agreement and they continued to apply.

The 2014 Amendment Regulations inserted a new reg 4A into the 2006 Regulations, so that collectively agreed rights which come into force after the date of transfer will not transfer if the transferee is not a party to the collective bargaining for that right. See too **7.6** on varying collectively agreed terms post-transfer.

7.4.1.3   Pensions

Regulation 10 provides that regs 4 and 5 do not apply to occupational pension schemes (although a contractual provision that an employer would pay a certain percentage of salary into a personal pension fund would transfer). However, separate regulations have been issued under the Pensions Act 2004, which provide that when a relevant transfer occurs and employees had the benefit of an occupational pension scheme (with employer contributions) before transfer, the transferee *must* provide membership of an equivalent scheme. The detail is beyond the scope of the book; see Transfer of Employment (Pension Protection) Regulations 2005 (SI 2005/649) (as amended) and <http://www.dwp.gov.uk>.

7.4.1.4 'Liability for failure to consult'

Regulation 15(9) makes the transferor and the transferee jointly and severally liable in respect of compensation payable as a result of a failure to consult (see **7.7**).

7.4.2 Rights and liabilities which are not assigned under the 2006 Regulations

The 2006 Regulations do not have the effect of assigning:

(a)   criminal liabilities (reg 4(6)); or

(b)   liability (in a health and safety context) under a continuation order.

7.5 DISMISSAL OF AN EMPLOYEE BECAUSE OF A RELEVANT TRANSFER

If an employee is dismissed, before of after a relevant transfer, the dismissal is effective and the contracts ends. Depending on the facts, liability may fall on the transferor or the transferee.

The 2014 Amendment Regulations, which came into force on 31 January 2014, made changes to reg 7 of the 2006 Regulations. The wording of reg 7(1)–(3A) is now:

> (1)   Where either before or after a relevant transfer, any employee of the transferor or transferee is dismissed, that employee is to be treated for the purposes of Part X of the 1996 Act (unfair dismissal) as unfairly dismissed if the reason for the dismissal is the transfer.
>
> (2)   Paragraph (1) does not apply to dismissals that may take place for economic, technical or organisational reasons entailing changes in the workforce of either the transferor or transferee before or after a relevant transfer.
>
> (3)   If a dismissal takes place for a reason referred to in paragraph (2), without prejudice to the application of section 98(4) of the 1996 Act (test of fair dismissal), for the purposes of sections 98(1) and 135 of that Act (reason for dismissal)—
>
> > (a)   the dismissal is regarded as having been for redundancy where section 98(2)(c) of that Act applies; or
> >
> > (b)   in any other case, the dismissal is regarded as having been for a substantial reason of a kind such as to justify the dismissal of an employee holding the position which that employee held.
>
> (3A)   In paragraph (2), the expression 'changes in the workforce' includes a change to the place (within the meaning of section 139 of the 1996 Act) where employees are employed by the employer to carry on the business of the employer or to carry out work of a particular kind for the employer.

This aims to clarify the definition of an 'economic, technical or organisational reason entailing changes in the workforce' ('ETO') and bring it more into line with the definition of redundancy. It also removed a phrase ('connected with the transfer') which had caused uncertainty as to its scope. This amended wording is intended to make it easier for employers to make post-transfer changes to contracts. This may give employers greater flexibility post-transfer, as a dismissal is now automatically unfair only if the reason or principal reason for the dismissal is the transfer itself, but the authors advise caution as the phrase 'the transfer' may yet be interpreted by courts to include 'transfer-connected reasons'.

If an employee is dismissed (whether actually (see **3.4.1**) or constructively (see **3.4.3**), or within the meaning of reg 4(9) (see **7.3.2.1**), and whether before or after the transfer), if the sole or principal reason for the dismissal is the transfer then, by reg 7 of the 2006 Regulations, the dismissal is automatically unfair (ie there is no need to consider whether the dismissal is reasonable in accordance with ERA 1996, s 98(4) (reg 7(1)). However, if the sole or principal reason for the dismissal is an ETO reason entailing changes in the workforce (of either the transferor or the transferee before or after a relevant transfer), there is no automatically unfair dismissal. The dismissal shall (without prejudice to the application of s 98(4) of the ERA 1996), for the purposes of ss 98(1) and 135 of the 1996 Act, be regarded as having been for redundancy where s 98(2)(c) of that Act applies (see **5.2.1**), or otherwise for a substantial reason of a kind such as to justify the dismissal of an employee holding the position which that employee held (reg 7(2)and (3)). The effect of this is that a presumption is created that ETO dismissals will be for the potentially fair reasons of either redundancy or some other substantial reason, and reasonableness will be determined in the usual way (see **Chapter 5**), liability lying with the employer who carried out the dismissals.

Regulation 7(4) states that reg 7 applies irrespective of whether the employee in question is assigned to the organised grouping of resources or employees that is, or will be, transferred. This means that the protection of reg 7 is available to *all* employees. It is important, therefore, that transferees are aware that their existing employees, as well as the transferring employees, are protected against transfer-related dismissal.

To bring a claim of unfair dismissal arising out of a transfer-related dismissal, an employee still needs to have a minimum of one or two years' continuous employment (dependent on when the employment commenced).

7.5.1   When is a dismissal by reason of the transfer itself?

It will be a question of fact for the tribunal to determine whether a dismissal is by reason of the transfer itself. The BIS Guidance gives the following example in connection with changing terms and conditions, but it is useful by way of analogy:

Q.   When is the sole or principal reason for a purported variation of contract the transfer?

A.   Where an employer changes terms and conditions simply because of the transfer and there are no extenuating circumstances linked to the reason for that decision, then the reason for the change is the transfer.

Where there are some extenuating circumstances, then whether or not the sole or principal reason for any purported variation is the transfer is likely to depend upon the circumstances.

If the new employer wishes merely to bring into line the terms and conditions of transferred staff with those of existing staff, then the transfer would be the reason for this change (due to the way in which the Courts have interpreted the Acquired Rights Directive).

In the authors' opinion, a dismissal following collusion between a transferor and a transferee with regard to dismissals (ie the transferee was involved in some way in the decision to dismiss) might be regarded as a dismissal by reason of the transfer itself, but as yet there is no authority supporting this proposition. In *Wheeler v Patel* [1987] IRLR 211 (a case decided under the old law), Mrs Wheeler was employed by the vendor of a shop in his business which he proposed to sell. Before the shop was transferred to a prospective purchaser, Mrs Wheeler was dismissed, in order to achieve agreement for sale. The EAT held (under the old law) that this dismissal was for a reason connected with the transfer, but it may be seen under the new law as a dismissal by reason of the transfer itself.

Although dismissals which occur shortly before or after the transfer are more likely to be by reason of it, an employee may have difficulty convincing the tribunal that a dismissal which took place weeks or even months before the transfer was by reason of the transfer, unless a court now determines that 'the transfer' includes 'transfer-connected reasons'.

One area of difficulty was whether it was sufficient for the employee to show that his dismissal was by reason of transfers generally as opposed to a specific transfer. There was a conflict of EAT decisions under the 1981 Regulations on this point. In *Ibex Trading Company Ltd v Walton and Others* [1994] IRLR 564, the EAT held that the actual transferee had to be identified. Dismissal in respect of transfers generally was not sufficient. The employees in this case were held to be dismissed by reason of 'a' transfer, rather than 'the' transfer.

However, in *Harrison Bowden Ltd v Bowden* [1994] ICR 186, and subsequently in *Morris v John Grose Group Ltd* [1998] IRLR 499 and *CAB Automotive Ltd v Blake and Others* (UKEAT/0298/07), the EAT held that the words 'the transfer' did not necessarily have to refer to the particular transfer that had actually occurred. That this is the correct approach was confirmed by the Court of Appeal in *Spaceright Europe Ltd v Baillavoine and Another* [2011] EWCA Civ 1565.

In the *Spaceright* case, the claimant was the managing director of a business which was up for sale. Although no buyer had been identified, a view had been taken that an incumbent managing director was too expensive for a purchaser. The claimant was dismissed, ostensibly on the grounds of redundancy, but the business was always going to need a managing director, and there was always going to be an ongoing business. The EAT agreed that the dismissal was connected with the transfer which was contemplated. The Court of Appeal agreed with this approach, holding that an ETO reason is not available where an employee is dismissed to make a business more attractive to prospective transferees.

This approach, said Mummery LJ, accords with the Acquired Rights Directive. The fact that no transferee can be identified at the moment of dismissal does not prevent employees' rights from being protected by the Directive.

In *Dynamex Friction Ltd and Another v Amicus and Others* [2008] IRLR 515, when the company got into difficulties, joint administrators were appointed. The administrators decided to dismiss the workforce on the basis that the company had no money to pay them. The Court of Appeal upheld the tribunal decision that the sole reason for the dismissals was economic, as there was no money to pay the workforce, and so was not transfer-related. It was the administrator's decision to dismiss, and just because there was collusion between the director of the insolvent company and the transferee did not make the dismissals transfer-related in circumstances where the administrator was not involved in the collusion.

For a recent decision, see *Hare Wines Ltd v Kaur* [2019] EWCA Civ 216 (below) where a tribunal found that the dismissal of an employee immediately before a transfer was automatically unfair because the principal reason was the transfer.

7.5.2 Establishing an ETO reason which entails a change in the workforce

If there is a pre-transfer dismissal because of the transfer, the transferee (ie the new employer) will be liable for all claims by the dismissed employee (reg 4(3)) unless the dismissal was for an ETO reason which entailed a change in the workforce, in which case liability for a pre-transfer dismissal will lie with the transferor (ie the old employer). Liability for a post-transfer dismissal will always lie with the transferee.

If there is an ETO reason, the dismissal will be either for redundancy, or for 'a substantial reason' under s 98(1) and s 135 of the ERA 1996. Even where the employer can show such a reason, the employment tribunal must still be satisfied that the employer has acted reasonably within s 98(4) of the ERA 1996.

The employer must show an ETO reason entailing a change in the workforce, otherwise the dismissal will be automatically unfair.

Note that the wording of reg 7 mirrors the wording of reg 4(4) (see **7.6** below) There is no statutory definition of an ETO reason. According to the BIS Guidance, it is likely to include:

(a)   a reason relating to the profitability or market performance of the transferee's business (ie an economic reason);

(b)   a reason relating to the nature of the equipment or production processes which the transferee operates (ie a technical reason); or

(c)   a reason relating to the management or organisational structure of the transferee's business (ie an organisational reason). (See below.)

Likewise there is no statutory definition of the phrase 'entailing changes in the workforce'. Previous interpretations of the phrase by the courts under the 1981 Regulations (see, eg, *Berriman v Delabole Slate Ltd* [1985] ICR 546 and below) restricted it to changes in the numbers employed, or to changes in the functions performed by employees. The BIS Guidance suggests a functional change could involve a new requirement on an employee who held a managerial position to enter into a non-managerial role, or to move from a secretarial to a sales position. The amendments made by the 2014 Regulations have added a further situation to be covered by the phrase, namely a change to the place where employees are employed to carry on the business of the employer or particular work for the employer.

Because the *Berriman* decision left little scope for a change of workplace to amount to an ETO reason (unless it was accompanied by a change in numbers or functions), the 2014 Amendment Regulations inserted the new subs (3A) into reg 7 of the 2006 Regulations (see **7.5** above for the new wording), which expressly expanded the definition of 'changes in the workforce' to include a change to the place of work and to refer specifically to the definition of 'redundancy' in s 139 of the ERA 1996. The aim of this is to ensure that dismissal due to changes in the location of a business, or part of it, will not automatically be unfair; instead, the fairness of such dismissals will be considered in accordance with the familiar test under s 98(4) of the ERA 1996. So, the employer will need to make sure as with dismissal for redundancy, that selection for dismissal is fair and not based simply on the fact that the person is a transferred employee. Dismissed employees may also be entitled to a redundancy payment if they have been employed for two years or more. Employers must further ensure that the required period for consultation with employees' representatives is allowed (see **7.7** below).

In *Osborne v Capita Business Services Ltd* (UKEAT/0048/16), Capita argued that there were 'economic, technical or organisational reasons' for its dismissal of a group of employees who had transferred to it under a TUPE transfer, and it succeeded in regard to all but two employees. Seven employees were dismissed because their job functions were split and redistributed across several different sites: this entailed changes in the job functions of the workforce. Two employees were relocated with no significant change to their function. As the transfer occurred before the 2014 amendments, Capita could not rely on relocation to meet the 'changes in the workforce' condition. These two were therefore automatically unfairly dismissed.

See also the Court of Appeal judgment in *Hare Wines Ltd v Kaur* [2019] EWCA Civ 216 where a dismissal was held to be related to the transfer and so was automatically unfair. Although proximity of dismissal to the date of transfer is not conclusive, it will be strong evidence. In this case, the transferor company dismissed the claimant at the request of the transferee company.

As it will sometimes be unclear whether the 2006 Regulations apply, and therefore whether the previous or the new employer is responsible for making redundancy payments (because if the 2006 Regulations do not apply then liability for the dismissals will not pass to the transferee but will remain with the transferor), employees are best advised to make any claims against both employers at an employment tribunal.

In certain circumstances, reg 9 allows for variations to be agreed to where a transferor is subject to 'relevant insolvency proceedings' (as defined). The detail of this is beyond the scope of this book.

7.5.3 Summary

In summary, therefore:

(a) Where the sole or principal reason for a dismissal is the transfer itself, the dismissal will be automatically unfair under reg 7(1). Irrespective of whether the dismissal occurred before or after the transfer, the claim will be against the transferee.

(b) Where the sole or principal reason for a dismissal is not the transfer itself but is an ETO reason, under reg 7(2) and (3) the dismissal will be potentially fair on the basis of either redundancy (in which case a redundancy payment may also be appropriate) or some other substantial reason, subject to the normal unfair dismissal tests. In this situation, while the transferee will remain liable for any post-transfer dismissals, the transferor will be liable for pre-transfer dismissals.

(c) Where the sole or principal reason for a dismissal is not the transfer, the usual unfair dismissal principles will apply.

(d) An employee who has been dismissed, or who has resigned in circumstances in which he considers he was entitled to resign because of the consequences or anticipated consequences of the transfer, needs to have the requisite continuous employment, although the qualifying period does not apply where an employee claims that he was dismissed for asserting his statutory rights under the 2006 Regulations (reg 19) (see **5.5.3**).

(e) Any complaints must be brought within three months of the date when employment ended.

(f) Because it may be unclear whether claims should be made against the previous employer or the new employer, employees should consider whether to claim against both employers.

7.6 POST-TRANSFER VARIATIONS TO TERMS AND CONDITIONS

One of the aims of the 2006 Regulations was to clarify what the position was post-transfer, where variations were made to contracts. The Regulations ensure that employees retain the same terms and conditions post-transfer as they enjoyed pre-transfer, and that they are not penalised when they are transferred by being given inferior terms and conditions. This is achieved by two routes. First, the 2006 Regulations state (reg 4(1)) that the contract of employment of any transferred employee 'shall have effect after the transfer as if originally made between the person so employed and the transferee'. This ensures that the pre-existing terms and conditions are transferred across on the first day of the employee's employment with the transferee. Secondly, by way of reinforcement, the Regulations also impose limitations on the ability of the transferee and employee to agree variations to those terms and conditions.

The 2014 Amendment Regulations, which came into force on 31 January 2014, made changes to reg 4(4) and (5). The new wording is now as follows:

(4) Subject to regulation 9, any purported variation of a contract of employment that is, or will be, transferred by paragraph (1), is void if the reason for the variation is the transfer.

(5) Paragraph (4) does not prevent a variation to the contract of employment—

(a) if the reason for the variation is an economic, technical or organisational reason entailing changes in the workforce; or

(b) if the reason for the variation is the transfer, provided that the terms of that contract permit the employer to make such a variation.

(5A) In paragraph (5), the expression 'changes in the workforce' includes a change to the place (within the meaning of section 139 of the 1996 Act) where employees are employed by the employer to carry on the business of the employer or to carry out work of a particular kind for the employer.

(5B) Paragraph (4) does not apply in respect of a variation of contract in so far as it varies a term or condition incorporated from a collective agreement, provided that—

(a)   the variation of the contract takes effect on a date more than one year after the date of the transfer; and

(b)   following that variation, the rights and obligations in the employee's contract, when considered together, are no less favourable to the employee than those which applied immediately before the variation.

(5C)   Paragraphs (5) and (5B) do not affect any rule of law as to when a contract of employment is effectively varied.

Any purported variation of a contract of employment that is transferred under reg 4(1) will thus be void if the reason for the variation is the transfer, but in certain situations (reg 4(5), (5B)) a variation may not be void, eg where there is an ETO or where a contract expressly permits changes. The definition of 'entailing changes in the workforce' will include changes to the place of work, as discussed in **7.5.2** above in connection with reg 7, so as to bring the definition more into line with the definition of 'redundancy' in s 139 of the ERA 199, and to take geographic or locational redundancies outside the scope of automatically unfair redundancies. Some caution is needed, as until the courts start interpreting the new wording, it is unclear how widely they will view 'the transfer'. The BIS Guidance suggests that where there are *transfer-connected* reasons for varying a contract, these might be caught by the phrase 'the transfer'. The advice currently therefore is that where there is a transfer-connected reason for varying contracts, it is sensible to ensure that there is also an ETO justification for it. Note that there are special provisions in reg 5B which relate to changes to terms incorporated from collective agreements.

Thus, reg 4(5) now permits a transferee or a transferor to agree to vary an employment contract with an employee where the sole or principal reason falls within the definition of an 'economic, technical or organisational reason entailing changes in the workforce' or the terms of the contract permit such a variation. Note that an employer cannot unilaterally change or impose new terms and conditions without the agreement of the employee (see *Regent Security Services v Power* [2008] IRLR 226). The BIS Guidance suggests that a reason unrelated to a transfer could include the sudden loss of an expected order by a manufacturing company, or a general upturn in demand for a particular service or a change in a key exchange rate.

Where a change occurs after the transfer, it will be a question of fact whether the change was related to the transfer. One relevant factor will be the length of time between the date of the transfer and the change, but the gap is only one factor. In *Taylor v Connex South Eastern Ltd* (UKEAT/1243/99), a case decided under the old law, the EAT held that there was still a connection between the transfer and an attempt to force changes in terms and conditions two years after the relevant transfer, because the subject matter of the insistence by the respondents on the contractual change was an important term which had been transferred across on the occasion of the transfer. However, in *Tabberer v Mears Ltd* (UKEAT/0064/17), the EAT upheld a tribunal's decision that the respondent's reason for ending an allowance was not connected with the transfer but, rather, because the allowance was 'outdated'.

It is unlikely that an attempt by a transferee to change the terms and conditions of a transferring employee in order to harmonise them with those of the existing workers would be covered by this wording. Any wish to harmonise terms and conditions is really a reason related to the transfer, and it is difficult to see how it could fall within the wording of reg 4(5). There is no hard-and-fast rule as to how long after a transfer it would 'safe' for the transferee to vary contracts because of the passage of time. The BIS Guidance points out that while there is likely to come a time when the link with the transfer can be treated as no longer effective, this must be assessed in the light of all the circumstances of the individual case, and will vary from case to case.

In summary, therefore, the Regulations draw a distinction between four situations:

(a) cases where the sole or principal reason for a purported contractual variation is the transfer itself (void);

(b) cases where the reason is entirely unconnected with the transfer (eg a misconduct dismissal) (valid);

(c) cases where the reason is an ETO reason (valid);

(d) cases where the terms of the contract permit the employer to make the variation (valid); and

(e) cases where the changes are made to a collective agreement term more than one year post-transfer where the changes are entirely to the benefit of the employee (valid).

In the first situation any purported variation will be void, but this will not prevent a valid variation being agreed in the remaining situations.

Some commentators have raised questions about the compatibility of reg 4(5)(a) with the Acquired Rights Directive. The Directive does not deal with post-transfer contract variations, but in *Foreningen af Arbejdsledere I Danmark v Daddy's Dance Hall A/S* [1988] IRLR 315, the ECJ held that changes made 'by reason of the transfer' are on the whole invalid. There is no mention of an ETO exception. The UK Government has taken the view that because the Directive creates an exception for dismissals due to the transfer, the same should logically apply to contractual variations, which are a 'lesser interference' with an employee's rights.

In *Regent Security Services v Power* (above), the Court of Appeal held that favourable transfer-related variations (where no ETO existed) are valid, notwithstanding the statutory language. The Court held that the employee does not waive his transferred rights but rather obtains an extra right which co-exists with the original right. On the facts, Mr Power could therefore choose to retire at 60 (the transferred right) or 65 (the additional right).

Note that reg 9 allows for variations to be agreed in certain circumstances where a transferor is subject to 'relevant insolvency proceedings' (as defined). The detail of this is beyond the scope of this book.

7.6.1 Practical advice

Where acting for a transferee, it is imperative to carry out full due diligence of all transferring employees' terms and conditions, since the transferee will inherit on those terms and conditions, and may not be able to vary the terms and conditions even with the employees' consent (see also **7.7.1**).

Where acting for the transferee, an indemnity should be gained from the transferor in the event of there being any difference between the terms and conditions detailed in the due diligence process by the transferor, and the actual terms and conditions on which employees transfer across.

A transferee who wishes to be sure that old terms and conditions do not apply, and/or to harmonise terms and conditions with the existing workforce, may dismiss those employees post-transfer or get the transferor to dismiss pre-transfer, with a view to re-engaging them on new terms. Such dismissals will be effective, but will give rise to the risk of unfair dismissal claims. Such dismissals will be 'automatically' unfair, unless there is an ETO reason. In *Berriman* (**7.5.2** above), the Court of Appeal held that an ETO reason entailing changes in the workforce involves more than a mere change in terms and conditions. If transferees wish to have contractually binding and harmonious terms, they will have to bear in mind the potential costs of any consequential unfair dismissal claims. Alternatively, they will have to try to ensure that changes are not connected with the transfer.

One area where post-transfer contractual variations can cause problems is in the 'offshoring of services' – ie where work is transferred from the UK to abroad. This was the scenario considered by the EAT in *Xerox Business Services Philippines Inc Ltd v Zeb* (UKEAT/0121/16). From

2009, Mr Zeb worked for a financial accounting team, and in 2011 his employment transferred under TUPE to Xerox UK. He was based in Wakefield. In 2014, the financial accounting team function was offshored to Xerox Philippines. Xerox believed that the place of work of employees would remain in Wakefield, and because Xerox Philippines had no need for staff based in Wakefield, there would be a genuine redundancy. It gave staff various options, including being made redundant by Xerox UK with an enhanced package, transferring via TUPE and being made redundant by Xerox Philippines with a standard package, or relocating to the Philippines on local terms and conditions (which were considerably less generous than those in the UK). Mr Zeb argued that he should be able to relocate on his existing terms, so he did not object to the transfer and was then made redundant by Xerox Philippines.

The EAT, overturning the employment tribunal's finding of an automatically unfair dismissal, said that, under TUPE, Xerox Philippines had been obliged to employ Mr Zeb at Wakefield and pay his UK salary but had not been obliged to employ him in Manila at the same salary. TUPE permits variation of contracts but such variations must be agreed. Here, there was no meeting of minds on terms, so there was no variation. TUPE did not permit Mr Zeb unilaterally to vary his place of work. The statutory definition of redundancy was met and it appeared to be an ETO reason for dismissal.

7.7 THE PROVISION OF INFORMATION AND CONSULTATION UNDER THE 2006 REGULATIONS

Regulations 11–16 of the 2006 Regulations impose duties upon both the transferor and the transferee to provide information to each other, and to provide information to and consult the representatives of employees who may be affected by the transfer.

7.7.1 The provision of employee liability information

Article 3(2) of the Acquired Rights Directive (as amended in 2014) gives Member States the option to introduce provisions 'to ensure that the transferor notifies the transferee of all the rights and obligations which will be transferred to the transferee … so far as those rights and obligations are or ought to have been known to the transferor at the time of the transfer'. As a result, from 6 April 2006, under reg 11 of the 2006 Regulations, transferors became obliged, for the first time, to give transferees written information about 'any person employed by [the transferor] who is assigned to the organised grouping of resources or employees that is the subject of a relevant transfer' and all the associated rights and obligations towards them, ie 'employee liability information'. This information includes, for example, the identity and age of the employees who will transfer, information contained in the employees' written particulars of employment under s 1 of the ERA 1996 (see *Born London Ltd v Spire Production Services Ltd* (UKEAT/0255/16)), any disciplinary and grievances procedures within the last two years, details of any claims that the transferor reasonably believes might be brought and information about any collective agreements. This is aimed at helping the transferee to prepare for the arrival of the transferred employees, and ensuring that it is fully aware of all its inherited obligations.

The obligation includes a duty to provide employee liability information relating to any person who would have been employed by the transferor and assigned to the organised grouping of resources or employees that is the subject of a relevant transfer immediately before the transfer if he had not been dismissed in the circumstances described in reg 7(1) (see **7.5**), including, where the transfer is effected by a series of two or more transactions, a person so employed and assigned, or who would have been so employed and assigned, immediately before any of those transactions (reg 11(4)).

The information, which need not be provided all in one go, should be given in writing or in any other form that is accessible to the transferee (eg as computer data files). The information may also be provided via a third party. For example, where a client is re-assigning a contract from an existing contractor to a new contractor, that client organisation may act as the third party in passing the information to the new contractor. The information must be provided not less than 28 days before the transfer or, if special circumstances make this not reasonably practicable, as soon as reasonably practicable thereafter (reg 11(6) and (7)). There is no provision entitling the transferor and the transferee to agree to contract out of the duty to supply the employee liability information.

If the transferor does not provide this information, within three months after the transfer the transferee may complain to an employment tribunal that the transferor has failed to comply with any provision of reg 11. The tribunal may make a declaration and award such compensation, as it considers just and equitable. Compensation starts at a minimum of £500 for each employee in respect of whom the information was not provided or was defective (reg 12).

7.7.2 The duty to inform and consult

Regulation 13 of the 2006 Regulations imposes duties upon both the transferor and the transferee to provide information to, and to consult, the representatives of employees who may be affected by the transfer.

An employer must inform and consult appropriate representatives, who may be:

(a)   elected employee representatives;

(b)   representatives of an independent trade union recognised by an employer. (Where there is a recognised trade union, the employer must consult with representatives of that trade union rather than with employee representatives.)

Regulation 14 lays down detailed requirements for the election of employee representatives. See the BIS Guidance for more information on how this works. Representatives and candidates for election have certain rights and protections to enable them to carry out their function properly. The dismissal of an elected representative will be automatically unfair if the reason, or the main reason, related to the employee's status or activities as a representative. An elected representative also has the right not to suffer any detriment short of dismissal on the grounds of his status or activities. Candidates for election enjoy the same protection.

The obligation to consult and provide information applies in relation to

> any employees of the transferor or the transferee (whether or not assigned to the organised grouping of resources or employees that is the subject of a relevant transfer) who may be affected by the transfer or may be affected by measures taken in connection with it; and references to the employer shall be construed accordingly.

Categories of 'affected employees' might include not only the individuals who are to be transferred, but also their colleagues in the transferor who will not transfer but whose jobs might still be affected by the transfer, and their new colleagues in employment with the transferee whose jobs might also be affected by the transfer.

In *I Lab Facilities Ltd v Metcalfe and Others* (UKEAT/0224/12), the EAT held that employees assigned to part of a business that was wound up, did not have to be consulted in respect of the transfer of the part of the business that was sold. The EAT held that those employees were not 'affected' by the transfer.

7.7.2.1 The duty to inform

The obligation to provide information arises whenever a relevant transfer is planned. The information must be provided 'long enough before a relevant transfer to enable the employer to consult with the employees' representatives' (reg 13(2)). There is no firm guidance on time limits. In particular, it is clear that they are not the same as redundancy time limits, ie 90 or 30 days. In practice, consultation under the Regulations often lasts for relatively short periods.

The information to be given to the representatives is to be delivered to them personally or by post, or (in the case of union representatives) sent by post to the union's head office.

The employer of affected employees must inform all the appropriate representatives of the following:

(a)   the fact that a relevant transfer is to take place;

(b)   when it is to take place (approximately);

(c)   the reasons for it;

(d)   the legal, economic and social implications of the transfer for the affected employees;

(e)   the measures which he envisages taking (eg if a re-organisation will result) in relation to those employees (and if no measures are envisaged, that fact);

(f)   if the employer is the transferor, the measures, in connection with the transfer, which he envisages the transferee will take in relation to any affected employees who will become employees of the transferee after the transfer (and if no measures are envisaged, that fact). The transferee must give the transferor the necessary information so that the previous employer is able to meet this requirement.

7.7.2.2   The duty to consult

If action is envisaged which will affect the employees, the employer must consult the representatives of the employees affected about that action. The consultation must be undertaken with a view to seeking agreement of the employee representatives to the intended measures (reg 13(6)). In practice, this means that the management must consider representations made and reply to the same; and if they choose to reject them, they should state the reasons for this. There is clearly an obligation to negotiate in good faith. The employer must consider any representations made by the appropriate representatives and reply to those representations; and if he rejects any of those representations, he must state his reasons (reg 13(7)). The employer must permit the appropriate representatives access to any affected employees, and must provide them with such accommodation and other facilities as may be appropriate (reg 13(8)).

The 2014 Amendment Regulations inserted a new reg 13A into the 2006 Regulations, which allows an employer with fewer than 10 employees to fulfil its reg 13 obligation by consulting directly with the workforce, provided there are no appropriate representatives (as defined by reg 13(3)). This change applies to transfers taking place on or after 31 July 2014.

It is a defence for the employer to show that there were special circumstances which rendered it not reasonably practicable to perform the duty in question, provided that he took whatever steps to perform that duty as were reasonably practicable in the circumstances. The tenor of the case law is that this defence is to be construed extremely narrowly. The circumstances must be out of the ordinary and relate to the particular situation and not merely to general circumstances which may create pressure or problems for the employer.

Confidentiality will not in itself be enough to invoke the defence. A mere desire to preserve confidentiality, rather than it being a prerequisite for the purchase to go ahead, will not be adequate.

With regard to a financial crisis in a redundancy situation, the tribunal will look to the practicability of consultation in light of the suddenness of the situation and the extent of prior knowledge.

There is no case law on the point which often arises in the context of listed companies, ie whether the defence is available where the disclosure of information would amount to a disclosure of price-sensitive information. In the authors' view, this argument is unlikely to persuade most employment tribunals. The tribunal would no doubt counter-suggest that appropriate representatives could have been asked to agree to confidentiality obligations and that the Listing Rules allow a company to disclose information about impending developments/negotiations to employee or trade union representatives.

7.7.2.3 Failure to comply

The relative inadequacy of the remedy for a failure to inform and consult means that many companies will probably opt to put other business concerns, such as confidentiality, ahead of their obligations under the 2006 Regulations.

Any of the affected employees, or their appropriate representatives, may bring a complaint (no later than three months after the date of the transfer) to an employment tribunal (reg 15). They can choose against whom they bring their complaint. Where either the transferor or the transferee is the sole defendant, he may seek to join the other employer to the case. The 2006 Regulations resolve one previous area of uncertainty, as to whether the transferor or the transferee was liable for any award made by a tribunal for a failure to comply: both the transferee and the transferor are now jointly and severally liable in respect of any compensation payable (reg 15(9)).

If a complaint is upheld, the tribunal must make a declaration and has a discretion to order the employer to pay appropriate compensation to such descriptions of affected employees as may be specified in the award. 'Appropriate compensation' in reg 15 means such sum not exceeding 13 weeks' pay for the employee in question as the tribunal considers just and equitable having regard to:

(a)   the seriousness of the failure of the employer to comply with his duty;

(b)   any loss sustained by the transferee attributable to the matters complained of; and

(c)   the terms of any contract between transferor and transferee under which the transferor may be liable to pay a sum to the transferee in respect of failure to provide such information (reg 16(3)).

The last provision is to prevent any element of double recovery. It is for a tribunal to decide when it would be 'just and equitable' to award less than the maximum, although the Government has commented that if a failure was 'minimal or trivial', the minimum award need not apply. Note that whether a week's pay for this purpose is subject to the statutory maximum (currently £479) imposed by s 227 of the ERA 1996 was the subject of an appeal in *Zaman v Kozee Sleep Products Ltd* (EAT/0312/10). The EAT said that even though reg 16 did cross-refer to s 227 of the ERA 1996, there was no intention to apply the cap. If there had been such intention, it would have been necessary either to amend s 227 to include a specific reference or include an express provision in the 2006 Regulations. The Court of Appeal confirmed in *Sweetin v Coral Racing* [2006] IRLR 252 (following *Susie Radin Ltd v GMB* [2004] IRLR 400 – see **4.8.1.2**) that where there is a complete failure to engage in the consultation process, a tribunal should start at the 13-week maximum and work down as appropriate (see eg *Cable Realisations Ltd v GMB Northern* [2010] IRLR 42 and *Todd v Care Concern* (UKEAT/0057/2010)).

Compensation for a failure to inform and consult cannot be set off against other obligations, for example damages for breach of contract or for a 'protective award' under the collective redundancy obligations.

In *Royal Mail Group v CWU* [2009] EWCA Civ 1045, Royal Mail was planning to franchise a number of post office branches to WH Smith. It believed, however, that there was no relevant transfer as a result because Royal Mail was offering voluntary redundancy and/or redeploying staff using an express contractual right. Because Royal Mail believed that there was no transfer, it believed that there was no need to inform and consult the union about the transfer. The CWU complained to an employment tribunal, which found that Royal Mail had failed to comply with the obligation to inform and consult. The EAT and the Court of Appeal disagreed and overturned the tribunal's decision. They accepted that where an employer genuinely believes that no transfer will take place, it will not be in breach of its obligations to inform and consult.

7.7.3   Other duties to consult and inform

In addition to the obligations under regs 11–16 of the 2006 Regulations, the Information and Consultation of Employees Regulations 2004 (SI 2004/3426) (implementing the EC Directive on information and consultation) apply to undertakings employing 50 or more employees. The Regulations provide for a comprehensive scheme of consultation and the provision of information to employees (see **4.8.2**).

Again, where there is an overlap, the 2004 Regulations cease to apply once the employer has notified the representatives that he will be complying with his duties under the 2006 Regulations.

Note: The 2014 Amendment Regulations, which became effective in January 2014, amended the Trade Union and Labour Relations (Consolidation) Act 1992 by inserting a new provision (s 198A), which allows pre-transfer consultation by the transferee to take place (where the transferor agrees) and for such pre-transfer consultation to count for collective redundancy consultation purposes (see **4.8** above).

7.8   FURTHER READING

BIS Guide, *Employment Rights on the Transfer of an Undertaking*.

Selwyn's Law of Employment, 22nd edn (OUP, 2022).

Blackstone's Employment Law Practice, 10th edn (OUP, 2019).

Wynn-Evans, *The Law of TUPE Transfers*, 3rd edn (OUP, 2022).

Harvey, *Industrial Relations and Employment Law* (LexisNexis), Div F.

Lewis, *Transfer of Undertakings* (Sweet and Maxwell, looseleaf).

McMullen, *Business Transfers and Employee Rights* (LexisNexis, looseleaf).

The blog <tupe.uk.net> endeavours to gather together information and case law on TUPE and contains a number of useful and updated resources. It is compiled by a practising barrister.

SUMMARY

At common law in the UK, the transfer of a business undertaking by one employer to another would automatically terminate the employee's contract of employment, ie there is a dismissal. The Transfer of Undertakings (Protection of Employment) Regulations 2006 alter the legal position by providing that where there is a 'relevant transfer', there will not be any automatic termination of the contract of employment simply by reason of the transfer. Where there is a 'relevant transfer', the employee will transfer to the new owner and will be employed by him on the same terms as under his original contract. If there are any dismissals, whether actual, constructive or deemed, and whether they are before or after the transfer of the business, if those dismissals are related to the transfer, they will be automatically unfair unless, effectively, there is a genuine redundancy situation (an economic, technical or organisational (ETO) reason for the dismissal; **7.1**).

For the 2006 Regulations to apply, there must be a transfer from one person to another; consequently, there must be a change in the employer, not merely in the ownership. The 2006 Regulations do not therefore apply to transfers by share takeover or to transfers of assets only, or to a situation where a purchaser buys a majority shareholding in a company, thereby gaining control. This is because there is no change in the identity of the employer – in all these situations it will remain the same company. The 2006 Regulations do apply to mergers, sales of part of a going concern, changes of franchisee, sale of a sole trader's business or partnership and to transfers between two companies belonging to the same group, or where one subsidiary subcontracts work to another, provided the transfer involves the transfer of an 'economic entity' (see *Allen and Others v Amalgamated Construction* (Case C-234/98) [2000] IRLR 119) (**7.2**).

Regulation 3 of the 2006 Regulations expressly covers 'service provision changes' such as contracting-out exercises (eg catering, cleaning, security) where services are outsourced, insourced or assigned to a new contractor. However, the Regulations will not apply to service provision changes that take place 'in connection with a single specific event or task of short term duration'.

Regulation 4(3) of the 2006 Regulations operates so as to transfer the contracts of any individuals who are:

(a)   employed by the transferor immediately prior to the transfer (or would have been had they not been dismissed for a reason related to the transfer – in this latter situation the dismissal will be effective but liability for any claims the dismissed employee may have may fall upon the transferee); and

(b)   assigned to the relevant grouping of employees that is transferred.

The Regulations state that there will be no transfer of employees who are only 'temporarily assigned' to a particular undertaking (**7.3** and **7.4**).

Regulations 4(5) and 7(1) clarify when the 'economic technical or organisational' (ETO) defence applies, and the ability to change terms and conditions on a transfer.

The 2006 Regulations permit variations of contract, which may be agreed between transferees and transferred employees, and which are done either for an ETO reason entailing changes in the workforce, or where the contract permits such variations. 'Entailing changes in the workforce' is not defined in the 2006 Regulations, but it has been interpreted by tribunals under predecessor Regulations as meaning changes in the 'numbers' employed. The 2014 Amendment Regulations have extended this meaning to include locational changes.

Regulation 4(7) and (8) allow an employee to object to a transfer, but specify that where this right is exercised, the employee shall be treated as having resigned (**7.5** and **7.6**).

Regulations 8 and 9 cover what happens where there is a rescue of failing businesses.

Regulations 11 and 12 create an obligation for the current employer to provide employee information to the transferee, so that the transferee is made fully aware of the employees' rights, obligations and liabilities upon transfer (**7.7**).

Flowcharts showing the steps to be taken to determine whether a dismissal before a relevant transfer or a dismissal on or after a relevant transfer is fair, are set out in **Figures 7.1** and **7.2** respectively below.

Figure 7.1 Dismissals before a relevant transfer

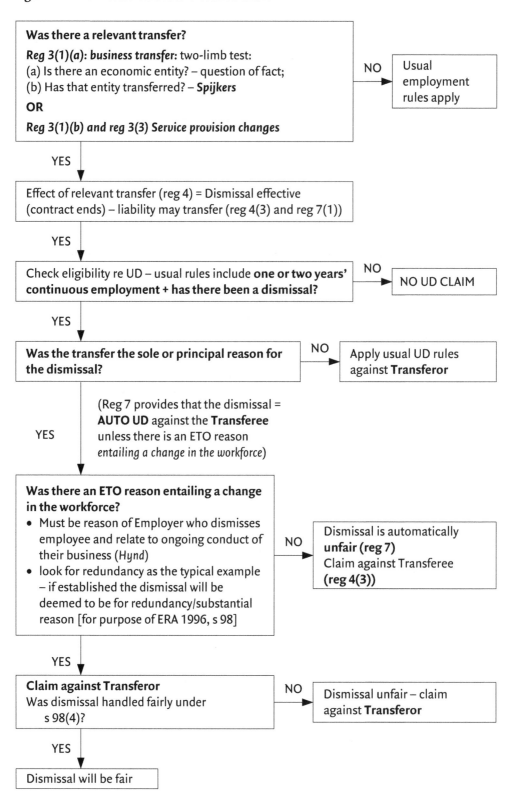

NB – ALSO check for redundancy payment claims and/or WD claims. Claim will be against the same party as the claim for UD.

Figure 7.2 Dismissals on or after a relevant transfer

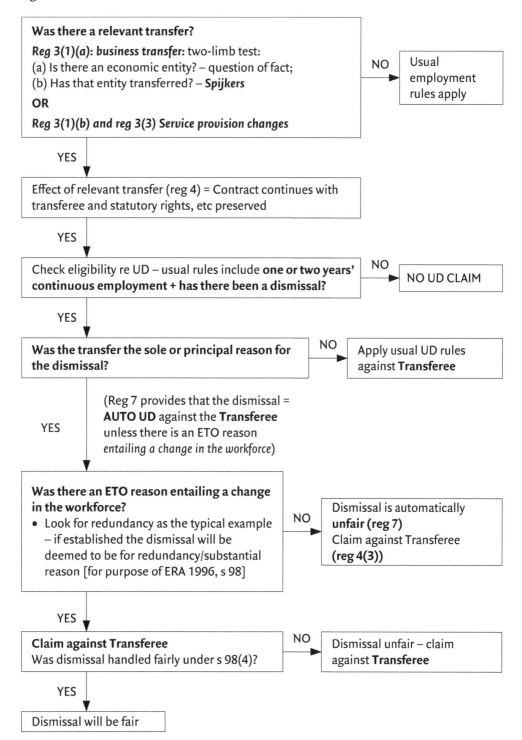

NB – ALSO check for redundancy payment claims and/or WD claims. Claim will be against the Transferee.

CHAPTER 8

DISCRIMINATION AND EQUAL PAY

8.1	Introduction	375
8.2	Protected characteristics	379
8.3	Prohibited conduct	388
8.4	Unlawful acts of discrimination – in the employment field	392
8.5	Occupational requirements	395
8.6	Vicarious liability	397
8.7	Retirement	403
8.8	Enforcement and remedies	403
8.9	Equal pay and the equality clause	412
8.10	Part-time workers	417
8.11	Fixed-term employees	419
8.12	Trade union membership or activities	419
8.13	Discrimination under the Human Rights Act 1998	420
8.14	Further reading	421
	Summary	422

LEARNING OUTCOMES

After reading this chapter you will be able to:

- understand the underlying principles of discrimination law and when and to whom it applies in an employment context
- list the grounds ('protected characteristics') in the Equality Act 2010 upon which discrimination is deemed unlawful
- describe and explain each of the protected characteristics
- list the four types of prohibited conduct
- understand the significance of occupational requirements and the reasonable steps defence
- describe the remedies available where a complaint of discrimination is made out.

8.1 INTRODUCTION

The first anti-discrimination legislation in the UK was passed in 1965. In 1975, Great Britain became a member of the European Community (which became the European Union in 1992 when the Maastricht Treaty was signed), but the then Government opted out of the Social Chapter provisions of the Treaty, which included anti-discrimination provisions. In 1997, the then Labour Government opted into the Social Chapter provisions of the Treaty. In 2000, the EU introduced a number of new directives protecting people on the basis of sexuality, religion, belief and age, as well as revising previous protections around disability, race and gender. Much of current UK anti-discrimination law mirrors these EU directives. Since the UK voted to leave the EU in June 2016, it remains uncertain what the position will be going forward as far as anti-discrimination law is concerned, as so much UK law in this area is EUgrounded. Although the UK has now left the EU, the UK–EU Trade and Cooperation Agreement, which was signed in December 2020, and came into effect in May 2021, meant that there was no immediate impact on discrimination law and that the UK courts still had to follow any case law of the European Court of Justice (ECJ) made before 31 December 2020, in respect of UK 'retained law'. The Government suggested in September 2021 that it 'intend[s] to remove the special status of retained EU law, so that it is no longer a distinct category of UK domestic law, but normalised within our law, with a clear legislative status'. In the May 2022 Queen's Speech, the Government said it would introduce a 'Brexit Freedoms Bill' to end the current legal status of EU law in UK domestic law and make it easier to amend or remove retained EU law. Time will tell what, if anything, this might mean for discrimination law in the UK.

The Equality Act 2006 received Royal Assent on 16 February 2006. It provided for the establishment of the Equality and Human Rights Commission (EHRC), which came into being in October 2007. The EHRC took on the work of the former equality Commissions (the EOC, the DRC and the CRE), and additionally assumed responsibility for promoting equality and combating unlawful discrimination in three new strands, namely sexual orientation, religion or belief, and age. The EHRC also has responsibility for the promotion of human rights. Section 64 of the Enterprise and Regulatory Reform Act (ERRA) 2013 curbed the EHRC's duties and powers. Whilst the Commission retains its 'general duty', its 'good relations duty' and 'power of conciliation for non-workplace disputes' were repealed from 25 June 2013.

The Equality Act 2010 received Royal Assent on 8 April 2010. The Act consolidated most of the previous discrimination legislation and, as well as codifying the different strands of the old statute-based law on discrimination (eg, direct discrimination still occurs when 'someone is treated less favourably than another person because of a protected characteristic'), also made a number of changes to the existing law (eg, employees may now complain about harassment even if it is not directed at them, if they can demonstrate that it creates an offensive environment for them). Additionally, it extended some aspects of the old law (eg, associative discrimination – direct discrimination against someone because he or she associates with another person who possesses a protected characteristic). Under the old law, discrimination by association applied only to race, religion and belief, and sexual orientation. It has now been extended to cover age, disability, gender reassignment and sex. Some entirely new concepts (eg, the concept of discrimination arising from disability, which occurs if a disabled person is treated unfavourably because of something arising in consequence of his or her disability) were introduced for the first time. Most of the employment provisions came into force on 1 October 2010.

The EHRC has created a series of non-statutory guidance documents to help explain the Act and provide practical examples. Its website <http://www.equalityhumanrights.com> has detailed guidance (running to hundreds of pages) for employers, workers, service providers, service users, education providers and public sector bodies. In line with its statutory powers (Equality Act 2006, s 14(1)), the EHRC has also published a code of practice on employment and one on equal pay. The purpose of these codes is to explain the statutory provisions of the Equality Act 2010. They draw on precedent and case law. The codes came into force on 6 April 2011. Courts and tribunals must take into account any part of the code that appears to them relevant to any questions arising in proceedings.

The Acas website <http://www.acas.org.uk> also contains a wealth of guidance on the Equality Act 2010.

This chapter and the following chapters on discrimination set out the current law. All the chapters on discrimination refer by way of illustration and example to the pre- and post-Equality Act 2010 case law. Although the Government believes, in many places, that there have been no changes, care is still needed where pre-Equality Act 2010 case law is relied upon as there are some nuanced differences.

In June 2020, the charity Business in the Community published a report, 'The Race at Work: Black Voices Report'. In her forward, Sandra Kerr, CBE, Race Director, says:

> We are living in challenging times. We have seen the disproportionate impact of COVID-19 on black, Asian and minority ethnic (BAME) people. And we witnessed the brutal killing of George Floyd and the resulting anti-racism protests in the US, UK and around the globe.
>
> I set out three priority areas for action for the business response to the Black Lives Matter anti-racism protests: leadership; allyship; and connecting to employees and communities ...
>
> The [Race at Work] Charter now has more than 400 employer signatories comprising many that want to focus on action and be employers that are truly inclusive of black employees.

The report finds that there has been 'little change in [the] number of black people in senior professional roles since 2014, representing just 1.5% of managers, directors and senior officials in the UK'; 'just 1% of journalists, senior civil servants, judges, academics and the police force are black'.

The Black Voices Report sets out actions that employers can take to support their BAME employees (<www.bitc.org.uk/report/race-at-work-black-voices-report/>).

8.1.1 Background

The general common law rule is that an employer is free to offer employment to whomsoever it chooses (*Allen v Flood and Taylor* [1898] AC 1). This common law freedom has been restricted by statute. The employer may be in breach of statutory requirements if it discriminates against a person on the following grounds (the 'protected characteristics'):

(a)   sex or marital status;

(b)   gender reassignment;

(c)   race;

(d)   religion or belief;

(e)   sexual orientation;

(f)   trade union membership;

(g)   part-time work;

(h)   age;

(i)   disability;

(j)   fixed (limited)-term work;

(k)   pregnancy and maternity.

In all areas of discrimination law it is important, for the time being at least, to appreciate the influence of EU law, in particular:

- the Equal Treatment Directive (76/207) (as amended);

- the Race Discrimination Directive (2000/43);

- Article 157 TFEU (ex 141 EC);

- the Framework Directive for Equal Treatment in Employment and Occupation (2000/ 78).

All references in **Chapters 8** to **13** to 'the Act' are to the Equality Act 2010.

8.1.2 Who is protected?

The Act protects, amongst others, employees (s 39), job applicants (s 39), contract workers (s 41), office holders (s 50) and trade union members (s 57). It also protects employees after their employment has ended (s 108). Section 83(2) of the Act defines 'Employment' as '(a) employment under a contract of employment, a contract of apprenticeship or a contract personally to do work'. This definition is wider than the definition of 'employee' in s 230(1) of the ERA 1996 (see **1.3.2** and **1.3.4.2** above).

Sections 39 and 40 make it unlawful for an employer to discriminate against, or to harass or to victimise employees and people seeking work. It applies where the employer is making arrangements to fill a job, and in respect of anything done in the course of a person's employment (see **8.4** below). Section 41 makes it unlawful for a person (referred to as a 'principal') who makes work available to contract workers to discriminate against, harass or victimise them (see *Leeds City Council v Woodhouse* [2010] IRLR 625).

Section 108 makes it unlawful to discriminate against or harass someone after a relationship covered by the Act has ended (see **8.4** below).

The Supreme Court held, in *Hounga v Allen & Another* [2014] UKSC 47, that the defence of illegality does not always defeat a discrimination complaint (see **5.4.2.4**).

There is a general interpretation section in s 212, and an index to defined expressions in s 214 and Sch 28.

8.1.3 Territorial jurisdiction

Unlike previous discrimination legislation, the Act does not deal with territorial scope. Most of the old legislation applied to employment 'at an establishment in Great Britain', and provided protection to those who worked 'wholly or partly' in Great Britain as well as to those who worked wholly outside Great Britain but fulfilled specific criteria. It is therefore left to employment tribunals to determine whether the Act applies in any given situation.

According to the Explanatory Notes, the decision to remove territorial scope from the Act follows the precedent of the ERA 1996 (s 196, which determined whether it applied to employees who ordinarily work outside Great Britain, was repealed by the ERA 1999). The EHRC Code states that discrimination protection is required where there is a sufficiently close link between the employment relationship and Great Britain (see *Lawson* and *Ravat* at **3.7** above).

In *Clyde & Co LLP and Another v Bates van Winkelhof* [2012] EWCA Civ 1207, the Court of Appeal upheld an employment tribunal's decision with regard to jurisdiction and agreed that it was right to apply the *Serco v Lawson* test to discrimination and/or whistleblowing claims (see **3.7**). In this case, Mrs Bates van Winkelhof spent the majority of her time working abroad. The Court confirmed that the test to be applied in that situation (ie where the person lives and/or works for at least part of the time in Great Britain) is whether an individual has a sufficiently strong connection with Great Britain. By contrast, in cases where the individual works *wholly* abroad, a comparative exercise will be appropriate (ie connections with Great Britain will need to outweigh connections with the other jurisdiction). Although the issue of whether the individual was a worker was appealed to the Supreme Court, the jurisdiction issue was not, and the Court of Appeal's analysis remains good law.

The High Court applied the *Lawson* test in *R (on the application of Hottak and Anor) v Secretary of State for Foreign and Commonwealth Affairs and Anor* [2015] IRLR 827, QBD. It held that two Afghan interpreters working for the armed forces in Afghanistan could not bring discrimination claims because they were not expat or peripatetic workers and did not have a closer connection to Great Britain than Afghanistan. In *British Council v Jeffrey* [2018] EWCA Civ 2253, the Court of Appeal held that the EAT was correct to recognise the 'very particular circumstances of the present case ... the only correct conclusion was that the factors connecting Mr Jeffery's employment with Great Britain outweighed the strong territorial pull of the place of work'. See too *FCO and others v Bamieh* [2019] IRLR 736.

8.1.4 Interpretation

Section 137 provides that any final finding in a claim brought under the previous discrimination legislation is to be treated as conclusive in proceedings under the Act. A finding is considered final when an appeal against it is dismissed, withdrawn or abandoned, or where the time-limit for appealing against it has expired. This is intended to prevent matters that were determined under the previous legislation being relitigated under the Act.

8.1.5 Scope of this and following chapters on discrimination

This chapter deals with the matters that are common to all the protected characteristics. It, together with **Chapters 9, 10** and **11,** deals with discrimination on the grounds of sex, race, religion or belief, marriage and civil partnership, pregnancy and maternity, and sexual orientation. This chapter also looks briefly at equal pay, discrimination against part-time workers and discrimination on grounds of trade union membership or activities.

Chapter 12 deals with age discrimination and **Chapter 13** covers discrimination on the ground of disability, because these follow slightly different regimes from the other protected characteristics.

8.2 PROTECTED CHARACTERISTICS

Section 4 of the Equality Act 2010 sets out certain 'protected' characteristics. These are the grounds upon which discrimination is deemed unlawful.

The characteristics relevant to this chapter and **Chapters 9–11** are:

- gender reassignment (s 7)
- marriage and civil partnership (s 8)
- race (s 9)
- religion or belief (s 10)
- sex (s 11)
- sexual orientation (s 12)
- pregnancy and maternity (s 18).

The characteristic relevant to **Chapter 12** is age (s 5) and to **Chapter 13** is disability (s 6 and Sch 1). The definitions in relation to the protected characteristics of age and disability are dealt with separately in **Chapters 12** and **13**. Pregnancy and maternity, which are discussed separately in s 18, are covered under direct discrimination (see **9.4**).

The EHRC Code of Practice on Employment contains a wealth of information, and tribunals are obliged to take it into account when it appears relevant. Readers should refer to the Code for further guidance on protected characteristics.

8.2.1 Sex

Sex is defined in s 11 of the Act:

> In relation to the protected characteristic of sex—
>
> (a) a reference to a person who has a particular protected characteristic is a reference to a man or to a woman;
>
> (b) a reference to persons who share a protected characteristic is a reference to persons of the same sex.

There appears to be a gap in sex discrimination protection for people who do not use the sex they were assigned at birth – the Act does not explicitly address this.

8.2.2 Race

'Race' is defined non-exhaustively in s 9 of the Act:

> (1) Race includes—
>
> (a) colour;
>
> (b) nationality;
>
> (c) ethnic or national origins.

(2)   In relation to the protected characteristic of race—

    (a)   a reference to a person who has a particular protected characteristic is a reference to a person of a particular racial group;

    (b)   a reference to persons who share a protected characteristic is a reference to persons of the same racial group.

(3)   A racial group is a group of persons defined by reference to race; and a reference to a person's racial group is a reference to a racial group into which the person falls.

(4)   The fact that a racial group comprises two or more distinct racial groups does not prevent it from constituting a particular racial group.

(5)   A Minister of the Crown may by order—

    (a)   amend this section so as to provide for caste to be an aspect of race;

    (b)   amend this Act so as to provide for an exception to a provision of this Act to apply, or not to apply, to caste or to apply, or not to apply, to caste in specified circumstances.

    …

The Explanatory Notes give the following examples:

- Colour includes being black or white.
- Nationality includes being a British, Australian or Swiss citizen.
- Ethnic or national origins include being from a Roma background or of Chinese heritage.
- A racial group could be 'black Britons' which would encompass those people who are both black and who are British citizens.

The Code of Practice also gives useful examples.

The courts have often had to consider the meaning of 'ethnic origins'. In *Mandla and Another v Dowell Lee and Another* [1983] 2 AC 548, HL, Lord Fraser identified two essential characteristics of an ethnic group:

(a)   a long shared history; and

(b)   a cultural tradition of its own.

On that basis, for example, Sikhs are a distinct ethnic group for these purposes.

In addition to these essential characteristics, his Lordship identified others which, although not essential, could be expected to be displayed, such as a common language, or a common geographical origin. The principles in *Mandla* have been applied in a number of cases, so, for example, gypsies have been held to constitute an ethnic group, but not Rastafarians.

In *BBC Scotland v Souster* [2001] IRLR 150, the Court of Session confirmed that the Scots and English are separate racial groups, defined by reference to their national origins (although not by reference to their ethnic origins).

In *Dizedziak v Future Electronics Ltd* (UKEAT/0270/11), the EAT upheld a decision that the claimant had been subjected to direct discrimination on grounds of her nationality when she was instructed by her line manager not to speak in 'her own language' at work (the claimant was a Polish national); but see too *Kelly v Covance* at **9.2.5.2**.

In *Moxam v Visible Changes Ltd and Another* (UKEAT/0267/11), the EAT confirmed that the phrase 'on racial grounds' protects a person against discrimination on grounds of race, not just on the ground of that person's race.

The Supreme Court held, in *Taiwo and Onu v Olaigbe and Akwiwu* [2016] UKSC 31, that mistreatment of a worker on the grounds of 'immigration status' was not race discrimination because immigration status could not be equated with nationality: while immigration status is a function of nationality, it is not so closely associated with it as to be indissociable from it. It was not direct discrimination because the mistreatment was due to their vulnerable migrant status, not because of their nationality. It was not indirect discrimination because no 'provision, criterion or practice' has been applied. (Baroness Hale suggested that Parliament might have to consider whether to give Employment Tribunals jurisdiction to award compensation under s 8 of the Modern Slavery Act 2015 where vulnerable migrant workers suffer ill-treatment.) See too *Mruke v Khan* [2018] EWCA Civ 280, where the Court of Appeal held that the claimant's socio-economic circumstances were the reason for the less favourable treatment and not her nationality.

In *Chandhok v Tirkey* (UKEAT/0190/14), the EAT found that, as many elements implicit in caste identity may reflect an employee's ethnic origin, caste will be covered by the broad protected characteristic of race (*Tirkey* was a trafficking case).

Section 97 of the ERRA 2013 (amending s 9 of the Equality Act 2010) came into effect on 25 June 2013, but the provision states only that a Minister must 'by order amend [the Equality Act] to provide for caste to be an aspect of race'. No draft Regulations have been produced yet. The EHRC published a report on the nature of caste prejudice and harassment in Spring 2014, and the Government consulted on prospective legislation from March–September 2017. The Government has said that, for now, it will not legislate but will keep cases under review to 'ensure the principles established by the *Tirkey* judgment [above] are upheld'.

8.2.3   Religion or belief

Religion or belief is defined in s 10 of the Act:

(1)   Religion means any religion and a reference to religion includes a reference to a lack of religion.

(2)   Belief means any religious or philosophical belief and a reference to belief includes a reference to a lack of belief.

(3)   In relation to the protected characteristic of religion or belief—

(a)   a reference to a person who has a particular protected characteristic is a reference to a person of a particular religion or belief;

(b)   a reference to persons who share a protected characteristic is a reference to persons who are of the same religion or belief.

The Explanatory Notes give the following examples:

- The Baha'i faith, Buddhism, Christianity, Hinduism, Islam, Jainism, Judaism, Rastafarianism, Sikhism and Zoroastrianism are all religions for the purposes of this provision.

- Beliefs such as humanism and atheism would be beliefs for the purposes of this provision but adherence to a particular football team would not be.

Note: Jews may also a constitute a racial group under the definition in s 9 (see **8.2.2**).

In *R v Secretary of State for Education and Employment & Others, ex parte Williamson & Others* [2005] 2 AC 246 (a case brought under Article 9 of the ECHR), the House of Lords considered the meaning of 'religious belief' and held that the court is concerned to ensure that the assertion of religious belief is made in good faith:

'neither fictitious, nor capricious, and that it is not artifice' … but emphatically it is not for the court to embark on an inquiry into the asserted belief and judge its 'validity' by some objective standard … Freedom of religion protects the subjective belief of an individual … The belief must be consistent with basic standards of human dignity or integrity … [and] possess an adequate degree of seriousness and importance … [and] be coherent in the sense of being intelligible and capable of being understood. But again, too much should not be demanded in this regard … Overall, these threshold requirements should not be set at a level which would deprive minority beliefs of the protection they are intended to have …

The Explanatory Notes state that the criteria for determining what constitutes a 'philosophical belief' are that it must:

(a)   be genuinely held;

(b)   be a belief and not an opinion or a viewpoint based on the present state of information available;

(c)   be a belief as to a weighty and substantial aspect of human life and behaviour;

(d)   attain a certain level of cogency, seriousness, cohesion and importance; and

(e)   be worthy of respect in a democratic society, compatible with human dignity and not conflict with the fundamental rights of others.

These criteria are founded upon the ECtHR's decision in *Campbell and Cosans v UK* (1982) 4 EHRR 293.

In *McClintock v Department of Constitutional Affairs* [2008] IRLR 29, the EAT said that to constitute a belief, there must be a religious or philosophical viewpoint in which one actually believes; it is not enough to have an opinion based on some real or perceived logic, or based on information or lack of information.

The EAT had previously endorsed the above criteria in *Nicholson v Grainger plc* [2010] IRLR 4 (a case decided under the old law), and it is clear that the criteria will also apply to religious beliefs.

In *Forstater v CGD Europe and others* (ET/2200909/19), the tribunal held that an *absolutist* belief that sex is biologically immutable was not a belief worthy of respect in a democratic society because it was incompatible with dignity and the fundamental rights of others. However, that decision was overturned by the EAT (UKEAT/0105/20). The EAT held that the belief was worthy of respect and that only extreme beliefs will fail to satisfy the test (eg beliefs akin to Nazism or totalitarianism). In summing up, the EAT said:

> In our judgment, it is important that in applying *Grainger* Tribunals bear in mind that it is only those beliefs that would be an affront to Convention principles in a manner akin to that of pursuing totalitarianism, or advocating Nazism, or espousing violence and hatred in the gravest of forms, that should be capable of being not worthy of respect in a democratic society. Beliefs that are offensive, shocking or even disturbing to others, and which fall into the less grave forms of hate speech would not be excluded from the protection. However, the manifestation of such beliefs may, depending on circumstances, justifiably be restricted under Article 9(2) or Article 10(2) as the case may be.

At a subsequent full merits hearing in March 2022, an employment tribunal upheld Ms Forstater's case, concluding that she had suffered direct discrimination on the basis of her gender critical beliefs.

8.2.3.1   Some other examples of what constitutes a religion or a belief

Religious belief

In *Trayhorn v Secretary of State for Employment* (UKEAT/0304/16) the EAT held that it was neither direct nor indirect discrimination to discipline an employee who was a Pentecostal Christian, who condemned homosexuality and spoke about repentance during a church service. The EAT said that it was not the manifestation of his belief that caused him to be disciplined but the way in which he had behaved.

The manifestation of religious beliefs can differ widely. The EHRC Employment Statutory Code of Practice states that 'a person does not have to prove that the manifestation of their religion or belief is a core component of the religion or philosophical belief they follow. It may instead be a means by which they choose to express their adherence to their religious belief.'

In *Gareddu v London Underground Ltd* (UKEAT/0086/16) the EAT emphasised that, to attract legal protection, the employee's expressed need to manifest their beliefs in a certain way must be genuine. On the facts (Mr Gareddu, who was a practising Roman Catholic from Sardinia, wished to take an extended five-week holiday to attend a number of religious festivals in Sardinia in August), while attendance at festivals in Sardinia was accepted as a manifestation of religious belief for Mr Gareddu, this was not the genuine reason for his extended holiday request. (Had it been genuine, the employer may have been able to justify refusing the request by showing that its practice of limiting holidays to a maximum of three weeks at a time was a proportionate means of achieving a legitimate end.)

In *Gan Menachem Hendon Ltd v De Groen* (UKEAT/0059/18), the EAT, relying upon the Supreme Court's decision in *Ashers* (see **9.2.5.3**), held that the claimant, who was dismissed because she was cohabiting with her boyfriend, contrary to the beliefs of some of those responsible for the management of her employer and because she would not (untruthfully) say she was no longer cohabiting, was not directly discriminated against because of her religion or belief, but rather because of the religion or belief of her employer. Both direct and indirect discrimination claims on this ground therefore failed. It remains to be seen whether the decision is correct. It is, in the authors' view, wrong to allow less favourable treatment because of the beliefs of the employer, and it and paves the way for employers to insist that its employees comply with their religious beliefs, without having to comply with the occupational requirement provisions in Sch 9 (see **8.5** below). (Findings of direct discrimination and harassment related to sex were upheld.)

Philosophical belief

In *Grainger plc v Nicholson* [2010] IRLR 4, the EAT adopted an expansive approach when it upheld a tribunal decision that an employee's belief that action was urgently needed to address climate change, could amount to a philosophical belief as it was cogent, serious, coherent and worthy of respect in a democratic society. The EAT rejected the argument that political or science-based beliefs could not fall with the meaning of 'philosophical belief', but any such belief must be 'worthy of respect in a democratic society'. *Grainger plc v Nicholson* established that to meet the definition, beliefs must:

(i)   be genuinely held;

(ii)   not be opinions;

(iii) be as to a weighty and substantial aspect of human life and behaviour;

(iv)   attain a certain level of cogency, seriousness, cohesion and importance;

(v)   be worthy of respect in a democratic society and not be incompatible with human dignity or conflict with the fundamental rights of others.

BNP members have not managed to persuade tribunals that their political belief amounts to a philosophical belief (see, eg, *Wingfield v North Cumbria Mental Health and Learning Disabilities NHS Trust* (ET/2510953/05) and *L'Anson v Chief Constable of West Yorkshire Police* (ET/1804854/09)). The ECtHR has previously distinguished between political opinions that are legal but extreme (eg the National Front) and those that are illegal (eg supporting terrorism). In *Redfearn v United Kingdom* [2012] ECHR 1878, the ECtHR was split 4:3 in Mr Redfearn's favour. It did not find that Mr Redfearn was either unfairly dismissed or discriminated against; it held that there was not a proper opportunity for him to argue his case. While s 10 of the Equality Act 2010 (replacing the Religion or Belief Regulations 2003) does not expressly include political beliefs, the Equality Directive 2007/78/ EC contains no such qualification. At the time the case was argued before the Court of Appeal, the BNP was characterised as a party that confined its membership to white people. Since then, following proceedings brought against the BNP by the EHRC, this is no longer strictly true, which may make it harder to dismiss BNP members from sensitive posts.

It is helpful to look at some employment tribunal decisions. In *Olivier v DWP* (ET/1701407/13), the tribunal held that a political belief (in this case a belief in democratic socialism (going beyond mere support for a political party) could amount to a philosophical belief, applying the *Grainger* criteria (above). In *Hashman v Milton Park (Dorset) Ltd* (ET/3105555/09), a gardener's belief in the sanctity of life, extending to a fervent anti-fox hunting stance, was held to be a protected philosophical belief; in *Lisk v Shield Guardian Ltd* (ET/3300873/11), a belief that individuals should wear poppies was held to be too narrow to constitute a protected belief; in *Maistry v BBC* (ET/1313142/10), a journalist's belief in the 'higher purpose' of public service broadcasting was a philosophical belief (that finding was not appealed, but the Court of Appeal held that the claimant was not dismissed because of his belief, in circumstances where those involved in the decision to dismiss were unaware that the claimant held such a belief);

in *Arya v London Borough of Waltham Forest* (ET/3200/396/11), the claimant's belief that 'the Jewish religion's professed belief in Jews being "God's chosen people" was at odds with meritocratic and multicultural society', and was not therefore capable of being a philosophical belief; in *Hawkins v Universal Utilities Ltd t/a Unicom* (ET/2501234/12), a tribunal held that a belief that 'it is wrong to lie under any circumstances' amounted to a philosophical belief; in *Dunn v University of Lincoln* (ET/2601819/17) the claimant's non-PC beliefs were held not to be a philosophical belief; in *McLeny v MOD* (ET/4105347/17), a belief in Scottish independence was held to amount to a philosophical belief; in *Tumenaite v PC Soho Centre Administration Ltd & Anor* (ET/2204607/18), the tribunal held that a waitress who was vegetarian for 'spiritual and ethical reasons' was protected by virtue of her philosophical belief; in *Casamitjana Costa v The League Against Cruel Sports* (ET/3331129/2018), the claimant's belief in ethical veganism was afforded legal protection as a philosophical belief.

But in *Conisbee v Crossley Farms Ltd* (ET/3335357/18) it was held that vegetarianism was not capable of amounting to a philosophical belief: it is not enough merely to have a belief relating to an important aspect of human life or behaviour, or to have an opinion based on logic, 'the belief must have a similar status or cogency to religious beliefs'. Most recently, in *Miles v The Royal Veterinary College* (ET/2206733/2020), a tribunal decided that a belief in ethical veganism, which encompassed an obligation to break the law in order to relieve animal suffering, did not amount to a philosophical belief under s 10. The claimant said her ethical veganism belief was that humans 'should not eat, wear, use for sport, experiment on or profit for animals' and that this extended to 'a moral obligation to take positive action to reduce or prevent the suffering of animals', even if this involves acting unlawfully. The tribunal said that had her belief been limited to the first part only, it 'would have had no reservation' in concluding that it amounted to a philosophical belief, but the belief here included acting in contravention of the law. As a result, it did not satisfy the fifth element of the test for a philosophical belief set out in *Grainger*.

In *Gray v Mulberry Company (Design) Ltd* [2019] EWCA Civ 1720, the Court of Appeal concluded that it was irrelevant whether the claimant's belief in statutory human or moral right to own the copyright and moral rights of her own creative works and output, except when that work or output is produced on behalf of an employer, was a philosophical belief because the dismissal was not connected to her refusal to sign the copyright agreement. The EAT had agreed with the tribunal that the belief did not attain a certain level of 'cogency, seriousness, cohesion and importance'

In *Mackereth v DWP* [2022] EAT 99, the EAT dismissed a claimant's appeal against a tribunal's finding that he had not been discriminated against for holding gender critical views. As in *Forstater*, the EAT was keen to acknowledge the 'issues of wider social concern and debate' that arose and to make clear that 'it expressed no view as to the merits of any side in that debate, it is not the role of the EAT to do so'. Although the claimant's Christianity was a protected characteristic, the question was whether his particular (lack of) beliefs fell within s 10. The claimant, who was a health and disabilities assessor, believed in the truth of Genesis 1.27, that a person cannot change their sex/gender at will. He also had a lack of belief in transgenderism. He refused to use the preferred pronouns of transgender patients he saw, which was against the DWP's policies. While the DWP was assessing whether the claimant's beliefs could be accommodated, the claimant left and brought claims of direct discrimination, harassment and indirect discrimination, which did not succeed before the tribunal. Applying *Forstater*, the EAT found that on several occasions the tribunal had erred in applying the *Grainger v Nicholson* criteria. The EAT held that the tribunal had been wrong to find that the claimant's beliefs did not relate to weighty and substantial aspects of human life and behaviour but accepted they did not meet the necessary level of cogency, seriousness, cohesion and importance. So, the claimant's belief in Genesis 1.27, and lack of belief in transgenderism, were protected beliefs under the Act. However, the EAT nonetheless upheld the tribunal decision and dismissed the appeal on direct discrimination and harassment based on the tribunal's factual findings relating to the 'lack of connection' between the claimant's beliefs and the respondent's conduct. The appeal against the failure of the indirect discrimination claim was upheld because the claimant accepted that not all Christians shared his beliefs. The EAT viewed this as a case where it was the manifestation of the claimant's belief that was really in issue, as opposed to the holding of the belief.

In the recent tribunal case of *Bailey v Stonewall and others* (ET/2202172/2020), the issue of an individual's gender critical beliefs was again considered in the context of a protected philosophical belief. The claimant was a barrister at Garden Court Chambers (GCC). She said on Twitter that she disagreed with the beliefs of those who said that a woman is defined by her gender, which may be different from her sex and is for the individual to identify. As a result of expressing this view, the claimant alleged that she suffered discrimination and victimisation by GCC's barristers and their staff because of her gender critical philosophical belief. The tribunal held that the Act protected both the belief that women are defined by their biological sex, not their gender identity, as well as the claimant's belief that 'gender theory as proselytised by [Stonewall] is severely detrimental' to women and lesbians. It found that the claimant suffered direct discrimination. Her indirect discrimination claim and her claim for loss of earnings due to her gender critical beliefs were dismissed.

There are two particularly tricky issues when looking at religion or belief discrimination. One concerns the extent to which law protects the manifestation of beliefs as opposed to the holding of them, particularly at work (see **10.2.3** below). There is a helpful ECHR Guidance Note on 'Religion or Belief and the Workplace', available at <http://www.equalityhumanrights.com/private-and-public-sector-guidance/employing-people/religion-or-belief-guidance-employers>. In May 2018, Acas issued new Guidance on Religion and Belief which, as well as providing an explanation of the law, contains practical guidance on talking about religion at work, food and fasting, and washing and changing rooms. Another difficult area is the apparent conflict with the protection of another characteristic, for example sexual orientation (see **9.2.5.2** below).

8.2.4   Sexual orientation

Sexual orientation is defined in s 12 of the Act:

> (1)   Sexual orientation means a person's sexual orientation towards—
>
> > (a)   persons of the same sex,
> >
> > (b)   persons of the opposite sex, or
> >
> > (c)   persons of either sex.
>
> (2)   In relation to the protected characteristic of sexual orientation—
>
> > (a)   a reference to a person who has a particular protected characteristic is a reference to a person who is of a particular sexual orientation;
> >
> > (b)   a reference to persons who share a protected characteristic is a reference to persons who are of the same sexual orientation.

The Explanatory Notes give examples:

- A man who experiences sexual attraction towards both men and women is 'bisexual' in terms of sexual orientation even if he has only had relationships with women.
- A man and a woman who are both attracted only to people of the opposite sex from them share a sexual orientation.
- A man who is attracted only to other men is a gay man. A woman who is attracted only to other women is a lesbian. So a gay man and a lesbian share a sexual orientation.

8.2.5   Gender reassignment

Gender reassignment is defined in s 7 of the Act:

> (1)   A person has the protected characteristic of gender reassignment if the person is proposing to undergo, is undergoing or has undergone a process (or part of a process) for the purpose of reassigning the person's sex by changing physiological or other attributes of sex.

(2)   A reference to a transsexual person is a reference to a person who has the protected characteristic of gender reassignment.

(3)   In relation to the protected characteristic of gender reassignment—

(a)   a reference to a person who has a particular protected characteristic is a reference to a transsexual person;

(b)   a reference to persons who share a protected characteristic is a reference to transsexual persons.

The Explanatory Notes give examples:

• A person who was born physically male decides to spend the rest of his life living as a woman. He declares his intention to his manager at work, who makes appropriate arrangements, and she then starts life at work and home as a woman. After discussion with her doctor and a Gender Identity Clinic, she starts hormone treatment and after several years she goes through gender reassignment surgery. She would have the protected characteristic of gender reassignment for the purposes of the Act.

• A person who was born physically female decides to spend the rest of her life as a man. He starts and continues to live as a man. He decides not to seek medical advice as he successfully 'passes' as a man without the need for any medical intervention. He would have the protected characteristic of gender reassignment for the purposes of the Act.

Readers should note that the language used in s 7 is considered by many to be outdated. This applies both to the term 'gender reassignment' as well as to the term 'transsexual'. The latter appears in a number of places in the Equality Act 2010 (eg ss 7, 16, 195 and Sch 9) and it has been widely acknowledged that people find it stigmatising. The preferred terminology is 'transgender'.

Note that the requirement that previously existed under the SDA 1975 of being under medical supervision has been removed. This is because gender reassignment is recognised as a personal process rather than a medical one.

It now appears that an individual who is living permanently as a person of the opposite sex from their birth sex will be covered by the s 7 protected characteristic; such an individual will not need to intend to have surgery, or indeed ever have surgery, in order to identify as a different gender to their birth sex. An area of longstanding uncertainty had been whether the Equality Act protection included those who temporarily adopt the dress or appearance of the opposite gender, intersex individuals who biologically have both male and female characteristics and who may have a gender assigned at birth which is different from the gender identity by which they live, and those who are non-binary, whose gender identity is not clearly male or female or who are gender fluid. The accepted interpretation had been that individuals in such groups would not be protected by virtue of their specific gender identity and would only be protected if they were also planning or undergoing gender reassignment. In *Taylor v Jaguar Land Rover Ltd* (ET/1304471/2018), the employment tribunal considered whether the Equality Act 2010 applied to those who are gender fluid or non-binary. The tribunal upheld claims for harassment, direct discrimination and victimisation on the grounds of gender reassignment brought by an engineer at Jaguar Land Rover who identified as gender fluid, and who usually dressed in women's clothing.

The employee claimed that they were subjected to insults and abusive jokes, had problems with the use of toilet facilities, and had a lack of managerial support. The employment tribunal said that it appeared that there was no binding legal authority, or even first instance decision, on what was covered by s 7. It pointed out that the definition in s 7, specifically the phrase 'proposing to undergo', could be interpreted in a number of ways, covering a spectrum encompassing 'is actively considering', 'intends to' and 'has decided to'. Consequently, it went on to consider what Parliament's intention had been and found (see para 174 onwards of the judgment) that Parliament intended the Act to protect those on a gender spectrum, concluding that a gender fluid or non-binary person falls within the definition of gender reassignment in the Act. It found that the intention of the Act was:

to make it clear that a person need not intend to have surgery, or indeed ever have surgery, in order to identify as a different gender to their birth sex. We consider that the words we have highlighted in paragraph 173 make it clear, and beyond dispute, that gender reassignment need never be a medical process.

It also found, referring in particular to remarks made by the then Solicitor General (who was the sponsoring Minister during the passage of the Equality Bill through Parliament) as reported in Hansard, that:

> It concerns a personal move away from one's birth sex, into a state of one's choice ... a personal process which may be proposed but never gone through. It may have happened. Its nature may be medical one. It may be choosing to dress in a different way, and moving a gender identity away from birth sex.

The tribunal concluded that:

> it was very clear that Parliament intended gender reassignment to be a spectrum moving away from birth sex, and that a person could be at any point on that spectrum. That would be so, whether they described themselves as 'non-binary' i.e. not at point A or point Z, 'gender fluid' i.e. at different places between point A and point Z at different times, or 'transitioning' i.e. moving from point A, but not necessarily ending at point Z, where A and Z are biological sex. We concluded that it was beyond any doubt that somebody in the situation of the Claimant was (and is) protected by the legislation because they are on that spectrum and they are on a journey which will not be the same in any two cases. It will end up where it does.

The employee in this case was awarded £180,000 in compensation.

Note: a trans worker may have a claim for disability discrimination if they have a physical or mental impairment which has a substantial and long-term effect on their day-to-day activities. Depending on the circumstances, for example, mental health difficulties associated with gender dysphoria could constitute a disability.

Employers should also be aware that the Gender Recognition Act 2004 allows an individual to change their legally recognised gender by the issue of a Gender Recognition Certificate and obtain a new birth certificate issued in the gender in which they identify. Staff who have a Gender Recognition Certificate should be treated in accordance with their acquired gender.

In addition to guidance in the Equality Act Statutory Code of Practice (published by the EHRC), Acas has published guidance on gender reassignment discrimination, and the Government's Equality Office published, in 2015, its own guidance on the recruitment and retention of transgender employees, available at <www.gov.uk/government/publications/recruiting-and-retaining-transgender-staff-a-guide-for-employers>.

8.2.6 Marriage and civil partnership

Marriage and civil partnership is defined in s 8 of the Act:

(1)   A person has the protected characteristic of marriage and civil partnership if the person is married or is a civil partner.

(2)   In relation to the protected characteristic of marriage and civil partnership—

(a)   a reference to a person who has a particular protected characteristic is a reference to a person who is married or is a civil partner;

(b)   a reference to persons who share a protected characteristic is a reference to persons who are married or are civil partners.

The Explanatory Notes give examples:

- A person who is engaged to be married is not married and therefore does not have this protected characteristic.
- A divorcee or a person whose civil partnership has been dissolved is not married or in a civil partnership and therefore does not have this protected characteristic.

Marriage and civil partnership does not include those who are single and cohabiting.

Civil partnerships were introduced into the UK on 5 December 2005. Paragraph 18 of Sch 9 to the Equality Act 2010 provides that it is lawful to discriminate against an employee who is in a civil partnership or same-sex marriage by preventing or restricting them from having access to a benefit, facility or service, the right to which accrued before 5 December 2005 or which is payable in respect of periods of service before that date. In *Walker v Innospec Ltd* [2017] UKSC 47, the Supreme Court upheld a discrimination claim from Mr Walker that this provision was incompatible with the Framework Directive (2000/78/EC), as it amounted to direct discrimination in that it permitted an employer to treat a same-sex partner less favourably than an opposite-sex spouse. If Mr Walker had been married to a woman, she would have been entitled to a pension of about £45,700 pa. The impact of para 18 of Sch 9 meant that Mr Walker's husband would be entitled to a pension of about £1,000 pa. The Supreme Court referred to two decisions from the CJEU on survivors' pension rights for same-sex couples (*Maruko v Versorgungsanstalt der deutschen Bühnen* (Case C-267/06) and *Römer v Freie und Hansestadt Hamburg* (Case C-147/08)) in declaring that para 18 of Sch 9 was incompatible with EU law and must be disapplied.

In *Gould v St John's Downshire Hill* (UKEAT/0002/20), the EAT upheld the tribunal's decision that whilst the claimant's marriage was part of the background to events, the dismissal of a vicar was due to his behaviour and a breakdown in trust and confidence, and was not significantly influenced by the belief that a minister cannot continue to serve if the marriage breaks down. If it had been, the discrimination claim would likely have succeeded.

8.2.7   Pregnancy and maternity leave

See **9.4** below.

8.3   PROHIBITED CONDUCT

The Act outlaws:

(a)   direct discrimination (s 13) (see **Chapter 9**);

(b)   indirect discrimination (s 19) (see **Chapter 10**);

(c)   harassment (s 26) (see **Chapter 11**);

(d)   victimisation (s 27) (see **Chapter 11**);

(e)   instructing, causing, inducing and helping discrimination;

in relation to each of the protected characteristics. There are some differences with regard to age and disability. These characteristics are therefore dealt with separately in **Chapters 12** and **13**.

Direct and indirect discrimination are two different causes of action. They are different statutory torts (see R *(on the application of Elias) v Secretary of State for Defence* [2006] IRLR 934 and *National Statistics v Ali* [2005] ICR 201).

The Act also outlaws discrimination where a person is absent from work because of gender reassignment (s 16) (see **9.3**) and discrimination where a woman is absent from work as a result of pregnancy or illness caused by the pregnancy (s 18) (see **9.4**).

The prohibited conduct gives rise to a cause of action only if it falls within an area that the Act makes unlawful. The relevant part of the Act for employment purposes is Part 5 'Work'. Section 120 provides that an employment tribunal has jurisdiction to determine complaints relating to a breach of Part 5 provisions (see **8.4** for the relevant unlawful acts).

The EHRC non-statutory core guidance on 'Recruitment' gives the following examples of the various types of discrimination:

- You must not treat a person worse than another job applicant because of a protected characteristic (this is called **direct discrimination**).

> **Examples**
> - An employer does not interview a job applicant because of the applicant's ethnic background.
> - An employer says in a job advert 'this job is unsuitable for disabled people'.

- You must not do something which has (or would have) a worse impact on a job applicant and on other people who share a particular protected characteristic than on people who do not have that characteristic. Unless you can show that what you have done, or intend to do, is **objectively justified**, this will be **indirect discrimination**. 'Doing something' can include making a decision, or applying a rule or way of doing things.

> **Example**
> A job involves travelling to lots of different places to see clients. An employer says that, to get the job, the successful applicant has to be able to drive. This may stop some disabled people applying if they cannot drive. But there may be other perfectly good ways of getting from one appointment to another, which disabled people who cannot themselves drive could use. So the employer needs to show that a requirement to be able to drive is objectively justified, or they may be discriminating unlawfully against people who cannot drive because of their disability.

- You must not treat a disabled person **unfavourably** because of something connected to their disability where you cannot show that what you are doing is **objectively justified**. This only applies if you know or could reasonably have been expected to know that the person is a disabled person. The required knowledge is of facts of the applicant's disability. An employer does not need to realise that those particular facts are likely to meet the legal definition of disability. This is called **discrimination arising from disability.**

> **Example**
> An employer tells a visually impaired person who uses an assistance dog that they are unsuitable for a job because the employer is nervous of dogs and would not allow it in the office. Unless the employer can objectively justify what they have done, this is likely to be discrimination arising from disability. The refusal to consider the visually impaired person for the job is unfavourable treatment which is because of something connected to their disability (their use of an assistance dog). It may also be a failure to make a reasonable adjustment.

- You must not treat a person worse than someone else because they are **associated with** a person who has a protected characteristic.

> **Example**
> An employer does not give someone the job, even though they are the best-qualified person, just because the applicant tells the employer they have a disabled partner. This is probably direct discrimination because of disability by association. Direct discrimination cannot be justified, whatever the employer's motive.

- You must not treat a person worse than another job applicant because you incorrectly think they have a protected characteristic (**perception**).

> **Example**
> An employer does not give an applicant the job, even though they are the best-qualified person, because the employer incorrectly thinks the applicant is gay. This is still direct discrimination because of sexual orientation.

- You must not treat a job applicant badly or **victimise** them because they have complained about discrimination or helped someone else complain or have done anything to uphold their own or someone else's equality law rights.

> **Example**
> An employer does not shortlist a person for interview, even though they are well-qualified for the job, because last year the job applicant said they thought the employer had discriminated against them in not shortlisting them for another job.

- You must not **harass** a person.

> **Example**
>
> An employer makes someone feel humiliated by telling jokes about their religion or belief during the interview. This may amount to harassment.

In addition, to make sure that disabled people have the same access to everything that is involved in getting and doing a job as a non-disabled person you must make **reasonable adjustments**.

If an applicant asks for information about the job and the application form (if there is one), in an **alternative format** which they require because they are a disabled person then you must provide this, so long as it is a reasonable adjustment – and it is likely to be.

If an applicant needs reasonable adjustments to participate in any interview or assessment process, then you must make them.

When you assess a disabled job applicant's suitability for the job, you must take account of any reasonable adjustments which are needed to enable them to do the job.

If, after taking reasonable adjustments into account, the disabled applicant would not be the best person for the job, you do not have to offer it to them.

But if they would be the best person with the reasonable adjustments in place, you must offer them the job. In any event, it would make sense for you to do this, as you want the best person for the job.

...

- You must not **discriminate** against a person or harass or victimise them even after your employment relationship with them ends if what you are doing arises out of and is closely connected to the employment relationship that you had with them.

> **Example**
>
> A job applicant complains that you treated them worse than others in an interview because of their ethnic background. In response you tell another employer with whom you do business that it would not be a good idea to offer the applicant a job and when the applicant applies to that employer, he is refused an interview because of what you have said. This will be unlawful victimisation.

Distinguishing between direct and indirect discrimination

Direct and indirect discrimination are mutually exclusive, in that a single act, if it is discriminatory, cannot be both. It can sometimes be hard to determine whether a complaint is of direct or indirect discrimination. Generally, a provision, criterion or practice (PCP) (which is a requirement of an indirect discrimination claim) must be apparently neutral (see *James v Eastleigh Borough Council* [1990] ICR 554). If a PCP is very closely linked to a protected characteristic of an individual, it is more likely to be a direct discrimination claim.

The distinction between direct and indirect can be significant because whereas indirect discrimination can be justified, in most cases (but see direct age discrimination, **Chapter 12**) direct discrimination cannot. In practice, most claimants would be advised, where it is not clear, to claim under both heads.

Lady Hale addressed the differences between direct and indirect discrimination in several Supreme Court cases. In *R (on the application of E) v Governing Body of JFS* [2009] UKSC 15, [2010] IRLR 136, she said:

> The rule against direct discrimination aims to achieve formal equality of treatment: there must be no less favourable treatment between otherwise similarly situated people on grounds of colour, race, nationality, or ethnic or national origins. Indirect discrimination looks beyond formal equality towards a more substantive equality of results: criteria which appear neutral on their face may have a disproportionately adverse impact upon people of a particular colour, race, nationality or ethnic or national origins. ... Direct and indirect discrimination are mutually exclusive. You cannot have both at once.

As Mummery LJ explained in *Elias* at para 117: 'The conditions of liability, the available defences to liability and the available defences to remedies differ.' The main difference between them is that direct discrimination cannot be justified. Indirect discrimination can be justified if it is a proportionate means of achieving a legitimate aim.

In *Homer v Chief Constable of West Yorkshire Police* [2012] UKSC 15, [2012] IRLR 601, Lady Hale said at [17]:

> The law of indirect discrimination is an attempt to level the playing field by subjecting to scrutiny requirements which look neutral on their face but in reality work to the comparative disadvantage of people with a particular protected characteristic ... The resulting scrutiny may ultimately lead to the conclusion that the requirement can be justified ...

In *Essop v Home Office; Naeem v Secretary of State for Justice* [2017] UKSC 27, [2017] IRLR 558, she said:

> Direct discrimination expressly requires a causal link between the less favourable treatment and the protected characteristic. Indirect discrimination does not. Instead it requires a causal link between the PCP and the particular disadvantage suffered by the group and the individual. The reason for this is that the prohibition of direct discrimination aims to achieve equality of treatment. Indirect discrimination assumes equality of treatment – the PCP is applied indiscriminately to all – but aims to achieve a level playing field, where people sharing a particular protected characteristic are not subjected to requirements which many of them cannot meet but which cannot be shown to be justified. The prohibition of indirect discrimination thus aims to achieve equality of results in the absence of such justification. It is dealing with hidden barriers which are not easy to anticipate or to spot.

Worked example (with thanks to the LSE-Featherstone Moot and Verity Bell)

Jessica is a transgender woman early in her transition and is employed as a receptionist at a city university. The university has a swimming pool which all employees are allowed to use. Jessica wanted to use the women only changing facilities but other pool users complained about a man using the changing rooms. When there was a complaint the lifeguard had to shut down the pool to investigate. The university then required Jessica to use the accessible staff changing facility and did not allow her to use the women's changing facility. Gender reassignment is a protected characteristic and is defined in section 7 of the Equality Act.

Should Jessica bring her claim of gender reassignment discrimination under section 13(1) or section 19(1) of the Equality Act?

Direct discrimination under section 13 occurs when, because of a protected characteristic, one party treats another less favourably. Direct gender discrimination cannot be justified. Here, Jessica would argue that being compelled to use the accessible changing facilities constituted less favourable treatment by reference to a comparator of someone who was not undergoing gender reassignment. The university would argue that their actions did not constitute less favourable treatment as all the facilities – male, female and accessible were equivalent in terms of the available facilities and ease of access to the pool.

An indirect discrimination claim under section 19 occurs where a provision, criterion or practice ('PCP') is applied, apparently neutrally to people, but which impacts on people with a relevant protected characteristic by putting them at a particular disadvantage when compared with persons who do not share that protected characteristic, and the individual claimant shares that protected characteristic. A discriminatory PCP can be justified if it is a proportionate means of achieving a legitimate aim. Here, Jessica would argue that the university was applying a PCP that the users of the gender-segregated changing facilities are 'somatically' consistent in appearance with the sex group of the facilities and that this puts those undergoing gender reassignment at a particular disadvantage. The university would most likely seek to justify any finding of indirect discrimination on the grounds that it had to consider the comfort and facility of all users and this included a convention that women were entitled to safe segregated spaces without physical male intrusion.

Although direct discrimination uses the term 'less favourable treatment' and indirect discrimination uses the term 'particular disadvantage', in practice the same factual matters are likely to be argued in support of both. So, for example, the requirement not to use the female only facilities / to use the accessible facilities. Direct discrimination requires a 'causal' link between the treatment and the protected characteristic, whereas indirect discrimination requires a 'causal' link between the PCP and the disadvantage. The PCP here is arguably so closely aligned to the protected characteristic of undergoing gender reassignment, that it in effect creates a closed category of potential users which only comprises those with the protected characteristic. If all of the people who suffer disadvantage share the same protected characteristic, the discrimination is going to be direct rather than indirect. If Jessica establishes that there is less favourable treatment which relates to the opportunity to use the changing rooms that match her gender identity, she should win. The university may argue, successfully, that it was not *because of* her gender identity but because of the physical manifestation (which might be related to the protected characteristic of sex), and / or that if the claimant was further down the line in her transition, it would allow her to use the women only changing rooms, and problems from public complaints and disruption. The case *of James v Eastleigh Borough Council* [1990] 2 AC 751 established that there will be direct discrimination if the PCP used exactly corresponds with a protected characteristic. If there was a finding that the PCP was not a closed category, and the case were to proceed as an indirect discrimination claim, justification would most likely be the main focus. That would involve considering whether the PCP was a proportionate means of achieving a legitimate aim. The university might seek to rely on the comfort of all the pool users, the claimant might counter that there are more proportionate options such as seeking to educate the public or installing private individual cubicles in the women's changing facilities.

Conclusion

Before looking in detail at each of these types of discrimination (in their individual chapters), we shall first consider what constitutes an unlawful act of discrimination. Discrimination is not in itself outlawed: it must be accompanied by an unlawful act.

8.4 UNLAWFUL ACTS OF DISCRIMINATION – IN THE EMPLOYMENT FIELD

Unlawful discrimination in the employment field against job applicants and employees/ workers is prohibited by ss 39 and 40 of the Act. These sections make it unlawful for an employer directly or indirectly to discriminate against, victimise or harass employees and people seeking work. They apply where the employer is making arrangements to fill a job, and in respect of anything done in the course of a person's employment. This can include the terms on which employment is offered as well as not offering employment. The definition of employer is contained in s 83 and is wide enough to include 'employees' and 'workers' as defined in the ERA 1996. Claims can therefore be brought again prospective, current or former (see s 105) employers and individuals.

Other sections create causes of action for contract workers (s 41), police officers (ss 42–43), partnerships (ss 44–46), barristers and advocates (ss 47–48), office holders (ss 49–52, Sch 6) and trade union members (s 57). Section 108 prohibits discrimination and harassment against former employees and other groups referred to in this section. For a pre-Equality Act 2010 decision on the meaning of 'contract worker' in discrimination legislation, see *Leeds City Council v Woodhouse* [2010] IRLR 625, where the Court of Appeal rejected a submission that it is necessary for the alleged contract worker to show that the respondent had control or influence over the work that he did.

8.4.1 Recruitment

Under s 39(1) of the Act:

An employer (A) must not discriminate against a person (B)—

(a)   in the arrangements A makes for deciding to whom to offer employment;

(b)   as to the terms on which A offers B employment;

(c)   by not offering B employment.

Section 39(3) contains an identical provision with regard to victimisation, and s 40(1) protects job seekers from harassment.

Whilst there is no general duty for an employer to advertise job vacancies, in order to avoid internal or external complaints, it is preferable to advertise all vacancies (while taking care to avoid using discriminatory language).

Readers should note that under the Immigration, Asylum and Nationality Act 2006, an employer is expected to ensure that any migrant workers whom it employs are eligible to work in the UK (the Asylum and Immigration Act 1996 applies to those employed pre-February 2008). Section 15 of the 2006 Act provides that an employer who employs a person subject to immigration control who does not have the right to take employment, shall be guilty of a civil offence and liable to payment of a civil financial penalty (see **1.2.6**). The 2006 Act allows employers to avoid the penalty if they have carried out specific checks on documents. Checking the documents of prospective employees provides an employer with what is known as a 'statutory excuse'. For workers with a time-limit on how long they can stay in the UK, employers must repeat the document checks at least once a year to retain the 'statutory excuse'. The 2006 Act also (s 21) makes it a criminal offence knowingly to employ someone who has no permission to work in the UK. (For a case where the EAT considered the immigration rules, see *Kelly v University of Southampton* (UKEAT/0295/07).)

Tough penalties are in force for anyone caught employing illegal migrants. However, an employer also needs to take care that, when implementing or exercising measures to prevent illegal working, he also avoids unlawful discrimination. While taking proper steps to ascertain that an employee does have a right to work, careful consideration must be given to when to ask questions of applicants to avoid discriminating on the grounds of race (see, eg, *Osborne Clarke Services v Purohit* [2009] IRLR 341). Guidance ('An employer's guide to right to work checks') and a Code of Practice (on preventing illegal working/avoiding discrimination) are available on the Home Office website (see <https://assets.publishing.service.gov.uk/government/uploads/system/uploads/attachment_data/file/773780/An_employer_s_guide_to_right_to_work_checks_-_January_2019.pdf> and <https://assets.publishing.service.gov.uk/government/uploads/system/uploads/attachment_data/file/774078/Code_of_practice_on_preventing_illegal_working_-_January_2019.pdf>).

The best way for employers to ensure that they do not discriminate is to treat all job applicants the same way at each stage of the recruitment process. In other words, to carry out document checks on all prospective employees and not make assumptions about a person's right to work based on that person's background, appearance or accent.

In 2013, the UK Border Agency, which had, inter alia, responsibility for immigration enforcement, was abolished. A new executive agency, Immigration Enforcement, under the supervision of the Home Office, is now responsible for enforcing the UK's immigration laws and targeting illegal working. The Criminal and Financial Investigation Department is responsible for investigating criminality surrounding immigration, including trafficking and modern slavery.

The various EU equality directives permit positive action. Section 159 of the 2010 Act allows (but does not require) an employer to take a protected characteristic into account when deciding whom to recruit, where persons who share a protected characteristic suffer a disadvantage connected to the characteristic, or participation in an activity by persons who share a protected characteristic is disproportionately low. This can be done only where candidates are equally qualified (it is colloquially known as the 'tie-breaker' provision). This does not allow employers automatically to prefer such candidates. Each case must be considered on its merits, and any action must be a proportionate means of addressing such disadvantage or under-representation. For a recent employment tribunal decision on this section, see *Furlong v Chief Constable of Cheshire Police* (ET/2405577/2018), where Cheshire Police were found to have acted unlawfully in a recruitment exercise for new police officers. The tribunal accepted that it was reasonable for the police to regard the protected group as under-represented, so taking positive action was legitimate, but the candidates were not all of equal merit.

8.4.2 Promotion and dismissal

Under s 39(2) of the Act:

> An employer (A) must not discriminate against an employee of A's (B)—
> (a)   as to B's terms of employment;
> (b)   in the way A affords B access, or by not affording B access, to opportunities for promotion, transfer or training or for receiving any other benefit, facility or service;
> (c)   by dismissing B;
> (d)   by subjecting B to any other detriment.

Section 70(1) of the Equality Act 2010 prevents successful reliance on the employment discrimination provision in ss 13 and 39(2)(a) in circumstances where the equal pay provisions apply (sex only). However, s 71 of the Equality Act 2010 provides that where the claimant is not able to identify an actual comparator and the complaint is one of *direct* sex discrimination, the claim may be brought under the equal treatment provisions (ss 13 and 39) (and reliance placed upon a hypothetical comparator).

Dismissal, for the purposes of the Act, includes constructive dismissal (s 39(7)). Detriment does not include conduct which amounts to harassment (s 212). This is because of the existence of explicit protection for harassment, and to avoid the possibility of a claim for direct discrimination by detriment being brought on the same facts. This means that harassment and direct discrimination claims are mutually exclusive.

The EAT confirmed in *Cordant Security Ltd v Singh & Another* (EAT/0144/15) that it is a necessary part of any discrimination complaint that an unlawful act is made out. In that case, the employee could not have suffered a detriment because if the complaint had been investigated, it would have been found to be untrue because it was entirely fabricated. The employee could not be said to have suffered any injustice as a result of the less favourable treatment he suffered because the grievance was fabricated. Of course, a genuinely believed grievance might turn out to be unsubstantiated but that grievance is still a detriment.

A dismissal, even if subsequently withdrawn, can give rise to a detriment (see *Jakkhu v Network Rail Infrastructure Ltd* (UKEAT/0276/18)).

Section 39(4) contains an identical provision with regard to victimisation.

Being subject to a detriment is an element of the statutory cause of action additional to and distinct from being treated 'less favourably', although there will be 'very few, if any cases, where less favourable treatment will be meted out and yet it will not result in a detriment. This is because being subject to an act of discrimination which causes, or is reasonably likely to cause, distress or upset will reasonably be perceived as a detriment by the person subject to the discrimination even if there are no other adverse consequences.' (Elias LJ in *Deer v University of Oxford* [2015] ICR 1213)

Detriment has subjective and objective elements. The EHRC Employment Code, at paras 9.8–9.9, says, 'Generally a detriment is anything which the individual concerned might reasonably consider changed their position for the worse or put them at a disadvantage ... However, an unjustified sense of grievance alone would not be enough to establish detriment.'

The House of Lords, in *Shamoon v Chief Constable of the Royal Ulster Constabulary* [2003] ICR 337, provides useful guidance on the scope of 'detriment'. Referring to the words of Lord Hoffman in *Chief Constable of the West Yorkshire Police v Khan* [2001] UKHL 48, [2001] 1 WLR 1947 that a 'person may be treated less favourably and yet suffer no detriment', Lord Hope pointed out:

> 33. ... Lord Mackay of Clashfern also noted, at p 1956F, para 37 that the word 'detriment' has been widely defined. He referred to *De Souza v Automobile Association* [1986] ICR 514. Bingham LJ's observation in *Barclays Bank plc v Kapur* [1989] IRLR 387, para 54, that the phrase 'subjecting him to any other detriment' in section 4(2)(c) of the Race Relations Act 1976 was to be given its broad, ordinary meaning is consistent with this approach. The decisions in *De Souza v Automobile Association* and *Barclays Bank v Kapur* predate the decision of the Court of Appeal in this case, but it appears that its attention was not drawn to these authorities.

> 34. The statutory cause of action which the appellant has invoked in this case is discrimination in the field of employment. So the first requirement, if the disadvantage is to qualify as a 'detriment' within the meaning of article 8(2)(b), is that it has arisen in that field. .... As May LJ put it in *De Souza v Automobile Association* [1986] ICR 514, 522G, the court or tribunal must find that by reason of the act or acts complained of a reasonable worker would or might take the view that he had thereby been disadvantaged in the circumstances in which he had thereafter to work.

Section 40(1) protects employees from harassment but does not refer to dismissal (see **11.3.1**).

8.4.3 Post-employment discrimination

Section 108 prohibits discrimination after the employment relationship has ended. Where an employment relationship has come to an end, it is unlawful for the employer to discriminate against the former employee or by harassing the former employee where the discrimination arises out of and is closely connected to that former relationship.

The Explanatory Notes give examples, one of which is:

> A[n] ... employer refuses to give a reference to an ... ex-employee because of his or her religion or belief. This would be direct discrimination.

Although s 108(7) of the 2010 Act states that post-employment victimisation is not covered, the Court of Appeal held in *Jessemey v Rowstock Ltd and anor* [2014] EWCA Civ 185 that this was a drafting error, and that post-employment victimisation is covered (see **11.7.2**).

8.4.4 Advertisements

Under the old discrimination legislation, there were specific provisions concerning discriminatory advertisements (for example in s 29 of the RRA 1976 and s 38 of the SDA 1975; there was never a specific prohibition in the now repealed Age Regulations). These were all repealed by the Act, along with the specific sections of the Equality Act 2006 which dealt with advertising. There is no specific provision in the Act regarding discriminatory advertisements, so publishers are no longer required to prove they relied reasonably on an assurance from the creator of an advertisement. Instead, s 13 of the Act, which prohibits direct discrimination, is intended to embrace discriminatory advertisements. The Explanatory Notes gives this as an example of direct discrimination:

> If an employer advertising a vacancy makes it clear in the advert that Roma need not apply, this would amount to direct race discrimination against a Roma who might reasonably have considered applying for the job but was deterred from doing so because of the advertisement.

In March and April 2016, the EHRC produced a guide to 'what equality law means for advertisers ...', which includes guidance in relation to, inter alia, advertising job opportunities.

The EHRC has enforcement powers that cover both direct and indirect discrimination, and may bring prosecutions against employers.

8.5 OCCUPATIONAL REQUIREMENTS

Schedule 9, Pt 1, para 1 to the Equality Act 2010 provides:

(1)   A person (A) does not contravene a provision [in relation to recruitment, training or dismissal] by applying a requirement to have a particular protected characteristic, if A shows that, having regard to the nature or context of the work—

(a)   it is an occupational requirement,

(b)   the application of the requirement is a proportionate means of achieving a legitimate aim, and

(c)   the person to whom A applies the requirement does not meet it (or A has reasonable grounds for not being satisfied that the person meets it).

The Act therefore provides a general exception to what would otherwise be unlawful direct discrimination in relation to work.

The exception in para 1 applies where being of a particular sex, race, religion or belief, sexual orientation or age – or not being a transsexual person, married or a civil partner – is a requirement for the work, and the person to whom it is applied does not meet it (or, except in the case of sex, does not meet it to the reasonable satisfaction of the person who applied it). The requirement must be crucial to the post and not merely one of several important factors. It also must not be a sham or pretext. In addition, applying the requirement must be a proportionate way of achieving a legitimate aim, ie it must be the least restrictive way of achieving the aim.

Examples of para 1 occupational requirements given in the Explanatory Notes to the Act include:

- The need for authenticity or realism might require someone of a particular race, or sex for acting roles (for example, a black man to play the part of Othello) or modelling jobs.
- Considerations of privacy or decency might require a public changing room or lavatory attendant to be of the same sex as those using the facilities
- Unemployed Muslim women might not take advantage of the services of an outreach worker to help them find employment if they were provided by a man.

In *Amnesty International v Ahmed* [2009] IRLR 884, the EAT suggested that Amnesty might have been able to rely on an 'occupational requirement' (under the predecessor law) when it refused to promote a North Sudanese woman to a post in Sudan because of fears for her and others' safety.

Schedule 9, Pt 1, para 2 to the Act provides for exceptions in relation to religious requirements relating to sex, transsexuals, married persons and civil partners, and sexual orientation:

(1)   A person (A) does not contravene a provision by applying [in relation to recruitment, training or dismissal] a requirement to which subparagraph (4) applies if A shows that—

(a)   the employment is for the purposes of an organised religion,

(b)   the application of the requirement engages the compliance or non-conflict principle, and

(c)   the person to whom A applies the requirement does not meet it (or A has reasonable grounds for not being satisfied that the person meets it).

...

(5)   The application of a requirement engages the compliance principle if the application is a proportionate means of complying with the doctrines of the religion.

(6)   The application of a requirement engages the non-conflict principle if, because of the nature or context of the employment, the requirement is applied so as to avoid conflicting with the strongly held religious convictions of a significant number of the religion's followers.

The exception in para 2 allows the employer to apply a requirement to be of a particular sex or not to be a transsexual person, or to make a requirement related to the employee's marriage or civil partnership status or sexual orientation, but only if:

(a)   appointing a person who meets the requirement in question is a proportionate way of complying with the doctrines of the religion; or

(b)   because of the nature or context of the employment, employing a person who meets the requirement is a proportionate way of avoiding conflict with a significant number of the religion's followers' strongly held religious convictions.

Examples of para 2 occupational requirements given in the Explanatory Notes to the Act include:

- a requirement that a Catholic priest be a man and unmarried.
- unlikely to permit a requirement that a church youth worker who primarily organises sporting activities is celibate if he is gay, but it may apply if the youth worker mainly teaches Bible classes.
- would not apply to a requirement that a church accountant be celibate if he is gay.

In *Pemberton v Inwood* [2018] EWCA Civ 564, a Church of England priest, who had married his same sex partner, was refused a licence to practise by reason of the same sex marriage. The Court of Appeal held that the employment tribunal was entitled to find that the doctrines, as in teachings and beliefs of the Church of England, were as stated in Canon B30 with specific regard in relation to same sex marriages to the statement of Pastoral Guidance from the House of Bishops, and that the priest had not therefore been discriminated against because of the occupational requirement exception set out in Sch 9 above. See too the ECJ's decision in IR v JQ (Case C-68/17).

In *Sheridan v Prospects for People with Learning Disabilities* (ET/2901366/06), a tribunal held that a Christian charity providing support services for people with learning disabilities could not rely on the (as it was then) 'genuine occupational requirement' exemption to operate a blanket 'Christians only' policy as the work was primarily secular in nature: it could not be said that being of a particular religion was essential for performing the functions of the post. See more recently *Pemberton v Former Acting Bishop of Southwell and Nottingham* (UKEAT/0072/16), where a refusal to grant an Extra Parochial Ministry Licence to a priest who had married his long-term, same-sex partner, because the view of marriage as between a man and a woman was part of the Church's doctrine, was held not to be unlawful direct discrimination, whether because of sexual orientation or marital status, relying on the religious occupation exception.

In the context of age, the ECJ held in *Vital Pérez v Ayuntamiento de Oviedo* (Case C-416/13) [2015] IRLR 158 that an age restriction of 30 to join the local police was not a genuine occupational requirement as the evidence was too weak. However, it upheld an age limit of 35 in *Salaberria Sorondo v Academia Vasca de Policia y Emergencias* (Case C-258/15) because the evidence was that the job was more physically demanding and dangerous.

8.6 VICARIOUS LIABILITY

Under s 109 of the Act, an employer is vicariously liable for acts of discrimination (including harassment) committed by his employees 'in the course of … employment', as are principals for the acts of their agents. An individual as well as the 'employer' can both be liable for acts of discrimination (see below re ss 110–112). An employer will be liable whether or not the acts were done with the employer's knowledge or approval. The Court of Appeal held in *Kemeh v Ministry of Defence* [2014] EWCA Civ 91 that an employee of an independent contractor is not an agent of the third party employer simply because he carries out work for the third party. However, it is a defence for the employer to show that he took such steps as were reasonable to prevent an employee doing the act complained of (s 109(4) – see below).

8.6.1 Course of employment

Determining whether an act of discrimination arises in 'the course of employment' is not always straightforward, particularly if the occasion on which it arises is out of normal work hours. An employer will be liable for such conduct if it occurs on an occasion that could be said to be 'an extension of their employment' (see *Chief Constable of Lincolnshire Police v Stubbs* [1999] IRLR 81).

In *Jones v Tower Boot Co Ltd* [1997] IRLR 168, CA, Mr Jones was subjected to acts of racial harassment by other employees, including having his arm burnt with a hot screwdriver; having metal bolts thrown at his head; having his legs whipped with a piece of welt; and being called 'chimp', 'monkey' and 'baboon'. The EAT held that the acts complained of could not by any stretch of the imagination be regarded as an improper mode of performing authorised tasks, and found for the employers. This decision initially caused much concern because no one is employed to harass another employee. However, the Court of Appeal reversed the decision because the EAT had erred in applying the old common law test of an employer's vicarious liability. The words 'in the course of employment' should be interpreted in the sense in which they are employed in everyday speech and not restrictively by reference to the old principles laid down for establishing an employer's vicarious liability for the torts committed by an employee. Otherwise, the more heinous the act of discrimination, the less likely it would be that the employer would be liable. Note, too, that the House of Lords reassessed the test used to establish the vicarious liability of employers at common law for the tortious acts of employees. The decision in *Lister and Others v Hesley Hall Ltd* [2001] IRLR 472 brings the statutory and common law approaches to vicarious liability more in line. (For an interesting, decision on the scope of vicarious liability – but not specifically in a discrimination context – see *Maga v Birmingham Roman Catholic Archdiocese Trustees* [2010] All ER (D) 141.) The EAT commented in *Livesey v Parker Merchanting Ltd* (UKEAT/0755/03) that the statutory test is to be regarded as at least as wide as, if not wider than, the *Lister* test.

In *Chief Constable of the Lincolnshire Police v Stubbs*, a police officer was found to be acting 'in the course of employment' when he subjected the applicant to inappropriate sexual behaviour, even though the incidents occurred at social gatherings either immediately after work or at an organised leaving party. They were not chance meetings. The officer's employer was, on the facts, held to be vicariously liable for his actions under s 41 of the SDA 1975.

In *Sidhu v Aerospace Composite Technology Ltd* [2000] IRLR 602, the Court of Appeal upheld the tribunal's decision that a racial assault upon the applicant by a colleague during a family day out organised by the employer had not taken place 'in the course of employment', since the outing was in a public place, the employees had attended during their own time, and the majority of those attending were family and friends of the employees as opposed to employees.

The Court of Appeal considered the matter in two joined cases in 2012. In *Weddell v Barchester Healthcare Ltd* and *Wallbank v Wallbank Fox Designs Ltd* [2012] EWCA Civ 25, the Court decided that the employer was not vicariously liable for the actions of an employee who attacked his manager at the workplace but whilst he was off duty (*Weddell*), but that the employer was liable for an employee's attack on his manager carried out during work in response to a lawful instruction (*Wallbank*). In the former case, the act was not so closely connected with employment as to render the employer liable; the act was an 'independent venture ... distinct from [his] employment'. In the latter case, the sufficiently close connection was established because reacting to instructions was part of the job.

The Supreme Court, in four cases, looked at the sort of relationship which has to exist between an individual and a defendant before the defendant can be made vicariously liable in tort. In *Cox v Ministry of Justice* [2016] UKSC 10, a sack of rice was accidentally dropped on the claimant's back, injuring her. The person who dropped the sack was a prisoner working in the prison kitchen. The question arose as to whether the Ministry of Justice was vicariously liable for the prisoner's negligence. The Court found that prisoners working in kitchens were integrated into the operation of the prison. They worked under the direction of prison staff. The prison service was therefore found liable to the claimant. (Contrast the facts with those in *Warren v Henlys Ltd* [1948] 2 All ER 935, where the relationship had changed from that of customer and representative of the company to complainant and subject of the complaint on the facts.) The Court referred to five factors (identified in *Various Claimants v Catholic Child Welfare Society* [2012] UKSC 56) which make it 'fair, just and reasonable' to impose tortious vicarious liability. This extended the scope for vicarious liability beyond the responsibility of an employer for acts and omissions of its employees 'in the course of their employment', but not so widely as to impose liability for acts of independent businesses or third parties.

In *Mohamud v WM Morrison Supermarkets plc* [2016] UKSC 11, the Supreme Court held that a supermarket was vicariously responsible for an employee's unprovoked attack on a customer because the act was sufficiently connected to the employee's employment – his job was to deal with customers and the violence was carried out whilst dealing with a customer. The Supreme Court's judgment in *Mohamud* provides a useful review of the legal principles.

There are, according to *Mohamud*, two questions to be considered:

(a) First, looking at matters broadly, what were the functions or what was the field of activities entrusted by the employer to the relevant employee, ie what was the nature of his or her job?

(b) Secondly, was there sufficient connection between the position in which the person was employed and his or her wrongful conduct to make it right for the employer to be held liable under the principle of social justice?

In *WM Morrison Supermarkets plc v Various Claimants* [2018] EWCA Civ 2239, the Court of Appeal held that an employer was vicariously liable for the actions of an employee who disclosed the personal information of colleagues on the internet and was later convicted of fraud and offences under the Computer Misuse Act 1990 and s 55 of the Data Protection Act 1998. Employees issued proceedings against Morrisons, seeking to hold it vicariously liable for the employee's misuse of their personal data. The Court of Appeal upheld the High Court's decision that Morrisons was liable. There was, said the High Court, 'a sufficient connection between the position in which [the employee] was employed and his wrongful conduct, put into the position of handling and disclosing the data as he was by Morrisons (albeit it was meant to be to KPMG alone), to make it right for Morrisons to be held liable "under the principle of social justice which can be traced back to Holt CJ"'. However, in April 2020, the Supreme Court unanimously allowed an appeal and held that the judge and the Court of Appeal misunderstood the principles governing vicarious liability in a number of respects (*WM Morrison Supermarkets plc v Various Claimants* [2020] UKSC 12). The online disclosure of the data was not part of the employee's 'field of activities'; it was not an act which the employee was authorised to do, which was to transmit the payroll data to auditors. The disclosure of the data was *not* so closely connected with that task that it could be fairly and properly be regarded as made by the employee acting in the course of employment. The Supreme Court said that Lord Toulson's comment, in relation to the facts of *Mohamud*, that 'motive is irrelevant' should not be taken out of context: whether the employee was acting on his employer's business or for personal reasons was important, but, on the facts of *Mohamud*, the reason why he had committed the tort could not make a material difference to the outcome ([29]–[30]).

In *Barclays Bank v Various Claimants plc* [2020] UKSC 13, the Supreme Court held that Barclays Bank was not liable for assaults perpetrated by a doctor in the course of the medical examinations he carried out for Barclays. The Supreme Court held that the doctor was not ever an employee or anything coming close to an employee. Barclays made the arrangements for the examinations and chose the questions to which it wanted answers, *but much the same would be true of window cleaners or auditors*. He was paid a fee for each report and was free to refuse to conduct an offered examination. The Supreme Court declined to align the common law concept of vicarious liability with the statutory concept of 'worker' (which the doctor might have been): it would be going too far down the road to tidiness for this court to align the common law concept of vicarious liability, developed for one set of reasons, with the statutory concept of 'worker', developed for a quite different set of reasons. Of course, on a different set of facts, a worker may be 'sufficiently akin to' an employee but not if acting as an independent contractor. On the facts, the doctor was used ad hoc by the bank, as one of his many clients and as part of his independent practice. The bank was not liable for his acts while doing so.

In *Bellman v Northampton Recruitment Ltd* [2017] ICR 543, the High Court held that the employer was not liable for one employee's violent attack on another during an 'impromptu drink' after the firm's Christmas party: the drinks were after the party and at a different location; partners and other guests were present, and the conversation was, in the main, non-work-related. The Court of Appeal overturned the decision ([2018] EWCA Civ 2214) and held that there was a sufficient nexus between the job and the act: the employee was senior, and the function was not purely social – it followed on from a work event where the company paid for taxis and drinks. In that case, the employee was the managing director and the other employee was left with severe brain damage. The Court noted the power and authority that the managing director had over his staff.

In *Forbes v LHR Airport Ltd* (UKEAT/0174/18), the EAT usefully reviewed the case law on vicarious liability, and the meaning of the course of employment, in a social media context. The EAT found that the posting of offensive images by an employee on a private Facebook account, which was shown to a work colleague, was not done in the course of employment. (See also **15.4.4** on employees' rights to freedom of expression.)

8.6.2   Reasonable steps' defence

Section 109(4) sets out the 'reasonably practicable' defence:

> In proceedings against A's employer (B) in respect of anything alleged to have been done by A in the course of A's employment it is a defence for B to show that B took all reasonable steps to prevent A—
>
> (a)   from doing that thing, or
>
> (b)   from doing anything of that description.

This defence is often unsuccessful. The employer must be able to show that it took preventative action, but it will also be necessary to consider any such steps in the context of what further steps it would have been reasonably practicable for the employer to take. A written equal opportunities policy alone is unlikely to succeed, unless it is actively implemented, employees are trained on it, and violations are seriously and constantly dealt with.

The European Recommendation and Code of Practice on the Dignity of Women and Men at Work (92/131/EEC) makes specific recommendations to employers on how to combat sexual harassment. The Code recommends that:

(a)   employers should issue a policy statement which expressly states that all employees have the right to be treated with dignity, that sexual harassment at work will not be permitted or condoned and that employees have the right to complain about it should it occur;

(b)   the policy should then be communicated to all employees so that they are aware that they have a right to complain and to whom they should complain. In this way, employees are made aware of the likely consequences of engaging in sexual harassment;

(c)   managers and supervisors have a particular duty to ensure that sexual harassment does not occur in the area for which they are responsible; they should explain the policy to their staff, and be responsive and supportive in confidentiality to anyone who complains;

(d)   managers and supervisors should be given training on their responsibilities in relation to sexual harassment and to ensure that they are aware of the factors which contribute to a working environment free from sexual harassment.

The Code also makes some recommendations as to the procedures which employers should follow when dealing with allegations of sexual harassment:

(a)   both formal and informal methods of resolving the problems created by harassment should be available;

(b)   employers should designate someone to provide advice and assistance to employees who are subjected to sexual harassment;

(c)   a formal procedure should specify to whom complaints should be brought, and also set out an alternative if complaining to that person would be inappropriate for the employee in question;

(d)   internal investigations of complaints should be seen to be independent, objective and handled with due respect for the rights of both the complainant and the alleged harasser. Those carrying out the investigation should not be connected with the allegations;

(e)   violations of the employer's policy on sexual harassment should be treated as a disciplinary offence.

The EHRC's Code of Practice suggests that reasonable steps will include training and implementation of an equality policy. An extract appears below:

> 18.5 It is essential that a written equality policy is backed by a clear programme of action for implementation and continual review. It is a process which consists of four key stages: planning, implementing, monitoring and reviewing the equality policy.
>
> ...
>
> 18.7 A written equality policy should set out the employer's general approach to equality and diversity issues in the workplace. The policy should make clear that the employer intends to develop and apply procedures which do not discriminate because of any of the protected characteristics, and which provide equality of opportunity for all job applicants and workers.
>
> *Planning the content of equality policies*
>
> 18.8 Most policies will include the following:
>
> * a statement of the employer's commitment to equal opportunity for all job applicants and workers;
> * what is and is not acceptable behaviour at work (also referring to conduct near the workplace and at work-related social functions where relevant);
> * the rights and responsibilities of everyone to whom the policy applies, and procedures for dealing with any concerns and complaints;
> * how the policy may apply to the employer's other policies and procedures;
> * how the employer will deal with any breaches of policy;
> * who is responsible for the policy; and
> * how the policy will be implemented and details of monitoring and review procedures.
>
> 18.9 It will help an employer avoid discrimination if the equality policy covers all aspects of employment including recruitment, terms and conditions of work, training and development, promotion, performance, grievance, discipline and treatment of workers when their contract ends. ...
>
> *Planning an equality policy – protected characteristics*
>
> 18.10 It is recommended that adopting one equality policy covering all protected characteristics is the most practical approach. Where separate policies are developed, such as a separate race equality or sex equality policy, they should be consistent with each other and with an overall commitment to promoting equality of opportunity in employment.
>
> *Implementing an equality policy*
>
> 18.11 An equality policy should be more than a statement of good intentions; there should also be plans for its implementation. The policy should be in writing and drawn up in consultation with workers and any recognised trade unions or other workplace representatives, including any equality representatives within the workforce.
>
> ...
>
> *Promotion and communication of an equality policy*
>
> 18.13 Employers should promote and publicise their equality policy as widely as possible and there are a number of ways in which this can be done. Promoting the policy is part of the process of effective implementation and will help an employer demonstrate that they have taken all reasonable steps to prevent discrimination.

18.14 Employers may use a number of methods of communication to promote their policy, including:

- email bulletins
- intranet and/or website
- induction packs
- team meetings
- office notice boards
- circulars, newsletters
- cascade systems
- training
- handbooks
- annual reports.

18.15 These methods of communication may not be appropriate in all cases.... Employers must also consider whether reasonable adjustments need to be made for disabled people so that they are able to access the information.

18.16 Promoting and communicating an equality policy should not be a one-off event. It is recommended that employers provide periodic reminders and updates to workers and others such as contractors and suppliers. Employers should also periodically review their advertising, recruitment and application materials and processes ...

Implementing an equality policy – training

18.18 Employers should ensure that all workers and agents understand the equality policy, how it affects them and the plans for putting it into practice. The best way to achieve this is by providing regular training.

18.19 Some workers may need more specific training, depending on what they do within the organisation. For example, line managers and senior management should receive detailed training on how to manage equality and diversity issues in the workplace.

18.20 The training should be designed in consultation with workers, their workplace representatives and managers and by incorporating feedback from any previous training into future courses.

18.21 Employers should make sure in-house trainers are themselves trained before running courses for other workers. External trainers also need to be fully informed about the employer's policies, including their equality policy ...

Monitoring and reviewing an equality policy

18.23 Equality monitoring enables an employer to find out whether their equality policy is working ...

Tribunals must take the Codes into account in cases involving areas they cover.

In *Caspersz v Ministry of Defence* (UKEAT/0599/05), the EAT held that the tribunal was correct to take the two-stage approach referred to in the earlier case of *Canniffe v East Riding of Yorkshire Council* [2000] IRLR 555, which is that a tribunal should:

(a) identify whether a respondent took any steps at all to prevent the employee from doing the act or acts complained of; and

(b) having identified what steps, if any, the employer took, consider whether there were any further steps that the employer could have taken that were reasonably practicable.

The EAT accepted in that case that the defence was satisfied: the employer had a 'Dignity at Work' policy that had been carefully implemented.

In *Zulu and Gue v MOD* (ET/2205687/2018 and ET 2205688/2018), nine of 11 steps put forward by the claimants were rejected as reasonable steps by the tribunal, but two were successful as being reasonable steps which the respondent failed to take (failure to maintain a comprehensive equality and diversity log having decided to keep a log (which is good practice) and failure to ensure that annual equalities training was done adequately and effectively (it was found to be a tick box exercise)). As a result (any single failure to take a reasonable step means that the respondent has failed to take 'all reasonable steps') the respondent had therefore failed to establish the statutory defence and was therefore liable for the proven allegation of harassment.

In *Allay Ltd v Gehlen* (UKEAT/0031/20), the tribunal had rejected the defence because the equality training had been a year earlier and was 'stale'. The EAT upheld the decision.

8.6.3 Personal liability of employees

By virtue of s 110 of the Act, the employee for whose act the employer is liable (or would be so but for establishment of a defence that he took all reasonable steps) is deemed to have aided that unlawful act. This means that the complainant may claim against both the employer and the employee who carried out the act of discrimination. It is not now necessary (as it was under the previous legislation) to show that the employee or agent knew that the act was unlawful. Section 111 covers instructing, causing or inducing contraventions of the Act, codifying the situation in *Weathersfield Ltd v Sargent* [1999] IRLR 94. It permits the intended victim to bring proceedings even if the instruction has not been carried out. Both the EHRC and B and/or C (if they are subjected to a detriment as a result of A's conduct, even where the instruction is not carried out) may bring enforcement proceedings in relation to any breach.

Note that if the employer is not vicariously liable for the acts of the employee because the acts did not take place during the course of employment, there can be no claim against the employee who carried out the discriminatory act. However, if the acts were committed during the course of employment then, even if the employer establishes the reasonably practicable defence, the employee may still be personally liable (*Yeboah v Crofton* [2002] IRLR 634). The Explanatory Notes give this example:

> A factory worker racially harasses her colleague. The factory owner would be liable for the worker's actions, but is able to show that he took all reasonable steps to stop the harassment. The colleague can still bring a claim against the factory worker in an employment tribunal.

The EAT held, in *Barlow v Stone* [2012] IRLR 898, that an employment tribunal had jurisdiction to consider a claim of victimisation brought by an employee against a fellow employee, even though no claim had been brought against their mutual employer, where the employer would have been liable under s 109 (see **8.6**).

8.7 RETIREMENT

The age at which the State retirement pension is payable is permitted to be discriminatory (EC Directive 79/7, Article 7). It is currently 65 for a man and between 60 and 65 for a woman. The State pension age for women has been increasing gradually since 2010, so that by 2018 it will be 65. By 2020 the State pension age for men and women will be 66, and by 2028 it will be 67. By the mid-2030s it is predicted to be 68, in the 2040s to be 69 and in the 2060s to be 70.

8.8 ENFORCEMENT AND REMEDIES

Enforcement proceedings may be brought either by an individual, or by the EHRC. The EHRC has power to investigate discriminatory practices and may serve a non-discrimination notice. Additionally, the EHRC can give assistance to an individual pursuing a claim.

The EHRC issued a Code of Practice which came into force on 6 April 2011. Whilst breach of the Code does not give rise to any legal liability, tribunals must take it into account if relevant.

The employment tribunal derives its jurisdiction from s 113 and ss 120–135 of the Act. An employment tribunal has jurisdiction, inter alia, to determine a complaint relating to a contravention of Pt 5 (work) (ss 39–83), s 108 (prohibited conduct where work relationships have ended). Note that members of the armed forces must have first utilised the armed forces procedure before they can complain to an employment tribunal under Pt 5 (s 121).

8.8.1 Enforcement by an individual

8.8.1.1 Time-limits

A complaint should be made to an employment tribunal within three months (less a day) of the act complained of or such other period as the tribunal thinks just and equitable (s 123). As with all time-limits, this three-month limit will need to take into account the early conciliation process. The burden of proof is on a claimant to show that it would be just and equitable to extend time. In considering whether to exercise its discretion and allow for a different period, the employment tribunal should consider the prejudice that each party would suffer as a result of granting or refusing an extension of time, and should have regard to all the other relevant circumstances. In *British Coal Corporation v Keeble* [1997] IRLR 336, the court said that a comparison with the checklist in s 33 of the Limitation Act 1980 might 'illuminate' the tribunal's task. The factors are:

- the length of and reasons for the delay
- the extent to which the cogency of the evidence is likely to be affected by the delay
- the extent to which the party sued had co-operated with any requests for information
- the promptness with which the claimant acted once he knew of the possibility of taking action
- the steps taken by the claimant to obtain appropriate professional advice once he knew of the possibility of taking action.

In *London Borough of Southwark v Afolabi* [2003] IRLR 220, the Court of Appeal held that a tribunal is not required to go through the matters listed in s 33(3) of the Limitation Act 1980 as a checklist in considering whether it is just and equitable to extend time, provided no significant factor has been left out of account by the tribunal in exercising its discretion. In *Adedeji v University Hospitals Birmingham NHS Foundation Trust* [2021] EWCA Civ 23, the Court of Appeal upheld a refusal to extend time for a race discrimination claim. The claimant had been warned by his legal adviser to bring his claims within the primary time limits and chose to ignore that advice. The Court of Appeal cautioned again against tribunals rigidly adhering to the checklist of potentially relevant factors in s 33 of the Limitation Act 1980 (see [37]–[38]).

The Court of Appeal confirmed in *Apelogun-Gabriels v London Borough of Lambeth* [2002] IRLR 116 that there is no general principle that it will be just and equitable to extend the three-month time-limit where the delay was caused by the applicant's seeking to deal with the matter internally. In *Robertson v Bexley Community Centre* [2003] IRLR 434, the Court of Appeal emphasised that there is no presumption that tribunals should extend time: the claimant must persuade the tribunal that it is just and equitable to do so. In *Pathan v South London Islamic Centre* (UKEAT/0312/13), the EAT held that the test is not, however, one of exceptional circumstances, it is whether it is 'just and equitable' to extend time. If the claim is brought against more than one respondent, the tribunal must decide whether it is just and equitable to extend time in each case separately (*Harden v Wootlif & Anor* (UKEAT/0448/14)).

In *British Transport Police v Norman* (UKEAT/0348/14), the EAT held that an employment tribunal had erred when it decided that it was just and equitable to extend the time-limit for a claim in circumstances where it had not first established the extent of and the reasons for the delay. The relevant questions were those proposed by Langstaff P in *ABM University Local Health Board v Morgan* (UKEAT/ 0305/13) (at para 52):

(a)   Why was it that the primary time-limit had been missed?

(b)   Why, after expiry of the primary time-limit, was the claim not brought sooner than it was?

The Court of Appeal explored the principles behind extending time-limits in *Abertawe Bro Morgannwg University Local Health Board v Morgan* [2018] EWCA Civ 640. The Court confirmed that, in a complaint about an omission to act, such as a failure to make reasonable adjustments, the time-limit does not run from the date when the breach occurred, but rather begins to run at the end of the period in which the employer might reasonably have been expected to comply with the relevant duty.

Identifying the specific 'act(s) complained of' is important. Sometimes this is a clear and obvious one-off act with a date, but the act may be occurring for a period which extends over some time. This is known as 'a continuing act'. Where there is a continuing act of discrimination, the three months do not start to run until the discrimination ceases (s 123(3)). The concept of 'continuing acts' of discrimination has generated much case law over the years and is a matter that requires very careful consideration. Continuing acts are distinguishable from one-off acts that have continuing consequences; time will run from the date of the one-off act complained of. Readers should refer to the Court of Appeal decision in *Hendricks v Commissioner of Police for the Metropolis* [2003] IRLR 96 on the question of continuing acts for further guidance. In that case the Court held that the test is whether the employer is responsible for 'an ongoing situation or a continuing state of affairs'. See also *Aziz v FDA* [2010] EWCA Civ 304 and *Okoro and anor v Taylor Woodrow Construction Ltd and Others* [2012] EWCA Civ 1590 for more recent Court of Appeal decisions. In *Veolia Environmental Services UK v Gumbs* (UKEAT/0487/12), two allegations of discrimination over a long period were held to be linked by the employee's manager, who had made decisions adverse to the claimant on both occasions. See too *Lyfar v Brighton and Sussex University Hospitals Trust* [2006] EWCA Civ 1548 and *Pugh v National Assembly for Wales* (UKEAT/0251/06). In *Pugh*, the EAT held that a tribunal should consider the allegations 'in the round', asking whether the employer was responsible for an ongoing state of affairs. In *Royal Mail Group Ltd v Jhuti* (UKEAT/0020/16), Mitting J said that whether or not there is a relevant connection is a question of fact. All the circumstances surrounding the acts will have to be considered. The EAT's decision was upheld by the Supreme Court (see **5.5.6.4**).

In *South Western Ambulance Service NHS Foundation Trust v King* (UKEAT/0056/19), the EAT reminds us that there cannot be a series of continuing acts if only one of them is discriminatory:

> ... reliance cannot be placed on some floating or overarching discriminatory state of affairs without that state of affairs being anchored by specific acts of discrimination occurring over time. The claimant must still establish constituent acts of discrimination or instances of less favourable treatment that *evidence* that discriminatory state of affairs. If such constituent acts or instances cannot be established, either because they are not established on the facts or are not found to be discriminatory, then they cannot be relied upon to evidence the continuing discriminatory state of affairs.

Where the discrimination consists of a failure to do something, the time-limit starts to run when the person decides not to do the thing in question. Note that the Act states (s 212(2) and (3)) that a reference (however expressed) to an act includes a reference to an omission; and a reference (however expressed) to an omission includes a reference to:

(a)   a deliberate omission to do something;

(b)   a refusal to do it;

(c)   a failure to do it.

Where an employer fails to make a reasonable adjustment for a disabled person, because it simply fails to consider doing so, time runs from a notional date – the date on which the employer might reasonably have been expected to make the adjustment. Given that a claimant will not know what that date is, one might expect tribunals to have 'sympathetic regard' to that difficulty in applying the just and equitable extension.

Readers should also remember that the Early Conciliation procedure must be complied with before a complaint is presented to the tribunal (see **6.3.7**).

8.8.1.2 Questionnaire procedure

Section 138 allowed a complainant to deliver a standard form of questionnaire to a respondent, to enable the complainant to decide whether to institute proceedings and, if so, how to present his case. Although a respondent was not obliged to reply to the questionnaire, failure to reply, or the giving of evasive replies, allowed a tribunal to draw an inference that discrimination had occurred. In *D'Silva v NATFHE* (UKEAT/0384/07), the EAT held that an employer's failure fully to answer a questionnaire did not automatically raise a presumption of discrimination. The real significance was whether the failure could support an inference that the employer committed the discriminatory act: there might be situations in which a failure to deal with a questionnaire, however reprehensible, had no bearing at all on the employer's defence.

The Government abolished the questionnaire procedure in April 2014. However, while removing the formal procedure, claimants will still be able to seek such information through pre-action requests, by asking questions of the employer or by making applications to tribunals for orders for further information or disclosure. Employers who refuse to answer will still run the risk that adverse inferences may be drawn. See, for example, *Dattani v Chief Constable of West Mercia Police* [2005] IRLR 327. Employees can also make data subject access requests, to see what information the employer holds about them. The Acas Guide recommends a six-step process for pre-action questions, and a three-step process for respondents to follow (see <www.acas.org.uk/media/pdf/m/p/asking-and-responding-to-questions-of-discrimination-in-the-workplace.pdf>).

8.8.2 Remedies

Under the previous discrimination legislation, tribunals' powers to award the same remedies were to be exercised where the tribunal considered it just and equitable to do so. Section 124 does not contain the words 'just and equitable', but because the words referred to the choice of remedy and not the amount of compensation to be awarded, the authors do not consider that the change of wording is significant.

Note: Unlike a whistleblowing claim, interim relief is not available for discrimination claims. In *Steer v Stormsure Ltd* [2021] EWCA Civ 887, the Court of Appeal upheld an employment tribunal's refusal to list an interim relief application in respect of certain discrimination allegations, holding that there is no such right provided for by the Equality Act 2010 and that the lack of provision for interim relief in discrimination and victimisation claims under the Equality Act 2010 does not breach the European Convention on Human Rights. The fact that a whistleblowing claimant can apply for interim relief, whereas a discrimination claimant cannot, does not constitute discrimination on the ground of sex.

8.8.2.1 Declaration, orders and recommendations

Under s 124 of the Act, if the complaint is well founded:

> (2) The tribunal may—
>   (a) make a declaration as to the rights of the complainant and the respondent in relation to the matters to which the proceedings relate;
>   (b) order the respondent to pay compensation to the complainant;
>   (c) make an appropriate recommendation.
>
> (3) An appropriate recommendation is a recommendation that within a specified period the respondent takes specified steps for the purpose of obviating or reducing the adverse effect on the complainant of any matter to which the proceedings relate.

Failure to comply with a recommendation in so far as it relates to the complainant, without reasonable excuse, can lead to an increase in the compensation ordered (s 124(7)).

The power to make a recommendation does not include a power to recommend that the employee should be promoted to the next suitable vacancy (*British Gas v Sharma* [1991] IRLR 101).

The Government removed the powers of tribunals to make 'wider' recommendations (ie that obviate or reduce the adverse effect on anyone other than the claimant) with effect from 1 October 2015. Since then, a tribunal can only make a recommendation relating to the claimant.

In *Lycée Français Charles de Gaulle v Delambre* (UKEAT/0563/10), the EAT upheld the tribunal's recommendations that the respondent circulate the judgment to the Governing Board and management team, that the respondent review existing equal opportunities policies, and that it undertake a programme of formal equality and diversity training.

In *Hill v Lloyds Bank* (UKEAT/0173/19), the EAT held that there can be no objection in principle to a recommendation that an employer give an undertaking in suitable (perhaps rare) cases. The EAT relied upon the fact that the tribunal had found that the step that was required to alleviate the disadvantage being suffered by Mrs Hill was an undertaking that she could rely upon. The failure to give that very undertaking was the basis for her success in her disability discrimination claim.

A declaration is an important statement of the decision. Most tribunals' findings result in a compensation order. The tribunal has power to order the respondent to pay compensation of an amount corresponding to the damages that could be ordered in a county court. There is no upper limit to the amount that may be ordered. Unlike compensation for unfair dismissal, compensation for discrimination is awarded on tortious principles. This means that the tribunal must, as far as it can, put the claimant in the position he would have been in 'but for' the discriminatory act. An employee has a duty to mitigate his losses. Although the Act no longer specifically refers to an award being made if the tribunal considers it just and equitable to do so, there is no reason to believe this will change the way in which tribunals make such awards.

There is some uncertainty as to whether a compensatory award for discrimination may be reduced to take account of contributory fault. In *Way v Crouch* [2005] IRLR 603, the EAT concluded that compensation in discrimination cases may be subject to a deduction for contributory conduct on the part of the claimant (although the EAT found no grounds for any such deduction on the facts of the case). However, more recently, in *First Great Western & Linley v Waiyego* (UKEAT/0056/18), the EAT held that contributory negligence will rarely, if ever, apply because it is difficult to attribute 'fault' to a victim of discrimination. Instead, contributory fault can, said the EAT, be treated as a failure to mitigate loss.

8.8.2.2 Assessment of compensation

Readers may find it useful to read *Michalak v Mid Yorkshire Hospitals NHS Trust* (ET/1810815/08) and *Lokhova v Sberbank CIB (UK) Ltd* (2015). The claimants were awarded £4.5 million and £3.2 million respectively in discrimination and harassment claims.

In deciding the appropriate level of compensation, the following matters will be taken into account:

(a)   Pecuniary loss arising directly from an act of discrimination, including past loss to the date of the hearing and future losses (to put the claimant in the position he would have been if the discrimination had not occurred). In *Secretary of State for Justice v Plaistow* (UKEAT/0016/20 & UKEAT/0085/20), the EAT upheld an employment tribunal's decision to calculate compensation for direct sexual orientation discrimination and harassment on the basis of career-long loss because, adopting the approach laid down by the Court of Appeal in *Wardle v Credit Agricole Corporate and Investment Bank* [2011] IRLR 604, the tribunal was entitled to find that it was very unlikely that the claimant would ever be able to return to any work before his retirement age. The claimant's medical evidence showed that the claimant's condition was likely to be life-long. As far as the duty to mitigate is concerned, see **5.6.2.2**.

(b)   Injury to feelings. Whilst an award for injury to feelings is not made automatically, in the majority of cases it will be almost inevitable. Awards for injury to feelings are compensatory: they should not be about punishment; they should be just to both parties. Awards need to be sufficient to command public respect for the policy underlying anti-discrimination legislation. The guidance in HM Prison Service v Johnson [1997] IRLR 162 gives a good summary of the approach to injury to feelings:

a.   Awards for injury to feelings are compensatory. They should be just to both parties. They should compensate fully without punishing the tortfeasor. Feelings of indignation ... should not be allowed to inflate the award.

b.   Awards should not be too low, as this would diminish respect for the policy of the anti-discrimination legislation. Society has condemned discrimination and awards must ensure that it is seen to be wrong. On the other hand, awards should be restrained, as excessive awards could ... be seen as the way to untaxed riches.

c.   Awards should bear some broad similarity to the range of awards in personal injury cases. We do not think this should be done by reference to any particular type of personal injury award; rather to the whole range of such awards.

d.   In exercising their discretion in assessing a sum, tribunals should remind themselves of the value in everyday life of the sum they have in mind. This may be done by reference to purchasing power or by reference to earnings.

e.   Finally, tribunals should bear in mind ... the need for public respect for the level of awards made.

In Vento v Chief Constable of West Yorkshire Police [2003] IRLR 102, the Court of Appeal handed down guidance on awards for injury to feelings. The Court said that the top band of awards should normally be between £15,000 and £25,000, and apply only to the most serious cases. The middle band of £5,000–£15,000 should be used for serious cases not meriting the top award, and awards of £500–£5,000 should be made for less serious cases (eg, an isolated incident). Awards of less than £500 should be avoided. The EAT set out new guideline figures in Da'Bell v NSPCC (UKEAT/0227/09) to take account of inflation. The ranges were:

(i)   The lower band – the upper limit for this band rose to £6,000.

(ii)   The middle band – the upper limit rose to £18,000.

(iii)   The upper band – the upper limit rose to £30,000.

Underhill P said in Bullimore v Pothecary Witham Weld Solicitors (No 2) [2011] IRLR 18 (EAT) that, '[a]s a matter of principle, employment tribunals ought to assess the quantum of compensation for non-pecuniary loss in "today's money"', although it would not be an error of law not to do so (see too AA Solicitors Ltd (t/a AA Solicitors) & Another v Majid (EAT/0217/15)).

The EAT decision in St Andrews School v Blundell (UKEAT/0330/09) reviews some post-Vento authorities.

The Court of Appeal held in Simmons v Castle [2012] EWCA Civ 1039 that general damages (which would include injury to feelings damages) should be increased by 10% after 1 April 2013. This was revised slightly a year later (see Simmons v Castle [2012] EWCA Civ 1288), to make clear that the 10% did not apply to claimants covered by s 44(6) of the Legal Aid, Sentencing and Punishment of Offenders Act 2012 (which applied to certain types of 'no win, no fee' agreements). The EAT held, in Cadogan Hotel Partners Ltd v Ozog (UKEAT/0001/14), Sash Window Workshop Ltd & Another v King (EAT/0057/14), Beckford v London Borough of Southwark (EAT/0210/14) and Olayemi v Athena Medical Centre & Another (EAT/0140/15) and again in AA Solicitors v Majid, that the 10% uplift applied to injury to feelings awards. Given that the Court of Appeal held in

Summers v Bundy [2016] EWCA Civ 126 (a non-employment case) that the uplift applies 'across the board' (save in s 44(6) cases), it seems likely that it applies to injury to feelings awards too. ET Presidential Guidance also supports an uplift of 10%. The Court of Appeal in *De Souza v Vinci Construction UK Ltd* [2017] EWCA Civ 879 held that the 10% increase should also apply to injury to feelings awards. In September 2017, the Presidents of the Employment Tribunals issued joint guidance on the bands for injury to feelings and psychiatric injury. The new bands for injury to feelings awards for claims presented from September 2017, to include the 10% uplift, were:

- lower: £800 to £8,400
- middle: £8,400 to £25,200
- higher: £25,200 to £42,000

These figures were upgraded with respect to claims presented on or after 6 April 2022 (as the fifth addendum to the September 2017 Presidential Guidance) as follows:

- lower: £990 to £9,900
- middle: £9,900 to £29,600
- upper: £29,600 to £49,300
- exceptional: above £49,300

In *AA Solicitors* (above), the EAT stated that appeals against amounts of awards for injury to feelings would rarely succeed unless the award was placed in the wrong *Vento* band. The EAT confirmed in *Base Childrenswear Ltd v Otshudi* (UKEAT/0267/18) that whilst a one-off event will often fall in the lowest band, that will not always be so, depending on the facts. See too *Komeng v Creative Support Ltd* (UKEAT/0275/18) (the focus should be on the actual injury suffered by the claimant and not the gravity of the acts of the respondent).

(c)   Aggravated damages where the respondent has behaved in a high-handed, malicious, insulting or oppressive manner. Aggravated damages, which are an aspect of the injury to feelings award, are compensatory in nature, not punitive (see *Commissioner of Police for the Metropolis v Shaw* (UKEAT/0125/11). The power to award aggravated damages is not statutory; it derives from other, non-statutory torts.

In *Shaw*, the EAT considered the three categories of circumstances identified in the Law Commission Report on Aggravated, Exemplary and Restitutionary Damages (1997) (Law Comm No 247) that may attract an award of aggravated damages. The first concerned the *manner* in which the wrong was committed. The distress caused by an act of discrimination may be made worse by its being done in an 'high-handed, malicious, insulting or oppressive' way (May LJ used this expression in *Alexander v Home Office* [1988] ICR 685). The EAT warned that this should not be treated as an exhaustive definition of the kind of behaviour which may justify an award of aggravated damages, pointing out that, as the Law Commission Report made clear, an award may be made in the case of any exceptional or contumelious conduct which has the effect of seriously increasing the claimant's distress. The second circumstance identified in the Report was the respondent's motive. The EAT said that conduct which is spiteful or vindictive, or based on prejudice or animosity, is more likely to cause distress. The third circumstance was the respondent's conduct after the tort which related to it. This might include, depending on the circumstances, a failure to apologise, or not taking a complaint seriously.

The EAT commented on the difficulty of distinguishing between the injury caused by the discriminatory act itself and the injury attributable to the aggravating elements: tribunals had to be aware of the risks of compensating claimants under both heads for the same loss. The ultimate question is whether the overall award is proportionate to the totality of the suffering caused. The EAT cautioned on the dangers of focusing too much on the conduct – which could lead down the dangerous route of equating damages with punishment. While the EAT expressed doubt as to the desirability of awarding aggravated damages as a separate head of compensation, as there was no 'bright line' by which to distinguish what part of the injury to the claimant's feelings resulted from the core act and what resulted from an exceptional feature, it felt the practice had been approved too many times to suggest that it was wrong, but suggested a better way of dealing with it might be to include it as a subheading of injury to feelings, ie 'injury to feelings in the sum of £x, incorporating aggravated damages in the sum of £y'. This might reduce the risk of a tribunal unwittingly introducing a punitive element into the calculation.

The employee must have some awareness of the improper conduct or motive (*Ministry of Defence v Meredith* [1995] IRLR 52). Conduct in the course of litigation may be taken into account (*City of Bradford Metropolitan Council v Arora* [1991] IRLR 165, CA). In *Tameside Hospital NHS Foundation Trust v Mylott* (UKEAT/0352/09 and UKEAT/0399/10), the EAT quashed a tribunal award of aggravated damages where the tribunal found that a manager had acted in a brusque and insensitive manner towards the employee, and that in giving evidence she was dismissive and evasive: none of these was sufficient to support the making of an award of aggravated damages.

In *Michalak* (above), the tribunal awarded £30,000 for injury to feelings and £56,000 for psychiatric damage but, despite being 'positively outraged' by the conduct of the employer, made no award for aggravated damages, in light of the guidance in *Shaw* (above). It did, however, award exemplary damages (see (d) below).

(d)   Exemplary damages may be awarded in discrimination cases but are rare. Exemplary damages punish the wrongdoer and should be awarded only for 'arbitrary and outrageous use of executive power' (see, eg, *Kuddus v Chief Constable of Leicestershire Constabulary* [2001] UKHL 29).

In *Ministry of Defence v Fletcher* (UKEAT/0044/09), the EAT looked at the relationship between aggravated and exemplary damages, and upheld the aggravated damages award but overturned the exemplary damages award, finding no 'conscious and contumelious' wrongdoing.

In *Michalak* (above), the employment tribunal awarded exemplary damages for 'oppressive, arbitrary or unconstitutional' behaviour. The NHS Trust had, the tribunal held, acted in such a manner when it failed to follow government procedures prescribed for NHS Trusts, in a deliberate attempt to deprive the claimant of her rights.

(e)   Compensation for personal injury (psychiatric or physical injury) caused by the discrimination can be awarded, for example, for depression or post-traumatic stress – see *Sheriff v Klyne Tugs (Lowestoft) Ltd* [1999] IRLR 481, CA. In *HM Prison Service v Salmon* [2001] IRLR 425, a female prison officer was awarded £21,000 for injury to feelings and £11,250 for personal injury in respect of psychiatric damage caused by sexual harassment. On appeal, the EAT recognised that there was a risk of double recovery, but that in principle injury to feelings and psychiatric injury are distinct, although in practice not always easy to separate.

In *Essa v Laing Ltd* [2004] IRLR 313, the Court of Appeal held that compensation for unlawful discrimination is not limited to cases of reasonably foreseeable harm. A claimant simply has to show that the discrimination caused the harm (it is sufficient to show that it was a substantial and effective cause, even if not the dominant cause). (See also *Taylor v XLN Telecom* (EAT/0383/09) for confirmation that a claimant is entitled to recover for injury (to feelings or personal injury) attributable to the act complained of (eg a racially motivated dismissal) and does not have to prove that the injury resulted from actual knowledge of the discrimination.)

In a case of psychiatric injury (and in some other cases where the claimant is 'only' seeking an injury to feelings award) medical evidence will normally be required (see **Chapter 6**), but see *Hampshire County Council v Wyatt* (UKEAT/0013/16) where the EAT held that an employment tribunal was entitled to make a personal injury award for depression in a disability discrimination case, despite no medical evidence being produced by the employee. The EAT did, however, confirm that it would be advisable for suitable medical evidence to be obtained by employees.

The Court of Appeal confirmed in *BAE Systems (Operations) Ltd v Konczak* [2017] EWCA Civ 1188 that where psychiatric injury is caused by an employer's wrongdoing, a tribunal needs to examine whether the harm suffered should be apportioned (where part was caused by the employer and part was not so caused).

(f)   In a case of indirect discrimination where the respondent proves that there was no intention to treat the claimant unfavourably, a tribunal cannot award damages to a claimant unless it has first considered making either a declaration or a recommendation (s 124(4) and (5)). The EAT held, in *JH Walker Ltd v Hussain and Others* [1996] IRLR 11, that a person will have intended an act if he intended the consequences of his act, ie he knew when he did the act that those consequences would follow and he wanted those consequences to follow. So, in this case, the company knew that the Islamic festival of Eid was important to Muslim employees, that only they were affected by prohibiting holidays from May to July, and that they were required to work on that day. Such discrimination was not, therefore, unintentional.

(g)   Pregnancy dismissals – loss of career prospects or congenial employment does not form a separate head of damage and should be catered for in the award for injury to feelings ((b) above). Estimated child-care costs should be set off against future loss of earnings.

(h)   Accelerated receipt – a discount should normally be applied (see **2.4.1.9**).

(i)   Section 207A of the TULR(C)A 1992 gives the tribunals discretion to increase or reduce awards by up to 25% where the employer or employee unreasonably fails to comply with the 2009 Acas Code.

(j)   Taxation – see **Table 5.1** at **5.6.2.5**. While the Court of Appeal in *Moorthy v Commissioners for HMRC* [2018] EWCA Civ 847 confirmed that awards for injury to feelings (under the Income Tax (Earnings and Pensions) Act 2003) are exempt from tax, it is of limited impact because, from 6 April 2018, s 406 of the 2003 Act has been amended to specify that a payment for injury to feelings in respect of discrimination connected with termination of employment now falls outside the tax free exemption for personal injury (unless it is a psychiatric injury). A payment for injury to feelings which is *not* related to termination can still be paid tax free.

(k)   Interest – tribunals must consider whether to award interest. Any award must be calculated in accordance with the Employment Tribunals (Interest on Awards in Discrimination Cases) Regulations 1996 (SI 1996/2803) and the Employment Tribunals (Interest on Awards in Discrimination Cases) (Amendment) Regulations 2013 (SI 2013/ 1669). Interest on past pecuniary losses will generally be awarded from the midpoint date between the act of discrimination and the date of the tribunal hearing. Interest on injury to feelings runs from the date on which the unlawful act took place to the date of leaving. The rate from 28 July 2013 is 8%.

Note that there is no upper limit on the amount of compensation which may be awarded.

8.8.2.3   Joint and several liability

Employees who are held to have knowingly aided the employer are treated as if they themselves did the unlawful act(s), and tribunals have power to make a separate award against each respondent (see *Gilbank v Miles* [2006] IRLR 538). In practice, tribunals often make substantial awards against an employer and a small award against any individual who has been found to have committed any actual acts of discrimination. Tribunals may also treat the parties as joint tortfeasors and make one award against all respondents jointly and severally.

In *Way and Another v Crouch* [2005] IRLR 603, the EAT held that it is proper to make both the employer and any individual who has been found to have committed any actual acts of discrimination liable on a joint and several basis. In practice this allows the employee to sue the individual harasser for the full amount of any compensation if the employer turns out to be insolvent. The EAT emphasised that when making joint and several awards, tribunals must apportion the respective shares, so that if a claimant chooses to enforce against only one respondent, that respondent can still seek a suitable contribution. Any apportionment should be on the basis of respective culpability (and not on the financial strengths of the parties).

In *Munchkins Restaurant Ltd and Another v Karmazyn and Others* (UKEAT/0359/09), the EAT said (casting doubt on *Way v Crouch*) that the appropriate principle where there is an award of joint and several liability is that any one of the respondents is liable for the full extent of the damages to the claimant. Although, as between respondents, a respondent may have a right to seek contribution from a co-respondent, depending upon the relative contribution and responsibility of each of the respondents to the wrong which has been done, that should not affect the position of a claimant, who is entitled, if the award is joint and several, to receive the full extent of his award from any of the respondents as he chooses. The EAT held:

> [A]s a matter of general approach, where there is more than one respondent to a claim ... a Tribunal will have to decide whether or not it is to make a joint and several award. In some cases the reason for it doing so will be obvious and need very little elaboration.

In *London Borough of Hackney v Sivanandan and Others* [2013] EWCA Civ 22 the employment tribunal found complaints of victimisation were valid, and determined that the respondents were jointly and severally liable to pay the claimant £421,415. The tribunal declined to apportion liability as between the respondents. The Court of Appeal held that the employment tribunal's decision not to apportion was correct, and that there is no power in law allowing employment tribunals to apportion damages. In *Brennan and Others v Sunderland City Council and Others* (UKEAT/0286/11), the EAT, following *Sivanandan*, said that the employment tribunal has no jurisdiction to determine claims for contribution under the Civil Liability (Contribution) Act 1978.

8.8.3 Removal of contractual term

Section 142 provides that a contractual term 'is unenforceable against a person in so far as it constitutes, promotes or provides for treatment of that or another person that is of a description prohibited by this Act'. The provisions also provide that a county court may, on the application of an interested party, make an order removing or modifying a term which is unenforceable against that party (s 143).

In *Mead-Hill v The British Council* [1995] IRLR 478, an employee sought to rely on these provisions in relation to a mobility clause. It was held that the insertion of the clause could amount to indirect discrimination against women, who form a higher proportion of secondary earners and, as such, are less likely to be able to relocate. However, it was open to the employers to show justification irrespective of sex.

8.9   EQUAL PAY AND THE EQUALITY CLAUSE

8.9.1 Introduction

What follows is merely a very brief introduction to this complex area of the law, the detail of which is beyond the scope of the book. The law was previously contained in the EPA 1970 as amended (principally by the SDA 1975); it is now contained in Pt 5 (work), Ch 3 (equality of terms) of the Equality Act 2010, which is designed to ensure that men and women within the same employment receive equal pay (and other contractual terms) for equal work. Note that the equal pay provisions render it unlawful for an employer to discriminate between men and women in relation to the *terms of their contracts of employment*. That is wider than just pay. The legislation implies a 'sex equality clause' into contracts. Section 66(2) of the Equality Act 2010 defines a 'sex equality clause':

(a)   if a term of A's [the claimant] is less favourable to A than a corresponding term of B's [the comparator of the opposite sex] is to B, A's term is modified so as not to be less favourable

(b)   if A does not have a term which corresponds to a term of B's that benefits B, A's terms are modified so as to include such a term.

Equal pay for men and women for equal work is a requirement of EU law under Article 157 TFEU (ex 141 EC). The law works by implying an 'equality clause' into a contract. Lord Nicholls, in *Glasgow City Council and Others v Marshall and Others* [2000] 1 WLR 333, set out what was regarded as the proper approach (under the old law as set out in s 1 of the EPA 1970) to equal pay claims.

It is important to consider whether the claim is one that should be brought under the equal pay provisions, or one that should be brought under the discrimination provisions (above):

*   If the less favourable treatment relates to the payment of money which is regulated by a contract of employment, only the equal pay provisions can apply.

*   If the employee is treated less favourably than an employee of the other sex who is doing the same or broadly similar work, or whose work has been given an equal value under a job evaluation, and the less favourable treatment relates to some matter which is regulated by the contract of employment of either of them, only the equal pay provisions can apply. However, if the less favourable treatment relates to a matter not included in the contract, only the sex discrimination provisions can apply.

*   If the less favourable treatment relates to a matter (other than the payment of money) in a contract, and the comparison is with workers who are not doing the same or broadly similar work, or work which has been given an equal value under a job evaluation, only the sex discrimination provisions can apply.

*   Lastly, if the complaint relates to a matter which is regulated by an employee's contract of employment, but is based on an allegation that an employee of the other sex would be treated more favourably in similar circumstances (ie it does not relate to the actual treatment of an existing employee of the other sex but rather requires a hypothetical comparator), only the sex discrimination provisions can apply (Equality Act 2010, s 71).

The distinctions are crucial in practice because there are different time-limits. In some cases, it may be advisable to bring a discrimination claim and an equal pay claim, in the alternative, to protect the client's position.

In *Birmingham City Council v Abdulla and Others* [2012] UKSC 47, the Supreme Court decided that equal pay claims, which would have been out of time in an employment tribunal, could be brought in the High Court.

8.9.1.1   The equality clause

Section 64(1) states that ss 66 to 70 apply where:

(a)   a person (A) is employed on work that is equal to the work that a comparator of the opposite sex (B) does;

...

By s 66:

(1)   If the terms of A's work do not (by whatever means) include a sex equality clause, they are to be treated as including one.

(2)   A sex equality clause is a provision that has the following effect—

(a)   if a term of A's is less favourable to A than a corresponding term of B's is to B, A's term is modified so as not to be less favourable;

(b)   if A does not have a term which corresponds to a term of B's that benefits B, A's terms are modified so as to include such a term.

This has the effect of implying an equality clause into the contract of employment of a woman (or man), so that she (or he) is entitled to be treated no less favourably than a man (or woman) in the same employment.

Section 65 deals with what is meant by equal work:

(1) For the purposes of this Chapter, A's work is equal to that of B if it is—

   (a) like B's work,

   (b) rated as equivalent to B's work, or

   (c) of equal value to B's work.

(2) A's work is like B's work if—

   (a) A's work and B's work are the same or broadly similar, and

   (b) such differences as there are between their work are not of practical importance in relation to the terms of their work.

It will be necessary for a claimant in an equal pay case to be able to point to an actual (not hypothetical) comparator in the 'same establishment' (Equality Act 2010, s 79), or at different establishments where common terms apply, or where there is a single source of pay and conditions of work between the claimant and the comparator (see *Lawrence v Regent Office Care Ltd* [2003] ICR 1092) (however, note that no comparator is needed if it can be shown that the reason for not paying a woman the same as a man is because she is pregnant – see *Alabaster v Woolwich plc and DWP* [2005] IRLR 576). In *Walton Centre for Neurology v Bewley* (UKEAT/0564/07), the EAT held that a woman's successor in the job cannot be used as a comparator for the purposes of an equal pay claim. The comparator must be employed contemporaneously or be a predecessor. If there is no actual comparator available, the woman must bring a claim of direct sex discrimination claim against the employer. The example given in the Explanatory Notes is as follows:

> An employer tells a female employee 'I would pay you more if you were a man' ... In the absence of any male comparator the woman cannot bring a claim for breach of an equality clause but she can bring a claim of direct sex discrimination ... against the employer.

For decisions on the meaning of 'same establishment', including common terms and conditions and a single source of pay and conditions, see *North and Others v Dumfries and Galloway Council* [2013] ICR 993 and *Fox Cross Claimants v Glasgow CC* [2013] ICR 954. These cases were decided under the old Equal Pay Act. Whilst the Equality Act 2010 is similar, there are subtle changes that readers will need to take into account. The EAT held in *Asda Stores Ltd v Brierley* (UKEAT/0092/16) that the '*North* hypothetical test remains good law' (see *North* above). In other words, where there is not a comparator at the establishment where the claimant works, comparison is permitted where common terms apply *or would apply* at those establishments. The Court of Appeal agreed ([2019] EWCA Civ 44) and set out a useful summary of the position at paras 66–73. The Supreme Court upheld the Court of Appeal's decision in 2021 ([2021] UKSC 10), allowing comparison of retail store employees and distribution depot employees, in spite of the latter working at different establishments. Lady Arden started by saying that the provision permitting cross-establishment comparison if 'common terms apply' is meant to *facilitate* comparison, not frustrate it.

8.9.1.2 Defences

It is a defence to an equal pay claim to show that the difference in pay is due to a material factor which is relevant and significant, and which does not directly or indirectly discriminate against the worker because of her sex (s 69) . If there is evidence that the factor which explains the difference in terms is not directly discriminatory but would have an adverse impact on people of her sex (that is, without more, it would be indirectly discriminatory), the employer must show that it is a proportionate means of meeting a legitimate aim or the sex equality clause will apply. For these purposes, the long-term objective of reducing pay inequality will always count as a legitimate aim.

The EAT provided a useful step-by-step summary of the defence in *Bury Metropolitan Borough Council v Hamilton and Others; Council of the City of Sunderland v Brennan and Others* (UKEAT/ 0413–5/09):

(1)   It is necessary first to identify the explanation for the differential complained of. (In the language of the statute, this is the 'factor' to which the differential is 'due'; but the terminology of 'explanation' used by Lord Nicholls in *Marshall* [*Glasgow City Council v Marshall* [2000] ICR 196] is generally less clumsy.) The burden of proof is on the employer.

(2)   It is then necessary to consider whether that explanation is 'tainted with sex'. What that not altogether happy metaphor means is that the explanation relied on must not itself involve sex discrimination, whether direct or indirect (see per Lord Browne-Wilkinson in *Wallace* [*Strathclyde Regional Council v Wallace* [1998] ICR 205], at pp 211H–212A and per Lord Nicholls in *Marshall*, at pp 202H–203A).

(3)   In considering whether the explanation involves direct or indirect discrimination, the ordinary principles of the law of discrimination apply. That means that:

(a)   if the differential is the result of direct discrimination (in the sense established in *Nagarajan v London Regional Transport* [1999] ICR 877) the defence under section 1(3) will fail;

(b)   if the differential involves indirect discrimination of either the 'PCP' or 'Enderby' type – as to this distinction, see para 16 below – the defence will fail unless the employer proves that the differential is objectively justified, applying the classic proportionality test;

(c)   if the employer's explanation involves neither direct nor indirect discrimination the defence will succeed, even if the factor relied on cannot be objectively justified – this is most vividly illustrated by the 'mistake' cases such as *Yorkshire Blood Transfusion Service v Plaskitt* [1994] ICR 74 and *Tyldesley v TML Plastics* [1996] ICR 356, approved in *Wallace*.

(4)   In conducting the exercise under (3), the ordinary principles governing the burden of proof in discrimination claims will apply. Thus if the claimant shows a prima facie case of discrimination (in the sense explained in *Madarassy v Nomura International plc* [2007] ICR 867), the burden shifts to the employer to prove the absence of discrimination.

In *Calmac Ferries Ltd v Wallace & Another* (UKEATS/0014/13) (see also **Chapter 6**), the EAT held that since the burden lies on the employer to prove a material factor defence, strike out of such claims is wrong at the preliminary stage.

In *Glasgow City Council v UNITE Claimants* [2017] CSIH 34, when the Council implemented a job evaluation scheme, it implemented a three-year pay protection system to protect bonuses and other payments for so-called 'red-circled' employees (employees whose roles had been downgraded) who were typically men and who would otherwise have seen their pay fall because of the changes. Other employees, who were predominantly female, were not red-circled because their jobs had not been downgraded. This had the effect of keeping men's overall pay higher than women performing equivalent roles. The Court of Session held that treating differently red-circled employees and the other employees whose work has been rated as equivalent could not be justified on the facts because there was no evidence before the employment tribunal that the appellant had even considered the position of the other employees who had not been red-circled. As was observed in *Bury MBC v Hamilton* [2011] ICR 655, at para 78:

[A] local authority cannot prove unaffordability by mere assertion. A case of justification on this basis can only be proved by adducing sufficiently detailed evidence, both of the costs themselves and of the financial context, to enable the Tribunal to reach an informed view … That need not involve an exhaustive review of the Council's finances, but the Tribunal must be put in a position where it can assess the broad picture.

The equality clause does not apply to any provision affording women special treatment in connection with pregnancy or childbirth.

Readers should note the EAT's comments in *McNeil & Others v Commissioners for HM Revenue & Customs* (UKEAT/0183/17) that, as the judgment of the Supreme Court in *Essop/Naeem* (below at **10.2.3**) held, in a claim based on unlawful indirect discrimination:

69.   (i)   once it has been established ... that a PCP places people with relevant protected characteristics at a particular disadvantage compared with others, that is sufficient to require objective justification ...;

(ii)   it is irrelevant whether or not the reason why the PCP puts that group at a particular disadvantage is itself related to the protected characteristic;

(iii)   the only required causal link is between the PCP and the particular disadvantage.

70.   [T]hose principles apply equally to an equal pay claim based on indirect discrimination.

71.   Accordingly, to the extent that the line of authority based on *Armstrong v Newcastle upon Tyne NHS Hospital Trust* [2006] IRLR 124 has been understood as holding that it is open to a respondent to rebut a finding made of particular disadvantage by showing that the underlying reason for the particular disadvantage was not itself related to the protected characteristic in issue, it is inconsistent with the ratio of *Essop/Naeem* and can no longer be regarded as good law.

The Court of Appeal upheld the employment tribunal and EAT decision but did not refer to *Armstrong* (see [2019] EWCA Civ 1112).

In *Co-operative Group v Walker* (UKEAT/0087/19), the EAT held that a material factor defence continues to apply unless and until there is a fresh decision or its equivalent by the employer which can no longer be justified and which displaces the original negotiated pay agreement.

8.9.1.3   Enforcement

In the event of a breach of the equality clause, the remedy is to present a complaint to an employment tribunal within six months of the end of the employment contract, or in some circumstances to bring a breach of contract claim in the civil courts within six years (*Birmingham City Council v Abdulla and Others* [2012] UKSC 47). The tribunal, if the complaint is well founded, may award arrears of remuneration and damages going back for up to six years for breach of the equality clause.

Note that unlike in sex discrimination claims, damages for non-pecuniary loss (such as injury to feelings and aggravated damages) cannot be recovered in equal pay claims (because such claims are based on contract and are not based on a statutory tort as in a discrimination claim) – see *Council of the City of Newcastle upon Tyne v Allan and Others* [2005] IRLR 504 and *BMC Software Ltd v Shaikh* (UKEAT/0092/16). Nor can tribunals make recommendations in equal pay cases.

8.9.1.4   Equal pay audit

The ERRA 2013, which received Royal Assent on 25 April 2013, enabled the Secretary of State to require tribunals to order an equal pay audit where an employer is found to have breached the equal pay provisions in the Equality Act 2010, subject to exemptions and exceptions. The Government introduced the power on 1 October 2014 (see Equality Act 2010 (Equal Pay Audits) Regulations 2014 (SI 2014/2559). The Regulations require a tribunal to order an employer found to be in breach of equal pay law to undertake an equal pay audit in certain circumstances.

8.9.1.5   Gender pay gap reporting

The Equality Act 2010 (Gender Pay Gap Information) Regulations 2017 (SI 2017/172) came into force on 6 April 2017. The Regulations apply to public sector employers with 250 or more employees (and include 'workers') (see **Chapter 1**). Employers have until 4 April 2018 to publish details of their gender pay gap.

8.10 PART-TIME WORKERS

The Part-time Workers (Prevention of Less Favourable Treatment) Regulations 2000 (SI 2000/1551) implement the European Part-time Work Directive (97/81/EC). Clause 4(1) of the Directive provides:

> In respect of employment conditions, part-time workers shall not be treated in a less favourable manner than comparable full-time workers solely because they work part time unless different treatment is justified on objective grounds.

What follows is a very brief overview.

The 2000 Regulations make it unlawful for employers to treat part-time workers less favourably than full-time workers on the ground that the worker is a part-time worker (unless different treatment can be objectively justified – reg 5) in their terms and conditions, in areas such as:

(a)   hourly rates of pay;

(b)   overtime rates;

(c)   access to occupational pension schemes;

(d)   training;

(e)   (pro rata) holiday entitlement;

(f)   (pro rata) maternity/paternal leave;

(g)   (pro rata) sick pay.

Part-time workers should also be treated no less favourably when being selected for redundancy, unless the different treatment can be justified objectively.

The 2000 Regulations apply to 'workers', not just 'employees'. A part-time worker who is treated less favourably than a full-time worker is able to bring a claim regardless of whether he or she is a man or a woman. Before the 2000 Regulations came into force, because part-time work is overwhelmingly done by women, claims of indirect sex discrimination were possible, but only by women part-time workers. If advising a woman, the adviser will need to decide whether to run claims under both the Equality Act 2010 and the 2000 Regulations. Readers should consult the Regulations for detailed guidance.

Key to claims under the 2000 Regulations is whether the part-time worker and his or her full-time comparator are employed by the same employer under the same type of contract and engaged in the same or broadly similar work (reg 2(4)). This has generated a fair amount of case law. Note that the part-time worker must identify a full-time actual comparator (a hypothetical comparator is not adequate in these claims) employed by the same employer.

The first UK case on what is required to make a part-time worker comparable with a full-time worker was decided by the House of Lords on 1 March 2006 (*Matthews v Kent and Medway Towns Fire Authority* [2006] IRLR 367). Retained firefighters (ie, part-time firefighters) claimed parity of employment terms with full-time, regular firefighters. They sought to belong to the pension scheme, and to be paid the same rate for additional duties and sick pay. Their Lordships said that the question is whether the main duties and responsibilities of the two jobs were the same or similar. This will involve looking at the work done by both groups, and taking into account similarities and differences. If the answer to the above question is 'Yes', the next stage is to look at the differences and decide whether they are so important as to prevent the work being regarded as the same or broadly similar. Their Lordships commented that just because the full-timers carried out some extra tasks, this would not prevent the jobs being the same or broadly similar. The case was sent back to the tribunal for reconsideration.

In *Roddis v Sheffield Hallam University* (UKEAT/0299/17), the EAT looked at whether an associate lecturer engaged on a zero hours contract was employed under the same type of contract as a full-time lecturer. The EAT said that the proper approach to reg 2(3) was to look at the 'comprehensive' list of categories of contract in reg 2(1), (2) and (4) and bear in mind that the purpose of the Regulations is to provide a threshold for comparison which is deliberately set not too high. Just because there are different terms and conditions or workers are treated differently does not automatically mean that they are not engaged in the same work. The EAT concluded that the permanent full-time lecturer was employed under the same type of contract as the part-time associate lecturer.

The Court of Appeal held in BA plc v Pinaud [2018] EWCA Civ 2427 that a part-time crew member who was required to be available for 53.5% of the full-time equivalent hours but was only paid 50% of the salary of the full-timer was treated less favourably.

In Forth Valley Healthcare Board v John Campbell (UKEAT/0003/21) the EAT held that the fact that the claimant did not receive a paid break of 15 minutes during certain shifts, whereas full-time workers did receive such breaks, did not amount to unlawful discrimination because the difference in treatment between the claimant and the full-time comparator was not 'on the ground' of the claimant's part-time status. It was an agreed fact before the tribunal that whether or not a shift included a break depended on the length of the shift in question.

Although the language used in the Regulations is the language of discrimination, there is no provision to make any award for injury to feelings. No adjustment to compensation for failure to comply with the 2009 Acas Code is possible, because a claim under the Regulations is not one of the listed Sch 2 jurisdictions.

The ECJ has ruled (see Istituto nazionale della previdenza social (INPS) v Bruno [2010] IRLR 890) on how the Part-time Work Directive applies to occupational pension rights. That case suggests that the protection goes beyond mere access to such schemes. In O'Brien v Ministry of Justice (Case C-393/10), the ECJ held that if fee-paid, part-time judges are workers, the national law that excludes fee-paid judges from the pension scheme is discriminatory, unless it can be objectively justified. The case was heard by the Supreme Court on 4 July 2012, and its reasons were given on 6 February 2013 ([2013] UKSC 6). The Supreme Court held that a part-time Crown Court recorder was a part-time worker for the purposes of the Part-time Workers Regulations, and that the differences in treatment between part-time, fee-paid recorders and full-time, salaried recorders regarding pensions was not objectively justified. Lady Hale gave the judgment of the Supreme Court on the justification issue. She referred (at [46]) to the opinion of Advocate-General Kokott, implicitly endorsed by the ECJ, that unequal treatment must be justified by

> the existence of precise, concrete factors, characterising the employment condition concerned in its specific context and on the basis of objective and transparent criteria for examining the question whether that unequal treatment responds to a genuine need and whether it is appropriate and necessary for achieving the objective pursued ...

Lady Hale emphasised that European case law clearly established that a discriminatory rule or practice could not be justified by reference to the simple saving of costs. The case was remitted back to the employment tribunal to determine the amount of pension to which the claimant was entitled. The EAT held that Mr O'Brien's pension should only be calculated with reference to his service after 7 April 2000 (the date the Part-time Workers Directive should have been implemented in the UK) (UKEAT/0466/13).

The issue of the amount of pension due to Mr O'Brien came before the Supreme Court at the same time as Walker v Innospec (see **8.2.6** above). A majority of the Supreme Court believed that the relevant date for the purposes of when discrimination occurred was not when the pension was earned but when it came to be paid. On this view, it would be the future effect of a past situation, in which case service before 7 April 2000 should be taken into account. The Court was unsure on this point and referred it to the CJEU, whose ruling was handed down on 7 November 2018. The CJEU (Case C-432/17) held that part-time work carried out before the deadline for implementing the Directive on 7 April 2000 must be taken into account.

In *Harpur Trust v Brazel* [2022] UKSC 21, the Supreme Court confirmed that all workers are entitled to 5.6 weeks and held that part-time workers engaged on permanent contracts who only work irregular hours for particular periods throughout the year (eg a teacher on a term-time contract) should have holiday pay calculated with reference to their average pay in the 52 weeks immediately prior to the statutory calculation date (multiplied by 5.6); the Working Time Regulations 1998 do not provide for the kind of pro-rating for which the respondent argued – being the application of the 12.07% of total (expected) hours worked per year formula.

8.11 FIXED-TERM EMPLOYEES

The Fixed-term Employees (Prevention of Less Favourable Treatment) Regulations 2002 (SI 2002/2034) work on a similar basis to the Part-time Workers Regulations 2000 (see **8.10**). However, there is one important distinction. The Fixed-term Employee Regulations apply only to employees, not to the wider category of workers.

Again, the detail of the legislation is beyond the scope of this book but, briefly, the 2002 Regulations cover the following:

(a)   A right for a fixed-term employee not to be treated less favourably than a comparable permanent employee (see *Carl v University of Sheffield* (**8.10** above)) on the grounds that he is a fixed-term employee, unless objectively justified. Objective justification is deemed to be made out where the fixed-term employee's contractual rights are, as a whole, at least as favourable as the permanent employee's. Otherwise, the employer will have to show that there is an objective reason for treating the fixed-term employee less favourably. Archived BIS Guidance gives an example an employee on a three-month fixed-term contract, who is not provided with a company car because the cost of doing so is so high, and the employee's travel needs can be met in another way.

(b)   An obligation on employers to advertise permanent vacancies in such a way as is reasonably likely to come to the fixed-term employee's attention.

(c)   A right to receive a written statement of reasons for treatment, if the employee believes less favourable treatment has occurred.

(d)   Provision that any dismissal for seeking to enforce these rights is automatically unfair.

(e)   Provision that a fixed-term contract will be converted to a permanent contract upon the next renewal/extension if the employee has been employed on a fixed-term contract for over four years (unless the employer can demonstrate an objective justification for continued fixed-term employment). The archived BIS Guidance gives as an example professional sports people, where it is traditional practice for employees to work on fixed-term contracts.

For some case law on the 2002 Regulations, see *Duncombe and Others v Secretary of State for Children, Schools and Children* [2011] UKSC 14, *The Manchester College v Mr M Cocliff* (UKEAT/0035/10), *Hall v Xerox UK Ltd* (UKEAT/0061/14) and *Ibarz v University of Sheffield* (UKEAT/0018/15) (time-limits).

8.12 TRADE UNION MEMBERSHIP OR ACTIVITIES

Section 137 of the Trade Union and Labour Relations (Consolidation) Act 1992 (TULR(C)A 1992) abolishes the pre-entry closed shop (ie the refusal to employ a person who is not a member of a trade union). It also prohibits an employer from refusing to employ someone because he is a member of a trade union or takes part in trade union activities.

8.12.1 Refusal of employment

It is unlawful to refuse to employ a person on the grounds that he is, or is not, a member of a trade union. It is also unlawful to refuse to employ a person if he does not agree to become, or remain or cease to be a member of a trade union (TULR(C)A 1992, s 137(1)).

8.12.2 Remedies

If a person has been refused employment on the grounds that he is, or is not, a member of a trade union, he may present a complaint to an employment tribunal within three months of the act complained of. The complainant may apply for interim relief (see **5.5.1**).

The tribunal may make an order for compensation, including injury to feelings, or a recommendation that the effect of the act be obviated or reduced. This could involve, for example, a recommendation that the complainant be offered employment. If a recommendation is not complied with, the compensation award can be increased. The maximum compensation currently awardable is £78,335 (at 6 April 2015).

8.13 DISCRIMINATION UNDER THE HUMAN RIGHTS ACT 1998

The ECHR ('the Convention') was incorporated into domestic law by the Human Rights Act (HRA) 1998. This means that individuals are able to enforce Convention rights in the UK's domestic courts and tribunals (see **Chapter 15**).

Article 14 of the Convention contains a wide prohibition against discrimination. It states that the enjoyment of rights and freedoms set forth in the Convention shall be secured

> without discrimination on any ground such as sex, race, colour, language, religion, political or other opinion, national or social origin, association with a national minority, property, birth or other status.

However, Article 14 does not create any 'freestanding' right to freedom from discrimination, and is thus limited to the right to enjoy the other Convention rights without discrimination. Protocol 12 prohibits discrimination in the enjoyment of any right granted by national law, but the UK has not ratified the Protocol.

There have been a number of cases before the ECtHR looking at violations of Article 14 (in conjunction with Article 2 (right to education)) by States in connection with education policies relating to the children of Roma parents (see, eg, *DH and Others v The Czech Republic* (App No 57325/00) and *Sampanis v Greece* (App No 32526/05), which contain useful statements on indirect discrimination and the shifting burden of proof).

Article 9 of the Convention contains the rights to freedom of thought and religion. It will cover, for example, religious groups who are not currently covered under the definition of 'race' under the Equality Act 2010 (eg Muslims; Rastafarians). If employers discriminate on grounds of belief or religion, that will be unlawful. However, the Court has been restrictive of these rights and has given only limited protection. See, for example, *Ahmad v UK* (1982) 4 EHRR 126, *Stedman v UK* (1997) 23 EHRR CD 168, ECtHR and *Kontinnen v Finland* (1996) 87 DR 68, ECtHR, where the ECtHR accepted that the right could be limited by contractual provisions. In these cases, the view taken was that if, for example, working hours conflict with religious convictions, the applicant is free to resign. However, the ECtHR held more recently in *Eweida & Others v UK* [2013] IRLR 231 that, given the importance in a democratic society of freedom of religion, rather than holding that the possibility of changing job would negate any interference with the right, the better approach is to weigh that possibility in the overall balance when considering whether or not the restriction is proportionate.

Even though discrimination on grounds of sexual orientation has, until very recently, not been covered by UK or EU law, sexual orientation has been recognised as part of an individual's private life under Article 8 of the Convention. If there is a dismissal on such grounds, Article 8 can be used to give strength to an argument that there is an unfair dismissal. If there is an act by a public authority, Article 8 will give rise to a direct cause of action. Article 8, in conjunction with Article 14, was significant in *EB v France* (App No 43546/02), where the ECtHR found breaches of the Convention when a lesbian's application to adopt a child was refused.

Particularly gross forms of harassment and discrimination may amount to inhuman or degrading treatment under Article 3 of the Convention.

8.14 FURTHER READING

Barnard, *The Substantive Law of the EU: The Four Freedoms*, 7th edn (OUP, 2022).

Barnard, *EU Employment Law*, 4th edn (OUP, 2012).

Wadham, Robinson, Ruebain and Uppal, *Blackstone's Guide to the Equality Act 2010*, 4th edn (OUP, 2021).

Harvey, *Industrial Relations and Employment Law* (LexisNexis), Divs K and L.

Hughes, *Discrimination Law* (looseleaf) (Bloomsbury Professional, 2019).

Tolley's Employment Handbook, 36th edn (2022).

Jackson and Banerjee, *Disability Discrimination: Law and Case Management*, 2nd edn (Law Society Publishing, forthcoming 2023).

Rubenstein, *Discrimination: A Guide to the Relevant Case Law*, 35th edn (2022).

The Government Equalities Office (GEO) website:
<http://www.gov.uk>.

The Advisory, Conciliation and Arbitration Service (Acas) Guidance at:
<http://www.acas.org.uk>.

See also the Acas advisory booklet, *Tackling discrimination and promoting equality – good practice guide for employers*, available from the Acas website at <http://www.acas.org.uk/publications>.

SUMMARY

The general common law rule is that an employer is free to offer employment to whomsoever he chooses (*Allen v Flood and Taylor* [1898] AC 1). This common law freedom has been restricted by statute. The EC Equal Treatment Directive (76/207) provides that there should be no discrimination on grounds of sex, either directly or indirectly, nor by reference to marital or family status, in access to employment, training, working conditions, promotion or dismissal. In the UK, under the provisions of the Equality Act 2010, an employer may be in breach of statutory requirements if he discriminates against a person on a large number of protected characteristics including:

(a)   sex, maternity, pregnancy or marital status;

(b)   gender reassignment;

(c)   colour, race, nationality or ethnic or national origins;

(d)   religion or belief;

(e)   sexual orientation;

(f)   age;

(g)   disability (**8.1**).

The Equality and Human Rights Commission (EHRC) has responsibility for promoting equality and combating unlawful discrimination on grounds of sex, race, disability, sexual orientation, religion or belief, and age. It also has responsibility for the promotion of human rights.

This chapter has looked at the matters which are common to all the protected characteristics. Provisions in the Equality Act 2010 relating to age and disability discrimination are in some ways different from the other protected characteristics, and so age discrimination (**Chapter 12**) and disability discrimination (**Chapter 13**) are dealt with separately.

Four main types of discrimination in the employment field are outlawed by UK legislation on these grounds. These are:

(a)   direct discrimination (ie being subject to less favourable treatment than others because of sex, race, religion or belief, sexual orientation, age, etc) (see **Chapter 9**);

(b)   indirect discrimination (ie the application of a provision, criterion or practice which disadvantages people of a particular sex, race, religion or belief, sexual orientation, age, etc) (see **Chapter 10**);

(c)   harassment (unwanted conduct that violates a person's dignity, or creates an intimidating, hostile, degrading, humiliating or offensive environment for him or her having regard to all the circumstances, including the perception of the victim) (see **Chapter 11**); and

(d)   victimisation (because the victim has been subject to a detriment because he has done a protected act) (see **Chapter 11**).

In most cases, indirect discrimination may be justified 'objectively' where the discrimination is a 'proportionate means of achieving a legitimate aim' (**Chapter 10**).

Discrimination is outlawed (Equality Act 2010, ss 39 and 40) in the employment field against job applicants (ie recruitment) and employees and former employees. It is unlawful for a person, to discriminate against a person employed by him (**8.4**):

(a)   in the way he affords him or her access to opportunities for promotion, transfer or training, or to any other benefits, facilities or services; or

(b)   by dismissing him or her, or subjecting him or her to any other detriment.

An employer may have a defence under the occupational requirements provisions of the Equality Act 2010 (**8.5**) and under the 'reasonable steps' defence (**8.6.2**), if he can show that he took such steps as were reasonably practicable to prevent an employee doing the act complained of. Employers may be vicariously liable for the acts of their employees during the course of employment (**8.6**).

Remedies and enforcement are dealt with at **8.8**. Tribunals may, on making a finding of discrimination, as they consider just and equitable, make:

(a)   an order declaring the rights of the complainant;

(b)   an order requiring the respondent to pay the complainant compensation; and/or

(c)   a recommendation that the respondent take, within a specified period, practicable action to obviate or reduce the adverse effect of any act of discrimination.

The general principle as far as compensation is concerned is that, as far as possible, complainants should be placed in the same position as they would have been but for the unlawful act (see *Ministry of Defence v Wheeler* [1998] IRLR 23). In addition to awarding compensation for foreseeable damage arising directly from the unlawful act, a tribunal has jurisdiction to award compensation for personal injury, including both physical and psychiatric injury, and for injury to feelings (**8.8.2.2**).

CHAPTER 9

DIRECT DISCRIMINATION

9.1	Introduction	425
9.2	Direct discrimination	425
9.3	Gender reassignment and absence from work	436
9.4	Pregnancy and maternity discrimination	437
9.5	Burden of proof	439
9.6	Remedies	443
9.7	Case study: direct race discrimination claim – burden of proof	444
	Summary	448

LEARNING OUTCOMES

After reading this chapter you will be able to:

- understand the definition of direct discrimination

- explain what is meant by 'less favourable treatment'

- describe how direct discrimination protects women who are pregnant or on maternity leave

- explain what is meant by the shifting burden of proof

- list the potential remedies that are available where a complaint of discrimination is made out.

9.1 INTRODUCTION

This chapter considers direct discrimination in respect of the following protected characteristics listed in s 4 of the Equality Act 2010 ('the Act') (see **8.2.1**):

- gender reassignment (s 7)

- marriage and civil partnership (s 8)

- race (s 9)

- religion or belief (s 10)

- sex (s 11)

- sexual orientation (s 12)

- pregnancy and maternity (s 18).

The protected characteristics of age (s 5) and disability (s 6) are dealt with in **Chapters 12** and **13** respectively.

This chapter refers, by way of illustration and example, to the pre- and post-Equality Act 2010 case law.

9.2 DIRECT DISCRIMINATION

9.2.1 Definition

Direct discrimination is defined in s 13 of the Act. It occurs where the reason for a person being treated less favourably than another is a protected characteristic listed in s 4 of the Act (see **9.1**). This definition is broad enough to cover cases where the less favourable treatment is because of the victim's association with someone who has that characteristic (eg is disabled – see **Chapter 13**), or because the victim is wrongly thought to have it (eg a particular religious belief) (see **9.2.2**). Note that men cannot claim the privileges for women connected with pregnancy or childbirth (s 13(6)(b)).

The definition of 'direct discrimination' is set out in s 13 of the Act:

(1)   A person (A) discriminates against another (B) if, because of a protected characteristic, A treats B less favourably than A treats or would treat others.

...

(4)   If the protected characteristic is marriage and civil partnership, this section applies to a contravention of Part 5 (work) only if the treatment is because it is B who is married or a civil partner.

(5)   If the protected characteristic is race, less favourable treatment includes segregating B from others.

(6)   If the protected characteristic is sex—

(a)   less favourable treatment of a woman includes less favourable treatment of her because she is breast-feeding;

(b)   in a case where B is a man, no account is to be taken of special treatment afforded to a woman in connection with pregnancy or childbirth.

(7)   Subsection (6)(a) does not apply for the purposes of Part 5 (work).

(8)   This section is subject to section ... 18(7) [see **9.4**].

The Explanatory Notes give examples:

- If an employer recruits a man rather than a woman because she assumes that women do not have the strength to do the job, this would be direct sex discrimination.

- If a Muslim shopkeeper refuses to serve a Muslim woman because she is married to a Christian, this would be direct religious or belief-related discrimination on the basis of her association with her husband.

- If an employer rejects a job application form from a white man who he wrongly thinks is black, because the applicant has an African-sounding name, this would constitute direct race discrimination based on the employer's mistaken perception.

- If an employer advertising a vacancy makes it clear in the advert that Roma need not apply, this would amount to direct race discrimination against a Roma who might reasonably have considered applying for the job but was deterred from doing so because of the advertisement.

In *Islington Borough Council v Ladele* [2009] ICR 387, the EAT explained direct discrimination as follows (para 32) (the case was appealed to the Court of Appeal but the explanation remains a valid one):

> The concept of direct discrimination is fundamentally a simple one. A claimant suffers some form of detriment (using that term very broadly) and the reason for that detrimental treatment is the prohibited ground. There is implicit in that analysis the fact that someone in a similar position to whom that ground did not apply (the comparator) would not have suffered the detriment. By establishing that the reason for the detrimental treatment is the prohibited reason, the claimant necessarily establishes at one and the same time that he or she is less favourably treated than the comparator who did not share the prohibited characteristic.

So, in most cases of direct discrimination, a comparator is required (see below). However, no comparator is needed if treatment can be said to be inherently discriminatory (see *Amnesty International v Ahmed* [2009] ICR 1450). An example might be exclusion from renting accommodation by a sign saying particular racial groups need not apply.

By virtue of s 70 of the Equality Act 2010, if the claim relates to terms of the contract of employment (see **Chapter 8** and in particular **8.9.1** on equal pay – the equal pay provisions make it unlawful for an employer to discriminate between men and women in relation to the terms of their contracts of employment), then the complainant must rely upon the equal pay provisions in the Equality Act 2010. It is important to bring a claim under the correct provisions. In some cases, it may be advisable to bring a discrimination claim and an equal pay claim, in the alternative, to protect the client's position.

Only direct discrimination because of age may be justified (Article 6 of the Framework Directive and Equality Act 2010, s 13(2); see, for example, *Seldon v Clarkson Wright and Jakes* [2012] UKSC 16, **Chapter 12.**)

9.2.2 Association and perception

Associative discrimination occurs when someone who does not have a protected characteristic themselves is discriminated against because of someone else's protected characteristic. Perceptive discrimination is discrimination against an individual because others think (wrongly) that they possess a particular protected characteristic.

The wording of the definition of 'direct discrimination' in the Act is wide enough to cover both associative and perceptive discrimination: the reference in s 13 (see **9.2.1**) is to treatment 'because of [protected characteristic]' as opposed to 'on grounds of' A's protected characteristic. This broader wording removes the need to consider whether the complainant's protected characteristic was the reason for the treatment complained of. It means that so-called 'associative discrimination' is covered. If A treats B less favourably because B cares for an elderly relative, A may be held to have discriminated against B *because of age*, even though B's age is not the reason for the treatment.

The Explanatory Notes state that direct discrimination occurs where the reason for a person being treated less favourably than another is a protected characteristic listed in s 4, and that the definition (save in the case of marriage and civil partnership) is broad enough to cover cases where the less favourable treatment is because of the victim's association with someone who has that characteristic (eg, is black) (association), or because the victim is wrongly thought to have it (eg, a particular religious belief) (perception).

Note that a different approach applies where the reason for the treatment is marriage or civil partnership, in which case only less favourable treatment because of the victim's status amounts to discrimination. It must be the victim, rather than anybody else, who is married or a civil partner, and a perception that the victim is married or a civil partner is not sufficient.

Until recently, it was thought that associative discrimination was limited to direct discrimination and harassment. However, three cases, *CHEZ Razpredelenie Bulgaria* (Case C-83/14), *Thompson v London Central Bus Company Ltd* (UKEAT/0108/15) and *Follows v Nationwide Building Society* (ET/2201937/18), suggest that it may also apply to cases of indirect discrimination and victimisation (see **10.2.4** and **11.9.1**).

See too the case of *Lee v McArthur and Ashers Baking Co Ltd* [2016] NICA 39, discussed at **9.2.5.3** below, which the Northern Ireland Court of Appeal held was a case of associative discrimination.

It is not clear how perception discrimination will work where the protected characteristic is disability (see **13.3.9**).

9.2.3 Reason for the less favourable treatment

Section 13 of the Act uses the words 'because of' where the previous legislation used the words 'on grounds of'. The Explanatory Notes state that this difference in wording does not change the legal meaning of the definition but rather is designed to make it more accessible to the ordinary user of the Act. In *Amnesty International v Ahmed* [2009] IRLR 884, Mr Justice Underhill stated that

> there can be no objection to the use of the phrase 'because of' if used as a synonym for the phrase 'on grounds of' as long as the phrase is not used to import a 'causation' (or a 'but for') test.

(For a case where the tribunal erroneously used the 'but for' test, see *Chief Constable of Greater Manchester Police v Bailey* [2017] EWCA Civ 425.)

9.2.4   What is less favourable treatment?

Less favourable treatment is a wide concept: it covers any 'disadvantage' (see, eg, *Jeremiah v Ministry of Defence* [1979] IRLR 436). It does not require any tangible loss (see *Chief Constable of West Yorkshire Police v Khan* [2001] IRLR 830). A mere deprivation of choice will be sufficient to found a claim of less favourable treatment (see, eg, *Gill v El Vino Co Ltd* [1983] QB 425 and *R v Birmingham City Council, ex p Equal Opportunities Commission* [1989] IRLR 173).

The wording in s 13 appears to suggest that the test is objective: the question is whether the complainant would have been treated:

(a)   differently; and

(b)   more favourably,

had it not been because of sex, race, religion or belief, sexual orientation, gender reassignment or marital/civil partnership status. The reason for the less favourable treatment must be because of sex, race, etc. The tribunal must ask what the 'conscious or subconscious reason for treating the claimant less favourably was'. If a protected characteristic was one of the reasons for the treatment, that is enough to establish direct discrimination. It need not be the sole or main reason, as long as it had a significant influence on the outcome. (See *Nagarajan v London Regional Transport* [1999] IRLR 572, HL.)

What amounts to less favourable treatment is for the tribunal to decide, but the hurdle is generally not a difficult one to satisfy. In considering the meaning to be given to 'less favourable', the courts have generally adopted the same test as that applied to determine whether a 'detriment' has occurred. In *Chief Constable of West Yorkshire Police v Khan* (above), the employer refused to give the claimant a reference, and he claimed that this was racially discriminatory. The employer argued that the claimant was better off without a reference, because any such reference would have been unfavourable and that there was, therefore, no less favourable treatment. The House of Lords held it was enough that the claimant 'could reasonably say that he would have preferred not to have been treated differently in this way'. In *Metropolitan Police v Keohane* (UKEAT/0463/12), the claimant was a police dog handler: the removal of her work dog when she went on maternity leave was not a detriment on its own, but the potential resultant loss of overtime and career disadvantage upon the claimant's return from leave was.

The judgment of the CJEU on headscarf bans illustrates how difficult it can sometimes be to determine what is less favourable treatment in a direct discrimination context. The judgment is also illuminating on how the lines between direct and indirect discrimination can get blurred. In the cases of *Achbita v G4S Secure Solutions* (Case C-157/15) and *Bougnaoui v Micropole Univers* (Case C-188/15), the CJEU found that prohibitions on wearing an Islamic headscarf do not constitute direct religious discrimination but may amount to indirect discrimination unless they are objectively justified by a legitimate aim. In these cases, before they reached the CJEU, two different Advocates General had expressed different views. In *Achbita*, one Advocate General gave an opinion that banning the wearing of an Islamic headscarf at work could be justified when an employer has a policy of neutrality and when the ban is applied equally to all visible signs of religious beliefs, ie not just where they relate to one religion. However, in *Bougnaoui*, a different Advocate General gave an opinion that it was unlawful to ban a Muslim employee from wearing her headscarf when in contact with clients. Both cases raised the question as to whether a prohibition for employees against wearing visible characteristics of political, philosophical or religious belief violates Directive 2000/78/EC.

In *Achbita*, Ms Achbita, a Muslim female, was hired as a receptionist at G4S Secure in Belgium. G4S had an unwritten rule (which subsequently became officially incorporated) that employees were not allowed to wear *visible characteristics* of their religious, political or philosophical convictions while working. In 2006, Ms Achbita informed her management that she would start wearing a headscarf during working hours. She was told this violated the company policy. She was eventually dismissed by G4S due to her firm intention to wear an Islamic headscarf. She sued G4S relying on the Directive and Belgian courts found for G4S. A Belgian court then referred the case to the ECJ. The Advocate General in her opinion stated that the main issue was whether the prohibition represented direct or indirect discrimination. She stated that there was no direct discrimination based on religion when an employee with Islamic faith was prohibited from wearing a headscarf at the workplace, if this prohibition was based on a general internal company rule which prohibits visible political, philosophical and religious symbols at the workplace and not on stereotypes or prejudices against one or more specific religions or against religious persuasions in general. She went on to say, however, that it might be indirect discrimination as there is a risk that the prohibition would particularly affect Muslim females more severely. On that basis, she considered whether the treatment was justified, concluding that:

> a prohibition as the one determined by G4S may be regarded as a regular, decisive and legitimate professional requirement as dealt with under Article 4 (1) of Directive 2000/78 which as a rule may substantiate unfair treatment – regardless it is of direct or indirect nature – due to religion provided that the principle of proportionality is complied with.

As an employee cannot leave his gender, his skin colour, his ethnic background, his sexual orientation, his age or his disability 'outside the door' when he enters the employer's premises, there may, according to the Advocate General in connection with the person in question exercising her religion at the workplace, however, be required a certain amount of restraint whether or not it involves religious practice, religiously motivated behaviour or – as in the matter in hand – the relevant person's clothing.

In *Bougnaoui*, Ms Bougnaoui was also a Muslim female. She was employed in France as a design engineer by Micropole SA, an IT consultancy company. She wore an Islamic headscarf whilst at work including when she was visiting clients at their premises. The headscarf covered her head but not her face. When Ms Bougnaoui had been recruited, she had been told that the company had a religious neutrality principle and that it 'entirely respect[ed] the principle of freedom of opinion and the religious beliefs of everyone, but that, since [she] would be in contact internally or externally with the company's clients, [she] would not be able to wear the [headscarf] in all circumstances'. Subsequently, a client complained about Ms Bougnaoui's headscarf saying it 'embarrassed a number of its employees' and asked Micropole that she not wear it on future visits. Micropole asked her to remove her headscarf when visiting clients. She refused to do so and was dismissed. She brought a claim for discrimination based on her religious beliefs. Two French courts held that the dismissal was well founded on the basis of a 'genuine and serious reason'. The matter was then referred to the ECJ for a preliminary ruling. The Advocate General decided that Ms Bougnaoui was treated less favourably on the ground of her religion, since a comparator (a design engineer who had not chosen to manifest their religious belief) would not have been dismissed. As such, therefore, her dismissal did constitute unlawful direct discrimination on the grounds of religion or belief. There was no occupational requirement on the facts of this case. For example, it was considered that it would be proportionate to exclude a Sikh who wore a turban from working in a post that required the wearing of protective headgear, for health and safety reasons.

The CJEU's substantive conclusion and analysis is found in *Achbita*. The CJEU in *Achbita* agreed with the Advocate General that her case did not meet the criteria for direct discrimination but held that it was capable of constituting indirect discrimination. In terms of justification, the Court accepted that there was a legitimate aim (wanting a neutral image) but had more difficulty with whether the ban was proportionate. In *Bougnaoui* the CJEU was asked to consider a much narrower question than in *Achbita*. The Court said that the absence of religious clothing could not be a genuine occupational requirement, and nor could a desire to accommodate the cultural expectations and prejudices of customers.

In the UK, employers are generally free to set whatever dress codes for staff that they wish, as long as the requirements are not discriminating. In May 2018, the Government Equalities Office and the Department for International Development issued guidance, entitled 'Dress codes and sex discrimination: what you need to know'. It advises that while dress codes do not need to be identical, gender-specific rules, such as any requirement to wear make-up, have manicured nails, wear hair in certain styles or wear specific types of hosiery, should be avoided. Requiring female employees to wear high heels but not having footwear requirements for men, for example, is likely to constitute direct discrimination. (It could also amount to indirect discrimination against disabled employees.) Having requirements to dress smartly, however, which are not gender-specific, would be lawful. While problems with dress codes tend to be associated with sex discrimination claims, rather than religion, restrictions on the display of religious symbols (see eg *Eweida v British Airways* at **10.2.3** below) can also be problematic, more particularly in the context of indirect discrimination. At the end of April 2017, the Government published its response to the House of Commons Petitions Committee and Women and Equalities Committee joint report on dress codes on the workplace. Guidance on heels, make-up, manicures, skirt length, and the like, is due shortly.

In *Wasteney v East London NHS Foundation Trust* (EAT/0157/15), the EAT held that an evangelical 'born again' Christian worker accused of 'grooming' a female Muslim member of staff had not been discriminated against nor harassed on the grounds of her religion or belief when she was disciplined for seeking to impose her religious views on her colleague, who complained that the claimant had tried to pray with her, made repeated invitations to her to attend her church and gave her a book concerning the conversion of a female Muslim to the Christian faith. The Trust found that this was misconduct, namely the blurring of professional boundaries and subjecting a junior colleague to improper pressure and unwanted attention. She was issued with a final written warning, which was reduced to a first written warning on appeal. The claimant complained to an employment tribunal of direct discrimination and harassment because of/related to her religion and belief, and the manifestation of her belief. The employment tribunal did not uphold her complaints. She appealed to the EAT on grounds including that Article 9 of the European Convention on Human Rights (see **Chapter 15**) protected her right to manifest her belief and that the sanction imposed was 'oppressive'. The EAT dismissed her appeal, pointing out that the rights under Article 9 are qualified and limited, and finding that the sanction imposed was proportionate.

Note that in *HM Chief Inspector of Education, Children's Services and Skills v The Interim Executive Board of Al-Hijrah School* [2017] EWCA Civ 1426, the Court of Appeal held that segregation of girls and boys in a mixed school from age 9 was direct discrimination against both girls and boys. Where there is mirror discrimination (ie both genders suffer a detriment), there can still be a finding of less favourable treatment under s 13, as that section protects the individual, so a group comparison is not relevant.

9.2.5 The 'reason why question'

9.2.5.1 Comparison by reference to circumstances

The Explanatory Notes explain that s 23 provides that like must be compared with like in cases of direct discrimination. The treatment of the claimant must be compared with that of an actual or a hypothetical person – the comparator – who does not share the same protected characteristic as the claimant but who is (or is assumed to be) in not materially different circumstances from the claimant.

The use of the words 'would treat' in s 13(1) (see **9.2.1**) allows for a hypothetical rather than an actual real life comparator. The relevant circumstances of the complainant and the comparative group should be the same or not materially different (s 23; *Shamoon*). In *Chief*

Constable of West Yorkshire v Vento [2001] IRLR 124, the EAT made an important point about comparing like with like and the use of hypothetical comparators where there is no actual comparator. In such cases, where the tribunal has to construct the probable treatment of a hypothetical comparator, it is legitimate to see how unidentical but not wholly dissimilar instances had been dealt with in the past. This would not infringe the principle of comparing like with like. For example, a woman might say that cases of alleged misconduct are investigated swiftly and in detail by the employer, whereas there was a slow and half-hearted investigation into her claim of sexual harassment. Thus, in the *Vento* case, the EAT held that the tribunal had not erred in constructing an inference from the hypothetical case of how the employers had treated four actual, unidentified but not wholly dissimilar comparators. The Court of Appeal approved *Vento* in *Balamoody v United Kingdom Central Council for Nursing, Midwifery and Health Visiting* [2002] IRLR 288, and ruled that the question of the correct comparator is a question of law.

The House of Lords emphasised the importance of the hypothetical comparator in *Shamoon v Chief Constable of the Royal Ulster Constabulary* [2003] IRLR 285. Their Lordships stated that 'in most cases a suitable actual comparator will not be available and a hypothetical comparator will have to constitute the statutory comparator'. As Michael Rubenstein notes in 'Highlights IRLR May 2003', 'the way others are treated whose circumstances are insufficiently similar to be actual comparators then becomes evidence of how a hypothetical comparator would be treated'. In *Shamoon*, the House of Lords also indicated that instead of relying on like with like comparators, a claimant may rely on the 'evidential significance' of non-exact comparators in support of an inference of direct discrimination, even though their evidential value will become weaker the greater the difference in circumstances. In that case, a Chief Inspector was removed from staff appraisal duties following complaints. The claimant sought to compare her treatment to that of two male officers who were in many respects directly comparable with her, save that no complaints had been made against them. That meant that they were inappropriate comparators. The comparator had to be a male officer against whom similar complaints had been made.

In *Olalekan v Serco Ltd* (UKEAT/0189/18), the EAT held that a tribunal was entitled to find that the circumstances of white prison officers were materially different to those of the claimant, especially in circumstances where the respondent's witness was not cross-examined, leaving unchallenged evidence. The tribunal was also entitled not to note the similarities between the claimant and those white comparators in order to construct a 'Shamoon style' hypothetical comparator. Whilst that was a course open to the tribunal, it was entitled to conclude that the differences were such as to 'render them of limited assistance in the tribunal's analysis'. The tribunal went on to construct a hypothetical comparator (a white male prison officer who had committed the same offence) and concluded that he would also have been dismissed. There was no error of law.

Where no actual comparator can be found, tribunals should consider the position of a hypothetical one. In *D'Silva v NATFHE* [2008] IRLR 412, Underhill P said at [30]:

> It might reasonably have been hoped that the Frankensteinian figure of the badly-constructed hypothetical comparator would have been clumping his way rather less often into discrimination appeals since the observations of Lord Nicholls in *Shamoon v Chief Constable of the Royal Ulster Constabulary* [2003] IRLR 285 (see in particular paragraph 11 at p.289) and the decision of this tribunal, chaired by Elias J, in *Law Society v Bahl* [2003] IRLR 640, at paragraphs 103–115 (pp.652–654). We regard it as clear, taking the reasons as a whole, that the tribunal made an express finding that the only reason why the union acted in the way complained of was that (as regards the initial decision and the first review decision) the appellant had expressed a lack of trust and confidence in his legal team and (as regards the subsequent review) that Mr Bryan had genuinely overlooked the appellant's further correspondence. Those findings necessarily exclude the possibility that the acts complained of were done, even in part, on racial grounds (or on grounds which would constitute victimisation). If that finding is unassailable it necessarily answers also the question whether he would have been treated

more favourably if he had been white or if he had not previously supported Mr Deman or complained of racial discrimination. It is accordingly unnecessary to consider in detail the passages in which the tribunal referred to the nature of the hypothetical comparator. We would however say that we can see no sign that it failed to appreciate any essential feature of the necessary comparison.

See also:

- *Amnesty International v Ahmed* [2009] IRLR 884 – consideration of what the characteristic of a hypothetical comparator should be is 'often a less useful way of addressing the questions raised by an issue of direct discrimination than focusing on the fundamental question of the reason for the act complained of' (para 25);
- *Aylott v Stockton-on-Tees Borough Council* [2010] IRLR 994 – 'there is no obligation ... to construct a hypothetical comparator in every case' (para 37); and
- *Cordell v Foreign and Commonwealth Office* [2012] ICR 280:

  [D]irect discrimination [requires answers to] two questions – (a) whether the Claimant has been treated less favourably than an actual or hypothetical comparator with the same characteristics [other than the proscribed ground] ('the less favourable treatment question'), and (b) whether that treatment was [because of the proscribed ground] ('the reason why question'). ... Where there is an actual comparator, asking the less favourable treatment question might be the most direct route to answer both questions; but where there is none it will usually be better to focus on the reason why question than to get bogged down in the often arid and confusing task of 'constructing a hypothetical comparator'.

See too *Martin v Devonshires Solicitors* [2011] ICR 352 for further discussion of some of these cases.

Note that the EAT held that a comparator was not required in a case where the woman alleged a breach of s 13 (it was agreed that the claim could not proceed under s 18 of the Equality Act 2010 (below)), when her employer refused to pay the London Allowance for the full period of her maternity leave (the allowance stopped when her maternity pay stopped). It was accepted that the same rules applied to male and female employees on sick leave but, applying the ECJ's decision in *Webb v EMO Air Cargo* (**9.4** below) to s 13 claims too, the EAT upheld the tribunal's conclusion that the claimant had been directly discriminated against on the grounds of her sex (*Commissioner of the City of London Police v Geldart* (UKEAT/0032/19)).

Note that a distinction is to be drawn between actual or hypothetical comparators and evidential comparators. Lord Scott in *Shamoon* at [109]–[110] noted:

109. ... comparators have a quite separate evidential role to play ... The victim who complains of discrimination must satisfy the fact-finding tribunal that, on a balance of probabilities, he or she has suffered discrimination falling within the statutory definition. This may be done by placing before the tribunal evidential material from which an inference can be drawn that the victim was treated less favourably than he or she would have been treated if he or she had not been a member of the protected class. Comparators, which for this purpose are bound to be actual comparators, may of course constitute such evidential material. But they are no more than tools which may or may not justify an inference of discrimination on the relevant prohibited ground, e.g. sex. The usefulness of the tool will, in any particular case, depend upon the extent to which the circumstances relating to the comparator are the same as the circumstances relating to the victim. The more significant the difference or differences the less cogent will be the case for drawing the requisite inference. But the fact that a particular chosen comparator cannot, because of material differences, qualify as the statutory comparator ... by no means disqualifies it from an evidential role. It may, in conjunction with other material, justify the tribunal in drawing the inference that the victim was treated less favourably than she would have been treated if she had been the article 7 comparator.

110. In summary, the comparator required for the purpose of the statutory definition of discrimination must be a comparator in the same position in all material respects as the victim save only that he, or she, is not a member of the protected class. But the comparators that can be of evidential value, sometimes determinative of the case, are not so circumscribed. Their evidential value will, however, be variable and will inevitably be weakened by material differences between the circumstances relating to them and the circumstances of the victim.

9.2.5.2 Reason for the treatment

Importantly, in *Shamoon* (**9.2.5.1** above) Lord Nicholls said (at para 11) that

> employment tribunals may sometimes be able to avoid arid and confusing disputes about the identification of the appropriate comparator by concentrating primarily on why the claimant was treated as she was. Was it on the proscribed ground which is the foundation of the application?

This approach has been adopted in a number of subsequent cases. In *London Borough of Islington v Ladele* (UKEAT/0453/08), Elias J (the then President) said that often, in practice, a tribunal will be unlikely to be able to identify who the correct comparator is, without first asking and answering the question why the claimant was treated as he was. Until that question is answered, he said, the appropriate attributes of the comparator will not be known. His conclusion was that whilst comparators may have evidential value, often they cast no light on the 'reason why question'. Elias J gave a useful example (at paras 36–37):

> A claimant alleges that he did not get a job because of his race. The employer says that it is because he was not academically clever enough and there is evidence to show that the person appointed had better academic qualifications. The claimant alleges this was irrelevant to the appointment; it was not therefore a material difference. The employer contends that it is a critical difference between the two situations. If the Tribunal is satisfied that the real reason is race, then academic qualifications are irrelevant. The relevant circumstances are not therefore materially different. It is plain that the comparator was treated differently. If the Tribunal is satisfied that the real reason is the difference in academic qualifications, then that provides a material difference between the claimant and the comparator.
>
> The determination of the comparator depends on the reason for the difference in treatment.

In *Ladele v The London Borough of Islington* [2010] IRLR 211, Ms Ladele was the registrar at Islington Council. She said that same-sex civil partnerships conflicted with her strict Christian beliefs, and refused to conduct same-sex civil partnership ceremonies. She was disciplined by the Council as a result. The EAT found that Ms Ladele was disciplined because she was refusing to carry out her duties, not because of her religious beliefs. Elias J said:

> The proper hypothetical or statutory comparator here is another registrar who refused to conduct civil partnership work because of antipathy to the concept of same sex relationships but which antipathy was not connected [to] or based upon his or her religious belief.

The Court of Appeal agreed with that view, and therefore held that there was no basis upon which the employment tribunal could have made a finding of direct discrimination ([2009] EWCA Civ 1357).

In *McFarlane v Relate Avon Ltd* [2010] ICR 50, EAT, the claimant entered into a contract of employment with the employer as a paid counsellor in August 2003. Upon doing so he expressly signed up to the employers' equal opportunities policy. The claimant is a Christian. In the course of his employment he experienced no difficulties of conscience in counselling same-sex couples where no sexual issues arose. At length, however, he sought to be exempted from any obligation to work with same-sex couples in cases where issues of psycho-sexual therapy ('PST') were involved. The EAT held that the tribunal was correct in its finding that there was no direct discrimination:

> [W]e concluded, firstly, that it was necessary for an actual or hypothetical comparator to be identified and, secondly, that an appropriate comparator would be another counsellor who, for reasons unrelated to Christianity, was believed by the respondent to be unwilling to provide PST counselling to same sex couples and therefore unwilling to abide by the respondent's Equal Opportunities and Ethical Practice Policies. The question, therefore, is whether the respondent would have treated [such] a comparator differently, and in our view it would not.

In other words, while religious belief was the claimant's motivation for his actions, the employer had dismissed him because he refused to comply with its equal opportunities policy.

See also *Sutton Oak Church of England School v Whittaker* (UKEAT/0211/18).

The clash between religious freedom and sexuality has manifest itself in a number of discrimination claims that are primarily based around religious objections to same-sex equality rights. There can seem to be irreconcilably conflicting rights. This has led to a distinction being drawn between the absolute right to hold a particular belief and the way in which that belief manifests itself. Manifestation is something that can and has been constrained by the law. Once religion enters the public domain, it effectively becomes a qualified right that is limited by other rights, which the law seeks to balance. (See *R v Secretary of State for Education and Employment, ex parte Williamson* [2005] UKHL 15, where the House of Lords held that freedom of religion was qualified when it came to manifestation by the need for a balance to be struck 'between the freedom to practise one's own religion and the interests of others affected by those practices'.) In addition to *Ladele* and *McFarlane*, see *McClintock v Department of Constitutional Affairs* [2008] IRLR 29 and *Lee v Ashers Baking Co Ltd and Others* [2018] UKSC 49 (**9.2.5.3** below).

In *Dziedziak v Future Electronics Ltd* (UKEAT/0270/11) the EAT upheld the tribunal's conclusion that the claimant, who is Polish, was subjected to direct discrimination on grounds of nationality when told by her line manager that she should not speak to colleagues 'in her own language', as those words demonstrated an 'intrinsic link' with her nationality. However, the EAT held in *Kelly v Covance Laboratories Ltd* (EAT/0186/15) that the 'intrinsic link' test in *Dziedziak* only went to shift the burden of proof to the respondent and that in *Kelly* the employer had a reasonable explanation for its actions unrelated to the claimant's race or national origins. The Court of Appeal held that the employment tribunal had been correct to focus on the decision maker's mental process in *CLFIS (UK) Ltd v Reynolds* [2015] EWCA Civ 549, because only he had taken the decision; none of the other players who influenced his reasoning were parties to the decision. Were it alleged that another player has provided tainted information, the correct approach is to treat that conduct as a separate act of discrimination from that of the person who acts upon it.

The EAT held, in *Grace v Places for Children* (UKEAT/0217/13), that the employment tribunal had been entitled to find that an employee was dismissed for the way in which she chose to manifest her religion, as opposed to her religious belief. There was therefore no direct discrimination. Paragraph 2.6.1 of the Employment Statutory Code of Practice issued by the EHRC states:

> Manifestations of a religion or belief could include treating certain days as days for worship or rest .... There is not always a clear line between holding a religion or belief and the manifestation of that religion or belief. Placing limitations on a person's right to manifest their religion or belief may amount to unlawful discrimination; this would usually amount to indirect discrimination.

The EAT agreed with that statement.

In *Page v NHS Trust Development Authority* (UKEAT/0183/18), the EAT held that the claimant was not directly discriminated against on grounds of religion or belief but, rather, because of the way he had expressed his views.

In *Gould v St John's Downshire Hill* (UKEAT/0002/20), the EAT upheld the tribunal's decision that whilst the claimant's marriage was part of the background to events, the dismissal of a vicar was due to his behaviour and a breakdown in trust and confidence, and was not significantly influenced by the belief that a minister cannot continue to serve if the marriage breaks down. If it had been, the discrimination claim would likely have succeeded.

In *Gan Menachem Hendon Ltd v De Groen* (UKEAT/0059/18), the claimant, who was employed by a Jewish nursery run in accordance with ultra-orthodox Chabad principles, was dismissed after it became known that she was cohabiting with her boyfriend and she refused to lie about that fact to parents. The respondent's reasons for dismissal included that the claimant was 'acting in contravention of the nursery's culture, ethos and religious beliefs'. The EAT held that the tribunal had erred in its conclusion that the claimant had been directly discriminated against on the grounds of religion or belief. Less favourable treatment because of the beliefs of the employer is not enough to make out a direct religion or belief discrimination claim.

9.2.5.3 Motive

The motive or intentions behind the action are irrelevant and there is no defence once direct discrimination has been proved (see *Birmingham City Council v EOC* [1989] AC 1155). For example:

(a) If the only woman remaining on a work experience scheme is withdrawn 'for her own good', this will be direct discrimination.

(b) If the temporary appointment of a black person as a refuse collector is withdrawn due to fear of industrial action by the other workers, this will amount to direct discrimination even though the employer's intention was not to discriminate but to avoid disrupting the service.

In *Amnesty International v Ahmed* (UKEAT/0447/08), Amnesty declined to appoint a northern Sudanese woman to the position of researcher because it was concerned that her ethnic origin might compromise her impartiality and her safety. The tribunal upheld the claim of direct discrimination, as 'but for' her Sudanese origins she would have been appointed. The EAT upheld the tribunal's finding and approach. It made clear that the explanation for the discrimination was irrelevant and that this was a clear case where the employer's decision was overtly made on basis of the claimant's race (see *James v Eastleigh BC* [1990] 2 AC 751). Underhill J referred to the 'reason why question' as the discriminator's 'motivation' and to the explanation for the discrimination as his 'motive'. He explained (at paras 33–34):

> In some cases the ground, or the reason, for the treatment complained of is inherent in the act itself. If an owner of premises puts up a sign saying 'no blacks admitted' race is, necessarily, the ground on which (or the reason why) the black person is excluded. *James v Eastleigh* is a case of this kind ... In cases of this kind what was going on inside the head of the putative discriminator – whether described as his intention, motive, his reason or his purpose – will be irrelevant. The 'ground' of his action being inherent in the act itself, no further inquiry is needed. It follows that, as the majority in *James v Eastleigh* decided, a respondent who has treated a claimant les favourably on the ground of his or her sex or race cannot escape liability because he had a benign motive.

> But that is not the only kind of case. In other cases – of which *Nagarajan* is an example – the act complained of is not itself discriminatory but is rendered so by a discriminatory motivation, ie by the 'mental processes' (whether conscious or unconscious) which led the putative discriminator to do the act ... Even in such a case, however, it is important to bear in mind that the subject of the inquiry is the ground of, or reason for, the putative discriminator's actions, not his motive; just as in the kind of case considered in *James v Eastleigh*, a benign motive is irrelevant.

What is important, therefore, is to discover what caused someone to act as he did, as opposed to a consideration of that person's motive, intention, reason or purposes; or to put it another way, in order to establish if direct discrimination has occurred, it is necessary to identify only 'the factual criteria that determined the decision made by the discriminator', as opposed to the motive for the discrimination. It is important therefore to identify why the alleged discriminator acted as he did; 'what consciously or unconsciously was his reason'? (See *Chief Constable of West Yorkshire Police v Khan* [2001] IRLR 830.) [Note: Motive may be relevant to remedy.]

In *Lee v Ashers Baking Co Ltd and Others* [2018] UKSC 49, the Supreme Court held that there was no unlawful discrimination, on grounds of sexual orientation, in a baker refusing to supply a cake iced with 'support gay marriage' because the objection was to the message, not to Mr Lee's sexual orientation (ie a distinction between the man and the message); the baker would have refused to supply the cake to anybody, whatever the characteristics. It was not therefore direct discrimination. Daphne Romney QC asks: 'Would it be different if the cake was to be iced with the words "Congratulations Bill and Ben or Congratulations Betty and Barbara"'?

See 'The Consequences of the Ashers Cake Judgment', Oxford Human Rights Hub, 12 October 2018 (http://ohrh.law.ox.ac.uk/the-consequences-of-the-ashers-cake-judgment/). The case is now awaiting a hearing date before the ECtHR. The case is brought against the UK, with Mr Lee claiming that, in reaching its decision, the Supreme Court failed to give appropriate weight to his Convention rights.

See *Bull and Another v Hall and Another* [2013] UKSC 73, in which a bed and breakfast's refusal to allow a gay couple a room was found to be discriminatory on sexual orientation grounds.

9.2.6 Irrelevance of alleged discriminator's characteristics

Section 24 of the Act provides that it is no defence to a claim of direct discrimination that the alleged discriminator shares the protected characteristic with the victim. The discriminator will still be liable for any unlawful discrimination.

The Explanatory Notes provide an example:

> An employer cannot argue that because he is a gay man he is not liable for unlawful discrimination for rejecting a job application from another gay man because of the applicant's sexual orientation.

9.2.7 Stereotypical assumptions

Stereotypical assumptions may amount to direct discrimination. For example:

(a)   Assuming that a woman with young children will be an unreliable employee is direct discrimination.

(b)   Assuming that the husband is the breadwinner and that his wife will resign and follow him, in the event of the husband being relocated, without asking the wife what her intentions are, also amounts to direct discrimination.

See *Commerzbank AG v Rajput* (UKEAT/0164/18) for a recent case in which the EAT considers stereotypical assumptions.

The courts have held that it is not discriminatory to take into account natural differences between the sexes, for example to tell men that their hair must be worn above the collar, whereas, although women are allowed long hair, they are also subject to a rule prohibiting 'unconventional hair styles'.

9.2.8 Illegality

Note that the Supreme Court held, in *Hounga v Allen & Another* [2014] UKSC 47 (see **5.4.2.4**), that the illegality defence did not defeat a discrimination claim, as there was no 'sufficiently close connection between the illegality [the claimant had no right to work in the UK] and the tort to bar the claim'.

9.3   GENDER REASSIGNMENT AND ABSENCE FROM WORK

Section 16 of the Act provides that it is also discrimination against transsexual people if they are treated less favourably for being absent from work because they propose to undergo, are undergoing or have undergone gender reassignment than they would be if they were absent because they were ill or injured. Transsexual people are also discriminated against in relation to absences relating to their gender reassignment if they are treated less favourably than they would be for absence for reasons other than sickness or injury and it is unreasonable to treat them less favourably.

The Explanatory Notes give an example:

> A female to male transsexual person takes time off work to receive hormone treatment as part of his gender reassignment. His employer cannot discriminate against him because of his absence from work for this purpose.

9.4 PREGNANCY AND MATERNITY DISCRIMINATION

Section 18 of the Act defines what it means to discriminate because of a woman's pregnancy or maternity, as distinct from her sex, in specified situations within work. It protects a woman from discrimination because of her current or a previous pregnancy. It also protects her from maternity discrimination, which includes treating her unfavourably because she is breast-feeding, for 26 weeks after giving birth, and provides that pregnancy or maternity discrimination as defined cannot be treated as sex discrimination. Maternity is defined in s 213 of the Act. There is no definition of pregnancy.

Section 18 provides as follows:

(1)   This section has effect for the purposes of the application of Part 5 (work) to the protected characteristic of pregnancy and maternity.

(2)   A person (A) discriminates against a woman if, in the protected period in relation to a pregnancy of hers, A treats her unfavourably—

(a)   because of the pregnancy, or

(b)   because of illness suffered by her as a result of it.

(3)   A person (A) discriminates against a woman if A treats her unfavourably because she is on compulsory maternity leave.

(4)   A person (A) discriminates against a woman if A treats her unfavourably because she is exercising or seeking to exercise, or has exercised or sought to exercise, the right to ordinary or additional maternity leave.

(5)   For the purposes of subsection (2), if the treatment of a woman is in implementation of a decision taken in the protected period, the treatment is to be regarded as occurring in that period (even if the implementation is not until after the end of that period).

(6)   The protected period, in relation to a woman's pregnancy, begins when the pregnancy begins, and ends—

(a)   if she has the right to ordinary and additional maternity leave, at the end of the additional maternity leave period or (if earlier) when she returns to work after the pregnancy;

(b)   if she does not have that right, at the end of the period of 2 weeks beginning with the end of the pregnancy.

(7)   Section 13, so far as relating to sex discrimination, does not apply to treatment of a woman in so far as—

(a)   it is in the protected period in relation to her and is for a reason mentioned in paragraph (a) or (b) of subsection (2), or

(b)   it is for a reason mentioned in subsection (3) or (4).

In *Webb v EMO Air Cargo (UK) Ltd* [1993] IRLR 27, the House of Lords held that to dismiss a woman because she was pregnant, or to refuse to employ her because she was or might become pregnant, was unlawful direct discrimination. In *Brown v Rentokil Ltd* [1998] IRLR 445, the ECJ held that dismissal during pregnancy for absences due to incapacity for work 'must … be regarded as essentially based on the fact of pregnancy'. The ECJ decided that since pregnancy can affect only women, action taken on the grounds of a pregnancy-related illness constitutes direct discrimination on the grounds of sex.

Section 18 of the Act codifies the *Webb* decision above and sets out the meaning of discrimination because of a woman's pregnancy or pregnancy-related illness, or because she takes or tries to take maternity leave. Under s 18, a person discriminates against a woman in relation to her pregnancy or maternity leave if, during the protected period of her pregnancy and maternity leave, he treats her unfavourably because of her pregnancy (or an illness resulting from it) or maternity leave. The period during which protection from these types of discrimination exists is the period of pregnancy and any statutory maternity leave to which the woman is entitled. Section 13 (see **9.2.1**) does not apply during these periods. Because the test is whether the woman has been treated unfavourably (not less favourably), there is no need for a comparator during the protected period. Where a woman is treated unfavourably because of pregnancy or a pregnancy-related illness, and the decision to treat her in that way was taken during the protected period but not implemented until after the end of that period, the treatment is regarded as occurring during the protected period (s 18(5)).

The Explanatory Notes give examples:

- An employer must not demote or dismiss an employee, or deny her training or promotion opportunities, because she is pregnant or on maternity leave.
- An employer must not take into account an employee's period of absence due to pregnancy-related illness when making a decision about her employment.

Section 18(7) means that a claim in respect of pregnancy and maternity discrimination during the protected period cannot be brought as direct sex discrimination under s 13. A claim for direct discrimination outside that protected period would fall under s 13. When a pregnancy-related illness arises during pregnancy or maternity leave (the protected period) and persists after the end of that leave, an employer is, however, permitted to take into account such absences after the maternity leave period in computing periods of absence justifying dismissal, in the same way that a man's absence for illness would be taken in to account (see *Larsson v Føtex Supermarked* (Case C-400/95) [1997] ECR I-2757 and *Lyons v DWP Jobcentre Plus* (UKEAT/0348/13)).

In *Eversheds v De Belin* (UKEAT/0352/10), the EAT held that the obligation to protect employees who are pregnant or on maternity leave is limited to treatment that is 'reasonably necessary [meaning proportionate] to compensate them for the disadvantages occasioned by their condition'. In this case, the claimant had been scored lower in a redundancy exercise than a colleague who was on maternity leave solely because the colleague was given a maximum notional score for one of the criteria. The EAT upheld the tribunal's finding of sex discrimination and unfair dismissal: the maternity benefit applied was disproportionate because there were less discriminatory alternative measures that could be adopted, such as measuring performance at a time when both candidates were still at work. Thus, the claimant who had been disadvantaged by this was entitled to claim sex discrimination. However, applying the approach in *Polkey* (see **5.6.2.2**), as there was cogent evidence that the claimant would have been made redundant in any event some nine months later, the claim was remitted to a different tribunal to consider whether the claim for loss of earnings should be capped or discounted on that basis.

In *CD v ST* [2014] EUECJ C-167/12, the ECJ held that a commissioning mother in a surrogacy arrangement did not fall within the scope of the Pregnant Workers Directive.

In *Interserve FM Ltd v Tuleikyte* (UKEAT/0267/16), the EAT emphasised the 'because of' question – the unfavourable treatment must be 'because of' maternity leave, etc (the 'reason why' question applies just as much here as it does under s 13 (see **9.2.5.2**)).

In *Really Easy Car Credit Ltd v Thompson* (UKEAT/0197/17), the EAT held that an employer must believe or know that the employee is pregnant if a claim for pregnancy discrimination (or a claim for automatic unfair dismissal because of pregnancy) is to succeed. The decision to dismiss in this case was taken before the employer had belief or knowledge of the pregnancy. There is no provision against less favourable treatment because of something arising from pregnancy (as there is with disability discrimination). The case was remitted back to the tribunal to determine whether, on the facts, the real reason for the dismissal was pregnancy.

In *South West Yorkshire Partnership NHS Foundation Trust v Jackson* (UKEAT/0090/18) the EAT held that sending an important email to an employee's work email while she was on maternity leave, and which she was not accessing, could amount to unfavourable treatment. (On the facts, as the employment tribunal had not considered whether the fact of the maternity leave was the reason why she had been treated unfavourably, the case was remitted back to the tribunal.)

Note that the sorts of discussions that preceded the introduction of s 18 of the Act and specific protection for pregnancy and maternity are now being heard in connection with the biological health change that occurs in women, known as the menopause. There is no guidance in the EHRC Code of Practice on the menopause. The symptoms arising from the menopause, which can be both physical and mental, can adversely affect some women's ability to work. Part of the debate centres around whether, if less favourable treatment is meted out because of menopausal symptoms, this should be seen as a disability issue, or dealt with under sex or age discrimination (see *Rooney v Leicester City Council* [2021] 10 WLUK 69, at **13.3.3** below). The House of Commons' Women and Equalities Committee has recently held an inquiry into the issue of the menopause. Research released by the Committee in February 2022, which polled 2,161 women all experiencing at least one symptom of the menopause, found that 31% had missed work because of their symptoms. The same poll found that one in 10 women (11%) had asked for workplace adjustments related to their menopause symptoms, with a quarter (26%) of those who said they had not asked for adjustments saying they were 'worried about the reaction of others'. The Women and Equalities Committee report was published on 28 July 2022. It calls on the government to amend the Equality Act 2010 to introduce menopause as a protected characteristic, and to include a duty for employers to provide reasonable adjustments for menopausal employees. To date, the government has indicated that it does not intend to take either of these steps, so it remains to be seen what will happen next in this area.

9.5   BURDEN OF PROOF

9.5.1   The shifting burden of proof

The legislation provides that where a complainant can establish facts from which the tribunal could decide that there has been a contravention of a provision of the Act, the tribunal *must* make a finding of unlawful discrimination *unless* the employer shows it did not contravene the provision (s 136). The Explanatory Notes explain that the burden of proving a case starts with the claimant. Once the claimant has established sufficient facts which, in the absence of any other explanation, point to a breach, then the burden shifts on to the respondent to show that it did not breach the Act. This has been held to mean that the complainant does have to establish some facts from which a tribunal could decide that there has been discrimination.

In some cases, it will be obvious what 'the reason why' is for the less favourable treatment, and in such cases it will not be necessary to engage in the burden of proof, but where 'the reason why' cannot be clearly determined on the evidence, there is an initial burden on a claimant to prove, on the balance of probabilities, a prima case of discrimination. The burden does not shift to an employer to explain the reason for its treatment unless the claimant can get over this initial evidential hurdle. There must be 'something more' than a bare assertion of discrimination or difference.

The EAT had the chance to consider the burden of proof in *Barton v Investec Henderson Crosthwaite Securities Ltd* [2003] IRLR 332 (a sex discrimination case decided under the old law). Ansell J gave guidance on the burden of proof in practice in direct discrimination claims. That guidance was amended by the Court of Appeal in *Igen Ltd and Others v Wong* [2005] IRLR 258 and approved again in *Madarassy v Nomura International plc* [2007] EWCA Civ 33. Although these cases involved sex or race discrimination, the Court of Appeal in *Igen* made it clear that they apply to all the discrimination strands. The guidance is as follows:

1.   [It] was for the claimant who complained of sex discrimination to prove on the balance of probabilities facts from which the tribunal could conclude, in the absence of an adequate explanation, that the respondent had committed an act of discrimination against the claimant which was unlawful ...

2.   If the claimant did not prove such facts he or she would fail.

3.   It was important to bear in mind in deciding whether the claimant had proved such facts that it was unusual to find direct evidence of sex discrimination. Few employers would be prepared to admit such discrimination, even to themselves. In some cases the discrimination would not be an intention but merely based on the assumption that 'he or she would not have fitted in'.

4.   In deciding whether the claimant had proved such facts, it was important to remember that the outcome at this stage of the analysis by the tribunal would therefore usually depend on what inferences it was proper to draw from the primary facts found by the tribunal.

5.   It was important to note the word 'could' in s [136]. At this stage the tribunal did not have to reach a definitive determination that such facts would lead it to the conclusion that there was an act of unlawful discrimination. At this stage a tribunal was looking at the primary facts before it to see what inferences of secondary fact could be drawn from them.

6.   In considering what inferences or conclusions could be drawn from the primary facts, the tribunal must assume that there was no adequate explanation for those facts.

7.   Those inferences could include, in appropriate cases, any inferences that it was just and equitable to draw in accordance with s [138] ... from an evasive or equivocal reply to a questionnaire or any other questions that fell within s [138] ...

8.   Likewise, the tribunal must decide whether any provision of the relevant code of practice was relevant and if so take it into account in determining such facts ... This meant that inferences might also be drawn from any failure to comply with any relevant code of practice.

9.   Where the claimant had proved facts from which conclusions could be drawn that the respondent had treated the claimant less favourably on the ground of sex, then the burden of proof moved to the respondent.

10.   It was then for the respondent to prove that he had not committed, or as the case might be, was not to be treated as having committed, that act.

11.   To discharge that burden it was necessary for the respondent to prove, on the balance of probabilities, that the treatment was in no sense whatsoever on the grounds of sex, since 'no discrimination whatsoever' was compatible with the burden of proof Directive (Council Directive 97/80/EC).

12.   That required a tribunal to assess not merely whether the respondent had proved an explanation for the facts from which such inferences could be drawn, but further that it was adequate to discharge the burden of proof on the balance of probabilities that sex was not a ground for the treatment in question.

13.   Since the facts necessary to prove an explanation would normally be in the possession of the respondent, a tribunal would normally expect cogent evidence to discharge that burden of proof. In particular, the tribunal would need to examine carefully explanations for failure to deal with the questionnaire procedure and/or code of practice.

To summarise, following *Igen*, it has become accepted practice that, in a discrimination case, a claimant must prove, on the balance of probabilities, facts from which a (reasonable) tribunal could conclude, in the absence of an adequate explanation, that the respondent has discriminated against the claimant. The claimant must produce some evidence of discrimination before the burden will pass to the respondent. If the claimant does this then the respondent must prove that it did not commit the act. This is known as the shifting burden of proof – once the claimant has established a prima facie case (which will require the tribunal to hear evidence from the claimant and the respondent to see what proper inferences may be drawn (see *Madarassy v Nomura International* above and below)), the burden of proof shifts to the respondent to disprove the allegations, which will require consideration of the subjective reasons that caused the employer to act as he did. The respondent will have to show a non-discriminatory reason for the difference in treatment.

On the facts of *Barton v Investec*, the EAT found that Mrs Barton had produced sufficient evidence of sex discrimination to shift the burden of proof to the respondent, but that the tribunal had not considered what the employer's explanation was. The EAT found that, in hearing her claim for equal pay, the tribunal erred in that it failed to take into account Investec's reluctance to answer Mrs Barton's questionnaire and provide her with the information she requested concerning pay and bonuses.

The Court of Appeal in *Madarassy v Nomura* (above) took a further look at the burden of proof in discrimination cases. Essentially, it upheld the approach of the Court of Appeal in *Igen* and said that 'the correct legal position' was made plain in paras 28 and 29 of the judgment. The material parts of those paragraphs stated as follows:

28.   ... It is for the complainant to prove the facts from which ... the employment tribunal could conclude, in the absence of an adequate explanation, that the respondent committed an unlawful act of discrimination. It does not say that the facts to be proved are those from which the employment tribunal could conclude that the [respondent] 'could have committed' such act.

29.   The relevant act is, in a race discrimination case ... , that (a) in circumstances relevant for the purposes of any provision of the ... Act ...(b) the alleged discriminator treats another person less favourably and (c) does so on racial grounds. All those facts are facts which the complainant, in our judgment, needs to prove on the balance of probabilities ...

The bare facts of a difference in status and a difference in treatment indicate only a possibility of discrimination: They are not, without more, sufficient material from which a tribunal 'could conclude' that, on the balance of probabilities, the respondent had committed an unlawful act of discrimination.

Evidence supporting a prima facie case might include gender stereotyping (see eg *Commerzbank AG v Rajput* (UKEAT/0164/18)), statistical evidence (see eg *West Midlands Transport Executive v Singh* [1988] ICR 634, *Rihal v London Borough of Ealing* [2004] IRLR 642 and *Home Office v Kuranchie* (UKEAT/0202/16)), breaches of the Codes of Practice (the tribunal must consider the reason for the failure – see *Tera (UK) Ltd v Mr A Goubatchev* (UKEAT/0490/08)), or a lack of transparency (see *EB v BA* [2006] EWCA Civ 132) or inconsistency in approach (see eg *Veolia Environmental Services UK v Gumbs* (UKEAT/0487/12)), or an evasive reply to questions asked or a witness's lack of veracity (*Solicitors Regulation Authority v Mitchell* (UKEAT/0497/12) (see **8.8.1.2**), or protected characteristic-related comments (*Cromwell Garage Ltd v Doran* (UKEAT/0369/10) and *James v Gina Shoes Ltd and Ors* (UKEAT/0384/11)), or an employer's failure to provide information about recruitment criteria (*Meister v Speech Design Carrier Systems GmbH* (Case C-415/10) [2012] ICR 1066). Evidence against a prima facie case might be, for example, evidence of how the respondent treats (or mistreats) others (and not just the complainant). In *Laing v Manchester City Council* [2006] IRLR 748, the claimant's case failed at the first stage because the respondent gave evidence that the claimant was treated in the same way as all subordinate employees.

Usefully, the Court of Appeal in *Madarassy* made it clear (at paras 56 and 70) that although s 136 involves a two-stage test, the tribunal does not hear evidence in two stages; rather, it will hear all the evidence in a case before applying the two-stage analysis. Readers should study the case carefully before advising in discrimination cases. In *Gay v Sophos plc* (UKEAT/0452/10) the EAT confirmed that the tribunal is not obliged to follow the two-stage approach: if it finds that the employer was motivated by non-discriminatory considerations, the burden of proof has been discharged.

The burden of proof was considered by the Supreme Court in *Hewage v Grampian Health Board* [2012] UKSC 37. The Supreme Court declined to give any further guidance beyond *Igen* and *Madarassy*. Lord Hope, giving the unanimous judgment, reiterated that a complainant must prove facts from which the tribunal could conclude, in the absence of an adequate explanation, that the respondent had committed an act of unlawful discrimination, 'so the prima facie care must be proved, and it is for the claimant to discharge that burden'. Lord Hope repeated (at para 32) what Underhill J had pointed out in *Martin v Devonshires Solicitors* [2011] ICR 352 (at para 39), to the effect that

it is important not to make too much of the role of the burden of proof provisions. They will require careful attention when there is room for doubt as to the facts necessary to establish discrimination. But they have nothing to offer where the tribunal is in a position to make positive findings on the evidence one way or the other.

The Supreme Court did say that inferences might be drawn by considering how others are treated, even if the situations compared are not exactly the same.

Some doubt was cast upon this previously accepted approach to s 136 by the EAT in *Efobi v Royal Mail Group* (UKEAT/0203/16) where the EAT said that there was no burden on claimants to prove facts from which a tribunal could decide that the employer has discriminated.

However, the Court of Appeal restored the orthodox position in *Ayodele v Citylink Ltd* [2017] EWCA Civ 1913 and held that the EAT's decision in *Efobi* should not be followed. Singh LJ held that the difference in wording between the old and the new was no more than a legislative 'tidying up' exercise. He approved the previous decisions in, for example, *Igen* and *Hewage*. The Court of Appeal in *Efobi* ([2019] EWCA Civ 18) held that the burden was on the claimant to prove his case at the first stage, ie to prove facts from which, on the balance of probabilities, an employment tribunal can infer an unlawful act of discrimination. In many cases, a tribunal will not need to have recourse to s 136 at all. As Lord Hope made clear in *Hewage*, s 136 and the shifting burden of proof rules have no relevance where a tribunal can make positive findings on the evidence one way or another as to whether a claimant was discriminated against. A respondent should not have to discharge the burden of proof unless and until a claimant has shown that there is a prima facie case of discrimination which needs to be answered. Section 136 has an important role to play in cases where there is room for doubt as to the facts necessary to establish discrimination. The Court of Appeal's decision in *Efobi* was upheld by the Supreme Court ([2021] UKSC 33).

In *Raj v Capita Business Services Ltd* (UKEAT/0074/19), the EAT makes it clear that there is no rule of law that a tribunal must reverse the burden if it disbelieves some of the respondent's evidence. In an appropriate case where a tribunal rejects aspects of a respondent's evidence as to what occurred, it is *open* to a tribunal take that into account under s 136, but it is not obliged to do so.

In *Governing Body of Tywyn Primary School v Aplin* (UKEAT/0298/17), the EAT held that a tribunal had been entitled to infer, on the basis of procedural failings by the school (the investigating officer's report was not objective), that the burden of proof had been reversed.

9.5.2 Case law – drawing inferences

9.5.2.1 Cases decided prior to *Barton v Investec*

In *Strathclyde Regional Council v Zafar* [1998] IRLR 36, the House of Lords held that mere unreasonable treatment by the employer 'casts no light whatsoever' on the question whether he has treated the employee 'unfavourably' (see also *Martins v Marks and Spencer plc* [1998] IRLR 326). In *Law Society and Others v Bahl* [2003] IRLR 640, the EAT agreed that mere unreasonableness is not enough. Elias J commented that

> all unlawful discriminatory treatment is unreasonable, but not all unreasonable treatment is discriminatory, and it is not shown to be so merely because the victim is either a woman or of a minority race or colour ... Simply to say that the conduct was unreasonable tells nothing about the grounds for acting in that way ... The significance of the fact that the treatment is unreasonable is that a tribunal will more readily in practice reject the explanation given for it than it would if the treatment were reasonable.

A tribunal must also take into consideration all potentially relevant non-discriminatory factors that might realistically explain the conduct of the alleged discriminator.

These cases are still useful and relevant.

9.5.2.2 Cases decided after *Barton v Investec*

In *Igen Ltd and Others v Wong* (see **9.5.1** above), the Court of Appeal stated: 'The finding of unexplained unreasonable conduct enabled the Tribunal to draw the inferences satisfying the requirements of the first stage.' So it seems that unreasonable behaviour by an employer, combined with a relevant difference (sex, race, etc) may lead to a finding that the claimant has satisfied the initial evidential burden. However, Gibson LJ warned tribunals against

> too readily infer[ring] unlawful discrimination on a prohibited ground merely from unreasonable conduct where there is no evidence of other discriminatory behaviour on such ground, [although on the facts] the tribunal was not wrong in law to draw that inference.

In *DKW Ltd v Adebayo* [2005] IRLR 514, a race case, the EAT gave guidance on the level of evidence that is required to establish a prima facie case so that the burden of proof passes to the employer. The claim in *Adebayo* followed the summary dismissal of an employee of black African origin, employed as a senior trader, for breach of trading guidelines. The claim for race discrimination was based on the fact that other traders who had breached the guidelines in the same way had not been disciplined. The EAT confirmed that the tribunal was correct to accept that the applicant had established a prima facie case not only because other, white traders had not been disciplined for the same offence, but also because there had apparently been a number of procedural failings in the way the employers dealt with the case. The employers had failed to put forward an adequate explanation, and the fact that they had a genuine belief in the applicant's misconduct was not sufficient. The case establishes that all that an applicant needs to do is to show some primary facts from which inferences could be drawn. The EAT emphasised that it is not sufficient at the first stage for an applicant to show simply that a comparator of a different race was promoted to a post for which the applicant had also applied – he would need to show that a comparator of a different race was promoted to the post *and* that he was at least as well qualified.

The Scottish Court of Session in *Bvunzai v Glasgow City Council* [2005] CSIH 85 upheld a tribunal's decision that it would be legitimate to draw an adverse inference that an interview panel's assessment of the claimant at interview was influenced by racial factors. That inference was based on the manner in which the claimant and another applicant for the job were scored, and the fact that the respondent was unable credibly to explain how it had scored the job applicants. Moreover, the respondent had also departed from its Code of Conduct and could not credibly explain why.

In *Iwuchukwu v City Hospitals Sunderland NHS Foundation Trust* [2019] EWCA Civ 498, the Court of Appeal held that the employment tribunal had been entitled to draw inferences of discrimination (race) from the employer's failure to investigate the employee's grievances. See too *Base Childrenswear Ltd v Otshudi* [2019] EWCA Civ 1648 where the Court of Appeal held that if a manager lies, even if in good faith about the reason for dismissal, that may be sufficient to shift the burden of proof.

9.6 REMEDIES

See **8.8**. An employment tribunal can order a respondent to pay compensation including interest. Compensation can include damages for hurt feelings and the loss of the job. The tribunal can also make declarations or recommendations as to what action an employer could take to limit or restrict any damage done. Exemplary damages may be available.

9.7 CASE STUDY: DIRECT RACE DISCRIMINATION CLAIM – BURDEN OF PROOF

Facts

(1)   C was employed as a cleaning supervisor by Veryclean Bus Services Ltd (R) at its main London depot, from 25 April 2019 until her dismissal on 30 September 2020. R's business is that of providing bus-cleaning services. R has over 500 members of staff across 15 sites. R issued an equal opportunities policy in 2010. R's workforce consists of people from a variety of racial and national origins. C worked 40 hours per week, from 6pm until 2.30am on each weekday night. Her job involved management responsibilities, supervising in total 30 night and day workers at the depot. C's main job role was to ensure the proper and adequate cleaning of buses that were bought to the depot as part of a weekly maintenance and service check. At the end of the maintenance and service work, R needed to clean the buses, prior to their being sent back into service. It was C's responsibility to oversee that cleaning operation. With effect from 1 June 2019, C's line manager changed. There was no evidence that, prior to X becoming C's line manager, there had been any concerns about the way in which C carried out her job. X became dissatisfied (based partly on comments that he said he received from London Underground about the state of some of the buses, and based partly on his own observations) about the standard of the cleaning, and spoke about this to C informally on two occasions, on 20 July and 11 August. C maintained she had given X legitimate explanations for what he had observed. X noted on the second of these occasions that C's perception was that he was picking on her.

(2)   In addition to the two incidents on 20 July and 11 August, there were a number of other criticisms recorded by X about C on 19/08, 22/08, 28/08, 4/09 and 20/10. The final incident (20/10) related to an occasion on which X recorded that when he arrived at the site, he was told by a cleaner that C had gone home, that she had not told him, that he had tried to phone her and that she had said that she was sick. C did not deny that she was at home sick on this date.

(3)   Following that incident, X hand-delivered to C's home a letter of termination giving C one week's notice. The letter set out no reasons for the termination. Notwithstanding that R had a disciplinary procedure which was stated to apply to all staff after the completion of their probationary period, there had been no investigation, and no disciplinary process or procedure was followed. Subsequently, in response to a suggestion by C's representative that the dismissal was discriminatory, X wrote:

> As you are aware, C's employment with Veryclean Bus Services was less than 24 months, therefore we are under no legal obligation to supply you with the reasons for her dismissal. However, in the interest of fairness, openness and to dispel any suggestion that there may have been discrimination of any description, I am prepared to do so on this occasion. During her employment with us the following issues in regard to her performance conduct were raised but failed to be adequately addressed:
>
> •   Failure to perform the necessary quality control measures that were fundamental to her role. For example, the completion and standard of the rota cleaning.
>
> •   Failure to take reasonable action to ensure that the staff reported to her while performing their duties adequately and conducting themselves properly.
>
> •   Failure to advise her area manager of absence from site.
>
> •   Complaints from clients regarding the standard of cleaning.
>
> Should C wish to exercise her right of appeal we are willing to extend the deadline for this request to 10 October 2020 as per your request.

(4)   C's representative responded, stating that his client believed that she had been dismissed on the grounds of her race and that, in particular, she believed that there was an informal policy of replacing black workers with white Portuguese workers.

(5)   On 11 October 2020, C submitted a race questionnaire to R; and on 26 October, she submitted an appeal against the termination of her employment. She made no mention of or nor complained about discrimination in that appeal. That appeal stated:

> I was not given any warning and carried out my duties to the best of my knowledge. We have to clean rota buses before they are inspected and before the engineers get to repair them and repair could last up to two days sometimes even longer and the buses are sent back during the day with oil/grease etc.

No appeal took place. R subsequently submitted additional information in response to the questionnaire.

(6)   After C was dismissed, her job was offered to M, a black African, who was a supervisor at an another of R's bus depots, who turned it down. Subsequently, a Portuguese worker, N, took over C's position.

Claims

(7)   C's complaint is that her dismissal amounted to direct discrimination under s 13 of the Equality Act 2010 on racial grounds. She is of black African origin. The alleged less favourable treatment is her dismissal and the manner of her dismissal. As C had less than two years' service with R, she was unable to bring an unfair dismissal claim arising out of her dismissal.

(8)   R says it has not discriminated against C. It says the dismissal was not because of C's race.

Evidence

(9)   Disclosure took place in the usual way and paginated bundles were prepared which included extracts from C's personal file, extracts from the staff handbook on *Disciplinary Procedures, Grievances and Appeals*, papers relating to the C's dismissal and a Schedule of Loss from C setting out her claim for compensation.

(10) Statistically, the evidence proved in response to the RRA questionnaire showed a total of 29 leavers between April 2019 and February 2020. There were 19 black leavers out of 29, which would be two-thirds of the total leavers. In terms of information relating to X, he supervised a total of nine sites. As regards the other site supervisors or managers, out of nine, one was Portuguese, two were South American, one was Asian and one was Eastern European. The remainder were black Africans.

(11) Witness statements were exchanged prior to the hearing. At the hearing all witnesses who gave oral evidence were cross-examined and the tribunal had the opportunity to ask questions of them.

(12) At the conclusion of the evidence, both sides made oral submissions on liability and remedy.

(13) All these matters were taken into consideration by the tribunal before reaching its decision.

The issues to be decided

(14) The tribunal will have to determine:
  (a)   Has C been treated less favourably than a real or hypothetical comparator?
  (b)   If so, is the comparator from a different racial group from C?
  (c)   If so, has C proved facts from which the tribunal could conclude that the difference in treatment was because of race?
  (d)   If so, has R proved that it did not treat C less favourably in any sense whatsoever because of race?

(15) Depending on the outcome of the matters, the tribunal will have to determine what amount of compensation, if any, should be awarded.

Submissions

(16) R submitted that the tribunal needed to take note that there was a very diverse ethnic pattern within R's workforce, which was also affected by influxes of different nationalities. It submitted that C was not doing her job. It accepted that if this was an unfair dismissal case, the dismissal would be unfair, but said that that was not relevant to this claim. R submitted that there was an informal practice with regard to employees with less than one year's service, but there was nothing in writing about that. R referred the tribunal to *Igen Ltd v Wong* [2005] IRLR 258, where the Court of Appeal set out a number of guidelines with regard to the burden of proof. R submitted that, in the first instance, the burden did not shift from C to R. In the alternative, it submitted that if the burden did shift, R had discharged its obligations in terms of showing that C's dismissal was not connected in any way whatsoever to her race. R said that the fact that it did not comply with its own disciplinary procedures could not shift the burden of proof on its own; even if there was unreasonableness, there needed to be something else to shift the burden. The evidence was that the post was initially offered to M, who was a black African like C. Alternatively, if the burden shifted then there was an adequate explanation, which was that provided by M.

(17) C submitted that the appropriate comparator was a white Portuguese person. In that context, it was submitted that N, who eventually took over the post, might well be a suitable actual comparator, but in any event, C said that a hypothetical white Portuguese comparator would suffice. She said that the tribunal needed to look at the imbalance between black non-Portuguese and white Portuguese/others. C's case was that X had a policy of dismissing black workers and replacing them with Portuguese workers, and that she had been a victim of this policy. C's evidence was that there had been mainly black Africans in the workplace before X started work. After X arrived, 22 out of 39 staff were white, of whom 16 were white European. C says she complained about race discrimination to X in August 2019. There was a suspicion that the notes of these meetings had not been recorded contemporaneously as X had claimed. R had not applied its own procedure. There was no reason for the dismissal. As far as *Igen v Wong* is concerned, C had been dismissed, no – and no fair – procedure had been followed, and C had been displaced by a Portuguese worker; these matters were, she said, sufficient to shift the burden of proof.

(18) As far as statistics were concerned, C relied upon the statistics which indicated that out of 10 white leavers, 6 had been dismissed and 4 had resigned (one of whom returned); and that there had been 17 black leavers, of whom only 2 had resigned. Proportionately, she said, it was significant that there had been a large number of black leavers over a relatively short period of time. C submitted that the burden of proof shifted to R, who needed to provide an explanation. She said that R had failed to show that in no way whatsoever was race the reason for C's dismissal.

Tribunal findings

(19) The unanimous judgment of the tribunal was that C's complaint of racial discrimination was not made out and it was dismissed.

(20) *Comparator.* C's chosen comparator was a white Portuguese person who would not have been dismissed in the way and in the circumstances that C was, and/or who was promoted when C was dismissed.

(21) *Has C proved facts from which the Tribunal could conclude that the treatment was because of her race?* The tribunal found as follows:

21.1 C had been treated unreasonably, in that no proper process had been followed with regard to any investigation or disciplinary hearing in connection with allegations about her conduct or capability; R had failed in that regard to follow its own procedures; however, the tribunal accepted the evidence advanced by both

R's witnesses, which the tribunal regarded as being supported by the documents, that R had in practice disregarded a fair procedure when it dismissed *anyone* who had less than two years' service. The tribunal noted in particular that the dismissal letter sent to C was in virtually identical terms to (i) that sent by X's predecessor, Y, who was white British [against whom no complaint was or had been made] and (ii) that sent by X to B, described as white European; and (iii) was not dissimilar in terms to that sent by X to D, described as white European. As indicated by the EAT in *Laing* and approved by the Court of Appeal in *Madarassy*, having regard to all the evidence, the treatment or mistreatment (of others by the alleged discriminator) can be a highly material fact. On balance, the tribunal did not believe that the unreasonable treatment meted out to C was aimed only at her or at individuals of her race; it believed that all employees with less than two years' service were treated in this dismissive and unfair way by R. The tribunal was not convinced on the evidence before it that M and/or the hypothetical comparator would have been treated differently from C in similar circumstances relating to dissatisfaction with the way they carried out their jobs. On that basis, the tribunal did not find that this amounted to a proven fact from which it could conclude that C's less favourable treatment was because of race.

21.2 R was inconsistent in the reason it gave for C's dismissal – it had originally given no reason for the dismissal; subsequently it had said it was for 'operational' reasons; later, the letter of explanation set out reasons relating to C's capability. The tribunal accepted that R knew staff with less than two years' service did not have to be given a reason for dismissal. On balance, the tribunal did not believe that this alleged inconsistency amounted to a proven fact from which it could conclude that C's less favourable treatment was because of race.

21.3 A white Portuguese person eventually got C's job. Having heard the sworn testimony of M, who was a black African, the tribunal was satisfied that he had been offered the job by R. The tribunal did not find that the eventual appointment of a white Portuguese man amounted to a proven fact from which it could conclude that C's less favourable treatment was because of race. Neither did it give rise to any inference that C's treatment was because of race.

21.4 *Statistical evidence.* As far as statistics were concerned, there had been mainly black Africans in the workplace before X arrived. After he arrived, 22 out of 39 staff were white, of whom 16 were white European. Out of a total of 29 leavers between April 2019 and February 2020, there were 10 (British and European) white leavers (6 of whom were dismissed and 4 of whom had resigned (one of whom returned)); in contrast there had been 19 (African, British and European) black leavers, of whom only 2 had resigned. Proportionately, C relied on these figures to support her allegation that X was dismissing black Africans and replacing them with white Europeans. There was no specific information available as to who, in terms of race, had replaced those who had been dismissed over this period, although by extrapolation from the information to answers in the Questionnaire, it would appear that out of a total of 69 staff recruited, 23 were black Africans, of whom 11 left [just under 50%] and 22 were white Europeans, of whom 6 left [just under 25%]. There is clearly, on any analysis, a very high turnover of staff – of 69 recruited, 30 had left and 39 had remained. The statistics relating to black leavers did on their face appear to be significant – there was a higher proportion of black leavers over that period, and particularly black leavers who were dismissed (17/29 compared to 6/29). R relied upon the fact that, out of the sites managed by X and/ or over which he had responsibility for recruitment, almost half of the managers who were in a position directly comparable to that of C were black African. There was only one Portuguese manager. Further, if the leaving figures were narrowed down from the broad groupings replied upon by C [all blacks against all whites], so as to focus on the treatment of black Africans against white Europeans, the apparent disparity between dismissals decreased quite significantly – 11 black Africans compared to 6 white Europeans. The statistics indicated that 6 out of 10 white people were dismissed rather than resigned, and that 17 out of 19 black people were dismissed rather than resigned. There was a slight weighting in favour of black people over white people in the tribunal's judgment, when looked at in the round; while the statistical evidence provided some support for C's thesis, it was not particularly determinative and was not, in isolation, sufficient to amount to a fact from which it could conclude that this dismissal was because of race. It was not enough to shift the burden onto R to give an explanation.

(22)   On balance, therefore, it was the tribunal's judgment that C had not succeeded in discharging the initial burden of proof to show facts from which the tribunal could conclude that her dismissal because of race, and she accordingly did not get to stage two, such as to require an explanation from R.

(23)   The tribunal added that in case it was wrong with regard to its assessment of the evidence at stage one, it would in any event have found that R had proved that it did not treat C any less favourably in any sense whatsoever because of race. In particular, the tribunal found R had proved to its satisfaction two matters, which it regarded as compelling, namely, that:

23.1   prior to the appointment of N, the job had been offered to M, who had turned it down;

23.2   R treated everyone with less than two years' service in the same unreasonable way.

(24)   On that basis, it was the unanimous decision of the tribunal that C's claim for race discrimination failed.

SUMMARY

This chapter has looked at direct discrimination in respect of the following protected characteristics listed in s 4 of the Equality Act 2010:

(a)   sex;

(b)   marriage and civil partnership;

(c)   pregnancy and maternity;

(d)   gender reassignment;

(e)   race;

(f)   religion or belief;

(g)   sexual orientation (**9.1**).

(Age and disability are dealt with in separate chapters.)

One of the four main types of discrimination in the employment field outlawed by UK legislation is direct discrimination. Direct discrimination occurs when the reason for a person being treated less favourably than another is because of one of the protected characteristics (sex, race, religion or belief, sexual orientation, age, etc). The definition of direct discrimination is set out in s 13 of the Equality Act 2010 (**9.2**).

Less favourable treatment is a wide concept, which covers any 'disadvantage' – it does not require any tangible loss (**9.2.5**). Motive or intention is irrelevant and there is no defence once direct discrimination has been proved (save for age discrimination). There are special rules relating to pregnancy and maternity (**9.4**).

The burden of proving discrimination is a shifting one. The burden starts with the claimant. Once the claimant has established sufficient facts that, in the absence of any other explanation, point to a breach, the burden shifts to the employer. Section 136 provides that where a complainant can establish facts from which a tribunal could decide that there has been a contravention of a provision of the Equality Act 2010, the tribunal *must* find unlawful discrimination, *unless* the employer shows that it did not contravene the provision (**9.5**).

Remedies and enforcement are dealt with at **8.8**. Tribunals may, on making a finding of discrimination, as they consider just and equitable, make:

(a)   an order declaring the rights of the complainant;

(b)   an order requiring the respondent to pay the complainant compensation; and/or

(c)   a recommendation that the respondent take, within a specified period, practicable action to obviate or reduce the adverse effect of any act of discrimination.

The general principle as far as compensation is concerned is that, as far as possible, complainants should be placed in the same position as they would have been but for the unlawful act (see *Ministry of Defence v Wheeler* [1998] IRLR 23). In addition to awarding compensation for foreseeable damage arising directly from the unlawful act, a tribunal has jurisdiction to award compensation for personal injury, including both physical and psychiatric injury, and for injury to feelings (**8.8.2.2**).

A flowchart summarising direct discrimination is set out at **Figure 9.1**.

Figure 9.1 Flowchart – Direct Discrimination

ELIGIBILITY

time-limit – within 3 months of act of discrimination

UNLAWFUL ACT

discrimination in recruitment, promotion, dismissal, harassment, post-employment matters or subjecting a person to detriment

TYPE OF CLAIM

[NB some situations can give rise to more than one type of discrimination claim]

DIRECT DISCRIMINATION

- Has C been treated differently and less favourably because of a protected characteristic?
- Need actual or hypothetical comparator (*Shamoon*)?
- 'Reason why question'
- *Barton v Investec/Igen v Wong*
  - initial evidential burden on C to prove facts from which ET could conclude that reason for less favourable treatment is because of sex, etc
  - legal burden passes to R to show cogent reason for less favourable treatment; it was in no way whatsoever to do with C's sex, etc
  - if R's explanation is inadequate, ET must find that R committed an act of unlawful discrimination
- Exception. Is there an occupational requirement (OR) exception?

NO DEFENCE

VICARIOUS LIABILITY

R will be vicariously liable for acts of employees committed in the course of employment (*Jones v Tower Boot Co/Chief Constable of Lincolnshire Police v Stubbs/Bellmann v Northampton* etc) unless R took all reasonably practicable steps to stop/avoid the discrimination (statutory defence – s 109(4))

REMEDIES

- declaration of employee's rights
- recommendation that employer take action to alleviate or reduce the effect of the discrimination on C or the wider workforce
- order for compensation (no maximum)
  - pecuniary losses
  - aggravated damages if employer has behaved in a high-handed, malicious, insulting or aggressive manner
  - injury to feelings (*Vento/Da'Bell*)
  - psychiatric or physical injury
  - possibility of exemplary damages
  - increase/decrease for any unreasonable failure to comply with the Acas Code of Practice

CHAPTER 10

INDIRECT DISCRIMINATION

10.1	Introduction	451
10.2	Indirect discrimination	451
10.3	Burden of proof	463
10.4	Remedies	464
	Summary	464

LEARNING OUTCOMES

After reading this chapter you will be able to:

- understand the definition of indirect discrimination
- explain what is meant by the shifting burden of proof
- describe how the justification defence works
- list the potential remedies that are available where a complaint of indirect discrimination is made out.

10.1 INTRODUCTION

This chapter considers indirect discrimination in respect of the following protected characteristics listed in s 4 of the Equality Act 2010 (see **8.2.1**):

- gender reassignment (s 7)
- marriage and civil partnership (s 8)
- race (s 9)
- religion or belief (s 10)
- sex (s 11)
- sexual orientation (s 12)
- pregnancy and maternity (s 18).

This chapter refers, by way of illustration and example, to the pre- and post-Equality Act 2010 case law.

10.2 INDIRECT DISCRIMINATION

10.2.1 Definition

Indirect discrimination occurs when there is equal treatment of all groups but the effect of the provision, criterion or practice (PCP) imposed by an employer has a disproportionate adverse impact on one group, unless the requirement can be justified. The definition of indirect discrimination is set out in s 19 of the Act:

> (1)   A person (A) discriminates against another (B) if A applies to B a provision, criterion or practice which is discriminatory in relation to a relevant protected characteristic of B's.
>
> (2)   For the purposes of subsection (1), a provision, criterion or practice is discriminatory in relation to a relevant protected characteristic of B's if—
>
> (a)   A applies, or would apply, it to persons with whom B does not share the characteristic,

(b)   it puts, or would put, persons with whom B shares the characteristic at a particular disadvantage when compared with persons with whom B does not share it,

(c)   it puts, or would put, B at that disadvantage, and

(d)   A cannot show it to be a proportionate means of achieving a legitimate aim.

Baroness Hale said in *Secretary of State for Trade and Industry v Rutherford and Another* [2006] IRLR 551, HL, that some points stand out:

(a)   the concept is normally applied to a rule or requirement which *selects* people for a particular advantage or disadvantage;

(b)   the rule is applied to a group of people who *want* something. The disparate impact complained of is that they cannot have what they want because of the rule, whereas others can.

The Explanatory Notes provide examples:

•   A woman is forced to leave her job because her employer operates a practice that staff must work in a shift pattern which she is unable to comply with because she needs to look after her children at particular times of day, and no allowances are made because of those needs. This would put women (who are shown to be more likely to be responsible for childcare) at a disadvantage, and the employer will have indirectly discriminated against the woman unless the practice can be justified.

•   An observant Jewish engineer who is seeking an advanced diploma decides (even though he is sufficiently qualified to do so) not to apply to a specialist training company because it invariably undertakes the selection exercises for the relevant course on Saturdays. The company will have indirectly discriminated against the engineer unless the practice can be justified.

Other examples include the following:

(a)   A Sikh boy who was refused entrance to public school unless he cut his hair and stopped wearing a turban was indirectly discriminated against (*Mandla (Sewa Singh) and Another v Dowell Lee and Another* [1983] 2 AC 548; see now the approach in *R (on the application of Watkins-Singh) v Aberdare Girls' High School and Another* [2008] EWHC 1865 (Admin) and *G v Headteacher and Governors of St Gregory's Catholic Science College* [2011] EWHC 1452 (Admin), discussed at **10.2.3** below). Readers should note that on 1 October 2015, the right for Sikhs to wear turbans instead of safety helmets was extended to most workplaces.

(b)   To impose a requirement that a job applicant must weigh at least 12 stone would be discriminatory against women unless the minimum weight was a genuine requirement of the job.

(c)   The imposition of an age requirement of 17½ to 28 for promotion to executive officer was held to be indirect 'discriminatory', as more women than men would be out of the labour market between those ages having children. It could also discriminate against immigrant applicants, who may obtain qualifications at a later age than those educated in the UK.

(d)   The requirement that an employee should work full time as opposed to part time may indirectly discriminate against women (*Home Office v Holmes* [1984] 3 All ER 549).

(e)   In order to increase efficiency a company decided that no holidays could be taken during the May to July peak period. When Eid fell in June 1992, the company refused to make any exceptions to its policy, even though its Muslim employees offered to work extra hours to compensate. The rule was indirectly discriminatory (*JH Walker Ltd v Hussain and Others* [1996] IRLR 11).

(f)   A requirement to be available for duty 24 hours a day, seven days a week, taken together with a restriction on bringing relatives abroad to facilitate childcare, was indirectly discriminatory on grounds of sex and race (*Ministry of Defence v DeBique* (UKEAT/0048/09)).

(g)   A height requirement for police was not justified (*Ypourgos Esoterikon and Another v Kalliri* (Case C-409/16)).

Elements of an indirect discrimination claim

To bring a claim of indirect discrimination, a claimant must first show that he belongs to a particular protected group. He must also show that he is put to the disadvantage to which the protected group to which he belongs is put. A provision, criterion or practice (PCP) must then be identified which is applied to the claimant and has or would have an adverse impact on the claimant. The PCP must be apparently neutral; if it is premised on a rule that is itself discriminatory, the claim is likely to be one of direct discrimination (*James v Eastleigh Borough Council* [1990] ICR 554).

The only defence to an indirect discrimination claim is justification, ie that the application of the PCP constituted a proportionate means of achieving a legitimate aim.

10.2.2 Meaning of provision, criterion or practice

The phrase 'provision, criterion or practice' (PCP) is not defined but must be apparently neutral and will cover informal and formal working practices, and will therefore allow for examination of, for example, recruitment and promotion policies and working practices that do not operate as absolute requirements for the job in question (see, eg, *BA plc v Sturmer* [2005] IRLR 862). The EAT held in *Nottingham City Transport Ltd v Harvey* (UKEAT/0032/12) that a one-off flawed disciplinary procedure did not amount to a PCP. A practice, it held, must have an element of repetition. See too *H Fox (Father of G Fox, deceased) v BA plc* (UKEAT/0315/14). However, it can be sufficient for it to be applied to just the claimant.

It is necessary to determine a PCP in order to assess whether something an employer does to its employees gives rise to a difference in outcome, or has an adverse disparate impact, depending on the characteristics of its employees. In indirect discrimination claims, the adverse disparate impact must be shown to affect one group (to which the claimant belongs) more than it does to another group. Defining the PCP is key to finding whether there has been indirect discrimination. The leading decision is *Environment Agency v Rowan* [2008] IRLR 20, which was approved by the Court of Appeal in *Newham Sixth Form College v Sanders* [2014] EWCA Civ 734 and in *Brangwyn v South Warwickshire NHS Foundation Trust* [2018] EWCA Civ 2235. See also *Unison v Lord Chancellor* [2017] UKSC 51 at [121]–[131].

For a recent useful decision in the context of disability discrimination (see **Chapter 13**), see the Court of Appeal's decision in *Ishola v Transport for London* [2020] EWCA Civ 112, where Simler LJ stated:

> In my judgment, however widely and purposively the concept of a PCP is to be interpreted, it does not apply to every act of unfair treatment of a particular employee. That is not the mischief which the concept of indirect discrimination and the duty to make reasonable adjustments are intended to address. If an employer unfairly treats an employee by an act or decision and neither direct discrimination nor disability related discrimination is made out because the act or decision was not done/made by reason of disability or other relevant ground, it is artificial and wrong to seek to convert them by a process of abstraction into the application of a discriminatory PCP.
>
> In context, and having regard to the function and purpose of the PCP in the Equality Act 2010, all three words carry the connotation of a state of affairs (whether framed positively or negatively and however informal) indicating how similar cases are generally treated or how a similar case would be treated if it occurred again. It seems to me that 'practice' here connotes some form of continuum in the sense that it is the way in which things generally are or will be done. That does not mean it is necessary for the PCP or 'practice' to have been applied to anyone else in fact. Something may be a practice or done 'in practice' if it carries with it an indication that it will or would be done again in future if a hypothetical similar case arises. Like Kerr J, I consider that although a one-off decision or act can be a practice, it is not necessarily one.
>
> In that sense, the one-off decision treated as a PCP in *Starmer* is readily understandable as a decision that would have been applied in future to similarly situated employees. However, in the case of a one-off decision in an individual case where there is nothing to indicate that the decision would apply in future, it seems to me the position is different. It is in that sense that Langstaff J referred to 'practice'

as having something of the element of repetition about it. In the *Nottingham* case in contrast to *Starmer*, the PCP relied on was the application of the employer's disciplinary process as applied and (no doubt wrongly) understood by a particular individual; and in particular his failure to address issues that might have exonerated the employee or give credence to mitigating factors. There was nothing to suggest the employer made a practice of holding disciplinary hearings in that unfair way. This was a one-off application of the disciplinary process to an individual's case and by inference, there was nothing to indicate that a hypothetical comparator would (in future) be treated in the same wrong and unfair way.

10.2.3   Impact of provision – group disadvantage

PCPS cannot be considered in isolation. The adverse disparate impact must also be established. Once a PCP has been established, the complainant must show that the PCP is to the disadvantage of his or her group. Before any assessment of the impact of the PCP can be made, the appropriate pool for comparison must be identified. There has been some doubt as to whether the identification of the appropriate pool for comparison is a question of fact or law for the tribunal. If it is a question of fact, that means that a tribunal's decision cannot easily be appealed.

However, in *Allonby v Accrington and Rossendale College and Others* [2001] IRLR 364, Sedley LJ characterised the identification of the pool as a 'matter ... of logic', such that once the PCP has been identified, 'there is likely to be only one pool which serves to test its effect'. If the wrong pool is used, this will probably now be an error of law.

In *Jones v University of Manchester* [1993] IRLR 218 (a claim under the SDA 1975), the University had advertised a post requiring a graduate aged between 27 and 35. Mrs Jones argued that this indirectly discriminated against women. She was aged 46. The pool for comparison, Mrs Jones argued, should be graduates who had obtained their degrees as mature students. The tribunal agreed and upheld her complaint, as statistics showed that the proportion of women graduates obtaining their degrees as mature students (aged over 25) who could comply with the requirement was considerably smaller than the proportion of male graduates who had obtained their degrees as mature students. However, the EAT held that the wrong pool for comparison had been chosen, and the Court of Appeal upheld this view. The Court held that the appropriate pool for comparison was all men and women with the required qualifications for the job, not including the requirement complained of (ie, all graduates with relevant experience, ignoring age, and not just those who had graduated as mature students).

It will often be the case in recruitment situations that the appropriate pool for comparison is all those who are qualified for the post in question, including all those who would be so qualified were it not for the alleged discriminatory requirement. In other cases, where the complainant alleges that a practice of the employer is discriminatory, the pool might be the workforce to whom that requirement applies (see, eg, *London Underground Ltd v Edwards* [1998] IRLR 364, where the pool was all London Underground train drivers). The EAT held, in *Naeem v Secretary of State for Justice* (UKEAT/0215/14) that the tribunal had erred in selecting a pool comprised of all prison chaplains to whom the PCP applied. To include pre-2002 chaplains, when no Muslim chaplains were recruited pre-2002, only 'served to highlight a material difference between the [two groups]'. The PCP could only be tested in relation to persons employed since 2002.

In *Dobson v North Cumbria Integrated Care NHS Foundation Trust* (UKEAT/0220/19), the claimant was employed as a community nurse; she worked fixed days per week. The Trust introduced a requirement to work flexibly, including weekends. Because of her caring responsibilities for three children, the claimant could not comply and she was dismissed. The EAT held that the tribunal had erred in limiting the pool for comparison to the team in which the claimant worked:

The provision, criterion or practice (PCP) in this case was the requirement to work flexibly, including at weekends. That PCP was applied to all community nurses across the Trust. Logic therefore dictated that the appropriate pool for comparison was all community nurses.

Once a pool for comparison has been established, the tribunal must consider whether the PCP *would* put persons of the group in question at a *particular disadvantage* when compared to persons of the other group. Thus, for example, in a indirect sex discrimination claim, the tribunal must compare the proportion of women within the pool who suffer a disadvantage with the proportion of men. Under the old law it was necessary to show that the proportion of one sex or one race *who could comply* with the requirement was *considerably smaller* than that of the comparative group. The change suggested that statistical evidence would not always be required to prove this.

In *Homer v Chief Constable of West Yorkshire Police* [2012] IRLR 601, the Supreme Court confirmed that the new formulation was intended to do away with statistical comparisons where no statistics exist, and that now what is required is a particular disadvantage when compared with others who do not share the protected characteristic in question. On that basis, the employer's introduction of the need to have a degree to reach a higher grade worked to the comparative disadvantage of persons approaching compulsory retirement age, and was indirectly discriminatory on the ground of age.

In *London Underground Ltd v Edwards* (above) (a sex discrimination case), London Underground imposed a requirement to work flexible hours. All 2,023 men could comply (100%) and 20 out of the 21 women could comply (95.2%). The Court of Appeal held that the requirement was indirectly discriminatory. The Court accepted that a percentage difference of no more than 5% would often lead a tribunal to the conclusion that the then 'considerably smaller' requirement had *not* been made out. However, by taking into account wider national statistics (10 lone mothers for each father), the Court of Appeal was able to uphold the tribunal's findings of indirect discrimination. A similar approach was taken by the EAT in *Chief Constable of Avon Constabulary v Chew* (UKEAT/503/00), [2001] All ER (D) 101 (Sep). The EAT held in *Dobson v North Cumbria Integrated Care NHS Foundation Trust* (above) that the fact that women still bear a greater burden of childcare is a matter of which judicial notice can (and should) be taken without further inquiry. For that reason, women are less likely to be able to accommodate certain working patterns than men, and group disadvantage was therefore established. The case was remitted on the question of justification (and unfair dismissal).

In *Cross and Others v BA plc* [2005] IRLR 423, the EAT upheld the tribunal's decision that the provision, providing for a compulsory retirement age of 55 for cabin crew and pilots, was to the detriment of a considerably larger proportion of women than men. The statistics presented to the tribunal showed that 90.28% of men were disadvantaged compared to 98.55% of women; and that 9.72% of men could comply with the provision, etc, compared to 1.45% of women. The employer argued on appeal that the tribunal should have ignored the smaller advantaged group and instead concentrated on the disadvantaged group statistics; it would, according to the employer, have been bound to find that there was no clear case of adverse impact. The EAT held that the tribunal was entitled to look at all the figures; and that in cases of less obvious adverse impact it should use more than one form of comparison.

In 1998, a challenge was launched to the UK's cut-off age of 65 for unfair dismissal claims and redundancy compensation (*Secretary of State for Trade and Industry v Rutherford and Another* [2006] IRLR 551, HL). In the absence of any age equality legislation at that time, the claim was brought based on indirect sex discrimination. Mr Rutherford had been made redundant in 1998 at the age of 67 by his employer, Harvest Town Circle Ltd. He claimed that the cut-off age of 65 indirectly discriminated against men, because more men than women continued to work past 65. Harvest subsequently went into liquidation and the defence of the claim was taken over by the Secretary of State. A tribunal held that the cut-off provisions did amount to indirect sex discrimination against men. It found, after a detailed statistical analysis, that in the pool of employees affected by the cut off, the proportion of men who were disadvantaged (ie all those over 65) was greater than the proportion of disadvantaged women. The EAT ([2001] IRLR 599 and [2003] IRLR 858) and the Court of Appeal ([2004] IRLR 892) disagreed with the way the tribunal had analysed the statistics. The case went to the House of Lords, which gave its decision on 3 May 2006. Unhelpfully, while there was a unanimous conclusion that there was no unlawful discrimination, each of their Lordships adopted a slightly different approach. However, the analysis in the House of Lords judgment of the principles of and the approach to the indirect discrimination claims is important, and should be considered fully by anyone wishing to bring or defend an indirect discrimination claim. The point to note here is that the House of Lords focused on relative proportions within the *advantaged* group in this case.

However, the Court of Appeal, in *Grundy v BA plc* [2007] EWCA Civ 1020, held that the employment tribunal did not err when it focused on the *disadvantaged* group, where the women disadvantaged outnumbered men 14:1, rather than on the make-up of the advantaged group, which contained 99% of all employees in the relevant pool, when deciding whether the practice disadvantaged considerably more women. The Court said that there is no rule that the focus should be on the advantaged or disadvantaged group. It depends on the facts. The pool, said the Court of Appeal,

> must be one which suitably tests the particular discrimination complained of; [there is no universal formula for locating the correct pool]. It needs to include, but not be limited to, those affected by the term of which complaint is made, which can be expected to include both people who can and people who cannot comply with it.

In *Eweida v British Airways* [2009] IRLR 78, the EAT said that a dress code that prevented an employee from wearing a visible cross was not unlawful indirect discrimination. British Airways' policy did not permit personal items of jewellery to be visible over a uniform unless they were mandatory religious items which could not be concealed. When E insisted on wearing her cross visibly, having been warned not to do so, she was sent home. She was offered an alternative job for which a uniform was not required, but she refused it. She said that the policy was indirectly discriminatory. The EAT said that the policy did not put Christians as a group at a *particular disadvantage*, as there was no evidence that other Christians felt disadvantaged, and this decision was upheld by the Court of Appeal ([2010] EWCA Civ 80). However, in *Eweida and Others v UK* [2013] ECHR 37 the ECtHR held that she had been indirectly discriminated against because the policy was not justified as her beliefs were not reasonably accommodated. The Court held that the domestic courts accorded too much weight to the employer's wish to project a certain corporate image.

In *Mba v Mayor and Burgesses of the London Borough of Merton* [2013] EWCA Civ 1562, when a practising Christian was rostered to work on Sundays, she brought an indirect discrimination claim. The Court of Appeal held that group disadvantage is required, even in cases where Article 9 is engaged because Article 9 is not directly enforceable in the employment tribunal. However, the Article 9 dimension meant that the employment tribunal should not have taken into account the fact that the claimant's religious belief was not a core belief of her religion when assessing justification.

The ECtHR has issued a guidance note on 'Religion or Belief and the Workplace', available at <http://www.equalityhumanrights.com>. There is also, separately, an Acas guidance note on dress codes, available at <http://www.acas.org.uk/dresscode>.

In *G v Headteacher and Governors of St Gregory's Catholic Science College* [2011] EWHC 1452 (Admin), the High Court had to consider whether a school's uniform and hair policy, which prohibited boys from wearing their hair in cornrows, was unlawful discrimination on sex and/or racial grounds. G, who was 11 and of African-Caribbean ethnicity, was due to start his secondary education at St Gregory's Catholic Science College, a strict but high-performing inner-London school. Since birth, G had not cut his hair and, in accordance with family tradition, kept his hair in cornrows. African-Caribbean girls were permitted to wear their hair in cornrows as the School recognised that this helped keep long hair neat and under control. The school's written uniform policy did not explicitly prohibit cornrows for boys, but the cornrow ban was outlined at an introductory meeting at the school in September 2009, which G missed. G was unwilling to comply with the school's policy and was therefore unable to take up his place at the school. He subsequently brought judicial review proceedings, alleging that the school's policy amounted to indirect race discrimination and sex discrimination. (He also launched a claim for damages in the county court alleging sex and race discrimination.)

The school had a strong Catholic ethos. One of its principal aims behind the ban on cornrows was to keep gang culture out of the school, to avoid ethnic tensions and violence. The school considered that distinctive haircuts could be 'badges of ethnic or gang identity in an aggressive or unwelcome sense and can help foster disunity rather than unity'. It therefore adopted a zero tolerance approach to all male hairstyles.

To prove indirect race discrimination, G had to show that the school's policy placed a racial group at a particular disadvantage and also that he, as an individual, suffered that disadvantage. The case is a good example of the difficulties of proving group discrimination where not all those who share a protected characteristic are equally affected by the policy. Compare *Mandla* (see **10.2.1**), where all Sikh men are required to wear their hair long and would be disadvantaged by a prohibition on wearing turbans, with *Eweida* (above), where the Court found that the employee's belief in the requirement to wear a visible cross was a personal one. The courts have been clear that 'the whole purpose of indirect discrimination is to deal with the problem of group discrimination' (per Elias J in *Eweida*), but there is no agreement as to how large or small a group must be to be protected. The Court of Appeal in *Eweida* expressed concern that a wide interpretation of 'group' risks placing 'an impossible burden on employers to anticipate and provide for what may be parochial or even factitious beliefs in society at large'.

In G's case, the judge concluded that the 'group disadvantage test' was satisfied as there was evidence that there were groups of African-Caribbean ethnicity who, for reasons based on their culture and ethnicity, regard the cutting of their hair to be wrong, so that it is necessary for them to keep their hair in cornrows. Collins J said:

> It may be that those who regard it as an obligation rather than a preference are in the minority, but on the material before me, I am satisfied that there is a group who could be particularly disadvantaged by a refusal to permit them to wear their hair in cornrows.

The judge also concluded that the school's refusal to allow G to attend school, and the trauma he suffered in being turned away on his first day, amounted to a sufficient individual disadvantage. The judge rejected the school's defence of justification, namely that its policy was a 'proportionate means of achieving a legitimate aim'. Collins J concluded that although the aim of the policy was legitimate, the school's argument that introducing exceptions would undermine the whole uniform policy was not a valid one. He concluded that a blanket policy without exceptions could not be justified.

The judge rejected G's sex discrimination claim. Applying *Smith v Safeway* [1996] ICR 868, he concluded a dress code will not be discriminatory where it enforces a common standard of conventionality for both men and women. On the facts, the school's rationale for permitting African-Caribbean girls to wear their hair in cornrows (keeping long hair neat and under control) was not evidence of sex discrimination.

The Supreme Court in joined appeals in *Essop v Home Office (UK Border Agency); Naeem v Secretary of State for Justice* [2017] UKSC 27 considered issues arising from claims of indirect discrimination on grounds of race and/or age and/or religion. Mr Essop was the lead appellant in a group of 49 people, six of whom had been chosen as test cases. They are, or were, all employed by the Home Office. They were required to pass a Core Skills Assessment (CSA) as a prerequisite to promotion to certain civil service grades. A report in 2010 established that

Black and Minority Ethnic (BME) candidates, and older candidates, had lower pass rates than white and younger candidates. No-one had been able to identify why this was. The claims alleged that the requirement to pass the CSA constituted indirect discrimination on the grounds of race or age. The Home Office argued that s 19(2)(b) of the Equality Act 2010 required the appellants to prove the reason for the lower pass rate. The Court of Appeal agreed, upholding the decision of the Employment Judge.

Mr Naeem is an imam who works as a chaplain in the Prison Service. Before 2002, Muslim chaplains were engaged on a sessional basis only, because it was believed that there were too few Muslim prisoners to justify employing them on a salaried basis, as some Christian chaplains were. Mr Naeem worked on a sessional basis from 2001 but in 2004 became a salaried employee. At this date the pay scheme for chaplains incorporated pay progression over time. The average length of service of Christian chaplains was longer, which led to a higher average basic pay. Mr Naeem argued that the incremental pay scheme was indirectly discriminatory against Muslim or Asian chaplains, resulting in lower pay in a post where length of service served no useful purpose as a reflection of ability or experience. Mr Naeem's claim was rejected by the employment tribunal which found that the indirect discrimination was justified. The EAT held that the scheme was not indirectly discriminatory at all because chaplains employed before 2002 should be excluded from the comparison between the two groups. The Court of Appeal held that it was not enough to show that the length of service criterion had a disparate impact upon Muslim chaplains: it was also necessary to show that the reason for that disparate impact was something peculiar to the protected characteristic of race or religion.

The Supreme Court unanimously allowed the *Essop* appeal. It unanimously dismissed Mr Naeem's appeal but confirmed the point that it is not necessary to answer the 'reason why' question. Mr Naeem lost because the employer had justified the PCP – the pay structure was a proportionate means of achieving a legitimate aim. The judgment makes clear that:

(a)   once it has been established (whether by statistical evidence or otherwise) that a PCP places people with relevant protected characteristics at a particular disadvantage compared with others, that is sufficient to require objective justification by a respondent of its use of the PCP;

(b)   it is irrelevant whether or not the reason why the PCP puts that group at a particular disadvantage is itself related to the protected characteristic;

(c)   the only required causal link is between the PCP and the particular disadvantage.

In the *Essop* case, it was irrelevant that some BME or older candidates could pass the CSA: the group was at a disadvantage because the proportion who could pass was smaller than the proportion of white or younger candidates. It is always open to a respondent to show that the PCP is justified. There may well be a good reason for it. A wise employer will, however, try to see if PCPs which do have a disparate impact can be modified to remove that impact while achieving the desired result. The disadvantage suffered by the individual must correspond with the disadvantage suffered by the group. The disadvantage in *Essop* was that members of the group failed the CSA disproportionately and the appellants suffered this disadvantage. However, a candidate who fails the CSA because he did not prepare or did not turn up for or finish the CSA has not suffered harm as a result of the PCP in question, and in such a case it is open to the respondent to show that the causal link between the PCP and the individual disadvantage is absent.

In Mr Naeem's case, the reason why the pay scale put Muslim chaplains at a disadvantage was known. It was because they have on average shorter lengths of service than Christian chaplains. The Court of Appeal was wrong to require the reason to relate to the protected characteristic. The pool of comparators comprises all workers affected by the PCP in question. In this case the incremental pay structure affected all chaplains in the Prison Service and this did put the Muslim chaplains at a disadvantage compared with the Christians. As regards justification, it was not in dispute that the pay scheme had a legitimate aim but the means adopted needed to be proportionate. The employment tribunal found as a fact that six years was the most required for newly appointed chaplains to have the skills and experience for reward at the top of the scale, but that in the circumstances the disadvantage suffered by Mr Naeem was no more than was necessary as the transition to a new shorter pay scale took its course. This Supreme Court said that was the correct test. It is not open to the courts on an appeal to disturb that finding, even if there were alternative means to reduce the disadvantage more quickly which could have been considered.

The decision in these two cases has been seen by commentators as helpful for both employers and employees. As far as employees are concerned, while a claimant will still need to show a causal link between the PCP and their own disadvantage, the Court stated that the purpose behind indirect discrimination legislation is to protect people with a protected characteristic from suffering disadvantage where an apparently neutral PCP is applied. It is about achieving a level playing field and removing hidden barriers. This makes it clear therefore that there is no obligation on an employee to explain why a PCP puts a group at a disadvantage when compared to others: it is enough simply to show that there is disadvantage. However, there is positive news for employers as well: the Court said that the requirement to justify a PCP should not be seen as placing an unreasonable burden on employers or as 'casting some sort of stigma upon them'. The Court also clarified that all workers affected by a PCP, whether positively or negatively, should be placed in the pool for comparison. There is a useful note about the cases on the 11KBW website by Sean Jones QC and Amy Rogers, entitled 'The Supreme Court makes indirect discrimination simple again'.

The EAT held in *Pendleton v Derbyshire CC & Another* (UKEAT/0238/15) that those who hold a religious belief in the sanctity of marriage face a particular disadvantage if forced to choose between their husband/wife and their career.

10.2.4 Complainant's disadvantage

The complainant must suffer a disadvantage and show why the PCP caused that disadvantage. Hypothetical cases cannot be brought. The House of Lords confirmed in *Shamoon v Chief Constable of the Royal Ulster Constabulary* [2003] IRLR 285 that, in order to qualify as a disadvantage, the disadvantage must arise in the employment field. But once this requirement is satisfied, as the House of Lords confirmed in *Shamoon*, the only other limitation that can be read into the words is:

> Is the treatment of such a kind that a reasonable worker would or might take the view that in all the circumstances it was to his detriment? An unjustified sense of grievance cannot amount to 'detriment' ... [b]ut ... it is not necessary to demonstrate some physical or economic consequence.

An obvious example of disadvantage in the employment context is not getting promoted or being dismissed.

In *Keane v Investigo and Others* (UKEAT/0389/09), the EAT dismissed the claimant's claims of age discrimination because she had applied for jobs only in order to claim compensation, and on that basis had not suffered a detriment (ie she had no interest in the job vacancies).

Readers should note the ECJ's decision in *CHEZ Razpredelenie Bulgaria* (Case C-83/14) (ECJ, 16 July 2015), which established that an individual may be able to claim indirect discrimination under the Race Discrimination Directive (2000/43) on the basis of associative discrimination. Section 19 of the Equality Act 2010 defines indirect discrimination: the complainant must share the same protected characteristic as the disadvantaged group. The ECJ decided in the *CHEZ* case that the Race Discrimination Directive does not require the complainant to share the protected characteristic (in this case, race) to bring a claim of indirect discrimination, as long as the complainant suffers the *same* disadvantage. The case illustrates the point: a utility company in Bulgaria had a practice of placing electricity meters at an unaccessible height in a district largely populated by people of Roma ethnic origin. The complainant was of non-Roma origin, but the ECJ held that she could allege indirect discrimination as she suffered the *same* disadvantage as those persons of Roma origin – namely, not being able to check electricity usage.

The judgment may mean that s 19 of the 2010 Act will need amending, but in the meantime employees could seek to rely directly or indirectly on relevant EU directives, to allege indirect discrimination (by association), where they do not share the protected characteristic.

10.2.5 Direct v indirect discrimination

Readers are referred to **8.3** above, the ECJ cases of *Achbita* and *Bougnaoui* and the judgment, in particular, of Lady Hale in *Essop and Naeem* (above) at [17]–[25].

10.2.6 Dual discrimination

In *Ministry of Defence v DeBique* (UKEAT/0048/09), the EAT held that the claimant, a female soldier from St Vincent with childcare commitments, had been the victim of sex and race discrimination by reason of two 'provisions, criteria or practices' (PCPs): one requiring that she be available for deployment on a 24/7 basis ('the 24/7 PCP'), which disadvantaged her as a female single parent; the second prohibiting her from inviting a member of her extended family not of British origin to stay with her in Services Family Accommodation (and thereby assist with childcare) ('the immigration PCP'), which disadvantaged her as a foreign national. On this basis, the EAT upheld the employment tribunal's conclusion that indirect discrimination claims under the RRA 1976 and the SDA 1975 were made out when the combined effect of the two PCPs were considered. The EAT commented that 'discrimination is often a multi-faceted experience' and should not be artificially compartmentalised. When the two PCPs were considered together, their discriminatory effect could not be justified.

10.2.7 Employer's defence

The employer must show that the PCP is 'a proportionate means of achieving a legitimate aim' (s 19(2)(d) of the Act). The Directive uses slightly different language: 'objectively justified by a legitimate aim and the means of achieving that aim are appropriate and necessary'. The (old) CRE commented as follows:

> It is our belief that the 'proportionality test' is a more limited test than that provided for by the Directive ie that the means used are 'appropriate and necessary'.

In *Chief Constable of West Midlands Police v Harrod* [2015] IRLR 790, the EAT emphasised that justification is an objective evaluation. Further what has to be justified is the outcome, not the process followed. In *Allonby v Accrington and Rossendale College and Others* [2001] IRLR 364, the Court of Appeal made it clear that

> once an employment tribunal has concluded that [the PCP] has a disparate impact on a protected group it must carry out a critical evaluation of whether the reasons demonstrate a real need to take the action in question. This should include consideration of whether there was another way to achieve the aim in question.

The EAT emphasised in *Rajaratnam v Care UK Clinical Services Ltd* (UKEAT/0435/14) that it is the rule that needs to be justified and not its application to the individual concerned.

Courts and tribunals must carry out a balancing exercise between the degree of discrimination caused and the object or aim to be achieved, taking into account the surrounding circumstances (*Cobb v Employment Secretary* [1989] IRLR 464).

The Supreme Court held, in *Homer v Chief Constable of West Yorkshire Police* [2012] UKSC 15, that to be proportionate, a measure must be an appropriate and necessary means of meeting the legitimate aim. The ECHJ held in *Dansk Jurist- og Økonomforbund v Indenrigs- og Sundhadsministeriet* [2013] EUECJ C-546/11 that actions will not be proportionate if less discriminatory means to achieve the result were available.

So, for example, a rule prohibiting beards in a chocolate factory may be considered a proportionate response and justifiable in the interests of hygiene; but rather than not employing bearded persons, the employer should look at other means of achieving the objective, such as the covering up of beards. The 'appropriate and necessary' test requires consideration of whether there are less discriminatory alternative measures to achieve the aim; the proportionality test requires the same consideration.

In *Hardys & Hansons v Lax* [2005] EWCA Civ 846, (a case under the SDA 1975), the Court of Appeal held that the 'range of reasonable responses' test (see **5.3.1.1**) does not apply when tribunals have to decide whether an otherwise discriminatory practice is objectively justified. (See too *Board of Governors of St Matthias Church of England School v Crizzle* [1993] ICR 401, *Azmi v Kirklees Metropolitan Borough Council* [2007] IRLR 484 and *Allen and Another v GMB* [2008] IRLR 690.) The Court in *Hardys* said that the principle of proportionality required the tribunal to take into account the reasonable needs of the business. But it had to make its own judgment, upon a fair and detailed analysis of the working practices and business considerations involved, as to whether the proposal was reasonably necessary. The reasonableness qualification did *not* permit the margin of discretion or range of reasonable responses for which the respondent contended. The Court also added that, where an employer is relying on the economic needs of the business, it would be expected to adduce sufficient evidence of that business need to enable the tribunal to 'set out at least a basic economic analysis of the business and its needs'.

In *XC Trains Ltd v CD* (UKEAT/0331/15) the EAT upheld the employment tribunal's decision that the requirement to work anti-social hours put women at a particular disadvantage, but held that the employment tribunal had failed to weigh the legitimate aims of the employer against the discriminatory impact of the requirement.

Examples of objective justification under the old and new definitions of 'indirect discrimination' include the following:

(a)   In *Panesar v Nestlé Co* [1980] ICR 144, a factory rule prohibiting beards and long hair had a disproportionate impact on Sikhs, but it was held to be objectively justified on the grounds of hygiene.

(b)   In *London Underground Ltd v Edwards* (a sex discrimination case) (**10.2.3** above), the EAT held that the tribunal was entitled to find that the employers had not justified the requirement to work flexible hours. There was good evidence that the employer could have made arrangements which would not have been damaging to its business plans but which would have accommodated the reasonable needs of its employees.

(c)   There is some conflicting case law on whether cost alone may be relied upon to justify an otherwise discriminatory policy. In *Cross and Others v BA plc* (**10.2.3** above), a case decided under the equivalent of the new law, the EAT held that the employment tribunal had been entitled to take the cost to the employer of changing the offending provision into account when deciding whether the employer could justify the provision. The EAT added that costs could not be the sole justification, but they were nevertheless a relevant factor. (See also *BA plc v Starmer* [2005] IRLR 862, where the employer failed in its attempt to justify a refusal to halve the hours of a full-time female airline pilot with childcare responsibilities.) In *Bressol v Gouvernement de la Communauté Française* (Case C-73/08) the ECJ considered a costs plus justification advanced by a State. In *Woodcock v Cumbria Primary Care NHS Trust* [2012] EWCA Civ 330, the Court of Appeal held that a dismissal carried out in such a way as to avoid additional costs to the Trust of the employee attaining the age of 50 years before the end of his notice period, and thus being entitled to enhanced redundancy payments, was justified because the decision to terminate his employment by reason of redundancy was genuine and legitimate, and it was a *part* of that aim to ensure that the Trust also saved money through the timing of the notice given (the 'costs plus' approach). See too *Kapenova v Department of Health*

(UKEAT/0142/13) where the Department of Health was able to rely on on a 'costs plus' justification on registration rules for trainee doctors (which operate to the disadvantage of medical students from some European countries).

(d)   In *Williams Drabble v Pathway Care Solutions Ltd and Another* (ET/2601718/04), the employment tribunal held that the employer had indirectly discriminated against a Christian employee when it imposed a requirement to work on Sundays. The employer had imposed a PCP on all staff, but it put practising Christians at a disadvantage and the employer was not able, on the facts, to show that the requirement to work on Sundays was a proportionate means of achieving a legitimate aim.

(e)   In *Azmi v Kirklees Metropolitan Borough Council* [2007] IRLR 484, the tribunal's finding was that refusing to permit a Muslim woman teacher to wear a full veil did not amount to indirect religious discrimination because the treatment was justified – the need to communicate effectively was a legitimate aim and was proportionate – the woman could wear a veil at all other times when not working directly with the children.

(f)   The ECtHR held in *Eweida & Others v UK* [2013] ECHR 37 that, while British Airways' wish to protect its image was legitimate, the policy interfered with Mrs Eweida's right to manifest her religion, and a fair balance was not struck by British Airways. Mrs Eweida's cross was discrete and did not encroach on others' interests. However, the ECtHR rejected complaints from three others (Mrs Chaplin – her cross interfered with health and safety and was therefore legitimately banned; Ms Ladele and Mr McFarlane's religious beliefs had to be balanced against competing Convention rights, and the Court allows a wide margin of appreciation when balancing competing rights).

(g)   In *Mayuuf v Governing Body of Bishop Challenor Catholic Collegiate School and Another* (ET/ 3202398/2004) (see <www.practicallaw.com/3-369-5996>), the claimant's beliefs required attendance at a mosque every Friday. The school required him to teach at that time (in 2003/04), and he brought a claim of indirect discrimination. The tribunal held that the school's actions were objectively justified, balancing the discriminatory effect on Mr Mayuuf against:

(i)   declining standards in maths and the new arrangements in place;

(ii)   the fact that all the Year 11 maths classes had to take place at the same time, so that pupils could be moved up or down between sets according to ability;

(iii) the fact that it was impossible to rewrite the timetable to free the relevant period; and

(iv)   the fact that providing a supply teacher would have affected the continuity of education and have been too costly.

(h)   In *Joseph Estorninho v Zoran Jokic t/a Zorans Delicatessen* (ET/2301487/06), the claimant was held to have been indirectly discriminated against when he was told that he would be required to work on Sundays. As a practising Catholic he attended church on a Sunday, and he was thereby placed at a 'particular disadvantage' compared with non-Catholics. Moreover, the employer had not considered other ways of arranging Sunday working, and thus had not adopted proportionate means.

(i)   In *Cherfi v G4S Security Services Ltd* (UKEAT/0379/10), the EAT upheld the tribunal's decision that a requirment that security guards be on site during the whole of their shift was a proportionate means of achieving a legitimate aim, in circumstances where the claimant had access to an on-site prayer facility and had been offered different shifts.

(j)   In *Mba v Mayor and Burgesses of the London Borough of Merton* (see **10.2.3** above), the Court of Appeal held that requiring all care workers at a children's home to work some Sundays in accordance with their contracts was objectively justified. Elias LJ pointed out in that case that the more widely shared the belief, the more difficult it may be for an employer to accommodate it.

(k)   In *Ypourgos Esoterikon and Another v Kalliri* (Case C-409/16), the ECJ held that the requirement for candidates for the Greek police academy to be at least 170cm tall amounted to indirect sex discrimination which could not be objectively justified. While ensuring operational capacity and proper functioning of the police force was a legitimate aim, maintaining a certain physical aptitude was not an appropriate way of achieving that aim.

(l)   In *City of Oxford Bus Services Ltd v Harvey* (UKEAT/0171/18) the EAT held that the employment tribunal had failed to balance the discriminatory effect of the PCP (requirement to work Fridays and Saturdays) on the claimant against the needs of the business (effects on efficiency, harmonious working, effects on others and union concerns).

(m)   In *Ix v WABE eV; MH Muller Handels GmbH v MJ* [2021] WLR(D) 399, the CJEU held that a ban on the wearing of any sign of political, philosophical or religious beliefs was capable of justification. However, a ban on wearing any 'conspicuous, large sized signs of political, philosophical or religious beliefs' was not. In the first situation, the ECJ held that a policy of 'neutrality' *could* be a legitimate aim, if there is a genuine need. In the latter case, the rule would have a greater effect on people with religious beliefs requiring larger sized signs of the belief (eg a headscarf cf a cross) and would therefore amount to direct discrimination or unjustifiable indirect discrimination. In relation to the first situation, the EHRC guidance states that 'it is very unlikely that a Tribunal would accept "neutrality" as a legitimate aim ...'. The employer would need to show that no less a restrictive way of achieving its aim was possible. Readers must also remember that CJEU decisions are no longer binding on UK courts.

10.3   BURDEN OF PROOF

The burden of proving objective justification is on the employer. The employer needs to produce cogent evidence that the justification defence is made out (see *British Airways v Starmer* [2005] IRLR 862 and *Osborne Clarke Services v Purohit* [2009] IRLR 341). However, the claimant has to show some evidence of disparate impact before the burden of proof is placed on the employer. The Court of Appeal held in *Bailey and Others v The Home Office* [2005] IRLR 369 that the tribunal had been entitled to conclude that there was a prima facie case of discrimination where the advantaged group was predominantly male but the disadvantaged group was mixed, containing both men and women. Waller LJ made clear the claimant's burden:

> [T]hus, where a difference in pay is established, and statistics seem to indicate a possibility of a disproportionate impact on women when looking at both the advantaged and disadvantaged groups as a whole, those statistics must provide sufficient evidence to get those carrying the burden over the hurdle of placing the onus on the employer ...

The Court of Appeal's judgment was given before a new definition of 'indirect discrimination' was brought into effect in October 2005 by the Employment Equality (Sex Discrimination) Regulations 2005. The definition in the Equality Act 2010 is identical. Commentators, at the time the new definition became law, queried *when* the burden of proof shifts in an indirect discrimination case. Taking the new definition into account, Claire Hockney of the EOC suggested that the burden of proof would transfer to the employer where the claimant could show:

(a)   the existence of a PCP; and

(b)   facts that 'indicate a possibility' that a particular group has been disadvantaged without the need to provide supporting statistics.

She said:

> [A]rguably, the intention of the legislation is that all the claimant is required to do is produce some evidence (even their own oral evidence) from which a tribunal could infer disparate impact. Once they do this the burden shifts to the respondent to show otherwise by cogent evidence.

A respondent could, at this stage, for example, put in evidence showing others are also at a disadvantage. This analysis still appears relevant today.

10.4 REMEDIES

See **8.8**. In a case of indirect discrimination, where the tribunal is satisfied there was no intent to discriminate, the tribunal must not award compensation without first considering whether to make a declaration or recommendation (s 124(4) and (5)).

SUMMARY

This chapter has looked at indirect discrimination in respect of the following protected characteristics listed in s 4 of the Equality Act 2010:

(a)   sex;

(b)   marriage and civil partnership;

(c)   pregnancy and maternity;

(d)   gender reassignment;

(e)   race;

(f)   religion or belief;

(g)   sexual orientation (**8.1**).

(Age and disability are dealt with in separate chapters.)

One of the four main types of discrimination in the employment field outlawed by UK legislation is indirect discrimination. Indirect discrimination occurs when there is equal treatment of all groups but the effect of a PCP imposed by an employer has a disproportionate adverse impact on one group, unless the requirement can be justified. The definition of indirect discrimination is set out in s 19 of the Equality Act 2010 (**10.2**).

Once a provision, etc has been established, the complaint must show that it is to the detriment of his group, ie it would put persons of the group at a particular disadvantage. The complainant must also suffer a disadvantage, so hypothetical cases cannot be brought (**10.2.3** and **10.2.4**). An employer has a defence to an indirect discrimination claim if he can show that the PCP is a 'proportionate means of achieving a legitimate aim' (**10.2.6**).

The burden of proving discrimination is a shifting one. The burden starts with the claimant. Once he has established sufficient facts that, in the absence of any other explanation, point to a breach, then the burden shifts to the employer. Section 136 provides that where a complainant can establish facts from which a tribunal could decide that there has been a contravention of a provision of the Equality Act 2010, the tribunal *must* find unlawful discrimination *unless* the employer shows it did not contravene the provision (**10.3** and **9.5**).

Remedies and enforcement are dealt with at **8.8**. Tribunals may, on making a finding of discrimination, as they consider just and equitable, make:

(a)   an order declaring the rights of the complainant;

(b)   an order requiring the respondent to pay to the complainant compensation; and/or

(c)   a recommendation that the respondent take, within a specified period, practicable action to obviate or reduce the adverse effect of any act of discrimination.

The general principle as far as compensation is concerned is that, as far as possible, complainants should be placed in the same position as they would have been but for the unlawful act (see *Ministry of Defence v Wheeler* [1998] IRLR 23). In addition to awarding compensation for foreseeable damage arising directly from the unlawful act, a tribunal has jurisdiction to award compensation for personal injury, including both physical and psychiatric injury, and for injury to feelings (**8.8.2.2**).

A flowchart summarising indirect discrimination is set out at **Figure 10.1**.

Figure 10.1 Flowchart – Indirect Discrimination

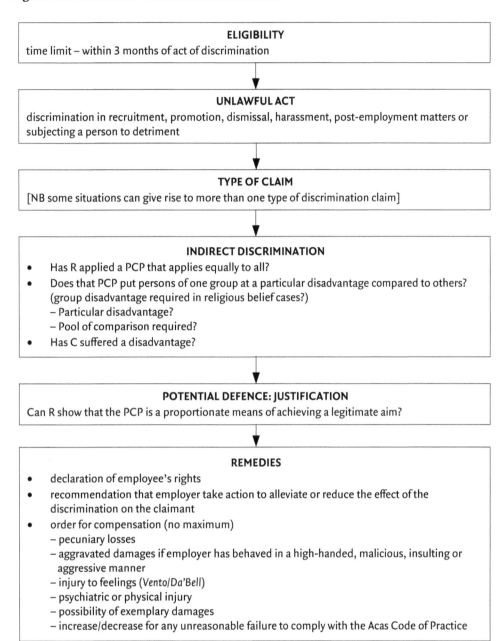

ELIGIBILITY

time limit – within 3 months of act of discrimination

UNLAWFUL ACT

discrimination in recruitment, promotion, dismissal, harassment, post-employment matters or subjecting a person to detriment

TYPE OF CLAIM

[NB some situations can give rise to more than one type of discrimination claim]

INDIRECT DISCRIMINATION

- Has R applied a PCP that applies equally to all?
- Does that PCP put persons of one group at a particular disadvantage compared to others? (group disadvantage required in religious belief cases?)
  - Particular disadvantage?
  - Pool of comparison required?
- Has C suffered a disadvantage?

POTENTIAL DEFENCE: JUSTIFICATION

Can R show that the PCP is a proportionate means of achieving a legitimate aim?

REMEDIES

- declaration of employee's rights
- recommendation that employer take action to alleviate or reduce the effect of the discrimination on the claimant
- order for compensation (no maximum)
  - pecuniary losses
  - aggravated damages if employer has behaved in a high-handed, malicious, insulting or aggressive manner
  - injury to feelings (*Vento/Da'Bell*)
  - psychiatric or physical injury
  - possibility of exemplary damages
  - increase/decrease for any unreasonable failure to comply with the Acas Code of Practice

CHAPTER 11

HARASSMENT AND VICTIMISATION

11.1	Introduction	467
11.2	Burden of proof	468
11.3	Harassment	468
11.4	Remedies for harassment	474
11.5	Employers' liability for the acts of employees	474
11.6	Employers' liability for the acts of third parties	474
11.7	Protection from Harassment Act 1997	476
11.8	Case study: harassment	476
11.9	Victimisation	481
	Summary	484

LEARNING OUTCOMES

After reading this chapter you will be able to:

- explain what is meant by harassment and what the different types of harassment are
- explain when employers are liable for the acts of third parties
- explain what is meant by victimisation
- list the potential remedies that are available where a complaint of harassment or victimisation is made out.

11.1 INTRODUCTION

This chapter considers harassment and victimisation in respect of the following protected characteristics listed in s 4 of the Equality Act 2010 (see **8.2.1**):

- gender reassignment (s 7)
- race (s 9)
- religion or belief (s 10)
- sex (s 11)
- sexual orientation (s 12).

Section 26 (harassment) does not include marriage and civil partnership, or pregnancy and maternity: this is because pregnancy and maternity are covered by harassment related to sex, and as there is no evidence that people have been harassed due to marriage and civil partnership, it was not considered necessary to include these characteristics. These grounds are not covered by European law. One view is that harassment relating to those matters may be brought under s 13 as direct discrimination; another view is that as s 26 does not specifically disapply those protected characteristics, they are still included.

In 2019, the Equality and Human Rights Commission published what it claimed to be 'the authoritative and comprehensive guide to the law and best practice' in tackling sexual harassment and harassment at work.

The Government published its response to a consultation on sexual harassment in the workplace on 21 July 2021. The Government said that it would introduce a duty requiring employers to prevent sexual harassment, 'as we believe that this will encourage employers into taking positive proactive steps to make the workplace safer for everyone'. It said it would also consider (re-)introducing protection from third party harassment (employer liability for this was contained in s 40 of the Equality Act 2010 but the relevant subsections were repealed in 2013; see **11.6** below) and whether to extend the time limit for bringing a claim to six months. In October 2022, a private members' bill, the Worker Protection (Amendment of Equality Act 2010) Bill, which introduces employers' liability for harassment of their employees by third parties and includes a duty on employers to take all reasonable steps to prevent sexual harassment of their employees, was debated for the second time in the House of Commons. This does not, however, contain any provisions relating to the extension of the time limit.

This chapter refers, by way of illustration and example, to the pre- and post-Equality Act 2010 case law.

11.2 BURDEN OF PROOF

The reversed burden of proof applies in both harassment and victimisation cases (s 136). Thus, where a prima facie case of harassment or victimisation is made out by a claimant, the tribunal will be required to find for the claimant unless the defendant can prove that his or her conduct was not unlawful (see **9.5** and **10.3**).

11.3 HARASSMENT

For a recent and thorough review of the case law on harassment, see IDS Employment Law Brief No 1151, July 2022.

11.3.1 Definition

The definition of harassment is set out in s 26 of the Act.:

(1)   A person (A) harasses another (B) if—

    (a)   A engages in unwanted conduct related to a relevant protected characteristic, and

    (b)   the conduct has the purpose or effect of—

        (i)   violating B's dignity, or

        (ii)   creating an intimidating, hostile, degrading, humiliating or offensive environment for B.

(2)   A also harasses B if—

    (a)   A engages in unwanted conduct of a sexual nature, and

    (b)   the conduct has the purpose or effect referred to in subsection (1)(b).

(3)   A also harasses B if—

    (a)   A or another person engages in unwanted conduct of a sexual nature or that is related to gender reassignment or sex,

    (b)   the conduct has the purpose or effect referred to in subsection (1)(b), and

    (c)   because of B's rejection of or submission to the conduct, A treats B less favourably than A would treat B if B had not rejected or submitted to the conduct.

(4)   In deciding whether conduct has the effect referred to in subsection (1)(b), each of the following must be taken into account—

    (a)   the perception of B;

    (b)   the other circumstances of the case;

    (c)   whether it is reasonable for the conduct to have that effect.

    ...

As with direct discrimination, s 26 prohibits harassment based on association and perception; to bring a claim, a victim of harassment does not have to possess the 'protected characteristic' himself: '... A engages in unwanted conduct *related to* a relevant protected characteristic' (s 26(1)(a)) (emphasis added).

Note that under the law, where the complaint is about harassment, the complainant cannot also claim direct discrimination, because 'detriment' does not include subjecting a person to harassment: see the definition of 'detriment' in s 212(1) of the Act: '"detriment" does not, subject to subsection (5), include conduct which amounts to harassment'. This is to avoid the possibility of a claim for direct discrimination by detriment being brought on the same facts. This means that harassment and direct discrimination claims are mutually exclusive, so while a claimant can plead both in the alternative, they cannot succeed on both.

There are three different types of harassment:

(a) 'Characteristic-related (or general) harassment' applies to all the protected characteristics listed in **11.1** above – it involves unwanted conduct which is related to a relevant characteristic and has the purpose or effect of creating an intimidating, hostile, degrading, humiliating or offensive environment for the complainant, or violating the complainant's dignity (s 26(1)).

(b) Sexual harassment is unwanted conduct of a sexual nature, where this has the purpose or effect of creating an intimidating, hostile, degrading, humiliating or offensive environment for the complainant, or violating the complainant's dignity (s 26(2)).

(c) The third type of harassment is treating someone less favourably because that person has either submitted to or rejected sexual harassment, or harassment related to sex or gender reassignment which had the purpose or effect of creating an intimidating, hostile, degrading, humiliating or offensive environment for the complainant, or violating the complainant's dignity (s 26(3)).

In practice, most claims relating to workplace harassment are brought under the 'general' harassment provision of s 26(1). The provisions of the Act which are relevant to harassment include:

- s 40: it is unlawful for employers to harass employees and job applicants;
- s 109(1) and (3): an employer is liable for acts of harassment carried out by its employees in the course of their employment, irrespective of whether they are done with the employer's knowledge or approval;
- s 109(4): an employer has a defence if it can show that it took 'all reasonable steps' to prevent the employee from either committing the particular act of harassment or committing acts of that description; and
- s 110(1): employees can be liable for harassment of their colleagues.

Each type of harassment will be dealt with in more detail below.

The EAT confirmed in *Timothy James Consulting Ltd v Wilton* (UKEAT/0082/14) that a resignation that amounts to a constructive dismissal does not of itself fall within the meaning of 'harassment', because s 26 of the Equality Act 2010 makes no reference to dismissal (cf s 39 of the Equality Act 2010 at **8.4.2**); it simply provides that employers must not harass employees and job applicants. However, prior acts which give rise to the constructive dismissal can be relied upon, and an actual dismissal can amount to something done 'in relation to employment' and therefore amount to harassment (see *Urso v Department for Work and Pensions* (UKEAT/0045/16)).

11.3.2 Characteristic-related (or general) harassment

European Union law defines harassment (Equal Treatment Directive (Recast) 2006/54) as:

> where unwanted conduct related to the [sex, etc] of a person occurs with the purpose or effect of violating the dignity of a person, and of creating an intimidating, hostile, degrading, humiliating or offensive environment.

To be unlawful under the previous law, harassment had to be 'on the ground' of sex, etc. In *Equal Opportunities Commission v Secretary of State for Trade and Industry* [2007] IRLR 327, the EOC successfully challenged the UK legislation (in so far as it dealt with harassment in sex cases) in judicial review proceedings. The EOC submitted that the use of the words 'on the ground of' in SDA 1975, s 4A imported causation into the Act, requiring an investigation of the reason for the conduct complained of, whereas the Directive, by referring to conduct 'related to' the sex, etc of a person, defined harassment by association with sex, etc. The High Court held:

> [T]he use of the words 'on the ground of her sex' impermissibly imports causation – the reason why issue – into the concept of harassment. There can be conduct which is related to sex, but not of a sexual nature, which has the effect of creating an offensive working environment for a woman ... That would not fall within [the law] on a straightforward reading, as it would not be conduct on the ground of the woman's sex.

The law was amended in 2008 where the characteristic was sex, which meant that there were different definitions depending on the characteristic in question.

The Equality Act 2010 follows through that change in respect of all the protected characteristics in **11.1**: harassment no longer needs to be 'on the grounds' of but rather should be 'related to' a protected characteristic. The view is therefore that causation is no longer relevant, and that no comparator is needed. This means that an employer can no longer rely on the *Brumfitt* type defence by arguing that its conduct was not discriminatory because it treated everyone alike (in *Brumfitt v MOD* [2005] IRLR 4 (a case decided under the old test), the complainant lost her case because the obscene language used by the alleged harasser was directed at both men and women). The unwanted conduct must 'relate to' the protected characteristics. The EHRC Code states (para 7) that 'related to' should be given a broad meaning, namely 'a connection with the protected characteristic'.

Section 26(1) of the Act provides that a person (A) harasses another (B) if A engages in unwanted conduct related to a relevant protected characteristic, and the conduct has the purpose or effect of violating B's dignity, or creating an intimidating, hostile, degrading, humiliating or offensive environment for B. This can be broken down into three essential elements that together make up a complaint of unlawful harassment under s 26(1), and this is how the courts have approached their analysis (see *Richmond Pharmacology v Dhaliwal* [2009] ICR 724 and *Bakkali v Greater Manchester Buses (South) Ltd t/a Stage Coach Manchester* (UKEAT/0176/17)):

(1)   Did the respondent engage in unwanted conduct?

(2)   Did the conduct in question either:

    (a)   have the *purpose* or

    (b)   have the *effect* of either (i) violating the claimant's dignity or (ii) creating an adverse environment for her ('the proscribed consequences')?

(3)   Was the unwanted conduct related to a relevant protected characteristic?

Unwanted conduct is broadly construed. The question of whether conduct is unwanted is largely assessed subjectively, ie from the employee's point of view. The word 'unwanted' means essentially the same as 'unwelcome' or 'uninvited' (*Insitu Cleaning Co Ltd v Heads* [1995] IRLR 4). Unwanted conduct can be a one-off or a series of events. It can cover anything from serious physical or verbal abuse to offensive jokes, insults, taunts and banter. 'Ordinary' acts can become unwanted if they are persistent and unwelcome; but it is not necessary for there to be an explicit rejection of conduct. The EHRC Statutory Code states that unwanted conduct includes spoken or written words or abuse, imagery, graffiti, physical gestures, facial expressions, mimicry, jokes, pranks, acts affecting a person's surroundings, or other physical behaviour (para 7.7). The Code recognises that victims of abuse do not necessarily readily complain (see also *Munchkins Restaurant Ltd v Karmazyn* (UKEAT/0359/09)). If a claimant genuinely did not welcome the conduct, the test will be met.

The definition covers both the situation where conduct is deliberate or intentional, ie the purpose (irrespective of the actual effect) is to violate the dignity of the claimant or to create an unpleasant environment for them (see *Finn v British Bung Manufacturing Co Ltd* (ET/1803764/ 21)), and also where, regardless of intent, the conduct does, in fact, have that effect, which will require assessment from the claimant's point of view. But note the qualification in s 26(4), which means the test has both subjective and objective elements, namely that the conduct must reasonably be considered to have violated the victim's dignity or created the unpleasant environment. See *Ahmed v The Cardinal Hume Academies* (UKEAT/0196/18).

The question of whether an act is sufficiently 'serious' to support a harassment claim is a question of fact and degree – see *Kirk v Citibank NA* (ET/3200291/18) where a one-off remark that the claimant was 'old and set in [his] ways' as part of the justification for not retaining him after a reorganisation was humiliating and insulting given his long and successful career with the bank, and it constituted harassment relating to his age.

The Explanatory Memorandum to the 2008 amendments gave an example which is still useful: where male colleagues dislike a female colleague and decide to put the office equipment on a high shelf to make it hard for her to reach it, the old definition would not help as the men are acting out of dislike rather than because their colleague is a woman, ie not on the 'ground of her sex'; under the new definition such conduct might be actionable because it is 'related to sex', ie woman are on average shorter than men. The term 'related to' does not require a direct causal link between the conduct and the protected characteristic. It is wider than the test which applies in direct discrimination cases, which requires less favourable treatment 'because of' a protected characteristic. For a recent case, see *Tees Esk and Wear Valleys NHS Foundation Trust v Aslam* [2020] IRLR 495.

However offensive or hostile the unwanted conduct is, it will not constitute harassment under s 26(1) unless it is related to a relevant protected characteristic (note that the protected characteristics of pregnancy and maternity and marriage and civil partnership are not covered by the 'general' definition of harassment in s 26(1)). However, it is not necessary for a claimant to have the protected characteristic in order to be covered by the protection (see *Hodgson v Martin Design Associates Ltd* (ET/1806368/19)). In *English v Thomas Sanderson Blinds Ltd* [2008] IRLR 342, Mr English complained about homophobic banter directed at him. He was not gay and his colleagues knew this. He found the banter degrading and offensive. The Court of Appeal concluded that he had been harassed within the definition: although the banter was not based on a perception or assumption that he was gay, it was enough that Mr English was taunted as if he were gay. The banter created a degrading and hostile working environment, on the grounds of sexual orientation.

The law also covers a person who is a witness to harassment (see *Gago v Uneek Clothing Co Ltd* (ET/1600212/16). The Explanatory Notes provide an example:

- A white worker who sees a black colleague being subjected to racially abusive language could have a case of harassment if the language also causes an offensive environment for her.

In *Raj v Capita Business Services Ltd and another* (UKEAT/0074/19) the EAT upheld the tribunal's decision that massaging the claimant's neck, whilst unwanted conduct, was unrelated to the claimant's sex – rather it was misguided encouragement on the part of the second respondent.

For a recent case on harassment related to the protected characteristics of race and disability, see *Evans v Xactly Corporation Ltd* (UKEAT/0128/18), a case where teasing and banter were common. The EAT found that, in that context, it could not be said that the comments directed against the claimant were unwanted (as he was such an active participant in the banter) and did not have, on the facts, the purpose or effect of creating an intimidating atmosphere or violating the claimant's dignity.

11.3.3 Sexual harassment

Sexual harassment encompasses any conduct of a sexual nature which has the purpose or effect of violating a person's dignity or of creating an intimidating, hostile, degrading, humiliating or offensive environment. Conduct of a sexual nature is not defined in the Act. The example given by the EHRC is unwelcome sexual advances – touching, standing too close, the displaying of offensive pictures.

The Explanatory Notes provide an example:

- An employer who displayed any material of a sexual nature, such as a topless calendar, may be harassing her employees where this makes the workplace an offensive place to work for any employee, female or male.

In August 2016, the Trades Union Congress (TUC) published a Report, 'Still just a bit of banter?'. See the Introduction for more details, but key findings included that more than half (52%) of all the women polled have experienced some form of sexual harassment, 28% of women have been subject to comments of a sexual nature about their body or clothes, and nearly one-quarter of women have experienced unwanted touching (such as a hand on the knee or lower back).

The Government published a response to a consultation on tackling sexual harassment on 21 July 2021. The Government proposed a new duty on employers to prevent sexual harassment and to (re)introduce protection against third party harassment (see **11.6** below). There was also a suggestion that the time-limit for all Equality Act 2010 claims will be extended to six months (from the current three months) (see **8.8.1.1**). As noted above, the Worker Protection (Amendment of Equality Act 2010) Bill proposes employers' liability for harassment of their employees by third parties and includes a duty on employers to take all reasonable steps to prevent sexual harassment of their employees. It does not, however, contain any provisions relating to the extension of time-limits.

11.3.4 Less favourable treatment

An employer may also be liable where there is less favourable treatment of a person by reason of that person's submission to or rejection of sex- or gender reassignment-related harassment or sexual harassment which had the purpose or effect of violating that person's dignity or of creating an intimidating, hostile, degrading, humiliating or offensive environment.

The Explanatory Notes provide an example:

- A shopkeeper propositions one of his shop assistants. She rejects his advances and then is turned down for promotion which she believes she would have got if she had accepted her boss's advances. The shop assistant would have a claim of harassment.

11.3.5 'Purpose or effect ...'

All three types of harassment require that the conduct has the purpose or effect of (s 26(1) – see **11.3.1**):

    (i)   violating B's dignity, or
    (ii)   creating an intimidating, hostile, degrading, humiliating or offensive environment for B.

If the conduct was intended to have the effect of violating dignity or creating a hostile, etc environment, it amounts to harassment whatever the actual effect. If there is no such intent then the conduct may be treated as having the effect of violating dignity or creating a hostile, etc environment only if 'it should reasonably be considered as having that effect'; as part of that assessment, the victim's perspective is a relevant circumstance to take into account (s 26(4)). It is therefore for the tribunal to decide, based on the evidence, whether the effect of the conduct was to create a hostile, etc working environment.

In *Richmond Pharmacology v Dhaliwal* [2009] IRLR 336, the EAT noted that the fact that, at least in some cases, there will be substantial overlaps between the questions that arise in relation to each element (eg, the question whether the conduct complained of was 'unwanted' will overlap with the question of whether it creates an adverse environment for the employee) and between the two defined proscribed consequences (many or most acts which are found to create an adverse environment for an employee will also violate her dignity). The EAT went on to state that

> 14. ... an employer may be held liable on the basis that the effect of his conduct has been to produce the proscribed consequences even if that was not his purpose; and, conversely, that he may be liable if he acted for the purposes of producing the proscribed consequences but did not in fact do so (or in any event has not been shown to have done so). ... In most cases the primary focus will be on the effect of the unwanted conduct rather than on the employer's purpose ... .

> 15. ... A respondent should not be held liable merely because his conduct has had the effect of producing a proscribed consequence: it should be reasonable that that consequence has occurred. That ... creates an objective standard. The proscribed consequences are, of their nature, concerned with the feelings of the putative victim: that is, the victim must have felt, or perceived, her dignity to have been violated or an adverse environment to have been created. That can, if you like, be described as introducing a 'subjective' element; but overall the criterion is objective because what the tribunal is required to consider is whether, if the claimant has experienced those feelings or perceptions, it was reasonable for her to do so. Thus if, for example, the tribunal believes that the claimant was unreasonably prone to take offence, then, even if she did genuinely feel her dignity to have been violated, there will have been no harassment within the meaning of the section. Whether it was reasonable for a claimant to have felt her dignity to have been violated is quintessentially a matter for the factual assessment of the tribunal. It will be important for it to have regard to all the relevant circumstances, including the context of the conduct in question. One question that may be material is whether it should reasonably have been apparent whether the conduct was, or was not, intended to cause offence (or, more precisely, to produce the proscribed consequences): the same remark may have a very different weight if it was evidently innocently intended than if it was evidently intended to hurt.

In *Pemberton v Inwood* [2018] EWCA Civ 564, Underhill LJ revised his guidance in para 15 above. He noted that under the predecessor law, 'Conduct shall be regarded as having the effect [of violating that other person's dignity, or creating an intimidating, hostile, degrading, humiliating or offensive environment for him] only if, having regard to all the circumstances, including in particular the perception of that other person, it should reasonably be considered as having that effect', so that it was a requirement of liability that it was reasonable that the conduct should have the effect in question. However, under s 26 (above), perception, circumstances and reasonableness are now expressed as matters to be taken into account in deciding whether the effect has occurred. He did not believe that the difference in the structure of the successor provision was intended to make any substantive difference, but he amended the guidance as follows:

> In order to decide whether any conduct falling within sub-paragraph (1)(a) has either of the proscribed effects under sub-paragraph (1)(b), a tribunal must consider both (by reason of sub-section (4)(a)) whether the putative victim perceives themselves to have suffered the effect in question (the subjective question) and (by reason of sub-section (4)(c)) whether it was reasonable for the conduct to be regarded as having that effect (the objective question). It must also, of course, take into account all the other circumstances – sub-section (4)(b). The relevance of the subjective question is that if the claimant does not perceive their dignity to have been violated, or an adverse environment created, then the conduct should not be found to have had that effect. The relevance of the objective question is that if it was not reasonable for the conduct to be regarded as violating the claimant's dignity or creating an adverse environment for him or her, then it should not be found to have done so.

In *Thomas Sanderson Blinds Ltd v English* (UKEAT/0316/10), the EAT held that a heterosexual employee who was subject to homophobic banter was not harassed because the banter did not have the effect of violating his dignity or creating a hostile etc environment – on the facts he had remained friends with his tormentors and had not complained.

In *Weeks v Newham College of Further Education* (UKEAT/0630/11), the EAT held that the word 'environment' is a 'state of affairs', which may be created by one incident if the effects are of longer duration.

In *Heathfield v Times Newspapers Ltd* (UKEAT/1305/12), the EAT upheld the tribunal's decision that offence caused by reference to 'the f***ing Pope' did not amount to harassment because, to the extent the claimant felt his dignity had been violated or a hostile environment created, that was not a reasonable reaction in the context of the case facts.

In *Betsi Cadwaladr University Health Board v Hughes and Others* (UKEAT/0179/13), a loss of status was held to amount to harassment related to the claimant's disability.

In *Ahmed v The Cardinal Hume Academies* (UKEAT/0196/18), the EAT held that the employment tribunal had correctly applied *Pemberton* (above) and that it was not reasonable for the conduct to be regarded as violating the claimant's dignity or creating an adverse environment.

11.4   REMEDIES FOR HARASSMENT

See **8.8**. The main remedy is compensation, although tribunals can also make declarations and recommendations. In the recent case of *AA Solicitors v Majid* (EAT/0217/15), the EAT (noting the contrary decision in *De Souza* which was pending appeal) confirmed that the 10% uplift to general damages introduced in *Simmons v Castle* applied to injury to feelings. It also added that employment tribunals should be entitled to take the effect of inflation into account when assessing damages going forward. The claimant won her claim of sexual harassment and was awarded £14,000 for injury to feelings amongst other awards, based on the middle *Vento* band. The respondent, while accepting that the award was within the correct band, appealed, arguing that the award was excessive (the claimant had been dismissed after six weeks in her job; she cited about 40 acts of sexual harassment including asking her out, touching, and attempting to hug her; the respondent said that this was a case merely of persistent unwanted attentions but without serious physical contact, that was no worse than gauche and insinuating). The EAT dismissed the appeal. The claimant's dignity as a worker had been violated and she had been subject to humiliation. The award was not, in the EAT's judgment, 'manifestly excessive'.

There is no legal limit on the amount of compensation that can be awarded. While the *Vento* bands (see **8.8.2.2**) set limits for injury to feelings, there is no limit on other awards, such as for loss of earnings. In *Lokhova v Sberbank CIB (UK) Ltd* (2015), an employment tribunal awarded an employee nearly £3.2 million for sexual harassment, of which £44,000 was awarded for injury to feelings and £15,000 for aggravated damages; the remainder consisted of compensation for future loss of earnings for the claimant (who had earned £750,000 a year in salary and bonuses, but who the tribunal found 'will never work in financial services again, on the basis of the medical evidence').

11.5   EMPLOYERS' LIABILITY FOR THE ACTS OF EMPLOYEES

Readers are reminded of the principle of vicarious liability, and should refer to **8.6** above.

11.6   EMPLOYERS' LIABILITY FOR THE ACTS OF THIRD PARTIES

Employers could, until 2003, be liable for the acts of a person who was not an employee. In *Burton and Another v De Vere Hotels* [1996] IRLR 596, the applicants were employed as casual waitresses at one of the respondent's hotels, working at a dinner organised by the City of Derby Round Table. The stand-up comedian Bernard Manning had been booked as the guest speaker. The two women were working in the banqueting hall where Mr Manning was speaking. He used words such as 'wog', 'nigger' and 'sambo', and said that 'darkies were good at giving blow jobs'. The applicants brought claims under the RRA 1976. The tribunal held that the respondent was not liable because it was not the respondent that had subjected the applicants to the racial harassment. The EAT held the respondent liable. The EAT said that an employer subjects an employee to racial harassment if he causes or permits racial harassment to occur in circumstances which he can control, whether it happens or not, and where an application of good employment practice would prevent or reduce the harassment. In the present case, it would have been good employment practice for the manager to warn his assistants to keep a look out for Mr Manning, and to withdraw the waitresses if things became unpleasant.

However, in *Macdonald v Advocate General for Scotland; Pearce v Governing Body of Mayfield Secondary School* [2003] IRLR 512, the House of Lords disapproved of the decision in *Burton*. Their Lordships stated that whilst an employer's failure to prevent third parties committing acts of sexual/racial harassment might amount to discrimination by the employer, it would do so only if the employer failed to take such steps *because* of the employee's sex/race.

In *EOC v Secretary of State for Trade and Industry* (**11.3.2** above), the High Court agreed with the EOC that the law needed to be re-cast so as to facilitate claims that an employer subjected an employee to harassment by knowingly failing to protect that employee from repetitive harassment by a third party, such as a supplier or customer. The High Court said that

> [s]o long as [the law] is framed in terms of unwanted conduct engaged in on the ground of a woman's sex by the employer, it is difficult to see how an employer could be held liable for the knowing failure to take steps to prevent harassment by others, since such knowing failure would have to amount to unwanted conduct by the employer on the ground of her sex.

Section 40 of the 2010 Act was aimed at dealing with this issue of protecting employees against persistent harassment by third parties (on at least two occasions). However, following a Government consultation in 2012, s 40 was repealed with effect from 1 October 2013 by s 65 of the ERRA 2013, because it was deemed unworkable. It is still open to employees to argue that an employer's failure to act in such circumstances amounts to unwanted conduct by the employer, relying on s 26 of the 2010 Act (see **11.3** above), as long as the tribunal is satisfied that the reason for the failure to act was 'related to' a protected characteristic. That may be easier to demonstrate than showing that the inaction is 'because of' the protected characteristic.

In *UNITE the Union v Nailard* [2019] ICR 28, the Court of Appeal considered the effect of the repeal of s 40(2)–(4) and held that: 'for better or for worse, [the Equality Act 2010] no longer contains any provision making employers liable for failing to protect employees against third party harassment as such, though they may of course remain liable if the proscribed factor forms part of the motivation for their inaction'. In *Bessong v Pennine Care NHS Foundation Trust* (UKEAT/0247/18), the failure to prevent third party harassment was found not to be related to the protected characteristic on the facts. In *BDW Trading Ltd v Kopec* (UKEAT/0197/19), the EAT held that the respondent was liable because its failure to take seriously enough the claimant's complaints about the two incidents in question here came within the meaning of 'conduct related to' race and sexual orientation. However, the EAT held that that there could only be liability if the employer's inaction was driven by a protected characteristic. That was not so, on the facts. As Underhill LJ's judgment in *Nailard* made clear:

> the mere use of the formula 'related to' is [not] sufficient to convey an intention that employers who are themselves innocent of any discriminatory motivation should be liable for the discriminatory acts of third parties, even if they could have prevented them. In my view the 'associative' effect of the phrase 'related to' is more naturally applied only to the case where the discriminatory conduct is the employer's own ...

Following the ruling by the Court of Appeal in *Nailard*, and criticism that the prior provisions relating to third-party harassment had been confusing, a private members' bill, the Worker Protection (Amendment of Equality Act 2010) Bill, was introduced. This Bill reintroduces employers' liability for harassment of their employees by third parties and includes a duty on employers to take all reasonable steps to prevent sexual harassment of their employees. The 'three strikes' formulation of the previous provision (which required two occasions of known harassment to have occurred before liability was triggered) will not be replicated and, instead, liability will be triggered without there needing to be a prior incident. This will bring being harassed by a third party, for example a customer or client, in line with being harassed by a colleague. In October 2022, the Bill was debated for the second time in the House of Commons.

11.7   PROTECTION FROM HARASSMENT ACT 1997

Additionally, an employee may be able to bring a claim under the Protection from Harassment Act 1997. This allows for victims of harassment to claim damages and/or injunctive relief in the civil courts and to prosecute in the criminal courts. To bring a claim under the 1997 Act, it is not necessary to show that the harassment was done on any particular prohibited ground or basis. Harassment is not defined in the Act, but it includes 'alarming [a]person or causing a person distress'. The Act prohibits a course of conduct (defined as at least two occasions of harassment) that amounts to harassment, or which a person knows, or ought to know, amounts to harassment. There is no statutory defence available to an employer under the Act, which enables victims of harassment in the workplace to pursue claims against their employer through the civil courts (through the principle of vicarious liability) and/or through the employment tribunal (see *Majrowski v Guy's and St Thomas's NHS Trust* [2005] IRLR 340, CA (upheld by the House of Lords [2006] UKHL 34) and *Banks v Ablex Ltd* [2005] IRLR 357 for two decisions in this area).

Claims under the 1997 Act have a number of advantages over other more traditional 'employment' routes such as discrimination or unfair dismissal. The provisions will apply to workers as well as to employees. Unlike an unfair dismissal claim, compensation for injury to feelings can be recovered as well as loss of earnings. Claims under the 1997 Act can be brought in the courts, so there is no three-month limitation on bringing the claim. However, the realisation that the Act might give rise to claims for damages for what might be viewed as relatively trivial acts of harassment, led the Court of Appeal to re-examine what amounted to harassment under the Act. In *Conn v Sunderland City Council* [2007] EWCA Civ 1492, the trial judge found that two incidents involving verbal threats amounted to harassment under the Act and awarded a small sum by way of damages. The Court of Appeal made it clear that 'bad-mannered' behaviour should not give rise to criminal penalties or a civil claim for damages. It held that for the Protection from Harassment Act to be engaged, harassment had to amount to conduct that is, viewed objectively, likely to cause distress to the victim and is unacceptable and oppressive, and probably criminal. There must be two or more incidents which are each sufficiently serious.

However, see now *Veakins v Kier Islington Ltd* [2009] EWCA Civ 1288, where the Court of Appeal provided guidance on the sort of conduct that would be needed before an employee could successfully bring a claim under the Protection from Harassment Act 1997. In the leading judgment given by Maurice Kay LJ, the Court emphasised that

> since *Majrowski*, courts have been enjoined to consider whether the conduct complained of is 'oppressive and unacceptable' as opposed to merely unattractive, unreasonable or regrettable. The primary focus is on whether the conduct is 'oppressive and unacceptable' albeit that the court must keep in mind that it must be of an order which 'would sustain criminal liability'.

One of the perceived limitations on a claim under the Protection from Harassment Act was the requirement for harassment to arise out of a course of conduct, ie conduct occurring on at least two occasions. However, the provisions implemented by the Act now import a similar requirement into claims of third party harassment.

11.8   CASE STUDY: HARASSMENT

Facts

(1)   R1 is the operator of an adventure park. R2 is an employee of R1. He is the operations manager of R1, and was the line manager of C, who was a member of his operations team. C had been in post for nine months. On a previous occasion, another member of the operations team, 'F', complained informally to 'S' (the managing director of R1) about R2's conduct towards her, following which she then submitted a formal grievance in writing. C says she had a number of informal conversations with R2, making him

aware that she was uncomfortable with his engaging her in conversations of an explicit sexual nature and/or making sexual innuendos. R2 says that staff accepted a level of ribald language and that swearing was common amongst all staff.

(2) Following one particular incident when R2 made further remarks that C regarded as lewd, C sent R1 a letter giving one month's notice of her intention to resign. In this letter she said she had recently 'found working conditions intolerable due to your apparent disregard for the welfare of staff and your resultant failure to appropriately address or bring about a satisfactory conclusion regarding my concerns about R2 and the sexist and abusive behaviour others females and I have repeatedly endured'. She enclosed a copy of a diary she had been keeping, which she said contained examples of R2's behaviour. R1 did not take her complaint seriously and did nothing about it. C subsequently left.

(3) C issued a claim form to the employment tribunal.

Claims

(4) C complained of harassment under s 26(1) and (2) and of direct discrimination because of sex under s 13.

(5) C claimed against R1 and R2.

(6) She indicated on the claim form that she only wanted compensation.

(7) R1 and R2 did not admit that the alleged incidents of discrimination relied upon by C took place, and denied that any incidents that did take place were acts of discrimination.

Evidence

(8) Disclosure took place in the usual way, and paginated bundles were prepared which included extracts from C's personal file, extracts from the staff handbook on *Grievances and Appeals*, papers relating to previous complaints and a Schedule of Loss from C setting out her claim for compensation.

(9) Witness statements were exchanged prior to the hearing.

(10) At the hearing all witnesses who gave oral evidence were cross-examined and the tribunal had the opportunity to ask questions of them. On C's behalf, oral evidence at the hearing was given by C and F. C also submitted witness statements from a number of former employees who did not appear to give evidence. As their evidence could not be tested by cross-examination, the tribunal gave their testimony less weight evidentially. For R1 and R2, oral evidence was given by R2, S, T, and W (a junior manager).

(11) At the conclusion of the evidence, both sides made oral submissions on liability and remedy.

(12) All these matters were taken into consideration by the tribunal before reaching its decision.

The issues to be decided

(13) C complained of both characteristic (sex)-related harassment and sexual harassment and direct sex discrimination. Where R1's conduct was directed at other female staff, it was characteristic-related harassment. R1 does not admit that the alleged incidents took place, and denies that any incidents that did take place were acts of harassment. The tribunal will need to determine:

13.1 whether R2 subjected C to harassment either by way of conduct of a sexual nature directed at her, or by way of conduct directed at other female staff;

13.2 whether R1 was responsible for any such harassment.

13.3 The direct discrimination claims related to the way R1 responded to C's complaints about R2 and to the act of C's resignation.

(14) Depending on the outcome of the matters, the tribunal will have to determine what amount of compensation, if any, should be awarded.

Tribunal findings

(15) The unanimous decision of the tribunal is that:

15.1 R1 and R2 unlawfully discriminated against C;

15.2 R1 and R2 are to pay C £7,419.77 by way of compensation.

Reasons

Harassment claim

(16) The tribunal took account of s 136 of the Equality Act 2010 on the burden of proof. It noted that in *Igen v Wong* [2005] IRLR 258 (a race discrimination case determined under pre-Equality Act 2010 legislation), subject to one amendment, the Court of Appeal upheld the guidance given by the EAT in a sex discrimination case, *Barton v Investec Securities Ltd* [2003] ICR 1205, in particular, to summarise that guidance, that it is for the claimant who complains of sex discrimination to prove on the balance of probabilities facts from which the tribunal could conclude, in the absence of an adequate explanation, that the employer has committed an unlawful act of discrimination against the claimant. Where the claimant proves facts from which inferences could be drawn that the employer has treated the applicant less favourably on the grounds of sex, then the burden of proof moves to the employer. It is then for the employer to prove that he did not commit, or, as the case may be, is not to be treated as having committed, that act. To discharge that burden it is necessary for the employer to prove, on the balance of probabilities, that the treatment was 'in no sense whatsoever on the grounds of sex', since 'no discrimination whatsoever' is compatible with the Burden of Proof Directive 97/80. That requires a tribunal to assess not merely whether the employer has proved an explanation for the facts from which such inferences can be drawn, but further that it is adequate to discharge the burden of proof on the balance of probabilities that sex was not a ground for the treatment in question. The tribunal also noted the decision of the Court of Appeal in *Madarassy v Nomura International plc* [2007] EWCA Civ 33, which emphasised that the court in *Igen* expressly rejected the argument that it was sufficient for the complainant simply to prove facts from which the tribunal could conclude that the respondent 'could have committed an unlawful act of discrimination'. It held that the bare facts of a difference in status and a difference in treatment only indicate a possibility of discrimination. 'They are not, without more, sufficient material from which a tribunal "could conclude" that, on the balance of probabilities, the respondent had committed an unlawful act of discrimination'.

(17) The tribunal also considered the definition of harassment set out in s 26(1) and (2) of the Equality Act 2010. It noted that both types of harassment required that the conduct complained of had the purpose or effect of violating C's dignity or creating an intimidating, hostile, degrading or humiliating or offensive environment for C. It noted the case of *Reid and Bull Information Systems Ltd v Stedman* [1999] IRLR 299 (a pre-Equality Act 2010 case but one which it considered remained relevant on overall approach). It noted that in *Wileman v Minilec Engineering Ltd* [1988] IRLR 144, the EAT acknowledged that a person may be happy to accept the remarks of A or B in a sexual context and be wholly upset by similar remarks made by C; and that in *Driskel v Peninsula Business Services Ltd* [2000] IRLR 151, the EAT had held that a tribunal should not lose sight of the significance of the sex of both the complainant and the alleged discriminator. Sexual badinage with a heterosexual male by another man could not be completely equated with like badinage by him with a woman.

Tribunal's findings

Workplace culture

(18) The tribunal found from the evidence of a number of witnesses that general ribald banter and mickey-taking was common in the workplace, and that there was a lot of sexual banter and swearing. It was not a 'cloistered' environment. There was also girly gossip about sex. R2 struggled with the 'overly emotional' reaction of some of the young women to his remarks, which left him bewildered. The tribunal noted that C was open in discussion about her relationship with her boyfriend. Overall it found C was uncomfortable with R2's conversations and behaviour, and R2 knew this but persisted with his conduct. This was backed up by the diary that C kept. The tribunal held that even in an environment where it was accepted that bad language was commonplace, the continued use of this sort of language when objection has been taken to it, particularly when it is used by a more senior manager to his junior staff, was not acceptable conduct. The tribunal found therefore that harassment was made out under s 26(2) but not under s 26(1). The tribunal did not believe that any of R2's language or behaviour was directed specifically at C because of her sex.

(19) It held S did not do enough to set standards for his staff about this. Neither did he really take it seriously. It found there was a stark contrast between the way he treated C and the way he responded to a previous complaint about another member of staff. The tribunal found that the different treatment was not, however, because of C's sex; it stemmed from the fact that S was not willing to tolerate any criticism of R2 because he considered him a valuable asset. The tribunal was not satisfied that this treatment fell within the definition of direct discrimination.

(20) On balance, the tribunal found that the comments made by R2 did amount to sexual harassment – his intention was irrelevant. It also found that given that C's resignation was caused principally by R2's remarks and S's failure to take her concerns seriously, those actions amounted to less favourable treatment because of her sex. An employer is vicariously liable for the acts of employees carried out within the course of their employment. R2 carried out these acts of harassment during the course of his employment. R1 had not sought to avail itself of the 'reasonably practicable steps' defence in s 109 of the Equality Act 2010. On that basis, the tribunal found R1 was liable for the acts of R2 and the omissions of S.

Remedies

(21) Section 124 of the Equality Act 2010 sets out the remedies available on a finding of discrimination. The general principle as far as compensation is concerned is that, as far as possible, complainants should be placed in the same position as they would have been but for the unlawful act (see *Ministry of Defence v Wheeler* [1998] IRLR 23). Another way of looking at it is to ask what loss has been caused by the discrimination in question. It is important to remember that the loss must be caused by the discrimination and, secondly, that the loss must not be too remote a consequence of the discrimination. In *Skyrail Oceanic Ltd v Coleman* [1981] ICR 864 (a pre-Equality Act 2010 sex discrimination claim), Lawton LJ explained this by saying that, 'Compensation is to be awarded for foreseeable damage arising directly from an unlawful act of discrimination'. Compensation for unlawful discrimination falls under two heads: financial loss, and non-financial loss. Financial loss covers matters such as loss of earnings, both past and future; while non-financial loss covers matters such as injury to feelings. In addition to awarding compensation for foreseeable damage arising directly from the unlawful act, an employment tribunal has jurisdiction to award compensation by way of damages for injury to feeling and personal injury, including both physical and psychiatric injury, caused by the unlawful discrimination. Where compensation is

assessed under the discrimination regime, the Employment Protection (Recoupment of Jobseeker's Allowance and Income Support) Regulations 1996 do not apply.

(22) Principles relating to compensatory awards for injury to feelings for unlawful discrimination are set out in *Armitage and HM Prison Service v Johnson* [1997] IRLR 162, *Vento v Chief Constable of West Yorkshire Police* [2003] IRLR 102 and *Da'Bell v NSPCC* (UKEAT/0227/09). *Da'Bell* set out new guideline figures which the tribunal inserted into the *Vento* guidance. In *Vento* (original figures now adjusted for inflation and for the 10% uplift in general damages (which took effect from 1 April 2013) and which the EAT confirmed in *Cadogan Hotel Partners Ltd v Ozog* (UKEAT/0001/14) applies to injury to feelings awards in discrimination cases – see *Simmons v Castle* [2012] EWCA Civ 1039 – but see now **8.8.2.2**), the Court of Appeal observed that there were three broad bands of compensation for injury to feelings, as distinct from compensation for psychiatric or similar personal injury: (1) The top band should normally be between £19,800 and £33,000. Sums in this range should be awarded in the most serious cases, such as where there has been a lengthy campaign of discriminatory harassment on the ground of sex or race. Only in the most exceptional case should an award of compensation for injury to feelings exceed £33,000. (2) The middle band of between £6,600 and £19,800 should be used for serious cases which do not merit an award in the highest band. (3) Awards of between £660 and £6,600 are appropriate for less serious cases, such as where the act of discrimination is an isolated one or a one-off occurrence. Defining injury to feelings is more a broadbrush exercise of estimation than of calculation, comparison with precedents or cold logic.

(23) Since the Court of Appeal's ruling in *Sheriff v Klyne Tugs (Lowestoft) Ltd* [1999] ICR 1170 (a race discrimination case), tribunals have jurisdiction to award compensation for personal injury arising out of unlawful sex, race or disability discrimination. This includes compensation for psychiatric illness. In *HM Prison Service v Salmon* [2001] IRLR 425, the EAT considered the possibility of overlap and double recovery where a tribunal awards separate sums for psychiatric damage and injury to feelings. The EAT accepted that injury to feelings can cover a wide range of injury, from minor upset to serious and prolonged feelings of humiliation and depression, and that in practice psychiatric damage may be compensated under this heading. It also accepted that there was a risk of double recovery where separate awards were made, and stated that tribunals should be aware of the risk.

(24) In *Snowball v Gardner Merchant Ltd* [1987] IRLR 397, the EAT said that evidence as to the complainant's attitude to matters of sexual behaviour was relevant and admissible for the purpose of determining the degree of injury to feelings that the complainant suffered as a result of sexual harassment. Compensation for sexual harassment must relate to the degree of detriment, and evidence as to whether she had talked freely to fellow employees about her attitude to sexual matters was relevant for determining whether the claimant was unlikely to be very upset by a degree of familiarity with a sexual connotation, so as to challenge the alleged detriment suffered and any hurt feelings

Tribunal's findings

(25) C had less than one year's continuous service. A sensible average weekly figure for her wages was £173.41. This was agreed by the parties. C did not have a job to go to when she resigned. She obtained some part-time work over the Christmas period. She later went full-time. That work is on-going. She set out in her Schedule of Loss the details of these earnings. In her current job she was getting paid more than she had earned with R1 (approx £202.00 per week). C said she was depressed as a result of her treatment. She referred to her GP's notes, indicating that she was struggling with money problems and had headaches, and continued to suffer anxiety and headaches. However, she was now working a 40-hour week without any sickness problems.

(26) The tribunal can make separate awards against R1 or R2. It is common in such cases to make a larger award against the employer and a smaller award against the individual harasser. The tribunal can also make one award and make both parties jointly and severally liable for that award. When making joint and several awards, tribunals must apportion the respective shares, so that if a claimant chooses to enforce only against one respondent, that respondent can still seek a suitable contribution from the other respondent. Any such apportionment should be on the basis of respectively culpability. The tribunal in this case made only one award. While R2 was the perpetrator, S's attitude was primarily responsible for what happened in allowing R2 to continue with his objectionable conduct. The tribunal concluded that S (and therefore R1) was substantially culpable for what happened. The tribunal apportioned blame on the basis of 20% to R2 and 80% to R1.

(27) *Compensatory element.* By the date of the hearing, taking account of C's actual earnings over the period against what she would have earned, her actual losses were £1,419.77. There were no future losses continuing to accrue.

(28) In terms of an award for *injury to feelings*, the tribunal felt that this case fell towards the top of the lower *Vento* band, in that it had not found there was any deliberate or ongoing campaign against C, but this was not just one isolated incident; a number of lewd remarks were made, which occurred as a result of a careless disregard for C's sensitivities once they had been made known. Judging from the medical evidence, there were no lasting effects suffered by C. In the circumstances, the tribunal made an award, inclusive of interest, of £6,000 for injury to feelings.

(29) Accordingly, the tribunal found that the respondents were to pay C a total sum of £7,419.77. The Recoupment Regulations do not apply to this award.

11.9 VICTIMISATION

The victimisation provisions aim to give protection to workers who bring complaints of discrimination or other proceedings aimed at enforcing compliance with equal treatment principles.

11.9.1 Definition

The definition of victimisation is set out in s 27 of the Act:

(1) A person (A) victimises another person (B) if A subjects B to a detriment because—

    (a) B does a protected act, or

    (b) A believes that B has done, or may do, a protected act.

(2) Each of the following is a protected act—

    (a) bringing proceedings under this Act;

    (b) giving evidence or information in connection with proceedings under this Act;

    (c) doing any other thing for the purposes of or in connection with this Act;

    (d) making an allegation (whether or not express) that A or another person has contravened this Act.

(3) Giving false evidence or information, or making a false allegation, is not a protected act if the evidence or information is given, or the allegation is made, in bad faith.

    ...

The Explanatory Notes make it clear that the Act changes the old law, in that there is no longer a requirement for the tribunal to construct a comparator. However, a comparison of the claimant's treatment with that of an appropriate comparator will often be an effective way of establishing the reason for the treatment. Was the treatment *because* the claimant had done a protected act?

The Explanatory Notes give examples:

- A woman makes a complaint of sex discrimination against her employer. As a result, she is denied promotion. The denial of promotion would amount to victimisation.

- A gay man sues a publican for persistently treating him less well than heterosexual customers. Because of this, the publican bars him from the pub altogether. This would be victimisation.

- An employer threatens to dismiss a staff member because he thinks she intends to support a colleague's sexual harassment claim. This threat could amount to victimisation.

- A man with a grudge against his employer knowingly gives false evidence in a colleague's discrimination claim against the employer. He is subsequently dismissed for supporting the claim. His dismissal would not amount to victimisation because of his untrue and malicious evidence.

Some of the case law based on the pre-Equality Act 2010 law is still relevant. In *Chief Constable of West Yorkshire Police v Khan* [2001] 1 WLR 1947, the House of Lords confirmed that the less favourable treatment must be by reason of the protected act (ie motivated by it). In this case, the reason the employer refused to provide a reference was to preserve his position in pending litigation and not the fact that the worker had commenced proceedings.

According to the Court of Appeal in *Nagarajan v London Regional Transport* [1998] IRLR 73, there must be *conscious motivation* by the discriminator to treat the employee less favourably because of the protected act. The case was appealed to the House of Lords. Their Lordships (Lord Browne-Wilkinson dissenting) held that the Court of Appeal had erred in holding that the alleged victimiser must have been consciously motivated by the race relations legislation. The question that must be asked, according to their Lordships, is 'Did the defendant treat the employee less favourably because of his knowledge of a protected act?'. If the answer to that question is yes, the case will fall within the law, even if the victimiser did not consciously realise that he or she was prejudiced by the defendant's having done the protected act (*Nagarajan v London Regional Transport* [1999] IRLR 572).

In *St Helens Metropolitan Borough Council v Derbyshire* [2004] IRLR 851; [2005] EWCA Civ 977; [2007] IRLR 540, the EAT upheld a tribunal finding that female catering staff who had brought equal pay claims had also been victimised. The employer wrote to all catering employees (not just the women who brought the claims) and said that if the claims were successful, the cost of a school meal would rise so as to 'make provision of the service wholly unviable', which might lead to large numbers of redundancies. The employer also wrote to the women concerned and said, amongst other things, 'I am greatly concerned about the likely outcome of this matter ... [I would urge you to consider] the original offer of settlement'. The EAT held that this constituted victimisation and stated that a direct threat of dismissal or other sanction made to the individual claimant is not a necessary element for establishing less favourable treatment.

This decision was upheld on appeal by the House of Lords, which held that while an employer may seek to dissuade an employee from bringing a claim, it must seek to avoid putting unreasonable pressure on the employee. In this case, the House of Lords held that the letter was not reasonable and therefore amounted to victimisation.

In *Martin v Devonshires Solicitors* (UKEAT/0086/10), the EAT upheld a tribunal's decision that the claimant's dismissal was 'properly and genuinely separable' from the fact of her complaints. The EAT held that in principle a distinction can be made between subjecting a person to a detriment by reason of a complaint which amounted to a protected act, and by reason of the facts and features of the manner in which it was made. In *Martin*, the claimant suffered from a mental illness that led her to make claims of discrimination, which she believed to be true but were false, and she could not accept that they were false. *Martin* was an exceptional case (see too *Micheldever Tyre Service Ltd v Burrell* (UKEAT/0427/12), *McIntosh v Governing Body of St Mark's Primary School* (UKEAT/0226/13), *Page v NHS Trust Development Authority* (UKEAT/0183/18) and *Page v Lord Chancellor* (UKEAT/0304/18)). In *Woodhouse v West North West Homes Leeds Ltd* (UKEAT/0007/12), the EAT held that the claimant's dismissal was victimisation and could not properly be separated from the claimant's complaints. In that case the employee's numerous grievances were dismissed by the employer, and the employee was then dismissed on the basis that their relationship had broken down as a result of the employee's 'uncurable disaffection'. The EAT overturned the tribunal's decision and held this was victimisation. The claimant was not mentally ill (cf *Martin*) and that grievance (past and future) caused the dismissal and therefore amounted to victimisation.

In *Chief Constable of Greater Manchester Police v Bailey* [2017] EWCA Civ 425, the Court of Appeal held that the tribunal had erred in law in applying a 'but for' test. The tribunal found for the claimant, stating that the treatment complained of was 'inextricably linked' to his previous protected act. The tribunal should, held the Court of Appeal, have asked whether the treatment complained of was by reason of the protected acts, which requires a consideration of the employer's motivation (conscious or unconscious). The tribunal's decision that the treatment 'flow[ed] from [the Claimant's] position under the Compromise Agreement, and hence also ... from his protected act' was:

> wrong in law – and, with all respect to the Tribunal, obviously so. It is self-evidently the case that there would have been no secondment to terminate if the Claimant had not brought his earlier claims, but that kind of 'but for' causative link does not mean that the termination was 'because of' his earlier claims in the relevant sense.

The Court of Appeal confirmed, in *Deer v University of Oxford* [2015] EWCA Civ 52, that the manner in which a grievance is treated by the employer can amount to victimisation if the grievance process is less favourable than it would have been were it not for an earlier claim brought by the employees, *even if* the grievance was bound to fail. That latter fact will be relevant to compensation, but it does not defeat the victimisation claim. (See too *A v Chief Constable of West Midlands Police* (UKEAT/0313/14).)

In *Thompson v London Central Bus Company Ltd* (UKEAT/0108/15), the EAT considered that associative discrimination (see **9.2.2**) could apply to a victimisation claim. The issue is not whether there is a relationship between the victim and the third party with the protected characteristic, or how close that relationship is – while the more tenuous the relationship is, the harder it will be to prove causation, as a matter of law there is no minimum degree of association that needs to be established. This therefore appears to increase the scope of protection available to employees and workers under the Equality Act 2010, even if they have not carried out a protected act themselves.

The EAT held in *Saad v Southampton Hospitals NHS Trust* (UKEAT/0276/17) that the claimant's subjective belief that he had carried out a protected act was sufficient to counter a suggestion of bad faith under s 27(3) of the Equality Act 2010. The EAT held that, in determining bad faith, the primary focus must be on the employee's honesty.

For a recent case on continuing acts and victimisation, see *South Western Ambulance Service NHS Foundation Trust v King* (UKEAT/0056/19).

In *Page v Lord Chancellor and another* (UKEAT/0304/18), the EAT upheld the employment tribunal's decision that a magistrate who was removed from office for publicly expressing his faith-based objection to the adoption of children by same-sex couples, in circumstances which indicated that he had been disciplined because of his religious views as a Christian, was an allegation that he had suffered religious discrimination that would constitute a protected act within s 27(2)(d). However, the EAT upheld the tribunal's decision that he was not unlawfully victimised on grounds of religion or belief. Bringing the judiciary into disrepute was separable from any protected act, as per *Martin* (above).

In *Warburton v Chief Constable of Northamptonshire Police* [2022] EAT 42, the EAT held that the correct question when considering whether a claimant had suffered detriment in a claim for victimisation was: 'Is the treatment of such a kind that a reasonable worker would or might take the view that in all the circumstances it was to his detriment?' This is the test set out by the House of Lords in *Shamoon v Chief Constable of the Royal Ulster Constabulary* [2003] ICR 337. This test sets a relatively low threshold for claimants to establish a detriment.

11.9.2   Remedies

See **8.8** above.

11.9.3   Protection of former employees

Section 108 protects against post-employment discrimination and harassment, but s 108(7) states expressly that 'conduct is not a contravention of this section in so far as it also amounts to victimisation of B by A' (see **8.4.3**). However, the Court of Appeal held, in *Jessemey v Rowstock Ltd and anor* [2014] EWCA Civ 185, that post-termination victimisation is proscribed by the 2010 Act, that s 108(7) was a 'plain case of drafting mistake', and that there was no reason why the Equality Act 2010 should not be construed to cover post-employment victimisation. At the time the Equality Act was drafted, post-termination victimisation was unlawful (see *Rhys-Harper v Relaxion Group* [2003] IRLR 484), and there was no indication that the Government intended to withdraw that protection in the Equality Act 2010.

See *Aston v The Martlet Group Ltd* (UKEAT/02274/18) for an interesting case where the EAT held that a claimant could not bring a victimisation complaint arising in consequence of being offered money to discontinue his disability discrimination complaint. The complaint fell outside s 108 because the offer arose during cross-examination (at a preliminary hearing) and was therefore protected by the common law principle of judicial proceedings immunity.

SUMMARY

This chapter has looked at harassment and victimisation in respect of the following protected characteristics listed in s 4 of the Equality Act 2010:

(a)   sex;

(b)   gender reassignment;

(c)   colour, race, nationality or ethnic or national origins;

(d)   religion or belief;

(e)   sexual orientation (**8.1**).

(Age and disability are dealt with in separate chapters.) Harassment does not include marriage and civil partnership, or pregnancy and maternity (**11.1**).

Two of the four main types of discrimination in the employment field outlawed by UK legislation are harassment and victimisation.

Harassment is unwanted conduct that violates a person's dignity, or which creates an intimidating, hostile, degrading, humiliating or offensive environment for that person having regard to all the circumstances including the perception of the victim. The definition of 'harassment' is set out in s 26 of the Equality Act 2010 (**11.3**).

There are three different types of harassment (**11.3**):

(a)   'characteristic-related harassment', which involves unwanted conduct which is related to a relevant characteristic and has the purpose or effect of creating an intimidating, hostile, degrading, humiliating or offensive environment for the complainant, or violating the complainant's dignity;

(b)   sexual harassment, which is unwanted conduct of a sexual nature, where this has the purpose or effect of creating an intimidating, hostile, degrading, humiliating or offensive environment for the complainant, or violating the complainant's dignity;

(c)   treating someone less favourably because that person has either submitted to or rejected sexual harassment, or harassment related to sex or gender reassignment which had the purpose or effect of creating an intimidating, hostile, degrading, humiliating or offensive environment for the complainant, or violating the complainant's dignity.

Employers will be vicariously liable for the acts of their employees, unless they have taken such steps as were reasonable to prevent an employee doing the act complained of (see **8.6**). They will also be liable for the acts of third parties in some circumstances (see **11.4.2**).

The victimisation provisions aim to give protection to workers who bring complaints of discrimination or other proceedings aimed at enforcing compliance with equal treatment principles. Victimisation occurs when a person has been subject to a detriment because he has done a 'protected act'. This may include bringing a tribunal claim or giving evidence in connection with such a claim. The definition of 'victimisation' is set out in s 27 of the Equality Act 2010.

The same shifting burden of proof applies in both harassment and victimisation cases (**11.2** and **9.5**). Section 108 protects against post-employment discrimination and harassment, and victimisation (**11.7.2**).

Remedies and enforcement are dealt with at **8.8** above. A flowchart summarising harassment and victimisation is set out at **Figure 11.1**.

Figure 11.1 Flowchart – Harassment and Victimisation

ELIGIBILITY

time-limit – within 3 months of act of discrimination

↓

UNLAWFUL ACT

discrimination in recruitment, promotion, dismissal, harassment, post-employment matters or subjecting a person to detriment

↓

TYPE OF CLAIM

[NB some situations can give rise to more than one type of discrimination claim]

HARASSMENT	**VICTIMISATION**
• character-related harassment – unwanted conduct related to a protected characteristic; or	• has C been subject to a detriment because C has done a protected act (eg brought/ intends to bring proceedings or has given/intends to give evidence or information in connection with such proceedings)?
• sexual harassment – unwanted conduct of a sexual nature; or	
• less favourable treatment – where C has rejected unwanted conduct of a sexual nature or conduct related to sex of gender reassignment;	
• which has the purpose or effect of violating C's dignity or creating an intimidating, hostile, degrading, humiliating or offensive environment for C;	
• if unintended, having regard to all the circumstances, including C's perception, should conduct be reasonably considered as having that effect?	• No comparator needed • No bad faith

↓

NO DEFENCE

↓

VICARIOUS LIABILITY

R will be vicariously liable for acts of employees committed in the course of employment (*Jones v Tower Boot Co/Chief Constable of Lincolnshire Police v Stubbs*) unless R took such steps as were reasonable to stop/avoid the discrimination (statutory defence – s 109(4))

↓

REMEDIES

• declaration of employee's rights
• recommendation that employer take action to alleviate or reduce the effect of the discrimination
• order for compensation (no maximum)
  – pecuniary losses
  – aggravated damages if employer has behaved in a high-handed, malicious, insulting or aggressive manner
  – injury to feelings (*Vento/Da'Bell*)
  – psychiatric or physical injury
  – possibility of exemplary damages
  – increase/decrease for any unreasonable failure to comply with the Acas Code of Practice

CHAPTER 12

AGE DISCRIMINATION

12.1	Introduction	487
12.2	The protected characteristic	488
12.3	Prohibited conduct	488
12.4	Unlawful acts of discrimination	489
12.5	Occupational requirements	489
12.6	Direct discrimination	489
12.7	Indirect discrimination	494
12.8	Harassment and victimisation	496
12.9	Exceptions	496
12.10	Vicarious liability	497
12.11	Burden of proof	497
12.12	Practical considerations	497
12.13	Enforcement and remedies	499
12.14	Further reading	499
	Summary	500

LEARNING OUTCOMES

After reading this chapter you will be able to:

- understand the underlying principles of age discrimination law, and when and to whom it applies in an employment context
- list the four types of prohibited conduct
- describe how the justification defence works in a direct age discrimination claim
- describe how the justification defence works in an indirect age discrimination claim
- explain how a compulsory retirement age may operate
- describe the remedies available where a complaint of age discrimination is made out.

12.1 INTRODUCTION

This chapter gives an overview of age discrimination. The Framework Directive for Equal Treatment in Employment and Occupation (2000/78) required Member States to implement legislation prohibiting discrimination on grounds of age by 2 December 2006. The UK enacted law to comply with its Community obligations by way of the Employment Equality (Age) Regulations 2006 (SI 2006/1031) ('the Age Regulations'), which were the last plank of the UK's implementation of the Equal Treatment Framework Directive. These have now been consolidated and harmonised in the Equality Act 2010. The EHRC has responsibility for the promotion of equality and combating discrimination on the grounds of age (see **8.1**).

The protection against discrimination because of age applies to all employers, private and public sector, and employment agencies, vocational training providers, trade unions, professional organisations, employer organisations, and trustees and managers of occupational pension schemes. It applies to employees, job applicants, ex-employees, contract workers, office holders and partners. The protection applies to a broad definition of workers and employees (see **1.3**). As with sex, race, disability, religious belief and sexual orientation discrimination, 'employment' is defined as 'employment under a contract of service or of apprenticeship or a contract personally to execute any work or labour' (s 83). This is a wider definition than that of 'employee' in the ERA 1996, and means that certain categories of individuals who are not covered by other statutory rights (eg job applicants, office holders, police officers and the self-employed) are covered by the Equality Act 2010.

Much of the terminology used is familiar discrimination terminology: under the Act direct age discrimination is prohibited (ie persons being subject to less favourable treatment than others because of their age) as well as indirect age discrimination (ie the application of a provision, criterion or practice which disadvantages people of a particular age), although (unlike other forms of discrimination) direct age discrimination can be justified 'objectively' where the discrimination is a 'proportionate means of achieving legitimate aim'. Both harassment (being unwanted conduct that violates a person's dignity, or creates an intimidating, hostile, degrading, humiliating or offensive environment for that person having regard to all the circumstances, including the perception of the victim) and victimisation (because the victim has brought proceedings under the Act, or has given evidence or information in connection with proceedings under the Act) are also prohibited.

12.2 THE PROTECTED CHARACTERISTIC

Section 4 of the Equality Act 2010 sets out certain 'protected' characteristics (see **8.2**). These are the grounds upon which discrimination is deemed unlawful. Age is listed as a protected characteristic in s 5:

(1)   In relation to the protected characteristic of age—

    (a)   a reference to a person who has a particular protected characteristic is a reference to a person of a particular age group;

    (b)   a reference to persons who share a protected characteristic is a reference to persons of the same age group.

(2)   A reference to an age group is a reference to a group of persons defined by reference to age, whether by reference to a particular age or to a range of ages.

This section establishes that where the Act refers to the protected characteristic of age, it means a person belonging to a particular age group. An age group includes people of the same age and people of a particular range of ages. Where people fall in the same age group, they share the protected characteristic of age.

The Explanatory Notes give the following examples:

•   An age group would include 'over fifties' or twenty-one year olds.

•   A person aged twenty-one does not share the same characteristic of age with 'people in their forties'. However, a person aged twenty-one and people in their forties can share the characteristic of being in the 'under fifty' age range.

Section 14 provides for the discrimination prohibited by the Act to include direct discrimination because of a combination of two protected characteristics ('dual discrimination'), eg age and gender, or disability and race (see **9.2.3**). The Government considers it too complicated and burdensome to allow claims on three or more different discrimination grounds.

12.3 PROHIBITED CONDUCT

As referred to at **12.1** above, there are four main types of age discrimination outlawed in the employment field by the Equality Act 2010 so far as the protected characteristic of age is concerned:

(a)   direct discrimination (s 13), eg refusing employment on the ground of a person's being too young or too old;

(b) indirect discrimination (s 19), eg refusing employment on the ground of a person's having too few or too many years' service;

(c) harassment (s 26);

(d) victimisation (s 27).

These will be dealt with in more detail below. Note that employers can defend claims of direct and indirect age discrimination by showing that their actions are a proportionate means of achieving a legitimate aim.

12.4 UNLAWFUL ACTS OF DISCRIMINATION

As with sex and race, etc, discrimination in the employment field against job applicants, employees and former employees is prohibited by ss 39 and 40 of the Act. These sections make it unlawful for an employer to discriminate against, victimise or harass employees and people seeking work. The prohibition applies where the employer is making arrangements to fill a job, and in respect of anything done in the course of a person's employment. The provisions apply to recruitment, terms and conditions, promotions, transfers, dismissals and training. See **8.4** for more details.

In *Keane v Investigo and Others* (UKEAT/0389/09), K a 51-year-old accountant with a number of years' experience, applied for a large number of positions that were advertised as being for a recently-qualified accountant with limited experience. She was not interviewed for these posts and brought tribunal proceedings against 11 agencies, a number of whom settled. There were five left by the time of the tribunal hearing. At the hearing it was argued that K had no genuine interest in the jobs and had brought the claims to make a broader point about age discrimination. The tribunal found that there was no direct or indirect discrimination as K did not want the jobs. The EAT upheld that decision, finding that there was no 'less favourable treatment' or 'disadvantage' caused to K:

> [W]e do not see how an applicant who is not considered for a job in which he or she is not in any event interested can in any ordinary sense of the word be said to have suffered a detriment – or to be more precise, to have been (comparatively) unfavourably 'treated' or put at a 'disadvantage'.

The imposition of age limits has proved particularly problematic in European law – whether as a minimum or maximum at point of entry for a particular career, or when employment automatically terminates, or for the availability of certain benefits. On their face, all these limits amount to direct age discrimination. This treatment can be justified (see below) (under the Equal Treatment Framework Directive 2000/78) if it is 'objectively and reasonably justified by a legitimate aim ... and if the means of achieving that aim are appropriate and necessary'. This is why some time-limits are permitted (see for example *Rosenbladt* (Case C-45/09), *Hornfeldt* (Case C-141/11), *Goergiev* (Cases C-250/09 and C-268/09) and *Fries* (Case C-190/16)) and others are not (see for example *Prigge* (Case C-447/09), *Petersen* (Cases C-229/08 and C-341/09) and *Commission v Hungary* (Case C-286/12)).

12.5 OCCUPATIONAL REQUIREMENTS

See **8.5** for a more detailed discussion of occupational requirements.

12.6 DIRECT DISCRIMINATION

12.6.1 Definition

Direct discrimination occurs where the reason for a person being treated less favourably than another is a protected characteristic listed in s 4 of the Act (see **9.2.1**).

The definition of 'direct discrimination' in connection with a person's age is the same as for sex, race, etc, and is set out in s 13 of the Act:

(1)   A person (A) discriminates against another (B) if, because of a protected characteristic, A treats B less favourably than A treats or would treat others.

(2)   If the protected characteristic is age, A does not discriminate against B if A can show A's treatment of B to be a proportionate means of achieving a legitimate aim.

The Explanatory Notes give the following by way of example:

If the manager of a nightclub is disciplined for refusing to carry out an instruction to exclude older customers from the club, this would be direct age discrimination against the manager unless the instruction could be justified.

Acas gives the following example of direct discrimination in its booklet *Age and the Workplace*:

Whilst being interviewed, a job applicant says that she took her professional qualification 30 years ago. Although she has all the skills and competences required of the job holder, the organisation decides not to offer her the job because of her age.

Note that, unlike the other types of protected characteristics, direct age discrimination can be justified (see **12.6.2**): for age, different treatment that is justified as a proportionate means of meeting a legitimate aim is not direct discrimination.

The definition is wide enough to cover discrimination by association, ie cases where the less favourable treatment is because of the victim's association with someone who has the protected characteristic. It is also (see **9.2.4**) wide enough to include discrimination on the ground of a person's apparent age; it will not be a defence for the employer to say that the person in question appeared to be older or younger than he or she in fact was. This would apply where, for example, someone is refused employment because he looks too old or too young.

It is therefore unlawful to decide not to employ someone on the ground of age, to dismiss him, to refuse to provide him with training, to deny him promotion, to give him adverse terms and conditions, or to retire him without an objective justification.

In *Swann v GHL Insurance Services UK Ltd* (ET/2306281/07), an employment tribunal decided (by a majority) that a flexible benefits package containing a medical insurance option, where the premium was calculated according to age, did not amount to unlawful age discrimination, because all the employees were given the same flexible benefits package and the calculation of the package was not age-related. (See also *Live Nation (Venues) UK Ltd v Hussain* (UKEAT/ 0234/ 08), where the EAT overturned the tribunal's funding of direct age discrimination.)

In *ABN Amro Management Services Ltd & Anor v Hogben* (UKEAT/0266/09), the EAT struck out Mr Hogben's claim for age discrimination on the basis that his prospects of success were no more than fanciful that he had not been offered an alternative position during a redundancy consultation because the successful candidate was nine months older than him. In *Citibank NA & Ors v Kirk* [2022] EAT 103, Mr Kirk was aged 55 and Ms Olive was aged 51. Mr Kirk was dismissed by reason of redundancy, following a consultation. Mr Kirk appealed the decision and his appeal was dismissed. Mr Kirk brought several claims against Citibank, including direct age discrimination. The EAT held that a small age difference must be carefully scrutinised before deciding that age was the reason for the treatment:

A small difference in age between protagonists in their 50s might, without more, render it implausible that age is the reason for any difference in treatment. That is not to say that age could not be the reason in such cases, but a claim that it is would be subject to careful scrutiny.

The Court of Appeal held in *Lockwood v DWP & Another* [2013] EWCA Civ 1195 that the protected characteristic cannot be used to argue that the circumstances of the claimant and the comparator are not materially similar. The discussion at **9.2.5.2** is relevant here.

12.6.2 Justification

One important distinction between direct age discrimination and most other forms of direct discrimination under UK law, is that direct age discrimination can be objectively justified if the treatment in question is shown to be a proportionate means of achieving a legitimate aim. The test is the same for both direct and indirect discrimination (see **12.6.1** above and **12.7** below) but the tests are slightly different in the Equal Treatment Framework Directive. In relation to direct discrimination, the question is whether the treatment is 'objectively and reasonably justified by a legitimate aim' (Article 6).

In *Seldon v Clarkson Wright & Jakes (A Partnership)* [2012] UKSC 16, the Supreme Court held that the test for justifying direct age discrimination is narrower than that for justifying indirect discrimination (see below). The case was brought by a partner in the respondent firm who was made to retire at 65. The Court held that direct age discrimination can only be justified if the employer's legitimate aim is a 'public interest' aim as specified in EU law, as opposed to purely individual aims being pursued by the business (eg redundancy costs). Lady Hale said, drawing from the ECJ's jurisprudence:

> If it is sought to justify direct age discrimination under article 6(1), the aims of the measure must be social policy objectives, such as those related to employment policy, the labour market or vocational training. These are of a public interest nature, which is 'distinguishable from purely individual reasons particular to the employer's situation, such as cost reduction or improving competitiveness'.

Lady Hale summarised the legitimate aims recognised by the ECJ in the context of direct age discrimination claims:

(i)   promoting access to employment for younger people (*Palacios de la Villa, Hütter, Kücükdeveci*);

(ii)   the efficient planning of the departure and recruitment of staff (*Fuchs*);

(iii)   sharing out employment opportunities fairly between the generations (*Petersen, Rosenbladt, Fuchs*);

(iv)   ensuring a mix of generations of staff so as to promote the exchange of experience and new ideas (*Georgiev, Fuchs*);

(v)   rewarding experience (*Hütter, Hennigs*);

(vi)   cushioning the blow for long serving employees who may find it hard to find new employment if dismissed (*Ingeniørforeningen i Danmark*);

(vii)   facilitating the participation of older workers in the workforce (*Fuchs*, see also *Mangold v Helm*, Case C-144/04 [2006] 1 CMLR 1132);

(viii) avoiding the need to dismiss employees on the ground that they are no longer capable of doing the job which may be humiliating for the employee concerned (*Rosenbladt*); or

(ix)   avoiding disputes about the employee's fitness for work over a certain age (*Fuchs*).

The Supreme Court accepted that staff retention and workforce planning were directly related to the legitimate social policy aim of sharing out professional employment opportunities fairly between the generations, and that the need to expel partners by way of performance management was directly related to 'dignity' aims accepted as legitimate by the ECJ in *Rosenbladt* and *Fuchs*.

As far as proportionality is concerned, this will involve an employer showing that what it is doing is necessary to achieve the legitimate aim and is the least onerous way of doing so. It will be open to employers to demonstrate that any aim they are pursing is legitimate. Examples of treatment that a court or tribunal may find to be a proportionate way of achieving a legitimate aim could include setting age requirements in order to ensure the protection of, or to promote the vocational integration of, people in a particular age group, or the fixing of a minimum age to qualify for certain advantages linked to employment in order to recruit or retain older people. Acas gives the following advice in *Age and the Workplace*:

•   if your aim is to encourage loyalty then you ought to have evidence that the provision or criterion you introduce is actually doing so;

•   the discriminatory effect should be significantly outweighed by the importance and benefits of the legitimate aim;

•   you should have no reasonable alternative to the action you are taking. If the legitimate aim can be achieved by less or non discriminatory means then these must take precedence.

Seldon returned to the employment tribunal to make a decision on the facts. The dignity justification was not actively promoted before the tribunal. On the intergenerational fairness justification relied upon, the tribunal held that while the firm might have selected other ages within a narrow band (64 or 66) to achieve the aims, 65 was proportionate to the aims of retention and workforce planning, so that the mandatory retirement age of 65 was justified overall (ET 1100275/07). Mr Seldon appealed this decision. The EAT held that the tribunal had applied the correct test (UKEAT/0434/13). The proper analysis was to consider whether the chosen retirement age was reasonably necessary to achieve the aims, given the realities of setting a bright-line date. The decision does not provide an unqualified authority for companies to justify a mandatory retirement age of 65: this was a fact-sensitive decision since there was an agreed retirement age in the partnership deed; Mr Seldon was a partner, not an employee; and the case was decided using statistics relating to 2006, before the abolition of the default retirement age in 2011.

The EAT set out a useful summary of the legal position in *Magoulas v Queen Mary University of London* (UKEAT/0244/15):

(1) an employee will only justify a PCP if it shows that the PCP is a proportionate means of achieving a legitimate aim; (2) the test is an objective test and not a band of reasonable responses test; (3) the Tribunal must not conflate legitimate aim and proportionality; (4) what amounts to a legitimate aim is not defined in the 2010 Act and is a question of fact for the Tribunal; (5) the measure must pursue the aim, but it is not necessary for this to have been specified at the time, and an *ex post facto* justification is possible (see *Seldon v Clarkson Wright & Jakes* [2012] IRLR 590); (6) an aim that is inherently discriminatory will not suffice and will not be a legitimate aim; (7) reducing cost can be a legitimate aim in some circumstances, for example in allocating resources between competing demands, but it cannot justify an otherwise discriminatory provision; (8) the principle of proportionality requires the Tribunal to strike an objective balance between the discriminatory effect of the PCP and the reasonable needs of the employer's business; (9) there is no guidance in the 2010 Act about this, and it is for the Tribunal to assess proportionality; (10) in general, the greater the disadvantage caused by the PCP, the more cogent the justification that is needed; (11) an employer can rely on a justification defence not thought of at the time of the discrimination (see *Cadman v Health & Safety Executive* [2004] IRLR 971); and (12) some evidence is required to establish the defence, but see the *Seldon* case per Elias P, as he then was, at para 73. There is an important citation from that decision at para 36 of the ET's Decision:

'We do not accept the submissions ... that a tribunal must always have concrete evidence, neatly weighed, to support each assertion made by the employer. Tribunals have an important role in applying their common sense and their knowledge of human nature ... Tribunals must, no doubt, be astute to differentiate between the exercise of their knowledge of how humans behave and stereotyped assumptions about behaviour. But the fact that they may sometimes fall into that trap does not mean that the Tribunals must leave their understanding of human nature behind them when they sit in judgment.'

The Court of Appeal held in *Woodcock v Cumbria PCT* [2012] EWCA Civ 330 that cost alone cannot justify discrimination, but that where there is another factor (here there was a redundancy situation too), the discrimination may be justified on a 'costs plus' basis. In *Sturmey v The Weymouth and Portland BC* (UKEAT/0114/14), the EAT held that *Woodcock* was not intended to lay down 'any general principle as to whether omitting or eliding stages in a redundancy process to save pension costs will always be a proportionate means of [achieving a legitimate aim]'. That will depend on the facts. The EAT held in *Heskett v Secretary of State for Justice* (UKEAT/0149/18) (an indirect discrimination case) that the employment tribunal had been entitled to find that changes to pay structures were required because of government financial constraints and that this went beyond cost alone. Mr Heskett's appeal was rejected by the Court of Appeal in November 2020.

In *Abercrombie & Fitch Italia Srl v Bordonaro* [2017] IRLR 1018, the ECJ held that the use of zero hours terms for people under 25 was justified because the rule sought to achieve a legitimate aim (help young people into jobs) and that it was a proportionate way of achieving the aim. Less rigid contracts of employment were an appropriate and necessary way to achieve labour market flexibility. See too *Air Products PLC v Cockram* [2018] EWCA Civ 346 for a decision of the Court of Appeal on objective justification. The aim of 'intergenerational fairness', achieved by limiting the advantage enjoyed by one age group over another, was a legitimate social policy. Balancing retention of employees and opportunities for younger employees with incentives for retirement after the age of 55 was a proportionate approach to the problem.

An area of particular difficulty is around the introduction by the Government of transitionary provisions seeking to make changes to public service pension schemes. These are often, by their very nature, age (and possibly sex and race) discriminatory, but the Government has argued that they are objectively justified.

In *Lord Chancellor and Secretary of State for Justice and another v McCloud and others; Secretary of State for the Home Department and another v Sargeant* [2018] EWCA Civ 2844, the Court of Appeal looked at the transitional provisions for two public sector schemes, for judges and firefighters. The *McCloud* appeal concerned judicial pension provisions introducing a less favourable pension scheme for judges which included transitional protection for those within 10 years of pensionable age. It was argued that this directly discriminated against those who were not protected by the transitional arrangements. The *Sargeant* appeal concerned transitional arrangements for pensions in respect of firefighters (but which also applied to other public sector workers such as the police).

The Court of Appeal held in respect of the judges' pension provisions (agreeing with the employment tribunal):

> an aim which protected older judges rather than younger judges when the older judges needed it least was irrational and that it did not help to expand that by saying that older judges would have less time to prepare for pension reform. It does not seem to us that it adds anything either to say that it was somehow fairer to older judges to give them protection which they needed less than younger judges .... The point is that there was just no evidence that older judges did need protection more than younger judges.

The Court of Appeal went on to say that, even if the Government had established a legitimate aim, the discriminatory effect of the reforms on the younger judges went beyond what was reasonably necessary either to achieve consistency or to protect those closest to retirement and was therefore disproportionate.

In the firefighters' case, the Court of Appeal said that it:

> 161 ... agree[d] with and accept[ed] counsel's] submission that the Governments' aims were ones whose claimed justification had to be supported by evidence. It was for the Governments to show that, despite the apparently discriminatory effect of their transitional protective measures as between the three groups of FPS members, their measures were a legitimate aim of social policy. In the event, they sought to do so by nothing more than assertions and generalisations. Even though governments are entitled to be afforded a broad measure of discretion, 'Generalised assumptions, not based on any factual foundation, are not good enough' (*Seymour Smith*, per Lord Nicholls of Birkenhead). We noted, at para 71 above, that Lord Nicholls was there addressing himself primarily to means. But the ECJ made the same point about aims in the *Age Concern England Case* C-388/07 [2009] ICR 1080, at paras 51 and 65:-
>
>> '51. Mere generalisations concerning the capacity of a specific measure to contribute to employment policy, labour market or vocational training objectives are not enough to show that the aim of that measure is capable of justifying derogation from that principle ...
>>
>> 65. ... However, it is important to note that the latter provision [Article 6(1) of Directive 2000/78] is addressed to the member states and imposes on them, notwithstanding their broad discretion in matters of social policy, the burden of establishing to a high standard of proof the legitimacy of the aim pursued.'

Put simply, the Government failed, in both cases, to demonstrate a legitimate 'public interest' aim. (For a recent case where the defence of justification failed, applying *Seldon*, see *National Union of Rail, Maritime and Transport Workers v Lloyd* [2019] IRLR 897 (EAT).)

In *Pitcher and Another v The Chancellor, Masters and Scholars of the University of Oxford and Another* (UKEAT/0083/20 and 0032/20), the EAT upheld two conflicting tribunal decisions on whether a compulsory retirement age was proportionate. The EAT held that the University had three legitimate aims: (1) inter-generational fairness; (2) succession planning; and (3) equality and diversity. In the *Pitcher* case, the EAT upheld the tribunal's conclusion that the policy was proportionate (the scheme was relatively new and there was therefore limited evidence demonstrating impact). In the second case, the EAT upheld the tribunal's conclusion that the discriminatory effect of the policy was 'severe'. The EAT's headnote states:

> Although reaching different conclusions on proportionality, neither ET erred in law. The nature of the proportionality assessment meant it was possible for different ETs to reach different conclusions when considering the same measure adopted by the same employer in respect of the same aims; the task of the EAT was not to strive to find a single answer, but to consider whether a particular decision was wrong in law. Although justification related to the policy and not its individual application, the presentation of the claims and the evidence before the ETs differed in material respects. Neither ET erred in the decisions reached.

12.7 INDIRECT DISCRIMINATION

Indirect discrimination occurs when there is equal treatment of all groups but the effect of the provision, criterion or practice imposed by an employer has a disproportionate adverse impact on one group, unless the requirement can be justified.

The definition of 'indirect discrimination' in connection with a person's age is the same as for sex, race, etc, and is set out in s 19 of the Act:

(1)   A person (A) discriminates against another (B) if A applies to B a provision, criterion or practice which is discriminatory in relation to a relevant protected characteristic of B's.

(2)   For the purposes of subsection (1), a provision, criterion or practice is discriminatory in relation to a relevant protected characteristic of B's if—

    (a)   A applies, or would apply, it to persons with whom B does not share the characteristic,

    (b)   it puts, or would put, persons with whom B shares the characteristic at a particular disadvantage when compared with persons with whom B does not share it,

    (c)   it puts, or would put, B at that disadvantage, and

    (d)   A cannot show it to be a proportionate means of achieving a legitimate aim.

For example, in *Kraft Foods v Hastie* (UKEAT/0024/10), Kraft had an 'exceptionally generous' contractual redundancy scheme. Because of the high levels of payment under the scheme, it capped redundancy payments at the sum that a redundant employee would have earned if he had remained in employment until normal retirement age. Mr Hastie, who was 62, had his redundancy payment capped at £76,560. This was what he would have earned if he had remained employed until 65. If no cap existed, he would have received about £90,000. He complained that the cap amounted to indirect discrimination on grounds of age, as it would only 'bite' against older workers. The EAT held that the cap was justified. The company's aim of preventing employees receiving a 'windfall' met a legitimate aim, namely giving appropriate payments to employees to compensate them for future loss of earnings. They said the cap was a proportionate means of achieving that aim.

In *Rolls Royce plc v Unite the Union* [2009] IRLR 576, an issue arose as to whether a collectively agreed redundancy selection matrix which included an award of points for length of service was indirect age discrimination. The Court of Appeal said that rewarding long service was a reasonable and legitimate policy. It held that, viewed objectively, including a length of service criterion amongst a substantial number of other criteria was proportionate. The legitimate aim was to reward loyalty, and to achieve a stable workforce in the context of a fair process of redundancy selection. (For cases looking at contractual redundancy schemes based on age, see *MacCulloch v ICI plc* [2008] IRLR 846 and *Loxley v BAE Systems (Munitions and Ordnance) Ltd* [2008] IRLR 853.)

In *HM Land Registry v Benson* (UKEAT/0197/11), the EAT said that an employer's decision not to select employees aged 50–54 for voluntary redundancy/early retirement because they were too expensive was justified indirect age discrimination. The selection of cheapness as a criteria, which allowed the release of as many employees as possible within budget, was a proportionate means of achieving this legitimate aim. The EAT, while considering that whether this was a 'costs plus' case was debatable, did not need to challenge the tribunal's finding of fact on that (see **10.2.6** above). See also *Harrod v Chief Constable of West Midlands Police* [2017] EWCA Civ 191, where the Court of Appeal held that the tribunal should not have rejected the 'justification case on the basis that the respondent should have pursued a different aim which would have had a less discriminatory impact'.

In *Chief Constable of West Yorkshire Police v Homer* [2009] IRLR 262, the EAT overturned a tribunal's finding of indirect age discrimination where an employer introduced a requirement that, to be graded at the top grade and to receive the higher salary linked to that grade, an employee had to have a law degree. The tribunal had concluded that there was discrimination directed against those without a law degree who were within the 60–65 age bracket. The tribunal considered the issue of justification but concluded that, although the employers were seeking to achieve a legitimate objective, namely the recruitment and retention of staff of an appropriate quality, nonetheless the imposition of this criterion was not a proportionate means of achieving it.

The EAT held that there was no age discrimination. It held that such a requirement did not put a 61-year-old employee at a particular disadvantage on the grounds of his age, even though he could not have obtained a degree (studying part-time) before he retired. He was treated in precisely the same way as everyone else. The requirement for a law degree was not something required only of those over a certain age. Neither was it in principle more difficult for an older person to obtain the qualification than it was for a younger person. Any disadvantage could properly be described as the consequence of age, but it was not the consequence of age discrimination (para 39). However, had the claimant been able to establish the requisite age group disadvantage, the EAT would have upheld the finding that any age discrimination was not justified, as the requirement was not a proportionate means of achieving the recruitment and retention of appropriately qualified staff. The Court of Appeal agreed with the EAT ([2010] All ER (D) 189) that the employee's problem was not his age per se, but rather that he would retire before he could get the necessary qualification.

The Supreme Court disagreed with the Court of Appeal and held that the employer did indirectly discriminate on grounds of age, subject to justification. Therefore, a requirement which works to the comparative disadvantage of a person approaching compulsory retirement age is discriminatory on grounds of age. The tribunal decided, when the question of justification was remitted back to it, that the respondent could not justify the policy of requiring a law degree to justify promotion to the highest grade – it was not a proportionate means of achieving a legitimate aim because the respondent could have treated new employees differently to existing employees ([2013] EQLR 295).

In *Braithwaite and Others v HCL Insurance BPO Services Ltd and Another* (EAT/152/14/DM; 0153/14), the respondent was facing financial difficulties and required employees to agree new terms and conditions or be dismissed. This put older employees at a disadvantage because they would lose contractual benefits built up through longer service. The tribunal found that the requirement to enter a new contract was objectively justified and dismissed the claim. The EAT held that the tribunal was entitled to find that the provision, criterion or practice (PCP) was justified as a proportionate means of achieving the legitimate. The respondent had a legitimate aim, namely reducing staff costs to ensure its future viability and to have in place a market-competitive, non-discriminatory set of terms and conditions.

The correct approach to an indirect age discrimination claim was explored by the EAT in *Ryan v South West Ambulance Services NHS Trust* [2021] IRLR 4.

See **Chapter 10** for more a more detailed analysis of the underlying principles of indirect discrimination. For a recent decision on justifying indirect age discrimination, see *Heskett v Secretary of State for Justice* [2020] EWCA Civ 1487.

12.7.1 Age groups

Bringing a claim for age discrimination will involve comparing the claimant's 'age group' with another group. Section 5(2) states that 'age group' means 'a group of persons defined by reference to age, whether by reference to a particular age or a range of ages'. There is no further definition of age groups in the Act. This was the same wording as used by the Age Regulations 2006. However, it is still unclear whether 'age group' will be interpreted widely or narrowly. Acas suggests that companies could undertake age monitoring using age bands 16–21, 22–30, 31–40, 41–50, 51–60, 60–65 and 65+. Whatever age group an employee chooses, it will still be open to an employer to challenge the group on the basis that it is not appropriate.

In *Lockwood* (**12.6.1** above), the Court of Appeal compared the circumstances of the claimant's age group (under 30) and that of the older age group (35 and over) to hold that the claimant had suffered less favourable treatment because of her age (a reduced redundancy award). However, the scheme rules were held to be objectively justified by social policy objectives (reflecting the extra difficulties faced by older workers on redundancy).

For a recent analysis, see *Donkor v Royal Bank of Scotland* (EAT/0162/15). The case is a useful reminder of the importance of the 'reason why' question (see **9.2.5**).

12.8 HARASSMENT AND VICTIMISATION

As with the other areas covered by discrimination legislation, harassment is a specific separate ground of complaint. The definitions used in connection with a person's age are identical to those used for sex, race, etc, ie harassment includes behaviour that is intimidating, hostile, degrading, humiliating or offensive.

The IDS Brief, *Focus on Age Discrimination* (805, May 2006), gave some useful practical examples of the protection against harassment provisions:

- an employee whose father works in the same office is subjected to jokes about the father's age. Even though the victim's own age is not the subject of the jokes, this behaviour may still qualify as harassment on the ground of age

- an older employee is not asked to after-work drinks and events as his younger colleagues believe he would not fit in with their social culture. As this is likely to make the older worker feel excluded, it could come within the definition of offensive conduct

- an older employee is subjected to jokes about baldness, wrinkles, etc. Any offensive behaviour based on physical traits that become apparent as one gets older could be argued to be on the ground of age.

In *Lambert v BAT (Investments) Ltd* (ET/3100897/08), the tribunal held that an e-mail entitled 'The perks of being over 50' amounted to 'unwanted conduct which had the effect of violating [the claimant's] dignity'.

The victimisation provisions aim to ensure that individuals are not discouraged from bringing complaints of age discrimination. The protected acts include bringing proceedings under the Act; giving evidence in connection with a case; and alleging that someone has done something which would be unlawful under the Act. Victimisation cannot be justified.

See **Chapter 11** for a more detailed analysis of the underlying principles of victimisation and harassment.

12.9 EXCEPTIONS

Many service-related benefits (see Sch 9, para 10) and the minimum pay rates applicable to younger workers under the minimum wage legislation (Sch 9, para 11) are exempt from the provisions of the Act. Schedule 9, Pt 2 also makes special provision for exemption of or modification to the normal rules in the case of retirement and enhanced redundancy payments (para 13). While certain age-related criteria have been removed (the upper and lower age limits for redundancy payments), the two-year qualifying service period, the length of service used to calculate the payment, and the age-based multipliers for unfair dismissal and redundancy payment awards all remain.

There are a number of other grounds set out in Sch 9, Pt 2 on which otherwise discriminatory acts are lawful: see, eg, para 14 (life assurance) and para 15 (childcare provision for children of a particular age group). The full details of these are beyond the scope of this book.

12.10 VICARIOUS LIABILITY

Section 109 provides that employers are vicariously liable for any acts of their workers, done in the course of their employment, that are unlawful under the Act. Likewise, it extends to the acts of agents. This is so whether or not the acts were done with the employer's knowledge or approval. However, it is a defence for the employer to show that he took such steps as were reasonably practicable to prevent an employee doing the act complained of. See **8.6** for a more detailed discussion of vicarious liability.

12.11 BURDEN OF PROOF

The burden of proof for age discrimination is the same as in all the other main areas of discrimination, as set out in s 136(2) of the Act, namely:

> If there are facts from which the court could decide, in the absence of any other explanation, that a person (A) contravened the provision concerned, the court must hold that the contravention occurred.

In other words, once a complainant has established facts from which a tribunal could conclude there has been discrimination, the tribunal will have to make a finding of discrimination, unless the employer proves he did not commit the act of discrimination (see **9.5**).

In *McCoy v McGregor & Sons Ltd, Dixon and Aitken* (IT/00237/07), the tribunal held that a job advert requiring 'youthful enthusiasm', taken in the context of other evidence, gave rise to a prima facie case of direct discrimination and therefore shifted the burden to the employer.

12.12 PRACTICAL CONSIDERATIONS

12.12.1 Advertising and recruitment

Care should be taken with the language used in job advertisements. Words such as 'mature', 'senior', 'energetic' and 'junior' could all be problematic. Advertisements should focus on the job requirement and the tasks, and not on the person. Consider why and, if so, what experience is needed. Care also needs to be taken about where job advertisements are placed. Recruitment criteria need to be looked at to see if they could have a discriminatory impact. Avoid focusing on a particular age group to satisfy customer prejudice or targets. Using an agency to recruit staff does not avoid the risk of age discrimination.

12.12.2 Application forms and interviews

The Acas booklet recommended banishing questions about age and date of birth from application forms, and suggests that this information could be collected through a separate diversity monitoring form. Application forms should also avoid requesting information from which a job applicant's age can be inferred, unless such information is necessary (eg the dates when an applicant attended school). Employers should consider why they need this information so that, if necessary, they can avail themselves of the justification defence. Interviewers should have had age diversity training. Make sure that each candidate is asked the same questions in the same order. Focus on the job requirement, the tasks involved and the competencies needed for the job.

12.12.3 Contracts

Employment contracts, policies and procedures, and terms and conditions all need to be checked to ensure that they comply with the Act. If any policies or practices are potentially discriminatory, consideration will need to be given as to whether they can be justified. The Act requires that if changes are to be made to the contracts of more than 20 employees, there must be collective consultation with either unions or employee representatives. Similar consultation obligations apply as are to be found in large-scale redundancy situations.

12.12.4 Pensions and insurance benefits

The provisions of the Act relating to pensions are set out in s 61. While the Act makes it unlawful for trustees and managers of occupational pension schemes to discriminate against members or prospective members on the ground of age, there are lots of exemptions (which are beyond the scope of this book) (see, eg, s 197 and Schs 7 and 9). BIS published 'Guidance on the Age Regulations and their impact on pension schemes' in December 2006, which is still a useful reference.

The Act, like the Age Regulations, outlaws age discrimination in respect of employment-related insured benefits (private medical, motor insurance, etc). The cost to employers of providing insured benefits in relation to older staff, particularly those over 65, can be very high. Insurance companies are free to impose age limits or higher premiums on insurance policies, as insurance providers are not covered by the age discrimination legislation. There is concern amongst both employer and employee organisations that the absence of any exemptions for insurance benefits may cause employers to level down or remove insured benefits for all staff.

The Government has not ruled out introducing an exemption for insured benefits, but to date no action has been taken.

12.12.5 Dismissal and retirement

If an employer wishes to retire an employee, the employer will have to ensure that a fair procedure is followed under the ordinary unfair dismissal rules. Retirement is no longer a potentially fair reason for dismissal, so employers will need to show that the dismissal was for one of the potentially fair reasons for dismissal set out in s 98 of the ERA 1996 (capability, conduct, illegality, redundancy or some other substantial reason). This will mean that if an employer feels that an employee is under-performing then the employer should deal with the employee in the same manner as any other under-performing employee, ie by following a fair capability process that focuses on the employee's performance and not on his age. There has been concern that older employees will be particularly sensitive to this, and employers will have to ensure that any such disciplinary/capability procedures are handled sensitively and fairly.

Employers may still be able to operate a compulsory retirement age, provided that they can objectively justify it. They must show that the discrimination is a proportionate means of achieving a legitimate aim (see **12.6.2**).

Commentators have advised that there are now broadly two options for employers – to have and operate a contractual retirement age and be willing and able to justify it (s 13(2) of the Act) if an employee complains of direct discrimination; or to treat retirement on a case-by-case basis using ordinary capability and disciplinary procedures; but otherwise to leave it up to employees to decide when they want to retire. Clauses in contacts specifying that the contract may come to an end automatically when the employee reaches his 65th birthday may need to reviewed.

With regard to the first option, as indicated above, there is a consistent body of decisions from the ECJ adopting a liberal stance towards justifying compulsory retirement ages. The EHRC's Code of Practice on Employment – which is admissible as evidence – should be referred to. In *Seldon* (**12.6.2** above) the tribunal accepted that the following aims were potentially legitimate aims:

- retention reasons – giving younger senior solicitors the opportunity of partnership so that they do not leave;
- facilitating partnership and workforce planning so as to provide promotion opportunities (and see the Acas booklet, *Working within the DRA*); and
- limiting the need to expel partners by way of performance management, including potential health and safety arguments.

In addition to being required to meet a legitimate aim, the retirement age will have to be a proportionate means of achieving that aim. The EHRC Code of Practice states (para 4.31) that:

> EU law views treatment as proportionate if it is an appropriate and necessary means of achieving a legitimate aim. ... [I]t is sufficient that less discriminatory measures could not achieve the same aim. A balance must be struck between the discriminatory effect of the practice and A's reasons for applying it, taking into account all the relevant facts.

Even where an employer can show that a compulsory retirement age is justified, it will still be necessary where an individual is to be dismissed to show that the dismissal was for a potentially fair reason. The most likely category of the five potentially fair reasons for dismissal that could be used here would appear to be some other substantial reason. Where there is no contractual date, an employer will have to rely on one of the other potentially fair reasons, from which capability seems to be the one most employers will probably rely on. For a detailed analysis of capability dismissals, see **5.2.2.1** and **5.4.2.1** above. It should be noted that in addition to capabilities and qualifications, the definition of capability includes skills, aptitude and health, as well as 'any other physical or mental quality'.

12.12.6 Redundancy

Note that enhanced redundancy schemes may be unlawful if they pay out based on differential age grounds (likely to be direct discrimination unless exempted under Sch 9 or objectively justified) or on length of service (indirect discrimination unless exempted under Sch 9 or objectively justified). Paragraph 13 of Sch 9 to the Equality Act 2010 allows for enhanced redundancy schemes that essentially mirror the statutory redundancy payment scheme, although employers can derogate from the statutory cap on a week's wage and/or the multiple used. See **12.6** and **12.7** above.

12.13 ENFORCEMENT AND REMEDIES

Chapter 3 of Pt 9 of the Act contains the enforcement and remedies regime. Readers are referred to **8.8** for a more detailed discussion of enforcement and remedies. In essence, the same regime applies as applies to the other grounds of discrimination. Section 124 permits the making of a declaration of rights, an order to pay compensation and a recommendation that the employer take, within a specified period, specific steps for the purpose of obviating or reducing the adverse effect on the complainant or any other person of any matter to which the complaint relates.

12.14 FURTHER READING

In February 2019, Acas released useful guidance on age discrimination, including fact sheets with key points for employers to consider in the workplace.

SUMMARY

Age is a protected characteristic under s 4 of the Equality Act 2010 (**12.2**). The provisions of the 2010 Act apply to employees, job applicants, ex-employees, contract workers, office holders and partners. They outlaw age discrimination in terms of recruitment, promotion and training, transfers and dismissals (**12.4**); ban all retirement ages below 65 (except where objectively justified); and remove the current upper age limits for unfair dismissal and redundancy (**12.12.5**).

Four main types of age discrimination in the employment field are outlawed by UK legislation. These are:

(a)   direct discrimination (ie being subject to less favourable treatment than others because of age) (**12.6**);

(b)   indirect discrimination (ie the application of a provision, criterion or practice which disadvantages people of a particular age) (**12.7**);

(c)   harassment (unwanted conduct that violates a person's dignity, or creates an intimidating, hostile, degrading, humiliating or offensive environment for him having regard to all the circumstances including the perception of the victim) (**12.8**); and

(d)   victimisation (because the victim has been subject to a detriment because he has done a protected act) (**12.8**).

Much of the terminology used is familiar 'discrimination' terminology. Unlike other forms of discrimination, both direct and indirect age discrimination may be justified 'objectively' where the discrimination is a 'proportionate means of achieving legitimate aim' (**12.6.2** and **12.7.2**). Harassment and victimisation cannot be justified.

The Equality Act 2010 also removes the age limits for statutory sick pay, statutory maternity pay, statutory adoption pay and statutory paternity pay. The Employment Equality (Age) Regulations 2006, Sch 6 further introduced a right for employees to request to be permitted to work beyond retirement age, and a duty on employers to consider that request, and a requirement for employers to give at least six months' notice to employees about their intended retirement date so that individuals might plan better for retirement and be confident that 'retirement' is not being used as a cover for unfair dismissal. The Regulations also made changes to the existing unfair dismissal regime. In particular, 'retirement' is now a potentially fair reason for dismissal. The Equality Act 2010 does not affect the age at which people may claim their State pensions.

Remedies and enforcement are dealt with at **8.8** above.

CHAPTER 13

DISABILITY DISCRIMINATION

13.1	Introduction	501
13.2	The protected characteristic	502
13.3	The meaning of 'disability' and 'disabled person'	502
13.4	Unlawful discrimination in employment	514
13.5	Types of discrimination	515
13.6	Burden of proof	538
13.7	Vicarious liability	538
13.8	Enforcement and remedies	538
	Summary	539

LEARNING OUTCOMES

After reading this chapter you will be able to:

- understand the underlying principles of disability discrimination and how it differs from other areas of discrimination
- explain the four cumulative elements that make up the meaning of 'disability'
- list the six types of prohibited conduct and explain how they differ from each other
- describe the remedies available where a complaint of disability discrimination is made out.

13.1 INTRODUCTION

This chapter considers disability discrimination. Traditionally, disability discrimination has been treated differently from discrimination because of sex, race, religion or belief, etc. The pre-Equality Act 2010 legislation, the Disability Discrimination Act 1995 (DDA 1995) (as amended by the Disability Discrimination Act 1995 (Amendment) Regulations 2003 and the Disability Discrimination Act 2005) was different from other discrimination legislation in a number of ways. In relation to sex, race, religion or belief, etc, the emphasis is on treating all people the same. In disability discrimination, the opposite is often the case – a person's individual circumstances have to be considered, and such consideration is crucial to avoid discrimination. Many of the differences that existed between the DDA 1995 and the rest of the UK anti-discrimination legislation have been maintained in the Equality Act 2010, eg the concept of 'reasonable adjustments' (see **13.5.2** below), whereby employers need to treat disabled people differently in order to achieve substantive equality.

The relevant parts of the 2010 Act in so far as they relate to disability discrimination were implemented in October 2010.

The EHRC has responsibility for the promotion of equality and for combating discrimination on the grounds of disability. The EHRC published a Code of Practice on Employment, which came into force on 6 April 2011.

The protection against discrimination because of disability applies to all employers, private and public sector, and employment agencies, vocational training providers, trade unions, professional organisations, employer organisations, and trustees and managers of occupational pension schemes. It applies to employees, job claimants, ex-employees, contract workers, office holders and partners. The protection applies to a broad definition of workers and employees (see **1.3**). As with sex, race, age, etc, 'employment' is defined as 'employment under a contract of employment, a contract of apprenticeship or a contract personally to do work' (s 83). This is a wider definition than that of 'employee' as contained in the ERA 1996, and means that certain categories of individuals who are not covered by other statutory rights (eg job claimants, office holders, police officers and the self-employed) are covered by the Equality Act 2010.

Much of the terminology used is familiar discrimination terminology; under the Act direct disability discrimination is prohibited (ie being subjected to less favourable treatment than others because of disability) as is indirect disability discrimination (ie the application of a provision, criterion or practice (PCP) which disadvantages the disabled person). Both harassment (being unwanted conduct that violates a person's dignity, or creates an intimidating, hostile, degrading, humiliating or offensive environment for him having regard to all the circumstances, including the perception of the victim) and victimisation (because the victim has brought proceedings under the Act, or has given evidence or information in connection with proceedings under the Act) are also unlawful. However, some of the terminology is new and relevant to disability discrimination only (eg the duty to make reasonable adjustments; discrimination arising from a disability).

13.2   THE PROTECTED CHARACTERISTIC

Section 4 of the Act sets out certain 'protected' characteristics (see **8.2**). These are the grounds upon which discrimination is deemed unlawful. Disability is listed as one of the protected characteristics in s 4.

13.3   THE MEANING OF 'DISABILITY' AND 'DISABLED PERSON'

13.3.1   Introduction

Crucial to the operation of the disability discrimination regime in the Act are the definitions of 'disability' and 'disabled person' in s 6 (see Lord Hope in *SCA Packaging Ltd v Boyle* [2009] UKHL 37). This section establishes who is to be considered as having the protected characteristic of disability and is a disabled person for the purposes of the Act. Unless the parties agree that a claimant is a disabled person at the relevant time, the burden of proof is on the claimant to show that they were a disabled person.

Section 6 provides as follows:

(1)   A person (P) has a disability if—

   (a)   P has a physical or mental impairment, and

   (b)   the impairment has a substantial and long-term adverse effect on P's ability to carry out normal day-to-day activities.

(2)   A reference to a disabled person is a reference to a person who has a disability.

(3)   In relation to the protected characteristic of disability—

   (a)   a reference to a person who has a particular protected characteristic is a reference to a person who has a particular disability;

   (b)   a reference to persons who share a protected characteristic is a reference to persons who have the same disability.

(4)   This Act (except Part 12 and section 190) applies in relation to a person who has had a disability as it applies in relation to a person who has the disability;

   accordingly (except in that Part and that section)—

   (a)   a reference (however expressed) to a person who has a disability includes a reference to a person who has had the disability, and

   (b)   a reference (however expressed) to a person who does not have a disability includes a reference to a person who has not had the disability.

A person has a disability, therefore, if he has:

- a physical or mental impairment, which has
- a substantial and
- long-term adverse effect on his ability to carry out
- normal day-to-day activities. (s 6(1))

A 'disabled person' means a person who has a disability (s 6(2)). In essence, s 6 requires a tribunal to look at four different (cumulative) conditions.

The burden is on the claimant to show that he is a disabled person. Section 6 replaces similar provisions in the DDA 1995. The stated intention was that the 2010 Act would make it easier for a person to show that he is disabled. It introduces one major change from the DDA 1995, by removing a previous requirement to consider a specific list of eight capacities (such as mobility or speech, hearing or eyesight) which were said to constitute 'normal day-to-day activities', when considering whether or not a person was disabled (see **13.3.3** below). This change is intended to make it easier for some people to demonstrate that they meet the definition of a 'disabled person'.

A number of other sources also provide assistance, including Sch 1 to the Act; the Equality Act 2010 (Disability) Regulations 2010 (SI 2010/2128); and the 'Guidance on matters to be taken into account in determining questions relating to the definition of disability' ('the Guidance') which came into force on 1 May 2011. The Guidance is published by the Office for Disability Issues (ODI) which is a cross-government organisation that works with government departments, disabled people and a wide range of external groups: see <http://www.officefordisability.gov.uk>. The Guidance does not impose any legal obligations in itself, nor is it an authoritative statement of the law. However, para 12 of Sch 1 to the Act requires that an adjudicating body which is determining for any purpose of the Act whether a person is a disabled person must take into account any aspect of the Guidance which appears to it to be relevant.

In *HK Danmark (acting on behalf of Ring) v Dansk almennyttigt Boligselskab* (Case C-335/11) [2013] IRLR 571, the ECJ held that the concept of 'disability' in the Equal Treatment Directive 2000/78 must be interpreted in a manner consistent with the United Nations Convention on the Rights of Persons with Disabilities approved by the EU in Decision 2010/48, and that accordingly 'disability' referred to a long-term limitation which results in particular from physical, mental or psychological impairments which in interaction with barriers may hinder the full and effective participation of the person concerned in professional life on an equal basis with others. See too *Chacón Navas v Eurest Colectivadades SA* [2006] IRLR 706, where the ECJ focused on whether the disability hinders a person's full and effective participation in society on an equal basis. The domestic definition of disability in the Equality Act 2010 will have to be interpreted in a manner consistent with this approach.

We look at each of the various elements of the definition of 'disability' in s 6 of the Act in more detail below. *Goodwin v Patent Office* [1999] ICR 302 sets out useful guidance on the proper approach to be adopted by employment tribunals when considering whether someone is a disabled person. Morison J stated that:

> The tribunal should bear in mind that with social legislation of this kind, a purposive approach to construction should be adopted. The language should be construed in a way which gives effect to the stated or presumed intention of Parliament, but with due regard to the ordinary and natural meaning of the words in question.

For a recent decision which provides a useful summary of the provisions below, see *Seccombe v Reed in Partnership Ltd* (UKEAT/0213/20).

13.3.2 The impairment condition

The claimant must have a physical or mental impairment. There is no definition in the Act of either physical or mental impairment. The Guidance states that the term should be given its natural and ordinary meaning (*McNicol v Balfour Beatty Rail Maintenance Ltd* [2002] EWCA Civ 1074). Examples given include sensory impairments, organ specific diseases such as asthma, progressive diseases such as MS, and mental health conditions such as depression, OCD and eating disorders. The Guidance states that if the condition amounts to an impairment, it is *not* necessary to consider how the impairment was caused, and confirms the case law reported at **13.3.2.1** below in this respect. It is not necessary to show that a mental impairment is a clinically well-recognised illness.

The Equality Act 2010 (Disability) Regulations 2010 provide that an addiction to alcohol, nicotine or any other substance will not be an impairment for the purposes of the Equality Act 2010. In addition, a tendency to set fires, a tendency to steal, a tendency to physical or sexual abuse of other persons, exhibitionism (a compulsive desire to expose one's genital organs publicly), voyeurism (obtaining sexual pleasure from the observation of people undressing and having intercourse) and seasonal allergic rhinitis (hay fever) (although it may be taken into account for the purposes of the Act where it aggravates the effect of any other condition) are not recognised as impairments. Of course, as explained in the statutory guidance on matters to be taken into account in determining questions relating to the definition of disability (para A13) and dealt with in the cases of *Edmund Nuttall Ltd v Butterfield* [2006] ICR 77, *Governing Body of X Endowed Primary School v Special Educational Needs and Disability Tribunal (No 1)* [2009] IRLR 1007 and *Wood v Durham CC* (UKEAT/0099/18), the employment tribunal must always determine the basis for the alleged discrimination. If the alleged discrimination was as a result of an excluded condition, the exclusion will apply. If, however, the alleged discrimination is related to a disability which gives rise to an excluded condition, the exclusion may not apply. So, in *Wood*, the claimant, who was dismissed for shoplifting, could not succeed with a claim for disability discrimination (although shoplifting was a manifestation of his post-traumatic stress disorder (a disability)), since the effective cause of the dismissal was the excluded condition.

The 2010 Regulations also confirm that people who are certified blind, severely sight impaired, sight impaired or partially sighted by a consultant ophthalmologist are deemed disabled, and will automatically qualify for protection under the Act.

13.3.2.1 Case law

The Guidance emphasises that it is not how an impairment is caused that is important, but rather the effect it has. In *Power v Panasonic UK Ltd* [2003] IRLR 151, the EAT said that where depression was caused by alcohol addiction, the fact that the *cause* of the impairment was an addiction did not mean it was not covered.

In *J v DLA Piper UK LLP* (UKEAT/0263/09) the claimant's job offer was withdrawn soon after she revealed a history of depression. She tried (unsuccessfully) to convince the tribunal that she was in fact disabled and so entitled to protection under the pre-Equality Act 2010 legislation (DDA 1995). She maintained that her disability consisted of clinical depression, being a 'mental impairment which has a substantial and long-term adverse effect on [her] ability to carry out normal day-to-day activities'. She asserted that the condition had an adverse effect on her ability to concentrate. The tribunal decided that J did not suffer from a sufficiently well-defined impairment. J appealed and submitted that the existence of an impairment will, in most cases, be evident from the existence of an adverse effect on a claimant's ability to carry out day-to-day activities, and so the tribunal should examine that issue first. The EAT accepted that there will be cases where identifying the nature of the impairment in question involves difficult medical questions and that, in most such cases, it will be easier and legitimate for the tribunal to 'park' that issue and first consider adverse effect: it will not always be essential to identify a specific 'impairment' (within the words of s 1 of the DDA 1995) if the existence of one can be established from evidence of an adverse effect on the claimant's abilities. In *Khorochilova v Euro Rep Ltd* (UKEAT/0266/19), one of the claimant's grounds of appeal was that the tribunal had erred in considering the issue of whether the claimant had an impairment before considering whether that impairment had an adverse effect. HHJ Choudhury P stated:

> It is possible that some personality traits are such that they amount to an impairment within the meaning of the 2010 Act. In the absence of an express conclusion that such personality traits do not amount to an impairment, the real question is whether or not there was evidence of a substantial adverse effect on the Claimant's ability to carry out normal day-to-day activities. If there was, then, as held in the *J v DLA Piper* case, the appropriate approach would be to consider the question of impairment in light of the evidence as to the adverse effect.

On the facts, however, there was no error of law because the tribunal had also gone on to rule out adverse effect.

Thus it may be easier to address the second and third conditions at **13.3.3** and **13.3.4** below first, ie whether there is a substantial effect on ability to carry out day-to-day activities. In the event that the tribunal decides that those conditions are made out, an impairment may be inferred. So if, for example, the claimant's symptoms have a substantial effect on normal day-to-day activities caused by symptoms characteristic of depression, the tribunal is likely to conclude that the impairment condition is also made out: that the claimant is suffering from clinical depression. In this case the medical evidence was ambiguous. The EAT stated that it remains good practice for the tribunal to state its conclusions on the issues of impairment and effect separately, as recommended in *Goodwin v Patent Office* (see **13.3.3.1**), but, in reaching those conclusions, the tribunal need not proceed by rigid consecutive stages. Specifically, where there may be a dispute about the existence of an impairment, it will make sense to make findings on the question of substantial adverse effect and then consider impairment in the light of those findings.

In *Walker v Sita Information Networking Computing Ltd* (UKEAT/0097/12), the EAT confirmed that the focus is on the effect of the impairment and *not* how the impairment was caused. The ECJ confirmed in *FOA, acting on behalf of Karsten Kaltoft v Kommunernes Lansforening (KL)* (Case C-354/13) [2015] ICR 322, that obesity does not, in itself, constitute a disability; but said that obesity can constitute a disability if it entails a limitation resulting from long-term physical or mental impairments that hinder the full and effective participation of that person in professional life. That accords with the UK case law. When the case was then remitted back to the Danish court, it held that:

(1) the employee's weight fulfilled the criteria for obesity, but obesity alone did not constitute a disability;

(2) the employee had not established on the evidence that he suffered from impairments that prevented him from fully and effectively performing his work on an equal basis with other employees;

(3) the discomfort described by the employee (which included restricted mobility) did not prevent him from carrying out his work (as a child minder). Accordingly, the court found that he was not disabled at the time of the dismissal.

13.3.3 The adverse effect on normal day-to-day activities condition

The tribunal must ascertain whether the identified impairment adversely affects the claimant's ability to carry out normal day-to-day activities. The focus of attention required by the 1995 Act is on the things that the applicant either cannot do or can only do with difficulty, rather than on the things that the person can do (*Goodwin* (above)). See too *Ahmed v Metroline Travel UK Ltd* (UKEAT/0400/10) and *Rooney v Leicester City Council* [2021] 10 WLUK 69. 'Normal day-to-day activities' are not defined in the Act. The Guidance states that they are things that people do on a regular or daily basis, such as shopping, reading, getting dressed, etc. The Guidance confirms that the term is not intended to include activities which are normal only for a particular person or group of people. In any individual case, the activities carried out may be highly specialised, for example the playing of a particular game, taking part in a particular hobby, playing a musical instrument, playing sport or performing a highly-skilled task. Impairments which affect only such an activity and have no effect on 'normal day-to-day activities' are not covered. Nevertheless, the EAT held in *Cruickshank v VAW Motorcast Ltd* [2002] IRLR 24 that if, while at work, a claimant's symptoms have a significant and long-term effect on his ability to perform day-to-day tasks, such symptoms should not be ignored simply because the work itself is specialised, so long as the effect of the disability can be measured in terms of the claimant's ability to carry out day-to-day tasks. The EAT confirmed in *Paterson v Commissioner of Police of the Metropolis* [2007] IRLR 763, that 'normal day-to-day activities', includes 'the activities which are relevant to participation in professional life'. The Guidance confirms this.

The Guidance says as follows:

> It is not possible to provide an exhaustive list of day-to-day activities, although guidance on this matter is given here and illustrative examples of when it would, and would not, be reasonable to regard an impairment as having a substantial adverse effect on the ability to carry out normal day-to-day activities are shown in the Appendix. In general, day-to-day activities are things people do on a regular or daily basis, and examples include shopping, reading and writing, having a conversation or using the telephone, watching television, getting washed and dressed, preparing and eating food, carrying out household tasks, walking and travelling by various forms of transport, and taking part in social activities.

> The term 'normal day-to-day activities' is not intended to include activities which are normal only for a particular person, or a small group of people. In deciding whether an activity is a normal day-to-day activity, account should be taken of how far it is normal for a large number of people, and carried out by people on a daily or frequent and fairly regular basis. In this context, 'normal' should be given its ordinary, everyday meaning.

> A normal day-to-day activity is not necessarily one that is carried out by a majority of people. For example, it is possible that some activities might be carried out only, or more predominantly, by people of a particular gender, such as applying make-up or using hair curling equipment, and cannot therefore be said to be normal for most people. They would nevertheless be considered to be normal day-to-day activities.

The Guidance gives these examples:

> A woman plays the piano to a high standard, and often takes part in public performances. She has developed carpal tunnel syndrome in her wrists, an impairment that adversely affects manual dexterity. She can continue to play the piano, but not to such a high standard, and she has to take frequent breaks to rest her arms. This would not of itself be an adverse effect on a normal day-to-day activity. However, as a result of her impairment she also finds it difficult to operate a computer keyboard and cannot use her PC to send emails or write letters. This is an adverse effect on a normal day-to-day activity.

> A man works in a warehouse, loading and unloading heavy stock. He develops heart problems and no longer has the ability to lift or move heavy items of stock at work. Lifting and moving such unusually heavy types of item is not a normal day-to-day activity. However, he is also unable to lift, carry or move moderately heavy everyday objects such as chairs, either at work or around the home. This is an adverse effect on a normal day-to-day activity.

> A man has had chronic fatigue syndrome for several years and although he has the physical capability to walk and to stand, he finds these very difficult to sustain for any length of time because of the overwhelming fatigue he experiences. As a consequence, he is restricted in his ability to take part in normal day-to-day activities such as travelling, so he avoids going out socially, and works from home several days a week. Therefore there is a substantial adverse effect on normal day-to-day activities.

13.3.3.1 Case law

In *Paterson v Commissioner of Police of the Metropolis* (**13.3.3** above), the EAT held, following an ECJ decision, that career exams and assessments could constitute normal day-to-day activities. In

Chief Constable of Lothian and Borders Police v Cumming (UKEATS/0077/08), the EAT held that the claimant's minor eyesight impairment did not have a substantial adverse effect on normal day-to-day activities, albeit that she could not progress in her job because of the stringent medical criteria. In *Chief Constable of Dumfries and Galloway Constabulary v Mr C Adams* (UKEATS/0046/08), the EAT held that normal day-to-day activities, albeit carried out during the nightshift, fell within the definition of 'normal day-to-day activities'.

In *Leonard v Southern Derbyshire Chamber of Commerce* [2001] IRLR 19, the issue for the EAT was whether the claimant's clinical depression had a substantial adverse effect on her ability to carry out normal day-to-day activities. The tribunal said she could catch a ball, and eat and drink, and weighed these against what she could not do, such as negotiate pavement edges safely. This, the EAT said, was inappropriate, since her ability to catch a ball did not diminish her inability to negotiate pavement edges safely. A tribunal should, the EAT repeated, concentrate on what claimants cannot do or only do with difficulty, rather than on things they can do (see *Paterson v Commissioner of Police of the Metropolis* (above) and *Aderemi v London and South Eastern Railway Ltd* (UKEAT/0316/12)). See too *Sobhi v Commissioner of Police of the Metropolis* (UKEAT/0518/12). In *Banaszczyk v Booker Ltd* (UKEAT/0132/15), the EAT provided some useful guidance as to the meaning of normal day-to-day activities in the context of work activities.

In *Rooney*, the EAT held that a tribunal erred in holding that an employee suffering from menopausal symptoms was not disabled under the Act, and it allowed her appeal against the dismissal of her claims of disability and sex discrimination, harassment and victimisation. The case sets out examples of the difficulties faced by menopausal women in the workplace and the difficulties they may face in establishing that their symptoms amount to a disability.

13.3.4 The substantial condition

Section 212(1) of the Act defines 'substantial' to mean 'more than minor or trivial'.

The Guidance states that this requirement 'reflects the general understanding of "disability" as a limitation going beyond the normal differences in ability which may exist among people'. The Guidance suggests a number of factors to consider, including the time taken to carry out an activity, the way in which an activity is carried out, the cumulative effects of an impairment, the effects of behaviour and the effects of the environment. In one case the EAT said, albeit *obiter*, that someone whose hearing impairment merely requires him to view the television with the volume up, and which results in occasional difficulty in hearing speech, may have difficulty in showing 'substantial adverse effect' (*London Underground Ltd v Bragg* (UKEAT/847/98)). In *Elliott v Dorsett CC* (UKEAT/0197/20), the EAT made it clear that if the effect is clearly more than minor or trivial, the Guidance should not be used to undermine that conclusion, noting that there may be inconsistency between an adverse effect that is more than 'minor or trivial' and 'limitation going beyond the normal differences in ability which may exist among people'. Furthermore, in that case, the Employment Judge erroneously focused on what the claimant could do rather than what he could not do.

The Guidance states that the time taken by a person with an impairment to carry out a normal day-to-day activity should be considered when assessing whether the effect of that impairment is substantial. It should be compared with the time it might take a person who did not have the impairment to complete an activity. It gives the following example:

> A ten-year-old child has cerebral palsy. The effects include muscle stiffness, poor balance and uncoordinated movements. The child is still able to do most things for himself, but he gets tired very easily and it is harder for him to accomplish tasks like eating and drinking, washing, and getting dressed. Although he has the ability to carry out everyday activities such as these, everything takes longer compared to a child of a similar age who does not have cerebral palsy. This amounts to a substantial adverse effect.

The Guidance states that another factor to be considered when assessing whether the effect of an impairment is substantial is the way in which a person with that impairment carries out a normal day-to-day activity. The comparison should be with the way that the person might be expected to carry out the activity if he did not have the impairment. It gives the following example:

> A person who has obsessive compulsive disorder follows a complicated ritual of hand washing. When preparing a simple meal, he washes his hands carefully after handling each ingredient and each utensil. A person without the disorder might wash his or her hands at appropriate points in preparing the meal, for example after handling raw meat, but would not normally do this after every stage in the process of preparation.

In relation to the cumulative effects of a condition the Guidance gives the following example:

> A man with depression experiences a range of symptoms that include a loss of energy and motivation that makes even the simplest of tasks or decisions seem quite difficult. For example, he finds it difficult to get up in the morning, get washed and dressed, and prepare breakfast. He is forgetful and cannot plan ahead. As a result he has often run out of food before he thinks of going shopping again. Household tasks are frequently left undone, or take much longer to complete than normal. Together, the effects amount to a substantial adverse effect.

In the Appendix to the Guidance, further illustrative and non-exhaustive examples are given of circumstances in which it would be reasonable to regard as substantial the adverse effect of the ability to carry out a normal day-to-day activity. In addition, illustrative and non-exhaustive examples are given of circumstances where it would not be reasonable to regard the effect as substantial. The EAT upheld the tribunal's decision in *Anwar v Tower Hamlets College* (UKEAT/0091/10) that the effect, although 'more than trivial', was still minor and therefore not substantial. With respect, it is hard to see how that interpretation can be correct – the test is whether the effect is more than minor or trivial. The EAT, in *Aderemi v London and South Eastern Railway Ltd* (UKEAT/0316/12), held that any matter that cannot be classified as 'trivial' or 'insubstantial' must be treated as substantial. See too *Parnaby v Leicester City Council* (UKEAT/ 0025/19).

If an impairment ceases to have a substantial adverse effect on a person's ability to carry out normal day-to-day activities, it is to be treated as continuing to have that effect if that effect is likely to recur (Sch 1, para 1).

Progressive conditions (eg rheumatoid arthritis) do not have to have a *substantial* adverse effect if the condition is *likely to* result in such an impairment (Sch 1, para 8). However, they need to have *some* effect. Therefore, once a person with a progressive condition experiences symptoms which have *any* effect on his normal day-to-day activities, he will fall within the definition of 'disability', so long as the effect of the impairment is likely to become substantial in the future (see *Mowat-Brown v University of Surrey* [2002] IRLR 235 and *Kirton v Tetrosyl Ltd* [2002] IRLR 840). As to whether type 2 diabetes falls under progressive conditions, see *Taylor v Ladbrokes Betting and Gaming Ltd* [2017] IRLR 312. (Note that the Act covers from the date of diagnosis people who have cancer, HIV/AIDS and multiple sclerosis – see **13.3.11**.)

An impairment which consists of a severe disfigurement is deemed to have a substantial effect on the ability of the person to carry out normal day-to-day activities (Sch 1, para 3). The Guidance indicates that assessing severity will be mainly a matter of the degree of the disfigurement. Examples of disfigurements include scars, birthmarks, limb or postural deformation, or diseases of the skin. The Equality Act 2010 (Disability) Regulations 2010 make clear (reg 5) that a severe disfigurement is not to be treated as having a substantial adverse effect on the ability of the person concerned to carry out normal day-to-day activities if it consists of either a tattoo (which has not been removed) or a piercing of the body for decorative or other non-medical purposes, including any object attached through the piercing for such purposes.

13.3.5　Medical evidence

Medical evidence has traditionally played an important role in disability discrimination cases. In *Kapadia v London Borough of Lambeth* [2000] IRLR 699, the tribunal discounted uncontested medical evidence and held that the claimant's medical condition did not have a substantial adverse effect on his ability to carry out day-to-day-activities. The Court of Appeal, agreeing with the EAT, held that the tribunal had erred in rejecting the medical evidence, and reversed the decision. Pill LJ said that uncontested medical evidence need not be accepted by the tribunal where the evidence, on the basis of which the doctor has formed an opinion, is rejected, or where the doctor has misunderstood the evidence he was invited to consider. Nevertheless, the Court of Appeal said the issue of whether an individual has a disability within the meaning of the DDA 1995 is a legal issue, and is one to be determined by the tribunal itself, in light of the medical evidence. In *Abadeh v British Telecommunications plc* [2001] IRLR 23, the EAT held that the tribunal had erred in deciding that an employee was not disabled within the meaning of the DDA 1995 by, in effect, adopting the doctor's assessment as to whether the adverse effects of the impairment were substantial, instead of making its own assessment based on the medical evidence. In *McKechnie Plastic Components v Grant* (UKEAT/ 0284/08), the EAT held that the tribunal had been free to reach a finding of discrimination when an agreed expert's medical report did not support such a finding, except that it had failed to apply the correct test with respect to whether the impairment was long-term.

The EAT confirmed in *Mutombo-Mpania v Angard Staffing Solutions Ltd* (UKEAT/0002/18) that the burden of proof is on the claimant to prove disability.

13.3.6　The long-term condition

Schedule 1, para 2 of the Equality Act 2020 provides as follows:

> **2　Long-term effects**
>
>　(1)　The effect of an impairment is long-term if—
>
>　　(a)　it has lasted for at least 12 months,
>
>　　(b)　it is likely to last for at least 12 months, or
>
>　　(c)　it is likely to last for the rest of the life of the person affected.
>
>　(2)　If an impairment ceases to have a substantial adverse effect on a person's ability to carry out normal day-to-day activities, it is to be treated as continuing to have that effect if that effect is likely to recur.

The question whether an impairment is 'long-term' should be answered as at the date of the alleged discriminatory acts, not with the benefit of hindsight at the date of the hearing (*Richmond Adult Community College v McDougall* [2008] ICR 431 and see too *All Answers Ltd v W* [2021] EWCA Civ 6060). In *Seccombe v Reed in Partnership Ltd* (above), the EAT stated that it 'is important to note that the long-term requirement relates to the effect of the impairment rather than merely the impairment itself. It is not sufficient that a person has an impairment that is long term, the impairment must have a substantial adverse effect on day-to-day activities that is long-term.'

It may be difficult, in the case of mental impairments such as stress or depression, to determine when they are likely to last for a year or more. In *Tesco Stores Ltd v Tennant* (UK/EAT/ 0167/19), the claimant brought proceedings in September 2017 for disability discrimination and harassment based on actions of her employer starting in September 2016. The tribunal held that the claimant suffered an impairment (namely depression) from 6 September 2016 which had a substantial adverse effect on her ability to carry out normal day-to-day activities and which was long term because by September 2017 it had lasted 12 months. Tesco appealed and the EAT granted the appeal on the basis that in order to claim disability discrimination or harassment, the claimant must be disabled at the time of the relevant act and could only therefore bring claims as from 6 September 2017. The claimant had also relied upon para 2(1)(b) in the employment tribunal but had not succeeded on that point either. However, the claimant could not rely upon an error of law in the EAT (either on the basis that the Employment Judge was wrong to say there was no evidence on which he could find that there was a likelihood of the effects lasting for 12 months or on the basis that he was wrong because he failed to deal with the submission at all and that his reasons were therefore deficient) because the claimant had not cross-appealed.

See *Parnaby v Leicester City Council* (UKEAT/0025/19) for an EAT decision on para 2(1)(b). The tribunal held that the effect of the claimant's impairment was not likely to last at least 12 months or to recur, because the claimant had been dismissed, which had removed the cause of the impairment – the work-related stress. Allowing an appeal, the EAT held that the tribunal should have considered the question of likelihood of the disability lasting 12 months and/or recurring at the time of the relevant decisions, which was before the decision to dismiss. The question as to whether the claimant's impairment was 'long term' for the purposes of Sch 1 was remitted.

In *Sullivan v Bury Street Capital* [2021] EWCA Civ 1694, the Court of Appeal upheld an employment tribunal decision that the claimant's impairment, while meeting the 'substantial and adverse effect' test, did not meet the 'long-term' element of the definition. Although there were two incidents, in 2013 and again in 2017, in the intervening years the paranoid delusions condition had not had an adverse effect and indeed had improved. The incidents had been triggered by 'life events' which were unlikely to recur.

In *Igweike v TSB Bank Plc* (UKEAT/0119/19), the EAT upheld an employment tribunal decision dismissing a claimant's disability discrimination claim following the claimant's bereavement after the death of his father. The tribunal found that the claimant's reaction to a 'life event' did not amount to a mental impairment, did not have a substantial adverse effect on his 'day-to-day' activities, and that there was no evidence to conclude that any disability he might have was likely to last a year or more.

In *SCA Packaging Ltd v Boyle* [2009] UKHL 37, the House of Lords held that the word 'likely' should be interpreted as meaning 'could well happen' rather than 'more likely than not'. Their Lordships rejected previous authority that 'likely' in the DDA 1995 was taken to mean a 51% chance, and applied a lower standard. The EAT held that to be the correct test more recently in *Martin v University of Exeter* (UKEAT/0092/18). For a recent case applying the test, see *Nissa v Waverly Education Foundation Ltd* (UKEAT/0135/18).

In *Burke v Turning Point Scotland* (ETS/4112457/2021), a tribunal held that an employee with long Covid symptoms came within the definition of disabled. Mr Burke was employed by Turning Point as a caretaker. In November 2020, he tested positive for Covid-19 and reported fluctuating symptoms including extreme fatigue, joint pain, severe headaches and sleeplessness. He was issued with successive fit notes which stated that he was unable to work and referred to the effects of long Covid and post-viral fatigue syndrome. However, two occupational health reports concluded that he was medically fit to work and that the disability provisions of the Equality Act 2010 were unlikely to apply. Mr Burke's sick pay ceased in June 2021, but due to relapses of his symptoms (fatigue) he never returned to work. He was dismissed in August 2021 on grounds of ill health. He brought a number of claims, including one for disability discrimination. As a preliminary issue, the tribunal had to determine whether Mr Burke was disabled during the relevant period. It concluded that he was. It held that he suffered from the physical impairment of post-viral fatigue syndrome caused by Covid-19. This impairment was found to have had an adverse effect on his ability to carry out normal day to day activities. He said he no longer felt able to walk to the shop 'at the end of my block to buy a newspaper' or help with the cooking or household chores. The effect was considered substantial even though his symptoms varied in severity, and it was found likely to be long-term on the basis that his symptoms were capable of lasting for at least 12 months.

The Act states that if an impairment has had a substantial adverse effect on a person's ability to carry out normal day-to-day activities but that effect ceases, the substantial effect is treated as continuing if it is likely to recur. Conditions with effects which recur only sporadically or for short periods can still qualify as impairments for the purposes of the Act in respect of the meaning of 'long-term' (Sch 1, para 2(2)).

The Guidance gives as an example a person with rheumatoid arthritis, who may experience substantial adverse effects for a few weeks after the first occurrence and then have a period of remission. If the substantial adverse effects are likely to recur, the Guidance says they are to be treated as if they were continuing. If the effects are likely to recur beyond 12 months after the first occurrence, they are to be treated as long-term. It should be noted that some impairments with recurring or fluctuating effects may be less obvious in their impact on the individual concerned than is the case with other impairments where the effects are more constant. Likelihood of recurrence should be considered taking all the circumstances of the case into account. This should include what the person could reasonably be expected to do to prevent the recurrence. See *Williams v Leukaemia and Lymphoma Research* (UKEAT/0493/13) and *Thyagarajan v Cap Gemini UK plc* (UKEAT/0264/14) for a recent cases on recurring conditions.

The Act provides that a person who has had a disability within the definition is protected from some forms of discrimination even if he has since recovered or the effects have become less than substantial. In deciding whether a past condition was a disability, its effects count as long-term if they lasted 12 months or more after the first occurrence, or if a recurrence happened or continued until more than 12 months after the first occurrence (s 6(4) and Sch 2, para 2). For a recent decision on timing, see *Parnaby v Leicester City Council* (UKEAT/0025/19).

13.3.7   Examples of disabilities under the Act

The Explanatory Notes to the Act give the following examples:

- A man works in a warehouse, loading and unloading heavy stock. He develops a long-term heart condition and no longer has the ability to lift or move heavy items of stock at work. Lifting and moving such heavy items is not a normal day-to-day activity. However, he is also unable to lift, carry or move moderately heavy everyday objects such as chairs, at work or around the home. This is an adverse effect on a normal day-to-day activity. He is likely to be considered a disabled person for the purposes of the Act.

- A young woman has developed colitis, an inflammatory bowel disease. The condition is a chronic one which is subject to periods of remissions and flare-ups. During a flare-up she experiences severe abdominal pain and bouts of diarrhoea. This makes it very difficult for her to travel or go to work. This has a substantial adverse effect on her ability to carry out normal day-to-day activities. She is likely to be considered a disabled person for the purposes of the Act.

- A man with depression finds even the simplest of tasks or decisions difficult, for example getting up in the morning and getting washed and dressed. He is also forgetful and can't plan ahead. Together, these amount to a 'substantial adverse effect' on his ability to carry out normal day-to-day activities. The man has experienced a number of separate periods of this depression over a period of two years, which have been diagnosed as part of an underlying mental health condition. The impairment is therefore considered to be 'long-term' and he is a disabled person for the purposes of the Act.

In the case of *Herry v Dudley Metropolitan Council* (UKEAT/0100/16) the EAT drew a distinction between a mental impairment, such as clinical depression or anxiety (which could be a disability), and stress caused by adverse life events (including difficulties at work), which will not be a disability without 'something more'.

In *Walker v Sita Information Networking Computing Ltd* (UKEAT/0091/10), the EAT held that while obesity is not a disability, the conditions caused by it are likely to render someone disabled. The claimant weighed over 21 stone and suffered from a number of conditions, including asthma, diabetes, high blood pressure, anxiety and depression. This resulted in various physical and mental symptoms which could not be attributed to any pathological or mental cause. The EAT emphasised that what was important was not the cause but the effect of the impairments on the claimant's day-to-day activities. However, the EAT said that obesity was not a clinically recognised condition which would itself justify a finding of disability. The EAT did recognise the possibility that an obese person who was determined to lose weight and return to normal weight levels within 12 months might not have a long-term impairment. What is important is that tribunals examine the impact of the obesity on the individual and his ability to carry out normal day-to-day activities, not the cause of any symptoms arising from it.

The ECJ reached the same conclusion in *Kaltoft* (Case C-354/13), see **13.3.2.1**. It held that obesity is not in itself a disability, but that if

> the obesity of the worker concerned entails a limitation which results in particular from physical, mental or psychological impairments that in interaction with various barriers may hinder the full and effective participation of that person in professional life on an equal basis with other workers, and that limitation is a long-term one, obesity can be [a disability].

Burke v Turning Point Scotland (ETS/4112457/2021) is a recent tribunal case considering whether the claimant who had long Covid was disabled. The tribunal decided that the claimant was a disabled person in the period 25 November 2020–13 August 2021, which included the relevant period of the alleged discriminatory acts. Readers might find it a useful case to read in order to see the application of the law to the facts.

13.3.8 The effect of medical treatment

Where measures are being taken to treat or correct an impairment that would be likely to have a substantial adverse effect on the ability of the person to carry out normal day-to-day activities but for the fact that measures are being taken to treat or correct the condition, the effects of treatment are disregarded and that impairment is still treated as amounting to a disability (save that spectacles and contact lenses are taken into account) (Sch 1, para 5). The Court of Appeal held in *Woodrup v London Borough of Southwark* [2003] IRLR 111 that clear medical evidence will be required in 'deduced effect' cases. However, the EAT observed in *Fathers v Pets at Home Ltd and anor* (UKEAT/0424/13), that relatively little evidence may be required in some cases, eg that to stop taking anti-depressants would lead to a serious effect on ability to carry out day-to-day activities.

Further analysis of the statutory provisions relating to the effects of medical treatment under the old law may be found in *Abadeh v British Telecommunications plc* [2001] IRLR 23.

The EAT held, in *Metroline Travel Ltd v Stoute* (UKEAT/0302/14), that the avoidance of sugary drinks was not sufficient to amount to a particular diet such that it would be ignored when considering the adverse effects of a disability.

13.3.9 Perceived disabilities

The new definition in the Act is wide enough to include people who are discriminated against because they are perceived to be disabled, ie where the discriminator thinks that a person has a disability which he does not have, and discriminates against him for that reason. This is achieved by the use of the terms 'because of' (direct discrimination, s 13) and 'related to' (harassment, s 26) – see **13.5** below. In *Chief Constable of Norfolk v Coffey* [2019] EWCA Civ 1061, the Court of Appeal held that the Equality Act 2010 also extends to cases in which an employer wrongly perceives that a disability might develop in the future.

Two pre-Equality Act 2010 cases looked at the issue of perception discrimination – see *J v DLA Piper UK LLP* (UKEAT/0263/09) and *Aitken v Commissioner of Police of the Metropolis* (UKEAT/0226/09). Although in neither case was the issue properly before the EAT, it made clear its rejection of the claimants' arguments. One of the reasons given by the EAT in *J v DLA Piper* for rejecting perception discrimination was the conceptual difficulty in fitting it into the framework of the DDA 1995. In particular, how would a tribunal establish that what the employer 'perceives' actually amounts to a disability? The Foreword to IDS Brief 905 (July 2010) suggested that similar difficulties might apply under the 2010 Act, which retains the same definition of 'disability' as the DDA 1995:

> For example, suppose an employer suspected a job applicant to be emotionally unstable and refused a job on that basis. Could the applicant bring a claim on the basis that the employer had discriminated on the basis of a perceived disability, such as depression? Or would the employer easily defeat the claim on the basis that, while he perceived that the claimant was irrationally and unpredictably moody and so would be difficult to work with, he was perceiving something less than an actual disability? Adopting a broad and purposive approach, tribunals might consider it sufficient that an employer declines to employ because he perceives some adverse effect on the employee's ability to do the job in question. This could be evidence that he perceived the employee's 'condition' to be serious enough to qualify as a disability. However, such an interpretation would deprive the word 'disability' of its specific, technical meaning. It would also potentially mean that any job applicant rejected because of the employer's perception that they would be difficult to work with would have an arguable claim.

In *Chief Constable of Norfolk v Coffey* [2019] EWCA Civ 1061, the Court of Appeal held that the Equality Act 2010 extends to cases in which an employer wrongly perceives that a disability might develop in the future. In this case, the parties agreed that in a perceived disability discrimination case, the employer must believe that the elements of the statutory definition of disability are present, although it does not have to attach the label 'disability'. So, for example, does the employer perceive the impairments at issue to be substantial and long term?

In this case the claimant was a police officer who suffered hearing loss. That did not prevent her from doing her job and did not require adjustment. However, when she applied to transfer to another region, her request was declined. The Court of Appeal held that the tribunal had been entitled to find that her application for a transfer to a different force had been refused because the Chief Inspector had perceived the claimant to have a progressive condition which was a potential future disability. The respondent had acted on the basis of a stereotypical assumption that the claimant's hearing loss would render her incapable of doing aspects of her job (front-line duties).

13.3.10   Past disabilities

Past disabilities, for example a mental illness which is now cured, are protected under Sch 1, para 9 to the Act. It provides that:

(1)   A question as to whether a person had a disability at a particular time ('the relevant time') is to be determined, for the purposes of section 6, as if the provisions of, or made under, this Act were in force when the act complained of was done had been in force at the relevant time.

(2)   The relevant time may be a time before the coming into force of the provision of this Act to which the question relates.

13.3.11   Certain medical conditions

The Act covers from the time of diagnosis people who have cancer (see *Lofty v Harris t/a First Café* (UKEAT/0177/17) where the EAT held that Sch 1, para 6 does not distinguish between invasive and other types of cancer), HIV/AIDS and multiple sclerosis (Sch 1, para 6). This means that such people do not have to rely on the condition having 'some' effect as a progressive condition (see **13.3.4**). Otherwise, conditions which will develop into a disability in the future are not protected until the person develops some symptoms, but those symptoms do not have to have a substantial adverse effect if the condition is a progressive one (Sch 1, para 8).

13.3.12   Relationship between the disability and the allegedly discriminatory act

The EAT, in *Cruickshank v VAW Motorcast Ltd* [2002] IRLR 24, held that the tribunal must assess, on the basis of the evidence available at that time, whether the claimant had a disability *at the time of the alleged discriminatory act*, rather than at the time of the hearing. That approach was confirmed by the Court of Appeal in *Richmond Adult Community College v McDougall* [2008] ICR

431 in the context of when to determine whether the effect of an impairment is likely to last for at least 12 months (see **13.3.6**). At the time the decision (not to employ) was taken, there was no evidence that the illness was likely to recur, and the tribunal held that it did not therefore have a long-term effect.

13.3.13   The definition of disability under the EC Equal Treatment Framework Directive

The EC Equal Treatment Framework Directive (2000/78) sets out a framework for eliminating employment and occupational discrimination in a number of areas, including disability. The concept of disability is not defined in the Directive. In *Chacón Navas v Eurest Colectividades SA* (Case C-13/05) [2006] IRLR 706, the ECJ had to decide if a sickness that might cause what might constitute a disability in the future, could be equated with disability. The ECJ said not. The ECJ's approach to what amounted to a disability was broadly the same as that contained in the DDA 1995, although interestingly the Court focused on the effect of any impairment on the employee's *professional* life, in contrast to the Act's focus on the impact on 'normal day-to-day activities'. (See also *HK Danmark (acting on behalf of Ring) v Dansk almennyttigt Boligselskab* (Case C-335/11) (**13.3.1** above) and *FOA, acting on behalf of Karsten Kaltoft v Kommunernes Lansforening (KL)* (Case C-354/13) (**13.3.2.1** above).)

13.4   UNLAWFUL DISCRIMINATION IN EMPLOYMENT

13.4.1   Recruitment

Under s 39(1) of the Act, it is unlawful for an employer to discriminate against a disabled person:

(a)   in the arrangements which he makes for the purpose of determining to whom he should offer employment;

(b)   in the terms on which he offers that person employment; or

(c)   by refusing to offer or deliberately not offering him employment.

There is a new provision in the Act (s 60) which prevents a prospective employer asking an applicant for work about his health before work is offered or he has been included in a pool of successful candidates to be offered a job when a vacancy arises. This is not, however, a blanket ban on pre-employment health enquiries. There is a limited set of circumstances in which health-related inquiries can be made. For instance, s 60 does not apply to questions that are necessary to establish whether the applicant will be able to carry out a function intrinsic to the work concerned. Only the EHRC can enforce a breach of this provision, but where the employer asks such questions and rejects the applicant, if the applicant brings a claim of direct discrimination, it will be for the employer to show that he has not discriminated against the applicant.

Section 159 allows an employer to take disability into account when deciding whom to recruit, where disabled people are at a disadvantage or under-represented. This can be done only where candidates are equally qualified. This does not allow employers automatically to prefer disabled candidates. Each case must be considered on its merits, and any action must be a proportionate means of addressing such disadvantage or under-representation.

13.4.2   Promotion and dismissal

Under s 39(2) of the Act, it is unlawful for an employer to discriminate against a disabled person whom he employs:

(a)   in the terms of employment which he affords him;

(b)   in the opportunities which he affords him for promotion, a transfer, training or receiving any other benefit;

(c)   by refusing to afford him, or deliberately not affording him, any such opportunity; or

(d)   by dismissing him, or subjecting him to any other detriment (dismissal, for the purposes of the Act, includes constructive dismissal (s 39(7)). Detriment does not include harassment (s 212).

Section 159 allows an employer to take disability into account when deciding whom to promote, where disabled people are at a disadvantage or under-represented. This can be done only where candidates are equally qualified. This does not allow employers automatically to prefer disabled employees. Each case must be considered on its merits, and any action must be a proportionate means of addressing such disadvantage or under-representation.

13.4.3 Post-employment discrimination

Section 108 prohibits discrimination after relationships have ended. Where an employment relationship has come to an end, it is unlawful for the employer to discriminate against the former employee or harass the former employee where the discrimination arises out of and is closely connected to that former relationship. This means, for example, that former employees are protected from being discriminated against on grounds of disability so far as references are concerned, or in a post-dismissal appeal (see also **8.4.3**).

Article 5 of the Equality Act 2010 (Consequential Amendments, Saving and Supplementary Provisions) Order 2010 made changes to s 108(4). The amendment was intended to ensure that the new provision replicated the 'old' law (ie, that even if a person becomes disabled after the relationship has ended, the duty to make a reasonable adjustment (see **13.5.2**) still applies). The original provision could have been interpreted as meaning that the duty arose only if the person already had a disability at the time the relationship ended.

13.5 TYPES OF DISCRIMINATION

There are six ways in which an employer may discriminate against a disabled claimant, employee or former employee. Each will be considered in more detail below. As a matter of ease of approach, the various heads have been considered in this order: direct discrimination, failure to make reasonable adjustments, discrimination arising from disability, indirect discrimination, harassment and victimisation. This approach has been adopted because discrimination arising from disability and indirect discrimination may be justified.

13.5.1 Direct discrimination

Section 13 provides:

>   (1)   A person (A) discriminates against another (B) if, because of a protected characteristic, A treats B less favourably than A treats or would treat others.
>
>   ...
>
>   (3)   If the protected characteristic is disability, and B is not a disabled person, A does not discriminate against B only because A treats or would treat disabled persons more favourably than A treats B.

Direct discrimination occurs where the reason for a person being treated less favourably than another is a protected characteristic listed in s 4. The language of s 13 explicitly involves a comparison between how the claimant and another person without that protected characteristic is treated – the less favourable treatment. Direct discrimination occurs where someone is discriminated against *because* he is disabled.

Therefore an employer's treatment of a disabled person will amount to direct discrimination if:

(a)   the treatment is because of his disability;

(b)   the treatment is less favourable in comparison to the treatment of a person not having that protected characteristic is (or would be); and

(c)   the relevant circumstances, including the abilities, of the person with whom the comparison is made are the same as, or not materially different from, those of the disabled person (but without the disability). See *Owen v AMEC Foster Wheeler Energy Ltd* [2019] EWCA Civ 822, where the employment tribunal used a hypothetical comparator who had the characteristics and same health problems as the claimant but fell short of having a disability. The Court of Appeal upheld that decision and held that the comparator with the requisite medical risk would have been treated in the same way.

The Code gives an example of treatment that might amount to direct discrimination:

> During an interview, a job applicant informs the employer that he has multiple sclerosis. The applicant is unsuccessful and the employer offers the job to someone who does not have a disability. In this case, it will be necessary to look at why the employer did not offer the job to the unsuccessful applicant with multiple sclerosis to determine whether the less favourable treatment was because of his disability.

Note that the tribunal case of *Attridge Law v Coleman* [2007] ICR 654 was referred to the ECJ for clarification as to whether the UK's then current discrimination legislation properly implemented the EC Equal Treatment Framework Directive. Mrs Coleman was not disabled, but her son was. She resigned after allegedly being refused flexible working. She claimed constructive unfair dismissal, direct discrimination and harassment related to disability under the DDA 1995. The ECJ ruled ([2008] IRLR 722) that the EC Framework Directive covers discrimination by association, and sent the case back to the tribunal to see if it could 'fit it into' the current UK law, ie whether the DDA 1995 could be construed to give effect to this interpretation (Case C-303/06). In *Coleman v EBR Attridge Law LLP and Another* (ET/2303745/2005) the tribunal held that the DDA 1995 was capable of an interpretation consistent with the Directive so as to include discrimination by association. The respondent appealed on the basis, inter alia, that the tribunal had 'distorted and rewritten' the DDA 1995. The EAT upheld the tribunal's decision (UKEAT/0071/09) and read words into the DDA 1995 to achieve 'the purpose and effect of the directive'. In *Follows v Nationwide Building Society* (ET/2201937/18), an employment tribunal held that the claimant had been indirectly discriminated against by reason of her caring responsibilities (see **13.5.5** below).

The definition of direct discrimination in the Act now states that direct discrimination occurs where the reason for a person being treated less favourably than another is a protected characteristic listed in s 4, and the definition is broad enough to cover cases where the less favourable treatment is because of the victim's association with someone who is disabled, or because the victim is wrongly thought to have a disability.

In *Coffey* (above), the Court of Appeal held, on the facts, that the Chief Constable *was* significantly influenced in her decision by a stereotypical assumption about the effects of what she perceived to be the claimant's (actual or future) hearing loss (cf the typical case where a person is refused a job – or indeed is dismissed or suffers any other detriment – because they are unable to meet a performance standard in consequence of a disability – in which case they would have to claim under s 15 (below) and the employer would be able to argue justification). Here the claimant was directly discriminated against.

There is a new exception to what would otherwise be direct disability discrimination in Sch 9, para 1 ('work occupational requirements'). Where being disabled is an occupational requirement for work and a person does not meet that requirement, it will not be discriminatory to reject that person. The requirement must be a 'proportionate means of pursing a legitimate aim', and the burden of showing that rests on those seeking to rely on it. An example might be where an organisation advertises for a deaf person who uses British Sign Language (BSL) to work as a counsellor for other deaf people who use BSL.

The wording used for direct discrimination because of disability is now identical to the wording used in connection with other protected characteristics, and readers are referred to **Chapter 9** for more details about direct disability discrimination, including:

(a) association and perception (see **9.2.3**);

(b) the interpretation of the phrase 'because of' (see **9.2.4**);

(c) what amounts to 'less favourable treatment' (see **9.2.5**);

(d) the use of comparators (the treatment of the claimant must be compared with that of an actual or a hypothetical person – the comparator – who does not share the same protected characteristic as the claimant (or, in the case of dual discrimination, either of the protected characteristics in the combination) but who is (or is assumed to be) in not materially different circumstances from the claimant. The Code gives an example in a disability case:

> A disabled man with arthritis who can type at 30 words per minute applies for an administrative job which includes typing, but is rejected on the grounds that his typing is too slow. The correct comparator in a claim for direct discrimination would be a person without arthritis who has the same typing speed with the same accuracy rate. In this case, the disabled man is unable to lift heavy weights, but this is not a requirement of the job he applied for. As it is not relevant to the circumstances, there is no need for him to identify a comparator who cannot lift heavy weights.

The Court of Appeal's judgment in *Aitken v Commissioner of Police of the Metropolis* [2012] ICR 78 provides useful guidance on how to construct the correct hypothetical comparator in a direct disability discrimination claim (see **9.2.5**). In *Cordell v Foreign and Commonwealth Office* (UKEAT/0016/11), the EAT re-emphasised that it will often be better 'to focus on the reason-why question than to get bogged down in the often arid and confusing task of "constructing a hypothetical comparator"' (see **9.2.5**). In *Aitken*, the Court of Appeal upheld the tribunal's decision that the proper hypothetical comparator was someone who did not have the claimant's disability but used aggressive words and behaviour frightening to a reasonable person; and

(e) motive (see **9.2.7**).

13.5.2 Failure to comply with the duty to make reasonable adjustments

An employer also discriminates against a disabled person if he fails (without justification) to make reasonable adjustments, in circumstances where it is under a duty to do so.

Sections 20 and 21 of the Act provide as follows:

20 Duty to make adjustments

(1) Where this Act imposes a duty to make reasonable adjustments on a person, this section, sections 21 and 22 and the applicable Schedule apply; and for those purposes, a person on whom the duty is imposed is referred to as A.

(2) The duty comprises the following three requirements.

(3) The first requirement is a requirement, where a provision, criterion or practice of A's puts a disabled person at a substantial disadvantage in relation to a relevant matter in comparison with persons who are not disabled, to take such steps as it is reasonable to have to take to avoid the disadvantage.

(4) The second requirement is a requirement, where a physical feature puts a disabled person at a substantial disadvantage in relation to a relevant matter in comparison with persons who are not disabled, to take such steps as it is reasonable to have to take to avoid the disadvantage.

(5) The third requirement is a requirement, where a disabled person would, but for the provision of an auxiliary aid, be put at a substantial disadvantage in relation to a relevant matter in comparison with persons who are not disabled, to take such steps as it is reasonable to have to take to provide the auxiliary aid.

(6) Where the first or third requirement relates to the provision of information, the steps which it is reasonable for A to have to take include steps for ensuring that in the circumstances concerned the information is provided in an accessible format.

(7) A person (A) who is subject to a duty to make reasonable adjustments is not (subject to express provision to the contrary) entitled to require a disabled person, in relation to whom A is required to comply with the duty, to pay to any extent A's costs of complying with the duty.

(8)   A reference in section 21 or 22 or an applicable Schedule to the first, second or third requirement is to be construed in accordance with this section.

(9)   In relation to the second requirement, a reference in this section or an applicable Schedule to avoiding a substantial disadvantage includes a reference to—

(a)   removing the physical feature in question,

(b)   altering it, or

(c)   providing a reasonable means of avoiding it.

(10)   A reference in this section, section 21 or 22 or an applicable Schedule (apart from paragraphs 2 to 4 of Schedule 4) to a physical feature is a reference to—

(a)   a feature arising from the design or construction of a building,

(b)   a feature of an approach to, exit from or access to a building,

(c)   a fixture or fitting, or furniture, furnishings, materials, equipment or other chattels, in or on premises, or

(d)   any other physical element or quality.

(11)   A reference in this section, section 21 or 22 or an applicable Schedule to an auxiliary aid includes a reference to an auxiliary service.

21   Failure to comply with duty

(1)   A failure to comply with the first, second or third requirement is a failure to comply with a duty to make reasonable adjustments.

(2)   A discriminates against a disabled person if A fails to comply with that duty in relation to that person.

Schedule 8, Part 3, para 20 provides a defence if the employer does not know and could not reasonably be expected to know of the disability (see **13.5.2.5** below).

13.5.2.1 Duty to adjust

Under ss 20 and 21 an employer can be liable for failing to take positive steps to help overcome the disadvantages resulting from disability. An employer is under a duty to make reasonable adjustments where a disabled person is placed at a substantial disadvantage in comparison with non-disabled people.

The first requirement (s 20(3)) covers changing the way things are done (such as changing a practice), the second (s 20(4)) covers making changes to the built environment (such as providing access to a building) and the third (s 20(5)) covers providing auxiliary aids and services (such as providing special computer software or providing a different service).

Where the first or third requirement involves the way in which information is provided, a reasonable step includes providing that information in an accessible format (s 20(6)). Under the second requirement, taking steps to avoid the disadvantage will include removing, altering or providing a reasonable means of avoiding the physical feature, where it would be reasonable to do so (s 20(9)). It also makes clear that, except where the Act states otherwise, it would never be reasonable for a person bound by the duty to pass on the costs of complying with it to an individual disabled person (s 20(7)).

The Court of Appeal in *Cave v Goodwin and Another* [2001] EWCA Civ 391 stressed that the duty does not arise where the disabled person is not placed at a substantial disadvantage. The Act defines substantial as more than minor or trivial (s 212).

The duty applies in recruitment and during all stages of employment, including dismissal (see *Aylott v Stockton-on-Tees Borough Council* [2010] EWCA Civ 910).

Section 21 makes clear that a failure to comply with any one of the reasonable adjustment requirements amounts to discrimination against a disabled person to whom the duty is owed. It also provides that, apart from under this Act, no other action can be taken for failure to comply with the duty.

The EAT held in *Environment Agency v Rowan* (UKEAT/0060/07) that a tribunal must identify:

(a)   the provision, criterion or practice applied, or the physical feature, or the auxiliary aid not supplied;

(b)   the identity of non-disabled comparators (where appropriate); and

(c)   the nature and extent of the substantial disadvantage suffered by the claimant.

The Court of Appeal endorsed this approach in *Newham Sixth Form College v Sanders* [2014] EWCA Civ 734.

Note that the duty applies to the disabled worker, and the principle of associative discrimination does not extend to the duty to make reasonable adjustments (*Hainsworth v Ministry of Defence* [2014] EWCA Civ 763).

Advisers are therefore required to consider these matters with their clients.

13.5.2.2   'Provision, criterion or practice'

The Code states that 'provisions, criteria and practices' (PCPs) should be construed widely and include formal and informal policies, rules, one-off decisions and actions etc. The duty to make reasonable adjustments will apply, for example, to selection and interview procedures as well as to job offers, contractual arrangements and working conditions.

Physical features, according to the Code, include, for example, steps, kerbs, parking areas, lighting, furniture etc. Auxiliary aids include, for example, specialist equipment, sign language interpreters and support workers.

In *Mallon v AECOM Ltd* [2021] IRLR 438, the EAT held that 'no consideration was given to whether the claim should be analysed on the basis that the claimant was contending that he needed an auxiliary service, by way of assistance in completing the online application form'. The EAT stated that:

> Tribunals should have in mind when determining the issues in reasonable adjustments claims that it may not be a PCP case but may be about physical features (including furniture etc) or auxiliary aids (including services). For example, it is all too common for claims in which an employee contends that s/he needed an ergonomic chair, or voice recognition software, for the claim to be incorrectly analysed in terms of PCPs.

It can sometimes be hard to identify and articulate a PCP; it is worth considering in such a case whether it might be better put as a s 15 case (see below). The following are examples of things found not to amount to a 'provision, criterion or practice':

(a)   inefficiency by an employer's human resources department (*Newcastle Upon Tyne Hospitals NHS Foundation Trust v Bagley* (UKEAT/0417/11));

(b)   a one-off flawed disciplinary procedure (*Nottingham City Transport Ltd v Harvey* (UKEAT/0032/12));

(c)   incompetently-run disciplinary proceedings (*Carphone Warehouse plc v Martin* (UKEAT/0371/12)).

In *Secretary of State for Justice v Prospere* (UKEAT/0412/14), the EAT re-emphasised the importance of the tribunal properly identifying the PCP at the outset of a case, since the steps which a respondent is under a duty to take must depend on the particular PCP applied.

In *Griffiths v Secretary of State for Work and Pensions* [2015] EWCA Civ 1265, the claimant was dismissed for sickness absence. She argued that the employer's sickness absence policy should be modified to allow her, as a disabled person, to have longer periods of illness absence before she faced the risk of sanctions than would be permitted for employees not subject to disability-related illnesses. Elias LJ held that the PCP was that 'the employee must maintain a certain level of attendance at work in order not to be subject to the risk of disciplinary sanctions. That is the provision breach of which may end in warnings and ultimately dismissal.'

In *Carreras v United First Partners Research* (UKEAT/0266/15), the EAT confirmed that an expectation that an employee would work long hours could be a PCP that puts a disabled employee at a substantial disadvantage compared to non-disabled employees. Mr Carreras was an analyst working for an independent brokerage and research firm. Initially, he worked long hours (often at least 12 hours a day). However, in 2012, he had a serious cycling accident. On his return to work he experienced dizziness, fatigue and headaches, had difficulty concentrating and found it difficult to work in the evenings. For the first six months after his return to work, he worked no more than eight hours a day. However, he then began to increase those hours, working from 8am until 6.30pm to 7pm until the end of 2013. From October 2013, he initially made some requests to work late but it became assumed that he would work late. In February 2014, Mr Carreras objected to being asked to work late and, following a heated dispute over this, resigned from his employment. He subsequently brought claims for constructive unfair dismissal and a failure to make reasonable adjustments. An employment tribunal dismissed both his claims. In relation to the reasonable adjustments claim, the PCP he was relying on was a 'requirement' that he work late hours. The respondent argued he had been asked, but not made, to work late. The tribunal agreed with the respondent. Because the PCP Mr Carreras was relying on as a 'requirement' was not made out, his reasonable adjustments claim failed.

Mr Carreras appealed. The EAT overturned the tribunal's decision and said that it had adopted 'an overly technical approach' to the PCP. The EAT referred to the EHRC Code of Practice, which made it clear that a PCP had to be construed broadly: 'Adopting a real world approach, whilst "requirement" might be taken to imply some element of compulsion, an expectation or assumption placed upon an employee ... might well suffice.' The EAT's judgment was approved by the Court of Appeal, which stated that a 'pattern of repeated requests' can be sufficient ([2018] EWCA Civ 323). The case was remitted back to the tribunal.

For a recent decision dealing with PCPs, see the Court of Appeal's decision in *Ishola v Transport for London* [2020] EWCA Civ 112. In that case, it was alleged that the respondent operated a PCP of requiring the claimant to return to work without concluding a proper and fair investigation into his grievances prior to his dismissal. The employment tribunal held that there was no PCP operated by the respondent because the alleged requirement was 'a one-off act in the course of dealings with one individual'. The EAT upheld that conclusion. The claimant appealed on the basis that an ongoing expectation that a person should behave in a certain manner (here, return to work despite the outstanding grievances) was a 'practice'. See **10.2.2** and in particular the findings of Simler LJ quoted there.

In *Martin v City and County of Swansea* (UKEAT/0253/20) the EAT emphasised that it is necessary to distinguish between the terms of an absence management policy and its application (the PCP may be one or both):

> A policy can result in a disabled person being put at a substantial disadvantage because the policy is more likely to be applied to a disabled person in comparison with people who are not disabled because of the greater likelihood of sickness absences, even if there is a discretion in the policy that could be exercised that would avoid the disadvantage.

13.5.2.3 Identifying the comparator and the substantial disadvantage

The s 20 duty arises when the PCP, or physical feature or failure to provide an auxiliary aid places the disabled person at a substantial disadvantage when compared with the non-disabled. 'Substantial' again means 'more than minor or trivial'. It is important that the disadvantage allegedly suffered is *identified* by the claimant or claimant's representative for the tribunal.

The House of Lords, in *Archibald v Fife Council* [2004] IRLR 651, identified how the non-disabled comparator should be identified. In that case, the employee had been a road sweeper with the Council. She had minor surgery which gave rise to complications, leaving her virtually unable to walk and therefore unable to do her job. The Council took various positive steps to seek to redeploy her, such as by retraining her and short-listing her for various posts for which she might be eligible. However, she was not appointed to an alternative post and was dismissed for failing to be able to carry out her job. She claimed that her employers had failed to make reasonable adjustments because she had still had to go through a competitive interview process. In the course of his speech, Lord Rodger identified the comparator as being those employees who were not disabled, could carry out the functions of their job and were therefore not at risk of dismissal.

In *Smith v Churchills Stairlifts plc* [2006] IRLR 41, the Court of Appeal considered the judgment in *Archibald* and concluded that 'the comparator is readily identified by the disadvantage caused by the relevant arrangements'. In that case the claimant was prevented from attending a training course because he could not carry a radiator cabinet, because of his disability. The Court of Appeal held that the correct comparators were the other candidates who attended the training course. On that basis, the claimant was placed at a substantial disadvantage compared to the comparators who could attend the course. As he could not attend, he could not be appointed to the position. The EAT made it clear in *Fareham College v Walters* (UKEAT/0396/08) that in many cases the facts will speak for themselves, and the identity of the non-disabled comparator will be clear from the PCP found to be in play. In that case, the PCP was conceded as the refusal to allow the claimant a phased return to work. The EAT held that the correct comparator group was non-disabled employees who could attend work forthwith. That placed the claimant at a substantial disadvantage compared to the comparators. The employees in the comparator group would not be dismissed because they could attend work without a phased return. That approach accords with the Court of Appeal's decision in *Smith v Churchills Stairlifts* (above).

A less generous approach to comparators was initially taken by the EAT in sickness absence cases. *Rider v Leeds CC* (UKEAT/0243/11) and *London Borough of Hillingdon v Bailey* (UKEAT/0421/12) concerned the enforcement of the respondents' respective sickness absence policies. In the *Rider* case, the EAT said that the correct comparator was someone who was not disabled but was subject to the policy because of illness. As such, the claimant was not at a disadvantage at all. In the *Bailey* case, the EAT held again that the correct comparators were employees who were ill and subject to the sickness policy but non-disabled. However, the Court of Appeal in *Griffiths* (above) held that the claimant was placed at a substantial disadvantage compared to non-disabled persons. The requirement to maintain a certain level of attendance at work in order not to be subject to the risk of disciplinary sanctions placed the claimant, whose disability led to disability-related absences which would not be the case with the able-bodied, at a substantial disadvantage. *Bailey* and *Rider* are therefore no longer good law.

As the EAT noted, in *General Dynamics Information Technology Ltd v Carranza* (UKEAT/0107/14), employees would also be well advised to bring a claim of discrimination arising from a disability in the alternative in circumstances where they are dismissed for poor attendance. Elias LJ noted in *Griffiths* that '[i]t would be open to a tribunal to find that the dismissal for disability-related absences constituted discrimination arising out of disability contrary to section 15, if, for example, the absences were the result of the disability and it was not proportionate in all the circumstances to effect the dismissal' (see **13.5.4**).

In *Rakova v London North West Healthcare NHS Trust* (UKEAT/0043/19), the tribunal accepted that the adjustments the claimant was seeking – a Livescribe pen, electronic sensitive paper and printer and software updates – would have made her more efficient. However, the tribunal decided that the claimant was not placed at a substantial disadvantage. The EAT held that the tribunal should not have simply assumed that there is 'necessarily a disconnect between seeking to be more efficient (thus acknowledging that one is less efficient) and claiming that that reflects a substantial disadvantage'. The tribunal should have asked itself 'whether the Claimant's disabilities placed her at a substantial disadvantage. Where she was seeking adjustments to improve her efficiency, the question was whether she suffered a substantial disadvantage in that regard. Ruling out a possible correlation between these matters meant that the ET thus failed to identify the nature and extent of any disadvantage claimed by the Claimant. That was an error of approach ....'

In *Mallon v AECOM Ltd* [2021] IRLR 438, the EAT reminds us that it is for the employer to make adjustments, not third parties (the tribunal had decided that the claimant did not succeed with his claim that an online form put him at a substantial disadvantage because he could have asked for assistance from a friend or family).

13.5.2.4 Has the employer made reasonable adjustments?

Once a comparison has identified a substantial disadvantage, the question will be whether the employer has made reasonable adjustments – the onus is on the employer to show this. This will depend on the circumstances of each case. That question has to be determined objectively. In the *Smith v Churchills Stairlifts* case (at **13.5.2.2** above), the position was summarised as follows (section numbers adjusted to reflect the amended legislation):

> There is no doubt that the test required by [s 20] is an objective test. The employer must take 'such steps as it is reasonable, in all the circumstances of the case ...' The objective nature of the test is further illuminated by [the draft Code]. Thus, in determining whether it is reasonable for an employer to have to take a particular step, regard is to be had, amongst other things, to ... the financial and other costs which could be incurred by the employer in taking the step and the extent to which taking it would disrupt any of his activities.
>
> It is significant that the concern is with the extent to which the step would disrupt any of his activities, not the extent to which the employer reasonably believes that such disruption would occur. The objective nature of this test is well established in the authorities: see *Collins v Royal National Theatre Board Ltd* [2004] EWCA Civ 144, [2004] IRLR 395 in which Sedley LJ said (at paragraph 20):
>
>> 'The test of reasonableness under [s 20] ... must be objective. One notes in particular that [s 21] speaks of 'such steps as it is reasonable ... for him to have to take.'

A duty is imposed on the employer only to take such steps as are reasonable in all the circumstances of the case. The employer can therefore undertake a cost–benefit analysis when considering reasonable adjustments.

The Code provides that, in determining whether it is reasonable for an employer to have taken a particular step in order to comply with the duty, the following factors *might be taken into account*:

(a)   whether taking any particular steps would be effective in preventing the substantial disadvantage;

(b)   the practicability of the step;

(c)   the financial and other costs of making the adjustment and the extent of any disruption caused;

(d)   the extent of the employer's financial or other resources;

(e)   the availability to the employer of financial or other assistance to help make an adjustment (such as advice through Access to Work); and

(f)   the type and size of the employer.

The following are examples of steps which an employer might take in relation to a disabled person in order to comply with the duty to adjust. The examples are from the Code:

•   making adjustments to premises;

•   providing information in accessible formats;

•   allocating some of the disabled person's duties to another worker;

•   transferring him to fill an existing vacancy;

•   altering his hours of working or training;

- assigning him to a different place of work or training or arranging home working;
- allowing him to be absent during working hours for rehabilitation, assessment or treatment;
- giving or arranging for training or mentoring (whether for the disabled person or any other person);
- acquiring or modifying equipment;
- modifying procedures for testing or assessment;
- providing a reader or interpreter;
- providing supervision or other support;
- allowing the person to take disability leave;
- employing a support worker;
- modifying disciplinary or grievance procedures;
- adjusting redundancy selection criteria;
- modifying performance-related pay arrangements.

The EAT held, in *Kenny v Hampshire Constabulary* [1999] IRLR 76, that the duty to adjust under the DDA 1995 was limited to job-related matters. So, in this case, the provision of a carer to assist a disabled person when using the toilet was not something the employer had to provide under the duty to adjust. However, the EAT thought that if the worker had his own personal carer then the employer would be expected to make physical arrangements to accommodate the carer at the workplace.

The obligation to make adjustments is an ongoing one (*Wilding v British Telecommunications plc* [2002] IRLR 524). For another decision on reasonable adjustments, see *Home Office v Collins* [2005] EWCA Civ 598.

The House of Lords in *Archibald v Fife Council* (see **13.5.2.3**) considered whether the duty to make reasonable adjustments applied to the position of a disabled employee who became totally incapable of doing the job for which she was originally employed but who could do another job in the same organisation. Mrs Archibald was interviewed for a sedentary post, but a more qualified person was appointed and Mrs Archibald was dismissed. The House of Lords held that there was a positive duty to make reasonable adjustments. Unlike sex and race discrimination, an employer was obliged to discriminate positively in favour of disabled people. The House of Lords gave a very wide meaning to the concept of 'arrangements'. In this case, there was, it said, an 'arrangement' which placed Mrs Archibald at a substantial disadvantage, namely that if she was physically unable to work as a road sweeper, she was liable to be dismissed. The positive obligation to make reasonable adjustments potentially includes allowing disabled persons to 'trump' candidates for other jobs, even if the disabled employee is not the best candidate, if the disabled employee is suitable to do that work.

As Baroness Hale said:

> [In the cases of sex and race discrimination] men and women or black and white, as the case may be, are opposite sides of the same coin. Each is to be treated in the same way ... Pregnancy apart, the differences between the genders are generally regarded as irrelevant. The 1995 Act, however, does not regard the differences between disabled people and others as irrelevant. It does not expect each to be treated in the same way. It expects reasonable adjustments to be made to cater for the special needs of disabled people. It necessarily entails an element of more favourable treatment.

This decision made clear that employers needed to take proper medical advice and consult with the employee before making decisions about reasonable adjustments (see, eg, *Southampton City College v Randall* [2006] IRLR 24). It is also clear that the need to make reasonable adjustments continues throughout the employment on an ongoing basis. In *Rothwell v Pelikan Hardcopy Scotland* [2006] IRLR 24, the EAT held that the employer's failure to consult with the employee (after having accommodated his disability for many years) before dismissing him on grounds of ill-health was a failure to make reasonable adjustments. In

Greenhof v Barnsley Metropolitan Borough Council [2006] IRLR 98, the EAT suggested that a serious failure to make a reasonable adjustment would almost inevitably amount to a breach of the implied term of trust and confidence, so entitling an employee to resign and claim constructive dismissal. The EAT confirmed in *Nottingham City Homes Ltd v Brittain* (UKEAT/0038/18) that:

> [a]n employer cannot benefit from their own failure to obtain evidence as to whether an employee with a disability can return to work with reasonable adjustments. As explained in *Doran*, whether the employer has complied with their duty to make reasonable adjustments will be judged not only on what they knew but on what should have been known to them had they made reasonable enquiries.

There have been conflicting decisions on whether an employer's failure to make an assessment of a disabled employee is of itself a failure to make a reasonable adjustment (see, eg, *Mid-Staffordshire General Hospitals NHS Trust v Cambridge* [2003] IRLR 566). However, in *Tarbuck v Sainsbury's Supermarkets Ltd* [2006] IRLR 664, the EAT said it was not. That approach was confirmed again by the EAT in *Spence v Intype Libra Ltd* (UKEAT/0617/06), where the claimant sought to argue on appeal that *Tarbuck* had been wrongly decided or could be distinguished on its facts. The EAT upheld the tribunal's decision. In *Scottish and Southern Energy plc v Mackay* (UKEAT/0075/06), the EAT said 'we follow the *Tarbuck* line'. In *Watkins v HSBC Bank plc* (UKEAT/0018/18), an occupational psychologist examined the claimant and recommended that his work activity and work flow be monitored. The employment tribunal struck out his claim on the basis that a failure to assess the claimant, following the *Tarbuck* line of authority, could not be a failure to make a reasonable adjustment. The EAT held that whilst a failure to carry out an assessment will similarly not of itself be a failure to make a reasonable adjustment because it will not remove any disadvantage, where there is a recommended course of action, that may well amount to a failure to make a reasonable adjustment. It goes beyond mere failure to consult/assess.

The EAT in *Tameside Hospital NHS Foundation Trust v Mr Mylott* (UKEAT/0352/09) (a case decided under s 4A of the DDA 1995) held that the duty to make reasonable adjustments involves taking steps to enable the employee to stay in employment, not to compensate him for having to leave it – so in Mr Mylott's case, there was no duty to offer him ill-health retirement.

The EAT held in *Salford NHS PCT v Smith* (UKEAT/0507/10) that a career break could not amount to a reasonable adjustment, because it would not have prevented the provisions, criteria and practices placing the claimant at a substantial disadvantage in comparison with persons who were not disabled. Reasonable adjustments are, the EAT held, concerned with enabling the disabled person to remain at or return to work (see also *Conway v Community Options* (UKEAT/0034/12)).

The EAT clarified in *Noor v Foreign and Commonwealth Office* (UKEAT/0470/10) that, 'although the purpose of reasonable adjustments is to prevent a disabled person from being at a substantial disadvantage, it is certainly not the law that an adjustment will only be reasonable if it is completely effective'.

The EAT gave guidance on the costs issue in *Cordell v Foreign and Commonwealth Office* (UKEAT/0016/11) and said that it must be weighed with the other factors, but that cost 'is one of the central considerations in the assessment of reasonableness'. It stated that tribunals 'must make a judgment, ultimately, on the basis of what they consider right in their capacity as an industrial jury'.

The EAT held in *Croft Vets Ltd v Butcher* (UKEAT/0430/12) that the respondent failed to make reasonable adjustments by refusing to pay for private counselling. The EAT held that the issue was not 'the payment of private medical treatment in general, but, rather, payment for a specific form of support to enable the claimant to return'.

The EAT confirmed in *Wade v Sheffield Hallam University* (UKEAT/0194/12) that the duty to adjust does not require an employer to redeploy a disabled employee to a role for which he does not meet most of the essential criteria. In *HK Danmark (acting on behalf of Ring) v Dansk almennyttigt Boligselskab* (Case C-335/11) (see **13.3.1** above), the ECJ held that reducing an employee's working hours could be a reasonable adjustment, though it would depend on the facts.

Elias LJ held in *Griffiths* (above) that whilst the sickness absence policy placed the claimant at a substantial disadvantage:

> the steps required to avoid or alleviate such disadvantages are not likely to be steps which a reasonable employer can be expected to take. The *O'Hanlon* case ... provides an example. The sick pay rules in that case were found to constitute a substantial disadvantage for reasons already discussed, but the Court of Appeal agreed with the EAT in holding that increasing the period during which the disabled claimant could claim full pay whilst sick would not be a reasonable step to expect the employer to take. ... Hooper LJ also approved an observation by the EAT that:
>
> > 'The Act is designed to recognise the dignity of the disabled and to require modifications which enable them to play a full part in the world of work, important and laudable aims. It is not to treat them as objects of charity which, as the tribunal pointed out, may in fact sometimes and for some people tend to act as a positive disincentive to return to work.'

Elias LJ upheld the employment tribunal's conclusion on the facts that modifying the policy to allow the claimant to have longer periods of illness absence before she faced the risk of sanctions than would be permitted for employees not subject to disability-related illnesses, was not a reasonable adjustment. He noted, however, that where periods of absence were limited and occasional, it might be possible to modify the policy in a principled and rational way, and it might be unreasonable not to do so. It will, of course, depend on the facts.

In *G4S Cash Solutions (UK) Ltd v Powell* (UKEAT/0243/15) the EAT held that an employer cannot impose as a reasonable adjustment something that is incompatible with the terms of the employment contract (the employee offered a job at a reduced rate of pay) unless the employee consents. There is no reason in principle why pay protection, in conjunction with other measures, cannot be a reasonable adjustment. The question would be whether it was reasonable for the employer to take that step. However, the EAT held that it might be a reasonable adjustment, where an employee is unable to continue in their original role, to move them to a new role and to maintain their former rate of pay, if that was higher than the usual rate for that role.

In *Linsley v Commissioners for Her Majesty's Revenue and Customs* (UKEAT/1050/18), the EAT held that a tribunal had erred in failing to give proper weight to a parking policy that was directly relevant to the question of reasonable adjustments (it said that priority to its car parks was to be given to staff requiring a space as a reasonable adjustment). The EAT said that an adjustment recommended by an employer's own policy was likely to be a reasonable adjustment to make. If it departs from such a policy, a cogent reason needs to be given (which was not the case on the facts here).

In *Hill v Lloyds Bank plc* (UKEAT/0173, 0174 and 0233/19), the EAT upheld a tribunal's decision that it was a reasonable adjustment to undertake that the employee concerned would no longer have to work with the employees who had harassed her and that, if there was no alternative, to undertake to offer a severance payment equivalent to a redundancy payment.

The EAT upheld the tribunal's decision that, on the facts, wage continuation was not a reasonable adjustment in *Aleem v E-Act Academy Trust Ltd* (UKEAT/0299/20 and 0100/20) (see too *O'Hanlon v HM Revenue & Customs* (UKEAT/0109/06), upheld by the Court of Appeal ([2007] ICR 1359)).

13.5.2.5   Knowledge of disability

Note that the duty in s 20 is not to make adjustments to facilitate the employment of disabled people generally. The duty arises only in relation to particular identifiable individuals. Schedule 8, Pt 3, para 20 states that an employer is not subject to a duty to make reasonable adjustments if the employer does not know, and could not reasonably be expected to know, that a person has (or has had) a disability and is likely to be placed at a substantial disadvantage. That language reflects wording that was used previously, where an employer was exempted from the duty to make reasonable adjustments if 'he did not know, and could not reasonably be expected to know, that someone was likely to be placed at a substantial disadvantage'. The burden of proof is on the employer to prove it did not have knowledge.

In *DWP v Alan* (UKEAT/0242/09) the EAT held that, to ascertain whether that exemption applies, two questions arise:

1. 'Did the employer know both that the employee was disabled and that his disability was liable to affect him in the manner set out in [s 20]'. If the answer is no, then the second question is:

2. 'Ought the employer to have known both that the employee was disabled and that his disability was liable to affect him in the manner set out in [s 20]'. If the answer to this question is also no, there is no duty to make reasonable adjustments.

(See too *Wilcox v Birmingham CAB Services Ltd* (UKEAT/0293/10).)

In *Department for Work and Pensions v Hall* (UKEAT/0012/05), the employer was held to have constructive knowledge of an employee's disability because, inter alia, the employee's manager had seen her application for disabled person's tax credit.

In *Wilcox* (above), the EAT held that the employer did not and could not have reasonably known about the claimant's disability until it had received a consultant's report that had been commissioned (on the order of the tribunal).

In *Gallop v Newport CC* [2013] EWCA Civ 1583, the Court of Appeal overturned a tribunal's finding that the employer did not have knowledge because it was entitled to rely on advice from an occupational health adviser that the employee was not disabled. The Court of Appeal held that the question was not what the occupational health department had reported, but rather whether the employer had actual or constructive knowledge of the facts constituting the claimant's disability. The employer does not also need to know that the consequence of those facts is that the employee is, as a matter of law, disabled. The case was remitted for a re-hearing. On remission, the employment tribunal held that the decision maker did not, nevertheless, have actual knowledge of the claimant's disability and that his decision was not because of an intention or motivation stemming from the claimant's disability, so there was no direct disability discrimination. That decision was upheld on appeal (UKEAT/0118/15). Note, however, the important clarification provided by the Court of Appeal in *Donelien v Liberata UK Ltd* [2018] EWCA Civ 129 (see too *Kelly v Royal Mail Group Ltd* (UKEAT/0262/18)) that the basis of *Gallop* was that an employer cannot simply rely on its own unquestioning adoption of occupational health's unreasoned opinion, which the Court said is a long way from saying that an employer may not attach great weight to the informed and reasoned opinion of an occupational health consultant:

> It seems that there was some concern following the decision in Gallop that it raised a serious question about whether employers in a case of this kind were entitled to attach weight to advice from occupational health consultants about whether an employee was suffering from a disability within the meaning of the 1995 Act. It was explicitly for that reason that Judge Richardson, when permitting the appeal in the EAT to proceed, directed that it be heard by a tribunal that included lay members. In my view it is plain that Rimer LJ did not intend generally to discount the value of such advice. The basis on which the employee's appeal was allowed was that the ET had found that the employer was entitled to rely, and rely exclusively, on the opinion of the occupational health advisers in circumstances where that opinion was worthless because it was unreasoned. That is perhaps most clear from para 42 of Rimer LJ's judgment ('relying *simply* on its *unquestioning* adoption of OH's *unreasoned* opinion') but equally from paras 40 and 43 ('he cannot simply rubber-stamp the adviser's opinion'). That is very far from saying that an employer may not attach great weight to the informed and reasoned opinion of an occupational health consultant. That was the view of the EAT, and in particular of the lay members, in the present case. Having expressed at para 30 of his judgment essentially the same view as me about

the ratio of *Gallop*, Langstaff J went on to say, at para 31, that while an ET will 'look for evidence that the employer has taken its own decision ... the lay members sitting with me in this case would wish to emphasise that in general great respect must be shown to the views of an Occupational Health doctor', though such views should not be followed uncritically.

The Code states that 'an employer must do all [it] can reasonably be expected to do to find out if a worker has a disability ... [and this is] an objective assessment'.

In *Abertawe Bro Morgannwg University Local Health Board v Morgan* [2018] EWCA Civ 640, the Court of Appeal held that the time by which an employer should comply with its duty to make reasonable adjustments is not the same as when a failure to comply with that duty begins. The duty to make reasonable adjustments begins as soon as an employer is able to take steps to avoid any relevant disadvantage to its employee, and that depends on its knowledge of an employee's disability. However, in assessing time, the Court said that the correct approach is to 'establish a default rule that time begins to run at the end of the period in which the respondent might reasonably have been expected to comply with the relevant duty' and that date must be assessed in light of the facts as they would reasonably have appeared to the claimant, including what the claimant was told by the respondent.

13.5.2.6 Concluding remarks

Schedule 8 to the Act sets out further guidance in respect of reasonable adjustments. If two or more people have a duty to make reasonable adjustments for the same person, each of them must comply with the duty in so far as it is reasonable for each of them to do so.

The Explanatory Notes to the Act give the following examples of reasonable adjustments:

- A utility company knows that significant numbers of its customers have a sight impairment and will have difficulty reading invoices and other customer communications in standard print, so must consider how to make its communications more accessible. As a result, it might provide communications in large print to customers who require this.

- A bank is obliged to consider reasonable adjustments for a newly recruited financial adviser who is a wheelchair user and who would have difficulty negotiating her way around the customer area. In consultation with the new adviser, the bank rearranges the layout of furniture in the customer area and installs a new desk. These changes result in the new adviser being able to work alongside her colleagues.

- The organiser of a large public conference knows that hearing-impaired delegates are likely to attend. She must therefore consider how to make the conference accessible to them. Having asked delegates what adjustments they need, she decides to engage BSL/English interpreters, have a palantypist and an induction loop to make sure that the hearing-impaired delegates are not substantially disadvantaged.

- An employee develops carpal tunnel syndrome which makes it difficult for him to use a standard keyboard. The employer refuses to provide a modified keyboard or voice-activated software which would overcome the disadvantage. This could be an unlawful failure to make a reasonable adjustment which would constitute discrimination.

- A private club has a policy of refusing entry to male members not wearing a collar and tie for evening events. A member with psoriasis (a severe skin condition which can make the wearing of a collar and tie extremely painful) could bring a discrimination claim if the club refused to consider waiving this policy for him.

- A visually-impaired prospective tenant asks a letting agent to provide a copy of a tenancy agreement in large print. The agent refuses even though the document is held on computer and could easily be printed in a larger font. This is likely to be an unlawful failure to make a reasonable adjustment which would constitute discrimination.

Note: In *Hainsworth v Ministry of Defence* [2014] EWCA Civ 763, the Court of Appeal held that employers are not obliged to consider making reasonable adjustments to accommodate employees who have an association with a disabled person (see *Coleman v EBR Attridge Law* at **13.5.1**, and **9.2.3**, where the claimant complained of direct discrimination by association). The claimant was employed by the Ministry of Defence in Germany. Her daughter had Down's

Syndrome, and the educational establishment provided by the Ministry of Defence in Germany did not cater for her educational requirements. The claimant requested a transfer to the UK to help her meet her daughter's needs. This was refused and she brought a claim under s 20 of the Equality Act 2010.

While the definition of harassment and direct discrimination in the Equality Act 2010 were changed so as to cover associative discrimination, the Act states only that reasonable adjustments must be made to assist the *disabled person* in question. This reflects the wording in Article 5 of the Equal Treatment Framework Directive. The tribunal rejected the claim, holding that the Equality Act only required an employer to make reasonable adjustments for an employee or job applicant who is disabled; it does not oblige an employer to make adjustments for a non-disabled employee who is associated with a disabled person. The EAT and the Court of Appeal upheld the tribunal's decision: the Equality Act 2010 did not entitle the claimant to any reasonable adjustments, and the EU Directive focused on disabled employees and not on others.

13.5.3   Background to discrimination arising from disability and indirect discrimination – disability-related discrimination and the House of Lords decision in *Malcolm*

Under the DDA 1995, an employer discriminated against a disabled person if, for a reason relating to the person's disability, he treated him less favourably than a person to whom that reason did not apply and he could not show that the treatment was justified. The reason for the less favourable treatment only needed to be related to the person's disability, not necessarily on the grounds of it.

In *Clark v Novacold Ltd* [1999] IRLR 318, the employee was dismissed after a period of long-term absence by reason of ill health following a work accident. The Court of Appeal held that he had been dismissed for a reason relating to his disability, and gave the following further example:

> If no dogs are admitted to a café, the reason for denying access to refreshment in it by a blind person with his guide dog would be the fact that no dogs are admitted. That reason 'relates to' his disability. ...

The House of Lords, in *London Borough of Lewisham v Malcolm* [2008] IRLR 700, overruled that analysis. Their Lordships held that 'a reason which relates to a person's disability' has to be construed narrowly. *Malcolm* was not an employment case.

The view of most commentators was that the effect of imposing a much stricter comparator test in these claims would be that claimants would rarely be able to clear the hurdle of showing less favourable treatment. The decision appeared to render the disability-related provisions of the DDA 1995 meaningless, and to make it extremely hard (if not impossible) for a claimant to succeed in a claim of disability-related discrimination which existed under the DDA 1995.

In late November 2008, the Government announced that it would be issuing a consultation document setting out its proposals for dealing with the problems posed by *Malcolm*. The Government published its response to the consultation in April 2009. In brief, it proposed removing disability-related discrimination as a concept, and replacing it with 'indirect' discrimination. The intention was that there would also be a provision requiring a duty-holder to fulfil the duty to make reasonable adjustments before he could seek objectively to justify indirect discrimination (see **13.5.5** below).

It is against this background that the measures in the 2010 Act relating to discrimination arising from disability and indirect discrimination were introduced.

13.5.4   Discrimination arising from disability

Section 15 of the Act was enacted with the intention of rebalancing the situation, post-*Malcolm*, which it was felt had restricted the wider purpose of the DDA. Section 15 provides:

> (1)   A person (A) discriminates against a disabled person (B) if—

> (a)   A treats B unfavourably because of something arising in consequence of B's disability, and
>
> (b)   A cannot show that the treatment is a proportionate means of achieving a legitimate aim.
>
> (2)   Subsection (1) does not apply if A shows that A did not know, and could not reasonably have been expected to know, that B had the disability.

The key elements of a s 15 claim are therefore (a) unfavourable treatment causing a detriment, (b) because of something, (c) which arises in consequence of the claimant's disability. The employer has a defence if it can show either that (a) the unfavourable treatment is a proportionate means of achieving a legitimate aim ('objective justification), or (b) it did not know and could not reasonably have been expected to have known that the claimant had the disability.

The explanatory notes state that s 15 is aimed at 're-establishing an appropriate balance between enabling a disabled person to make out a case of experiencing a detriment which arises [from] his or her disability, and providing an opportunity for an employer or other person to defend the treatment'. It provides that it is discriminatory to treat a disabled person unfavourably not because of the person's disability itself, but because of something arising from, or in consequence of, his or her disability, such as the need to take a period of disability-related absence. While the language of s 13 on direct discrimination explicitly involves a comparison with persons without the protected characteristic, s 15 only refers to 'unfavourable treatment' and does not therefore necessitate a comparator. It is, however, possible to justify such treatment if it can be shown to be a proportionate means of achieving a legitimate aim.

The EAT gave guidance on the meaning of 'unfavourable', which is not defined in the Act, in *Swansea University Pension Scheme Trustees v Williams* [2015] IRLR 885 and said that 'unfavourable' should be measured against an objective sense of that which is adverse as compared with that which is beneficial. On appeal (*Williams v Trustees of Swansea University Pension and Assurance Scheme* [2017] EWCA Civ 1008), the Court of Appeal held that an employee was not unfavourably treated because of something arising in consequence of his disability. The appellant suffered from a number of conditions, including Tourette's syndrome, obsessive compulsive disorder and depression. After having worked full time for a number of years, he asked to wok part time because of his disabilities: his hours (and pay) were reduced. He then applied for ill health retirement (at the age of 38). Under the Scheme's rules, he was provided with an enhanced benefit up to what would have been his normal retirement age. No actuarial reduction was made for early receipt; however, his enhanced benefits were calculated using his part-time salary at the date of his retirement, and the claimant complained under s 15 that this was unfavourable treatment because a person working full time would have had their pension calculated using their full-time pay. The Court rejected his claim: Mr Williams had actually been treated advantageously in consequence of his disability (although not as advantageously as a person with a different disability or medical history would have been treated). The Supreme Court agreed with the Court of Appeal ([2018] UKSC 65). The claimant had not suffered unfavourable treatment because the 'relevant treatment' was the award of a pension which he would not have received at all if he had not been disabled, and the award of a pension could not be regarded as unfavourable.

By contrast, in *Chief Constable of Gwent Police v Parsons and another* (UKEAT/0143/18), the EAT upheld the tribunal's decision that the application of a cap to a payment that would otherwise have been substantially larger, was distinguishable from *Williams*. In *Williams*, there was no unfavourable treatment because had the claimant not been disabled, he would not have received a pension at all. The issue on the facts of *Parsons* was one of justification (see below).

Discrimination arising from disability is different from direct discrimination in that the question is whether the person has been treated unfavourably *because of something arising in consequence* of his disability (cf direct discrimination which is *less favourable* treatment *because of the disability* and requires a comparator). So, for example, this section may be relied on by persons who are dismissed while on long-term sick leave; if the absence is due to a disability, the dismissal would appear to be potentially unlawful discrimination arising from the person's disability. In *Buchanan v Commissioner of Police of the Metropolis* (UKEAT/0112/16) the EAT emphasised that a key facet of s 15 (unlike s 19) claims is that it is individualised: it is not sufficient to show that there is a policy that has been considered and applied to everyone; it is the treatment arising from the policy in the individual case that needs to be justified. The EAT held in *Hall v Chief Constable of West Yorkshire Police* (UKEAT/0057/15) that a s 15 claim could succeed where the disability had a significant influence on, or was an effective cause of, the treatment.

In *Basildon and Thurrock NHS Foundation Trust v Weerasinghe* [2016] ICR 305, the EAT explained parts (b) and (c) of the s 15 elements and said that it did not matter in which order those elements were examined. It is easy to get confused between cause and effect – s 15 discrimination does not arise where the treatment complained about impacts on the disability, as opposed to the treatment being because of something arising in consequence of the disability.

In *Pnaiser v NHS England* [2016] IRLR 170, the EAT set out the correct approach (at para [31]):

(a)   A Tribunal must first identify whether there was unfavourable treatment and by whom: in other words, it must ask whether A treated B unfavourably in the respects relied on by B. No question of comparison arises.

(b)   The Tribunal must determine what caused the impugned treatment, or what was the reason for it. The focus at this stage is on the reason in the mind of A. An examination of the conscious or unconscious thought processes of A is likely to be required, just as it is in a direct discrimination case. Again, just as there may be more than one reason or cause for impugned treatment in a direct discrimination context, so too, there may be more than one reason in a s 15 case. The 'something' that causes the unfavourable treatment need not be the main or sole reason, but must have at least a significant (or more than trivial) influence on the unfavourable treatment, and so amount to an effective reason for or cause of it.

(c)   Motives are irrelevant. The focus of this part of the enquiry is on the reason or cause of the impugned treatment and A's motive in acting as he or she did is simply irrelevant: see *Nagarajan v London Regional Transport* [1999] IRLR 572. A discriminatory motive is emphatically not (and never has been) a core consideration before any prima facie case of discrimination arises ....

(d)   The Tribunal must determine whether the reason/cause (or, if more than one), a reason or cause, is 'something arising in consequence of B's disability'. That expression 'arising in consequence of' could describe a range of causal links. Having regard to the legislative history of s 15 of the Act (described comprehensively by Elisabeth Laing J in *Hall*), the statutory purpose which appears from the wording of s 15, namely to provide protection in cases where the consequence or effects of a disability lead to unfavourable treatment, and the availability of a justification defence, the causal link between the something that causes unfavourable treatment and the disability may include more than one link. In other words, more than one relevant consequence of the disability may require consideration, and it will be a question of fact assessed robustly in each case whether something can properly be said to arise in consequence of disability.

(e)   For example, in *Land Registry v Houghton* UKEAT/0149/14 a bonus payment was refused by A because B had a warning. The warning was given for absence by a different manager. The absence arose from disability. The Tribunal and HHJ Clark in the EAT had no difficulty in concluding that the statutory test was met. However, the more links in the chain there are between the disability and the reason for the impugned treatment, the harder it is likely to be to establish the requisite connection as a matter of fact.

(f)   This stage of the causation test involves an objective question and does not depend on the thought processes of the alleged discriminator.

...

(i)   As Langstaff P held in *Weerasinghe*, it does not matter precisely in which order these questions are addressed. Depending on the facts, a Tribunal might ask why A treated the claimant in the unfavourable way alleged in order to answer the question whether it was because of 'something arising in consequence of the claimant's disability'. Alternatively, it might ask whether the disability has a particular consequence for a claimant that leads to 'something' that caused the unfavourable treatment.

In *Hall v Chief Constable of West Yorkshire Police* (above) the EAT emphasised that it was not necessary for the disability to be the cause of the unfavourable treatment. The burden on a claimant to establish causation in a claim for discrimination arising from disability is low. It will be sufficient to show that there is a 'loose' causal link and that the unfavourable treatment has been caused by an outcome or consequence of the disability, and the employer's motivation is irrelevant. The EAT in *Charlesworth v Dransfields Engineering Services Ltd* (UKEAT/ 0197/16) said that s 15 requires unfavourable treatment to be 'because of something' arising in consequence of the disabled person's disability. If the 'something' is an effective cause – an influence or cause that operated on the mind of the alleged discriminator to a significant extent (whether consciously or unconsciously) – the causal test is satisfied. However, even if a claimant succeeds in establishing discrimination arising from disability, the employer can defend such a claim by showing either that the treatment was objectively justified or that it did not know or could not reasonably have known that the employee was disabled.

A similar approach was taken in *Risby v London Borough of Waltham Forest* (EAT/0318/15) where it was held that an employee's loss of temper, for which he was dismissed, arose from his disability because, although his loss of temper was unrelated to his disability per se, it arose from the employer's decision to hold a course in a venue the employee could not access because of his disability. The EAT provided a clear analysis of s 15 of the Equality Act 2010 in *T-Systems Ltd v Lewis* (EAT/0042/15) and made reference to some of the examples set out in the EHRC Code of Practice on Employment (see above).

In *City of York Council v Grosset* [2018] EWCA Civ 1105, the claimant was a teacher suffering from a disability (cystic fibrosis). He was employed by the respondent with full knowledge of this. The claimant's case was that he was subjected to an increased workload; he was unable to absorb the increased pressure of work by working in his own time, by reason of the time-consuming exercise regime he has to pursue to keep his disease under control. He became very stressed. Whilst subject to this high level of stress, the claimant showed a class of 15-year-olds an 18-rated horror film, *Halloween*. When the school learned about this, disciplinary charges were brought against the claimant. These resulted in his summary dismissal for gross misconduct. The claimant accepted at the disciplinary hearing that showing the film was inappropriate and maintained that it had happened as a result of an error of judgment on his part arising from the high level of stress he was under at the time in consequence of his disability.

The employment tribunal was satisfied that the error of judgment for which the claimant was dismissed arose in consequence of his disability. The respondent appealed to the EAT in relation to the finding of the tribunal that there had been a breach of s 15 in relation to the dismissal of the claimant. The EAT dismissed the appeal. The respondent argued in the Court of Appeal that the claimant had to show that the respondent itself appreciated that the claimant's behaviour in showing the film arose in consequence of his disability for the s 15 claim to succeed, and that he could not do so. The tribunal had accepted that the decision-makers for the respondent did not believe the claimant's claim that his behaviour was the result of a misjudgment caused by levels of stress arising in consequence of his disability.

The Court of Appeal pointed out that s 15(1)(a) requires an investigation of two distinct causative issues: (i) did A treat B unfavourably because of an (identified) 'something'? and (ii) did that 'something' arise in consequence of B's disability? The CA held:

> 37.　The first issue involves an examination of A's state of mind, to establish whether the unfavourable treatment which is in issue occurred by reason of A's attitude to the relevant 'something'. In this case, it is clear that the respondent dismissed the claimant because he

showed the film. That is the relevant 'something' for the purposes of analysis. This is to be contrasted with a case like *Charlesworth v Dransfields Engineering Services Ltd*, EAT (Simler J), UKEAT/0197/16/JOJ, unrep, judgment of 12 January 2017, in which the reason the claimant was dismissed was redundancy, so that no liability arose under section 15 EqA, even though the redundancy of the claimant's job happened to be brought into focus by the ability of the defendant employer to carry on its business in periods when he was absent from work due to a disability. In that case, therefore, the relevant 'something' relied upon by the claimant was the claimant's absence from work due to sickness, but he was not dismissed because of that but because his post was redundant.

38.   The second issue is an objective matter, whether there is a causal link between B's disability and the relevant 'something'. In this case, on the findings of the ET there was such a causal link. The claimant showed the film as a result of the exceptionally high stress he was subject to, which arose from the effect of his disability when new and increased demands were made of him at work in the autumn term of 2013.

39.   In my view, contrary to Mr Bowers' argument, it is not possible to spell out of section 15(1)(a) a further requirement, that A must be shown to have been aware when choosing to subject B to the unfavourable treatment in question that the relevant 'something' arose in consequence of B's disability (ie that A should himself be aware of the objective causation referred to in issue (ii) above).

The EAT referred to the Grosset case in *Sheikholeslami v University of Edinburgh* (UKEAT/0014/17) in deciding that the employment tribunal erred when it failed to consider the possibility that the causal connection between the something that causes unfair treatment and the disability may involve several links. See too *South Warwickshire NHS Foundation Trust v Lee and Others* (UKEAT/0287/17), *Dunn v Secretary of State for Justice* [2018] EWCA Civ 1998 and *iForce v Wood* (UKEAT/0167/18).

The Code gives an example of how this works:

An employer dismisses a worker because she has had three months' sick leave. The employer is aware that the worker has multiple sclerosis and most of her sick leave is disability-related. The employer's decision to dismiss is not because of the worker's disability itself. However, the worker has been treated unfavourably because of something arising in consequence of her disability (namely, the need to take a period of disability-related sick leave) …

It is irrelevant whether or not other workers would have been dismissed for having the same or similar length of absence. It is not necessary to compare the treatment of the disabled worker with that of her colleagues or any hypothetical comparator. The decision to dismiss her will be discrimination arising from disability if the employer cannot objectively justify it.

The Explanatory Notes give the following examples:

•   An employee with a visual impairment is dismissed because he cannot do as much work as a non-disabled colleague. If the employer sought to justify the dismissal, he would need to show that it was a proportionate means of achieving a legitimate aim.

•   The licensee of a pub refuses to serve a person who has cerebral palsy because she believes that he is drunk as he has slurred speech. However, the slurred speech is a consequence of his impairment. If the licensee is able to show that she did not know, and could not reasonably have been expected to know, that the customer was disabled, she has not subjected him to discrimination arising from his disability.

•   However, in the example above, if a reasonable person would have known that the behaviour was due to a disability, the licensee would have subjected the customer to discrimination arising from his disability, unless she could show that ejecting him was a proportionate means of achieving a legitimate aim.

In *Wood* (above), the claimant's belief (mistaken) that moving her workstation would exacerbate her osteoarthritis (which led to a written warning after refusing to obey the instruction) did not establish unfavourable treatment because of something arising from her disability under s 15 of the Equality Act 2010. The test is an objective one. Did the 'something' arise from the claimant's disability? On the facts, it did not because it arose from the claimant's mistaken belief that moving benches would worsen her condition and, on the facts, her mistaken belief did not arise because of impaired judgement (see *Grosset* above).

In *Cummins Ltd v Mohammed* (UKEAT/0039/20), the EAT held that the tribunal had failed to properly determine the decision maker's reason for dismissal. The tribunal decided that the 'something' arising from the claimant's disability was a trip to Pakistan (his GP had recommended a therapeutic holiday to the claimant who had anxiety and depression). The tribunal's decision failed to address what part the disputed permission or fitness to work played in the decision.

The fact that this is a complex area of the law, which creates difficulties in its application, is evident from the consistent number of cases that make their way up to the Court of Appeal. Although the 'but for' test has been discredited for some time, there was still uncertainty as to whether a claimant could say 'but for my disability I would not even find myself in this situation in the first place'. That issue was considered by the Court of Appeal in *Robinson v Department for Work and Pensions* [2020] EWCA Civ 859, where the Court emphasised that for a claim under s 15, a claimant cannot argue that 'but for' their disability they would not have been put in a situation that led to unfavourable treatment – rather the focus is on the reasons for the treatment itself. Tribunals must look at the motivation behind the treatment complained of. Ms Robinson worked for the DWP as an administrator in its debt management department, which required the use of a particular computer software. She began to suffer from blurred vision which was later diagnosed as a hemiplegic migraine. As a result, she struggled to undertake her work as the computer program she used worsened her symptoms. The DWP attempted various solutions to alleviate the substantial disadvantage caused but ultimately was not successful. This caused Ms Robinson considerable stress which led to lengthy sickness absences. Ms Robinson raised a grievance due to this and was then moved to a paper-based role. She brought two employment tribunal complaints: discrimination arising from a disability and a failure to make reasonable adjustments. She argued that had she not been disabled ('but for' her disability), there would not have been a grievance and so there would be no issue with the grievance being dealt with in a timely manner. The tribunal held that the DWP had made all possible reasonable adjustments, but that she had been treated unfavourably in the way in which her grievance had been dealt with and the delay in finding a solution to her problems. The DWP successfully appealed to the EAT, which held that the tribunal had adopted an incorrect approach to causation under s 15. Ms Robinson appealed, unsuccessfully, to the Court of Appeal, which said that the DWP's actions were not motivated by anything arising from her disability:

> [The] 'treatment' of [Ms Robinson] cannot, in my judgment, have been 'motivated' ... by the consequences of the disability. Only by applying the forbidden 'but for' test can it be said that [Ms Robinson's] symptoms caused her to be treated as she was. The finding was merely that an attempt was made to deal with the consequences of the disability, which did not succeed. In so far as the treatment was unfavourable at all, that was because the attempt to solve the problem failed, it took a long time and [Ms Robinson] suffered stress as a result ... there are no primary facts to connect [the DWP's] conduct resulting in those delays with the consequences of [Ms Robinson's] disability.

It was necessary to consider the thought processes of the managers dealing with Ms Robinson's grievances, to see whether there was any basis for concluding that they delayed resolution of the grievance 'because of' something arising from her disability. It was not enough for a claimant to show that 'but for' disability, she would not have been in the (unfavourable) situation complained of.

In *Stott v Ralli Ltd* (UKEAT/0223/20), the EAT reviewed the authorities in a case where the treatment was dismissal and the 'something arising in consequence of disability' was poor performance. The EAT held that the tribunal had erred by failing to consider whether the claimant's poor performance was something arising in consequence of her anxiety and depression. However, the claimant's appeal was dismissed because the EAT upheld the finding that the employer did not have knowledge at the time of the impugned treatment, and so the treatment was justified. At the time of her dismissal, the employer was unaware of the condition and was only informed of her mental health problems after she raised a grievance following her dismissal. The EAT also held that the employer's subsequent knowledge of the claimant's mental health issues at the time of her post-dismissal grievance was not relevant to her discrimination case. While in the context of an unfair dismissal claim the dismissal would include the process encompassing the appeal stage and outcome, this was not an approach that should be taken for disability claims.

13.5.4.1 Objective justification

The s 15 defence applies if an employer can show that the (unfavourable) treatment is a proportionate means of achieving a legitimate aim. Examples of legitimate aims could be business needs and health and safety concerns. Cost alone is not sufficient (see *Woodcock v Cumbria PCT* [2012] ICR 1126). See *Swansea University Pension Scheme Trustees v Williams* (above), *Griffiths v Secretary of State for Work and Pensions* [2015] EWCA Civ 1265 and *DL Insurance Services Ltd v O'Connor* (UKEAT/0230/17) for recent cases on how the justification defence is applied in a s 15 case. Whilst much of the case law on s 19 justification will apply here too, not all of it is relevant because s 15 does not involve the application of a PCP giving rise to group disadvantage (see **13.5.5** below).

The EAT held in *Dominique v Toll Global Forwarding Ltd* (UKEAT/0308/13) that there is no legal obligation to consider any failure to adjust before considering objective justification. However, the EAT held that any relevant failure to adjust will be pertinent to the necessary balancing exercise required. The EHRC's Code states:

> If an employer has failed to make a reasonable adjustment which would have prevented or minimised the unfavourable treatment, it will be very difficult for them to show that the treatment was objectively justified.

Proportionality involves carrying out a balancing exercise, weighing the needs of the employer against the discriminatory effect of the proposed action, which may involve consideration of whether lesser measures could have been deployed by the employer to achieve its aim. The treatment must be an appropriate means of achieving the aim identified and reasonably necessary to do so (see *Hardys & Hansons* at **10.2.7**).

In *Chief Constable of Gwent Police v Parsons* (above), the EAT summarised the relevant principles (at para 24):

(1) Once a prima facie case of discrimination arising from disability is shown the onus is on the employer to establish justification;

(2) This involves showing that the unfavourable treatment (ie in this case capping the payments to the Claimants) was a reasonably necessary and proportionate means of achieving a 'legitimate aim';

(3) Saving money is not in itself a legitimate aim but preventing a 'windfall' could in principle be one;

(4) Entitlement to receive immediate benefits from a pension fund might justify exclusion from (or a cap or limit on the amount of) a payment under a redundancy scheme but that is not inevitable in every case; it will depend on the nature of the redundancy scheme and the pension scheme and an analysis of the financial benefits which would arise under them (see: *Loxley* case at paras [37] to [41]); (Note that in *Loxley* the ET had found that exclusion from the redundancy scheme in question was justified but, although they had been provided with a lot of financial information they had failed to analyse it or the general issue of justification properly and the matter was remitted to a fresh ET.)

(5) However, a cap imposed to prevent an employee recovering more under a redundancy scheme designed to compensate him for loss of earnings than he would have received in earnings if he had remained in his employment and worked to retirement age will necessarily constitute a proportionate means of achieving the legitimate aim of preventing a windfall (see: *Loxley* at para [37] and the decision in *Hastie*).

On the facts, the EAT upheld the tribunal's decision that the Chief Constable had failed to justify a cap on the payments on the basis that the *Loxley* and *Hastie* cases did not assist him, and that the Chief Constable had not demonstrated any 'windfall' in fact or that applying the six months' cap was necessary to prevent any windfall.

In *Hensman v Ministry of Defence* (UKEAT/0067/14), the EAT overturned a tribunal's decision that the dismissal was disproportionate, holding that it had failed to carry out the necessary balancing exercise. The employment tribunal had focused on what the Crown Court had said about the actions of Mr Hensman in filming a colleague in the shower not being his fault because of his medical condition, rather than balancing that against the employer's concerns relating to trust and confidence.

The EAT held, in *Burdett v Aviva Employment Services Ltd* (UKEAT/0439/13), that the employment tribunal failed to balance the discriminatory impact of the measure (dismissal for sexual assault of two female employees when the claimant stopped his medication) against other options open to the employer (eg allowing the claimant to work from home). The employment tribunal had held that the discrimination was justified.

In *Birtenshaw v Oldfield* (UKEAT/0288/18), the EAT held that, in considering the issue of proportionality, whilst a tribunal's consideration of the objective question should give a substantial degree of respect to the judgment of the decision maker as to what is reasonably necessary to achieve the legitimate aim provided he has acted rationally and responsibly, the employment tribunal did not have to be satisfied that the identified and proportionate lesser measures would or might have been acceptable to the decision maker or otherwise caused him to take a different course. To do so would be at odds with the objective question which it had to determine; and would give primacy to the position of the decision maker.

In *Department of Work and Pensions v Boyers* (UKEAT/0282/19), the EAT held that the tribunal had erred in failing to carry out the balancing act between the needs of the employer, represented by the legitimate aims that the tribunal accepted were being pursued and the discriminatory effect on the employee (the tribunal did not, for example, set out the evidence about the level of strain placed on others; nor the impact on public funds). It had, instead, erred by focusing on the respondent's decision-making process.

In *Scott v Kenton Schools Academy Trust* (UKEAT/0031/19) and in *Department of Work and Pensions v Boyers* (UKEAT/0282/19), the EAT reminded itself that whilst the tests for reasonableness in unfair dismissal cases and for justification under s 15 will often lead to the same outcome (*O'Brien*), that will not always be so (*Grosset*). In *Iceland Foods Ltd v Stevenson* (UKEAT/0309/19), the EAT's judgment raised the question of whether the unfair dismissal reasonableness test and s 15 justification test outcomes are more likely to be the same in capability dismissals (see *O'Brien*), but less likely to be the same in misconduct cases (see *Grosset*). That is probably right in the authors' opinion. Underhill LJ said in *O'Brien* that: '... it would be a pity if there were any real distinction in the context of dismissal for long-term sickness where the employee is disabled within the meaning of the 2010 Act'.

Regard may also be had to the EHRC Code in relation to justification.

13.5.4.2   Knowledge of disability

For discrimination arising from a disability to occur, the employer or other person must know, or reasonably be expected to know, that the disabled person has a disability.

Section 15(2) states that 'subsection (1) does not apply if A shows that A did not know, and could not reasonably have been expected to know, that B had the disability'. That is the same wording used with regard to s 21, so readers should have regard to the interpretation given to the phrase in *DWP v Alan* (UKEAT/0242/09) and other cases (see **13.5.2.5**).

Where employers are dealing with misconduct issues with a disabled employee, they are advised to get informed medical advice on whether a link exists or is likely to exist between the conduct and the disability.

The EAT held in *Baldeh v Churches Housing Association of Dudley & District* (UKEAT/0290/18) that it was an error of law for the employment tribunal not to have considered whether the employer had acquired actual or constructive knowledge of the claimant's disability before the rejection of her appeal (it was accepted that the respondent did not have knowledge at the date of dismissal). In *A Ltd v Z* (UKEAT/0273/18), the EAT confirmed that there are two steps to the test: (1) what steps the employer could reasonably have been expected to take; and (2) whether, if it had taken those steps, the employer could reasonably have been expected to know of the claimant's disability.

The correct approach to adopt to actual or constructive knowledge was analysed by HHJ Eady QC in *A Ltd v Z*:

23. In determining whether the employer had requisite knowledge for section 15(2) purposes, the following principles are uncontroversial between the parties in this appeal:

(1)   There need only be actual or constructive knowledge as to the disability itself, not the causal link between the disability and its consequent effects which led to the unfavourable treatment, see *York City Council v Grosset* [2018] ICR 1492 CA at paragraph 39.

(2)   The respondent need not have constructive knowledge of the complainant's diagnosis to satisfy the requirements of section 15(2); it is, however, for the employer to show that it was unreasonable for it to be expected to know that a person (a) suffered an impediment to his physical or mental health, or (b) that that impairment had a substantial and (c) long-term effect, see *Donelien v Liberata UK Ltd* UKEAT/0297/14 at paragraph 5, per Langstaff P, and also see *Pnaiser v NHS England* [2016] IRLR 170 at paragraph 69 per Simler J.

(3)   The question of reasonableness is one of fact and evaluation, see *Donelien v Liberata UK Ltd* [2018] IRLR 535 CA at paragraph 27; nonetheless, such assessments must be adequately and coherently reasoned and must take into account all relevant factors and not take into account those that are irrelevant.

(4)   When assessing the question of constructive knowledge, an employee's representations as to the cause of absence or disability-related symptoms can be of importance: (i) because, in asking whether the employee has suffered substantial adverse effect, a reaction to life events may fall short of the definition of disability for [Equality Act] purposes (see *Herry v Dudley Metropolitan Borough Council* [2017] ICR 610, per His Honour Judge David Richardson, citing *J v DLA Piper UK LLP* [2010] ICR 1052), and (ii) because, without knowing the likely cause of a given impairment, 'it becomes much more difficult to know whether it may well last for more than 12 months, if it has not [already done so]', per Langstaff P in *Donelien* EAT at paragraph 31.

(5)   The approach adopted to answering the question thus posed by section 15(2) is to be informed by the Code, which (relevantly) provides as follows:

5.14 It is not enough for the employer to show that they did not know that the disabled person had the disability. They must also show that they could not reasonably have been expected to know about it. Employers should consider whether a worker has a disability even where one has not been formally disclosed, as, for example, not all workers who meet the definition of disability may think of themselves as a 'disabled person'.

5.15 An employer must do all they can reasonably be expected to do to find out if a worker has a disability. What is reasonable will depend on the circumstances. This is an objective assessment. When making inquiries about disability, employers should consider issues of dignity and privacy and ensure that personal information is dealt with confidentially.

(6)   It is not incumbent upon an employer to make every inquiry where there is little or no basis for doing so (*Ridout v TC Group* [1998] IRLR 628; *Secretary of State for Work and Pensions v Alam* [2010] ICR 665).

(7)   Reasonableness, for the purposes of section 15(2), must entail a balance between the strictures of making inquiries, the likelihood of such inquiries yielding results and the dignity and privacy of the employee, as recognised by the Code.

13.5.5 Indirect discrimination

Section 19 provides:

(1)   A person (A) discriminates against another (B) if A applies to B a provision, criterion or practice which is discriminatory in relation to a relevant protected characteristic of B's.

(2)   For the purposes of subsection (1), a provision, criterion or practice is discriminatory in relation to a relevant protected characteristic of B's if—

(a)   A applies, or would apply, it to persons with whom B does not share the characteristic,

(b)   it puts, or would put, persons with whom B shares the characteristic at a particular disadvantage when compared with persons with whom B does not share it,

(c)   it puts, or would put, B at that disadvantage, and

(d)   A cannot show it to be a proportionate means of achieving a legitimate aim.

The other provision, which was introduced as a consequence of *Malcolm* (above), is one familiar to employment lawyers in relation to discrimination on other grounds (see **Chapter 10**). Indirect discrimination occurs when a policy that applies in the same way to everybody has an effect which particularly disadvantages people with a protected characteristic. Where a particular group is disadvantaged in this way, a person in that group is indirectly discriminated against if he is put at that disadvantage, unless the person applying the policy can justify it. The 2011 Guidance on Disability states, by way of example, that a disabled person with a mobility impairment will have 'the particular characteristic of being mobility impaired' and 'would share the protected characteristic with other people who have mobility impairments'. Thus the focus should be on symptoms. Unlike discrimination arising from disability, there is no requirement in s 19 that an employer need know about an employee's disability.

Indirect discrimination may also occur when a policy would put a person at a disadvantage if it were applied. This means, for example, that where a person is deterred from doing something, such as applying for a job or taking up an offer of service, because a policy which would be applied would result in his disadvantage, this may also be indirect discrimination.

In order objectively to justify indirect discrimination, the employer will need to show that there is a legitimate aim and that the PCP is a proportionate way of achieving that aim.

The definition and interpretation of indirect discrimination in this context are identical to those set out in the Equality Act 2010 for the other protected characteristics (see **Chapter 10**). However, the reference in s 19 to persons who share a protected characteristic is defined as a reference to persons who have the *same disability* (s 6(3)) (the guidance suggests that this is assessed in terms of symptoms – eg mobility impaired). Indirect discrimination may cause difficulties for a disabled person who has to show a group disadvantage under this section. In *Russell v College of North West London* (UKEAT/0314/13), the EAT pointed out that to establish a claim it was necessary to show that a PCP caused a particular disadvantage to employees who shared the protected characteristic of the claimant. This is because s 6(3)(b) of the Equality Act 2010 makes it clear that the disadvantage has to apply to people who share the same disability rather than to disabled people as a whole. On that basis, the claimant failed because she had not put forward any evidence as to the impact the PCP had on people with Meniere's Disease. For a case on applying multiple choice tests in a recruitment exercise, see *GLS v Brookes* (UKEAT/0302/16).

Readers should refer to **Chapter 10** for more details. Readers should also note the decision in *Follows v Nationwide Building Society* (ET/2201937/18), where an employment tribunal held that the claimant had been indirectly discriminated against by reason of her caring responsibilities which meant she could not attend the office. The tribunal held that the claimant was put at a substantial disadvantage by the employer's requirement to be office-based, because of her family member's disability, and that the justification defence was not made out on the facts (see the CHEZ case above at **10.2.4**).

13.5.6 Harassment

The definition of 'harassment' (s 26) for disability discrimination is identical to that set out in the Act for the other protected characteristics. See **11.2** for more details.

The Code provides an example:

> A worker has a son with a severe disfigurement. His work colleagues make offensive remarks to him about his son's disability. The worker could have a claim for harassment related to disability.

Note that the Act prohibits harassment based on association and perception: the prohibition on harassment 'related to' disability can cover treatment of the employee based on the disability of a third party (see *Coleman v Attridge Law* at **13.5.1** above). The definition of 'harassment' may well also cover combined discrimination because the harassment 'relates' to each of the grounds (see the House of Lords debates on the Equality Bill, *Hansard HL*, cols 546–47, 13 January 2010). Harassment by an employer also covers harassment by a third party where the employer has failed to take such steps as are reasonably practicable to prevent the party from so acting. This will not apply unless the employer knows the employee has been harassed in his employment on at least two other occasions by a third party, although this does not have to be the same party on each occasion.

See *Peninsula Business Service Ltd v Baker* (UKEAT/0241/16), where a harassment claim based on a 'perception' of disability failed. The definition of actual disability in s 6 appears problematic in this type of case. In order to bring a successful disability discrimination claim, a disability need to be established, unless either (a) an individual is subjected to conduct related to a protected characteristic they are wrongly perceived to have, (b) an individual closely associated with someone with a protected characteristic suffers harassment related to that characteristic (even if they do not share it), or (c) a protected characteristic is attributed to someone and they are harassed because of it.

13.5.7 Victimisation

The definition and interpretation of victimisation (s 27) are identical to those set out in the Act for the other protected characteristics. If a worker or employee is treated less favourably as a result of complaining about discrimination, or raising the issue or doing any other 'protected act', the claimant will be able to complain to the tribunal of unlawful victimisation. See **11.3** for more details.

13.6 BURDEN OF PROOF

The burden of proof is on the employer (s 136). The legislation provides that where a complainant can establish facts from which the tribunal could decide there has been direct discrimination, the tribunal *must* make a finding of unlawful discrimination *unless* the employer proves that there is a non-discriminatory explanation. This means that the complainant does have to establish some facts from which a tribunal could decide that there has been discrimination before looking to the employer for a non-discriminatory explanation. See **9.5.10.3** and **11.2** for more details.

13.7 VICARIOUS LIABILITY

An employer is vicariously liable for acts of discrimination by its employees during the course of their employment by virtue of s 109 of the Act (see **8.6** for more details).

13.8 ENFORCEMENT AND REMEDIES

The employment tribunal has exclusive jurisdiction to consider claims of disability discrimination in the field of employment. The complaint must be presented within three months beginning with the date of the act complained of, unless the tribunal considers that it is just and equitable in the circumstances to hear the claim outside that period. In cases of failure to make reasonable adjustments, the Court of Appeal held in *Matuszowicz v Kingston upon Hull City Council* [2009] EWCA Civ 22 that the three-month period runs from the point at which the employer makes it clear that no adjustment or further adjustment can be made. In cases where the employer simply does nothing, time, said the Court, will run from when, if the employer had been acting reasonably, it would have made the adjustment. That will be an artificial date, and difficult to second-guess what the tribunal will conclude. It is unfortunate, in the authors' view, to impose a start date that the parties may not realise has begun. Of course, the employment tribunal retains a discretion to extend time if it considers it just and equitable to do so – where, for example, the employee did not realise time had begun to run.

Readers should have regard to the very useful decision of HHJ Auerbach in the remedy appeal in *Morgan v Abertawe BRP Morgannwg University Local Health Board* (UKEAT/0114/19), if permission of the tribunal is to be sought to rely upon expert evidence (see **Chapter 6**). See too *Heal v The Chancellor, Masters and Scholars of the University of Oxford and others* (UKEAT/0070/19) for guidance on disabled litigants seeking permission to audio record tribunal proceedings.

Enforcement proceedings may be brought by an individual or by the EHRC. The EHRC has power to conduct formal investigations and serve non-discrimination notices, and to give assistance to an individual pursuing a claim. The same principles apply to those in relation to sex, race, etc discrimination. Compensation may be awarded for injury to feelings. The EAT held in *Instant Muscle Ltd v Khawaja* (UKEAT/216/03) that the guidance in *Vento* should be applied to awards for injury to feelings in a case under the DDA 1995. See **8.8** for more details.

SUMMARY

Provisions relating to disability in the Equality Act 2010 are in some ways very different from other discrimination legislation, such as that relating to sex, race, religion or belief, sexual orientation or age, where the emphasis is on treating all people the same. In disability discrimination, the opposite may be true – a person's individual circumstances must be considered, and such consideration is crucial to avoid discrimination (**13.1**).

A person has a disability if he has a physical or mental impairment which has a substantial and long-term adverse effect on his ability to carry out normal day-to-day activities (s 6(1)). A 'disabled person' means a person who has a disability (s 6(2)). It also covers, from the time of diagnosis, people who have cancer, HIV/AIDS and multiple sclerosis (**13.3**).

Under s 39(1) of the Equality Act 2010, discrimination is outlawed in the employment field against job applicants, employees and former employees. It is unlawful (s 39(2)) for an employer to discriminate against a disabled person whom he employs in terms of access to opportunities for promotion, transfer or training, or other benefits, facilities or services; or by dismissing him or subjecting him to any other detriment (**13.4**).

There are six ways in which an employer may discriminate against a disabled applicant, employee or former employee.

(a) Direct discrimination (s 13). This is where someone is discriminated against because he is disabled. Such discrimination cannot be justified (**13.5.1**).

(b) Failure to make reasonable adjustments (ss 20–22). An employer may be liable for failing to take positive steps to help overcome the disadvantages resulting from disability. The defence of justification is not relevant here (**13.5.2**).

(c) Disability arising from disability (s 15). An employer may discriminate against an individual if he treats that individual unfavourably because of circumstances arising out of his disability (**13.5.4**). An employer may justify such treatment if he can show that it was a proportionate way of achieving a legitimate aim.

(d)   Indirect discrimination (s 19). This covers the application of a PCP that disadvantages a disabled person (**13.5.5**). An employer may justify such treatment if he can show that it was a proportionate way of achieving a legitimate aim.

(e)   Harassment (s 26). The definition is the same as for sex, race, religion or belief, etc (**13.5.6**).

(f)   Victimisation (s 55). The definition is the same as for sex, race, religion or belief, etc (**13.5.7**).

Remedies and enforcement are dealt with at **8.8**. A flowchart summarising disability discrimination is set out at **Figure 13.1**.

Figure 13.1 Flowchart: Disability Discrimination

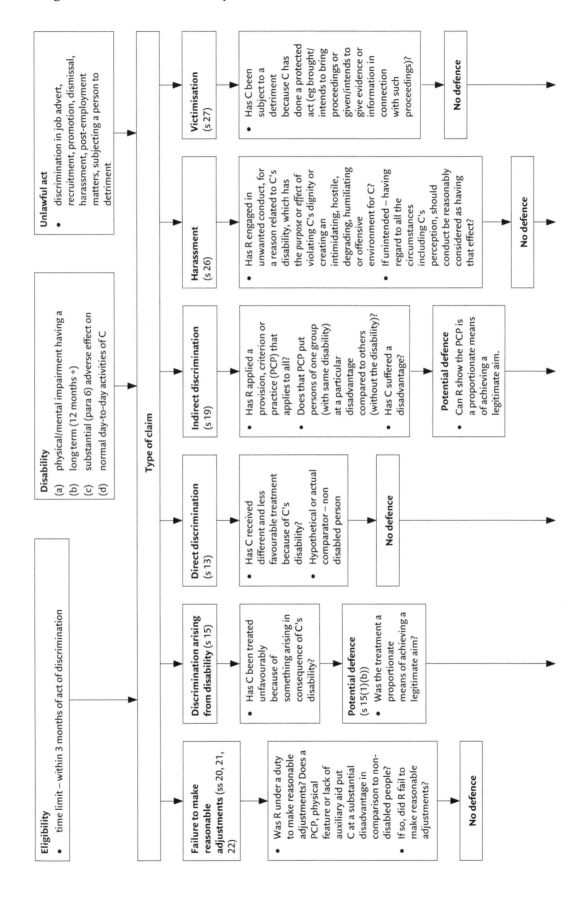

Vicarious liability

R will be vicariously liable for acts of employees committed in the course of employment (*Jones v Tower Boot Co/Chief Constable of Lincolnshire Police v Stubbs*) unless R took all reasonably practicable steps to stop/avoid the discrimination (s 109(4))

Remedies

- Declaration of employee's rights
- Recommendation that employer take action to alleviate or reduce the effect of the discrimination on the claimant or wider workforce
- Order for compensation (no maximum)
  - pecuniary losses
  - aggravated damages if employer has behaved in a high-handed, malicious, insulting or aggressive manner
  - injury to feelings (*Vento/Da'Bell*)
  - psychiatric or physical injury
  - possibility of exemplary damages
  - increase or decrease if employer or employee unreasonably fails to comply with Acas 2009 Code

CHAPTER 14

FAMILY-FRIENDLY RIGHTS AND THE RIGHT TO REQUEST FLEXIBLE WORKING

14.1	Introduction	543
14.2	Maternity leave	544
14.3	Ordinary and additional maternity leave	544
14.4	Compulsory maternity leave	548
14.5	Redundancy during maternity leave	548
14.6	Protection from detriment short of dismissal	548
14.7	Automatically unfair dismissal	549
14.8	Remedies for unfair dismissal	550
14.9	Redundancy payments	550
14.10	Wrongful dismissal	550
14.11	Pregnancy/maternity discrimination	550
14.12	Other maternity-related rights	551
14.13	Adoption leave	553
14.14	Paternity leave	555
14.15	Parental leave	555
14.16	Shared parental leave	555
14.17	Parental Bereavement Leave and Pay	557
14.18	Payments whilst on furlough	557
14.19	Right to request flexible working	558
14.20	Time off to care for dependants	560
14.21	Further reading	561
	Summary	562

LEARNING OUTCOMES

After reading this chapter you will be able to:

- describe the special rights afforded to pregnant women and women on maternity leave
- explain the differences between the ordinary and additional maternity leave regimes
- understand the significance of automatically unfair dismissal under s 99 of the ERA 1996
- list the other family-friendly rights.

14.1 INTRODUCTION

In this chapter we look briefly at family-friendly rights, including some of the special rights afforded to pregnant women. The chapter also briefly considers the laws which create other family-friendly rights such as adoption, paternity and parental leave, as well as the right to request flexible working arrangements and to unpaid time off work to deal with emergencies at home. Only employees working under contracts of employment (see **1.3**) are entitled to these rights (but note that workers do have protection from discrimination (see **1.3.4.2**)).

The law concerning maternity, paternity, and parental and adoption leave rights is contained in the ERA 1996, as amended. However, much of the detail in respect of maternity rights and parental leave, etc is contained in secondary legislation, the Maternity and Parental Leave etc Regulations 1999 (SI 1999/3312) (MPLR 1999), as amended by the Paternity and Adoption Leave Regulations 2002 (SI 2002/2788) and the Shared Parental Leave Regulations 2014 (SI 2014/3050). The European Commission published a 'Roadmap' for the formulation of proposals to improve women's participation in the labour market and enable parents and carers to better balance their caring and work responsibilities. More detail is expected in 2016.

Legislation relating to pay is contained principally in the Social Security Contributions and Benefits Act 1992, the Statutory Maternity Pay Regulations 1986 (SI 1986/1960) and the Statutory Paternity Pay and Statutory Adoption Pay Regulations 2002 (SIs 2002/2818, 2820 and 2822).

The detail about flexible working is contained in the ERA 1996 and the Flexible Working Regulations 2014 (SI 2014/1398).

The Government has started to consult on proposals to reform family leave provisions (including maternity leave, paternity leave, shared parental leave and pay, and a new right to neonatal leave and pay). The consultation will close on various dates between October and November 2019.

14.2   MATERNITY LEAVE

Only employees who work under contracts of employment are entitled to maternity leave. Workers who do not fit the definition of 'employee' set out in s 230(1) of the ERA 1996 (see **1.3**) do not qualify for the right to time off, but they do have protection from discrimination (see **1.3.4.2**, **Chapters 8** and **9** and **14.11**).

All pregnant women are entitled to up to 52 weeks' maternity leave. The first 26 weeks are known as 'ordinary maternity leave' (OML). The remaining period of up to 26 weeks is known as 'additional maternity leave' (AML), which commences on the day after the last day of a woman's OML. There are few differences between the two regimes which are dealt with below. Statutory maternity pay (SMP) is currently payable for 39 weeks to women with 26 weeks' service by the beginning of the 14th week before the expected week of childbirth (EWC).

Parents are able to share up to 50 weeks of this leave and 37 weeks' maximum pay (see **14.16**). (Mothers are still obliged to take two weeks' leave immediately after the birth – see **14.4**.)

14.3   ORDINARY AND ADDITIONAL MATERNITY LEAVE

Section 71 of the ERA 1996 (as amended) provides for ordinary maternity leave.

14.3.1   Notice provisions (MPLR 1999, reg 4(1))

No later than the end of the fifteenth week before the EWC, or, where that is not practicable, as soon as reasonably practicable, a woman should notify her employer of:

(a)   her pregnancy;

(b)   the EWC;

(c)   the date on which she intends to start her maternity leave. This part of the notice must be in writing if the employer so requests;

and in addition, if the employer requests,

(d)   provide him with a certificate from a registered medical practitioner or registered midwife stating the EWC.

A woman who has given notice under reg 4 can revise the date by giving further notice. If she wants to postpone the start date, she must give at least 28 days' notice before the date previously notified. If she wants to start leave earlier, she must give at least 28 days' notice before the new start date, unless it is not reasonably practicable to do so (eg, if the baby is born early).

If the woman fails to serve the correct notices, she may not be able to start her leave on the intended date.

14.3.2 When can a woman start her maternity leave? (MPLR 1999, reg 4(2))

A woman cannot start her maternity leave period earlier than the eleventh week before the EWC, unless the baby is born before the eleventh week; and the maternity leave cannot start later than the birth of the baby.

Subject to the above, a woman can start her leave when she chooses. So, for example, she could take 11 weeks before the birth of the baby and the remainder after, or she could take six weeks before and the rest after, or work up to the birth and take all her maternity leave after.

However, if a woman is absent from work wholly or partly because of pregnancy in the four-week period before the EWC, she may have to start her leave on that date (reg 6(1)). The woman must notify her employer as soon as reasonably practicable that she is absent for a reason related to pregnancy (reg 4(3)). The employer might agree to waive the pregnancy related absence. Additionally, maternity leave will be automatically triggered where childbirth occurs before the date she has notified, or, before she has notified a date. In that event, she must notify her employer as soon as reasonably practicable of the date of the birth (reg 4(4)).

14.3.2.1 Employer's notice

An employer who is notified of the date on which an employee's maternity leave will start or has started shall, within 28 days of notification, notify the employee of the date her AML will end (reg 7(6)).

14.3.3 Additional maternity leave (ERA 1996, s 73 as amended)

Additional maternity leave will commence on the day after the last day of a woman's OML period (MPLR 1999, reg 6(3)) and continue for *up to* 26 weeks from the day it begins.

The woman does not have to tell her employer that it is her intention to take AML when she gives her initial maternity leave notice.

14.3.4 Sickness at the end of maternity leave

Where a woman is unable to return to work at the end of her maternity leave, according to BIS guidance, the normal contractual arrangements for sickness will apply. She should be treated like any other sick employee. Generally, if an employee has a pregnancy-related sickness after the end of her maternity leave, she does not have *automatic* protection from sex discrimination (see **14.13**).

14.3.5 Rights and obligations during maternity leave (ERA 1996, s 71)

14.3.5.1 Rights

During the maternity leave period, the woman's contract of employment continues. A woman is entitled to the benefit of all the terms and conditions of employment which would have applied to her had she not been absent, including non-contractual benefits, except remuneration. The ECJ ruled, in *Gillespie v Northern Health* [1996] IRLR 214, that nothing in EU equal pay law requires that a woman on maternity leave should receive her normal full pay while on leave. The law only requires that the amount paid complies with the Pregnant Workers Directive and is adequate, and not so low as to jeopardise the general purpose of maternity leave. Remuneration is defined as 'sums payable to the employee by way of wages or salary' (MPLR 1999, reg 9). Thus, a woman on maternity leave is entitled to continue to receive benefits in kind, such as private medical insurance, the company car (if for company and personal use), club membership, subsidised loans, etc, and she will continue to accrue statutory and contractual holiday entitlement. The EAT held in *Peninsula Business Services Ltd v Donaldson* (EAT/0249/15) that childcare vouchers provided under a salary sacrifice scheme were part of an employee's remuneration under reg 9 and did not have to continue during maternity leave. The key distinction was that the vouchers were paid under a salary sacrifice scheme and not in addition to salary.

If the employer denies the woman such benefits, he will be acting in breach of contract, and such action will also be discriminatory if the denial is because of maternity leave or pregnancy (Equality Act 2010, s 18 – see **14.11** below). Section 47C of the ERA 1996 also protects the woman from being subjected to any detriment short of dismissal because she took maternity leave (see **14.6**).

The woman who takes maternity leave continues to be bound by express and implied contractual terms and conditions, for example the implied duty of good faith. The obligation does not extend to terms that are inconsistent with the right to maternity leave, for example the obligation to turn up and work.

14.3.5.2   Working during maternity leave

Regulation 12A of the MPLR 1999 enables an employee on maternity leave to agree with her employer to work for up to 10 days during the statutory maternity leave period without bringing that period to an end as a result of carrying out the work. For the purposes of that provision, 'work' may include training or any other activity undertaken to assist the employee in keeping in touch with the workplace. The provision also sets out that reasonable contact, which employers and employees are entitled to have with each other during the maternity leave period, does not bring that period to an end. Any such work must be by agreement between the parties, and there is no right for an employer to demand that an employee undertake any such work, nor for an employee to do such work. The regulation also provides that any such days' work shall not have the effect of extending the maternity leave period.

14.3.6   Right to return to what?

14.3.6.1   After OML

A woman who takes only OML is entitled to return to the job in which she was employed before her absence with her seniority, pension rights and similar rights as they would have been had she not been absent, and terms and conditions no less favourable than they would have been had she not been absent. The OML period counts towards the woman's period of continuous employment for both statutory and contractual rights. 'Job' is defined in MPLR 1999, reg 2(1) and has the same meaning as that described below in relation to AML (see **14.3.6.2**).

14.3.6.2   After AML

A woman does not have to give any notice if she simply intends to return at the end of the AML period. However, if she intends to return earlier than the end of the AML period, she must give her employer eight weeks' notice of the date on which she intends to return (reg 11(1)). If she fails to do so, the employer is entitled to postpone her return to work to a date that will ensure he receives eight weeks' notice, unless the employer has failed to comply with his duty under reg 7(6), in which case the employer cannot prevent her from returning early (see **14.3.2.1**).

The statutory right is to return to the job in which she was employed before her absence, or, if not reasonably practicable for the employer to allow her to return to that job, for a reason other than redundancy, to a suitable and appropriate job:

(a)   on no less favourable terms and conditions as to remuneration than those which would have been applicable had she not been absent;

(b)   with seniority, pension and similar rights preserved as they would have been if the period of employment prior to AML were continuous with her employment following her return to work.

So, for example, if all employees of her grade received a pay rise during her leave, the woman will be entitled to this higher rate of pay on her return. The AML period will not count towards service related contractual benefits, but will be counted for the purpose of statutory rights that depend on length of service.

'Job', for the purposes of AML, is defined as the nature of the work which she is employed to do in accordance with her contract and the capacity and place in which she is employed (MPLR 1999, reg 2(1)). So, if for example her contract provides that she can be required to work in one of three departments (A, B and C), although she actually worked in Department A, she could be taken back in Department B or C.

In *Blundell v Governing Body of St Andrew's Catholic Primary School* [2007] IRLR 652, the EAT gave guidance on what the 'same job' is, saying that a returner should come back to a work situation as near as possible to that which she left, but held that a teacher could not insist on returning to teach the same class after her leave.

If it is not reasonably practicable *for a reason other than redundancy* for the employer to let the woman return to the job in which she was employed before her AML (eg due to a business reorganisation or some other substantial reason), the employer must allow her to return to another job which is both suitable for her and appropriate for her to do in the circumstances (MPLR 1999, reg 18(2)) (see *Kelly v Secretary of State for Justice* (UKEAT/0227/13)). The terms and conditions of the job offered must not be less favourable than those that applied (or would have applied) to the old job. The BIS guidance states that if the offer is suitable and the woman refuses the job, she will have 'effectively resigned'. This view has not been tested, and in the authors' view she is more likely to have been dismissed. Such dismissal will not be automatically unfair but may be 'ordinarily' unfair, depending on the facts. If the offer is not suitable, the woman can bring a complaint of unfair dismissal (and perhaps pregnancy/maternity discrimination/wrongful dismissal (see below)).

Returning on different terms and conditions

An employee may wish to return to work on different terms and conditions, for example part time or working different hours to fit in with her family responsibilities. She has no such right under the existing statutory provisions. She may, however, be able to allege indirect sex discrimination if the employer refuses, for example, to allow her to return on a part-time basis (see generally **Chapter 8** and *Sibley v The Girls Day School Trust, Norwich High School for Girls* (UKEAT/1368/01)). In addition, employees have a right to request flexible working patterns (see **14.16**).

Failure to return at the end of AML

A failure to return at the end of AML will not of itself terminate the contract of employment. The court will look at the intention of the employee: if the employee intended her failure to return to end the contract then the court will interpret her act as terminating the contract. Failing any express intention, employers will need to take steps to discover the reason for any late return before deciding what action to take (eg whether to treat it as a disciplinary matter) (see *Rashid v Asian Community Care Services Ltd* (UKEAT/480/99). A failure to treat an AML late returner in the same way as any other late returner could also give rise to a potential discrimination claim under the general provisions of the SDA 1975 (see **14.11** and **Chapters 8 and 9** generally) or unfair dismissal (see **14.7**). Furthermore, if the employer has failed to specify the return date (see **14.3.2.1**) and the woman reasonably believed that her maternity leave had not ended, then any dismissal will be automatically unfair (see **14.7**).

14.4   COMPULSORY MATERNITY LEAVE

Section 72 of the ERA 1996 prescribes a mandatory period of maternity leave. An employer must prohibit a woman from returning to work during a two-week period from the date of childbirth. To allow her to return in that period is a criminal offence and the employer will be liable, on conviction, to a fine not exceeding level 2 on the standard scale (currently £500). This applies to employees and workers.

This period counts as time worked for the purposes of a discretionary bonus.

14.5   REDUNDANCY DURING MATERNITY LEAVE

Section 74 of the ERA 1996 provides that Regulations may be made to make provision about redundancy. Regulation 10 of the MPLR 1999 provides that if it is not practicable for the employer, by reason of redundancy, to continue to employ the woman under her existing contract of employment, she is entitled to be offered a suitable available vacancy before the contract ends, where there is a suitable vacancy (in priority to other employees). The new contract must be such that:

(a)   the kind of work to be done under it is both suitable in relation to the employee and appropriate for her to do in the circumstances; and

(b)   its provisions as to capacity and place in which she is employed, and as to other terms and conditions of her employment, are not substantially less favourable than her previous contractual terms and conditions (MPLR 1999, reg 10).

If the woman is dismissed by reason of redundancy and this provision is not complied with, the dismissal will be automatically unfair (MPLR 1999, reg 20, see **14.7**).

In *Simpson v Endsleigh Insurance Services Ltd* (UKEAT/0544/09) the EAT gave guidance on the right of employees facing redundancy while on maternity leave to be offered a 'suitable available vacancy'. The EAT held that the suitability of the vacancy is to be assessed by the employer, having regard to the employee's personal circumstances and work experience. In *Sefton BC v Wainwright* (UKEAT/0168/14), the EAT held that if there is a suitable vacancy, it should be offered to the woman, even if her (non-pregnant) colleague was the better candidate, unless the employer could offer the woman another suitable vacancy.

In October 2022, the Protection from Redundancy (Pregnancy and Family Leave) Bill had its second reading in Parliament and passed with government support. The Bill, if enacted, will amend the Employment Rights Act 1996 to enable the Secretary of State to make regulations to protect against redundancy 'during or after' an individual taking relevant leave, rather than just during that leave. The Bill will also introduce protection during or after a 'protected period of pregnancy', which may offer protection to a woman who has miscarried. The Bill has now been sent to a Public Bill Committee.

14.6   PROTECTION FROM DETRIMENT SHORT OF DISMISSAL

The ERA 1996, s 47C contains special protection from acts short of dismissal for pregnant/ maternity leave employees. The situations when that protection arises are set out in MPLR 1999, reg 19. They are similar to those set out in s 99 (see **14.7** below) relating to dismissal.

The woman can complain to the tribunal that she has been subjected to a detriment in contravention of s 47C under ERA 1996, s 48. Her remedies will be a declaration and/or compensation.

Note that no period of continuous employment is required to claim under the above provisions.

14.7 AUTOMATICALLY UNFAIR DISMISSAL

Under s 99 of the ERA 1996, a woman who is dismissed is entitled to be regarded as unfairly dismissed if the reason or the principal reason is connected, inter alia, with:

(a)   the pregnancy of the employee (MPLR 1999, reg 20(3)(a));

(b)   the fact that she has given birth to a child (reg 20(3)(b));

(c)   the fact that she is on maternity suspension under ERA 1996, s 66 (reg 20(3)(c));

(d)   the fact that she took OML, or sought to take OML or availed herself of the benefits of any of the terms and conditions of her employment preserved by ERA 1996, s 71 (reg 20(3)(d));

(e)   the fact that she took AML or sought to do so (reg 20(3)(e));

(f)   a failure to return after AML in a case where the employer did not give her notice of the date on which the AML would end and she reasonably believed that that period had not ended; or the employer gave less than 28 days' notice of the end of AML and it was not reasonably practicable for her to return on that date (reg 20(3)(ee));

(g)   the fact that she undertook, considered undertaking or refused to undertake work in accordance with reg 12A (reg 20(3)(eee)).

If the dismissal is shown to be for any of the above reasons, then the tribunal does not have to go on and consider whether the dismissal was reasonable in accordance with ERA 1996, s 98(4).

The MPLR 1999, reg 20(3)(b) applies only where the dismissal ends the employee's OML or AML period (reg 20(4)). This means that a woman will not be protected under this provision from a childbirth-related dismissal that occurs after the end of her maternity leave.

A dismissal is also automatically unfair under s 99 if the reason or principal reason for the dismissal is that the employee was redundant and that MPLR 1999, reg 10 has not been complied with (see above at **14.5**). In other words, she has not been offered suitable alternative employment before the end of her existing contract (where a vacancy exists) and the dismissal ends the woman's OML or AML period. The duty to offer a suitable alternative vacancy appears to be an absolute one; if a suitable vacancy exists, it must be offered to the woman on OML or AML in preference to any other affected employee.

If reg 10 has been complied with, the dismissal may still be automatically unfair, if the reason or principal reason for her dismissal is that the employee was redundant, and it is shown that the circumstances constituting redundancy applied to other employees who held similar positions and the reason for which the woman was selected for redundancy was for a reason in reg 20(3) (see (a)–(g) above).

The employee is not required to prove that her dismissal was for one of the above reasons. She only has to adduce some evidence to create a presumption and, if the employer is arguing that the dismissal was for a reason other than pregnancy, the burden is on him to prove this. If it is found that the reason for dismissal fell within the above provisions, there is no scope for the employer to argue that it was nonetheless reasonable in all the circumstances. The dismissal is automatically unfair.

Note again that no period of continuous employment is required to claim automatically unfair dismissal under the above provision.

If the woman's dismissal is not automatically unfair under the above provisions, it may still be unfair under the ordinary principles in ERA 1996, s 98(4) (see **Chapter 5**).

14.7.1 Exception to protection from automatically unfair dismissal

The automatic unfair dismissal protection contained in s 99 of the ERA 1996 does not apply where it is not reasonably practicable for a reason other than redundancy for the employer to allow the woman to return from OML or AML to a job which is suitable for the employee and appropriate for her to do in the circumstances, but an associated employer offers her a job of that kind and the employee accepts the job or unreasonably refuses that offer (MPLR 1999, reg 20(7)).

Of course, even where these exceptions apply, a woman could still claim that her dismissal was unfair under ERA 1996, s 98(4) (see **Chapter 5**).

14.7.2   Written reasons for dismissal (ERA 1996, s 92(4))

If a woman is dismissed while pregnant or during the OML/AML periods, she is entitled, without prior request, to a written statement giving the reason for her dismissal.

14.8   REMEDIES FOR UNFAIR DISMISSAL

A complaint must be brought within three months of the date of dismissal. If the complaint is upheld, the usual remedies are available. If reinstatement is ordered, it will be in the job to which the woman was allowed to return. If the dismissal occurred before the commencement of leave, the tribunal may include in the reinstatement order a declaration that all rights in connection with maternity leave are to be restored (see **Chapters 5** and **6**).

14.9   REDUNDANCY PAYMENTS

If no suitable alternative vacancy exists and the woman is genuinely redundant within the meaning of ERA 1996, s 139 (see **Chapter 4**) then, provided she is eligible, she will be entitled to a redundancy payment.

If a suitable alternative job is offered and she unreasonably refuses it, the right to a payment will be lost.

14.10   WRONGFUL DISMISSAL

If the woman is dismissed during pregnancy, OML or AML, or after she has returned from leave, she is entitled to receive proper notice, unless she has acted in repudiatory breach of contract. If the woman does not receive proper notice she will be able to claim wrongful dismissal. Even if she is on maternity leave, she is entitled to full pay if her notice period is the statutory period under s 86 (see s 87(4)).

14.11   PREGNANCY/MATERNITY DISCRIMINATION

In addition to the statutory right to leave described above and the right to pay described below, there is also protection from discrimination.

Section 18 of the Equality Act 2010 reads:

(1)   This section has effect for the purposes of the application of Part 5 (work) to the protected characteristic of pregnancy and maternity.

(2)   A person (A) discriminates against a woman if, in the protected period in relation to a pregnancy of hers, A treats her unfavourably—

(a)   because of the pregnancy, or

(b)   because of illness suffered by her as a result of it.

(3)   A person (A) discriminates against a woman if A treats her unfavourably because she is on compulsory maternity leave.

(4)   A person (A) discriminates against a woman if A treats her unfavourably because she is exercising or seeking to exercise, or has exercised or sought to exercise, the right to ordinary or additional maternity leave.

(5)   For the purposes of subsection (2), if the treatment of a woman is in implementation of a decision taken in the protected period, the treatment is to be regarded as occurring in that period (even if the implementation is not until after the end of that period).

(6) The protected period, in relation to a woman's pregnancy, begins when the pregnancy begins, and ends—

    (a) if she has the right to ordinary and additional maternity leave, at the end of the additional maternity leave period or (if earlier) when she returns to work after the pregnancy;

    (b) if she does not have that right, at the end of the period of 2 weeks beginning with the end of the pregnancy.

(7) Section 13, so far as relating to sex discrimination, does not apply to treatment of a woman in so far as—

    (a) it is in the protected period in relation to her and is for a reason mentioned in paragraph (a) or (b) of subsection (2), or

    (b) it is for a reason mentioned in subsection (3) or (4).

Section 18 makes it unlawful during the protected period to treat a woman unfavourably on the ground of her pregnancy, or on the ground that she is exercising or seeking to exercise a statutory right to maternity leave. No comparator is needed and no justification defence is available. Pregnancy or maternity leave must be a substantial reason for the treatment (see *O'Neill v Governors of St Thomas More* [1996] IRLR 372). Once the protected period has ended, a comparator will be needed. Note that as the right to maternity leave is generally statutory (unless an employer has a contractual scheme), only employees have the right to maternity leave, and therefore workers are not protected under s 18 (other than during their pregnancy or for their two weeks' compulsory leave after giving birth (see **14.4**)). Section 18 also covers less favourable treatment as a result of pregnancy-related illness. However, where a woman falls ill with a pregnancy-related illness, such as post-natal depression, after she returns from maternity leave, that illness is not subject to any special protection.

The protected period referred to in s 18 above is defined (following *Brown v Rentokil* [1998] IRLR 445, ECJ) as beginning with pregnancy and ending at the end of the maternity leave period or, if the woman returns to work before then, when she returns to work. It goes without saying that the employer must know that the woman is pregnant (actual knowledge) (*Ramdoolar v Bycity Ltd* [2005] ICR 368 and see too *Really Easy Car Credit Ltd v Thompson* (UKEAT/0197/17)).

For a useful recent summary of the law relating to pregnancy, maternity and sex discrimination, see *Commissioner of the City of London Police v Geldart* [2021] EWCA Civ 611.

14.12 OTHER MATERNITY-RELATED RIGHTS

14.12.1 Suspension from work on maternity grounds

It may happen that a pregnant woman cannot safely continue with her existing job. Her employer cannot simply dismiss her without falling foul of ERA 1996, s 99. He could, however, suspend her under s 66. This will amount to a suspension on maternity grounds if it is due to:

(a) any statutory requirement (eg Ionising Radiation Regulations 1985); or

(b) any recommendation contained in a Code of Practice issued under the HSWA 1974.

If an employer has available suitable alternative employment (on terms and conditions not 'substantially less favourable'), he must offer the pregnant woman such work on full pay before suspending her on maternity grounds (see *BA Ltd v Moore and Botterill* [2000] IRLR 296). A failure to make such an offer may result in the woman bringing a complaint to the employment tribunal.

A woman who is suspended on maternity grounds is entitled to be paid in full (see *Mahlburg v Land Mecklenburg-Vorpommern* [2000] IRLR 276, ECJ).

As both men and women are entitled to parental, paternity and adoption leave, it is unlikely that either sex will have a claim for direct sex discrimination if dismissed, or if subjected to any other detriment in relation to taking time off. If, however, it is less acceptable in a particular workplace for a man rather than a woman to take parental, paternity or adoption leave, and as a result he is treated less favourably, this would be direct discrimination.

14.12.2 Health and safety risk assessments

Regulation 3(1) of the Management of Health and Safety at Work Regulations 1999 (SI 1999/ 3242) imposes a general duty on an employer to safeguard the health and safety of its employees by making a suitable and sufficient assessment of the risks to which they are exposed at work. A failure to carry out a risk assessment may amount to a detriment under s 26 of the Equality Act 2010, as well as unlawful discrimination under s 18 of that Act (see **14.11**) (see *Day v T Pickles Farms Ltd* [1999] IRLR 217 and *Hardman v Mallon* [2002] IRLR 516).

The ECJ held in *Otero Ramos v Servicio Galego de Saúde* (Case C-531/15) [2018] IRLR 159 that the reverse burden of proof applies to the Pregnant Workers Directive where a worker is denied a risk assessment or a satisfactory risk assessment because any less favourable treatment of a female worker due to pregnancy or maternity leave, here due to her being a breastfeeding woman, constitutes direct sex discrimination. That meant that the woman had to present facts or evidence capable of showing that the risk assessment was not done properly and, if so, the burden was on the employer to prove no discrimination.

If there is a causally linked dismissal, it will be automatically unfair under ERA 1996, s 99 or reg 20 of the MPLR 1999 (see **14.7**).

14.12.3 Maternity pay

The ECJ ruled in *Gillespie v Northern Health and Social Services Board* [1996] IRLR 214, that nothing in EU equal pay law requires that a woman on maternity leave should receive her normal full pay while she is on leave. It requires only that she receives an amount that is adequate and not so low as to jeopardise the general purpose of maternity leave (see the Pregnant Worker Directive).

A woman on maternity leave may be entitled to receive statutory maternity pay (SMP). This is paid by the employer who recoups it from the State. It is paid for a maximum period of 39 weeks, which may begin at the start of the eleventh week before the expected week of confinement.

Statutory maternity pay is presently set at 90% of the woman's normal weekly earnings for the first six weeks, and for 33 weeks thereafter at £156.66 per week or 90% of the normal weekly earnings if this is less than £156.66 (for babies due on or after 4 April 2022).

14.12.4 Time off for ante-natal care (ERA 1996, s 55)

A pregnant woman has the right not to be unreasonably refused time off during her working hours to attend ante-natal appointments. She is entitled to be paid for such absence (ERA 1996, s 56). From 1 October 2014, partners are also entitled to time off to attend ante-natal appointments (and adoption appointments – see **14.13** below).

The right is available only to employees. Case law suggests that tribunals are reluctant to find refusals reasonable where appointments have been made on proper medical advice. The employer may ask for evidence of the appointment, except in the case of the first appointment (ERA 1996, s 55(2) and (3)).

An employee who is the husband, civil partner or partner of a pregnant women, the father or parent of a pregnant women's expected child or an intended parent in a surrogacy arrangement who meets specified conditions, has the right to take (unpaid) time off (up to a maximum of six and a half hours) during working hours to accompany the woman to up to two ante-natal appointments. Such employees are protected against detrimental treatment or dismissal in connection with the exercise of these rights (ERA 1996, s 57ZE, as inserted by the Children and Families Act 2014, s 127(1)).

14.12.5 Surrogacy and infertility

Most of the legal protections accorded to pregnancy and maternity do not currently apply to the commissioning parents in a surrogacy arrangement. While the surrogate mother will be entitled to the protections accorded to any pregnant woman, in *CD v ST* (Case C-167/12) the ECJ held that a mother who becomes the parent through a surrogacy arrangement (the 'commissioning' mother), even if she is the biological mother and even if she is treated in law (under s 54 of the Human Fertilisation and Embryology Act 2008) as the legal parent, is not entitled to the paid leave that other new parents are, although she may take unpaid parental leave (see **14.16** below) and, with an employer's consent, other periods of leave. In the instant case, the employee was heavily involved in the baby's life from the outset, and breastfed the baby within an hour of the birth and continued to so for three months, but the ECJ said the decision by the employer (an NHS Trust) not to pay either maternity or adoption pay was correct as neither applied to the employee. The ECJ also held that the refusal of the employer to provide maternity leave to a commissioning mother does not constitute discrimination on the grounds of sex contrary to the Equal Treatment Directive.

The Children and Families Act 2014, which came into force in December 2014 where the EWC was on or after 5 April 2015, includes provisions that enable the commissioning parents in a surrogacy arrangement to utilise adoption leave and pay (see **14.13** below).

The ECJ in *CD v ST* (above) also considered whether the employee's gynaecological condition amounted to a disability, but found it did not. Some care may be needed in this area, as infertility may be the result of or lead to a medical condition which may fall within the definition of disability.

Employees under going fertility treatment such as IVF also have limited legal protection. In particular, currently, a woman is not entitled to take paid or unpaid time off to undergo fertility treatments. A woman undergoing IVF does enjoy statutory protection from sex discrimination during a limited period of time when the ova are collected, fertilised and 'immediately' thereafter implanted. The position may be different where there is a gap between fertilisation and implantation. A woman also benefits from the protection of UK maternity laws, as being in a 'protected period', once a fertilised ovum is implanted (ie once the woman is regarded as being pregnant). If the implantation fails and the pregnancy ends, the protected period ends after a further two-week period. There is a Code of Practice issued by the EHRC which provides guidance in this area. The EHRC Code recommends that employers treat requests for time off for IVF treatment 'sympathetically'.

14.13 ADOPTION LEAVE

Employees have the right to take time off work after adopting a child. The statutory right is set out in the ERA 1996, ss 75A–75D, and the detail is contained in the Paternity and Adoption Leave Regulations (PALR 2002) (SI 2002/2788) (as amended). Until 5 April 2015, there was a requirement for 26 weeks' continuous service, but on 5 April 2015 the entitlement became a 'day one' employment right. The law is very similar to the law which applies to women taking OML and AML. The summary below sets out in outline only the legal framework.

As a basic proposition all employees are entitled to take up to 52 weeks' adoption leave if they:

- are matched for adoption;
- foster a child with a view to adoption;
- are intended parents in a surrogacy arrangement who have or intend to apply for a parental order.

An employee who is entitled to ordinary adoption leave (OAL) will also be entitled to 26 weeks' additional adoption leave (AAL), which will start on the day after the last day of the OAL period (reg 20). This is the same period as AML (**14.3.3**).

The employer must notify the employee of the date AAL will end, in the same way that an employer must tell a woman of the date her OML or AML will end (see **14.3.2.1**).

The terms and conditions of employment that apply during ordinary adoption leave (OAL) are exactly the same as those which apply to a woman during OML (see **14.3.5.1**).

The terms and conditions of employment which apply during AAL are exactly the same as those which apply during AML (see **14.3.5.1**)

Exactly the same rules that apply to women returning from OML or AML apply to employees returning from OAL or AAL (see **14.3.6.2**). In essence, eight weeks' notice must be given of any return to work if the employee intends to return earlier than the end of the AAL period (MPLPAL(A)R 2006, reg 15).

Returning employees are entitled to almost the same rights as those which apply to women returning from OML or AML (see **14.3.6**).

The rules which apply when a redundancy situation arises during an employee's OAL or AAL are the same as those which apply to redundancy situations which arise while a woman is on OML or AML (see **14.5**).

Employees who take or seek to take adoption leave are protected in the same way as women who take or seek to take maternity leave (see **14.6**; **14.7**) against detrimental treatment, and will be regarded as automatically unfairly dismissed if the reason for their dismissal was connected to the fact that they took or sought to take adoption leave.

Where a couple is notified of being matched with a child for adoption on or after 3 April 2011, additional paternity leave can be taken (Additional Paternity Leave Regulations 2010, reg 3(2)) – see **14.14** for more details.

As both men and women are entitled to parental, paternity and adoption leave, it is unlikely that either sex will have a claim for direct sex discrimination if dismissed, or if subjected to any other detriment in relation to taking time off. If, however, it is less acceptable in a particular workplace for a man rather than a woman to take parental, paternity or adoption leave, and as a result he is treated less favourably, this would be direct discrimination.

Adopters are entitled, since 5 April 2015, to paid time off work to attend appointments to have contact with the child prior to the adoption's taking place.

An employee who adopts a child and takes adoption leave may be entitled to statutory adoption pay (SAP). The qualifying conditions are set out in the Social Security Contributions and Benefits Act 1992 (as amended) and the Statutory Paternity Pay and Statutory Adoption Pay (General) Regulations 2002 (SI 2002/2822). Detail of the provisions are outside the scope of this book, but essentially an employee who is eligible for adoption leave and who takes that leave will normally be entitled to SAP.

Statutory adoption pay is paid for 39 weeks by the employer at a weekly rate of £151.97 (from 4 April 2021) or 90% of the employee's normal weekly earnings, whichever is the lower.

The administrative requirements which pertain to SAP are extremely complex; the rules are contained in the Statutory Paternity Pay and Statutory Adoption Pay (Administration) Regulations 2002 (SI 2002/2820).

Adoption leave can also be converted to shared parental leave (see **14.2** and **14.16** below).

In *Price v Powys County Council* (UKEAT/0133/20), the EAT upheld the decision of an employment tribunal that it was not direct discrimination under s 13 of the Equality Act 2010 for an employer to provide enhanced adoption pay but no enhanced shared parental leave pay. The underlying purposes of the two are materially different.

14.14 PATERNITY LEAVE

The Employment Act 2002 (EA 2002) introduced a new right for fathers and other eligible employees to take up to two weeks' paid paternity leave (ordinary paternity leave: OPL). The right is also available to foster parents and parents in a surrogacy arrangement. The EA 2002 introduced ss 80A–80D into the ERA 1996, which allows the Secretary of State to make Regulations governing the new right. Such Regulations have been made in the form of the PALR 2002, where the detail of how the right works is set out.

Statutory paternity pay is currently £156.66 (from 4 April 2022) a week or 90% of normal weekly earnings if less, and is payable for a maximum of 28 weeks.

Additional paternity leave has been abolished. Its place is taken by shared parental leave (see **14.16**).

The provisions and requirements that apply to employees taking paternity leave are exactly the same as those that apply to women taking OML (see **14.3**).

14.15 PARENTAL LEAVE

Parental leave is available to birth and adoptive parents, and to anyone with parental responsibility for a child. Eligible employees can take up to 18 weeks' leave (unpaid) for each child at any time before the child's fifth birthday. Parents of disabled children can take 18 weeks' unpaid leave until their child's 18th birthday. No more than four weeks' leave may be taken in any one year, and leave must be taken in one-week blocks.

During parental leave, the contract continues in a limited form, and the employee continues to accrue holiday. The employer will continue to be bound by its obligation of trust and confidence and any terms and conditions relating to (i) notice periods; (ii) contractual redundancy payments terms; (iii) disciplinary and grievance procedures. The employee continues to be bound by the implied term of good faith, and terms and conditions relating to, inter alia, (i) notice periods; (ii) confidentiality. Readers should consult the legislation for the details of parental leave.

The Government has passed the Parental Bereavement (Leave and Pay) Act 2018, which provides a right to two weeks' leave and pay to parents who lose a child under 18. It came into force in April 2020 and inserted s 80 of the EA 2002 into the ERA 1996. The 2020 Parental Bereavement Leave and Pay Regulations (SI 2020/249 and SI 2020/233) entitle a bereaved parent to at least two weeks' leave to be taken within 56 days of a child's death.

14.16 SHARED PARENTAL LEAVE

The Shared Parental Leave Regulations 2014 (SI 2014/3050) came into force on 1 December 2014, for babies expected on or after 5 April 2015 or matched/placed for adoption on or after 5 April 2015. They also apply to foster parents and intended parents in a surrogacy arrangement. They are aimed at allowing partners to be more involved in the first year, and at allowing mothers to return to work while ensuring that there is still parental care. Employees must have 26 weeks' continuous employment to be entitled to share the leave. Mothers must take a two-week compulsory maternity leave period. Save for that restriction, the Regulations allow parents to share the leave as they wish, but there are procedural requirements that must be complied with. Similarly, parents can share statutory pay.

The new shared parental leave rights allow eligible employees to share up to 50 weeks' leave and 39 weeks' pay in the year following a child's birth or adoption. The 50-week period starts two weeks after the birth and applies to children born/placed for adoption/placed with foster parents who are approved prospective adopters/placed with parents in a surrogacy arrangement who have or expect to acquire a parental order (under the Human Fertilisation and Embryology Act 2008) on or after 5 April. Parents can take the leave alternatively or simultaneously, the intention being to allow parents more flexibility in sharing the care of a child during the first year after its birth. Shared parental leave does not need to be taken as one consecutive period but can be taken in one block or several discontinuous blocks (up to a maximum of three blocks of leave per person, although an employer could voluntarily agree more), and employees can return to work between blocks. If a child's parents choose not to take shared parental leave then a mother's right to 52 weeks' maternity leave is unaffected.

Shared parental leave is available to the mother of the child and either the father or the person who at the date of the child's birth is the mother's spouse, civil partner or partner. 'Partner' is defined as the person who lives with the mother in an 'enduring family relationship' but is not a relative. Both parents must have shared responsibility for the care of the child.

The procedure to be followed, and the information that has to be provided, is complex, and a detailed analysis is beyond the scope of this work. However, it is the employee's responsibility to check eligibility. In broad terms, a mother must first curtail her maternity leave. To do this, a mother must give at least eight weeks' notice to her employer that she wishes to do so. Secondly, either the mother and/or the partner (depending on who is making the request) must serve a written (non-binding) Notice of Entitlement at least eight weeks before the first period of shared parental leave. The Notice of Entitlement must contain certain information, including the names of both parents, the start and end dates of maternity leave, and how much shared parental leave each intends to take and an indication of when they intend to take it. Both parents must also provide signed declarations to the relevant employer confirming that the information in the Notice of Entitlement is correct. Thirdly, and subsequently, a Period of Leave notice must be served on the employer, setting out the start and end dates of each period of shared parental leave. The Period of Leave notice must be served at least eight weeks before the start of the first period of leave. A maximum of three Period of Leave notices can be served. Provided these procedural requirements are complied with, and the request is for one or more periods of continuous leave, an employer must allow the request. However, an employer retains discretion to refuse or negotiate requests for discontinuous shared parental leave. Requests must be granted or refused within 14 days of the date of the Period of Leave notice.

Parents can also share statutory parental leave pay (£156.66 as of 4 April 2022) for up to 37 weeks. There are some employment and earnings tests where a partner is not employed.

An employee's rights during and on return from shared parental leave are similar to those enjoyed by mothers on maternity leave (see **14.3.5** and **14.3.6**).

Two useful Acas guides are available – 'Shared Parental Leave: a good practice guide for employers and employees' and 'Shared parental leave summary process' – as well as a BIS guidance note, 'Shared parental leave and pay: employer guide'. An online calculator is available at <http://www.gov.uk/government/news/calculate-your-leave-and-pay-when-you-have-a-child>. IDS Employment Law Briefs 1010 and 1011 also contain a detailed two-part analysis of the right and BIS has published an 'Employers' Technical Guide to Shared Parental Leave and Pay'.

Note: Concern has been expressed that where employees offer enhanced maternity pay, failing to offer enhanced shared parental leave pay may be discriminatory. The Government believes this is discretionary and not discriminatory. Two employment tribunals have looked at this and come to different conclusions. In *Hextall v Chief Constable of Leicestershire Police* (ET/2601223/2015), the tribunal found it was not a discriminatory practice (see too *NJ Shuter v Ford Motor Company* (ET/3203504/2013) where a similar outcome resulted). But in *Ali v Capita Customer Management Ltd* (ET/1800990/2016), the tribunal found that it was direct discrimination (which meant the employer had no opportunity to justify it) not to pay full salary to a father taking shared parental leave in circumstances where a mother on maternity leave during the same period would have received full pay.

The Court of Appeal has now considered the issue in the joined cases of *Ali v Capita Customer Management Ltd; Hextall v Chief Constable of Lincolnshire Police* [2019] EWCA Civ 900. The Court of Appeal concludes that to offer enhanced pay to women but not men is neither directly nor indirectly discriminatory: men and women are in different positions and are not comparable; the 'special treatment' exceptions for pregnancy and childbirth include enhanced maternity pay; and such a claim is in reality an equal pay claim, but there is a specific exclusion (Sch 7, para 2) in terms of 'special treatment' in connection with pregnancy or childbirth.

14.17   PARENTAL BEREAVEMENT LEAVE AND PAY

The Parental Bereavement (Leave and Pay) Act 2018 came into force in January 2020 and provides that employed parents who lose a child under 18 on or after 6 April 2020 can take two weeks' statutory paid leave to allow them time to grieve (ERA 1996, ss 80EA–80EE). Previously, employees had to rely either on contractual rights or employer goodwill in such situations. Although s 57A of the ERA 1996 allows an employee to take a reasonable amount of time off work to deal with an emergency, this is unpaid and there is no definition of reasonable. Mothers who lose a child after 24 weeks of pregnancy or during maternity leave will not lose their entitlement to maternity pay and leave.

As always, the detail is found in the secondary legislation:

*   Statutory Parental Bereavement Pay (General) Regulations 2020 (SI 2020/233);
*   Statutory Parental Bereavement Pay (Administration) Regulations 2020 (SI 2020/246);
*   Parental Bereavement Leave Regulations 2020 (SI 2020/249);
*   Statutory Parental Bereavement Pay (Persons Abroad and Mariners) Regulations 2020 (SI 2020/252).

In overview, the Regulations provide that the two weeks' leave can be taken at any time within 56 weeks of the death of the child, in two consecutive weeks, or in two periods of one week each. The employee will continue to enjoy the benefit of their terms and conditions, save in relation to remuneration. Employees with 26 weeks' continuous employment are entitled to statutory parental bereavement pay (£156.66 per week or 90% of the normal weekly earnings if this is less than £156.66 (from April 2022)). An employee has the right to return to the same job after two weeks' leave. If the leave follows maternity or parental or adoption leave, the right is to return to the same job or, if that is not reasonably practicable, to a suitable and appropriate job (see **14.3.6**).

Acas has produced guidance on managing bereavement in the workplace. This highlights some of the potential difficulties in this area:

*   Details of death are covered by data protection rights.
*   Religious observance rights need to be taken into account, or there is a risk that religious or racial discrimination may arise.
*   The impact of grief can have an effect on performance and behaviour.

14.18   PAYMENTS WHILST ON FURLOUGH

The Maternity Allowance, Statutory Maternity Pay, Statutory Paternity Pay, Statutory Shared Parental Pay and Statutory Parental Bereavement Pay (Normal Weekly Earnings, etc) (Coronavirus) (Amendment) Regulations 2020 (SI 2020/450) amended all of the relevant Regulations above to provide that where the person claiming the pay has been placed on furlough, their weekly pay for statutory purposes is to be calculated as if they had still been on their normal pay. These provisions came into force on 25 April 2020. The scheme ended in September 2021.

14.19　RIGHT TO REQUEST FLEXIBLE WORKING

Amended legislation concerning the right to request flexible working was brought into force on 30 June 2014. The scheme is set out in ss 80F–80I of the ERA 1996 and the Flexible Working Regulations 2014 (SI 2014/1398). In summary, all employees with at least 26 weeks' continuous employment can request to work flexibly if the change relates to hours, times or place of work. The employer must deal with an application 'reasonably', and can only refuse a request for one of eight statutory reasons. An employee can complain to a tribunal if, for example, the employer does not deal with her application reasonably or rejects it on a non-statutory ground. Acas has published a Code of Practice and guidance (see <http://www.acas.org.uk>). Employment tribunals must take the Acas guidance into account when considering relevant claims.

The Government announced a consultation on flexible working on 23 September 2021. It will close on 31 December 2021. The consultation sets out a number of proposals such as:

- whether to make the right to request flexible working a 'day one' entitlement;
- whether the eight business reasons for refusing a request all remain valid;
- whether to require the employer to suggest alternative proposals if the employer cannot accommodate the request;
- whether to change the three-month period employers have to respond to a request; and
- whether to permit employees the right to request a temporary flexible arrangement.

The current rules are set out below.

14.19.1　The application

A flexible working application must be in writing, state whether the employee has made a previous application (only one application per 12 months is permitted) and be dated.

14.19.2　Grounds for refusal

Employers are under a duty to consider requests reasonably and to notify the decision, including any appeal, within three months (or such longer period as agreed) (s 80G).

An employer can refuse an employee's request for flexible working only where one or more of the grounds in s 80G of the ERA 1006 applies, ie:

- additional costs
- detrimental effect on ability to meet customer demand
- inability to reorganise work among existing staff
- inability to recruit additional staff
- detrimental impact on quality
- detrimental impact on performance
- insufficiency of work during the periods the employee proposes to work
- planned structural changes.

The Acas Guide provides examples, and readers are recommended to read it before advising.

In *Whiteman v CPS Interiors Ltd* (ET/2601103/2015), a claim for breach of the flexible working legislation was rejected. The tribunal emphasised that there is no 'right' to work flexibly, only a right to request it and to have the request dealt with in a reasonable manner. Provided an employer follows the Acas Code and its approach is not discriminatory (see **14.19.6**), an employer is free to reject requests on one of the specified grounds. See also *Smith v Gleacher Shacklock LLP* (ET/2202747/2015), where a claim was also rejected, along with an indirect sex discrimination claim.

14.19.3   Complaining to the tribunal

If an employer refuses a request to work flexibly, an employee can complain to an employment tribunal on grounds that the employer:

- failed to deal with the application in a reasonable manner;
- failed to decide within the decision period (three months);
- rejected the application for a reason other than one of the statutory grounds;
- based its decision on incorrect facts.

Tribunals do not have the power to question the commercial validity of the employer's decision to refuse an application. The tribunal's role is essentially to ensure that the employer has taken the request seriously and that its refusal was based on the correct facts. Complaints must be brought within three months from the date on which the employee was notified of the decision. The tribunal may extend the deadline if it was not reasonably practicable for the employee to present the complaint within the three-month period.

14.19.4   Remedies

Remedies are dealt with under s 80I of the ERA 1996 and reg 6 of the Flexible Working Regulations 2014. The maximum compensation that a tribunal may award is eight weeks' pay (subject to the statutory maximum – currently £544 at 6 April 2021). The amount awarded will depend on what the tribunal considers just and equitable.

14.19.5   Detriment and automatic unfair dismissal (ERA 1996, ss 47E and ERA 1996, s 104C)

Employees who make an application to work flexibly, or who exercise their rights under the above provisions to work flexibly, are protected against detrimental treatment in the same way as women who take or seek to take maternity leave, and will be regarded as automatically unfairly dismissed if the reason for their dismissal was connected to the fact that they sought to work flexibly or exercised their rights under the above provisions. An employee who is dismissed because she tried to exercise the right to work flexibly may also bring a claim to have been dismissed for asserting a statutory right under s 104(1)(a) or (b) (see *Horn v Quinn Walker Securities* (ET/2505740/03) for an example).

So long as the employee has two years' service (or one year if employed before 6 April 2012), she could also bring a normal unfair dismissal claim (see, for an example, *Superdrug Stores plc v Fannon* (UKEAT/1190/96)).

If an employer acts perversely or unreasonably in dealing with or refusing a request, an employee may be entitled to resign and claim constructive dismissal (see *Clarke v Telewest Communications plc* (ET/1301034/04)).

14.19.6   Overlap with sex discrimination law

Where a woman returning from maternity leave asks to work part time, she may, if the employer refuses her request, have a claim of unlawful indirect sex discrimination. To bring a claim of indirect sex discrimination, an individual will need to establish a PCP that appears to be gender neutral, which puts a person of that sex at a particular disadvantage which cannot be justified. If she made the request under the above statutory provisions, she may also, depending on the facts, have a complaint under s 80H of the ERA 1996, for unjustified refusal of a request for flexible working (see, for an example, *Girvin v Next Retail Ltd* (ET/1900767/05)). A man may also be able to bring a direct sex discrimination claim if he can show that a woman's request would have been treated more favourably.

In *Thompson v Scancrown Ltd (t/a Manors)* (ET/2205199/19), the claimant, who was a sales manager, was denied flexible working following her return from maternity leave. She succeeded in a claim for indirect sex discrimination. The employment tribunal decided that the PCP (requirement to work 9am–6pm Mon–Fri) placed women at a substantial disadvantage and that the respondent had not shown that the refusal of the proposed reduction in hours of work was proportionate to the real need of the business to maintain successful relations with customers.

14.20   TIME OFF TO CARE FOR DEPENDANTS

As a basic proposition, all employees are entitled to reasonable unpaid time off work to look after a dependant (dependant care leave) (ERA 1996, s 57A).

14.20.1   Entitlement to dependant care leave

Section 57A(1) of the ERA 1996 states that an employee is entitled to be permitted to take a reasonable amount of unpaid time off work in order to take action necessary:

(a)   to assist a dependant who is ill, has given birth, is injured or assaulted;

(b)   to arrange care for an ill or injured dependant;

(c)   as a result of the death of a dependant;

(d)   due to care arrangements being disrupted or ending;

(e)   to deal with an incident at the child's school.

The amount of time the employee can take off work to care for a dependant is a reasonable amount of time to take *necessary* action. In *Royal Bank of Scotland plc v Harrison* (UKEAT/0093/08) the EAT gave guidance on what was meant by 'necessary'. It said that there was no justification for inserting words such as 'sudden' or 'emergency' into s 57A(1)(d).

In order to be entitled to take time off to care for a dependant, the employee must tell his employer:

(a)   the reason for his absence as soon as reasonably practicable; and

(b)   How long he expects to be absent (s 57A(2)).

'Dependant' is defined in s 57A(3), (4) and (5) as follows:

(a)   The employee's spouse, civil partner, child, parent or person who lives in the same household (but not a tenant, lodger or boarder). The definition clearly extends to non-married partners.

(b)   'Dependant' also includes anybody who *reasonably relies upon* the employee for help when a person is ill or injured or assaulted or to make arrangements for care. The BIS guidance states that this may be where the employee is the primary carer for another person, or is the only person who can help in an emergency: for example, an elderly neighbour living alone who falls and breaks a leg, where the employee is closest at hand at the time of the fall.

14.20.2   Meaning of reasonable amount of time off

The decision in *Qua v John Ford Morrison Solicitors* [2003] IRLR 184 was the first reported appellate decision on the right to time off to care for dependants. Ms Qua was absent from work for 17 days (over a period of eight separate occasions) as a result of her young son's medical problems.

The EAT considered the meaning of 'reasonable amount of time off work' and stated that when determining what is a reasonable amount of time off work, a tribunal should always take into account the circumstances of that individual and should ignore any disruption to the employers' business. The EAT pointed out that an employee is entitled to be permitted to take a reasonable amount of time off work to take the action needed to deal with a sick child. But, as the EAT indicated, the section is dealing with the unforeseen. Once a parent knows that a child is suffering from an underlying medical condition which is likely to cause further relapses, such a situation no longer falls within the section. The employee would, in such a situation, be entitled to a reasonable period off work to make arrangements for longer-term care. Thus the advice to the employer in respect of an employee who wishes to take three weeks off work to care for her sick child is that the employee cannot do this. She is entitled to take time off to make arrangements for his care, but not to take the three weeks and care for him herself.

In *Royal Bank of Scotland plc v Harrison* (UKEAT/0093/08) an employee learnt on 8 December that her childminder would be unavailable on 22 December and argued that the time she took off to look after her child was time off to care for a dependant under s 57A. The Bank argued that absence of anyone to care for her child was not unexpected and s 57A only applied to situations that arose suddenly or in an emergency. The EAT disagreed. It held that an event is 'unexpected' at the moment the employee learns of it. Once aware of it, he or she must try to make alternative arrangements, but if it is not possible to do so, it will become necessary for the employee to take time off under s 57A.

14.20.3 Detriment and automatic unfair dismissal (ERA 1996, s 99 and MPLR 1999, regs 19 and 20)

Employees who take or seek to take dependant care leave are protected in the same way as women who take or seek to take maternity leave against detrimental treatment, and will be regarded as automatically unfairly dismissed if the reason for their dismissal was connected to the fact that they took or sought to take dependency leave (MPLR 1999, regs 19 and 20(3)(e)(iii)). (See **14.6** and **14.7**.)

Similarly, an employee will be regarded as automatically unfairly dismissed if there was a redundancy situation and those circumstances (ie the redundancy situation) applied to other employees, and the reason the employee was selected for redundancy, was because he took or sought to take dependency leave (reg 20(2)).

In *Ellis v Ratcliffe Palfinger Ltd* (UKEAT/0438/13), the EAT upheld an employment tribunal decision that an employee had not been automatically unfairly dismissed for exercising his right to take time off for dependants because he had not told his employer the reason for his absence 'as soon as reasonably practicable'. Under the terms of his contract, Mr Ellis was obliged, if absent due to illness, to notify his line manager no later than 30 minutes after he should have started work and was required to stay in regular contact. As a result of attendance issues, Mr Ellis received a final written warning on 25 November 2011, which was to remain on his file for 12 months. On 6 February 2012, Mr Ellis took his heavily pregnant partner to hospital several times. However, he did not telephone his line manager. His father telephoned in later in the day. Mr Ellis did not attend work for the rest of the week and did not keep in touch with his employer. He was called to a disciplinary meeting on 12 February. He said his mobile phone battery had run out and he could not remember his employer's telephone number. He was dismissed and brought proceedings for automatically unfair dismissal under s 57A of the ERA 1996. The tribunal judge found that Mr Ellis could have made contact with his employer on a number of occasions and that he had not, therefore, told his employer the reason for his absence 'as soon as reasonably practicable', which is a mandatory requirement of s 57A. On that basis he was not covered by the automatically unfair dismissal protection.

14.20.4 Remedies

The remedies available to employees in relation to their right to take time off to care for a dependant are set out in s 57B of the ERA 1996. The time-limit for making a complaint is three months from the date of the refusal. If the tribunal decides that the complaint was well-founded, it may make a declaration and/or award compensation, of such amount as the tribunal considers to be just and equitable having regard to the employer's behaviour and any loss sustained by the employee.

14.21 FURTHER READING

Blackstone's Employment Law Practice, 10th edn (OUP, 2019).

Harvey, *Industrial Relations and Employment Law* (LexisNexis), Vol 2, Div J.

SUMMARY

The provisions relating to maternity rights have been implemented as a result of the Equal Treatment Directive 1976 and the Pregnant Workers Directive 1992. The law is contained in the ERA 1996, as amended. However, much of the detail in respect of maternity rights and parental leave is contained in the Maternity and Parental Leave etc Regulations 1999 (as amended) (**14.1**). The following checklist summarises points of importance when considering maternity rights:

- Length of service.
- Detrimental treatment.
- Dismissal.
- Reason for dismissal – ERA 1996, s 99/other.
- If not s 99, eligibility/fairness of employer's actions under s 98(4).
- Whether entitled to a redundancy payment and/or to claim sex discrimination and/or wrongful dismissal.

The main rights afforded to pregnant woman relate to the right to take maternity leave and to return to work after that leave expires. In most instances, some of that leave will be paid for. All pregnant women are entitled up to 52 weeks' maternity leave. The first 26 weeks are known as 'ordinary maternity leave' (OML) (**14.3**). The remaining period of up to 26 weeks is known as 'additional maternity leave' (AML) (**14.3.3**).

A woman who wants to take maternity leave must notify her employer of the fact of her pregnancy, the expected week of childbirth and the date she intends to start her maternity leave. There are rules about the time by which this must be done (**14.3.1**).

During maternity leave, the woman's contract of employment continues. A woman is entitled to the benefit of all the terms and conditions of employment which would have applied to her had she not been absent during the maternity leave period, including non-contractual benefits, except remuneration. A woman who takes OML is entitled to return to the job in which she was employed before her absence, with her seniority, pension rights and similar rights as they would have been had she not been absent, and on terms and conditions no less favourable than they would have been had she not been absent. The statutory right to return to a job after AML is more restricted than after OML. A woman on maternity leave may be entitled to receive statutory maternity pay (SMP), which is paid for a maximum period of 39 weeks (**14.12.3**). The maternity leave period counts towards the woman's period of continuous employment for both statutory and contractual rights (**14.3.6.1**).

An employee on maternity leave may agree with her employer to work for up to 10 days during her maternity leave without bringing that period to an end. 'Work' may include training or any other activity undertaken to assist the employee to keep in touch with the workplace (**14.3.5.2**).

Under ss 47C and 99 of the ERA 1996, pregnant/maternity leave employees have special protection from acts short of dismissal and/or dismissal (**14.6** and **14.7**). Section 18 of the Equality Act 2010 states that it will be sex discrimination where a woman is treated less favourably because she is pregnant or exercising or seeking to exercise, or has exercised her right to maternity leave (**14.11**).

Since April 2003, employees have the right to take time off work after adopting a child. The law is very similar to the law which applies to women taking maternity leave. An employee who adopts a child and takes adoption leave may be entitled to statutory adoption pay (SAP) (**14.13**).

The Employment Act 2002 (EA 2002) introduced a right for fathers and other partners to take up to two weeks' paid paternity leave. The Paternity and Adoption Leave Regulations 2002 set out the relevant details. Employees who take or seek to take paternity leave are protected against detrimental treatment in the same way as women who take or seek to take maternity leave, and will be regarded as automatically unfairly dismissed if the reason for their dismissal was connected to the fact that they took or sought to take paternity leave. An employee who takes paternity leave is entitled to statutory paternity pay (SPP) (**14.14**).

New provisions, which became effective from 5 April 2015, allow parents to take shared parental leave (**14.16**).

Under the Maternity and Parental Leave etc Regulations 1999 (as amended), an employee is entitled to take up to 18 weeks' unpaid parental leave (18 weeks for a disabled child). Employees who take or seek to take parental leave are protected against detrimental treatment in the same way as women who take or seek to take maternity leave, and will be regarded as automatically unfairly dismissed if the reason for their dismissal was connected to the fact that they took or sought to take parental leave (**14.16**).

The detail about flexible working is contained in the Flexible Working (Eligibility, Complaints and Remedies) and (Procedural Requirements) Regulations 2002. The right to request flexible working applies to carers of children and carers of adults (**14.17**).

Under the ERA 1996, s 57A, all employees are entitled to unpaid time off work to look after a dependant who is ill, has given birth, is injured or assaulted, or who has died, and to deal with an incident at a child's school. The amount of time the employee may take off work to care for a dependant is a reasonable amount of time to take necessary action (**14.18**).

Table 14.1 summarises the main rights and remedies available with regard to maternity leave, parental leave, time off for dependants, paternity leave, adoption leave and requests for flexible working.

Table 14.1 Summary of main rights and remedies

The right (primary jurisdiction in brackets)	Main features	Who qualifies?
Rights and remedies covering maternity leave, parental leave, time off for dependants, paternity leave, adoption leave, requests for flexible working (the detail is contained in the MPL, PAL and SPL Regs)		
Pregnancy/maternity discrimination (Equality Act 2010, ss 18 and 39)	Unfavourable treatment because of pregnancy/maternity leave	All female workers who are pregnant, employees on maternity leave & workers for 2 weeks after the birth
Sex discrimination (direct and indirect) (Equality Act 2010, ss 13, 19 and 26) and harassment	Where there is less favourable treatment on grounds of sex/marital status or unjustified PCP which disadvantages one sex	All workers, male and female
Automatic unfair dismissal (ERA ss 99 and 104C, MPL Regs 10 & 20, PAL Regs 28 & 29, APL Reg 34)	Automatic unfair dismissal if the only or principal reason is connected with a right to leave for family reasons, or requesting flexible work	All employees regardless of length of service
Protection from detriment (ERA s 47C & 47E)	Covers leave for family and domestic reasons and in relation to flexible working	All employees regardless of length of service

The right (primary jurisdiction in brackets)	Main features	Who qualifies?
'Ordinary' unfair dismissal (ERA s 98)	Where the dismissal is not fair. Note also the possibility of automatic unfair dismissal under ss 100 (H&S) and 104 ERA (asserting a statutory right)	Employees with two years' service (for those who start work on or after 6 April 2012)
Written reasons for dismissal (ERA 1996 s 92(4) & (4A))	Applies if s/he is dismissed when pregnant or on maternity or adoption leave	All employees whether or not they have requested the reasons in writing
Specific rights and remedies		
Time off for antenatal care (ERA ss 55–56)	Reasonable paid time off	All employees
Refusal of time off for antenatal care (ERA s 57)	Specific remedy in addition to protection from dismissal, detriment and discrimination	
H&S protection (Management of Health and Safety at Work Regulations 1999 and ERA ss 66–69)	Protection from risks is the employer's responsibility culminating in suspension on full pay	All employees, must notify pregnancy in writing to benefit from alternative work & paid suspension
Breach of H&S provisions	Compensation (ERA s 70), automatic unfair dismissal in relation to suspension (MPL Regs 20(3)(c)), sex discrimination	Note: a dismissed employee may have a claim under ERA s 100 and the employer is also liable to prosecution
Ordinary maternity leave (OML) (ERA s 71, MPL Regs 4–11)	26 weeks	All employees regardless of length of service
Additional maternity leave (AML) (ERA s 73, MPL Regs 5–12)	Starts when OML ends and runs for 26 weeks	All employees regardless of length of service
Refusal of maternity leave (ERA s 99 and 47C)	Automatic unfair dismissal or detriment	
Contractual rights during OML and AML (ERA s 71, MPL Reg 9)	All rights set out in contract continue to accrue apart from remuneration	
Parental leave (ERA s 76, MPL Regs 13–18)	Thirteen weeks for each parent for each child under 5 years old (18 weeks if the child is disabled)	Employees with responsibility for a child who have been employed for one year
Shared parental leave (SPL Regs)	Parents can share up to 50 weeks' leave	Employees with 26 weeks' continuous employment
Parental leave: unreasonable postponement or refusal (ERA s 80)	Declaration and compensation under ERA s 80	
Time off for dependants (ERA s 57A)	Time off to care for dependant in an emergency	All employees
Refusal of time off for dependants (ERA s 57B)	Declaration and compensation under ERA s 57B	
Paternity leave (ERA s 80A, PAL Regs)	2 weeks' leave to be taken together	Employees with 26 weeks' service by the 15th week before the EWC or the date of matching for adoption
Additional paternity leave	2–26 weeks paid leave	If partner returns to work before the end of their maternity (or adoption leave) period

The right (primary jurisdiction in brackets)	Main features	Who qualifies?
Refusal of paternity leave (ERA s 99 & 47C)	Automatic unfair dismissal or detriment	
Adoption leave (ERA s 75A, PAL Regs)	52 weeks' leave	All employees
Refusal of adoption leave (ERA s 99 and 47C)	Automatic unfair dismissal or detriment	
Redundancy during maternity or adoption or shared parental leave (ERA ss 74 and 75C, MPL Reg 10, PAL Reg 23, SPL Reg 39)	Right to be given first refusal of any suitable alternative job available	All employees on OML and AML and adoption leave
Return to work after OML (ERA s 71); up to 26 weeks' – SPL (SPL Reg 40); OAL (PAL Reg 26)	Right to return to the same job	
Return to work after AML (ERA s 73, MPL Reg 18); up to 26 weeks' – SPL (SPL Reg 40); AAL (PAL Reg 26)	Right to return to the same job. Only if that is not reasonably practicable may the employer offer a suitable alternative	All employees
Statutory Maternity Pay/Adoption Pay/SPL Pay)	90% of normal weekly earnings for 6 weeks, 33 weeks at £156.66 pw	All employees and other workers who have NI deducted at source and who have been employed for 26 weeks by the 15th week before the EWC & earn at least £120 a week in an 8 week 'relevant period'
Failure to pay SMP	Unlawful deduction from wages (see ERA s 27(1)(c))	Note: the employer is also liable to prosecution
Maternity allowance	£156.66 (or 90%, whichever is the lower) payable by the DSS for 39 weeks	Employed and self-employed workers who work during their pregnancy but do not qualify for SMP
Means tested benefits	Support from the welfare benefits safety net via DWP for women who cannot claim SMP or MA	
Statutory paternity pay	Fixed rate for 2 weeks of £156.66 or 90% gross earnings, if lower	Average earnings must be £120 pw (or more)
Refusal of paternity pay	Unlawful deduction from wages (ERA s 27(1)(ca))	
Additional statutory paternity pay	£156.66 pw or 90% gross earnings	26 weeks' continuous employment/£120 pw
Refusal of adoption pay	Unlawful deduction from wages (ERA s 27(1)(cb))	
Flexible working (ERA s 80F, FW Regs 2014)	The right to ask for flexible working for all employees	Employees with 26 weeks' service.
Refusal of FW	ERA s 80H and possibly indirect sex discrimination	

CHAPTER 15

HUMAN RIGHTS, MONITORING AND DATA PROTECTION

15.1	Human Rights Act 1998 – introduction	567
15.2	The existing scheme of the Human Rights Act 1998	568
15.3	Key definitions	569
15.4	Relevant Convention rights	570
15.5	Data protection	579
15.6	Monitoring in the workplace	586
15.7	Further reading	591
	Summary	591

LEARNING OUTCOMES

After reading this chapter you will be able to:

- understand how the Human Rights Act 1998 may influence UK law
- explain when Article 6 may impact upon internal disciplinary proceedings
- explain how Article 6 impacts upon employment tribunal hearings
- describe how Article 8 is relevant to employment tribunal claims
- describe the relevance of the Regulation of Investigatory Powers Act 2000 and of the Data Protection Act 1998.

15.1 HUMAN RIGHTS ACT 1998 – INTRODUCTION

The Human Rights Act (HRA) 1998 came into force on 2 October 2000. It incorporates into domestic law the European Convention for the Protection of Human Rights and Fundamental Freedoms 1950 ('the Convention' or 'ECHR'). The ECHR is an instrument of the Council of Europe, which has 47 Member States, including the UK and Russia. It is enforced by the European Court of Human Rights (ECtHR) based in Strasbourg. It is completely separate from the EU. The EU has its own Charter of Fundamental Rights, which is overseen by the Court of Justice of the EU (ECJ), based in Luxembourg. Although the UK was already a signatory to the Convention and was therefore bound by it as a matter of international law, until the HRA 1998 came into force the Convention was not directly part of UK domestic law and individuals could not enforce Convention rights in the domestic courts.

Following an earlier consultation and consideration of the responses thereto, the Government has introduced a draft Bill of Rights which is intended to replace the HRA 1998. This was given its First Reading in the House of Commons on Wednesday 22 June 2022. This is simply a formal stage and takes place without any debate. The Government has said that the Bill of Rights will reinforce the UK's 'tradition of liberty whilst curtailing the abuses of human rights, restoring some common sense to our justice system, and ensuring that our human rights framework meets the needs of the society it serves'. It says it is clear that it is committed to remaining party to the European Convention on Human Rights (ECHR). Amongst other things, the Government says the Bill will:

(1)   strengthen the right to freedom of speech;

(2)   limit courts' powers for certain rights, especially Article 8 (right to family life), which the government says has been 'used to frustrate the deportation of criminals';

(3)   reduce burdens on public authorities;

(4)   ensure that public protection is given due regard in interpretation of rights;

(5)   implement a permission stage to ensure trivial cases do not undermine public confidence in human rights;

(6)   recognise that responsibilities exist alongside rights;

(7)   strengthen domestic institutions and the primacy of UK law, so as to make explicit that the UK Supreme Court is the ultimate judicial arbiter;

(8)   increase democratic oversight.

In September 2022, in one of her first acts as Prime Minister, Liz Truss halted the plans to enact a Bill of Rights. Sources at the time said that the Bill was 'unlikely to progress in its current form' and that there would be a widespread review on the most 'effective means to deliver objectives through legislative agenda'. However, Justice Secretary Dominic Raab has said that the Bill will now be brought forward.

15.2   THE EXISTING SCHEME OF THE HUMAN RIGHTS ACT 1998

Schedule 1 to the HRA 1998 sets out the relevant Convention rights which are protected under the Act.

Section 3 of the Act states that 'so far as it is possible to do so' primary and secondary legislation must be read and given effect in a way which is compatible with the Convention rights; this includes (s 2) taking account of any judgments and decisions of the European Court of Human Rights. In order to give effect to the spirit of the Convention, UK courts and tribunals adopt a 'purposive' approach to the interpretation of such legislation. This is an area with which the UK courts are reasonably familiar, albeit in a different context, as they have been applying a purposive approach to EU Regulations and Directives for some time. For example, the House of Lords in *Litster v Forth Dry Dock and Engineering Co Ltd* [1989] IRLR 161 (see **7.3.2**) had to put a very strained interpretation on the Transfer of Undertakings (Protection of Employment) Regulations 1981 in order to make them comply with the (old) Acquired Rights Directive which they were intended to implement.

If any primary or subordinate legislation is found to be incompatible with a Convention right, the HRA 1998 provides that such legislation remains effective. In such a situation, certain courts (the Supreme Court and some named appellate courts, but not including employment tribunals or the EAT) can make (s 4) a 'declaration of incompatibility' in relation to that legislation, upon which Parliament may act if it wishes. (This allows for the sovereignty of Parliament to remain unchallenged.) The declaration does not affect the validity of the law and is not binding on the parties to the proceedings.

The HRA 1998 creates a new free-standing cause of action for the victims of unlawful acts by public authorities. Victims are entitled to rely on their Convention rights in proceedings brought against public authorities, or in conjunction with other existing causes of action – for example breach of contract or unfair dismissal claims. Public authorities are defined as 'including' the courts and tribunals, and 'any person certain of whose functions are functions of a public nature' (s 6). Section 6 provides that it is unlawful for a public authority to act in a way which is incompatible with Convention rights. It allows 'victims' who claim that a public authority has acted (or proposes to act) unlawfully to bring proceedings in the 'appropriate court or tribunal' (s 7). Section 8 deals with remedies.

The important Convention rights, from an employment perspective, are identified at **15.4**. Most of those rights are not absolute rights but are limited by counter-balances which permit legitimate interferences with those rights in certain situations. Most human rights cases are not about whether the right exists but whether there has been an interference with the right, and whether that interference is legitimate and necessary. That will involve questions of proportionality and relevance being considered (see **15.4** below).

15.3 KEY DEFINITIONS

The mainstay of the HRA 1998 is that it permits victims to sue public authorities.

15.3.1 Public authorities

Case law has considered the meaning of 'public authority' and recognised three categories of legal persons for the purposes of the Act:

(a) clear public authorities (eg central and local government, the police, HM Revenue and Customs, courts and tribunals);

(b) mixed authorities (eg privatised utilities like Railtrack, which retain some public functions, or private companies which carry out some public duties, like G4S);

(c) private persons.

The scope of the Act differs according to each category. Clear public authorities fall within the scope of s 6 (ie they have to act in a way which is compatible with the Convention rights) in relation to all their activities. Mixed authorities fall within the scope of s 6 in relation only to those acts they carry out which are of a public nature. Private persons are entirely outside the direct scope of s 6.

Defining within which category a particular body falls is a difficult area. As far as mixed authorities are concerned, determining whether acts are private acts or public acts is a distinction with which the UK courts are familiar, not least in determining whether bodies are susceptible to judicial review. The boundaries between public and private law continue to be hotly contested by parties in judicial review proceedings and are beyond the scope of this book, but we set out some of the HRA case law on this issue below.

In a case involving a housing association in Poplar (*Poplar Housing and Regeneration Community Association Ltd v Donoghue* [2002] QB 48), the Court of Appeal held that housing associations were not to be regarded as public authorities for all purposes. The fact that the association was a charity motivated by the public interest did not point towards it being a public authority. However, the Court said that an act which would otherwise be private, could become public if it had features that imposed a 'public stamp', and concluded, on the facts, that the role of the housing association was so 'closely assimilated' to that of the local authority that it should be regarded as a 'hybrid' public authority for the purposes of s 6. In (*R (Heather and Others) v Leonard Cheshire Foundation and Others* [2002] 2 All ER 936) the Court of Appeal decided that the Leonard Cheshire Foundation, which was a charitable voluntary organisation, was not performing a public function within the meaning of s 6(3) because the provision of care was not a 'public function', although the fees for the care were paid by the local authority.

Similarly, in *YL v Birmingham City Council* [2007] UKHL 27, the House of Lords held (3:2) that a private care home for the elderly under contract with a local authority was not exercising 'functions of a public nature'. Baroness Hale, dissenting, concluded that the fact the care was paid for by the local authority was supportive of the home's performing public functions.

In R (*on the application of Susan Weaver*) *v London and Quadrant Housing Trust* [2008] EWHC 1377 (Admin), a registered social landlord's management and allocation of housing functions were held to be functions of a public nature. The Court of Appeal upheld the High Court's decision ([2009] EWCA Civ 587) and the Supreme Court refused leave to appeal.

15.3.2 Victims

A 'victim' can bring proceedings against a public authority, relying on a Convention right.

A victim is defined (s 7(7)) to include a person, non-governmental organisation or group of individuals. Thus, in addition to individuals, victims may include companies, political parties, professional bodies and trade unions. Victims must be 'directly affected' by the act complained of (or at risk of being so affected). But note that in some situations the ECtHR has allowed those 'indirectly affected' (eg relatives of a dead victim) to bring a complaint. The ECtHR has not allowed pressure group claims, and the scope for representative actions is limited.

15.3.3 Reliance

Section 6 creates a free-standing cause of action for victims of unlawful acts done by public authorities (see **15.3.1** above). They do not need to 'hang' such a claim on any other existing cause of action. Such persons are therefore entitled to bring a claim under s 7 in the 'appropriate court or tribunal'. Employment tribunals and the EAT fall within that definition. They can adjudicate on free-standing claims under the HRA 1998, have to interpret any legislation in accordance with Convention rights (s 3) and, as they are themselves public authorities, are obliged to act in compliance with Convention rights in accordance with s 6.

Those persons who do not fall within the category of persons who may bring direct free-standing claims (eg private sector employees) will still be able to avail themselves of Convention rights but not as a free-standing claim. Because tribunals are themselves public authorities, and are obliged to act in compliance with Convention rights under s 6, and because they will have to interpret UK legislation in accordance with Convention rights under s 3, such other persons can rely on Convention rights to help in the interpretation and application of any existing causes of action (eg unfair dismissal or breach of contract claims).

15.4 RELEVANT CONVENTION RIGHTS

Identified briefly below are those Convention rights which may be of relevance to UK employment law. Reference is also made in other chapters, where appropriate, to specific employment law areas where the HRA 1998 may have application.

15.4.1 Article 4

Readers should note the Modern Slavery Act 2015, aimed at cases of slavery and human trafficking. The Act requires larger organisations to publish an annual slavery and trafficking statement (see **Introductory Note**).

15.4.2 Article 6

This creates a right to a 'fair and public hearing within a reasonable time by an independent and impartial tribunal established by law'. Article 6 may be used to challenge areas such as the following:

(a) *A right to legal representation at disciplinary hearings.*

There has been much discussion about whether Article 6 applies to employers' internal disciplinary procedures (see **15.3.1**).

In R (G) v The Governors of X School [2011] UKSC 30, the Supreme Court held (by a 4:1 majority) that a teaching assistant's rights under Article 6 of the European Convention on Human Rights had not been breached by the school's decision to prohibit legal representation at his internal disciplinary hearing. The claimant was employed as a teaching assistant at a primary school. He was accused of kissing and having sexual contact with a 15-year old boy, who was undergoing a period of work experience at the school. As a result of the accusations the claimant was suspended and disciplinary proceedings were commenced. Criminal proceedings were not brought against the claimant. The claimant asked for legal representation at the disciplinary hearing, which was to take place before the school's governors. This request was refused as the school's disciplinary policy provided for accompaniment only by a work colleague or union representative. The disciplinary hearing resulted in a finding that the allegations were substantiated, and the claimant was summarily dismissed.

Statutory provisions obliged the school, when it made a serious finding of misconduct, to make a reference to what became the Independent Safeguarding Authority (ISA) (originally the Secretary of State) to consider whether the claimant should be should be placed on the 'children's barred list' and prevented from working with children in the future. Under this statutory framework, the claimant would have a right to legal representation before the ISA; and if dissatisfied with its decision, there was a right of appeal.

The claimant appealed the decision of the school's disciplinary committee to the appeal committee of the school's governors. He requested permission to be legally represented at this hearing, but this was refused. He brought judicial review proceedings, alleging that the disciplinary proceedings were unfair and constituted a breach of his rights to a fair hearing under Article 6 of the Convention. His appeal to the appeal committee of the school's governors was stayed, pending the outcome of the civil proceedings.

The Court of Appeal held that where the consequences of an internal disciplinary proceeding were sufficiently linked to the determination of an individual's civil right to practise his chosen profession (in the sense of having a 'substantial influence or effect' on the outcome of a subsequent process which is determinative of civil rights (in this case the outcome of the ISA's process, which could have meant that the claimant's name was added to the register)), the school had to have regard to Article 6. Laws LJ said (para 47):

> It seems to me that there is every likelihood that the outcome of the disciplinary process in a case like this, where there has been a finding of abuse of trust by virtue of sexual misconduct, will have a profound influence on the decision-making procedures relating to the barred list ...

Having concluded that Article 6 was 'engaged', the Court of Appeal decided that Article 6 required that the claimant should be allowed legal representation in the disciplinary proceedings.

The Supreme Court agreed with the Court of Appeal on the appropriate test to be applied in determining whether Article 6 is engaged in the course of an internal disciplinary procedure. The Supreme Court, by a majority, applying the 'substantial influence or effect' test, overruled the Court of Appeal's finding that Article 6 required that the claimant should be allowed legal representation in the disciplinary proceedings

In its view, the fact that the ISA was required by statutory provisions and published guidance to 'exercise its own independent judgment both in relation to finding facts and making an assessment of their gravity and significance', before forming a view as to whether G should be placed on the barred list, was significant. The Supreme Court considered that the governors' determination that G had been guilty of gross misconduct would *not* have a 'substantial influence or effect' on the ISA's decision-making process. It followed that G's Article 6 rights were not engaged at the internal disciplinary stage, but only at the subsequent ISA hearing.

In his dissenting judgment, Lord Kerr considered that the ISA's decision in the barring procedure would inevitably be affected by the governors' report on the allegations. Accordingly, in Lord Kerr's view, Article 6(1) required that G should have been permitted legal representation by the school governors at the internal disciplinary hearing.

In *Mattu v The University Hospitals of Coventry and Warwickshire NHS Trust* [2012] IRLR 619, the Court of Appeal rejected the proposition that the fair trial guarantees contained in Article 6(1) were engaged at the stage of disciplinary proceedings brought by an employer that could lead to dismissal and career damage. This was a different situation from *R (G) v The Governors of X School* (above), as it was the effect of dismissal that could render the employee unemployable in the NHS thereafter. All three members of the

Court of Appeal agreed that Article 6 would not be engaged by the decision to dismiss. It also said that dismissal was a contractual matter, not the determination of a civil right.

Provided there is no contractual obligation to permit legal representation, it appears that, while employers should always consider in any particular case the gravity of the allegations and the possible implications of an adverse finding, the vast majority of employers will not need to be concerned by requests for legal representation at disciplinary hearings.

(b)   *Access to the courts.* In *Devlin v UK* [2002] IRLR 155, the ECtHR held that a total block on the applicant bringing proceedings for religious discrimination on grounds of national security, amounted to a disproportionate restriction on the applicant's right of access to a court and was therefore in breach of Article 6. By contrast, in *Fogarty v UK* [2002] IRLR 148, the same court held that excluding an employee of the US embassy from bringing discrimination proceedings did not breach Article 6 because there was a legitimate aim being pursued and the exclusion was proportionate, namely, the promotion of good relations between States through respect for State sovereignty.

In *Benkharbouche and Anor v Embassy of the Republic of Sudan* [2015] IRLR 301, the Court of Appeal held that immunity from proceedings conferred on two embassies by the State Immunity Act 1978 in respect of two members of staff (non-diplomatic) was contrary to Article 6 because there were no special features present in the case. The Supreme Court upheld that decision in *Benkharbouche v Secretary of State for Foreign and Commonwealth Affairs* [2017] UKSC 62.

(c)   *Limitation periods.*

(d)   *Qualifying periods.*

(e)   *Court fees.*

(f)   *Funding.* In *Airey v Ireland* (1979) 2 EHRR 305, the ECtHR found that while there is no general right to legal aid in civil cases, legal aid is required when legal representation is compulsory, because of the complexity or nature of the case or the ability of a person to self-represent. In *Steel and Morris v The UK* [2005] ECHR 103 (the 'McLibel' case), the ECtHR held that the lack of civil legal aid in this case was in violation of Article 6. The case was factually and legally complex, and 'equality of arms' was central to a fair hearing.

(g)   *Refusal to grant adjournments* (see *Teinaz v London Borough of Wandsworth* [2002] IRLR 721 and *Andreou v Lord Chancellor's Department* [2002] IRLR 728). In *Iqbal v Metropolitan Police Service & Another* (UKEAT/0186/12), the EAT held that a tribunal had been wrong to refuse an adjournment on medical grounds, referring to the guidance in *Teinaz*.

(h)   *Delays in hearings.* For example, Article 6 may allow a challenge to the lengthy delays in equal pay cases. In *Somjee v UK* [2002] IRLR 886, the ECtHR held that the delays caused by the conduct of the employment tribunal and EAT amounted to a breach of Article 6. It took eight and seven years respectively for the claimant's claims to be disposed of, and despite the fact that some of the delays were caused by the claimant herself and that the proceedings were complex, because the employment tribunal and EAT had contributed to the delays, there was a breach of Article 6. In *Kwamin and Others v Abbey National plc and other cases* [2004] ICR 841, the EAT held that excessive delay between hearing and decision renders the decision unfair. The EAT said that Article 6 requires a fair hearing to be conducted within a reasonable period. In *Elliot v Whitworth Centre Ltd* (UKEAT/0030/13), the EAT upheld an Employment Judge's decision to strike out the claimant's claim on the ground that a fair trial was no longer possible two years after the claim was issued. The tribunal had not communicated with either the claimant or the respondent, and the claimant did not chase the tribunal until nearly two years later.

(i)   *Independence and impartiality.* The House of Lords held in *Lawal v Northern Spirit Ltd* [2003] IRLR 538 that there is a real possibility of bias where counsel appears as representative in front of a division of the EAT where that person previously sat as part-time judge with one or both wing members. The House of Lords stated that '[they] consider that the present practice in the EAT tends to undermine public confidence in the system. It should be discontinued.' Part-time judges have now been phased out.

In *Breeze Benton Solicitors v Miss A Weddell* (UKEAT/0873/03), the appeal by the solicitors' firm was based on the refusal of the employment tribunal chairman to recuse himself following previous proceedings involving the same firm and the firm's complaint concerning the chairman's conduct. The EAT said with regard to the test of bias:

(i)   that the test properly applied requires the tribunal to recuse itself if there is a real possibility of bias. If such a risk is found, the tribunal is not entitled to balance against that risk considerations of prejudice to the other party resulting from delay,

(ii)   that if in any case there is a real ground for doubt, that doubt should be resolved in favour of recusal,

(iii)   that it is no answer to a recusal application to say that the chairman was only one of three members with an equal vote, given the important position of the legally qualified and presiding member of a tribunal of three members, and

(iv)   unless he admits to the possibility of bias, the claim of the person asked to recuse himself that he will not be or is not partial is of no weight because of 'the insidious nature' of bias.

Applying these principles to the facts, the EAT concluded that the fair-minded and informed observer, having considered all the facts, would decide that there was a real possibility of bias and that the chairman should thus have recused himself.

(j)   *Fairness in terms of 'equality at arms'* (eg the right of both parties to present their cases without being placed at a substantial disadvantage when compared to the means of and resources available to the other party).

(k)   *Use of a closed material procedure.*

In *Home Office v Tariq* [2011] UKSC 35, the Supreme Court held that the use of a closed material procedure in employment tribunal proceedings is compatible with Article 6 of the European Convention and EU law. Mr Tariq was suspended from his job as an immigration officer with the Home Office after the arrest of his brother and cousin as part of a major counter-terrorism investigation. There was no suggestion that Mr Tariq had been involved in any terrorism. He brought direct and indirect discrimination claims on the grounds of race and religion. The Home Office made an application for the use of a closed material procedure, on grounds of national security. The use of the procedure would mean that Mr Tariq and his representative would be excluded from certain aspects of the proceedings. His interests would be represented by the appointment of a special advocate, who is allowed to see the material but not to tell his client about it. The Court of Appeal dismissed Mr Tariq's appeal but held that Article 6 required Mr Tariq to be provided with the gist of the allegations made against him. The Home Office appealed against that decision and Mr Tariq cross-appealed against the conclusion that a closed material procedure could be used. The Supreme Court unanimously dismissed Mr Tariq's cross-appeal and by a majority of 8:1 allowed the Home Office's appeal. It held that ECtHR case law has established that national security may require the imposition of special systems whereby a party may not be permitted to know about secret material which is protected by national security. There were sufficient safeguards in the availability of special advocates. As far as the right to know the gist of the case was concerned, the Supreme Court said that ECtHR case law provides that where the liberty of the subject is involved, Article 6 requires the gist be provided, but this case did not involve the liberty of the subject.

15.4.3 Article 8

This provision gives a right to respect for private and family life, home and correspondence. Article 8(2) permits 'interference' by a public authority which is in accordance with the law and is necessary in a democratic society in the interests of national security, public safety or the economic well-being of the country, for the prevention of disorder or crime, for the protection of health or morals, or for the protection of the rights and freedoms of others. In *Botta v Italy* (1998) 26 EHRR 241, at para 32, the ECtHR said:

> Private life, in the court's view, includes a person's physical and psychological integrity; the guarantee afforded by [Article 8] is primarily intended to ensure the development, without outside interference, of the personality of each individual in his relations with other human beings.

See also *Niemietz v Germany* (1992) 16 EHRR 97, *Bensaid v UK* (2001) EHRR 205 and *Pretty v UK* (2002) 35 EHRR 1.

Common law in the UK had been moving towards protecting privacy through the law of confidence (see, eg, *Douglas v Hello!* [2005] EWCA Civ 595, *McKennitt v Ash* [2005] EWHC 3003 (QB) and *Browne v Associated Newspapers Ltd* [2007] EWCA Civ 295, as well as, more recently, *BC and Others v Chief Constable Police Service of Scotland* [2019] CSOH 48). In *Campbell v Mirror Group Newspapers plc* [2004] UKHL 22, the House of Lords held that where a person has a reasonable expectation of privacy, that engages the right to an action for breach of confidence, enshrined in Article 8. However, it has now been accepted (see eg *Vidal-Hall v Google* [2014] EWHC 13 (QB)) that misuse of private information is a separate and distinct tort from misuse of confidential information.

In the employment context, Article 8 may be used to protect employees' privacy. It may allow employees to challenge over-intrusive policies by employers. For example, if the employer opens 'private and confidential' mail addressed to an employee, the employee may be able to bring a claim under Article 8. If the employee is a public sector employee, he may (see **15.3.1**) have a free-standing claim under Article 8. If the employee is a private sector employee, he may be able to rely indirectly on Article 8 in an unfair dismissal or breach of contract context.

Article 8 has also been relied upon to protect the identity of an individual who was neither a party nor a witness in proceedings (see *Piepenbrock v London School of Economics and Political Science* [2022] EAT 119). The EAT found that the Article 8 rights of Ms D, against whom 'lurid allegations' were made by the claimant, outweighed the principle of open justice.

Note that Article 8 has been specifically relied upon by the courts in cases involving disabled persons (see, eg, *Price v UK* (2001) 34 EHRR 1285; *JAB and Y v East Sussex CC* [2003] EWHC 167 (Admin)) to recognise that the concept embraced in 'physical and psychological integrity', protected by Article 8, is the right of the disabled to participate in the life of the community.

In *Halford v UK* [1997] IRLR 471, Alison Halford, an Assistant Chief Constable with the Merseyside Police, brought an allegation that private conversations from a phone she had been given expressly for her private use had been intercepted. It was an extreme case and the ECtHR had no difficulty in finding that her rights under Article 8 had been violated. In *Copland v UK* [2007] ECHR 253, the ECtHR held that an employer risked breaching Article 8 if it monitored an employee's phone, email or Internet usage without having an 'acceptable use' policy in place or informing the employee of the monitoring. In *Atkinson v Community Gateway Association* (UKEAT/0457/12), the EAT held that accessing an employee's emails in the course of a disciplinary investigation into his conduct was not a breach of Article 8. There was no reasonable expectation of privacy where the employee sent emails from his work account in breach of the email policy. Further, such emails were not marked 'personal/private'.

See too *Barbulescu v Romania* [2016] ECHR 61 and *López Ribalda v Spain* [2019] ECHR 752 for confirmation that surveillance may or may not be justified and it will always depend on the facts. Certainly, there is no absolute right for employers to monitor their employees' emails without needing both adequate contractual cover (eg an appropriate policy) and proper justification.

Article 8 was used to protect the interests of gay service personnel in the armed forces. See *Lustig Prean v UK* [1999] IRLR 734, where the ECtHR held that the applicants' discharge from the armed forces as part of a blanket ban on gay persons infringed their right to respect for their private life. The internal investigation which was carried out prior to their discharge was also found to be a breach of Article 8. The UK Government was unable to show that either breach was necessary in a democratic society.

If an employer insists on pre-employment screening or testing without proper justification (eg there will be some groups of workers where there is a genuine risk that they could infect others – such as surgeons), or, for example, asks questions about whether an applicant/employee is HIV-positive, that may itself give rise to an Article 8 complaint. Article 8 may also be relevant to the question of whether employers can search their employees or test them for drugs (see *O'Flynn v Airlinks Airport Coach Company Ltd* (UKEAT/0269/01).

In *X v Y* [2004] IRLR 625, the Court of Appeal dealt with the question of whether tribunals must take account of Convention rights (in this case Article 8) when deciding unfair dismissal claims brought against private sector employers. Mr X was a charity worker and worked with young offenders. He was arrested after a 'passing' policeman discovered him and a man he did not know 'engaging in sexual activity' in the toilets of a transport café. Mr X accepted a caution, and his name was placed on the Sex Offenders Register. Subsequently, his employers, who worked closely with the Probation Service, discovered this and dismissed him on the grounds of gross misconduct. The tribunal found the dismissal was fair. The Court of Appeal had to decide whether a tribunal, when deciding whether a dismissal is fair or unfair, was bound to have regard to the right to respect for privacy in private life. The employer here, however, was a private sector employer. The EAT did not answer the question. It got round the point by holding that Article 8 was not engaged. The EAT considered that an act of 'gross indecency', committed in a public place, which attracted a caution, was a public matter not a private one. ('We are not persuaded that transitory sexual encounters between consenting male adults in public lavatories fall within the right to respect for private life enshrined in Article 8.')

The majority of the Court of Appeal (Mummery and Dyson LJJ) agreed with the EAT that Article 8 was not engaged. Brooke LJ doubted this (on the basis that acts in a secluded room in private could be private in nature), but thought that the acceptance of the caution by Mr X subsequently removed the private aspect of it. Mummery LJ went on to state that there should be no difference in approach whether the employer is private or public sector. He described the effect of the Convention as 'oblique', rather than horizontal. He said the HRA 1998 did not give an applicant any cause of action against a respondent that was not a public authority. In this sense, he said the HRA 1998 did not have full horizontal effect. However, he said the effect of s 6 in a case involving a claim against a private employer was to reinforce the strong interpretative obligation imposed on a tribunal by s 3. By a process of interpretation, the right to privacy was 'blended' with the law on unfair dismissal, but without creating new private law causes of action against private employers.

In *Williams v Architects Registration Board* (Administrative Court, 20 May 2016), Mr Williams, a registered architect, received a criminal conviction for a benefit fraud. He failed to attend any professional conduct hearings, was found guilty of misconduct as a result of his conviction and was struck off, with an order that the finding subsist for five years. He appealed to the Administrative Court, arguing that his Article 8 rights were breached because, under the Rehabilitation of Offenders Act 1974, his conviction would become spent after two years. The court accepted his Article 8 rights were engaged but held that any interference was necessary and proportionate. The 1974 Act did not bind disciplinary proceedings. Publishing a sanction was an important part of disciplinary proceedings and involved an element of public deterrence and maintaining standards.

The Supreme Court held, in R (*on the application of T and anor*) *v Secretary of State for the Home Department and Others* [2014] UKSC 35, that automatic disclosure of all spent convictions on an enhanced CRB check is incompatible with Article 8. The Government has introduced a 'filter', which results in certain old and minor offences not being disclosed, but only where a person has a single conviction, ie not for persons with more than one conviction.

In *Garamukanwa v United Kingdom* (Application No 70573/17) [2019] 6 WLUK 109, the employer relied on material found on the employee's phone during a police investigation into allegations of harassment made against the employee by a colleague. In a decision on admissibility, the ECtHR held that there was no breach of Article 8 on the facts. Whilst correspondence that covers both professional and private matters can fall within the protection given to private life, on the facts the employee could not have had a reasonable expectation of privacy. By the time of his arrest, he had been aware for almost a year that his colleague had raised concerns about his behaviour with the Trust, and the employer had a clear policy on monitoring social media activity

The Grand Chamber of the ECtHR considered the lawfulness of covert camera surveillance of employees at work in *López Ribalda v Spain* (Application Nos 1874/13 and 8567/13). The surveillance was carried out to monitor suspected thefts by employees, and on the facts it was held not to breach Article 8. While the Court said that a slight suspicion of wrongdoing could not justify the installation of covert video surveillance by an employer, it found that a reasonable suspicion of serious misconduct could be a justification, all the more so where there was a suspicion of concerted action. (Three judges disagreed with this finding, saying that it had failed to strike the right balance between the rights of the worker and employer and did not provide sufficient legal safeguards.) See too *Köpke v Germany* (Application No 420/17) where the surveillance of *one* employee suspected of theft was held not to breach Article 8. The difference between the two cases is that in *Köpke*, the surveillance was targeted at a particular employee; in *López Ribalda* it was not. See too *Antovic v Montenegro* (Application No 70838/13) where the Court held (by a majority of 4:3) that cameras in lecture theatres (installed to protect property and people and to monitor teaching) breached Article 8.

The EAT confirmed in *Q v Secretary of State for Justice* (UKEAT/0120/19) that whilst:

> ... at a doctrinal level [counsel] is right that *Hill* identifies that there is an additional legal consequence which applies where the [unfair dismissal] claim is against a public body. This is that, in addition to the Tribunal having a duty to weigh the impact of the dismissal upon Convention rights, and whether it is proportionate (which it must, whether the employer is a public or a private body), a public employer also itself has that same duty when taking its decision. However, while that is doctrinally correct, I am doubtful that this added feature makes any real difference in practice. When I raised this with [counsel] he was unable to give me an example of any scenario in which it would. I say this because, whether the case involves a public or a private employer, the Tribunal must, in deciding whether the dismissal is fair or unfair, come to its own view as to whether the imposition of the sanction of dismissal involved a disproportionate and unjustified interference with Convention rights, or not. If it did, then this will take the dismissal outside the band of reasonable responses. If not, then this feature of the case will not do so. That will be the position regardless of whether the employer had a duty of its own, whether, if so, it applied its mind to the question, and, if it did, whatever conclusion it came to. It is always the Tribunal's conclusion that, ultimately, must decide the point.

The issues raised by Article 8 are also reflected in two other pieces of legislation – the Regulation of Investigatory Powers Act 2000 (RIPA 2000) and the Data Protection Act 2018 (DPA 2018) (see **15.5**).

15.4.4   Articles 9 and 10

Article 9 protects freedom of thought, conscience, and religion. Article 10 gives the right to freedom of expression. Both these provisions are subject to restrictions similar to those contained in Article 8. These Articles are most likely to be relevant to, for example, employees' attendance at religious ceremonies and employers' imposition of dress codes. In terms of the latter, there would be no need for a comparison between the sexes as, under the Equality Act 2010, the issue would be simply whether the interference with the freedom could be justified by the employer (eg on health and safety grounds – but what about enhancing the employer's business reputation?). To a large extent the protection offered by Article 10 is mirrored in the Public Interest Disclosure Act 1998. Article 10 may also impact on confidentiality clauses in contracts (see also **1.8.6**).

In *Copsey v WWB Devon Clays Ltd* [2005] IRLR 811 (a case decided before the Religion and Belief Regulations 2003 came into force), the Court of Appeal considered the issue of whether and when a refusal to work on a Sunday is unfair. The case looks at the impact of Article 9 on UK unfair dismissal law. For different reasons (there are three separate judgments) the Court of Appeal held that such a dismissal was not unfair. However, the decision makes clear that employers must try to minimise the impact of changes to working hours (for example by offering alternative jobs) where employees hold strong religious beliefs.

In *Eweida & Others v UK* [2013] ECHR 37, the ECtHR held that the UK failed to comply with its legal obligation under Article 9 in respect of one of the four claimants – Ms Eweida – because although her right to manifest her religion by wearing a cross whilst at work on the check desk at British Airways (BA) was sufficiently protected, a fair balance was not struck between her rights and those of others, in circumstances where there was no evidence of any real encroachment on the interests of others – the cross was discreet and did not detract from her professional appearance. Moreover, BA had subsequently amended its uniform policy to allow for the visible wearing of religious symbolic jewellery. However, the other three claimant's all lost on the facts:

(a)   Ms Chaplin worked as a nurse on a geriatric ward, and the ban on jewellery was therefore proportionate, given clinical safety concerns.

(b)   Ms Ladele had objected to conducting same-sex civil ceremonies. The Court held that the UK was allowed a wide margin of appreciation in striking a balance between Convention rights, and that in this case the aim of providing access to services, irrespective of sexual orientation, was a legitimate aim and that the means used to pursue this aim (Ms Ladele was dismissed and the tribunal rejected her discrimination complaint) were proportionate, given the competing rights of freedom of religion and non-discrimination on grounds of sexual orientation.

(c)   Mr McFarlane refused to counsel safe-sex couples, and his complaint that his Article 9 rights had been breached was dismissed. The UK courts enjoyed a wide margin of appreciation in deciding where to strike the balance between the claimant's rights to manifest his religious beliefs and his employer's interest in securing the rights of others. It was not, on the facts, exceeded.

In *Mba v Mayor and Burgesses of the London Borough of Merton* [2014] IRLR 145, a case brought under what was reg 3(1)(b) of the Employment Equality (Religion or Belief) Regulations 2003 (now s 19 of the Equality Act 2010), the claimant, who was a Christian, was employed at a children's home. All full-time staff had to work on two of three weekends over a three-week period. After two years of accommodating the claimant's wish not to work on Sundays, the respondent required her to start working on Sundays. She refused, resigned and brought a discrimination claim. The employment tribunal found that she was put at a particular disadvantage, but that this was a proportionate means of achieving a legitimate aim. While the claimant's belief that Sunday should be a day of rest was deeply held, the tribunal said it was 'not a core component of the Christian faith', such that any group impact was limited. The Court of Appeal noted that where the right to religious freedom under Article 9 was engaged, it does not require a group disadvantage to be shown (see *Eweida* above). While the Regulations do require the group position to be considered, it is still possible to apply the concept of justification in a way that is compatible with Article 9. In that context, the fact that the claimant's beliefs were not more widely shared, or did not constitute a 'core' belief, could not weaken her case on justification.

In *Grimmant v Sweden* (Application No 43726/17), the ECtHR considered a case where the claimant midwife applied for but did not get a job after she told the potential employer that she was not prepared to assist in abortion procedures. The Court held that she satisfied Article 9(1) because her objection to assisting an abortion was a manifestation of her religion but that she failed under Article 9(2) which permits limitations 'prescribed by law and necessary in a democratic society':

> The requirement that all midwives should be able to perform all duties inherent to the vacant posts was not disproportionate or unjustified. Employers have, under Swedish law, great flexibility in deciding how work is to be organised and the right to request that employees perform all duties inherent to the post. When concluding an employment contract, employees inherently accept these duties. In the present case, the applicant had voluntarily chosen to become a midwife and apply for vacant posts while knowing that this would mean assisting also in abortion cases.

In *Matuz v Hungary* [2014] ECHR 1112, the EctHR held that the dismissal of a Hungarian State television journalist related to and interfered with the journalist's Article 10 rights. The journalist was dismissed after publishing a book, which breached his contractual duty of confidentiality, containing allegations of censorship against his employer.

In *Rubins v Latvia* [2015] ECHR 2, a majority of the ECtHR held that a Latvian university had infringed a professor's right to freedom of expression by dismissing him after his allegations of mismanagement were published in the national press. The case is controversial, as some commentators regard it not as a whistleblowing case but rather as a blackmail case, because the professor had offered to withdraw all his complaints if the university revoked a number of decisions concerning the merger of his Department or paid him compensation. When the university refused, the national news agency published his criticisms of the university's management.

One area where Article 10 is becoming increasingly prominent relates to the rights of employers to take action against employees who express their views and opinions on social media platforms such as Facebook and Twitter. According to an Acas Research Paper in 2010 ('Workplaces and Social Networking: The Implications for Employment Relations'), dismissals concerning employees' use of social media are increasing (see, eg, *Preece v JD Wetherspoons plc* (ET/2104806/2010), *Crisp v Apple Retail UK Ltd* (ET/1500258/11), *North West London Hospitals NHS Trust v Bowater* [2011] EWCA Civ 63, *Smith v Trafford Housing Trust* [2012] EWHC 3221 (Ch), *Redfearn v United Kingdom* [2012] ECHR 1878 and *Teggart v TeleTech UK Ltd* [2014] IRLR 625).

Tribunals have been slow to recognise that employees may have Article 10 rights in such situations, of which proper account will need to be taken when considering whether a dismissal is fair. There is a tendency, where the speech at issue is considered 'unimportant' or of low social value or public contribution, to belittle the Article 10 right, which may be relevant to the reasonableness of a dismissal but should not intrude into an assessment of the proportionality of the interference (interference with Article 10, as a qualified right is justified only when prescribed by law, where there is a legitimate aim (see Article 10(2)) and when it is proportionate to that aim), which is a separate issue. For example, in *Gosden v Lifeline Project Ltd* (ET/2802731/2009), the claimant's contract of employment stated that gross misconduct included 'any act which is or is calculated to or may damage the company's reputation or integrity'. The claimant had forwarded, while at home, an offensive e-mail from his private e-mail account to the private e-mail account of an acquaintance, who worked for his employer's biggest client. The employment tribunal found that dismissal was justified, as this was something that 'might' damage the employer's reputation, even though there was no clear evidence of actual harm and it had been the client's employee who had subsequently distributed the e-mail.

In *British Waterways Board v Smith* (UKEAT/0004/15) the EAT had to decide whether it was unfair to dismiss an employee who, it transpired, as a result of a separate and unrelated investigation, had two years previously made derogatory comments on his Facebook page about his colleagues and made comments about drinking while on standby. The employment tribunal held the dismissal was unfair. The EAT allowed the employer's appeal and substituted a finding that dismissal was not unfair. The EAT accept the submission for the respondent that there was no need for special rules in respect of cases relating to the use of Facebook. It relied on the EAT's decision in *Game Retail*. The EAT held that there had been a reasonable investigation, that the employer had lost confidence in the employee and that a fair procedure was followed, and said that in the circumstances the only decision an employment tribunal properly directing itself could make was that dismissal was not unfair.

It is clear from these decisions that it is important that employers have clear, effective and well-communicated policies around the use of social media, both within and outside the workplace. This will make it easier for employers to take disciplinary action if employees post negative or derogatory comments.

In *R (on the application of Miller) v College of Policing and another* [2020] EWHC 225 (Admin), the High Court held that the College infringed the claimant's Article 10 rights when it took action in response to a complaint by a member of the public about the claimant's tweets concerning transgender issues. The High Court held that the claimant's views were 'congruent with the views of a number of respected academics who hold gender critical views and do so for profound socio-philosophical reasons'. See too, by contrast, *Forstater* (at **8.2.3**) where an employment tribunal held that an *absolutist* belief that sex is biologically immutable was not a belief worthy of respect in a democratic society because it was incompatible with dignity and the fundamental rights of others.

In *Herbai v Hungary* (Application No 11608/15) [2019] IRLR 159, the ECtHR found that a dismissal by a private employer in respect of the claimant publishing a professional blog violated freedom of expression guaranteed under Article 10 on the facts. The lower court had failed to fairly balance the claimant's right to freedom of expression against the employer's legitimate business interests. The ECtHR provided guidance to be taken into account when carrying out the balancing exercise required (the nature of the speech, the employee's motive, damage caused to the employer and the severity of the sanction imposed by the employer).

15.4.5   Article 11

Article 11 protects the right to freedom of association, including the right to form and join a trade union, and is outside the scope of this book.

15.4.6   Article 14

This prohibits discrimination, but only in the context of other Convention rights (see **8.13** for more detail). For cases, see *Webster v The Attorney General of Trinidad and Tobago* [2015] UKPC 10, *R (JS) v Secretary of State for Work and Pensions* [2015] UKSC 16, *Mathieson v Secretary of State for Work and Pensions* [2015] UKSC 47 and *Boyraz v Turkey* [2015] IRLR 164.

For an interesting but ultimately unsuccessful case on pregnancy discrimination brought under Article 1 of Protocol 12 to the Convention, which relates to employment rights, see *Napotnik v Romania* [2021] IRLR 70.

15.5   DATA PROTECTION

Employers need to ensure that they comply with the law when they process their employees' data. All employers have data protection obligations and risk substantial penalties for non-compliance with their obligations.

What follows is a very brief overview. Readers are advised to consult the legislation and the Information Commissioner's Office for further information and guidance (https://ico.org.uk/). The Information Commissioner has responsibility for upholding information rights in the public interest, promoting openness by public bodies and data privacy for individuals.

On 3 October 2022, the Secretary of State for Digital, Culture, Media and Sport announced that the Government planned to replace the UK GDPR with a bespoke British data protection system. No further details were available at the time of writing.

15.5.1 The UK General Data Protection Regulation and the Data Protection Act 2018

The EU passed a new General Data Protection Regulation (GDPR) (Regulation (EU) 2016/679) (replacing the Data Protection Directive 95/46 on which previous UK law was based in the Data Protection Act 1998) relating to personal data processing (Article 2), which applies to all Member States from 25 May 2018. The GDPR has direct effect in each EU Member State without the need for further implementing legislation. However, Article 88 of the GDPR permits Member States to provide for more specific rules (by way of legislation or collective agreements) to ensure the protection of the rights and freedoms in respect of processing employees' personal data.

The European Data Protection Board will seek to ensure that the GDPR is applied consistently across the EU (see www.i-scoop.eu/gdpr/european-data-protection-board-edpb/#The_European_Data_Protection_Board_and_binding_decision_making). The European Commission has published guidance on its website (https://ec.europa.eu/commission/priorities/justice-and-fundamental-rights/data-protection/2018-reform-eu-data-protection-rules_en).

The UK Government passed the Data Protection Act (DPA) 2018 and the UK GDPR in order to implement the GDPR into UK domestic law. The DPA 2018 received Royal Assent on 23 May 2018. The Data Protection Act 2018 (Commencement No 1 and Transitional and Saving Provisions) Regulations 2018 (SI 2018/625) brought the majority of the provisions of the DPA 2018 into force on 25 May 2018 (on which date the DPA 1998 was repealed). The EU GDPR no longer applies to the UK. Employers need to comply with the UK GDPR and the DPA 2018.

The Information Commissioner's Office (ICO) is the UK's independent body, set up to uphold information rights. It will investigate complaints of GDPR breaches. The ICO has published guidance on the GDPR on its website (https://ico.org.uk/for-organisations/guide-to-the-general-data-protection-regulation-gdpr/). Employers will need to show that they have complied with the legislation when carrying out data processing and monitoring in the workplace and can demonstrate compliance. The ICO's Guide on the GDPR should help organisations comply with the GDPR/DPA 2018 requirements.

The Data Protection (Charges and Information) Regulations 2018 (SI 2018/480) require every employer who processes personal information to pay a data protection fee to the ICO unless they are exempt (see the self-assessment tool: <https://ico.org.uk/for-organisations/data-protection-fee/>).

Article 4 of the UK GDPR defines 'personal data' as:

> any information relating to an identified or identifiable natural person ('data subject'); an identifiable natural person is one who can be identified, directly or indirectly, in particular by reference to an identifier such as a name, an identification number, location data, an online identifier or to one or more factors specific to the physical, physiological, genetic, mental, economic, cultural or social identity of that natural person.

The ICO has issued guidance on what constitutes personal data, which includes many useful examples: <https://ico.org.uk/for-organisations/guide-to-data-protection/guide-to-the-general-data-protection-regulation-gdpr/key-definitions/what-is-personal-data/>.

Article 4 defines 'processing' as:

> any operation or set of operations which is performed on personal data or on sets of personal data, whether or not by automated means, such as collection, recording, organisation, structuring, storage, adaptation or alteration, retrieval, consultation, use, disclosure by transmission, dissemination or otherwise making available, alignment or combination, restriction, erasure or destruction.

Employers need to identify the types of processing that they carry out.

Article 5 of the UK GDPR sets out the principles of data protection with which data controllers (eg employers) must comply:

- lawfulness, fairness and transparency;
- purpose limitation ('collected for specified, explicit and legitimate purposes ...');
- data minimisation ('... limited to what is necessary ...');
- accuracy;
- storage limitation;
- integrity and confidentiality;
- accountability.

Article 6 sets out the (alternative) bases for processing data under the UK GDPR:

(a) *Consent* – the individual has given consent for their personal data to be processed for a specific purpose. The ICO states that '... employers and other organisations in a position of power over individuals should avoid relying on consent unless they are confident they can demonstrate it is freely given' because of the obvious imbalance of power in the relationship.

(b) *Contract* – the processing is necessary for performance of the contract or to take steps prior to agreeing the contract.

(c) *Legal obligation* – the processing is necessary to comply with the law.

(d) *Vital interests* – the processing is necessary to protect the vital interests of the individual.

(e) *Performance of a task carried out in the public interest* – processing is necessary to perform a task in the public interest or in the exercise of official authority, and has a clear basis in law.

(f) *Legitimate interests* – the processing is necessary for the purposes of the legitimate interests of the controller or a third party except where such interests are overridden by the fundamental rights of the individual.

It will be noted that all bar one of the above depend upon the processing being 'necessary'. The ICO suggests that this does not mean that processing always has to be essential but that it must be a targeted and proportionate way of achieving the purpose. A lawful basis will not apply if you can reasonably achieve the purpose by some other less intrusive means.

The ICO advises that employers may need to consider a variety of factors, including:

- What is your purpose – what are you trying to achieve?
- Can you reasonably achieve it in a different way?
- Do you have a choice over whether or not to process the data?
- Are you a public authority?

The ICO gives the following guidance:

> - You must have a valid lawful basis in order to process personal data.
> - There are six available lawful bases for processing. No single basis is 'better' or more important than the others – which basis is most appropriate to use will depend on your purpose and relationship with the individual.

- Most lawful bases require that processing is 'necessary'. If you can reasonably achieve the same purpose without the processing, you won't have a lawful basis.

- You must determine your lawful basis before you begin processing, and you should document it. Take care to get it right first time – you should not swap to a different lawful basis at a later date without good reason.

- Your privacy notice should include your lawful basis for processing as well as the purposes of the processing.

- If your purposes change, you may be able to continue processing under the original lawful basis if your new purpose is compatible with your initial purpose (unless your original lawful basis was consent).

- If you are processing special category data [see GDPR, Article 9 below] you need to identify both a lawful basis for general processing and an additional condition for processing this type of data.

- If you are processing criminal conviction data or data about offences you need to identify both a lawful basis for general processing and an additional condition for processing this type of data.

To lawfully process some 'special' categories of personal data (defined in Article 9 to include racial or ethnic origin, political opinions, religious beliefs, trade union membership, health data or data concerning sexual orientation), one of the Article 9 bases must be established (eg explicit consent, employment and social security law necessity, etc).

The GDPR provides the following rights for individuals:

(a)   the right to be informed (Article 13);

(b)   the right of access (Article 15);

(c)   the right to rectification (Article 16);

(d)   the right to erasure (Article 17);

(e)   the right to restrict processing (Article 18);

(f)   the right to data portability (Article 20);

(g)   the right to object (Article 21);

(h)   rights in relation to automated individual decision making, including profiling (Article 22).

The ICO suggests that there a number of steps that employers need to take to comply with the UK GDPR's accountability obligations, including:

- adopting and implementing data protection policies;

- taking a 'data protection by design and default' approach;

- putting written contracts in place with organisations that process personal data on your behalf;

- maintaining documentation of your processing activities;

- implementing appropriate security measures;

- recording and, where necessary, reporting personal data breaches;

- carrying out data protection impact assessments for uses of personal data that are likely to result in high risk to individuals' interests;

- appointing a data protection officer; and

- adhering to relevant codes of conduct and signing up to certification schemes.

Article 33 of the UK GDPR requires the data processor to notify the data controller on becoming aware of a data breach. The ICO states:

- The GDPR introduces a duty on all organisations to report certain types of personal data breach to the relevant supervisory authority. You must do this within 72 hours of becoming aware of the breach, where feasible.

- If the breach is likely to result in a high risk of adversely affecting individuals' rights and freedoms, you must also inform those individuals without undue delay.

- You should ensure you have robust breach detection, investigation and internal reporting procedures in place. This will facilitate decision-making about whether or not you need to notify the relevant supervisory authority and the affected individuals.

- You must also keep a record of any personal data breaches, regardless of whether you are required to notify.

The ICO goes on to say:

> When a personal data breach has occurred, you need to establish the likelihood and severity of the resulting risk to people's rights and freedoms. If it's likely that there will be a risk then you must notify the ICO; if it's unlikely then you don't have to report it. However, if you decide you don't need to report the breach, you need to be able to justify this decision, so you should document it.

Failing to notify a breach when required to do so can result in a fine of up to €10 million or up to 2% of global turnover, whichever is higher. The fine can also be combined with the ICO's corrective powers under Article 58.

Article 35 of the UK GDPR introduces the concept of a Data Protection Impact Assessment (DPIA) as a tool which can help employers. A DPIA will be required when data processing is 'likely to result in a high risk to the rights and freedoms of natural persons'.

The UK GDPR sets out the minimum features that must be included in a DPIA:

- a description of the processing operations and the purposes, including, where applicable, the legitimate interests pursued by the data controller;

- an assessment of the necessity and proportionality of the processing in relation to the purpose;

- an assessment of the risks to individuals;

- the measures in place to address risk, including security, and to demonstrate that the data controller is complying with the GDPR.

Before doing a DPIA, a data protection officer, if one has been appointed, should be consulted along with the views (where appropriate) of data subjects or their representatives. The views of the ICO may also need to be sought. Data controllers will be obliged to retain a record of the DPIA. Failure to carry out a DPIA when one is required can result in an administrative fine of up to €10 million or, in the case of an undertaking, up to 2% of the total worldwide annual turnover of the preceding financial year, whichever is higher.

15.5.2 Specific issues

15.5.2.1 Employee consent to data processing

The Information Commissioner has warned employers that consent may not be adequate in the employment context due to the imbalance of power inherent in an employment relationship. The ICO states:

> **What's new?**
>
> The GDPR sets a high standard for consent, but the biggest change is what this means in practice for your consent mechanisms.
>
> The GDPR is clearer that an indication of consent must be unambiguous and involve a clear affirmative action (an opt-in). It specifically bans pre-ticked opt-in boxes. It also requires distinct ('granular') consent options for distinct processing operations. Consent should be separate from other terms and conditions and should not generally be a precondition of signing up to a service.
>
> You must keep clear records to demonstrate consent.
>
> The GDPR gives a specific right to withdraw consent. You need to tell people about their right to withdraw, and offer them easy ways to withdraw consent at any time.

Public authorities, employers and other organisations in a position of power may find it more difficult to show valid freely given consent.

You need to review existing consents and your consent mechanisms to check they meet the GDPR standard. If they do, there is no need to obtain fresh consent.

Why is consent important?

Consent is one lawful basis for processing, and explicit consent can also legitimise use of special category data. Consent may also be relevant where the individual has exercised their right to restriction, and explicit consent can legitimise automated decision-making and overseas transfers of data.

Genuine consent should put individuals in control, build trust and engagement, and enhance your reputation.

Relying on inappropriate or invalid consent could destroy trust and harm your reputation – and may leave you open to large fines.

When is consent appropriate?

Consent is one lawful basis for processing, but there are alternatives. Consent is not inherently better or more important than these alternatives. If consent is difficult, you should consider using an alternative.

Consent is appropriate if you can offer people real choice and control over how you use their data, and want to build their trust and engagement. But if you cannot offer a genuine choice, consent is not appropriate. If you would still process the personal data without consent, asking for consent is misleading and inherently unfair.

If you make consent a precondition of a service, it is unlikely to be the most appropriate lawful basis.

Public authorities, employers and other organisations in a position of power over individuals should avoid relying on consent unless they are confident they can demonstrate it is freely given.

What is valid consent?

Consent must be freely given; this means giving people genuine ongoing choice and control over how you use their data.

Consent should be obvious and require a positive action to opt in. Consent requests must be prominent, unbundled from other terms and conditions, concise and easy to understand, and user-friendly.

Consent must specifically cover the controller's name, the purposes of the processing and the types of processing activity.

Explicit consent must be expressly confirmed in words, rather than by any other positive action.

There is no set time limit for consent. How long it lasts will depend on the context. You should review and refresh consent as appropriate.

How should we obtain, record and manage consent?

Make your consent request prominent, concise, separate from other terms and conditions, and easy to understand. Include:

- the name of your organisation;
- the name of any third party controllers who will rely on the consent;
- why you want the data;
- what you will do with it; and
- that individuals can withdraw consent at any time.

You must ask people to actively opt in. Don't use pre-ticked boxes, opt-out boxes or other default settings. Wherever possible, give separate ('granular') options to consent to different purposes and different types of processing.

Keep records to evidence consent – who consented, when, how, and what they were told.

Make it easy for people to withdraw consent at any time they choose. Consider using preference-management tools.

Keep consents under review and refresh them if anything changes. Build regular consent reviews into your business processes.

The Greek Data Protection Authority (Greek ICO) fined PwC €150,000 for using consent to process employees' data generally. The decision referred to the imbalance in the relationship and makes it clear that consent will rarely be appropriate as the lawful basis to process employee data.

Further guidance produced by the European Data Protection Board (EDPB) can be found here: http://ec.europa.eu/newsroom/article29/item-detail.cfm?item_id=623051.

15.5.2.2   Providing information to employees

Article 12(1) of the UK GDPR says that information collected must be provided to employees in 'a concise, transparent, intelligible and easily accessible form, using clear and plain language ...'. Articles 13 and 14 list the information that must be provided, depending on whether the data is collected from the employee or not.

The ICO states:

> You can provide this information through a variety of media:
> - Orally – face to face or when you speak to someone on the telephone (it's a good idea to document this).
> - In writing – printed media; printed adverts; forms, such as financial applications or job application forms.
> - Through signage – for example an information poster in a public area.
> - Electronically – in text messages; on websites; in emails; in mobile apps.

It is good practice to use the same medium you use to collect personal data to deliver privacy information. So, if you are collecting information through an online form you could provide a just-in-time notice as an individual fills in the form. You can combine this with more detailed information on your website, accessible through a clear and prominent link on the online form.

15.5.2.3   Data Protection Act 2018

The UK data protection regime is set out in the DPA 2018, along with the UK GDPR (above). The Act came into force on 25 May 2018.

The DPA 2018 contains four separate regimes:

- Part 2, Chapter 2 (GDPR): supplements the UK GDPR;
- Part 2, Chapter 3: extends a modified GDPR to some other (rare) cases;
- Part 3: sets out a separate regime for law enforcement authorities; and
- Part 4: sets out a separate regime for the three intelligence services.

For a useful overview of the DPA 2018, see <https://ico.org.uk/media/for-organisations/documents/2614158/ico-introduction-to-the-data-protection-bill.pdf>.

15.5.2.4   Subject access requests

Employees have the right (under the UK GDPR, Article 15 and the DPA 2018) to be told, upon request (requests must be dealt with without 'undue delay' and at the very latest within one month of receiving the request), whether personal data about them are being processed and, if so, to be told what the specific data are, why they are being processed and to whom they are going. This is known as a 'subject access request' (SAR). The DPA 2018 provides for some exemptions, eg confidential references given by the data controller but not received by the data controller; legally privileged information. If personal data on one employee contain personal data on another, the employer will, according to a majority decision of the Court of Appeal in *B v GMC* [2018] EWCA Civ 1497, have to consider if disclosure is reasonable having regard to all the relevant circumstances by considering the statutory balancing of interests test, including taking any objection into consideration. If an employee withholds consent, that might, in some situations, tip the balance against disclosure, according to the Court of Appeal, if other interests were balanced. Personal data may include copies of appraisals, disciplinary records, sickness/holiday forms, as well as informal notes/emails passing between managers about the employee. Generally, no fee is payable.

The right to make a SAR existed under the DPA 1998, but there are some changes, for example to the timeframe for responding (see above), and a fee can no longer be charged (unless the requests are 'manifestly unfounded or excessive' or for further copies, in which case a reasonable fee can be charged (UK GDPR, Articles 12 and 15)).

Employees sometimes use their right to make a SAR in the context of a dispute with their employer. A failure to respond by the employer could make a dismissal unfair (see the unreported employment tribunal decision in *McWilliams v Citibank NA*, 19 April 2016). If an employer refuses to comply with such a request, the employee can complain to the Information Commissioner. Alternatively, an employee could apply to the High Court for an order that the employer comply. In *Gurieva v Community Safety Development (UK) Ltd* [2016] EWHC 643 (QB), the High Court said that employees are not obliged to give reasons for making a SAR, and there is nothing inherently wrong with an employee using such a request for the purposes of obtaining early access to information that they might get later via disclosure in litigation.

In 2017, the ICO published a Code of Practice on SARs. On 21 October 2020, it was updated to take into account the DPA 2018 and responses to a consultation issued in December 2019. The Code reflected case law in the courts. Readers are referred, inter alia, to the Court of Appeal case of *Dawson-Damer v Taylor Wessing LLP* [2017] EWCA Civ 74 (impact of legal professional privilege on a SAR; disproportionate effect exemption) and the employment tribunal case of *McWilliams v Citibank NA* (above) (where a refusal to comply with a SAR contributed to the unfairness of a dismissal). See too, *B v GMC* (above).

15.6 MONITORING IN THE WORKPLACE

There are many reasons why businesses might wish to monitor or record telephone or email use. Some financial or insurance firms may be legally obliged to record calls when executing transactions over the telephone; others may wish to monitor calls for quality or compliance purposes. Monitoring may also be useful to ensure that employees are not misusing the communications facilities provided to them. The law looks to balance these objectives, which will generally be considered legitimate, against the need to protect the privacy of employees and external callers. Employers should always be up-front about what and when they are monitoring, and should have social media, internet and email policies in place. Employers should also seek to avoid breaching the implied duty of trust and confidence in some monitoring circumstances. See too cases decided under Article 8 ECHR above.

From 27 June 2018, monitoring and recording of electronic communications is regulated by the Investigatory Powers Act (IPA) 2016 and the Investigatory Powers (Interception by Businesses etc for Monitoring and Record-keeping Purposes) Regulations 2018 (SI 2018/356) (which replace the Regulation of Investigatory Powers Act (RIPA) 2000 and the Telecommunications (Lawful Business Practice) (Interception of Communications) Regulations 2000 (SI 2000/2699)), in addition to the GDPR and DPA 2018 (above). What follows is a very brief introduction to the provisions that currently apply in the workplace. Readers will need to keep up to date with the changing legal position, and this section will be fully updated in the next edition.

The IPA 2016 regulates when a person may make an 'interception of a communication in the course of transmission'. Interception includes 'monitoring or interference with a private telecommunication system which makes the communication available to someone other than the sender or the recipient'. While most of the Act is aimed at the security services and the State, the provisions on the interception of communications sent and received on public and private telecommunication systems, where they impact on aspects of the employment relationship, and the provisions on surveillance and covert sources (set out in Part II) are of much more general application. As far as the interception of communications is concerned, unless there is (expressly or by implication) consent (by both parties to the communication) to the interception, a criminal offence may be committed. An employer can lawfully intercept communications without consent (from both parties to the communication) only if it complies with the provisions of the 2018 Regulations. The Regulations create in effect a number of 'lawful purposes' whereby employers can monitor and record communications between parties without their consent, provided that the employer has made 'all reasonable efforts to inform' every person who uses the telecommunication system that their communications may be monitored and recorded. Lawful purposes are (reg 3):

(a)   to establish the existence of facts;

(b)   ensuring compliance with regulatory or statutory rules;

(c)   ascertaining or demonstrating employee standards;

(d)   national security;

(e)   prevention or detection of crime;

(f)   investigating the unauthorised use of the telecommunications system;

(g)   to secure the effective operation of the telecommunication system.

Note that the Investigatory Powers Tribunal ruled in *C v Police and Secretary of State for the Home Department* (November 2014, IPT/03/32) that not all covert surveillance of employees was covered by RIPA 2000, and that will continue to be the case under the revised legislation.

In practice, the RIPA 2000 caused few problems for employers, and that is likely to continue to be the case under the IPA 2016 – it permits most types of surveillance, provided they are for business-related reasons.

Readers should refer to the 2016 Act and 2018 Regulations for the detail.

15.6.1   Guidance

Part 3 of the ICO's Employment Practices Code contains guidance on monitoring at work. It provides that it will normally be intrusive to monitor workers; employers should normally carry out an impact assessment before monitoring and should be sure that the monitoring is justified by real benefits; workers should normally be told if and why they are being monitored; employers should be careful when monitoring personal communications such as emails that are clearly personal; employers should not undertake covert monitoring except in the rarest circumstances where there are grounds for suspecting criminal activity, it has been authorised at the highest level of the business, and where there is a risk that notifying workers of the monitoring would prejudice the prevention or detection of that criminal activity. At the heart of the Code is proportionality.

The Article 29 Working Party (now European Data Protection Board (made up of a representative from each EU Member State's data protection authority, together with the European Data Protection Supervisor and the European Commission)) has published both an Opinion on data processing at work and a set of Data Protection Impact Assessment (DPIA) guidelines which set out criteria for assessing when data processing is high risk. Whilst no longer applicable to the UK, the criteria are still useful.

The criteria for assessing when data processing will be considered to be high risk include:

(1)   any evaluation or scoring, especially based on a data subject's performance at work, economic situation, health, personal preferences or interests, reliability or behaviour, location or movements;

(2)   automated decision-making with legal or similar significant effects;

(3)   systematic monitoring of individuals;

(4)   sensitive data;

(5)   personal data on a large scale;

(6)   datasets that have been matched or combined;

(7)   data concerning vulnerable data subjects;

(8)   data transfers across borders outside the EU;

(9)   data that prevents data subjects from exercising a right or using a service or a contract.

Any sort of employee monitoring is very likely to be considered as high-risk processing (see criteria 3, 7 and 9).

Article 4(11) of the UK GDPR states:

> 'Consent' of the data subject means any freely given, specific, informed and unambiguous indication of the data subject's wishes by which he or she, by a statement or by a clear affirmative action, signifies agreement to the processing of personal data relating to him or her.

According to the ICO guidance on the GDPR:

> Freely given consent will also be more difficult to obtain in the context of a relationship where there is an imbalance of power, particularly for public authorities and employers.

It is unlikely therefore that employers will be able to rely on consent where surveillance is concerned. Given that surveillance is usually undertaken to prevent or detect crime or to detect or stop misuse of the employer's resources, an employer may be able to rely on Article 6(1)(f) – processing for 'the purposes of the legitimate interests pursued by the data controller or by a third party, except where such interests are overridden by the interests or fundamental rights and freedoms of the data subject which require protection of personal data, in particular where the data subject is a child'. However, there is a potential problem for local authority and government employers, as Article 6 states that the legitimate interests condition shall not apply to processing carried out by public authorities in the performance of their tasks. Such organisations may have to fall back on Article 6(1)(c) and 6(1)(e).

Employers, as data controllers, also have an obligation to ensure that they are transparent in terms of the how they use employees' information. Consideration will also have to be given as to what extent general information will have to be supplied to employees in respect of the employer's surveillance activities (see Articles 13 and 14 of the GDPR on privacy notices).

The Article 29 Working Party Opinion on data processing at work (now the European Data Protection Board) (Opinion 2/2017: http://ec.europa.eu/newsroom/article29/item-detail.cfm?item_id=610169) complements Opinion 8/2001 on the processing of data protection in the employment context and its 2002 Working Document on the surveillance of electronic communications in the workplace (http://ec.europa.eu/newsroom/article29/item-detail.cfm?item_id=611236). 'The Opinion makes a new assessment of the balance between legitimate interests of employers and the reasonable privacy expectations of employees by outlining the risks posed by new technologies and undertaking a proportionality assessment of a number of scenarios in which they could be deployed.' One matter the 2017 Opinion stresses is the need for transparency, so that employees are properly informed about any processing taking place in a clear and accessible manner. Another area that the Opinion identifies as potentially problematic is the tracking of employees across devices, and the potential for reducing anonymity that may impact on whistleblowing. It suggests that data collected during recruitment, for example, should be deleted as soon as it is clear that a candidate is not going to be employed. Key to all this going forward will be the understanding by employers that they can only collect data for legitimate purposes, with any processing taking place needing to be proportionate, necessary, for a real and present interest, and in a lawful, articulated and transparent manner. The fact that an employer may 'own' the electronic means does not mean that employees are not entitled to have their communications kept secret. If an employer has a policy of allowing employees to 'bring your own devices' into work, for example, employees should try to ensure that their devices have the ability to shield private communications from work-related monitoring.

15.6.2   Use of personal devices at work

Employers need to have in place proper measures to make sure that they secure and protect data that they process or retain, whether those data relate to employees or to third party customers/clients. Many employees use their own mobile devices to access their employers' corporate networks and systems. This can create potential problems, both in distinguishing between work information and personal information (eg, who 'owns' a contact list (see **1.8.6.2**)) and with regards to the access to, storage of, and processing and security of personal data (eg, customer or client profiles).

In March 2013, a YouGov survey found that while 47% of all UK adults were using personal devices at work, relatively few were given any guidance on their use. The ICO was concerned about the implications of employees using their own personal devices for the security of personal data. This includes employees' use of personal iPads, smartphones and other personal devices for work purposes. Often, personal devices are not very secure – even if they have passwords, they will not be using technologically secure methods to send and receive information – yet if used for work purposes, they will start to store data that it will be hard for employers to monitor properly. The use of own devices can also blur the line between work and private life. This may create problems not only regarding who 'owns' what information, but also about what rights the employer has to access information on the device. Travelling abroad with devices can constitute a transfer of data, which may cause problems with individual countries' data protection obligations. As all data controllers in the UK are responsible for ensuring that personal data are processed in accordance with the DPA 2018, this means that employers are responsible for ensuring that they take appropriate technical and organisational measures against accidental loss, destruction or damage. Employers should conduct an audit of what personal data are being processed, where such data are stored, which devices are being used and by whom, how data are accessed and transferred, and the potential for leakage, and how losses, theft, etc will be dealt with. Employers should then maintain an 'acceptable use' policy for BYOD. The ICO has issued guidance on 'Bringing Your Own Devices' (BYOD) to work.

Employers will need to consider, inter alia, whether to prohibit or limit personal activity on the use of company-owned devices and how to ensure company data on such devices is held securely. Practically, if employers are to include this in a policy, they will need to consider how they will monitor such use and enforce the policy. Where employees use their own devices and are allowed access to company systems and information, policies should clearly state how data and information are expected to be treated and protected. Clear information should be given as to what an employee should do if a device is lost or stolen. It will be necessary to delineate how the company will treat and have access to personal information (which should be private) and how it will treat and have access to work-related information. The policy should state what will happen on the termination of the employment, both with regard to the physical device *and* with regard to information stored on it.

15.6.3   Transfers of personal data outside the EU/UK

Until Brexit, one of the most vexing issues arising out of the GDPR (see **15.5.1**) related to the transfer of personal data outside the EU. Post-Brexit, regard should be had to the ICO's guidance about transferring data overseas from the UK. This can impact on UK companies who have EU or US subsidiaries or parents with regard to both customers'/clients' personal data as well as employees' personal data. They may be subject to EU and UK regulatory regimes.

The 1995 Data Protection Directive (no longer applicable) prohibited transfers of personal data outside the EU to a third country unless the country in question ensured an adequate level of data protection. In July 2000, the European Commission approved (executive decision 2000/520/EC) what were known as the Safe Harbor Principles, whereby the US provided safeguards for data protection. The Safe Harbor arrangements consisted essentially of American undertakings voluntarily self-assessing and self-certifying against an agreed set of principles. In October 2015, in a case decided under that Directive, the ECJ, in the case of *Schrems v Irish Data Protection Commissioner* (Case C-362/14), invalidated the Safe Harbor arrangements that had governed transfers of personal data between the EU and the United States.

Some or all of the data provided by subscribers to Facebook is transferred from Facebook's Irish subsidiary to servers located in the United States, where it is kept. Max Schrems, an Austrian citizen and privacy campaigner, had been a Facebook user since 2008. He lodged a complaint with the Irish data protection authority (the Data Protection Commissioner) against Facebook Ireland Ltd, contending that, in the light of the revelations made by Edward Snowden in 2013 concerning the activities of the United States intelligence services (including the National Security Agency (NSA)), the law and practices of the United States offered no real protection against surveillance by the United States of any data transferred to it. The Data Protection Commissioner rejected the complaint on the ground, in particular, that the European Commission had approved the Safe Harbor scheme. Mr Schrems appealed the decision to the Irish High Court, which referred various questions to the ECJ for a preliminary ruling. The ECJ held that the Safe Harbor arrangements failed to protect privacy, were inadequate and therefore invalid.

After the ruling, a number of American-based companies, such as Facebook and Microsoft, invoked template standard contractual clauses from the European Commission on the basis that these allowed them to continue to transfer data to the US. Schrems brought a further complaint to the Irish Data Protection Commission in respect of this usage. In May 2016, the Data Protection Commission referred the case to the ECJ.

On 2 February 2016, the European Commission and the US Government reached a political agreement on a new framework for transatlantic exchanges of personal data for commercial purposes to replace Safe Harbor: the EU–US Privacy Shield (IP/16/216). This was put before the Data Protection Board, the European Data Protection Supervisor and the European Parliament, and a number of clarifications and improvements were made. In July 2016, this was formally adopted by the European Commission and notified to Member States. US companies were able to certify with the US Commerce Department starting from 1 August 2016.

The European Commission believed that the EU–US Privacy Shield provided a robust new system that brought stronger data protection standards than under the Safe Harbor Principles, and which were better enforced, as well as providing safeguards on government access to personal data and easier redress for individuals in case of complaints. The General Data Protection Regulation (GDPR), like its predecessor, does not allow the transfer of data on EU citizens outside the EU unless that country has adequate data privacy laws. It is likely that being certified under the EU–US Privacy Shield will comply with most GDPR requirements, but it is not a substitute for GDPR compliance. It is likely that there will be challenges to its adequacy under the GDPR regime.

In a judgment issued by the ECJ in July 2020 (*Schems II* (Case C-311/18)), the ECJ said that standard data protection clauses were valid, subject to the existence of effective mechanisms to ensure compliance. It also stated that the revised EU–US Privacy Shield agreement was invalid. The ECJ has confirmed that EU standards of data protection must travel with data when it goes overseas. This means that the judgment has ramifications beyond just the EU and the US. It confirms the importance of safeguards for transfers of personal data outside the UK.

The US Department of Commerce has published guidance on the Privacy Shield and Brexit and made additional regulations to ensure that the Shield continues to cover UK to US transfers.

The ICO launched a consultation on 11 August 2021 on how organisations can protect data transferred outside the UK. The ICO suggests following *Schems II*.

Readers should note that the above is only a very brief overview of this complex area, and reference should be made to the legislation and the ICO website for further details.

15.7 FURTHER READING

Allen, Crasnow, Beale, McCann and Barrett, *Employment Law and Human Rights*, 3rd edn (OUP, 2018).

Carey, *Data Protection – A Practical Guide to UK Law*, 6th edn (OUP, 2020).

SUMMARY

The Human Rights Act 1998 incorporates the European Convention for the Protection of Human Rights and Fundamental Freedoms 1950 ('the Convention') into domestic law. Although the UK was already a signatory to the Convention and was therefore bound by it as a matter of international law, until the HRA 1998 came into force the Convention was not directly part of UK domestic law and individuals could not enforce Convention rights in the domestic courts (**15.1**).

Schedule 1 to the HRA 1998 sets out the relevant Convention rights that are to be protected under the Act:

*   Article 6 creates a right to 'a fair and public hearing within a reasonable time by an independent and impartial tribunal established by law'.

*   Article 8 gives a right to respect for private and family life and correspondence.

*   Article 9 protects freedom of thought, conscience and religion.

*   Article 10 gives the right to freedom of expression.

*   Article 11 protects the right to freedom of association, including the right to form and join a trade union.

*   Article 14 prohibits discrimination, but only in the context of other Convention rights (**15.2**).

The important Convention rights, from an employment perspective (eg Articles 6, 8, 9 and 10), are not absolute rights but are limited by counter-balances which permit legitimate interferences with those rights in certain situations. Most human rights cases are not about whether the right exists but whether there has been an interference with the right, and whether that interference is legitimate and necessary. That will involve questions of proportionality and relevance (**15.4**).

United Kingdom courts and tribunals must (HRA 1998, s 3) adopt a 'purposive' approach to the interpretation of UK legislation. If primary legislation is found to be incompatible with a Convention right, the HRA 1998 provides that such primary legislation remains effective but permits certain courts (the High Court and named appellate courts, but not employment tribunals or the EAT) to make (s 4) a 'declaration of incompatibility' in relation to that primary legislation, upon which Parliament may act if it wishes (**15.2**). (This allows for the sovereignty of Parliament to remain unchallenged.) Secondary legislation may, however, be struck down.

The UK GDPR and the DPA 2018 apply to the 'processing of the data'. This covers most of the routine personnel tasks, from the creation of personnel information to its filing, retention and storage. Personal data must be obtained only for specific and lawful purposes, must be processed fairly and lawfully, and must be kept accurate and up to date. There are special restrictions on the processing of 'sensitive' personal data – these include data about an employee's racial or ethnic origins, political beliefs, physical or mental health or sex life, and the commission of offences.

The Investigatory Powers Act 2016 and the Investigatory Powers (Interception by Businesses etc for Monitoring and Record-keeping Purposes) Regulations 2018 provide, as far as the interception of internal communications is concerned, that unless there is (expressly or by implication) consent (by both parties to the communication) to the interception, a criminal offence may be committed. The Regulations create in effect a number of 'lawful purposes' whereby employers can monitor and record communications between parties without their consent, provided that the employer has made 'all reasonable efforts to inform' every person who uses the telecommunication system that their communication may be monitored. These lawful purposes include:

(a)   ensuring compliance with regulatory or statutory rules;

(b)   ascertaining or demonstrating employee standards;

(d)   prevention or detection of crime.

The Information Commissioner has responsibility for the working and policing of the law. The Information Commissioner has published an Employment Practices Code, relating to recruitment and selection, employee records, monitoring at work and workers' health. Although the Code contains guidance and is not legally binding, it provides the benchmarks the Commissioner will use. It has not been updated post-GDPR/DPA 2018.

Appendix 1

Statement of Terms and Service Contract Examples

Example of Statement of Terms under the Employment Rights Act 1996, s 1

[Section 1 of the ERA 1996 requires an employer to give an employee or worker a written statement of terms and conditions not later than the beginning of employment and must set out certain matters relating to the employment relationship. If there is a separate written contractual agreement then it is not necessary also to provide a separate set of terms: see **1.4.2**. A written statement or contract – see below – can also contain additional matters that have specifically been offered to/accepted by the employee/worker.]

[In this example the employer is a limited company. The employee is a clerk.]

From [Employer   ]
To [Employee   ]

This statement sets out certain particulars, as at the date of the statement of the terms and conditions of your employment which are required to be given to you under s 1 of the Employment Rights Act 1996.

1. Your employment commenced on [   ]. No employment with a previous employer counts as part of your period of continuous employment.

[Length of service can be important in terms of determining unfair dismissal rights as well as in the calculation of notice and unfair dismissal awards. In this context, continuity can also be important, especially if, for example, someone has transferred as a result of a TUPE transfer: see **3.5**. If a probationary period is applicable, this should be set out.]

2. The title of your job is [   ]. [The duties which this job entails are set out in the attached job description [   ] and in addition to those duties you may be required to undertake additional or other duties as necessary to meet the needs of the business.

[It is important to be precise when defining the job description and duties. Job descriptions can be important, for example, when determining whether a redundancy situation has arisen: see **1.8.2** and **4.2.3**.]

3. Your place of work is [   ].

[Place of work can be important, for example, when determining whether a redundancy situation has arisen: see **1.8.2.3** and **4.2.2**.]

4. Your remuneration is [   ] per year, payable at [   ] intervals on [   ] directly into your bank account.

[The remuneration clause should specify how an employee's remuneration is calculated. Where appropriate, it should set out an hourly rate, when payment is due, whether it is paid in advance or in arrears, along with any fringe benefits. Consideration also needs to be given to the national minimum wage requirements and, where appropriate, the 'living wage' rate for over-25s: see **1.8.3.1**. Any fringe benefits should also be included.]

5. Your normal hours of work are from [   ] to [   ] Monday to Friday inclusive. A [   ] hour break may be taken for lunch.

[It may be useful to specify whether the lunch hour is included as part of the weekly hours worked and to make clear if it is unpaid.]

6. You are entitled to [   ] days paid holiday in each calendar year to be taken at times convenient to us, in addition to public holidays. During holidays you will be entitled to your normal basic remuneration. On termination of your employment your entitlement to accrued holiday pay will be in direct proportion to the length of your

service during the calendar year in which termination takes place. No holidays may be taken during a period of notice.

[Paid holidays can often be a source of confusion and dispute between employer and employee. Bearing in mind the statutory minimum (see **1.8.3.4**, **1.12**), it is important to set out clearly how much paid holiday an employee is entitled to, when it accrues from, and when the holiday year runs from/to: see **1.8.3.3**. Although certain minimum information must be set out in the written terms, it is acceptable to refer employees to a more detailed separate document that is reasonably accessible to the employee, such as a staff handbook. Such a document may allow an employer to give a much clearer account of how the holiday policy works in practice. It also allows, where an employee is part time, to set out how a pro rata entitlement is calculated and what the appropriate procedure is when time off is requested. Where additional documents are referred to setting out more fuller policy details, employers often include a sentence that says that the policy does not form part of the contract of employment, so as to give them flexibility to amend the policy. See **1.9** on variation of contractual terms. Any training that is to be provided should also be set out.]

7.   You will be paid your normal remuneration during absence through sickness or injury up to a maximum [   ] weeks in any period of 12 months, provided that you supply a medical certificate in the event of any such absence for seven or more consecutive days. Such remuneration will discharge our liability to pay you Statutory Sick Pay and you will be required to give credit for any other national insurance sickness benefits payable to you as a result of such absence.

[The contract terms should state whether the employer pays more than statutory sick pay (SSP). There is no legal right for an employee to be paid anything more than SSP. SSP is paid at a prescribed rate and is payable for up to 28 weeks. If additional ('enhanced') contractual sick pay is paid, the contract should set out whether a medical certificate is required, the period for which it is paid, the amount and whether SSP is deducted when calculating it. Although certain minimum information must be set out in the written terms, it is acceptable to refer employees to a more detailed separate document which sets out these matters: see **1.8.3.3**. In practice, employers will need to provide information about the entitlement to sick pay as well as sickness absence reporting procedures.]

8.   [You are eligible to join the [   ] pension scheme. Full details can be found in the booklet entitled [   ], a copy of which can be obtained from [   ]. [No pension scheme is applicable to your employment, but we shall provide you with access to a designated stakeholder pension scheme. We do [not] make contributions.]

[All employers will be obliged to offer eligible employees access to a workplace pension by 2018. Employees who qualify for a workplace pension will be those who are aged between 22 and the State Pension age, earn at least £10,000 a year and work in the UK. Employers must pay at least 1% of their employee's 'qualifying earnings' into their workplace pension. This will rise to 3% in 2019 if approved by Parliament. Employees can choose to opt out. If the employee has opted out, this should be reflected in the agreement. Employers are obliged to re-enroll eligible employees every 3 years. The contract terms should state the relevant details. Although certain minimum information must be set out in the written terms, it is acceptable to refer employees to a more detailed separate document which sets out these matters: see **1.8.4**.]

9.1   The disciplinary rules which will apply to you are set out in the booklet entitled [   ] [a copy of which can be obtained from   ]. The rules do not form part of your contract of employment.

9.2   If you are dissatisfied with any disciplinary decision relating to you, you may appeal to [   ] for the matter to be reconsidered.

9.3   If you have any grievance relating to your employment you may seek redress by applying to [   ]. The steps consequent upon an application of this kind are set out in the booklet entitled [   ] a copy of which can be obtained from [   ]. The rules do not form part of your contract of employment.

[Although certain minimum information must be set out about disciplinary procedures in the written terms, it is acceptable to refer employees to a more detailed separate document which sets out these matters: see **1.8.8**.]

10.1   The length of notice which you are obliged to give to us to terminate your employment is [   ].

10.2 The length of notice you are entitled to receive from us to terminate your employment is (subject to 10.3):

10.2.1 One week's notice if your period of continuous employment is less than two years.

10.2.2 One week's notice for each year of continuous employment, if your period of continuous employment is two years or more, subject to a maximum of 12 weeks' notice after 12 years' continuous employment.

10.3 You may be dismissed without notice in the event of your committing an act of gross misconduct.

[Although there are set statutory minimum notice periods, these must be set out in the contract. Employers can impose longer notice periods by contract if required. Following the decision of the Supreme Court in Haywood (2.3.3) that a term will be implied into all contracts of employment that notice will only start to run from the date an employee receives written notice and has had a reasonable opportunity to consider it, employers now need to make sure that their contracts of employment set out expressly how notice can be served and when it will be considered to have been received.]

11. There is no collective agreement in force which affects your terms and conditions of employment.

[Collective bargaining consists of negotiations between an employer and a group of employees so as to determine the conditions of employment. The result of collective bargaining procedures is usually reflected in a collective agreement. Employees are often represented in bargaining by a union or other labour organisation. Where there are collective agreements in place that regulate the terms and conditions of employees in their workplace, these must be stated.]

Dated [   ]

Signed Employee [   ]

For and on behalf of Employer [   ].

© The University of Law 2023

Example of Service Contract

[In this example the employer is a partnership. The employee is a member of the firm's middle management. In order to avoid the necessity of a separate statement of terms, the requirements of ERA 1996, s 1 have also been included. It has been shortened by incorporating a number of standard written policies around grievances and disciplinary hearings. Contracts should always be reviewed when employees are promoted. Commentary on the standard minimum terms as required by the ERA 1996, s 1 is included in the sample statement above; additional commentary has been added here only around additional clauses.]

THIS AGREEMENT dated [   ] [*year*] is made BETWEEN:

(1)   [   ] ('the Employer')

(2)   [   ] ('the Employee')

1. Definitions

'Business' the business carried on from time to time by the Employer

'Confidential Information' includes any trade secrets, secret manufacturing processes, technical data, know-how and all information relating to the affairs and finances of the Employer (including business contacts)

[One of the major advantages of tailored and agreed contractual terms is that express confidentiality clauses can be agreed. While all contracts will imply a duty of mutual obligation, fidelity and trust, that is of a narrow nature and limited, and it is always advisable, where employees have access to confidential information, to include carefully drafted and tailored terms: see **1.7.2.8**, **1.8.6.1** and clauses 5, 12, 13, 14 below. Including an express term allows an employer to make clear what sort of matters and information it considers to be 'confidential'.]

'Employment' the Employee's employment under this agreement

'Incapacity' any illness accident or similar reason preventing the Employee from properly carrying out the Employment

'Partner' any partner in the firm [   ]

'Partners' the partners for the time being of the firm [   ]

2. Job title and length of employment

2.1   Subject to clause 18, the Employer agrees to employ the Employee as [   ] from (and including) [   ].

2.2   No employment with a previous employer counts as part of the Employee's period of continuous employment with the Employer.

[2.3   Probationary period, if relevant.]

3. Duties

3.1   The duties which this job entails are set out in [   ] and in addition to those duties the Employee may be required to undertake additional or other duties as necessary to meet the needs of the Business.

3.2   The Employee must:

    3.2.1   perform to the best of his/her ability all the duties of the job,

    3.2.2   do all in his/her power to promote, develop and extend the Business,

    3.2.3   comply with the reasonable directions of the Partners.

4. Place of work

4.1   The Employee's usual place of work is [   ] but the Employee may be required to work in any place which the Partners may reasonably require.

4.2   The Employee may also be required to travel on the business of the Employer anywhere within the European Union.

[Express mobility clauses are sometimes included in contracts to allow employers to have the flexibility to move an employee to a different place of work. If there is no express mobility clause, an employer may be able to rely on an implied clause if relocation is still within reasonable travelling distance of an employee's home. Even if there is an express mobility clause, it must still be enforced reasonably (see *Courtaulds v Sibson* and *Kellogg Brown & Root (UK) Ltd v Fitton*). If an employee is senior, it can be important for the place of work ('mobility') clause to be widely drawn to allow flexibility. If an employee is expected to work outside the UK, this should be stated. For more junior employees, a narrower mobility clause may be preferable. Employment tribunals generally interpret mobility clauses restrictively – ie with ambiguities resolved in the employee's favour.]

5. To devote full time

5.1   The Employee's normal hours are [   ] to [   ], but he/she will be expected to work whatever other hours are necessary to meet the needs of the Business.

5.2   The Employee must (unless prevented by Incapacity) devote his/her whole time and attention to the Business.

5.3   The Employee must not without the prior written consent of the Partners:

(a)   take part in any other business or employment (of whatever nature), or

(b)   except where permitted by clause 5.4, have an interest in any other business which is similar to or competes with the Business.

5.4   The Employee may have an interest in shares or other securities which are quoted on a recognised stock exchange, so long as the interest does not extend to more than 2% of the total amount of the shares or securities of the company in question.

5.5   [Working time opt out if appropriate: see **1.11.3.4**.]

[This can enable an employer to be more specific about what constitutes fidelity and good faith. It may be helpful to identify where potential competition might be perceived and where financial or other conflicts of interest can arise.]

6. Remuneration

6.1   The Employer agrees to pay to the Employee a salary (accruing from day to day) at the rate of [£   ] per year payable in arrear by equal monthly instalments on the 5th day of each month directly into the Employee's bank account.

6.2   The Partners must review this salary annually and may increase the salary with effect from the review date.

[6.3   Include any other benefits that may arise]

7. Expenses

7.1   Subject to 7.2, the Employer agrees to repay the Employee for all reasonable hotel and other expenses wholly and exclusively incurred by him/her in the performance of the Employment.

7.2   The Employee must give the Employer receipts or other evidence of these expenses.

8. Company car

8.1   The Employer agrees to provide a car for the Employee in accordance with the Firm's car policy as published and varied by the Employer from time to time.

8.2   The Employee must:

8.2.1   take good care of the car,

8.2.2   comply with the provisions of any insurance policy relating to it, and

8.2.3   return the car and its keys to the Employer at its principal place of business (or any other place the Employer may reasonably specify) immediately upon the ending of the Employment.

9. Holidays

9.1   The Employer's holiday year runs from 1st January to 31st December.

9.2   The Employee is entitled to [   ] working days' paid holiday in each holiday year (in addition to the usual public holidays) to be taken when convenient to the Employer.

9.3   The Employee may not without the consent of the Partners carry forward any unused part of his/her holiday to a subsequent holiday year.

9.4   On termination of this employment, the Employee's entitlement to accrued holiday pay will be in direct proportion to the length of service during the calendar year in which termination takes place.

9.5   The Employee will be required to repay to the Employer pay received for holiday taken in excess of basic holiday entitlement accrued at termination.

10. Private health and permanent sickness insurance

The Employer agrees to cover the cost of the Employee's membership of an appropriate permanent sickness insurance and private patients' medical plan with such reputable insurance schemes as the Employer may decide from time to time.

11. Pension

On completion of [   ] months' employment the Employee may join the [   ] pension scheme. Details are set out in the booklet [   ]. A copy can be obtained from any Partner.

[Many employment contracts contain a reference to contracting out. However, this is no longer relevant as it ended in April 2016. In addition to the basic State Pension, the State previously provided a second-tier top-up pension, based on how much an employee earned. This was introduced in 1978 and was originally called the State Earnings Related Pension Scheme (Serps). It became State Second Pension (S2P) in 2002. Before rules were changed in 2012, employees were allowed to 'contract out' of this additional pension. In exchange for lower National Insurance contributions, they gave up part or all of it and received extra pension from their occupational scheme or personal/stakeholder pension instead. In April 2016, the Government introduced a raft of pension reforms, and contracting out was abolished. If employees still have these provisions in their contract, the statutory reform provisions automatically repealed them.]

12. Confidentiality during the Employment

12.1   The Employee is aware that in the course of the Employment he/she may be given or come across Confidential Information.

12.2   The Employee must not disclose or use any Confidential Information (except in the proper course of his/her duties).

12.3   The Employee must use his/her best endeavours to prevent the disclosure of any Confidential Information.

12.4   All notes of any Confidential Information which the Employee acquires or makes during the Employment belong to the Employer. When the Employment ends (or at any time during the Employment should any Partner so request) the Employee must hand over these notes to someone duly authorised by the Partners to receive them.

[One of the major advantages of tailored and agreed contractual terms is that express confidentiality clauses can be agreed: see **1.7.2.8**, **1.8.6.1** and see also clauses 5, 12, 13, 14 which may together make up a package of restrictions. During employment, there is always an implied term of 'fidelity' or good faith which can be replied upon to ensure an employee does not reveal confidential information. However, including an express term allows an employer, for example, to make clear exactly what sorts of information it considers to be 'confidential'.]

13. Confidentiality after the Employment ends

After the Employment ends, the Employee must not disclose or use any of the Firm's trade secrets or any other information which is of a sufficiently high degree of confidentiality as to amount to a trade secret.

[After employment, only very highly sensitive confidential information is protected by any implied term. An express term allows this cover to be widened. See **1.8.6.2**.]

14. Unfair competition after the Employment ends

14.1   The Employer is entitled to protect its Confidential Information, its goodwill and its trade connections from any unfair competition by the Employee.

14.2   Therefore

    14.2.1 For [   ] months after the Employment ends, the Employee agrees not to seek business from any person, firm or company who at any time during the [   ] months immediately preceding the ending of the Employment has been a customer of the Employer, or done business with it and with whom the Employee has had personal contact.

    14.2.2 For [   ] months after the ending of the Employment, the Employee agrees not to be associated with the business of [   ]

        (a)   within [   ] miles of the Employer's premises at [   ] or

        (b)   within [   ] miles of any other premises of the Employer where the Employee was employed for at least [   ] months in the last [   ] months of the Employment.

[In order to prevent unfair competition after employment ends, employers should consider inserting a restrictive covenant into an employee's contract. This can restrain an ex-employee from working in a competing business, soliciting customers or poaching other staff. Such clauses, to be enforceable and not to amount to an unlawful restraint of trade, must be clear, must be aimed at protecting a legitimate business interest and must not be over-restrictive or unduly onerous. See **1.8.7**. Not all employees will need such clauses. Most arguments about restrictive covenants arise at the end of the employment relationship. However, when a court is asked to determine the enforceability of a restrictive covenant, it will have to consider the job role of the employee at the point when the covenant was entered. Restrictive covenants should therefore be appropriate for the role in question or they risk being unenforceable (see *PAT Systems v Neilly*, *Bartholomews Agri Foods Ltd v Thornton* and *Egon Zehnder Ltd v Tillman*). What are known as 'garden leave' clauses may also be considered. These allow an employer to require an employee who has been given and paid notice to stay at home during the notice period rather than coming into work. This can prevent an employee immediately joining a competitor. See **1.8.7.3**.]

15. Incapacity

15.1   If the Employee cannot work because of Incapacity, he/she must immediately tell a Partner. The Employee must provide a medical certificate, specifying the nature of the Incapacity and its likely duration, within eight days of the start of his/her absence and then at weekly intervals.

15.2   The Employee will be paid during absence due to Incapacity (payment to be inclusive of statutory sick pay) for a total of up to [   ] weeks in any one calendar year of the Employment.

15.3   After that, the Employee will continue to be paid salary only at the discretion of the Employer.

15.4   The Employee must inform the Employer of the amount of any social security benefit he/she receives and the Employer may deduct this from the salary paid to him/her under this clause.

16. Grievance Procedure

A copy of the current edition of the Grievance Procedure is attached. The procedure is revised by the Firm from time to time and the Employee may apply to a Partner at any time to inspect the most recent copy.

17. Disciplinary Procedure

A copy of the current edition of the disciplinary procedure affecting the Employee is attached to this agreement, although it does not form part of this contract and will not have contractual effect. The procedure is revised by the Firm from time to time and the Employee may apply to a Partner at any time to inspect the most recent edition.

18. Collective Agreement

There is no collective agreement in force which affects your terms and conditions of employment.

19. Ending the Employment

The Employer may end the Employment without notice or pay in lieu of notice in the following circumstances:

19.1   If the Employee has committed a serious or repeated breach of any of his/her obligations under this agreement or the Employer has reasonable grounds for believing he/she has done so.

20. Notice of termination

20.1   The Employee is obliged to give the Employer [   ] weeks' notice in order to terminate this contract.

20.2   The Employee is entitled to receive [   ] weeks' notice from the Employer in order to terminate his/her contract (subject to clause 19.1).

[20.3   Consider including an option to make a payment in lieu of notice ('PILON' clause). See **2.3.3**.]

[20.4   Consider a fixed term as an alternative.]

[Although there are set statutory minimum notice periods, employers can impose longer notice periods by contract if required. 'Garden leave' clauses may also be considered. These allow an employer to require an employee who has been given and paid notice to stay at home during the notice period rather than coming into work. This can prevent an employee immediately joining a competitor. See **1.8.7.3**. A PILON clause allows an employer to protect against a wrongful dismissal claim (see **Chapter 3**) if it makes a payment instead of requiring an employee to work out his notice period.]

21. Notices

21.1   Notices by the Employee must be by letter addressed to the Employer at its principal place of business. Notices by the Employer must be by letter addressed to the Employee at his/her last known address in Great Britain.

21.2   Any notice given by letter will be treated as being given at the time at which the letter would be delivered in the ordinary course of second class post. Any notice delivered by hand will be treated as being given upon delivery. In proving service by post it will be enough to prove that the notice was properly addressed and posted.

[Following the decision of the Supreme Court in *Haywood* (**2.3.3**) that a term will be implied into all contracts of employment that notice will only start to run from the date an employee receives written notice and has had a reasonable opportunity to consider it, employers now need to make sure that their contracts of employment set out expressly how notice can be served and when it will be considered to have been received.]

SIGNED by ....

In signing this, the Employee acknowledges and confirms that s/he agrees that these terms constitute his/her contract of employment with the Employer.

[It is always useful to get the employee to sign a contract as then there is express evidence that he received and so was aware of the contractual terms and staff policies.]

[Note: This is not an exhaustive list. Increasingly contracts may include clauses relating to social media (including cyber-bullying), e-mail and Internet use (in order to comply with the notice requirements under the Telecommunications (Lawful Business Practice) (Interception and Communications) Regulations 2000), records and monitoring (see **Chapter 15**), bonuses, whistleblowing (see **5.6.5**), equal opportunities (see **Chapter 8**), health and safety, maternity, paternity and flexible working, etc (see **Chapter 14**). Consideration must be given as to whether such terms are to be contractual or not (see **1.8** and **1.9**).]

© The University of Law 2023

Appendix 2

Case Study

Employment Tribunal

Claim form

Official Use Only			
Tribunal office			
Case number		Date received	

You must complete all questions marked with an '*'

1 Your details

| 1.1 | Title | ☑ Mr ☐ Mrs ☐ Miss ☐ Ms |

1.2* First name (or names)

James

1.3* Surname or family name

Gold

1.4 Date of birth 　3　0　/　0　6　/　1　9　5　8　　Are you? ☑ Male ☐ Female

1.5* Address

Number or name 12

Street Douglas Crescent

Town/City

County Guildshire

Postcode G U 1 2 8 Q Y

1.6 **Phone number**
Where we can contact you during the day

011111 123456

1.7 Mobile number (if different)

1.8 How would you prefer us to contact you?
(Please tick only one box)

☑ Email ☐ Post ☐ Fax

Whatever your preference please note that some documents cannot be sent electronically

1.9 Email address

james.gould@hotmail123.com

1.10 Fax number

1.11 Would you be able to take part in a hearing by video?
(Requires internet access).

☐ Yes ☑ No

Further details on video hearings can be found on the following link https://www.gov.uk/guidance/hmcts-telephone-and-video-hearings-during-coronavirus-outbreak

2 **Respondent's details** (that is the employer, person or organisation against whom you are making a claim)

2.1* Give the name of your employer or the person or organisation you are claiming **against** (If you need to you can add more respondents at 2.5)

> Car Parking PLC

2.2* Address

Number or name

Street

Town/City

County | Guilshire

Postcode |___|___|___|___|___|___|___|

Phone number | 01234 567 789

2.3* Do you have an Acas early conciliation certificate number?

☑ Yes   ☐ No

Nearly everyone should have this number before they fill in a claim form. You can find it on your Acas certificate. For help and advice, call Acas on 0300 123 1100 or visit www.acas.org.uk

If Yes, please give the Acas early conciliation certificate number.

> Acas 1234

If No, why don't you have this number?

☐ Another person I'm making the claim with has an Acas early conciliation certificate number

☐ Acas doesn't have the power to conciliate on some or all of my claim

☐ My employer has already been in touch with Acas

☐ My claim consists only of a complaint of unfair dismissal which contains an application for interim relief. (See guidance)

2.4 If you worked at a different address from the one you have given at 2.2 please give the full address

Address

Number or name

Street

Town/City

County

Postcode |___|___|___|___|___|___|___|

Phone number

2.5 If there are other respondents please tick this box and put their names and addresses here. ☐

(If there is not enough room here for the names of all the additional respondents then you can add any others at Section 13.)

Respondent 2

Name

Address

Number or name

Street

Town/City

County

Postcode ☐ ☐ ☐ ☐ ☐ ☐ ☐ ☐

Phone number

2.6 Do you have an Acas early conciliation certificate number?

☐ Yes ☐ No

Nearly everyone should have this number before they fill in a claim form. You can find it on your Acas certificate. For help and advice, call Acas on 0300 123 1100 or visit www.acas.org.uk

If Yes, please give the Acas early conciliation certificate number.

If No, why don't you have this number?

☐ Another person I'm making the claim with has an Acas early conciliation certificate number

☐ Acas doesn't have the power to conciliate on some or all of my claim

☐ My employer has already been in touch with Acas

☐ My claim consists only of a complaint of unfair dismissal which contains an application for interim relief. (See guidance)

Respondent 3

2.7 Name

Address

Number or name

Street

Town/City

County

Postcode ☐ ☐ ☐ ☐ ☐ ☐ ☐ ☐

Phone number

2.8 Do you have an Acas early conciliation certificate number?

☐ Yes   ☐ No

Nearly everyone should have this number before they fill in a claim form. You can find it on your Acas certificate. For help and advice, call Acas on 0300 123 1100 or visit www.Acas.org.uk

If Yes, please give the Acas early conciliation certificate number

☐

If No, why don't you have this number?

☐ Another person I'm making the claim with has an Acas early conciliation certificate number

☐ Acas doesn't have the power to conciliate on some or all of my claim

☐ My employer has already been in touch with Acas

☐ My claim consists only of a complaint of unfair dismissal which contains an application for interim relief. (See guidance)

3 Multiple cases

3.1 Are you aware that your claim is one of a number of claims against the same employer arising from the same, or similar, circumstances?

☐ Yes   ☑ No

If Yes, and you know the names of any other claimants, add them here. This will allow us to link your claim to other related claims.

4 Cases where the respondent was not your employer

4.1 If you were not employed by any of the respondents you have named but are making a claim for some reason connected to employment (for example, relating to a job application which you made or against a trade union, qualifying body or the like) please state the type of claim you are making here. (You will get the chance to provide details later):

Now go to Section 8

5 Employment details

If you are or were employed please give the following information, if possible.

5.1 When did your employment start?

9/11/18

Is your employment continuing?

☐ Yes   ☑ No

If your employment has ended, when did it end?

30/04/21

If your employment has not ended, are you in a period of notice and, if so, when will that end?

5.2 Please say what job you do or did.

Team Leader

6   Earnings and benefits

6.1   How many hours on average do, or did you work each week in the job this claim is about?   `40`   hours each week

6.2   How much are, or were you paid?

Pay before tax   £ `1916.00`   ☐ Weekly   ☑ Monthly

Normal take-home pay
(Incl. overtime, commission, bonuses etc.)   £ `1482.00`   ☐ Weekly   ☑ Monthly

6.3   If your employment has ended, did you work (or were you paid for) a period of notice?   ☑ Yes   ☐ No

If Yes, how many weeks, or months' notice did you work, or were you paid for?   `2` weeks   ☐ months

6.4   Were you in your employer's pension scheme?   ☐ Yes   ☑ No

6.5   If you received any other benefits, e.g. company car, medical insurance, etc, from your employer, please give details.

7   If your employment with the respondent has ended, what has happened since?

7.1   Have you got another job?   ☐ Yes   ☑ No

If No, please **go to section 8**

7.2   Please say when you started (or will start) work.

7.3   Please say how much you are now earning (or will earn).   £

8 Type and details of claim

8.1*   Please indicate the type of claim you are making by ticking one or more of the boxes below.

[✓] I was unfairly dismissed (including constructive dismissal)

[ ] I was discriminated against on the grounds of:

    [ ] age   [ ] race

    [ ] gender reassignment   [ ] disability

    [ ] pregnancy or maternity   [ ] marriage or civil partnership

    [ ] sexual orientation   [ ] sex (including equal pay)

    [ ] religion or belief

[ ] I am claiming a redundancy payment

[ ] I am owed

    [ ] notice pay

    [ ] holiday pay

    [ ] arrears of pay

    [ ] other payments

[ ] I am making another type of claim which the Employment Tribunal can deal with.
    (Please state the nature of the claim. Examples are provided in the Guidance.)

8.2*   Please set out the background and details of your claim in the space below.

The details of your claim should include **the date(s) when the event(s) you are complaining about happened.** Please use the blank sheet at the end of the form if needed.

9 What do you want if your claim is successful?

9.1 Please tick the relevant box(es) to say what you
want if your claim is successful:

☐ If claiming unfair dismissal, to get your old job back and compensation (reinstatement)

☐ If claiming unfair dismissal, to get another job with the same employer or associated employer and compensation (re-engagement)

☑ Compensation only

☐ If claiming discrimination, a recommendation (see Guidance).

9.2 What compensation or remedy are you seeking?

If you are claiming financial compensation please give as much detail as you can about how much you are claiming and how you have calculated this sum. (Please note any figure stated below will be viewed as helpful information but it will not restrict what you can claim and you will be permitted to revise the sum claimed later. See the Guidance for further information about how you can calculate compensation). If you are seeking any other remedy from the Tribunal which you have not already identified please also state this below.

The claimant seeks loss of earnings from 30 April 2021 to the date of the hearing and future loss of earnings. The claimant seeks an uplift of any award because the respondent unreasonably failed to comply with Acas.

10 **Information to regulators in protected disclosure cases**

10.1 If your claim consists of, or includes, a claim that you are making a protected disclosure under the Employment Rights Act 1996 (otherwise known as a 'whistleblowing' claim), please tick the box if you want a copy of this form, or information from it, to be forwarded on your behalf to a relevant regulator (known as a 'prescribed person' under the relevant legislation) by tribunal staff. (See Guidance). ☐

11 **Your representative**

If someone has agreed to represent you, please fill in the following. We will in future only contact your representative and not you.

11.1	Name of representative	Fred McLean
11.2	Name of organisation	Collaws Solicitors LLP
11.3	Address	Number or name: 20
		Street: The Street
		Town/City:
		County: Guildshire
		Postcode: G U 1 2 1 G G
11.4	DX number (If known)	
11.5	Phone number	07777 123456
11.6	Mobile number (If different)	
11.7	Their reference for correspondence	FM/JG
11.8	Email address	fm@collaws.co.uk
11.9	How would you prefer us to communicate with them? (Please tick only one box)	☑ Email ☐ Post ☐ Fax
11.10	Fax number	

12 **Disability**

12.1 Do you have a disability? ☐ Yes ☑ No

If Yes, it would help us if you could say what this disability is and tell us what assistance, if any, you will need as your claim progresses through the system, including for any hearings that maybe held at tribunal premises.

13 Details of additional respondents

Section 2 allows you to list up to three respondents. If there are any more respondents please provide their details here

Respondent 4

Name

Address

Number or name

Street

Town/City

County

Postcode

Phone number

Do you have an Acas early conciliation certificate number?

☐ Yes   ☐ No

Nearly everyone should have this number before they fill in a claim form. You can find it on your Acas certificate. For help and advice, call Acas on 0300 123 1100 or visit www.acas.org.uk

If Yes, please give the Acas early conciliation certificate number.

If No, why don't you have this number?

☐ Another person I'm making the claim with has an Acas early conciliation certificate number

☐ Acas doesn't have the power to conciliate on some or all of my claim

☐ My employer has already been in touch with Acas

☐ My claim consists only of a complaint of unfair dismissal which contains an application for interim relief. (See guidance)

Respondent 5

Name

Address

Number or name

Street

Town/City

County

Postcode | | | | | **|** | | |

Phone number

Do you have an Acas early conciliation
certificate number?

☐ Yes   ☐ No

*Nearly everyone should have this number before they fill in a claim form.
You can find it on your Acas certificate. For help and advice, call Acas on
0300 123 1100 or visit www.acas.org.uk*

If Yes, please give the Acas early
conciliation certificate number.

If No, why don't you have this number?

☐ Another person I'm making the claim with has an Acas early conciliation certificate number

☐ Acas doesn't have the power to conciliate on some or all of my claim

☐ My employer has already been in touch with Acas

☐ My claim consists only of a complaint of unfair dismissal which contains an application for interim relief. (See guidance)

14 Final check

**Please re-read the form and check you have entered all the relevant information.
Once you are satisfied, please tick this box.** ☑

General Data Protection Regulations

The Ministry of Justice and HM Courts and Tribunals Service processes personal information about you in the context of tribunal proceedings.

For details of the standards we follow when processing your data, please visit the following address https://www.gov.uk/government/organisations/hm-courts-and-tribunals-service/about/personal-information-charter.

To receive a paper copy of this privacy notice, please call our Customer Contact Centre:

England and Wales: 0300 123 1024

Welsh speakers: 0300 303 5176

Scotland: 0300 790 6234

Textphone: 18001 0300 123 1024 (England and Wales)

Textphone: 18001 0300 790 6234 (Scotland)

Please note: a copy of the claim form or response and other tribunal related correspondence may be copied to the other party and Acas for the purpose of tribunal proceedings or to reach settlement of the claim.

15 **Additional information**

You can provide additional information about your claim in this section.

If you're part of a group claim, give the Acas early conciliation certificate numbers for other people in your group. If they don't have numbers, tell us why.

Please see separate sheet.

HM Courts & Tribunals Service

Diversity Monitoring Questionnaire

It is important to us that everyone who has contact with HM Courts & Tribunals Service, receives equal treatment. We need to find out whether our policies are effective and to take steps to ensure the impact of future policies can be fully assessed to try to avoid any adverse impacts on any particular groups of people. That is why we are asking you to complete the following questionnaire, which will be used to provide us with the relevant statistical information. **Your answers will be treated in strict confidence.**

Thank you in advance for your co-operation.

Claim type

Please confirm the type of claim that you are bringing to the employment tribunal. This will help us in analysing the other information provided in this form.

- (a) ☑ Unfair dismissal or constructive dismissal
- (b) ☐ Discrimination
- (c) ☐ Redundancy payment
- (d) ☐ Other payments you are owed
- (e) ☐ Other complaints

Sex

What is your sex?

- (a) ☐ Female
- (b) ☑ Male
- (c) ☐ Prefer not to say

Age group

Which age group are you in?

- (a) ☐ Under 25
- (b) ☐ 25-34
- (c) ☐ 35-44
- (d) ☐ 45-54
- (e) ☑ 55-64
- (f) ☐ 65 and over
- (g) ☐ Prefer not to say

Ethnicity

What is your ethnic group?

White

- (a) ☑ English / Welsh / Scottish / Northern Irish / British
- (b) ☐ Irish
- (c) ☐ Gypsy or Irish Traveller
- (d) ☐ Any other White background

Mixed / multiple ethnic groups

- (e) ☐ White and Black Caribbean
- (f) ☐ White and Black African
- (g) ☐ White and Asian
- (h) ☐ Any other Mixed / multiple ethnic background

Asian / Asian British

- (i) ☐ Indian
- (j) ☐ Pakistani
- (k) ☐ Bangladeshi
- (l) ☐ Chinese
- (m) ☐ Any other Asian background

Black / African / Caribbean / Black British

- (n) ☐ African
- (o) ☐ Caribbean
- (p) ☐ Any other Black / African / Caribbean background

Other ethnic group

- (q) ☐ Arab
- (r) ☐ Any other ethnic group

- (s) ☐ Prefer not to say

Disability

The Equality Act 2010 defines a disabled person as 'Someone who has a physical or mental impairment and the impairment has a substantial and long-term adverse effect on his or her ability to carry out normal day-to-day activities'.

Conditions covered may include, for example, severe depression, dyslexia, epilepsy and arthritis.

Do you have any physical or mental health conditions or illnesses lasting or expected to last for 12 months or more?

(a) ☐ Yes

(b) ☑ No

(c) ☐ Prefer not to say

Marriage and Civil Partnership

Are you?

(a) ☐ Single, that is, never married and never registered in a same-sex civil partnership

(b) ☐ Married

(c) ☐ Separated, but still legally married

(d) ☑ Divorced

(e) ☐ Widowed

(f) ☐ In a registered same-sex civil partnership

(g) ☐ Separated, but still legally in a same-sex civil partnership

(h) ☐ Formerly in a same-sex civil partnership which is now legally dissolved

(I) ☐ Surviving partner from a same-sex civil partnership

(J) ☐ Prefer not to say

Religion and belief

What is your religion?

(a) ☑ No religion

(b) ☐ Christian (including Church of England, Catholic, Protestant and all other Christian denominations)

(c) ☐ Buddhist

(d) ☐ Hindu

(e) ☐ Jewish

(f) ☐ Muslim

(g) ☐ Sikh

(h) ☐ Any other religion (please describe)

[   ]

(I) ☐ Prefer not to say

Caring responsibilites

Do you have any caring responsibilities, (for example; children, elderly relatives, partners etc.)?

(a) ☐ Yes

(b) ☑ No

(c) ☐ Prefer not to say

Sexual identity

Which of the options below best describes how you think of yourself?

(a) ☑ Heterosexual/Straight

(b) ☐ Gay/Lesbian

(c) ☐ Bisexual

(d) ☐ Other

(e) ☐ Prefer not to say

Pregnancy and maternity

Were you pregnant when the issue you are making a claim about took place?

(a) ☐ Yes

(b) ☑ No

(c) ☐ Prefer not to say

Thank you for taking the time to complete this questionnaire.

Employment Tribunals check list

Please check the following:

1. Read the form to make sure the information given is correct and truthful, and that you have not left out any information which you feel may be relevant to you or your client.
2. Do not attach a covering letter to your form. If you have any further relevant information please enter it in the 'Additional Information' space provided in the form.
3. Send the completed form to the relevant office address.
4. Keep a copy of your form posted to us.

If your claim has been submitted on-line or posted you should receive confirmation of receipt from the office dealing with your claim within five working days. If you have not heard from them within five days, please contact that office directly. If the deadline for submitting the claim is closer than five days you should check that it has been received before the time limit expires.

You have opted to print and post your form. We would like to remind you that forms submitted online are processed much faster than ones posted to us. If you want to submit your claim online please go to www.gov.uk/employment-tribunals/make-a-claim

A list of our office's contact details can be found at the hearing centre page of our website at – www.gov.uk/guidance/employment-tribunal-offices-and-venues; if you are still unsure about which office to contact please call our Employment Tribunal Customer Contact Centre (Mon – Fri, 9am – 5pm) they can also provide general procedural information about the Employment Tribunals.

Customer Contact Centre:

England and Wales: 0300 123 1024

Welsh speakers: 0300 303 5176

Scotland: 0300 790 6234

Textphone: 18001 0300 123 1024 (England and Wales)

Textphone: 18001 0300 790 6234 (Scotland)

IN THE Guildshire Employment Tribunal

Case Number 123456/2021

Mr J Gold (Claimant)

v

Car Parking PLC (Respondent)

Statement of Case

1. The Claimant was employed by the respondent as a Team Leader based at the Guildshire car park.

2. He started working in this role in November 2018. He was dismissed on the grounds of redundancy on the 30th April 2021 and was paid a redundancy payment.

3. The Claimant does not accept that there was a genuine redundancy situation and understands that a new employee is currently employed in his role at the car park.

4. The Claimant further argues that the selection criteria were unfair in that his level of experience and expertise was underscored.

5. He appealed his dismissal but was unsuccessful in the appeal which was heard on the 20th April 2021. The Claimant only saw the scoring for the first time after the appeal so he didn't have an opportunity to contest the score before the appeal, or at the appeal. The scoring was only forwarded to him after the appeal hearing was adjourned. The Claimant expected to return to the appeal to raise his complaints but this didn't happen and he received a letter confirming his dismissal. The Claimant has worked previously for the respondent for a number of years and was Tupe'd out to a different employer. He has worked in this industry for approximately 4 years. He argues the procedure adopted was unfair and predetermined.

6. On viewing the score he was horrified to see he had been scored 1 for his skills for the current position and job. He had no performance issues and had a good appraisal. There was simply no justification to score him one meaning 'not acceptable'.

7. In conclusion the respondent did not allow the claimant the opportunity to contest his scores. They concluded the appeal then sent him his score, and when he saw his score he found that the score was unfair and didn't reflect his skills and ability. The Claimant had no performance issues and was never advised that his performance was below par. He would have expected to score 4 'good' and not 1.

8. His comparators in the pool were 3. The Claimant asked for an alternative role locally. He was aware that two members of staff in a more junior role were leaving. His request was ignored by the contractor manager. These jobs were given to two more junior staff with no rail experience at all; they were only used to off street car parks. The machinery and procedures are very different in the rail track contract sites. The Claimant could easily have done either role. The respondents offered a junior role miles from his home and on less pay.

EMPLOYMENT TRIBUNALS

To: Car Parking PLC

e-mail: GuildshireET@tribunals.gsi.gov.uk

Case Number: 123456/2021

Mr J Gold	**Claimant**
v	
Car Parking PLC	**Respondent**

NOTICE OF A CLAIM

The Claim

The Employment Tribunal has accepted a claim for unfair dismissal against the above respondent. It has been given the above Case Number, which should be quoted in any communication relating to this case.

A copy of the claim is enclosed for the respondent.

The Response

To submit a response, a prescribed form must be used. Alternatively you may respond on-line at www.employmenttribunals.gov.uk. It must be received at this office by 26/07/2021. If a response is not received by then, and no extension of time has been applied for and given, the claim will proceed undefended, or a default judgment may be made.

Acas

Acas (whose services are free) may be able to help the parties resolve the matter at any time.

Representative

If you appoint a representative to act for you, please pass these documents to your representative as soon as possible. You remain responsible for ensuring that the representative deals with all matters promptly.

Enclosures

A copy of the claim

A prescribed response form

A copy of the booklet 'Responding to a claim' can be found on our website at www.employmenttribunals.gov.uk/Publications/publications.htm

If you do not have access to the internet, paper copies can be obtained by telephoning the tribunal office dealing with the claim

Signed *D Smith*

D SMITH

For the Tribunal Office

Guildshire ET

Dated: 28 June 2021

cc   Acas

RESPONSE TO AN EMPLOYMENT TRIBUNAL CLAIM

In the claim of:

Mr J Gold

-v-

Car Parking PLC

Case Number: 123456/2021
(please quote this in all correspondence)

This requires your immediate attention. If you want to resist the claim made against you, you must use the prescribed response form. Your completed form must reach the tribunal office within 28 days of the date of the attached Notice. If the form does not reach us by 26/07/2021 you will not be able to take part in the proceedings and a default judgment may be entered against you.

Please read the guidance notes and the notes on this page carefully **before** filling in this form.

By law, you **must** provide the information marked with ⋆ and, if it is relevant, the information marked with • (see guidance on Pre-acceptance procedure).

Please make sure that all the information you give is as accurate as possible.

Where there are tick boxes, please tick the one that applies.

If you fax the form, do not send a copy in the post.

You must return the full form, including this page, to the tribunal office.

ET3

Employment Tribunal

Response form

Case number	

You must complete all questions marked with an '*'

1 Claimant's name

1.1   Claimant's name   James Gold

2 Respondent's details

2.1*   Name of individual, company or organisation   Car Parking PLC

2.2   Name of contact   Mrs J Price

2.3*   Address

     Number or name   The Business Centre

     Street

     Town/City

     County   Guildshire

     Postcode   G U 1 2 8 Q Y

     DX number (If known)

2.4   Phone number
Where we can contact you during the day   01234 567789

     Mobile number (If different)

2.5   How would you prefer us to contact you?
(Please tick only one box)   [✓] Email   [ ] Post   [ ] Fax   Whatever your preference please note that some documents cannot be sent electronically

2.6   Email address   j.price@carparkingplc.co.uk

     Fax number

2.7   Would you be able to take part in a hearing by video?
(Requires internet access).   [ ] Yes   [✓] No   Further details on video hearings can be found on the following link https://www.gov.uk/guidance/hmcts-telephone-and-video-hearings-during-coronavirus-outbreak

2.8   How many people does this organisation employ in Great Britain?   1500

2.9   Does this organisation have more than one site in Great Britain?   [✓] Yes   [ ] No

2.10   If Yes, how many people are employed at the place where the claimant worked?   8

3 Acas Early Conciliation details

3.1 Do you agree with the details given by the claimant about early conciliation with Acas?   ☑ Yes   ☐ No

If No, please explain why, for example, has the claimant given the correct Acas early conciliation certificate number or do you disagree that the claimant is exempt from early conciliation, if so why?

4 Employment details

4.1 Are the dates of employment given by the claimant correct?   ☑ Yes   ☐ No

If Yes, please **go to question 4.2**

If No, please give the dates and say why you disagree with the dates given by the claimant

When their employment started   09-11-2018

When their employment ended or will end   30-04-2021

I disagree with the dates for the following reasons

4.2 Is their employment continuing?   ☐ Yes   ☑ No

4.3 Is the claimant's description of their job or job title correct?   ☑ Yes   ☐ No

If Yes, please **go to Section 5**

If No, please give the details you believe to be correct

5   Earnings and benefits

5.1   Are the claimant's hours of work correct?   ☑ Yes   ☐ No

If No, please enter the details you
believe to be correct.   [   ] hours each week

5.2   Are the earnings details given by the
claimant correct?   ☑ Yes   ☐ No

If Yes, please **go to question 5.3**

If No, please give the details you believe to
be correct below

Pay before tax   £ [   ]   ☐ Weekly   ☐ Monthly
(Incl. overtime, commission, bonuses etc.)

Normal take-home pay   £ [   ]   ☐ Weekly   ☐ Monthly
(Incl. overtime, commission, bonuses etc.)

5.3   Is the information given by the claimant
correct about being paid for, or working a   ☑ Yes   ☐ No
period of notice?

If Yes, please **go to question 5.4**

If No, please give the details you believe to
be correct below. If you gave them no
notice or didn't pay them instead of letting
them work their notice, please explain what
happened and why.

5.4   Are the details about pension and other
benefits e.g. company car, medical   ☑ Yes   ☐ No
insurance, etc. given by the claimant correct?

If Yes, please **go to Section 6**

If No, please give the details you believe to
be correct.

6 Response

6.1* Do you defend the claim?   ☑ Yes   ☐ No

If No, please **go to Section 7**

If Yes, please set out the facts which you rely on to defend the claim.
(See Guidance - If needed, please use the blank sheet at the end of this form.)

The respondent is the UK's leading provider of 'off-street' parking services. It has approximately 1,500 employees. The claimant worked as a Team Leader at its car parks in Guildshire, where about 8 people work. The Claimant was employed from 9th November 2018 until 30th April 2021, when he was dismissed by reason of redundancy. The Claimant's claims are denied in their entirety.

On 16th February, the Claimant and his colleagues were invited to a meeting on 21st February about proposed changes to the workplace. The Respondent operated what was known as the 'First Contract' at 3 railway stations. There were three Team Leaders, including the Claimant. In order to increase focus and accountability and to reduce the overhead cost, the business proposed to reduce the Team Leaders to two, who would be expected to cover the three stations. The three Team Leaders were told of the proposal and were informed that they were at risk of redundancy and would be consulted severally.

Martin Smith, the Contract Manager, and Jack Tawse, from the Human Resources department, conducted the first consultation with the Claimant on 23rd February. The restructuring proposed was discussed, along with the process of consultation and selection. The Claimant was told that a process of selection would determine which one of the three Team Leaders would be at risk of redundancy. The Claimant had no question or comment.

A second consultative meeting took place with the Claimant on 7th March. The Claimant was asked whether he had any questions or comments. He did not. He was given estimates of the payments that he would receive if he were made redundant. He was told about the internal vacancies. The Claimant had no questions outstanding.

A third meeting took place on 22nd March. The Claimant again had no comments or questions.

So, on 22nd March, Martin Smith undertook to score the Claimant and his two colleagues against the following criteria:
Skills for the current position/job:
   Performance; Skills for other positions/jobs with Car Parks PLC; Length of service; Disciplinary record.
   They were rated as follows:
   Not acceptable/incomplete 1; Acceptable 2; Good 4; Exceptional 5.
   The Claimant's colleagues scored 18 and 24.
   Unfortunately the Claimant's experience was at one of the three sites only. The other two Team Leaders had experience at the other sites.

At the next consultative meeting on 25th March the Claimant was told that, because he had recorded the lowest score, he was at risk of redundancy. He was served with the notice that his employment would be terminated on 30th April, unless alternative employment could be found. The Claimant was sent the company's weekly bulletin of internal vacancies and asked to indicate any that were of interest. This was confirmed to the Claimant in writing, including the Claimant's right of appeal, on 25th March.

The Claimant was off sick from 1st April.

The Claimant appealed by letters dated 5th April and 11th April. He said that:
   1 he had shown unquestionable loyalty
   2 he carried out all instructions, often going beyond what was asked of him
   3 he had built a strong team in the site where he worked
   4 he had had to query why a number of his staff were not receiving their expenses, some of which were outstanding
   5 he had supported the staff team at night and at weekends when proper cover could not be found
   6 he had been working 'on-call' without receiving any payment
   7 he had not been shown the scoring process
   8 he thought that there would be more work not less, so could not understand the reduction in the staff.

Alan Savage, the Head of Operations, conducted the appeal hearing on 20th April. Jack Tawse was present. The Claimant confirmed that he was satisfied with the process, but his main concern was not having received details of what he scored. These were given to him.

See continuation sheet

7　Employer's Contract Claim

7.1　Only available in limited circumstances where the claimant has made a contract claim. (See Guidance)

7.2　If you wish to make an Employer's Contract Claim in response to
the claimant's claim, please tick this box and complete question 7.3　☐

7.3　Please set out the background and details of your claim below, which should include all important dates
(see Guidance for more information on what details should be included)

8 Your representative

If someone has agreed to represent you, please fill in the following. We will in future only contact your representative and not you.

8.1 Name of representative

V Alavy

8.2 Name of organisation

Swallows & Co LLP

8.3 Address

Number or name   12

Street   High Street

Town/City

County   Guildshire

Postcode   G U 1 2 1 A B

8.4 DX number (If known)

8.5 Phone number

01999 234567

8.6 Mobile phone

8.7 Their reference for correspondence

8.8 How would you prefer us to communicate with them? (Please tick only one box)   ☑ Email   ☐ Post   ☐ Fax

8.9 Email address

v.alavy@swallows.co.uk

8.10 Fax number

9 Disability

9.1 Do you have a disability?   ☐ Yes   ☑ No

If Yes, it would help us if you could say what this disability is and tell us what assistance, if any, you will need as the claim progresses through the system, including for any hearings that maybe held at tribunal premises.

Please re-read the form and check you have entered all the relevant information. Once you are satisfied, please tick this box. ☑

Employment Tribunals check list and cover sheet

Please check the following:

1. Read the form to make sure the information given is correct and truthful, and that you have not left out any information which you feel may be relevant to you or your client.

2. Do not attach a covering letter to your form. If you have any further relevant information please enter it in the 'Additional Information' space provided in the form.

3. Send the completed form to the relevant office address.

4. Keep a copy of your form posted to us.

Once your response has been received, you should receive confirmation from the office dealing with the claim within five working days. If you have not heard from them within five days, please contact that office directly. If the deadline for submitting the response is closer than five days you should check that it has been received before the time limit expires.

You have opted to print and post your form. We would like to remind you that forms submitted on-line are processed much faster than ones posted to us. If you want to submit your response online please go to www.gov.uk/being-taken-to-employment-tribunal-by-employee.

A list of our office's contact details can be found at the hearing centre page of our website at – www.gov.uk/guidance/employment-tribunal-offices-and-venues; if you are still unsure about which office to contact please call our Customer Contact Centre - see details below

General Data Protection Regulations

The Ministry of Justice and HM Courts and Tribunals Service processes personal information about you in the context of tribunal proceedings.

For details of the standards we follow when processing your data, please visit the following address https://www.gov.uk/government/organisations/hm-courts-and-tribunals-service/about/personal-information-charter.

To receive a paper copy of this privacy notice, please call our Customer Contact Centre - see details below

Please note: a copy of the claim form or response and other tribunal related correspondence may be copied to the other party and Acas for the purpose of tribunal proceedings or to reach settlement of the claim.

Customer Contact Centre

England and Wales: 0300 123 1024
Welsh speakers only: 0300 303 5176
Scotland: 0300 790 6234

Textphone: 18001 0300 123 1024 (England and Wales)
Textphone: 18001 0300 790 6234 (Scotland)

(Mon - Fri, 9am -5pm), they can also provide general procedural information about the Employment Tribunals.

Continuation sheet

On appeal, the dismissal was upheld. Unfortunately, no alternative employment acceptable to the Claimant could be found. Before the employment tribunal the Respondent will argue:
  – that was a genuine reason for the redundancy
  – that the selection process was fair
  – that the dismissal of the Claimant by reason of redundancy was fair and reasonable in all the circumstances
  – that, contrary to his assertion, the Claimant has not been 'replaced'.

EMPLOYMENT TRIBUNALS

Case No. 123456/2021

Mr J Gold	Claimant
v	
Car Parking PLC	Respondent

ORDER FOR DIRECTIONS

An Employment Judge has directed that:

1 This case will be given a one day hearing.

1.1 The parties are required to prepare and present their cases to enable the Tribunal to deal with all the issues, and remedy if applicable, in that time.

1.2 You **must** inform the Tribunal **immediately** if you believe the hearing date, time or length is not appropriate and, if so, give detailed reasons why.

2 No later than **10 September 2021** the Claimant **must** send a **Schedule of Loss** to the Respondent and the Tribunal.

3 No later than **24 September 2021** each party **must** send to each other party a **copy of any document** it has relevant to the claims in the proceedings.

4 The parties **must** agree **a bundle** of **documents** for the tribunal hearing. The [First] Respondent **must** ensure that **six copies of the bundle** are available at the tribunal hearing.

5 **No documents or copy correspondence should be sent to the Tribunal before the hearing date unless a party is required to do so.**

6 Each party must prepare **six copies of a written witness statement** for each person who is to give evidence at the hearing. This includes the Claimant and any personal Respondent. The statements will normally be read aloud at the hearing and the person will then be questioned about the contents.

7 The statement shall contain **all** of that person's evidence. No person can give evidence without a statement unless the Tribunal agrees.

8 **Not later than 28 days before the hearing** there shall be simultaneous exchange of witness statements by each party providing to each other party one copy of each witness statement.

GUIDANCE ON THE ABOVE ORDERS IS GIVEN BELOW

GUIDANCE

Schedule of Loss

1   A Schedule of Loss **must** set out the money you want as compensation for each part of your claim and the way it has been calculated. You may find it helpful to use a spreadsheet program.

Documents

2   'Documents' includes letters, notes, emails, memos, diary entries, audio or visual recordings, text messages and any other legible records.

3   If extensive hand-written document/s are being relied on a typescript **must** be provided by the party relying on the document/s.

4   If a recording is being relied on a transcript **must** be prepared by the party relying on it. That typescript **must** be included in the bundle and sent to any other party, together with a copy of the recording.

Bundles of Documents

5   The bundle **must** contain a copy of any relevant document any party intends to use at the Tribunal hearing. Two-sided copying is encouraged.

6   The parties **must** agree on the inclusion of only relevant extracts of lengthy documents. A full copy of such a document should be brought to the Hearing.

7   All the documents **must** be in date order, with the oldest at the front.

8   Each page **must** be numbered.

9   The bundle **must** have an index showing the date, description and page number of each document.

10   The bundle **must** be held together so it opens flat.

11   Witness statements **must not** be included in a bundle.

Witness Statements

12   Each witness statement (including the claimant's) **must**:

12.1   have page numbers, be typed single-sided with double line spacing with at least 2.5cm page margins;

12.2   use a 'standard' (e.g. Arial, Times New Roman or similar) size 12 font;

12.3   contain **all** the evidence of the witness;

12.4   be laid out in short consecutively **numbered** paragraphs;

12.5   set out **in chronological order,** with dates, the facts which the witness can state;

12.6   not contain matters irrelevant to the issues;

12.7   refer **by page number in the bundle of documents** to any document mentioned in the statement;

12.8   be signed and dated;

12.9   not be contained in a bundle.

Case No. 123456/2021

NOTES

1   Failure to comply with an Order for DISCLOSURE/INSPECTION may result on summary conviction in a fine of up to £1,000 being imposed upon a person in default under section 7(4) of the Employment Tribunals Act 1996.

2   If a person does not comply with Orders made under the Employment Tribunals Rules of Procedure 2013, rule 8 of the Employment Tribunals (Levy Appeals) Rules of Procedure or rule 7 of the Employment Tribunals (Health and Safety – Appeals against Improvement and Prohibition Notices) Rules of Procedure an Employment Judge or Tribunal may:

2.1   make an order in respect of costs or preparation time (if applicable) under rules 74 to 84; or

2.2   at a Preliminary Hearing or a Final Hearing make an order to strike out the whole or part of the claim or, as the case may be, the response and, where appropriate, order that a respondent be debarred from responding to the claim altogether.

3   The Tribunal may also make a further Order (an 'Unless Order') providing that unless it is complied with, the claim or, as the case may be, the response shall be struck out on the date of non-compliance without further consideration of the proceedings under rule 38.

4   An Order may be varied or revoked upon application by a person affected by the Order or by an Employment Judge on his own initiative.

Dated: 18 August 2021

Employment Judge

ORDER SENT TO THE PARTIES ON

.......19 *August 2021*........

....

FOR THE TRIBUNAL OFFICE

[Guildshire Employment Tribunal]

To: Mr Fred Mclean
Collaws Solicitors LLP
20 The Street, Guildshire, GU12

V Alavy
Swallows & Co LLP
12 High Street, Guildshire GU12

Cc: Acas

EMPLOYMENT TRIBUNALS

To: Mr Fred Mclean
     Collaws Solicitors LLP
     20 The Street, Guildshire, GU12

     V Alavy
     Swallows & Co LLP
     12 High Street, Guildshire GU12

Case Number: 123456/2021

Mr J Gold	**Claimant**
v	
Car Parking PLC	**Respondent**

NOTICE OF HEARING
Employment Tribunals Rules of Procedure 2013

The claim will be heard by an Employment Tribunal at **Guildshire House, Guildshire**, on **29 October 2021** at **10:00 am** or as soon thereafter on that day as the Tribunal can hear it. The Tribunal may transfer your case at short notice to be heard at another hearing centre within the region.

The Hearing has been allocated **1 day** including remedy, if appropriate. If you think that is not long enough, you must give your reasons, in writing, and your time estimate within 14 days of this Notice.

Unless there are exceptional circumstances, no application for a postponement will be granted. Any such application must be in writing. The application should include any dates agreed for re-listing the case or should advise the Tribunal of your unavailable dates within two months of the original Hearing.

You may submit written representations for consideration at the hearing. If so, they must be sent to the tribunal and to all other parties not less than 7 days before the hearing. You will have the chance to put forward oral arguments in any case.

It is your responsibility to make sure that your witnesses come to the Hearing.

You must comply with any Case Management Order issued in relation to this case and refer to the guidance in the booklet 'The hearing'.

A copy of the booklet 'The hearing' and expenses leaflet can be found on our website at www.employmenttribunals.gov.uk/Publications/publications.htm

A location map for the office can be found at www.employmenttribunals.gov.uk/HearingCentres/hearingCentres.htm

If you do not have access to the Internet, paper copies can be obtained by telephoning the tribunal office dealing with the claim.

To   Mr Fred Mclean
      Collaws Solicitors LLP
      20 The Street, Guildshire, GU12

and

      V Alavy
      Swallows & Co LLP
      12 High Street, Guildshire GU12   Signed R Drummond
                                             For the Secretary of Employment Tribunals

      Dated: 20 August 2021

cc   Acas

Mr J Gold v Car Parking PLC

Case number: 123456/2021

SCHEDULE OF DOCUMENTS

Page	Description	Number of sheets
	Tribunal Papers	
1–11	Claim	11
12–18	Response	7
19–21	Order for Directions	3
22–23	Notice of Hearing	2
	Documents	
24–26	Offer letter dated 6th November 2018	3
27	Letter to the Claimant dated 16th February 2021	1
28	Announcement	1
29	Letter to the Claimant dated 21st February	1
30–33	Notes of first meeting dated 23rd February	4
34	Letter to the Claimant dated 25th February	1
35	Notes of second meeting dated 7th March	1
36	Letter to the Claimant dated 17th March	1
37	Notes of third meeting dated 22nd March	1
38–39	Blank criteria for selection	2
40–42	Criteria for selection – the Claimant	3
43–46	Criteria for selection – others	4
47	Letter to the Claimant dated 23rd March	1
48	Letter to the Claimant dated 25th March	1
49	Letter to the Claimant dated 25th March	1
50–51	Fit note dated 1st April	2
52	Letter from the Claimant dated 5th April	1
53	Letter to the Claimant dated 6th April	1
54	Letter from the Claimant dated 11th April	1
55	Letter to the Claimant dated 15th April	1
56–57	Fit note dated 18th April	2
58 – 61	Letter to the Claimant dated 20th April	4
62–64	Document headed 'Monday to Friday 17.00–08,00 (if no team leader)'	3
	Remedy	
65	Schedule of loss	1
66–94	Evidence of job searching	29
95–112	Payslips	18

Guildshire Employment Tribunal

Case Number 123456/2021

Mr John Gold (Claimant)

v

Car Parking PLC (Respondent)

CLAIMANT'S WITNESS STATEMENT

1. Prior to commencing employment with the respondent, I was in the army for 10 years. I was employed for 8 years of this in the transport section. I joined Car Parking PLC in March 2016 on the network rail contract; that contract covered 4 mainline stations and I was employed as a team leader managing 17 staff. I was transferred under the TUPE rules to a different employer in 2017. I remained in this role until I was made redundant in July 2018. This information is relevant because it shows I had previous service with the company with more responsibility and it also shows a degree of management experience and flexibility. I had 4 years experience managing staff in car parks.

2. I started working for the respondents as a team leader at the Guildshire Car Park. Guildshire is an International Station and as such the role and nature of the duties differed to that of the normal shopping type car park. There are security issues because of customs and immigration, there are terrorist issues and there is liaison with lots of other agencies. I commenced my employment in November 2018. I refer to my contractual offer letter (p 24–26). This is not accurate. I received this document having already started work.

3. The machinery and equipment differed, it was antiquated and prone to breakdowns, the staff were expected to provide more information to customers utilising the service, the staff had to be on the concourse near the car park machines to assist passengers to pay for their parking, car-parking could also be for longer periods than normal. There are two external car parks with 300 plus spaces. Then there is a six floors multi-storey car park with about 1200 spaces. The car parks are linked to the station. The car park is manned 24 hours a day all year round. There are two staff on days and two on nights. Other staff are on rest days and holidays. I covered a forty plus hours shift covering as and when required. I was on call when I was not working.

4. I was in charge of 8 staff based at this large car park. The car park is very busy and I certainly considered that I was busy and that the role I performed did not cease or diminish.

5. The normal car parks in Guildshire operate not on a 24 hour basis and they are closed in the evenings, they are primarily for shopping centre users and 9 to 5 staff working in the city centre.

6. On 16th February I received a letter (p 27). The letter invited me to attend a briefing. At this briefing I would then refer to the announcement document and point out that in this document it states 'we will comply fully with all our obligations for consultation'. The document also says that they will answer **'any questions or challenges which you may have'**. On 21st February the 30 day consultation started. I now refer to the various notes regarding the meetings. You will note that I am not provided any great detail on why the business has decided to remove my post. I am aware that I am entering an assessment process. I now refer to the selection criteria for the surviving positions. I do not recall seeing the criteria at all during the process. Looking at the criteria now under skills for my current position I had been doing the same job since 2018 and in fact my previous role was more complex and I had more staff to manage. I also had extensive management experience and that can be seen throughout my level of experience. I would challenge anyone who suggests that I am not qualified to do the role I was employed to do.

7. In relation to performance I prided myself on running an efficient service, we had very few customer complaints, the staff worked well with me and I worked well with them. My attendance was excellent, my service although broken was linked and I think that my previous service should have been taken into account as it was not my fault I was transferred under the TUPE process. I had no disciplinary history.

8. I can only describe the consultation process as a tick box exercise. I had nothing to say because I did not know how I was being scored and who was in my pool for redundancy. I now refer you to the document that I only received after my appeal hearing had concluded and when I was advised that I had no further right of appeal. I refer the appeal outcome letter that clearly shows this was the case. It scores me under the skills section not acceptable. The criteria is training courses or from experience with CP PLC or elsewhere. I had a great deal of experience with CP PLC previously and elsewhere doing the identical job at a much higher level. I would say my score should have been exceptional. I would also point out that it lists my job as a customer service advisor; that really worries me I am a team leader not a customer service advisor. It is dated 22nd March yet it takes them until 20th April to send it to me. My last consultation meeting took place on the 22nd March. That is the date when apparently I was scored. The question is did the scoring take place before or after this meeting. Mr Smith provides no information to me at this meeting about my scores, he asks me no questions about my experience.

9. How can this process I say amount to meaningful consultation?

10. I was in a position where I was fighting in the dark. I had no idea what reason I was scored down on to cause me to be made redundant. I only obtained this information after my appeal. It was in my view that they were deliberately concealing my scores because they could not fairly justify them until I had had my appeal.

11. Since I now have had sight of the criteria and my scores and the apparent reasons for the scores I would make the following comments under each criteria head;

12. **Skills and Knowledge for the current Position/Job**

I had several years experience in the role. So I clearly had the relevant skills to do the job I was employed to do at Guildshire. The criteria refer to experience with CP PLC or elsewhere. The criteria does not ask about performance in my role; it clearly excluded that the score should be based on the actual skills and experience in the role. I have skills and other positions that would cover knowledge of other systems in other sites (p 40). I refer to the reasons (p 41–42). I am scored down because of a perceived lack of knowledge on the different parking system at used at the other two stations. Firstly that was not the site I was employed at. If the other team leaders attended my site they couldn't operate the machines on my site easily either. The criteria are irrelevant to the job I was employed at. Secondly on the occasions I attended at these sites I gained a working knowledge of this system and familiarised myself with it. I just hadn't been formally trained on it because it was not my normal site. To score me at one was frankly an insult with my level of experience and cannot be justified according to the criteria. A fairer score would have been 4.

13. **Performance**

The site ran efficiently. Problems were always solved at the site without the need for outside help. No examples are given of how I do not solve problems. This is simply rubbish and is not supported by proof. I am scored 2 and yet if you now look at my Comparators you will note that basically this is an assessment based purely on the perception of the person scoring. It is not based on any evidence. I was well respected, problems solved and I always met what was asked of me yet I only score 2? (p 43–46).

14. **Skills for other positions and jobs**

I had done the job previously. I had helped set up the systems at one of the other stations and I was familiar with all necessary skills apart from being formally trained on the different parking system. Again a score of 4 would have been appropriate.

15.   In my view the scorer didn't apply the criteria correctly or provide evidence to support his conclusions. The scores were in effect one person's preferences.

16.   In relation to length of service they could for example have considered my previous service which was only broken because of Tupe. You will note that I am scored below Good on all aspects and only scored exceptional when all those comparators are scored the same.

17.   In conclusion the consultation process was in my view a tick box process, I expected to be given at some point my scores and the criteria and an explanation with evidence of how my scores had been arrived at. This didn't happen. I had been through a similar process in the past and it had happened on that occasion. My second one to one dealt with internal vacancies, how to apply etc. At this point though I was at risk I didn't know I was selected so I had no real comments. My third one to one dealt with the criteria that was to be used but the scoring was not yet done. It was on 25th March I was told I was selected for redundancy and that I was dismissed. At no time during the consultation could I know of or discuss my actual scores. I was shocked that I had been selected and became ill with stress at work. I appealed verbally and confirmed it in writing. I also applied for the more junior role at Ashford. I was unsuccessful despite having managed staff which really was humiliating. I submitted details of my appeal. You will note that I specifically refer in my appeal to not being shown the scoring. At the time of preparing this statement the respondents have not produced the minutes of the appeal. In the appeal I clearly said that I had no opportunity to put my case and that I should have the scores. Despite making this clear in my appeal letter they still had not bothered to show me my scores. The whole process was unfair and predetermined. At the appeal I recall being told that the appeal would be adjourned so I could get my scores and then once I had them it would be reconvened so that I could put my points.

18.   That's not what happened I get instead a decision with my scores and the letter makes it clear the process is over (p 58).

19.   I consider that the process was completely unfair and that if a fair process had taken place I would not have been selected for redundancy. I consider that when I received my scores after the process concluded it showed me that this was simply Mr Smith taking a personal view on me and it had little or nothing to do with the evidence.

20.   In relation to steps of mitigation I would say as follows. I was sick with work related stress for approximately 3 weeks after my dismissal. I then signed on for Job Seekers Allowance. I looked at various job agencies but I could find little to apply for so I decided to seek work via the Job Centre via newspapers and through online web sites.

21.   As you will see I looked at a wage spectrum of jobs in the junior management level. I have also obtained job details via an ex forces agency. I have had five interviews to date. The first was in mid-April with a security firm. I was then interviewed on 14th July for the position of Department Manager at Parkhome Leisure.

22.   The third was an interview for a company called Petrol Services as an account manager. The fourth was for the position of Facilities Manager at Dupont College Guildshire on the 3rd of August. I have also recently been interviewed on 20th September for the position of assistant Project Manager. I have been unsuccessful in all my interviews.

23.   I have tried for jobs with salaries as low as £14,000.

24.   I refer to the various positions I have applied for and the documents in support of the same.

25.   In conclusion this Statement is true to the best of my knowledge and belief.

Signed *J Gold*

25 October 2021

Mr J Gold v Car Parking PLC

Case number: 123456/2021

STATEMENT OF EVIDENCE OF MARTIN SMITH

My name is Martin Smith

1. I am employed by the Respondent as Contract Manager. I have worked in that capacity since November 2015. For 6 months prior to this I was acting as Duty Manager to become familiar with the role. At the time of the Claimant's dismissal I was responsible for the car parks attached to the 'First Contract' three rail stations. I have experience of the CP PLC dismissal procedures and have received a one day training course on the company dismissal procedures.

2. The claimant worked as a Team Leader at the CP PLC car parks in Guildshire International. The Claimant was employed from 9th November 2018 until 30th April 2021, when he was dismissed by reason of redundancy. His contract appears at page 24 to 26 of the bundle. The Claimant was always located at Guildshire International apart from when he was required to cover a Team Leader at one of the other sites. I am aware that the Claimant had previously worked for the Respondent but this was before my time.

3. On 16th February, I invited the Claimant and his two colleagues to a meeting on 21st February about proposed changes to the workplace. My letter appears at page 27 of the bundle.

4. There were three Team Leaders, including the Claimant. In order to increase focus and accountability and to reduce the overhead cost, the business proposed to reduce the Team Leaders to two. The two would be expected to cover the three stations. The three Team Leaders were told of the proposal and were informed that they were at risk of redundancy and would be consulted individually. The announcement appears at page 28 of the bundle. I read this out to them when they were all together.

5. I, along with Jack Tawse, from the Human Resources department, conducted the first consultation with the Claimant on 23rd February. My letter inviting the Claimant to that meeting appears at page 29 of the bundle.

6. The restructuring proposed was discussed, along with the process of consultation and selection. The Claimant was told that a process of selection would determine which one of the three Team Leaders would be at risk of redundancy. He was told the selection would be by way of a desk top exercise. In front of me during the meeting was the template criteria for selection for redundancy which appears at page 38-39 of the bundle. I explained the criteria that were to be used. The Claimant had no question or comment and in fact said he had been through the process four times before. To me that meant he was familiar with the process which is why he did not ask any questions. The notes of the meeting appear at page 30-33 of the bundle. I followed the same format for the other two Team Leaders who were at risk.

7. A second consultative meeting took place with the Claimant on 7th March. My invitation to him appears at page 34 of the bundle. At this point I had not conducted the desk top selection exercise. But I went through with him other opportunities that were available in CP PLC. It followed the same process with all three of the Team leaders who were at risk. The Claimant was asked whether he had any questions or comments. He did not. He was given estimates of the payments that he would receive if he were made redundant. He was told about the internal vacancies. The Claimant had no questions outstanding. The notes of the meeting appear at page 35 of the bundle. At that meeting we did not discuss the selection process any further.

8. A third meeting took place on 22nd March. The invitation appears at page 36 of the bundle. The Claimant again had no comments or questions. The notes of the meeting are at page 37 of the bundle. I confirmed to him and the other two Team Leaders that I would now conduct the desk top selection exercise.

9. So, on 22nd March, I undertook to score the Claimant and his two colleagues against the following criteria:

Skills for the current position/job

Performance

Skills for other positions/jobs with NCP

Length of service

Disciplinary record

They were rated as follows:

Not acceptable/incomplete   1

Acceptable   2

Good   4

Exceptional   5

The Claimant scored 16.

The Claimant's colleagues scored 18 and 24.

Whilst I was scoring the candidates I was looking at suitability for the job going forward. There was to be two team leaders covering the three sites. One of the requirements would be to produce compliance and audit documentation which unfortunately the Claimant did not do to the extent of the other Team Leaders. Unfortunately the Claimant's primary experience was at Ashford International only. The other two Team Leaders had experience at the other sites. In addition the Claimant had only been in post since November 2018.

The scoring charts appear at pages 40–46 of the bundle.

10. Before I met with the three Team leaders again I sent the scoring assessment that I had done on each to Dave Hirst, Head of Operations to review what I had done. He confirmed to me that it was in order and I arranged to see the three Team Leaders to confirm the outcome.

11. At the next consultative meeting on 25th March I informed the Claimant that, because he had recorded the lowest score, he was at risk of redundancy. He was served with the notice that his employment would be terminated on 30th April, unless alternative employment could be found. The letter inviting the Claimant to the meeting appears at page 47 of the bundle and the letters confirming that he was at risk of redundancy and giving notice of redundancy appears at page 48–49 of the bundle. I would have sent him both letters dated 25th March. One confirms that the position of Team Leader that he held was redundant and the other was a personal letter to the Claimant giving him notice of redundancy including details of his right of appeal.

12. At the meeting I told the Claimant he had been selected for redundancy. I had the scoring sheet in front of me. But unfortunately the Claimant said a few words and stood up and walked out of the office. I was unable to provide him with any more details of the scoring as he had left. Jack Tawse from Human Resources was also present during the meeting.

13. That was the last I heard until Dave Hirst asked me for the details of the scoring process and the consultation process. I gave Dave the relevant paperwork.

14. I understand that the Claimant has said that he was unable to challenge the scores that I gave him in the desk top selection exercise. Firstly I would say that the Claimant did not contribute to any of the meetings that I had with him. Secondly I would say that the scores would not have changed. His length of service is a fact. And it was a fact that he did not have certain skills required for the job going forward. So, even if he had raised an objection his scores would have remained the same.

15. This statement is true to the best of my knowledge and belief.

Signed   M Smith

Dated 27.10.21

Mr J Gold v Car Parking PLC

Case number: 123456/2021

STATEMENT OF EVIDENCE OF JACK TAWSE

My name is Jack Tawse

1. I am employed by the Respondent as Human Resources Business Partner. I have worked in that capacity for just over 4 years. I started with respondent around 2014 when I joined as Human Resources Policy Manager. As Human Resources Business Partner I provide HR support and advice to the managers in the area.

2. The Respondent does not have a Redundancy Policy. The approach adopted will depend upon the particular circumstances. We have been involved in situations which have required collective consultation as well as individual consultation in the past.

3. I provided Human Resources advice and assistance throughout the process of consultation, selection, dismissal and appeal in relation to the Claimant.

4. I am providing this evidence as the Employment Tribunal refused to postpone the hearing when it learnt that Dave Hirst, the manager hearing the appeal, was unavailable. I was present during the appeal hearing to provide HR advice to Dave Hirst.

5. I was involved in the first consultation meeting with the Claimant. I do recall Martin Smith going through the agenda items outlined at page 30 of the bundle. I also recall Martin Smith specifically explaining the desk top selection exercise to the Claimant and the other two Team Leaders. At that stage we were seeking comments from the Team Leaders about the proposal itself and selection methodology proposed. The Claimant had no comment to make.

6. I was also involved in the meeting on 25th March with the Claimant. Martin Smith confirmed that the Claimant had been selected for redundancy. The purpose of the meeting was to explain the selection process. But when the Claimant was informed that he had been selected, he said something along the lines of that he felt it had been a foregone conclusion and he left without Martin being able to explain his rationale and his scoring.

7. On 1st April, after the Claimant received notification of his redundancy, he was off sick. The sick notes appear at pages 50–51 of the bundle.

8. The Claimant appealed to Dave Hirst by letter dated 5th April. It appears at page 52 of the bundle. In preparing for the Employment Tribunal proceedings I have discussed matters with Dave Hirst. After the Claimant appealed on 5th April, he had been in touch with Dave Hirst and arranged to meet him informally. The Claimant was asking whether there were any openings in CP PLC in the south area. At that time all that Dave was aware of was a Mobile Support Officer. The Claimant said he would think about it and in the meantime confirmed that his letter of appeal dated 5th April should be ripped up. Dave Hirst became aware that the Claimant was not interested in the vacancy and wanted to pursue his appeal.

9. We then received the letter dated 11th April. He said that:
    (a) he had shown unquestionable loyalty
    (b) he carried out all instructions, often going beyond what was asked of him
    (c) he had built a strong team in Ashford with limited support from Ebbsfleet
    (d) he had had to query why a number of his staff were not receiving their expenses, some of which were outstanding
    (e) he had supported the staff team at night and at weekends when proper cover could not be found
    (f) he had been working 'on-call' without receiving any payment
    (g) he had not been shown the scoring process
    (h) he thought that there would be more work not less, so could not understand the reduction in the staff.

The Claimant's letter appears at page 54 of the bundle.

10.   Dave Hirst, the Head of Operations, conducted the appeal hearing on 20th April. The invitation appears at page 55 of the bundle. I was present.

11.   I accept that there are no notes of the appeal hearing. It was a quick meeting. During the appeal the Claimant confirmed that he was satisfied with the process, but his main concern was not having received details of what he scored. These were shown to him at the appeal hearing. But he said nothing. He said he did not have a copy so it was agreed a copy would be sent to him by post, which is what was done.

12.   I recall however that Dave did take the opportunity to review the scores not least because he was surprised that it had been the Claimant who had had the lowest score. But when looking at the scores and the rationale that Martin Smith had given, Dave was satisfied that they had been correct.

13.   So, on appeal, the dismissal was upheld. Unfortunately, no alternative employment acceptable to the Claimant could be found.

14.   The outcome letter appears at page 58 of the bundle.

15.   Overall, I would say that the Claimant was a good employee and had the business not been in a position where it needed to reduce numbers he would have still been employed. It had not been a foregone conclusion. It had been a fair process and each Team Leader was assessed objectively and fairly. It was unfortunate that the Claimant's score was the lowest.

16.   This statement is true to the best of my knowledge and belief.

Signed J Tawse

Dated 27.10.21

EMPLOYMENT TRIBUNALS

Case No. 123456/2021

BETWEEN

Mr J Gold   **Claimant**

and

Car Parking PLC   **Respondent**

Held at Guildshire on	29 October 2021
Representation	**Claimant:** Mr T Robinson, Non practising Barrister
	Respondent: Ms R Bates, Counsel
Employment Judge	Smith-Jones (sitting alone)

JUDGMENT

It was the unanimous decision of the Tribunal that the Claimant was unfairly dismissed by the Respondent.

REASONS

Introduction

1. The Tribunal convened on 29 October 2021 to hear the Claimant's claim, as set out in his ET1/Claim Form submitted on 22 June 2021 of unfair dismissal, namely that the Respondent had followed a flawed procedure when selecting him for redundancy, particularly with regard to the consultation and selection process adopted. The Respondent in its ET3 denied this claim. It submitted that the Claimant was dismissed for a fair reason, namely redundancy, following a reorganisation in response to a need to reduce operational costs. Further, it said that it acted reasonably within the meaning of section 98(4) ERA 1996. In particular, the Respondent said it carried out a fair consultation and selection procedure and explored options for alternative employment. There was no dispute that the Claimant had been dismissed. It was indicated at the commencement of the hearing by Mr Robinson that it was accepted that the dismissal was by reason of redundancy.

Issues

2. The matter was listed for a full merits hearing. The principal issues for us to determine were whether, in accordance with the principles set out in *Polkey v AE Dayton Ltd* [1988] ICR 142, the Respondent had:
   (a) Warned and consulted with the Claimant
   (b) Adopted a fair basis for selection, fairly applied
   (c) Taken such steps as may be reasonable to avoid or minimise redundancy
3. If we found that there was an unfair dismissal, then it would be necessary to consider what remedy was appropriate.

Witnesses/evidence

4. The Claimant provided a witness statement, which was taken as read. The Respondent's representative had the opportunity to cross-examine him and the Tribunal was able to ask questions of its own. On behalf of the Respondent, witness statements were

provided on behalf of Mr Martin Smith (Contract Manager) and Mr Jack Tawse (Human Resources Business Partner (South) who provided Human Resources advice and assistance to the Respondent with regard to the consultation, selection, dismissal and appeal of the Claimant). Both witness statements were taken as read by the Tribunal. The Claimant's representative had the opportunity to cross-examine them and the Tribunal was able to ask questions of its own.

5. The Tribunal also had an agreed paginated bundle of documents. Where a number appears in brackets in this Judgment [ ] that is a reference to a page in this bundle. There was also a separate bundle of additional documents provided relating to the Claimant's job search and the issue of mitigation.

6. Both representatives made short oral submissions at the close of the evidence. Both parties' submissions are summarised below. A brief oral judgment on liability and some matters of principle on remedy was given at the end of the hearing. This document formally records that judgment and gives the reasons for it. The parties subsequently agreed the remedy between themselves.

Brief Summary of Facts

7. Mr Gold was employed as a Team Leader at the Respondent's car park at Guildshire, with effect from 9th November 2018. The Claimant was primarily based at Guildshire but was one of three Team Leaders covering three stations. He was required to cover at the other sites from time to time. A different (and older) technology system was employed by CP PLC to manage the car parking at Guildshire than was used at the other two sites.

8. In early 2021, in order to increase focus and accountability and to reduce over head costs, a decision was taken by the Respondent to reduce the Team Leaders from three to two. On 16th February 2021, Mr Smith invited the Claimant and his two colleagues to a meeting on 21st February to discuss proposed changes to the workplace [27]. At that meeting, they were told of this proposal, informed that they were at risk and would be consulted individually [28]. The same procedure was followed with regard to each of the three Team Leaders.

9. On 23rd February, a first consultation meeting took place with the Claimant, conducted by Mr Smith, accompanied by Mr Tawse [29, 30–33]. At this meeting, the restructuring was discussed, along with the proposed process for consultation and selection. The Claimant was told what the selection criteria were [38–39]. These included skills for the current job, performance skills for other jobs within CP PLC, length of service and disciplinary record. The Claimant made no comment. A second consultation meeting with the Claimant took place on 7th March [34, 35]. Possible vacancies were discussed and the Claimant was given estimates of any payments he might receive were he to be made redundant.

10. A third consultation meeting took place on 22nd March [36, 37]. Following this meeting, Mr Smith conducted a selection procedure using the selection criteria referred to above. He carried out this exercise on his own using his personal knowledge and expertise of the three Team Leaders along with information from their personnel files. The Claimant was scored with the lowest mark of the three Team Leaders. Mr Smith's evidence was that while he was conducting the scoring he was looking at suitability going forward. There was not a revised job description for the new posts. Under the reorganised structure, it would however be necessary for a Team Leader to have responsibility for all three sites, and knowledge of and ability to use the system in place at the other two sites was deemed by Mr Smith to be essential. On any analysis. the Claimant had less experience of this system than the other two team leaders and would require training to operate it. Mr Smith thought such training might take a week and approximately a month on the job to assimilate it. He did not discuss this with the Claimant. The Claimant was given lower marks than his colleagues on the skills for the current job, performance, and skills for other jobs criteria. He also had less continuous service than the other Team Leaders [40–46].

11.   A further meeting was held with the Claimant on 25th March [27]. He was informed that he had received the lowest score and was therefore at risk of redundancy. He was subsequently sent letters confirming he was at risk of redundancy [48] and was given notice including his right of appeal [49]. The Claimant stood up and left the meeting shortly after being told he had received the lowest score. Mr Smith said he was ready to give the Claimant his score but was unable to because the Claimant left the meeting.

12.   The Claimant was signed off sick shortly afterwards [80–81]. He appealed the decision to dismiss him by letter dated 5th April [52] and subsequently by letter dated 11 April [54]. In his letter of appeal, the Claimant said, amongst a number of points, that he had not been shown the scoring process.

13.   An appeal hearing was conducted by Mr Hirst on 20th April [55]. There are no notes of this meeting. It was not disputed that the meeting did not last long. The Claimant was told his scores, and these were later sent to him by post. No alternative employment was available. The Claimant rejected a lower grade job and there were no other suitable internal vacancies.

Claimant's Submissions

14.   Mr Robinson submitted that the Respondent had not followed a fair and objective selection procedure. He submitted there was an unfair assessment of the Claimant's capabilities, and also that the consultation exercise was inadequate because no opportunity was given to the Claimant to discuss or challenge his scores. On this basis, he said the Claimant's dismissal was unfair. He had no issue with the pool of the three team leaders but said that the criteria were not fairly applied to the Claimant. The three consultation meetings all predated the scoring exercise. The meeting after it had been completed was a fait accompli – the Claimant was told he was dismissed. There was no meaningful consultation after the decision to dismiss had been taken. The Claimant was not shown the notes of the selection at the appeal and there was no opportunity given to him to embark on any meaningful review at that stage. Further, the scoring adopted was very subjective and appeared to be based on penalising the Claimant for lacking future skills, although the first criteria was only about his current skills. Although the Claimant was offered an alternative job this was a demotion and he was not obliged to accept it in order to mitigate his position.

15.   Mr Hughes referred the Tribunal to *E-ZEC Medical Transport Services Ltd v Gregory* (UKEAT/ 0192/08) (a case where the EAT upheld a finding by an employment tribunal that a subjective marking system without prior consultation had led to a finding of unfair dismissal; and where a tribunal had found on the facts that a meeting which had been described as a consultation meeting was in essence a meeting to impart the scores and not to review the process); and *Budenberg Gauge Co Ltd v Griffiths* (UKEAT/43/93 and 162/ 93) (an appeal against a tribunal finding of unfairness centering around the use of selection criteria used in a redundancy exercise, where the Claimant was not shown her scores and was therefore unable to comment on them).

Respondent's Submissions

16.   Ms Bates on behalf of the Respondent submitted that the Claimant was dismissed for a fair reason relating to redundancy. There was an economic/operational need to reduce the number of Team leaders from 3 to 2. The job had not changed but the individuals doing it needed to be more diverse. It was about capability going forwards. There was a group notification, followed by three separate consultation meetings. The selection criteria were put to Mr Gold and he raised no objection to them. They were objective. Mr Smith was the best placed manager to carry out the selection process. Unfortunately because the Claimant lacked experience of the newer parking system and he had less service, he was scored lower. Lack of experience on that system was a fair criteria for him to use. He had given Mr Gold proper credit for his previous experience. Because Mr Gold walked out of the meeting telling him about this, there was no opportunity to give him his scores. The issue was revisited on appeal but the decision was upheld by Mr Hirst. She submitted that there was a fair and reasonable procedure and proper

consultation and full discussion about all relevant matters. There were no other suitable equivalent vacancies but the Claimant had been offered employment, albeit of a lower status, but he had not wanted to take it. Ms Bates referred the Tribunal to the cases of *Buchanon v Tilcon* [1983] IRLR 417 and *British Airways v Greene.*

The law

Unfair dismissal – reason

17. Where there is a dismissal, an employer has to prove, in the sense that the burden of proof is on it, that the reason for the dismissal falls within one of the potentially fair categories listed in section 98 ERA 1996. These include redundancy. Where there is a potentially fair reason for dismissal, a tribunal must decide whether the employer acted reasonably or unreasonably in treating that as a sufficient reason for dismissal.

18. So far as material, section 98 ERA 1996 provides:

      '98   (1)   In determining for the purposes of this Part whether the dismissal of an employee is fair or unfair, it is for the employer to show–

               (a)   the reason (or, if more than one, the principal reason) for the dismissal, and

               (b)   that it is either a reason failing within subsection (2) ...

            (2)   A reason falls within this subsection if it ...

               (c)   is that the employee is redundant, ...'

19. It was said by Cairns LJ in *Abernethy v Mott Hay & Anderson* [1974] IRLR 213, at 215 that,

      'A reason for the dismissal of an employee is a set of facts known to the employer, or it may be a set of beliefs held by him, which cause him to dismiss the employee.'

    It is not for the employment tribunal to consider the substance of the employer's reasons at the section 98(1)(b) stage (provided they are more than *'whimsical or capricious'* [*Harper v National Coal Board* [1998] IRLR 260 at para 8, referred to in *Scott v Richardson* at paragraph 17]). As Griffiths LJ observed in *Kent County Council v Gilham* [1985] ICR 233, if on the face of it the employer's reason could justify the dismissal, then it passes as a reason and the enquiry moves on to section 98(4) and the question of reasonableness.

20. The definition of redundancy is set out at section 139 ERA. This provides, as far as relevant:

      '(1)   For the purposes of this Act an employee who is dismissed shall be taken to be dismissed by reason of redundancy if the dismissal is wholly or mainly attributable to–

               (a)   the fact that his employer has ceased or intends to cease–

                        (i)   to carry on the business for the purposes of which the employee was employed by him, or

                        (ii)   to carry on that business in the place where the employee was so employed, or

               (b)   the fact that the requirements of that business–

                        (i)   for employees to carry out work of a particular kind, or

                        (ii)   for employees to carry out work of a particular kind in the place where the employee was employed by the employer,

               have ceased or diminished or are expected to cease or diminish'.

Unfair dismissal – reasonableness

21. Where there is a potentially fair reason for dismissal, a tribunal must then go on to decide whether the employer acted reasonably or unreasonably in treating that potentially fair reason as a sufficient reason for dismissal of the employee. The material statutory provisions are set out in section 98(4) Employment Rights Act 1996, which, so far as relevant, are as follows:

      '(4)   Where the employer has fulfilled the requirements of subsection (1), the determination of the question whether the dismissal is fair or unfair (having regard to the reason shown by the employer)–

(a)   depends on whether in the circumstances (including the size and administrative resources of the employer's undertaking) the employer acted reasonably or unreasonably in treating it as a sufficient reason for dismissing the employee, and

(b)   shall be determined in accordance with equity and the substantial merits of the case.'

22.   *Iceland Frozen Foods v Jones* [1982] IRLR 439 (as confirmed by the Court of Appeal in the joined cases of *HSBC (formerly Midland Bank) v Madden and Post Office v Foley* [2000] IRLR 827), sets out that 'a decision to dismiss must be within the band of reasonable responses which a reasonable employer might have adopted'. Tribunals should not, when considering these matters, look at what they would have done but should judge, on the basis of the range of reasonable responses test, what the employers actually did. The appropriate test is whether the dismissal of the Claimant lay within the range of conduct that a reasonable employer could have adopted. The EAT, in *Sheffield Health and Social Care NHS Foundation Trust v Crabtree* (UKEAT/0331/09), reminded Employment Tribunals that the burden of proof under s 98 (4) is neutral.

Unfair dismissal – procedural fairness in a redundancy situation

23.   In a redundancy case, the procedural circumstances identified in numerous cases including *Williams v Compair Maxam* [1982] IRLR 83, *Polkey v A E Dayton Services Ltd* [1987] IRLR 503 and as emphasised by the EAT in *Mugford v Midland Bank plc* [1997] IRLR 208, need to be considered. The principles which were put forward in *Williams* as generally accepted principles (where employees are represented by an independent union but have since been recognised as having more general application – see for example *Freud v Bentalls* [1982] IRLR 443 where it was held that the same principles would apply to a workplace where there was no trade union) were –

'1.   The employer will seek to give as much warning as possible of impending redundancies so as to enable the union and employees who may be affected to take early steps to inform themselves of the relevant facts, consider possible alternative solutions and, if necessary, find alternative employment in the undertaking or elsewhere.

2.   The employer will consult the union as to the best means by which the desired management result can be achieved fairly and with as little hardship to the employees as possible. In particular, the employer will seek to agree with the union the criteria to be applied in selecting the employees to be made redundant. When a selection has been made, the employer will consider with the union whether the selection has been made in accordance with those criteria.

3.   Whether or not an agreement as to the criteria to be adopted has been agreed with the union, the employer will seek to establish criteria for selection which so far as possible do not depend solely upon the opinion of the person making the selection but can be objectively checked against such things as attendance record, efficiency at the job, experience, or length of service.

4.   The employer will seek to ensure that the selection is made fairly in accordance with these criteria and will consider any representations the union may make as to such selection.

5.   The employer will seek to see whether instead of dismissing an employee he could offer him alternative employment.'

24.   In particular, the appropriate test of fairness under s 98(4) ERA 1996 in a redundancy situation was that an employer would be expected to (i) sufficiently warn and consult affected employees (unless the tribunal finds that the employer acted reasonably in taking the view that, in the exceptional circumstances of the case, consultation or warning would be 'utterly useless'); (ii) adopted a fair (objective) basis on which to select for redundancy; and (iii) take such steps as may be reasonable to avoid or minimise redundancy by redeployment within its own organisation. A failure to act in accordance with one of these does not necessarily mean a dismissal is unfair: the tribunal must consider this in the light of the circumstances known to the employer at the time he dismissed the employee. Issues of fairness and reasonableness need to be

judged by reference to the 'range of reasonable responses' test (see *Beddell v West Ferry Printers* [2000] ICR 1263).

25. <u>Warning and consultation</u>. <u>Consultation</u> should be 'genuine and meaningful'. Case law has established that, for redundancy dismissals to be fair, the employer must usually warn employees of the possibility of redundancy and then consult individually with them before reaching any conclusion regarding their dismissal. This rule is not absolute, and the courts have repeatedly stressed that a procedural failure does not inevitably lead to a finding of unfair dismissal. Rather, tribunals must focus on the overall picture when determining whether, in the particular case, the employer has acted reasonably in dismissing.

26. It is unclear on the authorities as to whether there are separate obligations of warning and consultation. In *Rowell v Hubbard Group Services Ltd* [1995] IRLR 195, the EAT said there were separate obligations to warn and consult. However, in *Coney Island Ltd v Eikouil* [2002] IRLR 174, the EAT, which was referred to *Rowell* as well as to *Compair Maxam* and *Polkey*, held that there is no separate duty to warn and that warning and consultation are part and parcel of one single process of consultation which begins with the employee being given notice that he is at risk. On either analysis, whether these are separate duties or combined, it is clear that a tribunal should look at whether, in all the circumstances, adequate and reasonable warning of impending redundancy has been given and should consider whether there has been fair and adequate consultation.

27. Consultation involves giving the person consulted a fair and proper opportunity to understand fully the matters about which he is being consulted, and to express their views on those subjects, with the consultor thereafter considering those views properly and genuinely. It would appear that employees themselves may sometimes have a responsibility to ensure the effectiveness of such consultation as does take place.

28. <u>Criteria for selection</u>. In *Drake International Systems Ltd v O'Hare* (UKEAT/0384103), the EAT emphasised that tribunals should not impose their own views as to the reasonableness of the selection criteria or the implementation of the criteria: the correct question was whether the selection was one that a reasonable employer acting reasonably could have made.

29. One distinction which case law has determined since *Williams* is that there is a distinction between an exercise which is selecting for redundancy from within an existing group – ie is looking solely at reducing numbers and an exercise which is seeking to achieve that by selecting for a new role. Where an employer has to decide which employees from a pool of existing employees are to be made redundant, the criteria will reflect a known job, performed by known employees over a period. Where, however, an employer has to appoint to new roles after a re-organisation, the employer's decision must of necessity be forward-looking. It is likely to centre upon an assessment of the ability of the individual to perform in the new role. In *Akzo Coatings v Thompson* (EAT/117/94) His Honour Judge Peter Clark said:

> 'There is, in our judgment, a world of difference between the way in which an employer approaches selection for dismissal in a redundancy pool where some will be retained and others dismissed. It is to that exercise which points 2-4 in the *Williams* guidelines are directed. These observations have no application when considering whether the employer has taken reasonable steps to look for alternative employment.'

30. In *Ball v Balfour Kilpatrick Ltd* (EAT/823/95) His Honour Judge Smith said that there is no rule of law that selection criteria must be exclusively objective. He went on to say:

> 'It is clear on the authority of *Akzo Coatings Plc v Thompson and Others* [1996] EAT (unreported) that the touchstone in such a situation is reasonableness rather than the application of either agreed selection criteria for redundancy or the application of objective criteria.'

31. In *Darlington Memorial Hospital NHS Trust v Edwards and Vincent* (EAT/678/95) His Honour Judge Hull said:

> 'If these are new posts with a different job description from anything which the various Applicants brought to them, then it seems to us that the employer is most certainly not under a

duty to carry out something very like the exercise which he has to carry out in deciding who to select for redundancy. On the contrary, if he is to be allowed to manage his business, he must select as he thinks right. If he tells the employees that they will be allowed to apply for new jobs, as was manifestly the case here, then of course he will be required to carry out the exercise in good faith. If they are to be allowed to apply their applications must be considered properly. If the criteria are different from the old jobs so be it, that was part of the original occasion of redundancy, it was as much reorganisation as redundancy, although redundancy was the result. But to say that they are the same process and that it must be based on similar principles is quite simply, in our view, wrong. It may be, we are not going to decide this, that the duty goes beyond faith, and it may be said that there is some sort of duty of care, but there it is, it is something which the employer has said he will do and he must do it. He must consider the applicants.'

32. Another difficult question for tribunals is to decide the extent to which they should examine the marking that has been applied in a selection exercise. The EAT and the courts have considered on a number of occasions the principles that pertain to the investigation of marking and scores in a redundancy exercise and have made clear that close scrutiny is inappropriate. What is in issue is the question of fairness of the selection procedure and marking should only be investigated where there are exceptional circumstances such as bias or obvious mistake: see *Eaton v King* [1995] IRLR 75 (subsequently upheld by the Court of Session). Lord Coulsfield observed at paragraph 11 that:

'every redundancy situation is one of distress for employees who are affected: and every redundancy situation is one in which hard decisions have to be made. It is, however, essential to remember that what is required of the employer is that he should act reasonably'

33. Further guidance is to be found in *British Aerospace plc v Green* [1995] IRLR 433:

'13. The whole tenor of the authorities to which I have already referred is to show, in both England and Scotland, the courts and tribunals (with substantial contribution from the lay membership of the latter) moving towards a clear recognition that if a graded assessment system is to achieve its purpose it must not be subjected to an over-minute analysis. That applies both at the stage when the system is being actually applied, and also at any later stage when its operation is being called into question before an industrial tribunal. To allow otherwise would involve a serious risk that the system itself would lose the respect with which it is at present regarded on both sides of industry, and that tribunal hearings would become hopelessly protracted.'

34. The judgment of Lord Johnston in relation to the issue of fair consultation (again in the context of a trade union consultation) in *John Brown Engineering v Brown Ltd* [1997] IRLR 90 is frequently cited. He started by referring to the judgment of Glidewell LJ in *R v British Coal Corporation, ex Parte Price and Others* [1994] IRLR 72:

'Fair consultation means:

(a) consultation when the proposals are still at a formative stage;

(b) adequate information on which to respond;

(c) adequate time in which to respond;

(d) conscientious consideration by an authority of a response to consultation.

Another way of putting the point more shortly is that fair consultation involves giving the body consulted a fair and proper opportunity to understand fully the matters about which it is being consulted, and to express its views on those subjects, with the consultor thereafter considering those views properly and genuinely.'

35. Case law suggests that one of the requirements for fair consultation in a redundancy exercise involves giving an employee sufficient information about and explanation for his scoring so he understands it and has a meaningful chance to comment on and challenge it. See, for example, the two cases referred to by Mr Hughes (*E-ZEC Medical Transport Services Ltd v Gregory* (UKEAT/0192/08) and *Budenberg Gauge Co Ltd v Griffiths* (UKEAT/43/93 and 162/93). This was emphasised recently by the Court of Appeal in *Pinewood Repro Limited t/a County Print (County Print) v Page* (EAT/0028/10). In that case, the employer agreed the selection criteria (attendance, quality, productivity, abilities, skills, experience, disciplinary record and flexibility) with the trade union, ensured that the

scoring was carried out by two senior managers and gave the employee a right to appeal his selection for redundancy, but did not explain to Mr Page why he had received lower scores than the two other people in the selection pool. Mr Page was provided with a copy of his scores; he queried why he had been marked down for 'abilities, skills and experience' given his level of qualifications and 27 years experience. He also queried why he had been marked down for flexibility as he was 'as flexible as the next man.' He was given no explanation as to how the scores had been arrived at, being told only that 'we believe that the scores given by the assessors are responsible and appropriate'. On appeal, he was told that the employers were 'satisfied that the scoring was factual and correct'. A tribunal found that Mr Page had been unfairly dismissed. The EAT upheld their decision and took the opportunity to review the relevant authorities and, whilst cautioning against an impermissible 'microscopic analysis' of scoring by tribunals, indicated that, particularly with subjective criteria, employees should have sufficient information to understand their scores and an opportunity to challenge them. In *Dabson v David Cover & Sons*, (EAT/0374/2011), the EAT emphasised that when assessing the fairness of selection for redundancy, the marks awarded in the selection exercise should only be investigated in exceptional circumstances such as bias or obvious mistake.

36. Alternative employment. Following the principle in *Polkey*, dismissal will not normally be regarded as a reasonable step on the employer's part unless he takes such steps as would be reasonable to avoid or minimise redundancy by way of redeployment within his organisation. In *Thomas & Betts Manufacturing Ltd v Harding* [1980] IRLR 255, the Court of Appeal ruled that an employer should do what he can so far as is reasonable to seek alternative work. This does not mean, as the EAT pointed out in *MDFI Ltd v Sussex* [1986] IRLR 126, that an employer is obliged <u>by law</u> to enquire about job opportunities elsewhere, and a failure will not necessarily render a dismissal unfair. It is all a question of what is reasonable in the context. It was established in *Williams* that as a matter of good industrial practice, managers should make reasonable efforts to look for alternative employment for employees before making them redundant. The NIRC in *Vokes Ltd v Bear* [1973] IRLR 353, said that an employer who had failed to investigate whether there were job vacancies within the group which might have been offered to an employee as an alternative to making him redundant, had behaved unfairly:

> 'The employer had not yet done that which in all fairness and reason he should do, namely to make the obvious attempt to see if Mr Bear could be placed somewhere else in this large group'.

37. None of the cases go so far as to amount to a proposition that there was a duty to find alternative employment (see *Brush Electrical Machines Ltd v Guest* (1976) EAT 382/76). The duty under s 98(4) is to take reasonable steps to try and find alternative employment.

Conclusions

38. The Claimant's claim was that he had been unfairly dismissed contrary to ss 94 and 98 of the Employment Rights Act 1996. There was no issue about the dismissal or about the requisite length of service to bring this claim. The Tribunal is satisfied that the exercise was genuinely implemented in an honest belief that it was the sensible way forward in order to achieve efficiencies and cost savings and was based on genuine commercial and operational reasons. I am satisfied that the definition of redundancy as per the three stage test identified particularly by the House of Lords in *Murray and Another v Foyle Meats Limited* [1999] IRLR 562 was met. The Claimant did not, before the Tribunal, dispute the existence of a potential redundancy situation.

39. I then moved on to look at fairness in three main areas, consultation, selection and the adequacy of searches with regard to alternatives to redundancy. I looked at the overall picture up to the date of termination to ascertain whether the employer has or has not acted reasonably in dismissing the employee on the grounds of redundancy.

40. With regard to the consultation, and subject to what I have to say below on the selection scoring, my view was that what the Respondent did here was reasonable. Overall, I was satisfied that the efforts the Respondent made did fall within the range of reasonable responses. There was, I felt, adequate warning, consultation about the impending

redundancy situation, why it had arisen and how the Respondent was intending to deal with it and the opportunity was given to the Claimant to discuss these issues. There were several meetings about the redundancy situation with the Claimant. What was done, which is what I have to look at as far as the law is concerned, was not so inadequate in my judgment as to fall outside the range of reasonable responses test. So I did not feel that the consultation process per se was such as to give rise to unfair dismissal.

41. I then moved on to consider the selection process. It is not for me, when I apply the range of reasonable responses test, to say what I would have done. I must look at what the Respondent actually did. In my view, the failure by the Respondent to give the Claimant his scores and to allow him an adequate opportunity to discuss them before indicating the finality of the decision that he was the one to be dismissed was unreasonable and fell outside the range of reasonable responses test. I bore in mind the Claimant's reaction to the meeting after the selection process had been concluded but I nonetheless felt that this meeting was not designed to be a meeting to discuss the scores as opposed to a meeting to tell the Claimant he had been selected and would be dismissed. This was borne out by the letters of 25th March [48, 49] – for example 'This desktop exercise has now been completed and unfortunately you have been selected for redundancy'. The Respondent could for example, have written to the Claimant after this meeting enclosing his scores and giving him an opportunity to discuss them before sending the letter of dismissal. I felt the lack of opportunity allowed to the Claimant to have a meaningful opportunity to contest his selection was not remedied by the appeal process, which still failed to allow the Claimant to engage in the process. Lack of consultation implies a loss of opportunity, not that the opportunity, if given, would have made necessarily any difference. I have not engaged in a remarking process but it was also in my judgment unfair that, in the circumstances in this case, Mr Smith applied criteria relating to what he regarded as future skills needed, when these were not on the face of it one of the criteria he was selecting under, so no-one was aware this was a relevant criteria and therefore did not have the opportunity to engage or challenge or discuss it; and further (as indicated from the analysis of the cases above), while there is nothing wrong in using future skills as a criteria where a new job is being proposed in this case, here there was no new job just the same job going forward. This could put another way be said to be a failure of the consultation process, in that consultation involves giving the person consulted a fair and proper opportunity to understand fully the matters about which he is being consulted, and to express their views on those subjects, with the consultor thereafter considering those views properly and genuinely. This did not happen in this case.

42. In my assessment, what was done here was I felt sufficiently inadequate as to fall outside the range of reasonable responses test.

43. On the third and final area, ie whether consideration was given to seeing if there was an alternative to making the Claimant redundant, on the facts, I was satisfied that the Claimant was provided with a list of vacancies and that neither he nor the Respondent identified any that might amount to suitable alternative employment opportunities within the Respondent. The opportunity offered was a clear demotion and could not be said to be a suitable alternative; I was satisfied that the vacancies mentioned by the Claimant were not available as at the date of his dismissal. I was satisfied that what was done was reasonable in the circumstances and fell within the range of reasonable responses test.

44. Having looked at all these matters in the round, as well individually, on balance I was satisfied that the Respondent's failings in the areas identified above were such as to give rise to an unfair dismissal. On that basis, my overall finding was that this was an unfair dismissal on the grounds of redundancy.

45. I went on to consider whether there should be any sort of Polkey deduction, on the basis of considering whether there was a chance that even had a fair procedure been followed, the Claimant would still have been dismissed. This is always to some extent going to be

a hypothetical exercise. However, I bore in mind that any unfairness that I have identified above with regard to the approach to and application of the selection criteria and discussion thereon may have resulted in different marks being applied to the others in the pool. Further, there were only three in the pool and one had to go. In addition, Mr Smith sent his scoring assessment to a third party, who was standing in for Dave Hirst, to review. He raised no concerns. Further, Mr Hirst had reviewed it and had identified no concerns such as to overturn it. On balance, I felt taking these matters into account there was still a chance that the Claimant might have been dismissed. I assessed that risk at 25%.

46. In the light of the findings indicated above, the parties subsequently reached an agreement between themselves as to the appropriate remedy. It was agreed that the proceedings would be stayed for a period of 14 days with liberty to restore if necessary. The Recoupment Regulations do not therefore arise for consideration.

Employment Judge Smith-Jones

Judgment and Reasons sent to the parties on 23 November 2021 and entered in the Register.

.... for the Tribunal Office

EMPLOYMENT TRIBUNALS

To: Mr Fred Mclean
       Collaws Solicitors LLP
       20 The Street, Guildshire, GU12

       V Alavy
       Swallows & Co LLP
       12 High Street, Guildshire GU12

Date: 23 November 2021

Case Number: 123456/2021

Mr J Gold	**Claimant**
v	
Car Parking PLC	**Respondent**

EMPLOYMENT TRIBUNAL JUDGMENT

A copy of the Employment Tribunal's judgment is enclosed. There is important information in the booklet 'The Judgment' which you should read. The booklet can be found on our website at www.employmenttribunals,gov.uk/Publications/publications.htm. If you do not have access to the internet, paper copies can be obtained by telephoning the tribunal office dealing with the claim.

The Judgment booklet explains that you may request the employment tribunal to review a judgment or a decision. It also explains the appeal process to the Employment Appeal Tribunal including the strict 42 day time limit. These processes are quite different, and you will need to decide whether to follow either or both. Both are **subject to strict time** limits. An application to *review* must be made within 14 days of the date the decision was sent to you. An application to *appeal* must generally be made within 42 days of the date the decision was sent to you; but there are exceptions: see the booklet.

The booklet also explains about asking for written reasons for the judgment (if they are not included with the judgment). These will almost always be necessary if you wish to appeal. You must apply for reasons (if not included with the judgment) within 14 days of the date on which the judgment was sent. If you do so, the 42 day time limit for appeal runs from when these reasons were sent to you. Otherwise time runs from the date the judgment was sent to you or your representative.

For further information, it is important that you read the Judgment booklet. You may find further information about the EAT at www.employmentappeals.gov.uk. An appeal form can be obtained from the Employment Appeal Tribunal at: Fleetbank House, 2–6 Salisbury Square, London EC4Y 8AE or in Scotland at 52 Melville Street, Edinburgh EH3 7HF.

Yours faithfully,

....

MISS R SMITH

For the Tribunal Office

INTEREST ON TRIBUNAL AWARDS

GUIDANCE NOTE

1. This guidance note should be read in conjunction with the booklet, which you received with your copy of the Tribunal's judgment.

2. The Employment Tribunals (Interest) Order 1990, 2013 Amendment provides for interest to be paid on employment tribunal awards (excluding discrimination or equal pay awards* or sums representing costs or expenses) if they remain wholly unpaid from the day after the relevant decision day.

3. Time runs from the date on which the Tribunal's judgment is recorded as having been sent to the parties and is known as 'the relevant decision day'. The date from which interest starts to accrue is the day immediately following the relevant decision day and is recorded on the Notice attached to the judgment. If you have received a judgment and subsequently request a reasons (see 'The Judgment' booklet) the date of the relevant judgment day will remain unchanged.

4. If the full amount is paid within 14 days of the relevant decision day, no interest is payable.

5. 'Interest' means simple interest accruing from day to day on such part of the sum of money awarded by the tribunal for the time being remaining unpaid. Interest does not accrue on deductions such as Tax and/or National Insurance Contributions that are to be paid to the appropriate authorities. Neither does interest accrue on any sums which the Secretary of State has claimed in a recoupment notice (see 'The Judgment' booklet).

6. Where the sum awarded is varied upon a review of the judgment by the Employment Tribunal or upon appeal to the Employment Appeal Tribunal or a higher appellate court, then interest will accrue in the same way (from 'the calculation day'), but on the award as varied by the higher court and not on the sum originally awarded by the Tribunal.

7. The Judgment booklet explains how employment tribunal awards are enforced. The interest element of an award is enforced in the same way.

---

* The Employment Tribunals (Interest on Awards in Discrimination Cases) Regulations 1996 prescribe the provisions for interest on awards made in discrimination and equal pay cases.

NOTICE

THE EMPLOYMENT TRIBUNALS (INTEREST) ORDER 1990

Tribunal case number(s): 123456/2021

Name of case(s): Mr J Gold v Car Parking PLC

The Employment Tribunals (Interest) Order 1990 (as amended) provides that sums of money payable as a result of a judgment of an Employment Tribunal (excluding discrimination or equal pay awards or sums representing costs or expenses), shall carry interest where the sum remains unpaid on the day after the day ('*the relevant decision day*') that the document containing the tribunal's judgment is recorded as having been sent to the parties, but that no interest shall be payable if the full amount of the award is paid within 14 days after the relevant decision day.

The rate of interest payable is that specified in section 17 of the Judgments Act 1838 on the relevant judgment day. This is known as 'the stipulated rate of interest' and the rate applicable in your case is set out below.

The following information in respect of this case is provided by the Secretary of the Tribunals in accordance with the requirements of Article 12 of the Order-

'the relevant decision day' is: 24 November 2021

'the stipulated rate of interest' is: 8%

....

MISS R SMITH

For the Tribunal Office

Appendix 3

Presidential Guidance – General Case Management

1. This Presidential Guidance was first issued in England & Wales on 13 March 2014 under the provisions of Rule 7 of the First Schedule to the Employment Tribunals (Constitution and Rules of Procedure) Regulation 2013 ("the Rules"). It is now amended and reissued on 22 January 2018 to take account of the decision of the UK Supreme Court in R *(on the application of UNISON) v Lord Chancellor* [2017] UKSC 51 so as to remove all relevant and related references to Employment Tribunal fees. The opportunity has also been taken to make other editorial amendments.

Note

2. Whilst the Employment Tribunals in England & Wales must have regard to such Presidential Guidance, they will not be bound by it and they have the discretion available to them as set out in the Rules as to how to apply the various case management provisions.

3. This Presidential Guidance in relation to General Case Management matters does not supersede or alter any other Presidential Guidance.

Background

4. The overriding objective set out in Rule 2 applies.

5. Rule 29 of the Rules permits a Tribunal to make Case Management Orders. The particular powers subsequently identified in the Rules do not restrict the general power contained in Rule 29.

6. Any Case Management Order may vary, suspend or set aside any earlier Case Management Order where that is necessary in the interests of justice. In particular, this may be necessary where a party affected by the earlier Order did not have a reasonable opportunity to make representations before it was made.

7. Rule 30 specifies details of how an application for a Case Management Order is made generally. Rules 31, 32, 34, 35, 36 and 37 deal with specific instances where Case Management Orders may be made.

8. Rule 38 deals specifically with the situation where Unless Orders can be made.

9. Rule 39 deals with the provision relating to Deposit Orders.

10. The Rules generally contain other Case Management provisions: for example, Rule 45 in relation to timetabling.

11. In applying the provisions of the Rules this Presidential Guidance attempts to set out the procedure, processes and considerations that will normally apply in the circumstances specified below.

Action by Parties

12. While any application for a Case Management Order can be made at the hearing or in advance of the hearing, it should ordinarily be made in writing to the Employment Tribunal office dealing with the case or at a Preliminary Hearing which is dealing with Case Management issues.

13. Any such application should be made as early as possible.

14. Where the hearing concerned has been fixed – especially with the agreement of the parties – that will be taken into account by the Employment Judge considering the application.

15. The application should state the reason why it is made. It should state why it is considered to be in accordance with the overriding objective to make the Case Management Order applied for. Where a party applies in writing, they should notify the other parties (or other representatives, if they have them) that any objections should be sent to the Tribunal as soon as possible.

16. All relevant documents should be provided with the application.

17. If the parties are in agreement, that should also be indicated in the application to the Tribunal.

Examples of case management

18. These are examples of case management situations:
    - amendment of claim and response
    - adding or removing parties
    - disclosure of documents
    - preparation of hearing bundles

- witnesses and witness orders
- preparation and exchange of witness statements
- disability issues
- timetabling
- remedies
- costs
- concluding a case without a hearing

Further Guidance Notes on these matters are appended to this Presidential Guidance.

19. Where the parties' circumstances or contact details have changed, such changes should be notified to the Employment Tribunal office and to the other parties immediately.

Action by the Employment Judge

20. Where the appropriate information has been supplied, an Employment Judge will deal with the matter as soon as practicable. If any information has not been supplied, an Employment Judge may request further relevant information, which will have the effect of delaying consideration of the application.

21. The decision of the Employment Judge will be notified to all parties as soon as practicable after the decision has been made

22. Orders are important. Non-compliance with them may lead to sanctions. Therefore, if a party is having difficulty in complying with such an Order, they should discuss it with the other parties and then apply to the Tribunal to vary the Order.

Agenda for Preliminary Hearing

23. In preparation for a Preliminary Hearing concerned with Case Management matters, the Tribunal will often send out an agenda to the parties in advance of such a Preliminary Hearing. The agenda should be completed in advance of that Preliminary Hearing and returned to the Tribunal. If possible it should be agreed by the parties. A copy of the current form of agenda can be found at: https://www.judiciary.gov.uk/publications/employment-rules-and-legislation-practice- directions/.

Alternative dispute resolution

24. There is separate Presidential Guidance in respect of alternative dispute resolution (ADR) and, in particular, judicial assessments and judicial mediation at: https://www.judiciary.gov.uk/publications/employment-rules-and-legislation-practice- directions/.

Brian Doyle

Judge Brian Doyle
President
22 January 2018

GUIDANCE NOTE 1:
AMENDMENT OF THE CLAIM AND RESPONSE INCLUDING ADDING AND REMOVING PARTIES

Amendment

1. Amendment means changing the terms of the claim or response. This note concentrates on amendments to the claim. The Employment Tribunal can allow amendments, but it will generally only do so after careful consideration and taking into account the views of the other parties. In some cases a hearing may be necessary to decide whether to allow an amendment.

2. Generally speaking, minor amendments cause no difficulties. Sometimes the amendment is to give more detail. There may have been a typographical error or a date may be incorrect. The Tribunal will normally grant leave to amend without further investigation in these circumstances.

3. More substantial amendments can cause problems. Regard must be had to all the circumstances, in particular any injustice or hardship which would result from the amendment or a refusal to make it.

If necessary, leave to amend can be made conditional on the payment of costs by the claimant if the other party has been put to expense as a result of a defect in the claim form.

4. In deciding whether to grant an application to amend, the Tribunal must carry out a careful balancing exercise of all of the relevant factors, having regard to the interests of justice and the relative hardship that will be caused to the parties by granting or refusing the amendment.

5. Relevant factors would include:

    5.1 *The amendment to be made.* Applications can vary from the correction of clerical and typing errors to the addition of facts, the addition or substitution of labels for facts already described, and the making of entirely new factual allegations which change the basis of the existing claim. The Tribunal must decide whether the amendment applied for is a minor matter or a substantial alteration, describing a new complaint.

    5.2 *Time limits.* If a new complaint or cause of action is intended by way of amendment, the Tribunal must consider whether that complaint is out of time and, if so, whether the time limit should be extended. Once the amendment has been allowed, and time taken into account, then that matter has been decided and can only be challenged on appeal. An application for leave to amend when there is a time issue should be dealt with at a preliminary hearing to address a preliminary issue. This allows all parties to attend, to make representations and possibly even to give evidence.

    5.3 *The timing and manner of the application.* An application can be made at any time, as can an amendment even after Judgment has been promulgated. Allowing an application is an exercise of a judicial discretion. A party will need to show why the application was not made earlier and why it is being made at that time. An example which may justify a late application is the discovery of new facts or information from disclosure of documents.

6. The Tribunal draws a distinction between amendments as follows:

    6.1 those that seek to add or to substitute a new claim arising out of the same facts as the original claim; and

    6.2 those that add a new claim entirely unconnected with the original claim.

7. In deciding whether the proposed amendment is within the scope of an existing claim or whether it constitutes an entirely new claim, the entirety of the claim form must be considered.

Re-labelling

8. Labelling is the term used for the type of claim in relation to a set of facts (for example, "unfair dismissal"). Usually, mislabelling does not prevent the re-labelled claim being introduced by amendment. Seeking to change the nature of the claim may seem significant, but very often all that is happening is a change of label. For instance, a claimant may describe his or her claim as for a redundancy payment when, in reality, he or she may be claiming that they were unfairly dismissed.

9. If the claim form includes facts from which such a claim can be identified, the Tribunal as a rule adopts a flexible approach and grants amendments that only change the nature of the remedy claimed. There is a fine distinction between raising a claim which is linked to an existing claim and raising a new claim for the first time. In the leading case, the claimant tried to introduce an automatically unfair dismissal claim on the specific ground of his trade union activity in addition to the ordinary unfair dismissal claim in his claim form. The appeal court refused the amendment because the facts originally described could not support the new claim. Furthermore, there would be a risk of hardship to the employer by increased costs if the claimant was allowed to proceed with this new claim.

10. While there may be a flexibility of approach to applications to re-label facts already set out, there are limits. Claimants must set out the specific acts complained of, as Tribunals are only able to adjudicate on specific complaints. A general complaint in the claim form will not suffice. Further, an employer is entitled to know the claim it has to meet.

Time Limits

11. The Tribunal will give careful consideration in the following contexts:

    11.1 The fact that the relevant time limit for presenting the new claim has expired will not exclude the discretion to allow the amendment. In one case, a Tribunal allowed the amendment of a claim form complaining of race discrimination to include a complaint of unfair dismissal. The appeal court upheld the Tribunal's decision, although the time limit for unfair dismissal had expired. The facts in the claim form were sufficient to found both complaints. The amendment would neither prejudice the respondent nor cause it any injustice.

11.2   It will not always be just to allow an amendment even where no new facts are pleaded. The Tribunal must balance the injustice and hardship of allowing the amendment against the injustice and hardship of refusing it. Where for instance a claimant fails to provide a clear statement of a proposed amendment when given the opportunity through case management orders to do so, an application at the hearing may be refused because of the hardship that would accrue to the respondent.

Seeking to add new ground of complaint

12.   The Tribunal looks for a link between the facts described in the claim form and the proposed amendment. If there is no such link, the claimant will be bringing an entirely new cause of action.

13.   In this case, the Tribunal **must consider** whether the new claim is in time.

14.   The Tribunal will take into account the tests for extending time limits:

14.1 the "just and equitable" formula in discrimination claims;

14.2   the "not reasonably practicable" formula in most other claims;

14.3 the specific time limits in redundancy claims;

14.4 the special time limits in equal pay claims.

Adding a new party

15.   The Tribunal may of its own initiative, or on the application of a party, or a person wishing to become a party, add any other person as a party by adding them or substituting them for another party. This can be done if it appears that there are issues between that person and any of the existing parties falling within the jurisdiction of the Tribunal and which it is in the interests of justice to have determined in the proceedings.

Adding or removing parties

16.   These are some of the circumstances which give rise to addition of parties:

16.1   Where the claimant does not know, possibly by reason of a business transfer situation, who is the correct employer to be made respondent to the claim.

16.2   Where individual respondents, other than the employer, are named in discrimination cases on the grounds that they have discriminated against the claimant and an award is sought against them.

16.3   Where the respondent is a club or an unincorporated association and it is necessary to join members of the governing body.

16.4   Where it is necessary in order to decide a claim which involves a challenge to a decision of the relevant Secretary of State. The Secretary of State is responsible by statute for certain sums of money in different insolvency situations. The Tribunal decides if a refusal to pay is correct, provided conditions are met in relation to timing.

17.   Asking to add a party is an application to amend the claim. The Tribunal will have to consider the type of amendment sought. The amendment may deal with a clerical error, add factual details to existing allegations, or add new labels to facts already set out in the claim. The amendment may, if allowed, make new factual allegations which change or add to an existing claim. The considerations set out above in relation to amendments generally apply to these applications.

18.   When you apply to add a party you should do so promptly. You should set out clearly in your application the name and address of the party you wish to add and why you say they are liable for something you have claimed. You should further explain when you knew of the need to add the party and what action you have taken since that date.

19.   The Tribunal may also remove any party apparently wrongly included. A party who has been added to the proceedings should apply promptly after the proceedings are served on them if they wish to be removed.

20.   A party can also be removed from the proceedings if the Claimant has settled with them or no longer wishes to proceed against them.

21.   The Tribunal may permit any person to participate in proceedings on such terms as may be specified in respect of any matter in which that person has a legitimate interest. This could involve where they will be liable for any remedy awarded, as well as other situations where the findings made may directly affect them.

GUIDANCE NOTE 2:
DISCLOSURE OF DOCUMENTS AND PREPARING HEARING BUNDLES

1. The Employment Tribunal often requires the parties to co-operate to prepare a set of documents for the hearing. Even if no formal order is made, the Tribunal prefers that documentary evidence is presented in one easily accessible set of documents (often known as "the hearing bundle") with everyone involved in the hearing having an identical copy.

Why have an agreed set of documents?

2. Early disclosure of documents helps the parties to see clearly what the issues are. It helps them to prepare their witness statements and their arguments. There is no point in withholding evidence until the hearing. This only causes delay and adds to the costs. It may put you at risk of having your case struck out.

3. Agreeing a set of documents means that all parties agree which documents are relevant and the Tribunal will need to see. It does not mean they agree with what the documents contain or mean.

4. It avoids problems at a hearing when a party produces a document which the other party has not seen before. This is unfair and may lead to the hearing being delayed or adjourned. This is costly to all concerned and may result in the offending party paying the costs of the adjournment.

5. An agreed set of documents – rather than each party bringing their own set of documents to the hearing – prevents uncertainty and delay at the hearing.

What is the disclosure of documents?

6. Disclosure is the process of showing the other party (or parties) all the documents you have which are *relevant* to the issues the Tribunal has to decide. Although it is a formal process, it is not a hostile process. It requires co-operation in order to ensure that the case is ready for hearing.

7. Relevant documents may include documents which record events in the employment history: for example, a letter of appointment, statement of particulars or contract of employment; notes of a significant meeting, such as a disciplinary interview; a resignation or dismissal letter; or material such as emails, text messages and social media content (Facebook, Twitter, Instagram, etc). The claimant may have documents to disclose which relate to looking for and finding alternative work.

8. Any relevant document in your possession (or which you have the power to obtain) which is or may be relevant to the issues must be disclosed. This includes documents which may harm your case as well as those which may help it. To conceal or withhold a relevant document is a serious matter.

9. A party is usually not required to disclose a copy of a "privileged" document: for example, something created in connection with the preparation of a party's Tribunal case (such as notes of interviews with witnesses); correspondence between a party and their lawyers; correspondence between parties marked "without prejudice"; or part of discussions initiated on a "without prejudice" basis with a view to settlement of the matters in issue; or records of exchanges with ACAS.

How and when does disclosure take place?

10. The process should start and be completed as soon as possible. A formal order for disclosure of documents usually states the latest date by which the process must be completed.

11. In most cases, the respondent (usually the employer) has most or all of the relevant documents. This often makes it sensible for the respondent to take the lead in disclosure. Each party prepares a list of all relevant documents they hold and sends it as soon as possible to the other party.

12. Sometimes the parties meet and inspect each other's documents. More commonly, they agree to exchange photocopies of their documents in the case, which should be "clean" copies (that is, unmarked by later notes or comments, unless those notes or comments are themselves evidence).

How is the hearing bundle produced?

13. The parties then co-operate to agree the documents to go in the hearing bundle. The hearing bundle should contain only the documents that are to be mentioned in witness statements or to be the subject of cross-examination at the hearing, and which are relevant to the issues in the proceedings. If there is a dispute about what documents to include, the disputed documents should be put in a separate section or folder, and this should be referred to the Tribunal at the start of the hearing.

14. One party then prepares the hearing bundles. This is often the respondent because it is more likely to have the necessary resources. Whoever is responsible for preparing the hearing bundles prepares the documents in a proper order (usually chronological), numbers each page (this is called

"pagination") and makes sufficient sets of photocopies, which are stapled together, tagged or put into a ring binder.

15. Each party should have at least 1 copy. The Tribunal will need 5 copies for a full Tribunal panel or 3 copies if the Employment Judge is to sit alone. That is 1 copy for the witness table, 1 for each member of the Tribunal and 1 to be shown to the public or media, where appropriate. The copies for the Tribunal must be brought to the hearing. They should not be sent to the Tribunal in advance, unless requested.

Are the documents confidential?

16. All documents and witness statements exchanged in the case are to be used *only* for the hearing. Unless the Tribunal orders otherwise, they must only be shown to a party and that party's adviser/representative or a witness (insofar as is necessary). The documents must not be used for any purpose other than the conduct of the case.

17. Because it is a public hearing, the Tribunal will enable persons (including the press and media) present at the hearing to view documents referred to in evidence before it (unless it orders otherwise).

GUIDANCE NOTE 3:

WITNESSES AND WITNESS STATEMENTS

Witnesses

1. The parties should consider who they need to give evidence in support of their case at the Employment Tribunal hearing.

2. As part of the Case Management of the proceedings, the Tribunal will need to know how many witnesses are to be called, so that the required length of the hearing can be properly allocated and, if necessary, timetabled. The identity of the witnesses and the relevance of their evidence to the issues will also often be important.

3. Rule 43 provides that where a witness is called to give oral evidence, any witness statement of that person shall stand as that witness's evidence in chief unless the Tribunal orders otherwise. Witnesses are required to give their oral evidence on oath or affirmation.

4. The Tribunal may exclude from the hearing any person who is to appear as a witness in the proceedings, until such time as that person gives evidence, if it considers it in the interests of justice to do so. This is not the usual practice of the Employment Tribunal in England & Wales.

Witness orders

5. The Tribunal may order any person in Great Britain to attend a hearing to give evidence, produce documents or produce information (Rule 32).

6. If a party believes that a person has relevant information or evidence to give, but that they might not attend the hearing voluntarily, that party can apply to the Tribunal for a witness order. A witness order requires the witness to attend the hearing. It can also be useful where the witness is willing to attend, but their employer will not release them to attend.

7. An application for a witness order may be made at a hearing or by an application in writing to the Tribunal. In order that the Tribunal can send the witness order to the witness in good time before the hearing, it is important to make any application as early as possible. A witness order might be refused if the attendance of the witness cannot be ensured in time.

8. The application will need to give the name and address of the witness; a summary of the evidence it is believed they will give (or a copy of their witness statement, if there is one); and an explanation as to why a witness order is necessary to secure their attendance.

9. Exceptionally, an application for a witness order does not have to be copied to the other parties, unless the Tribunal considers that it is in the interests of justice to do otherwise. If the Tribunal grants a witness order, the other parties will then be informed that a witness order has been made and who the witness is, unless there is a good reason not to do so.

Witness statements

10. The Tribunal often orders witness statements to be prepared and exchanged. Even if no formal order is made, the Tribunal generally prefers evidence to be presented by means of written statements. These are normally read in advance by the Tribunal so that they stand as the evidence in chief (that is,

the main evidence of the witness before questions are put in cross-examination) without being read out loud by the witness.

Why prepare witness statements?

11.   It helps to write down what you have to say in evidence. You often remember much more and feel more comfortable when giving evidence having done so.

12.   Early exchange of witness statements enables the parties to know the case they have to meet and what the issues are going to be. All the relevant evidence will come out at the hearing. There is nothing to gain (and much to lose) by withholding it until then.

13.   Preparation of witness statements helps the Tribunal to identify the issues and to ensure that the case is completed in the time allowed.

14.   A witness statement should be prepared for each witness who is to give evidence. This includes the claimant (and the respondent where he or she is an individual).

How should a witness statement be set out and what should it contain?

15.   It is easier for everyone if the statement is typewritten or word-processed (although a clear and legible handwritten statement is acceptable) with each page numbered.

16.   The witness statement should be in a logical order (ideally, chronological) and contain numbered paragraphs. It should cover all the issues in the case. It should set out fully what the witness has to tell the Tribunal about their involvement in the matter, usually in date order.

17.   The statement should be as full as possible because the Tribunal might not allow the witness to add to it, unless there are exceptional circumstances and the additional evidence is obviously relevant.

18.   When completed, it is good practice for the statement to be signed, particularly if the witness is unavailable to attend the hearing. The Employment Tribunal Rules of Procedure do not require a witness statement to contain a "statement of truth" (such as "This statement is true to the best of my knowledge and belief" or "I believe the facts in this statement to be true") at the end. There is no objection to a witness statement that does or does not contain such a statement of truth.

19.   A copy of any witness statements should be provided to the other party. You should bring 5 copies with you to the hearing if there is a full Tribunal panel and 3 copies if the Employment Judge is to sit alone. That is 1 copy for the witness table, 1 for each member of the Tribunal and 1 to be shown to the public and media, where appropriate.

20.   If you realise that your statement has left out something relevant when you receive the other party's statements, you should make a supplementary statement and send it immediately to the other party. You do not need to comment on or respond to every point in the other side's statements or repeat what you said originally.

How should a witness statement be exchanged?

21.   When the witness statements are ready, a copy should usually be sent to the other side, whether or not their statements have been received or are ready to be exchanged.

22.   Exchange of witness statements at the same time is the norm, but it is not always appropriate. In some cases, it makes sense for the claimant's witness statement to be sent first. The respondent will then know exactly what case has to be answered. This avoids irrelevant statements being taken from witnesses who are not needed. In other cases, however, it may make sense for the respondent's statements to be sent first. Any particular directions made by the Tribunal must be followed.

23.   Unless there is a different date fixed, the exchange of witness statements should be completed by no later than 2 weeks before the hearing.

Inspection of witness statements

24.   Rule 44 provides that any witness statement, which stands as evidence in chief, shall be available for inspection during the course of the hearing by members of the public (that includes the media) attending the hearing. That is, unless the Tribunal decides that all or any part of the statement is not to be admitted as evidence. In that case, the statement or that part of it shall not be available for inspection.

25.   There are exceptions to this rule where the Tribunal has made an order protecting the privacy of a witness or restricting the disclosure of documents (rule 50) or in national security proceedings (rule 94).

GUIDANCE NOTE 4:
DISABILITY

1. The terms "disabled", "disabled person" and "disability" are words in common use. In disability discrimination cases in Employment Tribunals these terms have a particular meaning set out in section 6 of the Equality Act 2010 (and Schedule 1 to that Act) and regulations made under those provisions.

2. Reference should be made to those statutory provisions and to those regulations, as well as to the statutory *Guidance on matters to be taken into account in determining questions relating to the definition of disability* (2011) issued by the Secretary of State. That *Guidance* is available at: https://www. equalityhumanrights.com/en/publication-download/equality-act-2010-guidance-matters-be-taken-account-determining-questions.

Evidence of disability

2. A claimant who relies upon the protected characteristic of disability may be able to provide much of the information required without medical reports. A claimant may be able to describe their impairment and its effects on their ability to carry out normal day to day activities.

3. Sometimes medical evidence may be required. For instance, where there is a dispute about whether the claimant has a particular disability or whether an impairment is under effective control by medication or treatment.

4. The question then to be answered is what effects the impairment would have if the medication was withdrawn. Once more, a claimant may be able to describe the effects themselves, but respondents frequently ask for some medical evidence in support.

5. Claimants must expect to have to agree to the disclosure of relevant medical records or occupational health records.

6. Few people would be happy to disclose all of their medical records or for disclosure to be given to too many people. Employment Judges are used to such difficulties. They will often limit the documents to be disclosed and the people to whom disclosure should be made. Disclosure is generally for use only in the proceedings and not for sharing with third parties.

7. Even after a claimant's description of their impairment and disclosure of relevant documents in support, respondents may dispute that the claimant is disabled. If that happens the intervention of an Employment Judge may be necessary.

8. The following possibilities might arise, although there might be others:

9. That the claimant has to agree to undergo medical examination by a doctor or specialist chosen and paid for by the respondent.

   9.1 That the claimant agrees to provide further medical evidence at their own expense.

   9.2 That the claimant and the respondent may agree to get a report jointly. That would involve sharing the decision as to who to appoint, the instructions to be given and the cost of any report. This may be the most effective course, but neither party

   9.3 may in the end be bound by the findings of the report, even if they agree to this course of action.

10. It can be expensive to obtain medical evidence. Limited financial assistance may be available. Whether it is granted is a matter which only a member of the administrative staff of Her Majesty's Courts & Tribunals Service can decide. Any application for such assistance should be made to the manager of the relevant Employment Tribunal office.

11. Care should be taken to decide whether a medical report is necessary at all. For instance, if a claimant has epilepsy which is well-controlled by medication, then medical evidence may be unnecessary for a Tribunal to consider what effect would follow if the medication was not taken.

12. Claimants must remember that they have the burden of proving that they are disabled. They may be satisfied that they can do this, perhaps with the assistance of the records of their General Practitioner, their medical consultant and their own evidence.

Reasonable adjustments to the Tribunal hearing or procedure

13. If the disability of a party, representative, witness or other person might affect their participation in the Tribunal hearing or procedure, an application should be made to the Tribunal as soon as possible so that the Tribunal can consider what reasonable adjustments might be made.

GUIDANCE NOTE 5:

TIMETABLING

1. The overriding objective in Rule 2 of the Employment Tribunals Rules of Procedure means that each case should have its fair share of available time, but no more. Otherwise other cases would be unjustly delayed. Each party must also have a fair share of the time allowed for the hearing of their case.

What is timetabling?

2. Each party has a duty to conduct the case so that wherever possible the Tribunal can complete the case within the time allowed. Failing to do that may mean a delay of many weeks before the case can return for further hearing. It also means that other cases waiting to be heard might be delayed.

3. To avoid the risk of this happening the Tribunal sometimes divides up the total time allowed for a hearing into smaller blocks of time to be allowed for each part of the hearing. This is called "timetabling". It is necessary in particularly long or complicated hearings or sometimes where a party has no experience of conducting hearings.

4. Timetabling is permitted by Rule 45. It provides that a Tribunal may impose limits on the time that a party may take in presenting evidence, questioning witnesses or making submissions. The Tribunal may then prevent the party from proceeding beyond any time so allotted.

How and when is timetabling done?

5. Employment Judges estimate the amount of time to be allowed for a hearing based on all the information they have when the hearing is listed. In straightforward cases that might be when the claim first comes in or when the response arrives. In complex cases it is often done at a preliminary hearing as part of case management.

6. For very short cases it is rare for a formal timetable to be issued. Nevertheless, even for a hearing of one day it might be helpful for the judge and the parties to agree at the beginning of the hearing roughly how long they expect each of the various stages to take. For longer or more complex hearings a timetable is often decided in consultation with the parties at a preliminary hearing or at the start of the hearing itself.

7. Fairness does not always mean that the hearing time must be divided equally between the parties or each witness.

8. For example, the party giving evidence first – in unfair dismissal cases this is usually the employer, but in discrimination cases this is often the employee – will often have to explain the relevance of the documents referred to in the witness statements, which requires time. Also some witnesses might have to give evidence about many separate incidents, whereas others perhaps just one short conversation. If an interpreter is required extra time has to be allowed. The Tribunal will take these things into account when estimating how long the evidence and examination of each witness should take.

9. The Tribunal will set the timetable using its own experience, but the Employment Judge will often ask for the parties' views on how long each stage of the hearing might take.

10. The stages involved in a typical hearing are as follows:

    10.1 At the start of the hearing, if this has not already been done, the Tribunal should make sure that everybody understands the questions the Tribunal has to answer. This is about identifying the issues that are to be decided. The Tribunal will also check that everyone has copies of all of the documents, etc.

    10.2 Often the Tribunal will then read the witness statements and any pages in the agreed bundle of documents to which they refer.

    10.3 Each witness is then questioned on their own statement. This is called "cross–examination". The Tribunal may also ask questions of the witnesses. A specific time may be allocated for questions in respect of each witness and for the witness to clarify any points that have arisen from those questions (this is called "re- examination").

    10.4 When the evidence is finished, each party is entitled to make "submissions". This means that they may summarise the important evidence in their case and may highlight any weak parts of the other side's case. They may also refer the Tribunal to any legal authorities (statutory provisions or previous case law) which might be relevant. Although each party has the right to make submissions, they are not obliged to do so. Again, the Tribunal might timetable the amount of time for submissions.

    10.5 After submissions, the Tribunal will reach its decision. Sometimes it needs to "retire" or "adjourn" (which simply means to leave the hearing room) in order to consider everything that has been said. The length of time it needs to do this might just be a few minutes or an hour in a simple, straightforward case. It may be days or weeks in a very long or complex case, in which instance the parties will usually be sent away with an indication of when a decision might be expected.

10.6   The Tribunal will then tell the parties what has been decided and why. This is referred to as "delivering judgment". This might be done orally – that is, by telling the parties the decision in their presence in the hearing room. If the decision has been made later (a "reserved decision"), then it may be sent to the parties in writing.

10.7   After delivering judgment, the Tribunal will, if the claim succeeds, hear evidence about the claimant's loss. The parties may then make submissions on what award is necessary. The Tribunal may then have to retire or to adjourn again to decide on remedy. It will then deliver its judgment on remedy either orally or reserve it and send it later in writing.

10.8   Lastly, the Tribunal might have to consider orders in respect of any costs matters. Orders for costs are not the norm. The Tribunal will then give judgment with reasons on those matters, again either orally or in writing.

11.   If a party believes that the time estimate for the whole or any part of the hearing is wrong, the Tribunal will expect them to say so as soon as possible. Waiting till the day before the hearing or the start of it to ask for extra time is not helpful. It can save time to try to agree a more accurate estimate and then to ask the Tribunal to change the timetable.

What can a party do to assist the Tribunal to keep to the timetable?

12.   It is helpful for each party to make a list, for their own use, of the questions to be asked of the witnesses about each of the issues in the case. It is also useful to decide which of the questions are the most important, so that if time is running out the really important questions can be asked, even if others have to be abandoned.

13.   Being able to find and quote the page number of the relevant documents in the bundle can save a lot of time. Asking questions using words the witness will understand, so that less time is wasted having to explain what is being asked, also saves time. A series of short, precise questions is generally better than one long, complicated one. They take less time to ask and to answer, and are easier for the witness and the Tribunal to understand and for everyone to take a note of.

14.   There is nothing to be gained by asking the same question several times or to argue with the witness. That will just waste the time allowed. The purpose of asking questions is not to try to make the witness agree with the questioner, but to show the Tribunal which side's evidence is more likely to be accurate. If necessary, the Tribunal can be reminded in submissions at the end of the case that, for example, the witness would not answer a question or gave an answer which was not believable or which was not consistent with a document in the bundle, etc. An explanation of why your evidence is more reliable can be given at that stage.

What if the time allowed is exceeded?

15.   The parties must try to conclude their questioning of each witness, and their submissions, within the time limit allocated. Usually the Employment Judge will remind a party of how long they have left when time is nearly up. If a party does not finish in time, they run the risk that the Tribunal may stop their questioning of that witness (which is sometimes called "guillotining" the evidence). This is not a step the Tribunal likes to take. Sometimes it is necessary, especially if one side takes so long that they might prevent the other side from having a fair opportunity to ask their own questions.

16.   If later witnesses take less time than expected, it might be possible to "re-call" the witness who did not have enough time, if the Tribunal agrees.

GUIDANCE NOTE 6:

REMEDY

What is remedy?

1.   After an Employment Tribunal has decided whether the claimant's claim succeeds it will consider how the successful party should be compensated. This part of the judgment is called "Remedy". Sometimes it is done immediately after the merits or liability judgment, but in long or complex cases it may be adjourned to another day.

2.   The Tribunal has different powers for each different type of claim. It must calculate loss and order an appropriate remedy for each part of a successful claim. Accurate and often detailed information

from both parties is needed to make correct calculations and to issue a judgment which is fair to all. Sometimes the Tribunal can only estimate the loss: for example, for how long a party may be out of work.

Different types of remedy

3.   For some claims the only remedy is to order the employer/respondent to pay a sum of money: for example, wages due, holiday pay and notice pay.

4.   For unfair dismissal the Tribunal may:

4.1   Order the employer to "reinstate" the dismissed employee. This is to put them back in their old job, as if they had not been dismissed; or to "re-engage" them, which is to employ them in a suitable but different job. In each case the Tribunal may order payment of lost earnings, etc.

4.2   If those orders are not sought by the claimant or are not practicable, the Tribunal may order the employer to pay compensation. This is calculated in two parts:

- a "Basic Award", which is calculated in a similar way to a statutory redundancy payment; and

- a "Compensatory Award", which is intended to compensate the employee for the financial loss suffered.

5.   In claims of unlawful discrimination, the Tribunal may:

5.1   make a declaration setting out the parties' rights; and/or

5.2   order compensation to be paid by the employer and/or fellow workers who have committed discriminatory acts. If the employer can show that it has taken all reasonable steps to prevent employees from committing such acts (called the "statutory defence"), the only award which can be made is against the fellow worker, not the employer; and/or

5.3   make a recommendation, such as for the claimant's colleagues or managers to be given training to ensure that discrimination does not happen again.

Mitigation

6.   All persons who have been subjected to wrongdoing are expected to do their best, within reasonable bounds, to limit the effects on them. If the Tribunal concludes that a claimant has not done so, it must reduce the compensation so that a fair sum is payable.

7.   The Tribunal will expect evidence to be provided by claimants about their attempts to obtain suitable alternative work and about any earnings from alternative employment.

8.   The Tribunal will expect respondents, who consider that the claimant has not tried hard enough, to provide evidence about other jobs which the claimant could have applied for.

Statement of remedy

10.   The Tribunal will usually order the claimant to make a calculation showing how each amount claimed has been worked out. For example: x weeks' pay at £y per week. Sometimes this is called a "Schedule of loss" or a "Statement of remedy".

11.   Tribunals are expected to calculate remedy for each different type of loss – sometimes called "Heads of loss" or "Heads of damage". Therefore the statement should show how much is claimed under each head.

12.   If the claimant has received State benefits, he or she should also specify the type of benefit, the dates of receipt, the amount received and the claimant's national insurance number. (See also "Recoupment" below).

13.   Typical heads of loss include;

- wages due

- pay in lieu of notice (where no notice or inadequate notice was given)

- outstanding holiday pay

- a basic award or redundancy payment

- past loss of earnings

- future loss of earnings

- loss of pension entitlements.

14.   In discrimination cases, the heads of loss will also typically include:

- injury to feelings

- aggravated or exemplary damages (which are rare)

- damages for personal injury (but only when the act of discrimination is the cause of the claimant becoming ill).

15.   The Tribunal will usually order the statement to be produced early in the proceedings, as it can help in settlement negotiations, when considering mediation and when assessing the length of the hearing. It should be updated near to the hearing date.

Submissions on *Polkey* and contributory fault

16.   In an unfair dismissal claim, if an employee has been dismissed, but the employer has not followed a proper procedure (such as the ACAS Code), the Tribunal will follow the guidance in the case of *Polkey v AE Dayton Services Limited* and subsequent cases. The Tribunal will consider whether, if a fair procedure had been followed, the claimant might still have been fairly dismissed, either at all, or at some later time. This question is often referred to as the "Polkey" question or deduction.

17.   There are also cases where the dismissal may be procedurally unfair, but the employee's own conduct has contributed to the position they now find themselves in. This is called "contributory conduct".

18.   Where either or both of these are relevant, the Tribunal will reduce the compensation awarded by an appropriate percentage in each case. This means that there may be two reductions, which, where there has been really serious misconduct, could be as high as 100%, so that nothing would be payable.

19.   Generally the Tribunal will decide these issues at the same time as it reaches its decision on the merits of the claim. Sometimes this will be done at a separate remedy hearing. The Tribunal will usually explain at the start of the hearing which of those options it will follow. If it does not, then the parties should ask for clarification of when they are expected to give evidence and to make submissions on these matters.

Injury to Feelings

20.   In discrimination cases and some other detriment claims, Tribunals may award a sum of money to compensate for injury to feelings. When they do so, they must fix fair, reasonable and just compensation in the particular circumstances of the case. The Tribunal will bear in mind that compensation is designed to compensate the injured party rather than to punish the guilty one. It will also remind itself that awards should bear some relationship to those made by the courts for personal injury.

21.   The Tribunal will follow guidelines first given in the case of *Vento v Chief Constable of West Yorkshire Police* and in subsequent cases. These guidelines are referred to as the "Vento guidelines" or the "Vento bands". The President of Employment Tribunals will issue from time to time separate guidance on the present value of the Vento bands or guidelines.

22.   The Tribunal will expect claimants to explain in their statement of remedy which Vento band they consider their case falls in. They will also expect both parties to make submissions on this during the remedy part of the hearing.

Information needed to calculate remedy

23.   This varies in each case dependent on what is being claimed. Each party should look for any relevant information which could help the Tribunal with any necessary calculations in their case. They should provide copies of this information to each other and include those copies in the hearing bundle.

24.   The types of information that could be relevant include:
   - the contract of employment or statement of terms & conditions with the old employer
   - the date the claimant started work with that employer
   - details of any pension scheme and pension contributions
   - pay slips for the last 13 weeks in the old employment
   - any other document showing the claimant's gross pay and net pay
   - proof of any payments actually made by the old employer, such as a redundancy payment or payment in lieu of notice
   - any document recording the day the claimant last actually worked
   - any document explaining how many days and hours per week the claimant worked
   - any document explaining how overtime was paid
   - any document recording when the holiday year started
   - any document recording when holiday has been taken in that year and what has been paid for those days
   - any documents setting out the terms of the old employer's pension scheme
   - any documents showing the claimant's attempts to find new or other work
   - contract of employment and payslips for any new job with a new employer

- documents such as bank statements, if losses for bank charges are claimed
- medical reports or "Fit notes" if unable to work since dismissal
- any documents showing that jobs were or are available in the locality for which the claimant could have applied.

25. The witness statements should tell the Tribunal which parts of these documents are important and why. Providing enough information to the Tribunal at an early stage could help to promote a settlement and so avoid a hearing.

Is all loss awarded?

26. For claims such as unpaid wages, holiday pay and notice pay the Tribunal will order the difference between what should have been paid and what has actually been paid. Wages and holiday pay are usually calculated gross, but pay in lieu of notice is usually calculated net of tax and national insurance. The judgment should specify whether each payment ordered has been calculated gross or net.

27. In the case of unfair dismissal there are several limits (called statutory caps) on what can be awarded.

Grossing up

28. The rules on when tax is payable on awards made by Tribunals are too complex for inclusion here. When it is clear that the claimant will have to pay tax on the sum awarded, the Tribunal will award a higher figure, calculated so that tax can be paid and the claimant will receive the net sum which properly represents the loss. This calculation is called "grossing up".

Interest

29. There are two separate situations where interest is relevant.

30. First, when a Tribunal calculates compensation for discrimination, it is obliged to consider awarding interest. If it decides to do so, it calculates interest from the date of the act of discrimination up to the date of the calculation. The exception is for interest on lost wages, where the calculation is made from the middle of that period (as that is simpler than calculating interest separately on each missing wage, but leads to a roughly similar result). The Tribunal will then include that interest in the award made.

31. In addition, interest is payable on awards for all claims if they are not paid when due. A note accompanying the Tribunal's judgment will explain how interest has been calculated. In respect of all claims presented on or after 29 July 2013 interest is calculated from the day after the day upon which the written judgment was sent to the parties, unless payment is actually made within the first 14 days, in which case no interest is payable.

32. The Employment Tribunal plays no part in enforcing payment of the award it makes. That is done by the civil courts, who issue separate guidance on how to enforce payments.

Recoupment

33. For some claims, such as unfair dismissal, if the claimant has received certain State benefits the Tribunal is obliged to ensure that the employer responsible for causing the loss of earnings reimburses the State for the benefits paid. In those cases the Tribunal will order only part of the award to be paid to the claimant straightaway, with the rest set aside until the respondent is told by the State how much the benefits were. The respondent then pays that money to the State and anything left over to the claimant.

34. This is called "recoupment". The Tribunal should set out in the judgment whether or not recoupment applies, and if it does, how much of the award is set aside for recoupment purposes. If either party is in any doubt about recoupment, they should ask the Tribunal to explain how it affects them.

Costs

35. See the separate guidance on "Costs".

Pensions loss

36. The President of Employment Tribunals has issued separated guidance and principles on the calculation of pensions loss. See:

https://www.judiciary.gov.uk/wp-content/uploads/2013/08/presidential-guidance-pension-loss-20170810.pdf

https://www.judiciary.gov.uk/wp-content/uploads/2015/03/principles-for-compensating-pension-loss-20170810.pdf.

GUIDANCE NOTE 7:
COSTS

1. The basic principle is that Employment Tribunals do not order one party to pay the costs which the other party has incurred in bringing or defending a claim. However, there are a number of important exceptions to the basic principle, as explained below.

What are costs?

2. "Costs" means some or all of the legal and professional fees, charges, payments or expenses incurred by a party in connection with the Tribunal case. It includes the expenses incurred by a party or witness in attending a hearing.

What orders for payment of costs can be made?

3. There are three different types of payment orders: costs orders; preparation time orders (sometimes referred to as PTOs); and wasted costs orders. These specific terms have the following meanings.

4. A costs order generally means that a party is ordered to pay some or all of the costs paid by the other party to its legal representatives (barristers and solicitors) or to its lay representative. No more than the hourly rate of a preparation time order can be claimed for a lay representative. Separately, costs orders can be made for the expenses reasonably and proportionately incurred by a party or witness in attending a hearing.

5. Preparation time orders are for payment in respect of the amount of time spent working on the case by a non-represented party, including its employees or advisers, but not the time spent at any final hearing.

6. Wasted costs orders are for payment of costs incurred by a party as a result of any improper, unreasonable or negligent act or failure to act by a representative or for costs incurred after such act where it would be unreasonable to expect the party to bear them. They require payment by a representative to any party, including the party represented by the payer.

When may orders for costs and preparation time be made?

7. Apart from costs orders for the attendance of witnesses or parties at hearings, a party cannot have both a costs order and a preparation time order made in its favour in the same proceedings. So it is often sensible for a Tribunal in the course of the proceedings (for example, at a preliminary hearing) to decide only that an order for payment will be made, but to leave to the end of the case the decision about which type of order and for how much.

8. Orders for payment of costs or for preparation time may be made on application by a party, a witness (in respect of their expenses) or on the Tribunal's initiative up to 28 days after the end of the case. If judgment on the claims is given at a hearing, it will usually be sensible to make any application for costs or PTOs then, in order to avoid delay and the additional cost of getting everyone back for another hearing.

9. The circumstances when payment orders may be made are as follows.

10. If an employer in unfair dismissal proceedings requires an adjournment to obtain evidence about the possibility of re-employment, the Tribunal must order the employer to pay the costs of the adjournment provided:

    • the claimant notified the desire to be re-employed at least 7 days before the hearing;

    • the employer cannot prove a special reason why it should not pay.

11. A party may be ordered to pay costs or preparation time to the other party, without any particular fault or blame being shown, where:

    • the paying party has breached an order or practice direction; or

    • an adjournment or postponement is granted at the request of or due to the conduct of the paying party.

12. A party may be ordered to pay costs in the form of the expenses incurred or to be incurred by a witness attending a hearing, without any particular fault or blame being shown. The order may be in favour of or against the party who called the witness. It may be made on the application of a party, the witness or at the Tribunal's own initiative. It may be payable to a party or to the witness.

13. A party may be ordered to pay costs or preparation time to the other party where the Tribunal considers that:

    • a party has acted vexatiously, abusively, disruptively or otherwise unreasonably in bringing or defending the proceedings or in its conduct of the proceedings; or

- the claim or response had no reasonable prospect of success.

14. The circumstances described at paragraph 13 require a Tribunal to consider first whether the criteria for an order are met. Each case will turn on its own facts. Examples from decided cases include that it could be unreasonable where a party has based the claim or defence on something which is untrue. That is not the same as something which they have simply failed to prove. Nor does it mean something they reasonably misunderstood. Abusive or disruptive conduct would include insulting the other party or its representative or sending numerous unnecessary e- mails.

15. If the criteria are met, the Tribunal is at the threshold for making an order. It will decide whether it is appropriate to order payment. It will consider any information it has about the means of the party from whom payment is sought, the extent of any abusive or unreasonable conduct, and any factors which seem to indicate that the party which is out-of-pocket should be reimbursed. For example, sometimes it becomes clear that a party never intended to defend on the merits (that is, for example, whether the claimant was unfairly dismissed), but pretended that it was doing so until the last minute, causing the claimant to use his or her lawyer more, before conceding what was really always obvious.

When may a wasted costs order be made?

16. A Tribunal may consider making a wasted costs order of its own initiative or on the application of any party, provided the circumstances described at paragraph 6 above are established. This is a very rare event. When it happens, usually a party will seek costs from the other party and, in the alternative, wasted costs from that party's representative. The representative from whom payment is sought is entitled to notice and so is the party – because they may need separate representation at this costs hearing.

Amount of costs, preparation time and wasted costs orders

17. Broadly speaking, costs orders are for the amount of legal or professional fees and related expenses reasonably incurred, based on factors like the significance of the case, the complexity of the facts and the experience of the lawyers who conducted the litigation for the receiving party.

18. In addition to costs for witness expenses, the Tribunal may order any party to pay costs as follows:

    18.1 up to £20,000, by forming a broad-brush assessment of the amounts involved; or working from a schedule of legal costs; or, more frequently and in respect of lower amounts, just the fee for the barrister at the hearing (for example);

    18.2 calculated by a detailed assessment in the County Court or by the Tribunal up to an unlimited amount;

    18.3 in any amount agreed between the parties.

19. Preparation time orders are calculated at the rate of £33 per hour (until April 2014, when the rate increases by £1 as at every April) for every hour which the receiving party reasonably and proportionately spent preparing for litigation. This requires the Tribunal to bear in mind matters such as the complexity of the proceedings, the number of witnesses and the extent of documents.

20. Wasted costs orders are calculated like costs orders: the amount wasted by the blameworthy (as described at paragraph 6 above) conduct of the representative.

21. When considering the amount of an order, information about a person's ability to pay may be considered. The Tribunal may make a substantial order even where a person has no means of payment. Examples of relevant information are: the person's earnings, savings, other sources of income, debts, bills and necessary monthly outgoings.

GUIDANCE NOTE 8:

CONCLUDING CASES WITHOUT A HEARING

1. A claim or response which has been accepted may be disposed of by the Employment Tribunal at any point in any number of stages before the final hearing. This note sets out most of the situations generally encountered and refers you to the relevant rules.

Rejection at presentation stage

2. A claim may be rejected by an Employment Judge at the time of presentation under Rule 12 where there are certain substantive defects. A claimant may have a right to make representations and attend a hearing before this occurs.[2]

3.   The claimant may apply for reconsideration of that rejection by an Employment Judge within 14 days on the grounds that it is wrong or that the defect can be rectified. Unless the claimant asks for a hearing, the issue is decided on paper by the Employment Judge. If there is a hearing, only the claimant attends.

Failure to respond and Rule 21 judgment

4.   If no response to the claim is received from the respondent within the prescribed time, the Tribunal considers whether a judgment can be issued under Rule 21 on the available material. An Employment Judge may seek further information from the claimant or order a hearing. The respondent will receive notice of the hearing, but will only be allowed to participate in the hearing to the extent permitted by the judge.

Notice under Rule 26 after response received

5.   If a response to the claim from the respondent is accepted, the Tribunal conducts an initial consideration of the claim form and response form under Rule 26. If the Employment Judge considers that the Tribunal has no jurisdiction to hear the claim, or that the claim or the response has no reasonable prospect of success, notice will be sent to the parties setting out the judge's view and the reasons for it. The judge will order that the claim or response (or any part of it) shall be dismissed on a date specified unless the claimant or respondent (as the case might be) has before that date written to explain why that should not happen.

6.   If no representations are received then the claim or response or the relevant part will be dismissed. If representations are received, they will be considered by an Employment Judge, who will either permit the claim or response to proceed or fix a hearing for the purposes of deciding whether it should be permitted to do so. Such a hearing may consider other matters in relation to preparing the case for hearing.

Preparation for the final hearing

7.   If the Employment Judge directs the case is to proceed to final hearing, orders will normally be made under Rule 29 to prepare for the hearing which is listed. These may include disclosure of documents and exchange of witness statements. Failure to comply with these orders may lead to sanctions as set out below.

Striking out under Rule 37

8.   Under rule 37 the Tribunal may strike out all or part of a claim or response on a number of grounds at any stage of the proceedings, either on its own initiative, or on the application of a party. These include that it is scandalous or vexatious or has no reasonable prospect of success, or the manner in which the proceedings have been conducted has been scandalous, unreasonable or vexatious.

9.   Non-compliance with the rules or orders of the Tribunal is also a ground for striking out, as is the fact that the claim or response is not being actively pursued.

10.   The fact that it is no longer possible to have a fair hearing is also ground for striking out. In some cases the progress of the claim to hearing is delayed over a lengthy period. Ill health may be a reason why this happens. This means that the evidence becomes more distant from the events in the case. Eventually a point may be reached where a fair hearing is no longer possible.

11.   Before a strike out on any of these grounds a party will be given a reasonable opportunity to make representations in writing or request a hearing. The Tribunal does not use these powers lightly. It will often hold a preliminary hearing before taking this action.

12.   In exercising these powers the Tribunal follows the overriding objective in seeking to deal with cases justly and expeditiously and in proportion to the matters in dispute. In some cases parties apply for strike out of their opponent at every perceived breach of the rules. This is not a satisfactory method of managing a case. Such applications are rarely successful. The outcome is often further orders by the Tribunal to ensure the case is ready for the hearing.

13.   It follows that before a claim or response is struck out you will receive a notice explaining what is being considered and what you should do. If you oppose the proposed action you should write explaining why and seeking a hearing if you require one.

Unless orders under Rule 38

14.   The Tribunal may, in order to secure compliance with an order for preparation of the case, make an "unless order" under rule 38. This is an order that will specify that, if it is not complied with, the claim or response or part of it shall be dismissed without further order. The party may apply, within 14 days of the date that the "unless order" was sent, to have the order set aside or for time for

compliance to be extended. If the party does not comply with the order then the case is struck out without further order. A party may also apply after the strike out for the claim or response to be reinstated.

Deposit orders under Rule 39

15. The Tribunal has power under Rule 39 to order that a deposit be paid on the ground that a specific allegation or argument has little reasonable prospect of success. If such an order is made the deposit must be paid in the time specified as a condition of continuing to advance the allegation or argument. If the party fails to pay the deposit by the date specified, the allegation to which the deposit relates is struck out.

Withdrawal under Rule 51

16. When a claimant withdraws the claim it comes to an end. The Tribunal must issue a dismissal judgment under Rule 52, unless for some reason this is inappropriate. Often the settlement of a claim includes an agreement that the claimant withdraws the claim and that a dismissal judgment is made.

Compromise agreements and ACAS

17. Section 203 of the Employment Rights Act 1996 and section 144 of the Equality Act 2010 restrict any contracting out of the provisions of these two Acts. Claims can be settled using an ACAS conciliator to produce a COT3 agreement or, where legal advice is available to the claimant, a compromise or settlement agreement.

Conclusion

18. In the absence of one of the outcomes outlined above the case will be determined at a final hearing following consideration of the evidence and law by a Tribunal.

Index

ACAS
  arbitration 310–11
  codes of practice 164, 176–8, 181–4
    failure to comply 117, 231
  conciliation officers 305
  early conciliation scheme 250–4
  Equality Act guidance 376
  fire and rehire guidance 71
  parental bereavement 557
  recruitment and induction guidance 10
  settlements 305–6
  shared parental leave 556
account of profits 118–19
adoption leave
  additional 553–4
  detrimental treatment 554
  legislation 553
  notice requirements 554
  ordinary 553–4
  redundancy during 554
  return to work 554
  statutory adoption pay 544, 554
  summary 563–5
  unfair dismissal 554
age discrimination 487–99
  see also discrimination
  advertising 497
  age groups 496
  applicability 487–8
  application forms 497–8
  burden of proof 497
  contracts 498
  direct 427, 488, 489–94
  Directive 487
  employees 487–8
  enforcement 499
  exemptions 496–7
  harassment 489, 496
  indirect 488, 494–6
  insurance benefits 498
  interviews 497–8
  justification 490–4
  legitimate aims 490–4
  occupational requirement 489
  pensions 498
  prohibited conduct 488–9
  proportionality 490–4
  protected characteristic 488
  recruitment 497
  redundancy 499
  Regulations 487
  retirement 403, 498–9
    fair 498–9
  unlawful acts 489
  vicarious liability 497
  victimisation 489, 496
  workers 487–8

agency workers 32–5
  'Swedish derogation' abolition 35
annual leave 81, 85–95
  bank holidays 97
  carrying forward 94
  Covid-19 87
  current position in UK 94–5
  discrimination 97
  during furlough 87
  holiday pay 86–7, 112
  joiners 87
  Law Society practice note 97
  leave year 86
  leavers 87
  maternity/paternity leave and 94
  notice 87–8
  overtime and 89–90
  sanctions 97
  sickness and 93–4
  zero hour contracts 97
appeals
  employment tribunals 2, 301–2
  misconduct 191–2
apprenticeships 31
arbitration 310–11
armed forces
  gay service personnel in 575
  statutory dismissal exclusion 134
associated employer 147, 149

'balance of convenience' test 118
bank holidays 97
belief see religion or belief discrimination
benefits see remuneration; social security benefits
'blue pencil' test 62–3
breach of contract
  employee's 107–8
  employer's see wrongful dismissal
Brexit
  discrimination 375–6
  effect 4
  employment of EU citizens 6
'bumping' 147, 198
burden of proof
  age discrimination 497
  direct discrimination 439–43
  disability discrimination 538
  discrimination 463
  harassment 468
  public interest disclosure 217–18
  race discrimination 444–8
  victimisation 468
business efficacy test 45

case law
  direct discrimination 442–3
  disability discrimination 504–5, 506–7

case law – *continued*
  early conciliation 252–4
  source of law 2
Christian ministers
  as employees 35
civil courts 2
civil partnership discrimination 387–8, 396–7
codes of practice 3
  failure to follow 176, 178
  unfair dismissal 176–8
collective agreements
  transfer of undertakings 358
  working time 97
commission
  see also **remuneration**
  damages for lost commission 113
  express term 52
common law 2
  terms implied by 40–5
company directors
  as employees 36–7
compensation
  see also **damages**
  basic award 221–2
  compensatory award 222–32
    adjustments 232
      compulsory increase 226
      discretionary increase 226–8
  contributory fault 231
  discrimination remedy 407–11
  employment tribunals 312–13
  expenses 226
  failure to comply with ACAS code 231
  future loss of earnings 224–5
  harassment 474
  heads of loss 224–6
  immediate loss of earnings 224
  interest 232, 411
  loss of statutory rights 225–6
  maximum award 222–4
  mitigation 228–9
  non-economic loss 223
  payment in lieu 231
  pension rights 225
  'Polkey' deductions 229–31
  recoupment of social security benefits 232–3
  reducing factors 228–32
  taxation 233–6, 411
  unfair dismissal 221–36
competition
  employees' duty 44–5, 60–1, 65–6
compromise agreement 311
conciliation *see* **settlements**
conciliation officer 305
confidentiality
  after employment 57–8
  confidentiality clauses 304–5
  during employment 57
  employees' duty 45, 65–6
  employment tribunal disclosures 280–1
  non-disclosure agreements 56–7, 304–5, 308–9
  proposed reform 56–7
  restraint of trade clause 58–9

confidentiality – *continued*
  restrictive covenants 58–68
conflict of interest and duty 45
constructive dismissal 108
  ACAS code of practice 164
  breach of relationship 124–6
  change of terms and conditions 127
  cumulative effects 126–7
  job description 124
  reduction of pay 124
  repudiatory breach 125, 127–9
  resignation 123–4, 129
consultation
  redundancy
    collective redundancies 152–6
    Covid-19 procedures 201
    duty to consult 152–6
    protective award 155–6
    reasons to be given 153
    recognised trade union 152
    Secretary of State notification 157
    timing 152–3
    transfer of undertakings 156
    unfair dismissal 157
  transfer of undertakings
    duty to consult 367–9
    employee representatives 367
    failure to comply 369
    persons to consult 367
  variation of contract terms 69
continuing/continuous contract 38
continuous employment
  calculation 130–2
  change of employer 133–4
  continuity of employment 132–3
  effective date of termination 130–2
  industrial action 133
  relevant date 130, 132
  statutory dismissal requirement 129–30
contract of employment 37–40
  age discrimination 498
  continuing 38
  criminal record checks 8–10
  employees' duties *see* **employees' duties**
  employers' duties *see* **employers' duties**
  exchange of rights for shares 38
  express terms *see* **express terms**
  fixed-term 38, 48, 111, 123, 419
  flexibility clauses 69
  illegality 6–8
  implied 32–3
  implied terms *see* **implied terms**
  indefinite 38, 47
  induction 10
  pre-employment screening 8–10
  recruitment 10
  specimen 596–601
  spent convictions 10
  termination *see* **termination of employment**
  terms
    see also **express terms; implied terms**
    variation *see* **variation of contractual terms**
    written statement 37, 38–40, 593–5

contract of employment – *continued*
  tests for 11
  third parties 37
  transfer of undertakings 350–1
  working time *see* **working time**
  written contracts 46–7
  written statement of terms 37, 38–40, 593–5
  zero hours contracts 27–8, 38, 97
coronavirus *see* **Covid-19 pandemic**
Coronavirus Job Retention Scheme
  annual leave 87
  dismissal 169
  fire and rehire practices 71
  redundancy 201
  remuneration 52–3
  right to work and 41
  unlawful deductions from wages 73
costs
  amount 299–300
  deposit 276
  employment tribunals 294–301
  orders 295–9
  preparation time orders 300
  wasted costs orders 300–1
covert surveillance 574–5
Covid-19 pandemic
  see also **Coronavirus Job Retention Scheme**
  annual leave 87
  employees' duties 42, 44
  employers' duties 42, 44, 50
  employment tribunal procedure 285
  furlough *see* **furlough**
  mobility 50
  redundancy 169, 201–2
  safety and working conditions 42, 44, 50
  unfair dismissal 169–70, 201–2
  workplace risk assessment 42
criminal offences
  spent convictions 10
  unfair dismissal 193–5
custom and practice
  implied terms 45

damages
  see also **compensation**
  accelerated receipt 116–17
  accrued holiday pay 112
  additional loss 113–14
  benefits reducing loss 115–16
  discrimination remedy 408–10
  employer's remedy 117–18
  lost benefits 113–14
  lost commission 113
  lost net wages 111–12
  lost pension entitlement 113
  lost tips 114
  mitigation duty 115
  NI contributions 116
  non-pecuniary losses 114–15
  PILON and 116
  'stigma' 114
  taxation 116
  wrongful dismissal 111–17

data protection 579–86
  see also **Information Commissioner's Office**
  consent to processing 581, 583–5, 588
  data breach 582–3
  Data Protection Act 2018 580
  Data Protection Impact Assessment 583, 587
  fee 580
  individual's rights 582
  information provision to employees 585
  monitoring in workplace 586–91
  personal data 580
  personal devices at work 589
  pre-employment screening 8–10
  principles 581
  processing of data 581
  references 43
  'special' categories of data 582
  subject access requests 585–6
  transfer outside EU 589–91
  UK General Data Protection Regulation 580–3
Data Protection Act 2018 580, 585
deductions from wages 55, 73–4
  enforcement 76
  industrial action 76
  time limits 259–60
  unauthorised 73–7
dependant care leave
  detriment 561
  entitlement 560
  reasonable time off, meaning 560–1
  remedies 561
  summary 563–5
  unfair dismissal 561
'dependent contractor' 11, 23
detrimental treatment
  adoption leave 554
  dependant care leave 561
  flexible working 559
  maternity leave 548
  pregnancy 548
Directives 3–4
disability discrimination
  see also **discrimination**
  adjustments
    duty to adjust 518–19
    examples 522–5
    failure to make 517–28
    reasonableness 390, 522–5
  adverse effect condition 505–7
  applicability 501–2
  arising from disability 389, 528–36
  burden of proof 538
  case law 504–5, 506–7
  comparators 517, 520–2
  conditions developing into disabilities 513
  direct 502, 515–17
  Disability Discrimination Act 1995 501
  'disability' meaning 502–3
  disability-related discrimination 528
  'disabled person' 502–3
  dismissal 514–15
  dual discrimination 517
  effect of medical treatment 512

disability discrimination – *continued*
  enforcement 538–9
  Equal Treatment Framework Directive 514
  examples of disabilities 511–12
  flowchart 541–2
  harassment 502, 538
  impairment condition 504
  indirect 502, 537
  jurisdiction of tribunal 538–9
  knowledge of disability 525–7, 535–6
  legislation 501
  less favourable treatment
    adjustment and 517–28
    related to disability 528
  long-term condition 509–11
  Malcolm decision 528
  medical conditions 513
  medical evidence 509
  objective justification 389, 534–5
  past disabilities 511, 513
  perceived disabilities 512–13
  post employment 515
  progressive conditions 508
  promotion 514–15
  proportionate means of achieving legitimate aim 516
  protected characteristic 502
  provision, criteria or practice 519–20
  recruitment 514
  relationship with alleged discriminatory act 513–14
  severe disfigurement 508
  substantial condition 507–8
  unlawful discrimination 514–15
  vicarious liability 538, 542
  victimisation 502, 538
disciplinary procedures *see* **dismissal and disciplinary procedures**
disclosure
  whistleblowers *see* **public interest disclosure**
disclosure of documents
  confidentiality 280–1
  employment tribunals 276–82
  privilege 278–80
    advice 278–9
    legal professional 278–80
    litigation 279–80
    waiver of 280
  restrictions 287–9
discrimination
  see also **Equality Act 2010**
  ACAS guidance 376
  age *see* **age discrimination**
  annual leave and 97
  arising from disability 376
  associative 376, 389, 427
  background 377
  Black Voices Report 377
  burden of proof 463
  by perception 389, 427
  contract workers 31
  detriment or disadvantage 454–9
  direct 388, 389, 390–2, 488, 489–94, 515–17
    burden of proof 439–43
    case law 442–3

discrimination – *continued*
  case study 444–8
  comparator 426, 430–2
  definition 425–7
  dual discrimination 460, 517
  flowchart 450
  hypothetical comparator 430–2
  illegality 436
  indirect compared 460
  irrelevance of alleged discriminator's characteristics 436
  less favourable treatment 425–7, 428–30
  motive 435–6
  reason for 427–8, 433–5
  remedies 443
  stereotypical assumptions 436
disability *see* **disability discrimination**
dismissal 394–5
dual discrimination 460, 517
EHRC guidance 376, 379
employment tribunals 312
enforcement 403–6, 499, 538–9
  by individuals 404–6
  declaration 406–7
  orders 406–7
  questionnaire procedure 406
  recommendations 406–7
  remedies 406–12
  time limits 404–5
equal pay *see* **equal pay**
fixed-term employees 419
harassment *see* **harassment**
human rights prohibition 420–1, 579
indirect 388, 389, 390–2, 451–64, 488, 494–6, 537
  burden of proof 463
  complainant's disadvantage 459–60
  definition 451–3
  detriment or disadvantage 454–9
  direct compared 460
  elements of claim 452
  employer's defence 460–3
  flowchart 465
  group disadvantage 454–9
  provision, criterion or practice meaning 453–4
  remedies 464
inhuman or degrading treatment 421
joint and several liability 411–12
legislation 375–6
  employment defined 29–31
less favourable treatment *see* **less favourable treatment**
liability
  joint and several 411–12
  personal 403
  vicarious 474
migrant workers 393
non-statutory guidance 376
occupational requirement 395–7
part-time workers 417–19
personal liability 403
positive action 393–4
post employment 390, 395
pregnancy *see* **pregnancy**
prohibited conduct 388–92

discrimination – *continued*
   promotion 394–5
   protected characteristics 377, 379–88
   questionnaire procedure 406
   race *see* **race discrimination**
   recruitment *see* **recruitment**
   recruitment and induction 5
   religion or belief *see* **religion or belief discrimination**
   removal of contractual term 412
   sex *see* **sex discrimination**
   sexual orientation *see* **sexual orientation discrimination**
   time limits 259
   trade union membership 419–20
   unlawful acts 392–5
   vicarious liability 397–403, 474
      course of employment 397–400
      reasonable steps 400–3
   victimisation *see* **victimisation**
   voluntary workers 35–6
dismissal
   constructive *see* **constructive dismissal**
   contracting out of rights 139
   reasons for *see* **reasons for dismissal**
   statutory *see* **redundancy**; **unfair dismissal**
   summary 107–8
   unfair *see* **unfair dismissal**
   wrongful *see* **wrongful dismissal**
dismissal and disciplinary procedures 68
   fairness of dismissal 164
   grievances and 192
   human rights 570–1
dispute resolution *see* **dismissal and disciplinary procedures; grievance procedures**
duration clause
   continuous employment 48
   indefinite contracts 47

early conciliation 250–1
   case law 252–4
   errors 252
   procedure 251–2
   time limits 252, 260–4
effective date of termination
   extension 131
   unfair dismissal 130–2
employee liability information 366–7
employee representatives
   transfer of undertakings 367
employees
   see also **transfer of undertakings**
   definition 11–12
   duties *see* **employees' duties**
   statutory dismissal requirement 122
employees' duties
   competition 44–5, 60–1, 65–6
   confidential information 45
   conflict of interest and duty 45
   Covid-19 42, 44
   defined in contract 49
   fidelity 44
   good faith 44
   indemnity for employer 44
   mutual obligations 12–15

employees' duties – *continued*
   obedience to reasonable orders 43–4
   personal service 43
   qualification 49
   reasonable care and skill 44
   secret profits 44
   time devoted to 49
   trade secrets 45
employers' duties
   Covid-19 42, 44, 50
   data protection 582, 585
   indemnity for employee 41
   mutual obligations 12–15
   mutual trust and confidence 42
   notification of termination 43
   payment of wages 41
   provision of work 41
   reasonable care 41–2
   references 42–3
   safety and working conditions 41–2
Employment Appeal Tribunal 2, 301–2
employment law
   sources *see* **sources of law**
employment relationship 10–37
   apprenticeships 31
   breach of relationship 124–6
   considerations 16–18
   control 15–16
   mutual obligations 12–15, 42
employment tribunals 2
   additional information 276
   amendments to claim or response 271–3
   appeals 2, 301–2
   application 267–8
   attendance of witnesses 282
   awards 294
   bundle of documents 289
   case management 269–84
   compensation 312–13
   costs 294–301
   deductions from wages 259–60
   deposit requirement 276
   disclosure of documents 276–82
      confidentiality 280–1
      privilege 278–80
      voluntary 281
   discrimination 259, 312, 538–9
   early conciliation *see* **early conciliation**
   enforcement 303
   equal pay 259
   flexible working requests 559
   funding 303
   grievance procedures *see* **grievance procedures**
   hearings 284–6
      adjournments 291
      bundle of documents 289
      constitution of tribunal 289
      Covid-19 and 285
      decision 293–4
      evidence 292–3
      final hearing 289–94
      online 285–6
      postponement 289

employment tribunals – *continued*
    preliminary hearing 286–7
    preparations 289
    representation 291
  human rights 303–4
  initial considerations 269
  insolvency 255
  judicial assessment 284
  jurisdiction 250, 538–9
  legislation 249
  litigants in person 265–7
  overlapping claims and awards 311–13
  penalties for employers 236–7, 301
  preparation time orders 300
  public tribunal register 302–3
  'reasonable bounds test' 271
  reconsideration of decision 301
  redundancy 259, 312
  response 268–9
  restricted reporting orders 287–9
  rules 264–304
  settlements 304–10
  striking out 273–5
  time limits 252, 255–64
  unfair dismissal 312
  unless orders 283–4
  wasted costs orders 300–1
  withdrawal of claim 284
  'without prejudice' procedure 281–2
  witness statements 282
  witnesses, attendance 282
  'written answers' 276
  wrongful dismissal 312
enforcement
  age discrimination 499
  'blue pencil' test 62–3
  deductions from wages 76
  disability discrimination 538–9
  discrimination legislation 403
  employment tribunal awards 303
  equal pay 416
  public interest disclosure 218–19
  restrictive covenants 62–5
equal pay
  audit 416
  defences 414–16
  discrimination claims compared 413
  enforcement 416
  equality clause 412–14
  gender pay gap reporting 416
  time limits 259
Equality Act 2010
  see also **discrimination; harassment; victimisation**
  interpretation 378–9
  jurisdiction 378
  overview 376
  persons protected 377–8
  territorial scope 378
equality clause 412–14
Equality and Human Rights Commission
  age discrimination 487
  Code of Practice 376, 379, 403, 501
  harassment and 467

Equality and Human Rights Commission – *continued*
  non-statutory guidance 376
ETO reasons
  dismissal of employee 361–2
European Union law
  action against State 4
  agency workers 34
  collective redundancies 154–5
  data protection 580
  Directives 3–4
  interpretation of national legislation 4
  Regulations 3
  treaty provisions 3
  UK leaving EU *see* **Brexit**
expenses, overpayment 75–6
express terms 37
  benefits 51
  commission 52
  confidentiality
    after employment 57–8
    during employment 57
  disciplinary procedures 68
  discoveries 56
  duration clause
    continuous contracts 48
    indefinite contracts 47
  duties, defining 49
  employees' viewpoint 50
  'garden leave' clause 65
  grievance procedures 68
  human rights 72–3
  intellectual property rights 56
  inventions 56
  job title 48
  mobility 49–50, 144
  pension 56
  PILON clause 68, 105–7, 116
  place of work 49–50
  qualifications 49
  remuneration 51–5
  surrender of papers 68
  working time *see* **working time**

family-friendly rights
  adoption *see* **adoption leave**
  dependants *see* **dependant care leave**
  flexible work *see* **flexible working**
  maternity *see* **maternity leave**
  parental *see* **parental leave**
  paternity *see* **paternity leave**
fire and rehire
  ACAS guidance 71
  Statutory Code of Practice 71–2
fixed-term contract 38
  break clause 48, 111, 123
  less favourable treatment 48, 419
  termination 123
    by effluxion of time 111
    clause 48
flexibility clauses 69
flexible working
  application 558
  complaints to tribunal 559

flexible working – *continued*
  detriment 559
  eligibility 558
  government consultation 558
  grounds for refusal 558
  legislation 544
  reform 544
  refusal 558
  remedies 559
  right to request 558–60
  sex discrimination law and 559–60
  summary 563–5
  unfair dismissal 559
freedom of expression 578–9
frustration
  death of either party 109
  illness or injury to employee 109
  imprisonment of employee 109–10
furlough
  annual leave 87
  fire and rehire practices 71
  redundancy during 201–2
  statutory maternity pay 557
  statutory parental bereavement pay 557
  statutory paternity pay 557
  statutory shared parental pay 557

'gagging clauses' 304–5
'garden leave' clause 65
gay service personnel in armed forces 575
gender reassignment
  see also **discrimination; harassment; victimisation**
  discrimination 385–7, 388, 436
'gig' economy 23–6
good faith
  employees' duty 44
'Good Work Plan' 35
grievance procedures 68

harassment 390
  age discrimination 489, 496
  burden of proof 468
  case study 476–81
  characteristic-related 469–71
  compensation 474
  definition 468–9
  disability discrimination 502, 538
  EHRC guidance 467
  flowchart 486
  government consultation 467–8
  less favourable treatment 472
  promotion and dismissal 394, 395
  Protection from Harassment Act 1997 476
  purpose or effect 472–4
  recruitment 393
  remedies 474
  sexual 400–1, 471–2, 474
  third party acts 474–5
  vicarious liability 474
  witnesses to 471
health and safety
  disclosures *see* **public interest disclosure**
  unfair dismissal 207–9

holiday pay 55–6
  see also **annual leave**
  annual leave 86–7
  calculating 88–93
  case law 96
  commission 88–9
  damages for wrongful dismissal 112
  furlough and 87
  overtime and 89–90
  retrospective claims 90–3
  rolled-up 93
human rights
  association 579
  Convention Rights 570–9
  covert surveillance 574–5
  disciplinary procedures 570–1
  discrimination prohibition 420–1, 579
  drug searches or tests 575
  employment tribunals 303–4
  equality of arms 572, 573
  fair and public hearing 570–3
  freedom of expression 578–9
  private and family life 574–6
  public authorities 569
  public interest disclosure 219
  reliance 570
  slavery 570
  terms of contract 72–3
  thought, conscience and religion 576–8
  UK Bill of Rights 567–8
  unfair dismissal 175–6
  victims 569–70
Human Rights Act 1998 4–5, 303–4, 567, 568–9

Immigration Act 2014 5–6
Immigration, Asylum and Nationality Act 2006 5–6
implied terms 37, 40
  business efficacy test 45
  custom and practice 45
  employees' duties *see* **employees' duties**
  employers' duties *see* **employers' duties**
  equality clause 412–14
  implied by common law 40–5
  implied by statute 40
  intention to include 45–6
indefinite contract 38
  duration clause 47
indemnity
  employees' duty 44
  employers' duty 41
independent contractors 10
  IR35 legislation 12
industrial action
  continuity of employment 133
  official 206
  unfair dismissal 206
  unofficial 206
Information Commissioner's Office 580
  consent to processing 583–4
  data breaches 582–3
  guidance 580–3
  information provision to employees 585
  monitoring at work 587–9

Information Commissioner's Office – *continued*
   subject access requests 586
Information and Consultation of Employees Regulations 2004 156–7, 370
information to employees *see* **consultation**
injunctions
   'balance of convenience' test 118
   wrongful dismissal remedy 118
intellectual property rights 56
interception of communications
   private conversations 574
interpretation of legislation 4
inventions 56
Investigatory Powers Act 2016 586–7
IR35 legislation 12

job title 48
judicial mediation 284, 311

legal professional privilege 278–80
legislation 2–3
   see also **European Union law**
   interpretation 4
less favourable treatment
   arising from disability 528–36
   direct discrimination 425–7, 428–30
   disability discrimination 528
   fixed-term contract workers 48, 419
   harassment 472
   part-time workers 417–19
   reason for 427–8
   victimisation 481–4
limited-term contract *see* **fixed-term contract**
litigants in person 265–7
litigation privilege 279–80
lunch breaks 78

mariners
   statutory dismissal exclusion 134
marital status discrimination 387–8, 396–7
   see also **discrimination; harassment; victimisation**
maternity leave 544
   additional 544, 545
      commencement 545
      return to work after 546–7
      rights during 545–6
      working during 546
   annual leave and 94
   compulsory 548
   detriment short of dismissal 548
   general right 544
   notice provision 544–5
   ordinary
      commencement of 545
      employer's notice 545
      notice provisions 544–5
      return to work after 546
      rights during 545–6
      working during 546
   redundancy 548
   return to work
      after additional leave 546–7
      after ordinary leave 546

maternity leave – *continued*
      failure to return 547–8
      terms and conditions 547
      type of work 547
   shared parental leave 555–7
   sickness after 545
   summary 563–5
maternity rights 544
   health and safety risk assessment 552
   infertility and 553
   leave *see* **maternity leave**
   maternity pay 544, 552, 557
   surrogacy and 553
   suspension from work 551–2
   time off for ante-natal care 552
   unfair dismissal *see* **pregnancy**
menopause
   discrimination 439
misconduct 166–7, 180–97
   appeal 191–2
   characterisation 184–5
   discovered after dismissal 231
   investigations 188–9
   outside employment 167
   suspected 193
   suspension 186–8
   warnings 185–6
mitigation
   unfair dismissal compensation 228–9
   wrongful dismissal damages 115
mobility
   contract term 49–50, 144
   Covid-19 50
   'place of work' redundancy and 144
modern slavery 381, 393, 570
monitoring in workplace
   consent 588
   data protection 586–91
   guidance 587–9
   impact assessment 587
   Investigatory Powers Act 2016 586–7
   lawful purposes 587
   transparency 588
mutual trust and confidence
   employers' duty 42

national minimum wage 51–5
non-competition clause 60–1, 65–6, 66–8
non-dealing clause 62
non-disclosure agreements
   discrimination claims 308–9
   reform proposals 56–7, 304–5
   settlements 304–5
   sexual harassment claims 308–9
non-poaching clause 61, 65–6
non-solicitation clause 61, 65–6
notice
   insufficient 102
   PILON clause 68, 105–7, 116
   shared parental leave 556
   statutory minimum period 105
   termination of contract by 104–7

occupational requirements
　　race discrimination 396
　　religion or belief discrimination 396–7
　　sex discrimination 396–7
　　sexual orientation discrimination 396–7
Office for Disability Issues
　　Guidance 503
on-call time 78
　　sleeping time 53–4
overpayment
　　of expenses 75–6
　　of wages 75–6

parental bereavement leave 555, 557
parental bereavement pay 557
parental leave 544, 555
　　pay 556
　　shared 555–7
　　summary 563–5
part-time workers
　　less favourable treatment 417–19
partnerships
　　contract termination by dissolution 110
paternity leave 555
　　additional 555
　　annual leave and 94
　　shared parental leave 555–7
　　summary 563–5
pay see remuneration
payment in lieu of notice (PILON) 68, 105–7, 116
pensions
　　age discrimination 498
　　compensation for loss of rights 225
　　damages for lost entitlement 113
　　term of contract 56
　　transfer of undertakings 358–9
personal service 15, 44, 79
PILON clause 68, 105–7, 116
place of work
　　contract term 49–50
'place of work' redundancy 143–4
　　mobility clauses and 144
police service
　　statutory dismissal exclusion 134
'Polkey' deductions 229–31
pregnancy
　　detriment short of dismissal 548
　　discrimination 388, 411, 437–9, 550–1
　　　　see also discrimination; harassment; victimisation
　　health and safety 552
　　maternity leave see maternity leave
　　maternity pay 544, 552, 557
　　redundancy payments 550
　　suspension from work 551–2
　　time off for ante-natal care 552
　　unfair dismissal 549–50
　　　　exceptions 549–50
　　　　remedies 550
　　　　written reasons 550
　　wrongful dismissal 550
preparation time orders 300
privilege
　　advice 278–9

privilege – continued
　　employment tribunals 278–80
　　legal professional 278–80
　　litigation 279–80
　　waiver 280
privity of contract 37
promotion
　　disability discrimination 514–15
　　discrimination 394–5
Protection from Harassment Act 1997 476
public interest disclosure
　　burden of proof 217–18
　　causation 215–17
　　disclosure 210–11
　　employees and workers differentiated 29
　　enforcement 218–19
　　exceptionally serious material 214–15
　　good faith 215
　　human rights and 219
　　procedures for disclosure 214–15
　　protected disclosure 209–19
　　public interest requirement 211–13
　　qualifying disclosures 210–14
　　'reasonable belief' 213
　　relevant failures 213–14
　　unfair dismissal 209–19
　　vicarious liability 218
　　whistleblowers 209–19
public tribunal register 302–3

qualifications 49, 166, 178–80

race discrimination 379–81
　　see also discrimination; harassment; victimisation
　　burden of proof 439–40, 444–8
　　caste 381
　　ethnic origins 380, 381
　　immigration status 380–1
　　occupational requirement 396
　　racial groups 380
re-employment offers
　　acceptance 148
　　offer 148
　　re-engagement 147
　　redundancy 147–9
　　rejection 148
　　trial period 148–9
reasonable care and skill
　　employees' duty 44
reasons for dismissal
　　assertion of statutory right 206–7
　　capability 166, 178–80
　　conduct 166–7, 180–97
　　five permitted reasons 165–6
　　health and safety 207–8
　　illegality 167–8, 203
　　incompetence 179
　　industrial action 206
　　misconduct 166–7, 180–97
　　　　appeal 191–2
　　　　characterisation 184–5
　　　　discovered after dismissal 231
　　　　investigations 188–9

reasons for dismissal – *continued*
    outside employment 167
    suspected 193
    suspensions 186–8
    warnings 185–6
  other substantial reasons 168–9, 203–4
  potentially fair 164
  qualifications 166, 178–80
  redundancy 167, 197–202
  sickness 179–80
  statement of 171
  trade union reasons 205–6
  unfair dismissal 165–71
recoupment of benefits 232–3
recruitment
  advertisements 395
  age discrimination 497
  disability discrimination 514
  discrimination 392–4
  trade union discrimination 419–20
redundancy 103
  adoption leave 554
  age discrimination 499
  associated employer 147, 149
  'bumping' 147, 198
  cessation of business 143
  change of employer 133–4
    associated employer 149
    death etc 149
    transfer of undertaking 150
  consultation
    collective redundancies 152–6
    Covid-19 procedures 201
    duty to consult 152–6
    protective award 155–6
    reasons to be given 153
    recognised trade union 152
    Secretary of State notification 157
    timing 152–3
    unfair dismissal 157
  continuous employment requirement 130
  contracting out 139
  Covid-19 169, 201–2
  dismissal requirement 122–9
    actual dismissal 122–3
    constructive dismissal 123–9
  during furlough 201–2
  eligibility 121–2, 143
  'employee' requirement 122
  employment tribunals 312
  excluded employees 134
  fair reason for dismissal 167
  'job redundancy' 143
  lay offs 141–2
  maternity leave 548
  nature of payment 141–2
  notification to Secretary of State 157
  payment *see* **redundancy payment**
  place of employment 143–4
    mobility clauses and 144
  presumption of 147
  re-employment offers
    acceptance 148

redundancy – *continued*
    associated employer 147, 149
    offer 148
    re-engagement 147
    rejection 148
    trial period 148–9
  relevant date 130, 132
  short-time working 141–2
  statutory definition 143–7
  surplus employees 145
  time limits 259
  unfair dismissal reasons 197–202
  work of particular kind 144–7
redundancy payment
  case study 157–9
  computation 150–1
  employer's liability 151
  enforcement 151–2
  flowchart 161
  insolvency of employer 151–2
  pregnancy 550
  protective award 155–6
  reference to tribunal 151
references
  data protection 43
  employer's duty of care 42–3
  human rights and 43
Rehabilitation of Offenders Act 1974 10
reinstatement/re-engagement
  re-engagement offer 147
  unfair dismissal
    availability of order 219–20
    content of order 220
    non-compliance with order 220–1
religion or belief discrimination 381–5
  see also **discrimination; harassment; victimisation**
  comparators 433
  human rights 420
  occupational requirement 396–7
  philosophical beliefs 383–5
  political beliefs 383
remuneration
  commission
    damages for lost 113
    express term 52
  deductions from wages 55, 73–4
    time limits 259–60
    unauthorised 73–7
  express term 51–5
  failure to pay 73–7
  furlough and 557
  holiday pay *see* **holiday pay**
  itemised pay statements 39, 51
  meaning of 'wages' 74–5
  overpayment
    expenses 75–6
    wages 75–6
  penalties for underpayment 54–5
  protection of wages 73–7
  statutory adoption pay 544, 554
  statutory maternity pay 544, 552, 557
  statutory parental leave pay 556
  statutory paternity pay 544, 555, 557

remuneration – *continued*
  statutory sick pay 55
  tipping 114
  under CJRS 52–3
reporting restrictions
  employment tribunals 287–9
resignation 108
rest *see* **working time**
restraint of trade clause 58–9
restrictive covenants 58–68
  'blue pencil' test 62–3
  contents of clause 60–5
  employee's viewpoint 65
  employer's remedy 118
  enforcement 62–5
  'garden leave' clause 65
  non-competition clause 60–1, 65–6, 66–8
  non-dealing clause 62
  non-poaching clause 61, 65–6
  non-solicitation clause 61, 65–6
  restraint of trade clause 58–9
  review 66
  transfer of undertakings 358
  wrongful dismissal 64
retirement
  age discrimination 403, 498–9
  compulsory 498

safety *see* **health and safety**
secret profits 44
settlements
  ACAS code of practice 307
  compromise agreement 311
  conciliation officer 305
  confidentiality clauses 304–5
  'gagging clauses' 304–5
  infringement of statutory requirements 308
  non-disclosure agreements 304–5, 308–9
  pre-termination negotiations 309–10
  protected conversations 309–10
  record of 310
  relevant independent adviser 306
  waiver of statutory claim 305
sex discrimination 379
  see also **discrimination; harassment; victimisation**
  burden of proof 439–40
  equal pay *see* **equal pay**
  flexible working and 559–60
  occupational requirement 396–7
  pregnancy *see* **pregnancy**
  retirement age 403
sexual orientation discrimination 385
  see also **discrimination; harassment; victimisation**
  human rights 420
  occupational requirement 396–7
shared parental leave 555–7
  availability 556
  duration 555
  notice requirements 556
  pay 556, 557
  procedure 556
shareholders
  as employees 36–7

sick pay 55
social security benefits
  recoupment 232–3
sources of law
  case law 2
  codes of practice 3
  common law 2
  European Union law 3–4
  human rights 4–5
  legislation 2–3
specific performance 117
staff handbooks
  variations of terms and 68
statutory adoption pay 544, 554
statutory dismissal *see* **redundancy; unfair dismissal**
statutory dismissal and disciplinary procedures *see* **dismissal and disciplinary procedures**
statutory grievance procedures *see* **grievance procedures**
statutory maternity pay 544, 552
  furlough and 557
statutory parental leave pay 556
statutory paternity pay 544, 555
  furlough and 557
striking out 273–5
summary dismissal 107–8
surrender of papers
  term of contract 68

taxation
  discrimination compensation 411
  unfair dismissal compensation 233–6
  wrongful dismissal damages 116
Taylor Review 11, 23, 26, 27, 28, 35, 39
termination of employment 104–11
  breach of contract *see* **wrongful dismissal**
  breach of contract, employee's 107–8
  by agreement 104
  by notice 104–7
  constructive dismissal 108
  dissolution of partnership 110
  effective date of termination 130–2
  effluxion of time 111
  fixed-term contracts 48, 111, 123
  frustration 108–10
  redundancy *see* **redundancy**
  resignation 108
  unfair dismissal *see* **unfair dismissal**
  winding up of company 110
  wrongful dismissal *see* **wrongful dismissal**
third parties
  privity of contract 37
time limits
  discrimination enforcement 404–5
  employment tribunals 252, 255–64
trade secrets 45
trade unions
  discrimination for membership or activities 419–20
  freedom of association 579
  industrial action 206
  refusal of employment 419
  remedies 420
  unfair dismissal reasons 205–6

transfer of undertakings
advice 365–6
automatic transfer of contract 350–1
business transfers 338–43
collective agreements 358
consultation
    duty to consult 367–9
    employee representatives 367
    failure to comply 369
    persons to consult 367
contracts of employment 350–1
cross-border transfers 349
date of transfer 349–50
dismissal of employee 359–63
    on or after transfer flowchart 373
    before transfer flowchart 372
    by reason of transfer itself 360–1
    change in workforce 361–2
    connected with transfer 360–1
    ETO reason 361–2
    meaning 352–3
employee liability information 366–7
employee representatives 367
employees
    contracts otherwise terminated 353–5
    'immediately before transfer' 351, 357–9
    right of objection 355–6
    unfair dismissal 350
failure to consult 359
flowcharts 372–3
franchises 337
'immediately before transfer' 351, 357–9
information
    duty to inform 367–8, 370
    employee liability information 366–7
    employee representatives 367
    failure to comply 369
    persons to inform 367
insolvency 337
legislation 335–6
pensions 358–9
public authorities 338
redundancy and 150
Regulations 2006
    applicability 336–7
    variation of terms and conditions 363–5
relevant transfer 338–50
    dismissal of employee 359–63
    effect 350–6
rights transferred 356–9
    collective agreements 358
    failure to consult liability 359
    pensions 358–9
    restrictive covenants 358
    rights and liability not assigned 359
service provision change 337, 343–9
time of transfer 349–50
undertaking
    existence 339–40
    transfer 340–3
unfair dismissal 351–2, 359–63
variation of terms and conditions 363–6
    Regulations 2006 363–5

UK Bill of Rights 567–8
UK General Data Protection Regulation 580–3
bases for processing data 581
consent 588
data breach 582–3
Data Protection Impact Assessment 583, 587
individual's rights 582
principles of data protection 581
provision of information 585
transfers outside EU 589–91
unfair dismissal 103
absences 195
adoption leave 554
arbitration 310–11
breach of contract 174
case studies 237–45, 314–30
change of employer 133–4
codes of practice 176–8
compensation 221–36
    adjustments 232
    basic award 221–2
    compensatory award 222–32
    compulsory increase 226
    discretionary increase 226–8
    expenses 226
    future loss of earnings 224–5
    heads of loss 224–6
    immediate loss of earnings 224
    interest 232
    loss of statutory rights 225–6
    maximum award 222–4
    mitigation 228–9
    non-economic loss 223
    pension rights 225
    'Polkey' deductions 229–31
    recoupment of social security benefits 232–3
    reducing factors 228–32
    taxation 233–6
consistency 174–5
continuity of employment 132–3
continuous employment requirement 129–30
contracting out 139
Covid-19 169–70, 201–2
criminal offences 193–5
dependant care leave 561
disciplinary procedures *see* **dismissal and disciplinary procedures**
dismissal requirement 122–9
    actual dismissal 122–3
    constructive dismissal 123–9
effective date of termination 130–2
eligibility 121–2, 164
'employee' requirement 122
employment tribunals 312
equitable considerations 174
excluded employees 134
failure to consult about redundancy 157
fair reasons 164
    see also reasons for dismissal
fairness 164, 171
flexible working 559
flowchart 247
hearing

unfair dismissal – *continued*
    conduct 189–90
      failure to attend 190
    human rights 175–6
    information known to employer 173–4
    judicial mediation 311
    jurisdiction 134–9
    justifiable reasons 174
    misconduct 180–97
      appeal 191–2
      characterisation 184–5
      investigations 188–9
      suspected 193
      suspensions 186–8
      warnings 185–6
    on-going grievances 192
    penalties for employers 236–7, 301
    political reasons 208–9
    potentially fair reasons 164
    pregnancy 549–50
      exceptions 549–50
      remedies 550
      written reasons 550
    pressure on employer 174
    procedural unfairness 176–204, 229–31
    public interest disclosure 209–19
    reasonableness of dismissal 171–3
    reasons for dismissal
      assertion of statutory right 206–7
      capability 166, 178–80
      conduct 166–7, 180–97
      fair reasons 164
      five permitted reasons 165–6
      health and safety 207–8
      illegality 167–8, 203
      incompetence 179
      industrial action 206
      other substantial reasons 168–9, 203–4
      potentially fair 164
      qualifications 166, 178–80
      redundancy 167, 197–202
      sickness 179–80
      special cases 204–5
      statement of 171
      trade union reasons 205–6
    recoupment of social security benefits 232–3
    reinstatement/re-engagement
      availability of order 219–20
      content of order 220
      non-compliance 220–1
    remedies *see* compensation; reinstatement/re-engagement
    size of undertaking 174
    social media 192–3
    statement of reasons for dismissal 171
    time limits 255–9
    transfer of undertakings 350, 351–2, 359–63
    variation of contractual terms 69
unless orders 283–4

variation of contractual terms 68–72
    consultation 69
    employee's options 70

variation of contractual terms – *continued*
    express variation clauses 69
    staff handbooks 68
    unfair dismissal 69
vicarious liability 474
    age discrimination 497
    course of employment 397–400
    disability discrimination 538, 542
    discrimination 397–403
    harassment 474
    personal liability 403
    public interest disclosure 218
    reasonable steps 400–3
victimisation 389, 390
    age discrimination 489, 496
    associative discrimination 483
    burden of proof 468
    definition 481–4
    disability discrimination 502, 538
    discrimination 481–4
    flowchart 486
    former employees 484
    less favourable treatment 481–4
    promotion and dismissal 394
    recruitment 393

wages
    see also **remuneration**
    deductions from 73–4, 259–60
    duty to pay 41
    meaning 74–5
    overpayment 75–6
    'properly payable' 75
    protection of 73–7
wasted costs orders 300–1
whistleblowers *see* **public interest disclosure**
winding up
    employment tribunals 255
    termination of contract 110
work
    duty to provide 41
workers
    adult workers 80
    definition 10, 19–28, 79–80
    domestic servants 80
    excluded activities 80
    mobile workers 80
    personal service 79
    young workers 80
workforce agreements 97
    legal requirements 98
working time
    adequate records 80
    annual leave 81, 85–95
    'average working time' 81–2
    collective agreements 97
    daily rest break 81, 84–5
    daily rest period 81, 83–4
    enforcement 99
    exceptions 99
    excluded activities 80
    exclusion of rights/limits 97–8
    guidance 78–9

working time – *continued*
   lunch break 78
   meaning 78–9
   modification of rights/limits 97–8
   on-call time 53–4, 78
   'opt out' agreements 82–3
   'reference period' 81
   relevant agreements 97–8
   rest
      daily rest break 81, 84–5
      daily rest period 81, 83–4
      sanctions 85
      weekly rest period 81, 84
   sanctions 83
   summary 98–9
   travel 78–9
   'unmeasured' 82
   weekly rest period 81, 84
   weekly working time 80
      failure to observe 83
      maximum 81–3
   worker, meaning 79–80
   workforce agreements 97, 98
   Working Time Regulations 1998 77–95
   workplace meetings 79
written statement of terms 37, **38–40**, 593–5
   disputes 39–40
   exceptions 39
   failure to give 40
   written contracts 39
wrongful dismissal 101–2
   damages
      accelerated receipt 116–17

wrongful dismissal – *continued*
   accrued holiday pay 112
   additional loss 113–14
   discretionary contractual payments 113–14
   employer's remedy 117–18
   failure to follow ACAS code 117
   loss of benefits 113–14
   loss of net wages 111–12
   lost commission 113
   lost pension entitlement 113
   lost tips 114
   mitigation duty 115
   NI contributions 116
   non-pecuniary losses 114–15
   PILON and 116
   'stigma' 114
   taxation 116
  employment tribunals 312
  flowchart 120
  injunctions 118
  preconditions for tribunal claim 103–4
  pregnancy 550
  remedies
     see also damages
     account of profits 118–19
     employer's 117–19
     injunctions 118
     restrictive covenants 118
  restrictive covenants 64
  time limits 260

zero hours contracts 27–8, 38, 97